Purchasing and Materials Management

PURCHASING AND MATERIALS MANAGEMENT

WILBUR B. ENGLAND
Sebastian S. Kresge Professor of Marketing Emeritus
Graduate School of Business Administration
Harvard University

and

MICHIEL R. LEENDERS
Professor, School of Business Administration
University of Western Ontario

Sixth Edition   1975

RICHARD D. IRWIN, INC.   Homewood, Illinois   60430
Irwin-Dorsey International   London, England WC2H   9NJ
Irwin-Dorsey Limited   Georgetown, Ontario   L7G 4B3

Sixth Edition

Earlier editions of this book were published under the title
Procurement: Principles and Cases. The previous edition
was entitled *Modern Procurement Management: Principles and
Cases.*

First Printing, April 1975

ISBN   0-256-01635-6
Library of Congress Catalog Card No. 74–25937
Printed in the United States of America

PREFACE

BUSINESS CONDITIONS during 1973–74 placed as much, if not more, strain and pressure on the purchasing/materials management function as has occurred at any time in the 20th century. Critical material shortages, two digit inflation and arbitrary actions by governments seriously interfered with the orderly operation of business and the economy.

Many corporate managements have been made painfully aware of the shortcomings of the operations of their firms' purchasing/materials management functions. Past indifference to proper placement of the function in the organization structure and failure to staff with highly competent professional buyers have proved to be costly oversights. Those firms that have kept abreast of modern developments in organization concepts and manpower qualifications and requirements generally have had fewer interruptions in the continuity of supply and have obtained materials at competitive prices.

The objective behind the writing of earlier editions of this book initiated by the late Professor Howard T. Lewis[1] in the 1930s, 40s, and early 50s was to provide carefully researched text materials about the organization and operation of the procurement function along with cases detailing actual business experiences in procurement operations. This objective was continued from the middle 1950s to the middle 1970s by Wilbur B. England and is further strengthened in this edition by the work of coauthor Michiel R. Leenders.

The primary emphasis continues on the acquisition of materials, parts, equipment, and services for further manufacture or end use in the organization rather than a purchasing for resale. The authors are fully satisfied that the materials area will continue to provide exciting management career opportunities for university graduates who are able to bring imagination and aggressiveness to bear on the continuing challenges of marrying evolving needs with a capricious market.

The evaluation and feedback from educators who use this text and cases has always been a valuable guide in revisions. To this edition the authors would like to acknowledge especially the thoughtful and extensive comments by T. K. Lindsay. The comments of Harold F. Puff and Richard L. Shell were also much appreciated.

---

[1] Deceased 1973.

v

vi Preface

Major text revisions have been made in every chapter to reflect the changes which have occurred in the purchasing and materials management function since 1970. There are 48 new cases in this book, 40 of which have been researched and written within the past two years. The case problems are copyrighted by the President and Fellows of Harvard College and The University of Western Ontario and are used with their respective permissions.

Gratitude is expressed to Lawrence E. Fouraker of the Harvard Business School; to John J. Wettlaufer of the School of Business Administration, The University of Western Ontario; and to Andrew R. Towl, Director of Case Development, Harvard Business School, for assistance and understanding support.

Meaningful cases based on actual business situations are not possible without the wholehearted cooperation of many business executives. We are grateful for their help and cooperation as well as the assistance of many of our colleagues, past and present, especially the late Howard T. Lewis and Sterling Livingston, Jurgen Ladendorf, Stanley S. Miller, Robert R. Britney, Albert R. Wood, and David C. Shaw.

Our thanks go also to research assistants who aided in the collection and preparation of cases, including Douglas H. Clark, Richard G. Firth, Louise-Andree Godbout, Lawrence M. Jones, A. Rudi Kuhlmann, William A. Small, and Floyd T. Swann.

Much of the burden of the secretarial work and editorial assistance has been borne by Barbara G. Cunningham, and we are indebted to her for the dedicated manner in which she carried this responsibility. Peggy J. Bateman's help was also most welcome in the final stages along with Helen Murray's proofreading.

As is customary, the blame for any errors or shortcomings is the responsibility of the coauthors.

March 1975
WILBUR B. ENGLAND
MICHIEL R. LEENDERS

CONTENTS

*on people. Purchasing procedure for multinational companies. Informa-
tion systems: Internal information flows to purchasing. External information flows to purchasing. Internal information flows from purchasing to
the organization.*

CASES: Philadelphia Pharmaceuticals, Inc. (A), 178. Philadelphia Phar-
maceuticals, Inc. (B), 205. Mercury Oil Company, 217. Avco-Everett
Research Laboratory, 257. Victoria Hospital, 264. Vanier University, 276.
Canadian Liquid Air, Ltd., 282.

4. Quality and inspection   286

*Definition of need—function. Suitability. Reliability. Quality. Decision
on "best buy." Importance of service in determining quality. Responsibility for determining quality. Responsibility of purchasing personnel.
Purchase analysis section. Description of quality. Description by brand.
Description by specification. Specification by physical or chemical characteristics. Specification by material and method of manufacture. Sources
of specification data. Standard specifications. Standardization and simplification. Specification by performance. Specification to meet government
legal requirements. Description by engineering drawing. Miscellaneous
methods of description. Combination of methods of description. Metric
conversion. Control of quality—inspection: Purpose of inspection. What
is reasonable inspection? Specification of inspection method. Quality control department. Location of the quality control department. The quality
capability survey. Commercial testing labs and services. Inspection
methods. Process quality control. Output inspection—100 percent inspection and sampling. Operating characteristic curves. Sequential sampling.
Computer programs. Responsibility for adjustments and returns. Zero
defects programs. Importance of inspection records.*

CASES: Slagko Aggregate Company, 317. Kerr Life Insurance Company,
324. Northwest Division, 338.

5. Determination and control of quantity and inventories   349

*Quantity considerations. Forecasting. Forecasting techniques. The
moving average. Regression analysis. Exponential smoothing. Product
explosion and requirement accumulation. ABC analysis. Definition of inventory policy. Factors bearing on inventory control. Inventories: their
functions, forms, and control. Why do inventories exist? What functions
do inventories provide? Inventory forms. Inventory function and form
framework. Transit inventories. Cycle inventories. Buffer inventories.
Spare parts inventory. Decoupling inventory. Implications for the control
of inventories. The price-discount problem. Sample price-discount problem. Sample calculations for the price-discount problem. Inventory
models. Deterministic-fixed quantity models. Fixed period models. Probabilistic models. Service level. The fixed order quantity model with
variation in demand and buffer inventory. Use of integrated data
processing systems. Inventory management program and control tech-*

9. Price policies (continued)   623

Determination of most advantageous bid. Negotiation necessary between buyer and seller. Adjusting purchases to meet fixed costs. Guarantee against price decline and providing for escalation. Discounts. Cancellation of contracts. One-price policy. The problem of identical prices. Negotiation strategy.

10. Forward buying and speculation   687

Forward buying versus speculation: Is hand-to-mouth buying speculation? Speculation versus gambling. Objectives of forward and speculative buying. Costs of speculation. Control of forward buying. The commodity exchanges: Limitations of the exchanges. Hedging. Business cycles and price forecasting. Sources of information regarding price trends.

11. Procurement of major equipment   712

Definition of major equipment: Special problems of equipment buying. General principles which should control the selection of equipment. Importance of cost factors. Life cycle costing. Problem of engineering service. Timing of the purchase. Selection of the source. Some legal questions. Financing of the purchase. Disposition of obsolete or replaced equipment. Types of leases. Categories of leasing companies. Advantages used equipment comes on the market. Sales contract terms. Organization of used equipment market. Reasons for buying used equipment. Leasing equipment. Types of leases. Categories of leasing companies. Advantages and disadvantages. Evaluation of advantages and disadvantages.

12. Procurement by manufacture   771

Make or buy—the strategy. Direct control of sources of supply. Reasons for manufacture instead of purchase. Dangers involved in decision to manufacture. Some problems in costing.

1 THE MODERN MANAGEMENT OF MATERIALS AND PURCHASING

The effective management of materials and purchasing contributes significantly to the success of most modern organizations. In this text, the nature of this contribution and the management requirements will both be explored. The acquisition of space and equipment, materials, supplies and services—of the right qualities, in the right quantities, at the right prices, at the right time, and on a continuing basis—has long occupied the attention of many managers in both the public and private sectors. The rapidly changing supply scene with cycles of abundance and shortages, varying prices, lead times, and availabilities provides a continuing challenge to those organizations anxious to obtain a maximum contribution from this area.

Growing management interest through necessity and improved insight into the opportunities in the materials area has resulted in a variety of organizational concepts. Terms like procurement, purchasing, supply, logistics, materials management, and materiel are used almost interchangeably. No agreement exists on the definition of each of these terms, and it is possible to find managers in public and private institutions with identical responsibilities and yet with substantially different titles. Recognizing that this linguistic confusion does exist, the following definitions may be helpful in sorting out the more common understanding of the various terms.

In general usage, the term purchasing describes the process of buying: learning of the need, locating and selecting a supplier, negotiating price and other pertinent terms, and following up to ensure delivery. Procurement covers wider areas and may include the duties performed by purchasing, as well as such additional functions of materials supervision

1

and management as inventory control, traffic, receiving, incoming inspection, and salvage operations. When the procurement definition is expanded to include production planning and materials handling, the term materials management is often used to describe the broader concept. Occasionally shipping and management of finished inventories are also included in this definition.

Materiel has a military or governmental connotation and often includes the same functions as those identified under materials management. It is useful to note the difference between manufacturing concerns in which the bulk of purchases are further processed and subsequently sold as finished goods and nonmanufacturing organizations where the procurement process is primarily concerned with internal consumption. Supply is often used in North America by industrial concerns to cover the stores function of internally consumed items like stationery and office supplies. In the United Kingdom and Europe the term supply has a broader meaning to include at least purchasing, stores, and receiving. In the governmental sector supply also has this broader interpretation. In Canada, for example, the Department of Supply and Services is responsible for procurement in the federal government.

Logistics is claimed to have its origin near the year 1670.[1] A new staff structure proposed for the French army included the position of "Marechal General des Logis," who was responsible for supply, transportation, selecting camps, and adjusting marches. Although logistics has long been a military term, its application to nonmilitary management became known primarily in the 1960s. There it included: "the optimum co-ordination of the inbound raw material movements, raw material storage, work in process handling, and of the outbound packaging, warehousing of finished products, and movement of finished products to the customer."[2] Certain proponents of the logistics concept include in their definition the application of operations research concepts to the materials area. Harold Fearon[3] notes that, although the logistics concept is attractive from a theoretical point of view encompassing the complete systems approach, two major problems of implementation still exist. The first is the ability of a logistics manager to handle a job with this scope, crossing so many traditional lines of organizational authority and responsibility. The second is the current state of computer software systems.

This text will cover primarily those functions normally included in the procurement and materials management definition. The activities usually included in physical distribution management such as determin-

---

[1] J. D. Little, "The Military Staff, Its History and Development," 3d ed. (Harrisburg, Pa.: Stackpole Co., 1961), pp. 48–49.

[2] E. G. Plowman, "Elements of Business Logistics" (Stanford, Calif.: Stanford Graduate School of Business, 1964).

[3] H. E. Fearon, "Materials Management: A Synthesis and Current View," *Journal of Purchasing*, vol. 9 (February 1973), pp. 28–47.

ing finished goods inventory levels, determination of finished goods warehouse locations and levels of inventory, outbound transportation, packaging and customer repair parts, and warranty and installation service will receive no special coverage. It is the inflow of goods and services rather than the outflow, therefore, that forms our main concern. Even within the materials management area, greater emphasis will be placed on areas like source selection and determining the price to be paid than on inventory control and traffic which have already attracted a substantial volume of high-quality academic attention. The authors subscribe to an evolutionary systems approach to the management of materials in an organization. What is currently feasible or desirable in one organization may not be applicable in another for sound reasons. The relative importance of the area compared to the other prime functions of the organization will be a major determinant of the management attention it will receive. How to assess the materials needs of a particular organization in context is one of the purposes of this book. Cases are provided to illustrate a variety of procurement situations and to give practice in resolving managerial problems.

SCOPE OF PROCUREMENT

It is estimated that U.S. manufacturing and associated industries purchased materials totaling $356 billion in 1971.[4] Capital expenditures amounted to another $20 billion, and year-end inventories totaled $102 billion. The magnitude of these figures emphasizes the importance to the U.S. economy of performing the procurement function in the most effective manner possible.

Another and more specific measure of the importance of the procurement function in U.S. industry can be found in the figures showing the relationship between the cost of purchased materials and services and the total value of shipments of manufacturing companies. The U.S. Census of Manufacturers for 1967 reported that the cost of purchased materials and services from others averaged 57.8 percent of the total value of shipments of manufacturing companies for that year. Individual industries presented a broad spectrum of ratios of dollars spent for materials and services purchased from others. Companies specializing in research and development activities seldom have a ratio higher than 30 percent, while some companies in the basic metals and petroleum industries have ratios exceeding 70 percent. The great majority of industries spend between 40 percent and 60 percent of their sales income for materials and services from outside sources. Table 1–1 shows the ratios for selected industries each with sales exceeding $1 billion. It is expected

---

[4] *Annual Survey of Manufacturers, 1971,* General Statistics for Industry Groups and Industries, p. 3.

Table 1–1
VALUE OF SHIPMENTS, VALUE ADDED BY MANUFACTURE, AND VALUE OF PURCHASES BY VARIOUS U.S. INDUSTRY GROUPS, 1967*

Industry group	Value of shipments ($ millions)	Value added by manufacture ($ millions)	Value of purchases ($ millions)	Purchases as percent of shipments
1. Food and kindred products	83,978.2	26,620.9	57,357.3	68.3
2. Tobacco manufactures	4,903.6	2,032.0	2,871.6	58.6
3. Textile mill products	19,815.2	8,153.2	11,662.0	58.9
4. Apparel, other textile products	21,326.9	10,064.4	11,262.5	52.8
5. Lumber and wood products	11,203.7	4,973.4	6,230.3	55.6
6. Furniture and fixtures	7,749.8	4,169.5	3,580.3	46.2
7. Paper and allied products	20,969.9	9,756.3	11,213.6	53.5
8. Printing and publishing.	21,738.4	14,356.1	7,382.3	34.0
9. Chemicals and allied products	82,148.3	23,660.1	58,488.2	71.2
10. Petroleum and coal products	22,043.4	5,425.6	16,617.8	75.4
11. Rubber and plastics products, etc.	12,784.6	6,799.5	5,985.1	46.8
12. Leather and leather products	6,169.6	2,626.5	3,543.1	57.4
13. Stone, clay, and glass products	14,449.4	8,333.4	6,116.0	42.3
14. Primary metal industries	46,730.9	19,978.2	26,752.7	57.2
15. Fabricated metal products	34,577.6	10,042.6	24,535.0	71.0
16. Machinery, except electrical.	48,477.2	27,636.4	20,840.8	43.0
17. Electrical equipment, and supplies	43,361.0	24,487.3	18,873.7	43.5
18. Transportation equipment	68,512.3	28,173.9	40,338.4	58.9
19. Instruments and related products	9,907.2	6,418.4	3,488.8	35.2
20. Misc. manufacturing industries	8,310.7	4,599.4	3,711.3	44.7
21. Ordinance and accessories	9,267.7	5,587.8	3,679.9	39.7
	598,425.6	253,894.9	344,530.7	57.8

* Figures derived from: *1967 Census of Manufactures General Summary, December 1970;* U.S. Department of Commerce, Bureau of the Census; March 1971 Reader Microprint No. 4248, p. 28.

that today's ratios would be at least as high as those shown below because of the prevailing market conditions in the 1970s.

Decision making in the materials management context

One of the appealing aspects of the materials management function to its practitioners is the variety and nature of the decisions encountered on a daily basis. Should we make or buy? Must we inventory materials and how much? What shall we pay? Where shall we place this order? What should the order size be? When will we require what? Which alternative looks best as an approach to this problem? Should we hedge? Which transportation route should we use? Should we make a long- or a short-term contract? Should we cancel? How do we dispose of surplus material? Who will form the negotiation team and what shall its strategy be? How do we protect ourselves for the future? Shall we switch operating systems? Should we wait or act now? In view of the trade-offs what is the best decision? What stance do we take regarding our customers who wish to supply us? Do we standardize? Is systems contracting worthwhile here? Decisions like these may have a major impact on the organization. What makes the decisions exciting is that they are almost always made in a context of uncertainty. The uncertainty relates to both demand and supply creating "dynamic decisioning process involving diverse functional areas and hierarchical levels within an organization."[5]

Advances in management science in recent decades have substantially enlarged the number of ways in which materials decisions can be analyzed. Decision theory, gaming, simulation linear programming, queueing, Monte Carlo, linear programming, regression analysis and forecasting models have all found useful applications in procurement. The basic supplier selection decision is a classical decision tree model as shown in Figure 1–1. This is a choice between alternatives under uncertainty.

Figure 1–1
SIMPLIFIED ONE STAGE DECISION TREE SHOWING A
SUPPLIER SELECTION DECISION

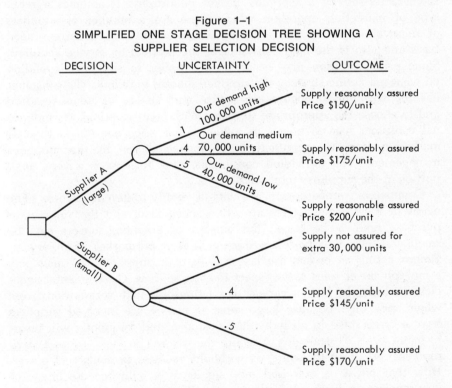

DECISION   UNCERTAINTY   OUTCOME

Our demand high
100,000 units
.1

Supply reasonably assured
Price $150/unit

Supplier A
(large)

.4   Our demand medium
70,000 units

Supply reasonably assured
Price $175/unit

.5   Our demand low
40,000 units

Supply reasonable assured
Price $200/unit

Supply not assured for
extra 30,000 units

Supplier B
(small)

.1

.4

Supply reasonably assured
Price $145/unit

.5

Supply reasonably assured
Price $170/unit

In the example shown, the uncertainty relates to our own demand, we are not sure if it will be high, medium, or low. The outcome is concerned with both price and ability to supply. Does the decision maker wish to trade a higher price against supply assurance under all circumstances?

[5] *Marketing Science Institute, Industrial Buying and Creative Marketing* (Boston, Mass.: Allyn & Bacon, Inc., 1967), p. 12.

That it is difficult to quantify all consequences reinforces the need for sound judgment in key decisions. It also means that the decision maker's perception of the risk involved may in itself be a key variable. Thus, the opportunity is provided to blend managerial judgment, gained through experience and training, with the appropriate mathematical concepts and techniques.

THE DIFFERENCES BETWEEN COMMERCIAL AND CONSUMER ACQUISITION

Procurement is a difficult function to understand because almost everyone is familiar in daily life with another version, that of personal buying. It is easy for one to presume a familiarity or expertise with the acquisition function for this reason. A consumer point of view is characterized by a shopping basket philosophy. It assumes a retail type of marketing operation where there are a number of suppliers of relatively common items. Every customer buys on a current need basis and also is the final consumer of the product or service acquired. Some price variation may occur from supplier to supplier depending on what marketing strategy the supplier chooses to follow. The consumer has the freedom to choose the nature and quality of items required and to choose the appropriate supplier. With few exceptions the individual consumer has no power to influence the price nor the method of marketing, nor the manufacturer or finance chosen by the supplier's management. The individual consumer's total business is a very small portion of the supplier's total sales.

Commercial procurement presents a totally different picture. The needs of most organizations are often specialized, and the volumes of purchase tend to be large. The number of potential sources may be small, and there may be few customers in the total market. Many organizations acting as buyers are larger than their suppliers and may play a multiplicity of roles with respect to their sources. Governmental agencies, for example, have a variety of relationships with corporations from whom they buy. Because large sums of money are involved suppliers have a large stake in an individual customer and frequently will resort to many kinds of strategies to secure the wanted business. In such environment, the right to award or withhold business presents real power. How that power is exercised may significantly influence the image of an organization in the industrial sector. This is no game for amateurs. Special expertise is required to assure proper satisfaction of needs on the one hand and the appropriate systems and procedures on the other to assure a continually effective and acceptable performance.

Suppliers spend large sums annually, using some of the brightest minds in our society, finding ways and means of persuading their customers to buy. Purchasing strength needs to be pitted against this marketing strength to assure that the buying organization's needs of the future are adequately met. The materials function needs to be staffed with people who can counterbalance this most impressive marketing force. It is not sufficient in this environment to be only reactionary to outside pressures from suppliers. Proaction in terms of foresight and a long-range planning outlook is vital so that future needs can be recognized and met on a planned basis.

THE POTENTIAL CONTRIBUTION

The performance of the materials function can be viewed in two contexts: trouble avoidance and opportunistic. The trouble avoidance context is the most familiar. Many people inside the organization are inconvenienced to varying degrees when the materials function does not meet with minimum expectations. Improper quality, wrong quantities, and late delivery may make life miserable for the ultimate user of the product or service. This is so basic and apparent that "no complaints" is assumed to be an indicator of good materials performance. The difficulty is that some users never expect anything more and hence may not receive anything more.

The second context is that of potential contribution to organizational objectives. At least six major areas of potential contribution are possible: dollar savings, internal image, external image, information source, training ground and organizational strategy, and social policy.

Dollar savings

In the first place, because large sums of money are involved, even a relatively small percentage saving can amount to a large dollar amount. For example, experience of others has shown that an effective procurement system may well contribute savings as high as 4 percent of annual purchases. Because most items are repetitive in nature, this contribution accrues year after year.

The large dollar volume spent in manufacturing concerns on materials and services gives considerable leverage to the acquisition function. A simple example illustrates how corporate profits may be increased in a variety of ways. In a manufacturing organization the following major sales-cost relationships exist:

$10,000,000 —total sales
$ 6,000,000 —purchases goods and services
$ 2,000,000 —labor and salaries
$ 1,500,000 —overhead
$ 500,000 —profit

To double the profit to $1,000,000 the following actions could be taken:

For profit to go up 100 percent we need:

a. Sales up 100 percent
b. Price up 5 percent
c. Labor and salaries down 25 percent
d. Overhead down 33 percent
e. Purchases down 8½ percent
f. A combination of the above.

A quick look at these figures should indicate the leverage potential of purchased goods and services. Every 1 percent decline in materials cost results in a 12 percent profit improvement! Most manufacturing organizations spend a substantial amount of money and managerial effort on increasing sales and controlling labor costs. A substantial opportunity exists in the materials area to contribute to the organization's profit potential.

Internal image

In addition, the materials function can add substantially to the internal image of how the organization's own employees view the total system. An effective materials system prevents comments like: "If this company can't even get me a simple item like this on time, how can it do anything else right?" Because the materials system is so internally visible, it can do much to assist in developing a positive employee morale.

External image

There is also an external image. In the eyes of its numerous suppliers, how does the organization compare with accepted business standards? Is it a slow payer and a nitpicker, or does it perform all functions effectively? Do supplier personnel see the buyer's business as desirable? Do they see the organization's personnel as competent, fair, and reliable? Similarly, does the public at large think that the organization's business is transacted honorably and above reproach? Public confidence can be boosted by evidence of a sound policy and fair implementation.

Information source

The contacts of the procurement function in the marketplace provides a logical base from which to act as a source of information for various functions within the organization. Primary examples include information about prices, availability of goods, new sources of supply, and new products, all items of interest to many others in the organization. New marketing techniques used by suppliers may be of interest to the marketing group. News about major investments, mergers, international political and economic developments, pending bankruptcies, major promotions and appointments, current and potential customers may be relevant to marketing, finance, research, and top management. New systems of distribution, payment, and materials management may affect the logistics function. Procurement's unique position vis-à-vis the marketplace provides a comprehensive listening post.

Training ground

The procurement area is also an excellent training ground for new managers. The needs of the organization may be quickly grasped. Exposure to the pressure of decision making under uncertainty with potentially serious consequences allows for evaluation of the individual's ability and his willingness to take risk and assume responsibility. Contacts with many people at various levels and a variety of functions may assist the individual in charting a career plan and will also be of value as the manager moves up the organization. A number of companies have found it useful to include the procurement area as part of a formal job rotation system for high potential employees. In one organization it is standard practice for bright young managers to spend one and a half to two years in the purchasing department. This continuing infusion of high-quality, capable, and motivated managers into the materials function has had a tremendous impact on its performance and acceptance in the organization.

Organizational strategy and social policy

The materials function can also be used as a tool of organizational strategy and social policy. Does the organization's management wish to introduce and stimulate competition? Does it favor some geographical representation, minority interest, environmental and social concerns? For example, are domestic sources preferred? Will a certain amount of money be spent on assisting minority suppliers? As part of an overall organization strategy the materials function can potentially contribute a great deal. Assurance of supply of vital materials or services at a time of general shortages can be a major competitive advantage. Similarly, access to a better quality or a lower priced product or service may represent a substantial gain. These strategic positions in the marketplace may be gained through active exploration of international and domestic markets, technology, innovative management systems, and the imaginative use of corporate resources in the materials area. Vertical integration and its companion decision of make or buy are ever present considerations in the management of procurement.

The potential contribution to strategy is obvious. Achievement depends on both top executive awareness of this potential and the ability to marshall corporate resources to this end. At the same time, it is the responsibility of those charged with the management of the procurement function to seek strategic opportunities in the environment and to draw top executive attention to them. This requires a thorough familiarity with organizational objectives, strategy, and long-term plans, and the ability to influence these in the light of new information.

This is briefly a capsule of the potential values of the function. It does not just happen, however. If full potential is to be achieved, users must consciously seek it. In some organizations the materials function is not management's prime concern. Continued lack of management interest and commitment can defeat the objectives of competent procurement performance, causing a weak link in the total chain. The experience of many companies has shown that a relatively small amount of time and effort in the procurement area will provide a substantial return on investment. This is an opportunity which should be brought to the attention of the key decision makers.

An effective materials function can and must be highly responsive to the users needs in terms of quality, quantity, price, and delivery. It can also contribute policy objectives as well as the overall public and internal image of the organization. Those in the materials function cannot accomplish this without assistance and cooperation from suppliers, users, and others involved in the total process.

Progressive managers have recognized these potential contributions of the materials area and have taken the necessary steps to assure results. The most important single step in successful organizations has been the elevation to top executive status of the procurement manager. This, coupled with the provision of high-caliber staff and the appropriate authority and responsibility, has resulted in an exciting and fruitful exploration of the potential of the materials function.

BIBLIOGRAPHY

ALJIAN, GEORGE W., ed. *Purchasing Handbook*. 3d ed. New York: McGraw-Hill Book Co., 1973.

AMMER, DEAN S. *Materials Management*. 3d ed. Homewood, Ill.: Richard D. Irwin, Inc., 1974.

ANYON, G. JAY. *Managing an Integrated Purchasing Process*. New York: Holt, Rinehart & Winston, Inc., 1963.

BALLOU, RONALD H. *Business Logistics Management*. rev. ed. International Management Service. Englewood Cliffs, N.J.: Prentice-Hall, 1972.

BARLOW, C. WAYNE. *Purchasing for the Newly Appointed Buyer*. New York: American Management Association, 1970.

BERRY, H. A.   *Purchasing Management.* Waterford, Conn.: Bureau of Business Practices, Division of Prentice-Hall, Inc., 1964.

BUCKNER, HUGH.   *How British Industry Buys.* London, Eng.: Hatchinson, 1969.

COLTON, RAYMOND B.   *Industrial Purchasing, Principles and Practices.* Columbus, O.: Charles E. Merrill, 1962.

DANIEL, NORMAN E. AND JONES, J. RICHARD.   *Readings in Business Logistics Concepts and Viewpoints.* Boston: Allyn and Bacon, Inc., 1969.

DOWST, SOMERBY H.   *Basics for Buyers: A Practical Guide to Better Purchasing.* Boston: Cahners Books, 1971.

ENGLAND, WILBUR B.   *The Purchasing System.* Irwin Series in Operations Management. Homewood, Ill.: Richard D. Irwin, Inc., 1967.

FEARON, HAROLD E.   *Purchasing Economics.* New York: American Management Association, Purchasing Division, 1968.

GRAVEREAU, VICTOR P. AND KONOPA, LEONARD J., ed.   *Purchasing Management: Selected Readings.* Columbus, O.; Grid, Inc., 1973.

HEDRICK, FLOYD D.   *Purchasing Management in the Smaller Company.* New York: American Management Association, Inc., 1971.

HEINRITZ, STUART F., AND FARRELL, PAUL V.   *Purchasing: Principles and Applications.* 5h ed. Englewood Cliffs, N.J.: Prentice-Hall, Inc., 1971.

HESKETT, J. L., IVIE, ROBERT M.; AND GLASKOWSKY, NICHOLAS A., JR.   *Business Logistics Management of Physical Supply and Distribution.* 2d ed. New York: Ronald Press, 1973.

HODGES, HENRY G.   *Procurement—The Modern Science of Purchasing.* New York: Harper & Bros., 1961.

LEE, LAMAR, JR. AND DOBLER, DONALD W.   *Purchasing and Materials Management.* 2d ed. New York: McGraw-Hill Book Co., 1971.

LINDSAY, TAMLIN K.   *How Small Manufacturers Buy.* 2 vols. Storrs, Conn.: School of Business Administration, University of Connecticut, 1964.

McCONAUGHY, DAVID, ed.   *Readings in Business Logistics.* Homewood, Ill.: Richard D. Irwin, Inc., 1969.

McELHINEY, PAUL T. AND COOK, ROBERT I.   *The Logistics of Materials Management: Readings in Modern Purchasing.* New York: Houghton-Mifflin Co., Inc., 1969.

McMILLAN, ARCHIBALD LIVINGSTON.   *Purchasing.* Scranton: International Correspondence Schools, 1969.

MAGEE, JOHN F.   *Physical-Distribution Systems.* New York: McGraw-Hill Book Co., 1967.

MAGEE, JOHN F.   *Industrial Logistics: Analysis and Management of Physical Supply and Distribution Systems.* New York: McGraw-Hill Book Co., 1968.

MANENTE, MANFREDO.   *The Functions of the Purchasing Manager.* AMA Management Bulletin 132. New York: American Management Association, Inc., 1969.

NATIONAL ASSOCIATION OF PURCHASING AGENTS, INC.   *Guide to Purchasing.* New York, 1965.

PEGRAM, ROGER M.   *Purchasing Practices in the Smaller Company.* New York: Industrial Conference Board, 1972.

POOLER, VICTOR H. JR. *The Purchasing Man and His Job.* New York: American Management Association, 1964.

ROBINSON, P. J. AND FAIRIS, C. W. *Industrial Buying and Creative Marketing.* New York: Allyn and Bacon, Inc., 1967.

SCIENTIFIC AMERICAN. *How Industry Buys/1970.* New York: Scientific American, Inc., 1970.

SMITH, ALTON E. *New Techniques for Creative Purchasing.* Chicago: Dartnell, 1966.

SUSSAMS, J. E. *Industrial Logistics.* Boston: Cahners Books, 1972.

WESTING, J. H.; FINE, I. V.; ZENZ, GARY JOSEPH ET AL. *Purchasing Management.* 3d ed. New York: John Wiley & Sons, Inc., 1969.

WILLETS, WALTER E. *Fundamentals of Purchasing.* New York: Appleton-Century-Crafts, 1969.

CASES FOR CHAPTER 1

GREGORY ELECTRONICS COMPANY*

The company and the industry

The Gregory Electronics Company was a medium-size manufacturer of highly specialized electronic instruments and instruments systems, formed in 1950 to capitalize on the talents of the president and the research director. The company had gained a reputation for singular competence in its field. The research director, an acknowledged leader in the industry, had brought together a group of outstanding engineers. By 1964, the company was securing contracts from large aerospace firms and the government for both exploratory research and actual development of instrument systems. Gregory installed and operated some of its more complex instruments during test flights of primary equipment built by its customers. In 1963, about half the company's income was from electronic instruments and systems and the balance from engineering services. Over 500 of the 2,100 employees of the company in 1963 were professionally qualified. The company had grown rapidly, as shown in the following table:

Year	Sales (in millions)	Employees
1950	—	12
1955	$ 3.6	700
1960	18.2	1,800
1963	40.0	2,100

Recognizing the desirability of some diversification while capitalizing on the company's strengths, the president in 1964 directed research studies into oceanography and into other possible applications of the company's basic equipment.

In 1961, and again in 1963, after the company's over-420 percent increase in sales in six years, the president directed studies resulting in significant organizational changes to strengthen the corporate structure. The corporate staff, the staff services to line supervision, and the training of line supervision were enlarged and realigned, and positive plans for future growth were made. One of the major changes was in the materials functions.

The purchasing department and purchasing officer

During the early growth of the company, the responsibility for the materials function was divided. The manufacturing manager controlled manufacturing materials inventories, both raw stock and in-process, and the research director and the maintenance engineer each controlled his own materials storeroom. The purchasing supervisor reported to the office manager, who also had such diverse duties as central office management, personnel management, and security of plant and records. In the 1961 reorganization, however, these and other related functions were placed under a vice president for administration. To assist the vice president for administration in the materials function, a young, aggressive executive named Roger Johnston was brought in from a major appliance manufacturer, where he had been a successful senior buyer in the purchasing department. He was named materials manager and designated as the company purchasing agent, with responsibility for the purchase and control of materials and inventories up to the point of entry into research or production. (See Exhibit 1 for organization chart.)

Johnston recognized the difficulties to be encountered before he could make substantial changes in the purchasing organization, which had been allowed to drift by lack of specific attention. Over the years, the Gregory Company had developed a paternalistic labor policy, and employees were not released if other jobs could be found for them. Production department and engineering department employees who were not productive in those departments were brought into the office as clerks, and several were in the purchasing department as buyers and expediters. Their lack of abilities in buying had led to the engineers' selecting the sources and, frequently, setting the price on major or technical purchases. Requisitions sent to purchasing included the names of the source or sources; and, in many instances, the engineers told the salesman or the supplier's representative to ship orders, or to start production, prior to purchasing's receipt of the requisition. In almost all instances, the engineers would accept no other sources than those designated by them.

Exhibit 1
ORGANIZATION CHART

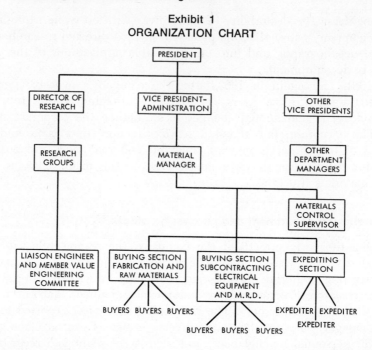

The buyers were thus reduced to order-placers in the buying of any important or technical material.

Johnston started a program to upgrade his purchasing personnel, along with changes to improve both the inventory control program and purchasing procedures. He revised job descriptions to state more specifically the duties of each position. He conducted a series of training sessions in purchasing procedures which served two purposes: it gave him information on the relative strengths of his people; and it gave them information on each other's abilities, making future changes more acceptable to each man and his associates. Based on this information, Johnston appraised each man and discussed the appraisal with him. Some of the less able men realized they were not qualified for the now more demanding jobs, and, as the company was still growing at a rapid rate, transfers were arranged to jobs for which they were better fitted. The personal appraisal discussions held by Johnston and the close cooperation of the personnel department made the transfers possible without dissatisfaction. Johnston also helped the more able men to design study programs to correct specific deficiencies. To fill vacancies, Johnston recruited college graduates with business degrees or men with engineering training. He had each new man spend a period as an expediter for technical material, while he studied both purchasing practices and company procedures. As soon as Johnston considered the man qualified for a buyer's position, he was promoted and placed in charge of purchasing for a category of materials.

Materials control

Along with this program of personnel improvement, Johnston revised materials control policies to reduce the volume of purchases required to service the expanded production and research facilities. An analysis of inventory characteristics and usage resulted in a new system of requisitioning and control of materials. About 300 items, representing 80 percent of the total dollar value of inventory, were to be closely controlled and frequently reviewed by one of Johnston's assistants, the materials supervisor. An inventory of government-owned materials would also be accounted for in detail, as required by government contractual practices. In the regular inventory, a second category of items, with monthly usage of $6 to $40, was to be reviewed monthly or at the time of a repurchase. A third category of items, with usage of less than $6 a month, was ordered by clerks using nomographs, the economic order points of which were based on a purchase order cost of $15 and a cost of possession of 2 percent of the inventory value. Any items of less than 19 cents cost per unit were carried in open bins on the production line or in the laboratories and used as needed by production and research personnel. For these materials, a two-bin system was used as a control device.

Better inventory control reduced the number of small purchases, as did maximum use of blanket purchase orders and period contracts. The smaller number of purchase actions gave the buyers time to pay particular attention to important or technically involved materials. As the purchasing organization, which included 2 senior buyers, 12 buyers, and 15 support personnel, began to provide prompt and knowledgeable service, the disharmony with engineering and research disappeared. The change was not immediate but came gradually as the result of the series of improvements in materials management. Eventually, Mr. Johnston was considered a member of the management team, and his advice, along with that of his key subordinates, was sought on appropriate questions. The choice of suppliers and the negotiation for price now became the responsibility of purchasing, though full consideration was given to source recommendations by engineering and research.

Technical information

In his efforts to further improve the support of engineering and research by his purchasing group, Johnston, in late 1963, made a study of the technical information flows into the materials department.

One source was the continual stream of industrial advertising and information material flowing into the company, which Johnston didn't think was very valuable as a source of technical information. Incoming mail was sorted in the administrative mail room. All mail, including commercial advertising, which was addressed to an individual or to a position, was distributed to the individual or the office. Johnston knew that much of this industrial advertising was discarded without being looked at by the receivers. Occasionally, a piece of advertising would be put on a route slip by one of the officers and addressed to several engineers or officers or both. In one instance he recalled, Johnston had received such mail from two different officers, after receiving directly and immediately discarding the same material. To get some "feel" as to the volume of this flow into his own office, Johnston saved all commercial advertising coming to his desk and those of his two principal assistants for four days and then summarized that accumulation of 112 pieces (see Exhibit 2 for summary). Two mailings were received in triplicate;

Exhibit 2
INDUSTRIAL ADVERTISING RECEIVED
DURING ONE FOUR-DAY PERIOD

No. of pieces	Type of information
33	Information about educational courses, books, and materials
7	Requests to be put on bidders' list
3	Requests for information about the company
52	Information about materials, processes, or equipment (exclusive of electronics)
17	Information about electronic materials, processes, or equipment
112	Total

one was in quadruplicate; and one was addressed to a purchasing agent who had left six years before. In addition, one list of contracts forwarded by a hopeful supplier as evidence of his capabilities was stamped "Confidential" in big letters on each page but was received without any explanation or instructions as to what his classification of "Confidential" meant. Johnston sent it back and remarked to the case writer that carelessness in marking or lack of specific attention in an advertising approach encouraged the recipient to throw it away without consciously absorbing the message. Seven pieces were from seven companies asking to be put on Gregory's bidding list, and one included the company's brochure listing firms now being supplied, with Gregory's name on the list as a current customer. Three pieces were requests for Gregory to supply information about the company, one being from *Thomas Register* and one from an institute interested in arranging management seminars. Fifty-two pieces were from companies giving information about materials, processes, or services; and 13 more pieces gave information about electronics.

As he had expected, the largest category of pieces concerned materials, processes, and services, but Johnston was surprised at the second largest category of mailings. It was composed of 33 pieces offering books, information, and programs about training sessions, educational courses, seminars, and conferences to be conducted by established organizations for the purpose of furthering the development of the active businessman. Most seminars were about purchasing or management, but one was about the writing of technical manuals, and one was about training for line supervisors. Johnston said he had noted there was some volume of this mail, but he had underestimated the number and the variety of offerings.

As to the value to the company of industrial advertising, Johnston said he considered the handling expense much larger than any value received. He knew that the engineers and other administrators must be getting similar quantities of mail, and he thought he might refer again to an article about a cost study on the receipt of industrial advertising made by a purchasing officer and reported in *Purchasing* magazine during early 1964.

Other sources of technical information flows using a written medium were supplier catalogs, trade journals, trade directories, and vendors' files. Johnston considered his coverage in these sources adequate, and he had them conveniently arranged for all users but had supplemented them with a VSMF (Vendors' Specifications Microfilm File) system. This was an information system, aimed at product data storage and fast retrieval, which had been on the market since 1960. The system consisted of a library of 16 mm. microfilm in cartridges, a printed product index, and a viewer with an automatic copy-making device. The library of information available applied to the aerospace and the electronic industries and included 100,000 pages of product data from over 3,100 vendors. The developers of the system were enlarging the number of suppliers covered. Included were specification sheets, engineering drawings, and catalog pages on components, materials, and equipment. A comprehensive index permitted very rapid search and retrieval for the information covered, and the automatic copy-making device permitted the engineer to take a copy of a print or specification back to his desk, if he so desired. The file was located in a room contiguous to the engineering and research departments on the floor above the purchasing department. Mr. Johnston said that it was used constantly by the engineers and scientists, looking for a piece of equipment or a component to satisfy a requirement in a design for a product or an experiment. The director of research was pleased with its use and said that its use resulted in many standard components being designed into new equipments, instead of special components being developed for the specific application. The designer could find quickly some adequate component already available in the market.

Johnston said his buyers seldom used the file, as the requisitions received usually had the file references listed as suggested sources. He considered that the best location for the file was next to the engineers. He related an experience of a friend of his wherein use of the file decreased considerably and the number of special purposes increased when the company's VSMF machine was relocated in the purchasing office.

In addition to the catalog and trade journal file in the purchasing office, most engineers had copies at their desks of these catalogs most useful to them.

Technical information from suppliers' representatives

Although the flow of industrial advertising was large and continuous, Mr. Johnston considered that the valuable flow of technical information from vendors came through contacts with vendors' sales and engineering representatives. When he was a buyer with his previous employer, Johnston was encouraged to visit the engineers in the laboratories once or twice a week to see what they were working on and ask what information about materials or processes would help them. These laboratory visits helped him to elicit information from salesmen or refer salesmen with valuable information to the engineer needing it. The buyers at the major appliance manufacturer were expected to be capable of recognizing the worth of new ideas and all suppliers' representatives were instructed to call on the purchasing department first.

At Gregory, however, Johnston found an added difficulty. Although some engineers were product-oriented and concerned with the redesign or design maintenance of a specific type of instrumentation, most of the scientists were oriented to a scientific discipline, and many of the materials and processes in which they were interested were unique or rare. The Gregory Company was recognized as a leader in new developments in two of its fields, and scientists working in these areas were concerned with concepts and material requirements three to five years ahead of present technology. They exchanged information with other scientists at scientific meetings and other professional gatherings and tried to stay current with other developments in their field through technical publications. These scientists and engineers, considering some sales representatives as sources of information on what other scientists were doing, scheduled their own appointments with suppliers salesmen and engineers.

As Mr. Johnston improved the service his department was giving to the research and engineering departments, the technical personnel began to have more confidence in the ability of the buyers; and fewer instances of violation of the company's policy on negotiations occurred. The policy was stated in a booklet called "How to Buy at Gregory," and a copy was given to each person who had authority to initiate a requisition. The last page of the booklet contained the following policy statement:

GENERAL

Authority to Negotiate—Only Purchasing Personnel are authorized to initiate, conduct, or conclude negotiations leading to a purchase order. Only such personnel can negotiate a change order affecting price, terms and delivery. Nonpurchasing personnel may make contacts with prospective vendors to secure technical information, but such contacts must not commit the company to a vendor directly or by inference.

The director of research was aware of the value of information to the creative process of his scientists, and he gave them various aids to stimulate the process. An extensive technical library, copies of professional and supplier's publications, attendance at professional meetings, and the Vendors' Specification Microfilm File were all available to the scientist. But he also realized that uncontrolled access to his scientists by suppliers' representatives would disrupt their creative efforts.

Security requirements made one control available. As the company was involved in work requiring information classified by the federal government, access of personnel to design and laboratory areas was restricted. Each supplier's representative called beforehand for an appointment, or the receptionist called the scientist and asked if he wanted to see the representative. But the director of research said he exercised no other control over appointments with his scientists.

Mr. Johnston was fully aware of the value to the company of technical information; and, as he considered commercial advertising ineffective, he wanted his department actively to contribute to the oral inflow of information from suppliers' representatives. He was encouraged by the increased confidence of the scientists in the buyers. Although the buyers made few visits to the laboratories to find out what the scientists were working on, Mr. Johnston himself sat in on planning meetings at which the future courses of major projects were charted and the present areas of problems and current needs, both material and informational, were considered. When such needs were specific, Mr. Johnston made contacts with possible suppliers or had his buyers do so. When the needs were not definite or immediate, he took no direct action but did discuss the direction of the company's efforts on the various projects with his buyers, and had the buyers keep looking for and asking about information in those fields.

Liaison engineer

As Mr. Johnston upgraded his buyers and the improved climate of confidence increased the use of the buyers by the scientists, the director of research assigned an engineer to act as liaison with the buyers, in addition to being the technical member in value engineering meetings.

The liaison engineer had broad engineering experience and was familiar with the various scientific fields. Whenever the buyer was uncertain about the value of information received from a supplier, he would arrange for the liaison engineer to meet with the supplier's representative to evaluate the value of this information.

About two years after the position of liaison engineer was created, the director of research was wondering about the value to research of the efforts of the liaison engineer and suggested that Mr. Johnston take him into the materials department. The director of research estimated that the annual cost to his department for the liaison engineer was $18,000.

The assignment as liaison engineer was the outgrowth of the engineer's effective performance as the technical member on the value engineering committee. The chairman of the committee was a production engineer who reported to the manufacturing manager, and both production and research engineers and buyers acted as members during discussions about these material questions with which they were knowledgeable. Although the scientists in research seldom attended value engineering meetings, the liaison engineer attended most meetings, and later he contacted those scientists who might have information about the product or material under analysis. He spent about 30 percent of his time in value engineering discussions or talking to scientists and engineers about products and research material problems and another 40 percent in talking to suppliers' representatives or discussing materials or processes with groups composed of scientists, buyers, production engineers, and suppliers' representatives. The remaining time was used on a specific design engineering project. Johnston knew that the liaison engineer had some experience in many design fields and that, with his pleasant personality, he was able to work with all categories of personnel. In fact, the engineer said he was spending so much time in liaison that his own design project was not progressing as rapidly as he would like.

Mr. Johnston knew of one instance in which the liaison function was valuable. In this instance, the liaison engineer and a buyer had been talking to a representative from a regular supplier about a change in the circuitry of an electronic component. The representative said that he did not think the change was feasible, unless the work being done by his company's engineers provided a better bond among one specific cluster of parts. The liaison engineer, recognizing the problem area as one which was troublesome to two Gregory scientists in the design of a new instrument, asked the representative to talk to the two scientists. The representative called his company and arranged a meeting among his company engineers, the two Gregory scientists, the liaison engineer, and himself. The supplier did additional research work, finally developing a satisfactory bond, and Gregory bought two special units to be used in the new instruments, as well as units of the new design for the production instruments.

In considering the suggestion of the director of research, Mr. Johnston was considering the liaison engineer's cost, how to evaluate his contribution to the company, and any changes that might occur as the consequence of a change in his organizational status.

LARIC CORPORATION INC.

Early in 1974, Mr. C. Moran, controller of A.G. Furniture, realized that he had accepted a substantial challenge in assuming the vice presidency of Laric Corporation. It was a new organization composed of ten small to medium furniture manufacturers located in Quebec, Canada. The corporation's principal objective was the pooling of its members' purchases in order to get better prices.

By January, 1974, only certain types of purchases had gone through Laric. Some of its members had not yet used Laric's services, as their own prices were equal to if not better than Laric's. In a market context of shortages and rising prices, Mr. Moran found it difficult to fulfill Laric's objectives.

Furniture industry

The Canadian furniture industry had broken the $1 billion sales mark in 1973. Quebec manufacturers accounted for about 40 percent of this volume, and Ontario supplied about 45 percent. Quebec produced 60 percent of the wooden furniture and Ontario 70 percent of the upholstered and about 80 percent of the metal furniture. There was some competition with U.S. firms but only at the higher price levels.

The Canadian industry included over 2,000 firms of which about 950 were furniture repair and upholstery shops. The household furniture manufacturing section numbered about 700, of which about 300 were located in Quebec. Household furniture manufacturers were typically small firms with limited capital. Furniture manufacturing was a small town industry because of its close association with lumbering and the continuing tradition of craftsmanship found in smaller centers.

Since the beginning of 1972, the industry was experiencing a boom period which was expected to continue through 1974. The Quebec manufacturers were reported as aggressive and fastest growing. One indication of the dynamism of furniture makers in Quebec was their sponsorship of not only the international furniture exposition in Montreal every year but the show in Toronto as well. There was also a trend towards merger into larger units able to finance sophisticated research, design, and marketing. Large Montreal companies, such as Warnock Hersey International and Molson Industries, had begun to put together a number of small producers into more efficient manufacturing complexes. Warnock Hersey, for example, bought seven companies with total sales of approximately $30 million. A smaller group of three companies located in Victoriaville was another example of merger but on a regional basis.

Total sales of the Quebec industry were estimated at $270 million in 1970 of which 60 percent were inside Quebec. The following exhibit shows the sales evolution since 1970.

Exhibit 1
SALES OF THE QUEBEC
FURNITURE INDUSTRY

Year	Sales ($ million)
1970	270
1971	290
1972	316
1973	400*

* Estimated.
Source: *Statistics Canada*, 1973.

Furniture sales were booming, but the industry was still beset by several problems. The Quebec industry was of high quality but still essentially conventional. In spite of major efforts in design modernization, it had not completed its evolution from a craft to a manufacturing process. It was facing problems in lumber procurement, technology, marketing, and labor. There were also difficulties with the rising prices of materials, slow deliveries, and the need to carry high inventories. Costs had escalated and since mid-1973, shortages were found in metal products and hardware, upholstery fabrics, and fuel oil. The immediate future of the industry was clouded by the shortage and price of lumber. For example, hardwood had more than doubled in price in the past 12 months. In August, 1973, in order to address the chronic lumber supply problem, the Quebec Furniture Manufacturers Association formed a purchasing consortium, St. Lawrence Wood Distributors, composed of 20 manufacturers. By January, 1974, it was still too early to determine what the outcome of this venture would be. Original plans for this consortium called for the purchase of 15 million board feet of lumber during its first year.

Laric's history

The original idea behind Laric had been conceived on a golf course after a game between Mr. B. Roy, president of Roy Furniture, an important manufacturer in the industry, and Mr. P. Labelle, promoter of a successful purchasing group in the furniture retailing area. They asked Mr. Dupre, a local lawyer, to join them and incorporated Laric in September, 1971. Quebec letters patent permitted the private company to dispense all services associated with the wood furniture industry and allied sectors like coffins, chesterfields, etc. The first directors were Mr. Roy, president, Mr. Labelle, vice president, and Mr. Dupre, secretary. They decided that the best way to approach prospective members would be the offering of a purchasing service for imported raw materials. To this end, they retained the services of an importer. As this man knew nothing about the industry, no concrete results were obtained. Nevertheless, they used the first year and a half to recruit seven members.

At the beginning of 1973, Mr. Moran, controller of A.G. Furniture, and Mr. Larue, president of Kay Furniture, whose companies were among the larger members of Laric, took the initiative to get Laric off the ground. In June, 1973, they both became directors, increasing the total to five, each one holding 20 shares of the corporation. The following month, the directors hired a competent purchasing agent, Mr. Proulx, to become the first full-time employee of the organization. (See Exhibit 2 for the organization chart.)

Exhibit 2
CORPORATION LARIC INC.
(organization chart)

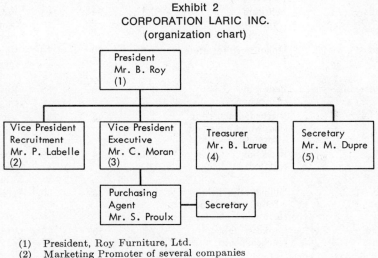

(1)   President, Roy Furniture, Ltd.
(2)   Marketing Promoter of several companies
(3)   Controller, A.G. Furniture, Ltd.
(4)   President, Kay Furniture, Ltd.
(5)   Lawyer

Laric's members

By the beginning of 1974, Laric totaled ten members. Most of them were small family enterprises. Total combined sales for Laric's members for 1973 amounted to $22 million and purchases to approximately $8 million. For 1974, an 18 percent sales increase was expected (see Exhibit 3 for data on each of the members). Anxious to ensure profitable operations, the board of directors chose its members carefully. Potential members were screened on the basis of their financial situation and willingness to cooperate.

Exhibit 3
LARIC CORPORATION INC.
(data on members)

Members*	Production (materials)	Sales for 1974 ($ million)	Raw materials sales %	Distance from Laric (miles)	Current buying done by (decision maker)
Roy Furniture, Ltd.	Bedroom, dining room (exotic veneers)	4.5	34	45	Buyer (president)
A. G. Furniture, Ltd.. . . .	Bedroom, dining-room (hardwood and exotic veneers)	6	34	25	Purchasing agent
Kay Furniture, Ltd.	Bedroom, dining-room (hardwood and exotic veneers)	4.5	34	0	Buyer (president)
Rempal, Ltd.	Bedroom (printed) (inferior category)	2.5	34	105	Production manager (president)
Suprem, Ltd.	Upholstered furniture	1.5	30	3	Buyer (general manager)
Bert Furniture, Ltd.	Bedroom (hardwood)	1	43	65	Buyer (president)
Touchette, Ltd..	Kitchen, dining-room (hardwood, plywood, formica, arborite)	1	48	280	Vice president
St. Jac, Ltd..	Bedroom (printed)	1.75	34	150	Buyer (general manager)
Paradis, Inc..	Dining-room, living-room, and bedroom (hardwood, plastic)	.75	36	80	Treasurer
Brossard, Ltd..	Bookcase, tables (particle board)	2.5	50	75	Vice president

* Names have been disguised.

The contract binding a member to Laric stipulated a corporation remuneration of 3 percent of the cost of the goods purchased through Laric (see Exhibit 4). In addition, an entrance fee of $3,000 was charged to cover the research done on a new member and to guarantee the member's seriousness. Members were not obliged to purchase through Laric. Mr. Moran expected future federal antitrust legislation forbidding an exclusive contract of that sort. In early 1974 it was still not clear

Exhibit 4
LARIC CORPORATION, INC.
MEMBERSHIP CONTRACT

Between: Laric Corporation, Inc., a legal body
                                             having its head office and main place of
                                             business in ....
And   herein called "Laric."
                                             herein called "Member."

Purpose: This contract is to make the members benefit from price reductions
while purchasing through Laric, as a consequence of the large volume transacted by the Corporation on behalf of all the members.

Fees: To become a member, a fee of three thousand dollars ($3,000.00)
must be paid to Laric, cash or convenient conditions acceptable by both
parties.

Duration: The present contract is for a period of three (3) years, said three
years beginning sixty (60) days after signing of the present agreement by
both, the member and Laric.

This contract will be renewed automatically for an additional period of
three years, without charge, unless a written notice is given to the Corporation,
by the member, ninety (90) days prior to the termination of the contract.

The member, who refuses or neglects to renew his contract, will have
to incur a new fee of three thousand dollars ($3,000.00) to be reinstated
as a member, except for special reasons over which only the board of directors
of Laric has jurisdiction.

Invoicing: The members will be invoiced at Laric's cost plus three percent
(3%) to cover administration expenses.

Payment: The members must pay their invoices as directed by Laric or
their subsequent orders may be refused.

In testimony whereof the parties have signed at   , this

Member   _____

                Laric Corporation, Inc.,
                By:
                _____

to Laric's management what percentage of member's purchases would
be channeled through Laric. An estimate of 40 percent was assumed
reasonable if Laric could get a well-organized service going.

Organization and functions

No director received direct payment for his services; consequently,
most of the daily work was executed by Mr. Proulx, the purchasing
agent. He and his secretary were the only two full-time employees.

After a contract was signed with a new member, Mr. Proulx had to make a detailed survey of the member's needs and means, involving transportation, receiving, stockroom, and production facilities, in addition to the financial and other management policies and procedures.

He had to obtain, or sometimes develop, forecasts for the production material requirements. He also inquired about the maximum and minimum levels of inventory the member wanted to keep in stock for its various commodities. Lastly, he tried to ascertain at what price the member would no longer be interested in dealing through Laric.

After he had surveyed the needs of every member, Mr. Proulx made a summary of the items common to all in order to find the potential amount of purchases for the group. Then quotations were sought. Mr. Proulx looked after all negotiations with suppliers. After he had obtained what he considered an acceptable price, he checked to see which members wished to take advantage of the offer. He sent copies of quotations to members by mail and received the same copy back with comments if a member wished to pursue the offer. He also telephoned members to inform them of a buying opportunity and to check whether they were interested. He was in touch by telephone with each member at least once a week, whether the member was currently using his services or not.

The purchase order form used by Laric was a standard three-copy document on which the Laric name was stamped. The first copy was sent to the supplier, and the two others were kept in Laric's files for alphabetical and numerical reference. Mr. Proulx did not consider the present form to be the best vehicle possible but used it in the short term for simplicity and economy. Goods purchased through Laric were invoiced and sent directly to the member. Mr. Proulx received a copy of the supplier's invoice and charged 3 percent of its amount to the member. An exception was lumber on which the commission was fixed at $6.00 for 1,000 board feet for all species. Laric had experienced some difficulties in getting suppliers to send a copy of the invoice back to Laric. Although the purchase order had a stamp requesting confirmation by return mail and a copy of the invoice, suppliers frequently ignored this. Consequently, Mr. Proulx had prepared a standard form letter, to accompany each purchase order, requesting invoice copies so that members could be properly charged (see Exhibits 5 and 6).

Laric's long-term prospects

Laric Corporation, according to its management, could be considered a type of endeavor to overcome the industry's main problems. "The small companies in grouping themselves," Mr. Moran said, "are able to get hospital prices instead of pharmacy prices on their raw materials. That way they can have at least the same advantages as our biggest members. This can mean, in certain cases, more than a 20 percent discount."

Exhibit 5
LARIC CORPORATION, INC.
(specimen purchase order)

CORPORATION LARIC Inc. C.P. 229 ARTAN, Que. Tel: (819) 321.8942	FACTURER &		**11500** VEUILLEZ MENTIONNER CE NUMÉRO SUR TOUS COLIS, FACTURES ET CORRESPONDANCE. THIS NUMBER MUST APPEAR ON ALL PACKAGES, INVOICES AND CORRESPONDENCE.

À / TO   TUC FOREST PRODUCTS LTD.   EXPÉDIER À / SHIP TO   KAY. FURNITURE LTD.
                                                                      12 RUE CÔTE,
454 OUEST, BEAUCHAMP   ARTAN, Que.
MONTREAL, QUE. ATT.:   JEAN VENNE   ATT.   DATE 21 JANVIER '74

VIA CAMION   PAYÉ / PREPAID [X]   CONTRE REMBOURSEMENT / COLLECT [ ]   F.A.B. / F.O.B. DESTINATION   CONDITIONS / TERMS 2%-30 JOURS

VEUILLEZ NOUS FOURNIR LES MARCHANDISES SUIVANTES SELON LES CONDITIONS CI-DESSOUS MENTIONNÉES   DATE DE LIVRAISON / DATE REQUIRED   2 SEMAINES OU MIEUX
PLEASE SUPPLY THE FOLLOWING GOODS SUBJECT TO THE CONDITIONS SPECIFIED BELOW

QUANTITÉ QUANTITY	DESCRIPTION		PRIX PRICE
18 à 20M	PMP Frêne*blanc 4/4 no. 2 Com. & Meilleur	FAS	$480./M'
	(2 voyages de trailer)	Select	$460./M'
		No. 1C	$380./M'
	PAS PLUS DE 10%	No. 2C	$225./M'
	CONFIRMATION DE NOTRE COMMANDE TELEPHONIQUE DE CE JOUR		
	REFERENCE NO. 11500 DOIT APPARAITRE SUR TOUS DOCUMENTS		
	VOTRE MESUREMENT NOTRE INSPECTION. POUR DECHARGEMENT		
	AVEC FORK LIFT TRUCK DONC PAQUETS DE 4' x 4'		
	L.T.V.F. No. S-48309		
	L.T.V.P. No. 209-MB-4720-1-PH		
	VEUILLER CONFIRMER CHAQUE POINT DE CETTE COMMANDE PAR RETOUR DE COURRIER. PLEASE CONFIRM BY RETURN MAIL EACH ITEM OF ORDER. *IMPORTANT:UNE COPIE DE FACTURE DOIT ÊTRE MALLEE A NOS BUREAUX. COPY OF INVOICE SHOULD BE MAILED AT ONCE OUR OFFICE.		

CORP. LARIC INC.

SIGNATURE   *Serge Proulx*

Laric continued to seek new members, and it was expected that, in the long run, at least 20 members might belong. Mr. Moran and Mr. Proulx were well aware that future growth was heavily dependent on the abiity to offer worthwhile services. As a first step, therefore, Mr. Proulx's current performance was a vital indicator to current and prospective members.

In addition to the possibility of getting better prices, the corporation

Exhibit 6
LARIC CORPORATION, INC.
(standard form letter)

January 21, 1974

Tuc Forest Products, Ltd.,
454 Beauchamp West,
Montreal, Que.

Attention: M. Jean Venne
Attention: Receivable Accounts

Dear Sir:
   You will find enclosed our purchase order no. 11500 to· be INVOICED
and shipped to Kay Furniture, Ltd.
   As requested on our purchase order, please send us a copy of the invoice
the same day that the original will be mailed to the member.
   As this is of prime importance for the smooth functioning of our system,
we rely on your cooperation.

Yours truly,
LARIC CORPORATION INC.

Serge Proulx

Serge Proulx,
Purchasing Agent.

SP/b

attempted to sell its members on the idea of a better purchasing service.
Only one member could afford a real purchasing agent. Mr. Proulx
offered more security of supply in raw materials, an increase in the
number of sources, a potential inventory reduction, and the opportunity
to relieve the members from the procedural tasks.
   In the long run, Mr. Moran considered the possibility of offering
financial or legal consulting services. The board of directors was well
endowed for this purpose, having as secretary a lawyer, specialist in
labor relations, and two others were experienced financiers. The corporation might eventually provide the services of a designer or an industrial
engineer. Most of the members did not need full-time employees in
these fields. Mr. Moran also foresaw the possibility of future mergers.
   In the short term, he expected that Laric would receive and pay
all supplier's bills itself. Mr. Proulx thought this would provide an opportunity for additional income, as the corporation could take advantage
of cash discounts. He said: "Presently about 80 percent of the raw materials suppliers are allowing cash discounts but nine of our ten members
are not taking them." Goods could eventually be delivered to Laric
which would then need stockroom, receiving, and shipping facilities
and also its own trucks. Mr. Proulx was aware that direct payment

of suppliers' bills and central receiving could not be done without: (1) a stronger financial position at Laric; (2) a well-established purchasing system; and (3) at least twice as many members.

Laric's first purchases

Until the beginning of 1974, 75 percent of Laric's purchases on behalf of its members had been of particle board. The remaining purchases had been primarily of species of lumber which were in short supply like walnut, elm, and ash. A few types of veneers, plywood, screws, and standard hardware had also been bought. Almost all purchases had been made from wholesalers with the exception of a few items like sandpaper and screws, which had been bought directly from manufacturers. Exhibit 7 shows the dollar volume of purchases and commissions from those members who used the corporation since August, 1973.

Laric's problems

In January, 1974, one of the main problems the corporation faced was the difficulty of obtaining interesting discounts. Because of rising demand and growing scarcities, almost all raw materials were in a seller's market. For example, 12 months previously, the price of particle board or "rip" was $95 for 1,000 board feet; by November, 1973, it was about $195, and it was expected to reach $210 by February, 1974.

Price at the Time of Shipment (PTS) stamps on confirmations of orders were becoming a current practice. Few suppliers could guarantee the price at delivery time. Two years earlier, it had been possible to confirm prices for materials to be delivered 12 months later.

Laric had to obtain at least a 5 percent discount in order to guarantee a justification for the member to adhere to the group. This discount was reduced to only 2 percent after the commission of 3 percent to Laric was deducted. Obtaining good discounts ran into the major problem of recognition by suppliers as an important buying group. Wholesalers were reluctant to cooperate with Laric, an eventual competitor, afraid that Laric would go directly to the mills. Their salesmen were afraid to lose their commission as Laric would become a house account. In the present market, many manufacturers were protecting their wholesalers and were actively discouraging distribution channel bypasses.

Attracting profitable new members into Laric was becoming increasingly difficult. The philosophy of the corporation was quite new in the industry. Many of the companies approached found the idea good on paper but were not convinced of its practicability.

The situation of the larger members in Laric was troublesome. A.G. Furniture, for example, of which Mr. Moran was the controller, had bought nothing yet through the corporation. It was the largest member

Exhibit 7

LARIC CORPORATION, INC.

(purchases—commissions)

1973	Brossard A	Brossard C	Touchette A	Touchette C	Bert A	Bert C	Kay A	Kay C	Rempal A	Rempal C	St. Jac A	St. Jac C	Total A	Total C
August......	—	—	662	21	—	—	—	—	—	—	—	—	662	21
September....	—	—	9,783	135	2,339	70	—	—	—	—	—	—	12,122	205
October.....	—	—	—	—	6,661	201	8,575	200	—	—	2,517	292	17,753	693
					5,310*	159*	15,566*	467*	3,375*	101*			24,251*	727*
November.....	8,871	265	156	4			6,325	111			3,206*	96	18,558	476
											58,620*	1,759*	58,620*	1,759*
December....	10,129	304	292	9	248	7					15,059	452	25,728	772
Paid........	136	4	10,601	161	9,000	271	10,479	236			9,797	292	40,013	964
To be received..	3,848	115	180	5	248	7					7,223	217	11,499	344
Orders not delivered......	15,016	450	112	3	5,310	159	19,987	542	3,375	101	62,382	2,090	106,182	3,345
Total $.......	19,000	569	10,893	169	14,558	437	30,466	778	3,375	101	79,402	2,599	157,694	4,653

* Blanket orders.

with purchases amounting to $2 million. As it had enough volume, it was able to get the same prices as Laric. In the long run, if Laric met its growth objectives, it could become interesting for A.G. Furniture. Recently A.G. Furniture had attempted to bring pressure on Laric, asking for compensation since it was because of its participation in the group that the others could get better prices. It had suggested that Laric's 3 percent charge should be dropped for A.G. Furniture. Mr. Proulx could not determine exactly why certain other members had not used Laric's services to date. His best information was that they apparently thought they could do as well or better on their own.

Mr. Moran hoped that Laric's financial picture in 1973 would show a break-even operation. He estimated that annual purchases of $1.5 million with a 3 percent commission would be enough to meet current expenses. He realized that break-even operation would not be acceptable to the directors in the longer run. Further financing would be required if Laric was to expand its range of services. Where such funds would come from was not clear to him yet.

Mr. Moran was convinced that if Laric Corporation reached a certain degree of maturity, it would be profitable for both its shareholders and its members. With Laric's present resources and problems, he was wondering what measures should be adopted to get through this difficult period.

BARBER BUILDING SUPPLIES

In July, 1973, Mr. Bill Hope was hired as general manager of Barber Building Supplies. During his first few months on the job he became very concerned about a number of problems in the organization, including the way purchasing functioned. Mr. Diamond, president and owner of Barber wanted to retire in a few years and wished to groom Bill Hope as his successor. He had given the new general manager free rein to do as he pleased. "You prove to me that you can handle this business, and it will be yours," he said. Bill Hope was a graduate of a well-known school of business administration. He was 34 years old and had several years retailing and marketing experience.

Company background

In November, 1973, Barber was celebrating its fifth year of operation. The company had grown from a small lumber yard to a combined retail lumber, building supplier, and home care center with annual sales of $1.6 million. In addition, the company had in 1972 invested $65,000 in the construction and equipping of a plant producing prefabricated trusses, a combination of wooden beams arranged in a group of triangles.

The beams formed a rigid framework and were used in house construction for supporting the roof. This operation now yielded $150,000 per year in additional sales.

Of the company's sales, 50 percent were to contractors in the form of rough lumber and associated construction materials. The remaining 50 percent were retail sales in the home center product line, including hardware, flooring materials, carpeting, lamps, ceiling fixtures, decorative wall paneling, room dividers and gardening utensils.

Barber employed 27 people in November, 1973, down from 39 in July. Bill Hope in the first few months weeded out what he called "fat in the system." He said: "When I arrived here, most people spent the day standing around looking at each other. Most of them had been with Barber from the start. I asked lots of questions for which there were no answers. Some quit because of the pressure; others, I fired. We still have too many people." (See Exhibit 1 for the current organization chart.)

Exhibit 1
BARBER BUILDING SUPPLIES
(organization chart)

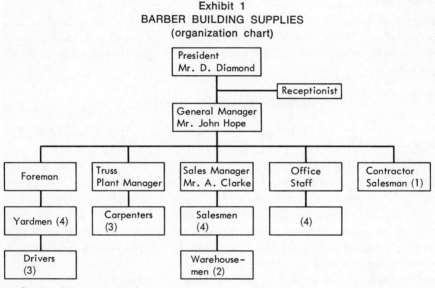

Source: Company records.

The retail building supply business

The retail building supply business in North America was undergoing rapid change. Bill Hope said: "According to a market study, Americans spend over $25 billion a year on their homes—building rumpus rooms, refinishing basements, and just puttering around. But instead of spending most of it in the retail lumber yards, as we used to, more Americans now take their do-it-yourself business to retail home centers. The growing market has attracted such concerns as K-Mart, Sears, and other large firms into the home care center business. Consequently, we are competing with large organizations with sophisticated mass merchandising techniques. These people have tremendous purchasing power which we smaller dealers don't enjoy. It seems to be an industry-wide trend for suppliers to try and take advantage of the lack of sophistication of the little guys—cute tricks like short shipping, double-invoicing, and the like. It's getting tougher to be in the business all the time."

Purchasing at Barber

In the 1972–73 fiscal year, sales totaled $1.6 million; purchases were $1 million and profit after tax was $28,000. Mr. Diamond said: "Because the industry is so price sensitive, and because mark-ups tend to be so low, purchasing is an essential ingredient of success in this business." Bill Hope added: "Lumber yards have always been based on sound purchasing. However, many times we worry so much about how much it costs us to put it on the shelf and about how many hot deals we get that we lose sight of the fact that we have to sell it. Because of the price sensitivity of the consumer and the apparent inability (at least at this point in time) to forecast customer demand with any reliability or accuracy, purchasing and inventory control can be key factors in generating profits for this company."

When Bill Hope arrived in July, 1973, he found the purchasing system strange. In his own words: "Anybody and everybody was purchasing, from the salesmen to the yard men and truck drivers. A person who wanted something simply picked up a purchase order, filled it in, and had it processed through one of the secretaries. Or worse yet, anybody could phone a supplier and not bother with a purchase order at all."

The purchasing situation will be described under the following headings:

1. Ascertainment of need.
2. Selection of source of supply.
3. The purchase order.
4. Follow-up.
5. Receiving and payment.
6. Problems in purchasing.

1. Ascertainment of need. The order procedure at Barber was informal and unstructured. In the absence of a defined inventory control system, the primary method of determining need was by periodic visual check. The check of items in stock on the shelves of the sales floor was carried out by the sales manager, Mr. Clarke, and to some extent by his staff of salesmen. There were no prescribed inspection cycles (one per week, one per month, etc.). The salesmen normally noticed low stocks after the sale of a particular item. At this point, they completed a "Low Stock Card" and forwarded it to Mr. Clarke. Depending on the urgency of demand for the item and the dollar value, these cards were accumulated by Mr. Clarke until:

1. A company representative visited Barber (there were normally eight calls by various salesmen per week); or
2. Sufficient quantity was generated to qualify for the prepaid shipping terms granted by supplying companies (normally a 200-pound minimum).

It was not unusual to run low of certain supplies unexpectedly, either in the truss plant or the sales floor. Then anyone could phone a supplier and ask for immediate delivery of the item in question. Mr. Clarke and Mr. Diamond had jointly looked after most of the lumber purchases and the acquisition of new lines. Mr. Diamond had traditionally been responsible for most capital investment and carload purchases. Mr. Clarke usually purchased for all 2,500 items carried on sales floor shelves.

2. Selection of source of supply.   The source of supply was determined by the class of item desired. Lumber was purchased primarily from brokers who periodically contacted Barber. If an urgent need existed for lumber to augment low stocks or to meet a large customer order, Mr. Diamond or Mr. Clarke would contact a number of brokers to obtain lumber. This process took up to a day for one carload. Lead time for delivery of shipments varied from three to four days if the car was on the rails, up to 16 weeks or longer on hard-to-get items.

In many cases, the purchase process was initiated by brokers who had lumber on hand for disposal. In this case, Barber management had to make an extremely fast analysis of stock on hand, demand (turnover), price trends, and the offered price. Often Mr. Diamond or Mr. Clarke had five minutes or less to make a purchase decision, particularly if the broker was calling from the West Coast and substantial long distance charges were involved. If, based on their analysis, the shipment was deemed to be a good deal, the purchase was made. Mr. Diamond estimated that most of their lumber business was carried out with ten brokers.

Most of the estimated 2,500 items displayed on the sales floor shelves were purchased from some 50 wholersaler and factory representatives. These representatives visited Barber at various intervals to take orders and to maintain and service their respective product displays. Three of the major wholesalers' representatives visited twice weekly. It had been Mr. Diamond's stated management policy that cordial relations be established and maintained with sales representatives.

For specialty items not normally carried by Barber, the sales department maintained a large collection of dealers' and manufacturers' catalogs for ordering references and prices. Mr. Clarke stated that very little "shopping" was done when purchasing most items. He placed a premium on supplier service and reliability and felt that these factors more than offset the small price savings he might realize through "shopping." The president, Mr. Diamond, also placed a premium on supplier service.

3. *Purchase order.* Over 70 percent of Barber's purchasing was carried out by telephone. The remaining orders were placed directly with salesmen calling on the firm. A purchase order was prepared by the receptionist or one of the three girls on the office staff. Because of the telephone ordering procedure, no copy of the purchase order was sent to the supplier. The prime purpose for purchase order preparation was to provide information for the cost book (see Exhibit 2). This

Exhibit 2
BARBER BUILDING SUPPLIES
(sample sheet from manual
cost book)

Date	Item	Supplier	Cost	Sc. & Freight	Total Cost	Prod. Code	Retail	Retail Code	Cash Price	Retail Code
July / 73	2 x 2 Spruce	Ore. Hard.	05½	P-5 8/10	05½	20	10	18	9½	15
July / 73	2 x 3 Spruce		07½	P-7 8/10	07½	20	12½	16	11½	14
July / 73	2 x 4 #1 Struct.	Ore. Hard.				21				
July / 73	2 x 4 Constr. R/L 2 x 4 Constr. to 14'	Ore. Hard.	152.50	P-13 3/10	12 6/10	21	16¢	10	15½	8
June / 73	2 x 4 Precuts 93"	Ore. Hard. Falcon	135.00 165.00	P-93	88	21	1.24	15	1.16 1.12	12 11
Feb / 73	2 x 4 Precuts 86½"	Falcon	132.00		70 4/10	21	1.24	15	1.16 1.00	12 6
July / 73	2 x 6 Constr. to 16'	Falcon	184.00	P-19 4/10	18 4/10	22	27	16	26 23	14 10

NOTES: The retail code columns were profit code figures used by Barber in pricing items. These were 25 profit codes, each one representing a percentage of selling cost above total cost. For example, on the sample sheet for 2 × 2 Spruce, the total cost was 05½¢. The selling price for a charge sale was 10¢ and the profit code was 18. For a cash sale the selling price was reduced to 9½¢ and the profit code reduced to 15.

book, kept manually, contained a record of all purchases and was used by Mr. Diamond and Mr. Clarke to determine prices in advance of delivery. When the occasion warranted, new price lists were prepared by the receptionist for use by the salesmen. When landed cost could not be determined at the time the purchase order was prepared, a pricing decision would be delayed until the supplier's invoice arrived.

One copy of the purchase order was filed on a spindle file in the sales area for reference by sales personnel. The second copy was filed numerically in a purchasing file.

4. *Follow-up.* There was no formal follow-up system to ensure on-time delivery of an order. When a "tickler file" of purchase orders arranged by due date was suggested as a possible method by one of the salesmen, Mr. Hope said that such a system had been tried elsewhere and that experience has shown that such a system required the full-time attention of one of his salesmen. Mr. Clarke said that his people were able to remember large orders and to initiate follow-up action on these orders when the due date drew near.

5. *Receiving and payment.* There were two principal receiving areas at Barber, the warehouse in the lumberyard where rail cars and large truckloads of lumber were received, and the small area at the back of the store for materials for the sales floor shelves and displays.

The yard foreman was charged with receiving lumber shipments, checking for quantity, and for informing Mr. Diamond, Mr. Clarke, or the office manager of any shortages, damage, or other discrepancies between the shipment and the shipping slip.

Shipments arriving at the rear of the store were checked in a similar fashion by the receiver. He, in turn, advised Mr. Clarke of any discrepancies between the shipment and the shipping slip.

If there were discrepancies between the shipping slip and the shipment received, Mr. Clarke noted the discrepancy and attached an information slip to the package. He also notified the supplier involved in order to obtain a credit note for the difference. Normally, no problems were involved in obtaining credit notes if the company involved was a regular Barber supplier.

When the supplier's invoice arrived, the bookkeeper looked after payment, making sure that cash discounts were taken. Approximately 600 invoices were processed a month, and the bookkeeper attempted to even out the work, avoiding a backlog.

Purchasing problems

The present purchasing system seemed to work well according to Mr. Diamond. It had served the organization during five years of substantial growth and was simple with a minimum of red tape and paperwork. Suppliers were generally reliable, and good relations existed with sales representatives and brokers.

Mr. Hope did not share this view and had a number of points of concern. Under the present system a number of orders were placed for which no purchase order was prepared. Thus, no record existed, creating the risk that a second order for the same item might be placed or that a supplier might send goods which had not been ordered. Moreover, anyone could initiate a purchase order, leading to confusion in responsibilities.

Purchase orders were not checked against invoices, because Mr. Clarke considered this a waste of time. Mr. Hope had recently spent several weeks at home at night and on weekends going over purchase orders and invoices placed during the first six months of 1973. He found that discrepancies in shipments, prices, shipping terms and double invoicing had cost Barber at least $50,000 during this period.

A recent incident with a lumber broker had placed in question the telephone ordering procedure. Barber had not received a carload of lumber containing 54,000 board feet ordered from a broker, because the $25,000 order had not been confirmed in writing. The load had been sold in advance of receipt, and Mr. Hope estimated it had cost Barber an additional $5,000 to secure an alternate supply at an inflated price in a hurry. Customer goodwill had also suffered from this incident because delivery was still a week late. Rapidly increasing prices, lengthening lead times, and shortages in the marketplace created further worries for Mr. Hope. He was not sure how much time he could spend personally on the purchasing function, because of the other duties of his position. He was not satisfied that the area was running smoothly and wanted improvements but was not sure where and how to begin.

JEAN PRINCE, LTD.

Jean Prince, Ltd., was an integrated producer of canned vegetables. Most vegetables were contracted by the company with local farmers. The company did most of its harvesting with its own equipment. Purchases accounted for an important part of the product cost and were decentralized.

The president, Mr. Lemay, looked after can purchases. He was also responsible for the purchases of cardboard and sugar. The sales manager bought the labels; and the production manager, an agronomist, negotiated the vegetable contracts with farmers and also bought the seeds, fertilizers, and all other factory and agricultural materials.

Spare parts for manufacturing and farming equipment represented an important expenditure. Each price of equipment had to be reconditioned during the off-season. Mr. Lemay suspected that most maintenance purchases were done in a haphazard manner as there was no purchasing agent nor stockkeeper in charge. He wondered if it would be advantageous for his company to hire a buyer/storekeeper for the management of spare parts.

Company background

Jean Prince, Ltd., was founded in 1929 by Mr. J. Prince, a northern Vermont farmer. In 1964 Mr. Prince sold his enterprise to a large financial organization for the sum of $4.5 million. Mr. Lemay, president of the company since 1964, bought the enterprise in 1972. Jean Prince, Ltd., was one of Vermont's largest canneries with sales amounting to $10 million in 1973.

The company produced many kinds of canned vegetables. Beans accounted for more than 50 percent of its sales. According to Mr. Lemay, the keys to the success of his enterprise were the first-rate quality of its products and a competitive pricing strategy.

Production facilities were located 35 miles north of Burlington. Headquarters, including the sales and accounting departments, were in Burlington (see Exhibit 1 for the organization chart). The seasonal nature

Exhibit 1
JEAN PRINCE, LTD.
(organization chart)

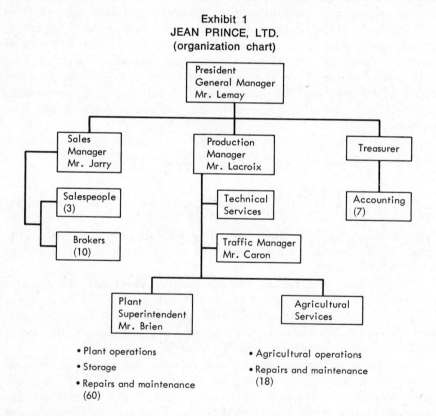

of the company's activities was reflected in the variation of the number of employees: from 100 during the winter season up to 450 in summer time. The company cultivated about 20 percent of its vegetables on rented lands; the balance was contracted with approximately 600 local farmers. In April, farmers sowed their fields with seeds supplied by Jean Prince, Ltd. Crops depended heavily on the farming conditions; for example, 1,000 acres could produce from 20,000 to 80,000 cases[1] of peas. The canning operations started at the end of June with peas and finished in late September or early October with carrots, potatoes, and beets. Seasonal employees were recruited among students and people normally on welfare. Total employee turnover reached 1,200 people during the summer. The short harvesting season necessitated intensive use of equipment and almost no machinery servicing. Approximately 80 people, mainly supervisory staff during the summer, stayed during the off-season and most of them were committed to the maintenance and reconditioning of agricultural and factory equipment.

The president said that sales had not been satisfactory because of poor crops in 1972 and 1973. However, prices had increased, and Jean Prince's profits had improved (see Exhibits 2 and 3). In 1974 Mr. Lemay

Exhibit 2

JEAN PRINCE, LTD.

Income Statement
Year ended December 31, 1973,
with comparative figures for 1972
(in $1,000)

	1973	1972
Net sales	$10,005	$10,493
Cost of goods sold	7,650	8,711
Gross margin.	2,355	1,782
Storage.	130	153
Distribution	9	13
Sales	446	530
Administration	679	615
Finance	218	253
Total expenses	1,482	1,564
Net operating profit	873	214
Other income	235	65
	1,108	279
Other expenses	71	36
Pretax profit.	1,037	243
Tax provision	484	99
Net profit	553	144
Depreciation.	333	312
Cash flows	$ 886	$ 456

expected to exceed the $11 million sales forecast. The profitability of the company during the past years had not been sufficient to pay dividends, finance inventories, and maintain adequate cash flows. Therefore, Mr. Lemay had to rely heavily on bank loans to meet his financial

---

[1] One case contains 24 cans of 19 ounces each.

Exhibit 3

JEAN PRINCE, LTD.

Balance Sheet
Year ended December 31, 1973,
with comparative figures for 1972
(in $1,000)

	1973	1972
Assets		
Current assets		
Cash	$ (84)	$ (164)
Accounts receivable	708	760
Inventory	5,424	4,476
Other.	348	456
Total current assets	6,396	5,528
Net fixed assets	2,346	2,541
Other assets	270	277
Total assets	$9,012	$8,346
Liabilities		
Current liabilities		
Bank loan	2,639	1,092
Notes payable		1,635
Accounts payable.	475	234
Other.	845	451
Total current liabilities	3,959	3,412
Long-term debt	850	964
Deferred income tax	430	431
Shareholders' equity	3,773	3,539
Total liabilities	$9,012	$8,346

obligations. "The canning industry is capital intensive," he explained, "with equipment working only a few weeks a year. Stock turnover is only about one and inventory costs are very high."

Production purchasing activities

Raw materials and packaging supplies accounted for more than 70 percent of the product cost (Exhibit 4 is a list of main purchases and their approximate value for 1973). Mr. Lemay explained that the highly seasonal nature of the business forced him to keep the number of permanent employees to a minimum. The company had no purchasing department nor any standard purchasing procedures. As there was no requisition form, internal purchasing communications were mostly verbal and done on a day-to-day basis during the canning period. The president was involved in strategic decisions concerning certain purchases. The production manager, Mr. Lacroix, was responsible mainly for determination of quantities, supplier choice, and price negotiations for purchases not looked after by the president or the sales manager, Mr. Jarry. Mr. Caron, traffic manager, prepared the purchase orders and did the expe-

Exhibit 4

JEAN PRINCE, LTD.

List of Main Purchases for 1973

Products	Approximate annual value (in $1,000)
Cans	$2,418
Vegetables	1,357
Seeds	624
Sugar	366
Spare parts.	264
Cartons.	216
Labels	158
Fuel	66
Starch	53
Fertilizers	46

diting during the summer season. The plant superintendent, Mr. Brien, was responsible for controlling inventories of materials according to minimum and maximum stock policies. Foremen sent daily inventory reports of the main materials to the superintendent who communicated his needs to Mr. Caron. Mr. Lacroix signed almost every purchase order.

Cans. Cans had always been a major purchase. For the past 30 years, the company had bought cans exclusively from American Can Company. The president explained that Jean Prince, Ltd., was tied to this supplier as it had been renting canning machinery from American Can since the founding of the enterprise. This machinery was worth $450,000 in 1974. Mr. Lemay said the purchasing process of cans was very simple, almost automatic year after year. He did not sign a contract. Mr. Lacroix established required quantities for each size of can for the complete season. These quantities were based on the sales manager's forecasts. Mr. Lacroix had given the responsibility for the day-to-day purchasing releases to Mr. Caron. The main decision Mr. Lemay had to make was to determine which quantity should be bought in the preseason. American Can offered an important discount on cans delivered before June. The company had traditionally taken delivery of almost half of its total can requirements in advance to take advantage of this discount.

Vegetables. Contract negotiations for vegetables were made in early spring and usually took a few days. Mr. Lacroix, agronomist by profession, was in charge of these negotiations. He dealt with 12 local or regional producers' representatives and their president. Mr. Lacroix proposed tariffs for each kind of vegetable. These tariffs were based on the real cost per acre for each type of culture. The company experimental farm provided these cost data. Mr. Lacroix added what he considered a reasonable profit and submitted tariffs to the negotiation committee.

Producers' representatives insisted that Mr. Lemay be present at these negotiations. Contracts were written only after an oral agreement was reached. Then, a Jean Prince representative visited each of the 600 producers to sign individual contracts. Jean Prince, Ltd., sowed on rented lands what producers did not want to grow on their lands.

Other purchases related to agricultural operations. Seeds had to be bought one year in advance. Mr. Lacroix thought negotiation for this purchase was not possible. The cost of seeds had risen 40 percent from 1973 to 1974. Mr. Lacroix expected prices to double in 1975. He dealt with two main suppliers and three secondary ones. Producers were required to buy their seeds from Jean Prince who sold the seeds to them at cost price.

Fertilizers and pesticides were also important items. Normally, Mr. Lacroix tried to obtain quotations from suppliers. However, in 1974 suppliers would not commit themselves for any price. Mr. Lacroix recommended to Mr. Caron what share of purchases to give to each supplier.

Other purchases related to the canning operations. Sugar was a highly speculative item mainly used in the canning of corn and peas, and the president felt he had to assume personally the risk associated with this purchase. Mr. Lemay's role was to determine when to buy and from whom. Normally, a contract was signed for the complete season with a provision made in case of a contract surplus at the end of the canning period. For the coming season, he was still unsure whether he should sign a contract or buy at market prices.

Mr. Lemay was also involved in the purchasing of corrugated cartons. He said that finding packaging at this time was as difficult as finding raw materials and that successful purchases depended on the company's relationship with its suppliers. Mr. Lemay tried to keep three carton suppliers: two sharing in equal parts the bulk of the cardboard requirements and the third as a watch-dog.

Mr. Lacroix looked after the other factory purchases like salt, starch, glue, etc. Most of these items were purchased only once a year. He said that normally these purchases were quite easy to handle.

The president had delegated responsibility for labels purchases to the sales manager. Mr. Jarry determined quantities based on his sales forecasts, asked for quotations, and gave his recommendations to Mr. Lemay for final approval. The sales manager usually dealt with two suppliers. He ordered labels only once a year. The purchase order had to be sent at least four months in advance because of the long lead time. The traffic manager looked after label delivery instructions during the canning season.

Mr. Lemay was quite happy with the present production purchasing system, which he thought was running smoothly considering available resources. However, he was concerned about the off-season purchasing activities.

Non-production purchasing activities

Jean Prince, Ltd., had $2.3 million (book value) worth of fixed assets (see Exhibit 5). Mobile equipment included over 375 vehicles: trucks,

Exhibit 5

JEAN PRINCE, LTD.

Fixed Assets
Year ended December 31, 1973,
(in $1,000)

	Cost	Accumulated depreciation
Land	$ 229	$
Drainage-farms	27	27
Plant	4,585	2,991
Agricultural machinery		
Various	578	429
Combines	963	728
Self-propelled vehicles	279	241
Rolling stock	105	75
Furniture	143	96
Residences.	51	27
Total	$6,960	$4,614
Less: Accumulated depreciation. .	4,614	
Net value of fixed assets	$2,346	

fork lifts, tractors, plows, harrows, seeders, watering machines, harvesters of all kinds, etc. Mr. Lemay estimated that each piece of agricultural equipment did in one season the normal work of a machine in five seasons. In the factory, salt and sugar had corrosive effects on the canning equipment. All machinery had to be completely overhauled at the end of the canning season. The plant superintendent inspected the equipment with machinists and estimated the repairs to be done on each piece. Estimation of required spare parts was made visually by the machinists, keeping in mind past repairs or considering weather conditions when the machinery had been working. The objective of these estimates was to produce a list of all necessary spare parts and to establish the amount of labor for the following year's budget. Agriculture and factory expenses were reflected on two different budgets. One machinist's team was assigned to the factory maintenance and the other to agricultural equipment reconditioning. However, this task division was flexible, and all maintenance personnel reported to the plant superintendent. Mr. Caron sent spare parts orders to the different dealers and suppliers as soon as the list of required spare parts was ready. Lead time could be several months. Every year, Jean Prince, Ltd., spent between $225,000 to $300,000 on spare parts (see Exhibit 6).

Exhibit 6

JEAN PRINCE, LTD.

Repairs and Maintenance Expenses
Year ended December 31, 1973,
with comparative figures for 1972
(in $1,000)

	1973	1972
Wages (agricultural).	$138	$109
Wages (plant)	66	28
Parts (agricultural)	160	114
Supplies (plant)	110	39
Supplies (workshop)	34	20
Tools	9	9
Welding materials	6	5
Cleaning stuffs	5	5
Sundry	6	1
Vehicles operation	13	10
Equipment lease	56	69
Indirect labor	136	132
Social benefits.	60	46
Total of repairs and maintenance expenses	$799	$587

During the winter the plant superintendent, Mr. Brien, helped by his best machinists, planned the general execution of the maintenance activities and submitted a weekly program to Mr. Lacroix. However, a day-to-day control of labor and materials used was not practiced. The repair and maintenance operations were spread throughout the plant as there was no specific repair shop. There was no central store; parts and supplies were kept in about six little stockrooms. There was no control over incoming and outgoing materials and parts. Inventory included approximately $90,000 worth of used and new parts. Any machinist could help himself in any of these open stock corners. No one had ever attempted to determine how much pilferage took place, but Mr. Lacroix estimated pilferage at 10 percent of the small items in inventory. The superintendent tried to keep in stock the majority of standard parts, but Mr. Lacroix was aware that quantities kept in inventory were not necessarily optimal. Purchasing procedures for these materials were as follows. Machinists made oral requisitions to their foreman, and Mr. Lacroix signed every purchase order written by Mr. Caron, the traffic manager.

The president was conscious of the weak control in this part of the operation. He suspected there were many excess parts in stock and that many had been poorly purchased. He wanted to know the reconditioning costs per machine. In 1973 he found out by accident that the cost of reconditioning five tractors purchased in 1950 exceeded the cost of buying new ones. He was wondering if it would be profitable to have a buyer/storekeeper in charge of the management of spare parts. In addition, this person could control incoming and outgoing materials and keep files on each asset (covering labor data, list of spare parts purchased, etc.). Mr. Lemay realized that the creation of this job could provide an opportunity to centralize all purchases and, therefore, to unburden Mr. Caron during the canning season.

Mr. Lacroix was aware that a central store would be required; however, presently there was no space available for this purpose. Another problem he anticipated concerned the status of this buyer/storekeeper. He thought he would have to pay him at a workman rate of $3.00 per hour, but he did not know how the union would react and accept this new job.

CUSSON KNITWEAR, LTD.

Mr. Dupuis, president of Cusson Knitwear, Ltd., was concerned about the purchasing operation in his firm. He had added the responsibility for purchasing to the plant manager's duties when the purchasing agent left the organization in 1973. The president thought the plant manager, who was also in charge of production and personnel, might be too busy to give proper attention to all of his tasks. In the spring of 1974 Mr. Dupuis knew that some action should be taken, but he was unsure about his best alternative.

Company background

Cusson Knitwear, Ltd., was originally a family-owned concern located since 1939 in the eastern townships of the province of Quebec. In 1964 Mr. Cusson sold his enterprise to a powerful financial organization. Subsequently, a new management was brought in, and in 1967 Mr. Robert Dupuis was appointed president. With sales of approximately $3.5 million the company was among the largest in the clothing industry. "This industry is a very tough one," Mr. Dupuis said, "where one must react very quickly to unpredictable fashion trends. We are one of the few French Canadian enterprises in this business." In the spring of 1974 stylists were giving the final touch to the 1975 spring collection.

Total number of employees varied from 250 at the end of September to 400 in the spring because of the seasonal character of the operations. The president said it was becoming more and more difficult to find suitable employees in the small town where the factory was located. He also said he tried as much as possible to involve each manager in the decision-making process. The factory, the warehouse, and the accounting department were situated about 100 miles east of Montreal;

the president's office and the sales and styling departments were in Montreal (see Exhibit 1 for the organization chart).

Exhibit 1
CUSSON KNITWEAR, LTD.
(organization chart)

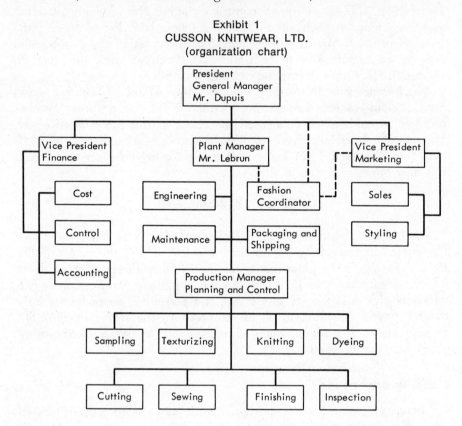

Until 1962, Cusson Knitwear produced only stockings. Then, the company started diversifying into all kinds of single knitted sportswear articles to the extent that, in 1974, the stocking line representing no more than 30 percent of total sales. The sportswear line included over 450 different styles of clothes (shorts, bathing suits, pants, etc.) for the spring collection and around 200 in the fall. Taking into account all sizes and colors for each style, the company produced over 15,000 different types of garments. Between 65 percent and 70 percent of its sales volume was realized from January to June. Mr. Dupuis said he wanted to reduce the seasonal character of the operations by enlarging his fall collection. He also wished to decrease the number of styles because of the administrative difficulties of managing such a wide variety.

Cusson Knitwear sold its products all over Canada at low or budget prices and under private labels mainly through chain and discount stores like Woolco, Woolworth, and Zellers. Promotion activities were confined to volume discounts. Major efforts had been made to sell through department stores, but the company seemed to be closely associated with a low-price type of distribution. "Department store distribution would have permitted us to increase our prices by one third," commented Mr. Dupuis. "Unfortunately, our attempt has been fruitless up to now, and I rather believe that it is impossible to make Cadillacs in a Ford plant."

Since 1969, sales followed a downward trend. Imports from Hong Kong, Taiwan, and other countries had severely affected Cusson's sales. However, Mr. Dupuis expected 1974 to be a better year which would provide an opportunity to reverse this trend. He anticipated 1974 sales to reach $4.5 million. Despite net losses incurred in the last two years, Mr. Dupuis believed the financial situation of his firm was quite favorable. He thought the company generated sufficient cash flows; its main shareholder was in a strong financial position; its bank credit line was good and its financial structure satisfactory. (See Exhibits 2 and 3.)

Production activities

Cusson Knitwear's operations were integrated, i.e., the company produced its own fabrics for all its garments. It manufactured about 80 kinds of fabric, in seven or eight colors, changing every six months. First, filaments (mainly synthetics) were textured to give the material its stretchability; second, yarn was knitted to form cloth; third, the yarn was dyed. Then, clothes were cut and sewn. Finally, the sewn articles went through the finishing operations and inspection.

"In this type of business, the purchasing function is closely related to the sales and styling departments," noted Mr. Dupuis. To prepare a new collection, the stylists first met with the supervisors of the knitting and dyeing departments to decide on a range of colors and choice of fabrics for the season in question. Availability of raw materials was considered at this point. The marketing vice president had the last word in this selection. Fabrics were developed in the factory while stylists designed their new models. Once fabrics were produced, seamstresses made two samples of each model: one for the Montreal showroom and the other for the factory. Detailed production specifications, like fabric number, description, and name of supplier for each material included in the garment, were attached to the factory sample. The collection was presented to management and salesmen who were sent right away to prospect the market and to get orders. Simultaneously, production activities were started. Basic clothes offering less risk were produced at first. The production manager, the marketing vice president, and the fashion coordinator established production forecasts for each garment. Subsequently, in the factory the production manager, with the help

Exhibit 2

CUSSON KNITWEAR, LTD.

Income Statement

Year ended December 31, 1973,
with comparative figures for 1972
(in $1,000)

	1973	1972
Sales	$3,472	$4,281
Cost of goods sold		
Raw materials.	1,085	1,359
Direct labor	836	1,019
External contracts	(2)	14
Manufacturing variable expenses	310	320
Decrease (increase) of inventories	(8)	233
Sales variable expenses.	182	251
Total cost of goods sold	2,403	3,196
Gross margin	1,069	1,086
Store net income	35	33
	1,104	1,119
Manufacturing fixed expenses.	385	409
Sales and administration fixed expenses		
Sales	207	260
Factory administration	122	135
General administration	267	332
Financial expenses	147	168
Total sales and administration fixed expenses	743	895
Income before depreciation and taxes	(24)	(185)
Depreciation.	150	178
Taxes to recover		(24)
Deferred tax credit	(22)	(151)
	128	3
Net income (net loss) before extraordinary item	(152)	$ (188)
Extraordinary item—loss.	37	
Net loss after extraordinary item	$ (189)	

of the different department supervisors, calculated quantities required for each kind of material. At the beginning of a season, production forecasts were readjusted once a week for each of the 450 styles, depending on market reaction and acceptation of the new collection.

Purchasing activities

The plant manager, Mr. Lebrun, was in charge of the purchasing activities in addition to his production and personnel responsibilities. The purchasing agent had left the organization the previous year and had not been replaced partly for economy reasons and partly because Mr. Lebrun had not been able to find a knowledgeable person with sufficient purchasing background.

Exhibit 3

CUSSON KNITWEAR, LTD.
Balance Sheet
Year Ended December 31, 1973
(with comparative figures for 1972, in $1,000)

	1973	1972
Assets		
Current assets		
Cash	$ 2	$ 2
Accounts receivable	277	695
Tax receivable.	2	24
Inventory	1,546	1,445
Other.	45	50
Total current assets.	1,872	2,215
Net fixed assets	1,022	1,143
Other assets	43	50
Total assets	$2,937	$3,408
Liabilities		
Current liabilities		
Bank loan	$ 768	$ 803
Accounts payable.	350	422
Other.	140	175
Total current liabilities.	1,258	1,400
Deferred income taxes		22
Long-term debt	999	1,109
Shareholders' equity	680	877
Total liabilities	$2,937	$3,408

Purchases consisted mainly of nylon filaments, yarns (polyester, nylon, cotton, and wool), dye stuffs, accessories (sewing threads, buttons, zippers, elastics, etc.), labels, packaging, machinery spare parts, etc. (see Exhibit 4 for the approximate value of each type of purchase for 1973.) For 1973, raw materials represented 31.25 percent of total sales.

Every purchase order passed through Mr. Lebrun's hands. Requisitions came from each of the production departments. However, there were no requisitions for large volume orders, like filaments, directly handled by the production manager. Mr. Lebrun negotiated all prices, searched for suppliers if they were not already specified, and looked after all other kinds of communication involved in purchasing. He was one of the few bilingual persons in the factory, and most suppliers were English-speaking. A secretary typed the purchase orders, but Mr. Lebrun personally checked each order before it was sent out.

Cusson Knitwear purchased nylon filaments exclusively from Du Pont. Mr. Lebrun did not sign a contract with Du Pont. Cussin was on a quota system because of the shortages in the nylon industry. However, Mr. Lebrun said this dependence could be reduced because he could still buy nylon in its yarn form. He purchased the other types of yarn

Exhibit 4

CUSSON KNITWEAR, LTD.
Main purchases and their approximative value
for 1973

Filaments (nylon)............	$ 260,000
Yarns:	
Polyester.............	260,000
Nylon	80,000
Cotton..............	110,000
Wool...............	45,000
Dye stuffs	75,000
Accessories:	
Threads	35,000
Buttons	30,000
Zippers..............	30,000
Elastics..............	80,000
Trimmings............	45,000
Etc..................	35,000
Labels	30,000
Packaging	40,000
Machinery spare parts	40,000
Etc..................	45,000
Total purchases.........	$1,240,000

from 12 different suppliers. However, 80 percent of these purchases were made with Du Pont and Dominion Textile. Mr. Lebrun also tried to buy on the free market, but he was often hampered by the difficulties of controlling the quality or making adaptability tests. "You never know the possible dyeing implications of yarn coming from a different supplier," he explained. However, the plant manager noted that large volume items were in general the easiest to purchase.

Dye stuff involved over 140 different products. Problems of color matching tied the company with certain suppliers. In that specialized area Mr. Lebrun relied mainly on the dyeing department supervisor.

According to the plant manager, most purchasing problems originated from small purchases like buttons, trimmings, and other accessories. These purchases were made on a weekly basis after the production program was established by the production manager. Mr. Lebrun thought that buttons and zippers, for example, could be bought three or four times per season, but he had no time to study the total corporate requirements for these materials with a view towards grouping these orders. These repetitive purchases involved a lot of work because there was a large number of suppliers, and, therefore, he had to ask for several quotes. Mr. Lebrun thought labels purchases were really a nuisance. Prices varied considerably with volume. In addition, marginal suppliers could price their products as much as 50 percent below the others. However, they were less reliable and could offer poor quality products.

The government required a label indicating the fabric content of each garment, which should resist at least ten washings, and should not vary from more than 5 percent of the real fabric content. Mr. Lebrun said he was forced to buy in large quantities to avoid excessive prices. "Demands in our industry are great," he added, "if you think that customers can choose any style, in any quantity, within a short delivery period."

Staffing options

The plant manager confessed that his purchasing responsibilities were the most time-consuming of all his duties. He found that the purchasing function required detailed knowledge of textile materials and technology. Presently, he was engrossed in labor contract negotiations and did not even have time to delegate some purchasing responsibilities to his subordinates. He wished he could get an assistant who could be used full time on purchasing activities. He knew it was almost impossible to hire an experienced person because of the diversification and complexity of the company's operations and also because of the failure of his attempts to replace the previous purchasing agent. Therefore, he wondered if he should get a younger person that he could train himself.

The president, on the other hand, considered decentralization of all purchasing activities. Mr. Dupuis thought that Mr. Lebrun could delegate the purchasing responsibilities to the main users of the different materials. Thus, the supervisor of the knitting department could look after filaments and yarns purchases. Responsibilities for dye stuffs could be given to the dyeing department's supervisor and labels and cardboard to the supervisor of the packaging and shipping department after consultation with the sales department. One of the stylists could purchase buttons, zippers, and other accessories. Mr. Dupuis was aware that Mr. Lebrun's load was quite heavy and that with the present raw materials market conditions efficient purchasing management had never been more desirable.

2 ORGANIZATION FOR EFFECTIVE PURCHASING AND MATERIALS MANAGEMENT

Introduction

Every organization in the public and private sector is in varying degrees dependent on materials and services supplied by other organizations. Even the smallest office needs space, heat, light, power, communication and office equipment, furniture, stationery, and miscellaneous supplies to carry on its functions. No organization is self sufficient. Procurement is, therefore, one of the basic common functions of every organization. Organizing the materials function to obtain the appropriate contribution to objectives is one of the challenges of management.

A large number of ideas regarding proper organization have been advanced over many years. That this is a continuing process is underlined by Chandler who identifies four evolutionary stages in organizational growth:

1. Initial expansion and accumulation of resources;
2. Rationalization of the use of resources;
3. Expansion into new lines and markets to ensure continuing use of resources; and
4. Development of new structures to allow continuing mobilization of resources to meet changes in both short-run and long-run demands and trends in markets.[1]

The process of building effective organizations involves innumerable activities, but none are more important at the outset than the relationship between strategies, structures, and delegation. Strategies, once devised, must be carried out in some structural framework; and no matter what organizational design is chosen, delegation takes place within it. Whether the organization structure

---

[1] A. E. Chandler, Jr., *Strategy and Structure* (Cambridge, Mass.: M.I.T. Press, 1972).

is based on building blocks, information flows, or people-oriented concepts is immaterial; what really matters is that work must be assigned and executed in accordance with strategic plans and organizational goals. It follows logically that organizational planning and delegation procedures are important segments of the integration of strategic goals and organizational designs.[2]

Jay Lorsch contributes the reminder:

. . . that the structure of an organization is not an immutable given, but rather a set of complex variables about which managers can exercise considerable choice. . . . It is useful to make a distinction between the basic structure and the operating mechanisms which implement and reinforce this basic structure. Design of the basic structure involves such central issues as how the work of the organization will be divided and assigned among positions, groups, departments, divisions, etc., and how the coordination necessary to accomplish total organizational objectives will be achieved. Choices made about these issues are usually publicized in organization charts and job descriptions. If we recognize that behavior in an organization is influenced by a system of variables (technical, individual, social, and organizational inputs), it is obvious that such formal documents are only one method of signaling to individuals what behavior is expected of them. Nevertheless, this method is important because it is so widely used by managers to define and communicate their expectations of other organization members.

Managers also can reinforce the intent of their basic structural design through what we call operating mechanisms. Operating mechanisms include such factors as control procedures, information systems, reward and appraisal systems, standardized rules and procedures, and even spatial arrangements. These structural variables can be used to more clearly signal to organizational members what is expected of them, to motivate them toward their assigned part of the organization's goal, and, as necessary, to encourage them to undertake collaborative activity.[3]

What makes the task of organizing the materials function particularly difficult is that not only corporate strategy and internal needs have to be considered but the outside world as well. Both the purchasing and traffic functions have daily contact with the marketplace and have to be responsive to market developments. The work of Chester Karrass[4] in negotiation shows that corporate status of the individuals charged with negotiating responsibilities significantly influences chances of success. If suppliers place high emphasis on marketing, staff the area with well-qualified, aggressive and imaginative personnel with high status, buying organizations must find a suitable way to counterbalance this outside force.

---

[2] John G. Hutchinson, *Management Strategy and Tactics* (New York: Holt, Rinehart and Winston, Inc., 1971), p. 205.

[3] Dalton, Lawrence, and Lorsch, *Organizational Structure and Design*, (Homewood, Ill., Richard D. Irwin, Inc. 1970), pp. 1–2.

[4] Chester Karrass, *The Negotiating Game* (New York: World Publishing Co., 1970).

How these organizational ideas and concepts are currently shaping managerial thinking is outlined by Feldman and Cardozo who perceive three models of buying behavior.

During the last decade, a virtual revolution has occurred in industrial buying. In an increasing number of companies, purchasing (exchanging money for goods) has become procurement (total responsibility for acquiring goods). Where the purchasing agent formerly influenced primarily routine repurchases of standard supplies, he now frequently exercises considerable influence not only in the routine purchase of highly important material but also in the decision to adopt entirely new products and processes. In many firms the purchasing "agent" has become a "manager," responsible for managing all phases of the supplier-buyer relationship. In short, the procurement department has taken over functions which formerly were performed by company departments other than purchasing.

To an increasing extent, procurement departments are headed by professional executives, rather than senior clerks whose role resembled that of foremen. These executives act more as administrators than as buyers and frequently are members of top company management.

The industrial buying process has changed much more rapidly than the literature on industrial buying would indicate. A major reason for this gap between current practice and ways of thinking about industrial buying is that these "ways of thinking," or "models," in general have not been clearly spelled out. Consequently, it has been impossible to appraise their usefulness or to update them.

The classical or simplistic model

This title seems appropriate for this oldest and crudest conception of industrial buying behavior. In this model, the buyer's job is to act as a clerk who receives requisitions from "management" and catalogs from suppliers. His sole duty is to buy what is specified, at the lowest price per unit.

The underlying assumptions of this model closely resemble classical economic buying motives under conditions of pure competition. The buyer is regarded as completely rational and adequately, if not fully, informed about available alternatives.

To sell this "honest clerk," marketers presumably need only a complete catalog and the lowest price. Market segmentation is limited to classify buyers by products and/or use and perhaps geography.

But many marketers and analysts recognized that this "honest clerk" has a greedy, self-serving brother whose goal was not to minimize expense to the firm but instead was to maximize personal gain. The marketing strategy adopted for this man stressed social activities between salesman and buyer and other personal side benefits to the purchasing agent.

The neoclassical model

The typical current conception of industrial buying behavior well could be called a much extended and modified version of the classical model. The inputs which the purchasing agent receives are not only routine requisitions, but also more complex requisitions which allow and require him to exercise greater discretion. The neoclassical purchasing agent performs cost and value analyses, in addition to seeing that routine purchases are made. His objective is to minimize total cost for the firm. Since shutting down an automated production line may be quite costly, the purchasing agent may choose a supplier because of his ability to meet delivery schedules or to deliver materials with zero defects, rather than because of his ability to offer the lowest price per unit.

The neoclassical model extends the "rational" portion of the simplistic model. In addition, some versions of the neoclassical model add specific provisions for "emotional" factors. One well-known text states that "a particular (industrial) purchasing decision is typically based upon several motives, both rational and emotional; some of them may even be conflicting. Often the underlying rational factors are so evenly balanced that the scales are finally tipped through emotional motivations." This more recent neoclassical model, indeed, could be stated as an equation:

Industrial Buying
   = f (Economic Rationality + Correction for Emotional Factors)

A new approach

As a first step in overcoming the limitations of earlier models, we suggest a new approach, which we have labeled a "consumeristic" model. This model is based on concepts drawn from consumer behavior research and on more than 100 hours of observing, interviewing, and analyzing the behavior of industrial purchasers. While it shares earlier models' emphasis on rationality, the consumeristic model also provides a framework for understanding "emotional," "social," and other "nonrational" behavior which the earlier models, in our opinion, did not handle satisfactorily. Figure 2–1 presents an outline comparison of all three models.

An overview of the model

The consumeristic model defines the purchaser as a procurement manager rather than a purchasing agent. The procurement manager's job is problem solving, not simply buying. To solve problems, procurement managers employ a variety of purchasing strategies. These strategies are sets of decision rules designed to solve particular problems within

Figure 2–1

COMPARATIVE ANALYSIS OF MODELS OF INDUSTRIAL BUYING

Purchasing process	Classical (simplistic) model	Neoclassical model	Consumeristic model
Inputs to buyers	From suppliers: Supplier catalogs and salesmen From management: requisitions for specific items	From suppliers: Catalogs, salesmen, advertising From management: Complex requisitions allowing discretion	From suppliers: Information sought by purchaser from periodicals, catalogs, advertising material, salesmen From management: Requisitions of all types, many of which will have been discussed with and initiated by purchasing
Buyer's activities	Clerical only	Initiates supplier contact; performs cost and value analyses plus clerical functions	Contacts suppliers and other departments within the firm; has several roles: buyer, manager, and perhaps member of top management team
Purchasing strategy	Objective: minimize cost to firm (or maximize personal gain)	Objective: minimize total cost and obtain emotional satisfactions from supplier relationships	Objective: solve wide variety of purchasing and management problems within acceptable levels of risk and resource expenditure; strategies vary by firm, situation, and individual buyer
Appropriate marketing strategy			
Market segmentation	Product and/or use, geography	Product and/or use, geography	Product and/or use, geography, purchasing strategies (which vary by firm and purchasing problem)
Communications:			
Selling	Stress low price (or personal benefits)	Negotiate terms in addition to price; enhance buyer's status	Provide detailed information on suppliers' capabilities and offerings
Advertising	Not applicable	Provide information on supplier capability; build favorable supplier image	Provide varying amounts and types of information on supplier capability
Other	Large and complete catalog	Catalog of capabilities, not just items	Catalog, stressing capabilities more than specific items
Price	Lowest possible or competitive	Offer lowest total cost, not necessarily lowest item price	Buyer's sensitivity to item price and total cost varies by product, firm, and individual
Follow-up service	None except, in some cases, social activities	Follow-up service part of contract or provided as customary practice; some "status enhancement" may be necessary	Service specified in contract or provided as customary practice; varies by market segment

acceptable limits of risk and resource allocation. Because this problem-solving activity occurs in a social context, it requires both analytical skills and skill in interpersonal relations.

The consumeristic model suggests that industrial markets usefully may be segmented on the basis of purchasing strategies. The model implies that salesmen, advertising, price, and service may have quite specific uses as marketing tools, which vary according to the segment (defined by purchasing strategy) of the industrial market to be reached.[5]

This interesting definition of three models of buyer behavior shows the evolutionary nature of the materials function. How to organize for the consumeristic model is still a problem. Decisions about the reporting level, functionalization, and degree of decentralization will determine the real effectiveness of the function.

The reporting level—decentralization from the chief executive

Decentralization is simply a matter of dividing up the managerial work and assigning specific duties to the various executive levels. . . . The central issue in decentralization, is this: How much of the managerial work—the planning, organizing, leading and controlling—should be done by the president himself and how much of it should he assign to executives at lower administrative levels? Should this work be done principally at the level of the vice president, or should its' decentralization be carried on down to first-line supervisors? In short, at what level should the various administrative chores actually be performed?

The greater the amount of managerial work the chief executive passes along toward the operating levels, the more decentralized an organization is said to be. By contrast, a centralized organization is one in which a relatively large portion of the management work is performed at the highest executive levels.

This allocation of managerial work is one of the most subtle aspects of the organizing process. The degree of decentralization may vary from department to department within a single company. The sales department, for example, may be highly decentralized. But the controller may hold to himself a great deal of the planning, organizing, and motivating of the operations under his direction. Even within a department, decentralization may vary. Thus, management work in the production department may be decentralized from the vice president down to the shop superintendent, but then the shop superintendent may delegate little authority to the foremen.[6]

The level at which a function is located within the organization usually indicates top management's appraisal of the importance of the func-

[5] W. Feldman and R. Cardozo, "The 'Industrial' Revolution and Models of Buyer Behavior," *Journal of Purchasing*, vol. 5, no. 4 (November 1969), pp. 77–88.

[6] William H. Newman, Charles E. Summer, and E. Kirby Warren, *The Process of Management* 2d ed. (Englewood Cliffs, N.J.: Prentice-Hall, Inc., 1967), p. 61–62.

Figure 2–2
WHO'S PURCHASING'S IMMEDIATE BOSS?

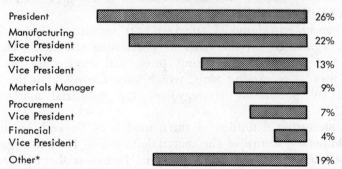

President	26%
Manufacturing Vice President	22%
Executive Vice President	13%
Materials Manager	9%
Procurement Vice President	7%
Financial Vice President	4%
Other*	19%

* Includes administrative services managers, general managers, etc.

tion. The functions of major decision-making importance usually report to a general management executive, the president, executive vice president, or general manager (see Figure 2–2).

Historically, in organizations where procurement was regarded as a subfunction, the manager reported most frequently to the executive in charge of production or manufacturing (see Figure 2–2) and less frequently to the chief financial officer. In recent years, some companies and many nonprofit organizations have created the position of vice president of administration on a coordinate level with marketing, production, and engineering. This organizational device is often used to group functions regarded as being service-oriented—rather than profit-oriented—under an executive who is on a coordinate level with the major functions.

The factors which influence the level at which the procurement function is placed on the organization chart cover a broad spectrum. Among the major factors are:

1. The amount of purchased material and outside services costs as a percentage of either total costs or total income of the organization. A high ratio emphasizes the importance of effective performance of the procurement function.
2. The nature of the products or services acquired. The acquisition of complex components or extensive use of subcontracting represents a difficult procurement problem.
3. The conditions in the marketplace for those products and services of vital importance to the organization.
4. The talent available for assignment.
5. The problems and opportunities present in the procurement area to achieve organizational objectives.

Where the procurement function reports within the organization has been the subject of a number of studies. A survey of 500 purchasing managers was made by *Purchasing Magazine*.[7] As part of its survey the procurement executives were asked to whom they reported. Aim of the question was to find out what level of management is responsible for interpreting the measurement criteria endorsed by top executives. The levels to which purchasing managers report, according to the poll, are shown in Figure 2–2.

A survey of 350 nationally recognized leaders of purchasing made by one of the editors of the *Purchasing Handbook* shows the following distribution of reporting levels and size of companies.[8]

Table 2–1
TO WHOM PURCHASING REPORTS, BASED ON COMPANY SIZE

	Under $5 million, percent	$5 to $50 million percent	Over $50 million, percent	Total percent
President.	56.1	30.8	19.0	34.7
Vice president	15.8	20.5	41.3	25.4
Executive vice president	5.3	10.2	27.6	13.9
General manager	8.8	13.0	1.7	8.3
Treasurer (or secretary and treasurer) . .	1.7	5.1	–	2.6
Others	12.3	20.4	10.4	15.1

Functionalization

Functionalization is defined by Newman as "concerned with bringing into a single unit all phases of a particular kind of work."[9] Functionalization in procurement has major advantages. The traditionally perceived contributions come through specialization which allows functional expertise to be brought to bear on decisions and problems in the procurement area. Since it is easier to talk about a single unit's organization rather than one that's geographically dispersed, let us confine our remarks at the start for a single plant manufacturing organization.

The advantages of functionalized procurement usually lead to lower costs. The consolidation of quantities, resulting in quantity discounts; prompt payment of bills to take advantage of cash discounts; the regulation and control of inventories, reducing storage and interest costs; the more accurate adaptation of purchases to needs, resulting in a better

[7] "To Whom Purchasing Reports." Reproduced by permission from *Purchasing Magazine*, December 9, 1971.

[8] George W. Aljian, ed., *Purchasing Handbook*, 3d ed. (New York: McGraw-Hill Book Co., 1973), p. 2–6. Reproduced with permission of McGraw-Hill Book Co.

[9] William H. Newman, Charles E. Summer, and E. Kirby Warren, *The Process of Management*, 2d ed. (Englewood Cliffs, N.J.: Prentice-Hall, Inc. 1967), p. 63.

product and lower cost and the elimination of suboptimization through the systems approach—these advantages derived from functionalized buying are too definite and too substantial to be disregarded. Indeed the full contribution of procurement to overall corporate success is not likely to be realized without functionalization. Some of these advantages, it will be noted, relate simply to matters of routine, others to broad policy determination, still others to policy administration. All are important. Certainly, so far as the individual company is concerned, lack of functionalization results in an uncoordinated and haphazard performance with many persons working at cross purposes; reasonable functionalization means presenting a unified policy and practice to competitors, suppliers, and customers alike. The result of the latter should be a sounder, broader, more enlightened procurement policy, resulting in improved contribution to organizational objectives.

If the contention that procurement is a major function holds, then organization must recognize it. There can be no more justification for investing the authority to make purchases in a dozen or more individuals in a company than there is for diffusing the responsibility for production or for sales or finance among a similar number of persons. The manager's responsibilities may be divided and apportioned among subofficials and departments, but the functional responsibility and authority of any department head should be definitely recognized. Moreover, functionalization implies that all the responsibilities reasonably involved in the procurement function must be given to the procurement officer as a major official. It is not sufficient to make his sole responsibility the placing of orders as a matter of clerical routine. There should be a clear and definite understanding of his responsibilities and authority. He must be given adequate assistance and must have the backing of executive management. Above all, throughout all procurement activities, the spirit of functionalization and cooperation, not merely the form, must prevail.

The difficulty, of course, is in determining exactly what are the procurement officer's responsibilities and what should be his authority. Certain duties are, for example, to interview all salesmen before they call on other members of the company personnel, to see that the goods purchased conform with the requirements or specifications, to select the source from which the purchase is to be made, to conduct all intermediate negotiations between the vendor and the buyer, and to consummate the purchase by actually placing the order. The additional responsibilities and duties may depend very largely upon circumstances. We are now interested only in the essential principles, namely, that there are certain universally recogized duties pertinent to this function and that these duties should be functionalized and definitely placed in a separate department coordinate in status with the other major departments of business.

Where procurement is functionalized under a competent director and where full cooperation with other departments is enjoyed, definite advantages may and do follow. The full weight of these advantages cannot be apparent so early in the discussion, but some appreciation of their significance can be gained at this point. Functionalization places the responsibility on officials who have the interest and the skill to do the work properly and whose primary concern is in the performance of this special task. It aids in fixing responsibility and in measuring the consequences of any given procurement policy. It permits setting up uniform policies for vendor relationships. It facilitates prescribing procedures, records and routine, and also expedites inspection and approval of materials and arranges payment. It encourages market analysis, study of price trends, and analysis of vendors' production costs, with the result that purchases are made under the most favorable conditions and at the most favorable times. It promotes economy by consolidating requirements and by setting up material standards for inventories. Through searching for substitute materials and materials exactly suited to the requirements demanded, it encourages reducing costs without impairing the quality of the product.

Degree of decentralization within procurement

Impressive as the arguments for functionalization are in the procurement field a narrow conclusion would lead to one procurement department within every organization. Such complete functionalization goes counter to some modern developments. According to Newman:

In recent years, however, two developments have tended to moderate emphasis on functionalization. One is the growing emphasis on team work. A manager must divide and subdivide operations so that he can promote team work and, at the same time, narrow the assignment of each individual. But teamwork (or the coordination of activities) becomes more difficult to stimulate when men concentrate on ever narrower specialties. A point is reached where the problems of coordination offset the benefits of functional specialization. Large companies often find that they can get better results if they first divide up their operations by product or territory and provide each department with its own sales, finance, production, and other functional divisions. . . . Let us simply note here that there is a strong trend toward creating small, self-contained operating units that are large enough to reap many of the benefits of functionalization; at the same time, the total operating departments remain of manageable size.[10]

To what extent the procurement function should follow this trend is an interesting question. Today so many organizations are spread geographically, have a variety of products and services to offer through

---

[10] William H. Newman, Charles E. Summer, and E. Kirby Warren, *The Process of Management*, 2d ed. (Englewood Cliffs, N.J.: Prentice-Hall, Inc. 1967) p. 51.

subunits, that centralized procurement may not be compatible with the general corporate philosophy. This raises questions such as:

1. Should there be a headquarters procurement organization and what should be its role?
2. Should a headquarters procurement organization buy the major raw materials for several or all of the divisions?
3. Where one division uses products manufactured by another division, should the using division be required to buy from the making division when an outside supplier can supply proper quality at a substantially lower price?
4. How far should the organization's chief procurement officer go in evaluating the performance of a divisional procurement executive?

Obviously, there are no ready-made answers to such decisions—much depends on the abilities and personalities of the executives in such an organization. One major difference between procurement and other functions lies in the area of headquarters' involvement in common purchases. This places an operating task at headquarters, creating a potentially strong communication channel with divisions or subunits. This tends to break down the "we-they" relationship so often created between functional units at headquarters and those in the field.

Insofar as divisions or geographically dispersed units are uniform in terms of common needs and services and deal with the same suppliers, centralized procurement may well make sense. It is important, however, that the procurement function fits reasonably with organizational policies regarding divisionalized responsibilities. Obviously, the greater the geographical spread and the greater the divergence in organizational needs the stronger the argument for procurement decentralization to distinct subunits becomes.

Problems arising in conglomerate organizations

Conglomerate types of organizations are usually large groupings of companies which have been acquired by a parent organization. In many instances, there is no direct relationship among the types of industries represented by the acquired companies, although there may be an underlying relationship centering on an area of science or technology. Because of the diversity of the member companies of a conglomerate corporation and in many cases the large size of each member company, the problems of developing any meaningful concept of corporate procurement are immense.

Any solution to the problem must be scheduled over long time periods to have any chance for success. Some conglomerate companies have found that one way to start to develop sound procurement policies and coordination among the member companies is to have a small headquarters group of highly competent procurement executives who are available to act as consultants on procurement problems when called on by the appropriate division executives. Needless to say, the success of the consultants' group will depend equally on their abilities in the human relations field and on their competence in the procurement function.

Several problems may be associated with complete functional decentralization without a corporate headquarters group. Where the decentralized units are small in size, they may become so involved in operating matters that the impetus for change and planning is overlooked. Status of such decentralized units may also be relatively low with the resulting problems of quality of personnel and identification of supply opportunities. No subunit may be large enough to justify functional expertise in areas such as customs, traffic, warehousing, inventory management, procurement research, materials handling, and value analysis. Corporate benefits may be lost, because of a low level of performance and lack of coordination in each of these areas. Even in those organizations where the individual units are large enough in size that the above problems are not serious, it may well be possible that they will compete with one another in the marketplace for the same suppliers or materials and may interfere with each other without knowing it.

Organization for materials management

The rationale of materials management may be better comprehended through understanding of the growth of a small firm through three separate stages. According to Harold Fearon these stages are complete integration, evolution of independent functions, and reintegration of related activities.

Complete integration

When an organization initially is established, almost all functions are performed by the chief executive (often the owner) or by a few key individuals who make up the management team. For example, the purchasing function might be performed by the chief executive, but since he also handles the scheduling of production and watches inventory levels closely, there will be no problem of coordination or control. This system works reasonably well, for the evidence shows that the materials-type functions (e.g., purchasing, inventory control, stores, and traffic) typically are grouped together and assigned to one person, whether he be president or some other key operating executive.

Evolution of independent functions

As the firm's business increases and additional personnel are added to the organization, it becomes evident that certain advantages would accrue if individual functions, such as purchasing, stores, traffic, production scheduling, inventory control, and quality control were separated and made full-time managerial assignments. The primary advantage, assuming the workload is sufficient to justify a full-time job assignment, is that of occupational specialization. The purchasing agent and later on the buyers that are added to the purchasing department (using that function as an example) become professional specialists. They bring to their function an expertise available only when an individual can devote his energies solely to one job. But with the emergence of these independent functions a problem of coordination develops.

The organizational assignment of individual functions to other major activities normally will be done on a "most use" criterion. Thus, purchasing might be assigned to the operations or production manager, since the major dollars are spent for raw materials; traffic might be assigned to the sales manager, since he would be responsible for delivery of finished items to customers. The "critical relationship" is a second criterion which might be used to assign certain functions. For example, inventory control might be assigned to finance, in view of the dollar investment involved. Other functions might be assigned on an "executive interest" basis. For example, the value analysis/engineering function might be assigned to engineering, since the engineering manager may be the one who has promoted and pushed this activity. The point is that the responsibility for different, but interrelated, functions becomes widely dispersed throughout the organization structure, creating very real problems of coordination and communication which prevent the organization from effectively and efficiently achieving its overall goals.

Reintegration of related activities

Eventually it becomes clear that substantial advantages, through the reduction of communication and coordination problems, could be obtained by bringing together again, under one responsible individual, all those functions which clearly are interrelated. This reintegration of interrelated materials functions is the basis of the materials management concept.[11]

If an organization adopted a "full-blown" materials management concept, following the principle of homogeneous assignment, the organizational structure might appear as in Figure 2–3.

Functions included in materials management

1. Production control. The production control manager plays an important part in establishing the total production schedule. Working with information inputs which either estimate future demands for a company's products or are based on the receipt of actual orders, or a combination of both, production control develops the time and quantity schedules for parts and materials to determine availability and amounts needed to facilitate the production schedule.

---

[11] Harold E. Fearon, "Materials Management: A Synthesis and Current View," *Journal of Purchasing,* vol. 9, no. 1 (February 1973), pp. 35, 36.

Figure 2–3
ORGANIZATION FOR MATERIALS MANAGEMENT

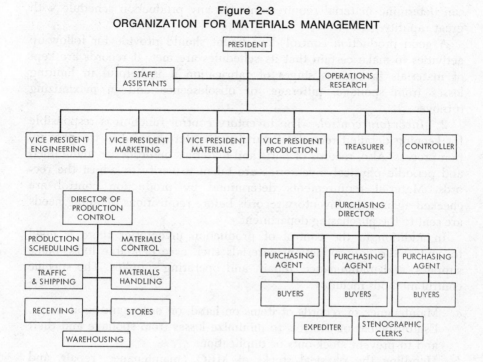

When a materials management concept of organization is used it is wise to consider production control separately from production scheduling. Under this form of division of responsibilities, production control is concerned with numbers of units to be produced, the time intervals over which production will occur, and the availability of materials. Production scheduling is concerned with allocation of work to men and machines to produce the number of units specified by production control within the scheduled time constraints.

Failure to recognize the subtle difference between production control and production scheduling has frequently caused major problems within an organization when the materials management concept was adopted. In highly automated manufacturing processes decisions about how men and machines are going to be used are normally made at the time the facilities are designed and installed and not as production orders are released.

Once the number of units to be produced within a specified time period is determined, production control is in a position to figure detailed requirements for parts and materials, both purchased and manufactured, by using bills of materials and specifications supplied by engineering. Companies with integrated data processing systems which have incorporated bills of material and specification requirements within the system can determine material requirements for any production schedule with great rapidity.

A good production control department should provide for follow-up activities to make certain that its schedules are met. If records are kept of materials in various stages of fabrication it is helpful in limiting losses from spoilage, pilferage, or obsolescence and in maximizing turnover.

2. *Inventory control.* The inventory control function is responsible for keeping detailed records of parts and materials used in the production process. Also, records of parts and materials on order are maintained and periodic physical inventories are taken to verify or adjust the records. Material requirements determined by production control are checked against the inventory records before requisitions detailing needs are sent to the purchasing department.

In addition to the control of production inventories there is need to control the nonproduction materials such as expendable tools, office supplies, and maintenance, repair, and operating supplies. The specific control methods include:

a. Maintenance of records of items on hand, on order, and total usage. Establishment of controls to minimize losses from spoilage and theft and to prevent stock-outs or duplication.

b. Handling the physical stocks of MRO (maintenance, repair, and operating supplies), items to be issued as needed for operations or maintenance.

c. Issuing requisitions to the purchasing department when stocks reach the reorder point or special needs arise.

Both production and nonproduction parts, materials, and supplies can be controlled through one inventory control department or they can be organized into two separate departments.

3. *Purchasing.* The purchasing department has the responsibility of buying the kinds and quantities of materials authorized by the requisitions issued by production control, inventory control, engineering, maintenance, and any other department or function requiring materials. Where the purchasing department has the right and the duty to advise, question, and even to challenge other departments on matters of material specification and selection, a dynamic value is added to the operation of the purchasing function and the firm.

The basic activities of purchasing can be grouped as follows:

a. Checking the specifications of materials which are requisitioned, in an endeavor to standardize where possible and to buy the materials which are the best values for the purposes intended.

b. Selecting the best available sources of supply, negotiating the terms of purchase, including delivery and performance, and issuing the proper purchase orders. Maintaining the necessary records to provide historical data on price trends, vendor performance, and the like.

c. Follow-up to ensure on-time delivery and receipt of the proper quality and quantity.

d. Acting as the company's "G2" or intelligence unit in the marketplace, constantly searching for new and more effective suppliers and new materials and products with the objective of reducing costs or improving the company's product.

e. Supervising or conducting all contacts between suppliers and all other company departments on all matters relating to the purchase of materials.

4. *Traffic.* Transportation costs have had an increasing influence on material costs in recent years. Also, types of transportation have had a major influence on inventory policy in some types of industry, i.e., the use of air freight and air express has reduced size of inventory stocks for certain items. There are two basic traffic activities:

a. Traffic control involves the selection of carriers, documentation of shipments, study of carrier services and rates, tracing shipments, audit and approval for payment of carrier charges, and the evaluation of carrier performance.

b. Traffic analysis is concerned with assessing the total cost of transportation including loading and unloading, methods of packaging, transit time, and thefts and other losses, and with developing techniques for reducing overall transportation costs.

5. *Materials handling.* The materials handling function is concerned with the movement of materials within a manufacturing complex. Development of special purpose equipment such as forklift trucks, pallets, and automated conveyor systems have revolutionized the physical handling of materials. These inventions and developments have been based on two objectives: reduced handling costs per unit of material and reduction in time required to move a unit of material from one location to another.

6. *Receiving.* The receiving department is responsible for the physical handling of incoming shipments, the identification of such material, the verification of quantities, the preparation of reports, and the routing of the material to the place of use or storage.

7. *Shipping.* The responsibilities for the packaging of finished products for shipment, the stenciling or labeling of the shipping instructions on the shipping containers, and the delivery to the carrier used for transportation are commonly delegated to the shipping department.

8. *Warehousing.* In the past the responsibility for the control of finished goods inventories and the warehouses in which they are stored

has generally been delegated to the sales or marketing function. Inventories of finished goods may represent a substantial portion of a company's investment in materials. Under a materials management concept of operation it is reasoned that a change in finished goods inventories may have a direct bearing on production material requirements. Therefore, better coordination and control of the total investment in materials can be accomplished if the materials manager has control over finished inventories.

9. *The disposal of scrap and surplus.* Traditionally this has been a function included with the responsibilities of purchasing. Aside from the desire to obtain good value for disposals, two major additional concerns stem from the environment and shortages of critical materials. Since suppliers are often interested in disposals inclusion with the materials function is sensible.

10. *Quality control.* Quality control continues to be a difficult function to place in many organizations. The responsibility for inspection of incoming raw materials and supplier's operations places it directly with materials management. The evidence is not conclusive on internal plant operations.

11. *Customs.* As international trade grows, customs, concerned with clearance across national borders, the tariffs applied, and extensive paperwork, grows in importance in the organization.

12. *Customer service.* Depending on the nature of the product and the warranty covering the product there may be substantial impact on parts inventories from time to time.

Purchasing in the materials management context

What happens to the purchasing function when it becomes part of a materials management concept in an organization? Will it lose status? Will the former purchasing manager become the new materials manager? These interesting questions were raised by G. J. Zenz in a research study involving almost 300 companies.

A survey of the functions included under the materials management umbrella showed purchasing to be the most frequently included function. See Figure 2–4.

Respondents from firms utilizing materials management showed that 60 percent thought purchasing's status would be unchanged, 24 percent expected an increase, and 16 percent a decrease. It may well be that in those organizations in which purchasing has relatively low internal status at the time of materials management introduction the renewed management awareness may result in substantial improvement. It has traditionally been argued that the purchasing manager should be a prime candidate for the position of materials manager. The research showed that 29 percent of the materials managers came from the purchasing

Figure 2–4
FUNCTIONS INCLUDED UNDER MATERIALS MANAGEMENT

Function	Percent of firms including under materials management
Purchasing	68%
Production control	61
Inventory control	51
Traffic (including shipping)	49
Stores	29
Schedules (and planning)	26
Receiving	16
Warehousing	10
Distribution	6
Customer service	6
Other	10

Source: *Journal of Purchasing,* vol. 4, No. 2 (May 1968), p. 41. Reproduced with permission of the *Journal of Purchasing* and *Materials Management,* National Association of Purchasing Management, Inc., 11 Park Place, New York, N.Y. 10007.

function, 33 percent from production control, and 38 percent from areas normally considered outside the materials management area. Apparently the growing sophistication of management concepts and techniques, including the use of the behavioral sciences as well as mathematical and EDP concepts in many of the materials management functions, puts a premium on managerial skill requirements.[12]

BIBLIOGRAPHY

ALJIAN, GEORGE W., ed. *Purchasing Handbook.* 3d ed. New York: McGraw-Hill Book Co., 1973.

AMERICAN MANAGEMENT ASSOCIATION. *Purchasing Department Organization and Authority.* Edited by George H. Haas et. al. Research Study No. 45. New York, 1960.

BROWN, ALVIN. *Organization of Industry.* Englewood Cliffs, N.J.: Prentice-Hall, Inc., 1947.

DRUCKER, PETER F. *The Practice of Management.* New York: Harper & Row, 1954.

DRUCKER, PETER F. *Technology, Management and Society.* New York: Harper & Row, 1970.

LEWIS, H. T., AND LIVESEY, C. A. *Materials Management: A Problem in the Air Frame Industry.* Research Studies No. 31. Boston: Harvard University, Graduate School of Business Administration, 1944.

NATIONAL ASSOCIATION OF PURCHASING AGENTS, INC. "Organization For Purchasing," *Guide to Purchasing.* New York, 1965.

[12] Gary J. Zenz, "Materials Management: Threat to Purchasing," *Journal of Purchasing,* vol. 4, no. 2 (May 1968), pp. 39–45.

PINKERTON, RICHARD L.   *A Curriculum for Purchasing.* Madison: University of Wisconsin, Bureau of Business Research & Service, 1969.

STUART, ROBERT DOUGLAS.   *Purchasing in Worldwide Operations.* New York: American Management Association, Purchasing Division, 1966.

WEBSTER, FREDERICK E. AND WIND, YORAM.   *Organizational Buying Behaviour.* Englewood Cliffs, N.J.: Prentice-Hall, Inc. 1972.

WESTING, J. H., FINE, I. V., ZENZ, GARY JOSEPH, ET AL.   *Purchasing Management.* 3d ed. New York: John Wiley & Sons, Inc., 1969.

CASES FOR CHAPTER 2

LOCKHURST RAILWAY COMPANY

Mr. Alex Jones, vice president of purchasing at Lockhurst Railway, faced the following decision. His chief purchasing agent, John Shipley, had received an offer of employment with another railway, at an increase in salary of $2,500 per year. John was well liked by all employees but was perhaps not quite as efficient as Mr. Jones would like him to be. Mr. Jones was, therefore, considering hiring Jim Martin, a materials manager in the transportation industry on the West Coast. Jim was well known for his technical ability, and Mr. Jones expected he could make improvements which might result in substantial savings. On the other hand, Jim had an abrasive personality, and he might antagonize supervisors and employees to such an extent that operations could deteriorate so that severe losses might occur. Should this happen, Mr. Jones would have no choice but to fire Jim and try to find someone else. Jim Martin would have to be paid $4,000 more than Shipley's current salary.

The last alternative was to let John go and replace him by his current subordinate, Don Mix. Don would require some further training and experience, but Mr. Jones thought that in a year or so Don could be just as effective as John Shipley. Don Mix would undoubtedly be happy to accept this promotion and would start at a salary of $1,300 below John Shipley's present level.

MICHIGAN PHARMACEUTICALS, LTD.

One afternoon in September, 1972, Mr. James Wilson, assistant purchasing manager of Michigan Pharmaceuticals Ltd. (M.P., Ltd.), was discussing the purchase of packaging materials and contract filling of tablet samples with a supplier's representative. When the details of the packaging purchase order were finalized, Mr. Wilson told the salesman, Mr. Fred Brown, of Christie Paper Box Company, that he would send him the purchase order for the packaging components and 25 percent of the contract filling. Mr. Brown replied that Mr. Peter O'Toole, of the marketing department, had promised him 100 percent of the contract filling. "This is the first I've heard of that," snapped Mr. Wilson. "It's not marketing's responsibility," he continued, controlling his temper, "to decide what percentages of contract filling a particular supplier will get. Purchasing arranges the contract filling with the suppliers that can give the best quality, delivery, and price."

Mr. Brown, an experienced salesman, remained unperturbed. He replied that he had always dealt with both marketing and purchasing and that sometimes purchasing was not involved at all in the projects. He said that in this case where both marketing and purchasing were involved that he was just keeping purchasing informed of what marketing wanted. Mr. Wilson closed the interview by politely telling the salesman that he would have to clear up the situation between the two company departments. He told Mr. Brown he would let him know how much of the contract packaging he would be getting.

Mr. Wilson, his immediate superior, Mr. Rose, and a senior buyer made up the total purchasing staff (see Exhibit 1). One of Mr. Wilson's

Exhibit 1
MICHIGAN PHARMACEUTICALS, LTD.
(organization chart)

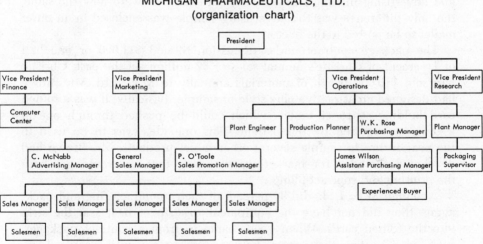

responsibilities was to handle the purchase of the marketing department's requirements. He also acted as liaison between that department and the production planning, manufacturing, and packaging departments. In recent weeks Mr. Wilson was finding the job more and more frustrating.

The company carried an extensive line of prescription and nonprescription items which were manufactured in Michigan. M.P., Ltd., had 10,000 drugstore customers plus hospital and government accounts. Annual sales of close to $10 million were handled by 50 sales representatives from coast to coast. Although the nonprescription items, known as over-the-counter (O.T.C.) products, were promoted directly to the drug stores, most business was generated by convincing the doctors to prescribe M.P., Ltd., products for their patients. No selling or advertising was directed at the consumer.

The basic idea was that the M.P., Ltd, salesmen would give samples to a doctor after getting a verbal promise that he would prescribe. These samples would be used to start the patient on an M.P., Ltd., product, and the doctor would write a prescription for the patient to pick up at the drugstore. With a large number of similar products on the market, it was a difficult marketing problem to keep M.P., Ltd.'s brand name in the doctor's mind, days or weeks after the salesman's visit. To help solve this problem, salesmen asked the doctors to sign forms requesting additional samples at spaced intervals.

The marketing department had been recently reorganized, and the two new men, Mr. P. O'Toole, sales promotion manager, and Mr. C. McNabb, advertising manager, were understandably anxious to do a good job. Both had made a lot of progress in working with Mr. Brown of Christie, standardizing the samples to be used for sales promotion and advertising mailings. Essentially, both samples were now the same, the only difference was the advertising sample was enclosed in an outer mailer to be posted to the doctor.

The package contract under discussion totaled $11,000 or one half of 1 percent of Christie's annual sales of $2 million. In the past, Christie had sold $10,000 worth of materials annually to M.P., Ltd. Mr. Brown had designed an attractive new style of sample. Basically, it was a folded card holding strips of tablets which could be pushed through one at a time, as required by the patient. This one idea was to be used in the near future to sample several other tablet products. Mr. Brown had developed the idea for marketing, expecting that he would get both the printing and contract filling.

Although M.P., Ltd., did 90 percent of their manufacturing and packaging, they did not have the equipment to strip or heat seal the strip into the folded cards. When goods came in from a contract packager, such as Christie, they were held in inventory until required by marketing.

While Mr. O'Toole and Mr. McNabb had been able to work well together, they were having their difficulties in getting the cooperation of other departments involved. Frequent instances of sample mailings being late or salesmen samples being out of stock continued to plague the success of their program. Delays had been caused by late ordering of components from outside suppliers, shortages of tablets, and computer mailing lists being incorrectly printed. In their attempts to remedy the situation, the marketing men had trampled on a few toes. During attempts to investigate the causes for these delays, the vice president of operations discovered that there were usually good reasons offered by the departments involved.

Purchasing, production, and the computer center pointed out that they could not drop their usual work "everytime marketing wanted something in a rush." The feeling expressed by the production planner was typical of most department supervisors. He commented, "It's fine to get out the samples but rather pointless if we are running out of trade size in the meantime. Some of those unusual sample carton constructions slow us up 50 percent."

While it was part of Mr. Wilson's job to coordinate marketing's sample requirements, he was not making much progress. His attempts to get each department to cooperate met with the usual arguments that marketing was only one department and had to wait its turn. Mr. O'Toole and Mr. McNabb at times grew impatient with Mr. Wilson's efforts, and they started to go directly to each department supervisor.

Mr. Wilson felt that the action taken by Mr. O'Toole in telling the supplier how much contract filling business he would get was the last straw. With this in mind he went to see his immediate superior, Mr. Rose, to try to get a policy statement on the matter. He wanted to know where the line was drawn between purchasing and marketing's responsibility in matters dealing with company suppliers.

Mr. Rose explained that, because marketing promotion expenditure totaled $2.1 million or 21 percent of sales, M.P., Ltd., as most other companies in the industry, faced similar purchasing marketing problems.

If marketing was responsible for their budgets, they had the right to spend $1 each for 10,000 items, or if they wanted they could buy 5,000 items at $2 each and still stay within their budget. It was a marketing decision whether they were getting better results from the $1 or $2 item. For these items purchasing merely typed a purchase order to confirm the deal already made by marketing with the supplier. This policy applied to nonproduction items, such as calendars, letter openers, diet sheets, patient history cards for doctors, or displays and posters for drugstores. In contrast, production and inventory purchases had last year reached 20 percent of sales dollars.

However, he pointed out that final selection of sources for any purchased items which had to be packaged by the plant had always been the responsibility of the purchasing department. In this particular case there was still a significant inventory of old style samples in the building, which marketing had not considered when they promised Mr. Brown 100 percent of the contract filling. Mr. Wilson felt that placing all the contract filling right away would build up the stock of samples unnecessarily. Besides this, he had negotiated a much better price from another reliable supplier and felt that he would give the balance of 75 percent to them.

Marketing, Mr. Rose explained, was only charged for samples as they were shipped to salesmen or mailed out to doctors. Therefore, marketing was not too concerned about inventory levels as long as there were no shortages. Packaging components and bulk products held in inventory were not segregated from trade sizes in the warehouse or in accounting records. Ony the finished samples were given a special account number so that the marketing budgets could be debited as the samples were sent out.

Mr. Rose suggested that a marketing-purchasing meeting be held so that each department could state its case. The main points brought up were as follows:

Marketing—Mr. O'Toole and Mr. McNabb

1. Samples were the keystone to the marketing program. M.P., Ltd., could not afford the delays which were depriving salesmen and doctors from receiving adequate supplies on time.
2. It was necessary to operate within their budgets, and therefore they should have a say in selecting suppliers.
3. Continual foul-ups had delayed marketing objectives because of the inability of purchasing, production-planning, packaging, and the computer center departments to meet deadlines set by marketing.
4. Since Mr. Brown had done so much development work to design the new sample, he was entitled to the printing as well as the contract filling business if his prices were reasonable.

Purchasing—Mr. Rose and Mr. Wilson

1. It was agreed that samples were very important but not at the expense of trade size production and general efficiency of the plant.
2. Marketing budgets were one thing, but all departments had budgets and one department could not be favored over another. Purchasing did not deny marketing a say in supplier selection, but the final selection had to be made by purchasing.
3. Why were there foul-ups? Did marketing allow these departments sufficient lead time? Did they familiarize other departments with their plans early in their development? Were these deadlines reasonable in light of other departments' schedules?
4. Purchasing had a corporate responsibility to see that the greatest possible value was received for each dollar spent. How did we know prices were reasonable without getting other quotations?

If Christie got the initial orders for the new sample program, how much of their price per M was actually the cost of their idea? If someone else quoted lower, what premium was marketing prepared to pay the originator of the idea?

Before these last questions could be answered by marketing, the meeting had to be adjourned because of a shortage of time. Before parting, all those involved felt that some progress had been made but that they still had a long way to go.

THOMAS MANUFACTURING COMPANY

"Delivery of our 412 casting is critical. Production just cannot be stopped for this casting, every time you have a minor pattern problem," said Mr. Litt, engineer for Thomas Manufacturing.

"I'm not interested in running rejects," answered Mr. James of A & B Foundry. "I cannot overextend my time on these castings when other jobs are waiting."

"If you can't cast them properly and on time, I'll just have to take our pattern to another foundry that can," retorted Mr. Litt.

"Go ahead! It's all yours. I have other jobs with fewer headaches," replied Mr. James.

Mr. Litt returned to Thomas Manufacturing with the 412 casting pattern.[1] He remembered that Mr. Dunn, vice president of manufacturing for Thomas, (see Exhibit 1) had obtained a quote on his casting

Exhibit 1
THOMAS MANUFACTURING COMPANY

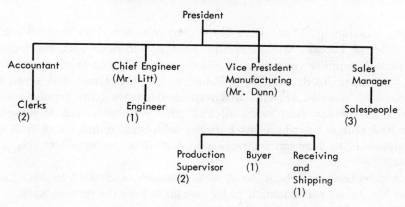

from Dawson, another gray-iron foundry, several months before. It seemed that Dawson had the necessary capabilities to handle this casting.

To Mr. Litt's surprise, Mr. Dunn was not entirely happy to find the 412 pattern back in the plant. Mr. Dunn contacted Dawson foundry who said that they could not accept the job because of a major, six-month facilities conversion. Locating another supplier would be difficult. Most foundries would only undertake complex casting if a number of orders for simple casting were placed at the same time.

---

[1] A pattern is used in making molds in which the gray iron is formed. The mold after cooling is broken off leaving the desired casting.

Mr. Dunn knew that gray-iron foundry capacity was tight. In general, foundries were specializing or closing down. Mr. Dunn had gathered some data on the gray-iron industry located within a 500-mile radius of his plant (see Exhibit 2), which highlighted the problems his com-

Exhibit 2

FOUNDRY DATA FOR AREA WITH A 500-MILE RADIUS
AT THE THOMAS PLANT

a.   Shipments of Manufactured Goods

Gray iron (commercial castings)	Quantity	Value
Previous year	280,000 tons	$65,000,000
Current year	243,000 tons	$54,000,000

b.   Number of Establishments

									Current year
140	133	131	134	137	134	134	128	126	116

|—————————— Ten-year history ——————————|

pany was facing. There were three gray-iron foundries located within 60 miles of Thomas Manufacturing. Thomas had dealt with one foundry until that supplier suffered a 12-month strike. Thomas then moved most of its casting needs to A & B Foundry, but Mr. Dunn had given the occasional order to Dawson and requested quotes quite regularly from them. In the last four years all had gone well with A & B Foundry. He had planned to share his business with both foundries. A & B was comparable to Dawson on price and had done an excellent job until now.

A telephone call back to A & B Foundry indicated to Mr. Dunn that Mr. James was adamant in his refusal to take the pattern back.

Thomas Manufacturing Company was a portable generator manufacturer with sales reaching the $1 million mark in 1971. Thomas employed approximately 160 people in a fairly modern plant. Many of its small portable generators were sold to clients all over North America.

The 412 casting

The 412 casting was part of the most popular "middle-of-the-line" generator. The casting weighed 70 pounds, cost approximately $30.00—and its pattern was worth $4,000. A run normally consisted of 100 castings, and Thomas usually received 100 castings every month. The 412 represented about 15 percent of Thomas's casting needs.

Normal lead time was at least eight weeks. When the supply problem arose, Thomas held six weeks inventory.

Mr. Litt, an expert in pattern work, explained that the pattern was tricky, but, once the difficulties were ironed out and the job set up, a hand molder could pour 50 castings in two days without any problems.

OLIN (A)*

Introduction

In December, 1965, top management of the Olin Mathieson Chemical Corporation (Olin) was reexamining the company's organization structure with a view of bringing about changes to reflect the needs of the company's highly diversified products and product markets. Mr. Gordon Grand, a Yale-educated tax lawyer, who had joined the company in 1953 as assistant to John M. Olin (then president of Olin Industries) and who had been elected president and chief executive officer in April, 1965, stated, "Olin Mathieson Chemical Corporation is engaged in five different business areas—different in terms of customers, markets, technology, production, and, indeed, geographical distribution." He believed that, because of the heterogeneous product lines, the company's operation should be organized into distinct industry groups functioning as autonomous and largely independent enterprises under the strategic guidance and overall control of the president's office with the assistance of a relatively small presidential staff. Mr. Grand stated that it was one of his objectives to give Olin "the flexibility of small business combined with the scale and economy of big business." Company executives quoted the president as referring at times to "the holding company concept" in discussing changes in the organization structure. In its 1964 Annual Report, Olin management stated, "Substantial progress was . . . made during the year toward the decentralization of the five areas of our business. We are now studying the management advantages to be gained by incorporating these related operations into separate subsidiaries."[1]

[1] In an address by Olin's president before the New York Society of Security Analysts in October, 1965, this statement led to the following question-answer exchange:

Question [from the floor]: Management has stated that it is "studying the management advantages to be gained by incorporating our five basic activities into five separate affiliates." This has given rise to occasional apprehension that Olin is planning to spin off all, or part, of certain divisions. Can management elucidate this for us?

Answer [Mr. Grand]: The statement referred to is a statement we made with deliberate care in last year's Annual Report. We said that we were studying the management advantages to be gained from incorporating our related businesses into separate subsidiaries. We have no present intention—no intention at all—of spinning off—splitting up—splitting off—or disposing of any of Olin's five businesses as a result of any incorporation which we may make.

In conjunction with the contemplated realignment of the Olin organization structure, the president had asked Mr. Ralph C. Phillips, corporate director of purchasing, to make recommendations as to how to organize the company's complex procurement activities in a way that would be consistent with the basic concept of organization envisioned by top management.

Company background

Olin Mathieson Chemical Corporation had been formed in 1954 through a merger of Olin Industries, Inc., and Mathieson Chemical Corporation. Both companies had been founded independently in 1892. Since 1892 each had actively sought and acquired numerous other firms, each had merged with several other companies, and each had entered a diversity of industries and product fields (see Exhibit 1 for table giving chronology and growth of Olin). Prior to the merger in 1954 Olin Industries, Inc., had been operating on a decentralized basis and

Exhibit 1
CHRONOLOGY OF GROWTH AND DEVELOPMENT

OLIN INDUSTRIES, INC.	MATHIESON CHEMICAL CORPORATION
Industrial Explosives—1892	*Company Formed—1892*
Began making blasting powder, East Alton, Ill.	Founded Mathieson Alkali Works, Saltville, Va.
Sporting Ammunition—1898	*First Production—1895*
Expanded operations to include ammunition.	Began to produce alkalis for industrial users.
Brass—1916	*Liquid Chlorine—1909*
Started fabrication of brass for cartridge cases.	Developed first commercial production in U.S.
Copper-Based Alloys—1918	*Synthetic Ammonia—1923*
Became large-scale producer of copper alloys.	Pioneered synthetic ammonia production in U.S.
Sporting Arms—1931	*Plant Foods—1949*
Entered sporting arms industry through Winchester.	Became major producer of chemicals for agriculture.
Packaging—1951	*Petrochemicals—1951*
Began production of transparent film and fine paper.	Began production of organic chemicals from natural gas.
Timberlands—1952	*Medicinal Chemicals—1952*
Acquired raw materials source for packaging expansion.	Expanded to pharmaceutical production through Squibb.
Aluminum—1953	*High Energy Fuels—1953*
Expanded metals fabrication to include aluminum.	Formed joint company with Olin to produce hydrazine.

Source: Company records.

was referred to by company personnel as a "holding company whose operating divisions knew little of each other's existence and whose management regarded centralized management through a central staff organization as a waste of money." The Mathieson Chemical Corporation, in sharp contrast, had been run on a highly centralized basis with directors of staff functions exercising strong influence on each division's operations through the setting of both long-range and short-range divisional objectives, formulating plans and programs to achieve these objectives, and initiating action and implementing decisions.

In 1964, Olin product lines included principally industrial and specialty chemicals, petrochemicals, plant food and pesticides, aluminum, brass, ethical and proprietary drugs, arms and ammunition, fine papers, cellophane, lumber, and kraft paper products. The company maintained over 40 geographically dispersed manufacturing facilities. Consolidated sales for 1964 were $816 million, with earnings (net after taxes) amounting to $41 million. Exhibit 2 gives a breakdown of sales by major product

Exhibit 2
SALES BY MAJOR PRODUCT DIVISIONS
(dollars in millions)

	1964	Percent	1963	Percent
Chemicals	$239.6	29.4	$241.2	30.9
Metals	160.2	19.6	147.9	19.0
Winchester-Western	117.1	14.4	103.4	13.3
Packaging	148.0	18.1	141.2	18.1
Squibb	150.8	18.5	145.5	18.7
Total	$815.7	100.0%	$779.2	100.0%

Source: Company records.

groups for the years 1963 and 1964. Exhibit 3 is a five-year financial summary, 1960 through 1964. The company employed approximately 40,000 persons. Commenting on Olin's growth and development since 1954, Mr. Grand said:

By mid-1963 Olin had passed through three distinct periods in its growth: a period of rapid external expansion—1954–1956; a period of severe financial strain created by entering the aluminum industry as an integrated producer—1956–1959; and, thirdly, a period during which capital funds were sufficient for only a limited program of modernization of existing facilities—1960–1962.

By mid-1963 the problems inherent in these three periods of growth into our five business areas were largely behind us. Management could now shift its emphasis from problem solving to exploiting opportunities—and it is, after all, top management's responsibility to make profits, not to solve problems.

The goal we established in 1963 was clear and precise—to maintain or to move each of our five businesses into the upper third of its competition

Exhibit 3
FIVE-YEAR FINANCIAL SUMMARY
(in millions of dollars)

	1964	1963	1962	1961	1960
Net sales and operating revenues	$815.7	$779.2	$737.3	$708.2	$674.2
Interest, dividends, and other income	13.2	8.0	7.1	7.7	7.8
	828.9	787.2	744.4	715.9	682.0
Cost of goods sold	550.6	530.2	493.8	475.2	449.5
Depreciation, depletion, and amortization	34.8	33.7	35.0	32.5	30.9
Administrative, selling, advertising, and research	147.9	139.1	135.6	127.5	119.4
Interest on long-term debt	13.9	14.1	14.2	14.3	14.4
Other deductions	7.2	4.4	3.5	7.1	1.3
Federal and foreign taxes on income	33.2	28.7	28.2	27.2	28.3
Net income	41.3	37.0	34.1	32.1	38.2
Dividends paid	17.0	12.9	13.0	12.9	13.4
Assets	960.6	916.0	878.3	867.6	873.8
Liabilities	496.5	476.7	464.7	457.1	462.6
Shareholders' equity	464.1	439.3	413.6	410.5	411.2
Working capital	296.7	292.3	270.2	245.2	258.7
Investments, advances, and receivables	86.0	95.6	99.3	126.5	105.6
Property, plant, and equipment: Expenditures for additions and replacements	65.1	57.9	53.7	36.9	48.9
Total property, plant, and equipment, at cost	806.7	755.4	711.7	685.1	676.0
Accumulated depreciation, depletion, and amortization	357.4	335.1	313.6	297.1	279.8
Long-term notes	211.0	220.7	224.2	227.6	231.0
Convertible debentures	100.0	100.0	100.0	100.0	100.0
Per share in dollars: Earnings	3.16	2.86	2.63	2.47	2.86
Dividends paid	1.30	1.00	1.00	1.00	1.00
Shareholders' equity	35.38	33.86	32.00	31.69	30.71
Average number of common shares in thousands	13,081	12,940	12,952	13,026	13,383
Number of holders of common stock	59,000	60,000	65,000	67,000	73,000

Source: Company records.

in terms of net profit and return on assets. All our assets susceptible to economic measurement throughout business in general, and within our specific businesses in particular, were analyzed in depth and placed into one of three categories—those assets earning 8 percent and above; those earning between 4 percent and 8 percent; and those earning below 4 percent.

To achieve our goals it was clear we had to:

a. Increase the earnings on existing assets by running what we had better —through modernizing facilities, reducing costs, improving systems.
b. Invest in opportunities with above-average potential due to significant Olin competitive advantages.

c. Expand from within our existing business areas by improved research, technology, and marketing.
d. Dispose of those assets which did not have the potential of meeting the company's return-on-assets criteria.
e. Conduct each of our five businesses on a worldwide basis.

We then determined that a management system of broader delegation of responsibility, authority, and personal accountability for profit results was required and now possible.

The task was clearly for the many and not for the few. And as it is frequently said, an organization structure is nothing more than the means of permitting common people to do uncommon things. Ours was an uncommon task and an uncommon opportunity.

In establishing an organization structure of broadened individual responsibility based on autonomous product groups, we recognized two requisites for success: first, the need for people equal to the new responsibility, and second, the need to maintain the essential balance between individual initiative and control of the total enterprise. Convinced that the people were available, we adopted two programs to fulfill the second need.

First was to install a comprehensive system of moving five-year plans, up-dated annually. Second was a coordinated and integrated system of financial controls designed to monitor progress against these plans, asset by asset.

Thus, in brief, Olin today is run with authority, responsibility, and accountability for profit results delegated to the appropriate executive vice presidents, and by them successively down the line to the 100 profit centers that have been established throughout the company.

Each segment of our business operates under its own five-year moving plan—the sum of which makes up the total approved corporate plan. These plans establish specific financial goals, purposes and strategies, capital and manpower requirements—all translated into a performance timetable of net profit and return on asset improvement.

Capital resources are allocated to each of our five businesses on a moving three-year basis. We are currently in the 1965–1967 period during which we will spend approximately $230 million.

When approved, the first year of our five-year plan becomes our performance control budget by months for the current year.

The corporate financial control system monitors the results of each profit center against the operating control budget, which is not changed. The first report showing variances from planned net profit is available the fifth working day of each month. Some 20 different monthly reports, each designed to show actual variances from the control budget and the reasons establishing future changes by month, quarter, and year, are prepared from financial information flowing up from our profit centers.

Marketing

In 1965, Olin marketed its highly diversified products under many different brand names, including Winchester (sporting arms and ammunition), Squibb (pharmaceuticals), Western (ammunition), Frost (forest products), Puritan (auto products), Ramset (fastening systems), Ecusta (paper products), Western (brass), Mathieson (industrial chemicals and plant foods), Olin (cellophane and aluminum), and Frostkraft (cartons and containers).

Olin sold to many different buyers—such as the government, industrial users, house contractors, physicians, and ultimate consumers—through many different distribution channels and by use of many different marketing techniques. Even within divisions, products were often sold to several markets by different marketing methods.

Late in 1961 a consulting firm retained by the company to study Olin's advertising and related communication policies had recommended the adoption of a "corporate identity system" which called for the incorporation of the name "Olin" in all product names, advertising, public relations material, stationery, and other communication media. Traditionally, each division had held complete responsibility and authority for the formulation and execution of its marketing policies in light of its own needs and with little or no reference to other divisions or to the parent company. The recommendation by the consulting firm to rename and market most of the company's products under the single brand name "Olin," or at least to give divisional brand names and trademarks strong corporate support and close tie-in with a corporate name, had been partially accepted. Some divisions had opposed the consulting firm's proposals on the ground that customers would no longer recognize the products affected by the proposal and that declining sales would result. These divisions had continued with their relatively autonomous marketing programs.

Corporate organization

In 1965 Olin's operations were organized along four broad product groups: metals, chemicals, packaging, and pharmaceuticals, each headed by an executive vice president. Each group consisted of several product divisions, which in turn consisted of numerous operating plants. Thus, for instance, the metals group encompassed the metals division with six plants producing brass and aluminum, and the Winchester-Western division with three plants manufacturing firearms, ammunition, powder-actuated tools, fasteners, and solid propellents. The chemicals group, divided into the chemicals division and the agricultural division, was the largest single group, operating over 20 geographically dispersed plants.

A group of seven staff vice presidents at Olin's executive offices had the following functions: accounting, corporate services, law and administration, marketing, production and engineering, research and development, and finance. Mr. Phillips, as corporate director of purchasing,

Exhibit 4
ORGANIZATION CHART AS OF DECEMBER, 1965

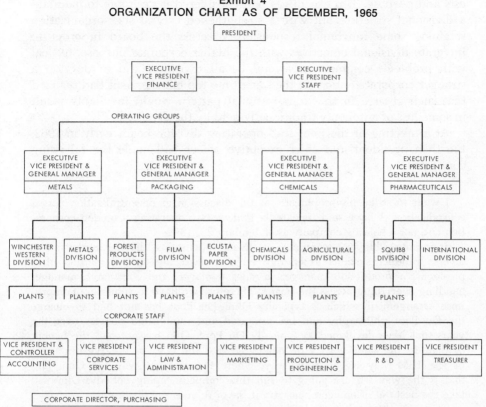

Source: Company records.

reported to Everett Bellows, vice president in charge of corporate services. A corporate organization chart is shown in Exhibit 4.

Prior to 1962 Olin divisions had operated essentially as autonomous units. Within wide limits division managers had been free to determine research and development priorities, to introduce new products and to determine the marketing and procurement mix. Division managers had been held fully accountable for results by top management, which operated with a relatively small corporate staff in New York City.

Between 1954 and 1960, as the size, complexity, and diversity of the company's operations grew, top management had realigned the organization structure by pulling together the numerous divisions into seven major product groups, each of which had continued to operate as a relatively autonomous organization.

In 1961, however, top management had become concerned with a need to combine maximum possible responsibility and authority for divisional performance at the divisional level with Olin's corporatewide interests and purpose. Top executives had considered it desirable to maintain a divisional structure but with a strengthened central staff organization retaining some functional responsibility across the board in order to integrate divisional objectives with the higher corporate purpose, to deal with problems common to several or all divisions, and to develop a stronger corporate entity. At the same time top management had realized that such change in the organizational pattern would inevitably result in some loss of autonomy traditionally held by the divisions.

At a meeting of the joint staff operating division heads early in 1962, the then president and chief executive officer had made the following comments:

I want to strike philosophically at the discussion of decentralization versus centralization. I have said repeatedly that we are operating a unified corporation and not a holding company as of January 23, 1962.

It is impossible in a company of diverse operations, diverse markets, and diverse product systems to operate on the classically unified method of a president, a production manager, a sales manager, and a research manager handling everything across the board. Therefore we have to come to a compromise arrangement which is typically Olin. Du Pont has not had to change the Du Pont philosophy and has operated and established policies over the years that have developed as typically Du Pont. Olin has not had the benefit of that. In the same way, I do not agree that the G.E. or the Westinghouse or the IBM way is the right way. There is one right way for Olin, and that is the way we are going to run this company, aping nobody. Olin will take the best out of one company, try it, savor it, and, if it fits, use it.

There are things that can better be done without taking one iota of responsibility from the general manager—can be better done by a unified Olin than can be done by seven separate units. Unfortunately, it isn't necessarily even seven separate units because there are divisions which have not been unified or integrated. Therefore, the company cannot go to just a classic decentralized holding company type of operation, because Olin loses the benefit of the intracorporate pollenization and of intracorporate buying and selling to each other. This is why we are operating a company called Olin. We will develop our own method.

Organization for procurement

Prior to 1962, Olin's procurement organization had reflected top management's strong belief in divisional operations on the basis of product groups, accompanied by maximum divisional autonomy. Each operating division had been purchasing all raw materials, parts, supplies, and services independently, with little or no reference to the procurement activities of other divisions. Following the gradual organization of Olin's previously totally unintegrated activities into seven major product divisions in the late 50s, most, but not all, of the divisions had maintained a divisional purchasing department and, depending on number of plants, material requirements, and related factors, one or more field purchasing departments. (See Exhibit 5.)

Mr. Phillips believed, however, that, with the exception of the chemicals, the organics, and the pharmaceutical divisions, an absence of a well-developed divisional purchasing management had continued. He commented:

For all practical purposes the other divisions went on with the purchasing function decentralized to the plant locations. In many of these instances purchasing was not under purchasing control. Purchasing agents merely wrote the orders or made commitments without analysis or evaluation. There was some centralized commodity buying at the divisional level, but not much. The divisions did not carry out purchasing research, or commodity or market analysis. Cost reduction programs and manpower development could be found nowhere.

The company, as indicated previously, had maintained a corporate staff purchasing organization at company headquarters in New York City. Beginning January, 1962, it was headed by Mr. Phillips, who was also purchasing manager of the chemicals and organics divisions. The emphasis of the work of the corporate purchasing staff prior to 1962 had been on the collection, analysis, and reporting to top management of statistical purchasing data for each division. The staff had provided assistance to the divisions in the procurement of materials, supplies, and services through sourcing studies and purchasing research. The staff also had rendered assistance to the divisions in disposing of excess and obsolete equipment, material, and real estate held by the divisions. Occasionally, the staff had performed special assignments for the divisions. Thus, for instance, the general manager of the pharmaceutical division had approached Mr. Phillips with the request to determine from the central purchasing statistics whether Olin could switch its purchases of flax used by the paper division from a domestic supplier to a Turkish supplier. The Turkish government had insisted that Olin buy some goods from Turkish companies in return for selling pharmaceutical products in Turkey. Mr. Phillips had, after first checking with the paper division, informed the pharmaceutical division that there would be no unusual problems taking business from the American flax supplier and that therefore the purchase of Turkish flax would be possible. He subsequently learned from the paper division, however, that the flax supplier was one of their subsidiaries and hence had to cancel the change from the domestic to a foreign supplier. This experience had prompted the corporate purchasing staff to search for and find other materials to be purchased from Turkish suppliers in order to comply with the Turkish government's request.

Exhibit 5
PURCHASING ORGANIZATION CHART, 1962

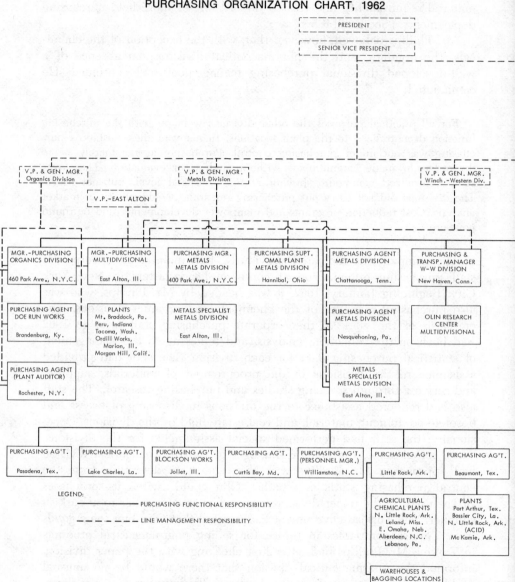

Commenting further on Olin's purchasing organization prior to 1962, Mr. Phillips said:

Purchasing was characterized by a lack of communication and coordination. There was no effective communication among the divisions, and there was little coordination of their purchasing activities. We had no corporatewide purchasing objectives, and no written policies or standards for purchasing performance. There wasn't a purchasing manual in existence. Training of

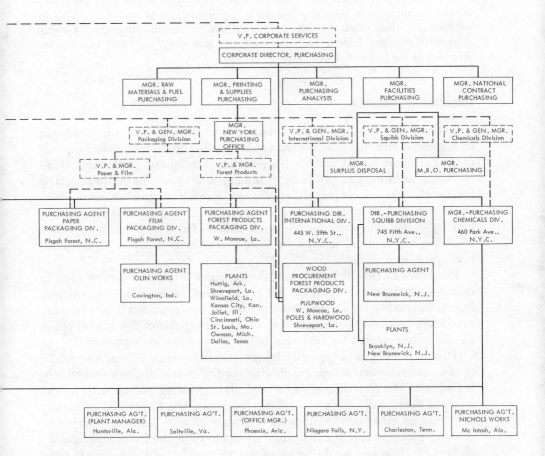

purchasing personnel was not done. Although there were other factors, this lack of attention to training led to an absence of a high level of competence of the purchasing personnel, both at headquarters and in the divisions.

In some plants it seemed everybody negotiated with the vendors except the purchasing agents. General managers, plant engineers, quality control people—everybody was in the act. Sometimes even the purchasing agent had a chance to negotiate. Little attention was paid to procurement problems affecting two or more divisions, such as national contracts. We had little coordinated overall corporate planning and procurement. Ordering procedures and terms and conditions varied from one division to the next, and most plants did not even put numbers on their purchase orders.

Of course, you must remember that Olin went through a tremendous growth period between the 1954 merger and the early 60s in which everybody's time was completely absorbed with the task of getting products out. There simply was not any time left for many of the difficult questions of organization and administrative procedures. Business was excellent, and our important job was to take full advantage of the extremely favorable economic climate. Each division had executives with great ambitions and a drive to grow and expand as rapidly as possible. Naturally top management wanted to put no restraint on that drive by giving more than minimum directions. I think there was also the feeling that the company was simply getting too big for any sort of centralized operation.

Purchasing activities

In 1961–62 Olin had spent annually over $300 million on purchases of materials, supplies, and services. Chemicals and allied products, products of primary metal industry, production machinery, paper and allied products, utilities, and products of mining and quarrying had accounted for nearly 60 percent of all purchases. Exhibit 6 gives a breakdown of the total dollar procurement volume by major commodity, cross-classified by major divisions, for the year 1962. (The composition of Olin's procurement volume, it may be noted, had not changed significantly between 1961 and 1965).

Purchases of the chemicals and the organics divisions together usually represented over one third of the corporation's annual buying volume. Purchasing activities by these two divisions were considered by company executives particularly important from the standpoint of the overall effect on the profit potentials and the interrelationships of suppliers.

The metals division typically bought annually over $50 million worth of raw materials and scrap. Purchasing for the metals division was closely linked with the flow of metals through the operating plants, with inventory positions, and with scrap tolling arrangements. Continuity of supply at minimum costs consistent with optimum balance between scrap and primary metal were critical factors, particularly in the brass mills' profitability. Fluctuations in the price of virgin metal and scrap also heavily influenced the division's profit level.

Olin's large purchases of timber, pulpwood, and flax were unique to the packaging division.

Each year the pharmaceutical division introduced several dozens of new products, potencies, and formulas in many size variations and distributed approximately 100 different types of samples' procedures involving new packaging and specialty containers. These promotional activities required particularly close cooperation between the purchasing and the marketing department. The pharmaceutical division's large volume of new and revised products and its promotions placed extreme timing pressure on the purchasing organization and made purchasing a vital and integral part of the division's procurement-manufacturing-distribution cycle.

Component parts and assemblies for firearms were an important part of the items bought by the Winchester-Western division. The volume of production parts purchased rather than made by the division had been gradually increasing for several years and was expected to reach ultimately 50 percent of all parts going into finished Winchester rifles and shotguns. This development was expected to require the division's purchasing organization to give increasing attention to the importance of costs, quality, and delivery. Production costs of the Winchester plants were generally regarded by company executives as extremely high. It was believed that close liaison between the purchasing department on the one hand, and the product design and production departments on the other, was essential in any attempt to reduce costs significantly.

In 1961–62 the company had employed, in over 30 divisional and field purchasing offices, close to 200 persons, of whom approximately 90 were buyers, assistant purchasing agents, purchasing agents, supervisors, and purchasing managers. The administrative budget for the purchasing organization had exceeded $1.5 million. The corporate purchasing staff had included, in addition to the director, six purchasing managers and several secretaries and clerk typists. (See Exhibit 7.)

The company issued annually over 200,000 purchase orders and maintained in excess of 250,000 items in inventory. The sum of the number of vendors used by each Olin plant amounted to over 40,000. No statistics were available on the number of different companies supplying material and services to the combined divisions of the firm.

Proposed reorganization of purchasing in 1962

The corporate organization planning department had undertaken a study of the company's organization for procurement and prepared a report of its findings and recommendations that had been presented to top management in January, 1962. Mr. Phillips stated:

This study was prompted by two major factors. First, our profits and return on investment had been unimpressive for some time, and one promising way to improve profits was to cut costs in procurement. Secondly, there had been the growing realization that customers also were insisting that they get an opportunity to sell to Olin. But in order to handle this customer-vendor relationship discreetly, one division must know what the other is buying and selling and who the suppliers and customers are. I think this activity brought some of our divisions more closely together than would have been possible under any other circumstances.

The recommendations made by the organization planning department had been preceded by the following observations:

There is no one set pattern or formula which will provide Olin with the most effective purchasing organization for its needs corporatewide or which

Exhibit 6
DOLLAR PROCUREMENT VOLUME BY MAJOR COMMODITY, CROSS-CLASSIFIED BY MAJOR DIVISIONS

	Total Corporate Purchases			Chemicals	
	$(000)	% of Total	Cumu- lative % of Total	$(000)	% of Total Cate- gory
Chemicals and allied products.........................	94,710	28.20	28.20	38,380	37.70
Products of primary metal industry....................	41,231	12.28	40.48	1,497	1.47
Production machinery (excluding electrical equipment).	28,675	8.54	49.02	2,263	2.22
Paper and allied products............................	26,880	8.00	57.02	1,734	1.70
Utilities, sanitary, and other services.................	19,090	5.68	62.70	12,020	11.82
Products of mining and quarrying of nonmetallic minerals, excluding fuel............................	18,729	5.58	68.28	18,485	18.16
Special trade contractors......................	14,096	4.20	72.48	2,102	2.06
Miscellaneous services and rentals...................	11,083	3.30	75.78	1,496	1.47
Fabricated metal products (excluding ordinary machinery and transportation equipment)...........	10,611	3.16	78.94	3,228	3.17
Construction—General contractors.....................	9,556	2.84	81.78	4,698	4.61
Electrical machinery, equipment, and supplies........	8,399	2.48	84.26	1,337	1.31
Lumber and wood products (excluding furniture)......	7,005	2.09	86.35	182	0.18
Miscellaneous manufactured items...................	5,739	1.71	88.06	800	0.79
Products of petroleum and coal......................	4,784	1.43	89.49	1,065	1.05
Stone, clay, and glass products......................	4,191	1.25	90.74	850	0.84
Bituminous and anthracite coal and lignite...........	3,589	1.07	91.81	2,271	2.23
Print, publishing, and allied products.................	2,978	0.88	93.73	318	0.31
Foods and kindred products, tobacco goods and cafeteria supplies...................................	2,509	0.75	94.48	799	0.78
Railroads...	2,464	0.73	95.21	2,279	2.24
Professional, scientific, and control instruments......	2,342	0.70	95.91	403	0.40
Textile mill products.................................	2,063	0.61	96.52	158	0.16
Transportation equipment............................	2,039	0.61	97.13	1,887	1.85
Rubber and synthetic rubber products................	1,803	0.54	97.67	445	0.44
Repairs and services.................................	1,735	0.51	98.18	582	0.57
Telecommunications utilities.........................	1,376	0.41	98.59	301	0.30
Products of metal mining.............................	1,338	0.40	98.99	418	0.41
Apparel and other finished products made from fabrics and similar materials........................	888	0.27	99.26	541	0.53
Products of fisheries.................................	851	0.25	99.51	851	0.84
Land, buildings, facilities, and farm products..........	615	0.18	99.69	146	0.14
Furniture and fixtures................................	382	0.12	99.81	41	0.04
Agricultural services, hunting, and trapping...........	174	0.05	99.86	*	*
Crude petroleum and natural gas.....................	149	0.05	99.91	149	0.15
Leather and leather products.........................	145	0.04	99.95	11	0.01
Forestry products....................................	8	0.00	99.95	*	*
Miscellaneous N.E.C.................................	173	0.05	100.00	47	0.05

* Not available.
Source: Company records.

Metals		Organics		Packaging		Pharma-ceuticals		Winchester Western		Research	
$(000)	% of Total Category	$(000)	% of Total Category	$(000)	% of Total Category	$(000)	% of Total Category	$(000)	% of Total Category	$(000)	Category
899	1.64	16,047	50.92	13,472	22.01	18,895	41.95	6,785	17.81	232	10.53
31,429	57.23	99	0.31	662	1.08	904	2.01	6,603	16.85	37	1.68
8,157	14.85	1,929	6.12	6,127	10.01	1,301	2.89	8,639	22.05	259	11.75
352	0.64	265	0.84	19,855	32.45	2,619	5.81	2,032	5.19	23	1.04
2,396	4.36	761	2.41	2,180	3.56	1,084	2.41	640	1.63	–	–
32	0.06	33	0.10	71	0.12	50	0.11	58	0.15	*	*
3,155	5.74	4,458	14.15	1,806	2.95	1,642	3.65	597	1.52	336	15.24
578	1.05	145	0.46	1,207	1.97	5,711	12.68	1,391	3.55	555	25.18
663	1.21	3,070	9.74	1,082	1.77	1,332	2.96	1,148	2.93	88	3.99
372	0.68	2,262	7.18	1,995	3.26	193	0.43	36	0.09	*	*
2,500	4.55	293	0.93	1,083	1.77	2,442	5.42	622	1.59	62	2.81
395	0.72	12	0.04	5,218	8.53	21	0.05	1,176	3.00	1	0.05
187	0.34	126	0.40	338	0.55	2,658	5.90	1,590	4.06	40	1.81
606	1.10	26	0.08	705	1.15	778	1.73	1,450	3.70	154	6.99
273	0.50	455	1.44	356	0.58	2,075	4.61	116	0.30	66	2.99
92	0.17	333	1.06	693	1.13	–	–	200	0.51	*	*
131	0.24	90	0.29	767	1.25	937	2.08	694	1.77	41	1.86
16	0.03	*	*	719	1.17	939	2.08	36	0.09	*	*
*	*	167	0.53	16	0.03	2	0.00	–	–	–	–
236	0.43	414	1.31	366	0.60	531	1.18	185	0.47	207	9.39
66	0.12	5	0.02	1,251	2.04	77	0.17	505	1.29	1	0.05
4	0.01	35	0.11	77	0.13	1	0.00	34	0.09	1	0.05
471	0.86	28	0.09	245	0.40	245	0.54	363	0.93	6	0.27
355	0.65	52	0.17	488	0.80	47	0.10	185	0.47	26	1.18
288	0.52	65	0.21	218	0.36	156	0.35	348	0.89	–	–
888	1.62	*	*	6	0.01	26	0.06	*	*	–	–
54	0.10	20	0.06	32	0.05	26	0.06	207	0.53	8	0.36
*	*	–	–	–	–	*	*	–	–	–	–
168	0.31	283	0.90	17	0.03	1	0.00	–	–	–	–
52	0.09	30	0.10	77	0.13	117	0.26	27	0.07	38	1.73
–	–	–	–	–	–	174	0.39	–	–	–	–
–	–	–	–	–	–	–	–	–	–	–	–
12	0.02	2	0.01	28	0.05	41	0.09	51	0.13	*	*
8	0.01	*	*	*	*	*	*	–	–	–	–
27	0.05	7	0.02	36	0.06	12	0.03	43	0.11	1	0.05

Exhibit 7

ORGANIZATION CHART, CORPORATE STAFF PURCHASING, 1961–62

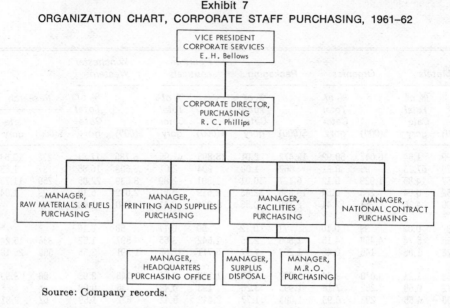

Source: Company records.

will assure Olin of the maximum value for its purchasing dollar in every instance.

This report sets forth a program tailored to the specific needs of the divisions and the overall advantage of the corporation.

It is essential to clarify the distinction between requisitioning and purchasing for full comprehension of the report which follows. As outlined in the following exhibit, requisitioning is the responsibility of line management and consists of establishing specifications, quantities, and delivery requirements. Purchasing is a service function and consists of obtaining quotations, negotiating, selecting the supplier, committing the corporation, and expediting delivery.

The corporation as a whole could provide commodity specialization in those areas which cross divisional lines and greater purchasing assistance in grouping materials common to more than one division; at the same time it could maintain a consistent commercial position with suppliers who are also major customers.

The recommendations appear below.

A. The president to delegate purchasing authority to the Corporate Director of Purchasing, who will, in turn, delegate appropriate purchasing authority to purchasing agents in the Operating Divisions. Such delegations will be made with the concurrence of the Operating Division General Managers. Delegations of purchasing authority should fit division needs and not follow any predetermined pattern of dollar or commodity limitations. [See Appendix A for the proposed plan.]

B. The president to delegate requisitioning authority to Operating Division General Managers, who will delegate appropriate requisitioning authority to key line management in each division.

C. Corporate Purchasing to prepare policy directives for issuance by the president. These will state the basic principles and guidelines within which all purchasing organizations shall operate. [See Appendix B for examples.]

D. Corporate Purchasing to provide functional guidance, assistance, and leadership to divisional and field purchasing departments. Operating Division and field purchasing departments to remain under local supervision and administration.

E. Corporate Purchasing to establish standards for purchasing performance, to train purchasing agents, and to physically audit purchasing performance in the field; Corporate Purchasing to be consulted in advance on the assignment and replacement of key purchasing personnel.

F. The organization structure of Corporate Purchasing to consist of commodity specialists who will negotiate and buy for the Operating Divisions in selected instances as directed by the Corporate Director of Purchasing, and who will also conduct purchasing research, sourcing studies (including emphasis on intracompany sources), value and market analysis, and develop intercorporate contacts to promote commercial intelligence and corporate commercial relationships.

G. Purchasing to coordinate with the Corporate departments.

H. Corporate Purchasing to plan negotiation strategy on major equipment purchases in conjunction with Corporate Engineering and the Operating Division personnel concerned; when called for by agreed plan, participate in negotiations for such purchases.

I. Division purchasing organizations to continue to purchase production materials and supplies. Corporate Purchasing to enter key commodity negotiations whenever circumstances dictate; i.e., market conditions, or other significant reasons. This will be done with concurrent notification to the Operating Division General Manager.

J. The Metals Division to assume the responsibility for the purchase of nonferrous metals and for continuing surveillance of metal markets.

K. An active and aggressive purchase-cost-reduction program to be undertaken throughout the corporation and directed by Corporate Purchasing. Specific objectives to be established and progress reported as to their attainment. Inherent in such a program is the understanding that price is not necessarily synonymous with cost. Therefore, savings must be emphasized through material substitution, quality, and performance as well as price.

L. Corporate Purchasing to continue to pursue, but on a more vigorous basis, the establishment of national contracts on common use items and to audit the use of such contracts by field purchasing agents.

M. All office equipment and machinery to be purchased or leased through national contracts by Corporate Purchasing. Each Operating Division to order against such contracts for this equipment.

N. Corporate Purchasing to assume active control over the screening and disposal of obsolete and excess asset equipment throughout the corporation.

O.   Following corporate approval of the above recommendations, convene New York meeting of key purchasing personnel to introduce new organization and explain program, functions, and relationships.

These recommendations had been presented at a meeting of the joint staff operating heads on January 23, 1962. They had drawn support from some vice presidents and opposition from others. Thus, for instance, the vice presidents of the chemicals, organics, and metal divisions, pointing to such companies as Du Pont, had been "generally in favor of centralizing Olin's purchasing to some degree," but had cautioned that such shift away from the company's existing decentralized operations could not be done overnight. The vice president of the packaging division had offered the practices of General Electric and Westinghouse as equally good evidence in support for decentralization, and had stated that the recommendations were in conflict with his responsibility for divisional profit performance. He said:

These recommendations constitute withdrawing essential responsibility for the division and putting it somewhere else. This not only makes the division head's responsibility much more difficult, but also it is an opening wedge to do it throughout the organization. If the company is centralizing the management to this degree in purchasing, it should do it on an overall basis for the entire organization. I see a great problem in setting up a new line of authority running from top management through the corporate purchasing department to the purchasing department in the divisions; the divisional purchasing department, either by delegation or practice, is going to take over control of purchasing that should reside with the division management.

The vice president and general manager of the paper and film division also expressed concern about a possible diffusion of responsibility. He commented:

There is a basic managerial issue involved in this process of putting an operating person in the very awkward role where he is not quite sure where the real responsibility lies for the performance of his job or to whom he looks for guidance and consultation. As to purchasing, I have no indication of where things are not working well, except in those instances where the division has accommodated to the overall corporate interest and has referred to corporate headquarters problems as to the supply of certain major items; and where there was a time lag and a confused atmosphere with respect to who does what and whether the division is free to make a commitment. The communication lag, which created added telephone expense, travel expense, and holding-up costs, has come from not being able to get an answer from headquarters.

In response to the divided opinions expressed by the vice presidents on the issue of how to organize the company's procurement activities, the president had stated:

The original delegation comes from the board, then from the president. I am not concerned with the mechanics of whether this delegation comes through the purchasing director of the corporation to the purchasing agents directly or through the general manager. I tend to agree that it might come through the general manager.

That the incursion on the part of corporate purchasing in the area of big dollar commitments, or of special deals, or of trade relations, is an extirpation of divisional management I do not see.

With $330 million worth of purchases in Olin, a 1 percent savings is worth 13 cents a share, after taxes, to this company. Therefore, a proper approach to the handling of our purchasing is mighty important to Olin.

Purchasing in today's economy is a highly professional operation just the same as is advertising. Each division used to want to control its own legal problems; but, as antitrust, Robinson-Patman, and other problems got more complicated, we had to get ever better experts and make an Olin policy. I don't think the fact that the lawyers get their policy and their delegation from the headquarters legal department is causing anybody any loss of prestige, loss of kudos, or loss of rights, because the general manager still has a lot to say and to do with that. The same applies to accounting, which is a professional operation.

The problem we have in purchasing is that if the general manager is negotiating a purchase of materials and supplies and doing all of this himself, then I don't think the general manager is necessarily doing his job. I think we do not have in this company, as do many other companies, as many professional people with professional ability in the purchasing field. I get this from the outside. This is why I say that we are not trying to interfere in the slightest degree with the rights to manage, to produce, to sell, to maintain quality, to find new products. These are the responsibilities of the general managers in this company.

I fail to see where the proposed purchasing policy will impair your ability to manage your division. If the problem is the *route* by which this delegation comes to you, I will not fight that. I am willing to have it channeled so that you are in control of the people having the purchasing authority in the division, but that does not mean the purchasing man in the division has the right to ignore corporate purchasing.

Mr. Bellows [vice president of corporate services] stated one of the responsibilities of corporate purchasing is to help the divisions to upgrade the performance of their purchasing people. It is the responsibility of the divisions purchasing man to see that the commercial terms and conditions of a contract are proper, but he will not settle the technical issues.

Mr. Bellows will incorporate as many of the ideas set forth at this meeting as are not in conflict with the theory and then will resubmit recommendations to the president.

On January 30, 1962, the president had approved the recommendations made by the organization planning department, which he then issued to the division general managers with the following memorandum:

By this memorandum, I am asking each of you to contribute your best efforts to put into effect the purchasing program which we discussed at our January 23rd meeting. I am aware that the report contained a novel proposal on the delegation of authority, but in all other respects I believe the report merely restated the kind of relationships which ought to obtain among management, technical, and purchasing people and which, in fact, has frequently been the case. Beyond this, the program calls for the establishment of purchasing standards and objectives, the upgrading of purchasing personnel, and the more effective coordination of corporate resources to gain maximum advantage for the divisions and the corporation as a whole. It is clear that no one opposes these purposes.

Returning to the one point of possible disagreement, it is obvious to me, as I believe it is to each of you, that you would want and I would expect that each general manager will personally play a determinant role in the acquisition of a critical commodity or critical equipment. To make this crystal clear, I shall delegate to each general manager purchasing authority.

However, I am asking that this authority not be redelegated for three reasons:

1. I think it is important that we establish clearly the responsibility of subordinate personnel in the line and technical staff areas for bringing division purchasing people into discussions with vendors early in the acquisition process.
2. At this time, I want to put squarely on the corporate purchasing staff the responsibility of assisting the general managers to improve the performance of purchasing people throughout the corporation.
3. I believe the redelegation of purchasing authority from corporate purchasing to purchasing agents, and only to those designated by the general manager, will provide an avenue of communication and a degree of responsiveness between the two, in both directions, which has not always been the case in the past.

It should not require further emphasis, but let me mention once again that any purchasing agent, including the corporate director of purchasing, will buy only what you have requisitioned or what you have authorized others to requisition.

On the foregoing basis, I am instructing Everett Bellows to proceed with the planning and administrative arrangements necessary to have this program in effect by April 1st.

Implementation of the 1962 purchasing reorganization program

In the months following the issuance of the memorandum by the president, Mr. Phillips had replaced nearly all the purchasing personnel at the corporate staff level with employees primarily from the various operating divisions. He had selected persons whom he considered adequately trained and experienced to perform highly specialized staff work, and sufficiently broad-gauged as managers not only to provide strong guidance and assistance to the divisional purchasing organizations, but also to assume direct responsibility for purchasing activities affecting more than one division. (See Exhibit 8 for organization chart of corporate purchasing staff.)

Having completed the regrouping of the corporate staff purchasing department, Mr. Phillips had designed and put into effect forms and procedures for the development by each operating division of annual forecasts to be submitted to the corporate purchasing office at the beginning of each planning period (calendar year). Together these forecasts were to form the "approved corporate purchasing plan." The instructions issued by Mr. Phillips to the divisional purchasing organizations for the preparation of the forecasts read in part as follows:

The corporate purchasing department will determine those items or services which are to be included as part of the corporate purchasing forecasts. Selection of the items will be on the following basis:

1. Items for which, on an overall corporate basis, purchases annually exceed $100,000, or, on an individual basis, exceed $50,000.
2. Items regardless of value which have a customer relationship.
3. Items or services on a special project basis which are expected to exceed $50,000.

The corporate purchasing department will specify the forms and the methods of preparing the local and divisional reports which are to be incorporated into the corporate purchasing forecasts.

For the annual forecast, it is anticipated that individual item cards as specified by the data processing department will be prepared for each using location. With these item cards, the data processing department can prepare such division or corporate purchase forecast data as needed, and division reports will be furnished to the division general manager and division purchasing department.

For the special project, equipment, services, construction, or engineering items, an individual report will be furnished to the corporate purchasing department at the time plans are in preparation. This report will itemize the contemplated major equipment and contracts, the estimated value of each, and the suppliers or contractors who will be on the bid list. The reports will be incorporated into the special projects purchasing forecast.

The purchasing forecasts submitted by the divisions for incorporation into the corporate purchasing forecast are to be considered as the division's plan of action *as of the time of submission*. The division is to advise the corporate purchasing department immediately if any change in the forecast is contemplated. The corporate purchasing department will coordinate overall corporate purchasing interests and obtain division concurrence of any changes to the division forecast. Once the corporate purchasing department and the division concur in the purchasing forecast and it is then approved by the division general manager and corporate director of purchasing, it becomes an "approved purchasing plan" subject to commitment action, and any changes thereto

Exhibit 8
CORPORATE PURCHASING ORGANIZATION STAFF

DIRECTOR OF PURCHASING

1. Directs the development of policies on basic Corporate Purchasing matters.
2. Reviews Purchasing plans and makes sourcing recommendations to assure a sound corporate buying pattern including Olin manufactured items.
3. Plans overall Purchasing strategy and assists the Operating Divisions as required in negotiation.
4. Purchases raw materials, supplies, and equipment in selected instances.
5. Trains and recommends placement of Division Purchasing personnel.
6. Directs research in buying and cost reduction techniques.
7. Directs the corporate purchase of major commodities as necessitated by market conditions or corporate interests.

PURCHASING MANAGER CHEMICALS AND FUELS

1. Recommends policies on the purchase of chemicals, coal, and petroleum products, and provides guidance to the Operating Divisions.
2. Develops and recommends sources of supply for chemicals, coal, and petroleum products.
3. Conducts research in buying and cost reduction techniques and commodity markets.
4. As directed by the Director of Purchasing, negotiates and purchases major chemicals, coal, and petroleum products.

MANAGER SURPLUS DISPOSAL

1. Recommends policies on the screening and sale of excess and obsolete equipment, spare parts, and real property.
2. Coordinates the corporate-wide screening of excess and obsolete asset equipment.
3. Sells surplus asset equipment and real property.
4. Maintains surveillance over excess equipment; keeps informed of corporatewide requirements for new equipment in order to assure maximum use of surplus equipment and spare parts.

PURCHASING MANAGER EQUIPMENT

1. Recommends policies on the purchase of equipment, including electrical and office equipment. Confers with Corporate Engineering and Operating Divisions on procurement strategy for major equipment.
2. In accordance with agreed upon strategy, participates in the review of bids and in negotiations with Operating Division personnel.
3. Conducts research in buying and cost reduction techniques.
4. Develops information concerning suppliers.
5. Reviews construction projects with Corporate Engineering, and specifies sources for commercially important items after conferring with the Vice President – Marketing.

PURCHASING MANAGER PACKAGING

1. Recommends policies on the purchase of packaging, and provides guidance to the Operating Divisions.
2. Develops specific commodity information.
3. Develops value analysis studies, and makes recommendations.
4. Reviews captive packaging sources.
5. Conducts research in buying and cost reduction techniques and commodity markets.
6. Develops new techniques and use of materials for shipping, packaging, and palletizing. Transmits pertinent information to Divisions Packaging personnel

PURCHASING MANAGER PRINTING

1. Recommends policies on the purchase of printed matter, and provides guidance to the Operating Divisions.
2. Develops specific commodity information.
3. Conducts research in buying and cost reduction techniques and commodity markets.
4. Purchases all printed matter for Corporate Staff at 460 Park Avenue.
5. As directed by the Director of Purchasing, assists the Operating Divisions in the purchase of printed matter.

PURCHASING ANALYSIS MANAGER

1. Develops Purchasing procedures, and provides guidance to the Operating Divisions.
2. Analyzes Corporate Purchasing statistics.
3. Conducts research in buying and cost reduction techniques and commodity markets.
4. Audits purchasing performance in the Operating Divisions, and makes recommendations to the Director of Purchasing.
5. Conducts special studies of a general purchasing nature.

Source: Company records.

must be with the concurrence of the corporate purchasing department and the division.

For special project items, the corporate purchasing department and division will prepare an "approved purchasing plan" as soon as purchase action on a specific item or service is imminent. The division general manager or corporate director of purchasing may delegate others to approve special project purchasing plans. It is recognized that some special project purchasing forecasts may never require further action but will remain in the corporate purchasing forecast until the project is abandoned.

At the time the "approved purchasing plan" is agreed upon, the corporate purchasing department and division will prepare, if needed, a plan of purchasing action which includes the participation, if any, of corporate or other staff or operating departments.

The "approved purchasing plan" for any given item is an agreement to take action subject to the policies, procedures, and authorities of the corporation and the division.

In conjunction with the purchasing plan, Mr. Phillips had considered it important to define purchasing authority. He wrote:

The requisition or other approved document is the instruction to the purchasing department to purchase on behalf of an authorized person. The requisition must be signed by the person who has been given the requisitioning authority for the type and value of material or service on the requisition. Only the division general manager, or those specifically authorized by the president, *can have both requisitioning authority and purchasing authority.*

Only those authorized by the president (division general managers) or the corporate director of purchasing may commit the division or the corporation to purchase items, materials, or services. *All* personnel purchasing on behalf of a division are responsible for their actions both to the division general manager and to the corporate director of purchasing. Delegations and limits of purchasing authority to division personnel by the corporate director of purchasing are to be made with the concurrence of the division general manager.

In general, subject to division general manager approval, it is anticipated that personnel within the division, dependent upon scope of operations, will be authorized to purchase materials, services, and supplies *not on* the "approved purchasing plan" up to $50,000 in value. For items *on the "approved purchasing plan,"* division personnel will be authorized to purchase up to $500,000 in value subject to specific stipulations, type and length of contracts, and corporate and division purchasing procedures.

Mr. Phillips had believed that in order to permit the corporate purchasing department to discharge its new responsibility and obligations properly, it was necessary to formulate and disseminate to the divisional purchasing departments policy statements delineating as precisely as possible the future relationships of the corporate purchasing department with the offices of the division general managers, the division purchasing departments, and other corporate staff departments. He therefore had drafted and circulated through his own and other departments what he believed to be reasonable guidelines:

Purchasing relationships

Division General Manager—Corporate Director of Purchasing

Any purchasing action affecting the operation of the division must be in accordance with corporate policies and procedures or must be in accordance with division policies and procedures and be approved by the division general manager. The corporate director of purchasing is responsible for providing certain purchasing services to the division general manager and will assist the general manager to develop an effective purchasing organization, policies, procedures, etc. It should be an exception rather than the rule for the division general manager or his immediate management subordinates to participate in purchasing negotiations. Similarly, the corporate director of purchasing is to coordinate those purchasing activities and interests which are multiple-division or corporate in nature. Circumstances may make it logical for the division general manager to ask the corporate director of purchasing to negotiate purchases, and similarly the corporate director of purchasing could recommend to the division general manager that corporate purchasing negotiate certain division purchases. The division general manager and the corporate director of purchasing are expected to cooperate with and assist each other to achieve the most effective purchasing for the division and the corporation.

Corporate Purchasing Department—Division Purchasing Department

The corporate staff purchasing managers are responsible for the purchasing functions in their assigned areas of responsibility. They will work closely with division purchasing personnel to assist, guide, and train them, and coordinate their purchasing actions. The corporate purchasing staff and division purchasing staffs of necessity must work as a team to help each other accomplish their specific goals. It is the responsibility of the corporate purchasing staff to provide the basic policies, procedures, and guidelines. The division purchasing personnel are to function within these policies, procedures, and guidelines. It will be through close association that each will be able to represent the interests of the other in accomplishing a good purchasing job. Division purchasing organization will vary from division to division. Corporate purchasing contracts will normally follow established purchasing channels. However, those persons signing purchase commitments are responsible directly to the corporate director of purchasing for compliance with policies, procedures, and stipulations affecting purchase commitments.

Purchasing Department—Other Departments (Engineering, Production, Transportation, etc.)

Purchasing department representatives, both division and corporate, are required to utilize the service, guidance, or obtain concurrence of other departments and staff members as a purchasing situation requires. Regardless of other department participation, the purchasing department representative who signs a commitment must make certain that all necessary factors have been considered—e.g., the engineering department may have selected a supplier or a certain piece of equipment on the basis of technical evaluation, but the purchasing agent must have an adequate analysis supporting the decision in the purchasing file. Even though direct technical contact between a supplier and other departments are to be encouraged, the purchasing agent must make sure that purchase terms and other such considerations are handled by the purchasing department.

Corporate Purchasing Department—Corporate Staff Departments

The corporate purchasing staff members will maintain close contact with other corporate staff departments so that purchasing policies, procedures, and actions at corporate and division levels are properly coordinated, and legal, tax, insurance, financial, and accounting matters which are pertinent to purchasing actions will be administered consistently.

Corporate Purchasing—Corporate Marketing

The corporate director of purchasing and corporate purchasing managers will consult with and obtain the advice of the corporate marketing department on all purchasing plans or actions which may affect customer relations. Division purchasing must refer all purchase actions based on customer relations to the corporate purchasing office for approval prior to commitment.

As a next major step, Mr. Phillips had conferred extensively with the division managers on the selection of key divisional purchasing personnel. He had reached agreement with the general managers to place heavy emphasis on college education as a general requirement for the job of purchasing agent. As a result, the company in 1962–63 had appointed or hired more than 20 purchasing agents holding bachelor degrees, notably in engineering and chemical engineering, to replace retiring or leaving personnel.

In cooperation with nearly all division managers, Mr. Phillips and his staff had spent considerable time on the drafting of basic procurement policies and procedures, major project purchasing procedures, surplus disposal policies and procedures, research purchasing procedures, supplier relationships policies, purchasing directories, standard lump sum and standard cost-plus construction contracts, purchasing savings report procedures, and other documents related to procurement matters. (For the table of contents of the Purchasing Policy Manual, see Exhibit 9.)

Subsequent to the issuance of these policies and procedures, Mr. Phillips had set up and conducted two one-week purchasing conferences attended by all divisional purchasing personnel. During these conferences members of the corporate purchasing department had explained and discussed at length the major aspects of the purchasing reorganization as well as other subjects such as "the function and use of a purchasing manual," "cost reduction programs," "engineering-purchasing-production team work," and "elements of negotiation." As an outgrowth of the conferences, the staff department had continued to assist the divisions in preparing divisional training outlines, training data, and seminar pre-

Exhibit 9
PURCHASING POLICY MANUAL TABLE OF CONTENTS: 1964

SECTION I
  A. Objectives
     1. Profit motivated
     2. Optimum value
     3. Assurance of supply
     4. Utilization of supplier technology
  B. Responsibilities
  C. Organization
  D. Purchasing personnel
  E. Purchasing reviews
SECTION II
  A. Relationships
     1. Interdepartmental
       a. General
     2. Interdivisional
       a. Purchasing quotations affecting interdivisional transfer prices
     3. Suppliers
       a. Obligation to suppliers
       b. Over-dependency of suppliers
       c. Supplier profit
       d. Supplier cost information
       e. Communication with suppliers and service contractors
  B. Personal
     1. Personal conduct and ethics
       a. General
       b. Outside business interests of employees
     2. Corporate policies
       a. Compliance with antitrust laws
       b. Supplier relations
       c. Delegation of authority
SECTION III
  A. Purchasing practices
     1. General
     2. Bids
     3. Negotiation
     4. Price increases
  B. Control of negotiation
  C. Sourcing
  D. Speculation
  E. Standard purchase order form
     1. Use of the standard purchase order form
     2. Legal department coordination
  F. Fixed price facility contracts
  G. Purchasing for government reimbursement contracts
    Source: Company records.

sentations. The staff department also had continued to hold, at more or less regular intervals, purchasing seminars on such topics as purchasing by objectives, purchasing performance measurement, equipment purchasing methods and negotiations, and value analysis.

Mr. Phillips and members of his staff had devoted a great deal of time to reviewing and changing purchasing procedures at both plant and divisional levels in the Winchester-Western division, the metals division, the chemicals division, and the pharmaceuticals division. Thus, for instance, surveys made of various Olin print shops resulted in the closing down of such shops and the establishment of a number of purchasing offices in which the procurement of all printed items and graphic arts items was concentrated. Other reviews had led to the reorganization or to the formation of new purchasing offices at the plant level. Upon request, the staff department had conducted special purchasing studies involving major procurement items, such as bulk chemicals and paper. Many of these studies had resulted in renegotiations of buying contracts by the divisional purchasing departments or in the establishment of long-range divisional procurement plans. In what Mr. Phillips considered to be an important phase of the purchasing reorganization, the corporate staff purchasing department had negotiated approximately 25 national and area contracts covering such products as sulfur, fluorspar, phosphate rock, alcohols, hydrogen, nitrogen, coke, oxygen, lime, carbon, glycol ethers, propylene and office paper and supplies. Plants had released orders against these contracts.

Because of a shortage of managerial purchasing personnel qualified to develop an effective divisional purchasing organization in the organics division Mr. Phillips had continued to direct the divisional procurement function and, with the aid of his corporate staff, had handled the major purchasing activities for that division's plants. The staff also had begun to participate actively in the evaluation of negotiations for major production equipment and facilities for the metals division, the Winchester-Western division, the chemicals division, and the forest products division.

Other major activities that the staff had developed in the course of implementing the purchasing reorganization program included the sale of surplus equipment, land, and facilities for all divisions, the purchase of special equipment of high dollar value, such as phosphate rock barges for the chemicals division and a Sabreliner jet aircraft, the negotiation of a national auto-lease plan, and the expediting of special engineering and construction projects.

Mr. Phillips had begun to draft procedures for corporatewide programs of cost reduction, value analysis, purchasing reviews, purchasing by objectives, performance measurement, and purchasing research. These programs, with the exception of cost reduction, had been held in abeyance, however, because the purchasing director did not believe that his staff was of sufficient size for effective implementation and follow-up.

Review of purchasing reorganization by Mr. Phillips in 1964

In April of 1964, two years after the purchasing had been reorganized, Mr. Phillips prepared a memorandum in which he commented as follows on each point of the program put into effect in 1962:[2]

---

[2] See pages 92 and 93 for the specific recommendations made in 1962.

A.   Delegation of purchasing authority to the corporate director of purchasing and redelegations of this authority to the lowest levels in the purchasing organization have been accomplished.

B.   Redelegation of requisitioning authority to the division general managers has been accomplished, but down the line redelegations have been spotty. Audit reports indicate a number of areas where buyers do not have any lists or adequate lists of authorized requisitioners.

C.   Policy directives have been issued.

D.   Functional guidance, assistance, and leadership have been given to division and field purchasing departments in the metals division, the Winchester-Western division, the chemicals division and the pharmaceuticals division. The purchasing service function has been very effective in promoting and developing divisional procedure, organizational studies, and purchasing plans.

E.   Written standards in the form of definitive purchasing policies, purchasing procedures, and purchasing audits have been established. Typical buyer, purchasing agent, and purchasing manager job descriptions have been drafted but not issued. Corporate purchasing department either prepared or assisted in the preparation of job descriptions, methods, and objectives in the Winchester-Western division, chemicals division, pharmaceuticals division, and metals division. However, the follow-through by the locations has been disappointing. A training program has been established and purchasing personnel have been assigned to attend NAPA and AMA purchasing courses. Corporate purchasing managers have been active as instructors or speakers in NAPA and AMA courses, seminars, and conferences. Purchasing audits have been conducted in the Winchester-Western division, the metals division, the chemicals division, and the pharmaceuticals division. Manpower limitation has restricted this program. The effort expended with corporate and divisional management has resulted in a willingness to hire into the purchasing function personnel more highly educated and trained. In most instances the director of purchasing has participated in the establishment of key purchasing positions and in the selection of key personnel.

F.   The director of purchasing was unsuccessful in obtaining a budget to support true commodity specialists, although some commodity buying by corporate staff personnel was accomplished. Purchasing research, sourcing studies, value and market analysis, and the development of intercorporate contacts to promote commercial intelligence and corporate commercial relationships were done on a very small scale.

G.   Coordination with the corporate marketing group to further marketing and customer interest has been effective on the whole. While most of the coordination is by means of purchasing plans, there is considerable continuing activity on a day-to-day basis. There are problems involving division marketing personnel making purchase-sales arrangements on contacting local purchasing departments direct.

H.   Corporate purchasing coordination with corporate engineering and division engineering and purchasing has been very effective to the extent of available manpower. Excellent results were obtained in the metals division, the forest products division, and the Winchester-Western division.

I. With the exception of the organics division, corporate purchasing did little negotiation on behalf of the divisions. Corporate purchasing did assume responsibility for major raw material purchasing for the organics division after it was reorganized and contributed considerably to the improved profit status of the division. Corporate purchasing continues to function as the organics division purchasing office.

J. The metals division assumed the nonferrous metals purchasing, developed a most professional and effective department, and cooperated fully with the corporate purchasing department.

K. A cost reduction program has been started under frustrating conditions. Manpower limitations did not permit a thorough indoctrination of the plan at all levels of management; it was discussed at the purchasing conferences and explained in writing. However, the plan has been all but scuttled by the reluctance of both division management levels and operating levels to accept the fact that good purchasing can result in cost reduction and profit improvement. Close control and evaluation are also required to keep the data reliable and the program effective. At the present time the program is just coasting.

L. Personnel assigned to the national contract function have been reassigned to higher priority tasks. Accordingly, the national contracts, while fairly numerous, are relatively ineffective.

M. A program of purchasing or leasing all office equipment and machinery through national contracts has not progressed, primarily because of ineffective action by the responsible purchasing manager in the staff department.

N. The surplus disposal department has functioned primarily as a disposal office for the divisions with significant success.

Commenting further on the success of the reorganization of the purchasing function, Mr. Phillips expressed the belief that one of the continuing problems was the wide difference in the evaluation of the role and importance of purchasing from one division manager to the next and also among plant managers. Mr. Phillips said:

Some believe that the primary purposes of purchasing are to order material and to expedite delivery. Many feel that the big dollar items are for division managers to handle. Corporate management supports a strong purchasing function but does not seem to realize that there is little general agreement at the division general manager's level or below as to who is to purchase or just what is to be expected from the purchasing function.

Mr. Phillips believed that the work of the corporate purchasing staff had led to effective individual purchasing effort at the plant level but to little effective purchasing management at the divisional level. He explained:

There are flashes of excellent buying, but analysis shows that the most capable people are so overloaded with people and detail that they have little time for truly effective efforts. While most management groups have accepted the need for better personnel, the fact remains that few managers are yet willing to let their purchasing personnel handle the "prestige" or high dollar commitments. There are attempts at commodity buying, but little time is available for study or evaluation. For instance, the chemicals division had one purchasing specialist trying to handle $50 million worth of chemicals involving complex procurement problems. The metals division, by contrast, devotes three highly qualified people to relatively few items totaling approximately $35 million. Needless to say, they do a better job.

Mr. Phillips thought that another major hurdle to a further effective implementation of the purchasing program was the resistance to corporatewide cost reduction programs shown by some divisions.

A start has been made to define purchasing savings or cost reduction and to report successful efforts. Most purchasing locations have made individual efforts to reduce costs. But management has generally not accepted and in some instances ridiculed the idea of cost reductions through better purchase.

Mr. Phillips was convinced that further significant progress in the reorganization of purchasing would require dispelling the notion held by many divisional people that corporate staff and the division are two separate entities. He said:

Top management's recognition of purchasing as a management function, recognition by the division managers that the corporate director of purchasing and the general manager have a joint procurement responsibility, and recognition of the importance of competent division directors of purchasing are three keys to a full implementation of the reorganization program.

After extensive consultation between Mr. Phillips and Mr. E. H. Bellows, vice president of corporate services, the latter sent a memorandum to top management that contained an appraisal of the status of the purchasing reorganization as of August, 1964, and a series of recommendations for further action. The memorandum dated August 12, 1964, read in part as follows:

The purpose of this memorandum is to outline for corporate management's understanding and endorsement a redirection of the purchasing effort within Olin. This proposal is based on a reassessment of purchasing practices in the light of our experience since the study submitted in January, 1962.

Since that date, our prime effort has been to upgrade and professionalize purchasing in Olin. To that end, we can cite some major achievements.

Nonetheless, I am far from satisfied that we have been able to get from our management generally a consensus as to the importance of purchasing as a profit contribution factor, or a consensus as to how purchasing should be performed, and by whom. It is in this light that I ask you to consider this memorandum.

A. Our reappraisal of the purchasing function throughout Olin was accompanied by a survey of Dow, Monsanto, Union Carbide, Du Pont, R.C.A., and American Cyanamid, plus having available the results of a detailed purchasing study of 25 companies by Standard Oil of Indiana. This survey disclosed the following to be characteristic of those companies generally reputed to have the most effective purchasing organizations.

1. Purchasing is regarded by top management to be a function significantly contributing to profit; it is therefore staffed in quality and at a level in the organization commensurate with this responsibility.

2. All purchasing is under purchasing control. This is usually achieved by placing the purchasing function under straight-line direction from top-purchasing management at corporate headquarters but with plant purchasing agents administratively assigned to operating locations.

3. Commodity buying by specialists is centralized, usually at corporate headquarters.

4. Purchasing research and analysis by commodities, by markets, and in cost reduction and value concepts is a discreet function within the top-purchasing managemant staff.

5. Specific profit-improvement objectives are established by categories or organizational units and performance against these objectives is regularly measured. These objectives are jointly arrived at with responsible levels of management, including the controller, and of course performance is similarly reviewed.

6. There is a highly developed application of EDP to reduce the manpower requirements for order processing, inventory control, and competitive bid evaluation, and to gather data essential to purchasing management and measurement promptly.

7. There are highly developed and intensively used techniques to minimize paper work and to free the time of the purchasing staff for truly professional effort. These include such systems as the "invoice approval slip"; the postauditing of invoices (which have been used somewhat in Olin but not nearly so widely as we should) and blanket orders with subsequent releases issued by the using department; and a telephone order system.

B. Measured against criteria such as these, Olin is clearly not in the major leagues.

1. No one in Olin would deny that purchasing should be a significant factor contributing to profit, but by and large we have not supported this view aggressively. We are not using our purchasing staffs effectively. Excessive paper work and routine ordering prevents smart buying. Some areas still suffer from inadequate quality of staff.

2. We have given official recognition to the need to have all purchasing under the control of purchasing departments, but this is by no means universally observed. (And let me add parenthetically, I am not concerned that it should be a matter of exclusive interest for purchasing, but rather I am concerned that purchasing is frequently informed after the event and this impairs the ability to do a thorough job.)

3. We have made a pass at centralized commodity buying at the corporate level and with some success, especially for organics, but we

have lacked the number of people necessary to do this on an informed basis for more than a very few items; and we do not have full agreement as to policy and purpose among divisions and corporate staff.

4. Purchasing research and analysis is in part an elaboration of point three in commodity buying but it goes further; with the exception of the nonferrous metals market where we do have three professional people continuously involved, there is no one in the corporation devoting his time *solely and in depth* to commodity and commodity market studies. Moreover, and beyond this obvious need, the corporation has not invested the time and money necessary to support profit improvement, make or buy, and other rational programs in purchasing that are open to us.

5. To my knowledge the purchasing units of the divisions are not required to have formal and fixed profit-improvement objectives and in consequence they also do not have performance reviews against such objectives.

6. The state of the art on EDP within Olin has not been sufficiently advanced to make materials control and hence purchasing within Olin what it needs to be—namely, part of an integrated Production-Sales-Inventory system, division by division. Remedial steps are underway, but this is necessarily a slow process.

7. We have attempted, at least in some locations, to get simplified methods adopted and installed, but we have discovered (*a*) this is not possible without management understanding and explicit support, and (*b*) installation requires a dramatic overhaul of present practices anl this in turn requires more days and weeks at a location than the local staff or the corporate staff could allocate to the task. Accordingly, little has been achieved, and purchasing staffs in the divisions and at the plants manufacture and massage excessive paper, (*c*) for example, a review made by Squibb of their purchasing operations for 1963 indicated that 2,790 orders were placed per month (average) and that these orders generated 6,194 invoices for a total dollar expenditure of $4,085,000. Of prime significance is the breakdown of the value of these orders:

   a. 61 percent of the orders and 60 percent of the invoices were for under $100; further,

   b. 83 percent of the orders and 80 percent of the invoices were for under $500 but covered only 10 percent of the dollars committed.

   c. This specific Squibb data is representative of what we would find in most other purchasing operations. (Procedures which would eliminate a very substantial part of this paper blizzard are incorporated in a revised Standard Procedure No. 2 distributed for comment to all financial officers on June 26.)

In the light of this summary I should like to restate for your endorsement and support what we believe should be the guidelines for purchasing in Olin—guidelines more commensurate with the proper protection of the $300 million we reinvest in materials and supplies annually.

1. Purchasing should be fully recognized as a function with an obligation to contribute affirmatively to profit. (It should not be a ministerial function of processing paper to legalize the real buying decisions wherever and by whomever they happen to have been made; neither does this mean that purchasing is an exclusive function: management, engineering, legal, and others must participate at the proper times and in the proper roles.)

2. Consequently every purchasing location should establish annually, in conjunction with its immediate management, a profit improvement target, and performance should be reviewed periodically against that target. (This is a line management function; however, corporate purchasing staff can assist in helping to set realistic targets and in advising on ways and means to achieve them.)

3. The professional purchasing *time* that must be devoted to achieve profit improvement goals can only come out of present staff if the present purchasing methods around the circuit are drastically overhauled. (The corporate purchasing staff will work with division and plant personnel to this end; but for this to be a successful effort in anything like a reasonable time period, we must have the explicit endorsement of the executive vice presidents and of their general managers; *time* must be devoted to this effort and the present cumbersome paper work and procedures *must* be changed.)

4. Through the installation of modern techniques and through training sessions (both formal and on-the-job) the quality of our purchasing performance can be greatly enhanced. We must be in agreement now, however, that progressively successful performance will be rewarded and that the lack of it will occasion attention and corrective action.

5. The bulk of the purchasing for raw materials and production supplies should continue to be done in the operating divisions. This means that the purchasing function in each division should be staffed and organized to perform the buying functions peculiar to that division without duplicating the specialty functions, training, and other administrative resources of the corporate purchasing staff. Further, the buying performed in each division will be based on an annual purchase plan approved by the division general manager concerned and the corporate director of purchasing. Purchase plans for significant equipment and contractors should similarly be prepared and approved.

6. To support this delegation of major purchasing activities to the divisions, the corporate purchasing staff should do these things:

    a. Coordinate the annual purchase plans of the several divisions through:

    (1) Identifying common items of genuine significance and arranging for corporate contracts against which any buying office can release. (Note: the corporate contracts on behalf of all users may be negotiated by a division purchasing office upon direction from corporate.)

    (2) Recommending additions to and deletions from vendor list or possible allocations among vendors.

    (3) Unless otherwise indicated on specific items, approval of the annual purchase plan constitutes delegation to purchase in ac-

cordance with specific grants of purchasing authority up to $500,000 per item and per vendor.

b. Functionally supervise project purchasing agents assigned to construction projects. The same technique of an approved purchase plan for each project will be followed in the same manner as in a division's equipment and contractor purchase plan.

c. In conjunction with construction and division staff, plan strategy and negotiate on major equipment and engineering and construction contracts.

d. In conjunction with division staff, plan strategy and negotiate raw material and supply contracts for selected items from annual purchase plans. Negotiate national and area contracts for standard equipment and MRO [maintenance, repairs, and operating] supplies (or assign corporatewide responsibility for particular actions to major interested division). Corporate purchasing specialists should participate *with* division personnel in negotiations for the most significant common-use items; examples, electric power, natural gas.

e. Conduct purchasing research and analysis on behalf of operating divisions and the corporation generally; for example but not limited to:
    (1) Major commodities and markets.
    (2) Vendor capabilities and performance.
    (3) Value analysis and other profit improvement techniques.
    (4) Statistical data.
    (5) EDP and systems applications.

f. Develop and recommend to the president major purchasing policy; develop and issue purchasing procedures and systems, manuals, and training material.

g. Establish personnel qualification standards for purchasing personnel, consult with division management on selection and assignment of key purchasing personnel, train purchasing agents and physically audit purchasing performance, and make recommendations for improvement to division management.

h. Provide technical and purchasing assistance when and where needed.

i. Maintain relations with major suppliers on a continuing basis.

j. Delegate purchasing authority with concurrence of division management.

Appendix A: Proposed grant of operating authority to corporate director of purchasing: 1962

The Corporate Director of Purchasing is hereby authorized to execute, or appoint purchasing personnel within the operating division to execute all purchases for the corporation.

Redelegations of authority and all notifications and revocations thereof made pursuant to this grant must be filed with the financial officer concerned, the vice president and controller, the secretary, the manager of organization planning, and others whose responsibility requires it.

Classifications	Limits (up to and including)	Stipulations
1. Capital equipment	Per stipulation	Approved capital appropriation requests.
2. Sale or retirement of capital assets	Per stipulation	Capital assets may be disposed of by the local purchasing agent after the availability of such assets has been made known throughout the corporation, and the person with the authority to approve the requisition of such assets has approved its disposal.
3. Leases	Per stipulation	Approved lease and rental requests.
4. Materials and supplies for normal business operations including production and maintenance	$500,000	Over $500,000, submit to the president for approval.
5. Construction contracts	$500,000	Construction contracts in excess of $500,000 submit to the president for approval after technical clearance by corporate engineering.
6. Service and utility	$100,000	Initial service and utility contracts in excess of $100,000, submit to the president for review prior to commitment.

S. DE J. OSBORNE
President

Source: Company records.

Appendix A (continued): Proposed redelegation of grant of operating authority to manager of purchasing—film operations, packaging division: 1962

Pursuant to the Grant of Operating Authority made to me by the president under date of January 8, 1962, I hereby redelegate to the Manager of Purchasing—Film Operations, Packaging Division, authority to execute all purchases for the film operations, packaging division. This authority may be redelegated to other purchasing personnel within the film operations, packaging division, with the prior concurrence of the director of purchasing.

Redelegations of authority and all notifications and revocations thereof made pursuant to this grant must be filed with the financial officer concerned, the vice president and controller, the secretary, the manager of organization planning, and others whose responsibility requires it.

Classifications	Limits (up to and including)	Stipulations
1. Capital equipment	Per stipulation	Over $10,000 consult with the corporate director of purchasing prior to issuance of invitations to bid; advise the corporate director of purchasing if negotiation with single supplier is necessary for proprietary items.
2. Sale or retirement of capital assets	Per stipulation	Capital assets may be disposed of by the local purchasing agent after the availability of such assets has been made known throughout the corporation, and the person with the authority to approve the requisition of such assets has approved its disposal.
3. Leases for equipment and facilities	Per stipulation	As authorized by approved lease and rental requests. If in excess of $50,000 or 5 years, inform the corporate director of purchasing prior to issuance of invitations to bid.
4. Materials and supplies for normal business operations including production and maintenance	Per stipulation	Annual requirements for all materials and supplies unless in excess of $500,000. Over $500,000, refer to the corporate director of purchasing for review and recommendation to the president.
5. Construction contracts	$500,000	Construction contracts in excess of $500,000, submit to the corporate director of purchasing for review with the vice president—production and engineering prior to commitment.
6. Service and utility contracts	$100,000	Initial service and utility contracts in excess of $100,000, submit to the corporate director of purchasing prior to commitment.

Appendix B: Sample policy—purchasing objectives: 1962

The primary objective of Olin purchasing is to assure a short- and long-range supply of quality materials, parts, and equipment at the maximum value to the corporation.

Inherent in this objective are the timely delivery of materials and parts and the establishment and maintenance of sound supplier relations. While price is an important aspect of value, net worth to the corporation is a more important consideration, and for this reason supplier performance, service, reliability, and know-how must be equally important factors in the purchasing decision.

In order to obtain maximum value for each dollar spent, it is necessary that we establish the additional objective of using our supplier's technology and development ability to the fullet extent possible in improving products and processes and in reducing costs.

Sustained and imaginative effort toward these objectives will fulfill the purchasing mission of supporting production and marketing to the greatest extent possible.

Appendix B (continued): Sample policy—Olin purchasing practices

"To buy without prejudice, seeking to obtain the maximum
ultimate value for each dollar of expenditure."

This statement from the Code of Ethics of the National Association of Purchasing Agents is the keystone of Olin purchasing practices. In accordance with this code, the following guides are established for all Olin purchasing personnel:

Suppliers. All representatives of suppliers and potential suppliers should be treated with courtesy, honesty, and tact. In fact, it should be our constant objective to treat salesmen from other firms as we would wish Olin salesmen to be treated.

Quotations. All suppliers who are asked to quote will receive identical information in terms of specifications and supplementary data so that they will have every opportunity to quote on a common basis of understanding.

During the bid process or negotiations, Olin purchasing personnel will not divulge a supplier's price.

Negotiation. Olin will negotiate with a single supplier or selected group of suppliers in those instances where it is determined that the most favorable terms, conditions, and prices cannot be obtained from straight competitive bidding. However, all purchasing agents should be aware of and review periodically those instances in their organizations where competitive bids are not being obtained.

Speculation. Purchases at Olin are made to support and sustain production and marketing. Olin will not speculate in commodity markets.

Gifts. No gifts from suppliers or potential suppliers will be accepted by Olin purchasing personnel unless they are under $5 in value and are clearly imprinted with the name of the donor firm.

Outside Business Interests of Purchasing Personnel. It is in conflict with the company's interest for any personnel, or their immediate family, to have a significant* business interest in any of Olin's suppliers or potential suppliers.

Source: Company records.

OLIN (B)†

In December, 1965, top management of the Olin Mathieson Chemical Corporation (Olin) was reexamining the company's organization structure with a view of bringing about changes to reflect the needs of the company's highly diversified products and product markets. Mr. Gordon Grand, who had joined the company in 1953 as assistant to John M. Olin (then president of Olin Industries) and who had been elected president and chief executive officer in April, 1965, stated: "Olin Mathieson Chemical Corporation is engaged in five different business areas—different in terms of customers, markets, technology, production, and, indeed, geographical distribution." He believed that, because of the heterogeneous product lines the company's operation should be organized into five industry groups functioning as autonomous and largely independent enterprises under the strategic guidance and overall control of the president's office, supported by a relatively small central staff. The president was frequently heard to speak of using the holding company concept in discussing changes in the organization structure. In its 1964 Annual Report, management stated: "Substantial progress was . . . made during the year toward the decentralization of the five areas of our business. We are now studying the management advantages to be gained by incorporating these related operations into separate subsidiaries."

In conjunction with the contemplated realignment of the Olin organization structure, Mr. Ralph C. Phillips, corporate director of purchasing, was asked to make recommendations as to how to organize the company's complex procurement activities in a way that would be consistent with the basic concept of organization envisioned by top management.

Changing role of corporate staff purchasing

In pondering an organizational structure for purchasing compatible with the reorientation of the entire corporate organization toward a

---

* "Significant interest" means any financial interest which may influence the judgment or action of any employee in the conduct of the company's business. Without limiting the generality of the foregoing, ownership of more than 3 percent of any class of stocks, bonds, debentures, or other securities; an option or warrant to purchase any of the foregoing types of securities which if exercised would result in ownership of more than 3 percent of any class; a partnership interest of more than 3 percent; or any loan to a supplier; shall be deemed a "significant interest."

† © by the President and Fellows of Harvard College; all rights reserved.

holding type of company, as contemplated by Olin's new president in the winter of 1965, Mr. Phillips said:

If you read Mr. Bellow's memorandum carefully,[1] you will notice that it already reflects a slight departure from the purchasing reorganization program that we developed in 1962. It is perhaps the first indication of my growing belief that, with some notable exceptions, the divisions' basic resistance against any sort of strong central purchasing staff organization has not materially changed since 1962, or, for that matter, since formation of O.M.C.C. in 1954. Some of our division managers as a matter of principle do not want the help of a corporate purchasing staff. They want to run their own show. They want no interference with their profit responsibility.

It is true, of course, that we have been involved in direct buying on behalf of the divisions, as in the case of the organics division. But that was not done under a concept of "centralized buying." It was done because of lack of certain capability, such as buying chemicals and major equipment in some divisional purchasing departments. And for all practical purposes some of the divisions still have no central divisional purchasing management office, and the purchasing function continues to be performed primarily at the plant level such as the aluminum division, the brass division, and the Winchester-Western division.

The concept of centralized buying, I think, involves the negotiation by a central purchasing organization of all orders for material and services requisitioned by the divisions. This we have never done. Olin could not logically operate under such a concept. Some people will say that we are now on the verge of decentralizing purchasing, along with the rest of the company. The fact is that we never had centralized purchasing. We only bought on behalf of some of the divisions.

True, we developed a very strong functional staff and provided very direct staff guidance or functional supervision. Over the past three years we have told the purchasing people in the plants in specific terms how to organize their work and how to run their departments. Maybe we developed symptoms of staff bureaucracy that tended to do too much of the purchasing job more properly performed by the divisions. But I don't think that there was much choice in the absence of a professional purchasing organization in many areas at the divisional level.

At any rate, I think that the divisions have recently begun to energize their efforts to bring about the changes necessary to effect modern-day professional purchasing techniques. Perhaps it is good that with the appointment of a new president the push toward a more centralized corporate organization came to an end. You can't swim upstream forever.

Mr. Phillips believed that, in order to be compatible with the president's concept of Olin's future organization, the size of the corporate purchasing staff should be reduced to a minimum, focusing its activities entirely on what he described as "corporate entity functions" and ceasing to perform "service functions" for the divisions. He explained:

---

[1] See the Olin (A) case for Mr. Bellows' memorandum dated August 12, 1964. Mr. E. H. Bellows was vice president of corporate services.

The corporate purchasing staff should probably consist of no more than two professional persons with support staff to be included in the budget of the president's office. The responsibility of this new corporate staff unit would be confined to the formulation and recommendation to the president of corporatewide procurement policy and procedures, the coordination of purchasing plans, the review of purchasing performance, the maintenance and periodic analysis of vital internal and external purchasing data, the participation in divisional purchasing activities if corporatewide interests are involved, and the maintenance of external relations, including high-level contacts with major suppliers, with trade and professional associations, and with government agencies.

As to the rest of the corporate staff purchasing department, it would be up to the divisions to decide what to do with it; if the divisions wanted to have the staff's service functions continued, they would have to share the costs. If the divisions wanted no corporate staff service, most of the staff department as it now exists would be dissolved.

The important change would be that the new corporate staff purchasing unit would no longer do any buying or negotiating. We would not set up purchasing objectives for the divisions nor programs to achieve these objectives. We would no longer recruit purchasing personnel or assist the divisions in establishing methods, systems, purchasing research, training programs, etc. We would no longer provide any other direct technical purchasing assistance to the divisions with respect to raw material and other supply contracts. We would no longer make detailed, on-the-spot reviews of divisional purchasing procedures or make detailed recommendations for improvement to divisional management. All of these tasks would be the responsibility of divisional purchasing management. In other words, our main responsibility would be to advise the Olin management, including division general managers, on all important matters and issues regarding purchasing, to recommend procurement policies and directives to the chief executive for issuance to the divisions, and to review and evaluate divisional purchasing performances. If performance turned out to be unsatisfactory against set standards, we would no longer go to work at the divisional level, setting up programs, reorganizing, restaffing, and doing whatever else might be necessary to improve purchasing performance. We would simply present the facts, point to the corporatewide purchasing objectives and policies and, in our role as agent or staff extension of the chief executive, advise divisional management that it was expected to do better.

INTERNATIONAL DIGITAL CORPORATION*

Introduction

Mr. Harvey F. Linscott, director of purchases in the corporate staff purchasing department of the International Digital Corporation (IDC), was concerned with the advisability of a reorganization of the company's foreign procurement activities. (See Exhibits 1, 2, and 3 for organization

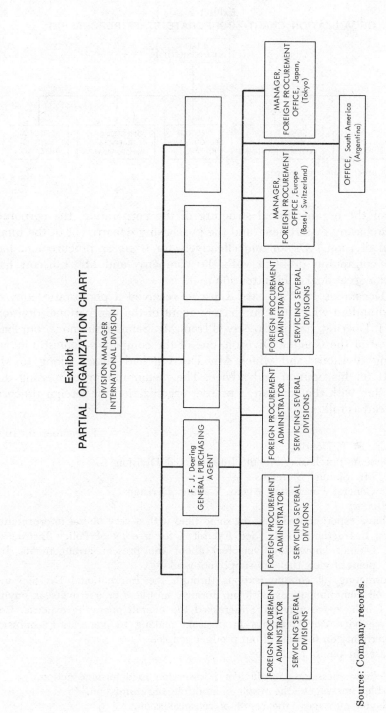

Exhibit 1
PARTIAL ORGANIZATION CHART

DIVISION MANAGER
INTERNATIONAL DIVISION

F. J. Doering
GENERAL PURCHASING
AGENT

FOREIGN PROCUREMENT
ADMINISTRATOR
SERVICING SEVERAL
DIVISIONS

FOREIGN PROCUREMENT
ADMINISTRATOR
SERVICING SEVERAL
DIVISIONS

FOREIGN PROCUREMENT
ADMINISTRATOR
SERVICING SEVERAL
DIVISIONS

FOREIGN PROCUREMENT
ADMINISTRATOR
SERVICING SEVERAL
DIVISIONS

MANAGER,
FOREIGN PROCUREMENT
OFFICE, Europe
(Basel, Switzerland)

MANAGER,
FOREIGN PROCUREMENT
OFFICE, Japan,
(Tokyo)

OFFICE, South America
(Argentina)

Source: Company records.

Exhibit 2
ORGANIZATION CHART—CORPORATE STAFF PURCHASING

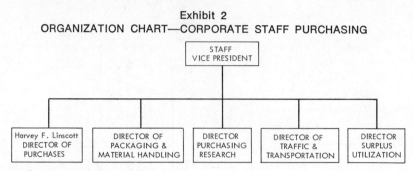

Source: Company records.

charts of the organizational structure of the corporation, the corporate staff purchasing department, and the purchasing department of the international division.) Organizing effectively for overseas procurement had been a continuing problem with the company, and Mr. Linscott had devoted a great deal of his attention to it.

On December 10, 1964, Mr. Linscott received a photostatic copy of a memorandum which the purchasing agent of the international division, Mr. F. J. Doering, had just received from Mr. Samuel Simmons, purchasing agent of the Gamma Division, one of the company's domestic manufacturing divisions, and which Mr. Doering had passed along to Mr. Linscott for his opinion and advice. The memorandum, expressing dissatisfaction with the company's present organization for foreign procurement, read as follows:

December 9, 1964

To: Mr. F. J. Doering
      General Purchasing Agent, International Division
From: Mr. Samuel Simmons
      General Purchasing Agent, Gamma Division
Dear Frank:

We have experimented now for some time with a very liberal interpretation of Policy Instruction P-111. [See Exhibit 4 for a copy of Policy Instruction P-111.] I don't know how you feel about the present arrangements, but from my point of view they are simply not working.

By directing all communications through the International Division and cutting off communications with our foreign suppliers or our overseas buying offices, I believe we may have increased the overall operating expense. Certainly, we have caused delays in decision making by generating confusion and uncertainty on the part of our product people.

In cases in point, I refer to:

a.   Indefinite messages—insufficient information to determine action.
b.   Garbled messages—the result of multiple retransmission.
c.   Delayed messages—the result of retransmission.
d.   Overlapped messages—the result of "too many cooks."

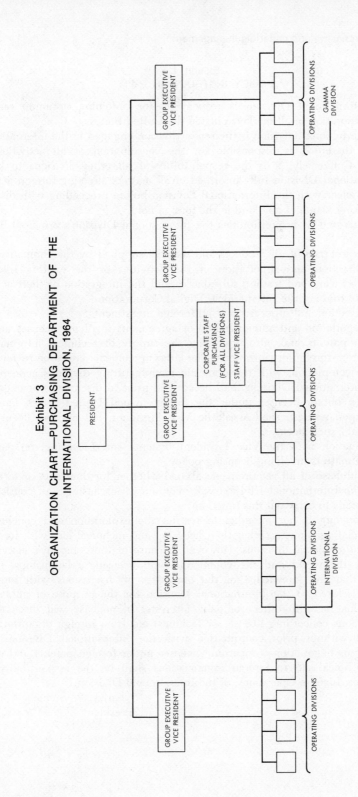

Exhibit 3

ORGANIZATION CHART—PURCHASING DEPARTMENT OF THE
INTERNATIONAL DIVISION, 1964

Exhibit 4
POLICY INSTRUCTION P-111

The International Division is responsible for obtaining optimum results for the Corporation in all markets outside the United States.

The International Division is the senior division engaged in the international field and, therefore, is responsible for the coordination of all activities in that field. Conversely, it is the responsibility of all other divisions to keep the International Division fully informed of all matters affecting foreign activities and to clear with the International Division before proceeding with discussions or taking action of any kind in the foreign field.

In discharging its responsibilities the International Division's principal functions are:

1. The export sale of all products and services supplied by the company.
2. The direction and supervision of the activities of the existing foreign manufacturing and trading subsidiaries and the integration of their activities into those of the International Digital Corporation.
3. The direction and supervision of all foreign investments.
4. The negotiation and administration of agreements involving licenses under foreign patents and, also, involving the supply of technical information to or from foreign organizations. The latter agreements are to be reviewed, before completion, with the domestic manufacturing divisions concerned. The International Division shall be advised prior to discussions or negotiations to obtain licenses under the foreign-owned United States Patents and, upon request, shall assist the Vice President, Patents and licensing, to obtain such licenses.
5. Coordination with the Vice President, Patents and Licensing, on patent license matters involving licensing policy.
6. The purchase of all requirements abroad whether for domestic, or foreign use. The International Division will maintain a purchasing staff consistent with needs to carry out this function.

The foregoing is not intended to restrict the exploration and conclusion of commercial agreements, other than licensing and technical aid, with foreign firms by the domestic divisions. However, because of the company's activities throughout the world and the commercial and licensing relationships, it is necessary that full knowledge of the objectives of discussions with foreign firms be disclosed to the International Division for the purpose of guidance and coordination with other company interests. In no case will discussions or negotiations concerning licenses or technical aid from foreign organizations take place without prior coordination with the International Division. All discussions or negotiations concerning licenses under foreign patents and concerning technical aid to foreign organizations shall be the responsibility of the Director, License Operations, of the International Division.

Charles P. Steele
President

And so on. In point of fact, almost every transaction now is a source of some confusion. Each case may be very minor in itself, but the accumulation has become worrisome.

I am sure you would be the first to agree that the intention of your implementation of Policy Instruction P-111 was to assist the divisional purchasing people and not to make the performance of their duties more hazardous. I believe these conditions have arisen from the introduction of an additional, nonfunctional step in the communication cycle between our foreign vendors and the purchasing agents in our operating divisions. There are enough problems in this communication cycle at the best of times.

As far as I can see, there is nothing in Policy Instruction P-111 that makes this present arrangement mandatory. It says that you "shall be responsible" and "maintain a purchasing staff consistent with *needs*." In my view, being responsible does not necessarily mean performing the act itself; as with all managerial jobs, it means coordinating, supervising, guiding. Likewise, in my view, the foreign procurement staff is not "consistent with needs" necessarily required at the international division. The provision and supervision of foreign buying offices would seem to fulfill this requirement.

Accordingly, I propose that we revert to our former basis of operations. This would mean that we would handle our own communications direct with our foreign buying offices and/or foreign suppliers, as the case may be, and that we would place our own purchase orders. This will let us exercise our product responsibilities with a much surer sense of effectiveness and with greater economy; and, since we will, of course, keep you fully informed with copies of everything we do, it will allow you to continue to exercise your coordinating function described in Policy Instruction P-111.

Please let me have your comments.

Kindest regards,

/s/ SAM

Since Mr. Linscott, prior to his promotion to the position of director of purchases of the corporate staff purchasing department, had held Mr. Doering's position for about three years, he was thoroughly familiar with the problems associated with the foreign procurement activities of IDC. One of the primary problems accompanying the utilization of overseas sources of supply for domestic operating divisions was how to fit the foreign procurement function effectively into the company's organizational structure. As director of corporate staff purchasing, Mr. Linscott maintained close working relationships with the general purchasing agents throughout the company's operating divisions, and he knew there was considerable aversion by many of these divisional purchasing executives to the international division's involvement in foreign procurement for the manufacturing units. The international division was primarily engaged in export operations, international licensing arrangements, and supervision of foreign subsidiaries. Although no formal organizational relationships existed between corporate staff purchasing and the international division, Mr. Doering frequently consulted with Mr.

Linscott on matters relating to the procurement of foreign-made materials for the domestic operating divisions. Knowing that the type of criticism reflected in Mr. Simmons' memorandum had occurred from time to time in many of the operating divisions and that, as a result, the company had not fully realized the potential material costs savings of foreign buying, Mr. Linscott wondered whether the time had come to recommend to top management a shift of the overseas procurement function from the international division to corporate staff purchasing.

Company background

International Digital Corporation, with headquarters in Chicago, was a large multidivision manufacturing organization producing a wide variety of equipment and appliances for consumer and industrial markets, with annual sales and other revenues of $1.4 billion and net earnings of $66 million in 1964. (See Exhibit 5 for a 10-year financial review.) The company employed over 100,000 persons in nearly 50 domestic and overseas manufacturing and distribution facilities.

The company's research, production, and marketing activities were devoted primarily to consumer products—such as kitchen ranges, refrigerators, washing machines, and small electrical kitchen appliances—and partly to industrial products—such as turbines, generators, transformers, switchgear, and circuit breakers. The percent of sales in 1963 for each of these two broad categories of products was as follows: consumer products and services, 66 percent; industrial products, 34 percent. The company's sales volume had grown over a ten-year period from less than $1 billion in 1955 to $1.4 billion in 1964. Profits after taxes had increased from less than $40 million to $66 million during the same period, although profits after taxes as a percentage of sales had remained essentially unchanged (see Exhibit 5).

As a percentage of total manufacturing cost, the material content of IDC's products varied from 15 percent in some electronic parts and components to 60 percent to 65 percent in home appliances. On the average, approximately 45 percent of sales income was spent for materials and services purchased from outside suppliers.

Overall company organization

As a result of the considerable diversity of its product lines, International Digital Corporation was organized under five groups, which could be classified as consumer products, industrial products, components, specialty products, and international operations. The five groups, comprising over 50 divisions and subsidiaries, were headed by group execu-

TEN-YEAR FINANCIAL REVIEW
(dollar amounts in $1,000)

	1964	1963	1962	1961	1960	1959	1958	1957	1956	1955
Sales and Earnings										
Products and services sold	$1,499,967	$1,431,422	$1,401,317	$1,236,730	$1,195,917	$1,116,496	$940,875	$941,022	$902,219	$844,213
Profit before federal taxes on income	122,156	108,506	86,348	51,929	53,534	62,834	48,354	61,639	64,059	80,086
Percent to sales	8.4	7.6	6.2	4.2	4.5	5.6	5.1	6.5	7.1	9.5
Profit after federal taxes on income	$ 65,996	$ 52,826	$ 41,228	$ 28,409	$ 28,094	$ 32,114	$ 24,754	$ 30,839	$ 32,025	$ 38,020
Percent to sales	4.6	3.7	2.9	2.3	2.3	2.9	2.6	3.2	3.5	4.5
Per common share*	1.21	0.96	0.76	0.52	0.56	0.70	0.54	0.68	0.70	0.84
Special items—net of taxes and expenses	$ 9,096	$ —	$ 5,568	—	—	—	—	—	—	—
Per common share	0.18	—	0.11	—	—	—	—	—	—	—
Dividends Declared										
$3.50 preferred stock—cash	$ 2,029	$ 2,522	$ 2,522	$ 2,522	$ 2,522	2,522	$ 2,522	$ 2,522	$ 2,522	$ 2,522
Common stock—cash	29,406	20,887	13,556	13,237	12,265	11,114	16,586	16,604	16,650	16,721
Per share—regular	0.48	0.40	0.26	0.26	0.26	0.26	0.26	0.26	0.26	0.26
Per share—special	0.08	—	—	—	—	—	—	—	—	—
Total cash dividends	31,435	23,410	16,078	15,759	14,787	13,636	19,109	19,127	19,172	19,243
Stock dividends on common stock	10%	—	2%	2%	2%	2%	—	—	—	—
Financial Summary at Year End										
Current assets	$ 637,761	$ 653,827	$ 595,085	$ 495,552	$ 410,456	433,622	$ 386,211	$ 377,430	$ 362,788	$383,932
Current liabilities	246,198	245,775	230,538	196,499	174,292	180,740	139,825	132,964	120,241	122,192
Net working capital	391,562	408,052	364,546	299,053	236,164	252,882	246,386	244,456	242,547	261,740
Current ratio	2.6	2.7	2.6	2.5	2.4	2.4	2.8	2.8	3.0	3.1
Additions to plant and equipment for year	$ 67,942	$ 48,025	$ 44,714	$ 45,026	$ 47,334	$ 34,590	$ 19,854	$ 28,474	$ 46,014	$ 24,831
Depreciation of plant and equipment for year	40,844	37,233	32,782	27,258	21,691	18,739	17,450	18,819	18,087	15,298
Net plant and equipment	234,937	215,423	211,512	205,866	191,631	168,209	158,863	159,665	151,978	126,395
Total assets	$ 905,378	$ 903,589	$ 847,118	$ 754,962	$ 652,402	$ 648,956	$ 589,005	$ 576,618	$ 522,446	$541,205
Reinvested earnings	107,144	240,426	211,010	195,987	197,066	198,049	105,026	189,382	177,670	164,816
Shareholders' equity	417,958	424,604	391,528	359,359	346,331	258,362	236,351	230,706	219,002	206,146
Taxes										
Federal income taxes	$ 56,160	$ 55,680	$ 45,120	$ 23,520	$ 25,440	$ 30,720	$ 23,600	$ 30,800	$ 32,042	$ 42,066
Social security taxes	17,022	18,765	18,257	15,347	14,547	11,474	8,430	8,224	7,707	6,854
State, local, and foreign taxes	13,097	11,494	10,690	8,923	7,474	6,615	5,823	5,178	4,765	4,369
Total	86,279	85,938	74,067	47,790	47,462	48,809	37,855	44,202	44,506	53,289

* Computed on average number of common shares outstanding during the respective years.

Source: Company records.

tive vice presidents. Division managers reported to one of the five group executive vice presidents, who, in turn, reported to the president. The operating divisions maintained their own production and engineering departments, performed the marketing function, and assumed full responsibility for the profitability of their operations. Major decisions of corporate strategy and policy were made at IDC's headquarters in Chicago, where the president and the members of the board's executive committee maintained offices. Because of the diversity, complexity, and geographical separation of divisional operations, top management's policy was to delegate as much responsibility as possible to IDC division managers and, except for matters relating to issues of corporate policy, to interfere as little as possible with the management of the divisions.

Organization of purchasing for divisional and staff level

In line with the company's policy of decentralization, each operating division maintained its own purchasing organization, headed by a divisional general purchasing agent, who reported to the division manager. Each general purchasing agent was responsible for the procurement of all materials, supplies, and services for the division's operations. (See Exhibit 6, Section C, for a description of the duties and responsibilities of the divisional purchasing organizations.)

Although IDC's procurement function was organized on a decentralized basis, the company maintained a purchasing department at the corporate staff level, which, in addition to such tasks as formulating and implementing companywide procurement policies, purchased all major materials common to two or more operating divisions. (See Exhibit 6, Section B, for a description of the duties and responsibilities of the corporate staff purchasing.)

Corporate staff purchasing was headed by a staff vice president, who reported to a group executive vice president (see Exhibit 1). Mr. Linscott, as director of corporate staff purchasing, carried staff responsibility for the company's general purchasing policy, central procurement activity, and supervision of divisional purchasing activity relative to mechanical and electronic parts, heavy components, and raw materials. Mr. Linscott reported to the staff vice president (see Exhibit 2).

Despite the widespread location of some of the operating divisions, Mr. Linscott tried to visit with the divisional general purchasing agents as frequently as possible, because he considered it essential to have the thorough insight into divisional purchasing problems possible only by maintaining effective personal communications with the purchasing agents. Mr. Linscott, however, was extremely conscientious not to interfere with the line responsibility of the division managers and the divisional purchasing executives and to stay out of their operations as much

Exhibit 6
PURCHASING STAFF-LINE RESPONSIBILITIES
(excerpt from company purchasing manual)

A. *Relationship between Line and Staff Responsibilities*

In keeping with IDC's concept of line and staff organization, each major operating unit has a purchasing organization which is responsible to the head of the major operating unit for procurement of all materials and supplies necessary to the conduct of its operation.

Staff responsibility for purchasing policy has been assigned to Corporate Staff Purchasing, which exercises necessary controls to assure compliance with approved purchasing policies and techniques by the purchasing organizations of each major operating unit.

The purchasing organization of each major operating unit is expected to develop detailed procedures suited to its requirements; however, such procedures shall conform to the policies established by Corporate Staff Purchasing to assure uniformity of purchasing practices throughout the Corporation.

B. *Duties and Responsibilities of Corporate Staff Purchasing*

1. Define purchasing policies, objectives, and responsibilities and interpret them for the major operating unit purchasing organizations.

2. Develop standardized procedures, basic forms, and record-keeping methods for purchasing organizations.

3. Examine general practices and internal procedures of major operating unit purchasing organizations to assure compliance with approved methods.

4. Make available to purchasing organizations, as requested, the services of purchasing specialists to assist in solving operational and procurement problems.

5. Approve prior to placing, all contracts and all purchases exceeding $25,000 made from outside suppliers.

6. Approve all requests for cancellation of commitments when the cancellation charges exceed $10,000.

7. In collaboration with appropriate general—purchasing agents, select items purchased by two or more operating units which offer opportunities for combining requirements to obtain better service and prices. Negotiate appropriate contracts to achieve this objective and inform interested purchasing organizations of contract terms. It is the responsibility of Corporate Staff Purchasing to originate all contracts which are established for more than one major operating unit.

8. Maintain records of purchases and contracts.

9. Analyze records of purchases and advise major operating unit purchasing organizations of opportunities to improve sources, distribution of business, prices, and terms and to assure compliance with current purchase contracts.

10. Consult with major operating unit general purchasing agents on market trends and the advisability of extending or contracting commitments.

11. Guide and assist major operating unit purchasing organizations in negotiating major purchases, consulting with the accounting, finance, and law activities when necessary.

Exhibit 6 *(Continued)*

12. Collaborate with staff standards group and other standardizing activities to promote standardization of common items throughout the Corporation.
13. Develop policies governing the disposal of surplus inventories, scrap materials, and excess facilities.
14. Accumulate statistics and prepare reports on purchasing performance throughout the Corporation.
15. Assure that competent, promotable people are selected and developed in purchasing organizations throughout the Corporation, and review the selection and proposed transfers of purchasing personnel.
16. Perform special assignments for the Staff Vice President.

C. *Duties and Responsibilities of Divisional Purchasing Organizations*

1. Initiate, conduct, and conclude all purchases of materials, equipment, services, and supplies necessary to the major operating unit's business in accordance with the approved policies of the major operating unit and Corporate Staff Purchasing.
2. Define purchasing objectives and policies for the approval of the appropriate major operating unit management.
3. Participate in the development of major operating unit policies and interpret such policies throughout the purchasing organization.
4. Interpret and administer programs and procedures in accordance with approved policies of the major operating unit.
5. Maintain lists of approved sources for materials used by the major operating units.
6. Explore markets for new sources of supply, new materials, processes, and ideas which may reduce costs and improve quality of products.
7. Consult with Corporate Staff Purchasing on market trends, seasonal changes, business conditions, and the advisability of extending or contracting commitments.
8. Collaborate with Corporate Staff Purchasing in the preparation of contracts.
9. Sell all scrap, excess and obsolete materials, machinery, and equipment of the major operating unit.
10. Participate in all investigations and decisions concerning whether to make or buy component parts or materials.
11. Recommend to the unit management modification of ordering quantities of raw materials, standard parts, and maintenance, repair, and operating supplies intended for general manufacturing purposes to obtain the best possible return on investment. Also, make recommendations to management on ordering of all other materials.
12. Submit to the major operating unit management and to Corporate Staff Purchasing periodic and special reports and statistics pertaining to the performance of the purchasing organization.
13. Cooperate with Corporate Staff Purchasing in the examination of purchasing practices and procedures throughout the major operating unit.
14. Maintain an adequate staff and provide the means to perform purchasing functions.
15. Establish budget objectives and appraise performance.

as possible. He believed that by this approach he had developed close and very satisfactory relationships with the divisional purchasing agents.

International operations

For some years the company had manufactured and distributed many products in foreign markets. In 1964, IDC maintained production, distribution, and research facilities in Canada, Mexico, Venezuela, Honduras, Brazil, Chile, Uruguay, Argentina, Great Britain, West Germany, Holland, Italy, Switzerland, Spain, India, Australia, and Japan. The company's international division, located in Aurora, Illinois, supervised the activities of the foreign subsidiaries, conducted all export operations, and granted licenses to foreign manufacturers under IDC's foreign patents. Licensing arrangements, which provided the company with substantial royalty revenues, involved, in many instances, complex problems of foreign taxation and international business relations. Frequently the exact nature and scope of such arrangements were treated as confidential matters and generally remained unknown to executives outside the international division.

The international division's general responsibility was outlined in Policy Instruction P-111 (as shown in Exhibit 4).

Foreign procurement

In 1958–59, top management became concerned with a marked intensification of price competition for some of the company's consumer products in world markets. As a result, the international division adopted, among other measures, a policy of purchasing certain consumer products such as kitchen appliances directly from overseas sources, rather than from IDC's domestic divisions or from domestic suppliers, for sale to overseas customers if significant cost savings could be realized. "This policy enabled us to meet competition by some of the large European and Japanese producers in our foreign markets," said Mr. Linscott. He added, "Of course, our domestic divisions did not like it, because they believed such policy would take factory orders away from them."

In the summer of 1959, after having gained initial experience with purchasing such consumer products in West Germany, Japan, and Chile at cost savings of approximately 30 percent, the management of the international division decided to investigate expansion of its foreign purchasing activities to cover a number of IDC-designed products for sale abroad and a number of foreign-made finished products, materials, parts, and components for IDC's domestic operating divisions.

In order to accelerate investigating the feasibility of establishing such a comprehensive foreign procurement program, Mr. Linscott toured England, Germany, France, Norway, Sweden, Austria, Switzerland, Italy, Mexico, Chile, Argentina, and Japan. In the course of this trip, he visited 52 vendors that he regarded as potential sources of supply. He also held extensive meetings with IDC officials at the company's research laboratories in Basel, Switzerland, and Tokyo, Japan, to explore their potential role as the company's overseas sourcing, purchasing, and inspecting offices within a comprehensive foreign procurement system.

Upon returning from his trip, Mr. Linscott prepared a report for the management of the international division that read, in part, as follows:

. . . currently, the International Division has established foreign procurement of Japanese and German frying pans and is finalizing both the buying of small kitchen appliances from Chile and the buying of European-type coolers from Great Britain. These commitments are being made at reduced purchase costs of 25 percent to 30 percent.

. . . Further investigation in the evaluation of a foreign procurement program was necessary in the following areas:

1. Is it possible to procure IDC-designed items in Europe, South America, and Japan? If so, would the potential savings be greater or less than the savings in buying non-IDC-designed items?
2. How could quality assurance be maintained? Would it be possible to utilize either the Basel or Tokyo laboratories of IDC? Would use of these laboratories jeopardize our relationships with foreign licensees?
3. What are the possibilities of development engineering in Europe, South America, and Japan?
4. What is the best method of providing production support, such as replacement parts, instruction booklets for technical equipment, and instructional literature? Where would spare parts be inventoried and what additional investment in inventory is required?
5. In our approach to foreign procurement, what are the benefits to the overall corporation?
6. What additional costs are required in carrying out the overall foreign procurement program and what are the overall savings to the division and to the corporation?
7. What are the necessary operating procedures in administering such a program and what type of organization is required?

The report then continued:

. . . ten individual equipments were sourced in Europe and/or Japan and cost indications obtained. Table 1, below, indicates the equipments sourced and the potential gross savings. Reductions in potential purchase costs range from 14.5 percent on a generator unit to 52.5 percent on an SS–99 Direction Finder. If these ten items were purchased abroad in 1960, the purchase costs based on historical yearly quantities would be reduced from $1,492,000 to $957,000 for gross savings of $535,000.

Table 1

Description	Present unit cost ($)	Foreign vendor unit cost indication ($)	
1. LL–6r Switchgear	$29,065	$19,600	
2. RR–1402 Switchgear	21,514	16,200	
3. FGH–707 Diesel engine	3,010	2,130	(50 units)
		1,896	(100 units)
4. SS–99 Direction finder	1,475	700	
5. RGB–420 Switchgear	22,000	14,990	
6. SG–12 Medium power transmitter	7,421	3,611	
7. JL Mark 16	710	475	
Outside Purchased Items			
8. WEE–78 Electric range	$ 198	$ 160	
9. Generator unit	263	225	(250 units)
		210	(500 units)
10. X–100 Field intensity meter	495	325	

The items surveyed represented more than one third of the 27 IDC-designed items, valued at $4,368,000 at purchase costs, which the marketing managers of the International Division have indicated would lend themselves to overseas procurement in 1960. On the basis of this sampling, it appears that overall purchase costs could be reduced by 35 percent before consideration of expense factors, which are detailed below. Utilizing a cost reduction factor of a conservative 30 percent to cover all contingencies, the gross savings in cost on 27 items in 1960, assuming all items were purchased, would amount to approximately $1,300,000. On 31 items, which could be sourced overseas in 1961, the gross reduction in cost might project to $1,800,000.

It should be borne in mind that these approximate costs were obtained from outside vendors in Europe, South America, and Japan. In actual practice, the foreign companies with which we have license agreements will be developed as potential suppliers, and price alone will not be the sole determining factor. It would be the policy of the International Division on foreign procurement to utilize commercial vendors only when it is not feasible to employ the services of a licensee.

My sampling of potential commercial suppliers indicates that it is possible to locate suppliers who can produce our type of appliances and equipment. However, because of the widespread distribution of possible suppliers and because of the competition from large manufacturers, such as Phillips and Siemens, any European procurement would probably be done with middle- or small-size vendors. Locating potential suppliers in Europe is considerably more difficult than in Japan, where, because of the concentration of manufacturers in two areas, the task of locating a potential supplier is much easier.

. . . The IDC laboratories in Basel are currently forming a unit of two professional engineers and a technician to encompass the following three areas:

1. Product development.
2. A technical production evaluation service for the International Division to determine suitability for possible procurement.
3. A technical quality control service in support of overseas procurement activities of the International Division.

The director of licensing is also checking the practicability of using this engineering group at Basel as an applications laboratory service in support of our components marketing activities and/or exploitation of highly technical IDC products at Basel, which are most effectively marketed by customer inspection and demonstrator. In Japan essentially the same procedures will be adhered to except that it is necessary to use the facilities of an outside testing agency, such as the Tokyo Testing Company (TTC) in Japan.

. . . An integral part of the foreign procurement program is its close relationship with IDC Canada, Ltd., our Canadian subsidiary. A branch office at Basel, Switzerland, has already been established by IDC Canada, Ltd., through which it is anticipated that all commitments, both European and Japanese, will eventually be placed. At the present time, the shipment and billing for IDC Canada, Ltd., is being handled by Export-Import, G.m.b.H. of Hamburg, Germany. The China Trading Company of Hong Kong has been performing the same function for Japanese equipment. Stella Internacional, S.A., of Panama, has recently been established for the importation of products from our Brazilian subsidiary, and for the possible distribution of components from Chile and Japanese equipment for the South American market. The means is thus provided through Export-Import, China Trading, and Stella Internacional to receive, ship, and process customer orders for selected foreign manufactured products. Our existing experience with IDC Canada, Ltd., in the handling of Japanese products, indicates that use of this vehicle results in an operating profit of 9.3 percent compared with an operating profit for the International Division of 1.5 percent.

. . . To obtain the profits on foreign procurement, it will be necessary to increase certain expenses. These costs will be incurred in the following areas:

Fixed expenses

1. IDC Canada, Ltd., buying services in Japan and Europe $20,000
2. Additional buyer in the International Division $10,000

	Percentage of overall purchasing costs
Variable expenses	
1. Testing of components and manufactured products (based on quotations)	1
2. Replacement parts investment (based on marketing approximation).	1
3. Reproduction of specifications; shipment of samples; increased use of cables, postage, etc..	3 Est.
4. Foreign procurement travel	.05

. . . A summary of the gross potential savings for 1959, 1960, and 1961 through foreign procurement, using a cost reduction factor of 30 percent, appears below:

	Procurement potential		
Product line	1959	1960	1961
Industrial products—Minimum	$ 145,740	$4,437,500	$6,282,500
—Maximum	145,740	4,962,500	6,807,500
Components.	1,125,000	1,685,000	Undetermined at this time
Consumer products.	500,000	1,000,000	1,500,000
Totals—Minimum.	$1,770,740	$7,122,500	$7,782,500
—Maximum	1,770,740	7,647,500	8,307,500

	Gross savings potential		
Product line	1959	1960	1961
Industrial products—Minimum	$ 43,722	$1,331,250	$1,884,750
—Maximum	43,722	1,488,750	2,042,250
Components.	377,500	505,500	Undetermined at this time
Consumer products.	150,000	300,000	450,000
Totals—Minimum.	$ 571,222	$2,136,750	$2,334,750
—Maximum	571,222	2,294,250	2,492,250

. . . Before proceeding on a full-scale foreign procurement schedule, it is necessary that the International Division receive a corporate policy decision pertaining to IDC-designed items. The necessary procedures to implement this program will be invoked based on the outcome of the corporate policy.

Presently, the determination of whether a specific foreign commitment is processed through IDC Canada, Ltd., is made by the marketing manager involved. A policy decision is necessary decreeing that all foreign manufactured equipment sold abroad must automatically flow through IDC Canada, Ltd.

There are numerous export, import, and currency restrictions which impede, to some degree, ready procurement and shipment of overseas purchases when handled from a U.S. location. It has been recommended to establish a worldwide procurement and finance group in Basel, Switzerland (similar to those operated by Du Pont, Radio Corporation of America, Chrysler, General Electric, and Westinghouse Electric), which would perform the following functions:

1. Consolidate foreign procurement in Basel for IDC Chicago, IDC Canada, Ltd., and any other affiliate engaged in world trade.
2. Provide Basel office with qualified banking facilities.
3. Allow Basel office to use, when necessary, other financial institutions that could facilitate switch transactions, settlement of exchange in restricted currencies, etc.

. . . Specific responsibilities of the International Division's purchasing department in overseas procurement are:

1. Based on requirements and specifications submitted by the International Division's marketing department or by any of the domestic manufacturing divisions, purchasing will explore the facilities of our licensees and other possible sources of foreign supply, using IDC Canada, Ltd., procurement facilities where available. As a matter of general policy, prime consideration should be given to IDC licensees.

2. All quotations from our licensees and other foreign vendors will be analyzed and submitted to the manufacturing divisions with recommendations. Purchase commitments together with the related manufacturing and test specifications will be placed on receipt of a properly authorized purchase requisition.

3. Purchasing will be the sole contact in dealing with IDC laboratories at Basel or with the Tokyo Testing Company on the specific inspection or test applicable to each transaction.

4. Purchasing will be responsible for the delivery of all commitments.

.   .   .   .   .

. . . Although there are many details to be ironed out, the basic procedures to be followed in the overseas buying and shipping are as follows:

1. Operating units will request International Division's purchasing to investigate foreign procurement of equipment, providing the necessary preliminary specifications, quantities, etc.

2. Purchasing will conduct negotiations with our licensees and will use IDC facilities in Europe, South America, and Japan to locate vendors and quotations.

3. When quotations from offshore suppliers are received, purchasing will compare costs, consult with the administrator, foreign exchange, and submit information to the requesting operating unit with recommendations.

4. If the operating unit decides to place the commitment abroad, they will create a purchase requisition.

5. International Division's purchasing will place orders with the foreign vendors through the foreign buying offices, if possible, which will handle the transaction with vendors, including payment, etc. . . .

.   .   .   .   .

Organization of purchasing for international division

The purchasing department of the international division, headed by Mr. Linscott in 1959–62, had been principally engaged in the domestic procurement of finished products for shipment overseas. The department bought from the company's manufacturing divisions and from outside suppliers. It was generally recognized by company executives that the department, in performing this function, not only had gained extensive and diversified experience in the field of procurement, but also had acquired valuable skills in handling international business transactions.

Exhibit 7
ORGANIZATION CHART—PURCHASING DEPARTMENT OF
INTERNATIONAL DIVISION, 1959-62

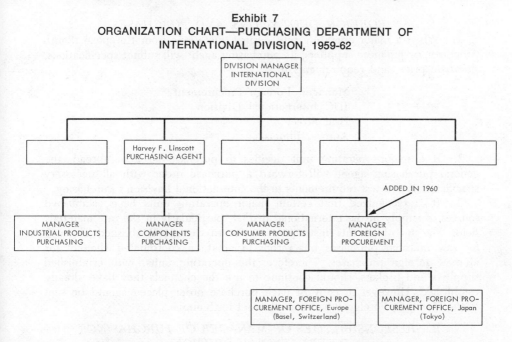

The formal organization of the department during the years 1959 to 1962 is shown in Exhibit 7.

Following approval by top management of the major recommendations that had been made by Mr. Linscott in the report on his survey of IDC's foreign procurement potential, the international division added in 1960 a foreign procurement section to its purchasing department. The department negotiated a contract with the Tokyo Testing Company, an independent Japanese testing organization, and assigned an IDC employee of the international division's licensing department, who was of Japanese origin, to the Japanese firm to perform the following functions: (1) exploration of sources of supply for IDC, (2) placement of purchase orders, (3) follow-up on purchase orders and collection of information on material and product developments in Japan. The first order placed by the international division through the Japanese buying office called for hot plates to be used in conjunction with the marketing of portable ranges in West European countries.

In order to carry out the same function in Europe, the purchasing department of the international division next assigned, in the fall of 1960, a staff member with extensive experience in purchasing and in international business to the company's subsidiary in Basel, Switzerland.

In March, 1961, the company's general purchasing manual outlined the procedures to be followed for overseas purchases. Excerpts appear below:

A. FOREIGN QUOTATIONS AND PURCHASES

1. When a major operating unit desires quotations from European, South American, or Japanese suppliers, its purchasing agent will submit specifications, domestic price, and requirements to:

> Manager, Foreign Procurement
> IDC International Division
> Hull Street
> Aurora, Illinois

2. If a major operating unit decides to purchase an item abroad, the general purchasing agent will forward a purchase order with all necessary specifications and test requirements to the International Division's Purchasing.

3. It is recognized that certain major operating units have established sources of supply in the international market, particularly in the raw materials field. The intent of this instruction is not to disrupt established channels for raw material purchases but rather to create a coordinated channel for all new foreign purchases. Therefore, the operating units, with established suppliers and brokers, should continue to use the channels they have already established. However, a copy of each purchase order placed should be sent to the Manager, Foreign Procurement, as set forth above.

B. RESPONSIBILITIES OF MANAGER OF PURCHASING, INTERNATIONAL DIVISION

IDC Purchasing, International Division, will:

1. Review all requests for quotations to assure clarity and completeness of information.

2. Place requests for quotations through the established IDC purchasing representatives abroad, and follow up to ensure prompt transmittal of desired information to the inquiring activity.

3. Arrange to place the commitment and letter of credit upon receipt of an approved purchase order, and check import and export license requirements, overseas traffic requirements, etc.

4. Disseminate source information pertaining to common items to all major operating units concerned, in order that full advantage may be taken of overseas buying opportunities.

5. Serve as a reference point for foreign source data.

6. Assume responsibility for the performance of the IDC purchasing representatives abroad.

Development of foreign procurement activities, 1961–64

Following the addition of a foreign procurement section to the international division's purchasing department and the establishment of the three overseas procurement branches, the volume of IDC-designed products bought from overseas suppliers upon request by the international division's marketing departments rose rapidly and in accordance with the expectations of Mr. Linscott. The volume of orders placed by the company's domestic manufacturing divisions through the foreign procurement section with overseas vendors, however, remained "disappointingly low," as Mr. Linscott phrased it. Looking back at the time when he held the position of purchasing agent at the international division and when foreign procurement was in his area of responsibility, he said:

To carry out the foreign procurement charter assigned to the international division by the corporation, I had to develop foreign procurement programs, within the various manufacturing divisions. But to gain acceptance by the line general purchasing agents or, for that matter, by the general managers, was initially next to impossible. The purchasing agents knew little about the executive order and furthermore could not have cared less to know anything about it. When I first visited the plants and talked to them about foreign procurement, about the policy instruction, and about the organizational and procedural setup, the typical answer was, "What in — is this? Policy order, so what! Why should I come to you to purchase when I am perfectly satisfied with my domestic suppliers?"

When I ran into this opposition in a number of divisions, I approached the man who was then staff vice president for procurement to enlist his support. But he took the position that, since the executive order had assigned foreign procurement to the international division, corporate staff purchasing had no business getting into the act. He did agree to discuss the matter of purchasing abroad with divisional purchasing agents but offered no other help.

Faced with this lack of interest in foreign buying by many of the operating units, Mr. Linscott and his staff began to select specific parts and components which, in their view, could be purchased at significant cost advantages in Japan, South America, and Europe. He obtained samples from foreign vendors, arranged for extensive testing, and assembled comprehensive information on costs and cost differentials, quality, performance, delivery, and service. Armed with such data, Mr. Linscott appeared at meetings and conferences of divisional purchasing agents to demonstrate, on the basis of concrete examples, the cost savings possible by shifting the purchase of certain materials from domestic suppliers to overseas suppliers. Mr. Linscott commented:

The evidence was hard to ignore. We finally succeeded in impressing at least some of the previously uninterested general purchasing agents and also in changing to some extent the attitude of corporate purchasing. The vice president warmed up a bit and gave his informal backing to the development of foreign procurement programs. He started telling the purchasing agents that IDC was a worldwide company and that procurement should therefore take place on a worldwide basis. But it required an enormous effort and a hard selling job just to get a foot in the door. We still did not succeed in inducing the general purchasing agents to come to us on their own initiative with a foreign sourcing request. Whatever we purchased for the divisions from abroad was accomplished after we had approached the general purchasing agents, although there were some sporadic attempts by one or two divisions to deal directly with foreign suppliers. This we had to stop because of established procedures. And some divisions still abstained completely from making any request of us.

Another major problem that the management of the international division encountered in its efforts to develop foreign procurement programs was the resentment of many of the divisional purchasing agents against being charged with a portion of the administrative costs incurred by the foreign procurement staff, including the company's three overseas buying offices.

As an operating unit, the international division, in accordance with general company procedure, assessed other operating units and corporate staff departments with the costs of services performed for such units and departments. By contrast, the operating costs of the corporate staff departments were treated as corporate assessments and not charged to any of the operating divisions.

In 1961 the international division assessed each domestic manufacturing division with a minimum of $200 per month, regardless of whether the division made use of the foreign procurement staff. The balance between the total amount thus assessed and the actual total expenses incurred was partly assessed to the four operating divisions making the largest use of the foreign procurement staff, and partly borne by the international division itself.

By 1964 the minimum assessment for each domestic manufacturing division has increased to $750 per month, reflecting the growth in the division's foreign purchasing activities. The major share of the foreign procurement staff's budget, which had increased to over $200,000 from less than $50,000 in 1961, was still carried by the international division and the four operating divisions mentioned above. Mr. Linscott said:

The problem of assessment invoices bouncing back to us was particularly acute with those divisions that made no use at all of the foreign procurement organization. It was not the dollar amount involved but the principle to which the purchasing agents objected. Each time they returned our invoices they told us that they would pay the invoices only if they had made use of our services but would refuse to pay for services not received. Of course, this is the way purchasing agents are trained to think. And, once they had taken this position, which naturally created some sort of interdivisional squabble, they made very sure they did not use us. Even today, after five years of operation, some divisions will send back our invoices. I believe that part of this resentment grew out of the general purchasing agents' feeling that they had no opportunity to audit the figures appearing in the invoices. Also, the arguments for not paying our assessments varied at time from one division to the next, as, for instance, in the case of one industrial products division whose purchasing agent told us that using foreign materials conflicted with U.S. government policies and that the governmental procurement agencies would not accept any charges for foreign procurement activities when auditing the division's books and records.

In 1964 the task of purchasing products in the domestic market for overseas shipment was transferred by executive order from the international division to the domestic manufacturing divisions. According to Mr. Linscott, this change was undertaken to stop an "increasing duplication of efforts." Following this transfer, the purchasing department of the international division became exclusively concerned with foreign procurement. (The department's revised formal organization chart is given in Exhibit 3.) Each of the department's four foreign procurement administrators serviced a group of operating divisions.

Toward the end of 1964, the company's overseas purchasing office in Tokyo was staffed with a manager, two buyers, an engineer, and a secretary. The staff of the Basel buying office included a manager, a buyer, and two secretaries. The Argentine office was represented by a buyer and an administrative assistant.

Mr. Linscott estimated that, by the end of 1964, the international procurement staff would have placed approximately 1,300 purchase orders with 120 foreign suppliers, covering materials, parts, components, and assemblies for the domestic manufacturing divisions, at a value of about $3 million for a total gross cost savings of about $1.3 million when compared with prices of U.S. suppliers prevailing for the same products at the time of ordering. Mr. Linscott commented:

These savings are impressive. But the problem of persuading the divisional purchasing agents throughout the organization to develop comprehensive foreign procurement programs, with the help of the international purchasing staff but otherwise on their own initiative, is not solved. At the start of the program of foreign buying, we had to choose a specific item, go to the purchasing agent buying the item, and do some hard selling to induce him to place an order through us with a foreign vendor. With minor exceptions, the same is still true today. Instead of assisting the manufacturing units in exploring systematically the entire range of products lending themselves to foreign buying—and there are many that do not—the foreign procurement people take on one little job at a time and start running with it. They must still spend so much time on selling foreign buying to the divisions that they cannot concern themselves with a methodical determination of the critical areas of foreign buying.

The great advantage that I can see in assigning international procurement to corporate staff purchasing rests on our intimate familiarity with what goes on at the divisional purchasing level: We know what the divisions buy, where they buy, how they buy, and at what prices they buy; we are familiar with the relationships they maintain with their suppliers; and we have full access to the details of every transaction. Orders in excess of $25,000 are always examined and approved by us; and, of course, we do a good deal of buying ourselves. All these things the international division cannot do. Unlike the international division, we could with great ease build a thoroughgoing foreign procurement program for each and every division. And we could do this not only methodically but also with fewer people, because we would not have to spend so much time selling the idea of foreign buying to the purchasing agents. I believe that we would be able to increase substantially the volume of offshore procurement.

In addition, Mr. Linscott thought that establishing responsibility for foreign buying at the corporate staff purchasing level also offered the advantage of eliminating assessing the manufacturing divisions with the costs of operating the international purchasing organization, thus removing what he believed to be a major source of the resentment by the general purchasing agents against foreign buying. Mr. Linscott commented:

These factors—access to all purchasing information at the operating level, ability to systematically develop foreign buying programs, and removal of the assessment issue—would enable us, I believe, to increase our foreign commitments to perhaps as much as 10 percent of the operating divisions' total disbursements for materials, parts, and supplies to outside vendors. Of course, there are many items we will never be able to buy overseas. Plastics, for instance, for which we spend over $30 million each year, are priced lower in Europe; but, by the time you add packing and transportation costs and duty, and, more importantly, when you become aware of the fact that most European plastic makers have licensing arrangements with certain American companies, you are better off buying in the United States. But these things you don't know until you set out to explore and determine with great care all specific areas of foreign buying.

We might be able to go beyond the 10 percent mark, though this would probably require a great deal of reorientation of the general purchasing agents. It would require changes in production planning and scheduling and therefore affect the purchasing agents' buying habits quite a bit. Quality problems would be amplified, because you cannot phone your supplier and get another shipment in a week. And, perhaps more importantly, if we kept increasing the usage of foreign-made parts and components, I would expect at some point renewed resistance by the divisional people for such reasons as loyalty to long-term domestic suppliers with a good performance record, prejudice against certain foreign nations, and fear of eliminating jobs in production, engineering, and even purchasing itself.

But, while Mr. Linscott saw significant advantages in shifting the foreign procurement function from the international division to corporate staff purchasing, he was also acutely aware of at least two weighty disadvantages that he believed to be inherent in such an organizational change. He commented:

First, there is no question in my mind that our licensing operations in foreign countries are extremely important to the corporation, not only from an income point of view, but also from the viewpoint of the corporation's long-range strategy and policy. Licensing involves many intricate and sensitive business relationships and calls for a careful protection of these relationships. For instance, if we have a choice among several suppliers for an item in

Europe, one of whom is a licensee, the placing of a substantial order with one of the nonlicensees might create considerable problems. On the other hand, placing the order with the licensee might jeopardize preferential tax rates associated with licensing operations in Europe. Protection of our trademark rights, which might be affected when we buy IDC-designed equipment abroad, is another problem area. Our international division, after having handled all of our foreign activities for many years, including licensing, is greatly experienced in these matters. From this point of view, it seems very desirable to keep foreign buying in the international division. It also helps the corporation to present a unified bearing overseas.

Second, I firmly believe that efficient and effective foreign procurement requires great experience and skill in international business affairs. The international division meets this requirement unequivocally.

This viewpoint was also expressed in the 1965 budget proposal for the international division's foreign procurement organization, which was prepared by Mr. Doering with the help of Mr. Linscott. The proposal read, in part, as follows:

The nature of the duties and the responsibilities of the U.S.-based foreign procurement administrators not only involves the activities normally attributed to sound domestic purchasing operations but also calls for skills, judgment, and knowledge of foreign markets and vendors, import-export customs and legal regulations, means and methods of transportation and packaging, payment terms (such as letters of credit), and foreign business practices.

An additional consideration, of which Mr. Linscott was not unmindful, centered on the allocation of the administrative costs of the foreign procurement operation. Toward the end of 1964, the major officers of corporate staff purchasing were much concerned with reducing the costs of the staff department from $250,000 to $200,000 in the next fiscal period without jeopardizing its effectiveness in "bringing the advantages of centralization to a decentralized procurement organization," as Mr. Linscott phrased it. He believed that in the midst of such cost-cutting efforts there was little enthusiasm among the executives of the department for adding over $200,000 to the budget for the administrative costs of foreign procurement. Mr. Linscott remarked:

Maybe this is merely a matter of timing, but we would look a little foolish to top management if we more than doubled our budget while trying at the same time to squeeze out $50,000. Also, following a recent change in management of the international division, there is an increased awareness by the new people that the extremely high return on investment involved in foreign buying and the resulting contribution to overall corporate profits cannot remain unnoticed by any chief executive. I don't think the international division is about ready to give up.

As Mr. Linscott was thus pondering the feasibility of shifting the foreign procurement function to the corporate staff purchasing, he received from Mr. Doering on December 17, 1964, another photostatic copy of a letter written by a general manager of the International Division to the general manager of the Gamma Division. This letter read as follows:

December 14, 1964

To: John Donnell [General Manager, Gamma Division]
FROM: L. D. Wesley [General Manager, International Division]
RE: Purchasing—Samuel Simmons, Letter of 12–9 to F. J. Doering

I have noted the December 9 letter written by Samuel Simmons to F. J. Doering.

We have recently had a series of discussions in the international division with respect to foreign procurement. It has been reaffirmed that the foreign procurement organization under the direction of Frank Doering will be responsible for all foreign vendor contracts and purchases. This means that the operating divisions will continue to work through Mr. Doering's organization, and I am sure that you will find the service satisfactory.

When and if you have complaints with respect to the type and quality of services which you are receiving, please feel free to bring such matters to my attention. It is important that anyone in your organization who is concerned in this area be made aware of the requirements to channel all foreign procurement matters into Mr. Doering's organization. There are to be no exceptions to this requirement.

LDW

cc: F. J. Doering

3 PROCEDURES, COMPUTERIZATION, AND INFORMATION SYSTEMS

The materials management area has a wide range of standard operating procedures to deal with the normal daily tasks. The large volume of items, the large dollar volume involved, the need for an audit trail, the severe consequences of unsatisfactory performance, and the potential contribution to effective corporate operations inherent in the function are five major reasons for sound system development. The acquisition process is not only closely tied to almost all other functions included in an organization but also to the external environment, creating a need for information systems development of a complex nature. The introduction of data processing has had a substantial impact on the acquisition process and its management. The need for systems and procedures which satisfactorily meet the materials and information requirements of the organization is obvious. Considerable management skill is required to assure continuing effectiveness.

Steps of procurement

We are interested only in a simple statement of the broad outlines of any system of sound purchasing procedure. We shall give little attention to the seemingly infinite variety of detail both as to the steps followed and as to the forms and records used.

The essential steps of procurement procedure are as follows:

1. The ascertainment of the need.
2. An accurate statement of the character and amount of the article or commodity desired.
3. The transmission of the purchase requisition.
4. Negotiation for the possible sources of supply.
5. The analysis of the proposals, the selection of the vendor, and the placing of the order.
6. The follow-up on the order.

7. The checking of the invoice and payment of the supplier.
8. The receipt and inspection of the goods.
9. The completion of the record.

Ascertainment of the need

It is, of course, obvious that any purchase originates with the recognition of a definite need by someone in the organization. It is one of the duties of the person responsible for a particular activity to know what the individual requirements of the unit are: what and how much and when it is needed. This may result merely in the sending of a material requisition to the stores department. Occasionally, such requirements may be met by the transfer of surplus stock from another using department. Sooner or later, of course, the procurement of new supplies will become necessary. Some purchase requisitions originate within the production or using department. Requests for office equipment of all sorts normally would come from the office manager or from the controller of the company. Some requests may come from the sales or advertising departments or from research laboratories. Frequently, special forms will indicate the source of requisitions, and where this is not the case, distinctive code numbers may be used. A typical requisition is shown in Figure 3–1.

It is, of course, also the responsibility of the procurement department to anticipate the needs of using departments. It is part of the procurement manager's work to urge not only that the requirements of other departments be as nearly standard in character as possible and that a minimum of special or unusual orders be placed, but also that requirements be anticipated far enough in advance to prevent an excessive number of "rush" orders. Also, since the procurement department is closely in touch with price trends and general market conditions, the placing of forward orders may be essential to the organization to protect against shortage of supply or increased prices.

Emergency, rush, and small orders

A problem which frequently arises in connection with the issuance of purchase requisitions is that of an excessively large number of "small orders" and of requests for material marked "rush." The two may overlap, although not necessarily. A small order may be marked "rush," and it may, in fact, represent a real emergency item and justify all possible haste; on the other hand, a rush order may quite conceivably call for a very large amount of material. A distinction, therefore, needs to be drawn between these two terms.

It is not to be expected that rush orders can always be avoided; emergencies do arise which justify their use. Sudden changes in style

Figure 3-1
PURCHASING REQUISITION
(8½ × 5½ in.)

F 60 AB

PURCHASE REQUISITION

No. 35851

Purchase Order No.

Order Date   Vendor

Charge Symbol

Del.   F.O.B.

Date
Notify

Deliver to ☐ Archer
☐ Riverdale
☐ See below

Send Via

Terms

Quantity	Unit	No. or Size	Description	When Material is Received
				Price

Confirmation ☐

Suggested Vendor

Wanted

Requisitioner.
Do Not Specify the Vendor Unless Absolutely Necessary. Only One Item to a Requisition Unless All Items Will Be Bought From the Same Source.

Approved
Approved   Date

Buyer

THE SHELBY SALESBOOK CO., SHELBY, OHIO —37606△

or design and unexpected changes in market conditions may upset a most carefully planned material schedule. Breakdowns are seemingly inevitable, with an accompanying demand for parts or material which it would be quite unreasonable to carry in stock regularly.

There are, however, so-called rush orders that cannot be justified on any such basis. They consist of those requisitions which arise because of (a) faulty inventory control, (b) poor production planning or budgeting, (c) an apparent lack of confidence in the ability of the purchasing department to get material to the plant by the proper time, and (d) the sheer habit of marking the requests "rush." Whatever the cause, such orders are costly. This higher cost is due in part to the greater administrative expense involved in proportion to the size of the order and in part of the greater chance of error when the work is done under pressure. Rush orders also place an added burden on the seller, and this burden must directly or indirectly find its way into the price paid by the buyer.

What can be done to reduce the seriousness of this problem? For an excessive number of rush orders that are not actually emergency orders, the solution is a matter of education in the proper purchasing procedure. In one company, for example, a ruling has been made that when a "rush" requisition is sent to the purchasing department, the department issuing such an order has to explain to the general superintendent the reason for the emergency and secure approval. Furthermore, even if the requisition is approved by the superintendent, the extra costs are, so far as they can be determined, charged to the department ordering the material. The result has been a marked reduction in the number of such orders.

Small orders

Small orders are a continuing matter of concern in every organization. Most requisitions follow Pareto's law so that about 70 percent of all requisitions only amount to about 10 percent of the total dollar volume. One important consideration then becomes the cost of the system set up to handle small orders versus the cost of the items themselves. Since the lack of a small item may create a nuisance totally out of proportion to its dollar value, assured supply is usually the first objective to be met. A number of approaches need to be used continuously to address the small order question. A few examples are:

a. If the fault lies with the using department, perhaps persuasion may be employed to increase the number of standardized items requested, as contrasted with unclassified items.

b. Another possibility is for the purchasing department to hold small requisitions as received until a justifiable total, in dollars, has been accumulated.

c. A third method is to establish a requisition calendar, setting aside specific days for the requisitioning of specific supplies, so that all requests for a given item are received on the same day. As an aid to the storeskeeper, the calendar also may be so arranged that practically all the supplies secured from any specific type of vendor are requisitioned on the same day.

d. Still another method of procedure is to make use of the "stockless buying" or "systems contracting"[1] concept. This concept has been used most widely in the purchase of MRO (maintenance, repair, and operating supply) items. (See explanation later in this chapter.)

Accurate description of commodity desired

No purchaser can be expected to buy without knowing exactly what the using departments want. For this reason, it is essential to have an accurate description of the need, the article, the commodity, or the service which is requested.

It is the responsibility of the purchaser to question a specification if it appears that the organization might be better served through a modification. An obvious case is the one where market shortages exist in the commodity requested and a substitute is the only reasonable alternative. Since future market conditions play such a vital role, it makes sense to have a high degree of interaction between the purchasing and specifying groups in the early stages of need definition. A number of writers strongly advocate a general problem solving approach to this area, advising careful definition by users and procurement and bringing this problem to the attention of suppliers. This approach would solve some of the traditional problems encountered when goods or services are specified without careful attention to the real performance required or the market's capability. This approach sounds sensible enough and will undoubtedly continue to gain popularity. Nevertheless, the bulk of today's requirements are still specified in the traditional manner and the need for accuracy in input data is obvious. At best, an inaccurate description may result in some loss of time, at worst it may have serious financial consequences, cause disruption of supply, hard feelings internally, and loss of supplier respect and trust.

Since the purchasing department is the last one to see the specification before it is sent on to the supplier, the need for a final check here is clear. Such a check is not possible if purchasing department personnel have no familiarity with the product or service requested. Any questions regarding the accuracy or adequateness of the requisition should, of course, be referred back to the requisitioner and should not be settled unilaterally in the purchasing department. The variety of ways in which specifications may be set is covered in Chapter 4.

---

[1] Systems contracting is a term registered by the Carborundum Company.

Standardization of requisition form

It is important that there be as substantial uniformity as possible in the use of terms to describe desired articles.[2] The importance of proper nomenclature as a means of avoiding misunderstanding cannot be overemphasized. The most effective way to secure this uniformity is to maintain in the purchasing office a proper file listing the articles usually purchased. Such files may be kept in various ways. Some organizations have found it worthwhile to maintain a general catalog, which lists all the items used, and a stores catalog, which contains a list of all of the items carried in stock. Such catalogs may be kept in loose-leaf form or in a card index. Provided that such catalogs are adequately planned and properly maintained, they tend to promote the uniformity in description which has been indicated as so essential. They have, of course, certain other advantages. They tend to reduce the number of odd sizes or grades of articles which are requisitioned, and they tend to facilitate accounting and stores procedure. It is probably needless to add that, unless such catalogs or their equivalent are properly planned, maintained, and actually used, they are confusing and expensive beyond any benefits which could be derived from them. A comprehensive commodity code is essential when DP equipment is used.

The description of the articles or commodities desired is, of course, indicated in some manner on the requisition forms. There is no standard form of requisition in common use. To serve the purpose for which it is intended, a requisition should be designed to provide space for the following:

To be filled in by requisitioner:
a. Date.
b. Number (identification).
c. Originating department.
d. Account to be charged.
e. Complete description of material desired and quantity.
f. Shipping instructions including date material is wanted.
g. Signature of person(s) authorized to issue requisition.

To be filled in by purchasing personnel:
a. Purchase order number.
b. Delivery dates specified on order.
c. Buyer's signature.

Transmission of purchase requisition

Although less than 25 percent of purchasing departments notify the requisitioner of the receipts of a requisition, it is good practice to make

---

[2] See also Chapter 4.

two copies of the requisition: one to be retained by the issuer and filed numerically and one to be forwarded to the purchasing department. Another practice is that of requiring the general stores department to keep or make out a list in duplicate of the requisitions sent each day (or at any one time) and to send one copy of the list to the purchasing office. When the requisitions are received by the purchasing department they may be time-stamped and checked against the list, which is then signed and returned to the stores department as a notification that the requisitions so listed has been received. It will be noted that neither of these two procedures provides the requisitioner with information as to the subsequent disposition of the requisition, which may be done at some future time.

It is a common practice to request that but one item may appear on any one purchase requisition, particularly on standard items of stores carried regularly in stock. In the case of some special items, such as plumbing fittings not regularly carried in stock, several items may be covered by one requisition, provided they are likely to be purchased from one vendor and are for delivery at the same time. This simplifies record keeping since various items are secured from various suppliers, call for different delivery dates, and in other ways require separate purchase orders and different treatment.

From the standpoint of good procedure, it is important for the purchasing department definitely to have established who has the power to requisition. Under no circumstances should the purchasing department accept requisitions from anyone other than those specifically authorized. This is just as important as it is for all salesmen to know definitely that a requisition is not an order. Much confusion, waste, and ill will could be avoided if all departments insisted upon this rule.

All requisitions should be carefully checked before any action is taken. The requested quantity should be based upon anticipated needs and should be checked against economical purchasing quantities. The dates requested should allow for sufficient time to secure quotations and samples, if necessary, and to execute the purchase order and obtain delivery of the materials. If insufficient time is allowed, or the date would involve additional expense, this should be brought immediately to the attention of the requisitioner.

The procedure of handling requisitions upon receipt in the purchase office is of sufficient importance to warrant citing an example:

Upon receipt of the requisitions in the central purchasing office after being time-stamped, all requisitions are turned over to the order typist or clerk, who will have charge of all the specification cards and who will attach the proper specification card to each individual requisition, being careful to see that the proper card is attached to the requisition according to the symbol given and the size. The requisitions are then turned over to the buyer, who will immediately mark up all contract items, showing the name of the firm with which the order is to be placed, also the word "contract" on the requisition, the price, the terms, the f.o.b. point, the total value, and the payment date, for the controller's information. The requisitions will then be turned back to the order typist, who will type the order, after which it will be carefully checked with the specification card, the price, terms, etc., before the order is finally mailed to the vendor.

When items are not covered by contract and therefore carry no price agreement, request for quotations will be dictated or sent out on standard inquiry blanks provided for this purpose. In cases where quotations are to be requested, a list of the names of potential vendors will be written on the back of the requisitions. The requisitions will then be turned over to the typist, who will make out standard inquiry forms and turn them over to the buyer, who will check and sign before mailing.

A quotation sheet will be filled out and attached to the requisition, which will show the date, vendor's name to whom the inquiry is sent, the list price, discount, net price, f.o.b. point, and cash terms.

When the quotations are received from the various vendors to whom the inquiries are sent, the quotations will be entered on the quotation sheet by the clerk designated to do this work and then turned over to the buyer, who will determine the vendor with whom the business is to be placed. The buyer will show on the requisition the total value and the payment date. The buyer then initials the requisition and turns it over to the order typist who will type the order.

The use of the traveling requisition

In the search to reduce operating expenses some companies have found it desirable to use the so-called traveling requisition for recurring requirements of materials and standard parts. One convenient form for this is the Kardex® type of record card. One side of the card provides for the following information:

Across the top of the card:
a. Part number or description of item or material to be covered and where it is used.
b. Maximum stock; ordering point; and minimum stock.

Lower portion of the card:
a. At the left an "Ordered" section provides for the date; purchase order number; date required; the department for which the requisition is placed; the quantity required; and a space for an authorized signature of approval.
b. On the right a "Received" section provides for recording the date; purchase order number; quantity; and the cost of the ordered item when received.

The reverse side of the card provides for the purchase order description of the item and part number, if any; a list of approved vendors including the cash discount terms and f.o.b. point for each; and columns to show which vendor received the order, the purchase order number, the quantity, required date, unit price, and a place for the name of the buyer and date.

When parts or material covered by the traveling requisition are being ordered, the inventory control clerk inserts the date, the date required, the name of the department for which the request is made, and the quantity, and obtains an authorized signature prior to sending the requisition to the purchasing department. After selecting the vendor, the buyer fills in the vendor's code number, quantity, required date, unit price, and his name and date, and returns the card to the inventory control department.

Inasmuch as all required information is on a single card which can be reused many times, the entire transaction can be handled with speed and a minimum of clerical paper work.

Stockless buying or systems contracting[3]

This technique is relatively new and has been used most frequently in buying stationery and office supplies, repetitive items, maintenance and repair materials, and operating supplies (MRO). This latter class of purchases is characterized by many different types of items, all of comparatively low value, and needed immediately when any kind of a plant or equipment failure occurs. The technique is built around a blanket-type contract which is developed in great detail regarding approximate quantities to be used in specified time periods, prices, provisions for adjusting prices whether as an increase or a decrease, procedures to be followed in picking up requisitions daily and making delivery within 24 hours, simplified billing procedures, and a complete catalog of all items covered by the contract.

Generally the inventory of all items covered by a contract are stored by the supplier, thus eliminating the buyer's investment in inventory and space. Requisitions for items covered by the contract go directly to the supplier and are not processed by the purchasing department. The requisition is used by the supplier to pull stock, to pack, to invoice, and as a delivery slip. The streamlined procedure reduces paper-handling costs for the buyer and the seller and has been a help in solving the small-order problem.

Systems contracting has become popular in nonmanufacturing organizations as well. It is no longer confined to MRO items and may well

---

[3] For a full description see *American Management Association, Systems Contracting*, Management Bulletin 63, New York, 1965; and Ralph A. Bolton, *Systems Contracting* (New York: American Management Association, 1966).

include a number of high-dollar volume commodities. The shortening of the time span from requisition to delivery has resulted in substantial inventory reductions and greater organizational willingness to go along with the supply system. The amount of "red tape" has become minimal. Since the user normally provides a good estimate of requirements and compensates the supplier in case the forecast is not good, the supplier risks little in inventory investment. The degree of cooperation and information exchange required between buyer and seller in a systems contract often results in a much warmer relationship than normally exhibited in a traditional arms length trading situation; an interesting result of a system originally designed to cut paper-handling costs and time delays!

Negotiation for sources of supply

Since negotiation with vendors is discussed at some length elsewhere in this book[4], only incidental reference needs to be made at this point. Negotiation constitutes an important part of the procurement function. It involves essentially the location of qualified sources of supply and a satisfactory agreement as to delivery and price of the desired material. In preparation for negotiation, among the basic records in a well-organized purchasing office are three of great value:

1. A record of outstanding contracts against which orders are placed as required;
2. A commodity classification of items purchased; and
3. A classified record of vendors.

Often, too, other records are kept such as catalog files. Here we are concerned less with the basis upon which the selection is made than with the strictly procedural problems.

Negotiations with suppliers always involve consideration of price. With many commodities which are in constant use by an organization, particularly those for which there is an open and free market on which quotations can be obtained at practically any hour of the day, no market problem is involved. Bids are often called for, however, on merchandise of common use, such as stationery. Frequently, contracts covering goods and periods of time are drawn up and then quotations or bids are usually necessary. A typical form of inquiry is illustrated by Figure 3–2.

Analysis of bids; placing order

The analysis of the proposals and the selection of the vendor lead naturally to the placing of an order. Since problems of negotiation and analysis and the selection of the vendor are matters of judgment, it is necessary only to indicate here that they are logical steps in purchas-

---
[4] See Chapter 9.

ing. A form is used by many firms to assist in making an analysis of the proposals, but there is no uniformity of practice. Purchase orders may at times be placed without securing quotations at all.

The placing of an order usually involves the use of a purchase order (see Figure 3–3) unless it becomes necessary to use the vendor's sales

Figure 3–2
QUOTATION REQUEST

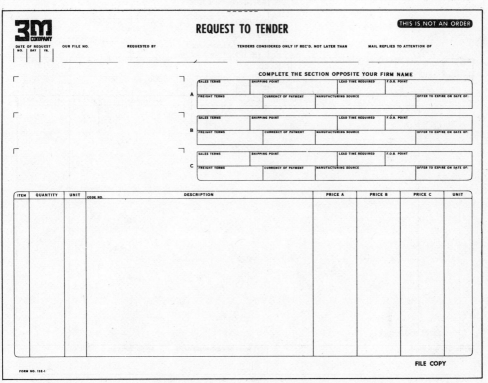

agreement instead or if a stockless buying contract is used. Failure to use proper contract forms may result in serious legal complications. Furthermore, the transaction may not be properly recorded. Therefore, even where an order is placed by telephone, a written order should follow for purposes of confirmation. At times, when emergency conditions arise it may be expedient to send a truck to pick up parts without first going through the usual procedure of requisition and purchase order. But in no instance—unless it be for minor purchases from petty cash—should materials be bought without a written order of some sort.

Actually, all companies have purchase order forms; in practice, however, all purchases are not governed by the conditions stipulated on the purchase order but rather are governed by the sales agreement sub-

Figure 3–3
PURCHASE ORDER

RAYTHEON									**PURCHASE ORDER**	

RAYTHEON
10-5083 (3/68)

PURCHASE ORDER

NO.

THIS NUMBER MUST APPEAR ON ALL PAPERS, PACKAGES AND INVOICES,

MAJOR PROG. CODE	COMPANY WIDE AGREEMENT NO.	REQ. NO.	ORIG. P.O. DATE		CHANGE ORDER NO.	C.O. DATE		ACCOUNT NO.

TO:

REFER ALL QUESTIONS TO BUYER — EXT.

REQUISITIONED BY

SHIP MATERIAL TO

ACCOUNT NO.

AT ABOVE ADDRESS UNLESS SPECIFIED OTHERWISE BELOW

CONTRACT NO.

DELIVER MATERIAL TO (INTERNAL)

SHIP VIA	SELL DEL	REA EXP	P.P	UPS	TRUCK	OTHER	DEST.	F.O.B. POINT	TRANSPORTATION TERMS P. & C.	COL.	F.A.	PPD.	VENDOR CODE NO.	MATERIAL CODE

CASH TERMS	CERT. FOR NAT'L DEFENSE USE DMS REG-1	GOVERNMENT SOURCE INSPECTION REQUIRED	YES	NO	CERT. OF COMP. ANAL	TAXABLE YES	NO	USE/RESALE EXEMPTION NO.	PRINTS/SPECS. ATTACHED	YOU HAVE

ITEM	QUANTITY	DESCRIPTION	PART NUMBER	REV	SFX	NET UNIT PRICE	I/C

DELIVERY AT DESTINATION

"X" INDICATES CONFIRMING ORDER   DO NOT DUPLICATE

DATE   YOUR

TOTAL

ITEM	QTY. REC'D	DATE REC'D	BALANCE DUE	REC'G LETTER	CHK. BY	I.D. TAG NO.	PACKING SLIP NO.	TYPE AND NO. CONT.	GROSS WEIGHT	REC'D VIA	W/B NO.	TRANS. CHG.

REJECTION REPORT NO.	QUANTITY REJECTED	QUANTITY ACCEPTED	INSPECTED BY	DATE	STANDARD PRICE

mitted by the seller. A comparison of the sales agreements and the purchase order forms of the same company may be interesting. Since every company naturally seeks to protect itself as completely as possible, responsibilities which the purchase order form assigns to the source of supply are, in the sales agreement, often transferred to the buyer. Naturally, therefore, a company is anxious to use its own sales agreement when selling its products and its own purchase order form when buying.

Some purchasing officers assert that they refuse to permit any of the men in the department who have authority to place orders to sign any sales agreements or orders other than the company's own official order. This restriction, of course, refers to purchase orders and salesmen's order blanks and not to contract forms. If the seller strenuously objects to any of the conditions contained in the order forms and can present good reasons for the modification of such provisions, a compromise is effected. In a strong sellers' market, however, it may be difficult to adhere to this rule. Also, some suppliers refuse to sell except when the buyer signs their sales order form. If there is no alternative source, as, for example, when an electrical company holds a patent on an article, the value of which is so outstanding that no substitute is acceptable, then the purchasing officer has no choice in the matter. But ordinarily the choice as to which document shall actually be used depends somewhat upon the comparative strength of the two parties, the character of the commodity being purchased, the complexity of the transaction, and the strategy used in securing or placing the order.

Before leaving this point, it may be said that a good deal of confusion seems to prevail on this whole matter. A purchasing agent may freely sign a salesman's order blank (which, though it may well bind the purchaser, legally is not likely to be binding upon the vendor until later confirmed by his home office) and then send a purchase order to the vendor, expecting it to govern. Or a purchasing agent, subsequent to the mailing of a purchase order, may receive in reply not an acceptance but a sales order erroneously considered an acceptance instead of the counteroffer that it really is. In view of the too common confusion on these points and of the possible legal complications that may ensue, purchasing personnel need to be reasonably clear on what they are doing. See Chapter 14 for a more detailed discussion of this point.

Form of the purchase order

Purchase order forms vary tremendously as to their format and routing through the organization (see Figure 3–3). Several studies have been made of purchase order forms, and one made by Professor W. B. England indicates a variance of from two to eleven in the number of copies. The movement to secure a standard purchase order form has not gained much headway. Quoting from the study:

It seems reasonable to suppose that, if all purchase order forms had the necessary information in approximately the same position, misunderstandings and clerical errors could be reduced greatly; that shipments would be expedited; that standard sizes would use standard paper stock without waste; that printing costs would be reduced; that the actual handling and filing of the forms would be facilitated; that litigation would be lessened; and that business in general would gain because of greater simplicity, uniformity, and economy.[5]

It is interesting that one of the first uniform purchase order forms in the world was adopted by the airline industry where the need for such a form was obvious. Probably the real reason that standardization of form has not been more generally accepted is that the purchase order is essentially a legal document.

It should, of course, be noted in this connection that standardization of the form by no means implies standardization of the conditions stipulated as governing the purchase.

There are certain generally accepted essential requirements to be looked for in any satisfactory purchase order form. These are the serial number, the date of issue, the name and address of the firm receiving the order, the quantity and description of the items ordered, the date of delivery required, the shipping directions, the prices, the terms of payment, and the conditions governing the order.

These conditions governing the relations between the buyer and the seller are extremely important, and the question of what should and what should not be included is subject to a good deal of discussion. What actually appears on the purchase order form of any individual company is usually the result of experience. The study[6] indicated that of the 237 purchase order forms examined, 22 percent were without conditions of any sort; in most instances, this characteristic applied to the forms used by small companies. The fact that most large companies include conditions specifying certain rights of the buyer would indicate that they believe it worthwhile. The character of these conditions, however, varies widely:

43%   contain provisions to guard the buyer from damage suits caused by infringement.

36%   contain provisions concerning prices, such as, "If the price is not stated on this order, material must not be billed at a price higher than last paid without notice to us and our acceptance thereof."

52%   contain clauses stating that no charges will be allowed for boxing, crating, or drayage.

37%   contain stipulations stating that the acceptance of the materials is contingent upon inspection and quality.

---

[5] W. B. England, *Purchase Order Forms*, NAPA Pamphlet no. 16.

[6] Ibid.

 4% require in case of rejection that the seller receive a new order from the buyer before replacement is made.

18% mention rejection because of quality without mentioning inspection rights.

33% provide for cancellation of the order if deliveries are not received on the date specified in the order and agreed to by the seller.

17% contain conditions stating that the buyer refuses to accept drafts drawn against him.

17% are estimated to have some mention of quantity, presumably relating to overshipments or undershipments of the quantities called for. The explanation of this provision is probably to be found in the fact that in certain industries it is hard to control definitely the amount obtained from a production run, and in such instances overruns and underruns are usually accepted within certain limits.

Several of the purchase order forms have special clauses to provide for matters of special interest to the companies issuing the forms, governing such matters as arbitration, the disposition of tools required in making parts, acceptance of the acknowledgment, change of waiver conditions governing the order, etc.

Individual companies differ widely both in the number of copies of a purchase order issued and in the method of handling these copies. In a typical example, the distribution may be as follows: The original is sent to the supplier, sometimes accompanied by a duplicate copy to be returned by the vendor as an acceptance. One copy is sent to the stores or other requisitioning department to serve as notice that the order has been placed, to give an opportunity to check it against the corresponding requisition, and, if necessary, to furnish a purchase order number which is entered on the copy of the requisition held by stores. Two copies may be retained by the purchasing department for its own use. One copy is sent to the accounting department. Sometimes a copy is sent to the receiving department (particularly if receiving and stores are organizationally separate) where it may be filed alphabetically by vendor until the goods arrive.

All the copies of the purchase order, though essentially identical and all typed at one operation, are by no means identical in form. For instance, the vendors' acceptance copy may contain an acceptance statement not reproduced on any of the other copies. So, too, only the receiving department's copy may provide for entering the receiving data. The purchasing department copies may provide space for data regarding delivery promise, invoices, and shipments. Pricing information is often limited to a few copies.

Reference has already been made to the filing of the requisition. As might be expected, purchase orders are filed in various ways in various companies. The really important thing is to be able to locate the documents any time they are wanted. So far as possible, too, all papers relating to a particular purchase order should be attached to one copy or, if necessary to file some elsewhere, cross-referenced so they can be found at a moment's notice. Nothing reflects more unfavorably on a purchasing department than to have inquiries made by users, production, stores, engineering, or accounting personnel concerning information answerable only from the purchase order and to find the purchasing personnel cannot answer the questions promptly and authoritatively.

One method of filing the purchase orders, where two are kept, is to file one numerically by purchase order number or by department and purchase order; and to file the second, together with the accompanying requisition and correspondence, alphabetically by vendor's name.

Still another procedure is to file one alphabetically by vendor and the second copy is a tickler file under the date the acceptance should be received from the vendor. In case acceptance is not received according to the time allowed, this fact is noted on this copy of the purchase order, follow-up instituted in an effort to get the acceptance, and the purchase order moved ahead to a second "acceptance date." When the order is finally accepted, the tickler copy is again moved, this time being filed under the date either by which final follow-up is desirable or by which the shipment is due.

Giving or sending a purchase order does not constitute a contract until it has been accepted. It appears to be true (unfortunately) that the usual form of acceptance requested is that of an "acknowledgement" sent by the vendor to the purchasing department. Just what does constitute mutual consent and the acceptance of an offer is primarily—perhaps it can be said entirey—a legal question into which we cannot delve extensively here. Generalizations concerning the acceptance of offers, as any lawyer will indicate, are likely to be only generalizations with many exceptions.

In bilateral contracts, acceptance is indicated by agreeing to do the thing requested, and the acceptance must be transmitted to the offeror. In unilateral contracts, the acceptance is manifested by doing (that is, completing) the act requested by the offeror. (See Chapter 14 for a more detailed discussion on the legal implications.)

One further fact needs to be kept in mind that argues for insisting upon securing an acceptance of the purchase order, quite aside from any question of law. Unless the order is accepted, the buyer can only assume that delivery will be made by the requested date or that price will be as hoped for. When delivery dates are uncertain and prices are likely to fluctuate widely, definite information in advance is most important if the buyer is to plan operations effectively, and within planned cost objectives.

Blanket and open-end orders

The cost of issuing and handling purchase orders may be reduced when conditions permit the use of blanket or open-end orders. A blanket order usually covers a variety of items. An open-end order allows for addition of items and/or extension of time. Maintenance and repair items and production line requirements used in volume and purchased repetitively over a period of months may be bought in this manner.

All terms and conditions involving the purchase of estimated quantities over a period are negotiated and incorporated in the original order. Subsequently, releases of specific quantities are made against the order. In some instances it is possible to tie the preparation of the releases into the production scheduling procedures and forward them to the purchasing department for transmission to the vendor. It is not unusual for an open-end order to remain in effect for a year, or until changes in design, material specification, or conditions affecting price or delivery make new negotiations desirable or necessary. (See also systems contracting.) Figure 3–4 shows a form used to authorize release of materials on a blanket order.

Figure 3–4
BLANKET ORDER RELEASE

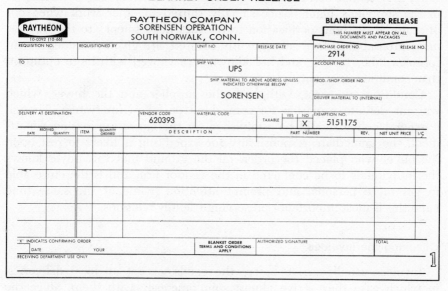

Follow-up on the order

One important reason for securing an acceptance of the buyer's order is to get some definite statement on the delivery date. The majority of buyers specify a delivery date on the purchase order.

The importance of knowing whether or not the requested delivery date is acceptable to the seller and, if not, what date can be met, particularly on critical materials, is of such importance that carelessness is inexcusable. Yet it is surprising how many purchasing agents do not ask for assurance on a delivery date and naively assume that the requested date will be met.

Even after a delivery date has been secured, a definite follow-up is often called for, not only on emergency and rush orders but also on critical material, the date of delivery of which has been somewhat vague (see Figure 3–5).

Theoretically, no special expediting procedure should be needed. If good planning is the rule in the buyer's organization, if engineering changes are rare and always kept to a minimum, if an adequate system of inventory control is operative, if the purchase order was properly prepared, if a reliable supplier has been selected and a delivery date given, and if reasonable tolerance and mutual helpfulness exist on the part of both, then no particular follow-up device would have to be resorted to. But a Pollyannish attitude that such conditions always obtain is either sheer bravado or a silly display of ignorance. Even if conditions at the buyer's organization are all that could be desired (and, of course, they often are not), it is still true that all suppliers do not cooperate fully; they do not bother to give or to observe delivery dates. Production in the supplier's plant is occasionally shifted to other work when out of material, without notification to its sales department (to the buyer); more profitable orders, subsequently secured, are given precedence; unforeseen labor trouble and breakdowns are viewed with more optimism than conditions warrant.

Conditions do exist, with both the supplier and the buyer, which warrant definite provision for some kind of follow-up system. Though a general policy should be established for the entire purchasing department, the immediate responsibility for expediting is likely to rest upon the buyer who placed the order, on the ground that this buyer knows the individuals to be contacted in the vendor firm and is therefore able to get more personal and prompt attention, while at the same time (and this is most important) preserving friendly relations.

Checking the invoices

Invoices usually arrive before the goods, except on local deliveries, in which case they arrive almost simultaneously with them. Since the invoice constitutes a definite claim against the buyer, it needs to be handled with great care, and the form of the invoice, the responsibility for handling, and the procedures involved in handling these documents are matters of importance.

Invoices are commonly requested in duplicate. In addition, it is not uncommon to find such statements as "invoices must show our order number and itemized price for each article invoiced."

Procedure relating to the invoice is not uniform. In fact, there is difference of opinion on whether the checking and approval of the in-

Figure 3–5
FOLLOW-UP ON ORDER
(8½ × 11 in.)

Purchasing Department

Date_____

_____

_____

_____

We are trying to conserve your time as well as ours by using this form. It is sent you in duplicate to enable you to use one copy for a REPLY and keep the other for your files.

Gentlemen:
    This is an IMPORTANT REQUEST for INFORMATION concerning SHIPMENTS against our

Order No._____   Dated_____   Please answer items checked.

SHIPMENTS			
1. When will you ship?			
2. In what quantity will you ship?			
3. Did you ship on date shown on order? How?			
4. Can you advance promised shipping date?			
5. Why did you not ship as promised?			
6. Make your delivery promise more specific.			
7. Please start tracer on shipment made.			
8. Release shipments as shown under remarks.			
9. Give us forwarding reference so we can trace.	Date shipped		
	From		
	Consignee		
	Car initials and number		
	Waybill reference		
	Carding Points		
	Remarks		
10. When will you ship balance of order?			
11. Advise present status of order and when you expect to complete.			

REMARKS

_____

_____

Mail Reply to _____   Yours truly,

_____

_____

voice is a function of the purchasing department or of the accounting department. Clearly, the invoice must be checked and audited. Many concerns maintain that since the work is accounting in character, the accounting department should do it. In such companies, approval for delivery, quality, and condition is given by the receiving department, and prices, terms, and extensions are checked in the accounting department. For this purpose a copy of each purchase order, as has already been indicated, is filed in the accounting department. The arguments for this procedure are that such checking is essentially an accounting function, that it relieves the purchasing department of the performance of a task not essential to procurement, and that it concentrates all the accounting work in a single office. It is also said that this practice constitutes a safeguard against dishonesty in the purchase or receipt of goods that might lead to some irregularities in billing. On the other hand, sending the invoices to the accounting department for checking and auditing unquestionably complicates the procedure, results in an additional administrative cost, and tends to slow down the clearing of the transaction. Occasional "spot-checking" may well serve the purpose of removing any temptation toward collusion between buyer and vendor.

The prime reason for having invoices checked in the purchasing department is that this is where the original agreement was made. If discrepancies exist, immediate purchasing action can be taken. It is probably true, in spite of the controversy that has been and still is being waged over this issue, generally the purchasing department checks the invoice.

Where the invoice is normally handled by the accounting department, the following procedure is typical:

1. All invoices are mailed in duplicate by the vendor directly to the accounting department, where they are promptly time-stamped. The accounting department checks all invoices and certifies them for payment to the controller's department without reference to the purchasing department, except where the purchase order and the invoice differ.
2. Invoices at variance with the purchase order on price, terms, or other features are referred to the purchasing department for approval.

If any of the information necessary is not on the invoice or if the information does not agree with the purchase order, the invoice is returned to the vendor for correction. Ordinarily, the buyer insists that, in computing discounts, the allowable period dates from the receipt of the corrected invoice, not from the date originally received.

In every instance of cancellation of a purchase order involving the payment of cancellation charges, the accounting department requires from the purchasing department a "change notice" referring to the order and defining the payment to be made before passing an invoice for such payment. In addition, the invoice division will secure the written approval of the director of purchases on the invoice for cancellation charges if the amount is over a specified dollar amount like $100.

In cases where purchasing does the invoice checking the following procedure applies: after being checked and adjusted for any necessary corrections the original invoice is forwarded to the accounting department to be held until the purchasing department authorizes its payment. The duplicate invoice is retained by the purchasing department until the receiving department notifies it of the receipt of the materials. As soon as the purchasing department obtains this notification in the form of a receiving report, it checks that report against the invoice. If the receiving report and invoice are found to agree, the purchasing office keeps both documents until it receives assurance from the inspection division that the goods are acceptable. The purchasing department then forwards its duplicate copy of the invoice and the report from the receiving department to the accounting department, where the original copy of the invoice is already on file. The original is then paid in due course, and the duplicate invoice is returned to the purchasing department to be filed with the other records of the order. Some companies file the invoices separately, a common practice being to file them alphabetically by date.

The purchasing department's checking of the receiving report occurs in cases in which the receiving department has made a blind check of the goods received, without reference to the original purchase order. In companies which follow a practice of having the receiving department compare the merchandise received with the purchase order, the purchasing department does not check the receiving report; upon receipt of this report and of a favorable report from the inspection division, it simply sends the receiving report with the invoice to the accounting department as authorization for payment.

Sometimes suppliers are negligent about invoicing goods shipped, and it may be necessary to request the invoice to complete the transaction. On the other hand, payment of an invoice prior to the receipt of the material is often requested. The question then arises: When invoices do provide for cash discounts, do you pay the invoice within the discount period, even though the material may not actually have been received, or do you withhold payment until the material arrives, even at the risk of losing cash discounts?

The arguments for withholding payment of the invoice until after the goods have arrived are as follows:

a. Frequently the invoice does not reach the buyer until late in the discount period and, on occasion, may even arrive after it. This situation arises through a failure on the part of the vendor (1) to mail the invoice promptly, especially where due allowance is not made for the Saturdays, Sundays, or holidays which elapse between the dating of the invoice and the processing and mailing of it, and (2) where the vendor is, in terms of "mailing time," several days away from the buyer.

b. It is unsound buying practice to pay for anything until an opportunity has been given for inspection. The transaction has not, in fact, been completed until the material or part has actually been accepted, and payment prior to this time is premature. In fact, legally, the title of the goods may not have passed to the buyer until acceptance of them.

c. In any event, the common practice of dating invoices as of the date of shipment should be amended to provide that the discount period runs from receipt of the invoice or the goods.

The arguments in favor of passing the invoice for payment without awaiting the arrival, inspection, and acceptance of the material are several:

a. The financial consideration may be substantial.

b. Failure to take the cash discounts as a matter of course reflects unfavorably on the credit standing of the buyer.

c. It is inconsistent, as a matter of general company policy, to hold its customers to the stipulated discount period while at the same time trying to take the discount from a supplier after the period has elapsed.

d. By purchasing from reputable and known vendors, mutually satisfactory adjustments arising out of unsatisfactory material will always be made, even though the invoice has been paid.

Receipt and inspection of goods

The proper handling of receiving materials and other items is of vital importance. The great majority of firms have, as a result of experience, centralized all receiving under one department, the chief exceptions being those large companies maintaining more than one plant. So closely is receiving related to purchasing that, in probably 70 percent of the cases, the receiving department is either directly or indirectly responsible to the purchasing department.

The arrival of the goods always involves one additional step, and sometimes two. All incoming shipments must be checked by the receiving department. In practice, receiving is not always provided with a copy of the purchase order. This way the check by receiving against the goods on receipt is a completely independent one, commonly reported on a "materials received" form and transmitted to the stores division. This report, an example of which is found in Figure 3–6, gives the vendor's name; the order number; the quantity received; the quantity rejected, if any; and the quantity provisionally accepted. Three or four copies of this report are commonly made: one is sent to the purchasing department to be checked against the invoice; one, as already described, to

Figure 3–6
MATERIALS RECEIVED RECORD

121 D-F110

WHITE—Accts. Payable
CANARY—Receiving Dept.,
PINK—Stores Dept.
BLUE—Purch. Dept.

Nº 833602

RECEIVING SLIP

RECEIVING DEPT.   Date_____19____

Received for_____

Shipped by_____

P. O._____Req._____Dept._____

Rolls	Bundles	Boxes	Crates	Pkgs.	Drums	Reels	Bbls.

Via _____ Charges _____ Pro. _____ Date

Car No. _____ Seals

Our Weight_____

Carrier's Weight_____   For { Weights and Chgs. } See
                                                            { Bal. of Shipment }
Pack. Slip No._____

Case Nos._____   R. S. No._____

Delivered to_____   Card No._____

Charges Carried $_____	Z Order No_____
Invoice No._____Date_____	Mat'l._____
Amount_____Date Passed_____	Billed—CONTRA
Passed by_____As Checked_____	NO CHARGE_____
For balance of shipment see R. S._____	_____
Complete File R. S._____Auditor	_____

the stores department; one to the using department for its files; and sometimes one is also sent to the traffic division.

Aside from the checking of goods received, there is the problem of inspection. What has been said up to this point relates to checking for quantity; inspection for quality is a matter handled by various concerns in their own individual ways. Some merchandise is not inspected for quality at all, some is inspected only by sampling, and some is checked by the laboratory. For example, a concern may have a quality control department which determines the question as to how much and how frequently and in what manner inspection shall be made. Following inspection, it may be necessary to return some of the material to the supplier. The problem of inspection is discussed in more detail in Chapter 4.

In checking the goods received, it will sometimes appear that shortages exist either because material has been lost en route or because it was short-shipped. Occasionally, too, there is evidence that the shipment has been tampered with or that the shipment has been damaged in transit. In all such cases, full reports are called for, going either to the traffic department, to the purchasing department, or (and a much-to-be-preferred procedure) to both.

Completion of the record

After having gone through the steps described, all that remains for the disposal of any order is to complete the records of the purchasing department. This operation involves little more than assembling and filing the purchasing department's copies of the documents relating to the order and transferring to appropriate records the information the department may wish to keep. The former is largely a routine matter. The latter involves judgment as to what records are to be kept and also for how long.

Most companies differentiate between the various forms and records as to their importance. For example, a purchase order constitutes evidence of a contract with an outside party and as such may well be retained much longer than the requisition, which is, after all, an internal memorandum. Lawyers, perhaps understandably, often argue for keeping all records indefinitely; but such a practice would be an unnecessarily extreme form of protection, costing far more than it would be worth.

There are, of course, many specific issues, both of organization and procedure, which our survey has not covered. Most of them will be taken up later in connection with the various problems out of which they arise.

Use of data processing

Up to this point the discussion and the analysis of the procedures needed and used in performing the procurement function have been based on the use of traditional office equipment and clerical methods. Within the past 20 years, however, we have witnessed the innovation of the truly remarkable development of data processing equipment in aiding recording, analysis, and reporting of information in the operation of complex business systems, scientific research, and the military.

When data processing equipment is installed to assist in performing the procurement function, the essential steps of good procurement remain much the same as those of the manual methods. The procedure change in performing the procurement function occurs only in the way the essential steps are performed. When it is economically feasible to introduce data processing equipment, four basic benefits are obtained:

1. The mechanized handling of procedures reduces clerical manual effort to a minimum.
2. Information from records becomes available almost instantly.
3. Control over operations is improved, not only by the timely availability of the information for sound decision making, but also by the flexibility afforded by the ease of handling vast quantities of detail, thus providing new tools for the buyer and manager.
4. Operating performance is improved by the availability of information and the improved control of operations.

At the beginning of this chapter, the essential steps of procurement were listed. It is our purpose at this point to consider briefly how integrated data processing equipment and procedures apply to each step.

1. Ascertainment of the need. When used properly, computers can be of great assistance in analyzing information pertaining to past usage, markets, economic factors, prices, and expected usage to the end that forecasts can be made with promptness and improved accuracy. Computers can assist in translating forecasts into estimates of requirements and of the required materials, quantities, and delivery dates.

2. Accurate statement of the character and amount of article or commodity desired. The responsibility for developing an accurate statement or specification for the article or the commodity used in the firm normally rests with the engineering or the using departments. After determination, the specification can be made readily available for use by data processing equipment by recording the specification on cards, tape, disc, or any of the various devices for storing information.

The quantities of the items required to be purchased are determined after obtaining the breakdown of the information mentioned in step 1 and after having the bill of materials processed by the computer to determine the effect of existing inventories and open orders on the specific requirements.

3. Transmission of purchase requisition. The requisition for the specific requirements, which may be on a card, tape, or other storage device, can be fed into the computer for an economical purchasing quantity analysis to weight such things as acquisition costs (including costs of placing an order, quantity discounts, transportation costs, and the like) against inventory carrying costs.

4. *Negotiation for possible sources of supply.* As the requisition is processed by the computer, information regarding suppliers, previously stored in the memory devices of the computer, can provide lists of vendors and their past prices and record of performance.

5. *Analysis of proposals, selection of vendor, and placement of order.* While it is possible to analyze vendors' proposals by programming them into a computer, it is probably not practical to do so except in situations in which there are many variable factors present, such as quantity discounts, transportation allowances, multiple plants to be supplied, and numerous suppliers scattered widely geographically. Usually, human judgment is used in making the final selection of the vendor. Once the final selection is made, the computer can prepare the purchase order automatically.

6. *Follow-up the order.* When the purchase order is placed, an order status record is created. This record is kept up to date by recording the receipts of the ordered material, the invoices, the change orders, and the expediting data, thus providing the current status of each open order. This record becomes the basic file for the invoice and receiving audit, the follow-up procedures, and some of the management and operations reports.

7. *Checking the invoice.* When invoices are received, the computer matches the invoices to the purchase orders, and the computer can be programmed to audit price, quantity, extension, discounts if any, routing, and transportation terms. Where everything is in order, a check for the proper payment can be written automatically and held for the payment due date. Any required accounting distribution can be made.

8. *Receipt and inspection of the goods.* Receiving and inspection reports can be fed into the order status record as received and used in auditing the invoice, in keeping inventory records, and in compiling quality reports.

9. *Completion of the record.* Closed orders are usually carried in the order status record for a period to allow adequate time for any rejections or adjustments.

Figure 3–7 shows a simple flow chart of an automated purchasing system.

There are a larger number of potential uses to which the computer may be put and a number of research studies have attempted to determine the nature of current application. The first question deals with what is being done. Secondly, what are the implications of using computer-based systems?

Figure 3–7
SIMPLIFIED FLOW CHART OF AN AUTOMATED PURCHASING SYSTEM

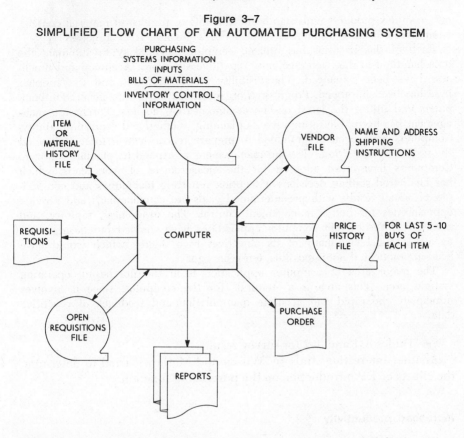

Computerized operating systems

A study by D. L. Moore and H. E. Fearon was useful in determining the status of well-developed computer operating systems.

This study was done to determine how the computer is being used to aid purchasing in two specific application areas: (1) computer operating systems, and (2) computer management-reporting systems. With the background information from a number of articles which have been written on what several companies have done in computer applications principally during the decade of the 1960s, 15 firms or divisions of a larger firm were selected as a survey group to determine specifically how the computer currently is being used. These operations, geographically located in all parts of the United States, were selected on the basis of their having a sophisticated purchasing organization and sophisticated computer systems.

Based on the interviews in these 15 operations, it was concluded that purchasing can benefit substantially from use of the computer. Major organizations processing tens of thousands of orders involving thousand of suppliers and items could not administer the purchasing function competitively without computer assistance. For the manufacturing firm that produces high-technology, complex products with significant amounts of purchased material content, computer assistance cannot be considered a luxury. It is a necessity.

Each of the 15 firms has utilized computer technology to automate the data handling in most large-volume, repetitive situations. Accuracy and timeliness have been enhanced. The visibility of expenditures and the supplier base has been improved. Progressive organizations have third-generation computers and utilize the latest on-line communication devices. Purchasing management has been able to improve its planning, staffing, and controlling ability. Computers have been programmed to prepare reports which forecast beyond the order release period, allowing management to expand its planning horizon. Computers have been adopted for the measurement of work-loads, which has facilitated staffing decisions. Exception reporting techniques and comparison of actual results with predetermined goals are commonplace and provide opportunities for better management control. The orderliness, rapidity, and accuracy of the current computer applications have enabled purchasing management to achieve many of its objectives to a degree which would have been impractical, if not impossible, ten years ago.

The major area of computer application is in the purchasing operating systems area. This area is a "natural" for the computer, since it involves principally the rapid and accurate manipulation and feedback of repetitive data.[7]

See Tables 3–1 and 3–2 for survey results.

Another interesting study by Wilson and Mathews[8] tried to determine the effects of DP introduction on the purchasing function.

Increased productivity

First, and foremost, improved purchasing information systems are creating a new class of purchasing people whose responsibilities are to structure and analyze purchasing problems. As routine tasks are taken over by the computer, it was anticipated that the purchasing manager's time, or a larger share of his time, would be devoted to increased use of creative decision-making techniques and problem solving. This trend is occurring slowly. Our data indicate that productivity, in terms of increased workload of the purchasing manager, has been tremendous. In other words, while we expected to find more time being spent in the creative aspects of decision making, it appears that the net result has been the more efficient use of time in much the same type of activities as before. In some instances, the productivity of a purchasing department was doubled through the use of a computer. While the computer does not replace the buyer, it does reduce the clerical support necessary to operate the department. In one large firm, two girls and the computer do the work that previously required 67 typists and file clerks. Not all of

---

[7] D. L. Moore and H. E. Fearon, "Computer Operating and Management Reporting Systems in Purchasing," *Journal of Purchasing*, vol. 9, no. 3 (August 1973), pp. 13–39, 38–39.

[8] D. T. Wilson and H. L. Mathews, "Impact of Management Information Systems Upon Purchasing Decision Making," *Journal of Purchasing*, vol. 7, no. 1 (February 1971), pp. 53–54.

Table 3–1

ORGANIZATION AND SYSTEM CHARACTERISTICS

Characteristics	Case 1	Case 2	Case 3	Case 4	Case 5	Case 6	Case 7	Case 8	Case 9	Case 10	Case 11	Case 12	Case 13	Case 14	Case 15
1. Number of different items purchased annually	10,000	20,000	25,000	10,000	122,000	25,000	25,000	30,000	(1)	50,000	31,000	16,000	(1)	90,000	(2)
2. Annual sales	$100–200 Mill	$50–100 Mill	$100–200 Mill	$40 Mill	$700 Mill	$70 Mill	$1,000 Mill +	$300 Mill (3)	(1)	$300 Mill	$200 Mill (3)	$200 Mill	$1,300 Mill	$500–1,000 Mill	$200 Mill (3)
3. Annual value of purchased materials and services	$45 Mill	$23 Mill	$71 Mill	$9 Mill	$155 Mill	$25 Mill	$500 Mill +	$100 Mill (3)	(1)	$120 Mill	$70 Mill	$80 Mill	$700 Mill	$230,000	$80 Mill
4. Number of personnel in purchasing organization	46	24	92	20	28	35	95	60	(1)	300	125	60	800	600	50
5. Annual computer system operating cost	$50,000	(2)	(2)	$70,000 (3)	$100,000 (3)	$120,000	$100,000 +	$300,000 (3)	(1)	$80,000	$200,000 (3)	$300,000 (3)	(1)	$3,000,000	(2)
6. Purchase orders issued annually	25,000	40,000	30,000	20,000	60,000	50,000	(2)	70,000	(1)	100,000	50,000 (3)	40,000	(1)	60,000	(2)
7. System design responsibility in purchasing															
In materials	•						•	•					•		
In other organizational units		•	•	•	•	•			•	•	•	•		•	•
8. Purchasing within a materials management organization?	Yes	Yes	No	No	No	Yes	No	No	(1)	Yes	Yes	No	No	Yes	Yes
9. System installation date	1966	1960	1960	1969	1967	1965	1965	1960	1970	1967	1968	1972	1965–1970	1960	(1)
10. Primary file updating method batch	•	•	•		•	•	•	•	•	•		•		•	
Online				•							•				
11. Online enquiry capability	•	•	•	•		•		•	•		•	•			•

(1) Not applicable
(2) Not available
(3) Estimated

Source: D. L. Moore and H. E. Fearon, "Computer Operating and Management Reporting Systems in Purchasing," *Journal of Purchasing*, vol. 9, no. 3 (August 1973), p. 25.

Table 3-2
RESEARCH FINDINGS—UTILIZATION OF COMPUTER OPERATING SYSTEMS

Computer applications found in purchasing	Case 1	Case 2	Case 3	Case 4	Case 5	Case 6	Case 7	Case 8	Case 9	Case 10	Case 11	Case 12	Case 13	Case 14	Case 15
1. Receiving status systems	*	*	*	*	*	*	*	*	*	*	*	*	*	*	
2. Schedule control and expediting systems	*	*	*	*	*	*	*	*	*	*	*	*	*	*	
3. Open purchase order status systems	*	*	*	*	*	*		*	*	*	*	*	*		
4. Commodity expenditure profile systems	*	*	*			*	*	*	*	*		*	*	*	
5. Vendor expenditure profile systems	*	*	*			*	*	*	*	*		*		*	
6. Price and source history systems	*			*		*		*	*	*		*	*		*
7. Material requisition status systems	*	*				*	*	*	*		*	*	*		
8. Supplier delivery rating systems				*		*	*	*	*			*			*
9. Department and buyer workload measurement systems	*		*			*				*			*	*	
10. Supplier quality rating systems		*		*		*	*	*	*						
11. Forecasting systems			*		*	*	*					*			
12. Analysis of degree of competition systems		*								*			*		
13. Invoice exception systems					*		*	*							
14. Material price analysis systems						*			*				*		
15. Long-term contract status systems	*														
16. Subcontract management status systems														*	*

Source: D. L. Moore and H. E. Fearon, "Computer Operations and Management Reporting Systems in Purchasing," *Journal of Purchasing*, vol. 9, no. 3 (August 1973), p. 27.

this reduction of staff is savings, since there are additional costs such as key punching and programming. Nevertheless, the computer does increase buyer productivity. Unfortunately, in our estimation, the average buyer appears not to have increased the time allocated to activities such as supplier development and value analysis.

Buying environment

A second area of change involves the structure of the buying environment. Our data showed that companies which had become involved in DP purchasing actually were using fewer suppliers than previously. A close analysis indicated that they were concentrating orders with fewer suppliers. The search of potential sources appeared to increase, but larger orders were placed with fewer vendors. The computer permits multiplant companies to accumulate their corporate purchasing requirements by item or commodity. It appears that the computer will stimulate systems or contract purchasing.

These forces also tend to increase the role of the corporate or staff purchasing group, since the development and maintenance costs of computer systems legislate against each plant unit independently developing its own system. These high costs encourage central coordination of computer activities to develop compatibility between the computer systems of the different corporate units.

Effect on people

A third area of major importance is the effect of DP on the people currently in purchasing. The buyer's role is one of increased frustration. Instead of handling routine tasks, he now is confronted constantly with a new crisis or a problem from the management by exception system that the computer necessitates. Our data indicate that it is very disturbing for a buyer to view his personal relations with the marketing, production control, and production people as a constant series of problems. In other words, with the computer system, the buyer interacts with production or production control people only when a problem has arisen. It takes time for all parties to recognize the change in their interaction pattern and to adjust.

Purchasing procedure for multinational companies

As U.S. companies have expanded their operations to foreign countries, often on a worldwide basis, more and more attention has been given by managements to coordinating purchasing activity on a global basis. While the managements of most multinational companies recognize the importance of granting a large degree of local autonomy to their foreign subsidiaries and affiliates, they also are aware of the savings which can be achieved by coordinating the total corporate purchasing power in world markets.

The development of procedures among the various units of a multinational company starts with the recognition of several fundamental needs:

a. The need for full and understanding communications between the purchasing department of the parent company and the purchasing departments of the various units throughout the world.

b. The need to coordinate procurement planning. Without adequate budget systems and forward planning of material requirements the benefits to be obtained through a worldwide purchasing operation are difficult to accomplish.

c. The need for a continuing intracompany educational and training program for all key procurement personnel regardless of geographical location.

d. The need for the development of complete manuals to define policies, procedures, and objectives. Provision must also be made to keep all manuals current.

An excellent example of the development of a program to coordinate worldwide procurement operations in a multinational company is described in the Mercury Oil Company case.

INFORMATION SYSTEMS

Purchasing procedures are established basically to process inputs of information from outside the procurement function and to produce outputs of information needed by other functions and institutions outside the purchasing function. Few business functions have the breadth of contacts both within the firm and with the external environment that the well-operated procurement function has.

Internal information flows to purchasing

Every functional activity within the firm generates information to, and/or requires information from, the purchasing system. Figure 3–8

Figure 3–8
INTERNAL INFORMATION FLOWS TO PURCHASING
COMPUTER OPERATIONS

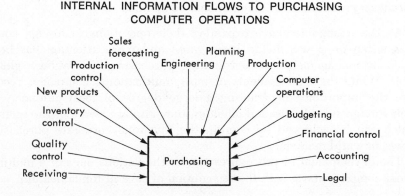

diagrams the information flows to purchasing. Essentially the information sent to purchsing breaks down into the following two major categories.

a. Statements of needs for materials and services obtained from outside the firm.
b. Requests for information available within purchasing or obtainable from outside the firm.

A brief description of the information flows charted in Figure 3–8 follows.

Planning. This function provides purchasing with information important in the orderly preparations to obtain the long-term future requirements of the firm for facilities, materials, and outside services. Competent planning is of special importance in preparing for future construction needs and for raw materials in tight or diminishing supply.

Sales forecasting. Well-developed sales forecasts are one of the most helpful tools available to purchasing in planning procurement strategies for periods up to 12 months in advance. Business operations usually achieve the greatest degree of operating efficiency when orderly planning permits orderly acquisition and scheduling of requirements. When purchasing has adequate advance notice of kinds of materials likely to be required and approximate quantities, it is in a favorable position to obtain the optimum balance between the conditions in the marketplace and the needs of the firm.

Budgeting and financial control. The information provided by the budgeting function helps in coordinating the information from planning and sales forecasting and brings into focus any constraints imposed by the financial control function. Such constraints may apply to the operating expenses of the purchasing system as well as to the possibilities of following other than a buy-as-required inventory policy.

Accounting. The accounting function supplies information on payments to suppliers, cost studies for make-or-buy decisions, comparison of actual expenditures to budget, and the like.

Legal. Inasmuch as the purchasing function is the major activity authorized to commit the firm legally to contracts for materials and outside services, the legal function provides information regarding contracts, procedures, and so forth.

Engineering. The basic responsibility of engineering is to provide information on what types of materials are needed and the specification of the qualities needed. As discussed in Chapter 4 the acknowledged right of purchasing to challenge specifications usually promotes more effective operation of the purchasing function for the benefit of the firm.

Production and production control. The production function frequently provides information on the quality requirements for materials. The production control and scheduling function provides information on what materials are needed and in what quantities for a given time period covered by a production cycle. Properly compiled, such information provides a useful tool in planning purchasing operations.

Inventory control. This function provides basic information on what needs to be purchased or ordered at any given time. The use of economic order quantities will be determined by the inventory policy which governs the investment in inventory at any given period. An inventory policy may be influenced by the financial resources of the firm, future plans, current market conditions, lead time in the procurement of materials, and so on.

Quality control and receiving. Both of these functions provide information which determines if the suppliers have furnished materials of the quality and quantity bought by the purchasing function. Such information is essential to the proper performance of the purchasing function.

New products. The importance of new products development to the success of a company has increased greatly in recent years. Unless information about new product development projects reaches purchasing at the inception of the project, the full contribution possible from purchasing will seldom be realized.

External information flows to purchasing

The efficiently operated purchasing department is one of the firm's major contact points with the external world and as such is a receiving point for a flow of information from sources outside the firm. Much of this information is essential to the operation of the firm. Figure 3–9

Figure 3–9
EXTERNAL INFORMATION FLOWS TO PURCHASING

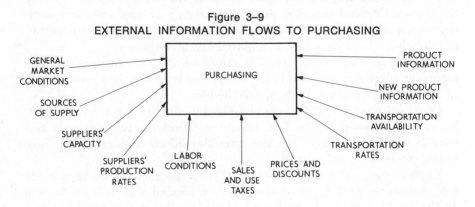

shows the nature of the information. A brief explanation of each of the major types of information coming from external sources follows.

General market conditions. Competent purchasing executives and buyers become specialists on general market and business conditions.

Suppliers' salesmen, purchasing trade publications, various National Association of Purchasing Management's publications and services, local purchasing agents' association meetings and publications provide a constant stream of information about prices, supply and demand factors, and competitors' actions.

Sources of supply. Suppliers' salesmen, advertising media of all types, special promotions, exhibits at trade shows and conventions, and credit and financial reports create information initiated by vendors and aimed at their customers and potential customers. Frequently when new products are under development, purchasing or engineering will have to initiate action to locate sources of supply which have not for any of a number of reasons beamed their information to the interested potential customers. Chapter 8 describes in detail the great importance of locating the best possible sources of supply.

Suppliers' capacity, suppliers' production rates, and labor conditions in the suppliers' plants and industries. Information flows on these factors are of great importance in determining inventory policy and assuring continuity of production as far as materials are concerned.

Prices and discounts, customs, sales and use taxes. All information of any nature regarding prices is important to the effective functioning of the purchasing job. Much of the price information is obtained directly from suppliers or salesmen representing potential suppliers. The services of consultants specializing in economic trends are frequently useful in determining price trends, particularly of commodities. Both the customs and tax fields are rapidly changing, requiring continuous monitoring.

Transportation availability and rates. The types, availability, and rates of transportation services have had an increasingly important bearing on the cost of materials within recent years. Whether problems involving transportation are the direct responsibility of a traffic department is not the critical point. It is how the information is used by purchasing which is of importance in its effect on costs of material.

New product and product information. The great emphasis in U.S. business on creating new products has placed a heavy burden on the purchasing function. Purchasing must process the information about products received from the outside in such a way that the appropriate function within the firm will be alerted to any product information, whether it be new or old, which can be useful in improving effectiveness, reducing costs, or aiding in developing new products for the firm.

Internal information flows from purchasing to the organization

There are very few functions of a business which are not concerned to some degree with the information which flows or can be generated from purchasing. Figure 3–10 diagrams the major types of information which flow from purchasing to the organization. A brief description

Figure 3–10
INTERNAL INFORMATION FLOWS FROM PURCHASING

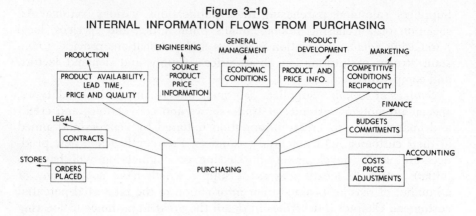

of these information flows to the personnel in the major functions follows.

General management. Purchasing personnel have daily contact with a wide spectrum of the marketplace, and if properly qualified by education, ability, and experience are in an advantageous position to collect up-to-the-minute information about current market and business conditions. This information when correlated and refined can provide top management with information valuable in the operation of the company.

Engineering. The engineering function requires much information from the marketplace. While there are situations which warrant the engineers making their own direct contacts with suppliers in order to obtain product and/or price information or place orders, such situations should be exceptional. Competent purchasing specialists can provide more effective service by better sourcing and negotiation of lower prices than an engineer whose special competence is concerned with an engineering specialty.

Product development. Product development departments, regardless of whether they are part of the engineering or the marketing functions, benefit from new materials information, price information, and the like which the purchasing function can provide from its contact in the marketplace. A purchasing function which recognizes its obligation to maximize information flow to new products activities performs a valuable service.

Marketing. The purchasing department is a target for the sales and promotion plans and devices of many different suppliers from many industries. Perceptive purchasing personnel can frequently provide information on new types of selling campaigns which have value to the marketing function of their own firm. Properly kept purchase records are essential in the implementation of a trade-relation program.

Production. The production function depends on purchasing for information about materials, material availability, material delivery lead times, material substitutes, and help in locating sources of supply for production equipment. Production can also be aided by purchasing with information about maintenance, repair, and operating supply items.

Legal. The purchasing department furnishes the legal department with all the information needed for drawing contracts for all types of materials purchased under a blanket contract or a stockless buying type of contract.

Finance and accounting. Purchasing is in a position to provide the financial and accounting functions with information which is basic to planning budget development and administration and determining cash requirements. Material and transportation costs and trends in costs, need for forward buying because of possible shortages resulting from greater demand, or anticipated interruption of supply such as happens during a major strike are some of the kinds of information purchasing provides to aid in planning financial operations.

Stores. The formulation of an inventory policy for a stores department is dependent in major part on information concerning lead times and availability of materials, price trends, and developments that may provide substitute materials. The purchasing department is the best source of such information.

BIBLIOGRAPHY

ALJIAN, GEORGE W., ed. *Purchasing Handbook.* 3d ed. New York: McGraw-Hill Book Co., 1973.

BAILEY, PETER J. *Design of Purchasing Systems and Records.* London: Gower P., 1970.

BAILEY, PETER J. AND FARMER, DAVID. *Purchasing Principles and Techniques.* London: Pitman for the Institute of Purchasing and Supply, 1968.

BLITZ, JACK FRANCIS. *Policies and Techniques for Progressive Purchasing.* London: Industrial and Commercial Techniques, 1971.

CANTOR, JEREMIAH. *Evaluating Purchasing Systems.* New York: American Management Association, 1970.

ENGLAND, WILBUR B. *The Purchasing System.* Homewood, Ill.: Richard D. Irwin, Inc., 1967.

FABRYCKY, WOLTER J. AND BANKS, JERRY. *Procurement and Inventory Systems; Theory and Analysis.* New York: Reinhold, 1967.

INTERNATIONAL BUSINESS MACHINES CORPORATION. *General Information Manual: Industrial Purchasing.* No. E20-8054. White Plains, N.Y., 1960.

INTERNATIONAL BUSINESS MACHINES CORPORATION. *General Information Manual: Industrial Purchasing.* General No. E20-007-0. White Plains, N.Y., 1965.

INTERNATIONAL BUSINESS MACHINES CORPORATION. *General Information Detail: Industrial Purchasing.* No. E20-0074-0. White Plains, N.Y., 1965.

KOLLIOS, A. E. AND STEMPEL, J. S. *The Application of EDP to the Purchasing*

Function. Management Bulletin 83. New York: American Management Association, 1966.

KOLLIOS, A. E. AND STEMPEL, J. S.   *Purchasing and EDP.* New York: American Management Association, 1966.

MURKICK, ROBERT G., AND ROSS, JOEL E.   *Information Systems for Modern Management.* Englewood Cliffs, N.J.: Prentice-Hall, Inc., 1967.

NATIONAL ASSOCIATION OF PURCHASING AGENTS, INC.   "The Processing of Data," *Guide to Purchasing.* New York, 1965.

WIDING, J. W., JR., AND DIAMOND, C. G.   "Buy by Computer." *Harvard Business Review*, March-April 1964, pp. 109–20.

CASES FOR CHAPTER 3

PHILADELPHIA PHARMACEUTICALS, INC. (A)*

Introduction

In the fall of 1965, Mr. Harry Wilson, manager of staff purchasing services of Philadelphia Pharmaceuticals, Inc., was concerned about the adequacy and timeliness of purchasing information generated periodically by the purchasing division's electronic data processing system. This computer output consisted basically of a "purchasing follow-up report," a "purchasing vendor performance report," a "purchasing buyer performance report," a "purchasing commodity report," and a "purchasing cash commitment report." These reports were designed to support and improve the buyers' decision making and also to aid management in evaluating the performance of purchasing.

When Mr. Wilson assumed his position as manager of staff purchasing services in March, 1965, the director of purchasing had expressed his dissatisfaction with the effectiveness of the reports. He had asked Mr. Wilson for a study of what changes should be undertaken to improve these reports. Following several months of observation and analysis of the company's purchasing system, Mr. Wilson believed the time was approaching when he should sum up his findings and make recommendations to the director of purchasing.

Company background

Philadelphia Pharmaceuticals, with headquarters and principal plants in Philadelphia, Pennsylvania, was a large international manufacturer and distributor of pharmaceutical products. The company manufactured over 500 different products, including such diverse items as drug extracts, vitamins, insect sprays, inorganic fertilizers, antibiotics, measles virus

---

vaccines, drops with fluoride for the prevention of tooth decay, compounds for the alleviation of arthritis and other inflammatory diseases, and drugs for the control of conception.

In 1965, consolidated sales were in excess of $172.5 million and net earnings were over $29.9 million. The company employed approximately 13,000 persons in over 20 manufacturing facilities located in the United States and abroad.

Organization of procurement

The purchasing division of Philadelphia Pharmaceuticals was organized into four sections: production materials purchases, nonproduction materials purchases, consolidated contract purchases, and purchasing services. (See Exhibit 1 for an organization chart of the purchasing division.) Procurement activities were divided mainly between production materials purchases (for such materials as commodity chemicals and chemical intermediates) and nonproduction materials purchases (for such materials as hardware and mill supplies, animal cages, and laboratory instruments). The third section, consolidated contract purchases, was concerned with the consolidation of material requirements common to two or more of the company's domestic and overseas production units. The fourth, purchasing services, was headed by Mr. Wilson, who had assumed the position of manager of purchasing services in June, 1965, after having worked for several years as a systems analyst in the company's inventory control division. Each of the four sections was headed by a purchasing manager reporting to the director of purchasing. The director of purchasing reported to the president of the company.

Procurement activities

Purchases in 1964 for the company's U.S. operations amounted to about $48.3 million. Of this total, approximately $25.5 million was spent for materials used in the production of pharmaceuticals and approximately $14.1 million for nonproduction requirements. Purchases of production materials for agricultural chemicals totaled approximately $8.7 million. A breakdown of purchases by major material categories is given in Exhibit 2. Major procurement items included antibiotics, steroids and hormones, crude drugs, oils, flavors, perfumes, gelatins, sugars, chlorides, esters, phenols, acid, gases, alcohol and solvents, bottles, vials and ampules, paper packaging, graphic arts, laboratory chemicals and supplies, laboratory animals, and a large variety of maintenance, repair, and operating supplies (MRO). A total of 15 kinds of chemicals and other raw materials used in the production process accounted for approximately 40 percent of dollar procurement volume.

Exhibit 1

ORGANIZATION OF THE PURCHASING DEPARTMENT, 1965

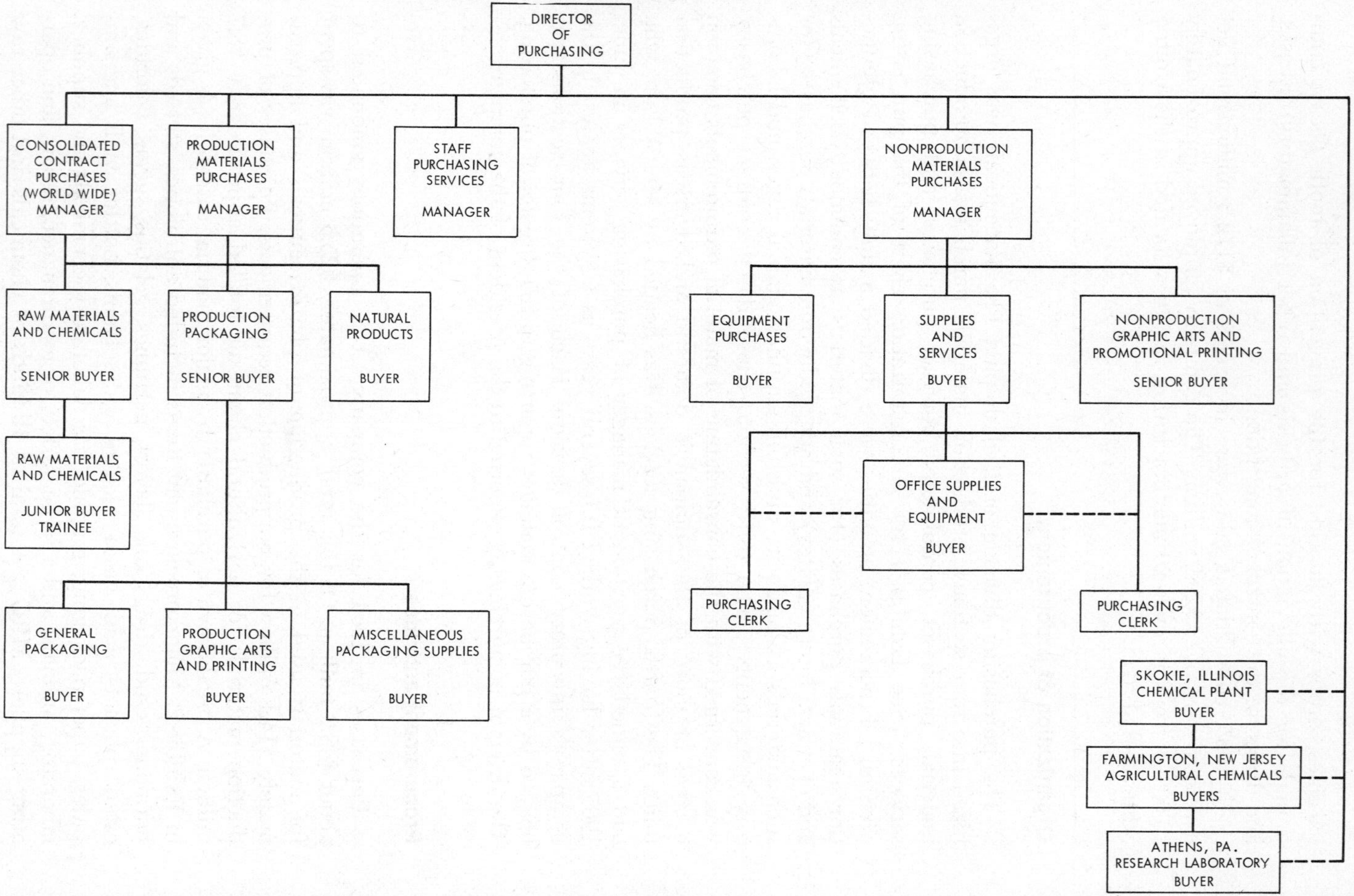

DIRECTOR OF PURCHASING

- CONSOLIDATED CONTRACT PURCHASES (WORLD WIDE) MANAGER
- PRODUCTION MATERIALS PURCHASES MANAGER
- STAFF PURCHASING SERVICES MANAGER
- NONPRODUCTION MATERIALS PURCHASES MANAGER

Production Materials Purchases

- RAW MATERIALS AND CHEMICALS SENIOR BUYER
  - RAW MATERIALS AND CHEMICALS JUNIOR BUYER TRAINEE
- PRODUCTION PACKAGING SENIOR BUYER
  - NATURAL PRODUCTS BUYER
- GENERAL PACKAGING BUYER
- PRODUCTION GRAPHIC ARTS AND PRINTING BUYER
- MISCELLANEOUS PACKAGING SUPPLIES BUYER

Nonproduction Materials Purchases

- EQUIPMENT PURCHASES BUYER
- SUPPLIES AND SERVICES BUYER
  - OFFICE SUPPLIES AND EQUIPMENT BUYER
  - PURCHASING CLERK
  - PURCHASING CLERK
- NONPRODUCTION GRAPHIC ARTS AND PROMOTIONAL PRINTING SENIOR BUYER

Plant Buyers

- SKOKIE, ILLINOIS CHEMICAL PLANT BUYER
- FARMINGTON, NEW JERSEY AGRICULTURAL CHEMICALS BUYERS
- ATHENS, PA. RESEARCH LABORATORY BUYER

Exhibit 2
BREAKDOWN OF PURCHASES BY MAJOR MATERIAL
CATEGORIES FOR THE YEARS 1962–64
(domestic operations)

	Purchases		
	1964	*1963*	*1962*
Production Requirements:			
Raw materials & chemicals	$17,875,896	$16,133,995	$16,580,823
Printed & packaging	7,673,536	6,715,701	8,094,400
	$25,549,432	$22,849,696	$24,675,223
Nonproduction Requirements:			
Graphic arts	$ 3,559,682	$ 3,732,241	$ 3,782,550
Equipment, supplies, services	7,786,167	7,313,065	7,287,664
Construction	2,827,098	803,249	3,322,350
	$14,172,947	$11,848,555	$14,392,564
Subtotal	$39,722,379	$34,698,251	$39,067,787
For agricultural chemical use	8,848,422	8,622,680	6,066,250
Total purchases for U.S. operations.	$48,570,801	$43,320,931	$45,134,037

The general quality standard set by the purchasing department for satisfactory performance by the company's vendors was "99 percent of delivered items accepted upon proper inspection." In recent years this standard had been consistently met or surpassed by the suppliers of what the company had classified as "raw materials and chemicals." Officials in the procurement department ascribed this satisfactory performance in large measure to the "long-term relationships" developed between Philadelphia Pharmaceuticals and its several suppliers of production materials. Quality performance by the suppliers of labels and circulars had been at or above "99.5 percent of delivered items accepted." Quality performance by the vendors of packaging supplies had been at or slightly above "98 percent of delivered items accepted." In March, 1965, the procurement department informed management that "as a result of our suppliers' consistent ability to meet our quality standard, consideration is being given, subject to the approval of the quality control division, to the institution of a vendor certification program under which we would accept the test results of the vendor, thus eliminating our sampling and testing of certain incoming materials."

Acceptable delivery performance was defined by the purchasing department as "90 percent on-time deliveries." Although improvements had been made since 1961, when only 75 percent of all deliveries had been on time, the purchasing department had not yet achieved the 90 percent standard. In 1964, approximately 15 percent of all deliveries had been late. A total of 12.5 percent of these overdue deliveries was 11 or more days late, 18.7 percent was 6 to 10 days late, and 68.8 percent was 5 days or less behind schedule. Partial deliveries had decreased by about 50 percent between 1961 and 1964. The company's receiving department had handled in excess of 70,000 deliveries in 1964.

Cost reductions reported by the purchasing department in 1964 under the department's "profit improvement plan" were $726,800, or 132 percent of the objective set by the department for the year. These savings were achieved primarily through improved methods of buying, such as the use of blanket purchase orders, and through the development of new sources of supply providing lower net cost. The department also reduced its operating costs from approximately $348,450 in 1963 to approximately $338,100 in 1964, despite an increase in the work load due to increased company sales.

Training of purchasing personnel

For several years, in order to "improve buyer performance, buyer understanding of the buying function, and performance of the individual," the purchasing department had held monthly in-house training sessions. The emphasis of these sessions, which were directed by supervisory personnel of the purchasing department and other departments, was on such subjects as value analysis, purchasing objectives, negotiations, legal aspects of purchasing, relations of purchasing to inventory control, tax situations relating to purchasing, and individual purchasing problems. From time to time purchasing agents and buyers had participated in purchasing seminars sponsored by the American Management Association and by the National Association of Purchasing Agents.

Purchasing practices prior to 1958

Although Philadelphia Pharmaceuticals had been using computers in the performance of some administrative functions since the early 1950s, management had given no attention to the utilization of electronic data processing in the purchasing department prior to 1958. "Purchasing simply was not on the list of EDP applications," commented Mr. S. Stanley, director of purchasing. Mr. Wilson said, "The focal points of our early EDP efforts were accounting and inventory control. The initial system was designed primarily to serve accounting. Most of the information needed by purchasing was not essential for the accounting function and of only partial usefulness to the inventory control function. Purchasing was therefore looked upon as 'not fitting into the system.'"

Traditionally, the purchasing department had not received as much attention from corporate management as had other major activities such as marketing and production. Consequently, the company's purchasing policies, procedures, and techniques had not been developed fully. This was particularly evident in the fact that the department was operating essentially without any formalized information system. Thus, for instance, management found it difficult, if not impossible, to obtain answers to such questions as: "Who are the current suppliers for a given commodity?" or "What is the performance record of a given supplier?" or "How much money has been and is being spent on a given item or with a given supplier?"

Mr. Wilson observed:

In addition to, or perhaps partly as a result of, the lack of information critical for the performance and evaluation of the purchasing function, the buyer's job was pretty much confined to reacting to a requisition that would come across his desk. He would spend most of his time with the preparation, writing, and recording of purchase orders, and the expediting work. Most of the sources of supply were preselected by the quality control department. Standard orders, particularly for nonproduction materials, were issued without any policy guidelines and without subsequent periodic reviews. Sometimes we continued to receive materials or services for which there was no longer a need or for which more competitive sources of supply were available. There was no control over the payments against these orders.

Generally speaking, we were in a vacuum with respect to what we were buying, how much was being spent, and with what vendors. If someone had asked the purchasing department, "How much do you spend for bottles?" there would not have been a readily available answer. There just was no organized system that told management what was bought, how much was spent for each commodity, how well the buyer handled his job, what the buyer's work load was, and how well the vendors were performing.

Mr. Stanley added:

The department had no commodity coding system. This made it difficult to analyze the considerable volume of materials that we were purchasing and to determine whether we were buying properly. Take, for example, folding cartons. We were buying over 300 different cartons without any real analysis, coordination, or planning of our carton requirements. When a buyer received the requisition he went out and filled it. We never saw the whole picture. There was little control over our buying activities. Management was not able to evaluate buyer performance, and our assessment of vendor performance was based strictly on personal opinions. The development of a purchasing management information system was too monumental a task to be accomplished on a manual basis in view of the size of our purchasing volume.

Developments in 1958 and subsequent years

In 1958, management had called in a consulting firm to study the company's purchasing function. One of the major recommendations made by the consultants was to create a "staff purchasing services" function and to assign a systems specialist to this function on a permanent basis. Two objectives were to be sought: the development of a purchasing information system, and the introduction of effective purchasing procedures and practices. Following the consultant's recommendation, Mr. Stanley had appointed Mr. F. Nutter, an employee with several years' experience in the firm's methods division, to the new post in the purchasing department.

The director of purchasing also had reorganized the purchasing department by assigning buying responsibilities more distinctly on the basis of production materials versus nonproduction materials and by substituting the new position of "purchasing manager" for that of "purchasing agent."

Mr. Wilson observed:

Prior to the reorganization, the department's supervisory personnel consisted of purchasing agents who were really full-time buyers and who exercised few or no managerial functions. Also there were many gray areas and much horse-trading as to who bought what. The reorganization necessitated some painful personnel changes, but it was an essential first step towards improving the department's performance. There was much clarification of what constituted production materials and nonproduction materials, and each buyer was given a clearly defined group of commodities. By changing the position of purchasing agent into purchasing manager we emphasized that this job involved little buying and plenty of managing. [For further details of the reorganization of the purchasing department, compare Exhibits 1 and 3.]

Exhibit 3
ORGANIZATION OF THE PURCHASING DEPARTMENT PRIOR TO 1958

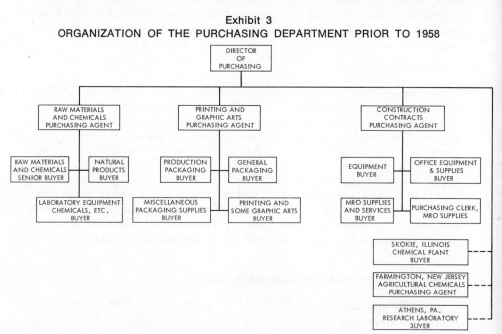

Source: Company records.

Commenting on the initial staff work performed in the purchasing department, Mr. Wilson said:

Given the situation with which my predecessor was faced, he had no choice but to start with such basic items as preparing job descriptions and developing a material-coding system—a coding system for purchase orders, purchasing forms, and so on. He began to collect manually two kinds of information on purchasing activities. First, he tried to obtain data on buyer work load to find out how much one buyer was being asked to do in relation to others. He wanted to be able to answer the questions: "How well is the buyer handling the volume?" "What happens when there is a rearrangement of assignments?" "Is management being fair to each buyer?" Purchasing needed standard job descriptions and a basis for determining the work force needed. Secondly, after developing commodity card codes for raw materials, packaging supplies, and so on, Nutter began to prepare manually reports on our monthly purchasing activities, listing the purchases in commodity code sequence and by descending dollar volume.

Early in 1960, Mr. Nutter had decided to utilize an IBM 632 electronic typing calculator as a first step toward computerized purchasing. Mr. Nutter believed this equipment would provide a basis for reducing much of the buyers' routine work by preparing purchase orders centrally and semiautomatically. A further advantage would be the generating of a set of purchasing reports useful to the buyers in their decision making and to management in evaluating the performance of the purchasing department.

Prior to his decision to start automating the purchasing function with a typewriter card-punch application, Mr. Nutter had had discussions with staff members of the methods division to determine the feasibility of this approach and to work out the basic procedures for semiautomated purchase order writing. With the advice of the tabulating section of the methods division, he also determined the content of the purchasing reports and the frequency of their preparation. Because the purchasing personnel had not had any exposure to automated data processing, Mr. Nutter decided to design the order writing system in detail before introducing it to the buyers and the purchasing managers. He believed this approach would not only reduce to a minimum the time required for the design work, but also would result in less misunderstanding and quicker acceptance than could be expected if he involved the purchasing personnel in the detailed and often frustrating design work.

Mr. Wilson commented:

The benefits from having a machine system were quite obvious. The amount of work being expended to gather manually the information required for current reports was an indication that some machine system would be economical for these and for additional reports as they became needed. A machine system that would also write purchase orders seemed highly desirable. There was a great deal of variation in the way in which purchase orders were prepared. The whims of the buyer had a strong influence on the format; there was no standard way of stating requirements. Purchasing needed better paper work control. There was need for a follow-up system that was common to all areas of activity. Centralized purchase order writing would free the buyers' secretaries so that they could provide the buyers with more assistance in doing a better buying job.

The 632 typewriter calculator was chosen because of its flexibility. It could be used as a typewriter controlled directly by the operator or it could be actuated by punched cards. In addition to performing calculations and listing the results, it could produce punched cards which, in turn, could be used as a basis for computer-prepared reports. This equipment situated in the purchasing division was preferred to using punched cards on a centrally located printer. The justification for the installation of the machine was considered to be the freeing of the buyer from much detail work of a clerical nature so that he could spend more time on creative buying.

The "632" order writing system

The "632" order writing system had, as basic sources of input, material requisitions from various departments of the firm for production and nonproduction materials. Depending on the nature of the material requisitioned (i.e., production materials, nonproduction materials, recurring requirements, nonrecurring requirements, etc.), a requisitioner used one of several requisition forms which, while serving the same purpose, varied slightly according to the manner in which each was processed in the system. Each requisition was first checked against inventories and then sent to the appropriate buyer for review, and, if incomplete, for further processing. Each buyer normally grouped his requisitions to the maximum extent possible to enable the preparation of consolidated orders. Individual or grouped requisitions for which purchase orders were to be prepared by the IBM 632 equipment were then sent to the purchasing department's machine room. Any purchase orders containing lengthy specifications and conditions of purchase, however, were prepared manually by the buyers' secretaries, duplicate copies being sent to the data processing division.

The 632 equipment consisted of an IBM typewriter calculator which could be actuated either by punched cards, an operator, or a combination of the two. The preparation of hard-copy[1] purchase orders from requisitions involved some automatic input from punched cards and some input by a machine operator. Fixed information, such as vendor number, commodity code, stock number, and item description, generally could be automatically provided by punched master cards. Variable information, such as quantity, price, and delivery dates, was generally entered by the machine operator.

---

[1] "Hard-copy" refers to any printout on paper.

As the purchase orders were prepared on the IBM 632, there was a simultaneous generation of punched cards, each card containing data for one "line item"[2] entered on the purchase order. Similar cards were manually keypunched from the data on the manually prepared purchase orders. All punched cards for items in the purchase orders were submitted daily to the central data processing division for entry into an "open order file" and were held for further processing.

As ordered materials were received, the central data processing division keypunched cards for the goods flowing in, using documents prepared by the receiving department. These punched cards for receipts were then processed against the open order file. Although other information was read into the system, the two types of input from punched cards—orders and receipts—provided the basis for the five purchasing reports mentioned in the introduction and more fully described below.

Upon the buyer's review and approval of a purchase order prepared by the IBM 632 machine, copies were generally released and passed as shown in Exhibit 4.[3] The information contained in a purchase order is described in Exhibit 5.

Computer-prepared purchasing reports

1. Purchasing follow-up reports. A comprehensive follow-up report was prepared weekly for each buyer (see Exhibit 6). In designing the format and content of this report, Mr. Nutter intended to give the buyers an effective working tool for expediting purchase orders. Buyers received a report each Wednesday showing all on-order items for which the data processing department had not obtained a receiving report as of the preceding Friday. Mr. Nutter believed that the follow-up report provided each buyer with the means to perform each week a complete open-order analysis, to expedite overdue orders efficiently and with up-to-date information and, if warranted, to follow up on open-orders prior to their due dates. The purchasing procedure manual dealing with the 632 system contained the following reference to the follow-up report:

Buyer Follow-Up Report
This report lists for each buyer, in due-date sequence, all of the on-order items for which data processing has not received a completed receipt.

---

[2] Each line of printout referring to an item of material is called a "line item," regardless of the quantity involved.

[3] The systems procedures set up by the staff assistant relating to the purchasing department's use of a semiautomated order writing machine and the company's control computer facilities comprised a multitude of details, such as provisions for purchase order changes, reconciliation of purchase order numbers issued twice or duplicate receipt listings, handling of receipt listings unmatched by purchase orders, item or stock numbers, and handling of partial deliveries and rejection adjustments. For the sake of simplicity these details—which required substantial systems analysis prior to the programming work for the 632 system—are not described here.

As delegated by the buyers, the secretaries, will follow up on routine requirements, referring the others to the buyer.

I.   Identification of special conditions.
    A.   A box □ in the quantity column indicates a partial shipment has been made against the item. The quantity reported is the balance due.
    B.   A "9" in the terms column indicates that a change of some sort has been made to the item as originally ordered.

II.   Order and item identification using the release number field.

To facilitate the identification of truck or carload shipments and items for scheduled engineering jobs or appropriations, the release number field of such orders is assigned a special identifying release number.
    A.   An 888 release number indicates materials ordered for scheduled engineering work. These orders are to be followed up before the due date. Any change in scheduled due dates should be communicated immediately to the engineering division's planning and scheduling department.
    B.   A 7XX release number is used to identify truckload shipments. The last two digits to be completed using the appropriate sequential release number. If an order, and not a release, is issued, the last two positions are to be zero filled.

Exhibit 4
PURCHASING DATA PROCESSING SYSTEM—IBM 632 PROCEDURE

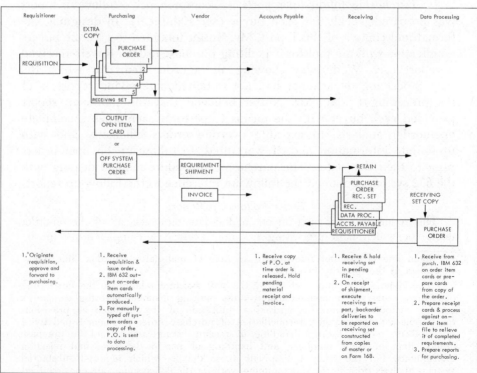

Exhibit 5
CONTENT OF PURCHASE ORDERS

Purchase Orders must contain the following information:

A. *Header Information*

   1. Purchase Order Number

This is a six-digit number, the first two of which designate the responsible buyer, and the next four are sequentially assigned by the buyer. The first number in each buyer's series is 1001 and sequentially, thereafter, to 8999 and then are recycled.

Release numbers are used as a suffix to Blanket Purchase Order Numbers to identify individual releases. This is a three-digit number which is sequentially assigned to each blanket order beginning with the number 001.

To facilitate the identification of certain types of orders, the following indicator numbers are entered into the release field of the order number:

     999—Standing Orders

     7XX—Truckload Shipments

     8XX—Carload Shipments

   2. Vendor Number

This is a four-digit number that is to be entered on the order form immediately to the left of the vendor's name. The assignment of vendor numbers is covered in a separate section of this report.

   3. Ship to

This space is to be left blank unless another location is specified.

   4. Mark for

Each page of any order must indicate where the requirements on the page are to be delivered. This is necessary as Receiving treats each page essentially as a separate order.

   5. Purchase Order Date

This is to be entered as a six-digit number signifying the day the order is prepared.

   6. Delivery Required Date

The date by when the material must be delivered. This must be a realistic date for the vendor as delivery performance will be assessed on the basis of this date.

Only one delivery date is to be entered on an order or release. On period orders where multiple deliveries for a series of items are scheduled for a given period of time the last delivery date is entered. The delivery dates prior to this are typed in the body of the order. If a period order runs from one year into the next, the quantity received during the year ended is to be marked complete and the balance of the order reentered as a new order.

In the event the delivery required date is unknown, the field is to be left blank and the following statement entered in the body of the order: "Delivery Date to Be Specified Later."

   7. Ship Via, F.O.B. Point, Terms

These fields of information to be completed with the appropriate information.

Exhibit 5 (*Continued*)

B. *Line Items*

Line item entries must be triple-spaced to provide Receiving space to enter the Receiving Report data immediately below each line item entry.

1. Requisition Number

   Requisition numbers must be shown on all purchase orders for production materials. The use of requisition numbers by other locations are optional; whenever they are available, they should be included on the order. If a requisition number is not available, the requisition date should be used for this field; i.e., July 3, 1964—0703.

   The maximum number of spaces available for requisition numbers is four.

2. Accounting Number

   Account numbers must be specified by the requisitioner on each requisition. Purchasing is responsible for transferring the account number to the Purchase Order.

   A normal accounting number has seven digits and is written continuously, without dashes.

   Example: 0705000

   An appropriation number should be preceded by an A, zero filled to make it seven digits, and written continuously, without dashes.

   Example: A3008001

   The first number denotes the year. The next three numbers denote the appropriation number and the last three numbers, the phase of the appropriation. Therefore, zeros should be placed in front of the last two groups to make them three digits each. In the number mentioned above, the appropriation number is 8 and the phase number is 1.

   Job numbers are preceded by a J and must have two numbers, a dash, and four numbers.

   Example: J10-9987

   It is most important that the J and the dash be present.

   On machine-written purchase orders, a dash preceding the accounting number takes the place of the A and J on manually written orders.

3. Commodity Code

   A three-digit commodity classification number must be assigned to each item ordered. The responsible buyer should refer to Purchasing's Master List of Commodity Codes for the appropriate numbers.

4. Stock or item Number

   Stock numbers are to be used wherever possible. If an item being requisitioned does not have a stock number, it is to be assigned a sequential item number. In those instances where item numbers are assigned, they should be entered in the stock number field so they align in the last digit position of the field, such as:

Stock Numbered Item	710 235 863221	
Item Number	710	1

   A stock number or item number may only be used once on the same order or release. If the quantity required is to be split between two delivery dates, either a separate order number or a release number must be assigned, thereby making it, in effect, two separate orders.

Exhibit 5 (*Concluded*)

5. Description

   Repetitively ordered items for which input cards are prepared to actuate Purchasing's data processing equipment should whenever possible be limited to 48 digits of description to minimize the use of trailer input cards.

   Nonrepetitive items should be described in sufficient detail, regardless of their length, to ensure the vendor's understanding what is required.

6. Unit of Purchase

   This field of information is limited to three digits. The abbreviated descriptions are to be taken from Purchasing's Master List.

   The Unit of Purchase used for any item should be the lowest common unit in which the material will normally be required.

7. Quantity

   The quantity must be stated in terms of the Unit of Purchase. No provisions have been made in the automated system for the incorporation of decimal or fractional amounts.

   This field is limited to seven-digit positions.

8. Unit Price

   The net Unit Price of an item must always be used and must be stated in terms of the Unit of Purchase and carried to three decimal places. This field is limited to seven-digit positions, $9,999,999. If the unit price is more than seven digits, the order must be manually typed, the data processing copy destroyed and the item entered into the system by the 3210 form.

   Nominal charges, such as setup charges and federal excise tax, should be stated in the description field and not brought out into the price field.

9. Extension

   The line items on purchase orders prepared on Purchasing's data processing equipment automatically extend the item and enter the total in the extension field. This field will accept an extended total of nine digits, $9,999,999.99.

   At the close of each order, the equipment automatically computes and enters the total value of all of the purchase commitments on the order. In those instances on manually typed orders where it is impossible to specifically identify an "each" price to an item, a lot price may be used. In this case the word "lot" is typed in the unit of purchase field, the quantity ordered remains the same and the total price is entered in the price field. The lot price should only be extended two decimal places.

   Example: Lot   160,000 $2,678.40

   On machine order the "lot price" should be specified on the requisition. In these cases, the machine operator types the quantity in the body of the order and in the quantity field the number "1" is used.

   Example:

   28mm caps, aluminum
   500/lot   Lot   1 $3.950

10. Tax Exemption

   Purchasing is responsible for determining and entering the tax status of the requirements on the orders.

Exhibit 6

PURCHASING FOLLOW-UP REPORT

DATE _____

DUE DATE (MO DAY YR)	REQ. NO.	COM. CODE	PREFIX	ITEM OR STOCK NO. / MATERIAL	ACCOUNTING DISTRIBUTION OR APPROP. NO.	VENDOR	BUYER	PURCHASE ORDER NO.	REL.	ORDER DATE (MO DAY YR)	QUANTITY ORDERED	PURCHASE COMMITMENT	ITEMS	QUANTITY RECEIVED	REMARKS
08 30 65	6639	2	105	166290	07 01 000	8261	11	7009	1	06 29 65	2,000	2,400.00	9		
08 30 65	6673	2	105	166290	07 01 000	9999	11	1092		08 16 65	250	375.00			
08 31 65	6617	2	105	22095	07 01 030	7465	11	6825	1	03 30 65	350	122.50	9		
08 31 65	6681	2	105	89900	07 01 000	643	10	1098	1	08 23 65	150	2,775.00	9		
09 3 65	6621	2	110	65956	07 01 000	5075	10	3324		03 30 65	36	5,760.00	9		
09 10 65	6682	2	105	88900	11 03 000	8680	16	1136		09 02 65	30	105.60	9		
09 17 65	6655	2	105	89900	07 01 000	643	16	1098	2	08 23 65	150	2,775.00			
09 17 65	6643	2	105	22300	07 01 000	7730	16	1016		07 16 65	5,800	783.00			
09 17 65	6642	2	105	166290	07 01 000	7730	11	7010		06 29 65	5,000	6,250.00			
09 17 65		2	105	166292	07 01 000	7730	11	7013		06 30 65	3,500	14,875.00			
09 20 65	6674	2	105	166290	07 01 000	9999	16	1092	2	08 16 65	500	750.00			
09 24 65	6649	2	105	56870	07 01 000	643	11	7054		07 07 65	1,400	210.00			
09 30 65	6647	2	105	20500	07 01 000	7730	11	7025		07 02 65	200	1,600.00			
10 1 65	6641	2	105	166290	07 01 000	6915	11	7011		06 29 65	4,000	4,800.00			
10 1 65	6640	2	105	166292	07 01 000	6915	11	7014		06 30 65	400	960.00			
10 1 65	6622	2	110	65956	07 01 000	5075	10	3325		03 30 65	36	5,760.00	9		
10 15 65	6664	2	105	22300	07 01 000	7730	16	1087		08 10 65	5,800	783.00			
10 15 65	6650	2	105	56870	07 01 000	643	11	7055		07 07 65	1,400	210.00			
10 15 65	6653	2	105	166290	07 01 000	9999	11	7043		07 08 65	1,000	1,200.00	9		
10 15 65	6654	2	105	166292	07 01 000	9999	11	7042		07 08 65	1,000	2,400.00			
10 15 65	6685	2	105	194772	07 01 001	8680	16	1127		09 02 65	300	8,775.00	9		
10 22 65	6661	2	110	65956	07 01 000	5075	11	1116		08 06 65	36	5,760.00			
10 25 65	6675	2	105	166290	07 01 000	9999	16	1092	3	08 16 65	500	750.00			
10 29 65	6644	2	105	166292	07 01 000	8261	11	7000		08 06 65	900	2,160.00	9		
11 12 65	6662	2	110	65956	07 01 000	5075	11	1117		08 06 65	36	5,760.00			
11 12 65	6651	2	105	56870	07 01 000	643	11	7056		07 07 65	1,100	165.00			
11 26 65	6676	2	105	166290	07 01 000	9999	16	1092	4	08 16 65	500	750.00			
11 29 65	6679	2	105	22095	07 01 000	7465	16	1104		08 24 65	2,000	700.00			
11 30 65	6663	2	110	65956	07 01 000	5075	11	1118		08 06 65	36	165.00			
12 10 65	6652	2	105	56870	07 01 000	643	11	7057		07 07 65	1,100	5,760.00			
12 17 65	5272	2	105	129980	07 01 000	5242	11	6585	5	01 26 65	5,130 □	125,685.00	9		
12 27 65	6677	2	105	166290	07 01 000	9999	16	1092		08 16 65	500	750.00			
12 27 65	6539	2	105	116090	07 01 000	6915	11	6529		12 18 64	24,627 □	6,403.02	9		
12 31 65	6583	2	105	116090	07 01 000	7730	11	6555		01 07 65	3,000 □	795.00	9		
12 31 65	6584	2	105	116090	07 01 000	643	11	6556		01 07 65	25,216 □	6,556.16	9		
12 31 65	6579	2	105	128260	07 01 000	643	11	6561		01 07 65	40	1,500.00			
12 31 65	6580	2	105	128260	07 01 000	7730	11	6571		01 07 65	169	6,337.50			
12 31 65	6645	2	105	166290	07 01 000	8261	11	6999		06 29 65	5,000 □	6,000.00			
12 31 65	6540	2	105	172895	07 01 000	6915	11	6530		12 18 64	6,490 □	9,735.00			
12 31 65	6582	2	105	172895	07 01 000	7730	11	6559		01 07 65	5,696 □	8,544.00			
12 31 65	6587	2	105	172895	07 01 000	6997	11	6590		01 14 65	7,540	11,910.00	9		
12 31 65	6581	2	105	172895	07 01 000	643	11	6560		01 07 65	2,682 □	4,023.00	9		
12 31 65	5125	2	150	130000	07 01 000	1115	11	6722		03 07 65	386 □	5,018.00	9		
02 25 66	6634	2	105	159905	07 01 000	7750	11	7003		06 28 65	80,000 □	10,200.00			
03 31 66	6636	2	105	130100	07 01 000	7750	16	1034		07 21 65	144,000	36,720.00			
											349,986	325,215.78 *			

C. An 8XX release number is used to identify carload shipments. The last two digits to be completed using the appropriate sequential release number. If an order, and not a release, is issued, the last two positions are to be zero filled.

III. Procedure for using the follow-up report.
The secretaries will:

A. Pull from their open-order files all orders covering past due items based on the cutoff date of the report. The cutoff date is normally the Friday of the preceding week.

B. Follow up on these items for which receipts have not been received, checking with receiving and the suppliers.

C. For those items on the report for which a completed receipt has been received, the back of purchasing's copy of the receiving report should be checked for a "punched and verified date."

1. If the date that it was punched is after the date of the report, disregard the item as it will be processed the following week.

2. If the date that the receipt was punched by data processing was before the cutoff date, the reason the receipt did not match up against the purchase order should be determined. Adjustments, if necessary, should be made using the appropriate form.

3. If the receipt is not stamped on the back "punched and verified" either detach the receipt and give it to the staff assistant's secretary for forwarding to data processing or enter it on the should-read line of the appropriate adjustment form. The action taken should be noted on the file copy of the order.

D. In the case of production materials, for which purchasing is notified daily of materials received by a special listing from the receiving department, the receipt information should be noted on the buyer's current follow-up report. This action provides a means for an effective day-to-day follow-up.

E. The follow-up report may be destroyed as soon as a new one is received. The staff assistant will keep copies of all buyer follow-up reports for approximately five weeks for referral.

IV. Procedure for using the follow-up report for delivery check.
The secretaries will:

A. Check the follow-up report for all items to be delivered the following week. These orders should be checked with the supplier, if necessary, to ensure that delivery will be on time.

2. *Vendor performance report.* The vendor performance report and, for that matter, all other purchasing reports prepared by the central data processing department were based on the information gathered for the follow-up report (see Exhibit 7). The vendor performance report was prepared quarterly, summarizing for each vendor the purchase order line item activity, the dollar commitments, and the delivery performance on a year-to-date basis. Items were arranged in commodity code and stock number sequence. With the exception of the year-end report, each quarterly report was based on commitments made year-to-date plus open

Exhibit 7

PURCHASING VENDOR PERFORMANCE REPORT

DATE _____

COM. CODE	ITEM OR STOCK NO. PREFIX	MATERIAL	VENDOR	BYR.	NO. OF LINE ITEMS ORDERED	DOLLAR VALUE	NUMBER OF DELIVERIES	NUMBER OF LATE DELIVERIES	% LATE DELIVERIES	REMARKS

commitments carried over from the preceding year. The year-end report included only information on items closed out during the year.[4] The two major objectives of the vendor performance report was to give a means by which to evaluate each vendor's delivery performance and to provide information on the company's volume of business with each vendor. The utilization of the vendor performance report was described in the purchasing department's 632 procedure manual as follows:

Uses of the Report

A. Operational uses include:
   1. Identification of purchasing's activity with a vendor and the distribution of business between the commodity groups and stock numbered items.
   2. Identification of a vendor's delivery performance by item, commodity group, and in total. By examining a vendor's delivery performance by commodity group and item, it is possible to isolate problem areas and items which can then receive the buyers' and vendors' attention.
   3. Vendor to vendor comparison of performance and activity.
   4. Used as an aid by the buyer in deciding on the future allocation of business.
B. Control uses of the report include:
   1. Purchasing management's identification of relative commitment levels with vendors.
   2. Identify those vendors whose delivery performance is unsatisfactory.

Note: The staff assistant prepares summary reports identifying on an exception basis those vendors whose delivery performance is unsatisfactory.

3. Buyer performance report. The buyer performance report was prepared and distributed every four weeks to the director of purchases and to the purchasing managers (see Exhibit 8). Information was arranged in buyer, commodity code, and stock number sequence. The utilization of the report was described as follows:

Uses of the Report

A. This is essentially a control report to be used by the purchasing agents and director to identify:
   1. Purchasing's line item and dollar volume commitment levels.
   2. Shifts in line item . . . work load between areas.
   3. Delivery performance.
B. From this report, the director of purchases' secretary prepares a statistical summary of delivery performance by month and year-to-date for each of the purchasing areas of responsibility.

4. Commodity report. The commodity report summarized, by commodity group, stock number, and vendor, the line item order activity and dollar commitments on a year-to-date basis (see Exhibit 9). Dollar subtotals were shown by stock number, within each stock number by vendor, and for each commodity group. The report was prepared quar-

---

[4] The same procedure was followed in preparing the buyer performance report and the commodity report described below.

Exhibit 8

PURCHASING BUYER PERFORMANCE REPORT

DATE

COM. CODE	ITEM OR STOCK NO.		VENDOR	BYR.	NO. OF LINE ITEMS ORDERED	DOLLAR VALUE	NUMBER OF DELIVERIES	NUMBER OF LATE DELIVERIES	% LATE DELIVERIES	REMARKS
	PREFIX	MATERIAL								

Exhibit 9

PURCHASING COMMODITY REPORT

DATE_____

COM. CODE	ITEM OR STOCK NO.		VENDOR	BYR.	NO. OF LINE ITEMS ORDERED	DOLLAR VALUE	NUMBER OF DELIVERIES	NUMBER OF LATE DELIVERIES	% LATE DELIVERIES	REMARKS
	PREFIX	MATERIAL								

terly, and copies were distributed to the purchasing managers and the buyers. It contained no information on delivery performance. The procedure manual described the use of the commodity report as follows:

With the exception that this report does not provide delivery performance statistics, it has broad applications:

a. Identification of those commodity groups which have the highest dollar commitment level and, therefore, offer the greatest potential for profit yielding exploitation.

b. Comparison of vendor to vendor activity by item and within commodity groups.

c. Permits purchasing to analyze and make recommendations concerning ordering and inventory practices based on the number of times an item is ordered compared to the total commitment value.

d. Provides the buyers and purchasing managers with a basis for examining actual allocations of business for the top dollar value items.

5. *Cash commitment report.* The cash commitment report, shown in Exhibit 10, was issued at the close of each month and submitted by the purchasing department to the treasurer as input for a monthly cash forecast. According to the procedure manual the report served "essentially as an encumbrance report listing all on-order material commitments by the month in which delivery was requested." On-order items were arranged in due date, commodity code, and stock number sequence.

Receiving operations

When a shipment was received, the receiving clerk pulled the copy of the purchase order, compared the order copy with the packing slip, inspected and counted the received material, wrote into the order copy the quantity received and the date of receipt, and forwarded the order copy to the data processing department.[5] Information included in the receiving report prepared by the receiving department included the purchase order number, the commodity code, the item or stock number, the quantity received, the receiving date, the receiving number, and the type of shipment (partial or complete). Handling a volume of several hundred material receipts daily, the receiving dock generally forwarded receiving reports to the data processing division within two days of a material receipt.

---

[5] Although time-consuming, the inspection work performed by the receiving department was largely perfunctory in the absence of any technical personnel. Indeed, even a determination as to whether the content of the documents accompanying incoming shipments corresponded with the content of the purchase orders was difficult at times because of the technical complexity of some of the materials received. Traditionally, however, the controller's office had insisted on the performance of the inspection function by the receiving department as a control measure. Primary inspection work was performed by the requisitioning departments and/or the quality control department.

Exhibit 10

PURCHASING CASH COMMITMENT REPORT

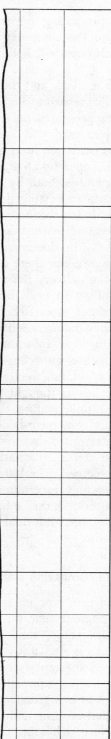

DUE DATE			REQ. NO.	COM. CODE	ITEM OR STOCK NO.		ACCOUNTING DISTRIBUTION OR APPROP. NO.	VENDOR	PURCHASE ORDER			ORDER DATE			QUANTITY ORDERED	PURCHASE COMMITMENT	TERMS	QUANTITY RECEIVED	REMARKS
MO.	DAY	YEAR			PREFIX	MATERIAL			BUYER	NO.	REL.	MO.	DAY	YEAR					

DATE _____

The data processing department keypunched receipt cards, which were read into the computer and processed against the on-order file. When a match occurred, both the open-order card and the receipt card dropped out of the system. If the order was complete the receiving report was so marked, and the two sets of receipt and order cards were held for use in preparing the purchasing reports. In the event the quantity received represented only a portion of the quantity ordered, a new open-order item card was created for the balance due. Keypunching of the receipt cards required generally one day, though there had been times when this operation had absorbed two days.

The time required both by the receiving dock for the inspection work and by the data processing division for the keypunching operation had made it difficult for the buyers to rely on the weekly follow-up report for their expediting work. Because each weekly report included all open purchase orders, the document received by the buyers consisted of over a hundred pages. Since there was no provision to enter into the punched-card system the delivery information obtained by a buyer in the course of his daily follow-up work, buyers making use of the centrally prepared report transferred manually from one weekly report to the next the information they themselves had secured.

In order to have information available on received shipments as quickly as possible, some buyers had made arrangements with receiving dock clerks to obtain directly from the dock a copy of each receiving report. These buyers thought that their follow-up work was made more effective by supplementing the tabulated follow-up report with their own informally kept records on material receipts. The buyers' follow-up work was interrupted by frequent telephone calls from requisitioners desiring order status information. It was estimated that the purchasing department received over 100 such calls daily. Thus, the buyers or their secretaries not only ascertained delivery information from the vendors but also transmitted this information to the requisitioners, who as a rule also maintained informal records on the delivery status of requisitioned materials.

Corrections to purchasing statistics

During the first year of operations with the 632 purchasing system, it became apparent that the purchasing reports frequently contained incorrect dollar value, vendor numbers, commodity code numbers, or stock numbers. It was also discovered that rejected items were often not reflected in the reports because of inaccurate rejection adjustments. In addition, buyers complained that the reports on many occasions showed orders as being delivered late when, in fact, vendors were found to have shipped on time and delays had occurred in transit. The buyers argued that late deliveries resulting from such in-transit delays were beyond their control and therefore should be treated statistically as on-time deliveries.

In order to improve the accuracy of the purchasing reports, the staff assistant consequently devised a procedure by which the buyers could prepare corrections which could then be keypunched and read into the system. Under this procedure a buyer wanting to make corrections filled out a form (see Exhibit 11), which he submitted to a purchasing man-

Exhibit 11
CORRECTIONS TO PURCHASING STATISTICS

CORRECTIONS TO PURCHASING STATISTICS THE USE OF THIS FORM IS RESTRICTED TO CHANGES ON CLOSED OUT ORDERS										Period Number_____	
+ —	BUYER	VENDOR	NUMBER OF LATE DELIVERIES	SOURCE CODE	COMM. CODE	ITEM OR STOCK NUMBER		NUMBER OF DELIVERIES	DOLLAR VALUE		
						PREFIX	MATERIAL				
CARD COLUMNS	(1—2)	(10—13)	(14—19)	(27)	(39—41)	(42—44)	(45—50)	(51—57)	(64—73)	P.O. NO.	REMARKS
TO ADD OR SUBTRACT DOLLAR VALUE				6							
x	x	x		6		x	x	x		x	x	x
TO SUBTRACT LATE DELIVERIES				6							
x	x	x	x	6		x	x	x			x	x
TO SUBTRACT A COMPLETE ITEM THAT HAS BEEN REJECTED				6							
x	x	x	(x)	6		x	x	x	x	x	x	x
TO CHANGE A VENDOR NUMBER, COMMODITY CODE, OR STOCK NUMBER											
—	x	x	(x)	6		x	x	x	x	x	x	x
+	x	x	(x)	6		x	x	x	x	x	x	x
				6							
				6							
				6							
				6							
				6							
				6							
				6							
				6							
(x) = optional, depending on whether or not it was late								For Punched Card Operations Department use only			
Compiled by: _____											
Transmittal Date: _____											

ager for approval and to the staff assistant for review and forwarding to the central data processing division. Commenting on the procedure for correction of data on which purchasing reports were based, Mr. Wilson said:

The input for the system was prepared by the buyers' secretaries, who really were never instructed in any formal and organized way in how to do it. Prior to the 632 system we had a typing pool where purchase orders were prepared. The pool was supervised by one person who monitored the accuracy of the purchase order details. When the 632 was introduced, the pool girls were assigned to individual buyers, who generally believed that it was more important to get out requisitions than to be concerned with coding details. Well, it didn't take the girls very long to realize that missing or inaccurate EDP input didn't bother their superiors very much, and this is now clearly reflected in their attitude toward preparing accurate input.

Corrections that were made by the buyers to the statistics on delivery performance could not be identified in the purchasing reports. Mr. Wilson observed:

There is only one exception: when an overzealous buyer removes a late delivery that was not recorded by the system as a late delivery. In this case, a minus sign appears on the report.

A yearly average of 10 percent late deliveries was considered acceptable by the director of purchases. In checking the performance reports for 17 buyers for January–March, 1965, Mr. Wilson found these data:

	Percentage of late deliveries (cumulative)		
Buyer	January	February	March
A	20	15	15
B	22	17	21
C	20	6	8
D	25	23	22
E	53	44	42
F	33	31	33
G	42	30	24
H	13	6	4
I	23	10	9
J	13	23	24
K	11	14	14
L	23	5	5
M	36	36	27
N	27	29	31
O	41	32	29
P	32	29	26
Q	13	12	11

Production material inventory control

In 1962, the methods division in cooperation with the production materials control department developed and installed—independently of the 632 purchasing system—a computerized inventory control system for production materials. Stored in the system were, among other things, bills of materials for each product specifying each ingredient and the quantity required to produce one manufacturing batch. Production plans, prepared manually by the production department on the basis of sales forecasts and desired inventory levels of finished products, were fed into the computer system and applied against the master bills-of-materials tape to produce detailed lists of production material requirements. Following the consolidation of ingredients commonly used in two or more products scheduled for manufacturing, the requirements lists were applied against inventory balances to produce material requisitions. These requisitions were reviewed by the materials control department and then forwarded to the purchasing department for the preparation of purchase orders within the 632 purchasing system. The materials control department was authorized to change any computer-prepared production material requisition if it was warranted by circumstances that were not reflected in the source data from which the requisition was generated. Thus, the purchasing department received from the materials control department both handwritten and computer-prepared requisitions.

Nonproduction material inventory control

In 1964, the methods department, in cooperation with the purchasing division and the nonproduction materials department, designed and installed—independently of the production material inventory system and the 632 purchasing system—a computerized system for a continuing monitoring of the stores for nonproduction materials and for an automatic preparation of replenishing orders by computer. Under this system, the data processing division maintained, for each repetitive nonproduction item, a master file containing such information as stock number, item description, dispensing unit, reorder point, current inventory level, purchasing unit, and delivery quantity. For most, but not all items, the master file also contained lead items in working days, vendor identification number, and prices in terms of purchasing units as well as dispensing units. The master file was designed to accommodate as many as three vendors for each item. The data processing division's 1401 IBM computer that was utilized for nonproduction materials inventory control was programmed to cycle progressively in the order-writing routine, selecting for each new order the next vendor and recycling to the first vendor.

Once each week the computer updated the inventory of each item included in the nonproduction materials files. If the inventory of an item was at or below the reorder point, the computer prepared automatically a purchase order or a purchase order requisition, depending upon the degree of completeness of information contained in the master file. For items covered by blanket purchase orders, the computer prepared a purchase *release* order. The issuance by the purchasing division of purchase orders to vendors for nonproduction materials items included in the system followed the inventory updating cycle; such orders were sent out to vendors once a week. Reorder points were set to take into account, among other things, the fixed reorder cycle of one week.

If the information contained in the master file for an item to be ordered was incomplete, as, for instance, in the case of a missing vendor identification, a missing price, or a missing lead time, the document generated by the computer served as purchase requisition rather than as purchase order.

For releases of items included in blanket purchase orders, the computer entered the blanket order number that was assigned at the time the blanket order was issued and entered into the master file. For items not covered by blanket purchase order, but for which a vendor had been designated, the computer developed a purchase order number. For items not covered by blanket purchase order and without vendor designation, the computer specified no purchase order number. These items were issued by the computer as requisitions to be completed manually by the buyer into purchase orders, or to form the source document for the preparation of the necessary purchase orders.

Commenting on the development of the computer-oriented inventory control and purchasing systems, Mr. Wilson said:

Whether or not the use of a 632 order-writing machine was a good choice as a primary means of introducing automatic data processing into purchasing may be open to question. But the company's central computer facilities were not available to purchasing at the time and purchasing had to do something. The 632 application was not the best solution, but it was better than what we had. I believe we have made great progress in the purchasing department over the past three or four years.

The decision to develop a production materials inventory control system as an independent system was made, I believe, in recognition of what was most urgently needed and also in recognition of the fact that one can rarely computerize a great many interrelated functions at the same time. There is great appeal in the "total system" approach that calls for the computerization of the total procurement cycle from the creation of a purchase requisition, through ordering, receiving, inspecting, inventory control, the accounting process, and vendor remittance. The design of a system that optimizes the inter-functional work process and flow of data among all procurement sections is relatively easy. It's the installation, implementation, and acceptance by the people that pose monumental problems. From this point of view, much has been said for an approach that converts a section of the procurement cycle at a time to EDP, beginning with those areas where the need for improvement is the greatest. By the same token, such an approach creates compatibility problems in any attempt later on to integrate the subsystems. In our case, for instance, the coding systems developed independently for production materials and nonproduction materials are incompatible in terms of prefixes, number of digits, meaning of digits, and so on. The accounting department has used for a number of years a coding system for EDP that is at least partially incompatible with the nonproduction material coding system.

The decision to integrate our subsystems rests with the methods division. There has to be a determination of the feasibility, the economics, and the desirability of combining the three systems into an integrated system for materials control, purchasing, receiving, inspecting, and accounts payable, which would cover all aspects of the procurement cycle and provide for more effective management information reporting.

One of the major trouble spots is the receiving section, where the personnel is totally unfamiliar with EDP. The procedures followed there are antiquated; and yet it's difficult to make any drastic changes that may be in conflict with the company's well-established control concepts.

A great deal of systems analysis and work simplification remains to be done in order to develop the essential elements of an integrated system. In fact, at this point nothing short of a very elaborate and comprehensive study of the total procurement cycle will suffice. We have come a long way in the use of computers within some phases of this cycle since the late 50s. The question now is: how high a level of sophistication in terms of systems integration does management want to achieve? I believe this question goes beyond achieving streamlined procurement procedures, improved operating performance, and better management control over the procurement activities. At issue now is the procurement concept that management wants to choose for this company. That is, how far do we want to go in applying the concept of material management with all its implications regarding organizational structure, interdepartmental relationships, and operating responsibilities?

PHILADELPHIA PHARMACEUTICALS, INC. (B)*

Introduction

In January, 1966, Mr. Harry Wilson, manager of purchasing services for Philadelphia Pharmaceuticals, Inc., was considering the question of whether to recommend to the director of purchasing that the use of dataphone in purchasing be discontinued. Early in 1965, the company had installed an IBM 1001 data transmitting terminal and a Bell System 401 dataphone for the placement of purchase orders with local suppliers over regular telephone lines.

Company background and organization for procurement

As reported in Philadelphia Pharmaceuticals, Inc. (A), the company was a large international manufacturer and distributor of pharmaceutical and agricultural chemical products with consolidated 1965 sales of $172.5 million and net earnings of more than $29.9 million.

The purchasing division was organized into four sections: production materials purchases, nonproduction materials purchases, consolidated contract purchases, and purchasing services (see Exhibit 1).

Exhibit 1

ORGANIZATION CHART—PURCHASING DIVISION AS OF JUNE, 1965

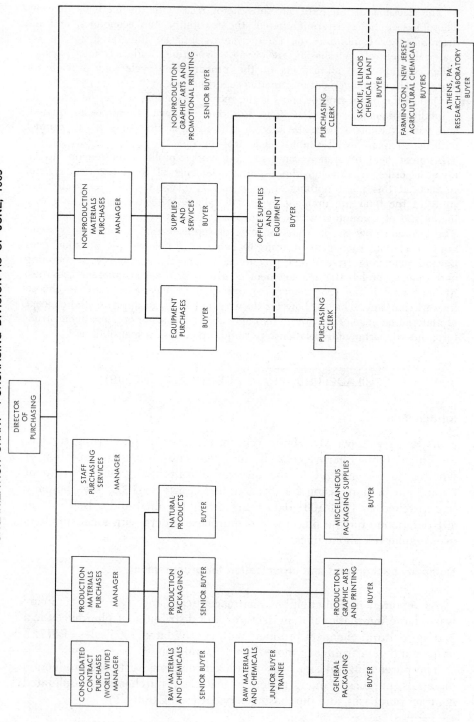

Source: Company records.

Purchases in 1964 for the company's U.S. operations amounted to approximately $48.3 million. Of this total, approximately $25.5 million was spent for the production materials for pharmaceuticals; and approximately $14.1 million for nonproduction requirements, including laboratory equipment, production machinery, and certain building construction. Purchases of production materials for agricultural chemicals totaled approximately $8.7 million. Major procurement items included antibiotics, steroids and hormones, crude drugs, oils, flavors, perfumes, gelatins, sugars, chlorides, esters, phenols, acids, gases, alcohol and solvents, bottles, vials and ampules, paper packaging, graphic arts, laboratory chemicals and supplies, laboratory animals, and a large vriety of maintenance, repair, and operating supplies (MRO).

Procurement procedures for nonproduction materials

In 1964 the company's methods department, in cooperation with the purchasing division, designed and installed a system for a continued monitoring of the stores of nonproduction materials (hereafter referred to as MOR stores) and for an automatic preparation of replenishment orders by computer.

Under the system, the company's data processing division maintained for each repetitive MRO item a master file containing such information as stock number, item description, dispensing unit, reorder point, current inventory level, purchasing unit, and delivery quantity. For most, but not all items, the master file also contained lead times in working days, vendor identification number, and prices in terms of purchasing units as well as dispensing units. The master file was designed to accommodate as many as three vendors for each item. The data processing division's 1401 IBM computer utilized for MRO inventory control was programmed to cycle progressively in the order-writing routine, selecting for each new order and next vendor and then recycling to the first vendor.

Once each week the computer updated the inventory of each item included in the MRO master file. If the inventory of an item was at or below the reorder point, the computer, depending upon the degree of completeness of information contained in the master file, automatically prepared a purchase order requisition. For items covered by a blanket purchase order, the computer prepared a purchase *release* order. The issuance of purchase orders to vendors by the purchasing division for MRO items included in the system followed the inventory updating cycle; that is, such orders were sent out to vendors once a week. Reorder points were set to take into account, among other things, the fixed reorder cycle of one week.

If the information contained in the master file for an item to be ordered was incomplete, as, for instance, in the case of a missing vendor identification number, a missing price, or a missing lead time, the document generated by the computer served as a purchase requisition rather than as a purchase order.

For releases under blanket purchase orders, the computer entered a blanket order number assigned at the time the blanket order was issued and entered into the master file. For items not covered by a blanket purchase order, but for which a vendor had been designated, the computer developed a purchase order number. For items not covered by a blanket purchase order and without a vendor's designation, the computer specified no purchase order number. Items in the last category were issued by the computer as requisitions that were to be completed into a purchase order manually by the buyer or were to form the source document for the preparation of purchase orders by an IBM 632 electronic typing calculator with punched card input and output maintained in the purchasing department. (See Exhibit 2 for description of IBM 632 calculator.)

Items to be ordered were accumulated by the computer according to vendor, blanket purchase order number, and lead time. As long as these three specifications were identical for any group of items, items were accumulated on the same purchase order or purchase release order. There were three possible conditions the computer could encounter in preparing to order or requisition material:

1. *Vendor and blanket purchase orders were specified in the master item file.* When this condition existed the computer grouped the items under the purchase release order specifying the vendor and the blanket order number (along with a release number).

2. *Vendor, but not purchase order number, was specified in the master item file.* When this condition existed the computer grouped the items in one order so long as the vendor and lead time were common. As indicated earlier, in writing such orders the computer developed a purchase order number.

3. *No vendor or purchase order was specified in the master file.* When this condition existed, grouping was restricted to items with the same lead time. As indicated earlier, these "orders" were treated as requisitions.

Simultaneously with the preparation of purchase orders or purchase release orders, the computer produced two punched cards for each ordered item. One of these cards was transferred to an existing on-order ("open") item file maintained by the data processing division for the purchasing department. The second was forwarded to MRO stores to be used later for reporting material receipts to the data processing division.

When neither a vendor nor a purchase release order was designated, the computer did not prepare these item cards. In such a case, it was the responsibility of the buyer processing the computer-prepared requisi-

Exhibit 2

The IBM 632...cuts clerical costs, reduces typing mistakes, and eliminates manual accounting steps.

Programmed to fit your accounting needs, the 632 types and calculates quickly to give you accuracy in invoices, forms and records...in less time and with less effort.

With the 632, your operator can now combine typing and calculating operations in one smooth procedure. Result: increased accounting efficiency.

Punched card input/output offers additional accuracy and reliability. One input card can contain customer information, such as name and address, discount, and salesman's number. Line items, including item number, description and price, can be read from separate input cards containing product information. The operator enters only a few variables, such as quantities ordered. Simultaneously, output cards are produced as a by-product of these operations. Much repetitive work is eliminated and the likelihood of manual errors is greatly reduced, thus leading to savings in your overall operation.

Typing of figures is done automatically. Mistakes occur most often in typing of figures. You greatly reduce such errors with automatic typing.

Computations are made electronically. The 632's electronic calculating unit assures accuracy and reliability.

Manual steps are virtually eliminated. Your operator—teamed with the IBM 632— produces work in one smooth, continuous flow. It's no longer necessary to pass papers back and forth, desk to desk, employee to employee.

tions to provide for the entry of the items involved into the on-order item file. The buyer could accomplish this in two ways:

1. When the requisitions form prepared by the computer could be completed manually by the buyer, so that it would be used as a purchase order, the buyer could submit a copy of the document to the data processing division for entry of the information into the system.

2. When one or more purchase orders needed to be prepared from a computer-generated requisition, the buyer could have the order writing done semiautomatically by the IBM 632 typing calculator which generated open-order item cards as a by-product. He then forwarded these cards to the data processing division for entry into the system.

All purchase orders, purchase release orders, and requisitions prepared by the computer were forwarded to MRO stores along with the second of the two punched item cards. Following approval by MRO stores of the orders and requisitions as written by the computer, the documents were forwarded to the purchasing division for approval, completion (or preparation of a new purchase order), and transmission to the supplier. The punched cards were retained by MRO stores pending receipt of the ordered or requisitioned material. (For a summary presentation of the purchasing data processing system for nonproduction materials, see Exhibit 3.) The company was not making use of stockless buying techniques.

Exhibit 3
SUMMARY PRESENTATION OF THE NONPRODUCTION MATERIALS

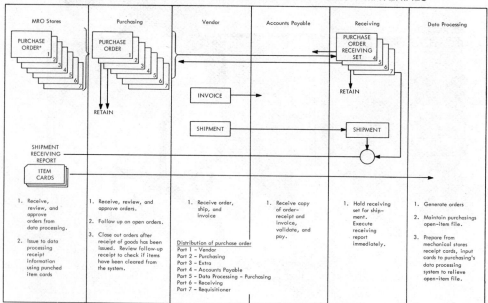

* Completely prepared by computer.

Source: Company records.

Upon receipt of material, personnel in the MRO stores department checked the quantities received to make sure they were correct. They then entered the data and quantity received, along with a receiving number, on the appropriate item card, which was then forwarded to the data processing division to report the addition to inventory. The data processing division prepared a duplicate card containing all receiving information. This duplicate card was then processed against the on-order item file to relieve the file of open items as they were received.

Utilization of dataphone

Early in 1965, one of the company's local suppliers of nonproduction materials suggested that the purchasing division install an IBM transmission terminal and Bell System dataphone for the transmission, over regular telephone lines, of purchase order information from prepunched cards. The supplier had been operating with an IBM 1001 receiving station (a 26 printing card punch) for several years in conjunction with a computerized system of order processing and inventory control. Representatives of the vendor emphasized that a transmission of purchase orders from Philadelphia Pharmaceuticals to the supplier by dataphone would enable the supplier to deliver ordered material within 24 to 48 hours of receipt of an order transmission. They pointed to the relatively low cost of operating an IBM 1001 data transmission terminal and a Bell System 401 dataphone.

The monthly rental for both devices was under $40. The supplier's representatives also stressed that the use of dataphone would eliminate paper work, reduce inventory, and avoid duplication of effort. See Exhibit 4 for a flow diagram showing the operations of the IBM 1001 data transmission system.

In response to the proposal, the director of purchasing argued that the use of dataphone by Philadelphia Pharmaceuticals would reduce the supplier's costs of doing business by simplifying his order processing procedures. This, the director held, should induce the supplier to offer to Philadelphia Pharmaceuticals an across-the-board price cut as an incentive to accept dataphone. When the supplier offered a general price reduction of 5 percent on all MRO items to be ordered by dataphone, the director of purchasing agreed to install the necessary equipment. On the basis of past business volume with the supplier, the director of purchasing estimated that this price reduction would save the company approximately $3,000 annually. Philadelphia Pharmaceuticals and the vendor determined the items to be put on dataphone and the information to be contained in the dataphone punched cards, such as material description, price, supplier stock number, Philadelphia Pharmaceuticals' accounting charge number, and other data relevant to the supplier's processing procedures. Philadelphia Pharmaceuticals made available to

Exhibit 4
EXCERPTS FROM "IBM APPLICATION BRIEF"
(on "IBM 1001 Data Transmission System for Industrial Purchasing at Beals, McCarthy & Rogers"*)

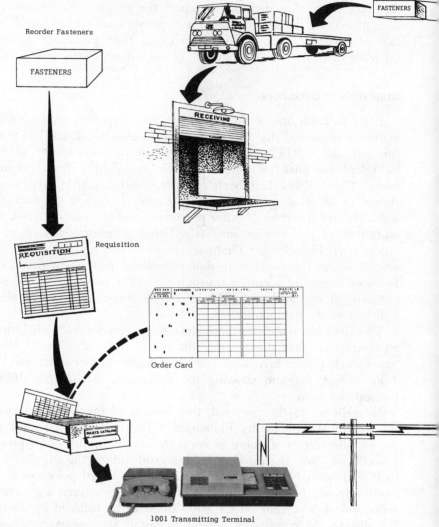

Reorder Fasteners

FASTENERS

Requisition

Order Card

1001 Transmitting Terminal

* Beals, McCarthy & Rogers is a large industrial supply firm in Buffalo, New York.

IBM 1001 DATA TRANSMISSION SYSTEM

The data transmission system consists of a receiving station (IBM 24 Card Punch or 26 Printing Card Punch) and any number of data transmitting terminals (1001). The receiving station is installed at Beals, and the data transmitting terminals, each containing a card reader and numerical keyboard, are installed on the customers' premises. Beals arranges for the installation

Exhibit 4 (*Continued*)

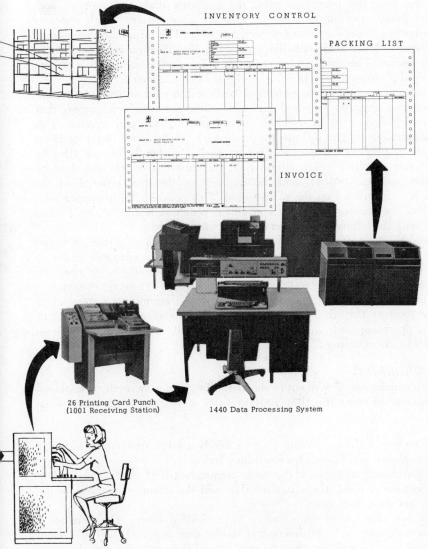

INVENTORY CONTROL

PACKING LIST

INVOICE

26 Printing Card Punch
(1001 Receiving Station)

1440 Data Processing System

Telephone Operator

of the transmitter and supplies the customers with prepunched cards coded with the identification information on items frequently or routinely ordered by the customer. The information on the card includes the item description, the account number, the unit price, the location of the part in Beals' warehouse, Beals' part number, and the customer's identification number.

The data transmitting terminal is connected to a telephone, and the receiving station is connected to Beals' switchboard. To transmit purchase order

Exhibit 4 (*Concluded*)

information over the telephone lines, the customer dials the supplier and, when the Beals' operator answers, he asks for an extension which connects the transmitting terminal to the receiving station. The customer then inserts a prepunched card coded with the exact item identification information into the card reader. The card reader transmits this information to Beals, where another card is automatically punched with the same information.

The customer now uses the numerical keyboard to send additional information, including quantity required and any other pertinent information that the customer desires to be printed on the packing list and invoice. This added information might include the customer's job or work order number. (The date is prepunched on the card at Beals.) Either before or after he transmits this purchase order information, the customer writes the date on which the part was ordered and the quantity of the item ordered on the convenient form printed on the master card. This provides the customer with a record of the transaction and a convenient purchase history which he can compare with the billing sheet when it arrives with the order.

An audible tone from the transmitting device signifies to the customer that the information has been received correctly. If the customer makes a mistake while operating the numerical keyboard, he can notify Beals' operator, or he can automatically reject the error card at the receiving station.

The customer, in taking advantage of this data transmitting system, automatically receives the advantages of reducing his inventory investment, optimizes his operating costs, reduces his clerical detail, and improves the level of service to his customers.

RAPID ORDERING

The accompanying flow diagram shows the fast and easy method employed by a customer in using the IBM 1001 to order a critically needed item from Beals.

1. The factory foreman, finding that he needs a large number of fasteners to complete a job, fills out his requisition form.
2. The purchasing agent pulls the Beals prepunched IBM card corresponding to the item in need. He writes the date and the quantity required on the card and then dials Beals.
3. Beals' operator connects the line to the receiving station. The purchasing agent transmits the item description on the card and adds any additional information. An audible signal informs him of the successful completion of the transmission.
4. The newly punched card is inserted in Beals' data processing system. The data processing equipment prepares order-filling papers, packing list invoice, and data for Beals' own inventory control.
5. The item is shipped to the customer by the fastest possible method.

the supplier information on past and projected usage of these items. The purchasing division obtained a verbal commitment from the supplier to make an all-out effort toward achieving delivery of all requirements ordered by dataphone within 24 to 48 hours of the order transmission.

Specific procedures were established for dataphone ordering; these covered such matters as the number and the content of the shipping slips to accompany each shipment and the monthly invoicing in the form of tally sheets. The vendor then supplied Philadelphia Pharmaceuticals with a deck of prepunched cards covering the agreed-upon items, and Philadelphia Pharmaceuticals began to place orders by dataphone.

The dataphone equipment was set up in the purchasing division next to the IBM 632 electronic typing calculator and was operated by the clerk-typist for the 632 system.

The basis for placing purchasing orders via dataphone consisted of the order documents prepared by the data processing division's IBM 1410 computer or by the IBM 632 typewriter calculator. Having determined that a purchase order could be transmitted by dataphone, the clerk-typist pulled from the supplier-prepared deck of punched cards, the card(s) corresponding to the specification(s) shown on the hard-copy purchase order or purchase requisition, dialed the telephone number of the supplier, asked for an extension connecting the transmitting terminal with the supplier's receiving station, and inserted into the cardreader of the terminal the selected card for data transmission. The clerk-typist then used the keyboard of the transmitting terminal to transmit variable purchase information contained on the hard-copy or requisition, such as order quantities, purchase order number, and work order number.

During 1965 the purchasing division extended the use of dataphone to five additional suppliers of nonproduction materials. Attempts by Philadelphia Pharmaceuticals to negotiate general price reductions as a condition of the firm's agreement to place orders by dataphone, however, had been unsuccessful in all but one case. Mr. Wilson commented:

One supplier offered a 10 percent across-the-board discount, which saves us about $5,000 per year; but the others told us that they already were making full use of electronic data processing and that any cost savings through computerized order processing and inventory control were reflected in their current prices.

There was a lack of uniformity among the vendors in the layout of the punched cards used. Consequently, none of these item cards could be used directly as input for Philadelphia Pharmaceuticals' computer system.

In January, 1966, Philadelphia Pharmaceuticals transmitted weekly approximately 100 line items via dataphone. Between 1,500 and 2,000 items were covered by the dataphone setup. Mr. Wilson estimated that between 50 percent and 60 percent of the different items ordered from the five suppliers was ordered by dataphone; he further estimated that approximately 60 percent of the suppliers' total dollar volume was Philadelphia Pharmaceuticals resulted from such orders.

Mr. Wilson noted that by January, 1966, all the items ordered by dataphone were covered by blanket purchase orders. He said:

Prior to dataphone our use of blanket purchase orders was confined to production materials. As we began to work with dataphone, we also began to set up this type of order for repetitive nonproduction materials. Today blanket purchase orders include most of the dataphone items. We have cut down on the total number of vendors of these nonproduction materials, as we were anxious to include as many items as possible under blanket order with few vendors. So I would say that the suppliers now on dataphone have picked up business due not to dataphone but to blanket purchase orders. I might also add that we have lost some of our flexibility in vendor selection since the adoption of dataphone.

Because of a large increase in the number of customers transmitting orders by dataphone, two of five suppliers found it necessary early in 1966 to allot a specific period of time to each customer during which orders could be transmitted. Thus, Philadelphia Pharmaceuticals could send orders only between 9 A.M. and 11 A.M. to one of the suppliers, and between 12 P.M. and 2 P.M. to the other.

Mr. Wilson's evaluation of dataphone

Mr. Wilson believed that aside from the initial 5 percent price cut negotiated, the use of dataphone was difficult to justify economically He said:

Dataphones are designed to transmit information with great speed and accuracy from one location to another. In themselves, that is all they do; instant and accurate transmission of data between distant points. I do not think that we have had any particular problem in the past on either count with the transmission of manually prepared purchase orders. As far as clerical cost savings are concerned, it is the vendor who benefits from dataphone; he gets the order in the form of punched cards, a method that eliminates a substantial number of clerical functions and provides for a great deal of administrative efficiency. As far as we are concerned, speed of order transmission, at least to local vendors, can be achieved in other ways if necessary. One supplier who heard that we were using dataphone came to us and expressed some fear that he might lose our business because of his inability to receive orders in the form of punched cards. I explained to him that by using dataphone we were adding just one extra step in our ordering procedure to provide the supplier with punched cards that he could feed into a data processing system. This moderate change came as a rather big surprise and relief to the supplier who had been convinced that the use of dataphone involved great systems improvements in our company. I told him that from an operating efficiency viewpoint it made no difference to us whether we sent orders by dataphone or by mail. The supplier proposed anyway to send a man each morning to pick up orders and to try to make delivery within 24 hours, and we told him that this would be fine with us. As it worked out, we are presently sending our orders by mail.

Mr. Wilson thought that the usefulness of dataphone was limited by the fact that the company's internal procurement cycle for nonproduction materials had not been fully automated. He said:

As long as our computer control system for nonproduction requirements involves hard-copy with punched cards, we are not really automated. And at the present time we need hard-copy output for the performance of various functions such as receiving and invoice validation. For example, we must prepare hard-copy purchase orders or some document that is tantamount to a written purchase order, so that the receiving department has a basis for properly receiving incoming shipments of materials. This, incidentally, is quite a curious thing that I have noticed in the sales presentations by companies pushing dataphone equipment. One of the big selling points invariably is the elimination of paper work. Well, it is true that when we use dataphone we eliminate the need to write out the purchase order for the vendor, but the receiving department still must write a complete receiving report for the accounts payable department. So what we are doing now on the IBM 632 typewriter is to write a complete set of purchase orders, destroy the original for the vendor if dataphone is used, and distribute the remaining copies to various departments, such as the receiving department. We are, in essence, writing the receiving report in advance and I believe that we do it quite efficiently. If we did not do it here in the purchasing division but went directly from a requisition to a dataphone punched card, the receiving department would have to create a receiving report manually. So, even if we were able to eliminate paper work in the purchasing division by use of dataphone, we would create some paper work elsewhere in the organization.

While Mr. Wilson found little justification for using dataphone on the basis of achieving reduction in paper work, clerical detail, lower inventory investment, or faster delivery, he thought that the device had some value in orientating the company's personnel as well as the vendors' toward modern data handling equipment and purchasing techniques. "I have serious doubts about any tangible dollar-and-cents operating benefits that we derive from dataphone under the present setup," said Mr. Wilson. He continued:

But this doesn't mean at all that I see no value in the dataphone concept. In fact, I believe that it is a fundamental step toward computer-to-computer communication. I believe in progressive purchasing, and I'm a strong advocate of making full use of electronic data processing in purchasing. I hope that within some years we will be able to achieve a computer-to-computer linkup with at least some of our major suppliers, particularly if industry can agree on a standard format for the transmission of data by dataphone. In this context, dataphone is valuable, but I am not sure that this is a sufficient reason to keep the equipment for the time being. Just the other day the manager of the nonproduction materials purchases told me that he thought a termination of dataphone would not affect the discounts originally received from two suppliers in conjunction with our use of the equipment.

MERCURY OIL COMPANY*

In the spring of 1966 Mr. Edward Exelbert, director of purchasing of the Mercury Oil Company, of San Francisco, California, was reviewing the progress his department had made since 1963 toward establishing what he termed a "worldwide procurement system" for the company's multinational oil producing, refining, and marketing operations. In 1963 the purchasing department, under the direction of Mr. Exelbert, had undertaken a comprehensive study of the procurement activities of Mercury's overseas operating units. In the course of this study, executives of the purchasing department had visited over 30 subsidiaries and affiliates in foreign countries for the purpose of examining and evaluating existing purchasing practices and procedures. These executives had also visited other major U.S. oil companies and several large manufacturing companies operating in international markets, to study their respective organizational and procedural arrangements for worldwide procurement.

The central recommendation emanating from this study had been the creation of a system by which the parent company purchasing department in San Francisco was to "preplan and coordinate the organization's purchasing activities throughout the world through issuance of basic procurement policies, development of a management-reporting system, establishment of commodity buying guides, development of joint procurement programs, and any other reasonable guidance initiated by the parent company purchasing department." The objective of such a procurement system was described as "providing the best total value to the entire Mercury group and thus making the maximum contribution to total corporate profits and earnings per share through worldwide purchasing." The question Mr. Exelbert posed to himself was whether this objective had been reasonably well accomplished between 1963 and 1966.

Company background

Mercury Oil Company was a large, U.S.-based corporation engaged primarily in the business of producing, transporting, refining, and marketing oil on a worldwide basis. In 1966 the company maintained wholly or partly owned subsidiaries and affiliates in over 100 foreign countries or territories. Consolidated revenue from sales and services was over $5 billion in 1965, with net income after taxes of over $300 million. In the period 1963–66, net income from overseas operations had averaged about 60 percent of total company net income. The company employed approximately 50,000 persons, of whom nearly 55 percent were foreign nationals attached to overseas operating units.

The domestic marketing of gasoline and other refined products was nationwide. U.S. and Canadian oil reserves were held in almost every oil-producing area. The company's domestic refineries, with a combined daily crude oil capacity of over 350,000 barrels, were located near the major producing or marketing centers. Refineries, storage, and tidewater terminals maintained in many states were connected with the company's principal oil fields by a large pipeline system. The company was also a large producer of natural gas. Major refinery sites were in New Jersey and California. As of 1965 the company operated in the United States approximately 8,000 oil wells, 900 gas wells, over 1,800 wholesale bulk plants, over 6,000 miles of pipelines for gathering crude oil and natural gas, over 1,300 miles of pipelines for distributing products, and approximately 14,000 retail outlets.

Mercury had entered into the field of petrochemicals in 1959. Three years later, sales of high purity olefins, aromatics, and terephthalic acid, as well as plastics, plastic resins, paint and chemical coatings, fertilizers, and other phosphate-related agricultural and industrial chemicals, accounted for over $200 million. Major domestic chemical facilities included 23 fertilizer plants, 11 chemical-coating plants, 2 petrochemical plants, 3 plastic plants, 2 phosphorus-related chemical plants, and 1 phosphate mining operation.

In 1965 Mercury's international subsidiaries and affiliates operated approximately 500 oil wells and 18 gas wells, 6 refineries (located in West Germany, Ireland, Holland, Sweden, Spain, and Venezuela), over 800 wholesale bulk plants, and approximately 13,000 retail outlets. The company owned 20 oceangoing tankers totaling close to 1 million dead weight tons. Major overseas chemical facilities, some of which were partly owned, included six chemical-coating plants, one fertilizer plant, two petrochemical plants, and two plastic plants. In addition, the company owned interests ranging from 5 percent to 85 percent in nine overseas refineries in Africa, the Near East, and the Far East. Mercury's share of crude oil capacity in these refineries was approximately 180,000 barrels per day.

Petroleum operations in the United States and Canada were carried out mainly by the Mercury Oil Company, the parent organization. Mercury International, a division, coordinated the petroleum operations of the company's operating units in Latin America, Europe, Africa, and Asia. Mercury Chemical, also a division, had worldwide responsibility for the company's chemical interests. (See Exhibits 1 and 2 for organization charts of the corporate organization and international operations.)

Mercury Oil Company had begun marketing operations abroad in the late 19th century. Commenting on the company's history of overseas interests and on the parent's financial policy with respect to its foreign subsidiaries and affiliates, one executive observed:

Because we evolved into an international organization, we have been able to avoid some of the organizational problems that other companies have faced in changing their orientation almost overnight from strictly domestic to a broader international outlook. . . . According to our concept of financial management, policy can be best coordinated by . . . Mercury with the broadest possible latitude for affiliates to exercise their judgment with respect to specific financial problems affecting their areas. However, we follow a practice of

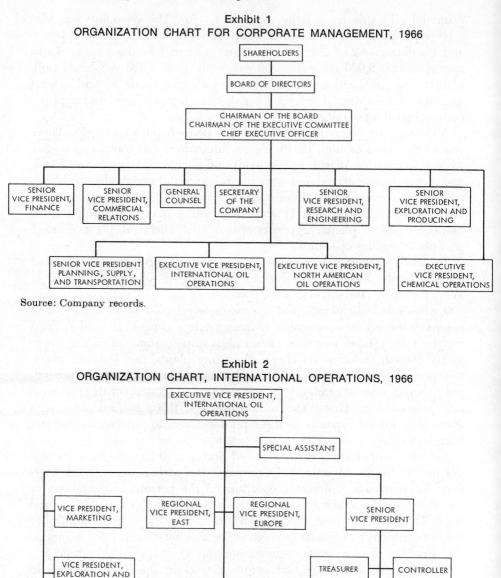

Exhibit 1
ORGANIZATION CHART FOR CORPORATE MANAGEMENT, 1966

Source: Company records.

Exhibit 2
ORGANIZATION CHART, INTERNATIONAL OPERATIONS, 1966

Source: Company records.

providing central assistance and coordination wherever this would be helpful to our affiliates.

Organization of the purchasing department in 1966

In the spring of 1966, the purchasing department of the Mercury Oil Company in San Francisco included, in addition to Mr. Exelbert, an assistant general manager, an assistant manager, two regional (domestic) managers, a manager for planning and analysis, a manager for foreign purchases, a manager for purchasing and traffic services, a materials-management coordinator,[1] and five commodity coordinators. Mr. Exelbert, who reported to the company's senior vice president for finance, was assisted by the assistant general manager and the assistant manager. The executives primarily concerned with international procurement were Mr. G. B. Snow, the manager of foreign purchases, who was directing the development of a worldwide procurement system; and Mr. R. R. Siegel, the commodity coordinator for exports, who was responsible for purchases of materials from U.S. sources of supply for export to Mercury's overseas subsidiaries and affiliates. (See Exhibit 3 for the organization chart of the purchasing department.)

Procurement activities

In 1962 Mercury spent over $250 million for the purchase of materials, equipment, parts, and supplies to support the company's petroleum and chemical operations throughout the world.[2] Exhibits 4 and 5 show breakdowns of these purchases by the firm's major business activities and major material categories. Overseas purchases of material for use by overseas subsidiaries and affiliates accounted for approximately 40 per-

---

[1] The position of materials-management coordinator was established in 1963 "to provide a focal point to coordinate materials studies and inventory control programs." Emphasizing that tied-up capital, storage, surplus, obsolescence, deterioration, insurance, and taxes would "equal 15 percent to 30 percent of the value of the inventory investment," the San Francisco purchasing department advised other Mercury purchasing units throughout the world that the materials-management section was "staffed to provide consulting and advisory assistance in all matters pertaining to materials and supplies inventories." These matters included warehousing, materials handling, record keeping, economic requisitioning, analysis of inventory values, development of inventory-elimination and inventory-reduction programs, control procedures, utilization and disposal of surpluses, commodity cataloging, and data processing of materials inventories. It was pointed out that "each affiliate purchasing office should be sufficiently aware of Mercury's materials-management group to be able to recognize this function as a purchasing service, which may be recommended to their management whenever a need arises for analysis of materials or inventory control problems."

[2] Not included were purchases of crude oil and petroleum products, insurance, utilities, land and buildings, services, art work, and layout space, none of which came within the scope of responsibility of the purchasing organization.

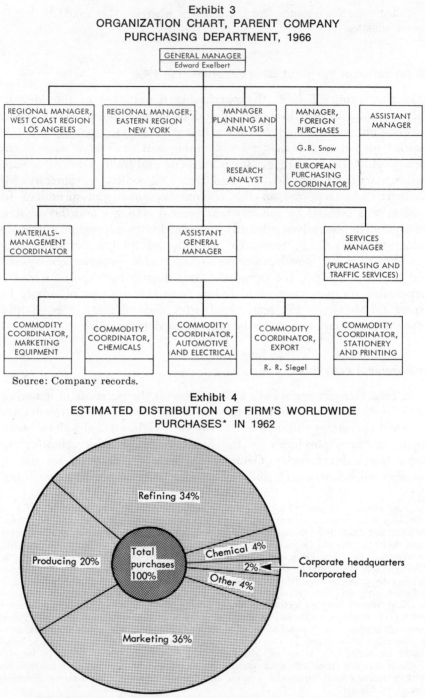

Exhibit 3
ORGANIZATION CHART, PARENT COMPANY
PURCHASING DEPARTMENT, 1966

GENERAL MANAGER
Edward Exelbert

REGIONAL MANAGER, WEST COAST REGION LOS ANGELES

REGIONAL MANAGER, EASTERN REGION NEW YORK

MANAGER PLANNING AND ANALYSIS

RESEARCH ANALYST

MANAGER, FOREIGN PURCHASES

G.B. Snow

EUROPEAN PURCHASING COORDINATOR

ASSISTANT MANAGER

MATERIALS-MANAGEMENT COORDINATOR

ASSISTANT GENERAL MANAGER

SERVICES MANAGER

(PURCHASING AND TRAFFIC SERVICES)

COMMODITY COORDINATOR, MARKETING EQUIPMENT

COMMODITY COORDINATOR, CHEMICALS

COMMODITY COORDINATOR, AUTOMOTIVE AND ELECTRICAL

COMMODITY COORDINATOR, EXPORT

R. R. Siegel

COMMODITY COORDINATOR, STATIONERY AND PRINTING

Source: Company records.

Exhibit 4
ESTIMATED DISTRIBUTION OF FIRM'S WORLDWIDE
PURCHASES* IN 1962

Refining 34%

Producing 20%

Total purchases 100%

Chemical 4%

2% — Corporate headquarters Incorporated

Other 4%

Marketing 36%

* Purchases of crude oil and petroleum products, insurance, utilities, land and buildings, art work, and layout space are excluded.

Source: Company records.

Exhibit 5
DISTRIBUTION OF FIRM'S PURCHASES BY
MAJOR MATERIAL CATEGORIES IN 1962

	Percent of total dollars spent
Chemicals	
Processing	
Additive	
Drilling muds and chemicals	
Fats	
	13.3%
Containers	
New drums	
Reconditioned cans, cartons	
	14.6%
Electrical equipment	1.3
Instruments and parts	1.1
Pumps and compressors	0.7
Service stations	9.6
Tanks	5.5
Tools	0.6
Tubulars and pipe	3.5
Valves and fittings	1.1
Vehicles	4.5
	27.9%
Total	55.8%

Source: Company records.

cent of the company's total dollar procurement volume. Overseas purchases for use by U.S. operating units were insignificant in relation to the total dollar procurement volume. A breakdown of the company's overseas purchases by major geographical areas, cross-classified by major business activities, is given in Exhibit 6.

Findings and recommendations of the 1963 procurement study

On the basis of questionnaires distributed in 1963 by the San Francisco purchasing department, the group conducting the study of overseas purchasing activities estimated that 86 percent of all purchases by the company's overseas subsidiaries and affiliates were made "without coordinated preplanning, pooling of purchasing power, or exchanges of purchasing knowledge and techniques." That is, the study group found that only in about 14 percent of all purchases by the company's foreign subsidiaries and affiliates was there any coordination among the purchasing departments involved. This finding led the study group to formulate the following three research questions: (1) Is one affiliate spending money for items that might be available from surplus at another affiliate? (2) Does each affiliate purchase material that represents the best total value to the Mercury organization? (3) How much of the company's

Exhibit 6

DISTRIBUTION OF ESTIMATED OVERSEAS PURCHASES BY REGION IN 1962
(total overseas purchases = 100%)

Region	Market-ing	Refining	Pro-ducing	Chem-ical	Shipping	Total
Inner Europe	7.97%	15.01%	4.57%	–	–	27.55%
Australia, New Zealand, and the Philippines	12.05	8.58	–	–	–	20.63
North and Southeast Europe.	11.42	5.87	1.55	1.05%	0.74%	20.63
Japan, Hong Kong, Taiwan, and South Korea	5.37	6.80	–	–	–	12.17
Latin America.	3.03	1.05	5.31	–	–	9.39
East and Southern Africa . . .	1.79	1.48	0.43	–	–	3.70
Mediterranean West Africa	4.57	–	0.99	–	–	5.56
South and Southeast Asia	0.37	–	–	–	–	0.37
	46.57%	38.79%	12.85%	1.05%	0.74%	100.00%

Source: Company records.

money might be saved or how much additional profit might be generated by a continuing purchasing program with reasonable guidance by the San Francisco purchasing department? Mr. Exelbert commented, "We wanted to learn through the study how the organization's purchasing actually operated both within the United States and overseas. We wanted to isolate the major universal problems confronting the company's purchasing function."

The study group engaged in a series of field trips to both domestic and foreign operating units to analyze and evaluate their purchasing practices and procedures. Subsequently, the group prepared for top management a report in which five problem areas were identified: (1) ineffective purchasing planning, (2) inconsistent purchasing policies, (3) weak purchasing procedures, (4) insufficient purchasing communications among affiliates, and (5) inadequate purchasing statistics. On the several points the study group made the following summary comments:

1. *Ineffective purchasing planning.* Purchasing now lacks knowledge of significant forthcoming events and therefore does not adequately plan even within most affiliates. Overall planning of the type needed to generate savings through joint procurement is virtually nonexistent.
2. *Inconsistent purchasing policies.* Individual affiliates have their own purchasing policies which are not coordinated and at times are inconsistent. The last policy guide was issued in 1955 and does not reflect corporate developments over the past eight years.

3. *Weak purchasing procedures.* As an example, competitive quotations
   are a basic tool of good purchasing. Yet there are no guidelines in existence
   which request buyers to obtain competitive quotations on a consistent
   basis.
4. *Insufficient purchasing communications among affiliates.* Little guidance
   has been given affiliates by the parent company's purchasing department,
   and there has been little interchange of ideas between affiliates relative
   to best known purchasing practices.
5. *Inadequate purchasing statistics.* It is not enough to know just the total
   value of purchases. Instead one must know how much has been spent
   for specific commodities. This knowledge is needed at various levels in
   order to concentrate purchasing manpower in those areas with the maximum cash-conservation potential.

In discussing these findings, Mr. Snow observed that the Mercury
subsidiaries and affiliates overseas traditionally had been "completely
autonomous entities" and that much of what the staff conducting the
procurement study regarded as shortcomings had to be seen against
"Mercury's long-standing management philosophy of maximum decentralization." Mr. Snow then went on to say:

This company has a long history of making the foreign affiliates self-contained and of giving each operating facility a high degree of autonomy. Basically, this history is still with us. But, as new managerial and administrative
concepts have emerged and as the need to give each affiliate a national
identity has somewhat receded with increasing internationalization of business
in recent years, a fairly strong tendency toward integrating a company's worldwide interests has emerged. This is the case with Mercury.

Fifteen years ago it would have been absolutely impossible to develop
a worldwide procurement system guided by a central purchasing department.
I have been with Mercury for 40 years and have had several occasions in
the past to suggest bringing together the purchasing departments of our affiliates. The answer was always, "it couldn't be done." Of course, another major
reason for the traditional absence of any sort of coordination and direction
of our global purchasing activities is the fact that the potential profit contribution of this function was simply not recognized.

We are fortunate in that Mr. Exelbert, who took over a general manager
in 1962, was basically marketing oriented and had little exposure to procurement. He questioned long-established policies and procedures that people
with a long working experience found difficult to question. Exelbert was
just not going to be satisfied by maintaining the status quo.

But the greatest single obstacle was the autonomy held by each foreign
affiliate, an autonomy which still exists today. Except for requisitions that
our overseas affiliates placed with the San Francisco purchasing department
for materials and equipment to be bought from U.S. sources of supply, purchasing was done largely within national boundaries. For instance, prior to 1963
the purchasing departments of our North African affiliates would not have

thought of placing requisitions with the purchasing departments of our German or British affiliates.

In fact, as a rule the purchasing people in one country did not even know the names of their counterparts in another country. There was generally no communication among purchasing departments beyond national borders. Even within a country, communication among purchasing units was poor. Although some significant changes in the company's overall management philosophy have occurred since 1963, changes which enabled us to make much progress toward establishing a worldwide procurement system, the basic autonomy with which each affiliate in operating remains unchanged.

In its report to top management the study group emphasized four "key themes": (1) effective decentralization by better preplanning and improved communications; (2) management by "exception," concentrating on high-dollar-value transactions; (3) concentration on how purchase dollars are spent for high-dollar-value commodities; and (4) maximization of purchasing's cash-conservation potential by management's aggressively motivating and supporting its purchasing function at all organization levels.

The study group made the following nine recommendations:

RECOMMENDATIONS

1. Redefine Mercury's purchasing objectives.
2. Restructure the organization of the parent company purchasing department.
3. Define the role of the purchasing organization.
4. Improve communications between the parent company purchasing department and those personnel concerned with purchasing in overseas affiliates.
5. Preplan purchasing activities including development of joint procurement programs.
6. Promote maximum desirable degree of interation between purchasing and other materials-management functions, including the development of an improved requisitioning system using economic purchase order formulas.
7. Promote the development of procedure and commodity buying guides.
8. Exchange commodity purchasing data.
9. Minimize clerical work.

The study group elaborated on each of these recommendations as follows:

1. Redefine Mercury's purchasing objectives. A total of nine broad purchasing objectives were suggested by the study group:

a. To purchase within the best total value concept all of the materials, equipment, and supplies to meet operating requirements.
b. To play a key role in Mercury's Materials-Management Program.
c. To develop on a worldwide basis sufficient and reliable sources of supply to assure satisfaction of present and future needs.
d. To negotiate the most advantageous types of purchasing arrangements (including joint procurement), emphasizing the best total value concept.

e. To develop new or substitute materials consistent with good quality and best total value.

f. To relieve operating personnel of the time-consuming activities attendant to purchasing.

g. To demonstrate that purchasing has a cash conservation function.

h. To promote and develop good vendor relations.

i. To train and maintain a specialized staff to achieve these objectives economically.

2. *Restructure the organization of the parent company purchasing department.* This recommendation was aimed primarily at the company's European purchasing staff group (EPSG) attached to the company's Dutch affiliate in Amsterdam, Holland. This advisory group, consisting at one time of 10 purchasing officers and supporting staff, had been established in the early 50s in order to utilize sales receipts in nondollar currencies for the local purchasing of materials, equipment, parts, and supplies. These purchases had been made for Mercury's Dutch affiliates or for affiliates in certain non-European countries other than the United States. The study concluded that effective use should be made of the purchasing staff group as a European procurement research unit and as a coordinating office for Mercury affiliates in Europe, the Middle East, the Far East, and Africa. The group, to be reduced in size, was not to perform actual purchasing functions but was to concentrate exclusively on rendering "staff assistance to the affiliates in developing and using sources of supply on a truly worldwide basis."

The recommendation was also aimed at creating the position of "manager of foreign purchases" with full authority and responsibility for the development of a worldwide procurement system. Finally, the recommended organizational change provided that all activities within the parent company purchasing department relative to the procurement of materials from U.S. sources of supply for overseas use be concentrated under the responsibility of an export coordinator.

3. *Define the sole of the purchasing organization.* The definition of the purchasing function offered by the study group consisted of three parts:

a. Procure necessary and suitable materials, supplies, and equipment through use of the most advanced purchasing techniques.

b. Assist in negotiations of contracts to assure that the most suitable purchasing methods are used in obtaining the necessary materials included in such contracts.

c. Utilize or dispose of surplus, obsolete, and scrap materials, supplies, and equipment.

This definition of the role of the purchasing organization was supplemented by the proposal that the parent company purchasing department would "provide advice and counsel and would recommend use of the best known methods to help each affiliate purchasing department to fulfill its role."

4. *Improve communications between parent company purchasing department and those personnel concerned with purchasing in overseas affiliates.* In order to improve communications between the San Francisco purchasing department and the purchasing organizations of the overseas affiliates, the study recommended (*a*) the development of procedure and commodity buying guides by the parent company purchasing department to "promote the use of the most effective purchasing practices on a worldwide basis," (*b*) the development of regular visitation programs between the parent company purchasing department and the overseas affiliates as well as among the overseas affiliates to "establish personal contact and gain a proper understanding of common purchasing problems as related to local operating requirements," and (*c*) the participation of affiliate purchasing executives in management operating and planning meetings. It was believed that the last recommendation would provide purchasing personnel with "advanced knowledge of operating requirements" and allow the purchasing organization to "fully contribute to the company's total cash conservation effort."

5. *Preplan purchasing activities including development of joint procurement programs.* The study group recommended that the San Francisco purchasing department obtain thorough knowledge of the affiliates' budgets well in advance of each planning period in order to develop procurement plans. It was proposed that such plans form the basis for an organizationwide procurement plan, with the objective of achieving the most effective worldwide purchasing of equipment and materials. The study group emphasized that such a corporate procurement plan was to be "reviewed with the operating affiliates affected, obtaining their approval and cooperation"; and that portions of the plan were to be delegated "to appropriate affiliate buying personnel for action." In further commenting on the need for a corporatewide procurement plan the study group observed that the absence of such a plan "permits uneconomical practices to be unnoticed" and prevents the use of the joint procurement principle whereby the requirements for several units are combined to generate significant dollar savings." The study group noted that the affiliates possessed "adequate planning data in prepared or available form for all functions served by purchasing to provide a firm basis for effective planning."

6. *Promote maximum desirable degree of interaction between purchasing and other materials-management functions, including the development of an improved economic requisitioning system.* The focal point of this recommendation was the creation and use of an "improved economic requisitioning system which demonstrates to management the need to consider all elements of cost related to purchasing transactions." The study group emphasized that "purchasing costs, both material and

administrative, are virtually uncontrollable without an economic requisitioning system." Concluding that "local determination of total costs of acquisition and possession is not desirable without guidance from a group trained in this specialty and possessing overall knowledge of the subject," the study group made three specific recommendations:

1. Distribute to all key requisitioning affiliates copies of the economic ordering guide prepared by the parent company purchasing department. This guide illustrates points to consider—eliminating, where practical, the need to warehouse materials; reducing cost of possessing materials; reducing cost of acquiring materials; maintaining necessary inventories at minimum cost levels.

2. Require the parent company purchasing department materials-management group to conduct on-site economic surveys in cooperation with major requisitioning affiliates to assess:

a. Local availability of key commodities.

b. Total cost of possession.

c. Total cost of acquisition.

d. Local government, public, or trade relations aspects.

3. Encourage affiliate managements to be guided in making important purchasing decisions by the following manuals, issued by the parent company purchasing department. These encompass the basic elements of an economic requisitioning system:

a. Economic ordering guide.

b. Foreign purchasing procedure guide.

c. Internal purchasing procedure guide.

d. Worldwide comodity buying guide.

Acceptance of these recommendations was considered important in order to "achieve the total cash-conservation benefits potentially available to the organization." "The absence of a standard of performance for economic requisitioning," it was noted, "allows uneconomic practices to go unnoticed." The recommended guidance from the parent company purchasing office was believed to be essential "if the affiliate purchasing organizations were to achieve maximum reductions in the costs of materials and inventory investment."

Finally, the members of the study group regarded as desirable "a high degree of interaction between purchasing and other elements of materials management." They wished, for instance, to "avoid expenditures of new capital by transfers of surplus articles from one location to another" and to "cooperatively exploit value analysis and standardization techniques to lower materials costs."

7. *Promote the development of procedure and commodity buying guides.* The development of a "foreign procurement buying guide" and a "worldwide commodity buying guide" was regarded by the study group as a critical element in any attempt to give the firm's procurement function an international orientation and to ensure that major procurement decisions be made on the basis of multinational rather than national

alternatives. Thus, the study group recommended that the parent company purchasing department "be responsible for issuing and maintaining guides, which will delineate procedures recommended to overseas affiliates in (a) establishing the economic implications of ordering requirements from foreign versus domestic locations, (b) requisitioning requirements from foreign locations, (c) fulfilling documentation requirements, and (d) expediting activities." Such a guide, it was argued, would "provide overseas affiliates with a single reference for handling transactions with other affiliates of the parent company and create standardized worldwide procedural practices resulting in lowering the total cost of purchases."

The development of a worldwide commodity buying guide was seen as a "cooperative effort involving the parent company purchasing department, the European purchasing staff group (EPSG), and affiliates. The parent company purchasing department was to be responsible for the issuance and maintenance of this guide. It was suggested that the department "build into the guide maximum flexibility consistent with sound purchasing practices, and maintain it on a current basis through perpetual market research and exchanges of information between affiliates and the department."

In addition to the development of a foreign procurement procedure guide and a commodity buying guide, the study also recommended that each affiliate create "internal purchasing procedure guides" under the guidance of the parent company purchasing department. It was noted that certain affiliates were operating without "any formal purchasing policy of their own," whereas in other cases some existing policies were inconsistent from one affiliate to another. The group concluded that the issuance and maintenance of procurement guides by the parent company purchasing department for the affiliates would not only "promote the use of improved purchasing practices on a worldwide basis," but also "provide an improved method of communication between the affiliates and the parent company purchasing department and give the affiliate managements a standard of performance for evaluating the effectiveness of purchasing practices."

8. *Exchange commodity purchasing data.* The report by the purchasing study group recommended that the parent company purchasing department be required to (a) "conduct a perpetual program of price comparison inquiries as a cooperative effort with EPSG and the affiliates, (b) limit price comparison inquiries to known key high-annual-value items, (c) submit resultant commodity reports to the affiliates, and (d) explore the possibilities for cost reduction through joint procurement agreements promoted by the department or through price reductions negotiated by the affiliates based on the knowledge of what other affiliates are paying." Without a formal data exchange program, it was argued, "no overall commodity knowledge is achievable."

9. *Minimize clerical work.* The focal point of this recommendation was the development of a "blanket purchase" system for the overseas affiliates under the guidance of the parent company purchasing department. The study group emphasized that "very little use has been made of the blanket order principle overseas although this system provided several benefits to key locations within the U.S.A. and in at least two overseas affiliates."

In demonstrating the cash-conservation potential of the purchasing function in overseas affiliates, the study group stressed that according to estimates made in 1962 "each dollar of savings in purchasing equals $15 of new sales." (See Exhibit 7.)

Exhibit 7
CASH-CONSERVATION POTENTIAL OF PURCHASING ON
PERCENTAGE DISTRIBUTION OF REVENUE
(Mercury International, 1962)

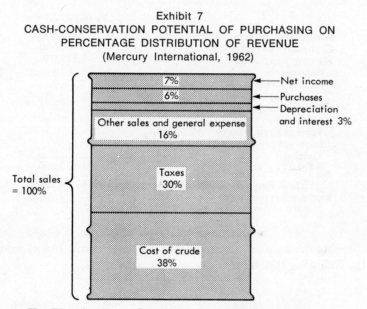

Key Thought: $1 saved in purchasing = $15 of new sales
Source: Company records.

In urging acceptance of the study's conclusions and recommendations, the group summarized the expected benefits of the recommendations as follows:

More effective utilization and control of the purchasing dollars, resulting in:
1. Conservation of working capital through:
   a. Utilizing surplus material.
   b. Lowering material costs and freight charges.
   c. Releasing valuable warehouse space.
2. Reduced construction, maintenance, and operating expenditures through:
   a. Lowering material costs and freight charges.
   b. Standardizing as much as possible.

     c. Providing effective communications.
     d. Facilitating logical field purchasing activities.
     e. Assuring availability of material.
     f. Expediting delivery.
3. Improved vendor relations.

    Based on the best judgment available, the study group projected savings of $1.24 million for the first year following the implementation

Exhibit 8
ESTIMATE OF DOLLAR SAVINGS TO BE REALIZED FOLLOWING IMPLEMENTATION OF 1962 RECOMMENDATIONS*

Estimated savings

Pooling of purchasing activities	$ 25,000
Commodity buying guides	80,000
Efficient purchasing	1,135,000
Planning	
Formal purchasing agreements	
Commodity analysis	
Competitive quotations	
Negotiation	
Value analysis	
Improved procedures	
Training	
Total	$1,240,000

* These estimates were based on informed guesses made by headquarters purchasing executives.
Source: Company records.

    of the recommendations. (See Exhibit 8.) The study report concluded with the following timetable:

Action Plan 1963

Action	*Completion date*
1. Approve organizational changes	September 1
2. Approve objectives and basic overseas concept	October 15
3. Present worldwide program to executive committee	December 1
4. Issue basic policies	December 15
5. Coordination visits to regional service companies	January, 1964
6. Purchasing seminar in Europe	January, 1964
7. Issue competitive quotation guide	February, 1964
8. Issue worldwide commodity buying guide	April, 1964

Implementation of study recommendations as of spring 1966

    The findings and recommendations of the study were approved by the company's executive committee in December, 1963. Messrs. Exelbert and Snow then undertood a series of visits with the managing directors and chief procurement officers of foreign affiliates to explain and discuss the recommendations, solicit the affiliates' advice and criticism, work out changes, and seek the affiliates' approval and cooperation in implementing the recommendations. Mr. Snow commented:

Shortly before the study was conducted, Mercury had set up so-called regional service companies at various strategic points in world markets, including London, Amsterdam, and Lausanne. These regional service companies offered management services to our overseas affiliates. They were in effect consulting organizations helping our affiliates to solve problems when they were asked by the affiliates to do so. These service companies had been accepted by our autonomy-conscious affiliates and had created the necessary climate for us to get the kind of cooperation from the affiliates that we needed if the recommendations were to be implemented at all.

Implementing the recommendations required a certain change in the affiliates' operating philosophy and a reconciliation between each affiliate's desire for maximum possible autonomy and the need for an effective coordinating function by the parent company. It was perfectly plain that unless we sought and obtained the affiliates' active participation and cooperation, achieving our objectives would be difficult. In our meetings we spent a great deal of time discussing the study, answering questions, and making concessions on specific items and on language, without changing the underlying organizational and administrative concept. Each affiliate was extremely sensitive to matters affecting its autonomy. The first joint meeting of the purchasing directors of the major affiliates was like a conference of foreign ministers concerned first and foremost with the interests of their countries rather than like a conference of executives working for the same organization.

Mr. Exelbert believed that the second major step toward gaining acceptance of the idea of a centrally coordinated worldwide purchasing system by the affiliate purchasing executives was the initiation of intensive and continuing in-house purchasing seminars. Recognizing that the imbuing of Mercury overseas affiliate executives—nearly all of whom were foreign nationals—with new organizational concepts and management techniques required a continuing educational effort, Mr. Exelbert decided to hold purchasing training programs for an indefinite length of time once the framework and content of such programs were determined.

In preparation for a planned series of international purchasing seminars, several purchasing managers of the parent company worked during an extended period with Mercury's educational director to develop and program a wide variety of purchasing topics. Seminars were then held in 1963, 1964, and 1965 in Paris, Lausanne, and London. These several seminars, conducted primarily by executives of the parent company purchasing department, were attended by purchasing executives from Australia, Spain, Holland, Germany, Japan, the Philippines, South Africa, Switzerland, and the United Kingdom. (Agendas for these seminars are shown in Exhibit 9.) In addition, over 20 affiliate purchasing managers were invited on an individual basis in 1964 and 1965 to spend several weeks at the parent company purchasing department in San

Exhibit 9

AGENDA FOR WORLDWIDE PURCHASING SEMINARS 1963, 1964, 1965

I. Amsterdam, Holland: February 11–13, 1963

1. Background of Worldwide Purchasing Study
2. Conferees and Agenda
3. Reports
   Greetings by G. B. Snow, Manager of Foreign Purchases, Mercury Oil Company
   Presentation of Purchasing Study
   Responsibilities of Manager of Foreign Purchases
   Presentation of Traffic Concepts
   Auditing Viewpoint—Internal Control
   Purchasing within Mercury Oil, N.V.
   Functions of Mercury European Purchasing Staff Group
   Functions of the Corporate Systems Department
   Briefing on Scandinavian Purchasing Survey
   Purchasing within Mercury Oil, A.G., Switzerland
   Purchasing within Mercury Oil, Spain
   Purchasing within Mercury Oil, Spain—Madrid Refinery
   Purchasing within Mercury Oil, A.G., Frankfurt
   Purchasing within Mercury Oil Company, Ltd., London
4. Discussion Topics
   a. Purchasing Guides
      Development of a Single Purchasing Guide for Use by User and Supply Affiliates
      Development of a Price Comparison Guide—To Minimize and/or Equalize Prices Paid for Major Commodities
   b. Competitive Quotations
   c. Elimination of Useless Paperwork
   d. Preplanning Based on Budgets
   e. Expansion of Cooperative International Joint Procurement Program
   f. Topics To Be Developed by Participants for Future Discussion
      Trade Relations
      Internal Control
      Traffic
5. Key Questions and Responses
6. Summary by Manager of Foreign Purchases, G. B. Snow

II. Lausanne, Switzerland: January 28–31, 1964

January 28

9:00 a.m.	Welcoming by G. B. Snow, Manager of Foreign Purchases
9:30–10 a.m.	Opening Remarks, President of Inner European Services Company
10–11:15 a.m.	Overseas Program for Purchasing Improvement
11:15 a.m.-12 noon	Preplanning—Purchasing Activities
2–2:45 p.m.	"What the Common Market Means to Purchasing"
3–3:45 p.m.	Purchasing Progress—Mercury Oil Holland
3:45–4:30 p.m.	Purchasing Progress—Mercury Oil Spain
4:30–5:15 p.m.	Purchasing Progress—Mercury Oil, Ltd.
5:15 p.m.	Summing-Up, G. B. Snow

January 29

9–9:20 a.m.	"How Purchasing Can Help Manufacturing Reduce Costs"
9:20–10:10 a.m.	Purchasing Progress—Mercury Oil Australia Pty., Ltd.
10:10–10:30 a.m.	"How Purchasing Can Help Marketing Reduce Costs"
10:45–11:05 a.m.	"How Purchasing Can Help Producing Reduce Costs" (with special emphasis on the off-shore drilling operations in the North Sea)
11:05–11:45 a.m.	Purchasing Progress—Mercury Oil A.G.
11:45 a.m.-12:15 p.m.	Service Station Equipment Manual
2–2:45 p.m.	Foreign Procurement Guide
3–3:30 p.m.	Purchasing Progress—Mercury Oil, N.V.

Exhibit 9 *(Continued)*

3:30–4:15 p.m. . . . . Purchasing Progress: Marketing–Mercury Oil Southern Africa
Pty., Ltd.; Manufacturing–Mercury Refining Southern
Africa Pty., Ltd.
4:15–4:40 p.m. . . . . Purchasing Progress–Mercury Tokyo
4:40–5:05 p.m. . . . . Purchasing Progress–Mercury Oil Germany A.G.
5:05–5:30 p.m. . . . . Purchasing Progress–Mercury Oil Switzerland A.G.
5:30 p.m. . . . . Summing-Up

January 30
9–10 a.m. . . . . Highlights of Scandinavian Joint-Procurement Program
10–10:45 a.m.. . . . . What Is Materials Management?
10:45–11:45 a.m.. . . . . . . Competitive Quotations
11:45 a.m.–12:30 p.m.. . . . Internal Control
2–2:45 p.m. . . . . Exchange Commodity Data
3–5 p.m. . . . . Value Analysis–Standardization
Film Demonstrating Principles
Actual Case Histories by Each of the Participants

January 31
9–10 a.m. . . . . Worldwide Buying Guides
10–10:30 a.m.. . . . . Utilization of Surplus Materials
10:45–11:45 a.m.. . . . . . . Economic Ordering Guide
11:45 a.m.–12:30 p.m.. . . . Minimize Clerical Work
2–2:45 p.m. . . . . 1964 Objectives
3:00 p.m. . . . . Closing Remarks

III. London, England: October 4–8, 1965

Subject
Welcoming
Mercury's Global Approach to Purchasing–Purchasing–Materials Management
Opportunities in Purchasing
Purchasing Progress Reports
The Companies Represented at the Seminar
Preplanning
The Art of Listening
Value Analysis
A Controller's Viewpoint of the Purchasing Function
Mid-Week Welcome on Behalf of Mercury Oil Co., Ltd.
Computer/Data Processing Program
Impact of Data Processing on Purchasing
Foreign Procurement Manual
Open Discussion
Art of Negotiation
Cost Price Analysis
Care and Handling of Buyer/Salesman
The Service Aspects of Purchasing
A Look at the Mercury World Served by Purchasing
Comparison of European/U.K. and U.S. Business Methods
Measuring Purchasing Performance
1966 Objectives
Closing

Francisco and at the office of the European purchasing staff group in
order to become acquainted with the executive personnel and to gain
familiarity with the major operations performed.

Mr. Exelbert planned to hold further seminars during 1966 in Australia, Germany, Scandinavia, South Africa, England, Turkey, Libya, Nigeria. These subsequent seminars were to be conducted either by affiliate purchasing managers who had previously participated in seminars or by personnel from the European purchasing staff group in Amsterdam. The format and content of the seminars, however, were developed by the parent company purchasing department.

The need for executive development in domestic plants also had been recognized. The parent company purchasing department had begun to conduct periodic seminars for purchasing personnel of U.S. plants in San Francisco.

Considered to be two key elements in the development of a centrally coordinated worldwide procurement system were a so-called foreign procurement guide and a worldwide buying guide, (mentioned earlier in the recommendations of the study group, and described in more detail below). The parent company purchasing department had commenced work on both guides early in 1964. By the spring of 1966, after lengthy consultations with the overseas affiliates, the purchasing staff had completed and issued a foreign procurement guide. The buyers' guide had also been started, but company officials estimated that this document was still several years away from completion.

A. *The foreign procurement guide.* The foreign procurement guide, issued to each overseas affiliate, was a comprehensive document of several hundred pages with exhibits covering such subjects as Mercury's purchasing objectives,[3] division and coordination of procurement responsibilities; definition of Mercury's purchasing terms; material coding framework; general communication procedures; requisitioning procedures; selection of supply sources; preparation of purchase orders and purchase change orders; expediting, shipping, and payment procedures; handling of claims; disposing of surplus; keeping of purchasing records and files; and evaluating purchasing performance. (See Exhibit 10 for the table of contents of the document.) Attached to the guide were samples of each purchasing form, use of which was recommended by the parent company purchasing department.

The purpose of the procurement guide, according to management officials, was "to implement worldwide standardization of purchasing practices and the utilization of modern purchasing techniques," allowing "a requisitioner or a buyer in any part of the world to have the purchasing procedure answers at his fingertips." Although the guide was concerned primarily with policies and procedures to control the procurement of material by the overseas affiliates from outside the respective countries in which they were located, a number of sections of the guide were addressed to such general purchasing problems as buyer and vendor

---

[3] The purchasing objectives set forth in the guide were identical with those recommended in the 1963 Procurement Study previously outlined.

Exhibit 10
FOREIGN PROCUREMENT GUIDE: TABLE OF CONTENTS

Purchasing Objectives: Purchasing Objectives Guide.

Division of Responsibilities: Coordinating Offices and Approved Supply Affiliates; Materials Management; Shipping.

Definitions: Definitions of Purchasing—Materials Management Terms.

Communications: General Correspondence (including Cables); Worldwide Buying Guide; Transmittal of Requisitions; Authorized Signatures; Identification of Materials and Supplies by Cataloging; Purchasing's Relationships with Other Departments.

Requisitioning Procedures: Foreign Purchase Requisition Forms—Described; Foreign Purchase Requisition Forms—Preparation; Requisition Symbols (Order Number Prefixes); How Much to Order—Use of Economic Ordering Guide; Cabled Requisitions; Distribution of Requisitions; Revisions to Requisitions; Publications and Subscriptions; Requests for Catalogs, Parts Lists, Manuals, Etc.; Requisitioning Services of Foreign Vendors' Employees.

Selection of Supply Sources and Vendors: Requests for Quotations and/or Proforma Invoices for Licensing or Budget Purposes; Competitive Quotations; Foreign Vendor Contacts.

Purchase Orders and Change Orders: Preparation of purchase Orders; Worksaver Forms and Checklists; Requisition Instruction Sheets; General and Special Requirements of Ultimate Consignee; Direct Purchase Order Placement on Foreign Vendors; Materials Inspection; Change Orders or Correction Notices.

Status Control: Expediting Procedure; Advice of Delivery.

Shipping Procedures: Shipping Insurance; Return of Materials.

Payment Procedures: Invoices, Commissions, and Handling Charges; Invoice Verification; Payment and Intercompany Reimbursement for Materials and Supplies Expenditures; Fees For Purchasing and Handling Services.

Claims: Claims against Vendors and Transportation Companies.

Surplus: Disposal of Surplus Materials and Supplies.

Records and Files: Purchasing Records and Files.

Evaluation Factors: Evaluation of Purchasing Performance; Purchasing's Profit Improvement Plan.

Forms: Purchasing and Shipping Forms.

Alphabetical Index: Alphabetical Index of Topics Covered.

evaluation, internal purchasing administration, and cost reduction programs. The preface of the foreign procurement guide read as follows:

The purpose of this guide is to provide a single reference which all purchasing personnel of the Mercury group companies can use as a guide to the best currently known purchasing techniques. It is designed as a tool for motivating good purchasing performance. It covers the purchasing functions which relate to acquisition of materials, supplies, and equipment which are to be exported or imported. In addition, it assists in establishing standards of performance which can be used to measure purchasing's performance.

It behooves the user affiliate to initiate great care in placing a requisition on the proper supply affiliate.[4] In the cases of competitive items or where there are questions of supply source, requisitions should be routed to San Francisco or EPSG, as outlined in this guide.

The magnitude of our purchasing function can best be illustrated by the fact that the purchasing departments of affiliates are responsible currently for the careful and proper expenditure annually of approximately $500 million. This figure covers the acquiring of materials and services, nearly one half of which applies to overseas activities.

It is therefore imperative that each purchaser make use of the best knowledge and tools which become available to him and perform his assignments carefully, intelligently, and diligently to the best interest of the Mercury group of companies.

It is our belief that generally material may be purchased more economically and efficiently within the countries of the origin of the material by affiliates in those countries. Accordingly, it is general policy to have affiliates requiring imported materials to so channel their requirements. This concept makes the user affiliate and the supply affiliate partners in good purchasing.

Good communications between user and supply affiliates are of paramount importance and are the keys which provide the best purchasing services to operating units. We feel confident, therefore, that effective use of this guide will provide an improvement in our overall purchasing effectiveness. We urge all purchasing people to take advantage of the effort expended on their behalf and make use of this foreign procurement guide.

The following Mercury affiliates were designated as "supply affiliates" able to handle the procurement and shipment of materials requisitioned by "user affiliates" (see footnote 4).

Material origin	Supply affiliate
U.S., Canada, Spain, Western Hemisphere	Mercury Oil Company Purchasing Department San Francisco
United Kingdom	Mercury Oil Company, Ltd. London, England
Germany	Mercury Oil, A.G. Frankfurt, Germany
Holland and Belgium	Mercury Oil, N.V. Amsterdam, Holland
Denmark, Norway, and Sweden	Mercury Oil Company Goteborg, Sweden
Switzerland	Mercury Oil, A.G. Lausanne, Switzerland
Japan	Mercury Oil Tokyo, Japan
Hong Kong	Mercury Oil Hong Kong, Ltd. Hong Kong
Australia	Mercury Oil Australia Pty., Ltd. Sydney, Australia

---

[4] "User affiliate" was defined as any affiliate "requiring material for its operation." "Supply affiliate" was defined as "any Mercury group office, which by location within a country or manufacture or production can supply material requirements."

As of the spring of 1966, the purchasing department of each overseas affiliate determined its choice of sources of supply without coordination. In other words, although the parent company purchasing department strongly encouraged and facilitated foreign procurement, no affiliate was under any obligation to make use of vendors outside its national market. However, if the executives of the purchasing department of an affiliate decided to purchase material from outside the country in which the affiliate was located, they were requested, but not required, to adhere to the directives contained in the foreign procurement guide. A section called "Basic responsibilities of coordinating offices and approved supply affiliates" read in part as follows:

A.   There are two coordinating offices for purchasing matters, namely, San Francisco and EPSG.

B.   1.   San Francisco guides, counsels, and coordinates purchases for all affiliates worldwide and is the primary coordinator for all affiliates.

      2.   San Francisco also functions as a supply affiliate and purchases U.S. and Canadian origin materials for user affiliates.

      3.   San Francisco administers the operations of EPSG.

C.   1.   At the direction of San Francisco, the European purchasing staff group performs an advisory and coordinating function for all affiliates in the countries within the regions specified elsewhere.

      2.   EPSG does not perform the actual purchasing function as European purchases are made by the supply affiliate located in the country in which purchase is to be effected.

      3.   The countries serviced by EPSG are described in this guide as being in the "EPSG service area." EPSG services both supply and user affiliates in this area.

D.   Approved supply affiliates are those affiliates who by location within a country of manufacture or production can supply material requirements.

E.   Requisitions received by San Francisco from user affiliates when procurement is to be finalized in Europe will be sent directly to the appropriate European supply affiliate, and the supply affiliate selected will be responsible for negotiating the purchase order. If there is no approved supply affiliate in the particular country, San Francisco will draw the order on the vendor and send to EPSG for transmittal to vendor.

F.   When requisitions are transferred to EPSG by San Francisco for source development, they will be sent under cover of a requisition transmittal letter.

G.   EPSG and European supply affiliates should forward to San Francisco, under cover of a requisition transmittal letter, requisitions covering materials to be procured in the U.S. or Canada for other than their own operation.

H.   Supply affiliates (including San Francisco) and EPSG may therefore receive requisitions from the following sources:

      1.   Direct from user affiliates.

      2.   From user affiliates via San Francisco.

      3.   From user affiliates via EPSG.

I.   Supply affiliates, San Francisco, and EPSG, receiving a requisition are expected to:

      1.   Develop proper or appropriate sources of supply—the first step under

this action involves determining whether the material is available from company surplus.

2. Issue purchase order on vendor or transmit to a supply affiliate as appropriate for placement of such order.

3. Include on purchase orders clear and sufficient instructions and all pertinent information needed for the particular requisition series involved.

4. Obtain early acknowledgment of order receipt by vendor.

5. Distribute purchase order copies (and inspection certificates if called for) in accordance with requisition instruction sheet for the requisition series involved.

6. Diligently follow-up for delivery to destination on the date specified by user affiliate; forward by air to user affiliate one copy of either vendor's invoice *as soon as received* so that user affiliate will be aware of material readiness, or other *advice of delivery readiness.*

7. Keep appropriate shipping group or freight forwarder and user affiliate closely advised of delivery situation.

8. Arrange for inspection if called for on requisition and forward necessary copies of purchase order to the inspection agency.

9. Receive and distribute invoices and packing lists as called for on the requisition instruction sheet for the requisition series involved.

10. Properly check, approve, and, in accordance with instructions from the appropriate controller's departments, arrange for payment of invoices and charging to user's appropriate account.

11. Correspond with user affiliate on any routine matter concerning any requisition received for action, until any problems relating to the requisition are resolved.

12. Keep a user affiliate regularly advised on status of any group of orders for a special project for which the user, EPSG, or San Francisco requests a progress (status) report.

13. Cooperate with the shipping group or freight forwarder to the maximum extent possible to enable arrival in the user's area as near as possible to the date requested.

14. Notify user affiliate of the earliest shipping date if the arrival date requested by it cannot be met.

15. Forward to the vendor through EPSG any order drawn by San Francisco on a Spanish vendor. (EPSG shall in this case be responsible for giving the vendor invoicing instructions, selecting the freight forwarder, and giving him documentation instructions.)

Speaking of the foreign procurement guide, Mr. Exelbert said:

We can't dictate these or any other terms to any affiliate, and we must never give the impression that we consider our affiliates to be merely branches. But we can point to the fact that the guide was clearly understood and accepted by each affiliate management when we presented it in various stages during our overseas seminars and in sessions with affiliate managers.

If a user affiliate goes outside the country for the purchase of material without going through a supply affiliate, the purchasing job is not only infinitely more difficult, but it's also significantly less effective because the user affiliate is generally unfamiliar with the foreign market. Furthermore, such approach might also be detrimental to the supply affiliate and the organization as a whole if a direct contact by the user affiliate with a foreign vendor upsets certain relationships existing between the vendor and the supply affiliate.

When this happens, the supply affiliate will invariably complain. This not only is the way we learn about direct contacts by an affiliate with a foreign supplier, but it also gives us a good argument for insisting that adherence to the guide is essential. Sometime user affiliates bypass a supply affiliate in order to save the commission which the supply affiliate charges for purchasing services performed for the user affiliate.[5] If this is the case, the parent company tax department, which has prepared guidelines in this area, will point out that what may be good for any one affiliate may not be good for the organization as a whole. Since the tax department reports to the same senior vice president for finance to whom we report, we have good cooperation.

Reflecting the potential difficulties seen by the parent company purchasing department in direct negotiations by an affiliate with a foreign vendor, the foreign procurement guide contained under the heading "Foreign Vendor Contacts" the following passage:

In the Preface to this guide is the statement: "It is our belief that generally material may be purchased more economically and efficiently within the countries of the origin of the material by affiliates in those countries. Accordingly, it is general policy to have affiliates requiring imported materials to so channel their requirements. This concept makes the user affiliate and the supply affiliate partners in good purchasing."

Most other international oil companies subscribe to this philosophy as it results in several advantages to both the user and supply affiliates.

Supply affiliates may make contractual arrangements and agreements in their country with reputable suppliers on whom the user affiliates may place directly their orders for specified materials. User affiliates placing such authorized orders should take care to issue required copies of these orders to the supply affiliate, which is accountable for payment and expediting of the order. The responsibility for supplier reliability rests with the supply affiliate. This activity is covered in more detail in the section entitled "Direct Purchase Order Placement on Foreign Vendors"[6] of this guide.

A user affiliate requiring catalogs, literature, material, or supplies should utilize the supply affiliate in the country of origin as the logical place to go for such a requirement. User affiliates should bear in mind the fact that supply affiliates treat a user's requirement as their own.

---

[5] The foreign procurement guide contained under the heading "Fees for Purchasing and Handling Services" the following statement:

It is recognized that purchasing and shipping services performed by one affiliate for another incur costs within the supply affiliate. For this reason, it is generally customary of the supply affiliate to charge the user affiliate the cost of procurement. The calculation of fees are charged to user affiliates to recover costs attendant to the purchasing, shipping, and accounts payable functions of supply affiliates should be in accordance with the most recently issued guide on this subject.

[6] This section is described below.

Supply affiliates are very familiar with legal, customs, and financial regulations in their countries and can be counted upon to protect the user's interests.

Invariably difficulties have been encountered when the above procedures were not followed. Some of the difficulties experienced in the past were as follows: material was ordered by unauthorized personnel; material was ordered from other than the most economical source of supply; adjustments were extremely difficult when requirements were incorrectly supplied; complaints were incorrectly registered and could have resulted in legal action; documentation requirements were not fulfilled; orders were not afforded needed or proper expediting effort; currency and payment problems were almost universal.

User affiliates will recognize that they would not like another affiliate to order material from within their country without their assistance or knowledge. Failure to follow these principles therefore may obviate an opportunity to promote sale of products.

Executives of the parent company purchasing department recognized that user affiliates "have the right to the knowledge that their requirements will be provided at the lowest cost consistent with proper quality and delivery." The purchasing department staff at headquarters, therefore, urged the purchasing personnel of each supply affiliate in a foreign market to seek competitive quotations as a matter of policy. In its foreign procurement guide, the parent company purchasing department formulated "guidelines to be used to define when and when not to obtain quotations for specific requirements by user affiliates." These guidelines are shown in Exhibit 11.

Exhibit 11
FOREIGN PROCUREMENT GUIDE:
SOLICITATION OF COMPETITIVE VENDOR QUOTATIONS

A. Competitive quotations, from experience in all areas, have been found to yield the greatest cost savings, provided judgment is used in bidding practices. This section of the foreign procurement guide suggests the guidelines to be used to determine when and when not to obtain quotations for specific user requirements.

B. "Competitive bidding should generally be practiced wherever it is practical and economically beneficial, regardless of the monetary consideration involved," is a philosophy to which most would subscribe. It is more practical, however, to recognize that quotations solicited on low-value items may not yield savings proportionate with the amount expended in time or material) to obtain such quotations. It is therefore recommended that supply affiliates establish a minimum bid value below which quotations are not mandatory. This figure, which may vary from affiliate to affiliate, is called "minimum bid value" hereafter in this section.

C. 1. For economical buying, a minimum of three competitive written quotations should normally be solicited for all purchase requisitions, renewal or new contracts, spot blanket purchase orders, and purchase agreements, whenever the value of the order will exceed the "minimum

Exhibit 11 (Continued)

bid value" when it is believed that there is an opportunity for significant savings.

2. Emergency purchases are justified when failure to obtain quickly an item could result in life or property being endangered, or cause the company an unnecessary expense or loss of revenue. In such instances, quotations need not be obtained unless in the judgment of the buyer they may be obtained on a verbal basis without any undue loss of time.

D. Processing requests for quotations:
1. Utilize the principles contained in the "Guide to Obtaining Quotations" (see paragraph "L" below).
2. Request quotations only from reputable suppliers with whom you would be willing to place the order.
3. Search for new sources of supply.

E. Handling suppliers' quotations:
1. Date or time stamp all quotations immediately upon receipt.
2. Prepare a competitive bid comparison and post results from quotations. Quotations received after the deadline date are to be recorded but annotated to show "Late." Late quotations, i.e., received after final date, shall not normally be considered unless significantly low. In such cases, it is advisable to allow other bidders an opportunity to requote.

F. Analyzing suppliers' quotations:
1. Is delivery specified timely? If not, does the difference in net delivered price warrant communicating with user for an extension of the date [on which] material is required at destination?
2. Consider the quality of the material offered by the vendors. Give attention to items offered as "equal to" the material described on the requisition. If supply affiliate is not familiar with the quality offered and if price quoted on an "equal to" article is attractive, communicate with the inquiring office for agreement on substitution, either on the requirement involved or on future requirements.
3. Study the effects on delivered cost as a result of trade discounts, cash discounts, freight terms, and other cost factors.
4. Keep confidential to company parties involved all prices and specific information received from the vendor.

G. Selection of vendor:
1. Balance all cost factors. Recognize here that low operating cost is achieved by best total value and give proper consideration to quality and service, as well as price. Consult user for advice on technical requirements and specifications.
2. With delivery and quality being acceptable, the vendor whose delivered quotation is the lowest should be awarded the order. If among the acceptable bids, other than the low cost quotation is being considered, approval from user affiliate should be obtained prior to placement.
3. Retain the original of the bid comparison as part of the regular purchase order file.

H. Supply affiliates *may* desire to code purchase orders for audit or control purposes when the particular requirement is over the "minimum bid value"

Exhibit 11 (*Continued*)

and no quotation has been obtained. In such cases it is suggested codes be shown on the order (in a place selected by the supply affiliate) substantially as follows:

BP   —Best Price
SS   —Sole Source
E   —Emergency
DEL—Delivery
DB   —Distribution of Business
MO   —Policy or Management Option
RPS —Reliability and Past Service
CON—Contract Commitment Letter, Blanket Order
COR—Confirming Order—Source Selected by Requisitioner
COP —Source Preselected by Purchasing (a result of previous quotations)

I.   Quotations should generally be obtained in the following situations:

1.   Items Not Previously Purchased—This should not be interpreted so specifically as to include items falling into natural groupings where we have ample experience. For example, a new screw size is not a new item to a buyer of hardware, nor is a new stationery item necessarily a new item to a stationery buyer.

2.   Items To Be Specially Fabricated to a Design—In general, this might include signs, light poles, machine parts, and complete devices where more than one vendor is competent to produce the item.

3.   Items for Which the Price Varies from Period to Period and between Vendors—There is a broad category of materials and parts where vendor pricing is unstable because of market or competitive conditions. Inedible animal oils are a good example of this category in that their prices vary from day to day and from vendor to vendor. It should be general practice to take advantage of these variations through the uniform procedure of obtaining multiple quotations prior to commitment.

4.   Items for Which the Requirement is Sufficient to Excite Special Price or Service Concessions Not Ordinarily Given—In such cases, we should seek such price advantage through the technique of requesting multiple quotations.

5.   Items on Which Competitive Quotation Should Be Obtained Periodically—On items where the solicitation of multiple requests for quotations on every purchase is not warranted (for example, automotive spare parts), it should be regular practice to make periodic reviews to insure complete familiarity with current market conditions.

J.   In many cases the use of multiple quotations may be unproductive or impractical. Examples of such cases may be found in the following categories:

1.   Low-Dollar-Value Transactions Involving Items of a Standard Nature for Which Published Price Lists Exist and Are Available from Several Sources—This type of item is characterized as the so-called catalog item where the transaction is of small dollar value. Its price is usually determined by broader forces of competition than created by

Exhibit 11 (*Continued*)

any single request for quotation. Prices are published and adhered to by reliable vendors and are frequently identical between all such vendors. In these cases competitive quotations may be used periodically as a tool, but placing low-value orders with vendors of known reliability and integrity without requesting competitive quotations is the general practice.

2. Items Whose Prices are Determined by Broad Competition and Where It Is Customary Industry Practice to Price Deliveries "at the Time of Shipment."

3. Items Specified in Such a Manner That Only One Source is Available—The specification of any item in such a way as to limit the purchase to a single source seriously limits a supply affiliate's ability to negotiate the most advantageous price. Example: A pump specified and labeled as "Do Not Substitute." Supply affiliates are urged to carefully evaluate such requests and to develop and suggest potential alternates to the user whenever there is a distinct price or quality advantage to be gained through use of an alternate.

4. Items Where the Vendor Is Specified by the User Affiliate as the Only Suitable Source—As in the case of a tightly written item specification, such a practice definitely limits the effectiveness of negotiation by the supply affiliate. A buyer is obtained to question such requisitions and is responsible for ascertaining that requirements so specified constitute "the best buy."

5. Items Being Reordered in a Reasonable Period after an Original Order Is Placed Based on Obtaining Competitive Quotations—Having placed an order for a given item on the basis of competition, it should not be mandatory to repeat the process of obtaining quotations for each subsequent purchase in a stable market. Buyer's judgment should prevail in the determination of when bids should be obtained again. Normally, such items should be resolicited on a competitive quotation basis at least quarterly.

6. Items Being Reordered Where the Initial Order Involved Tooling or Other Fixed Start-up Costs—Having established a given vendor as the logical source for a given part and having underwritten initial tooling or other start-up costs, solicitation of multiple quotations for subsequent orders is usually unproductive. The supply affiliate is expected, however, to continue to negotiate the best possible price on subsequent purchases or formal contractual arrangements. Additionally, the supply affiliate should give continuous consideration to the advantages and disadvantages of establishing alternate sources or transferring any owned tooling as additional requirements or contracts develop.

7. Items with Insufficient Lead Time—Supply affiliates are expected to advise user affiliates of the excessive costs incurred by failure to allow sufficient lead time. Where purchases of this type can be placed with vendors of known reliability at prices believed to be competitive and where the probable savings from multiple quotes or other approved practices seem small compared to the cost of delays, such orders may

Exhibit 11 (*Continued*)

be placed without competitive quotations. The use of telephone quotations, however, should be considered particularly when substantial sums of money are involved.

8. Items of Such Low Cost as to Make Potential Savings out of Proportion with the Cost of Processing Quotations—As recognized in paragraph "C" above, it is not recommended that supply affiliates obtain competitive quotations for purchases under the "minimum bid value." In some instances, however, the supply affiliate's judgment and knowledge of market conditions must be the determining factor in deciding whether or not to obtain competitive quotations.

9. Items of a Type Where Alternate Vendors Are Available but Where One Vendor Is Obviously Superior—The typical example of this situation is the case of repair of a proprietary item. Usually the repair of a proprietary item is best placed with the original manufacturer. In other instances where a vendor has established a superior record for performance and is known to be fair and reasonable in his pricing, it can be completely justified to place the business with this vendor without obtaining competitive quotations.

10. Item Where Favorable Warehousing and Handling Arrangements Have Been Established—This instance is best illustrated by some of the stockless purchasing arrangements negotiated by operating units as part of an overall cost reduction program. Such arrangements are usually made on the basis of indefinite time periods and a change in program or vendor would require a considerable amount of analysis and study.

11. Services Agreements Where Favorable Pricing Arrangements Exist—This instance is illustrated by the various valve-reconditioning programs, replacement pump-parts program, tube-bundle repair, etc. Once again such arrangements are usually entered into with a particular vendor on a reasonable long-term basis because of the circumstances involved.

K. Virtually every requisition has a potential for improved order placement. Observation of the following guide points should aid supply affiliate in obtaining quotations:

1. Surplus stock—Alertness to utilize existing surplus is necessary. Use of surplus liquidates frozen assets and forestalls the expenditure of new funds. Company surplus can often be the most *profitable* source of supply.

2. Substitute usage of surplus—Do not hesitate to suggest to user the importance of utilizing surplus through substitution. For example, use of surplus galvanized pipe for black pipe.

3. New source of supply—Endeavors should be made to test at least one new vendor against each requisition of considerable value.

4. Best net delivered price—Look for the best net delivered price. Have vendor state actual or estimated freight charges on quotations to guard against hidden costs.

5. Query handling cost—Query also the fairness of vendor's packing, handling, and minimum value order charges.

Exhibit 11 (*Concluded*)

6. Solicit vendor suggestions—for methods of lowering costs; lower priced equivalents; better terms; lower cost shipping methods, etc.

7. Be alert for quantity discounts and term discounts—Caution should be exerted to avoid increasing warehouse stocks.

8. Spare parts from distributors—Obtain quotations for spare parts from the prime manufacturer of the equipment, from distributors (if available), and *when feasible,* from reputable fabricators.
   Note: Substantial savings can sometimes be achieved by utilizing reputable fabricators of spare parts. Manufacturer's drawings should not be utilized for this purpose, however, without the written permission of the manufacturer.
   Example: In some areas fabricators will physically examine major repair parts, prepare drawings, and submit quotations on the cost of fabricating.

9. Spare parts, which may be purchased by the equipment manufacturer, should be critically studied for possible placement of order with prime manufacturer.
   Example: bearings, gaskets, carburetors, motors, pumps, etc.

10. Purchase "Delivered Ex-Stock"—Develop possible deliveries from vendor's stock "as-and-when required" on minimum notice to reduce user's inventory investment.

11. Purchase in reconditioned drums other than new drums when feasible and permissible.

12. Schedule periodic deliveries of large quantities of bulk products for resultant reduction of immediate cash layout and inventory investment.

13. Substitute lower specification material for savings after user approval. Review each requisition as a potential for possible savings through the effectiveness of the supply affiliate's buying skill.

14. "Equal to"—When a requisition specifies a trade or brand name, add to the quotation request the term "or equal." This then enables comparison of the cost of the brand product requisitioned against the "or equal" cost which may be furnished by a vendor. If the "or equal" cost is lower, this information should be passed on to the user before the final order is placed.

15. Die or pattern costs—When such costs are involved, such as in the fabrication of signs or castings, require that these costs be quoted separately from the cost of the item being made to the specification. This then enables proration of the cost over each item purchased and makes it much simpler to compare accurately quoted prices as well as to change vendors if a more competitive source develops at a later date.

Although the foreign procurement guide specified that foreign buying by any known user affiliate should, as a matter of policy, be done through supply affiliates located in the foreign market under consideration, Mercury's purchasing executives believed this policy should be flexibly interpreted. The foreign procurement guide therefore contained the following guidelines for the placement of purchasing orders by a user affiliate *directly* on a foreign vendor:

To expedite movement of materials and supplies to various users, a supply affiliate may elect to negotiate contractual arrangements with selected reputable vendors within its country with whom user affiliates can place direct orders for specified materials.

Under this procedure the supply affiliate, which receives a copy of the order bearing an authorized signature, is responsible for expediting and shipping the order and for payment of the vendor's invoice. User affiliates utilizing the direct order placement procedure are obligated to follow the regulations established by the supply affiliate, which set up the particular vendor as capable of handling direct orders.

Supply affiliates should determine material and/or equipment suitable for inclusion in the direct ordering program; solicit from reputable vendors competitive quotations, on the designated material or equipment; select vendor based on price, delivery, service, etc.; place a blanket order on the vendor, specifying (a) materials involved, (b) the Mercury group companies which will utilize the arrangement, (c) prices, delivery terms, payment terms, and delivery time from receipt of release order, (d) standing instructions for packing, shipping, and invoicing—instructions which will meet the specific needs of the users involved, (e) the person within the supply affiliate with whom all questions should be raised for clarification.

Dependent on location, notify the San Francisco purchasing department (or European purchasing staff group for affiliates in the EPSG service area) of direct ordering arrangements by submitting a draft World-Wide Buyer's Guide Card for issuance by the New York purchasing department.[7]

User affiliates should review World-Wide Buyer's Guide Cards to determine which items may be procured by them under this program, prepare purchase orders as required in accordance with the cards for direct submission to vendor with a copy to the appropriate supply affiliate, limit use of direct ordering methods to those arrangements specified in the World-Wide Buyer's Guide, and limit all correspondence concerning the order to the supply affiliate. Under no circumstances should user correspond directly with the vendor after placement of the order.

User and supply affiliates are cautioned to research thoroughly the capabilities of vendors selected for this program to ascertain if they will be capable of handling direct orders.

Cabled orders on vendors selected for this program should be confirmed immediately with a copy of the order to the supply affiliate.

A sample format of a direct purchase order is available. This has been designed specifically to meet U.S. requirements and may therefore vary for other supply affiliates. A sample format of a draft blanket order is also available.

Mr. Snow emphasized that although the foreign procurement guide contained comprehensive and detailed instructions not only for each affiliate's foreign purchasing activities but also for many of its general

---

[7] Details of the World-Wide Buyer's Guide are presented below.

purchasing procedures and internal purchasing operations, adherence to the guide by the affiliates was strictly voluntary. He said:

Each member of Mercury's worldwide network of affiliates is autonomous, and original requisitions for foreign buying must come from the affiliates. None of the affiliates is under any obligation to buy outside its national borders. Similarly, if a supply affiliate receives a requisition from a user affiliate in a different country, no attempt is made to justify the requisition because of each affiliate's autonomy. The same concept of autonomy applies to the purchasing practices, methods, and techniques, such as using economic ordering quantities or establishing profit improvement plans, which we recommend for adoption to our affiliates overseas. We aim to achieve a worldwide standardization of purchasing practices and the utilization of modern purchasing techniques by each affiliate, but we can only suggest and recommend. Basically, we function as a service organization.

Since the San Francisco purchasing department had no formal means of monitoring the procurement operations of the foreign affiliates, feedback on whether the affiliates had adopted any of the purchasing procedures and techniques detailed in the guide was generally not available, except on a random basis through personal visits and informal observations. Similarly, the department had no systematically collected information available as to the extent to which overseas affiliates had begun to utilize international sources of supply since the 1963 study. Mercury purchasing executives in San Francisco believed that the volume of orders placed by foreign affiliates on the parent company purchasing department had grown. According to these executives, however, foreign affiliates had always placed orders with U.S. suppliers via the parent company purchasing department.

B. *The World-Wide Buying Guide.* The stated purpose of the World-Wide Buying Guide was "to provide an improved means of communication between the parent company purchasing department supply affiliates and user affiliates and to establish a single reference for purchasing knowledge." San Francisco purchasing executives believed that the guide would (1) enable user affiliates to "buy their requirements in the best possible manner on the best total value basis," and (2) give user affiliates "a direct channel to enable requisitioning from the proper supply affiliates and, in some selected cases, place orders directly on specified foreign vendors with whom contractual arrangements have been made."

The World-Wide Buying Guide was being developed in the form of a loose-leaf book containing cards arranged alphabetically by material categories. (See Exhibit 12 for a card sample.) Each card covered a repetitively purchased item and not only gave specific information as to the best international source of supply known to the parent company purchasing department, but also listed recommended alternate supply sources. This information generally included prices, terms of payment,

Exhibit 12
SAMPLE OF WORLD-WIDE BUYING CARD

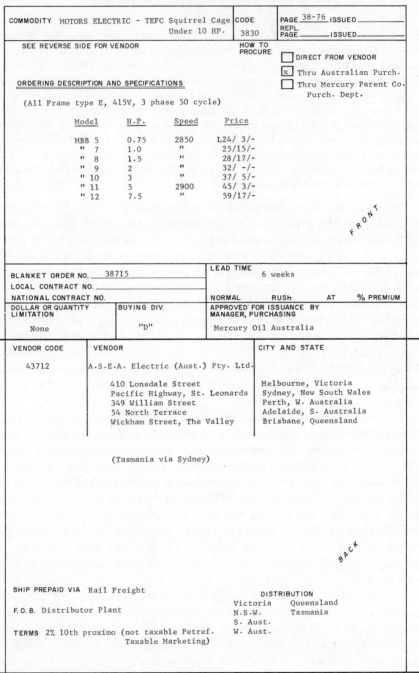

COMMODITY. MOTORS ELECTRIC - TEFC Squirrel Cage Under 10 HP.	CODE 3830	PAGE 38-76 ISSUED REPL. PAGE ____ ISSUED ____

SEE REVERSE SIDE FOR VENDOR

HOW TO PROCURE

☐ DIRECT FROM VENDOR
☒ Thru Australian Purch.
☐ Thru Mercury Parent Co. Purch. Dept.

ORDERING DESCRIPTION AND SPECIFICATIONS

(All Frame type E, 415V, 3 phase 50 cycle)

Model	H.P.	Speed	Price
MBB 5	0.75	2850	L24/ 3/-
" 7	1.0	"	25/15/-
" 8	1.5	"	28/17/-
" 9	2	"	32/ -/-
" 10	3	"	37/ 5/-
" 11	5	2900	45/ 3/-
" 12	7.5	"	59/17/-

FRONT

BLANKET ORDER NO. 38715	LEAD TIME 6 weeks
LOCAL CONTRACT NO.	
NATIONAL CONTRACT NO.	NORMAL RUSh AT % PREMIUM

DOLLAR OR QUANTITY LIMITATION	BUYING DIV.	APPROVED FOR ISSUANCE BY MANAGER, PURCHASING
None	"D"	Mercury Oil Australia

VENDOR CODE	VENDOR	CITY AND STATE
43712	A.S.E.A. Electric (Aust.) Pty. Ltd.	
	410 Lonsdale Street	Melbourne, Victoria
	Pacific Highway, St. Leonards	Sydney, New South Wales
	349 William Street	Perth, W. Australia
	54 North Terrace	Adelaide, S. Australia
	Wickham Street, The Valley	Brisbane, Queensland

(Tasmania via Sydney)

BACK

SHIP PREPAID VIA Rail Freight

F.O.B. Distributor Plant

TERMS 2% 10th proximo (not taxable Petref. Taxable Marketing)

DISTRIBUTION

Victoria	Queensland
N.S.W.	Tasmania
S. Aust.	
W. Aust.	

Source: Company records.

lead times, ordering procedure, specifications, blanket order or contract number, shipping instructions, and other pertinent items.

When sufficient material was organized to warrant its general distribution, a copy of the buying guide was issued to each requisitioning point throughout the Mercury organization. Each card was updated by the parent company purchasing department every three months, and new cards were added. As of spring of 1966, cards had been issued for such items as gasoline pumps, additives, catalysts, clutches, compressors, couplings, various electric parts, drilling and production equipment, gasoline engines, legends, and signs. Mr. Snow commented:

Although we are making progress, my guess would be that we have covered less than one fifth of all items that ultimately will be covered by the buying guide. Each item really means a complete survey of European, Japanese, American, and Eastern markets. Before we issue a buying card, we must find the best supplier and negotiate a contract either directly or through an appropriate supply affiliate. We have a long way to go before the guide will be anywhere near completion.

But despite the magnitude of the job, we believe it is worth it. Certainly the success of the guide is apparent from the fact that after more than one year of operation not one better deal on a standard item has been reported by an affiliate anywhere in the world.

Of course we welcome and solicit suggestions from all affiliates on better or more economical sources of supply. We would immediately incorporate any new and better sources into the buying guide.

The company's foreign procurement guide specified that the new parent company purchasing department "will (a) issue buying guide cards, covering items for which firm commitments have been made in San Francisco or by the supply affiliates, and (b) research and evaluate within 30 days all communications received from user or supply affiliate purchasing managers proposing changes to the existing buying guide cards." According to the guide, "supply affiliates should (a) assist the San Francisco purchasing department in establishing those sources of supply capable of providing the best total values to the user affiliates. Supply affiliates in the Eastern Hemisphere should route this information through EPSG in Amsterdam. Supply affiliates elsewhere should send information directly to San Francisco purchasing department; (b) furnish commodities to user affiliates in the manner prescribed in the buying guide and the foreign procurement guide; (c) develop new and better sources of supply within their countries and communicate such developments to offices outlined above." Finally, the guide provided that "user affiliate purchasing managers should (a) purchase imported items as prescribed in the appropriate buying guide cards, (b) check arrangements specified in buying guide cards against possible local arrangements and immediately advise San Francisco (or EPSG in the case of affiliates in Europe) of sources of supply, price structure, and/or procurement methods which are believed to be capable of providing better total value to the user affiliate concerned."

Executives of the parent company purchasing department stated that as a matter of policy the overseas affiliates were not compelled to use the sources of supply recommended by the buying guide. They emphasized, however, that if the department had worked out arrangements with a given vendor on the basis of Mercury's global requirements for a purchase item at favorable laid-down prices, the overseas affiliates were expected to take advantage of such arrangements unless valid reasons for national preference existed. Mr. Exelbert commented:

We may have to use a little persuasion at times, but there are procurement situations where joint purchasing is in the best interest of the group and where we all have to look to Mecca, irrespective of the autonomy which the foreign affiliates otherwise maintain. Platinum is a case in point; prior to the development of the World-Wide Buying Guide most of our affiliates used to pay over $170 per ounce. When supply was short, our affiliates were outbidding each other. After we had pooled our requirements and coordinated our purchases by negotiating a contract to benefit the organization as a whole, we paid less than $95 per ounce. In this type of situation we cannot leave the affiliates much choice in their source selection, but we certainly had no problem at all to convince the various foreign purchasing people involved about the soundess of taking a coordinated approach to purchasing materials of significant value.

We don't want to fool around with the nickel and dime stuff, and we must never create the impression that we treat our affiliates as if they were branches. We must not give the impression that we issue edicts in San Francisco, but we want to pull together and coordinate in a sensible way those 20 percent of all purchased items that account for 80 percent of the dollar spent. Yet decisions as to what to pull back to coordinated buying and what to leave to the affiliates are extremely sensitive and difficult to make. I think our balancing of worldwide contracts with local buying, a balancing which raises all the fundamental conflicts involved in coordinated decision making versus the idea of decentralized profit centers, will work as long as we can show that we are able to contribute substantially to the affiliates' profits.

Our buying guide is a critical element in our efforts to build a truly worldwide procurement system, but I think that it will still take many years before we achieve full administrative integration of our global purchasing operations. I think that the integrative tendencies will become stronger as new management concepts and techniques emerge and as we are able to put these concepts and techniques across to our overseas affiliates.

Foreign buying activities of Mercury's U.S. divisions and subsidiaries

While corporate management had given strong endorsement to the parent company purchasing department's efforts to internationalize the purchasing operations of the company's overseas affiliates, they had not generally encouraged foreign buying by the domestic operating units and affiliates. Mr. Exelbert, however, stated that if needed materials were unavailable within the domestic market, if the lead times of domestic vendors were unacceptable, or if unusually large price differentials between U.S. and foreign suppliers existed, management would not hesitate to suspend the company's "buy American" philosophy. He commented:

We could not justify to our stockholders paying substantially more for domestic materials. If the utilization of foreign vendors becomes necessary, we bring it to the attention of the corporate executive committee and get a decision from them. We should not and we do not shut our eyes to foreign materials. After all, organizations cannot, as a matter of policy, make a major portion of their purchases outside the United States. We cannot import a great deal of materials, parts, and supplies. There is, as you know, a balance-of-payment problem with which we are concerned.

But quite apart from these two considerations, one must remember that low foreign unit prices are meaningless unless tight delivery schedules and comprehensive service requirements are consistently met by the foreign suppliers. Excessive inventories are costly enough, but the costs of down-time in any of our operations are staggering. If delivery and service are a problem with foreign vendors, although you may be paying a premium to domestic suppliers, that premium may be very small compared with the potential loss through late deliveries or insufficient service backup.

Worldwide procurement planning

As of spring of 1966, Mercury's international buying activities were carried on without centrally coordinated materials and purchasing budgets. Important among the tasks of the European purchasing staff group at the time, according to parent company purchasing executives, was the development of budgetary procedures and of methods for gathering, on a continuing basis, information required for centrally coordinated procurement plans. Mr. Snow commented:

We don't know enough about what is being bought overseas. We don't receive sufficient planning data from our overseas affiliates to develop a worldwide materials purchasing plan. Although some of our affiliates do an outstanding planning and budgeting job for purchasing, many others have yet to develop a certain level of sophistication in the use of the technique.

The problem is that we cannot tell any affiliate to install a budgeting system. All we can do is remove certain misconceptions of the nature and purpose of purchasing budgets. We cannot force the development of procurement plans in our overseas affiliates any more than we can force them to submit such plans to us if they are developed. But improvements in this area will come as time goes by and as our teaching and coaching efforts will increasingly yield results.

Parent company purchasing executives believed that progress had been made between 1963–66 in developing global purchasing plans for certain individual items, involving capital investment. The San Francisco purchasing department, for instance, had succeeded in 1965 in placing service station pumps on a worldwide contractual basis at considerable overall cost savings. This pooled contract had been made possible by the receipt from major affiliates of capital appropriation plans for marketing operations. The department had distributed copies of the analysis of Mercury's worldwide pump requirements and also of the ensuing contract to all purchasing departments to "motivate profit improvements based upon preplanning of purchases." In his 1965 purchasing department progress report, Mr. Exelbert noted that "results have been most favorable primarily at the local division level and in the following overseas affiliates: Australia, U.K., South Africa, and Spain." He added, "But we still have a long way to go."

Coordination of surplus disposition

In developing a worldwide procurement system, the parent company purchasing department gave considerable attention to coordinating the utilization or disposition of surplus material, equipment, and supplies by Mercury affiliates throughout the world. To accomplish this task, the department asked major domestic and overseas affiliates to prepare regularly in reproducible form lists of such surplus. These reports were to be submitted to the purchasing department in San Francisco and also to the European purchasing staff group for distribution to other operating units. The lists gave detailed material descriptions and indicated, among other things, the quantities available, the original unit costs, the net book values (if any), and the countries of origin. Purchasing agents in affiliates throughout the world were asked to look first at surplus lists before requisitioning new material.

In order to facilitate quick reference to the list by affiliate purchasing personnel, surplus items were arranged by major activities, such as drilling and production, marketing, marine transportation, and manufacturing. In addition, the lists were supplemented by various specialty lists drawn up as a result of changes of program. For instance, if a refinery of an affiliate in a given country was to be shut down, a special list of the installation's assets was circulated, so that equipment to be dismantled could be placed into service by affiliates in other countries. As one executive put it, "We find that it is often cheaper to ship an item, say from San Antonio to South America, rather than order a new item."

The foreign procurement guide emphasized that "surplus must be considered the basic responsibility of the unit where the surplus exists," and that the unit "should be considered the preferential source of supply" by purchasing agents of the company's worldwide affiliates. Affiliate purchasing agents were asked to identify "the originally intended end use of each item declared surplus" to determine the following:

a. How could the surplus item possibly be used to the company's advantage?
b. Has the item a substitute usage?
c. Can it be utilized to cover a requirement of inferior specifications (i.e., using corroded furnace tubes for fence posts)?

d. Can it be disposed of logically? To another oil company; by sale outside the company?

e. Can the surplus be returned to the original vendor economically, after considering all possibilities and the cost of restocking and return freight, if any?

f. Is the surplus item of such a category that write-off and disposal as junk is the only practical alternative?

According to calculations by the parent company purchasing department, savings realized through coordinated utilization of surplus grew from $500,000 in 1963 to nearly $1.8 million in 1965. The breakdown of the 1965 savings by major geographical location of operating units was as follows:

Location	Dollars
San Francisco	$ 2,798
New Jersey	1,410,288
Los Angeles	79,816
Mercury Oil Canada	6,927
United States field units	233,372
Overseas affiliates	13,944
	$1,747,145

Mr. Exelbert commented:

In a sense we will always be in the "secondhand" business. If we let excess inventories merely gather dust, it would cost the Mercury organization large sums in caretaking activities. When you add the direct cost savings of using existing material, the Mercury companies save money two ways. In actual bookkeeping, one affiliate "purchases" the material, while another writes it off its books. But we have not added another item to inventory.

Worldwide profit contributions by purchasing, 1963–65, and objectives of the San Francisco purchasing department for 1966

Identifiable profit contributions by the purchasing function between 1963 and 1965 were calculated at $12.3 million (excluding savings through surplus utilization). A breakdown of these profit contributions by domestic and overseas affiliates is shown below.

	Profit contribution			Total
Affiliates	1963	1964	1965	(millions)
Domestic	$1.5	$3.0	$5.2	$ 9.7
Overseas	–	1.6	1.0	2.6
	$1.5	$4.6	$6.2	$12.3

The sources for the 1965 profit contribution by purchasing and the percentage of preset targets achieved during the year are indicated in the following table:

Source of profit contribution	Domestic units	Overseas units	Total
Value analysis/standardization	$ 954,907	$ 267,221	$1,222,128
More economical source of supply	901,930	154,152	1,056,082
Improved methods	696,110	133,177	829,287
Favorable price negotiation	2,424,157	360,529	2,784,686
Judicious buying	154,710	35,051	189,761
Other	50,147	59,836	109,983
Total	$5,181,961	$1,009,966	$6,191,927
Target for 1965	$3,210,000	$1,500,000	$4,710,000
Percent of target achieved	161.4%	67.3%	131.4%

A breakdown of purchasing's 1965 profit contribution by major organization activity, cross-classified by major operating groups, is given in Exhibit 13.

Exhibit 13
PROFIT CONTRIBUTION BY PURCHASING
(classified by major function and operating groups, 1965)

Activity	Major operating groups			
	Mercury North American	Mercury International	Mercury Chemical	Totals
Producing	$ 893,590	$ 194,331		$1,087,921
Refining	762,390	337,830		1,100,220
Marketing	698,950	655,214		1,354,164
Products	21,910			21,910
Manufacturing		637	$1,873,569	1,874,206
Chemical plants			216,344	216,344
Pipeline	417,010	301		417,311
Marine	1,704			1,704
Administrative	46,050	643		46,693
Research and development	69,096		2,358	71,454
Totals	$2,910,700	$1,188,956	$2,092,271	$6,191,927
Percentage of Total	47.01	19.20	33.79	100.00

Source: Company records.

In his annual report to top management in the spring of 1966, Mr. Exelbert stated that, despite changing business conditions that might make its achievement difficult, the worldwide profit contribution objective for 1966 was set at $4.7 million. Other procurement objectives for 1966 were described as follows:

Our 1966 program has been built around a new concept of improving purchasing's planning, profitability, productivity, performance (servicewise), and personnel development.

Concisely stated, this new concept is designed to force us to consider all of the important aspects of the management process as applied to the purchasing function.

As previously reported, we have carefully constructed our objectives so as to generate significant benefits for the major profit centers of the organization, which are:

U.S.	Overseas
Mercury Oil Marketing	Mercury International
Mercury Oil Manufacturing	
Mercury Oil Exploration and Producing	
Mercury Chemical	

Our 1966 objectives are designed to sustain the good work initiated and to push us forward to new achievements in 1966.

Those objectives which will be given concerted attention by our purchasing management team are as follows:

1. *Profit Improvement Program.* We'll strive to achieve or exceed our goal of $4.7 million. The value analysis technique will be given special emphasis.

2. *Chemical Planning Council.* We have Mercury Chemical's concurrence to create this council. Its purpose will be to improve the coordination between all purchasing people who are engaged in purchasing chemicals valued in excess of $170 million annually.

3. *Area Supply/Training Programs.* Will be fully launched this year after testing this principle in the Philadelphia area. Its purpose is to motivate all Mercury purchasing personnel located in the same geographical area to pool their mental, physical, and financial resources.

We expect to conduct this program in six domestic areas and nine overseas areas.

Training packages and concepts developed by the parent company purchasing department will be used to conduct these programs in a consistent manner. Ample latitude will be allowed to give proper weight to area factors.

4. *Contractor Coordination Program.* 1966 will see us involved in coordinating the contractors' purchases of materials, supplies, and equipment for at least three major construction projects.

5. *Formal Staff Training Program for the Parent Company Purchasing Department.* Fourteen new topics have been programmed for 1966 in our continuing effort to upgrade our personnel.

AVCO-EVERETT RESEARCH LABORATORY*

The company and the industry

The Avco-Everett Research Laboratory was organized in early 1955 and formally became a division of the Avco Corporation in 1957–58.

Early efforts involved the exploration of reentry problems for intercontinental ballistic missiles. By 1964, the laboratory had established an international reputation for advanced work in high-temperature gas dynamics, magnetohydrodynamic generation of electricity, plasma propulsion, and reentry phenomena. The laboratory, employing 750 people including 39 scientists with doctorates, had an academic atmosphere, as all the activities of the laboratory were directed toward original research. The basic products of the laboratory were technical reports and professional papers. Actual production was limited, and even the nose cone resulting from the early work in the laboratory was developed at another plant 20 miles away.

Laboratory personnel stated that there was no "organization chart," although a definite social order existed. At the top of the laboratory's organizational structure were the senior scientists, who composed the three key research committees that set the general areas of research and formed the groups that continually reviewed and examined the current work. All members of these committees could keep informed on the work in progress and exchange ideas. Committee membership, however, was not clearly defined, and meetings were attended by other scientists and other staff members. In addition to providing direction to research efforts, the committees generated reports on their findings and suggested possible applications. If any such application proved of interest to the parent corporation or to the government, it might be set up as a project, with a project director and a definite organization to carry through the work entailed.

The two other major groups in the laboratory organization were the administrative and the technical services, together employing over 450 persons. Their major function was to conduct the business aspects of the laboratory, including contracting, finance, public relations, and administration. The latter served to free the technical and professional staffs from nontechnical duties by providing the many services needed. The technical services group performed such various tasks as glassblowing, model-making, and electronic repair; and the administrative group took care of such activities as housekeeping, office work, computing, finance, technical library work, and procurement and handling of materials.

Technical library

An extensive technical library was maintained as a reference center for all scientific and technical needs. Over 6,000 books covering the fields of physics, mathematics, chemistry, gas dynamics, mechanical and electrical engineering, photography, and other areas of interest were supplemented with subscriptions to over 275 periodicals. Over 20,000 technical reports were also available, and reciprocal agreements were maintained with other university and industrial libraries in the area. The library was staffed with 15 librarians, most of whom were involved in technical searches.

Specific efforts were made to keep the available information before the scientists. A listing of the periodicals regularly received had been printed and circulated within the laboratory. A list of scientific conferences or meetings, with latest dates for submission of papers and reservations, was printed each month, including all known meetings for the next 10 months. The tables of contents of periodicals were reproduced, and packets of all those received each week were circulated to most technical personnel.

The purchasing department and purchasing officer

The head of the purchasing department was the matériel manager who directed and supervised the entire materials function up to the point of use. He said that the laboratory had only one product, knowledge generated by the scientists, and he had oriented his department to assist in its production. He visualized his department's function as performing such services as it could perform relatively effectively and economically, thus freeing the scientists for their technical endeavors. He was active in the local purchasing agents' professional association and was familiar with and used in his department the latest purchasing and inventory control techniques and mechanical aids. But he considered that his unique contribution to the laboratory was the flow of up-to-date, pertinent technical information through his department from suppliers and other sources.

Technical information

The life blood of the laboratory was technical information. The scientists were frequently in communication with each other and with other scientists. Members of the professional staff were encouraged to attend scientific meetings, especially if prepared to present papers. The laboratory research committee meetings were well attended, and there was a continuous flow of internal discussions. The technical library was busy with the circulation of books, periodicals, and reports; and the librarians were involved in hunting for written material relating to special fields of interest to the several researchers. The matériel manager said his department contributed to this flow of technical data by making readily available to the scientists information received from the many sources or potential sources of laboratory supplies. Such information was received through industrial advertising, suppliers' catalogs, and visits by suppliers' representatives.

Industrial advertising

The matériel manager thought that industrial advertising did not contribute much to the information used by the scientists. Much of this literature came by mail directed either to individuals or to the laboratory, the pieces not specifically addressed being sent to the matériel manager. He, in turn, routed those pieces that he considered might be of interest to his buyers or to specific technical or administrative personnel. Most of the rest of the direct-mail advertising he discarded immediately. The manager stated that in most instances the scientists also discarded the industrial advertising sent directly to them, since they were looking for unique types of materials and processes and found that the advertising messages usually were too general to be helpful. He estimated that less than 5 percent of industrial advertising received was useful in any way.

Catalogs

On the other hand, the matériel manager considered suppliers' catalogs valuable as sources of information, and he had assembled a large group of those covering all the fields of interest to the laboratory staff. He had made it his business to obtain up-to-date catalogs, either from visiting salesmen or by mail from the suppliers; and when these books were received he had them indexed both by material covered and by company. Although many of the technical personnel had at their desks duplicate copies of some catalogs of particular interest, these scientists and engineers frequently consulted the 70 feet of open-shelf space filled with catalogs in the purchasing department. The matériel manager stated that the scientists found the file useful, not only when looking for a particular product or material reference but also when trying to determine which companies might have the capability to produce an article with some unique characteristic.

Special vendor files

The information in the catalog file was supplemented with two special reference services: the visual search microfilm file (VSMF) and the *Thomas' Register* microfilm service. VSMF was an information system, aimed at product data storage and fast retrieval, which had been on the market since 1960. The system consisted of a library of 16 mm. microfilm in cartridges, a printed product index, and a viewer with an automatic copy-making device. The library of information currently available applied to the aerospace and the electronic industries. Over 100,000 pages of product data from over 3,100 vendors were indexed, and the developers of the system were continuously enlarging the number of suppliers covered. Included were specification sheets, engineering drawings, and catalog pages on components, materials, and equipment. A comprehensive index permitted very rapid search and retrieval for the information covered, and the automatic copy-making device permitted the engineers to take a copy of a print or specification back to their desks, if they so desired. The file was located in the back of the purchasing department office space and was accessible to scientists, buyers, and engineers. The matériel manager said that his buyers seldom used the equipment, as they had desk notes, catalogs, and references on the requisitions to direct their efforts; but scientists and engineers came down and spent hours looking through a section of the file when they were looking for a particular material or component. They would usually take one or more reproductions back to their desks with them for further study. He knew of specific instances wherein a scientist was saved the time of designing a component because he found one already available. He estimated that the file was in use about 30 percent of the time.

The second service, the *Thomas' Register* microfilm service, was used little by buyers or scientists. About 40 catalog pages were reduced to one $5'' \times 8''$ film card, and the cards were filed in a card box. A product index was provided to enable selection of the card desired, but the product coverage and cross-classification was not complete enough for effective use. The reader was adequate, but there was no printing device to permit reproduction of pages to take back to the user's desk.

Supplies' representatives

"There is a new breed of salesmen calling on Avco now, men who know their products, something of our needs, and have new ideas to present," said the matériel manager when asked about suppliers' representatives as a source of information. Elaborating further, he explained:

Of course, many suppliers' representatives are technically trained and make appointments directly with the scientists to discuss the latest offerings, but our people are very good about getting purchasing into the act before any negotiation occurs. Our purchasing department brochure, given to all suppliers' representatives, says: "The Purchasing Department buys all goods, materials, and services required to support this research effort." And most laboratory personnel let us do it. Any salesman without an appointment is referred to us, and most others call on us after seeing the scientist. We interview about 300 salesmen a month with our six buyers.

The matériel manager also discussed a recent procurement in these terms:

Here is an instance which I would classify as "a state-of-the-art buy," illustrating how an alert buyer saved money and time for the requisitioner and obtained better information on material:

A requisition for two infrared detector cells was filed by Dr. X in a memorandum stating that only one company in the United States was capable of manufacturing these exact units. Specifications were so stringent that these units were considered beyond the present technical knowledge in this field, beyond the so-called state of the art.

Upon receipt of this request, the buyer contacted the suggested source requesting price and delivery information along with information concerning any anticipated difficulty in the manufacture of these detectors. The supplier quoted a price of $1,475 for each detector with a delivery period of six weeks from the date of the receipt of order. The bidder further stated that the firm would experience no difficulty in producing the units. With this assurance from the manufacturer, the buyer thought it logical to assume that, if one firm could make the item without trouble, other companies also might be capable of producing it and that inquiries should be initiated.

After checking reference files—the *Optical Industry Magazine* and the *Thomas' Register*—solicitations for bids were mailed to 12 manufacturers of similar units. In addition, two local sources, qualified in the infrared detector field, were contacted by telephone.

These telephone calls resulted in information that lead to two additional telephone calls to out-of-state suppliers. As a result of the latter two conversations, it became quite evident that these units were very much beyond the present state of the art. Also brought to light was the information that two scientists working at a certain university were considered the top men in this field and that their research had covered much more than anything so far produced by any manufacturer.

A telephone call was placed to Dr. Q at the university mentioned. His answer to the request for a supplier of these detectors was very much a repetition of what was already known, except that he was able to recommend two definite sources. The first was the original company selected by the requisitioner as the sole source; the second, as the university doctor put it, "is right in your own back yard." But these were the only two in the United States.

The buyer then contacted the "backyard" firm, which submitted an estimate of $1,027 per item with a delivery period of 30 days. After checking the matter with the requisitioner, the buyer awarded the order to the second firm.

This search thus resulted in two beneficial savings to the laboratory: first, a quicker delivery of approximately two weeks; and, second, an overall savings of $900. In addition to the saving in money and time, more thorough information was gained about capabilities in this field, knowledge that would assist the laboratory in future procurements.

Period contracts and mechanization

A several step plan to reduce the number of small-dollar buys was under way, with the goal of freeing the buyers from unnecessary routines for more productive time on bigger and more important buys. Period contracts were being used for most maintenance, repair, and operating (MRO) items, and purchase order preparation was being mechanized.

Also, plans had been made to push mechanization back into inventory control and receiving, as part of an automatic inventory-control-and-purchasing system.

Program for information awareness

In addition to making available the catalog file, the vendors' information services, and the salesmen's referrals, the matériel manager used many methods to keep his buyers alert to the current informational needs and to keep the channels of communication open between the buyers and the scientists. Each one of the six buyers was responsible for several categories of material and hence could not be expected to be expert on all related materials and processes. However, with close attention to the requirements of his requisitioners and a constant program of familiarization with developments, each buyer had become sufficiently expert to be able to talk to the scientists whom he served and be responsive to their demands.

"This is a major part of our effort, to be able to help and then do it. So we must make time to prepare ourselves," said the matériel manager.

All buyers had been through a two-week indoctrination assignment, which included attendance at committee meetings, talks with scientists, visits to the laboratories to watch experiments, and a visit to the library for familiarization with the types of information used by the laboratory.

When a buyer was assigned to a project as a material representative, he became a part of the project team and presented the material status at the project meetings. He also brought information as to project goals and the direction of the research back to the buyers meetings for the other buyers' information. At these same buyers' meetings all the known informational needs of the laboratory were considered. After each project buyer discussed his projects and how they were developing, the matériel manager or those buyers who had attended the senior research committee meetings presented their analyses of the direction in which the committees were steering research efforts.

The buyers were urged to maintain contact with the scientists and researchers. They were encouraged to visit the laboratories and observe experiments being performed and to ask about ways they could help. Each buyer was expected to check equipment buys with the related laboratory head, using him as a consultant on equipment uses. On some complex purchases, the buyer set up a prebidding conference and discussed both technical and administrative implications with the scientists and the vendors' representatives. The buyers also invited technical personnel to come to the purchasing department when they wanted any kind of purchasing service, including information and service on personal needs. The matériel manager looked upon the assistance of the buyers in purchase of personal items for the scientists as another means of keeping communication channels open between the scientists and the buyers.

Evaluation of buyers

As the utilization of all available technical information was of prime importance to the laboratory, the matériel manager had included this factor in his indoctrination and training program for his staff. He wanted to educate his buyers not only to detect information which would be of value to the laboratory but also to be able to communicate with the researchers. Since these skills were so important, the matériel manager attempted to appraise them when evaluating the members of his staff. He believed that the buyers, knowing they were being judged on their ability to recognize and then exchange pertinent information with salesmen and scientists, would have a continuous incentive for intelligent performance of their work.

The matériel manager said:

Evaluation of buyers is a complex task in a regular plant. Comparisons of price changes, deliveries, and quality variations present enough variables; but, in our business, we must add the factor of technical information flow and communications to our evaluation technique. I use a rough measure by noting the number of technical people visiting a buyer for information and weighing the comments of the scientists about the contributions of the several buyers to their research. But I am still looking for a better way to evaluate my people's efforts in picking up technical information, as well as for new ways to increase the flow of technical information.

VICTORIA HOSPITAL

In November, 1971, Mr. Don Palmer, director of management services, received a request to study and recommend improvement to the Victoria Hospital purchasing department functions (Exhibit 1). After completing the study of existing methods early in 1972, he was considering ways in which the operations might be streamlined. Given the hospital's operating needs in relation to budget increase restrictions, Mr. Palmer presumed that any cost-reducing steps would be considered favorably by the administration. However, he also knew that service levels would have to be maintained or improved and that only limited amounts of funds could be allocated for any alterations he might recommend.

Background

The purchasing department was one of the nine service functions under the control of the director of hospital services. This department was responsible for:

1. Purchasing all hospital supplies (capital and noncapital),
2. Receiving, storage and distribution of supplies,
3. Maintenance of inventory control over all capital and noncapital stock items,
4. The billing of requisitions and recording any cost revisions,
5. Maintenance of forms control (designing and revising printed forms), and
6. Printing services.

Purchasing was responsible for the supply of about $550,000 of capital supplies and $5–6 million of noncapital supplies during 1971. Inventory records were kept for 8,000 to 10,000 individual items and about 120,000 requisitions were processed during 1971. Forms control and printing

Exhibit 1
VICTORIA HOSPITAL

Memorandum

To: Mr. D. F. Palmer   Date: November 9, 1971
     Director of Management Services

From: Mr. J. Schram
       Administrator

Request for Study—Purchasing/Accounting Departments

Subject: A systems and procedures study is requested to examine the paperflow of purchasing requisitions, purchase orders and associated forms, through the purchasing and accounting departments. Additionally, methods employed by the two departments in the handling of purchase orders should also be examined.

Background: The accounting department has a requirement to submit a financial statement to the finance committee by the third Wednesday of each month and the present flow of information between purchasing and accounting makes it impossible to achieve this deadline without staff working overtime. This, in turn, creates a staff morale problem.

Aim: To speed up the flow of purchasing orders and associated data by elimination of unnecessary delays and/or institution of alternative flow patterns. Where possible to improve methods employed in handling of purchase orders and materials.

Limitations: The actual study should be limited to purchasing and accounting departments but should include a review of all directives from higher authority pertaining to the study and requisitions from all departments which may affect the study.

JS:lm

c.c.: Mr. H. Whittle
       Mr. W. Berkley
       Mr. H. Haskell

represented about 12 percent of the work of this department. Although the total level of services provided by Victoria Hospital had been rising steadily and total hospital employees had increased from 2,000 to 2,650 since 1965, purchasing and stores had operated with the same work force.

Organization

The department was under the direct supervision and control of Mr. Sid Loucks, purchasing agent in the organization shown in Exhibit 2. The four main functions were considered by Mr. Palmer to be purchasing, receiving, storing and issuing, and controlling. Since the forms control function had no effect on purchasing procedures, he did not take it into consideration in the study. The purchasing agent was responsible for 25 people in these four main functions.

Purchasing responsibilities were divided as follows:

1. Purchasing agent—capital equipment, blanket laboratory orders.
2. Assistant purchasing agent—operating room orders, special telephone orders.
3. Buyer—food, stationery, maintenance supplies.

The stores were considered as two sections—wholesale and retail—though there was no physical isolation of the two types of stock. Wholesale activities included receiving all supplies and maintenance of adequate stock levels. The stock control clerks kept the wholesale inventory records up-to-date by posting orders, receipts, and issues. The retail stores received regular issues from wholesale and was responsible for distribution throughout the hospital. There were no inventory records for retail stores—requisitions filled could be balanced against issues from wholesale.

Requisitions normally would be filled from retail stock. If there was none of a particular item in "retail," the storeman could issue it from "wholesale" and stamp the requisition accordingly. "Wholesale" requisitions were sent to the stock control clerks for recording. However, under that system, Don Palmer pointed out that it was very easy for a storesman to issue some item from wholesale without stamping the requisition.

Another potential error source was that of routine transfers from wholesale to retail. Storesmen recorded issues in a book that was sent to stock control daily. Transfers could be made without being recorded. Don felt these factors could explain many of the frequent discrepancies between stock control records and actual stock. There were two counts during the year that revealed a total of approximately $100,000 in wholesale shortages. With no evidence of theft, the most reasonable explanation Sid Loucks could provide was that storesmen likely depleted whole-

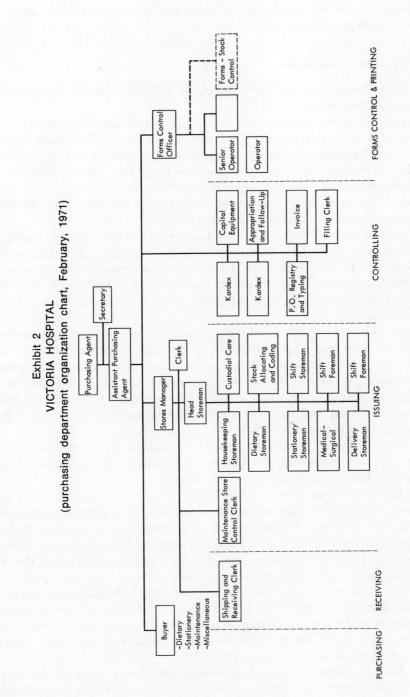

Exhibit 2
VICTORIA HOSPITAL
(purchasing department organization chart, February, 1971)

PURCHASING   RECEIVING   ISSUING   CONTROLLING   FORMS CONTROL & PRINTING

sale stocks to fill requisitions without noting the issue information for stock control and accounting.

Requisition procedures

There were two methods for wards and departments to requisition supplies from stores.

A.   Traveling requisitions.   Traveling requisitions were used by the wards to request recurring items such as stationery, daily food supplies for ward kitchens, cutlery and crockery, and medical and surgical supplies. These requisitions were kept in book form and completed by the requisitioner using the appropriate catalog number and goods descriptions. The requesting department would send the requisition to stores to have the order filled and the goods delivered.

Filling and delivering the daily food orders and the weekly stationery orders was particularly time-consuming for the stores. Don Palmer also found wards frequently would submit a supplementary food order, in addition to their daily traveling requisition, for food stuffs they had either omitted on the original order or had not ordered in sufficient quantity.

At the end of the month each ward or department was issued a new 25-page traveling requisition for the next month as they returned the filled ones to the purchasing office for costing. Costing was a time-consuming process as not all traveling requisition books were submitted on the date requested, and it was often necessary to obtain the books from the ward and then tally and price the entries. The list was then sent to accounts payable.

The traveling requisition procedure had been introduced by Mr. Loucks, as a temporary fact-finding document, since no suitable catalog existed. The system had become permanent.

B.   Stores requisitions.   (See Exhibit 3.) To obtain items other than those specified on the traveling requisition, a requesting department first had to complete four copies of a stores requisition (see Exhibit 4). That department would retain one copy and forward three to stores for action. Each requisition was date-stamped on receipt and directed for action appropriate to stock or nonstock items.

a.   In stock items.   These would be filled directly from retail or wholesale stores, with the supplies and third copy of the requisition being sent to the requesting department. If issued from "retail," the first copy would be stamped to indicate this and then sent directly to the filing clerk.

After "wholesale" issues had been made, copies one and two of the requisition were sent to the appropriate stock control clerk. She would check for accuracy and completeness, enter the prices of items on copy one, control stamp and sign that copy, and forward it to the filing clerk

Exhibit 3
VICTORIA HOSPITAL PURCHASING DEPARTMENT
(Stores requisition flow diagram)

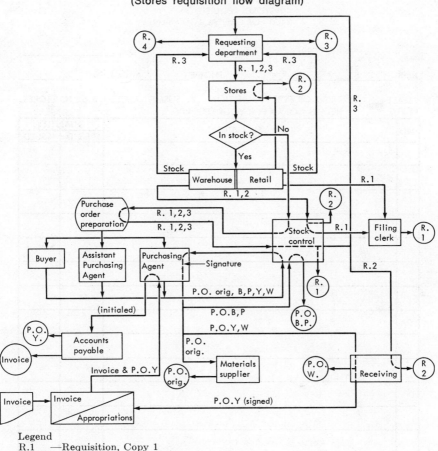

Legend
R.1   —Requisition, Copy 1
P.O.B.—Purchase Order, Copy Blue

for filing under the appropriate account number. Stock control retained copy two of the requisition.

At the beginning of each month, the filing clerk would send the previous month's completed requisitions to accounts payable. There each requisition would be checked for account and subaccounts number accuracy. Errors or omissions were frequently made, and accounts payable would return the forms to stock control or stores. When assured of the accuracy, the charges would be posted against the appropriate account.

b. Not in stock items. Requisitions were routed to the stock control office. Stock control passed the stores requisitions to the person responsible for purchase order preparation. The secretary would type purchase

Exhibit 4

VICTORIA HOSPITAL

STORES REQUISITION
(NOT FOR CAPITAL EQUIPMENT)

Date_____

DEPT._____ PHONE_____ ACCT. NO._____

PLEASE ► 1. PRINT OR TYPE REQUISITION   2. SUBMIT COPIES 1,2,&3 TO STORES.
NOTE   3. RETAIN COPY 4 FOR YOUR RECORDS.

Item	ITEM DESCRIPTION	QUANTITY	
		REQ'D	ISSUED

REQUISITIONED BY:

Requisitioner ....

Dept. Head ....

PURCHASING & STORES USE ONLY:	ITEM		ISSUED BY:
	NO.	COST	
ITEM NO.			
P.O. NO.			RECEIVED BY:
CONTROL NO.			
DATE			

orders to be handled by the purchasing agent, while the purchase order registry clerk would type purchase orders for the assistant purchasing agent and the buyer.

Purchase orders were passed to the appropriate stock control clerk to enter the order on the inventory control card. After entry, she would stamp and initial the purchase orders. Subsequently, all purchase orders were recorded in a register (which contained the date of the order, the supplying company, the purchase order number, and the originating department) and then were passed to the purchasing agent for signature.

Purchase orders were prepared in five copies. After being signed, the copies were separated and distributed as follows:

1. White original—to supplier.
2. Blue and pink copies—filed together in a bin in the stock control office.
3. Yellow and white copies—to receiving.

When stock control received its copies, the purchase order number and date would be entered on the stores requisition, and the third copy of the requisition would be sent to the requesting department. Reasons for returning a copy to the departments were: (a) it notified them that their request had been received and actioned, (b) and if they had queries to direct to purchasing, they had available the purchase order number (there were many queries). The second requisition copy was sent to receiving to be held with the yellow and white purchase order copies. Stock control held the first requisition copy on separate file for use in the event of a query from any requesting department. These requisition copies would be destroyed periodically.

Receiving functions

Receiving maintained a book record of all purchase orders as outgoing copies arrived. Photocopies were made and held for the 40 percent of all purchase orders that were likely to be back orders or partial shipments.

Part of the book record was the date on which an order was completely received, and the packing slip(s) and purchase order tallied. Receiving filed the complete order packing slip and the white purchase order copy together. The yellow copy would be signed by the stores manager and sent to the invoice clerk. The goods would be sent to the requesting department or placed in stores and a purchase order copy would be sent to stock control for recording.

Receiving handled an incomplete, or partial, shipment in much the same way. However, only a photocopy of the purchase order, indicating quantity received, was forwarded to invoicing, stock control, and the requesting department for direct deliveries. The purchase order record would be kept open until all items had been received.

Follow-ups were also a receiving responsibility. The purchase order registry was checked on a regular basis for orders outstanding one month or more (regardless of the promised delivery date). The clerk would first check the white purchase order copies of any such orders to see if partial deliveries had been received. If no partial orders had been received, she would complete a follow-up form to be signed by the stores manager. The details would be entered in a back-order ledger and a copy forwarded to the supplier to expedite the order. When a reply was received from a supplier, the receiving clerk would check to see if the order had been completed in the meantime and close the record if it had. If the order was not yet complete, further follow-up action might be taken.

Invoicing, appropriations and accounts payable

The invoicing clerk held the purchase order pending the invoice receipt. When the invoice arrived, it would be verified, the extensions would be checked, and invoice and purchase order copies would be sent to the appropriations clerk. She would check the invoice against the original requisition, verify the accuracy of tax charges, and sign and return copies of the purchase order and invoice to the invoice clerk. The appropriations clerk would next update the purchase order ledger and pass the documents to the purchasing agent. He would initial the documents and forward them to accounts payable.

Accounts payable processed all complete and incomplete order receipts as invoiced. Each would be checked for accuracy, correct appropriation, discounts where appliable, and the purchasing agent's initials. A machine remittance would then be made and checked against the invoice before being passed to the accountant for final approval and payment.

Exchanges, miscellaneous, and books

If a department wished to return goods that were "unsatisfactory" (for any reason), the department called or wrote a memo to the purchasing department. Purchasing would check with the supplier to determine the best method of return. Then purchasing would complete a "Return Goods Memorandum" and send it and the goods to shipping for packaging and shipment. The goods would then be returned to the supplier for an exchange or credit. Separate ledgers were kept for exchange items and for credit items. An exchange required only a record on its completion and a receipt for goods when forwarded to the requesting department. Any credits received had to be posted to the requesting department's account and to accounts payable. Don Palmer found that the procedures tended to be time-consuming but caused few problems except when goods returned for exchange and replacement items were not of equal value—an infrequent occurrence. (It was later determined that accounting did not always post credits or returns to accounts).

The miscellaneous returns could cause many difficulties. Shipping maintained a ledger for miscellaneous returns such as furniture sent for recovering. Such goods were sent out with the purchase order attached. Don Palmer found that miscellaneous items often were returned and the purchase order processed without the completion being noted in the shipping ledger.

Another problem area was the receipt of books. If the original supplier was out of stock, he would frequently refer the order to another supplier, and, when the shipment was received, the packing slip would refer to an unknown supplier who could not be matched with a purchase order. Even more frequently departments would order books direct from the publisher, and, when they were received, much time would be spent by receiving trying to find first a purchase order and then the original requisitioner.

Expanding the study

Mr. Palmer had been assigned the task of examining and improving the information flows in the purchasing and accounting system. However, he found it impossible to do this without examining the work environment. Touring the facilities in the stores building left him with the impression that the operation was crowded and likely inefficient. Don Palmer, therefore, felt a work study might indicate some potential for change. Accordingly, a work sample was taken over a period of five days between 6:30 A.M. and 4:00 P.M. The sampling did not cover the stores manager, receiving, stationery storesmen, and the night and weekend shifts. The results of Mr. Palmer's work sampling are shown in Exhibit 5.

The sampling indicated that storesmen were engaged in productive activities 70.9 percent of the time. This included 1.6 percent of supervisory time. Don Palmer suggested, "The small percentage of supervisory time (due largely to the illness of the supervisor during the time study) could be the reason for the level of productivity. More supervision could bring about higher productivity." Counting delivery of pharmacy supplies, 20.4 percent of the storesmens' productive time (81 man-hours in the sample period) was used portering or delivery stocks.

Mr. Palmer continued, "The assignment of specific responsibilities to supervisors and the development of job descriptions for all could bring about better supervision and greater productivity. The sampling

Exhibit 5

ACTIVITY SAMPLING STUDY—CENTRAL STORES

Total number of man hours sampled:

7 Storesmen × 8.5 hours per day × 5 days = 297.5 hours
1 Storesman × 8.5 hours per day × 3 days = 25.5 hours
1 Storesman × 8.5 hours per day × 4 days = 34.0 hours
2 Storesmen × 4.0 hours per day × 5 days = 40.0 hours

Total   397.0 hours

Element description	Percent of observation	Man-hours
Major Element Breakdown		
1–1 Nonproductive elements.	29.1	115.5
1–2 Productive elements (indirect)	8.1	32.2
1–3 Productive elements (direct)	62.8	249.3
Totals	100.0	397.0
Detailed Element Breakdown		
2–1 Nonproductive elements		
1–Personal	1.4	5.5
2–Break and/or lunch period	14.7	58.4
3–Idle	9.4	37.3
4–Away from work place	3.6	14.3
Totals	29.1	115.5
Productive Elements (Indirect)		
1–Give or receive instructions		
A. Given by supervisors	1.6	6.4
B. Received by storesmen	1.8	7.1
2–Talk to salesmen	0.3	1.2
3–Walk empty handed	1.2	4.8
4–Operate photocopier	0.4	1.6
5–Talk to supervisor	0.1	0.4
6–Receive or make telephone call	0.9	3.6
7–Routine clean-up of work area	1.8	7.1
Totals	8.1	32.2
Productive Elements (Direct)		
1–Prepare pharmacy supplies	2.6	10.3
2–Deliver pharmacy supplies	1.2	4.8
3–Price pharmacy supplies	0.7	2.8
4–Prepare medical and surgical supply orders	10.4	41.3
5–Prepare dietary supply orders	2.6	10.3
6–Prepare housekeeping supply orders	0.5	2.0
7–Porter	19.2	76.2
8–Stock returned items from floors	0.7	2.8
9–Stock wholesale supplies	4.9	19.5
10–Stock retail supplies	3.0	11.9
11–Stock dietary supplies to refrigerator	1.5	5.9
12–Serve at issuing window	3.1	12.3
13–Code cases and/or individual items	1.2	4.8
14–Unpack cartons and check contents against packing slip	2.4	9.5
15–Miscellaneous paper work	2.9	11.5
16–Receive	1.8	7.1
17–Obtain supplies from supply houses	0.3	1.2
18–Package items for repair or return to supplier	0.4	1.6
19–Load and/or operate conveyor	1.0	4.0
20–Prepare stock orders	1.5	5.9
21–Assemble travelling requisition books	0.9	3.6
Totals	62.8	249.3

indicated about 115 nonproductive hours which amounts to almost three men."

The supervisor and his responsibilities

The purchasing agent, Mr. Loucks, was responsible for the overall supervision and functioning of the department. The main functions involved were purchasing, stores, stock control, appropriation, forms control and printing.

Don Palmer's assessment was:

Apart from purchasing and stock control, these functions appear to be incompatible with the role of a purchasing agent. Appropriation could be an extension of accounts payable. Forms control (which includes forms design), although it appears to function well, is not normally a part of the purchasing organization and could function under medical records or management services. Similarly, apart from the passing of documents between receiving and stock control, the stores and printing functions are compatible to each other and could be completely dissociated from purchasing.

In a hospital the size of Victoria, the duties of purchasing agent alone could be a full-time function, whereas the present organization has the purchasing agent responsible also for another full-time function—stores.

Record keeping functions

The purpose of stock control was to ensure the maintenance of adequate bulk or wholesale supplies. However, the stock control system at Victoria Hospital exhibited many discrepancies between stock and records for which exact causes could not be defined. Don Palmer thought the problem could be due to over-control (or overly complex control). There were eight books for recording transfers from wholesale to retail stores—three for medial/surgical supplies, two for dietary, one for housekeeping, one for paper, and one for stationery. When making transfers from wholesale to retail, the storeman had to ensure details were entered in the appropriate book. Records also had to be kept separately when stores requisition forms were filled direct from wholesale rather than retail stores.

The record keeping was complicated because transfers of stock from wholesale to retail normally occurred daily. The retail stores were not stocked to any standard daily levels either, so extra transfers could be needed for any item at any time. Don Palmer wondered what effects this compounding of transfers could have on the accuracy of records. He also wondered if it might be better to stock retail stores to a standard level of items based on weekly consumption. He did not feel that adequate space was available in retail to accommodate the inventory that would be required, however.

The records kept and procedures for purchasing stock also varied.

Don Palmer found that some orders were made through purchase orders, others by stock requirement sheets, and still others by telephone (blanket orders). The paper work also varied. Purchase orders were kept as described previously. The stores requisition was used for telephoning blanket contract orders. And when a stock card indicated replenishment was needed, a stock requirement sheet would be made up to place an order.

VANIER UNIVERSITY

In August, 1973, Mr. Emery, newly appointed executive assistant to the vice president of administration and finance of Vanier University, assumed the responsibility for the purchasing department. Previously, it had been under the comptroller's authority. In discussions with purchasing personnel, Mr. Emery found out that the receiving processes on the campus were a source of annoyance. For example, lost orders, missing goods, and delays seemed to occur frequently.

University background

Vanier University was a large, well-known Louisiana university. Like most universities, it expanded rapidly in the 60s, and by 1973 it included over 200 administrative and academic departments. More than 14,000 full-time students were registered in its faculties. Vanier's total budget amounted to approximately $65 million a year.

Five access roads led to the 500-acre campus site which included over 50 buildings. Each building could be considered as a receiving center for the university's various requirements. More than half of the buildings had special delivery facilities like unloading docks.

Purchases

The nature of purchases was very broad and varied from mice to computer equipment. The purchasing department grouped products and services in 83 different classes of expenses. Thirty-nine classes of these 83 had annual expenditures of $75,000 and over (see Exhibit 1). Forty-nine percent of all classes used 94 percent of the total dollars recorded. For the 1972–73 period, 32,000 purchase orders were issued on 4,000 account numbers. Records from purchasing's 1972–73 Annual Activity Report indicated a total of $16.6 million spent with 9,345 different suppliers. This amount did not include $3.8 million for three types of goods purchased independently: books for the libraries, food for the cafeterias, and supplies to be resold by the bookstore.

Exhibit 1

SELECTED LIST OF PRODUCT CLASSES BY SUPPLIER FOR YEAR 1972–73

Product class	Class title	Suppliers	Purchase orders	Average $ per each supplier	Average $ per each p.o.
A045	Decor.	33	163	$ 3338.00	$ 676.00
A060*	Electrical supplies & equipment.	100	604	970.00	161.00
A070*	Heating.	100	390	5798.00	149.00
A080*	Plumbing.	57	128	428.00	191.00
A090	Clean supplies & equipment	112	757	1507.00	223.00
A100	Contracts	−	(Range too Wide)		−
A110	Construction	1	1	−	−
C020	Furniture	116	687	6826.00	1153.00
C030	Class supplies & equipment	32	112	5146.00	1470.00
D010	Lab chemicals	252	1987	646.00	82.00
D020	Lab glass	93	651	891.00	127.00
D030	Lab supplies	1281	5401	495.00	118.00
D035	Lab electronics	112	495	764.00	173.00
D040	Scientific equipment	441	1088	3192.00	1294.00
D070	Surgical supplies & equipment.	105	476	1888.00	417.00
D100	Scientific maintenance	161	451	551.00	197.00
D120	Physical education	95	225	840.00	355.00
E010	A/V supplies & equipment.	406	1175	770.00	266.00
E030	Photo supplies.	137	894	686.00	105.00
H010*	Computers.	103	292	7198.00	2539.00
H020	Business supplies & equipment	66	470	6347.00	891.00
H030	Business maintenance	51	734	1508.00	105.00
H040*	Copier supplies & equipment	38	181	2704.00	568.00
H050	Printing maintenance.	31	102	3567.00	1084.00
K020	Forms	29	144	3831.00	771.00
K030	Printing	79	331	3374.00	805.00
K040	Printing M & S.	78	549	3276.00	465.00
K050	Books.	1276	3879	97.00	32.00
K060	Journals	1126	2080	78.00	42.00
K080	Stationery	173	1178	972.00	143.00
M020	Staff−temporary	40	202	757.00	150.00
M025*	Professional fees.	97	158	1310.00	804.00
M030	Travel expenses	93	522	1811.00	323.00
M040*	Telephone & telegraph	−	(No Range)	−	−
M050	Entertainment.	72	210	2085.00	715.00
M060*	Miscellaneous	303	601	672.00	339.00
M085	Insurance	7	15	12295.00	5737.00
M090*	Taxes−property.	−	(No Range)	−	−
M130*	Dues, memberships	219	298	306.00	225.00

* Extraordinary high value, monopoly, or public service suppliers have been extracted from these classes to reduce distortion.

Responsibility and authority

Each department at Vanier had its own budget for capital and current expenditures. Over the years a variety of operating policies and procedures had evolved, many of which were not in written form. The purchasing department was no exception in this respect. Regarding its role, the university's standard administration manual said: "The Board of

Governors established the policy that all purchasing for the university be centralized for the sake of economy, budgeting control, and accounting" and "direct ordering from supplier by any department or person is not permitted and the University will not accept responsibility for goods so ordered." These statements were not fully accepted by many departments, and it was not unusual for individual professors, secretaries, technicians, or administrators to establish supplier contacts and make commitments without purchasing's knowledge or involvement.

For example, in June, 1973, Mr. Thompson, one of the assistant purchasing agents, received an order requesting confirmation for the purchase of a $140 piece of photographic equipment. He quickly found out that the price for the same product from the same catalog of the same company was $110. The 21 percent saving was never realized as the head of the requesting department politely told Mr. Thompson to mind his own business with the justification that he could spend the department's own money in his own ways.

Another incident involved printing and Mr. David, another assistant purchasing agent. Without reference to purchasing, the assistant dean of one of the faculties contacted a printing supplier and obtained a verbal quotation to perform an important printing job. He instructed the supplier to proceed and issued a requisition based on the original verbal quotation. No competitive quotation was sought. The supplier was advised to send the invoice to the faculty. Unexpected changes occurred which increased the costs of the job, raising the actual price 75 percent higher than the estimated one. Mr. David's first indication of this transaction appeared when he received a requisition with the invoice attached and a request for help from the assistant dean.

Mr. Emery suspected that examples like these were common in the whole university. He also knew that certain departments were taking full advantages of the purchasing services, while others seemed to accomplish a reasonably conscientious buying job, even though they bypassed purchasing or used it only for confirmation and paper work.

Purchasing department

Since August, 1973, the purchasing department reported directly to Mr. Emery, the excecutive assistant of the vice president of administration and finance. Mr. Martin, purchasing agent, was helped by four assistants specializing in different areas. Their principal functions were to place orders within authorized budget allowances, to secure quotations on goods and services required, to coordinate the purchases of commonly used items, to negotiate with suppliers, to interview sales representatives, and to maintain records of quotations and purchases. The total purchasing department staff amounted to 14 people (see Exhibit 2).

Exhibit 2

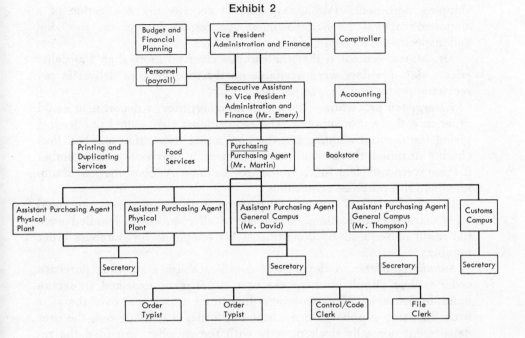

Purchasing had completed in 1971 a changeover to computerized operations to produce purchase orders and to gather statistical information.

Normal procedure. When university personnel requested goods, the following normal steps took place:

1. A department secretary prepared a purchase requisition and sent it by campus mail to purchasing.
2. In purchasing, the code clerk verified the account number validity, checked if sufficient funds were available in the budget allotment of the requisitioning department, and passed the requisition to Mr. Martin (or one of his assistants).
3. Mr. Martin completed delivery, shipping, and terms details; he entered commitment amount and follow-up date; he checked for tax exemptions as applicable and initialed the requisition.
4. An order typist produced a purchase order from the requisition.
5. A secretary checked the order and passed it to Mr. Martin for approval.
6. Mr. Martin returned the signed order to the secretary for mailing.
7. Finally, the file clerk distributed copies of the order to the accounts payable section, the requisitioning department, and the purchasing files.

The vendor subsequently delivered the goods to the requisitioning department. Then someone in this department was asked to sign the shipping documents. Purchasing did not receive any notification of a shipment's arrival. Each department was responsible for the receiving and inspection of its own goods.

Mr. Martin estimated that the campus received more than 150 deliveries a day. No data were available on the frequency of deliveries per receiving center, per day, or per year.

Emergency procedure.   In case of an emergency, a department could order directly from a supplier. The requisitioner then called purchasing, giving the account number and the purchasing requisition number. Purchasing scanned the account and assigned a purchase order number if there were sufficient funds in the free balance. A "confirmation" stamp identified this purchase requisition.

During the 1972–73 period, 30 percent of all requirements processed were marked confirmation; 16 percent of all requisitions handled were the result of requests by departments via telephone for purchase order numbers.

Standing orders.   A department could establish a standing purchase order with a supplier where the user department expected to secure multiple deliveries of various repetitive items or services over the year from the same supplier. Once a standing order was made out, the user department normally dealt directly with the supplier, provided the requests did not exceed the terms and conditions set out in the standing order. To initiate a standing order the requesting department had to complete the normal requisition form with mention of time and total dollar limits.

Systems contracting.   In 1970, Mr. Martin introduced the use of systems contract purchasing; for the 1972–73 period, systems contracting represented less than 1 percent of total purchases. It was confined to electrical, plumbing, and fasteners requirements.

Receiving problems

In October 1973, Mr. Emery initiated an inquiry into the newly renovated Central Administration Building to study the need for a centralized mailing, shipping, and receiving center in this building. It included 18 administrative departments. Excerpts from this inquiry were self-explanatory:

Stuff gets all over.

We have to bring dozens of boxes up, and we don't think this should be our job.

Hard to know if we've got everything.

Material can be here for two or three days, and we don't even know it's here.

Delivery men are wandering all over looking for someone to sign.

Delivery men can't find the room numbers of departments.

In discussion with Mr. Martin and his assistants, Mr. Emery learned that these findings could be a revealing sample of the receiving situation throughout the campus.

With budget cuts, limited personnel, and real building limitations, many departments had not placed someone in charge of the reception of goods. Therefore, no formal inspection was done. Purchasing's only involvement in the receiving process came when Mr. Martin or one of his assistants received calls to handle the problems caused by loss or damage. On occasion the shipper or the supplier dismissed any responsibility, arguing that materials had been delivered a week previously and that damage must have occurred afterwards. When a shipment was lost, purchasing had to reorder it, and it was quite possible that the university had to pay twice. Sometimes, when a follow-up order was delivered, it was found that the original need no longer existed.

Shippers were required to obtain a signature on their bill of lading. Delivery men often had difficulties finding someone willing to sign for a shipment. As a result, technicians, maintenance employees, and even students were approached by truckers. Sometimes a driver would get so frustrated that he dropped the goods off without a signature.

Even in those buildings where someone was placed in charge of receiving, truckers were often confused by the lack of signs and inconsistency of room numbers (e.g., Room 248 beside Room 232 and 234).

Because of the university's receiving arrangements, all kinds of situations could happen. For example, at the Business School, as in most departments, nobody was in charge of the reception of goods because of the relatively low number of orders. In September, 1972, a problem cropped up with the university directories. According to the supplier, the directories had been shipped; but nobody could find them. Finally, someone discovered that the garbage men had picked them up and that directories were missing throughout the campus. The university was obliged to reprint the order.

Sometimes it could take a long time to find out who owned parcels. A new receiver had been assigned at the physical plant department. In a dusty corner of the stockroom, he discovered two shipments dated August, 1972. The receiver called Mr. Thompson, the assistant agent, who checked all requests of the previous year and wrote to the supplier. But he had not been able to trace or identify the requisition. It was possible that a department had paid for it. Nobody knew.

The purchasing department had no record to indicate the frequency and the dollar value these incidents represented. Mr. Martin had no idea of how they related to total purchases, as most of the time each department found it easier to take care of its own problems. He estimated that such incidents might happen at least once a week in each receiving center. Nevertheless, he had never found out about an official claim from any supplier related to the receiving situation.

Mr. Emery was puzzled about improving the receiving situation as no proof existed that these unidentified but surely significant costs would be reduced if the receiving processes were changed. He wondered what steps could be undertaken to address this issue.

CANADIAN LIQUID AIR, LTD.

In early March, 1973, Mr. John Walton, vice president of Canadian Liquid Air, Ltd., was reviewing a proposal to introduce a four-day flexible working hour program in the company's head office purchasing department.

The company had adopted a similar program in the computer programming department in June of 1972. Preliminary results from both management and the department's employees' point of view were very favorable.

Due to the different nature of work in the purchasing department, Mr. Walton was unsure of the successful transferability of such a program.

The Company

Canadian Liquid Air, Ltd., with its head office in Montreal, has been engaged in the industrial gas and welding products business since 1911. It is a subsidiary of Liquid Air Corporation of North America, who also own Liquid Air, Inc., in a similar business based in San Francisco, and U.S. Divers Co., Santa Ana, California. Captain Jacques-Yves Cousteau is chairman of U.S. Divers Co., which is the leading manufacturer and distributor in the United States of underwater diving equipment, selling under the name Aqua-Lung.

L'Air Liquide of Paris, France, is the controlling shareholder of Liquid Air Corporation of North America. It was founded in 1902 to commercialize three fundamental discoveries of several French scientists: a process for separating air into its component parts, a process for storing acetylene under pressure, and the oxy-acetylene welding and cutting torches. L'Air Liquide, operating through over 100 subsidiaries with 330 plants in 53 countries, is one of the world's leading producers of industrial gases and welding products. It is also a leader in the engineering and construction of air separation plants and in the development of applications in the field of cryogenics.

Canadian Liquid Air, Ltd., has two main fields of activity:

1. The production and distribution of industrial and medical gases such as oxygen, nitrogen, argon, hydrogen, carbon dioxide, and acetylene, involving seven air separation plants and 21 other gas plants located from St. John's, Newfoundland, to Victoria, B.C.

2. The production and distribution of gas and electrical cutting and welding equipment and welding consummables. Four plants in the Montreal area produce electrical power sources, oxy-acetylene apparatus, welding electrodes, and welding wires.

The company is organized in seven operational units, two production and five regional. All operational units are supported by functional staff departments in the company's head office. Regional units include 27 branch sales and distribution locations and a network of over 80 specialized distributors. The company employs about 1,150 individuals, the majority being technically oriented male workers showing a low turnover and a high degree of company loyalty.

The company's sales reached the $65 million mark in 1973. Sales had grown 11 percent per year, in both gases and welding products over the last five years, whereas the number of employees grew 2 percent per year over the period.

The purchasing department

The department presently employs 15 people. Mr. E. Moffat, manager—purchasing and traffic, as three supervisors reporting directly to him. The rest of the department is made up of three buyers, three

Exhibit 1

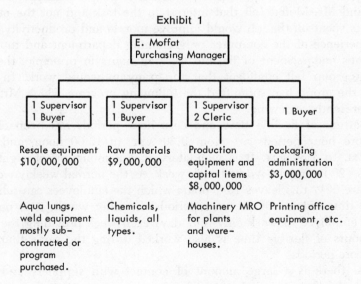

clerical staff, two secretaries and three more clerical people in the traffic and customs. (See Exhibit 1 for organization chart.)

The major purchases of the department are raw materials for the production of welding products and gases. The rest of the purchases are in the nature of welding equipment for resale and MRO items for the gas plants. Approximately 45 percent of each sales dollar is purchased at Canadian Liquid Air. The department has about $10 million in purchases of resale items on a computer record which is tied to an inventory control system. The other $20 million is for raw materials and for capital equipment used primarily in the distribution and storage of the company gas products. The department also deals with about 200 suppliers at least once a month and 300 at least once a year.

The purchasing department does not keep track of the number of calls or inquiries it handles on a daily basis. Mr. Moffat estimates that the volume is about equally divided between telephone and mail. Recent shortages in supply have increased the use of the telephone. Usually computer releases, blanket orders, and high-dollar value capital equipment purchases form the bulk of the mail items. The purchasing department sends out almost all orders and releases for the company and also audits invoices while much of the follow-up work is done by people at the local plants across the country.

The flexible working hour program

The purchasing department met in late January to discuss flexible working hours in the department. A number of people were very enthusiastic, and Mr. Moffat felt that interest in the task and not the number of hours spent on the job would improve morale and productivity. With the experience of the computer programming department and top management's endorsement of flexible working hours in principle, the purchasing group felt confident that the program would work. In early March the group had submitted the following program which Mr. Walton is presently reviewing.

A pattern of flexible time and core hour periods has been chosen. The core hour periods are from 9:30 A.M. to 12:00 noon, and from 2:00 P.M. to 4:30 P.M. It is mandatory that a minimum of eight core periods (20 hours) be worked each week. As the normal weekly working hours are 36¼ this leaves 16¼ hours which the employees can schedule at any time outside of the core periods. In other words, it is possible for an employee to work only four days each week providing the extra 16¼ hours of flexible time is also worked during the same four days as the core periods.

Since there is a large amount of contact with suppliers and sales people, all jobs in the department have to be covered five days a week. To solve this problem, the group decided to split into teams, with one team covering the jobs for the other during flexible hours and the fifth day of the week. A number of people would have to learn a second job to cover well, and planning the next week work schedule had to be done. A clock recording the number of hours worked would also be placed in the department. Four people in the department optioned to remain working the 8:40–5:00, five-day week.

Mr. Moffat listed a few of the potential benefits for his people:

1. Commuting time to work is reduced due to travel outside of congested rush hours.
2. Personal work habits are satisfied.
3. Education, formal and on-the-job, can be continued and facilitated by rescheduling hours.
4. Personal matters, i.e., dentist appointments can be scheduled outside of working hours.
5. A great deal of regimentation is taken out of the job, and cooperation with fellow workers is encouraged.

The company benefits were seen as:

1. A worker's work schedule establishes his own performance measure; thus, his competence is highly visible to management.
2. Lost time from sickness or absenteeism can be covered by other employees in the department.
3. Unnecessary procedures and routines can be spotted and eliminated.
4. Training will be shorter for job switches and for new employees.
5. Communication with employees is increased and strengthened.

Mr. Moffat felt that since the department built the plan and felt committed to it, the results should prove favorable. The department's efficiency could be improved, and the capabilities of the employees strengthened.

Mr. Walton felt that it was a matter of allowing employees to "think for themselves or not." Management had to be comfortable with that and not rely on managing by presences. His greatest reservation concerning the flexible working hour program was the ability of the employees to get along in such a seemingly free work environment.

4 QUALITY AND INSPECTION

The first step in any acquisition is to determine what is needed. This is followed by a decision on the quality of the material or item required and the control and measurement of this quality.

Definition of need—function

The term "need" is still a nebulous one. Every item to be purchased must perform a function. It must perform certain tasks. If it does not perform the function intended, the purchase may be a totally useless one and a waste of time, money, and effort. Similarly, quantity and price needs exist which are discussed in later chapters.

The function need requires some clarification. We seldom bother to think of the basic function the item must perform. We tend to speak of "a box" instead of "something to package this in;" "a bolt" instead of "something that fastens." We think of a steak, instead of something to eat; a bed, instead of something to sleep in; and a house, instead of a place to live. Note, that even when we issue an engineering drawing for a part, we really just say to a supplier, "Make this." And presumably, in our wisdom we have already made the decision that if the supplier makes the part as specified, it will perform the intended function. Seldom in our purchases do we dwell on this basic function aspect.

Why make an issue of this? It seems so simple and basic as to be hardly worth mentioning. But, actually, this is the heart of a sound purchasing system. Here lie the clues for improving the profitability of purchasing operations. A few simple examples will illustrate what is meant. A casual bypassing of the function need frequently results in improper specification. For example, a hose will be too short, a lining will shrink, a bolt shear, a motor burn out, a paint peel, a machine vibrate, a vessel burst, a part won't fit, an insurance policy won't cover, and a host of other troubles of this sort arise. Many of these troubles will result from underestimating the function required or from negli-

286

gence, error, or oversight, because certain functional needs have been forgotten or overlooked. We all laugh when we hear the story about the fellow who built the speedboat in the basement but couldn't get it out of the door. Yet, every day many people make this kind of mistake, perhaps not as glaring, or obvious, but often just as painful.

The answer to this problem, one will say, is to buy quality. As long as you buy good quality material you can't go wrong. Quality is really part of our function need. If the item is not of sufficient quality to perform the task required of it, it does not fulfill our function. Moreover, quality can be a cloak for various inadequacies. Buying the best quality, high alloy ½″ screws will not help if ⅝″ screws were needed in the first place. Buying high alloy screws when plain carbon mild steel ones will do is also going to increase costs unnecessarily.

If we define our basic functional need as a self-tapping or sheet metal screw, instead of a need to fasten together two sheets of metal of certain physical and chemical characteristics, we miss the first basic step in purchasing. We also miss the opportunity to investigate such alternatives as bolts, rivets, and spot welds, to name just a few. Frequently, and perhaps understandably, the tendency is to forget about the basic function need and to purchase something that will do the job for better or worse. This may become a dangerous guessing game that can lead to much trouble and cost a lot of extra money.

It is proper to emphasize here that in almost all industrial organizations the final responsibility for specifications lies with engineering.

Suitability

There is no such thing as quality divorced from an intended use. "Suitability" is more accurate.

The relationship between technical quality, on the one hand, and cost, on the other, is subject to a good deal of misunderstanding. Some persons appear to believe there are just two classes of goods in the market: one class purchased on the basis of quality and another in which quality is no considerable factor and which is sold entirely on a price basis. Such a conception is not sound. In every transaction, questions of price and quality are interrelated. The purchases made solely on a quality basis and with absolutely no reference to the price involved are so few both in number and in value as to make them practically negligible. On the other hand, goods in the so-called price class must have certain attributes of value or they could not command any price at all. The most that can be said, therefore, is that in some cases high quality is not as important as in other cases, and in some cases low-price merchandise is just as satisfactory to the buyer as high-price merchandise.

Reliability

In an effort to describe quality by a number the engineering profession has developed the concept of reliability: the mathematical probability that a product will function for a stipulated period of time. Originally, calculations like this were used in complex military electronic systems, but their use has spread into almost all types of products. The design of components in harmony with this concept allows for pre-determination of service calls and of what type at the design stage of equipment and, hence, the need for training of repair personnel and the size of spare parts inventory prior to actual manufacture. Complex military equipment is notoriously expensive to maintain with annual maintenance costs ranging from 60 percent to 1,000 percent of initial purchase cost.

Complexity is the enemy of reliability because of the multiplicative effect of probabilities of failure of components.

Consider a piece of equipment in which all parts have a reliability of 99.99 percent. If there are 100 parts, the overall reliability is reckoned to be 99 percent; 1,000 parts, 90 percent; 3,000 parts, 75 percent; 10,000 parts, 36.8 percent. The Telstar communication satellite has more than 10,000 electronic parts.

Such calculations are not entirely realistic, for they depend on two assumptions: first, that the failure of a single component causes failure of the whole system and, second, that failure of one component does not hasten or delay the failure of another. But designers often take pains to compensate for the partial or complete failure of some critical components, so that the whole equipment is not put out of action. In many instances the second assumption is nullified by the fact that the failure of one component changes the environment so greatly—e.g., by overheating—that nearby parts are likely to be affected.

The only way to get an entirely accurate reliability figure for a system is to build a number of the systems and test them until they fail. Unfortunately, in practice, the engineer can seldom do enough testing to get a figure that he can trust. It may be economically out of the question to fire off dozens of missiles or burn out many large radar receivers just to make a reliability prediction.

So usually the engineer must depend on what he knows about the reliability of components and synthesize a mathematical model that he hopes will enable him to predict accurately the reliability of the whole system. Fortunately, it is generally possible to get precise reliability measurements of most components by testing hundreds or thousands at a time. Sprague Electric Company, for example, has accumulated more than 200 million part-hours of test data on a top-grade capacitor developed for Minuteman. Such exhaustive testing is essential for developing what statisticians call a "confidence level"—the extent to which the reliability figure can be trusted. "Without high confidence levels, all calculations of system reliability are risky."[1]

---

[1] G. A. W. Boehm. "Reliability Engineering," *Fortune Magazine*, April 1963, pp. 7–8.

The distribution of failures is normally considered to be exponential, with failures occurring randomly. This facilitates calculations by making the reliabilities of the components additive. Testing is also more flexible because of the time-numbers trade-off. The same inference may be drawn from 20 parts tested for 50 hours as for 500 parts tested for 2 hours. Exceptions like the Weibull distribution (which accounts for the aging effect) and the bath tub curve (which recognizes the high probability of early failure, a period of steady state and a higher probability of failure near the end of the useful life) can also be handled, but they require more complex mathematical treatment.

From a procurement standpoint it is useful to recognize the varying reliabilities of components and products acquired. Penalties or premiums may be assessed for variation from design standard depending on the expected reliability impact.

Quality

"Quality" is a combination of characteristics, not merely one. The specific combination finally decided on is almost always a compromise, since the particular aspect of quality to be stressed in any individual case depends largely upon circumstances. In some instances the primary consideration is reliability; questions of immediate cost or facility of installation or the ease of making repairs are all secondary. In other instances the lifetime of the item of supply is not so important; efficiency in operation becomes more significant. Certain electrical supplies suggest themselves as illustrations. While a long life is desired, it is more important that the materials always function during such life as they may have than that they last indefinitely. Assuming dependability in operation and a reasonable degree of durability, the ease and simplicity of operation may become the determining factor. For instance, it is well known that the mechanism of the modern typewriter makes it dependable under all ordinary usages but that it is not essential for a typewriter to last indefinitely. Given these two factors more or less standardized among various types of machines, the determining factor is the ease with which the machine can be operated. What constitutes a satisfactory quality, therefore, depends largely on what a person is seeking in particular goods.

Perhaps an illustration will be helpful:

Paper towels come under the classification of bibulous papers, which are characterized by absorptiveness, loose formation, and softness. Blotting paper is a well-known example of a paper in this group. Towel and blotting papers are similar in their absorptive requirements, but the former must possess much greater strength than blotting papers. Unlike the latter they must be comparatively thin to have the required flexibility and yet must possess much greater strength than blotting paper so that they will not break under the severe conditions of usage. A good grade of paper toweling has two or three times the strength of blotting paper of the same fiber composition. In evaluating paper towels, therefore, the main consideration, in addition to absorptiveness and softness, is the strength. It is difficult to secure such a combination of desirable properties in the same sheet of paper.[2]

Decision on "best buy"

The decision on what to buy involves more than balancing various technical considerations. The most desirable technical quality or suitability for a given use, once determined, is not necessarily the desirable quality to buy. The distinction is between "technical" quality, which is strictly and entirely a matter of dimension, design, chemical, or physical properties, and the like, and the more inclusive concept of "economic" quality. Economic quality assumes, of necessity, a certain minimum measure of suitability but considers cost and procurability as well.

If the cost is so high as to be prohibitive, one must get along with an item somewhat less suitable. Or if, at whatever cost or however procurable, the only available suppliers of the technically perfect item lack adequate productive capacity or financial and other assurance of continued business existence, then, too, one must give way to something else. Obviously, too, frequent reappraisals are necessary, although a workable balance between technical and economic quality has been established. If copper rises from $0.70 a pound to $1.00 or more its relationship to aluminum may change.

The decision on what constitutes the best buy for any particular need is as much conditioned by procurement considerations as by technical quality. "Best quality" and "best buy" are one and the same. It should be clear that neither the engineer, the user or the production man, on the one hand, nor the purchasing officer, on the other, is qualified to reach a sound decision on the best buy unless they work closely together. The ability and willingness of all parties concerned to view the trade-offs in perspective will significantly influence the final decisions reached.

Importance of service in determining quality

Surely, with many items the service the vendor performs in connection with these items is quite as important as any attribute of the product itself. Many goods bought require no service; standard basic raw materials passing into manufacture are usually in this class. Many machines are so simple in construction that any ordinary mechanic can make repairs. At the other extreme are machines so complicated and delicate in adjustment that the manufacturer believes he can warrant satisfactory

---

[2] Bourdon W. Scribner and Russell W. Carr, *Standard for Paper Towels.* Circular C407 of the National Bureau of Standards.

performance of the machines only if his trained employees service them. One reason why the International Business Machines Corporation and the United Shoe Machinery Corporation originally had a policy of leasing many of their machines instead of selling them outright is that these companies wished to control the servicing of machines. The vendor feels that in his own interests he should supervise installation of the equipment, train the operators to be engaged on it, and perhaps provide occasional inspection afterward. Servicing may include expert repair, as in typewriters. To cover some types of service, vendors issue guarantees, covering periods of varying length. The value of such guarantees rests less upon the technical wording of the statement itself than upon the goodwill and reliability of the seller. Service, however, extends to considerations other than those of the type mentioned. Service by vendor may properly be said to include willingness to make satisfactory adjustments for misunderstandings or clerical errors.

Many vendors specifically include the cost of service in the selling price. Others absorb it themselves, charging no more than competitors and relying for the sale upon the superior service. One of the difficult tasks of a buyer is to get only as much of this service factor as is really needed without paying for the excessive service the vendor may be obliged to render to some other purchaser. In many instances, of course, the servicing department of a manufacturing concern is maintained as a separate organization. The availability of service is an important consideration for the buyer in securing the proper quality at the outset.

Responsibility for determining quality

It is generally accepted that the final verdict on technical suitability for a particular use should rest with the using department. Thus, questions on the quality of office supplies and equipment may be settled by the office manager; the quality of advertising material by the advertising department; maintenance supplies by the maintenance department; and operating supplies by the production department.

The ultimate responsibility for the quality of manufactured items should rest primarily with the engineering department charged with design and standards involving raw or semiprocessed materials and component parts. Basically, the immediate decision is an engineering-production decision. The person responsible for converting primary materials or semimanufactured articles into the finished product is the person who should have the authority to determine what is to be required. It is the purchasing agent's task to keep the cost of material down to the lowest point consistent with the standard quality required in the completed product. Purchasing's right to audit, question, and suggest must be recognized if this task is to be successful.

Purchasing fails to live up to its responsibility unless it insists that technical quality factors be considered and unless it passes on, to those immediately responsible for quality, suggestions of importance that may come as a result of its normal activities. The procurement officer is in a key position to present the latest information from the marketplace which may permit modifications in design, more flexibility in specifications, or changes in manufacturing methods which will reduce the cost of materials without detracting from their performance. Unless the engineer and the production executive are willing to consider the information presented by the procurement officer in attempting to determine the "best buy," the full benefits of effective operation of the procurement function are lost to the firm.

Responsibility of purchasing personnel

The trend toward securing full and active cooperation between the engineering, using, and procurement departments places a heavy responsibility upon purchasing men themselves, for unless they are well qualified to make real contributions toward determining the best buy, their suggestions are not likely to be considered seriously.

There are several ways this responsibility can be met. All of them or the uses to which the items are put, know as much as possible about the products they purchase. Of course, an adequate technical knowledge of maintenance, repair, operating, and other supplies is much more easily acquired than that for highly technical products, particularly those still in the developmental stage. The amount and character of the technical background required of a qualified buyer will therefore depend upon the nature of the commodities for which he is responsible. Likewise, the number of engineering qualified buyers in a department will vary from one type of company to another. This needs to be kept in mind by the reader evaluating the following alternatives.

The purchasing department may seek to increase the ability of its buyers to be of service in selecting the best quality in various ways:

1. *Select only persons with engineering training to fill buyers' jobs.* It is argued that an engineer has an advantage over a nontechnical person in buying because the basic engineering training and experience have given a thorough knowledge of materials, manufacturing methods, and inspection procedures. Thus equipped, the engineer commands the respect of those in the engineering and production departments and is able to "talk the language" of the designer and vendor.

There appears to be a trend toward employing engineers as buyers, although few purchasing departments are entirely so staffed, and many seriously question the necessity or desirability.

2. *Employ one or more engineers in the purchasing department to serve in a staff capacity as advisors to the various buyers in cases in*

which their advice and help are useful and to serve in a liaison capacity between the purchasing and engineering departments. This procedure can be helpful. Its value may be limited by the great variety of engineering problems with which they may be called to deal. It does not ensure that the buyer is qualified to know when and how best to use the services of these advisors.

3. *A third alternative is to transfer physically some of the purchasing personnel to the engineering department, where they are assigned desks adjacent to the engineers working on the same class of items as those in which the buyer is interested.* The reverse of this procedure is also followed at times, in which engineers (in some cases on a part-time basis) are assigned to purchasing departments for the purpose of furthering coordination between the two departments. Both these alternatives have obvious limitations, but they are steps in the right direction.

4. *Without making any changes in organization or personnel, buyers, assistant buyers, and others are encouraged to take advantage of night courses in blueprint reading, design, machine tool operations, cost accounting, engineering, materials, and similar studies.* Supervised plant visitations, films, and organized reading also may be used to advantage. Many executives feel this type of training is for most purposes entirely adequate, particularly when employees are brought into the purchasing department after plant experience. They feel that much of the work in the usual engineering school is of no special value to a buyer. They think that an alert, serious, conscientious person can gain an adequate background in those aspects of engineering and production necessary for satisfactory purchasing performance, particularly where a spirit of cooperation prevails.

Purchase analysis section

A development further emphasizing the effort to equip the purchasing department to deal more adequately with these technical problems is creating a purchase analysis[3] section within the department. The basic aim of purchase analysis is to determine what constitutes good value to assist in negotiations. In this respect there is nothing new about the idea. What is new is the increased emphasis placed on purchase analysis using a separate group of purchase analysts to coordinate this particular activity into an organized program. They work constantly in close cooperation with the engineering and production units of their own company and with vendors to determine designs, processes, and materials resulting in optimal value. These analysts are part of the purchasing department and are trained materials men and experienced engineers. In such companies as the Ford Motor Company, General Elec-

---

[3] Other terms in common use include: value analysis, value engineering, and purchase research.

tric Company, and others, they evaluate each product or component, piece by piece. They are concerned primarily with two questions: is its usefulness proportionate to its cost, and is a new or lower cost equivalent material or process available?

It should be emphasized that final responsibility for applying purchase analysis rests with the buyer. What an analyst seeks to do is to combine information on products, manufacturing methods, costs, prices, and markets, furnishing skilled advisory service to the buyer, who in turn coordinates the whole pricing operations and negotiates with vendors. (See also purchasing research and value analysis in Chapter 15.)

Description of quality

In any company it is not sufficient for the using department merely to know what quality is desired; that quality must be capable of reasonably accurate description. In no other way can the using department be assured of getting exactly what it wants. Although the responsibility for defining the quality needed usually rests with the using department in the first instance, the purchasing department has a very direct and immediate responsibility in checking the description given. The purchasing department should not, of course, be allowed to exercise its authority arbitrarily or to alter the description and change the quality or the character of the item being procured. It should, however, have the authority to insist that the description be sufficiently accurate and detailed to be perfectly clear to the supplier with whom the purchasing department must place the order. The purchasing officer has the direct responsibility of calling the attention of the using department to the added expense resulting when the description calls for an article not standard and likely to be more expensive for that reason.

The description of an item may take any one of a variety of forms or, indeed, may be a combination of several different forms. For our discussion, therefore, "description" will mean any one of the various methods by which a buyer undertakes to convey to a seller a clear, accurate picture of the required item. The term "specification" will be used in the narrower and commonly accepted sense of referring to one particular form of description.

The methods of description ordinarily used may be listed as follows and will be discussed in order:

1. By brand.
2. By specification:
    a. Description of physical or chemical characteristics;
    b. Material and method of manufacture;
    c. Performance.
3. By engineering drawing.

4. By miscellaneous methods, such as:
   a. Market grade;
   b. Sample.
5. By a combination of two or more of the above.

Description by brand

There are two questions of major importance in connection with the use of branded items. One relates to the desirability of using this type of description and the other to the problem of selecting the particular brand. Both these questions call for some detailed consideration.

Description by brand or trade name indicates a reliance upon the integrity and the reputation of the supplier. It assumes that the supplier is anxious to preserve the goodwill attached to a trade name and is capable of doing so. Furthermore, when a given supply is purchased by brand and is satisfactory in the use for which it was intended, the purchaser has every right to expect that any additional purchases bearing the same brand name will correspond exactly to the quality first obtained. The brand name is put upon an article to identify its origin. The manufacturer uses a brand name so that any goodwill cultivated among satisfied customers may redound to his benefit and profit and not to that of the distributor or of some other person. To protect this goodwill, however, it is essential that consistent quality be provided. Failure to maintain a consistent quality results in loss of confidence in the article by the users and, consequently, in ill will rather than goodwill.

There are certain circumstances under which description by brand may be not only desirable but also necessary:

a. When, either because the manufacturing process is secret or because the item is covered by a patent, specifications cannot be laid down.
b. When specifications cannot be laid down with sufficient accuracy by the buyer because the vendor's manufacturing process calls for a high degree of that intangible labor quality sometimes called "workmanship" or "skill," which cannot be defined exactly.
c. When the quantity bought is so small as to make the setting of specifications by the buyer unduly costly.
d. When, because of the expense involved or for some similar reason, testing by the buyer is impractical.
e. When the item is a fabricated part so effectively advertised by the maker as to create a real preference or even insistence on the part of the purchaser of the article in which it is incorporated.
f. When operating men often develop very real, even if unfounded, prejudices in favor of certain branded items, a bias the purchasing officer may find almost impossible to overcome.

On the other hand, there are some definite objections to purchasing branded items, most of them turning on cost. Although the price may often be quite in line with the prices charged by other vendors for similarly branded items, the whole price level may be so high as to cause the buyer to seek unbranded substitutes or even, after analysis, to set its own specifications. There are a great many articles on the market which, in spite of all the advertising, have no brand discrimination at all. Thus, the purchaser may just as well prefer using trisodium phosphate at 14 cents per pound as a branded cleaning compound costing 20 to 24 cents per pound.

A further argument, frequently encountered, against using brands is that undue dependence on them tends to restrict the number of potential suppliers and deprives the buyer of the possible advantage of a lower price or even of improvements brought out by competitors through research and invention.

If a purchase is to be made on the basis of brand, how is one to select the particular brand to buy? The buyer is, of course, confronted by many questions, of which quality, although primary, is but one. Testing provides an answer.

Brand testing. The original selection of a given brand may be based either upon a specific test or a preliminary trial. Once selected, it may or may not be subjected to periodic comparative tests. The brand tests are, in most instances, brought to the attention of the buyer by salesmen, although the purchasing officer may initiate an inquiry.

When salesmen offer samples for brand testing, the general rule apparently followed by purchasing men is to accept samples only of brands that have some chance to be used, although if there is any question about possible use, purchasing officers are more likely to accept samples than to reject them, since they are always on the lookout for items that may prove superior to those in current use. For various reasons, however, care does have to be exercised. For one thing, the samples cost the seller something, and the buyer will not wish to raise false hopes on the part of the salesman. Sometimes, too, the buyer lacks adequate facilities for testing.

To meet these objections, some companies insist on paying for all samples accepted for testing, partly because they believe that a more representative sample is obtained when it is purchased through the ordinary trade channels and partly because the buyer is less likely to feel under any obligation to the seller. Some companies pay for the sample when the value is substantial; some follow the rule of allowing whoever initiates the test to pay for the item tested; some pay for it only when the outcome of the test is satisfactory. The general rule is for the seller to pay for the sample on the theory that, if he really wants the business and has confidence in his product, he will be willing to bear the expense.

Use and laboratory tests. The type of test given also varies, depending upon such factors as the attitude of the buyer toward the value of specific types of tests, the type of item in question, its comparative importance to the company, and the buyer's facilities for testing. At times a use test alone is considered sufficient, as with paint and typewriter ribbons. One advantage of a use test is that the item can be tested for the particular purpose for which it is intended and under the particular conditions in which it will be used. The risk that failure may be costly or interrupt performance or production is, however, present. At other times a laboratory test alone is thought adequate and may be conducted by a commercial testing laboratory. Frequently, a preliminary laboratory test is given to determine whether or not a use test is worthwhile.

The actual procedure, in accordance with which samples are handled, need not be outlined here. It is important that full and complete records concerning each individual sample accepted should be made out and filed. These records should include not only the type of test but the conditions under which it was given, the results, and any representations made about it by the seller.

Description by specification

Description of desired material on a basis of specifications constitutes one of the best known of all methods employed. Like many of the other methods, it is used at one time or another by probably the great majority of manufacturing companies and governmental agencies for at least some part of their requirements. A great deal of time and effort has been expended in making it possible for purchasing officers to buy on a specification basis. Closely related to these endeavors is the effort toward standardization of product specifications and reduction in the number of types, sizes, and so on, of the products accepted as standard.

These efforts have been expended in the belief that, regardless of the particular type of specification, there are advantages in buying on specifications. Among them may be mentioned the following:

1. Adequate specifications are evidence that thought and careful study have been given to the need for which the material is intended and to the particular characteristics of the material demanded to satisfy this need.

2. Specifications constitute a standard for measuring and checking materials as supplied, preventing delay and waste that would occur with improper materials.

3. They are of definite value to the large consumer wishing to purchase identical material from a number of different sources of supply, either because no one manufacturer possesses the productive capacity

to meet all the buyer's requirements or because the buyer considers it good policy. To ensure identity of materials secured, adequate specifications are almost indispensable.

4. Purchase on a basis of specification tends toward ensuring more equitable competition. This is why governmental agencies place such a premium on specification writing. In securing bids from various suppliers, a buyer must be sure that the suppliers are quoting for exactly the same material or service.

5. When the buyer specifies performance, the seller will be responsible for performance.

While there are certain distinct advantages in buying on specification, using specifications does not constitute a panacea for all difficulties involving quality. The limitations involved in using specifications fall into seven classes:

1. There are many items for which it is practically impossible to draw adequate specifications.

2. Although a saving may sometimes be realized in the long run, the use of specifications adds to the immediate cost. If, therefore, the article desired is one not purchased in large quantities and does not need to conform particularly to any definite standards, it is frequently inadvisable to incur the additional expense of attempting to buy such materials on a specification basis. Some purchasing directors, when sending specifications for a special item, request the vendor to quote on the basis of the specifications and at the same time to indicate whether or not a standard article closely approaching the one specified is available and, if so, to quote a price on the standard article, indicating how it differs from the specifications submitted.

3. Compared with purchase by brand, the immediate cost is also increased by the necessity of testing to insure that the specifications have been met.

4. One of the difficulties arising from the use of specifications come from carelessness in drawing them when they are likely to give the purchaser a false sense of security.

5. At the opposite extreme is setting up specifications so elaborate and so detailed as to defeat their own purpose. Unduly elaborate specifications sometimes result in discouraging possible suppliers from placing bids in response to inquiries.

6. Unless the specifications are of the performance type, the responsibility for the adaptability of the item to the use intended rests wholly on the buyer, provided only that the item conforms to the description submitted.

7. The minimum specifications set up by the buyer are likely to be the maximum furnished by the supplier.

If after weighing these advantages and disadvantages, the buyer decides to purchase on a specification basis, four major choices are available: specification by physical or chemical characteristics, by material or method of manufacture, by standards, or by performance.

Specification by physical or chemical characteristics

Specification by physical or chemical characteristics or "dimensional specification" provides definitions of the properties of the materials the purchaser desires. They represent an effort to state in measurable terms those properties deemed necessary for satisfactory use at the least cost consistent with quality. They often include information on methods of test and disposition of material in case of failure to meet requirements. Little more need be said concerning this type of specification. Most buyers use it to some extent for such items as oil, paint, and cotton gray goods, although this usage varies widely from company to company.

Specification by material and method of manufacture

The second type of specification includes those prescribing both the material and method of manufacture. Outside of some governmental purchases, such as those of the armed forces, this method is used when special requirements exist and when the buyer is willing to assume the responsibility for results. Many organizations are not in this position, and as a result, comparatively little use is made of this form of specification.

It is with particular reference to the two methods of specification just considered that most of the well-known "standard" specifications apply. Some attention, therefore, may well be given to the matter of sources of specifications before considering other methods of quality description.

Sources of specification data

Speaking broadly, there are three major sources from which specifications may be derived: (1) individual standards set up by the buyer; (2) standards established by certain private agencies—either other users, suppliers, or technical societies; and (3) governmental standards.

Individual standards require extensive consultation between users, engineering, purchasing, quality control, suppliers, marketing, and, possibly, ultimate consumers. This means the task is likely to be arduous and expensive.

A buyer needs to be quite sure not only that it is best to acquire a given item on the basis we are now considering but also that there is no standard specification available serving this purpose equally well.

A common procedure is for the buying company to formulate its own specifications on the basis of the foundation laid down by the governmental or technical societies. To make doubly sure that no serious errors have been made, some companies mail out copies of all tentative specifications, even in cases where changes are mere revisions of old forms, to several outstanding manufacturers in the industry to get the advantage of their comments and suggestions before final adoption.

Standard specifications

If an organization wishes to buy on a specification basis, yet hesitates to undertake to originate its own, it may resort to one of the so-called standard specifications. These have been developed as a result of a great deal of experience and study by both governmental and nongovernmental agencies, and substantial effort has been expended in promoting them. They may be applied to raw or semimanufactured products, to component parts, or to the composition of material. The well-known SAE steels, for instance, are a series of alloy steels of specified composition and known properties, carefully defined, and identified by individual numbers. When they can be used, standard specifications have certain definite advantages. For one, they are widely known and commonly recognized. This makes them readily available to every buyer. Furthermore, this standard should have somewhat lower costs of manufacture. Finally, because they have grown out of the wide experience of producers and users, they should be adaptable to the requirements of a great many purchasers.

On the other hand there are certain disadvantages limiting the value of standard specifications. One of the most commonly urged objections is that just because they are standard, some of them are of necessity so broad as to be unsuited to the requirements of particular users. In some instances, too, certain so-called standard specifications have not been, as yet, sufficiently well accepted to warrant such designation.

Standard specifications have been developed by a number of nongovernmental engineering and technical groups. Among them may be mentioned the American Standards Association, the American Society for Testing Materials, the American Society of Mechanical Engineers, the American Institute of Electrical Engineers, the Society of Automotive Engineers, the American Institute of Mining and Metallurgical Engineers, the Underwriters Laboratories, the National Safety Council, the Canadian Engineering Standards Association, the American Institute of Scrap Iron and Steel, the National Electrical Manufacturers' Association, and many others.

While governmental agencies have cooperated closely with the above mentioned organizations, operations for compiling specifications have been conducted independently in developing standards for use in purchasing for the various governmental departments and agencies. The National Bureau of Standards in the U.S. Department of Commerce compiles commercial standards. The General Services Administration coordinates standards and federal specifications for the nonmilitary type of items used by two or more services. The Defense Department issues military (MIL) specifications for items involving all types of military equipment.

Standardization and simplification

No consideration of specifications would be complete without some reference to the efforts to standardize and simplify them. Some comments need to be made on this movement from a procurement angle, although no extended discussion is possible here.

In many discussions of this subject, these two terms are used as meaning much the same thing. Strictly speaking, they refer to two different ideas. "Standardization" means agreement upon definite sizes, design, quality, and the like. It is essentially a technical and engineering concept. "Simplification" refers to a reduction in the number of sizes, designs, and so forth. It is a selective and commercial problem, an attempt to determine the most important sizes, for instance, of a product and to concentrate production on these wherever possible. Simplification may be applied to articles already standardized as to design or size, or it may be applied as a step preliminary to standardization.

There are several sales aspects to the simplification-standardization movement. To the extent that standardization occurs, the salesman is compelled to stress not diversity in production as much as better product or service at the same price or of the same product at a lower price. It is just at this same point that a problem is created. If the product the buyer is purchasing is itself a completed product consumed in its finished form, then some reasonable measure of diversity in suppliers' offerings may well be desirable to get as large a degree of suitability for his particular use as possible. As N. F. Harriman has so aptly said in his *Standards and Standardization:* "Standardization is a useful servant but a bad master." That variations in completed products may have embodied a substantial measure of standardized components is no drawback to the buyer. Because it facilitates replacements, it becomes a positive advantage. The problem from a selling angle becomes one of how to secure all the advantages of technological improvement, of originality and advanced design, to have "something better" to sell, while at the same time securing the economies of production.

For the industrial product the answer to this dilemma is probably to be found in two different areas. The first is in the large measure of cooperation among the production, procurement, and sales divisions that we have stressed so continually.

A second part of the answer is to be found in stressing not standard-ization and simplification in the end product but the component parts. By so doing, the production economies are combined with individuality of end product. So, too, can be obtained the procurement advantages of low initial cost, lower required inventory, and diversity in selection of source.

Specification by performance

Performance specification is a method employed to considerable ex-tent, partly because it throws the responsibility for a satisfactory prod-uct back to the seller. Performance specification is results and use ori-ented, leaving the supplier with the decisions on how to make the most suitable product. This enables the supplier to take advantage of the latest technological developments and to substitute anything that exceeds the minimum performance required.

The satisfactory use of a performance specification, of course, is abso-lutely dependent upon securing the right kind of supplier. There are also some buyers who may resort to such specifications as an alibi for not going to the trouble of getting an exact method of description or of locating more satisfactory sources. Finally, particularly because of the difficulty of comparing quotations, the price paid may prove rather high.

Specification to meet government legal requirements

Recent federal legislation concerning employee health and safety and consumer product safety requires increased vigilance on the part of purchasing personnel to be sure that products purchased meet the gov-ernment requirements. The Occupational Safety and Health Administra-tion (known as OSHA) of the U.S. Department of Labor has broad powers to investigate and control everything from noise levels to sanitary facilities in places of employment. The Consumer Product Safety Act gives broad regulatory power to a commission to safeguard consumers against unsafe products. Purchasing people have the responsibility to make sure that the products they buy meet the requirements of the legislation. Severe penalties both criminal and civil can be placed on violators of the regulations.

Description by engineering drawing

Description by a blueprint or dimension sheet is very common and may be used in connection with some form of descriptive text. It is particularly applicable to the purchase of machine parts, forgings, castings, and punchings. It is an expensive method of description not only because of the cost of preparing the print itself but also because it is likely to be used to describe an item which is quite special as far as the vendor is concerned and, hence, expensive to manufacture. However, it is probably the most accurate of all forms of description and is particularly adapted to purchasing those items requiring a high degree of manufacturing perfection and close tolerances.

Miscellaneous methods of description

Description by market grades. Purchase on the basis of market grades is confined to certain primary materials. Wheat and cotton[4] have already been referred to in this connection; lumber, butter, and other commodities will suggest themselves. Purchase by grade is for some purposes entirely satisfactory. Its value depends upon the accuracy with which grading is done and the ability to ascertain the grade of the material by inspection. Setting up a definite series of grades sufficiently numerous to cover all major and perhaps minor divisions and the common acceptance of these grades by the trade are, of course, essential. The grading, furthermore, must be done by those in whose ability and honesty the purchaser has confidence. It may be noted that even for wheat and cotton, however, grading may be entirely satisfactory to one class of buyer and not satisfactory to another class. The differences between the upper and the lower limits of the recognized grades of wheat are such as to make possible delivery of wheat not at all suited to the user's requirements. It is for this reason that millers buy only by sample or after physical examination of the wheat. Another difficulty arises in cases in which cotton is bought on the cotton exchange contracts permitting delivery of various grades of cotton and adjustment of payment on a basis of the commercial differences in price between the grades delivered. Although this method may be satisfactory for a cotton merchant, it will not serve a cotton manufacturer.

Description by sample. Still another method of description is by submission of a sample of the item desired. Almost all purchasing officers use this method from time to time but ordinarily—there are some exceptions—for a minor percentage of their purchases and then more or less because no other method is possible.

Good examples are: items requiring visual acceptance, e.g., wood grain, color, appearance, etc.

---

[4] For agricultural raw materials, such as wheat and cotton, the grades are established by the U.S. Department of Agriculture. These include all food and feed products, the standards and grades for which have been established in accordance with the Federal Food and Drugs Act, the Grain Standards Act, and other laws enacted by Congress. As will be noted later, establishing grades acceptable to the trade is essential to the successful operation of a commodity exchange.

Combination of methods of description

A company frequently uses a combination of two or more of the methods of description already discussed. The exact combination found most satisfactory for an individual organization will depend, of course, upon the type of product made by the company and the importance of quality in its purchases. There is no one best method applicable to any single product, nor is there for any particular company a best method of procedure. The important thing for the individuals is to keep in mind that the objective of all description is to secure exactly the right quality, neither better nor worse, at the best price that can be secured.

Metric conversion

North America is currently engaged in a major planning program to convert to the metric system of measurement. Plans call for industry-wide changes in stages and a high degree of participation and consultation between companies and government. The International System of Units or "SI" in abbreviated form has the advantage of simplicity and universality. It is expected that the conversion will be largely accomplished over the next ten years. Since the conversion of industries and individual organizations is expected to follow voluntary lines, metric conversion committees of national associations are expected to play a major role. The National Association of Purchasing Management recommends that every corporation form a metric conversion committee to plan for orderly internal change. The materials manager and purchasing manager are obvious candidates to head such a committee.

CONTROL OF QUALITY—INSPECTION

Purpose of inspection

Just as the purpose of adequate description is to convey to the vendor a clear idea of the item being purchased, so the purpose of inspection is to assure the buyer that the supplier has delivered an item which corresponds to the description furnished. Regardless of how reliable the purchaser may have found the seller to be in the past and regardless of the care with which a manufacturer may inspect his product before he ships it, mistakes and errors of various sorts do occur. No such body of past experience exists when new suppliers are being tried, and their products must be watched with particular care until they have proved themselves dependable. Unfortunately, too, production methods and skills, even of old suppliers, change from time to time; operators become careless; and occasionally a seller may even try to reduce production costs to the point where quality suffers. Thus, for a variety of reasons, it is poor policy for a buyer to neglect inspection methods or procedures. There is no point to spending time and money upon the development of satisfactory specifications unless some adequate provision is made through inspection to see that the specifications are lived up to by vendors.

The type of inspection and the frequency and thoroughness with which it is conducted clearly vary with circumstances. In the last analysis, this problem resolves itself into a matter of comparative costs, the question at issue being, how much must the company spend in order to ensure proper compliance with its specifications?

What is reasonable inspection?

What is reasonable inspection? No formula will give the answer. The importance of inspection is in proportion to the importance of the quality. Even a small quantity of a material in which quality is highly important may call for very rigid inspection, and permissible variations from standard may be very small. Generally speaking, when quantities are small and considerable variations of quality are permissible, inspection is of less importance than when the contrary conditions prevail. Merchandise which is bought by brand may call for occasional inspection to ensure consistency of quality, but it is more than likely that a check on the results obtained by the using department would be satisfactory for this purpose. Products bought on the basis of grades must be checked as to their compliance with the grade specified. The same rule applies to purchases made on a basis of samples. Products which are bought on a specification basis are usually sufficiently important to require rather close checking.

While it is true that on items of major equipment and, in some cases, on fabricating parts, a very careful and detailed inspection is called for on every item delivered, inspection based on a test of samples taken from the shipment should, in the main, prove adequate. In all cases, of course, where the purchaser has any reason whatsoever to question the condition of an incoming shipment, inspection is necessary.

Specification of inspection method

In setting specifications, it is sometimes the practice to include the procedure for inspection and testing. This leaves the method of testing within the discretion of the buyer. Since methods may vary widely, they can be made unfair to the seller and be made grounds for rejection of merchandise almost at the whim of the purchaser. Specifying the inspection method is a protection to the buyer, since the vendor cannot refuse to accept rejected goods on the ground that he did not understand the type of inspection to which the goods would be subjected or that the inspection was unduly rigid. Instructions which indicate merely that a specified number of samples of a shipment are to be tested may have little value unless it is made clear how these samples are to be chosen. For instance, if all the samples are taken from the top of a certain solution, the results are likely to be very different from what they would be if the samples were taken from the bottom. Similarly, samples chosen from the beginning of a run from a die are likely to be different from the one-thousandth or one-millionth sample from the same die.

In such a situation, not only the method of selecting the sample but also the statistical limits (as distinct from the so-called engineering limits) to be imposed should be indicated. Indeed, it may be well for a company doing a large amount of buying of items that require statistical methods in sampling to work out in some detail a standardized statement of procedure, perhaps even with some discussion of the theory and practice involved. Such a statement placed in the hands of a supplier might avoid considerable misunderstanding.

Quality control department

Up to this point we have assumed that the responsibility of a quality control group is narrowly confined to the technical task of submitting incoming material to certain definite tests in order to answer the one question, does this item comply with the description as defined in the purchase order?—the answer always being a definite Yes or No. Granting that the primary objective of inspection is to answer this one question, does it follow that management has no right to expect more? If we are considering the function of inspection, more may very well be expected. If, on the other hand, we are considering the place of inspection in a particular company, then the answer will depend upon such factors as the organization of the company, its ability to maintain inspection facilities, and the character of the material used.

Actually, a number of duties other than straight testing of incoming material may be undertaken by the quality control group and very properly so. Thus, the quality control department should assist in setting specifications, if for no other reason than to pass upon the company's ability to test for compliance with them. Clearly, it is useless to call for characteristics the presence or absence of which cannot be determined. Again, the quality group can initiate material studies. It can be called upon to pass on samples left by salesmen. Frequently it must investigate claims and errors, both as to incoming items and as to outgoing or finished products. It may pass upon material returned to stores to determine its suitability for reissue. Similarly, it may be called upon to examine salvage material and to make a recommendation as to its disposition. It may also assist in assessing the quality assurance programs in supplier's plants.

Location of the quality control department

The location of the quality control department constitutes a relevant problem of administration. In most cases the work of inspection is performed by a separate department. The department's work may be divided into three parts: the inspection of incoming materials, the inspection of materials in process of manufacture, and the inspection of the finished product. The assignment of this work in such cases to a separate department is supported partly on the ground that if the inspectors of materials in process and of the finished product report to the executive in charge of production, there may be occasions when inspection standards are relaxed in order to cover up defects in production which, if discovered, would affect adversely the record of the production department. If the inspectors of incoming materials were under the administration of the purchasing director, there might, on some occasions, be a tendency to relax inspection standards in order to pass materials which the purchasing director had procured because of a substantial reduction in price but which did not meet the quality standards specified.

Since the production department is frequently expected to discover defects in materials during the manufacturing process, the contention is often held that it should also have responsibility for the inspection of material before it enters the manufacturing process. However, the inspection of incoming materials by a purchasing department is not parallel to this. The test being made is not of the purchasing department's own work but rather of that of the vendors. It is true that an undue number of rejections may reflect upon the buyer's selection of a source, but no one is more interested in eliminating unreliable vendors than the purchasing officer. The only exceptions to this statement are those cases in which collusion or dishonesty exists or the purchasing officer is buying on a price basis.

The really important things to keep in mind are:

1. Inspection involves not only purchased material and parts but also work in process and finished goods.
2. Inspection at any stage is a technical problem of where, when, how much, and how to inspect. Also, it frequently requires the use of more or less technical equipment.
3. The importance of quality varies from industry to industry and from company to company. This fact has direct bearing on the inspection problem.
4. Inspection should be remedial and preventive as well as negative. As has been pointed out, the constructive aspects of inspection are as important as that of testing.
5. Any organization for inspection involves intraplant administrative problems pertaining to personnel, cost control, and relations with

various departments, such as stores and production units, records, and so forth.

6. The real purpose of all inspection is to get materials and parts of the sort needed. This cannot be attained in the long run without good vendor relations and a sound purchasing policy.

Occasionally, the inspection is conducted by the buyer (or under his auspices) in the plant of the vendor. A great proportion of the procurements by the armed services are so inspected. Inspection at the supplier's plant is undertaken for several reasons. The usual methods of inspection of the finished item may not be adequate. Latent defects not determinable may appear only after the purchaser has further processed the material or part. Again, the correction of defects, if attended to as soon as possible, avoids the additional costs of carrying the work on to completion, only to find the end result unacceptable. Furthermore, transportation charges incident to the return to the vendor of rejected material, especially on heavy material or that shipped long distances, can be avoided. On the other hand inspection at the plant has two definite disadvantages, even where otherwise apparently desirable. One is the heavy cost of securing, training, and supervising an inspection staff. The second is that the presence of inspectors in his plant may be strongly resented by the supplier.

A different kind of buyer inspection at the seller's premises takes place when selection, rather than production of a commodity, determines the quality and when price varies accordingly. Examples would include but are not limited to: veneer and saw logs, pulp wood, livestock, land, feed and mixed grains, used equipment, antiques, paintings, scrap, and professional contracts. Furthermore, on premise buyer inspection almost always applies in conventional auctions but almost never in the case of dutch auctions.

The quality capability survey

The increased emphasis on reliability brought on by space age technology has created the requirement that suppliers be evaluated prior to the placing of an order and that continuous subsequent monitoring take place. This "quality capability survey" has become especially widespread in the aero space and military industry with a reported use in excess of 80 percent of all cases. It is interesting that despite widespread use of this technique, recent research findings show the survey's results to be statistically questionable.[5,6] This is unfortunate, because the ability to determine, a priori, whether one supplier has a better chance than

[5] R. W. Olive, "The Quality Capability Survey: A Procurement Quality Management Control," *Journal of Purchasing*, vol. 5 no. 1 (February 1969), pp. 5–22.

[6] R. W. Olive, "The Quality Capability Survey: Results, Reliability and Recommendations," *Journal of Purchasing*, vol. 5, no. 2 (May 1969), pp. 15–42.

another of meeting the desired quality standards is highly desirable. Since the principle is obviously attractive, the real question deals with our future ability to develop a better test instrument.

Commercial testing labs and services

The type of inspection required by a company may, in fact, be so complicated or so expensive that it cannot be performed satisfactorily in the company's own organization. In such cases some companies employ the services of commercial testing laboratories, particularly in connection with new processes or materials or for aid in the setting of specifications. The use of these agencies by manufacturers for any other purpose is limited; most companies do not use them at all and others only under unusual circumstances.

It is possible that the services of commercial testing laboratories are not used by some companies as much as they should be. Many of these laboratories are very dependable. They employ capable staffs and own the most modern of photometric, X-ray, electrical, chemical, and physical testing equipment. Their charges are commonly not unreachable for manufacturers in a position to use them. Standard testing reports of commonly used items are available from several commercial testing laboratories. They are the commercial equivalent of consumer's reports and can be a valuable aid. (See the Kerr Life Insurance Company case for a sample report on service contracts.)

Inspection methods

Although it is not the purpose of this text to cover the choice of inspection methods extensively, it is proper to mention them briefly here in the recognition that procurement costs and performance may be significantly affected by this decision. The same inspection methods may be used by either the manufacturer or the purchaser. Since almost all output results from a manufacturing or transformation process of some sort, process quality control will be the first item discussed. This will be followed by screening and sampling which deal with items already produced. All quality control can be divided further into observations of attributes and variables. Attributes usually observed are whether the product is acceptable or not. For example, for an automobile assembly line, is the paint acceptable or not? In a hotel, have the rooms been properly cleaned or not? This type of yes or no inspection is usually based on the binominal distribution. The generating function for this distribution is:

$$P(r) = \frac{n!}{r!(n-r)!} P^r (1-p)^{n-r} \text{ [7]}$$

---

[7] M. F. Spiegel, *Theory and Problems of Statistics* (New York: Schaum Publishing Co. 1961), p. 122.

Figure 4–1
FILLER CONTROL CHART, SUMMARY, AND EXPLANATIONS

A–2R	UCLR AA	LCLX ,,	X	UCLX ..
□	A	* ,	4	.
	A	* ,	1	.
	A	* ,		. # 2
	A	* ,		.
□	A	* ,	3	.
	A	* ,	4	.
	A	* ,	1	.
	A	* ,	2 #	.
□	A	* ,		. 3
	A	* ,	4	.
	A	* ,	1	.
□	A	2 * , #		.
	A	3 * ,	4	.
	A	1 * , #	2	.
□	A	3 * ,	4	.
	A	* ,	1	.
	A	* ,	# 2	.
	A	* ,	3	.
□	A	1 * , #	2	.
	A	3 * ,	4	.
	A	* ,	1	.
	A	* , #	2	.
	A	3 * ,	4	.
□	A	* ,	3	. 1
	A	4 * ,	2 #	.
	A	* ,	3	.
	A	1 * ,	#	.
	A	2 * , #	1	.
	A	* ,	4	. 4
□	A	3 * ,	1	.
	A	2 * , #		.
	A	* ,	1	.
	A	3 * ,	4	.
□	A	1 * ,	2 #	.
	A	* ,	3	.
	A	* . ,	1	4 .
	A	* ,		. 2
	A	* ,	3	.
□	A	* , # 2	4	.
	A	* ,	1	.
□	A	3 * ,		.
	A	4 * ,		. 1
	A	* ,	2 #	.
	A	3 * ,	4	.
	A	2 * ,	#	.
□	A	* . ,	4	.
	A	* ,	3	.
	A	* ,	4	. 1
	A	2 * , #		.
	A	4 * ,		.
	A	* ,	2 #	.
	A	3 * ,		. 3
	A	* ,	4	.
□	A	* ,		.

Partial Control Chart
(Average & Range)
Filler

CASE & LINE	HEAD	CAPABILITY	PACKAGE WEIGHT	PACKAGE WEIGHT	CONTROL	CHART	SUMMARY
AB 3	4	.026000	11.00		JANUARY 20		
	DAY					DAY	MONTH
A–2R		MONTH	DAY	MONTH		PKGS	WEIGHT	WEIGHT	PKGS
STD DEV.		.037960	% VAR FROM CAPABIL.		LIGHT			4.90–	126
UCLR AA		.025255	100.00000	2.86538	% LIGHT				6.73
LCLX ..		.118560			TOTAL NA			75.06	1872
X 5% CTL		.003584			AV OVERWT			.04010	
UCLX ..		.041544			% OVERWT			.36455	
		.079504			TOTAL NR			23.70	1824

Figure 4–1 (Continued)

Terminology:

A-$2R$—$(A_2\bar{R})$ where A_2 is a constant for a sample of 4 and $\bar{\bar{X}}' \pm A_2\bar{R}$ gives the upper and lower control limits.

$UCLR$—(UCL_R) Upper control limit, range

$LCLX$—$(LCL_{\bar{X}})$ Lower control limit, average

$X\ 5\%\ XTL$—$(\bar{X}')_1$ point at which average is set to insure that 95 percent of packages will equal or exceed stated net weight (CTL—control limit)

$UCLX$—$(UCL_{\bar{X}})$ Upper control limit, average

Capability—Capability of machine under control conditions

% Var. from capability—A percent by which the daily or month to date capability varies from the capability under control conditions

Package weight—Package weight (net) in ounces

Light—Number of packages under net weight

% Light—Percent of packages under net weight

Total NA—Total sample size

Av overwt.—Total overweight divided by the total sample size (gives average weight over net weight)

% Overwt.—Average overweight divided by the package weight

Total NR—The Total NR figure is similar to the Total NA figure except that the computer rejects samples which have "gone wild." These are removed and the Total NR figure is used to calculate the standard deviation

Note: Figure 4–1 is a composite of two control charts. The two columns on the left refer to the range control chart while the remaining three columns represent the weight control chart. The symbols 1, 2, 3 and 4 on the weight control chart refer to the observation number and the sample average is designated by the symbol #.

where p is the probability that the event associated with r will occur on any single trial and n is the number of trials.

Observation by variables tries to determine by how much the sample varies from the specification or from other units. How many paint defects on this car? How many things are wrong with the way this hotel room has been cleaned? Observation by variables is usually based on the normal distribution.

Process quality control

In processes using repetitive operations, the quality control chart is often valuable. Management attempts to produce a satisfactory output population which can be measured by an acceptable mean and dispersion. The $\bar{X}$ chart is useful for charting the population mean and the $\bar{R}$ chart the dispersion.

One key decision in using the $\bar{X}$ and $\bar{R}$ charts involves the choice of upper and lower control limits. The tighter these limits are placed, the greater the probability of rejection and, hence, the larger the manufacturing cost will become. Normally, a plus or minus range of two to three standard errors of the mean is used. The desired population mean is drawn horizontally (or vertically) as the central line on the chart. See Figure 4–1.

Inspectors or operators make random checks of the variables to be controlled and plot the results on the graph. If the average of the samples fall within the limits of the control chart the process is allowed to continue. If the averages fall outside the control limits, the process is normally stopped, and action is taken to determine the cause for the shift so that corrections can be made. The control chart uses random sampling techniques and is well suited to most manufacturing operations of large output and where it is not necessary to screen every item produced. This raises the decision regarding inspection of output.

Output inspection—100 percent inspection and sampling

There are basically two major types of quality checks on output. One is to inspect every item produced. The other is to sample.

100 percent inspection or screening. It is traditionally held that 100 percent inspection, or screening, is the most desirable inspection method available. This is not true. Experience shows that 100 percent inspection seldom accomplishes a completely satisfactory job of separating the acceptable from the nonacceptable or measuring the variables properly. Actually, 200 percent or 300 percent inspection or even higher may have to be done to accomplish this objective. Depending on the severity of a mistake, an error of discarding a perfectly good part may be more acceptable than passing a faulty part. In some applications the use of such extreme testing may increase the cost of a part enormously. For example, a 5¢ part may well end up costing $3.00.

If the test is destructive, 100 percent testing is impractical. The cost of 100 percent testing is frequently high. The testing is seldom fully reliable, because of worker boredom or fatigue, or inadequate facilities or methods, and, therefore, it is not often used in high-volume situations.

Sampling. The alternative to inspection of every item produced is to sample. How a sample is taken will vary with the product and process. The purpose is always to attempt securing a sample that is representative of the total population being tested. Random sampling is one commonly used technique.

The method of taking a random sample will depend on the characteristics of the product to be inspected. If it is such that all products received in a shipment can be thoroughly mixed together, then the selection of a sample from any part of the total of the mixed products will represent a valid random sample. The careful inspection of the sample will indicate what may be expected of the entire lot. For example, if a shipment of 1,000 small castings of supposedly identical characteristics are thoroughly mixed together and a random sample of 50 castings is picked from the lot and inspected and 5 are found to be defective, it is probable that 10 percent of the shipment is defective.

If the product has characteristics which make it difficult or impractical to thoroughly mix together, consecutive numbers can be assigned to each product, and then, through the use of tables of random sampling numbers (of which there are several) or a standard computer program, a sample drawn by number is chosen for detailed inspection.

The general rule which the statisticians believe should be observed when drawing a random sample is: adopt a method of selection that will give every unit of the product to be inspected an equal chance of being drawn.

Operating characteristic curves

Operating characteristic (OC) curves are used to see how well a sampling plan distinguishes between acceptable and nonacceptable product. In procurement the purchaser has to determine what the probability is of accepting goods that do not meet the minimum level of quality specified. This is called the consumer's risk with a percentage β. There is a parallel risk α for the producer that work may be rejected at the plant when it is in reality acceptable. See Figure 4–2.

Figure 4–2
TYPICAL OC CURVE
(data showing probability of rejecting bad lots by the producer with $\alpha = .10$ and the probability of accepting bad lots by the purchaser with $\beta = .10$)

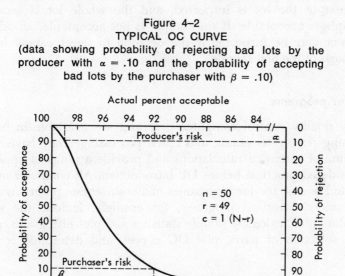

Source: R. B. Chase and N. J. Aquilano, *Production and Operations Management*, (Homewood, Ill.: Richard D. Irwin, Inc., 1973), p. 156.

In the example shown, the purchaser and the producer must select a sampling plan which relates the desire for risk, accuracy, and inspection cost. Usually, as the number of samples is increased additional accuracy is obtained, but sampling cost is also increased. Theoretically, in the selection of any sampling plan the cost of sampling must be weighed against the losses that would be incurred if no sampling were done. It is unfortunate that the sampling cost is normally easier to determine than the losses arising from not sampling.

Sequential sampling

Sequential sampling may be used to reduce the number of items to be inspected in accept-reject decisions without loss of accuracy. It is based on the cumulative effect of information that every additional item in the sample adds as it is inspected. After each individual item's inspection three decisions are possible: to accept, to reject, or sample another item. A. Wald[8] was one of the pioneers of sequential sampling development, and he estimated that using his plan the average sample size could be reduced to one half, as compared to a single sampling plan.

In a simple version of sequential sampling, often used by the military, 10 percent of the lot is inspected, and the whole lot is accepted if the sample is acceptable. If the sample is not acceptable, an additional 10 percent may be inspected if the decision to reject cannot be made on the basis of the first sample.

Computer programs

Many quality control computer programs are available in both real time, using remote terminals, and batch processing. They have resolved the tedium of extensive calculations and provide a range of applications not considered practical before DP introduction. All computer manufacturers and many service companies maintain these programs for use by customers. Standard programs, for example, include the selection of sampling plan, calculate sample statistics and plot histograms, produce random selection of parts, plot OC curves, and determine confidence limits.

Responsibility for adjustments and returns

Prompt negotiations for adjustments and returns made necessary by rejections are a responsibility of the purchasing department, aided by the using, the inspection, or the legal departments.

The actual decision as to what can or should be done with material that does not meet specifications is both an engineering and a procurement question. It can, of course, be simply rejected and either returned to the supplier at his expense or held for his instructions as to its disposition. In either case it is incumbent upon the buyer to inform the supplier

---

[8] A. Wald, *Sequential Analysis* (New York: John Wiley & Sons, 1947).

whether the shipment is to be replaced with acceptable material or to consider the contract canceled. Not infrequently, however, a material may be used for some other than the originally intended purpose or substituted for some other grade. At any rate, it is altogether probable that some private readjustment is called for. A third alternative sometimes open to buyers is to rework the material in their own plant, deducting from the purchase price the cost of the additional processing involved. Finally, particularly in the case of new types of equipment or new material to which the purchaser is not accustomed, the vendor may send a technical representative to the buyer's organization in the hope that complete satisfaction may be provided.

A final problem growing out of inspection is that of the allocation, as between buyer and seller, of costs incurred in connection with rejected material. The following statement indicates the nature of the problem and the various practices in dealing with it:

The costs incurred on rejected materials may be divided into three major classes:

1. Transportation costs.
2. Cost of testing.
3. Contingent expense (for work done on defective material before discovery of defect, handling, loss of production because of delay in receiving proper material, etc.).

The practice of allocating these costs varies considerably with various purchasing departments. The practice is affected to some degree by the kind of material rejected, trade customs, the essential economies of the situation, and the buyer's cost accounting procedure.

In practically all cases reported, transportation costs both to and from the rejection point are charged back to the supplier.

Very few companies report inspection or testing costs as items to be charged back to the supplier. Such costs are ordinarily borne by the buyer and considered by him as a part of his purchasing or inspection costs.

In a great many cases contracts or trade customs provide definitely that the supplier will not be responsible for contingent expense, yet this is perhaps the greatest risk and the most costly item of all from the buyer's standpoint. Incoming materials which are not of proper quality may seriously interrupt production; their rejection may cause a shortage of supply which may result in delay or actual stoppage of production, extra handling, and other expense. Labor may be expended in good faith upon material later found to be unusable, and not only the material but the labor thus expended is a total loss to the buyer. It is, in general, however, not the practice of buyers to allocate such contingent costs to the vendor. There is, however, a considerable minority practice in this respect upon the part of buyers who insist upon agreements with their vendors under which the vendor does assume a fair share of the responsibility for such contingent costs. This, it is true, is largely limited to that particular type of contingent cost which has to do with labor expended upon the material before discovery of its defective character.

Zero defects programs

Starting in the late 1950s, the U.S. Department of Defense encouraged many of its suppliers to install incentive programs aimed at defect prevention. These "Zero Defects Programs" had the objective to reduce to zero the rejection rates resulting from failure to meet quality standards. Benefits achieved from the successful operation of these programs included:

a. "On-time" delivery of products and materials which meet all quality specifications.
b. Lower costs because of less wasted materials.
c. Lower costs of inspection.

These motivational programs generally rely on moral suasion. PRIDE (Personal Responsibility in Daily Effort) and various other titles have been applied to these programs. It is useful to recognize that zero defects is usually not a process design possibility or a quality control system target. Machines are designed to operate within certain ranges, and all sampling plans are based on a certain percentage of consumer's risk and a probability of nonacceptable product. It is through the special care taken by operators, inspectors, and assemblers that better than design performance is obtained.

Purchasing managers have used the concept of "zero defects" in nondefense industries to encourage suppliers to provide defect-free materials and products.

Importance of inspection records

Complete and well-documented records of the results of the inspection of materials and products received from suppliers are an essential element of any formal method of evaluating suppliers. In companies where the nature of the products produced requires strict control of quality, it is of great importance to the proper performance of the procurement function to select suppliers who can deliver materials and products of the specified quality.

A supplier who submits the lowest bid but furnishes materials which fail in part to pass inspection for quality may actually be a high-cost supplier. Interruptions of production schedules caused by lack of material which meets quality standards can be very expensive. The time required of purchasing personnel to obtain replacement and other adjustments for materials which fail to pass quality inspection also adds to costs.

BIBLIOGRAPHY

ALFORD, LEON P., ed. *Cost and Production Handbook.* 2d ed. New York: Ronald Press, 1955.

ALIJIAN, GEORGE W., ed. *Purchasing Handbook.* 3d ed. New York: McGraw-Hill Book Co., 1973.

AMERICAN STANDARDS ASSOCIATION. *Company Standardization.* A survey of extent, costs, and results of standardization in industry. New York, 1959.

BRADY, G. S. *Materials Handbook.* 10th ed. New York: McGraw-Hill Book Co., 1973.

CROSS, H. E. "Standardization," *Guide to Purchasing.* New York, 1965.

DESMOND, DAVID J. *Quality Control Workbook.* Boston: Cahners Books, 1971.

DUNCAN, ACHESON J. *Quality Control and Industrial Statistics.* 3d ed. Homewood, Ill.: Richard D. Irwin, Inc., 1965.

FETTER, ROBERT B. *The Quality Control System.* Irwin Series in Operations Management. Homewood, Ill.: Richard D. Irwin, Inc., 1967.

HEINRITZ, STUART F., AND FARRELL, PAUL V. *Purchasing: Principles and Applications.* 5th ed. Englewood Cliffs, N.J.: Prentice-Hall, Inc., 1971.

NATIONAL ASSOCIATION OF PURCHASING AGENTS, INC. *Standardization Manual.* 4th ed. New York, 1964.

OLIVE, RUSSELL W. "The Quality Capability Survey Results, Reliability, and Recommendations," *Journal of Purchasing,* vol. 5, no. 2 (May 1969).

STUGLIA, ERASMUS J., ed. *Standards and Specifications Information Sources,* Detroit: Gale Research Co., 1968.

"Zero Defects—Making the Concept a Two-Way Street," *Purchasing Week,* March 22, 1965, p. 1.

CASES FOR CHAPTER 4

SLAGKO AGGREGATE COMPANY

Mr. T. Bolton, director of purchasing for Slagko, was wondering whether he should set up a test trial to evaluate a proposal for tire chain nets for the company's six large slag loaders. The rubber tire loaders used in hot, sharp slag beds currently showed a disappointing tire life of 600 operating hours.

Company background

Slagko converted steel slag which was crushed, screened, and mixed with other aggregates to provide paving materials for use in the construction and building trade. Sales in 1972 had reached $85 million. The company was rapidly expanding in all areas of the construction trade. Recently the company's slag pit operation had moved from one to two shifts to increase production.

Slag association

Slagko was a member of the National Slag Association which met periodically to share information on equipment problems, maintenance and safety programs, tire damage and manufacturer's warranties.

Steel crawler tracks were exclusively used by all members in slag beds until 1963. A number of operators in that year began using rubber tire loaders because of their better maneuverability and greater output. Output with rubber tires was reported to have increased two- and three-fold per loader. Adoption by most association members was gradual, however, due to the substantial tire damage reported by the early trials. Tires costing $2,000 to $3,800 each were lasting from 5 minutes to 1,000 hours in the slag pit. Tire manufacturer's investigations of the problem could only offer a range of tire qualities and options such as extra heavy treads or steel belts as a solution. Further studies conducted for the Slag Association reported an increased safety hazard in the rubber tire loaders. Depending upon the terrain and movement of the loader, a tire when pierced would tilt the loader dangerously or tip it over. Guidelines were then established for traveling speed and speed of turning for loaders with rubber tires. Operators were warned of loader operations involving very uneven surfaces. Despite continued Slag Association concern over the safety issue and the high tire operating cost, equipment manufacturers and tire producers had not come up with any worthwhile solutions.

Slagko's present slag pit operation

Slagko operated six 61-ton rubber tire loaders on two shifts five days a week. The loaders, costing anywhere from $150,000 to $190,000 each were from six months to eight years old. Total operating costs were kept for each machine showing a cost from $26–$38 per operating hour. (See Exhibit 1.) Tire costs of $100,000 per year for each loader in the slag pit made a solution minimizing tire damage and costs very attractive. The critical problem in tire life was that sharp slag cut the tread or the vulnerable side wall. Slag material was also very hard and abrasive, compounding the problem. Average tire life on some loaders varied as much as 40 percent, depending upon the location in the slag pit that the loader was operating in. Tires costing $3,500 with steel belts had prolonged tire life by a multiple of two over less expensive

Exhibit 1
SLAGKO AGGREGATE COMPANY
(loader cost breakdown)

The company kept a total maintenance record of costs for the life of each loader and used this to calculate the hourly operating cost for each loader. A computer record was kept for every machine. Actual and allocated costs were combined. For example, garage wages were actual wages paid out to date, but tire costs were allocated over the six company loaders on a monthly basis.

The following costs were for a loader which cost $180,000, was seven years old, and had operated for 31,200 hours. The other five loaders had operated from 3,000 to 35,000 hours.

Garage labor	$ 12,000
Parts	122,400
Outside repairs	27,600
Direct garage costs	67,200
Garage overhead	49,200
Total garage	$278,400
Gas, oil	38,400
Operating wages	170,400
Depreciation:	
Standard amount continued after end of estimated loader life	193,200
Tires (loader had been in slag pit for two yrs, five years in gravel operation)	213,600
Other	4,560
Total costs	$898,560
Cost per hour	$28.80

tires costing $2,300. Nevertheless, Slagko's tire life with the $3,500 tires still varied between 600 and 700 operating hours.

In most cases once a tire was damaged, it could not be repaired. Rear mounted tires where tire damage was less severe could be recapped. Front tire damage was nearly twice as much as rear tire damage. Presently, loaders were averaging 600 hours on front tires and 1,000 hours for rear tires.

Downtime, due to damaged tires, took one to two hours in the slag pit. The pit foreman would radio the maintenance shop which would send a new tire on a rim out to the site.

The chain net proposal

Mr. Bolton had always practiced an open-door policy to suppliers and had actively searched for ways to improve tire performance. A foreign sales representative from Europe contacted Mr. Bolton in regard to his company's tire chain nets, which it hoped to introduce and market in the United States. Since 1970 a number of open pit mines in Europe had adopted the tire chain net idea. Loader maneuverability and output remained constant while tire wear and damage was significantly reduced.

According to the salesman, the tire chain nets also eliminated most un-scheduled tire-related downtime and increased the operator's confidence, resulting in improved machine performance when working in sharp frag-mented materials.

The chain net was a series of interlocking rings and links which covered the complete tire including the side walls. (See Exhibit 2.) The net would minimize overheating of the tires and add a margin of safety to the loader's operation. Tire wear under the chain was esti-mated at 10 percent per 1,000 operating hours. Each chain net for Slagko's heavy loaders would cost $5,084 and came with a reasonable supply of extra links and rings. A number of emergency links were also supplied that could be bolted quickly by the loader operator to prevent net tear and unnecessary tire exposure at a break point. After the loader's shift these emergency links could be properly replaced. A chain net for Slagko's loaders would last approximately 2,500 operating hours. The salesman claimed chain tension, inspection, and replacement of broken links was estimated at one hour for every 40 operating hours for each net. He said unscheduled maintenance would come to no more than one hour for every 200 operating hours. Regular preventive mainte-nance was stressed as instrumental in good results from the chain nets. The salesman supplied a sample calculation of the potential savings with the use of chain nets which looked very promising (See Exhibit 3.)

Mr. Bolton approached the tire department superintendent, Mr. Knight, and the slag pit foreman, Mr. Kitson, to obtain their views on the chain net proposal. Mr. Knight said that hard steel belted tires were cut with a 61-ton loader carrying a one-ton full shovel when moving in the pit. What difference would a chain net make? Either the tire of the net or both would have to be repaired. He thought maintenance of the net could be critical if tension slipped during operation or chain links broke. He saw his maintenance costs increasing significantly. Mr. Knight was also worried that a broken chain link might not be detected as easily as a damaged tire unless a periodic visual inspection was made. Undetected chain damage would cause unequal net stress and result in further chain link breaks plus tire damage.

Mr. Kitson's only concern was with the operation of the loaders in the pit. Would the operators, not fearing tire damage be less careful? Would chain breaks result in more pit downtime? Was the speed or operation of the loader restricted with the tire chain nets? As long as production could be increased or maintained, Mr. Kitson was in favor of the idea.

Conclusion

With so little to go on in making an evaluation of the chain nets, Mr. Bolton contemplated a test of the chain nets in the slag pit. He

Exhibit 2

Loader with chain net mounted on front wheels.

Ring & link
(actual size)

did not know how many nets to buy, how long the trial run should be, what it would cost, or how the results should be interpreted. He also knew that it was up to him to suggest a reasonable test format

Exhibit 3
EXAMPLE OF ESTIMATED OWNING AND OPERATING COMBINED CHAIN/TIRE COST IN A TYPICAL OPEN PIT OPERATION

1. Your machine was delivered new with four (4) L–5 extra deep tread tires, size 37.25–25 (36 ply), worth $4,000 each, including tax, on a replacement tire basis.
2. Recaps are worth $2,000 each.
3. In 6,000 hours machine operating time you have consumed eight new tires on the two front wheels (including the two original tires), 1,500 hour average tire life, with no recaps possible.
4. In 6,000 hours machine operating time you have consumed four new tires and two recaps on the two rear wheels (including the two original tires), 4,000 hour average tire life *including one recap,* before new tire replacement is necessary.
5. At 6,000 hours, front tires are ready for new tire replacement; rear tires are ready for recapping.

Front Wheels:
8 new tires @ $4,000 = $32,000 (including two original tires)
Total front tire cost   = $32,000 (two front wheels)

Rear Wheels:
4 new tires @ $4,000   = $16,000 (including two original tires)
2 recap tires @ $2,000 =   4,000
Total rear tire cost   = $20,000 (two rear wheels)

Hourly Tire Cost in 6,000 Machine Operating Hours:
Two front wheels: $32,000 ÷ 6,000 hr. = $5.33/hr. (8 new tires)
Two rear wheels: 20,000 ÷ 6,000 hr. = $3.33/hr. (4 new tires & 2 recaps)
All four wheels: $52,000 ÷ 6,000 hr. = $8.66/hr. (12 new tires & 2 recaps)

---

6. The material the chain will work in is soft and low in abrasions. The material is sharply fragmented. Standard Service, Rock Super × 15, close mesh (4 × 4) Tire Protection Chain is selected for use.
7. The initial price for Erlau Rock Super × 15 is $5,084 each chain (U.S. Suggested List Price, Effective October 15, 1972).
8. Estimated average life of Rock Super × 15 in soft and low abrasive material is 6,500 hours.
9. Average cost of parts' consumption for 6,500 hours' service on a double shift, 2,000 hour work year basis ($16.00/mo. × 39 mos.) is $624.
10. Labor cost is figured as 4 hours/mo. × $6.00/hr (example only) × 39 months = $936.
11. Tire tread wear under the chain is figured as 65 percent tread wear (10%/1,000 hours' chain use). 65 percent of recap cost $2,000 = $1,300.

Exhibit 3 *(Continued)*

12. Freight is 2,487 lbs. (RS × 15, 37.25–35 shipping weight) × $2.00/cwt. = $50.
13. Installation cost is $75.00 (average dealer cost each chain).

New Erlau Rock Super × 15, size 37.25–35	$5,084.00 each chain
Freight: 2,487 lbs. @ $2.00/cwt.	50.00 each chain
Dealer installation	75.00 each chain
Parts cost	624.00 each chain
Labor cost	936.00 each chain
Tire tread wear under the chain:	1,300.00 each tire
Total estimated owning & operating combined chain/tire cost	$8,069.00 each wheel

Hourly Estimated O&O Combined Chain/Tire Cost Each Wheel:

Total estimated O&O chain/tire cost $8,069 ÷ 6,500 hrs. = $1.24 each wheel

Two wheel chain/tire O&O cost = $2.48/hr. 2 wheels
Four wheel chain/tire O&O cost = $4.96/hr. 4 wheels

Comparisons with Existing Tire Costs:

Using tire costs developed in the example and estimated O&O chain/tire costs, we have the following comparative example to prove, or disprove, economic justification for the use of Erlau Tire Protection Chain.

Two Front Wheels:

Existing unprotected tire cost = $5.33/hr. (8 new tires)
Estimated chain/tire O&O cost = 2.48/hr. (2 chains/2 tires)
Estimated cost reduction by
Erlau Chain   = $2.85/hr. (2 wheels)

**Two Rear Wheels:*

Existing unprotected tire cost = $3.33/hr. (4 new tires/2 recaps)
Estimated chain/tire O&O cost = 2.48/hr. (2 chains/2 tires)
Estimated cost reduction by
Erlau Chain   = $ .85/hr. (2 wheels)

All Four Wheels:

Existing unprotected tire cost = $8.66/hr. (12 new tires/2 recaps)
Estimated chain/tire cost   = 4.96/hr. (4 chain/4 tires)
Estimated cost reduction by
Erlau Chain   = $3.70/hr. (4 wheels)

In 6,500 hours of anticipated average chain life, the total estimated tire-related operating cost reduction through the use of Erlau Tire Protection Chains, installed on all four wheels, would be $3.70/hr. × 6,500 = $24,050.

---

* Combined O&O chain/tire cost can be considered the same for front wheel and rear wheel installations.

since no one else at Slagko seemed particularly interested in following up the chain net idea.

KERR LIFE INSURANCE COMPANY

Through 1971 Mr. Hansen, director of purchasing for the Kerr Life Insurance Company, had become increasingly doubtful about the need for annual maintenance contracts on electronic calculators. With the intention of reassessing the situation, an arrangement was made with all present manufacturers and distributors to terminate maintenance contracts for all calculators on a common date, December 31, 1972. At the same time, Mr. Hansen had removed ten machines from contracts in order to test the cost and reliability of maintenance service for calculators without contracts. By December 31, Mr. Hansen hoped to have his evaluation complete enough to make a decision on whether or not he should renew the contracts.

Current service contract policy

No formal policy had been established beyond ensuring that regional offices, because of their remoteness and the small amount of equipment involved, should automatically have all equipment serviced under contract.

The head office, with a variety of 430 mechanical and 200 electronic calculators, had its own in-house service man for mechanical calculators and typewriters. Mechanical calculators were expected to last much longer but were gradually phased out and replaced with the more versatile electronic units. Approximately 20 percent of the machines were specialized and had cost about $1,200. The rest of the machines were fairly standard ranging in price from $500 to $1,000 each. Until 1972 all electronic calculators had been purchased with service contracts. The suppliers were a mixture of manufacturers and independent local distributors.

The service contract

In Mr. Hansen's experience, the major differences between annual maintenance contracts from various sources were substantial and emphasized the difficulty of any clear analysis. (See Exhibit 1.) Service contracts cost the company up to $75 annually for some machines, averaging $27 for all electronic calculators.

During 1972 no service was required on the ten calculators he had removed from service contracts. A service call if required for a calculator would have cost $14 plus parts. Contract coverage, therefore, seemed

Exhibit 1
KERR LIFE SERVICE CONTRACT EXPERIENCE

	Manufacturers		Independent distributors	
	On contract	Off contract	On contract	Off contract
A. Quantity discount	Yes, on 40 units+	n.a.	No	n.a.
B. Cost (new machine)	10 percent purchase price	n.a.	Less than 10 percent purchase price (varies)	n.a.
C. Cost (starting second year)	More than B machine charge	n.a.	More than B	n.a.
D. Cost (starting third year or later)	C+ major overhaul charge	n.a.	C+ major overhaul charge	n.a.
E. Service calls	Included	Min. $25 + parts	Included	Min. $25 + parts
F. Major accidental damage, e.g., dropping	Not covered	n.a.	Not covered	n.a.
G. Replacement for machines under repair	Yes—at contract premium	Ordinary rental—if available	Yes—at contract premium	Ordinary rental—if available
H. Servicemen's training	Generally good	Generally good	Generally fair	Generally fair
I. Quality of service	Reliable	Reliable	Generally reliable	Variable
J. Promptitude of service	Generally good	Fair	Variable but good	Fair to poor
K. Inspection and cleaning	Regular no charge	As ordered	Regular no charge	As ordered

wasteful, but Mr. Hansen was not sure if it was not good value over the long term. Was a service contract really maintenance or insurance?

Choosing the right calculator

The operator and the department manager assessed the requirements to be performed by a calculator on a specific job. (Mr. Hansen was seriously considering a proposal from a major supplier to perform this service for all operations, feeling that more objectivity and better utilization might result.)

A number of well-established larger firms were then invited to quote, demonstrate their machines, and leave them for testing on the job. The operator's preference was then accepted if all other aspects of the purchase were relatively equal.

Purchasing of new machines

Mr. Hansen estimated the average life of his electronic calculators at ten years and that most of them were presently less than five years old.

The practice had been to introduce more sophisticated electronic units as jobs became too complex for the existing electronic calculators. The "old" units then superseded aging mechanical machines on other jobs throughout the head office.

Under this system, Mr. Hansen had been buying 30–60 electronic calculators annually, depending upon the need and how advantageous a purchase he could negotiate.

By the end of 1972, the calculator market had been drastically shaken up by the entry of mass-produced models sold in department stores for a low price of $270. These calculators were equal in quality to what Mr. Hansen had been paying long-established manufacturers $800 for just the previous year. Most manufacturers gave quantity discounts on 40 or more machines but never to the extent of the price differential currently seen with the new machines.

These lower priced machines carried a warranty but could only be serviced if returned to the store. The stores did not offer service contracts.

Opinion versus experience

In Appendix A are outlined the reasons by a major supplier of electronic calculators for retaining service contracts. Appendix B reports the experience of one insurance company after removing service contracts on varied office equipment including electronic calculators. Mr. Hansen concurred with those findings in his own trial run. Appendix C-G outlines the dimensions of the service contract evaluation by an independent research house.

Mr. Hansen found it very difficult to establish the priorities of his purchasing policy for electronic calculators. He was interested in generating the largest potential savings for the company but was continually perplexed by the hidden cost surrounding service contracts.

In talking with the company's chief accountant over lunch, Mr. Hansen was made aware of the high cost to the company of every purchase order issued and executed by his department. The chief accountant expressed concern with the number of purchase orders that machines without service contracts would generate. Mr. Hansen realized that costs and speculations as indicated by the chief accountant would be never-ending and exceedingly hard to pinpoint.

Appendix A: Should I place my electronic calculator under a maintenance guarantee service contract?*

This is a question many people are asking.

All of us have read and heard about space age reliability and troublefree electronic products. Here are some facts that may be helpful regarding electronic calculators.

1. Electronic calculators are not infallible.

Rumors to the contrary have been initiated by companies and dealerships who do not have adequate service facilities and by eager salesmen whose only concern is to make a sale. Even the billions of dollars worth of almost perfect electronic equipment used in our nation's space program continually undergoes servicing and testing by trained technicians.

2. Solid-state components do fail.

Although there are no moving parts in a transistor, an IC (integrated circuit) package or an MOS (metal-oxide semiconductor) unit, they do fail. Periodic voltage and circuitry inspection by a qualified technician can extend the life of electronic calculator equipment.

3. Electronic calculators are not as uncomplicated as they appear.

Even though they weigh less than 15 pounds and are small in size, the circuitry and function of a typical electronic calculator is *considerably* more complex than a color TV set. You expect solid-state products to be more reliable than their mechanical counterparts, and our relatively limited experience (in terms of years) has shown that your problems will be fewer; but, when they do occur, they will be more expensive to correct. Electronic parts are more expensive than mechanical ones; also elaborate test equipment is needed to properly service electronic equipment.

4. Periodic inspection will reduce trouble on electronic calculators.

Components blanketed by dust could overheat and fail prematurely. Dust is also responsible for "bridging" close tolerance connections and causing shorts in circuitry.

5. Trouble shooting.

The cause of most mechanical calculator failures can be detected visually and corrected in a relatively short period of time. The same is not true with electronic calculators. It normally involves an intermittent problem that requires time-consuming testing to locate the weak or faulty component.

6. I do not have a service contract on my TV: therefore, I don't need one for my calculator.

A calculator cannot be almost right. It must be perfect. Many of us watch TV pictures that are far from perfect, but we accept this until something really serious happens. However, the slightest malfunction of a calculator results in a wrong answer. Therefore, the analogy is not a good one.

7. The maintenance guarantee rates for electronic and mechanical calculators are comparable.

---

* Source: Monroe Business Machines

Monroe maintenance guarantee rates for its electronic calculators are comparable to the rates charged on our mechanical machines. Therefore, the maintenance guarantee contract on your Monroe electronic calculator is a good buy.

Appendix B: Service contracts versus actual costs*

Electric Typewriters—Adders—Printing Calculators

During 1971 American United conducted studies on several desk machines to determine if they should be removed from the Service Contract Maintenance Program. The studies included IBM Selectric, IBM, and Olympia electric typewriters, and Remington Rand and Victor adding machines and printing calculators. Attached are charts summarizing our findings to support our decision to remove the equipment from service contracts.

Exhibit 2

	Purchase year	Age (years)	Number of machines	Annual contract cost ($)	'71 actual repair cost ($)	'71 average actual repair cost ($)
28 Remington Rand Adding	1968	3	3	99.15	0	—
Machines	1967	4	6	198.30	46.11	7.69
(removed from contract	1966	5	2	62.79	0	—
January 1, 1971)	1965	6	2	59.50	0	—
	1964	7	0	0	0	—
	1963	8	2	66.10	31.32	15.66
	1961	10	3	99.15	21.88	7.29
	1960	11	3	99.15	16.07	5.36
	1959	12	1	33.05	6.25	6.25
	1956	15	2	66.10	0	—
	1955	16	1	33.05	0	—
	1953	18	2	60.05	0	—
	1952	19	1	33.05	28.06	28.06
			28	909.44	149.69	5.35
12 Remington Rand	1966	4	2	111.00	12.50	6.25
Printing Calculators	1965	5	2	105.45	46.75	23.38
(removed from contract	1964	7	5	271.95	44.13	8.83
January 1, 1971)	1962	9	1	49.95	9.39	9.39
	1961	10	1	55.50	12.50	12.50
	1957	14	1	55.50	3.13	3.13
			12	649.35	128.40	10.70
9 Victor Adding Machines	1971	0	1	36.90	0	—
(removed from contract	1964	7	1	25.20	0	—
January 1, 1971)	1962	9	7	244.98	77.77	11.11
			9	307.08	77.77	8.64

* Source: American United Life

Exhibit 2 (*Continued*)

	Purchase year	Age (years)	Number of machines	Annual contract cost ($)	'71 actual repair cost ($)	'71 average actual repair cost ($)
17 Victor Printing	1963	8	4	180.00	85.67	21.42
Calculators	1962	9	13	639.00	53.12	4.09
(removed from contract			17	819.00	138.79	8.16
January 1, 1971)						
Total Remington Rand and						
Victors			66	$2,684.67	494.65	7.49
17 Olympia Electric Type	1970	1	4	Not	28.40	7.10
(never placed on contract)	1969	2	4	on	70.25	17.57
	1968	3	7	contract	133.88	19.13
	1967	4	2		15.15	7.58
			17		247.68	
69 IBM Electric Type	1971	0	1	42.00	9.38	9.38
(removed from contract	1970	1	11	462.00	387.97	35.27
January 1, 1971)	1969	2	1	42.00	20.62	20.62
	1968	3	4	168.00	93.62	23.41
	1967	4	10	420.00	274.25	27.43
	1966	5	7	294.00	90.13	18.03
	1965	6	6	252.00	94.03	15.67
	1964	7	3	126.00	86.38	28.79
	1963	8	4	168.00	37.14	9.29
	1962	9	5	210.00	68.28	13.66
	1961	10	3	126.00	77.67	25.89
	1960	11	4	168.00	129.69	32.42
	1959	12	1	42.00	16.92	16.92
	1957	14	3	126.00	38.25	12.75
	1956	15	1	42.00	18.75	18.75
	1955	16	2	84.00	0	0
	1954	17	2	84.00	0	0
	1951	20	1	42.00	0	0
			69	2,898.00	1,443.08	20.91

	Purchase year	Age (years)	Number of machines	Annual contract cost ($)	1971 Number of calls	1971 Contract $ average/call
24 IBM Selectric	1971	0	4	168.00	13	12.92
Typewriters	1970	1	7	294.00	14	21.00
(removed from contract	1969	2	3	126.00	7	18.00
January 1, 1972)	1968	3	4	168.00	2	84.00
	1967	4	1	42.00	0	42.00
	1963	8	1	42.00	3	14.00
	1962	9	4	168.00	10	16.80
			24	1,008.00	49	20.57

In using these charts for company comparison it should be noted that some of the low actual figures for the older machines are influenced by downgrading them to a "light usage" basis when repair cost were unduly high. In only a few cases were high maintenance cost machines traded in for new machines.

Significant to note is the higher cost for typewriters in the first through fourth year and the Olympia versus IBM comparison. Based on the IBM electrics 1971 actual cost and the per call cost on the Selectric, it was decided to remove the Selectrics from contract this year even though actual costs will not be available until next January.

Other reasons involved in our decision was the poor quality of contract service work and security consideration. We have cut in half the number of different servicing people coming up to the building. We had noted a heavy turnover in persons assigned to come in and do the scheduled maintenance work.

Appendix C: What the service contract is*

The service (or "guaranteed annual maintenance") contract may be broadly defined as an agreement for a specified annual fee, providing periodic inspections and cleaning and emergency service and repairs as required. Some contracts cover the cost of all parts where replacement is required; others do not. Service contracts are available not only from manufacturers and authorized distributors, but also from many independent machine repair organizations.

For machines located more than a specified distance from the repair center, the base cost of a service contract may be increased, or the number of inspections per year may be reduced. Many service organizations offer discounts on contracts covering more than a certain minimum number of machines at the same location. A typical contract provides for three (occasionally two or four or some other number) inspections a year, at specifically stated intervals, plus required service and replacement of parts in the machine owner's office. Some contracts specify that the machine be brought to the manufacturer's service center for repair, though this requirement is generally waived unless the service location is at a considerable distance.

Appendix D: Service contracts—pros and cons

In favor of contracts
Among the major arguments offered in favor of service contracts are the following:

1. *"Insurance"*
By paying a fixed fee in advance, the user avoids the risk of high costs of repairs made on a call basis.

2. *Less "downtime"*
Even more important than the potential saving in out-of-pocket repair costs, according to this argument, machines will operate more efficiently as a result of regular inspection and cleaning and breakdown will occur less frequently,

---

* Appendix C-G taken from *Buyer's Laboratory Study-Report on Service Contracts.*

thus reducing downtime. Less downtime, in turn, means less personnel time lost while machines are inoperable.

3. *Longer useful life*
Periodic inspection and cleaning, it is claimed, extend the useful life of a machine; without a service contract, essential cleaning and other maintenance are likely to be neglected.

4. *Fixed expense*
The cost of service contracts is a fixed expense which can be budgeted in advance; it is impossible to budget quite so precisely on a pay-as-you-go repair basis.

5. *One annual bill*
One bill covers one or more machines and all repairs. Without a service contract, it may be necessary to issue individual purchase orders each time repairs are required, with resultant increase in bookkeeping expenses.

6. *Faster service*
Under service contracts the machine operator or his supervisor can call for service as required. Without service contracts, in many organizations at least, all requests for service must go through channels, taking up someone's time and delaying service.

7. *No minimum charge per call*
Almost all service organizations make a minimum charge per call in the absence of a contract. The charge typically will be for either a half hour or one hour's service. Thus, a minor adjustment requiring only a few minutes to make may be expensive. In the absence of a contract, especially in a small office where only one machine of a kind is likely to need adjustment at one time, and cost may discourage calls for adjustments and reduce the quality of the work performed.

Against contracts
Among the arguments against service contracts and for service on a call basis are the following:

1. *Economy*
The cost of a typical service contract is likely to be greater than the cost of service on an individual call basis.

2. *Less downtime*
Today's basic office machines are generally well designed and durable. A machine may be functioning perfectly and actually be thrown out of adjustment in the course of a routine inspection, causing subsequent breakdown. Furthermore, inspection calls disrupt work and sometimes interfere with the work of a group of people in an office.

3. *Limitations on contracts*
The fine print on many service contracts often limits their value more than the purchaser realizes. In many service contracts the manufacturer reserves the right not to renew the contract, unless the machine is subjected to shop overhaul. Even if his own service employees were responsible for inadequate maintenance of a machine, the manufacturer can still require the user to pay for a major overhaul before continuing a service contract.

4. Poor service

Some members of manufacturers' maintenance staffs are incompetent, and frequently they are slow in answering calls for service because it has already been paid for. Without a service contract the machine owner can use either the manufacturer's servicemen or, often at lower hourly cost, independent service organizations that may provide better service. And if he is not satisfied with one service organization, he can change to another.

Appendix E: Service contracts as insurance

Despite the fact that service contracts are often described as insurance, they lack an essential feature of true insurance—they protect not against potentially catastrophic losses, but only against minor losses. It is this lack which accounts for the difficulty many organizations have in deciding whether or not to purchase service contracts. The need for fire insurance requires no debate; but a service contract on, say, an electric typewriter provides at best a low order of protection, since costly repairs such as might be needed if a machine were dropped would not be covered.

Even though the protection afforded by service contracts is limited, however, the question of whether or not they should be purchased cannot be passed off as unimportant. The manager of a small office with a single manual typewriter may not wish to risk annual repair bills of as much as $50 when a service contract, where there may be hundreds or thousands of machines, the decision as to whether or not to have them covered by service contracts, can mean a difference in annual service costs of many thousands of dollars.

Appendix F: Preventive maintenance

Preventive maintenance is regarded by many as the chief value of service contracts, but the quality of preventive maintenance provided by different service organizations and by different service groups and servicemen within the same organization varies enormously. Good preventive maintenance, involving not only thorough cleaning but also careful inspection with detailed checking of operation, can mean at the least more satisfactory performance and at the best fewer service calls, less downtime, and perhaps longer machine life. Both from its own experience and from its surveys, however, Buyers Laboratory has learned that all too often "periodic inspection and cleaning" are hastily and indifferently performed and of little, if any, value. A number of BLI clients have complained that so-called inspection and cleaning, carelessly performed under a service contract, have been responsible for subsequent breakdowns and service calls instead of preventing them.

Quality of service

BLI knows of no nationwide service organization in the office machine field that provides uniformly satisfactory service. In the answers to the questionnaires there were words of praise and of harsh condemnation from different users of the same machine as a result of differences in the service received. A major manufacturer of office machines among BLI's clients complained of the lack of promptness of service on various machines used in its offices, but the same company's own servicemen were the subject of many similar complaints.

The fact is, of course, that competent, conscientious men who can be trained to do a thoroughly satisfactory job of maintenance and repair are as difficult to find as competent and conscientious people in all other fields and that a service organization, whatever the desires or policies of the company, will at best vary in the quality of service it renders. The significance of this variability is that the manufacturer's local service set-up should, if possible, be appraised before a service contract is purchased. If service provided by the manufacturer on a call basis is poor, an independent service organization can be tried, but a contract does not permit such flexibility.

The *competence* of servicemen employed by manufacturers of the machines serviced was rated somewhat higher on the average than that of independent service organizations; nevertheless, in a particular locality independent organizations may be superior, and, if the manufacturer's service is unsatisfactory, the independent organizations should be investigated.

Appendix G

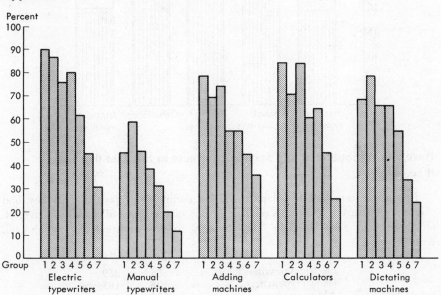

Percentage of machines under service contract

The chart shows the percentage of machines under service contract in each of the seven groups of companies. As the chart indicates, companies with many office machines generally make less use of service contracts than those with relatively few machines; this generalization holds for all the types of machines covered. Except for manual typewriters more than half of all the machines owned by companies in groups 1 through 5 were under service contracts. In groups 6 and 7 (over 1,000 machines) less than half were under contract.

Group 1	0– 50 machines
2	50– 100
3	100– 200
4	200– 500
5	500–1,000
6	1,000–1,500
7	1,500–

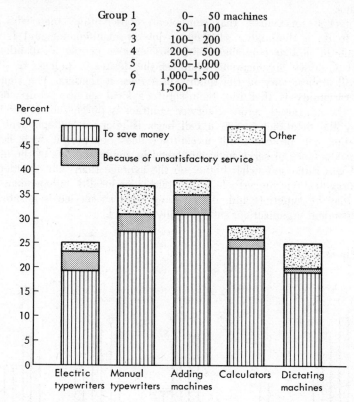

Have you discontinued any service contracts in the past five years? If so, why?

Just about one half of all participating companies reported that they had discontinued service contracts on at least one of the types of machines covered. Of those who gave "yes" or "no" answers to this question, the breakdown was:

	Yes	No
Electric typewriters	85	259
Manual typewriters	108	185
Adding machines	126	209
Calculators	96	245
Dictating equipment	74	220

The chart shows these figures as percentages, with the reasons given for discontinuing service contracts indicated by the divisions in each bar. The great majority felt that money could be saved by substituting per-call or in-plant service for service on a contract basis. A small percentage, as the chart shows, attributed the discontinuance of contracts to unsatisfactory service. Some indicated that they had discontinued contracts without giving the reasons.

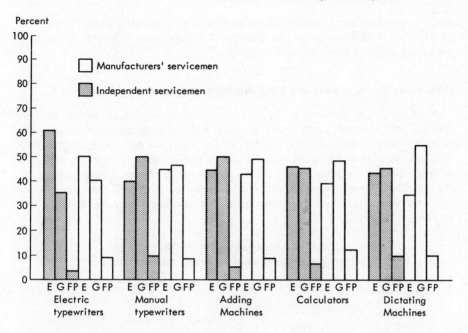

How capable are the servicemen?

Organizations participating in the survey were asked to rate the competence of servicemen as *excellent* (E), *good* (G), or *fair* or *poor* (FP). The chart shows the percentage of companies rating servicemen in each category. As it indicates, the great majority of companies considered both manufacturers'

PERCENTAGE OF COMPANIES REPORTING EACH NUMBER OF INSPECTIONS

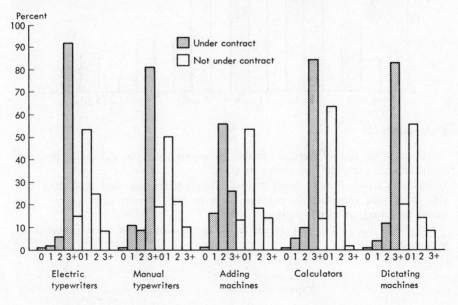

and independent servicemen to be either excellent or good. The replies showed no significant difference in the ratings of competence between companies with contracts and those without contracts.

How many times a year are your machines inspected and cleaned?

Most machines covered by service contracts as the chart shows, are inspected and cleaned three times a year; with adding machines, inspection twice a year is most common. The figures for machines not covered by service contract show that 13 to 20 percent of the participating companies reported no inspection or cleaning during the year; in most of the remaining companies, the machines were inspected and cleaned only once during the year. (Very few companies reported more than three inspections per year; the 3+ bar represents mainly 3's.)

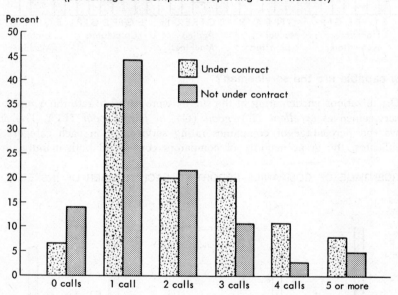

CALCULATORS—NUMBER OF REPAIR CALLS
(percentage of companies reporting each number)

Calculators

About what is the average number of repair calls per calculator per year under service contract? Not under contract?

Calculators needed more repairs than adding machines, but well over half the companies reported an average of only one or two calls a year, with many reporting no repair calls.

Average of the number of repair calls per machine per year reported by all companies:

With contract 2.3
With per-call service. 1.7

Maximum number of repair calls for a single machine reported by any company:

With contract 17
Without contract 20

AVERAGE NUMBER OF REPAIR CALLS: CUMULATIVE PERCENTAGES OF REPORTING COMPANIES

	With contract	*Without contract*
0 calls	7%	14%
0 or 1	42	59
2 or less	62	81
3 or less	82	92
4 or less	92	95
5 or more	8	5
4 or more	18	8
3 or more	38	19
2 or more	58	41
1 or more	93	86

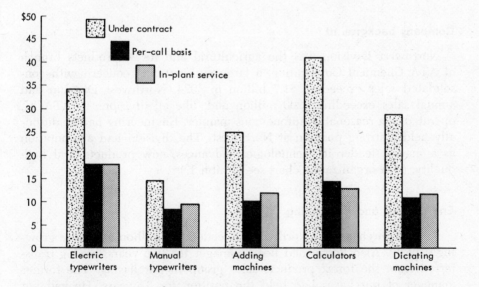

What is your approximate average annual cost per unit for servicing?
(A) Machines under contract (B) Machines not under contract

The chart shows the amount paid by the average company for service on each type of machine with and without service contracts. As with the other charts, the figures have not been weighted for the number of machines; if they had been, the average cost of service *without contract* would have been substantially lower for electric typewriters and a little lower for the other types of machines. The average cost of repairs without contract was lower than the average cost of contracts, not only for all five types of machines covered in the survey, but also for all groups of companies, from those with a total of fewer than 50 office machines of the types covered to those with more than 2500 machines. The potential saving without contracts appears to be least with manual typewriters, the machine least often covered by contract, and greatest with calculators—next to electric typewriters, the machine most often covered by service contract.

NORTHWEST DIVISION

Alec Perrin, manager of corporate purchases for Northwest Division, had long been concerned about the engineering-purchasing relationship in Northwest Division. He had asked his assistant to prepare a set of suggestions on how the two functions might cooperate better in the future. His assistant, Ted MacDonald, had prepared a set of guidelines and had given these to Alec with the words: "If these rules can't fix it up, nothing can." Alec was not sure how he might assess the guidelines and what action to take subsequently.

Company background

Northwest Division was the agricultural and forest products branch of ATA Chemical Corporation, a large multinational concern with consolidated sales exceeding $1.7 billion in 1974. Northwest Division had annual sales exceeding $200 million and, like all divisions in ATACC, operated in a reasonably autonomous manner. Engineering had traditionally held a strong position at Northwest. The division had a reputation as a market leader in technological advances, new products, and high quality. (For organization chart see Exhibit 1.)

Engineering and purchasing

Annual purchases for Northwest exceeded $80 million and were growing rapidly. Alec Perrin had been manager for two years, having transferred from the forest products sales group to purchasing. The former manager of purchases had held the position for 37 years. He had not been successful in obtaining engineering cooperation. During his stay in forest products sales Alec Perrin had gained the impression that engineers preferred to bypass purchasing because they thought they could cut the red tape and do a better job.

As manager of purchases Mr. Perrin had spent the first two years becoming better acquainted with the job, looking after the most pressing crises and the building of a stronger and more capable staff. The new group consisted primarily of university graduates in science, engineering, or business administration. About half had worked in other areas of Northwest Division prior to joining the new purchasing team. He found

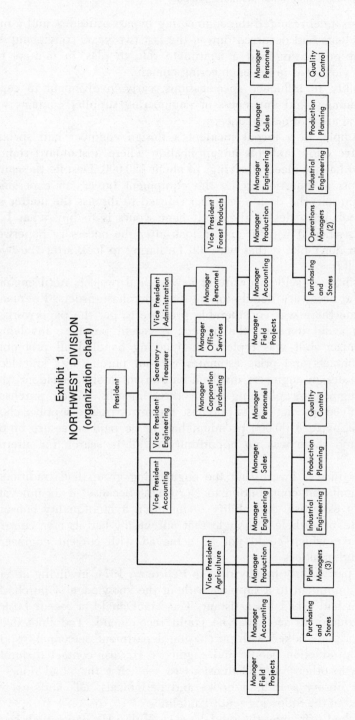

Exhibit 1
NORTHWEST DIVISION
(organization chart)

that his personnel resented the engineering bypass attitudes, and a number of incidents had occurred during the last two years convincing Alec Perrin that purchasing had a legitimate role to play in matters now apparently viewed as in the engineering domain.

The ability to influence specifications, early involvement in capital project planning, and awareness of engineering supplier contacts were three typical areas of major concern.

For example, in a recent incident a design engineer had specified an expensive alloy tank for an application where a standard stainless steel would have sufficed at savings of about $20,000. Despite the courteous attempts at questioning by the equipment buyer, an experienced engineer himself, the design engineer refused to discuss the matter saying: "My job is to design the equipment, yours is to buy what I tell you to get, where I want it and to look after the necessary paperwork. And if you don't like it that way, I'll be happy to look after the whole thing myself."

Purchasing was seldom aware of new capital projects until engineering sent the necessary details for the final purchase orders. Frequently, by that time there was considerable pressure to get the paperwork out quickly to avoid delaying the project. A recent purchase involving a $750,000 mixer unit was typical. Engineering handled all preliminary supplier contacts and price estimates without purchasing's knowledge. One of the design engineers involved had an automobile accident which delayed engineering planning about three months. When purchasing finally received instructions to purchase the mixer from a supplier chosen by engineering, a $100,000 premium had to be paid to assure on-time delivery, and there was no opportunity at all to search for alternate sources.

Alec Perrin was aware that the engineering group had traditionally made a significant contribution to Northwest because of its innovative role, strong expertise, and ability to maintain a high-quality consumer product. He, nevertheless, thought that purchasing had its own contribution to make which could not be achieved with current engineering attitudes and practices.

After a particularly touchy deal in February, 1974, involving an engineering commitment to a supplier without the knowledge of purchasing, Alec Perrin had asked his assistant, Ted MacDonald, a recent business school graduate, to see what he could recommend. Ted immediately went to work. He talked with purchasing department personnel, supplier personnel, production people and engineers. He also contacted purchasing people in other ATACC divisions to see what they had done. He also did a library search of books and periodicals. His findings were summarized in the following set of guidelines.

Alec wished to review the guidelines carefully. He had a high regard for Ted MacDonald and knew that Ted expected action quickly. Nevertheless, he wanted to be absolutely sure he had a sound plan and approach before he committed himself.

GUIDELINES FOR ENGINEERING/PURCHASING RELATIONSHIP

1. Project planning and estimates

Collection of data and prices for project planning and preliminary estimating requires flexibility and cooperation between the engineering and the purchasing departments. Care should be taken to prevent individual suppliers from doing considerable work to supply initial estimates to us. Care should also be taken that specifications are not written to fit one supplier's product to the exclusion of other suppliers in the field.

All requests by engineering for commercial information from suppliers will be made through the purchasing department on form "Request for Information," copy attached. The proper use of this form will ensure that all of the data required for estimating and purchasing is obtained from the vendor.

2. Vendor contacts

Vendor contacts by the engineering department prior to the awarding of a contract or the placing of a purchase order require cooperation between the two groups. It is recognized that at times the engineering department will, of necessity, discuss preliminary information or technical aspects with a vendor. It is the responsibility of the engineering department to keep the purchasing department informed of the discussion and direct the vendor to send a copy of any pertinent correspondence to the purchasing department. The engineering department must not solicit bids from the representatives. If a quotation is required, a Request for Information should be filled out and the vendor's representative referred to the purchasing department.

After awarding of the contract, technical contracts may be made by engineering with a copy of any pertinent correspondence to purchasing. All commercial contacts must be made by the purchasing department with a copy of any pertinent correspondence to engineering. Assigned inspectors or expediters may contact the supplier in carrying out their respective responsibilities.

3. Bid lists

a. Bid lists for engineering consultants. The engineering department has the prime responsibility for the bid lists for engineering consultants after evaluating their personnel, facilities, and experience. If the project is particularly large or includes an arrangement for the consultant to do project purchasing, the purchasing department should be involved.

b. Bid lists for contractors. Preparation of bid lists for contractors is a joint responsibility of engineering and purchasing. Engineering should investigate technical ability, experience, and personnel. The purchasing department should investigate commercial standing, obtain financial data and suitability from past performance.

Exhibit 2

REQUEST FOR INFORMATION

TO: Mr._____   FROM: _____
     Purchasing Department   Engineering Department

DATE:_____   SUBJECT:_____

                                 _____

                                 Project_____W.O._____

Please obtain the following information on the subject item(s):

_____

_____

FOR ESTIMATING PURPOSES ☐   FOR PURCHASE ☐

Secure bids   ☐

Price   ☐

Shipping weight   ☐

Estimated freight   ☐

Taxes applicable   ☐

Duty (if imported)   ☐

Current delivery   ☐

Literature   ☐

Sample(s)   ☐

Arrange meeting with representative   ☐

List of recommended spare parts   ☐

Time required to supply approval drawings ☐

Time required to supply certified drawings ☐

Enclosed are_____ sets of specifications and/or drawings.

SUGGESTED VENDORS

_____   _____

_____   _____

_____   _____

INFORMATION/BIDS REQUIRED BY_____

ESTIMATED VALUE $_____

Copies to: Signature_____

c. *Bid lists for major equipment.* Preparation of bid lists for major equipment is the joint responsibility of engineering and purchasing. Engineering will prepare detailed specifications of their requirements and provide purchasing with a list of suggested suppliers. Purchasing should take this original list and endeavor to find or develop other sources of supply until an adequate number for competitive bidding is obtained. In the case of noncompetitive or single supplier products, the engineering department must provide the purchasing department with the reason for handling in this manner. Purchasing may suggest that engineering rewrite specifications to enable them to obtain competitive bids.

d. *Bid lists for minor equipment and construction supplies.* The engineering department will prepare specifications for miscellaneous equipment and supplies. The preparation of the bid list is the prime responsibility of the purchasing department. Engineering department will comment, if necessary, on any particular item and supplier.

4. Bid transmittal and comparison

Purchasing will prepare for Engineering a "Bid Transmittal and Comparison" and "Engineering Equipment Comparative Bid Sheet," forms attached. After complete technical analysis by engineering, the Bid Transmittal and Comparison form will be returned to purchasing—the bottom half completed, accompanied by an approved purchasing requisition. Engineering will make recommendations for preferred supplier and reason for same. Purchasing will negotiate the best commitment for the item or service.

5. Supplier selection

Recommendation of the contractor, consultant, and supplier of major equipment and justification for the recommendations will be provided by the engineering department. The final decision on the contractor, consultant, or supplier is a joint responsibility of the two departments.

6. Notification

The purchasing department will notify, in writing, the unsuccessful bidders on all major items and contracts.

7. Specifications

Engineering specifications must be precise to prevent misunderstanding after the contract is let. In addition to details of buildings and equipment, items such as company's safety policies, work rules and restrictions, availability of utilities, and other items affecting contractor's cost should be included in the specifications. Care should be taken to see that items placed in the specifications conform with the requirements of standard Northwest Division documents such as contract forms, purchase orders, etc., to prevent undue costs due to ambiguity in specifications. Specifications should be reviewed

Exhibit 3

```
                                                    Project:_____
                                                    Item No._____
                                                    360 Work Order:_____

               BID TRANSMITTAL AND COMPARISON

    TO:  Engineering – Attention:

         Attached are Bids and Bid Comparisons covering




                                                    Buyer:_____


    To be completed by Engineering

               RECOMMENDATION FOR PURCHASE

    TO:  Purchasing – Attention

    c.c.

         Attached is approved Requisition No.

         Recommended Vendor:

         Reason:




                                                    Engineer:_____
```

by the plant management for the areas affected by the construction or installation. This is an engineering department responsibility.

8. Contract preparation

It is the responsibility of the purchasing department to prepare the contracts. Contracts should include warranties, guarantees, payment schedules,

Exhibit 4

ENGINEERING EQUIPMENT

COMPARATIVE BID SHEET

BIDDERS

QTY.	ITEM					
	QUOTED PRICE					
	F.O.B.					
	TAXES					
	DUTY					
	ESTIMATED FREIGHT					
	TERMS					
	DELIVERED PRICE					
	DELIVERY					

COMMENTS:

PREPARED BY: DATE:

holdbacks, bonus/penalty clauses, etc. Purchasing department must consult with engineering, legal department, etc., regarding their phases of the contract.

9. Commitments

All commitments must take the form of a purchase order or purchase contract placed by the purchasing department. Field change orders may be committed in writing by the designated project engineer/manager. All additions or deletions including field changes must be confirmed by the purchasing department on a purchase order change notice.

10. Noncompetitive purchasing policy

a. Lowest cost, commensurate with quality and service, can only be achieved by competitive bidding from qualified suppliers. Vendors' qualifications and performance must be continually updated and new suppliers sought out and evaluated from three viewpoints: quality, price, and service, which includes meeting schedules. The purchasing organization and the engineering department share the evaluation requirements, with purchasing being responsible for permanent files.

b. There are occasions when noncompetitive purchases must be made; for example, compressor parts, custom machine parts, instrument parts. However, ball bearings, seals, packing, gaskets, etc., do not normally fall in this category. Requisitions for noncompetitive materials must clearly identify the vendor's part number, vendor's serial or shop number, and Northwest's original purchase order number if needed by the vendor for identification purposes. The purchasing organization is authorized to make these purchases with normal approvals.

c. Any purchase requisition originating in the engineering department, limiting the purchase to one supplier, other than Statement *b.* materials, will require the approval of the engineering manager if the purchase value exceeds $500. Multiple requisitions will not be used to circumvent this policy, and this aspect will be monitored by purchasing.

d. The local purchasing manager will define the approval requirements for noncompetitive purchases less than $500. This may vary with locations in order to be compatible with the staffing at that location. The purchasing managers will also establish a maximum purchase value, whereby it costs more to obtain competitive prices than the potential saving of competitive bids.

11. Contractor's performance report

The manager of engineering or his designate will prepare a "Contractor's Performance Report," from attached, at the completion of the contract and forward to the local purchasing department. This department will make comments on commercial matters and forward a copy to the head office purchasing and engineering department.

12. Equipment performance report

Due to the wide variety of equipment and applications it is not practical to have a standard single report. The local purchasing and engineering departments are responsible to report supplier and equipment performance in a similar fashion to contractor's performance. Such report would include all types of performance such as delivery, quality, service facilities, and costs of spare parts, etc.

13. Expediting/inspection

The importance of expediting depends on the need for the particular item. Expediting of major or long-term items should be combined with inspection.

Exhibit 5

| CONTRACTOR'S PERFORMANCE REPORT | Contractor's Name |
| Product group and location | Contractor's representative |

Project identification

Type of contract

☐ Lump sum   ☐ Unit price   ☐ Cost plus fixed fee   ☐ Cost plus percentage fee

| Contract amount | Final total payments | Reason for additional payments in excess of contract amount |
| $ | $ | |

Contractor's claims for extras reasonable

☐ YES   ☐ NO

Unreasonable number of petty extras submitted

☐ YES   ☐ NO

| Job progress – scheduled start | Scheduled completion | Actual start | Actual completion |

Cause of delays (if any)

PERFORMANCE RATING	EXCELLENT	ADEQUATE	UNSATISFACTORY
Quality of subcontractors			
Scheduling and coordination			
Workers			
Labor relations			
Materials procurement and delivery			
Quality and supply of tools and equipment			
Cooperation with owner and/or owner's rep.			
Cooperation with other contractors			
Safety record			
Quality of field supervision			
General housekeeping of construction site			

Contractor recommended for future work   ☐ Yes   ☐ No (if no, give reason)

| Submitted by | Date | Title |

It is usually necessary to inspect the fabrication or construction to assess properly accuracy of the vendor's delivery promise. On large projects, expediting and inspection may be a full-time job for a member of the project team. Outside inspectors and/or expediters may be hired for these projects by the project manager.

On all other items, expediting will be done by the purchasing department on an exception basis. These exceptions are in two classes:

a.   When the time is late,
b.   On a special request basis.

Request for expediting should accompany the purchase requisition to the purchasing department and indicate the minimum frequency of the expediting contacts.

Purchasing, with the approval of the engineering manager, may retain outside expediting/inspection services on major project items or on any items where delivery could affect the manufacturing operation. Purchasing should also notify the engineering manager when, in its opinion, expediting and inspection may be required.

14. Equipment delivery

Purchasing will endeavor in all cases to procure equipment when stated on requisition and will advise engineering prior to placing order if the requested delivery date is unattainable.
March 27, 1974

5 DETERMINATION AND CONTROL OF QUANTITY AND INVENTORIES

Quantity considerations

Quantity is a logical consideration after quality. "How much?" is the proper question after, "What is required?" There are various aspects to decisions concerning quantity. Forecasting will be covered first. This will be followed by product explosion and ABC analysis. The management and control of inventories will be introduced next with a new framework based on the functions and forms of inventories. Special coverage on inventory models and the price-break-quantity trade-off is followed by discussion of the stores function. In materials management quantity considerations are a vital part of the total system and present a number of interesting trade-offs.

Forecasting

Forecasting is very much a part of the materials management picture. Forecasts of usage, supply, market conditions, technology, or price are always necessary, whether they be implicit or explicit. How to plan to take care of the needs of the future is the problem. As far as quantity required and usage is concerned, the real question exists where the responsibility for forecasting should lie. In addition, should the materials management group be allowed to second guess sales, production, or user forecasts? In so far as forecasts are shared with suppliers, the interest of the procurement group is direct. Should the supplier be held responsible for performance to forecast or to actual requirements? A similar situation exists inside the organization. Should the procurement manager be held responsible for satisfying internal needs or internal forecasts? Since missed forecasts are quickly forgotten but substantial shortages or overages are long remembered, the above questions are largely rhetorical. In most manufacturing organizations the need for production materials and parts is usually derived from a sales forecast which is the responsibility of marketing. In service organizations and public agencies the materials function finds itself often in the position of having to both forecast and acquire.

The real problem with forecasts is their reliability. To what extent will actual requirements fall short of or exceed forecasted needs? In a chemical company the following forecast was made by the marketing group for a consumer product requiring the following purchase of a basic petrochemical commodity.

Year 1	70,000 barrels
Year 2	120,000 barrels
Year 3	190,000 barrels
Year 4	280,000 barrels
Year 5	390,000 barrels

The cost per barrel was close to $25.00 making this a significant purchase. Further discussions with the marketing group revealed that considerable uncertainty existed regarding this forecast. (See Figure 5–1.)

Figure 5–1
FORECAST SHOWING UNCERTAINTY

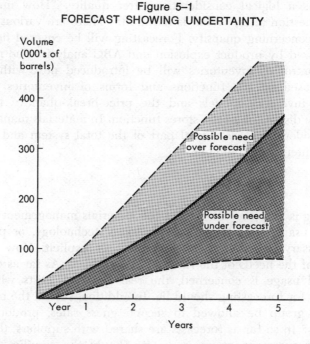

It might be possible for demand to be as low as 70,000 barrels five years later, and it might be as high as 600,000 barrels. This spread between high and low estimates made the procurement plan far more difficult, because it had to be prepared recognizing the full range of possible outcomes. For example, a take-or-pay commitment for 100,000 barrels per year after the first year was obviously not acceptable because of the possibility that actual demand might be well below 100,000 barrels per year. Simultaneously, provisions had to be found for substantial increases in requirements should actual volume exceed forecast.

To a supplier a substantial variation from forecast may appear as a procurement ploy. Should actual demand fall below forecast, the supplier may suspect that the original forecast was an attempt to obtain a favorable price. If substantial increases beyond forecast are demanded, supplier's costs may well increase because of overtime, rush buying, and changed production schedules. There is a need to share forecast uncertainty information with suppliers so that their quotations may take this into account. Such sharing is obviously impossible if the procurement managers themselves are not aware of the uncertainty and its potential impact on the supplier.

Forecasting techniques

No matter where the forecasting is done in the organization, a number of techniques are available to assist in making better forecasts. They fall into two broad classes. The first presumes that past history is indicative of future expectations. By applying statistical techniques to known data forecasts may be made. The second class includes activities such as marketing research, intention surveys of customers, consensus, correlation with economic indicators which are forecast separately, and salesmen's reports. Often both classes are used in combination and reconciled with each other. At this time we will concern ourselves primarily with the first class, the statistical methods which may be used on past data.

Past usage data may be examined for six significant components which are: average period usage, seasonality, trend, cyclical aspects, and autocorrelation. Average usage is calculated by dividing the total usage by the number of periods. Seasonality shows regular changes which recur at certain times of the year. For example, heating oil usage is highly seasonal. Trend shows a general overall direction. For example, the trend in power consumption is up over many years. Cyclicality relates to variations caused by outside influences like the state of the economy, wars, and inflation rate but may also be of shorter duration and difficult to identify. Random variations, on the other hand, are those left over when seasonality, trend, and cycle have been accounted for. When there is no apparent reason for any deviation, the result may well be due to straight randomness. Lastly, autocorrelation describes the property whereby variation in usage in any one period is affected by the usage in the preceding periods. Power consumption tends to be highly autocorrelated as are many items normally carried in the supply category.

The moving average

One of the least complex forecasting techniques is the moving average. The simple moving average is well known to most people. It works well in removing random variations when seasonality is not significant. The simple moving average tends to lag the trend line and may require the carrying of data for a large number of periods. How many periods the moving average should include will affect its ability to smooth random variations and to follow the trend. The more periods it includes the smoother the line but the larger the trend lag becomes.

The weighted moving average makes it possible to put different weights on past periods. For example, it can put a heavier emphasis on the more recent periods, something that cannot be done with the simple moving average.

Regression analysis

There are three major types of regression analysis, linear, curvilinear, and multiple regression. All are more difficult to calculate than the moving average, but they are also more powerful.

Linear regression is particularly useful when the data appear to lie close to a straight line. One variable regresses on another and the fit is computed as part of the procedure.

Normally, the "least squares method" is used to determine the best fit.

For example, the normal mathematical expression for a straight line is $y = a + bx$ and the problem is to define a and b where:

y (the dependent variable) = usage or sales
a = the y intercept
b = the slope of the line
x = (the independent variable) like sales in each period
y = the y value at each data point
$\bar{x}$ = the average of all x's
$\bar{y}$ = the average of all y's
n = number of data points
Y = the value of the dependent variable computed with the regression equation

and

$$a = \bar{y} - b\bar{x}$$

$$b = \frac{\Sigma xy - n\bar{x}\bar{y}}{\Sigma x^2 - n\bar{x}^2}$$

and the fit of the line is given by the standard error of the estimate:

$$Syx = \sqrt{\frac{\sum_{i=1}^{n} (y_i - y_i)^2}{n}}$$

An example using linear regression follows. Five years of usage data are available and we are trying to predict usage in the sixth year. (See Figure 5–2.) Usages are:

Year 1	Year 2	Year 3	Year 4	Year 5
4	7	12	16	25

y	x	xy	x^2	y^2	$Y = a + bx$
4	1	40	1	16	2.6
7	2	14	4	49	7.7
12	3	36	9	144	12.8
16	4	64	16	256	17.9
25	5	125	25	625	23.0
64	15	243	55	1,090	

$$\bar{x} = \frac{\Sigma x}{n} = \frac{15}{5} = 3$$

$$\bar{y} = \frac{\Sigma y}{n} = \frac{64}{5} = 12.8$$

$$b = \frac{\Sigma xy - n\bar{x}\bar{y}}{x^2 - n\bar{x}^2} = \frac{243 - 5(3)(12.8)}{55 - 5(9)} = \frac{51}{10} = 5.1$$

$$a = \bar{y} - b\bar{x} = 12.8 - 5.1(3) = -2.5$$

Therefore:

$$Y = a + bx = -2.5 + 5.1(x)$$
$$\text{for } x = 1 \qquad Y = 2.6$$
$$\text{for } x = 5 \qquad Y = 23$$

$$Syx = \sum_{i=1}^{n} \frac{(y_i - Y_i)^2}{n}$$

$$= \frac{(4 - 2.6)^2 + (7 - 7.7)^2 + (12 - 12.8)^2 + (16 - 17.9)^2 + (25 - 25)^2}{5}$$

$$= \frac{10.90}{5} = 2.18$$

The forecast usage for the sixth year using the calculations then is:

$$Y = -2.5 + 5.1(x)$$
$$Y_6 = -2.5 + 5.1(6) = 28.1$$

The standard error for this forecast is 2.18.

In curvilinear regression a curve is fitted to the data instead of a straight line. In multiple regression a number of variables are considered simultaneously. Data gathering and computation are more complex. As in many forecasting models, standard computer programs are available for multiple regression greatly facilitating the calculation requirements.

Figure 5–2
ILLUSTRATION OF LINEAR REGRESSION OVER
A FIVE-YEAR USAGE PERIOD

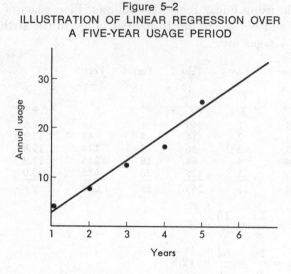

A typical multiple regression model might look like this:

$$R = U + U_c(C) + U_d(D) + U_e(E)$$

where: R = requirements

U = base usage
C, D and E are variables affecting requirements U_c, U_d and U
are influences on requirements due to C, D and E, respectively

All forecasting models discussed so far have the one disadvantage that substantial amounts of past data need to be carried continuously. As new data become known they are added to the data base and old pieces of information will be dropped. Since frequently in forecasting the most relevant information is the most recent information, the value of past data may be fairly small and exponential smoothing may be a suitable method to consider.

Exponential smoothing

In exponential smoothing only three pieces of data are required for any forecast, the actual usage for the most recent period, the forecast which was made for that period, and a smoothing constant α. Thus, calculations are considerably simplified and the data base reduced to a minimum. The factor α, called the smoothing constant, determines the reaction rate to differences between forecast and actual usage. The higher α becomes the more responsive to recent information the new forecast becomes and the less smoothing will take place. It is a managerial decision as to what value should be assigned to α. The more stable the usage, the lower α may be used, for example .04 or .05.

The following example illustrates a single exponential smoothing forecast. The basic equation is:

$$UF_t = UF_{t-1} + \alpha(UA_{t-1} - UF_{t-1})$$

where: UF_t = usage forecast for period t
   UF_{t-1} = usage forecast for previous period t–1
   α = smoothing constant
   UA_{t-1} = actual usage for previous period t–1

Let us assume a monthly forecasting procedure and that the forecast made for the previous month was 200 units and actual usage of 180 units. For an α of .10 the forecast for the next month would be:

$$UF_t = 200 + .10(180-200)$$
$$= 200 - 2 = 198 \text{ units.}$$

Double or triple exponential smoothing may be used to reduce the lag effect to trend changes in usage produced by single exponential smoothing. Seasonality and cyclical effects can also be accounted for in conjunction with exponential smoothing, creating a particularly powerful forecasting tool.[1] A recent simulation study of short-range forecasting effectiveness[2] compared exponential smoothing models and summarized best applications for forecasting as related to inventory requirements.

Product explosion and requirement accumulation

The translation of sales or use forecasts into procurement plans requires identification of individual component or material needs and the accumulation of individual needs into total requirements for a specified time period.

Most manufacturers use product explosions to identify all components for a certain end product. For example, every automobile produced needs one steering wheel, five tires, and thousands of other parts. These requirements are normally listed on parts lists or bills of materials, and computerized files can be readily totaled with the necessary sales forecasts. Often, standardized components are common to a variety of end products requiring further combination to establish a total requirement.

For supplies and nonproduction materials the estimated requirements

[1] Robert Goodell Brown, *Smoothing, Forecasting and Prediction of Discrete Time Series* (Englewood Cliffs, N.J.: Prentice-Hall, Inc., 1963).

[2] Genek Groff, "Empirical Comparison of Models for Short Range Forecasting," *Management Science*, September 1973.

of organizational subunits need to be accumulated by materials management personnel.

ABC analysis

A good starting point in developing an inventory system is to classify purchasing items into three groups: *A, B,* and *C* on the basis of the number of dollars spent annually for each item. (See Figure 5–3.)

Figure 5–3
A, B, C CLASSIFICATION OF INVENTORY

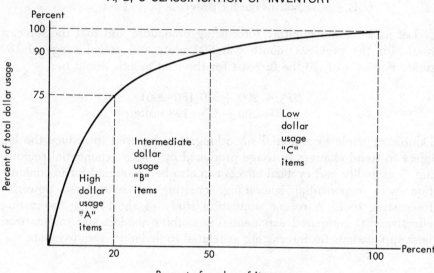

For example, a manufacturing firm with a total dollar volume of purchases annually of $30.4 million had the following breakdown of purchases:

Number of items	Percent of total items	Annual dollar purchases	Percent total purchases
521	4.8	$15,400,000	50.7
574	5.3	6,200,000	20.4
1,023	9.4	3,600,000	11.8
1,145	10.5	2,300,000	7.6
3,754	34.0	1,800,000	5.9
3,906	36.0	1,100,000	3.6
10,923	100.0	$30,400,000	100.0

As can be seen 10.1 percent of purchases (the *A* items) account for 71.1 percent of all the dollars spent. The following 19.9 percent of the number of items (the B category) accounts for 19.4 percent of the dollars, and 70.0 percent of the number of items (the C category) account for only 9.5 percent of the dollar value.

In so far as dollar investment in inventory is concerned, it pays to spend far more managerial time and effort on A and B items than on C items. Since supply assurance is usually equally critical for all categories, it is common to carry sufficient inventories of C items to give a high service level, to create a minimum of paperwork, or to have stockless buying agreements, like systems contracting which provide a high service level.

Since annual purchase volume is a combination of usage volume and unit price, it is not sufficient to call A items high dollar value and C items low dollar value. Actually the following combinations are likely to result in the following classes.

Dollar value/unit	Volume/year	Category
High	High	A
High	Medium	A
Medium	High	A
High	Low	B
Medium	Medium	B
Low	High	B
Medium	Low	C
Low	Medium	C
Low	Low	C

A items are particularly critical in terms of dollar investment and are, therefore, barring other considerations, normally carried in small quantities, ordered and reviewed frequently. B items fall between the A and C category and are well suited to a systematic approach with less frequent review than A items.

This discussion has centered on dollar impact alone, thus far. Certain C items may well require A type inventory care because of their special nature, perishability, or other considerations. For example, the flowers for the president's desk may require special attention.

Definition of inventory policy

While it may be more practical to discuss inventory policy in terms of days' supply or of physical quantities—and, after all, the two are inseparable—yet, in the last analysis, the question of what constitutes the proper inventory to carry resolves itself into a matter of dollars. "Too much" or "too little" or "badly balanced" inventories are all to be avoided because they "cost too much." They are expensive on many counts. "Too much" is "too much" because of undue carrying charges in the form of taxes, insurance, storage, obsolescence, and depreciation. They may be excessive because an undue proportion of the company's total working capital is invested in them. When material shortages exist, certain portions of the inventory may be too large, and capital may be frozen because other portions of the inventory cannot be maintained in proper proportion to them. On the other hand, "too little" is "too little" because of the costs of too frequent reordering, loss of quantity discounts, or higher transportation charges. Inventory may be too small in the face of probable price increases and subsequent higher material costs. It may be too low in view of likely shortages in the future, with a consequent costly "slowdown" resulting from delayed deliveries. In short, it is the inventory costs that are ultimately significant.

But, however measured, what is the proper size of inventory? This, after all, is the crux of the matter. What is "too little" at one time can be very quickly "too much" in a subsequent period. When general business deteriorates, any particular manufacturer is likely to find that he, like other businessmen, is threatened with reduced sales volume, lower production, and, therefore, markedly reduced material requirements. Moreover, such a condition is commonly accompanied by falling prices; hence, such quantities of material as the manufacturer does require can be purchased more cheaply, the lowered prices being reflected, of course, in lowered costs. These factors tend to reduce the size of forward commitments, to necessitate smaller stocks on hand, and to stress hand-to-mouth buying. Clearly, too, inventory purchased at higher prices remaining unused in stock or in uncancelable order represents some loss, even though subsequently used. To any manufacturer, therefore, an inventory which was, under one set of conditions, too small—or even just right—under altered conditions might, perhaps within a matter of weeks, become quite excessive. But the whole question as to when business conditions will begin to deteriorate and of the extent to which the less satisfactory general situation will affect any individual industry or business becomes a matter of judgment.

Factors bearing on inventory control

Any attempt to get a clear picture of the inventory management problem of an individual organization must, therefore, start with a classification of the factors which bear upon the particular problem of that organization. In so doing, we must recognize three things: first, that there are certain elements necessarily related to inventory in any organization; second, that, relative to one another, these factors vary in importance; and, third, that these variations depend on the type of merchandise bought, the conditions under which it is supplied, and the conditions under which it is used.

The elements which are common to all companies must be reviewed. They may be listed as follows:

a. Stocks on hand. The maximum amount which is desirable to be carried as an inventory item or the amount needed for any particular production or maintenance project which is in prospect is a combination of the amount already on hand and the amount which is procured and added to stocks on hand.

b. The time and extent of probable use. This is based on the production or other planning data which offer facts as to the time at which use is to be made of the material, the amount which is to be used, and the stability of that use.

c. Obsolescence. In determining how much of any given material or supply is to be purchased, due weight should be given to the possibility of change in production plans or specifications or developments from research which may render the material obsolete.

d. Quantity price differentials.

e. Market conditions and price trends.

f. Time required for delivery or lead time

g. The various costs associated with inventory. These normally include:

Set-up costs. For manufacturing the set-up cost is often a significant consideration. It may include such learning curve related factors as early spoilage and low production rate until standard is reached as well as the more common considerations such as the set-up man's cost, the machine downtime, the extra tool grinding, the parts damaged during set-up.

Stock-out costs. These are the costs to the organization of not having the required parts or materials on hand when they are needed. They may include lost contribution on lost sales, both present and future, change-over costs necessitated by the shortage, substitution of less suitable or more expensive parts or materials, rescheduling costs and management labor and machine idle time. Occasionally, penalty costs may have to be paid, and often goodwill of users or customers may be affected.

Carrying, holding or possession costs. These include handling charges, the cost of storage facilities and warehouse rentals, insurance, breakage, pilferage, taxes, obsolescence depreciation, and investment or opportunity costs. G. Aljian[3] presents the following detailed list:

Capital costs:
    Interest on money invested in inventory
    Interest on money invested in land and building to hold inventory
    Interest on money invested in inventory handling and control equipment

---

[3] G. W. Aljian, ed., *Purchasing Handbook*, 3d ed. (New York: McGraw-Hill Book Co., 1973), pp. 11–14, 11–15.

Storage space costs:
  Rent on building
  Taxes and insurance on building
  Depreciation on building
  Depreciation on warehouse installation
  Cost of maintenance and repairs
  Utility charges, including heat, light, and water
  Salaries of security and maintenance personnel
Inventory service costs:
  Taxes on inventory
  Labor costs in handling and maintaining stocks
  Clerical expense in keeping records
  Employee benefits for warehouse and administrative personnel
Handling-equipment costs:
  Taxes and insurance on equipment
  Depreciation on equipment
  Fuel expense
  Cost of maintenance and repairs
Inventory risk costs:
  Obsolescence of inventory
  Insurance on inventory
  Physical deterioration of inventory
  Losses from pilferage

Ordering or purchasing cost. These include the preparation costs for a purchase or production order. They include managerial clerical, material, and mailing costs and may be divided into line and header costs. Line cost refers to the computing cost per line item from a vendor. Header cost refers to the costs of identifying and placing an order with a vendor. In any purchase order where more than one item is acquired from one vendor, there should be several line costs and one header cost.

The identification of the above costs suggests the difficulty of properly identifying and collecting at least some of them in real life situations. The relevant cost principle should hold, but often for one particular item some marginal or relevant costs may be meaningless. For example, the set-up man is normally hired for a full work week, and one small set-up more or less may have no impact on what the set-up man is paid. An organization owns and operates its own warehouse and adding or removing a few individual items may have no effect on handling, depreciation, insurance costs, or taxes.

Stock-out costs present their own difficulties, because even at different times their impact may vary. In a seller's market an unsatisfied customer will not be lost as easily as in a buyer's market, and who will say what the cost of not satisfying this customer at this time will be in the long run? When a plant is operating well below capacity, changing over and set-up costs may not be as significant as when operating at capacity.

Two approaches may be used to address some of these difficulties. It is possible to trace and cumulate the individual costs attributable to individual items and use these for decision making. For example, what is the cost of issuing a purchase order for this item? Hopefully, such tracing would be applicable to a class or a number of different items and might, therefore, have broader applicability.

The second approach would be to forecast the impact of a major change in operations and predict the impact on various cost centers. For example, if for half of the C items we use systems contracting, what will the impact on the stores operation be? Or, if we introduce a new way of calculating order quantities order points and safety stocks, what will be the impact of the larger or smaller number of orders on the purchasing group? Since most inventory models and theory is based on finding an optimal cost level, weighing carrying costs against ordering costs or stock-out costs, the quality and availability of cost data are relevant considerations.

Professor Robert Britney has developed an interesting framework for identifying and managing inventories The authors gratefully acknowledge his contribution in the next section of this chapter, which is largely based on a paper presented by him.[4]

Inventories: Their functions, forms and control

Of all the many aspects of business administration, few are more perplexing than inventories. Basically they are necessary for prompt customer service, and yet they always seem to be too high, too low, or of the wrong kind. When business activity slows down, the first economic move taken is management's edict to cut all inventories. As business picks up once more, a flurry of activity begins to rebuild inventory stocks on hand. This volatility contributes little to the enhancement of our understanding and control of inventories.

Although the economic order quantity (EOQ) was first introduced in 1915 by Harris, many companies today do not purchase or manufacture in EOQs. This model has not yet achieved the level of success of other management models such as critical path scheduling introduced as recently as 1957.

Inventories may be viewed in terms of the functions they provide and the forms in which they emerge. Within this framework, the potential role of "rules of thumb" and models such as "EOQ" can be assessed.

---

[4] R. R. Britney, "Inventories: Their Functions, Forms and Control." Paper presented to the Canadian Association for Production and Inventory Control, May 1971.

Before doing this, one question should be considered: Why do inventories exist?

Why do inventories exist?

Inventories are important for many reasons, a few include:

1. Provide and maintain good customer service;
2. Smooth the flow of goods through the production process;
3. Provide protection against the uncertainties of supply and demand;
4. Obtain a reasonable utilization of equipment and manpower.

What we really mean is that the costs of not having inventories are usually greater than the costs of having them. They exist for this reason and for this reason alone.

Often these costs are difficult or impossible to obtain, and we simply may say that inventories are needed to do business. The implications here are that the costs associated with production inefficiencies, lost sales, and customer ill-will arising from not stocking inventories are perceived to be greater than the cost of maintaining stocks. If we are uncertain as to customer behavior, we then talk about the expected costs of inventories, combining probability estimates of customer demand with inventory costs.

This simple but effective definition of why inventories exist is intuitively reasonable and very useful. For example, the familiar EOQ formula can be derived directly from this definition.

Consider the situation where the yearly demand is R units, the cost purchase (or set-up) is S dollars, and the percentage annual cost of carrying inventory is K, and the purchase price (or cost) is C dollars per unit. We could look at a variety of lot sizes ranging from one unit lots up to large quantity lots. Let's assume that we know that a lot of some quantity Q is economical. Should we consider the next lot size larger by some small quantity q? The cost of not including q in the lot size will leave the number of orders required per year at R/Q with an annual purchase cost of $S(R)/Q$. If q is included the number of set-ups will fall to $(R)/Q + q$ with a cost of $S(R)/Q + q$ dollars. But the cost of having q will save $S(R)/Q - S(R)/Q + q$ dollars. The cost of having q in the lot size will increase the average level of inventory $q/2$, at an additional yearly carrying cost of approximately $KC(q)/2$. This will include q only if the cost of not having it is greater than the cost of having it. Further we would be indifferent when the costs are just equal. Equating these costs we obtain the equation:

$$S\frac{(R)}{Q} - S\frac{(R)}{Q+q} = KC\frac{(q)}{2}$$

Simplifying:

$$SR \frac{(q)}{Q(Q+q)} = KC \frac{(q)}{2}$$

Canceling q gives:

$$SR \frac{(1)}{Q(Q+q)} = \frac{KC}{2}$$

Rearranging:

$$Q^2 + Qq = \frac{2RS}{KC}$$

As q becomes rather small we consider the addition of an elemental quantity q only, then as q approaches a very small value so does Qq. This leaves: $Q^2 = 2RS/KC$. Thus the economic order quantity Q is:

$$Q = \sqrt{\frac{2RS}{KC}}$$

The economic order quantity is usually developed using calculus; however, it is important to see that it is really selected according to the simple definition of the existence of inventories. Let's now briefly review the functions of inventories.

What functions do inventories provide?

Regardless of their form (raw material, work in process, and finished goods), all inventories may be further described as performing one or more of transit, cycle, buffer, seasonal, and decoupling functions.

1. Transit inventories. These are primarily pipeline inventories, their existence arising because of the need to transport inventories from point A to point B in the production inventory system. Since this transit time is not instantaneous in most situations; significant quantities of transit inventories result.

2. Cycle inventories. These exist because of management's attempt to produce in lot sizes, either EOQs or other reasonable lot sizes. In order to facilitate such a plan, inventories accumulate at points in the system.

3. Buffer. Inventories in this classification arise mainly from decisions regarding risk. The higher the service level (the lower the risk we set of running out of stock) the greater are the quantities in buffer inventories required.

4. Anticipation inventories. Anticipation inventories exist because of expected changes in demand, supply, or price. A simple demand example would be a seasonal expectation for high requirements such as heating oil in the winter time. If supply shortages are expected or prices expected to rise, inventories may be acquired in anticipation of these developments.

5. *Decoupling.* Decoupling inventories provide the function of separating dependent production centers. The independent operation of these centers may be achieved over a limited period of time by the use of decoupling inventories.

A reasonable question at this time would be to ask why one would want to distinguish between five functions of inventories? At any one time, a transit, buffer, and decoupling inventory will all appear exactly the same, or one step further a single unit of inventory may in reality support all functions at once. One reason for dwelling on the functions of inventories as we have is to identify and highlight those inventories which are controllable and those which are essentially noncontrollable. The controllable/noncontrollable concept, of course, must pertain to a reasonable time period, for all inventories are controllable in the long run.

Before looking at management's decision variables which control these various inventories, let's first add the form dimension to these functions.

Inventory forms

Inventories can be classified by form as well as function. The three commonly recognized forms for production material are raw material, work in process, and finished goods. Scrap, or obsolete materials, although technically a form of inventory, will not be included in these basic forms here. (See Chapter 13 which deals with disposal.)

Supplies or MRO items are also a form of inventory and lend themselves to the same framework. In most manufacturing companies the size of the supplies inventory is relatively small compared to the other forms. The identification of inventory forms are relative in that the finished goods of one company often become the raw materials of the next company. This total system interdependence is well illustrated by Forrester's[5] interesting approach to industrial dynamics. However, within one organization they are easily distinguished.

Raw material inventories for manufacturers represent stocks of the basic material inputs into a company's production process. As material and labor is added to these inputs, they are combined and transformed into work-in-process inventories. When completed and stocked they become finished goods inventories.

[5] J. W. Forrester, "Industrial Dynamics," *Harvard Business Review*, July-August 1968.

In general, these inventory forms are distinguished by the amounts of materials and labor added by the organization. Finished goods inventories have more material and labor added than do work-in-process inventories. Again within any organization these forms are usually well defined.

For nonmanufacturing organizations other than retail institutions finished goods may not be a significant form and many of the inventories carried may properly be classified as supplies. Two main classes may be recognized here prior to use and in service.

Inventory function and form framework

Pulling together the five functions and three forms, we have the 15 potential kinds of inventory making up the total inventory profile of a company. Figure 5–4 illustrates these, together with brief descriptions

Figure 5–4

INVENTORY FORM

		Raw material 1	Work-in-process 2	Finished goods 2
INVENTORY FUNCTION	1 Transit (pipeline)	Logistics decisions		
		Design of supply system, supplier location, transportation mode	Design of layout and materials handling system	Design of plant location and product distribution system
	2 Cycle (EOQ, lots)	Product/Process Design Decisions		
		Order size, order cost	Lot size, set-up	Distribution costs, lot sizes
	3 Buffer (uncertainty)	Management Risk Level Decisions & Uncertainty		
		Probability distribution of price, supply & stock-out & carrying costs	Probability distribution of machine and product capabilities	Probability distributions of demand and associated carrying and stock-outs costs
	4 Anticipation price shortage	Price/Availability/Decisions & Uncertainty, Seasonality Capacity		
		Know future supply & demand price levels	Capacity, production costs of hire, fire, transfer, overtime, idle time, etc.	Demand patterns (seasonal)
	5 Decoupling (interdependence)	Production Control Decisions		
		Dependence/ independence from supplier behavior	Dependence/ independence of successive production operations	Dependence/ independence from market behavior

of the key management decision variables affecting the existence of these different kinds of inventories. All may not be present to the same degree in any one organization; however, those that are present in significant numbers exist because the cost of having them are less than the cost of not having them. It is useful to discuss some of the more common kinds of inventory at this point.

Transit inventories

In order to sustain operations, transit inventories are employed to stock the supply and distribution pipelines linking a company to its suppliers and customers respectively. On the procurement side some of the more common decisions affecting the size of this inventory deal with the supplier's location and the transport mode selected. A decision to use a supplier a long distance away and to use rail transportation may create far greater raw materials transit inventories than using a local supplier with daily truck deliveries. Trade-offs exist between transportation and inventory carrying costs as well. Obviously, a decision here may have further impact on the other functional inventories for the same material. If the likelihood of a rail strike is high, anticipation stocks may be forced up. And if the chances of variation in lead time are high, buffer stocks also may have to be enlarged. Total system design should recognize these trade-offs and assure their consideration in the decision making. Work-in-process transit inventories are determined by such factors as process design and plant layout as materials flow from operation to operation. Finished goods transit inventories are likewise related to marketing policies and channels of distribution. All are characterized as inventories in transit from one point to another.

For some organizations being located close to the source of raw materials is important. Others have to be close to markets. For others again location is less sensitive. Once an organization's site is established, however, operational decisions involving transit inventories must be made with the locational context as given. For example, a number of steel companies situated on the Great Lakes use water transport for raw materials and find that during the winter this facility is not possible. They are, therefore, forced to build an anticipation or seasonal inventory. So long as the cost of building up this inventory and carrying it over the winter is lower than the cost of switching to alternate means of transport in the winter, this practice will continue.

Cycle inventories

Rather than purchase, produce, or even transport inventories one unit at a time, we may choose to work in lots. As a direct result, inventories tend to accumulate at various points in the system. These are called cycle inventories, inventories required to support our decision to function in lot sizes. Although lot sizes may be determined in many ways, one lot size of special interest is the so-called economic order quantity. There are a large number and variety of economic order quantity models to take account of variations in demand, supply, or production rate, lead time, and costs. The derivation of the simple model $Q = \sqrt{2RS/KC}$ has been provided in an interesting way at the beginning of this chapter. This model presumes instant replenishment, standard usage throughout the year, and costs which do not change. From the procurement side the cost of ordering in itself is not easily determined. The principle behind almost all mathematical inventory models involves relevant or marginal costs which are balanced against carrying costs. Most accounting systems do not readily supply the necessary information for such calculations, and it is foolish to base extensive models and fancy systems on shaky cost foundations. The theoretical trade-off between ordering cost and carrying cost is readily seen from Figure 5–5. As the order

Figure 5–5
MATERIAL CARRYING AND ORDER COSTS

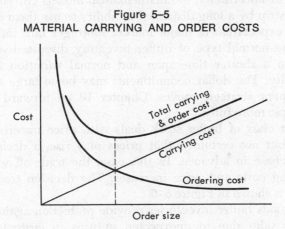

quantity increases ordering cost decreases (because fewer orders are placed), and carrying cost increases (because the average inventory increases). Not all costs will behave as shown in Figure 5–4. It is proper to determine the costs relevant to the particular situation studied. Not all total cost curves are smooth parabolas with a nice flat bottom and little sensitivity to the lot size over a wide range of values.

Buffer inventories

The term buffer inventory or safety stock is undoubtedly familiar to many of us, each with our own concept of what it means. However, let us reserve this definition to represent inventories that exist at a point in a company as a result of uncertainties of the demand or supply of units at that point. Raw material buffer stocks give some protection against the uncertainties of supplier performance due to such factors as lead time, variation, shut-downs, strikes, late deliveries, and poor quality units that cannot be accepted. The determination of the level of buffer inventory carried may be of significant financial consequence to the organization. The average inventory carried is close to the sum of all of the buffer inventory but only half of the EOQ. If the level of buffer stock is at all large in relation to the EOQ very special attention may have to be paid to it. Since the normal reason for carrying buffer stock is to protect against uncertainties of demand or supply, management efforts to reduce these uncertainties may have substantial pay-off. For example, switching from one supplier to another with a more predictable lead time may make a lot of sense. The buffer inventory level should be determined by balancing carrying cost versus stock-out cost. Since our ability to measure stock-out costs is not particularly advanced, possibly because few managers are willing and able to think negatively and in terms of uncertainty, the mathematical models currently available generally outstrip by a long distance our ability to use them effectively.

Buying in expectation of major market shortages falls into a different class from the normal type of buffer inventory discussed so far, which is oriented to a shorter time span and normal variation in lead time and availability. The dollar commitments may be so large as to require top management strategic moves. Chapter 10 on forward buying discusses this topic more fully.

A different class of buffer stock deals with price uncertainty. In the expectation, but not certainty, that prices may rise, a decision may be made to purchase in advance. In this case, the trade-off would be between carrying costs and price increases. The decision tree illustrating this situation is shown in Figure 5–6.

Finished goods buffer inventories provide protection against the possibility of lost sales due to unexpected upturns in customer demands. The location and quantities of buffer stocks are related to the risks and costs of being out of stock. These stocks provide a margin or safety and are often called safety stocks.

Anticipation stocks are accumulated for a well-defined future need. The difference between buffer and anticipation inventory is that the latter is committed in the face of reasonable certainty and, therefore, has far less risk attached to it. Seasonal inventories are an excellent example; the summer work-in-process stocking of tomato paste for further processing during the winter is a typical case. Anticipation stocks of raw materials may include availability reasons like strikes, or definite shortages, or price when definite increases are announced. The managerial decision is considerably simplified, however, compared to the buffer situation, because the model becomes a simple deterministic one without probabilities attached. Unfortunately, in periods of shortages and rapidly

Figure 5–6
DECISION TO INVENTORY IN ANTICIPATION OF
POSSIBLE PRICE INCREASE

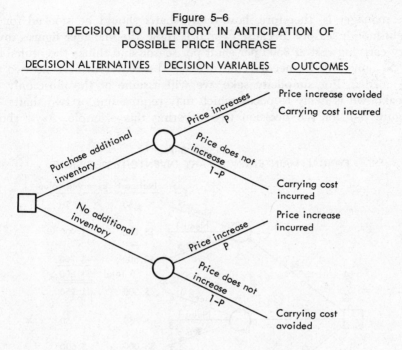

rising prices, although the need to increase inventory in the form of buffer and anticipation stocks is clear, the ability of the organization to commit the necessary funds may be severely taxed. Public organizaions working under control of regular budgets may find it difficult to obtain authorization and funds, and many private organizations short of working capital may be frustrated in their attempts to find the money.

Spare parts inventory

A form of buffer and anticipation inventory related to capital equipment is that of spare parts. This topic is more extensively covered in Chapter 11, but one simple example will illustrate the basic decision format.

In a certain factory one of the major pieces of equipment has two main shafts. If either shaft wears out, the machine has to be shut down and with it the whole plant. If new shafts are in stock, the machine can be repaired in four hours. Without sufficient stock it will take 48 hours to get emergency replacements and repairs. Each shaft costs $2,000. The additional cost of factory shutdown in excess of four hours (for 44 hours) is $2,500, and additional emergency costs for transportation, etc., are $500 per shaft. The factory normally operates for eight months a year. During the remaining four months maintenance and repairs and equipment replacements are performed. The decision facing the manager is, therefore, how many shafts should be stocked for the eight-month season? Because capital is tight, the manager figures inventory carrying cost at $500 per shaft per season and thinks the probability is .50 none will be needed; .30 one will be required; and .20 two will be needed. For simplicity sake, we will assume at the most only one breakdown is likely to occur which may require one or two shafts. See Figure 5–7 for the decision tree covering this example. As it shows,

Figure 5–7
TYPICAL MAINTENANCE PART INVENTORY DECISIONS

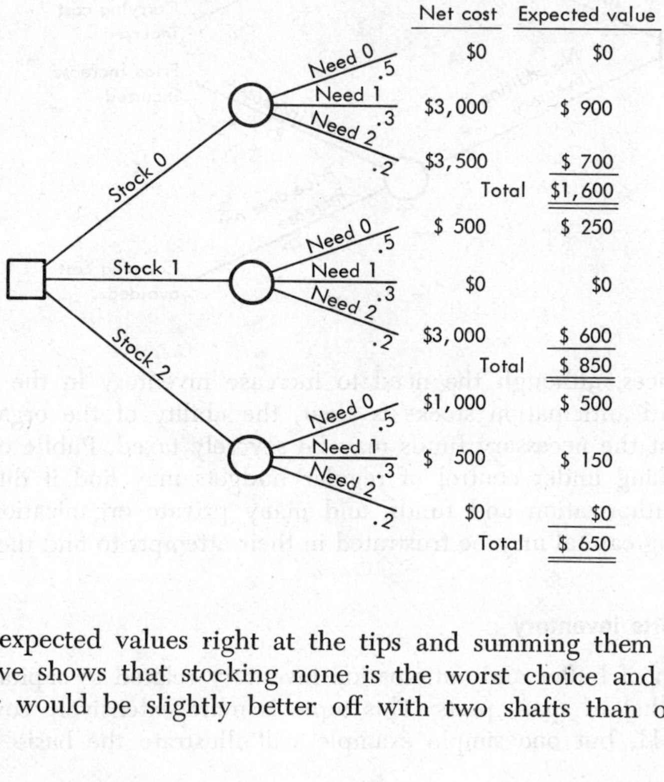

	Net cost	Expected value
Need 0 .5	$0	$0
Need 1 .3	$3,000	$ 900
Need 2 .2	$3,500	$ 700
	Total	$1,600
Need 0 .5	$ 500	$ 250
Need 1 .3	$0	$0
Need 2 .2	$3,000	$ 600
	Total	$ 850
Need 0 .5	$1,000	$ 500
Need 1 .3	$ 500	$ 150
Need 2 .2	$0	$0
	Total	$ 650

putting expected values right at the tips and summing them for each alternative shows that stocking none is the worst choice and that the manager would be slightly better off with two shafts than one shaft in stock.

Decoupling inventory

Finally, the existence of inventories at major linkage points makes it possible to carry on activities on either side of the point relatively independently of each other. These inventories tend to reduce the dependence of one activity on the other. The amounts and locations of raw material, work-in-process, and finished goods decoupling inventories depend upon the relative advantages of increased flexibility in operations over the costs of maintaining these inventories. The ability to plan the plant's operations independent of suppliers short run behavior is highly valued by most managers. Many contracts specify that the supplier shall maintain an inventory for just this reason. The size of such inventory and its appropriateness will vary from situation to situation. It is possible that a transit, cycle, buffer, or anticipation inventory may perform the double function of decoupling at the same time. It may be just as much in the supplier's interest as the purchaser's that decoupling inventory exists. It gives flexibility and independence to both parties and is an excellent area for negotiation. Work-in-process decoupling inventory may become substantial in situations where a large number of operations are planned for the same product. One reason for the line as opposed to the process layout in plants is to cut down on this type of inventory. The trade-off lies between carrying cost and operations costs and/or flexibility. One of the costs of flexibility is decoupling inventory. Since degree of flexibility is clearly a managerial decision and frequently a strategic one, decoupling inventories tend to play a larger role than may at first glance be apparent.

By examining the functions of inventories, it is now clear that inventories are the result of many interrelated decisions and policies within an organization. A management directive to reduce total inventories by 20 percent could, because of purchasing and marketing policies and a prior commitment on cycle and seasonal inventories, cause the virtual elimination of all decoupling and buffer inventories with potentially disastrous results.

Implications for the control of inventories

Because we are now dealing with up to 15 different kinds of inventories, the problem of control becomes a little more complicated. First, we should recognize that the behavior of inventories is the direct result of diverse policies and decisions within a company. Marketing, production, finance, and purchasing decisions directly influence the level of inventories throughout the organization.

For example, an inventory control manager within a staff production planning and control group may have little control over finished goods transit (marketing) and raw material cycle (purchasing) inventories. Thus, many firms have created material control executives to improve the coordination of marketing, purchasing, and production activities with respect to inventories.

Second, not all inventories are equally controllable for other reasons. Long-term marketing commitments in terms of distribution networks may render transit finished goods inventory levels quite inflexible, whereas the relatively shorter term production scheduling plans may provide a great deal of flexibility in the control of decoupling work-in-process inventories. Consider another case. Short-term production scheduling may provide a great deal of flexibility in work-in-process cycle inventories; relatively longer term supplier development and purchasing commitments may result in rigid raw material cycle and transit inventories. How often has the total value of inventories risen due to the unavoidable accumulation of raw materials as production schedules and product demand drop rapidly? To be effective inventory control managers must recognize the controllability of each kind of inventory in the short and long run.

Third, why haven't EOQs worked? Very simply, EOQs are cycle inventories and may be only a small part of the total inventory picture. Managers who produce only in EOQs are ignoring the potential benefits of transit, anticipation, and decoupling inventories. Often the production in noneconomic order quantities may be more profitable.

Finally, let's consider the simple "rules of thumb"—for example, turnover defined as the ratio of total sales to average inventory. Acceptable turnover values can be obtained from past performances or industry norms. Assume a company has $1 million annual sales and an average inventory level of $250,000 creating a turnover of four. If this is acceptable now, then as sales double inventories should rise to $500,000. However, let's take a closer look at the components of the inventory.

Cycle EOQ inventories vary as the square root of demand, so that as demand doubles EOQ rises by the square root of two which is less than doubling. In addition raw materials (purchasing in EOQ) need not be the same. The costs of carrying raw materials versus finished goods may be quite different. Thus, cycle inventories, if doubled, may not be optimal.

Further, transit inventories are more dependent upon the supply and distribution network than simply annual sales. A change in the distribution system to accommodate the doubled sales could result in more than a double finished goods transit inventory.

Anticipation finished goods stocks depend more upon the pattern of demand, rather than its total value. Decoupling stock requirements may remain unchanged and so on through the list.

The point that should be stressed here is this. Although a turnover of four was desirable for a sales level of $1 million the optimal turnover could legitimately drop to two for an annual sales of $2 million. All 15 kinds of inventories do not vary directly with sales volume, and therefore the rules of thumb can often be misleading.

During the 13th Annual International Conference of the American Production and Inventory Control Society, Professor Richard Shell[6] put it this way.

For a long time top executives of certain companies have used the inventory ratio as a "standard measurement" to determine if inventory levels are "proper." The inventory ratio is obtained by simply dividing the total dollar value

---

[6] Richard L. Shell, "Principles of Inventory Control," *Proceedings, International Technical Conference, American Production and Inventory Control Society,* 1970.

of inventory by the total dollar asset value of the company. Within a company, comparisons can be made between the inventory ratio for one year and the inventory ratio for another year. It is absurd to consider this relative comparison a true standard of measurement. Yet today many inventory control managers are in-part evaluated on this ratio. Countless other ratios have been devised in an attempt to quickly "evaluate" inventory levels within a particular company. These include such questionable values as the total number of parts produced divided by the total number of parts in inventory and the total physical area occupied by inventory divided by the total manufacturing area. Even the time tested number of inventory "turns" each year is not a fair measure of correct inventory level. This discussion might lead to the conclusion that we should not use ratios or rules of thumb to evaluate inventory levels. Generally, this is true. However, it is suggested that the inventory ratio can be useful in evaluating total inventory levels within a specific company if the ratio is properly developed. Proper development consists of determining individual product inventory levels, raw material through finished goods, and then summing their dollar value equivalent and dividing by total dollar assets. Stated another way, the inventory ratio is obtained after all individual requirements have been properly assessed as compared to the traditional method of obtaining the inventory ratio before assessing individual item requirements.

Most executives have rules and have learned from experience that desirable outcomes result as these rules are followed. The danger is, of course, that executives never know if the rules they have are the best available. Any set of rules used for inventory control should be reevaluated regularly.

The control of inventories is complex because of the many functions and forms. Inventory levels are the result of many short- and long-term decisions and policies of all functional areas (i.e., production, marketing, purchasing) within the organization. The control of inventories represent a shared responsibility and must be viewed as such.

The price-discount problem

A normal situation in purchasing occurs when a price discount is offered if purchases are made in larger quantities. Acceptance of a larger quantity provides a form of anticipation inventory. The problem may be solved in several ways. Marginally, the question is: should we increase the size of our inventory so that we obtain the benefits of the lower price? Put this way, it can be analyzed as a return on investment decision. The simple EOQ model is not of much assistance here since it cannot account for the purchase price differential directly. It is possible to use the EOQ model to eliminate some alternatives, however, and to check the final solution. Total cost calculations are required to find the optimal point.

The following problem is illustrative of the calculation.

Sample price discount problem

R = 900 units (annual demand)
S = \$50 (order cost)
K = .25 (carrying cost) or 25 percent
C = \$45 for 0–199 units per order
    \$43 for 200–399 units per order
    \$41.50 for 400–799 units per order
    \$40.00 for 800 and over units per order

Sample calculations for the price discount problem

	100	200	400	800
Total annual price paid	40,500.00	38,700.00	37,350.00	36,000.00
Carrying cost	562.50	1,075.00	2,075.00	4,000.00
Order cost	450.00	225.00	112.50	56.25
Total cost	41,512.50	40,000.00	39,537.50	40,056.25
Average inventory	2,250.00	4,300.00	8,300.00	16,000.00
EOQ	89.00	92.00*	93.00*	94.00*

* Not feasible

A simple marginal analysis shows that in moving from 100 per order to 200 the additional investment is \$4,300 — \$2,250 = \$2,050. The saving in price is \$40,500 — \$38,700 = \$1,800, and the order cost saving is \$450 — \$225 = \$225. For an additional investment of \$2,050 the savings are \$2,025 which is almost a 100 percent return and is well in excess of the 25 percent carrying cost. In going from 400 to 800 the additional investment is \$7,700 for a total price and order savings of \$1,406.25. This falls below the 25 percent carrying cost and would not be a desirable result. The total cost figures show that the optimal purchase quantity is at the 400 level. The largest single saving occurs at the first price break at the 200 level.

The EOQs with an asterisk are not feasible because the price range and the volume do not match. For example, the price for the second EOQ of 92 is 45. Yet for the 200–400 range the actual price is \$43.00. The EOQ may be used, however, in the following way. In going from right to left on the table (from the lowest unit price to the highest price) proceed until the first valid EOQ is obtained. This is 89 for the 0 to 199 price range. Then the order quantity at each price discount above this EOQ is checked to see whether total costs at the higher order quantity are lower or higher than at the EOQ. Doing this for the example shown gives us a total cost at the valid EOQ level of 89 of:

Total annual price paid	\$40,500
Carrying cost	500
Order cost	500
Total cost	\$41,500

Since this total cost at the feasible EOQ of 89 units is above the total cost at the 200 order quantity level and the 400 and 800 order levels as well, the proper order quantity is 400, which gives the lowest total cost of all options.

The discussion so far has assumed that the quantity discount offered is based on orders of the full amount, forcing the purchaser to carry substantial inventories. It is preferable, of course, from the purchaser's standpoint to take delivery in smaller quantities but to still get the lower discount price. This could well be negotiated through annual contracts, cumulative discounts or blanket orders. This type of analysis can also identify what extra price differential the purchaser might be willing to pay to avoid carrying substantial stocks.

Inventory models

Most procurement inventory models fall into four basic classes.

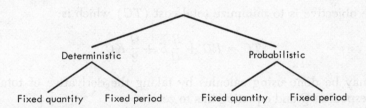

Deterministic models are different from probabilistic models in that they assume conditions of certainty regarding demand, price, and costs. For example, demand is 900 units, not 900 ± 200; prices and costs are similarly fixed at specified dollar amounts which do not change over time. These conditions seldom prevail in reality; nevertheless, deterministic models are useful in conceptualizing the problem and in a large number of low-cost situations where the additional accuracy of probabilistic models is not worth the extra effort. Fixed quantity models use a standard order quantity but vary the time between orders. The reorder point depends on usage. Fixed period models use a standard time between orders but vary the order quantity. All four models attempt to minimize cost (or maximize contribution) through trading off carrying costs, order costs, and stock-out costs.

Deterministic-fixed quantity models

One of the simplest deterministic fixed quantity models is shown in Figure 5–8.

In this example demand (R), lead time (L), price (C), order or set-up (S), and carrying cost (K) are all constant. When the inventory drops to the reorder point (P) a fixed order quantity Q is ordered which arrives after a lead time (L). There are no stock-outs and no back orders.

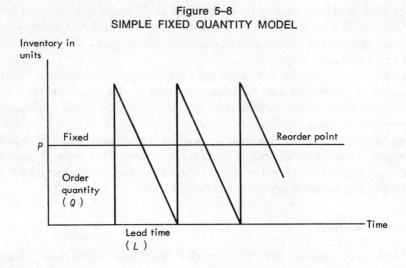

Figure 5–8
SIMPLE FIXED QUANTITY MODEL

The objective is to minimize total cost (TC) which is:

$$TC = RC + \frac{R}{Q}S + \frac{Q}{2}KC$$

This may be done using calculus by taking the derivative of total cost with respect to Q and equating this to zero.

$$\frac{dTC}{dQ} = 0 + \frac{(-RS)}{Q^2} + \frac{KC}{2}$$

This is equal to zero when:

$$Q = \frac{2RS}{KC} \text{ or } EOQ = \frac{2RS}{KC}$$

This is the EOQ (Economic Order Quantity) or Qopt (Optimal Order Quantity). (See also the different derivation of EOQ shown under the heading "Why Do Inventories Exist?" in this chapter.) The cost curve for this model are shown in Figure 5–9.

An example of the calculations that may be performed using this model follows:

R = Annual demand   = 900 units
C = Delivered purchase cost = \$45 unit
K = Carrying cost   = 25 percent
S = Order cost   = \$50 order

$$EOQ = \sqrt{\frac{2RS}{KC}} = \frac{2 \times 900 \times 50}{.25 \times 45}$$

$$= \sqrt{8,000} = 89$$

Figure 5–9
INVENTORY COSTS

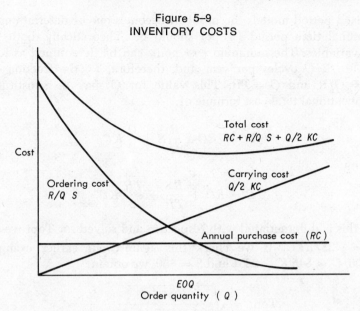

Order quantity (Q)

The daily demand is 4 units for 225 working days per year. The lead time (L) is 30 working days. The reorder point (P) is, therefore, $30 \times 4 = 120$ units. The average inventory carried is $89/2 = 44\frac{1}{2}$ units at an average investment of $44.5 \times \$45 = \$2002$ and annual carrying cost of $.25 \times \$2002 = \$500$.

Further deterministic models exist to account for usage during replenishment and stock-outs. A price discount deterministic model is discussed elsewhere in this chapter.

Fixed period models

There are many situations where fixed period models are more desirable from an operations management point of view than fixed order quantity models. The scheduling of tasks for employees is facilitated when, for example, they know they can be assigned to check on certain classes of inventory items with a predetermined time span of a day, a week, two weeks, a month, and so on.

Fixed period systems tend to require a higher safety stock level than fixed order quantity systems, because they receive less monitoring. In a fixed order quantity system a new order is theoretically placed the moment the reorder level is reached. In fixed period systems the inventory level is recorded only at review time. The inventory on hand must, therefore, cover against stock-outs during the review period and also the lead time which follows the placing of an order.

In fixed period models the problem becomes one of determining what the optimal time period (Topt) should be. Theoretically, both T and Q are variables. The minimum cost point can be determined as follows. There are R/Q cycles per year and, therefore, T (the fraction of the year) = Q/R and $Q = TR$. This value for Q may be substituted in the conventional total cost formula of:

$$TC = RC \; \& \; \frac{R}{Q} S + \frac{Q}{2} KC$$

giving:

$$TC = RC + \frac{RS}{TR} + \frac{TR}{2} KC$$

When this is differentiated with respect to and solved for Topt we obtain Topt = $\sqrt{2S/RKC}$. If we check this against our earlier example of $R = 900, C = \$45 \; K = \$25\%$ and $S = \$50$, we obtain:

$$\text{Topt} = \sqrt{\frac{2 \times 50}{900 \times .25 \times .45}}$$

$$= \sqrt{\frac{100}{10,125}} = \sqrt{.01} = .10$$

for 225 working days. This is once every $22\frac{1}{2}$ days and EOQ = RTopt = $900 \times .10 = 90$. The proper decision, then, would be to order 90 units every $22\frac{1}{2}$ days. This is the same decision as reached in the earlier example.

Probabilistic models

Probabilistic models take into account variations in the model variables. This increases their complexity but also their accuracy. To illustrate the principle involved, the fixed order quantity model with variation in demand (usage) will be discussed in some detail. A buffer stock needs to be maintained to give protection against stock-outs. This raises the question on the criterion to be used for safety-stock level and stock-out policy. Shall it be minimization of cost or maximization of service level?

Minimization of cost for buffer inventory would seek the point at which total cost of carrying the inventory and stock-out costs would be lowest. This, in turn, would require some reasonable knowledge of stock-out costs, something which, as discussed earlier in this chapter under buffer inventory still leaves much to be desired. The principle is clear, however, and parallels the ordering cost versus carrying cost situation discussed under the fixed order quantity model. As buffer inventory decreases stock-out costs soar; as buffer inventory increases holding costs go up and stock-out costs drop.

Service level

The service level is another method of describing the performance management expects from a buffer inventory. How many stock-outs are acceptable? A prominent manufacturer of sewing machines, for example, set a policy that 94 percent of all orders coming in for spare parts for commercial machines should be filled from stock on hand. A 92 to 96 percent service policy is relatively common in most industries. Experiments have shown that increasing the service level above 95 percent tremendously increases holding costs. A 100 percent service level is not only very difficult to achieve but also extremely expensive. A further refinement in definition of service level should be made. It can be defined as the ratio of users (customers) who are fully satisfied to the ratio of total users asking for the item. Suppose there are 400 using department requests for a certain item during a year, and 372 were immediately satisfied. This would amount to a 93 percent service level.

A second way of defining service level would be the ratio of number of units supplied versus the number of units demanded. For example, if in the 400 requests the 372 which were met were all for one unit each, while the 28 which were not met were all for five units each, the service level would be:

$$\frac{372 \times 1}{28 \times 5 + 372 \times 1} = \frac{372}{512} = 73 \text{ percent}$$

As long as we are discussing inventory levels internal to the organization and excluding finished goods, the customers are internal departments, and service level can be used as one measure of materials management's effectiveness. It is useful to stress that service level and investment required are not independent of each other, and a high expectation of the first without the financial back up for the second can only lead to frustration. Procurement is, of course, very interested in service levels as they pertain to supplier performance.

The fixed order quantity model with variation in demand and buffer inventory

In this model uncertainty exists only with regard to demand, costs, and lead time, and order quantity are all constant. The buffer inventory is necessary to protect against stock-out during the lead time between the time an order is placed and received. Figure 5–10 illustrates the situation.

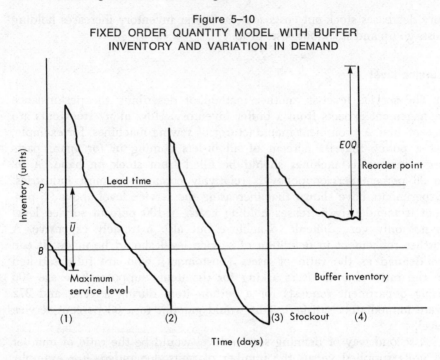

Figure 5–10
FIXED ORDER QUANTITY MODEL WITH BUFFER
INVENTORY AND VARIATION IN DEMAND

Let: P = reorder point
 B = buffer inventory
 L = lead time
 u = random variable, usage during lead time
 $\bar{u}$ = average usage during lead time
 σ_u = standard deviation of usage during lead time
 r = average daily demand
 σ_r = standard deviation of daily demand
 α_r = number of standard deviations needed for a specified confidence level

The service level will be defined as percentage of satisfied customers. As can be seen from the diagram, the variation in demand can lead to four different positions of buffer inventory at the time of replenishment. They are from left to right in Figure 5–10.

1. There is buffer inventory remaining, but some has been used.
2. There is no buffer inventory remaining and no stock-outs.
3. There is no buffer inventory remaining and a stock-out.
4. All buffer inventory remains.

The reorder point P is equal to the average usage during lead time $\bar{u}$ plus the buffer inventory B. $P = \bar{u} + B$. The average usage during the lead time L is $\bar{u} = \bar{r}L$. Buffer inventory $B = \alpha\sigma u$. Assume the demand is normally distributed and a 94 percent service level is desired. This corresponds to 1.555 standard deviations resulting in a reorder point $P = \bar{r}L + 1.555\ \sigma_u$. The standard deviation of usage during the lead time depends on the variance of the individual days. If we assume each day's demand is independent, the standard deviation of the sum of the days demand is equal to the square root of the sum of the variances.

Thus:

$$\sigma_u = \sqrt{\sum_{i=1}^{n} \sigma r_i}$$

The complexity of probabilistic models increases as more variables are allowed to change under conditions of uncertainty. If the variations are all continuous distributions, joint probability distributions may be used to solve the problem. For discrete variations tables may be built showing the range of outcomes. The interaction between variables may require a number of iterations until convergence is achieved. The $EOQ = \sqrt{2RS/KC}$ where R is the average annual demand.

Let us use the same example as for the fixed quantity uniform demand situation. The additional information is that daily usage is normally distributed with a mean of 4 and a standard deviation of 1.5 units. The lead time is 10 working days and there are assumed to be 225 working days evenly spaced during the year. Stock-out costs are assumed to be zero and back orders are filled as soon as the new order arrives.

Thus: $\bar{R} = 900 \qquad \bar{r} = 4$

$\qquad C = \$45 \qquad\quad \sigma\bar{r} = 1.5$

$\qquad K = .25$

$\qquad S = \$50$

$\qquad L = 10$ days

$$\text{The EOQ} = \sqrt{\frac{2\bar{R}S}{KC}} = \sqrt{\frac{2 \times 900 \times 50}{.25 \times 45}} = 89$$

$$\sigma u = \sqrt{\sum_{i=1}^{10} \sigma r i} = \sqrt{10(1.5)^2} = \sqrt{22.5} = 4.75$$

$$P = \bar{r}L + 1.555\sigma u$$
$$= 4 \times 10 + 1.555 \times 4.75 = 47.4$$
$$B = 1.555\sigma u = 1.555 \times 4.75 = 7.4$$

Therefore, the buffer inventory should be 7 or 8 units, and an order for 89 units should be placed whenever the total inventory drops to 48 units.

Use of integrated data processing systems

The computer and its associated hardware and software has aided greatly in good inventory management. All of the concepts mentioned previously in this chapter can be applied in developing programs for computer-based inventory recording and control systems. Economic order quantity formulas can be programmed into the computer so that when reorder points are reached purchase orders will be prepared automatically. Because of fantastic speeds of operation of the computer even the most complex inventories including tens of thousands of items can be maintained on a basis which permits a daily report showing items on hand, on order, withdrawals, additions, and any other information needed for control purposes. On-line terminals and visual displays may be effectively used in situations where continuous monitoring is desirable.

Most of the computer manufacturers make available software packages which provide sound inventory control programs. Examples are IMPACT and PICS.

Inventory management program and control techniques (IMPACT)

IBM's Inventory Management and Control Techniques software system (IMPACT) was designed for firms whose main concern is the distribution phase of a production/distribution system.[7] Wholesalers, for example, are prime users. In these applications the basic decisions of order size, order points, etc., become of paramount importance since they are an essential rather than a peripheral feature of the firm's mission as a supplier. In this section the theoretical bases of the IMPACT system will be presented, along with discussion on various aspects of the computer program itself.

Functions and objectives of IMPACT

The goal of IMPACT is to provide operating rules to minimize cost. In order to do this, the following functions must be performed.

1. Forecast future demand.
2. Determine the safety stock required for a specified level of service.
3. Determine the order quantity and time for reorder.
4. Consider the effects of freight rates and quantity discounts.
5. Estimate the expected results of the inventory plan.

The IMPACT system does all this in two phases: a start-up phase and an operating phase. The start-up phase (Figure 5–11) consists of

---

[7] This section is based on the following IBM publications: *Inventory Control*, 520-14491; *Introduction to IBM Wholesale IMPACT*, E20-0278-9; *Basic Principles of Wholesale IMPACT*, E20-8105-1; *Wholesale IMPACT—Advanced Principles and Implementations Manual*, E20-0174-0. Reproduced with permission from IBM and R. B. Chase and N. J. Aquilano, *Production and Operations Management* (Homewood, Ill., Richard D. Irwin, Inc., 1973), pp. 358–74.

Figure 5–11
IMPACT START-UP: INITIALIZING AND ESTIMATING

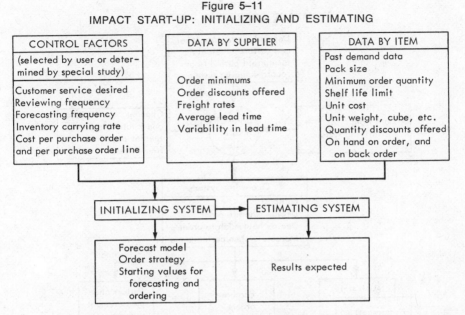

the initializing and estimating segment, which sets up the system and is brought into play whenever conditions or objectives change. The basic functions in this phase are:

1. Select the forecasting model and ordering strategy.
2. Calculate starting values for factors used in forecasting and ordering.
3. Estimate the results.

Once the system has been initialized, the operating phase takes over (see Figure 5–12). On a day-to-day basis, the operating system does the following:

1. Decides when and how much to order.
2. Makes new forecasts of demand and forecast error.
3. Keeps records of issues, receipts, inventory status, etc.
4. Collects data to measure performance of the system.

Figure 5–13 is the workflow of the IBM IMPACT system. In this diagram, the solid black line indicates that transactions are entered. They may occur at any time.

The solid color line indicates functions that are performed every review period. If a periodic plan is used, items are reviewed each week, biweekly, or monthly. In a reorder point system, the inventory status is reviewed after each transaction to see if the stock on hand has dropped to the reorder point, justifying placement of a new order.

Figure 5–12
IMPACT OPERATING SYSTEM

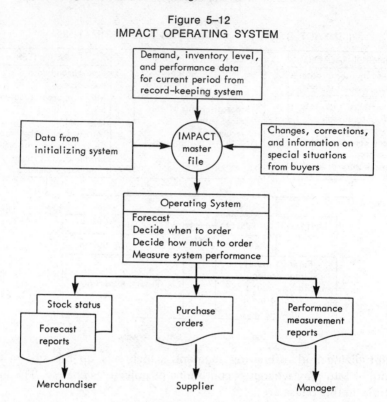

The dashed color line indicates that new forecasts are made. Typically, demand forecasts are made for periods of one, two, or four weeks.

The dashed black line shows initialization or reinitialization. This occurs when the program is started and whenever the conditions or objectives are changed.

The flows in the figure are typical, although differences may appear in individual applications because of various program options.

To operate the system, the user provides his own program routines, which are to be used in combination with the IMPACT program. He writes his own program for record keeping, updating the master file, forecasting, performance measurement, order follow-up (preparing purchase orders, status listings, etc.), and linkages between his programs and IMPACT library functions. (The IMPACT library provides programs for initializing, estimating, and ordering.)

To get an idea of the detailed operations carried out by IMPACT, we have summarized (below) the way it treats forecasting and ordering.

Forecasting. The forecasting models used in IMPACT are horizontal, trend, and seasonal (or cyclical) models.

The *horizontal* model represents demand about the average value which contains only random variation. Exponential smoothing is used

Figure 5–13
WORKFLOW AND FUNCTIONS PERFORMED IN A TYPICAL IMPACT SYSTEM

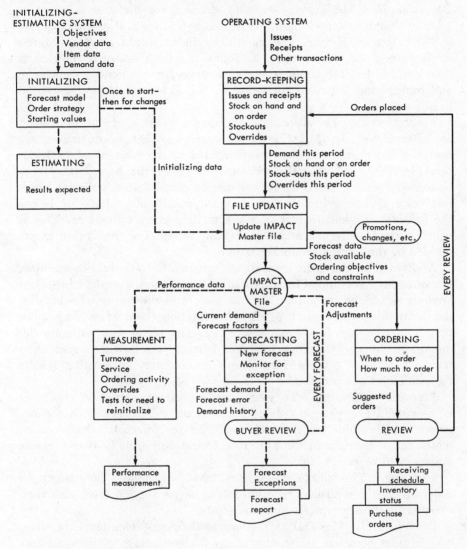

to forecast demand, thereby placing more emphasis on recent history. The *trend* model looks for an increasing or decreasing demand over time. Trends may be determined in a variety of ways, although the IMPACT program itself uses double exponential smoothing.

The *seasonal* model can be used when there is some logical reason for upswings and downswings. The model can be used for prediction only if the cause is identifiable or if it is repetitive over time. IBM suggests that the peaks and valleys should vary by at least 30 to 50 percent to justify the expense of using the seasonal model. Seasonal items are handled by applying a multiplier to each period of the year. For example, if the average monthly demand for the year is taken as a base value of one, each month is related to that base. If August demand is twice that of the average month, its index would be 2. If March is 60 percent of the average, its index is 0.6. A seasonal forecast is then derived by forecasting average demand by exponential smoothing and multiplying the resultant value by the index value for the period to be forecast.

Forecast error. Deviations are expected regardless of the forecasting model employed. In IMPACT the assumption is that the deviations are normally distributed and can be represented by the mean absolute deviation (MAD).[8] The program recommends either the horizontal, trend, or seasonal model, based on its calculation of the minimum mean absolute error. When errors in forecasts are consistently above or below the forecast, a measurement is made to help correct this bias. This is called a *tracking signal,* and algebraically is equal to the sum of errors divided by the mean absolute deviation.

Additional inputs to the forecast are optional to the user. For example, if a promotion is planned for a particular time period, a straight historical analysis would be incomplete in this case, and the buyer who handles the promotion must, therefore, insert information about when the promotion is to start and how long it will last. The buyer may estimate demands, or he can utilize a program feature which will provide him with an estimate. Figure 5–14 shows the monthly forecasting results for a ballpoint pen promotion.

Forecast monitoring. To guard against errors, exception reporting is provided. The program detects significant differences both for demands which differ from the forecast and for forecasts which consistently differ from demand. This monitoring will usually detect errors in data or in keypunching.

Ordering. This phase determines what, when, and how much to order. It is accomplished by establishing some service level and then considering the appropriate inventory costs.

Service level. The IMPACT program defines service level the same way as does common usage; that is, as the percentage of demand that is filled from stock on hand. A 98 percent service level means that 98 units can be offered directly from stock for each 100 demanded.

Order strategy. Items may be ordered independently (without regard for other items) or jointly (to take advantage of quantity discounts or transportation savings). The costs that are considered are (1) the cost of ordering (clerical and handling costs), (2) inventory carrying

---

[8] MAD is the average of the differences between the forecast sales and the actual sales, disregarding the plus or minus signs.

Figure 5-14
EXAMPLE OF FORECASTING AN ITEM WITH MACHINE COMPUTATION OF PROMOTION ESTIMATES (STAGE 3)

$\alpha = 0.1$
Tracking Signal Limits = ±6

Item #4364
Description: Bargain Ball Point Pens

Period	Demand	Forecast (made previous period)	Error	MAD	Error SUM	Tracking Signal	This Period Promotional Effect	Error from old Promotional Forecast	New Promotion Index	Promotion Forecast MAD	Next Month Forecast
Initial Values				(329)	(-125)				(900)	(500)	(Index) (2750)
June	3285	2750	+535	350	+410	+1.17					2804
July	3047	2804	+243	339	+653	+1.93					2828 (+900)
*Aug.	3873	2828 (+900)	**	**	**	**	+1045	+145	915	(464)	2828 (***)
Sept.	2661	2828 (***)	-167	322	+486	+1.51					2811
Oct.	2806	2811	-5	290	+481	+1.66					2810
Nov.	2514	2810	-296	291	+185	+.64					2780
Dec.	2909	2780	+129	275	+314	+1.10					2793 (+915)
*Jan.	3889	2793 (+915)	**	**	**	**	+1096	+181	933	(436)	2793 (***)
Feb.	2873	2793 (***)	+80	255	+391	+1.55					2801
Mar.	2659	2801	-142	244	+252	+1.03					2787
Apr.	3133	2787	+346	254	+598	+2.35					2822
May	2729	2822	-93	238	+505	+2.12					2813

* Promotion month.
** Not calculated: use value for former period.
*** Use same forecast and MAD as for previous month but exclude promotional corrections.

Figure 5–15

ADV. X ①	S.S. ②	COST ③	C/D ④	RECEIPTS ⑤	CODE ⑥	DESCRIPTION ⑦	PACK & SIZE ⑧	4 WEEKS SALES ⑨	LAST WKS. SALES ⑩
	356	356			3750	Purina Dog Chow	12 2 LB	116	26
	626	626		20	3752	Purina Dog Chow	10 5 LB	352	89
	548	548			3754	Purina Dog Chow	5 10 LB	228	57
	490	490			3756	Purina Dog Chow	2 25 LB	579	160
	455	455			3757	Purina Dog Chow	1 50 LB	56	12
	365	365			3930	Purina Cat Chow	12 22 OZ	141	36
	890	890			3932	Purina Cat Chow	12 4 LB	42	10
	604	604			5335	Ral Corn Chex	24 13 OZ	105	42
	515	515			5337	Ral Wheat Chex	24 12 OZ	144	51
	602	602			5339	Ral Rice Chex	24 9 OZ	137	49
	483	483			5341	Instant Ralston	18 18 OZ	112	33
	276	276			6099	Ry Krisp	12 81/2 OZ	30	13

THIS ORDER TO VENDOR 6262 INCLUDES 1005 ㉒ SELLING UNITS AND THEY TOTAL TO 41657 ㉓ POUNDS.

㉕ 4061   ㉖ 125   ㉗ 12

costs, and (3) opportunity costs (for example, savings or avoidable expenditures available but not taken, such as quantity discounts or lower freight rates).

When to order. The program decides the time for order placement, based on individual or joint order placement, and the forecasted demand, error, and lead time.

Order quantity. For individual items, the classic economic order quantity model is used:

$$Q = \sqrt{\frac{2DS}{H}}$$

where:

Q = Economic order quantity
D = Annual demand
S = Cost for handling and processing an order
H = Inventory carrying costs, such as insurance, taxes, depreciation, etc.

If discounts are available for larger quantity purchases, the program computes the additional feasible order quantities and selects the lowest cost.

When several items are ordered at the same time (termed a *joint ordering strategy*), the total must meet some quantity range (such as

INV. ON HAND	ON ORDER	CALC. ORDER	TIE	WEIGHT	ORDER	CODE	C D	PO GROUP CODE	DAY	MDSR
⑪	⑫	⑬	⑭	⑮	⑯	⑰	⑱	⑲	⑳	㉑
54	72	S 32	08	32.		3750	7	6262	4	5
111	192	S 224	16	51.		3752	3	6262	4	5
30	133	S 136	04	51.		3754	9	6262	4	5
156	297	S 280	04	53.		3756	4	6262	4	5
55	20	S 21	03	51.		3757	2	6262	4	5
64	88	S 40		18.		3930	5	6262	4	5
77	40	S ㉘	05	52.		3932	1	6262	4	5
23	51	S 45	05	22.		5335	5	6262	4	5
80	64	S 70	07	23.		5337	1	6262	4	5
41	57	S 63	07	14.		5339	7	6262	4	5
44	41	S 78	06	24.		5341	3	6262	4	5
24	9	S 16		8.		6099	6	6262	4	5

㉔
TO ARRIVE 12 20 63

a carload lot) while at the same time satisfying individual item service level requirements. This is accomplished by an "allocation" subroutine which adjusts the total order up or down, based on individual economic order quantities and desired service levels.

Overrides in order placement are always allowed. This may be purely a management decision, for whatever purpose, or may be aimed to correct such things as erroneous data.

Two outputs of the IMPACT program are the status report and the suggested order quantities, which are shown in Figures 5–15 and 5–16 with the report descriptions. This report may be further modified, or if it is satisfactory, a purchase order is directly written to the particular vendor.

Results from using the IMPACT system

Among the results claimed by users of IMPACT are:

1. Reduced inventory costs because:
   a. Either inventory size is reduced with no loss in service to customers or service levels have increased with no additional inventory stocking.
   b. Buyers can spend more time in problem areas or in developing new strategies since they have been relieved of routine purchasing decisions.

Figure 5–16

Column Headings	Description
① ADV.X	X in this column if item is on newspaper advertisement
② S.S.	Cost in dollars and cents to member retailer
③ COST	Cost of item in dollars and cents
④ C/D	Cash discount: 1 = 1 percent, A = 1-1/2 percent, 2 = 2 percent, B = 2-1/2 percent, etc. An & means that the item is on hand but not yet listed for sale
⑤ RECEIPTS	Receipts (in units) during this past week
⑥ CODE	Item card number
⑦ DESCRIPTION	Item description
⑧ PACK AND SIZE	Number of cans, jars, etc., in shipping unit, and size of the cans, jars, etc.
⑨ 4 WEEKS SALES	Number of units sold during past four weeks
⑩ LAST WEEKS SALES	Sales this past week
⑪ INV. ON HAND	Inventory on hand
⑫ ON ORDER	Units currently on order
⑬ CALC. ORDER	Suggested order quantity
⑭ TIE	Vendor pack, cases in a layer on a pallet, cases in a pallet, etc. (order quantities should always be in multiples of this number)

Column Headings	Description
⑮ WEIGHT	Shipping weight per unit in pounds
⑯ ORDER	Quantity to be ordered this reviewing cycle. This is written in by the merchandiser if he chooses to alter the suggested order quantity under heading no. 13
⑰ CODE	Item code number (repeated for convenience in key-punching purchase order cards if the actual amount ordered deviates from suggested order)
⑱ CD	Check digit for item code number
⑲ P.O. GROUP CODE	Purchase order group code, used to group items shipped and invoiced together
⑳ DAY	The day in the cycle when item is reviewed
㉑ MDSER	Identifying number of merchandiser who reviews this item
㉒	Total number of units to be ordered from this vendor
㉓	Extended pounds, dollars, etc., of suggested order
㉔	Specified delivery date for this suggested order
㉕	Dollar value of current inventory for this vendor
㉖	Dollar value of receipts this past week for this vendor
㉗	Number of items carried under this vendor number
㉘	An S in CALC. ORDER field indicates that item is being handled by system. Any item without the S is a new item, a discontinue-when-out item, etc., and must be controlled by the merchandiser.

2. Improved management control because:
   a. The specified rules and objectives are consistent.
   b. Rules and objectives can be easily revised.
   c. Effective measures of system effectiveness are available.
   d. Service is more stable.
   e. There is a smoother work load for personnel.
   f. Awareness of inventory concepts brought out by this program brings improvement in other areas.
   g. The process of data gathering needed to set up the program

points out unprofitable product lines and abnormally slow-moving items.

h. The costs output from the program are valuable for profit analysis and planning.

i. A framework is created which can be expanded to include potentially valuable applications, such as automatic generation and order placement with the vendor and providing forecasts and other information directly to the retailer.

Production and information control system (PICS)

Whereas the IMPACT system is intended for the distribution phase of a productive system, the Production and Information Control System (PICS) is designed for fabrication and assembly types of manufacturing.[9] The IMPACT system, for instance, concentrates on the problems of a wholesaler who must interpret customer demands and make inventory stocking decisions in light of the relevant costs involved. The PICS system does not directly include sales forecasting but uses this forecast to plan production requirements. These requirements are then used for raw material purchasing and control of product flow throughout the process.

PICS was prompted for two reasons: (1) the recognized need for a central information system in a fabrication and assembly plant and (2) the desire for a framework to facilitate computerization of the information system.

A major problem in any production system is that data and information about the system is dispersed throughout the operation. For efficient operation, a central records location is most desirable since more concentrated effort can be devoted to maintaining this file with accurate and up-to-date data, but it must, be easily accessible to the appropriate users.

Figure 5–17 shows the basic structure and information flow of the PICS system. The entire system is linked together by immediate access to a common data file that contains the firm's operational records. With only a part number, for example, the product description, standard routing, purchase order status, job order summary, and even the work center in which the job is being performed may be identified.[10]

In PICS, each functional area has been developed as an independent subsystem. Not only is this more practical from a computer system development aspect, but it is highly beneficial for implementation into an ongoing production system. The user can, at his own discretion, decide which subsystems he would like to incorporate first and in what se-

---

[9] IBM, *The Production Information and Control System*, GE20–0280–2.

[10] Each file contains varied data of interest. The "item master" is the master file, and it contains 117 fields which tell all about the item: its description, cost, structure, routing, order policy, forecast, lead time, usage history, stock on hand, projected orders, committed units, items on order, and engineering change status. The master file directs further search to specific files for more detailed information.

Figure 5–17
INTEGRATED PRODUCTION AND INFORMATION CONTROL SYSTEM
(PICS) WITH ACCESS TO CENTRAL DATA FILES

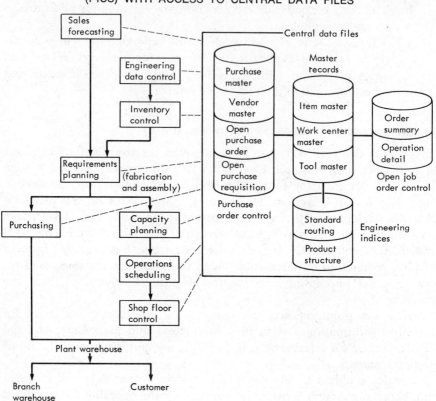

quence. In practice, the user would not try to put all products and all functional areas into use at the same time; he gradually builds this up with a small number of products and develops one area at a time.

Information flow begins from two directions: (1) sales forecasting and (2) engineering data control. Figure 5–18 lists the subsystems, along with some of the main features of each.

The sales forecasting subsystem analyzes historical data and inputs a sales forecast to requirements planning. The mission of engineering data control is to organize and maintain the basic records: item master, product structure, standard routing, and work center master.[11] The inventory control subsystem computes inventory on hand and on order, and usage rates. The inputs from inventory control and sales forecasting are combined to determine the net requirements of finished goods projected over future time periods. Product structure records then break

---

[11] This is accomplished by a separate program, the IBM System/370 Bill of Material Processor.

Figure 5–18
FEATURES OF PICS SUBSYSTEMS

Sales forecasting	Model selection
	Forecast plans
	Evaluation and measurement
Engineering data control	Basic records file organization
	Engineering drawings
	Engineering changes
	Production structure and standard routing
	Records maintenance
Inventory control	Stock status report
	ABC inventory analysis
	Order policy
	Inventory maintenance and update
	Physical inventory
Requirements planning	Finished product requirements gross to net
	Component requirements gross to net
	Special features:
	Lot sizing
	Offset requirements
	Net change
	Pegged requirements
Purchasing	Requisition and purchase order preparation
	Purchase order followup
	Purchase evaluation
	Vendor evaluation and selection
Capacity planning	Projected work center load report
	Planned order load
	Order start date calculations
	Load leveling
Operations scheduling	Dispatching sequence
	Order estimator
	Load summary by work center
	Priority rules
	Queue time analysis
	Tool control
Shop floor control	Labor reporting
	Material movement
	Work-in-process feedback
	Creation of control forms
	Machine utilization

this requirement down into components to be directed to purchasing and assembly and fabrication.

The flow continues as purchasing prepares purchase orders and receiving cards, based on item identification and the vendor master. An open purchase order is created so that the order will be followed up.

Assembly and fabrication order requirements are used in capacity planning for facility and manpower needs. Order start times are computed from the standard routing records and the available capacity as given by the work center master record. Operations scheduling takes the order released by capacity planning and makes short-range schedules for work centers. An analysis of work loads and completion dates is then conducted, based on various dispatching sequences and priority rules. The tools needed in production are designated in this step.

Shop floor control is the last phase of this system. It prepares shop packets and other factory documentation, open job order summaries, and operation detail records for monitoring and reporting work progress. The output of purchasing, assembly, and fabrication converges at the plant warehouse.

Inventory control subsystem of PICS

There are eight subsystems of the Production and Information Control System, and we will extend our coverage of PICS by discussing the inventory control subsystem, since that is the main emphasis in this chapter. There are four modules or subparts of the inventory control subsystem: inventory analysis, order policy, inventory maintenance and update, and physical inventory count.

Inventory analysis. This is performed by using the ABC classification (described earlier in this chapter). This method points out which items are the most important and should be most closely controlled.

Order policy. The order policy module computes order point and order quantity. The mean absolute deviation is used here, as in the IMPACT program, to provide safety stock for demand variation. The user must specify either the safety factor or the service level he desires. Order quantity run sizes are then computed by the classical formulas and by the least-cost-unit run size. Although the relatively flat dish shape of the EOQ total cost curve allows some flexibility in rounding to convenient sum sizes, EOQ formulas are based on average demands. Thus, if the forecasted product requirements vary in future periods, some additional cost benefits may be possible. The procedure is to try various order quantities to search for the least cost run. Figure 5–19 demonstrates the least-unit-cost run size technique.

Inventory maintenance and update. Three types of inventory are used here:

1. On-hand (or in-stores) inventory. These items are physically in the stockroom.
2. In-process inventory. These items are in the production stage.
3. On-order inventory. These items have not yet been received.

On-hand inventory is the responsibility of the stockkeeping area until stock is physically issued. The stockroom, on its own, places orders for standard items. For those items which are normally stocked, replenishment orders are placed on a simple order-point order-quantity basis. Orders which result from the requirements planning subsystem so as to meet planned needs are not initiated here. Whenever orders are received and stock is issued, a "transaction" is issued to inform the computer-based record-keeping system that a change has taken place. This entry may be in the form of a punched card or typewriter entry.

Figure 5–19
LEAST-UNIT-COST RUN SIZE

	Period	1		2	3	4	5	. . . . . . n
Line 1	Period	1		2	3	4	5	. . . . . . n
Line 2	Requirement	50		60	70	70	80	. . . .
Line 3	Possible run quantity and associated unit cost	50	.12	60	70	70	80	. . . .
Line 4		50+60	.065	0	70	70	80	. . . .
Line 5		50+60+70	.055	0	0	70	80	. . . .
Line 6		50+60+70+70	.056	0	0	0	80	. . . .

Inventory Carrying Rate = .02 (2%) per period, and the unit cost is $1.00

Possibility 1: Line 3 illustrates the possibility of running each requirement as a separate run. The unit cost of running 50 in period 1 is computed as follows:

$$\text{Unit Cost} = \frac{\text{Setup Cost} + \text{Carrying Cost}}{\text{Quantity}} = \frac{\$6.00 + \$0}{50} = \$.12$$

The next solution to this problem is combining other requirements with the 50 of period 1 to determine whether anything can be saved.

Possibility 2: If period 2 (60) is combined with period 1 (50) to yield a run of 110 (line 4), the unit cost drops:

$$\text{Unit Cost} = \frac{\text{Setup} + \text{Carrying Cost}}{\text{Quantity}} = \frac{6.00 + 60 \times 1.00 \times .02 \times 1 \text{ period}}{110}$$

$$= \$.065$$

Possibility 3: If this procedure is repeated, it is found (line 5) that a run of 180 in period 1 costs $.055 each.

$$\text{Unit Cost} = \frac{\text{Setup} + \text{Carrying Cost}}{\text{Quantity}}$$

$$= \frac{6.00 + 60 \times 1.00 \times .02 \times 1 + 70 \times 1.00 \times .02 \times 2}{180}$$

$$= \$.055$$

Possibility 4: Running 250 (line 6) in period 1 costs $.056 each.

Conclusion: The most economic quantity to be run in period 1 is 180.

The same problem is restated below assuming this run of 180 in period 1.

Period	1	2	3	4		5	. . . . n
Requirement	180 (run)			70		80	
Possible run quantity and associated unit cost				70	.086	80	
				70+80	.051	0	

The procedure would be repeated using period 4 as the base in an attempt to find its best run size.

Inventory status reports are generated in the form and at the times specified by the user. For example, Figure 5–20 shows the on-hand part

Figure 5–20
ON-HAND INVENTORY FIELDS IN THE ITEM MASTER

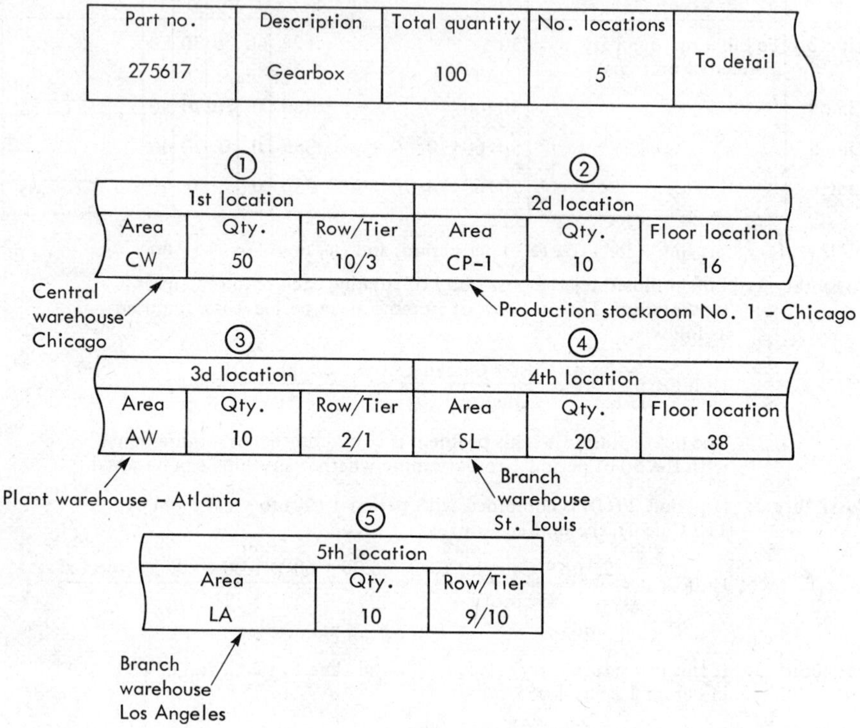

Part no.	Description	Total quantity	No. locations	
275617	Gearbox	100	5	To detail

①   ②

1st location			2d location		
Area	Qty.	Row/Tier	Area	Qty.	Floor location
CW	50	10/3	CP-1	10	16

Central warehouse Chicago

Production stockroom No. 1 – Chicago

③   ④

3d location			4th location		
Area	Qty.	Row/Tier	Area	Qty.	Floor location
AW	10	2/1	SL	20	38

Plant warehouse – Atlanta

Branch warehouse St. Louis

⑤

5th location		
Area	Qty.	Row/Tier
LA	10	9/10

Branch warehouse Los Angeles

of the item master record for part 275617. This identifies all the locations in the same record, whether in the stockroom, on the plant floor, in the central warehouse, or at a branch warehouse.

In-process inventory record keeping must account for all items withdrawn from stock. This record can terminate in two ways: first, by an item's return to the stockroom (even if some operations have been performed on it) and, second, when the item loses its identity by being incorporated into a larger assembly.

On-order inventory is responsible for keeping track of open purchase orders (ordered items not yet received) and open shop orders (items not yet released to production).

Physical inventory count. Occasionally an actual physical count of stock must be made to assure that the records and stock agree, and the records must be adjusted for any discrepancy. If a period for inventory counting has been predetermined, a notice will automatically be generated when the time has arrived. On completion of the account, a report is generated informing management of the results; exception reports are produced to emphasize unusual conditions.

Inventory control subsystem summary

Figure 5–21 shows in tabular form the four modules of the subsystem, their inputs, outputs, and other characteristics.

Figure 5–21
INVENTORY CONTROL SUBSYSTEM SUMMARY CHART

SUBSYSTEM: Inventory Control

Module name	Input	Processing routines	Data base		Output
			Record title	Record fields	
A-B-C inventory analysis	Parameter specifications	A-B-C analysis	Item master	Item number Parts usage history Unit costs Unit price	Analysis by investment Analysis by net return

Order policy	Percent carrying cost
	Order cost
		Calculations:
		(1) Order pt./order up-to-qty.
		(2) EOQ
			Item master	Order policy
				  Order code
				  Order point
				  Order qty. or order-up to level
				  Safety stock
				  Minimum
				  Maximum
				  Multiple
				Parts usage history
				Unit costs-std.
					Order point—order quantity

Inventory maintenance and update	Issues
	Receipts
	On order
	Cancellations
	Adjustments ±
	Transfers ±
	Scrap ±
		Inventory update	Item master	Inventory on hand
				  Total qty.
				  Area qty.
				Allocated qty.
				Back orders qty.
				Current period
				  Beginning inventory
				  Transfers & adjusts.
				  Receipts
				  Issues
				  Demand
				On order-purchasing/production
				Requirements-gross
					Stock status summary
					Transaction logs
					Order notice for order point items

Physical inventory count	Inventory count
	physical inventory adj. ±
		(1) Physical inventory notification
		(2) Physical inventory validation
			Item master	Physical inventory
				  Type
				  Qty. count
				  Checker no.
				  Date last count
				  Date of next count
				Inventory on hand
				  Total qty.
				  Area qty.
					Inventory discrepancy list
					Inventory adjustment report

CONCLUSION

Today's inventory systems are in the midst of great change. Early applications centered on the determination of order size and order points, sometimes using theoretical models, though more often than not using "seat of the pants" analysis. In any event, it was all done by hand, using a series of cards and files. Now, however, the field is changing to computerized record keeping and computer-aided decisions.[12]

In taking over many of the inventory decision chores, computer procedures have progressed from simple data processing tabulations to large-scale information systems encompassing the entire firm. This evolution from simple hand methods to an integrated computerized system seems to develop along the following lines. First, data processing is introduced and is applied to record keeping, the primary output being printouts of inventory status. Then some elementary forecasting and inventory rules are incorporated into a simple computer program. Next is the inclusion of more sophisticated forecasting techniques, refinement of ordering rules, and programmed monitoring of the form and location of inventory items.

From here on the system begins to overflow into other functional areas. Inventory control becomes part of the production-inventory program, which specifies material requirements and schedules the order of work to be done. As the system's size expands further, central files are formed which give ready access to complete item description, engineering changes, costs, vendors involved, and production schedules, as well as complete stock data. Ultimately, the company might consider a system in which the production-distribution system is integrated with finance, marketing, and personnel along the lines of the modular simulation approach discussed in the supplement to this chapter.

While on the surface this computerization may seem to indicate that the production manager is losing his decision-making area, in reality it is quite the opposite. The production manager will more frequently be freed to break new ground, find new ways to do things, and take a bigger hand in determining policy.

Stores

Stores are often placed under direct purchasing responsibility. This is normal for hospitals, educational and public institutions, and 15 percent–45 percent of manufacturing firms place stores under purchasing.

Emphasis needs to be placed on the importance of good storeskeeping as distinct from inventory control. After all, the only material that can

---

[12] Of all business fields, inventory control is probably the first to use computers. Inventory control and production control have also been the first to be studied by operations research and management science groups.

be used is that which is "on hand" in stores—not what the inventory control records say is available. It is always to be hoped that the stores and the inventory records will agree, as theoretically they always should, and it is for ensuring they do agree that physical stock inventory must be taken periodically. If the two records do not agree, then the inventory record must be adjusted. True as this is, decisions as to when and how much to order are based on the inventory record. And, regardless of how carefully, accurately, and adequately these records may be kept, their value is vitiated if the storeskeeping is badly handled. If stock records are inadequate or poorly kept; if material is withdrawn from stores without the proper notations being made; if items, though in stores, cannot be located or, if located, cannot be obtained; if stock clerks are dishonest, incapable, or just simply careless—if these conditions prevail, quite regardless of whose fault it may be—then the storeskeeping function is not carrying its share of the load.

Certain conditions are essential to good storeskeeping. These indicate the need for adequate and qualified personnel for centralizing responsibility for all stores in a chief storeskeeper and for adequate physical facilities.

The problem of the extent to which all stores should be kept in a central storesroom is often perplexing, particularly with reference to the matter of centralizing or decentralizing stores. The tendency toward decentralizing stores is quite widespread. Every effort is made, consistent with economical purchasing, materials handling, and storage, to keep materials as close to the machines or users as possible. This may be done by a series of shop storesrooms adjacent to the centers; sometimes no storesrooms may be maintained, but here also the material is kept near the point where it is to be used. Needless to say, control must be exercised even under these circumstances to show definitely what is on hand. In many cases, shop storesrooms are used only for storing material released on requisition for a definite factory order and not part of unassigned raw material. Obviously, there are limits beyond which decentralization must not be carried, however advisable it may be under other circumstances. Some materials may require special warehousing facilities because of the difficulties inherent in their handling, because of their perishable character, or because of some other characteristic that may necessitate special storage facilities. Regardless, however, of where stores are kept or the conditions under which they are kept, proper classification of stores is a prerequisite to good storeskeeping. Standard nomenclature is also essential. With carefully classified stores, designated by standard items or symbols, a system of records can be established which will indicate at all times what material is on hand, what is expected, and where it is. Only in this manner can close cooperation between stores and production, on the one hand, and stores and purchasing, on the other, be maintained.

Stores should be carefully classified into major groups. Although the actual classification of stores used must of necessity vary tremendously from one industry to another and from one company to another in the same industry, such a classification might be made on the following basis: (1) raw materials, (2) material parts, (3) supplies, (4) in-process material, (5) tools, (6) miscellaneous stores, and (7) finished goods. Each of these groups would be divided into subgroups according to the nature of the stock, and, finally the subgroups might be broken down into types and sizes. Each of the groups might be assigned a series of numbers, such as 100–199, 200–299, and the subclasses be numbered 100–109, 110–119, and so forth. In this way, each item of stock would be identified by a number. Instead of assigning numbers, many persons prefer to use the letters of the alphabet. Under such a system, all stores are represented by capital letter "S." "SM" may stand for maintenance stores, "SP" for production material stores, and so forth. In the symbol, "SMA," "SM" would stand for maintenance stores and "A" for the supplies. Usually, figures are combined with the letters to designate sizes.

Practically, the method of classification used in stores should correspond as closely as possible with that followed by those in charge of inventory. The actual arrangement of the stock in the storesroom, however, need not and usually does not follow this same arrangement. The nature of the item, its accessibility, and the frequency with which it is called for will obviously affect the decision on where the stock itself is placed.

Stores may be priced in any one of several ways, the choice of method being a matter for top management to decide. (1) One method is to use the average unit price paid for the material. Thus if, of the stock on hand, 100 units were bought for $50 and subsequently 500 units were purchased for $225, the entire lot would be valued at $45.83 per 100 units. (2) A second method is to value the stock in accordance with a standard cost figure set by the cost accounting department. (3) Some companies use the well-known first-in, first-out method commonly referred to as "Fifo." (4) Others use "cost or market," whichever is lower. (5) A method which has grown in popularity in recent years is "Lifo," or last-in, first-out.

A discussion of the relative merits of these various methods would carry us too far afield of our present purpose. Furthermore, the particular manner in which stores are valued has but little bearing on the actual operation of the storesroom.

BIBLIOGRAPHY

ALJIAN, GEORGE W., ed.   *Purchasing Handbook.* 3d ed. New York: McGraw-Hill Book Co., 1973.

BAILEY, PETER J. *Purchasing and Supply Management.* 3d ed. London: Chapman & Hall, 1973.

BALLOT, ROBERT B. *Materials Management.* American Management Association, 1971.

BROWN, ROBERT G. *Decision Rules for Inventory Management.* New York: Holt, Rinehart and Winston, 1968.

CURLEY, THOMAS J. *Purchasing and Supply Management.* Sydney: West Publishing Corp., 1968.

ENRICK, NORBERT LLOYD. *Inventory Management.* San Francisco: Chandler Publishing Co., 1968.

FETTER, ROBERT B., AND DALLECK, WINSTON C. *Decision Models for Inventory Management.* Homewood, Ill.: Richard D. Irwin, Inc., 1961.

HANSSMAN, F. *Operations Research in Production and Inventory Control.* New York: John Wiley & Sons, Inc., 1962.

HEINRITZ, STUART F., AND FARRELL, PAUL V. *Purchasing: Principles and Applications.* 5th ed. Englewood Cliffs, N.J.: Prentice-Hall, Inc., 1971.

JOHNSON, LYNWOOD A., AND MONTGOMERY, DOUGLAS C. *Operations Research in Production, Planning, Scheduling and Inventory Control.* New York: John Wiley & Sons, Inc., 1974.

KIMBALL, DEXTER SIMPSON, JR. *Control of Materials.* Scranton: International Correspondence Schools, 1968.

LEE, LAMAR, JR., AND DOBLER, DONALD W. *Purchasing and Materials Management.* 2d ed. New York: McGraw-Hill Book Co., 1971.

NATIONAL ASSOCIATION OF ACCOUNTANTS. *Techniques in Inventory Management* Reprint No. 40. New York, 1964.

STELZER, WILLIAM R., JR. *Materials Management.* Englewood Cliffs, N.J.: Prentice-Hall, Inc., 1970.

WELCH, W. EVERT. "Use These Nomographs to Help Solve Inventory Management Snags," *Purchasing Week,* July 6, 1959.

WELCH, W. EVERT. *Tested Scientific Inventory Control.* Greenwich, Conn.: Management Publishing Corp., 1959.

CASES FOR CHAPTER 5

MYERS DIVISION (R)*

On August 15, 1974, the Myers Division of the Young Corporation began negotiating the annual contract with its employees' union representatives. In 1973 and 1974 Myers had refused to accept the union's demands, and the union bargaining committee had advised the workers to strike. In each instance, however, the workers had voted against the committee's recommendation and had accepted the company's contract terms. For the third consecutive year, neither the union nor company representatives seemed willing to accept the others' demands. In preparing for the negotiation of the 1974 contract, however, the union bargaining committee had received a vote of confidence from the employees previous to the negotiations which, for all practical purposes, gave the committee the authority to call a strike against Myers without another employee vote. Therefore, a strike commencing October 1 appeared to be a foregone conclusion. Myers' management notified all excecutives of the situation and added that in their opinion, "the strike would probably be a long, drawn-out affair . . . possibly lasting several months."

The Myers Division was one of the major producers of dictating machines, with 1973 sales approximating $19,800,000 and profits after taxes of $1,006,000. Approximately 66 percent of the company's sales volume came from the sale of dictating machines, 13 percent from government contracts, 12 percent from repair parts and supplies, and 9 percent from repair service.

To Mr. Arthur, the manager of purchases, a potential, work stoppage presented several problems regarding outstanding purchase orders and future purchasing commitments. He believed that if the strike became a reality the entire inventory investment excluding finished goods would be largely under his control. The finished goods inventory would probably be depleted during a strike because all sales orders would have to be shipped from inventory since there would be no production. With the production lines shut down, there would be no problems concerning work-in-process inventory. Consequently, the raw materials inventory would not be reduced by production requirements but would be continually increased by the material flowing in from suppliers if the company continued its normal purchasing operations. He realized if a strike was called it would have to be determined for how long the company could finance an inventory accumulation and what action the purchasing department could take to limit its purchases during work stoppage. Limiting purchases presented two additional problems to Myers' manager of purchases: what effect will canceling outstanding purchase orders and delaying future purchases have on the relationship between Myers and its suppliers? and, how will cancellations and delays affect the availability to the company of critical materials after the strike ends? Mr. Arthur also understood that the truck drivers might refuse to deliver and unload incoming material at Myers' plant, which introduced the problem of what effect action taken by the purchasing department would have on strike activities. Since Mr. Arthur's decisions involved considerations of finance and labor relations, he felt he should bring the problem of inventory control during a strike to the attention of management. However, he realized that he was probably better acquainted with the details of the problem than any other executive and that management would expect a recommendation from purchasing on what action would be most appropriate under the circumstances.

Mr. Arthur first attempted to analyze the outstanding purchase orders. For his purposes, he separated the orders into three categories: basic raw materials such as steel, aluminum, magnesium, and so on; purchased parts such as small castings, forgings, circuit boards, transistors, injection molded parts and assembled controls of various types, and so on; and miscellaneous materials such as office supplies, maintenance supplies, and standard items that were usually procured from the stocks of local sales branch offices, mill supply houses, and so on. The breakdown was as follows:

Raw materials	$1,200,000
Purchased parts	400,000
Miscellaneous materials	75,000
Total	$1,675,000

Mr. Arthur also determined that Myers' normal monthly purchases totaled $750,000. He separated these purchases into the same classifications and found that each month the following materials were purchased from suppliers:

Raw materials	$300,000
Purchased parts	375,000
Miscellaneous materials	75,000
Total	$750,000

By reviewing the previous six months' inventory levels, Mr. Arthur found that Myers' inventory excluding finished goods and work-in-process had averaged $1.5 million. However, he estimated that the inventory was approximately $1 million on September 1, a month before the date the strike would probably begin. The normal inventory and August 15 inventory were broken down as follows:

	Normal inventory	Inventory on August 15
Raw materials	$ 700,000	$ 600,000
Purchased parts	520,000	320,000
Miscellaneous materials	80,000	80,000
Total	$1,300,000	$1,000,000
Work-in-process	$1,000,000	$1,000,000

After investigating the company's balance sheet (see Exhibit 1), Mr. Arthur believed that if normal buying operations continued during a work stoppage, Myers would be able to finance the normal inventory level for about two weeks but afterward would be forced to borrow money to cover the increasing investment in inventory.

EXHIBIT 1
MYERS DIVISION (R)
(balance sheet as of August 15, 1974)

Assets

Current Assets:

Cash	$ 1,163,313
Securities	4,200
Accounts receivable—net.	3,015,961
Inventories (raw materials; work-in-progress; finished goods and branch sales offices' stocks).	4,190,381
Total current assets	$ 8,373,855
Investments	397,110
Sinking fund	75
Land, buildings, and equipment.	1,455,467
Prepaid expenses	85,563
Patents.	1
Total assets	$10,312,071

Liabilities

Current Liabilities:

Notes payable.	$ 350,000
Accounts payable.	838,580
Sinking fund payments	140,000
Accrued liabilities	566,599
Accrued taxes.	1,661,376
Advanced payments received	47,681
Total current liabilities	$ 3,604,236
Sinking fund note at 4% interest	980,000
Capital.	5,727,835
Total liabilities and capital	$10,312,071

Myers' production process normally required about $750,000 of purchased materials a month. The requirements included approximately 40 percent raw materials, 50 percent purchased parts, and 10 percent miscellaneous materials. Since the sales department would probably deplete the inventories of finished goods during the strike, Mr. Arthur understood that management was scheduling an increased rate of production after the strike ended to rebuild sales inventories. The increased manufacturing schedules would, according to Mr. Arthur, probably require $1,125,000 of purchased materials per month until normal operations could be resumed.

It was expected that overtime would be used until finished goods inventories were built up to prestrike levels. Mr. Arthur also knew that substantial increases in future sales were expected. Forecasts for 1975 and 1976 called for annual increases of about 20 percent per year.

What made Mr. Arthur's planning task difficult was that a strike was not a foregone conclusion. There could be no strike at all, a short strike, or a long one. The purchasing department was expected to assure sufficient supply of raw materials and parts and supplies no matter what happened. Availability of equipment was one of the key sales factors of success in the dictating machine business.

The buyer of raw materials informed Mr. Arthur that he had been experiencing difficulty in procuring items in tight supply such as steel, copper, and magnesium. Purchase orders were being issued for these materials at least five months before the material was required for production schedules. The buyer had been informed by the suppliers that if the orders scheduled to be shipped within the next few months were canceled, it would be about four months after reinstatment before Myers' requirements could be fulfilled. Mr. Arthur believed that to be conservative, all basic raw material purchases should be regarded as in tight supply. If the outstanding orders for critical materials were canceled, the buyer informed Mr. Arthur, the cancellation charges would only be about ½ to 1 percent of the value of the orders.

This cancellation charge was not to reimburse the producer for work invested in manufacturing Myers' orders, since these orders called for basic raw materials and the suppliers would have no difficulty with the tight market situation in selling the canceled material to other users. However, a trade practice had existed for many years in the basic raw material industry stipulating that any orders canceled within two months of delivery would be penalized with a nominal cancellation charge. Mr. Arthur also considered placing orders for raw materials in the normal pattern and then canceling the orders just before delivery if the strike was still continuing. However, the raw material suppliers were strongly opposed to such a policy, and Mr. Arthur decided not to buy in this manner because of the necessity of maintaining excellent relationships with the raw material suppliers if Myers was to be assured a supply of these materials once the strike ended.

Mr. Arthur also learned that the buyer of purchased parts was concerned about the effect of cancellations and delays on many of his suppliers. Most of these orders were placed with relatively small, local firms that had scheduled a large part of their facilities to fulfill Myers' requirements. The buyer felt that most of his suppliers were so dependent on Myers' business that they would be forced to locate other work to fill the void resulting from cancellations or delays in future purchases. The only other alternatives for these companies, in the buyer's opinion, would be to close a portion of their factories—a costly process—or go completely out of business. Because of market shortages of raw materials in 1972, 1973, and 1974 many of these smaller sources had committed substantial amounts of working capital to raw material inventories to be able to supply Myers' rapidly growing needs. In any case the buyer believed that the relationships established between Myers and many of these suppliers would be endangered or eliminated. The company would, therefore, be forced to develop several new sources of supply which might prove to be a costly and time-consuming procedure. The purchased parts buyer was not convinced that Mr. Arthur's suggestion that Myers could probably work with these suppliers in an attempt to reduce these orders by 20 percent and still save the suppliers from large-scale inactivity would be successful. From past experience Mr. Arthur estimated that the cancellation charges on the orders for purchased parts would approximate 10 percent of the total price.

The final classification of purchases presented few if any problems concerning cancellation in Mr. Arthur's opinion. He estimated that 20 percent of the miscellaneous materials would be required by the office force and maintenance personnel irrespective of a work stoppage. The buyer for miscellaneous materials believed that the remaining 80 percent could be canceled without any complications. Since these orders called for items stocked by local suppliers, delivery could be obtained in two weeks or sooner if the strike ended abruptly and certain materials were required immediately.

Mr. Arthur next discussed the strike situation with the industrial relations manager and was told that there was a definite possibility that the union would not allow incoming material to be unloaded at Myers' plant. If a picket line were established around the receiving docks, the truck drivers' union would probably refuse to handle Myers' shipments. The only alternative available, if all orders were not canceled, was to receive and store all shipments at independent warehouses within the city. Mr. Arthur estimated that the additional costs accruing from this arrangement would average approximately $3,000 a week.

Before Mr. Arthur had determined what action the purchasing department should take if the union decided to strike, he received the following memorandum from the company's treasurer:

All company executives should attempt to keep the expenses of the operations under their direction at a base minimum for the duration of a work stoppage. A strike is always costly to everyone involved, and it is extremely important that Myers refrain from absorbing any unnecessary costs which would prevent the company from pursuing the contract negotiations to a successful conclusion.

DEANS BREWERY (B)

Early in 1968 Mr. Tony Benson was wondering how many bottles he should purchase in the coming year. During 1967 the market had leveled off, and 1968 sales predictions were difficult. On the one hand Mr. Benson wished to be sure sufficient bottles were available to supply 1968 sales levels, yet he also wanted to minimize year-end inventories as covered storage space for empty bottles was tight and a bottle change-over seemed possible for 1969 or 1970.

Company background

Deans Brewery was located in the southern Caribbean island of Trinidad. Founded by John Deans in 1924, the company had established a high reputation. Deans beer had also become a favorite with tourists, and as a result a modest export business to the United States had started in 1959. In February, 1968, sales reached the highest level in the company's history. However, in 1967 the sales increase had been well below the trend average (See Exhibits 1 and 2). Four sales peaks occurred

Exhibit 1
SALES 1957–1962
(thousands of cases—24 bottles/case)

Year	1957	1958	1959	1960	1961	1962
Sales	1,086	1,336	1,404	1,589	1,785	2,189

during the year: Carnival[1], Christmas, Easter, and Independence[2]. Carnival was the highest sales period, but each peak caused the company to operate on tight schedules, and Deans hired more labor and scheduled extra shifts.

Beer brewing started with extraction of sugar from malt by an enzymic process. This sugar was then boiled with hops, producing a sterilized and concentrated solution. The resins extracted from the hops during boiling acted as a preservative and gave the beer its bitter flavor. The hops were then removed, and the solution was cooled to optimum temperature ($50°F$) for bottom fermentation lasting seven days, during which yeast converted the sugar to alcohol and CO_2. After fermentation the beer was cooled to $30°F$ and stored for ten days (during which the yeast dropped out) and then roughly filtered through diatomaceous earth. After 24 hours storage it was put through a polish filtration process. By this time the beer had been artificially carbonated ready for bottling. After bottling and case packing the beer was stored in the finished goods warehouse ready for delivery to retail outlets.

Sales projections for 1968

Mr. Benson had difficulty forecasting sales for 1968, particularly because of the 1967 slump, government excise taxes, and other factors.

---

[1] Carnival took place two days before Ash Wednesday, which normally occurred during February and occasionally in early March.

[2] Trinidad gained its independence from Britain on August 31, 1962.

Exhibit 2
MONTHLY SALES JANUARY 1963–FEBRUARY 1968
(thousands of cases—24 bottles/case)

Month \ Year	Jan	Feb	Mar	Apr	May	June
1963	162	260	147	148	106	114
1964	188	310	164	188	118	150
1965	224	297	255	214	122	161
1966	244	362	247	247	158	259
1967	250	390	236	263	199	225
1968	259	407				

In November, 1962, the government had placed an additional excise tax of 50¢[3] on each case of beer. The company passed this tax on to the consumer, raising the retail price from $6.25 to $6.75 per case, including a bottle deposit of 72¢. During 1963 sales slumped almost 13 percent below the 1962 level. Again in July, 1965, a further tax of 75¢ per case was levied and the company raised the retail price to $7.50. Sales growth slumped to a 4.5 percent increase. In July, 1967, another tax of $1.00 raised the retail price to $8.50 per case. Mr Benson was reasonably certain that government would not levy additional taxes during 1968, but he wondered if the full effect of the tax had been reflected in 1967 sales.

Most of the Caribbean area was currently experiencing a serious drought. In Trinidad expected rainfall had not occurred, and, although water restrictions were not yet in effect, lack of rain would put the country in a serious state. Mr. Benson knew that a drought would reduce agricultural production which could affect consumer expenditures for liquor, beer, and entertainment.

Locally produced rum had always competed with beer. In bars the most popular white rum drink sold for less than a bottle of beer. In 1966 a Trinidadian company began producing gin. This didn't seem to affect beer sales at first as the gin product didn't receive widespread consumer acceptance. However, in early 1967 the popular Gordon's Gin was produced locally at competitive prices and seemed to enjoy increased sales.

An additional factor which might result in a tighter economy and reduced consumer spending was a partially published government report. It dealt with the productivity of the country's agricultural sector

[3] In 1968: $2.00 Trinidadian = $1.00 U.S.

July	Aug	Sept	Oct	Nov	Dec	Total
158	188	126	154	158	176	1,897
178	247	255	190	180	337	2,505
158	280	202	215	217	210	2,555
218	283	230	255	230	270	3,023
300	252	232	232	244	281	3,104

and basically concluded that increased mechanization was necessary for the loal producers to increase operating efficiencies. Because of the widespread rumors that labor would be reduced, Mr. Benson had learned of a particularly difficult but typical situation of one relatively small sugar cane producer. In January, 1968, at the start of the cutting season, only a handful of cutters showed up for work. The grower's normal weekly payroll of $50,000 was reduced to $10,000. Mr. Benson knew this kind of situation would result in drastic reductions in consumer take-home pay, and, until the report proposals were fully published and action programs resolved, beer sales would likely be affected.

Perhaps the biggest question mark facing the Trinidad economy was the effect of devaluation. In November, 1967, Great Britain devalued the pound by 14.3 percent. Although Trinidad was not on the pound sterling system, its economy was still closely tied to the U.K., and it devalued shortly afterwards. Mr. Benson was not at all certain what effects this might have on beer sales during 1968.

Beer bottle purchases

Mr. Benson joined the company in 1963 as purchasing manager. He was responsible for all goods and materials used in the company's production processes. This included the purchase of new bottles and the scheduling of deliveries. Local bottle producers were equipped to manufacture only clear glass bottles. Deans therefore had to import their standard 10 oz. dark amber long-necked bottle. The company's brand name was etched in the glass which eliminated replacing the label after each filling.

For many years Deans had imported bottles from a German manufacturer. Mr. Benson had continued buying from this supply and to the present had found the service excellent. The German company was one of the largest glass companies in Europe, and Deans' purchases represented less than 2 percent of the supplier's 30 percent export sales. The supplier allowed a minimum order quantity of 12,600 cases per year with minimum deliveries of 4,200 cases per month and always quoted prices c.i.f. This price excluded import duties and could vary during the year depending on fluctuations in shipping rates. The c.i.f. price gave the supplier the option of shipping and deliveries via any number of freighters in any one month. Quantity discounts were not given on orders below 200,000 cases. Mr. Benson had always found the price competitive compared to quotes received from South American companies.

Mr. Benson was responsible for setting the delivery schedule. He had found the supplier quote reliable in this regard. "If new bottle stocks are too low," Mr. Benson said, "it's my fault for not ordering in sufficient quantities or not scheduling properly." When the freighters arrived at the docks in Port-of-Spain, Deans assumed wharfage charges plus the four-mile transportation cost to the company premises. Wharfage charges varied based on space used and time held on the dock. Under normal circumstances stock remained at the dock three to four days while the company's broker cleared the goods through customs. When quick expedition was necessary, the broker could clear the papers in less than a day if they arrived ahead of the shipment. For transportation to Deans, Mr. Benson had chosen a local delivery service. Charges were $12.00 per truck load of 300 cases (24/case).

During the last six years, packaging had changed twice. Prior to 1964, the supplier packed the bottles in straw and burlap bales (one gross per bale). Breakage during ship transit, delivery to Deans, and outside exposed storage at the company was as high as 5 percent per year. In 1964 packaging changed to corrugated cardboard cartons (48 bottles per carton). Breakage was reduced to an average of 3 percent per year, and this rate was primarily due to outside exposed storage at Deans. Starting in 1967, the supplier began to palletize these cartons and wrapped the pallets with a plastic cover (see Exhibit 3). This cover gave added protection in transit and during the exposed storage period at Deans. Mr. Benson said breakage had now been reduced to less than 1 percent per year.

Empty bottle flow

Empty bottles were either returns from the trade or new bottles. The warehouse superintendent was responsible for control and storage of all returned bottles. Every day delivery salesmen returned truck loads of empty cases. These printed corrugated cardboard cases were imported from the United States and contained 24 bottles. The warehouse crew

Exhibit 3
A TYPICAL VIEW OF NEW BOTTLES IN OUTSIDE STORAGE

checked and pallet loaded the empties (40 cases per pallet) and delivered the pallets to the covered warehouse. Because of the potential weather deterioration with the printed cartons, empty returns received covered space priority over new bottles. Normally space in the warehouse was barely sufficient to store the returned empties.

Mr. Benson found it very difficult to determine the turnaround time for bottles (time taken from storage to processing to finished goods to retailer to customer to retailer to storage). The warehouse superintendent thought it was between two and three months. Empty bottle stocks were lowest just after Carnival and did not build up to normal levels until late April or early May. One executive estimated that every eight years the total stock of in-service bottles was completely replaced with new bottles, but another thought that at least 80 percent of the bottles were replaced in two to three years.

The warehouse superintendent sent empty bottles into the bottling shop as production demanded. When the empty stocks were low and returns not sufficient to meet production requirements, the warehouse superintendent requested new bottles from Mr. Benson. When Mr. Benson received the warehouse order, he had a crew of five men "pick" the new bottles. Picking consisted of removing the plastic cover from the pallets, unpacking the new bottles from the plain cardboard containers, and repacking the bottles in the printed company case. The men repalletized the cases, and a fork lift truck transported the pallets to the warehouse.

Order procedure

Each year at the end of February, Mr. Benson reviewed the stock control sheets showing empty bottle stocks, finished goods stocks, new bottle purchase and delivery records (see Exhibits 4 and 5). He then

Exhibit 4
INVENTORY POSITION ENDING FEBRUARY
(cases—24 bottles/case)

Year	Full goods	Warehouse empties	New bottle inventory (1)	New bottle order placed (in March)
1959	0	4,000	N.A.	74,000
1960	9,000	8,000	N.A.	54,000
1961	15,000	8,000	N.A.	95,000
1962	14,000	14,000	N.A.	55,000
1963	31,000	7,000	300 (2)	56,000
1964	18,000	6,000	560	51,000
1965	500	50	100	140,000
1966	18,000	23,000	13,000	150,000
1967	10,000	48,000	41,000	94,000
1968	22,000	26,000	29,000	To be decided

(1)   Although new bottle inventories and new bottle purchases were physically in 48 bottle cartons, the figures shown have been factored to coincide with normal company practice of working in terms of 24 bottles per case.
(2)   New bottle inventory equals inventory at beginning of period plus deliveries minus breakage and transfers to warehouse.

compared these stocks with the sales trends and projected his new bottle order quantities for the next year. He had to order in March for delivery in July to October. Cancellation charges were high; thus, it was not practical to try to reduce the order once it had been placed. Increases were possible, provided minimum order quantities and lead time were met. It had been standard practice to order 75 percent of yearly requirements in March followed by another order in August.

The situation would be different when Deans requested a change in the bottle design. In this case mold design costs increased, and the supplier would require a minimum of six months notice. Mr. Benson was aware that there was a 50 percent possibility the company would change the bottle design at the end of 1969, and it certainly would

Exhibit 5

C.I.F. Price Per case (as of Mar)	Year		Jan	Feb	Mar	April	May	June	July	Aug	Sept	Oct	Nov	Dec	Total
$2.40	1965	(2)			—	—	—	—	$2.68	$2.68	$2.58	$2.78 (5)	$2.70 (6)	$2.68	$2.68 Ave.
		(3)	N.A.	N.A.	—	—	—	—	14	14	10	47	28	14	127
		(4)	N.A.	N.A.	N.A.	N.A.	N.A.	N.A.	N.A.	N.A.	N.A.	N.A.	N.A.	N.A.	N.A.
$2.55	1966	(2)	$2.66		—	—	—	—	$2.76	$2.90	$2.80	$2.95	$3.00	$2.85	$2.89 Ave.
		(3)	13	—	—	—	—	—	6	16	12	20	45 (6)	14	126
		(4)	N.A.	N.A.	4	—	—	—	8	6	15	25	14	7	79
$2.70 Devalued Price Dec $3.08	1967	(2)	$2.98						$3.12		$3.09	$2.95	$2.86	$3.42	$3.14 Ave.
		(3)	37 (6)	—					16	—	13	9	7	27 (6)	109
		(4)	25	12					21	12	14	—	—	14	98
$3.15 Quoted	1968	(2)	—	$3.40											
		(3)	—	22 (6)											
		(4)	27	17											

(1) See footnote (1) in Exhibit 4.
(2) Landed cost per case (c.i.f. + wharfage + transportation to Deans).
(3) Deliveries to new bottle inventory from supplier.
(4) Transfers from new bottle inventory to warehouse.
(5) Four shipments during the month.
(6) Two shipments during the month.

change in 1970. At change-over time all remaining old-type bottles, new or used, would be scrapped.

Past bottle purchases

Prior to 1963, because of a tight working capital situation, the plant manager budgeted expenditures for new bottles closely so that just enough were available to meet demand. In 1964, extra funds became available and this policy was relaxed. Because of an unexpectedly large increase in sales during 1964, however, Mr. Benson's new bottle order of 51,000 cases was barely large enough. By mid-February of 1965, the company ran out of finished goods and empty bottles in the warehouse. Although Mr. Benson had 7,500 cases of new bottles on hand, they were still packed in the cartons received from the German supplier. Bottling operations were cut back in the plant, and capacity depended on the speed at which laborers picked the new bottles, and at which daily empty returns were washed. Delivery salesmen waited for the finished goods to load their trucks. February sales suffered with this bottle shortage crisis and were 13,000 cases less than in February of 1964. In 1965 Mr. Benson made sure sufficient bottles would be available and ordered 140,000 cases and in 1966, 150,000 cases. Empty bottle stocks at the end of February, 1967, were the highest in the company's history, and Mr. Benson reduced his order for 1967 to 94,000 cases.

Mr. Benson always met with the plant manager and the sales manager before placing the bottle order. He had already discussed the forecast problem informally with both and found that neither was confident in his predictions. He wanted to suggest a buying strategy that made sense to both production and sales, but he could not delay ordering past March 8, 1968. He had therefore requested a meeting for March 6 with both executives and knew he would have to have his proposals straight by then.

SAMPSON GAME

Background

In this game you will have the chance to try your skill at inventory management using information similar in type to that available to Mr. Marino, the general manager of Sampson Sewer Tile Works. Every two weeks in the summer sales period Mr. Marino had to decide how many tiles of each type and size should be produced by Sampson during the coming two weeks. In doing this, he took into account sales trends, the time of the year, the capacity of Sampson's tile making machinery, the stock of the various size tiles on hand, the cost of overtime production, and the cost of missed deliveries. In this game you will be able to make similar decisions although the game will be a simplified version of the actual situation. The most important feature of this simplification is that you will be dealing with only two sizes of sewer tile—the 18″ diameter size and the 36″ diameter size. Mr. Marino, in contrast, had to decide on production levels for 13 different sizes of tile.

Sales patterns

Company sales, and industry sales in general, were very much influenced by seasonal factors. Since weather affected tile laying conditions and the number of construction starts, sewer tiles exhibited a yearly sales trend of the following general shape (see Exhibit 1). Sales were

Exhibit 1

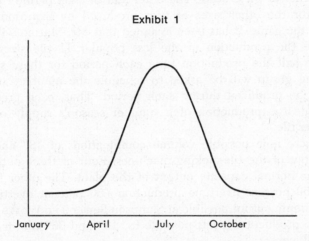

| January | April | July | October |

low for six months from October 1 to March 1 and rose rapidly in the spring to a summer peak and then tapered off again. About one third of all annual sales were made in the two middle months of the year while about three fourths were made in the summer sales season. However, it should not be thought that there was necessarily a smooth rise and fall in sales in any particular year. The curve shown is only the average of the experience of many years. In any given year, biweekly sales might vary ±25 percent from levels they would assume if a smooth sales curve existed. The maximum number of 18″ tiles sold in any two week period between April and October of last year was 455. The similar fiigure for 36″ tiles was 200.

In the game you are about to play, Period 1 refers to the first two weeks in April. Thus, company sales are just leaving the low part of the annual swing. The game culminates in Period 12, the last two weeks in September. At this point sales are reentering the low winter period. Between Periods 1 and 12, sales follow the general shape of the curve shown in Exhibit 1.

All sales made by Sampson Sewer Tile Works are booked for delivery within the period being considered. That is, there is no advance ordering.

Mr. Marino has no idea what the sales for any coming period will be other than from judgment of the sales level of prior periods and from consideration of the general shape of the sales trend curve.

Production constraints

The most popular sizes of concrete tile sold by Sampson Sewer Tile Works were the 18″ diameter and the 36″ diameter sizes. Mr. Marino had found that together these tiles accounted for a large part of tile sales; in fact, roughly one half of each period's production was devoted to one or other of these sizes. The other half of each period's production was used for the other sizes of tiles produced by Sampson. In order to simplify the game, it has been assumed that Mr. Marino will continue to schedule the production of the less popular 11 tile sizes and that he will use half the production time each period for these sizes. Each participating group will be asked to schedule the numbers of 18″ and 36″ tile to be produced during each period. Thus, each group will in fact schedule the production of a summer season's supply of 18″ and 36″ diameter tile.

There were nine possible volume combinations of 18″ and 36″ tile for the output of the tile-making machines. Four of these output values involved the normal capacity output of the plant. The other five values called for 50 percent overtime production (50 percent overtime represented maximum output possible at Sampson Sewer Tile Works).

The nine production levels possible for 18″ and 36″ tile in each two-week period were:

Normal capacity		50 percent overtime	
18″ tiles	36″ tiles	18″ tiles	36″ tiles
600	0	900	0
400	60	700	60
200	120	500	120
0	180	300	180
		100	240

Please notice that trade-offs are involved in choosing a production level for a period. If the number of 18″ tiles to be produced is increased, the number of 36″ tiles that can be produced will necessarily decrease unless overtime is used.

Costs involved

Inventory costs. In deciding on production alternatives, Mr. Marino bore in mind several costs which he knew to be fairly accurate. For instance, storage costs of 18″ tile for one period were an average of $.20. This amount took into account interest on tied-up capital, insurance against breakage, and direct handling expense. The inventory carrying costs on each 36″ tile were higher and averaged $.60 per tile per period.

Mr. Marino had found that, over the period of a season, inventory carrying charges could reasonably be calculated on the basis of inventory on hand at the end of each period.

Stock-out costs. Stock-out costs also had to be considered by Mr. Marino. A stock-out occurred whenever a sales in a particular period could not be filled because there were insufficient tiles of the required diameter on hand or in production during that period. For instance, if 10 tiles were on hand at the beginning of a period, 200 tiles were produced during the period, and sales during the period totaled 220, then a stock-out of 10 tiles would occur. When such a stock-out occurred there was a chance that a future customer of Sampson Sewer Tile Works would be lost. Furthermore, Sampson lost the profit potential on the missed order. Mr. Marino had assessed the risks and costs involved and thought that a stock-out cost Sampson Sewer Tile Works $2 for each 18″ tile and $6 for each 36″ tile. This figure took into account the fact that the larger the number of tiles that could not be delivered, the more apt the customer was to take future business elsewhere. Stock-outs could not be made up in subsequent periods. If a stock-out occurred, the sale was lost forever to the firm and the above costs were incurred.

Overtime costs. If overtime was used in any period, a fixed charge of $200 was incurred. This charge was used mainly to pay extra wages to the employees. The amount was fixed because the employees had been guaranteed a minimum amount each period overtime was used in the plant.

How to play the game

In the actual conduct of this game, teams will be used to make the production decisions normally made by Mr. Marino regarding the 18″ and 36″ diameter tile. Before each period each team will be required to decide on the production level that will be used in the plant. This decision will be made by the team by whatever means it chooses. Thus, a prediction from a plot of past period sales might be used by some teams, a pure guess by others. In making the decision, teams will want to consider both the possibilities of future sales and the inventories of tiles now on hand.

After each team has decided on the production level it desires for the coming period, the instructor will announce what the period sales have been. Given this information, teams will then be able to calculate inventory on hand, inventory, stockout, and overtime costs. These add up to a total period cost which is added to a cumulative total of costs.

The object of the game is to keep the total costs incurred over 12 periods to a minimum. This means that teams will have to decide whether it would be cheaper in the long run to incur overtime costs, inventory carrying costs, or stock-out costs. It is impossible to avoid all three. However, it is possible to cut costs considerably by using inventory management to advantage. At the end of the 12th period the game will be stopped and final costs figured. Your team's results will be compared to those of other teams. During subsequent discussions the merits of various inventory and production policies can be evaluated. Teams will probably find it advantageous to split the work of making sales estimates, calculating costs, and keeping records among the various members.

Result form used

To make the keeping of results easier for each team, a form similar to Exhibit 1 has been distributed. The exact steps in using this form are:

1. Decide on the production level to be used in the forthcoming period.
2. Enter number of tiles to be produced in columns A (18") and J (36").
3. Fill in stock on hand at start of period in columns B (18") and K (36"). These figures come from columns E (18") and N (36") of the previous period.
4. Enter total stock available for sale in the period in columns C and L.
   Entry in column C (18" tiles) = entry in column A + entry in column B.
   Entry in column L (36" tiles) = entry in column J + entry in column K.
5. Obtain actual sales in period from instructor. Enter in columns D (18") and M (36").
6. Compute inventory remaining at the end of the period. Enter in columns E and N.
   Entry in column E (18" tiles) = entry in column C − entry in column D.
   Entry in column N (36" tiles) = entry in column L − entry in column M.
   Enter zero if an entry is calculated as negative. There can be no negative inventory on hand.
7. Compute inventory carrying costs and enter in columns F and O.
   Entry in column F (18" tiles) = \$.20 × no. in column E.
   Entry in column O (36" tiles) = \$.60 × no. in column N.
8. Compute stock-outs incurred in period, enter in columns G and P if zero or a positive number. Enter zero if an entry is calculated as negative; there can be no negative stock-outs.

Entry in column G (18″ tiles) = entry in column D — entry in column C.

Entry in column P (36″ tiles) = entry in column M — entry in column L.

9. Compute stock-out costs, enter in columns H and Q.

Entry in column H = \$2 × no. in column G.

Entry in column Q = \$6 × no. in column P.

10. Compute total period inventory cost, enter in column R.

Entry in column R = entry in column F (18″ tiles) + entry in column O (36″ tiles).

11. Compute total period stock-out costs, enter in column S.

Entry in column S = entry in column H (18″ tiles) + entry in column Q (36″ tiles).

12. If overtime was used, enter \$200 in column T. If no overtime used, enter zero.

13. Compute total period cost and enter in column U.

Entry in column U = entry in column R (total period inventory cost) + entry in column S (total period stock-out cost) + entry in column T (overtime cost).

14. Compute cumulative total to date, enter in column V.

Entry in column V = entry in column U for current period + entry in column V for last period.

Example

Each team member should carefully trace the proceedings as outlined in the following example so that he fully understands all of the steps involved in playing and recording the game.

Mr. Marino has already used the form to record the operating results of the two periods prior to the first period for which you will be required to decide the production level (Period 1). Sampson Sewer Tile Works started Period 1 with 40 18″ tiles (column B) and 10 16″ tiles on hand (column K). Because he suspected that a special, large order for 18″ tiles would be placed in Period 1 (a most unusual size of order at this time of year), Mr. Marino decided to go to overtime and to produce 700 18″ tiles (column A) and 60 36″ tiles (column J). Thus, 740 18″ tiles (column C) and 70 36″ tiles (column L) were available for sales during Period 1.

In actual fact the special order was smaller than Mr. Marino had anticipated, and total sales turned out to be 600 for the 18″ tiles (column D) and 80 for the 36″ tiles (column M). Because inventory available for sale exceeded sales, Mr. Marino entered 140 in column E, to show there was inventory remaining at the end of the period, and then entered zero in column G, to show that there had been no stock-out of 18″

tiles. Column F then shows the inventory cost incurred by having 140 18″ tiles on hand at the end of the period ($.20 × 140 = $28). Column H shows that no stock-out cost was incurred. Because demand for the 36″ tiles (80) exceeded the total available for sale (70), a stock-out of 10 occurred, and no tiles were left in inventory at the end of Period 1. To show this, zero was entered in column N and 10 was entered in column P. There was a zero inventory carrying cost entered in column O while a stock-out cost of $60 was entered in column Q ($6 × 10 = $60).

The total inventory carrying cost was entered in column R ($28 + 0 = $28) and the total stock-out cost in column S (0 + $60 = $60). Two hundred dollars was entered in column T because overtime was used. The total period cost was calculated to be $28 + $60 + $200 = $288. This amount was then entered in column U and also column V.

Sampson Sewer Tile Works began Period 0 with 140 18″ tiles (column B) and zero 36″ tiles on hand (column K). These totals had been brought down from columns E and N respectively of Period 1. At the beginning of Period 0, Mr. Marino elected to produce 200 18″ tiles (column A) and 120 36″ tiles (column J). No overtime was called for. Thus, there were 340 18″ tiles (column C) and 120 36″ tiles (column L) available for sale in Period 0.

In Period 0, sales totaled 140 18″ tiles (column D) and 50 36″ tiles (column M). Thus, the inventory remaining at the end of the period was 200 18″ tiles (column E) and 70 36″ tiles (column N). There were zero stock-outs (columns G and P). Inventory carrying costs were computed to be $.20 × 200 = $40 (column F) and $.60 × 70 = $42 (column O). There were no stock-out costs (columns H and Q) because stock-outs equaled zero in this period.

The total inventory carrying cost for Period 1 was $82 ($40 + $42). This amount was entered in column R, while zero was entered in column S since there had been no stock-outs in the period. There was no overtime used, consequently a zero was entered in column T. The column U entry shows that the total period costs incurred were $82. The column V entry was $288 + $82 = $370. Since your team did not incur these costs we will wipe them off the slate and have you start with a zero cost at the beginning of Period 1 in column V.

Start of game

The game proper starts in Period 1. At the beginning of the game there are 200 18″ tiles on hand (brought down from column E of Period 0) and 70 36″ tiles on hand (brought down from column E of Period 0). It is now up to each team to pick the production level most appropriate for Period 1 and thus start the playing of the game.

Exhibit 2

Period	(A) Number produced	(B) Stock on hand at start of period	(C) Total available for sale C = A + B	(D) Sales in period	(E) Inventory remaining at end of period E = C-D (minimum = 0)	(F) Inventory carrying cost $.20 × E	(G) Number of stock-outs G = D-C if greater than 0	(H) Stock-out cost H = $2 × G	(J) Number produced	(K) Stock on hand at start of period	(L) Total available for sale L = J + K	(M) Sales in period	(N) Inventory remaining at end of period N = L-M (minimum = 0)	(O) Inventory carrying cost $.60 × N	(P) Number of stock-outs P = M-L if greater than 0	(Q) Stock-out cost Q = $6 × P	(R) Total inventory cost R = F + O	(S) Total stock-out cost S = H + Q	(T) Overtime cost $200 (if used)	(U) Total period cost U = R + S + T	(V) Cumulative total to date
					18" Tiles							36" Tiles					TOTALS				
March – 1	700	40	740	600	140	$28	0	0	60	10	70	80	0	0	10	$60	$28	$60	$200	$288	(288)
March 0	200	140	340	140	200	$40	0	0	120	0	120	50	70	42	0	0	$82	0	0	$ 82	(370)
April 1		200								70											
April 2																					
May 3																					
May 4																					
June 5																					
June 6																					
July 7																					
July 8																					
August 9																					
August 10																					
September 11																					
September 12																					
Total																					

ADAMS FARM EQUIPMENT, LTD.

During his first year of employment with Adams Farm Equipment, Ltd., Mr. Blyth learned that a major problem in the production department was shortage of parts on the assembly lines. To get an idea of how serious the problem was, Mr. Blyth got from one of the assembly line foreman some figures for the two-week period from April 3, 1972, to April 19, 1972. During this time only 15 out of the 282 tractors produced on one line in the factory were assembled without shortages of component parts. The other tractors had been set aside in the assembly area awaiting additional supplies of parts, either manufactured or purchased. The resulting extra assembly costs for that period amount to $2,810. Total assembly costs in the same period were $11,270. The foreman pointed out that shortages during these two weeks had been unusually acute but that the problem was almost as bad throughout the year. To illustrate, he showed Mr. Blyth his labor costs sheet for the three month period February 1, 1972, to April 30, 1972. The labor cost of installing missing parts after they had been either manufactured or purchased during this time was $12,840.

Not only were assembly costs inflated by these shortages but manufacturing costs were increased by the extra set-ups to make the few pieces that were short. When the assembly department discovered that there was an insufficient quantity of a part a rush order for the missing quantity was issued. Sometimes when this rush order was completed it too was found to be short a few pieces and a second rush order would have to be issued. This had recently happened with Part ETR 309, the standard cost of which was 96 cents including labor (30¢), material (36¢) and burden (30¢).

The original order called for 930 pieces. The first shortage order called for 35 pieces. The second shortage order called for 15 pieces. There were seven operations on this part which required a total of 7.20 hours set-up time worth $6.00 per hour. These last 50 pieces then cost $86.40 more than they should have plus lost production time on the machines during set-up.

The company

Adams Farm Equipment, Ltd., employed about 1,500 production employees, many of whom were skilled machinists. The company produced a full line of farm implements including tractors, combines, plows, and drills. They manufactured almost all component parts for the machines with the exception of electric starters, spark plugs, tires, batteries, and lights. The machinery department contained lathes, forges, drill presses, milling machines, and automatic screw machines. A batch of parts after being machined were sent to a temporary storage area where it waited until the assembly department required it. It was then taken to the assembly area where the parts were assembled into farm implements.

David Blyth

Mr. Blyth had joined the firm after graduating from college in the spring of 1971. He had been hired by the manager of the purchasing department who had explained that his first task would be to investigate the company's make or buy decision procedure with the object of finding ways of improving it. The benefits were to be twofold. First, the company would get a fresh, unbiased look at its make or buy decisions and, second, conducting the study would rapidly acquaint Mr. Blyth with the company, the purchasing department, and the other employees.

Mr. Blyth started his investigations in the accounting department but soon found that he would have to get actual out-of-pocket costs of manufacturing from the production department. There he was told that actual costs of parts varied considerably from one run to another for several reasons, the main one being that when it came time to assemble an implement seldom was there a sufficient number of all of the parts. The result usually was a shcedule-upsetting rush order through the machining department to make the few parts needed. Believing that he could do nothing about make or buy decisions without accurate actual costs, Mr. Blyth decided to try to track down the causes of the parts shortages on the assembly lines in hope that what he found might be useful for predicting shortages and, in turn, costs. Mr. Blyth could then proceed with his study with more accurate cost information. He spent the next few days in the plant talking to the workmen and the foremen, learning how things were done.

He learned that about nine months in advance of requirements the merchandising department estimated sales of all implements and repair parts for the coming year. The production control office then prepared a list of all parts required and, to the quantities needed, added a manufacturing spoilage allowance based on the following:

1. Large items or those with few operations 1 percent with a minimum of one and a maximum of two.
2. Costly or intricate parts 2 percent with a minimum of two and a maximum of ten.
3. All other parts 3 percent with a minimum of three and a maximum of ten.

The quantities of parts in inventory were compared with the requirements as shown on the list (including spoilage allowance). When requirements exceeded inventory, either purchase requisitions or manufacturing orders were placed for the difference.

The engineering department attempted to standardize parts as much as possible and with a fairly high degree of success. Frequently the same part would fit on all models of tractors and perhaps on some of the combines as well. Consequently, very long production runs of parts occasionally were required in which case the production control office split the lot into two batches in an effort to reduce the length of the runs.

Mr. Blyth got the impression that the problem of shortage had been in existence for some time because the cost accounting department actually budgeted for excess labor costs resulting from shortages at assembly. Thus, the only cost that showed up in the variance account was that which was in excess of "budgeted cost."

After a few days in the plant Mr. Blyth prepared a list of 12 reasons why there were parts shortages on the assembly lines.

1. Inadequate spoilage allowance

The spoilage allowance was set by a clerk in the production control office by first considering the appropriate percentage spoilage allowance and then adjusting it in light of his experience. If there were very few machining or fabricating operations on a part, the allowance was low, but, for parts requiring six or eight operations, the allowance was higher.

Some of the machinists told Mr. Blyth that for most set-ups two or three parts were spoiled before the machine was running properly, and even then another one or two parts in each batch were usually found to have been spoiled during each run.

On inquiring further about Part ETR 309 which had required two shortage orders (mentioned earlier), Blyth found that while this particular part had been used for many years it was not expected to be used in next year's models. Consequently, the production control office had allowed only ten for spoilage, hoping that when the implements were assembled and repair parts requirements deducted there would be none left in inventory. The foreman of the machining department, after checking his personal records, said that never had that part been made with only ten pieces spoiled. He estimated that in all the times they had run that piece through the shop about 10 percent of the times 15 pieces were spoiled; about 20 percent of the time 14 were spoiled; about half of the times, 13 pieces were spoiled; and in the remainder, 12 pieces were spoiled. He felt that one of the reasons that spoilage allowances were too low was that accurate information on actual spoilage was seldom transmitted back to the production control office.

2. Errors in annual physical inventory count

Each year the plant was closed down for a two-week period to count the inventory of parts. This work was performed by the most senior men in the plant in accordance with the agreement with the union (United Auto Workers). The procedure was for the workers to move through the various storage areas counting the number of parts in the tote boxes and bins and recording their findings on forms provided. Each bin and tote box had a tag attached showing in pencil the part number and the quantity in it. The quantities as determined by this count were then recorded in the perpetual inventory records.

Mr. Blyth, on questioning some of the workmen who had performed this work, discovered that the job was not taken too seriously by the workers. Sometimes the part number written on the tag was obliterated, in which case the worker took a guess at it. At other times a worker might, instead of actually counting the parts in a bin, just read the quantity on the tag and record it. As the total number of part numbers in the company's records exceeded 20,000, the counting of this inventory was no small task.

While he did not know how numerous inventory errors were, Mr. Blyth did know that they appeared frequently enough to warrant corrective action. One example he unearthed happened on April 1, 1972. A shortage of 195 pieces of Part FB-S3001 was reported by the assembly department and a rush order initiated for their manufacture. Several weeks later investigation revealed that there were 195 pieces of Part FB-S3001 in the warehouse but that none had been reported by the annual physical count.

3. Incorrect count of parts put into production

The shear room contained various saws, shears, and other cut-off equipment and was the place where the first operation was performed on most parts. It was there that the greatest responsibility lay for counting the work going into production.

A shop order told the workers in the shear room the number of pieces of steel to cut for each part, and it was up to them to cut that number. They were paid on piece rate according to a labor ticket on which they wrote the number actually produced. Most machines in this department had counters on them that showed the number of times the machine had performed its cutting operation. Mr. Blyth found that the counters were not used and that frequently no count of work pieces was made. However, sometimes after the first operation the workers determined the quantity they produced by weighing the lot and dividing by the weight of one. On May 26, 1972, Mr. Blyth asked one of the workers in the shear room if he was counting or weighing his output and was told that neither was being done. The worker reported that he was too busy.

After each operation the worker who performed it turned in to the production control office a card which showed the quantity ordered into production and the quantity he claimed to have processed. If it was found later that a worker had reported and been paid for a larger quantity than he had actually produced (called overbooking), then his earnings were supposed to be reduced by the amount he overbooked. This, of course, hinged on management's ability to prove that the parts claimed to be overbooked could not have become lost while being moved to subsequent operations. As there was usually no further count, over-booking was not easy to prove. Multiple shift operation further compli-cated the problem.

Mr. Blyth, while talking to the clerks in the payroll office uncovered several examples of overbooking. For example, 470 pieces of Part NIS 3000 had been ordered into production, but the quantities reported at each of the ten operations are shown below.

Operation	1	2	3	4	5	6	7	8	9	10
Booking	490	524	524	524	524	669	522	522	300	281

Mr. Blyth was interested to note that all ten workers involved in making the part had been paid for exactly the quantity reported. On checking further, he was unable to discover a single example of where a worker had been paid for an amount less than he had originally booked.

While talking to the foreman of the shear room Blyth learned that there were two chronic offenders in that department. They had been repeatedly warned about overbooking and had been threatened by the foreman with dismissal for a repetition. Consequently, when they were later caught overbooking, the foreman called the plant superintendent, and the four of them marched over to the personnel office. There the two workers were told that they must not overbook and were instructed to return to work. The foreman and the plant superintendent were told by the personnel manager to "take it easy" because it was contract negotiating time, and they did not want to upset the union.

4. Scrap control

The workers throughout the plant were told that if they made an error and had to scrap one or several pieces, they were to report it to their foreman who then sent the rejected pieces to the inspection department where a decision was made as to whether the faulty pieces should be reworked or scrapped and arrangements made for additional pieces to be made to make up the quantity required. All rework and scrap was charged against the department reporting the error.

Mr. Blyth discovered that sometimes the workmen, instead of report-ing the faulty pieces, buried them in machine cuttings and had them sent out to the scrap iron pile. The foremen tolerated this practice be-cause this way they avoided having the scrap or rework costs charged to their departments. In such cases the card showing the quantity produced was in error by at least the number scrapped. If a worker and the foreman did report faulty pieces as instructed, the worker did not get paid for the work he did on them.

5. Inaccurate stores records

Theoretically, all completed parts had to go to the stores area before being delivered to the assembly departments. However, Mr. Blyth discovered that occasionally if the assembly department was in a hurry for a part, a fork lift truck operator was persuaded to deliver the box of parts directly from the manufacturing area to the assembly area and instructed to ". . . tell the boys over in stores the next time you are over that way." If the driver neglected reporting the move, then the records in the production control office indicated that a quantity of the part had been manufactured, but there was not sufficient in stores to assemble the required number of machines. On more than one occasion this had resulted in a second batch of a part being rushed through manufacturing when the original batch was already assembled. Mr. Blyth was unable to determine the frequency with which this happened but did know that it had happened several times in the previous six months.

6. Tool repair charges

If a production tool was in need of repair, it was to the foreman's advantage to encourage the workman to use it as long as possible before sending it for repair even at the risk of a greater scrap rate. This was because all tool repairs were charged to the departments, and the foremen were judged partially by their ability to keep such costs to a minimum. If he was able to dispose of the scrap produced, it was to both the worker's and the foreman's advantage to get the maximum usage from a tool, dispose of the scrap by devious means, and report the same number produced as was recorded on the tag accompanying the parts. Mr. Blyth reported observing a gang drill being used with one drill burned so badly that the work piece was beyond repair. The operator said that he was near the end of the run and did not want to take the time to get a new drill for just a few pieces. He did not disclose how he intended disposing of the pieces he spoiled.

7. Tolerances on drawings not always specified

The standard drawings used in the plant had printed in the upper right hand corner "Tolerances unless specified $\pm$ .010" on all machined surfaces, angles $\pm$ 1°." Mr. Blyth found that sometimes the draftsmen neglected indicating tolerances on dimensions where the allowable tolerance was actually much greater than .010″. This caused a higher scrap rate in the plant with its resulting shortages.

8. Defective castings

Frequently while machining a casting, a machinist discovered that there was a flaw in it, making it useless. If he reported it, the production control office issued a new shop order to the foundry to cover a few castings of the type required. This resulted in delays of the original order or in making special set-ups for a few pieces.

9. Machine loading

When the production control clerk was arranging the manufacturing schedules he ordered parts into production in such manner that they would be completely manufactured at least two weeks before the date assembly was to begin. He issued a shop order for each part to the foreman of the first department to work on the part. The shop order gave the date that the part was required for assembly but did not give the foreman a date by which the part was required by another department. Consequently, parts were often delayed in a department to the point that they could not be completed in time for assembly to begin. Particularly troublesome were three machines that usually had a backlog of work of eight weeks. These three machines were a gear hobber, 14-foot shear, and a 400-ton forming press. There was no way of determining in advance when a part could be produced by a bottleneck operation. It just had to wait for its turn.

Mr. Blyth felt that this large backlog on some machines indicated that the shop was not balanced. He felt too that the fact that nobody knew when a part was supposed to leave each department aggravated the problem of shortages at time for assembly.

10. Insufficient raw materials purchased

Steel suppliers, when shipping steel to users, charged by weight but only guaranteed their count of the number of bars to be within 10 percent of that specified by the customer. It sometimes happened that Adams Farm Equipment, Ltd., ordered a quantity of steel bars only to find that they received an insufficient number to make the part required. One example of this unearthed by Mr. Blyth occurred when 81 steel bars of a certain size were ordered from a steel supplier and only 79 were delivered. This was within the allowed 10 percent, but it meant that Adams had to order an additional two bars and hold up manufacture on the part until they arrived. The steel suppliers imposed a penalty of $1.50 per hundred pounds on orders for less than two tons.

11. Inefficient lengths of raw material

Theoretically the length of raw material ordered was supposed to be that which would cut up with a minimum of waste. However, this did not always happen. For example Part NS-T57 was to be cut from steel bar stock and was to be $1\frac{1}{8}''$ in length. The quantity required was 1,026 pieces. To make them, 19 bars were ordered, each $5'4''$ in length, with the expectation that 54 pieces would be cut from each bar. However, when the bars were cut it was found that an extra $\frac{1}{8}''$ was required for each piece by the cut-off saw and an additional four inches was required for each bar for chucking. The net result was a shortage of 114 pieces before the first operation was performed.

12. Foremen performing clerical tasks

In discussing the problem of shortage with the department foremen, Mr. Blyth learned that they were usually too busy to track down all the causes of shortages in their respective departments. Because indirect labor was measured as a percentage of direct labor, when production workers were laid off through seasonal or other factors, the clerical force was reduced accordingly. Since the indirect labor work load was not correspondingly reduced, this sometimes burdened the foremen to the point where they had little time remaining to supervise.

McARTHUR MIRROR COMPANY

Early in 1973, the president of McArthur Mirror began questioning the value of the inventory control system which had been instituted by a consulting firm in 1970. The inventory as recorded seldom agreed with the physical count. Shipments of mirrors were delayed through a lack of cartons. Additional checks and inspection were required to prevent glass deterioration from excessive storage. The president wondered whether he should revert to the old system or make further changes in the present inventory control method.

The McArthur Mirror Company manufactured mirrors which it sold to furniture manufacturers, department stores, and hardware stores. The company employed about 50 workers and had annual sales amounting to about $1.5 million. Sales of mirrors had at one time been highly seasonal, but in the past ten years management had been able to make a number of off-season deals with certain customers enabling the company to level out production throughout the year.

In December, 1969, the president of the McArthur Mirror Company read an article about inventory control in one of the trade journals that passed regularly over his desk. The article stressed the need for regular reviews of a company's inventory control system. The president knew that no such a review had ever been made in the McArthur company. He therefore instructed the factory manager to study the inventory control system in use at McArthur Mirror and to make any suggestions for improvements. Soon after, the factory manager submitted the following memo to the president:

Memo to: The President   January 12, 1970
From: Factory Manager
Subject: Inventory Control

Recommendation: That a consultant be called in to set up a new system of inventory control.

Analysis: Our company carries an inventory of about 800 different items amounting to over $450,000. The major portion of our inventory consists of glass, much of which is imported from England and France, and of finished mirrors. Inventory control now rests mainly with the stores clerk. When he notices that the stock of a particular item is getting low, he orders more from the appropriate supplier. All inventory records are kept by the stores clerk, who makes an entry on a stock card whenever an item is taken into or out of stores. The purchasing agent also orders raw materials and supplies when he considers it necessary or when he is offered a good deal. Little consideration is given to inventory balance; the prime object is to have an ample supply of all materials on hand at all times.

It seems very likely that the company is tying up too much capital in inventory. There is also duplication of the purchasing function, and the stores clerk has the only inventory record available. For these reasons and because no one in our plant is technically qualified, it is suggested that a consultant be called in to set up a new system of inventory control.

The president approved the factory manager's proposal and engaged a management consulting firm to study the problem. By mid-February the two consultants assigned to the job had prepared a list of the items used in the process plus all sizes of finished mirrors, showing the quantities of each item to be kept in stores. These quantities were determined by the consultants after they had agreed upon an order point and an order quantity for each item.

Order point

The order point was a point in the diminishing stock of material at which consideration was to be given to ordering an additional quantity. The order point was based on the time it took to secure additional supplies and the quantity likely to be used during that time. The time needed to secure a new supply covered the period from placing the requisition with the purchasing department through to receipt of the material at the plant. To this was added a safety factor to cover unusual delays in shipping or, in the case of glass, the time required to make up a carload order. If the order point was reached on one or two glass items on which replacement did not represent a carload, the purchase requisition was held up roughly four to eight days until additional sizes reached order point. To arrive at the quantity likely to be called for during the time needed to secure a new supply, it was necessary to know how much had been used in the past and whether future usage was likely to differ from the past. For example, the annual usage of one particular size of plate glass was 2,400 lights,[1] and six weeks were needed to secure an additional supply. The order point was set at 300. For mirrors the order point was set by considering the time it usually took to manufacture a batch and the expected demand during that time.

Order quantity

The order quantity was the amount of a material the purchasing department had to order. The order quantity depended on price reductions due to quantity purchases, possible savings in transportation charges, the annual volume used, interest on investment, space limitations in stores, and the cost of storage and obsolescence. The order quantity for a special order mirror was, of course, the quantity in the order, but for stock mirrors the number ordered into production was usually a quantity that would satisfy several weeks expected demand.

Incoming material

Under the new system of inventory control, the purchasing department prepared a receiving memo showing codes and quantities of materials to be delivered to stores. The stores clerk verified the actual quantities received and indicated this on the receiving memo before forwarding it to the balance of stores clerk.

Production orders

On being notified by the balance of stores clerk that a particular size and style of mirror had reached the order point the production planner issued a production order which authorized the manufacturing of the required mirrors. When the batch of mirrors was manufactured the production order was sent to the balance of stores clerk who recorded the number manufactured on the appropriate card and adjusted the balance accordingly.

---

[1] A light is any pane of glass regardless of size. In ordering glass lights it was, therefore, essential to specify all dimensions.

Stores issue

When material was required for manufacture, it was requested on a stores requisition which described the material wanted, showing codes and quantities. To draw material from stores, the stores requisition was usually prepared by the production planner, attached to the production order, and sent to the foreman. When the foreman was ready to use the material, he or one of his men presented the stores requisition to the balance of stores clerk. Small items, such as buffing rouge and small nuts and bolts for assembly, were ordered by the foremen in bulk from the stores. The foremen had a supply of stores requisitions which they used for this purpose.

Balance of stores

The balance of stores clerk was asked to keep accurate and up-to-date records in order that the management could:

1. Help prevent running out of stock.
2. Know what was in stock.
3. Know what the stock cost.
4. Know what was on order.
5. Know what stock had been received, and when.
6. Know what stock had been issued, and to whom.

These records took the form of balance of stores cards, one of which was made out for each separate material, the name, description, and code numbers appearing on each card. The order point, order quantity, and standard cost were also shown on each card. Receipts and issues were posted and the current balance calculated each day from receiving reports and stores requisitions delivered by the stores clerk. When the balance on hand, which was the amount available for issue, reached the order point as shown on the balance of stores card, the production planner was notified by the balance of stores clerk on a handwritten memo. The production planner then authorized the purchase of new supplies by sending a purchase requisition to the purchasing department or, for mirrors, he issued a production order.

Developments after 1970

In 1973, three years after the new system of inventory control had gone into effect, the president tried to determine to what extent it had been successful. His investigation brought out the following facts.

Each year the plant manager and the production supervisor prepared estimates of the mirror sales they expected for the following year in terms of the number of lights of each size. Following this, the production supervisor reviewed the order points and order quantities of all raw materials and finished mirrors. He had not changed any of these in the three years since the system's inception in 1970. Sales for those years were:

1970 . . . . 109,000 lights
1971 . . . . 88,000 lights
1972 . . . . 74,000 lights
1973 (est.) . . . . 54,000 lights

While the numbers of mirrors sold had declined, the profits of the company had not shown a comparable reduction, because customers had demanded a substantial increase in size and grade of mirror.

There seemed to be a problem of accuracy with the balance of stores clerk. Under the system of inventory control in use prior to 1970, the stores clerk kept the inventory records in the stores warehouse, making entries himself whenever anything was brought in or taken out. When the new system was instituted early in 1970, it was proposed to permit the stores clerk to continue keeping his records until the new balance of stores card system was established in the office and working properly. It was found, however, to be virtually impossible to get the balance of stores cards to balance with the actual physical count. As the records kept by the stores clerk nearly always agreed with the physical count, the stores clerk had been permitted to continue to keep his own records. Reasons for this failure of the new cards to agree were considered by the production supervisor to be:

1. There was a relatively rapid turnover in balance of stores clerks.
2. The balance of stores clerks were usually girls and their interest in the job was low.
3. As the balance of stores cards did not indicate the source of the figures used, it was impossible to check back for errors.
4. Sometimes stores requisitions were lost during their trip through the plant thus upsetting the balance on the balance of stores cards.

Whenever the balance of stores clerk had a few spare minutes, she took a handful of the cards from her file and checked them against the physical count in the warehouse. If an error was discovered, she changed the balance on her card. It was rarely that the raw materials inventory did not balance with her cards. The finished mirror count was usually found to be in error, possibly because the number of entries on these cards exceeded by far the number of entries on raw materials cards.

The president also found that the inventory control of cartons was a problem. Each mirror was packaged in an individual carton prior to shipping. Because the demand for cartons of all types was highly seasonal, the company at certain times of the year could expect to get cartons two weeks after ordering while at other times two months were required. Rather than change the order points and order quantities on approximately 100 cards every few months, it was left to the purchaser to order cartons as he saw fit. The company seldom ran out of raw materials or finished goods but did find itself occasionally in the position of having to delay a shipment of mirrors because it had run out of cartons.

Glass inventory had always received special attention at McArthur Mirror because of its deterioration in storage. With the exception of glass, incoming shipments of raw materials were not marked to indicate their order of arrival, but the workers were instructed to use the oldest stock first. Cases of glass were marked and materials requisitions for glass indicated the number of the case to be used. Sometimes, however, because of space limitations and the crowded condition of the warehouse, the workers found it difficult to get at the case designated. At such times they might change the number on the requisition and substitute glass from a newer shipment. Glass deteriorated in storage by staining, and it was found that, if stored for more than a year, it was almost useless for mirror manufacture. Because of the potential loss from glass deterioration, the production supervisor made a periodic check of the warehouse to ensure that old stocks were being used first.

On a request from the president, the purchasing agent supplied the following breakdown of purchases during 1972:

Item	Value of purchases in 1972
Glass	$500,000
Hardware	49,000
Chemicals	67,000
Cartons	61,000
Buffing rouge	18,000
Grinding wheels and belts	22,000
Fibreboard backing panels	14,000
Other supplies	30,000
	$761,000

After his investigation, the president realized that over $9,000 and a great deal of time and effort had been spent to install a system that was not working properly. He wondered whether the company should discontinue the new system and revert to the old system or change the new system.

One possible change he thought was worth considering was to have different people in the company responsible for different items in inventory. Another was to provide a check on the balance of stores clerk so that even when she was behind in her work the company would not run out of essential items.

6 SELECTING ADEQUATE SOURCES OF SUPPLY

Introduction

The selection of sources of supply is a key decision area in the acquisition process. It is highly visible and the culmination of frequently extensive preparation. The expressed purpose of industrial marketing is to influence this decision in favor of one source over another. Supplier selection is purchasing's most important responsibility. The purchasing department must be able to locate dependable and progressive sources of supply and to secure and maintain their active interest and cooperation. All other purchasing contributions to the organization are secondary to the competent selection of suppliers.

Even though in sequence of preparation it is logical to consider matters of quality and quantity first, these can seldom be settled without appropriate consideration of available sources. One of the signs of a good supplier is the ability to be of assistance to the purchaser in establishing what constitutes the proper quality and quantity for the intended use.

In this chapter the topics of supplier goodwill, supplier evaluation, relationship satisfaction and stability, sources of information, foreign suppliers and supplier development will be discussed. The next chapter will cover problems in source selection such as concentrating orders with one source, supplier size, geographical and social implications, and reciprocal trading.

The supplier selection decision

The decision to place a certain volume of business with a supplier is always based on some rationale. The art of good purchasing is to make the reasoning behind that decision as sound as possible. An interesting study by G. W. Dickson listed 23 factors which might be considered in evaluating potential vendors. (See Figure 6-1.)
That the type of product purchased influenced the ranking of importance of these factors was clear. (See Figure 6-2.)

Figure 6–1
AGGREGATE FACTOR RATINGS

Factor	Mean rating	Evaluation
Quality.	3.508	Extreme importance
Delivery	3.417	
Performance history	2.998	
Warranties and claims policies	2.849	
Production facilities and capacity.	2.775	Considerable importance
Price	2.758	
Technical capability	2.545	
Financial position.	2.514	
Procedural compliance	2.488	
Communication system	2.426	
Reputation and position in industry	2.412	
Desire for business	2.256	
Management and organization.	2.216	
Operating controls	2.211	
Repair service	2.187	Average importance
Attitude	2.120	
Impression.	2.054	
Packaging ability	2.009	
Labor relations record	2.003	
Geographical location	1.872	
Amount of past business	1.597	
Training aids.	1.537	
Reciprocal arrangements.	0.610	Slight importance

Source: G. W. Dickson, "An Analysis of Vendor Selection Systems and Decisions," *Journal of Purchasing,* vol. 2, no. 1 (February 1966), p. 11.

Figure 6–2
THE MOST IMPORTANT FACTORS BY SITUATION

Importance rank	Case A: paint	Case B: desks	Case C: computer	Case D: art work
1	Quality	Price	Quality	Delivery
2	Warranties	Quality	Technical Capability	Production Capacity
3	Delivery	Delivery	Delivery	Quality
4	Performance History	Warranties	Production Capacity	Performance History
5	Price	Performance History	Performance History	Communication System

Source: G. W. Dickson, "An Analysis of Vendor Selection Systems and Decisions," *Journal of Purchasing,* vol. 2, no. 1 (February 1966), p. 10.

The supplier selection decision may be modeled using a decision tree format as shown in Figure 6–3.

This is, obviously, a very simple, one-stage situation with only two suppliers seriously considered and two possible outcomes. It illustrates,

Figure 6–3
A SIMPLE ONE STAGE SUPPLIER
SELECTION DECISION

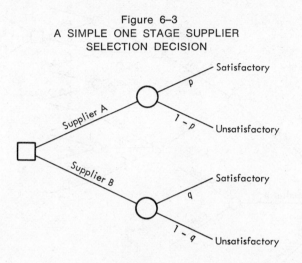

however, the uncertain environment present in almost every supplier choice and the risk inherent in the decision. David Wilson[1] conducted his thesis research on the treatment of this risk factor. He tried to relate personality variables of the purchasing agents to their willingness to take risks and their need to seek additional information. His work and that of a number of others show that the perceived risk of placing substantial business with an untried and unknown supplier is high. A distinction between routine repetitive purchases and less standard acquisitions needs to be made. The risk is seen higher with unknown suppliers as well as unknown materials, parts, or equipment and with increased dollar amounts. Purchasers attempt to share the risk with others by asking for advice, such as engineering judgment, and by seeking additional information which includes the placing of a trial order.

The more normal situation is shown in Figure 6–4 where a continuing need for the product or service exists. Whether the chosen source performs well or not, the future decision on which supplier to deal with next time around may well affect the present decision. For example, if we place the business with supplier C and C fails, then this may mean that only A could be considered a reasonable source at the next stage. If we don't like the idea of being tied to supplier A by necessity, without alternatives, we may not choose C as the supplier at the first stage.

[1] D. T. Wilson, An Exploratory Study of the Effects of Personality and Problem Elements upon Purchasing Agent Decision Styles, Unpublished doctoral thesis, London, Ontario, Canada, The University of Western Ontario, 1970.

Figure 6–4

SIMPLIFIED THREE STAGE DECISION TREE FOR SUPPLIER SELECTION

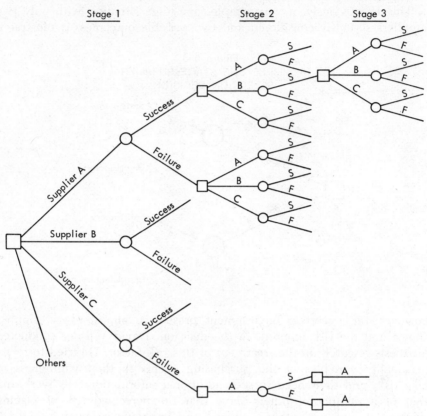

Necessity for supplier goodwill

It has long been considered sound marketing policy to develop good-will on the part of customers toward the seller. This goodwill has been cultivated through the development of trademarks and brands, through extensive advertising, through missionary efforts as well as through regular calls by salesmen, and through the many other devices which have appealed to the imaginations of marketing managers. Sellers are jealous of this goodwill, considering it very properly as one of their major assets. It has real commercial value and is so recognized by courts of law. Goodwill between a company and its suppliers needs to be just as assiduously cultivated and just as jealously guarded. When purchasing directors and the management behind such directors are as aggressive in their attempts to maintain proper and friendly relations with suppliers as sales managers are in their relations with customers, many a costly error will be avoided. Failure to maintain these relations is often more serious than is sometimes believed. Concerns have even been forced to engage in the manufacture of their own supplies because of an unwise attitude toward former sources of supply. Since corporate strategic plans are so often based on the assumption that supply sources will be cooperative, it makes sense to assure that such cooperation will be forthcoming.

No matter how carefully a purchasing, using, or production department may plan, it is inevitable that emergencies will arise and that actual needs will be different from anticipated requirements.

The shortages of many basic materials in recent years had the most serious effects on companies which had ignored developing good vendor relations during past periods of a buyers' market.

The purchasing manual from a very large corporation states: "The Purchasing Department has more contacts with other companies than any other department except sales. An opinion of a company is formed by contacts with its employees. The buyer has it in his hands to enhance or detract from the Company's good name in his relations with vendors and their salesmen and has a major responsibility to form a good reputation for the Company and for the goodwill it commands." Another manual states: "Friendship can be cultivated even through the very manner in which a salesman is told that he has lost, or cannot have, an order. These may seem small things, but courtesy, square dealing, honesty, and straightforwardness beget friendship. They are appreciated by sellers, and the buyer benefits largely from them."

Qualifications of a good supplier

The selection of a supplier will in no small measure be influenced by the purchaser's conception of what a good supplier is. On this point, there should be little serious disagreement. What, then, is a good supplier?

A good or preferred supplier should be one which does the following for its customers. It provides the quality specified and deliver on time as promised; has an acceptable price; reacts to unforeseen needs such as suddenly accelerated or decelerated volumes of business, changes in specifications, service problems, and any other legitimate requests. The good supplier takes the initiative in suggesting better ways of serving customers and attempts to find new ways of developing products and services which will allow customers to perform its operations more economically. The good supplier will warn ahead of time of material shortages, strikes, and anything else that may affect their operations. It will provide technological and other expertise when requested by customers. It will remain competitive on a continuing basis. Suppliers like this are extremely hard to find. In many industries there may only be one, two, or three that fit this bill. The art of a good purchasing department is to find and keep top suppliers over time. Many of the qualities listed in the above mentioned requirements create additional cost for the supplier in the short run. To make it worthwhile for the supplier to incur these costs, he must have the assurance that special care will be rewarded with additional future business. The greatest reward a customer can give is assurance of future business in response to satisfactory performance. It is important to avoid a very high and rapid supplier turnover. Occasionally, preferred suppliers have been given the axe on the basis of incomplete information. The reaction of a supplier is understandable if he loses the next order after he has gone to great lengths to please a customer's special demands in terms of over-time, quick delivery, unusual quality and special preference because someone else bids a few hundred dollars below him. Every supplier switch costs the customer something. Quality assurance needs to inspect the new premises, new contacts need to be established with supplier personnel, and new data inputs are required for the various computer systems. A supplier switch may well have substantial costs attached, depending on the commodity and supplier. If a supplier does not have the expectation of getting a contract renewal it may well choose not to make long-term raw material commitments so necessary to the continued running of the business. If purchasing is late in terms of contract renewal, even continuing with the same source may result in a period of stock-outs. Althought uncertainty regarding future business is certainly one of purchasing's powerful tools to keep suppliers on their toes, it does have its drawbacks. Should some of the current predictions regarding shortages of basic raw materials hold up, some customers may well be in a very difficult position when suppliers establish priorities of customers on vital requirements.

Suppose that the above premise is granted. The real danger clearly lies in becoming puppets of suppliers. They know that the customer depends on them, and they will charge excessively. This is where very careful supplier management becomes important. In the first place it requires an understanding and identification of value. Value is the ultimate long-term cost to the user of the product or service acquired. It does not mean lowest purchase price, or lowest investment in inventory, or fastest delivery time, or lowest delivery cost, or longest life, or highest disposal value, or even the highest attainable quality; it is an optimal amount cutting across all of these. The purchase price frequently is one very important part of this total. It is the duty of the purchasing department to make sure that the price quoted is reasonable in view of the total set of circumstances surrounding the purchase of the particular product. If the purchasing department cannot put a cost on the various services provided by the supplier and has no idea what the cost of the product or service should be the only alternative left is to ask for quotations and pick the lowest bid. This can be done by computer as well as by people. Fortunately, a variety of tools are available to assist in this procedure. Cost analysis, value analysis, competitive quoting, and a host of other means are available to assess value and to assist in keeping existing suppliers competitive pricewise. Furthermore, information is required on the actual performance of the supplier. Is his quality acceptable? Does he deliver on time? Does he bring in suggestions for changes and improvements? Do the quantities delivered conform with those requested? Without such information supplier management is impossible. Action needs to be taken immediately in response to feedback. Frequently, the marketing people of the supplier do not know what is going on with individual customers. Letting them know quickly that problems exist can solve many future headaches. This requires a good supplier performance record. Subsequently, at quotation time purchasing can make a good case for one supplier versus another, and it is illogical to let price have an unusually large bearing. In all fairness in some markets the segments do exist where the lowest bidder can be given the business in the expectation that he will perform satisfactorily. The problem is that even here the market segment may change, conditions may vary, and what is satisfactory one year may not be satisfactory at a future time.

Good sources of supply are one assurance of good quality production today, and their progressive thinking and planning is a further assurance of improved quality tomorrow. Good sources of supply, therefore, are an important company asset that no one individual, no emergency of the moment, no opportunity of the moment should be allowed to jeopardize. As a means of carrying out this policy, one company's bulletin states that it intends:

. . . to give full management support and authority to our Director of Purchasing so that he may carry out to the fullest degree the purpose and spirit of our source relationship policy and to maintain a *Source Relationship Committee* consisting of Director of Purchasing, Director of Research, Treasurer, Vice President in charge of Marketing, Vice President in charge of Production, Vice President in charge of Paper Mill Operation, and the President. It will be the responsibility of this committee to periodically review our source relationships with the continuing aim to improve present relationships, review any deficiencies, and recommend corrective action. Occasional reports on our source relationships will be made to the Board of Directors.

In a similar effort to strengthen its source relationships, Pillsbury Company, of Minneapolis, engaged an outside consultant to interview the company's suppliers to learn what the vendors thought of the company's purchasing policies and procedures and what complaints the suppliers had either of the Pillsbury Company or of its buying habits. The interviews covered salesmen who had personal contact with the company's purchasing agents and also the top management of the supplier companies. It was hoped that the results would show a mass-attitude answer to the question of how Pillsbury stood with its suppliers and provide a guide to its future purchasing policies and to the building of good supplier relationships.

Supplier evaluation—existing and potential sources

The evaluation of suppliers is a continuing purchasing task. Current suppliers have to be monitored to see if expected performance materializes. New sources need to be screened to see if their potential warrants serious future consideration. Since most organizations tend to place a significant portion of repetitive business with the same suppliers, evaluation of current sources will be discussed first.

Vendor rating and evaluation

Some procurement executives have attempted to establish formal vendor rating procedures as an aid in selecting suppliers. Inasmuch as price can usually be determined objectively if a way can be found to measure quality, delivery, and service, the attempt at rating is usually confined to these three factors.

One method which has been found effective in rating quality is to make a monthly tabulation of the invoices from each supplier and the value of the supplier's materials which were rejected during the month. This latter figure is then divided by the value of the materials shipped, and the resulting percentage indicates the rate of rejection.

Comparison of rejection rates among competing suppliers or against an average of the rejection rates shows those suppliers who are providing the proper quality.

Delivery and service can be rated by having whoever does the expediting keep a continuing tabulation for each supplier covering the following points:

Top rating:	a.	Meets delivery dates without expediting.
	b.	Requested delivery dates are usually accepted.
Good:	c.	Usually meets shipping dates without substantial follow-up.
	d.	Often is able to accept requested delivery dates.
Fair:	e.	Shipments sometimes late, substantial amount of follow-up required.
Unsatisfactory:	f.	Shipments usually late, delivery promises seldom met, constant expediting required.

In addition to the above tabulation the buyer records an opinion of the technical help the supplier is able to furnish, the willingness to furnish such help, and the general attitude in meeting any situation which may arise.

Point ratings can be applied to any of these factors and are used by a number of computer based systems. G. W. Dickson in his study[2] found that over one third of the responding firms in his sample did not retain formal records on actual supplier performance. For those who did, the most common types of information retained were:

Delivery experience	45.8%
Defective material experience	44.6%
Repair service rendered	22.6%
Technical service rendered	20.8%
All service rendered	17.8%
None of the above	35.0%

Some companies have found it advisable to inform the chief executives of the suppliers periodically on how their companies stand on the rating scale. Improved performance on the part of the supplier often results from the knowledge that its rating is lower than some competitors.

Each vendor is rated either by formal or informal methods. Where formal methods can be established at reasonable costs, results probably warrant the expenditure.

Evaluation of potential sources

In evaluating potential sources, the four most common major factors are technical or engineering capability, manufacturing strengths, financial strengths, and management capability.[3] Potential sources need to be examined to determine their suitability as future sources of supply. A list of 23 common evaluation factors has already been discussed in this chapter. (See Figure 6–1.) The quality capability survey was covered in Chapter 4. Price will be discussed separately in later chapters. The use of trial orders has been mentioned as a popular means of testing a supplier's capability, but, popular as this may be, it still begs the question as to whether the trial order should have been placed with a particular source at all. Even though a supplier may complete a trial order successfully, it may not be an acceptable source in the long run. Two prime reasons may be its doubtful financial and management capability.

Financial evaluation

The financial strengths and weaknesses of a supplier obviously affect its capability to respond to the needs of customers. There are often

---

[2] G. W. Dickson, "An Analysis of Vendor Selection Systems and Decisions," *Journal of Purchasing*, vol. 2, no. 1 (February 1966), pp. 5–17.

[3] M. G. Edwards and H. A. Hamilton, Jr. (eds.), "Guide to Purchasing," vol. 1 (New York: National Association of Purchasing Management Inc., 1969).

substantial opportunities for negotiation if the purchaser is fully familiar with the financial status of a supplier. For example, the offer of advance payment or cash discounts will have no appeal to a cash rich source but may be highly attractive to a firm short of working capital. A supplier with substantial inventories may be able to offer supply assurance and a degree of price protection at times of shortages which cannot be matched by others without the materials or the funds to acquire them.

A study at the Bell Helicoper Company showed that purchasing managers ranked financial evaluation third in importance, behind management and manufacturing, but ahead of technical and other considerations. Special factors considered included:[4]

	Importance ranking percentage
Net worth	8.5
Profitability	6.9
Bid rates	12.0
Working capital	10.7
Current ratio	9.0
Net quick assets ratio	6.5
Capitalization	5.8
Equity of business	5.8
Past financial record	9.5
Debt structure	7.7
Ability to finance contracts	17.7

This study was done in conjunction with a supplier classification system.

In reviewing procurement policies, practices, and procedures and the controls and requirements of the different governmental agencies, it was readily apparent that the most-stringent requirements were for suppliers which furnished materials to design criteria. This, then, comprises one classification of suppliers for which the most-stringent evaluation techniques and monitoring policies are required. These will be known as Class I suppliers.

The second most-important items procured are those purchased for production, and not necessarily to a design criterion. Generally speaking, these will be supplier-designed items requiring little or no modification. This group will be known as Class II suppliers.

The third and largest classification is for those suppliers which furnish non-production items, such as MRO materials, supplies, and services. This group will be known as Class III suppliers.

By segregating proposed suppliers into these three classifications, it becomes apparent that the Class I supplier requires the most-thorough evaluation and the greatest amount of control. The purpose of this study, then, was redefined as a concentrated effort to improve the techniques utilized in the evaluation, control, and monitoring of Class I suppliers.

According to A. K. Stewart there is a similarity between credit rating and financial analysis of supplier.

---

[4] H. L. Payne, "Development of a Supplier Evaluation Technique Utilizing Financial Information," *Journal of Purchasing*, vol. 6, no. 4 (November 1970), p. 23.

Combining the implications of the recommendations already made suggests an area where additional research would be of value. The basis for a vendor rating should be an evaluation of his technical, financial, production, and managerial ability. The credit rating makes an evaluation of financial and managerial ability. If technical and production ability are mainly dependent on the ability of the managers, the evaluation of financial and managerial ability, made for credit rating, would provide a very accurate estimate of the company as a supplier. If actual performance data on suppliers could be gathered from purchasing agents and if the credit rating of the supplier could be obtained from a credit reporting service (such as Dun and Bradstreet), a correlation analysis could be made. Such an analysis would show the reliability of the credit rating as an indicator of vendor performance. If reliability could be established, it would save many man-hours now spent in vendor surveys.[5]

Management evaluation

There is general agreement among purchasing executives that a supplier's management capability is a vital factor in source evaluation and selection. According to M. G. Edwards there is also general agreement that supplier management is considered most significant in high-risk, large dollar volume, and long-term situations. Few formal management evaluation systems exist and considerable work still needs to be done in this area. Three normal sources of information are: personal visits, financial reports, and credit reports. An interesting formal program is one initiated by the Boeing Company named the "Supplier Performance Evaluation and Rating System (SPEAR)."[6]

A brief description of this plan by their director of material follows:

On major subcontracts we appoint a Source Selection Board which establishes the criteria and subcriteria which will be used in the evaluation, and determines the weight factors for the major elements of consideration.

The supplier is requested to submit as part of his proposal a management plan covering: plan of management, organization of management, corporation structure and relationship, plan of assignment of personnel, and management controls. In addition to the proposal, a source selection survey is conducted which, among other things, evaluates the effectiveness of the supplier's management. As a result of discussions with supplier's management, the Boeing team completes a summary in which they are required to:

1. Discuss the company organization and staffing structures for the potential contract.
2. Evaluate planning and program control for the project, including its integration with present work.

---

[5] A. K. Stewart, "Vendor Rating and Credit Rating: A Comparison and Analysis," *Journal of Purchasing*, vol. 4, no. 3 (August 1968), p. 69.

[6] M. G. Edwards, "Supplier Management Evaluation," *Journal of Purchasing*, vol. 3, no. 1 (February 1967), pp. 28–41.

3. Generally evaluate management, particularly the personnel to be assigned to the project, with emphasis on approach to and knowledge of the project, past performance, and other aspects pertinent to accomplishment of the contract.

The results of the survey and the team summaries are used during the evaluation process.

Also, management is one of the factors evaluated and rated regularly during the life of purchase orders of $25,000 or more. Each six months, and at the time of order completion, the buyer rates the supplier's management performance as excellent, good, fair, poor, or not acceptable.

The total SPEAR program is quite elaborate, with considerable emphasis placed on management and its ratings. One of the first steps is for the source selection board to establish the criteria to be used in the evaluation. Although this will vary from one procurement to another, the major elements which likely are to be considered are engineering, management, finance, material, manufacturing, quality, and reliability. Each of these six major elements will have appropriate subelements, and under management the five subelements are:

1. Plan of management
2. Organization of management
3. Corporate structure and relationship
4. Plan of assignment of personnel
5. Management controls

A typical management evaluation summary is shown in the accompanying exhibit.

Figure 6–5
TYPICAL MANAGEMENT EVALUATION SUMMARY*

Company	Plan of management 20	Organization of management 30	Corporate structure and relationship 10	Plan of assignment of personnel 10	Management controls 30	Total 100
A	19	27	9	9	28	92
B	20	30	10	9	28	97
C	18	28	7	10	20	83
D	17	24	10	10	18	79
E	18	23	10	8	19	78
F	19	22	10	7	18	76

* In this particular supplier evaluation example, of the six elements included in the total evaluation, management was assigned a weight of 100 out of a total of 500 points.

Although this has been a rather brief explanation of the Boeing SPEAR system, it seems clear that its main points are:

1. A systematic check list of factors to be considered regarding each procurement and each supplier.
2. Flexibility to provide weights for each factor in accordance with its importance as decided by the source selection board.[7]

Performance information is fed into a data processing system and periodic reports are prepared.

Some questions which may be raised with respect to management evaluation follow. Is the purchaser's viewpoint of management the same as a stockholder's or creditor's? Should management attitudes be measured? What weight should management be accorded in relation to other factors? Should the purchaser try to overcome a supplier's management deficiencies? There are no easy answers to these questions, and their resolution will depend to a large extent on the quality of purchasing personnel assigned to this task.

Many examples exist illustrating the need for supplier management strength. Many of these are those normally related to the long-term survival of the company. Small suppliers are frequently dependent on the health, age, and abilities of the owner-manager. Every time this individual steps into an automobile the fate of the company rides along. The attitudes of this individual to certain customers may be very important in supply assurance.

Most long-term and significant supplier-purchaser relationships are highly dependent on the relationships and communication channels built by the respective managers in each organization. Unless each side is willing and able to listen and react to information supplied by the other side, problems are not likely to be resolved to mutual satisfaction.

Satisfaction and stability in purchaser—supplier relationships

Certainly one of the major assessments a purchaser must make is whether the current relationship with a supplier is a satisfactory one or not. This relationship is highly complex and different people inside the purchasing organization may have different perceptions of it. In the simplest form, with a new supplier just after a relatively small order has been placed but no deliveries have yet been made, it may consist only of an assessment of the agreement just reached and the buyer's quick impression of the sales representative. For a long-term supplier of major needs the assessment will be based on past and current performance, personal relationships with a number of personnel in both organizations, and even future expectations. Such assessments may well change as a result of competitive action in the marketplace. What may look like a good price deal today may not look so attractive when information comes to light that a fully competent competitor could have supplied the same materials or items for substantially less.

---

[7] Ibid., pp. 34–35.

Figure 6–6
A SIMPLE PURCHASER–SUPPLIER SATISFACTION MODEL

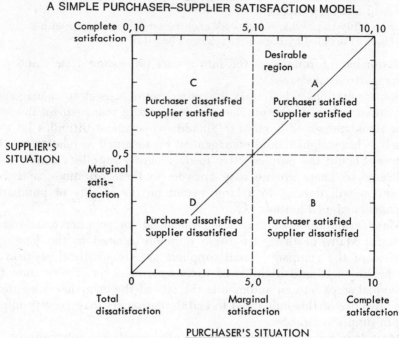

PURCHASER'S SITUATION

The following model (Figure 6–6) attempts to provide a simple framework for clarifying the current purchaser-supplier relationship in terms of satisfaction and stability. The assumptions behind it are:

1. That satisfaction with a current supplier relationship can be assessed, however crudely, at least in macro-terms, whether it is satisfactory or not.
2. That an unsatisfied party (seller or purchaser or both) will attempt to move to a more satisfactory situation.
3. That attempts to move may affect the stability of the relationship.
4. That attempts to move may fall in the win-lose, as well as the lose-lose, lose-win, and win-win categories.
5. That purchaser and seller may well have different perceptions of the same relationship.
6. That many tools and techniques and approaches exist which will assist either party in moving positions and improving stability.

A. The upper right hand quadrant. (5,5–10,5–10,10–5,10) Region. Considerable satisfaction exists on both sides and stability is likely. Long-term relationships may be built on this kind of foundation. Considerable room for improvement is still possible within this quadrant in moving from a (5,5) situation toward a (10,10) objective.

B. The lower right hand quadrant. (5,0–10,0–10,5–5,5) Region. In this region the buyer is at least marginally satisfied, but the seller is not. This is the mirror image of the *C* region, and the seller is likely to initiate action for change which may end up subsequently in any of the four regions. Stability is not likely over the long run.

The above comments are, of course, general in nature. It is entirely possible for a powerful purchaser or a powerful supplier to maintain a *B* or *C* region position respectively for a long time with a weak counterpart.

C. The upper left hand quadrant. (0,5–5,5–5,10–0,10) Region. The supplier is at least marginally satisfied, but the purchaser is not. The purchaser will attempt to improve the buying situation. If this is done at the expense of the seller, a see-saw may be created whereby the purchaser's efforts result in the supplier's moving down the satisfaction scale into the *D* region. The assumption is that the most dissatisfied party is the most likely instigator of change. It is also possible that such instigations may reduce satisfaction for both parties so that both end up in the *D* region. Hopefully, changes might result in both parties moving into the *A* region.

D. The lower left hand quadrant. (0,0–0,5–5,5–5,0) Region. Both parties agree that significant dissatisfaction exists on both sides. This kind of situation is not likely to be stable for any length of time, since each side will be striving to improve at least its own satisfaction.

The diagonal line. The diagonal in the diagram may be seen as a "fairness or stability" line. As long as positions move along this line both purchaser and supplier are at least equally well off. Its end points of (0,0) and (10,10) represent two extremes. The (0,0) position is completely undesirable from either standpoint and is a "total war" picture which is extremely unstable. It represents an unlikely starting point for any long-term stable position since memories of this unhappy state of affairs are likely to prevent substantial improvements. The obvious solution is disassociation and the seeking of a new source by the purchaser.

The (10,10) position represents a utopian view rarely found in reality. It requires a degree of mutual trust and sharing and respect that is very difficult to achieve in our society of "buyer beware" and where competition and the price mechanism are supposed to work freely. Perhaps, as more and more governmental controls are imposed on both purchasers and sellers, the (10,10) state may become more approachable. In some systems contracting situations a relationship close to the (10,10) state has been developed. Buyers are willing to share risks and information with the seller, and the seller is willing to open the books for buyer inspection. Problems are ironed out in an amicable and mutually acceptable manner and both parties benefit from the relationship.

The middle position of (5,5) should really be considered as a minimum acceptable goal for both sides, and few agreements should be reached by the purchaser without achieving at least this place. Adjustments in positions should, hopefully, travel along the diagonal and towards the (10,10) corner. Substantial departures from the diagonal raise the difficulty that the agreement may be seen as less beneficial to one party than the other, with the possibility of jealousy and the attempt by the less satisfied party to bring the other down to a more common denominator. The region of greatest stability will, therefore, lie close to the (5,5)-(10,10) portion of the diagonal line.

Perceptions

This model becomes more complex when the perceptions of both parties are considered, both with respect to their own position as well as the other side's. For example, the purchaser's perception may be that the relationship is in the A region. The supplier's perception may or may not match this view. Let us look at the congruent side first.

Congruent situations

Where both buyer's and supplier's perceptions agree, congruence exist and both parties would record their own and the other side's satisfaction on the same place on the chart. This does not necessarily mean that both parties are satisfied with the situation. Both at least have the same starting point, and mutual agreement on this is useful. For example, take a (8,6) situation, and both buyer and seller agree that the buyer is better satisfied with the current arrangement than the seller. Chances that both will be willing to work towards a corrective solution are reasonable (see Figure 6–7).

Noncongruent perceptions

Lack of congruence in perceptions of relative positions will present a problem in itself. Take, for example, the situation where the buyer's perceptions of the situation is (2,8), but the seller's perception is (9,1). (See Figure 6–7.) The buyer thinks the supplier has a pretty good deal but is quite dissatisfied with the purchaser's situation. The seller's opinion is the exact opposite. So both parties are dissatisfied, but their actions are likely to lead to even further dissatisfaction on the other side. This would normally be a highly unstable situation. It may be possible to settle differences of perception through discussion among the managers involved. Such resolution will be necessary before any attempts can be undertaken to improve the position of either side.

Figure 6–7
PURCHASER—SUPPLIER SATISFACTION MODEL
SHOWING (1) CONGRUENT (2) NONCONGRUENT
PERCEPTIONS

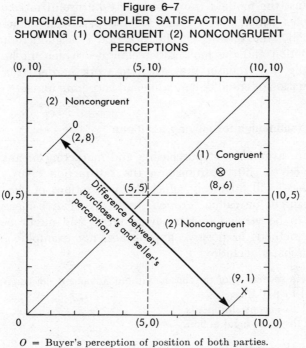

O = Buyer's perception of position of both parties.
X = Seller's perception of position of both parties.

Using the framework

The model is based on the assumption that both purchaser and seller are capable of expressing a view on the degree of satisfaction that exists with a relationship. Essential elements of this relationship would include perceptions on prices paid, service, delivery, and quality performance, and whether the demands and cooperation of the other party are reasonable in view of the circumstances. Personality factors are also a likely component. These measures are, of course, difficult to quantify, but ranking of relative positions compared to other suppliers (or customers) may well be possible. For example, Boeing's SPEAR system attempts to quantify the management component. Even though absolute quantification is difficult, this model may be useful in a number of ways.

From a purchasing point of view it is possible to assess the total package of current supplier relationships and to determine how many fall inside the desirable region and how many outside. A significant percentage of unsatisfactory or marginal situations will mean a substantial amount of work to restructure current arrangements. The purchasing perception of a relationship may be shared with a supplier to check on congruence and as a starting point for mutual diagnosis and plan for change. Even the process of attempting to assess contracts and suppliers against the model's framework may be useful in establishing the key variables which are relevant for the particular commodity under study. Finally, the severity of the situation is a good indicator of the need for action and the tools and techniques which might be applied. For example, a purchaser may wish to work harder at a (1,5) than a (5,5) situation of equal dollar value and corporate impact.

Tools and techniques for moving positions

There are a number of purchasing and marketing means which may be employed to shift positions on the satisfaction chart. The use of some of these will adversely affect the perceptions of the other party, and these might be called "crunch" tools or negative measures. Others are likely to be viewed in less severe terms and might be considered "stroking" methods or positive approaches. For example "crunch" tools for the purchaser include:

1. Complete severance of purchases without advanced notice.
2. Refusal to pay bills.
3. Refusal to accept shipments.
4. Use or threat of legal action.

For the supplier examples would include:

1. Refusal to send shipments as promised.
2. Unilateral substantial price increase without notice.
3. Insistence on unreasonable length of contract, take or pay commitments, escalation clauses, or other terms and conditions and use of take it or leave it propositions.

"Stroking" techniques by the purchaser would include:

1. Granting of substantial volumes of business or long-run commitments of 100 percent requirement contracts.
2. Sharing of internal information on forecasts, problems, and opportunities to invite a mutual search of alternatives.
3. Evidence of willingness and ability to work towards changed behavior in the purchasing organization to improve the seller's position.
4. Rapid positive response to requests from suppliers for discussions and adjustments in price, quality, delivery, and service.

On the marketing side examples could be:

1. Willingness and ability to make rapid price, delivery, and quality adjustments in response to purchasing requests without a major hassle.
2. Invitation to the purchaser to discuss mutual problems and opportunities.
3. The giving of notice substantially in advance of pending changes in price, lead times, and availability to allow the purchaser maximum time to plan ahead.

It is interesting that "stroking" techniques are more likely to be used in the A region, further strengthening the stability of the relationship, whereas the use of "crunch" tools may well accomplish short-term objectives but may impair future chances of a desirable stable relationship.

The perception of a relationship is based on both the results obtained as well as the process by which they have been achieved. For example, a price concession extremely grudgingly granted by a supplier and continually negatively referred to by supplier's personnel may create less satisfaction for the purchaser than one more amicably reached. "Crunch" methods pleasantly applied may be far more palatable than the same tool used in a hard-nosed way. For example, an unavoidable price increase can be explained in person by a supplier's sales manager well in advance more palatably than by circular letter after the increase has been put into effect. A purchasing manager can visit a supplier's plant to determine ways and means of solving a quality problem and explain that no deliveries can be accepted until the problem is solved, instead of sending back shipment after shipment as unacceptable. The results process combination puts a heavy emphasis on managerial judgment and capability to accomplish change effectively.

Supplier development[8]

Supplier selection is an important procurement task Supplier development implies a degree of executive involvement not normally encountered in supplier selection. For example, it frequently places a purchasing manager in a position where a prospective supplier must be persuaded to accept an order.

The need for supplier development

That purchasing executives need to find new sources of supply and to develop such sources when there are none available is a topic that has been discussed for many years. The classical point of view about this need for supplier development has been well expressed by S. F. Heinritz and J. Farrell in *Purchasing*. They state:

Products or parts that have not previously been made, intricacies of special design, unusual requirements in the specification or difficult conditions and use, and the utilization of unfamiliar materials for which there is little precedent in treatment and fabrication are some of the factors that may lead to a situation for which no established supply source stands ready to hand. Or from the standpoint of practical procurement, the only available sources may be too distant, prices may be exorbitant or out of line with budgeted costs for the product, production capacity may already be fully occupied

---

[8] M. R. Leenders, *Improving Purchasing Effectiveness through Supplier Development* (Boston, Harvard University, 1965).

so that no new customers may be accommodated, or the potential suppliers may simply be unwilling or uninterested in additional business.

Under any of these circumstances, the buyer's responsibility is not to select, but to create a satisfactory source.[9]

This point of view may be summarized as stating that the development of new sources of supply may be forced on the purchaser by circumstances beyond direct control. The purchaser does not initiate supplier development as an appropriate technique or tool; it is the only alternative other than making the part himself.

Our definition of supplier development takes a broader point of view. It defines the need for developing new suppliers as follows: the purchaser is aware that benefits will accrue to both the supplier and the purchaser, benefits of which the supplier may not be aware. These benefits may be limited to the particular order at hand, or they may include more far-reaching results, such as technical, financial, and management assistance; future business from the same purchaser as well as from others; training through learning about new manufacturing processes, skills, or quality levels; reduction of marketing effort; use of long-term forecasts permitting smoother manufacturing levels and a minimum of inventory; and so on.

It is true that this wider view includes all the factors for supplier development advanced by Heinritz and Farrell. In contrast with the view that this is the last resort of the purchasing executive, however, the broader definition allows for opportunities inherent in the method itself to give it greater scope.

It is the aggressiveness and initiative by the purchaser that makes the difference (see Figure 6–8). In the normal market context the pur-

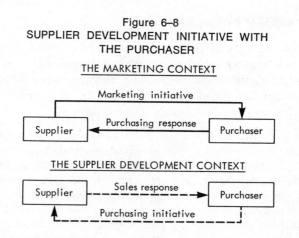

Figure 6–8
SUPPLIER DEVELOPMENT INITIATIVE WITH
THE PURCHASER

THE MARKETING CONTEXT

Marketing initiative

Supplier ← Purchasing response ← Purchaser

THE SUPPLIER DEVELOPMENT CONTEXT

Supplier - - - Sales response - - → Purchaser

Purchasing initiative

[9] S. F. Heinritz and P. J. Farrell, *Purchasing*, 5th ed. (Englewood Cliffs, N.J.: Prentice-Hall Inc., 1971), p. 236.

chaser responds to marketing efforts. In supplier development, the purchaser, not the marketer, has the initiative and may quote prices, terms, and conditions as part of the aggressive role. Numerous examples show that high pay-offs are possible from this purchasing initiative and that suppliers of all sizes may be approached in this fashion.

A further reason for supplier development not advanced by Heinritz and Farrell is that there are bound to be deficiencies in the normal industrial marketing-purchasing process in which the marketer traditionally takes the initiative. Numerous examples of such deficiencies exist. Even when a supplier and a purchaser have entered into a regular vendor-vendee relationship, often neither party is fully aware of all the opportunities for additional business which may exist between them. This might arise because of salesman and buyer specialization, a lack of aggressiveness by the salesman, or a lack of inquisitiveness by the purchaser.

If gaps are evident even where an established vendor-vendee relationship exists, there must be even greater shortcomings where no such relationship has yet been established. For example, a company may be unable to cover its full market because of geography, limited advertising, or lack of coverage by its sales force, distributors, or agents. Most companies have lines of products which receive more management attention and sales push than other products also made by the same company. It is always difficult to keep entirely up to date. A time lag may exist between the time of product introduction and the time the purchaser finds out about it. By filling these gaps through his own initiative, the purchaser effectively strengthens this whole process.

One of the most important arguments in favor of supplier development not yet mentioned arises from future considerations. If the procurement role is envisaged as encompassing not only the need to fill current requirements but also the need to prepare for the future, supplier development can be valuable in assuring future sources of supply.

There are at least two outside forces which would suggest the increasing necessity for purchaser involvement in the creation of future sources of supply. One of these forces is technological. The increasing rate of development of new products, materials, and processes through research will tend to make the industrial marketing task even more complex and more open to shortcomings. In addition to this, the stepping up of international trade will tend to widen supplier horizons and may create a need for purchaser aggressiveness in the development of foreign sources of supply. One of the most demanding and important tasks of management of a subsidiary in an underdeveloped country is the problem of supplier development.[10]

---

[10] C. W. Skinner, *Production Management of U.S. Manufacturing Subsidiaries in Turkey.* Published doctoral dissertation, Harvard Business School, 1961.

The supplier development decision

The nature of supplier development is such by definition that the responsibility for the decision of whether to engage in this development rests with the appropriate executives of the vendee company. This decision should be made on the basis of conscious analysis. Actual field research indicated, however, that this decision is seldom consciously made by the buyer. Apparently most source development decisions are still the result of a negative rather than a positive approach. "It is the only alternative left open to us" seems to be the general attitude. Recent market shortages, however, have reawakened purchasing's interest in aggressive acquisition.

Ideally, the choice of whether or not to engage in supplier development should be based on a sound analysis of the alternatives available. Were this the case, it would seem that far more frequent use of supplier development could be made. The examples near the end of this study show the successful use of supplier development by several purchasing executives in other than "avenue of last resort" situations. The analysis of the alternatives should be made on a basis similar to an investment or a make-or-buy decision. The problem is to select the alternative giving the best return for the investment in time, money, and effort involved.

When viewed in this way the supplier development decision involves the evaluation of many opportunity costs. The effort expended in developing one new source might have been used to develop another source, to encourage manufacture in the purchaser's own plant, or to sharpen internal control within the purchasing department. The decision not to engage in supplier development, so often made without full appreciation of its possibilities, presumes that another alternative will be in the end bring better over-all results.

Sources of information about suppliers

Having in mind the characteristics of a supplier, the next step is to ascertain the available sources. Knowledge of sources is a primary qualification for any efficient purchasing director. Some purchasing officials rely solely upon their experience and memory for their knowledge of sources. Perhaps in a very limited number of instances this practice may be satisfactory; when the requirements are exceedingly simple, obtainable from a strictly limited number of sources, or not large in any event, it may not be worthwhile to maintain any very elaborate record of sources of supply. These cases, however, are so few as to be almost negligible; in fact, one may say that even under the circumstances described, a record of actual and potential sources is a necessity for the efficient operation of the purchasing office.

In addition to mere memory, what are the sources from which the purchasing officer can secure information as to potential suppliers? The principal sources consist of catalogs (both printed and microfilm), trade journals, advertisements of various sorts, vendor and commodity directories, salesmen's interviews, and the purchasing department's own records.

We are not concerned with the question of which of these various sources is most important. In some instances salesmen's contacts are thoroughly satisfactory if supported by a record of relationships with vendors in the past. In some instances catalogs are extremely useful, as, for example, in the case of the purchase of many types of general supplies. In other instances a catalog is practically useless, as, for example, in the purchase of a commercial or transport airplane.

Catalogs.   Catalogs of the commonly known sources of supply, covering the most important materials in which a company is interested, are properly considered essential in any well-managed purchasing office. The value of such catalogs depends largely on the form in which they are presented (a matter for the most part beyond the control of the purchasing officer), the readiness with which the material contained in them is available, and the use which is made of such information. Although some vendors' catalogs are of little use to the industrial buyer, speaking broadly, most of them are of real value as one source of information on suppliers. The majority of the purchasing officers utilize them for that purpose with considerable frequency, and all resort to them occasionally for a number of reasons. Jobbers' catalogs contain a great many items from a variety of manufacturing sources and offer, to a certain extent, a directory of available commodities within the jobbers' fields. Equipment and machinery catalogs are an important source of information as to the specifications of, and the location of a source of supply for, replacement parts as well as new equipment.

Catalogs are a necessary part of the purchasing agent's library of price information; indeed, many supplies and materials are sold from standard list prices, and quotations are made by quoting discounts only. Catalogs also are important reference books for information called for by department heads and engineers.

The availability of the material in the catalogs is largely a matter of the manner in which they are indexed and filed. The indexing and filing of catalogs is not so simple a matter as it may appear to the casual observer. Catalogs are issued in all sorts of sizes and in binders which make them difficult to handle. Even when problems of filing have been met, the indexing of such catalogs is by no means an easy task.

In some cases all catalogs, regardless of size, thickness, or specification are filed together. In other cases catalogs are grouped and filed in comparable sizes, as nearly as may be. The identification of individual catalogs is commonly achieved by numbering them consecutively, frequently with the number pasted on the back of the catalog. A number of influential associations have endorsed a standard size of 7¾ × 10⅝, among them the National Association of Purchasing Management, American Society of Mechanical Engineers, Southern Supply and Machinery Dealers Association, and Automotive Jobbers Association. There is no doubt that the general use of a standard size would be of value in simplifying the filing problem.

Proper indexing of catalogs is essential. Some firms use loose-leaf ledgers with sheets especially printed for catalog filing; others use a form of card index. The information should be indexed both according to the names of the suppliers and according to the various products and items listed in the catalog. It should be specific, definite, and easily understandable. It should avoid generalities and broad statements. When possible, records of performance are desirable. Many companies undertake to invite a more frequent reference to their catalogs by including general trade or product information frequently called for by any purchaser or manufacturer. A catalog of the proper sort has the advantage of being a permanent record, always in the office of the buyer. Salesmen are not always present; advertisements are frequently forgotten; but the catalog is an ever-present reminder of the existence of the vendor issuing it and a source to which the purchaser should be able to go on many occasions.

Microfilm files.   Several companies have issued catalogs of suppliers with all information recorded on microfilm. An example of this service is that provided by VSMF (Visual Search Microfilm File). Information about more than 3,100 suppliers and their products serving the aerospace and electronics industries has been recorded on over 100,000 frames of 16 mm. microfilm. A comprehensive indexing system, a reader for the films, and a printer which permits a full-size sheet reproduction of the information on the film are included in the service.

Trade journals.   Trade journals also are a valuable source of information as to potential suppliers. The list of such publications is, of course, very long, and the individual items in it vary tremendously in value. Yet, in every field there are worthwhile trade magazines, and buyers read extensively those dealing with their own industry and with those industries to which they sell and from which they buy. These various trade journals are utilized in two ways. The first use is made through a study of the text of the magazine, which not only adds to buyer's general information but suggests new products, substitute materials, and the like. The trade gossip provides information as to suppliers and their personnel. The second use made has to do with advertising. While it is true that many suppliers spend a great deal of money for advertising in trade journals with no definite value to themselves, yet a consistent perusal of the advertisements in such publications is a worthwhile habit cultivated by all keen buyers.

Industrial advertising. As a general source of information to the purchasing officer, the exact value of industrial advertising is a matter of dispute. Advertising men generally, even professional teachers of the subject, are very definite in their opinion that in spite of many weaknesses, industrial advertising has great value; buyers generally read it and, although perhaps unconsciously, are largely influenced by it. In spite of much that has been said in support of this contention, there is some question as to whether such advertising is as good or as useful as is often claimed.

Trade directories. Trade directories are another useful source of information.

Trade registers, or trade directories, are volumes which list leading manufacturers, together with information as to their addresses, number of branches, affiliations, products, and, in some instances, their financial standing or their position in the industry of which they may be a part. Such trade registers also contain listings of the trade names of articles on the market with the names of the manufacturers, and classified lists of materials, supplies, equipment, and other items offered for sale, under each of which is given the name and location of available manufacturing sources of supply.

These registers, then, are so arranged that they may be consulted either from an approach by way of the commodity sought to be obtained, or by way of the manufacturer about whose product information is desired, or by way of the trade name or trade-marked description of the item about which information is sought.[11]

Such standard directories as, for example, *Thomas' Register of American Manufacturers* and *MacRae's Blue Book* and the Kompass publications in Europe, not to mention the more specialized directories, serve an extremely useful purpose, and no purchasing officer's library is adequate that does not contain a reasonably complete file of the more standard directories. The Yellow Pages of telephone directories provide lists of local suppliers. Trade directories vary widely, however, as to their accuracy and usefulness, and hence care must be exercised in their use.

Sales representation. Needless to say, sales representation may constitute one of the most valuable sources of information available to the purchasing manager, with references to sources of supply, types of products, and trade information generally. Today an alert purchasing official makes it a point to see as many sales representatives as possible without neglecting other duties. It is essential to develop good supplier relations which begin with a friendly, courteous, sympathetical, and frank attitude toward the vendor salesman. The buyer endeavors not to waste any time. After the visit a record is made of the call, together with such informa-

---

[11] *N.A.P.M. Handbook*, vol. 1, p. 409.

tion as promises to be of future value. Some purchasers make it a point to see personally every sales representative who calls at the office; others, because of lack of time and the pressure of other duties, are unable to follow such a rule, but they do make sure that someone interviews every visitor in order that no one may go away feeling rebuffed. The representative who receives brusque treatment is not likely to make any extra effort to render special services, to offer new ideas readily, or to speak so favorably of the manufacturer as he would if he felt that he had been given fair attention.

Some companies have placed in the hands of their buying personnel worthwhile suggestions concerning the relations between the purchasing office and the vendors' representatives. One such statement may be cited:

In negotiating with vendors and their sales representatives, there are certain points of personal character and ethical conduct that are requisites of a good purchasing agent or buyer. Courtesy, honesty, and fairness each has its place in this activity.

To the Sales Representative:

1. See them without delay. If, however, someone has violated routine rules, call the matter to his or her attention.
2. Let them tell their story and analyze it while listening.
3. Talk business.
4. Answer ethical questions.
5. Be truthful in all statements.
6. In all negotiations cover all elements of purchasing in order that the final understanding may be complete.

To the Vendor:

1. Do not ask any vendor to quote unless you conscientiously expect to consider the supplier at final determination.
2. Keep specifications fair and clear.
3. Keep competition open and fair.
4. Respect the confidence of vendors and sales representatives in all quotations and other confidential information.
5. Do not take improper advantage of sellers' errors.
6. Discourage revision of bids by insisting on best price on first bid. If, however, second bids are accepted, all bidders must have equal opportunity.
7. Cooperate with vendor in solving vendor's difficulties.
8. Negotiate prompt and fair adjustment in handling material below quality.
9. Be courteous in stating rejection of bids with explanations that are reasonable but do not betray confidential information.
10. Answer letters promptly.
11. Handle samples, tests, and reports concerning them with prompt, complete, and truthful information.
12. Submit shipping schedule to vendor and follow up efficiently.
13. Avoid all obligations to seller except strict business obligations.

Were we concerned primarily with industrial marketing instead of industrial buying, a great deal would be said at this point concerning the mistaken attempt on the part of both sales representative and sales managers to bypass the purchasing executive. Such attempts are unfortunate from everyone's point of view. But in this present discussion we are forced to omit an extended analysis of this problem. However, this much must be said. Although the purchasing executive is expected to be well acquainted with the company's operation, equipment, materials, and production and to be qualified to pass on the practicality of suggestions and proposals that may be made by sales representatives and technical people, the purchaser does not, as a rule, have the background that constitutes the basis for the technical person's special knowledge. Therefore, it is often necessary for the purchasing agent to refer such proposals to technical plant people better qualified to handle them. The best way to reach the right technical people in any company is through the purchasing agent. One sales manager said in effect:

It is easy for a sales manager to ask the question, "What does the Technical Service Department do to help me get the business?" The average sales manager would answer the question quickly by giving this definition of technical service: It is the means of selling the customer's technical people without hurting the purchasing agent's feelings. . . . But this is a misconception of the true situation. Centralized purchasing is based on management policies that channel all procurement through the purchasing department. This is indispensable if a company is to reap the full benefit of controlled purchasing. In order that the purchasing agent may function in the best interests of the company and its departments, all transactions must be screened through the purchasing department from their inception. Suppliers find that adherence to this policy best serves their interests. Bypassing the purchasing agent is not a matter of hurting feelings. It is a matter of violating sound rules of procedure and company policies that experience has proved to be of greater value to all concerned—buyer and seller alike.

There are scores of sales representatives, sales engineers, technical experts, and others making "cold" calls who fail to recognize that the head of today's modern purchasing department is fully conversant with the company's production and material requirements and is quite capable of determining whether a new product has potential use in the firm. The purchasing agent is one of a cooperative group within a company, made up of engineering, planning, production, procurement, and sales and is duty-bound to see to it that technical people or sales representatives with products of interest are given a full hearing and referred to technical department heads when necessary and not otherwise.

Vendor files. Information from any source, if of value, should be recorded. One such record has already been mentioned, the index accompanying the catalog file. Another common record is that of the vendor file, which consists of a record, commonly on small cards or simple computer file, classified by the names of the vendors. Such files contain information concerning the address of the vendor, past orders placed with the company, data concerning its general fitness and reliability and the company's willingness to meet the particular requirements of the purchaser, and other pertinent information of any sort that might be of value to the buyer. A third record of importance kept in many companies is a commodity file, in which material is classified on the basis of the product. The information on such cards relates to the sources from which the product has been purchased in the past, perhaps the price paid, the point of shipment, and a cross-reference to the vendor file. Miscellaneous information is also given, such as whether specifications are called for, whether a contract already exists covering the item, whether competitive bids are commonly asked for, and such other data as may be of importance. Accompanying such files as those dealing with sources are, of course, those relating to price and other records. Some of these have already been discussed in earlier chapters, and others will be discussed later. Proper use of DP equipment facilitates the compilation of the above records.

From any or all of these various sources of information, the purchasing officer is able to make up a list of available vendors from whom the items required can be acquired. The next step is to reduce this list to a workable length, retaining only the most likely sources of supply. From the resulting list, usually a comparatively small one, the best source (or sources, if more than one are to be used) must be selected. Obviously, the extent to which the investigation and analysis of sources are carried will depend upon the cost and the importance of the item involved. A large number of items which the purchasing department is called upon to buy are so inexpensive and are consumed in such small quantities as to render any studied investigation clearly unwise.

In reducing the number of potential suppliers to a practical list or in passing upon the desirability of a new supplier (either for a new product or for one already being used), it is obvious that an adequate study must be made of each vendor's qualifications. The points to check have already been listed and will not be repeated. The investigation required may be fairly long drawn out and extensive. It may well require joint inquiry by the purchasing executive, cooperating with representatives of the engineering and production departments.

Personal visits to suppliers' plants. In some instances, a representative of the procurement department may visit the potential supplier in order to, through actual observation, form an opinion as to the supplier's equipment, personnel, and similar matters. Few purchasing managers or buyers follow a practice of making such visits regularly, but the percentage of those who do no visiting whatsoever is equally small. It is good practice to "team visit" with technical and financial experts where a major corporation assessment needs to be made. There are, of course, a number of reasons for plant visits other than merely to check up on a potential supplier. Visits to suppliers already being utilized are sometimes equally worthwhile, perhaps to learn why delivery promises are not being kept, to settle an adjustment that has long been pending, to discuss the terms of an important order or contract with some major executive. Another very important objective is that of getting personally acquainted with the personnel and habitat of a firm with which the purchasing officer is doing business.

In this connection it should be pointed out that some purchasing executives feel that visits to suppliers are particularly useful when there are no difficulties to discuss. By such friendly visits the purchasing officer frequently can talk with higher executives rather than confining himself to someone who happens to be directly responsible for handling a specific complaint. This helps to cement good relations at all levels of management and may reveal much about a supplier's future plans that might not otherwise come to attention. Such a visitation policy does raise certain problems not found in the more routine types of visits, such as who should make the visits, how best to get worthwhile information, and the best use to put the data to, once obtained. Experience has indicated that in order to get the best results from such trips, it is desirable (1) to draw up in advance a general outline of the kinds of information to be sought; (2) to gather all reasonably available information, both general and specific, about the company in advance of the trip; and (3) to prepare a detailed report of the findings, once the visit is completed.

Such visits, if not overdone and provided that the visitor has some real idea of what to look for, are definitely worthwhile. When the visits are carefully planned, the direct expense incurred is small as compared with the returns.

Motion-picture films or video-tapes of suppliers' plants. Profitable use can be made of well-selected motion-picture films as an aid in adding to a buyer's general fund of knowledge about major commodities and sources of supply. One of the reasons for plant visits is to learn more about commodities and manufacturing processes. Visits for such purposes are to be commended. Actual visits, however, have their limitations. They may be expensive or, if not, may be available to but a portion of the procurement staff of a particular company. They are also frequently very fatiguing physically. Much of the process may not be observable because it goes on hidden from the observer's sight. The visitor may not know what should be looked for, or what questions should be asked. Many of these difficulties are overcome with a good film. Cross-sections of machines and diagrammatic presentation of processes, coupled with actual "shots," can tell a most informative story. Needless to say, films by themselves can never tell the whole story—the plant itself must be visited in addition to viewing the film if the very maximum is to be gotten from the study. Of course, too, the film or tape tells little or nothing of the reliability of a vendor or of prices. It is limited by its very nature to a fairly brief presentation. It shows to the observer only what the sponsor wants. However, in spite of these disadvantages, properly used, well-chosen, properly presented films add tremendously to a purchaser's fund of knowledge.

Samples. In addition to the usual inquiries concerning the potential supplier and to a plant visit, samples of the vendor's product can be tested.[12] Some thought may well be devoted, therefore, to the problem of how to handle what may be called the "sample problem." Very frequently a sales representative for a new product urges the buyer to accept a sample for test purposes. This raises questions as to what samples to accept, how to ensure a fair test of those accepted, who should bear the expense of testing (see Figure 6–9), and whether or not the vendor should be given the results of the test.

Figure 6–9
ENGINEERING TEST AND ANALYSIS

Engineering Test and Analysis No. M 14051

Sample: ________ Part No. ________

________ Spec. No. ________

Substitute for: ________

Supplier: ________ Quantity ________

Information: ________

____

Requested by ________ Division ________ Date ________ Report by ________

Checked by ________ Book ________ Page ________ Report Issued ________

Report:

Company practice on all these matters differs widely. The following statements, therefore, are, at best, generalizations. Since buyers are usually on the watch for worthwhile items, they are more likely to accept a sample than to reject it. The acceptance of a sample should imply an obligation to test it, but unfortunately the acceptance of samples without thought to their disposition is widespread. Generally speaking, samples are provided at the vendor's expense, though this rule is by no means universal, some companies refusing to accept any free samples at all. Tests are either laboratory or in use and sometimes both, particu-

[12] For a discussion of the use of samples in connection with quality, see Chapter 4.

larly where a laboratory test is favorable. Careful records of all samples accepted are desirable, especially where tests are conducted on them. Generally speaking, the buyer feels obligated to inform the seller of the results of whatever tests are made and sometimes will permit observation of tests.

Foreign sources of supply

Until comparatively recent times, industrial buyers have sought sources of supply outside of the United States only when the products needed were not readily available domestically. Since the close of World War II, many different events and forces have set in motion developments aimed at expanding world trade. In the efforts to build the economies of Western Europe and Japan after the war's massive destruction, international agreements included provisions for encouraging trade between the free nations. U.S. government leaders played a major role in working for the reduction of tariffs and other commercial restrictions among the countries of the free world.

The introduction of the jet airliner with its ability to cover vast distances in hours rather than days makes it possible for American businessmen to make foreign business trips in a few days rather than a few weeks. American soldiers who had served in foreign countries returned to civilian life and in due course became managers and executives of companies aware of foreign opportunities.

The large expenditures for research and development during wartime established new attitudes toward such expenditures, and consequently sums spent for research continued a steady growth in the postwar period. As a result, American technology gained worldwide attention.

Many American companies became multinational in capitalizing on their technical know-how in foreign markets. Licensing agreements, joint ventures, acquisitions, and mergers led many companies into worldwide operations.

Competitive pressures stimulated many executives of American companies to seek new and lower cost sources of supply in order to protect or increase profit margins. Many foreign manufacturers had modern plants built after the end of the war, and foreign labor rates were substantially lower than American labor rates. American purchasing executives investigating the possibilities of using foreign suppliers found that it was often possible to save 30 percent to 50 percent by buying in foreign markets.

While problems of communication, language, differences in cultural background, and the metric system of measurement create some difficulties, the benefits to be obtained more than compensate for the difficulties—especially as expertise and business friendships are developed.

Large companies with ownership interests in foreign companies have frequently found it desirable to establish a purchasing office in a foreign country. Other companies have worked through the purchasing departments of their foreign subsidiaries.

Small American companies have been able to obtain most of the benefits of buying from foreign sources of supply by using the services of importers, trading companies, or the agents representing foreign manufacturers.

There are a number of significant obstacles and constraints to international trade. The different languages, customs, red tape, long lead times, and transportation modes as well as the uncertainties of the international monetary market are real difficulties for the novice. P. Combs[13] advises a two-step approach. First, use an importer to get started and to answer questions of quality, availability, corporate acceptance, etc. Then, subsequently, deal directly with foreign sources.

Foreign trade zones

Foreign trade zones provide an interesting opportunity for channeling foreign trade.

How foreign-trade zones function

Geographically, a foreign-trade zone is located in a designated area(s) or its port of entry (see Figure 6–10). Each zone differs in character depending upon the functions performed in serving the pattern of trade peculiar to that trading area. The major functions which may be conducted within a zone are:

1. *Transshipment.* Goods may be stored, repackaged, assembled or otherwise manipulated while waiting shipment to another port, without the payment of duty or posting a bond.

2. *Storage.* Part or all of the goods may be stored at a zone indefinitely. This is especially important for goods being held for new import quotas or until demand and price increase.

3. *Manipulation.* Imported goods may be manipulated, or combined with domestic goods, and then either imported or reexported. Duty is paid only on imported merchandise.

4. *Refunding of Duties, Taxes, and Drawbacks.* When imported merchandise that has passed through customs is returned to the zone, the owner immediately may obtain a 99 percent drawback of duties paid.[14] Likewise, when products are transferred from bonded warehouses to foreign-trade zones, the bond is cancelled and all obligations in regard

---

[13] P. H. Combs, *Handbook of International Purchasing* (Boston: Cahners, 1971.)

[14] Under the drawback arrangement, exporters may apply for a refund of 99 percent of the duty paid on imported material used in the manufacture of exported products.

Figure 6-10
HOW FOREIGN-TRADE ZONES WORK

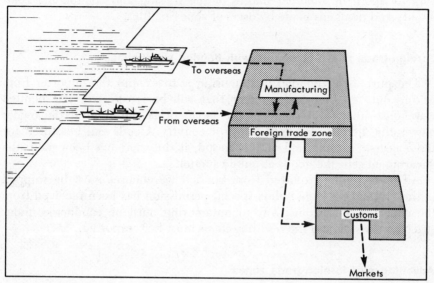

Source: M. B. Neace, "Foreign Trade Zones: Circumventing Barriers to Overseas Sources of Supply," *Journal of Purchasing*, vol. 1, no. 3 (November 1965), pp. 6–9.

to duty payment and time limitations are terminated. Also, exporters of domestic goods subject to internal revenue taxes receive a tax refund as soon as such products move into a foreign-trade zone.

5. *Exhibition and Display.* Users of a zone may exhibit and display their wares to customers without bond or duty payments. They can quote firm prices (since they can determine definite duty and tax rates in advance) and provide immediate delivery. Duty and taxes are applicable only to those goods that enter customs territory.

6. *Manufacturing.* Manufacturing involving foreign goods can be carried on in the zone area. Foreign goods can be mixed with domestic goods and, when imported, duties are payable only on that part of the product consisting of foreign goods. This activity, made possible by the 1950 amendment to the original Celler Act, offers an excellent opportunity for use of foreign-trade zones.

If the purchasing executive has large overseas suppliers or is contemplating importing substantial amounts of dutiable products, savings can be realized on duties or drawbacks, and on the cost of shipping both imported materials to plants in the hinterland and manufactured products back to the same port for export.[15]

---

[15] William A. Dymsza, *Small Business Opportunities in Foreign-Trade Zones and International Business,* Small Business Administration Management Research Summary (Washington: U.S. Government Printing Office, 1964), p. 2.

The functions actually performed in any zone, in the last analysis depend upon the inherent nature of the trading and commercial community and demands made by users of zone facilities.

Foreign-trade zones compared with bonded warehouses

The purpose of bonded warehousing is to exempt the importer from paying duty on foreign commerce that will be reexported. The bonded warehouse allows for delay of the payment of duties until the owner moves the merchandise into the host country. Goods can be stored for three years.[16] At the end of the period, if duty has not been paid, the government sells the goods at public auction.

All merchandise exported from bonded warehouses must be shipped in the original package unless special permission has been received from the collector of customs. Any manufacturing must be conducted under strict supervision and the resulting items must be reexported.

Advantages of foreign-trade zones

Although bonded warehouses and foreign-trade zones serve similar purposes, greater freedom is permitted the user of the zones, as illustrated by the following comparisons between them:

1. An importer may lease space in the zone where he can establish his own office and use his own employees. In a bonded warehouse, the proprietor furnishes the labor and charges for handling merchandise, unless the merchandiser also operates the warehouse.

2. A customs entry or bond is not required for merchandise entering the zone. In a bonded warehouse, the proprietor must furnish a bond and each warehouse entry must be covered by a single entry or term bond.

3. Merchandise may be stored in the zone for an unlimited time. In a bonded warehouse, the period is for three years, although that time may be extended, upon application for one or more years.

4. In a foreign-trade zone, merchandise may be manufactured and thereafter withdrawn for consumption. Merchandise may be manufactured in a customs bonded manufacturing warehouse but withdrawn only for export.

5. Specific-rate merchandise withdrawn after storage in the zone is subject to duty on the weight at the time of withdrawal. In a bonded warehouse, duty is charged on the landed weight with no allowance for shrinkage, loss, or breakage.

6. When merchandise in the zone is given a foreign privileged status, it is subject to the rate of duty in effect at that time, although the

---

[16] Extensions may be granted upon application.

rate may have been increased by time of withdrawal. In a bonded warehouse, merchandise is subject to duty at the rate in effect at the time of withdrawal for consumption.

7.   Merchandise brought into the zone in packages may be withdrawn therefrom in pieces. A withdrawal from a bonded warehouse may not cover less than one package.

8.   Small quantities of merchandise in a zone may be withdrawn without delay under an informal entry prepared in the zone. If in a bonded warehouse, such merchandise must be covered by a warehouse withdrawal for consumption, which must be passed in the customhouse.

9.   Because he filed no bond, an importer is not responsible under a bond for any losses of merchandise in the zone. Under a warehouse entry the importer is liable for such losses under his bond.

10.   Bond charges may be canceled and drawback paid on imported merchandise which later has been transferred to the zone for future exportation, and it may remain in the zone for an unlimited time period. The merchandise otherwise would have to be laden on the exporting vessel or vehicle within the time limits provided by law.

11.   Merchandise in the zone may be examined by the importer prior to customs entry to determine its condition.

12.   Fumigation facilities are available at most zones. These are not usually available at bonded warehouses.

13.   Any kind of commodity can be handled in a zone and any kind of facility installed which will promote international trade. Subzones may be established adjacent to the area or miles away—whichever best serves the purpose.[17]

In summary, the following are the main advantages of a foreign-trade zone: various operations permitted; low cost services; reduced capital outlay; no sale—no duty; less insurance costs; and no time limit on storage.

Major zones in the U.S.A. are in New York, New Orleans, San Francisco, Seattle, Mayaguez, Puerto Rico, and Toledo.

As of 1974 worldwide inflation the devaluation of the U.S. dollar, greatly increased foreign labor rates, and rapid changes in foreign exchange rates have reduced substantially many of the advantages of buying in worldwide markets.

Sourcing in the multinational company

The multinational company is automatically involved in worldwide procurement through the location of its various subsidiaries. It is practically impossible to supply every subsidiary need through the parent

---

[17] Taken primarily from: *22nd Annual Report of the Foreign-Trade Zones Board*, op.cit., p. 27.

company. A relevant problem, then, becomes what should be purchased where and for whom. That many multinationals still fail to recognize the problems and opportunities of operating in worldwide markets is evident from a number of writers. R. C. Acknoff said:

. . . it is not uncommon for firms to assume, even implicitly, that there will always be enough raw material and other required supplies at an acceptable price. Sometimes this leads to lack of anticipation of major changes in the "supply picture." . . .

In short, a firm should have some understanding of the markets in which it operates as a consumer. Perception of impending changes in these markets and its suppliers' activities can indicate either the need for research and development, acquisition of sources of supply, redesign of old products, or design of new ones."[18]

D. H. Farmer adds:

"That an increasing number of constraints are affecting the scope of action of the multinational company in this area; if they are to be mitigated, careful planning of sourcing decisions will be required.

Governmental intervention

An illustration of the constraints upon multinational companies relates to the increasing intervention of governments in the business patterns of their countries. Transfer of funds and "arms length" pricing are two of the areas where governmental attention has been directed. Now as more governments face up to economic and socio-political pressures, the scope of their search for greater inputs increases.

This is particularly true in the developing countries and soft currency areas where there is competition to attract larger contributions from the multinational companies. In looking for this larger share, an obvious area of considerable significance is the supply market of the multinational company. On the average in a manufacturing company, over 50 percent of the gross money received by the concern is disposed of in purchasing raw materials and components. Clearly, by directing a flow of business of that extent into their own economy a government could make a worthwhile contribution to is gross national product and to the prosperity of its people.

The traditional method of "encouraging" such action was to manipulate tariffs to make importing unattractive. While not abandoning this ploy, many governments now are taking a more positive line; they are soliciting reciprocal business. In effect they are saying to the multinationals, "If you wish to sell a large volume of goods in this country, then you must manufacture here and purchase components or materials from our national sources."

Where suitable sources do not exist, governments appear to be setting out to persuade the international companies to develop local sources. And where that is not feasible, they encourage the current source of supply of major items to set up a factory in the country.

---

[18] Russell L. Ackoff, *A Concept of Corporate Planning* (New York: Wiley-Interscience, 1970), pp. 48–49.

In Eastern Block countries the previous preparedness to exchange things like fresh fruit for manufactured goods is now being superceded by requests to make purchases equal to the sales in the area concerned. One European coordinator of procurement for a multinational company told the writer that once sales equal to 1 million per annum were achieved the pressure for reciprocal business increased.

One author has suggested that "these new efforts (pressures from governments) tend to influence the initiative that the international manufacturer can take to plan and control the availability and the flows of his nonmonetary (as well as financial) resources"[19] Developments since then have heightened these pressures, particularly in certain countries. For example, supplies executives in seven multinational companies recently have reported to this author approaches from the Spanish government regarding their requirements of reciprocal business.[20]

Supply market differences

It is a common marketing concept that marketing approaches be planned to suit the various market segments, while maintaining an integrity with the overall marketing plan. International procurement needs to be approached in much the same way, in full recognition of the differences between various markets, particularly their opportunities and constraints. David Farmer prepared an interesting table listing the constraints under the headings of internal, economic, sociological, market size, political and legal. (See Figure 6-11.)

The opportunities stem from differences in price, availability, and the various cost components of any material or product, as well as different levels of constraint. Theoretically, a multinational company should be in a much better position than a national organization to purchase intelligently on the international market. It is surprising how few multinationals use local contacts as information about local opportunities.

The idea of bringing together those who head purchasing operations in subsidiaries is still relatively new. Even where such corporate conferences have been held, they've often tended to focus on communicating the parent's will rather than the subsidiary's input.

An interesting development arose at one such conference for a multinational company with at least one common raw material used extensively throughout the world. This material was supplied by another large multinational firm at substantially different prices in different world markets. It was agreed to purchase the total corporate requirements in the most favorable market. Clearly, these requirements were far too

---

[19] Robert E. McGarrah, "Logistics for the International Manufacturer," *Harvard Business Review*, vol. 44 (March-April 1966), p. 154.

[20] D. H. Farmer, "Source Decision-Making in the Multi-National Company Environment," *Journal of Purchasing*, vol. 8, no. 1 (February 1972), p. 6.

Figure 6–11
CONSTRAINTS AFFECTING THE MULTINATIONAL
COMPANY SUPPLY MARKET COMPLEX

Internal	*Sociological*	*Political*
Make or buy	Attitudes toward	National defence and
Effectiveness of	authority	military policies
communications and	Attitudes to status of	National foreign policies
interrelationships	delivery/quality	Union strengths
Creativity and general	specifications	Political stability
effectiveness of	Attitudes to work and	Government intervention
procurement staff	wealth	re:
Forecasting and planning	Attitudes toward inter-	Markets (sales &
effectiveness	company cooperation	supply)
Finance	(buyer-seller)	Imports (licenses &
Plant location decision	Religious and ethical	permits)
Nature of product line	beliefs	Location of industry
(e.g., volatile)	*Market Size*	Fund management
Manufacturing strategy	Sales market size and	Reciprocal business
Attitude to risk taking	extent of competition	demands
Economic	Supply market size and	Political/economic
National economic frame-	extent of competition	alliances
work and system	Skills available in supply	*Legal*
Economic stability	market	National legal rules
Organization of capital	Technical	International legal rules
markets	Management	
Social overhead(s)	Support research	
Political/economic		
alliances		

Source: D. H. Farmer, "Source Decision-Making in the Multi-National Company Environment," *Journal of Purchasing*, vol. 8, no. 1 (February 1972), p. 12.

large for that market, so that extensive negotiations were started in both multinationals in an attempt to resolve their differences. Developments like this might well lead to different pricing behavior. David Farmer quotes four interviews with supplier executives showing that increased interest is being shown in the opportunities of international markets by multinationals.

Interview 1:
Until 1965 there was no attempt even to co-ordinate purchases where there was commonality. In one case we discovered, just in time, that we had been bidding against our French associate for a parcel of a certain material which was then in short supply. As a result of this and of a number of similar happenings there was an attempt to set up a European office in 1966. This was closed in 1967 because "its presence was not justified by events." Only in 1971 has the idea been revived and now on a far broader scale.
Interview 2:
Until this year (1971), all our companies throughout the world were independent of our U.S. parent, save for financial control. Now we are organized into three zonal areas: Europe, The Americas, and Asia. In each area there is a purchasing controller among whose functions it is to utilize our purchasing power in that region to the full, while maintaining local flexibility.

Interview 3:

In the late 50s our policy was to buy for our European factories from the U.S. This was changed in 1961 to allow local purchasing, but it was then carried on by each plant in isolation. In 1966 we realized that we were not using our corporate purchasing strength to the full and, in 1968, following a survey, this office [that of the European Procurement Controller] was set up.

Interview 4:

There was no coordination between our U.S. headquarters and the rest of the world on purchasing. As a matter of fact, there was some animosity and distrust about what we were doing in trying to bring some kind of cohesion to the European end. Only in 1970 did the first break appear in the ice and that was when our East European sales started to go well. Only last month (April, 1971) we held our first corporate supplies meeting and we are now at the stage of putting forward draft procedures for collaboration. But we have a long way to go.[21]

Developing countries

In developing countries sourcing problems are particularly difficult. D. H. Farmer lists eleven areas:

1. Lack of local technological back up.
2. License and foreign exchange difficulties.
3. Poor service from indigenous supply sources (e.g., poor delivery schedule performance, quality failure, limited variety, etc.).
4. Political instability or risk, affecting investment (either with respect to the company itself or potential suppliers).
5. Tariffs and host government pressure to buy within the country.
6. Governmental pressures regarding their own purchasing from the company.
7. Necessity for carrying higher inventories.
8. Necessity for intensifying goods inwards inspection activity.
9. "Home" derived specifications not available from local supply markets.
10. Quality inconsistency with certain imported components.
11. Lack of trained local staff, affecting supply department performance. (Even though this could be said to apply to all company staff, it was said in more than one case to affect purchasing in particular.)[22]

Apparently, few companies recognize these difficulties at the project planning stage, and operations of subsidiaries may be severely hampered by this lack of adequate concern.

BIBLIOGRAPHY

ALEXANDER, RALPH S.; CROSS, JAMES, S.; AND HILL, RICHARD M. *Industrial Marketing.* 3d ed. Homewood, Ill.: Richard D. Irwin, Inc., 1967.

[21] D. H. Farmer, ibid., page 8.
[22] D. H. Farmer, ibid., pp. 9–10.

ALJIAN, GEORGE W., ed.   *Purchasing Handbook*. 3d ed. New York: McGraw-Hill Book Co., 1973.

AMMER, DEAN.   "What Do Your Suppliers Think of You?" *Purchasing Magazine*, April 20, 1964.

COMBS, PAUL H.   *Handbook of International Purchasing*. Boston: Cahners Books, 1971.

DAND, RICHARD, AND FARMER, DAVID.   *Purchasing in the Construction Industry*. London: Gower Publishing, 1970.

DICKINSON, ROGER A.   *Buyer Decision Making*. Berkeley, Calif.: Institute of Business and Economic Research, 1967.

LEENDERS, MICHIEL R.   *Improving Purchasing Effectiveness through Supplier Development*. Boston: Division of Research, Graduate School of Business Administration, Harvard University, 1965.

NATIONAL ASSOCIATION OF PURCHASING AGENTS, INC.   "Vendor, Supplier Evaluation," *Guide to Purchasing*. New York, 1967.

CASES FOR CHAPTER 6

ABC METAL WORKS, INC.*

Introduction

In late fall of 1964 Mr. Charles M. Linscott, purchasing agent of the ABC Metal Works, Inc., a fabricator of quality steel products in Baltimore, Maryland, felt the need for a review of his procurement policy for stainless steel, which constituted the largest single item going into the company's manufacturing process. Approximately 45 percent of sales income was spent for materials and services purchased from outside suppliers. Stainless steel accounted for about 12 percent of the total dollar purchasing volume. In 1963, ABC Metal Works, Inc., bought between $500,000 and $550,000 worth of domestic and foreign stainless steel for its production and inventory requirements. Prior to 1959 Mr. Linscott had purchased stainless steel entirely from domestic sources. But to meet vigorous competition and to maintain an adequate profit level, the company searched for lower material costs, and, as a result of this effort, in 1959 to 1960 Mr. Linscott added certain foreign steel mills to his vendor list. Since then, the company's foreign imports of stainless steel were steadily rising and in 1964 accounted for nearly 25 percent of its annual purchases of stainless steel. Since the company's production volume was continuing to expand rapidly and the percentage of imported steel kept going up, Mr. Linscott thought an appraisal of steel procurement was called for. He anticipated he would conclude such appraisal with a report to top management, in which he would either reaffirm his present policy or recommend certain changes with the objective of achieving further material cost reductions. He knew such reductions would be welcomed by management, as new pressures upon the company's level of profits were expected from stiffening competition. The purchasing agent thought he should give particular attention to his buying channels for foreign steel and to finding a balance between domestically and internationally procured steel.

History

• ABC Metal Works, Inc., was organized in the late 1800s in Baltimore, Maryland, to manufacture various iron products used in storage and warehousing for local wholesale and retail merchants. Around 1910 the company began to fabricate metal bins and lockers. Six years later it added a line of fabricated metal products for the construction industry. By 1929, sales reached $600,000 annually, and the company employed close to 100 persons. It was about that time the company began to undertake fabrications in stainless steel. During World War II the skills and knowledge that the company had developed in working with stainless steel became very much in demand for the production of war materials. Employment rose to over 500 workers. The end of the war left the company with considerable overcapacity and no products other than those made prior to the war, for which an extremely competitive market developed. High fixed cost and declining sales forced the company into the red. In 1948, the founder was replaced by a younger president. The company gradually changed from a job shop operation to one making several lines of standardized products. The impact of this change on company organization, as well as on management thinking and action, was felt throughout the organization for the next 12 years. Rather than being mostly concerned with keeping the shop filled with contract work, executives now turned their full attention to such matters as long-range product development, sales programs, procurement, and production plans. ABC Metal Works changed from a production-oriented company to an organization in which the sales function assumed a dominating role.

In 1952, sales were $3.8 million, with net earnings of $22,000 after taxes. By 1958 the sales volume had grown to $5.8 million and net earnings stood at $60,000. In November, 1964, management projected sales for 1964 in excess of $12 million and net earnings in the vicinity of $200,000. The company employed between 300 and 350 people at that time.

Overall organization

Following the decision to develop standardized end products, the company's sales organization, which had been one unit under one sales manager, was reorganized and set up on a divisional basis, each division handling a group of related products. There were four such divisions. (See Exhibit 1 for organization chart.) One production organization, headed by a works manager, served all divisions. Engineering, personnel,

Exhibit 1
FORMAL ORGANIZATION CHART

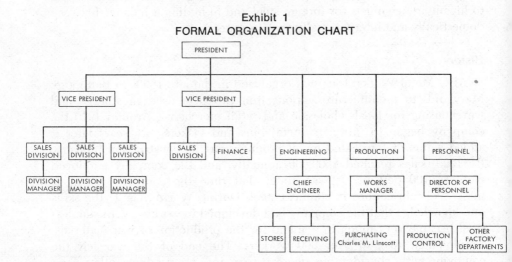

and finance were organized in separate departments, each department head reporting to the president. The purchasing department, along with production control, receiving, and stores, reported to production. The purchasing agent reported formally to the works manager. While a formal organization structure was created, the company was small enough to retain many informal relationships not shown on the organization chart.

Competition

Competition was described by management as extremely strong in some areas and relatively mild in others. Overall profit margins were narrow. ABC Metal Works was one of a few large companies in the fabrication of bins and lockers, and competition was largely confined to quality and service. In other areas, such as industrial and institutional kitchen equipment, the company faced intense competition from large-scale corporations. In still others, such as products from the construction industry, the company had to compete with many small metal fabricators with work forces of less than a dozen people, which frequently offered their products at lower prices. Generally speaking, management did not consider ABC to be a low-cost producer and believed the company's competitive strength was in its reputation for quality and service built up over the years.

Production and production control

The manufacturing skills of ABC Metal Works were concentrated in sheet metal fabrication and production stampings. Typically, the operations performed included stamping, shearing, coping, bending, forming, welding, grinding, and polishing. Such parts as fittings, valves, and all electrical components were purchased from the outside. Production operations were performed in a central multistory plant, divided into 22 "feeder" (pressing, machining, welding, and so forth) and "assembly" departments. The plant was over 50 years old.

Although there was a marked trend toward producing standard parts for inventory, about 40 percent to 50 percent of the company's assembly operations were still completed for firm orders only, resulting in relatively short production runs.

Orders to produce or to order parts were initiated as the on-hand figures on inventory control cards fell to the reorder point. Minimum stock quantities were based on sales forecasts made by all sales divisions at six-month intervals. Once a minimum was established, it was entered on an inventory card and served as the reorder point until it was changed by a new and different sales forecast six months later. Altogether, there were usually some 5,000 parts in stock; half of these parts were produced by the plant and half were purchased from the outside. As reorder points were reached, the production control department issued material requisitions, which were sent to the purchasing department if they were for parts to be purchased or to the factory department if they were for parts to be made. Factory orders also served as operations sheets. They were combined with blueprints and bills of material and sent to the foremen of the production departments involved. The department to perform the first operation used the bill of material as a requisition for raw materials from inventory. When all production operations were completed, the original factory order was returned to production control, which closed the order out. At times, parts went directly from "feeder" to assembly areas without being recorded on inventory by production control, and, occasionally, parts were taken from stock for emergency orders without requisition, practices that disrupted the parts inventory control system.

Expediting of factory orders and requisitions for outside parts was not formalized and was set in motion only in case of actual shortages. Plans, however, were being made by production control to install a more comprehensive inventory control system, except for steel inventories which were handled by the purchasing department. Similarly, production control was in the process of setting up a central production scheduling system, rather than letting each foreman decide within monthly due dates when to work on factory orders. This latter procedure sometimes resulted in shortages of parts needed for assembly and in delayed deliveries.

Purchasing

In 1964, ABC Metal Works purchased raw materials, parts, and supplies in the amount of approximately $5 million to $6 million. The company's vendor list comprised approximately 1,500 firms, but the bulk of purchases was made from about 400 to 500 suppliers. In addition to the purchasing agent the purchasing department was staffed with an assistant purchasing agent and three clerk-typists who also performed purchasing functions. Mr. Linscott, the purchasing agent, had been with the company for 17 years. Prior to the transition from job shop to batch production of standardized end products in 1948, no purchasing department existed as such. The president had been in charge of steel procurement because of the large dollar value involved, and Mr. Linscott had had responsibility for all other purchases. Inventories had been kept at nominal levels as the company bought most of its materials as they were needed.

In the early 1950s, the president relinquished his steel buying activities to Mr. Linscott, who then organized purchasing as a separate and distinct function. According to the formal organization chart, Mr. Linscott reported to the works manager. But, because of the president's experience in steel procurement and the relative importance of steel in the company's profit levels, and also because the president had trained Mr. Linscott, all major matters relative to the purchasing function that needed attention beyond Mr. Linscott's responsibility were handled by the president. Thus, until recently, the relationship between the purchasing agent and the works manager had been confined to such matters as late deliveries and missing purchased parts. The task of the purchasing department was defined by management in the following way: (1) to make company purchases at the best possible price; (2) to get purchased parts delivered in the proper quantity and at the proper time; (3) to review costs continually, and also to review quality and service of vendors to obtain better values for ABC Metal Works; and (4) to supervise payments for purchased materials.

Purchases of materials other than steel were initiated by requisition from production control. Procurement of steel was handled without participation by production control.

Basic to the purchasing of steel were forecasts developed on a six-month basis by three of the sales divisions and on a monthly basis by the fourth sales division, which dealt with metal specialties. The forecasts developed on a monthly basis by the metal specialties division were necessitated by the heavy and sudden fluctuations in demand for that division's products. The forecasts were converted into monthly production schedules and material requirements by the production control department. The six-month forecasts served Mr. Linscott as the most important tool in determining the steel quantities to be purchased, though other considerations such as price trends, breakpoints, and the company's liquidity entered into the picture. In addition to the forecasts, Mr. Linscott made use of the steel inventory cards maintained in the purchasing department. The steel inventory cards gave him a historic view of the company's usage of steel and helped him in combining various sheet sizes within one gauge for economical ordering quantities.

The purchasing agent had authority to determine not only the sources of supply for steel but also the quantities to be bought at a given time, as well as the timing of the orders. All price negotiations were conducted by him. He usually informed the president when large orders were awarded. Because of the vital importance of stainless steel in the manufacturing process, Mr. Linscott spent a good deal more time on the procurement of stainless steel than on carbon steel. Altogether, steel procurement activities absorbed over 60 percent of Mr. Linscott's time. He thought his annual volume of stainless steel purchases was extremely attractive to any mill, whereas the volume of carbon steel purchases was too small to provide him with any bargaining power.

Foreign buying

Beginning in 1958–59, ABC received from a large number of American import brokers offers to sell Japanese-made stainless steel with qualities comparable to American products and at delivered prices up to 30 percent below U.S. prices. The company had had no experience in purchasing from overseas suppliers except for a very brief period during the Korean War, when U.S. mills were unable to meet the company's requirements and the company was forced to take in foreign steel at a premium price.

This lack of experience in buying foreign steel—and the knowledge that the large majority of importers originally offering steel were new firms that had no operating history but had been set up to take advantage of the substantial price differentials between American and Japanese stainless steel—led ABC initially to ignore offers of foreign steel. In addition, management was extremely uncertain whether the quality of the Japanese product would match that of U.S. mills. Inferior quality, it was reasoned, would not only disrupt production schedules and create rejection problems but also jeopardize the company's carefully built image as a quality producer.

In 1959, however, management, to protect the company's profit margins, decided to implement a cost reduction program and to investigate material costs. Attracted by the possibility of cutting costs for stainless steel by up to 30 percent, Mr. Linscott began to study the Japanese situation carefully. He made the following comments:

Generally speaking, the growth of this company, or any company, is dependent not only on sales but also on how well we buy. So our salesmen are able either to sell a better quality or sell at lower prices. In our efforts to reduce material costs, we became extremely sensitive to new supply sources, including foreign vendors.

Because of the total lack of experience in buying directly from overseas suppliers, management decided early in the exploratory stage to deal with U.S. importers only. The company spent considerable time checking out the reputation, the size and type of business, the financial capacity, and related matters of these importers before contacting them. Following extensive investigations, a Baltimore broker who had been in business for over 40 years was selected for concrete negotiations.

As these negotiations progressed, the company heard many rumors that Japanese stainless steel failed to meet chemical specifications by American fabricators and that it was just not good enough for a quality product. "These rumors may have been partly true, particularly because a very large number of foreign mills were shipping, and because of the circulation of rumors by American steel mills," said Mr. Linscott.

He continued:

At any rate, they made us extremely cautious. In addition, we were worried that, even if the chemical specifications were all right, the steel might crack because of shortcomings in the way the Japanese rolled it. This had happened to domestic material some years back. Unfortunately, the folding operations in our plant come after a great deal of labor has been put into a work piece. It is usually the last or next to the last operation. So, on the one hand, we were terribly cautious and had little enthusiasm to buy from Japan, but, on the other, we realized that there was a tremendous saving possible.

In 1959, the company placed its first order for a nominal volume of stainless steel with the Baltimore importer, after having spent considerable time and effort in drawing up a comprehensive purchase contract. The order specified, among other things, that the importer would stand any losses ABC might suffer from faulty steel. Thus, the company eliminated the possibility of having to deal directly with the Japanese mill if quality trouble developed. The purchase contract further specified that payment was to be made on terms of 30 days net, which would give the company sufficient time to put the material through the fabrication process and examine the results.

As the first shipment went into the plant, some difficulty was experienced in the welding and finishing operations. The problem, however, was not considered serious and was remedied in subsequent shipments by communication with the Japanese mill via the importer and by a direct visit of a Japanese mill representative to the plant to clarify specifications. Mr. Linscott noted that, as the first lot went through, some workmen complained that such imports would "defeat American Labor." "This, we had to expect, as some of our people are well schooled by the union," he went on to say. "But most of the employees felt that our company was growing and that the use of the material that was much cheaper than American stainless steel would make their jobs safer and benefit all of us." The purchasing agent also noted that the workers were initially very suspicious of the quality and somewhat hesitant to work with it. As experience established that the quality was equal to what they had been using, these suspicions quickly disappeared. Nevertheless, the company's quality inspection personnel continued to spend considerably more time examining Japanese steel than steel from American mills.

In 1960, ABC was buying about 3 percent of its stainless steel requirements from Japan. Thereafter, the figure jumped to 8 percent in 1961, 12 percent in 1962, 18 percent in 1963, and close to 30 percent for the first 10 months of 1964.

Beginning in 1956–57 domestic prices for stainless steel had started to drift downward. As a typical instance, the representative base price for sheets "AISI No. 304" had declined from 55.50 cents per pound in December, 1957, to 41.75 cents per pound in December, 1963. Mr. Linscott noted, "American prices today are lower than those I paid originally for Japanese steel, and the Japanese prices I am paying today are lower than the Japanese prices I paid four years ago. The Japanese mills have become a very important factor in the domestic price level for stainless steel." (For information on foreign imports of stainless steel, see the Appendix to this case.)

ABC continued to buy directly from the American import house, which, in turn, placed orders with Japanese trading firms in New York representing Japanese steel mills. The prices paid by the company to the importer were for delivery f.o.b. plant. Shipments came directly from the Japanese mills to ABC, but all matters relative to ocean transportation, entry of material into the United States, docking, wharfing, transportation from port of entry to ABC, as well as all dealings with banks, marine insurance agents, customs, and shipping companies, were shifted to the importer.

In the fall of 1964, Mr. Linscott thought that, after almost five years of working experience with Japanese steel and in the face of a still rising volume of imports, a decision needed to be made, first, on whether to start by passing the importer in order to save the brokerage commission, which he estimated to be somewhere between 6 percent and 8 percent on the net price. Mr. Linscott said:

As of now, importers do not carry any inventories but place each order as they receive it. It is my understanding that the importers cannot order directly from the Japanese steel mills but must go through the Japanese trading firms, although I heard from one source recently that you can buy directly from a few Japanese mills. At any rate, I am thinking about eliminating the importer and dealing directly with the Japanese trading companies having offices in New York City. Of course, the savings will have to be weighed against additional handling costs, and also against any risks that we may have to bear. If I decided to go ahead and buy directly from the trading firms, they will have to handle all the technical details up to the point where the steel is docked, and we will merely arrange for the trucking from the dock to the plant. Also, the trading firm will have to guarantee to pay for any losses we might have from defective materials. It is all a matter of dollars and cents and of whether the money I will save from the brokerage commission would be worth the additional work. We are not afraid of taking on the job if it will reduce cost.

During the years the company had been buying Japanese steel, no defective materials were recieved. But, on one occasion, sheets in wrong dimensions were delivered. In this case, ABC bought an equivalent quantity in correct lengths from a U.S. mill, used the Japanese material for another product, and charged the increase in scrap loss, but not the price differential, to the importer. As the question of buying channels was being pondered by the purchasing agent, he received two offers from American importers to supply Japanese steel from their own stock at previous prices plus a warehousing charge of between 1 cent and 2 cents per pound. One of the offers proposed putting steel into the company's warehouse under consignment. Then, too, Mr. Linscott was wondering whether he should also explore if, and to what advantage, he would be able to buy straight from a Japanese mill, thus eliminating not only the importer but also the trading firms.

ABC bought stainless steel in about 30 different sizes and in half a dozen or more different gauges. For the three-month period August–October, 1964, Mr. Linscott placed domestic orders of 285,882 pounds and international orders for 92,311 pounds in close to 100 dimensions, which he considered typical for the company's overall needs. He estimated that, by buying close to 25 percent of his stainless steel requirements from Japan, he would save approximately a net sum of $25,000 for 1964. Despite such cost savings, Mr. Linscott nevertheless thought there were limits to the percentage of Japanese steel in his total steel purchases. He explained:

Because of the large number of products we make, and because of the many models we have in each product line, we buy a large quantity of special size sheets. Now, the sales volume of many of our products varies and deviates from our forecasts quite a bit. And even if the forecasts by the sales divisions were fairly accurate for a product line, they still would be off for the various models within that line. But different models require different size sheets. That's why, in general, I buy from Japan only standard sizes, which can be used for several products, and from American mills special sizes, which we need for quite a few of our products and which we need on short delivery because they are ones that fluctuate in volume. If I bought from Japan standard size material for products requiring special sizes, the increase in waste or drop-off would absorb the savings from buying Japanese steel at the lower prices. For example, a 48 × 120 sheet would be considered standard size. If I need material that is 42 × 80, there is a 40-inch cutoff. Sure, I can use the 40 inches, but not 100 percent, because it is unlikely that you have many pieces that take exactly 40 inches. So my waste factor starts to creep up, and, instead of its being a nominal figure, it is all of a sudden 20 percent—which may be just what we are saving from the price differential. On the other hand, if I bought special sizes from Japan in sufficient quantity to get good prices, I might wind up with a lot of material on my hands for models that are not selling at a particular time, while the sizes we do need are not in stock.

Long lead times, caused by the Japanese mills' heavy production schedules and by the time needed for ocean transportation as well as customs clearance, were another consideration in the purchasing agent's attempt to determine a proper ratio between domestic and foreign buying.

To buy substantially all material from Japan would be extremely dangerous. Stainless steel is the heart of our products. As of early October, 1964, the importer was asking me to place orders, for manufacture in Japan, for December, 1964–January, 1965, shipments from Japanese ports. Then, from the Japanese ports, it takes five to six weeks longer to get the material here, meaning that I would not receive the material before early March. As a result, my needs would have to be determined about five and a half to six months in advance. An that is very, very difficult. So, although I do buy a substantial amount in Japan, I must counter it with buying a still larger amount in the American market because of the long lead times required for foreign buying and the impossibility of our forecasting our requirements accurately six months in advance—our needs change too quickly. Then, again, the percentage of steel that we would buy from Japan would depend on the extent to which we were able to standardize our products.

Directly associated with relatively long lead times was the fact that, since the company's decision to buying from overseas, stainless steel inventories were increasing at a much faster rate than production volume. Although Mr. Linscott recognized the need to balance the lower acquisition cost for Japanese steel against the heavier inventory position, the company had not attemped to look thoroughly into the problem of "cost of possession" and to determine the actual savings from buying foreign steel. Information on the exact extent of enlarged inventories—stemming from increased output, on the one hand, and from foreign buying, on the other—and on inventory turnover rates was not available. Mr. Linscott commented, "The price savings we make are reduced by the costs of increased inventory, extra inspection, extra handling, extra inventory control, extra moving, and storage. We have not made an economic analysis, because the difference between domestic and Japanese prices was so large that it did not really matter, though there were times when the price differential dropped below 10 percent, depending on how American mills adjusted their prices." He placed the value of his stainless steel inventory, composed, roughly, of 65 percent Japanese and 35 percent U.S. material, at approximately $100,000 as of November, 1964. He estimated that the inventory would drop to about $60,000 if he replaced all Japanese steel with U.S. material.

Mr. Linscott thought that, in addition to long transportation time for foreign steel, the hazards involved in ocean shipping were much greater than those involved in transporting steel by truck or rail from a domestic mill to his plant. The greater hazards in ocean shipping, he thought, increased the risk of rupturing the flow of production, and, thus, constituted another reason for limiting foreign buying.

Stoppages in the supply from American mills are usually caused by strikes, which you know of far in advance and take into consideration in your planning. If you give an American supplier four to five weeks, delivery is very good. But, with steel from Japan, you may have strike problems unknown to you, dockage problems you don't know of, unavailability of ships when the material leaves the mill, unexpected calls on ports by the ships en route, dockage problems in U.S. ports, problems with the customs people, and what not. Accuracy of delivery time is a real problem. Sometimes the shipments are two to three weeks early, sometimes two to three weeks late, and very seldom at the specified time. We have little control over these factors.

ABC had received sales literature on stainless steel from other countries, particularly France and Sweden, and the prices of Swedish and French steel were in line with Japanese prices. Mr. Linscott said, "We have not turned to any sources outside of Japan, because we are not yet using the Japanese mills to the fullest extent possible." Although the purchasing agent was maintaining files on other foreign supply sources and compiling comparative price data, he had not looked into the matter of lead times and delivery schedules.

Maintaining strong domestic sources backstopping the company's steel needs was of dominant concern to Mr. Linscott in trying to decide how much to buy from overseas. "I would never be caught in a situation in which this company is dependent upon foreign supplies," he said. "It is much too dangerous. We know there can be fluctuations in the stream of supply from Japan—for example, the Japanese government might restrict exports to the United States to avoid higher tariffs—and we just cannot afford to be sitting here with no supplies." In addition to procuring all the company's carbon steel from U.S. mills—which, according to Mr. Linscott, was not adaptable to foreign purchasing for lack of significant cost advantages—the purchasing agent believed strongly that he should continue to cover a large portion of his annual stainless steel needs from domestic mills. He thought that the objective of keeping U.S. sources fully available would itself limit foreign buying to 50 percent, at the most, leaving enough business for U.S. mills to avoid any discriminatory treatment in the domestic market in times of serious shortages.

In negotiatons with salesmen from U.S. mills, Mr. Linscott generally made it a point to avoid references to his foreign steel buying. He said, "If I am asked directly if and how much we purchase from abroad, I always reply by saying 'We are trying it out.' " Although he was aware of the strong "Buy American" attitude of American mills, he had never felt any pressure not to buy foreign-made steel. "In fact," he said, "some months ago I had a call from our receiving department to come and look at a shipment of carbon steel that had just come in from an American mill. I went down and the fellows pointed to prints on some of the packing material that said 'Made in France.' "

Appendix: Foreign imports of stainless steel

In June, 1964, the American Iron and Steel Institute reported that 44 percent more foreign steel mill products came into the United States during the first quarter of 1964 than in the same period of 1963. The 1.4 million net tons imported nearly equaled the volume of steel imports in the first three months of 1960, a period following a strike in the U.S. steel industry, when demand for any kind of steel was held to be exceptionally high. In 1956, by comparison, first-quarter steel imports came to slightly over 200,000 net tons. By 1959, this figure had risen to 800,000 net tons. For the full year of 1964, the Institute projected a record level of close to 5.6 million tons, as compared with a high of 5.5 million tons set in 1963.[1]

Although by October, 1964, it became evident that steel imports for the first seven months of 1964 were only 22 percent above the 1963 level[2] and that further declines were expected in the second half of the year, a heated debate continued among U.S. steel producers, U.S. steel importers, the government, and other interested groups about the significance, causation, and consequences of steel imports.

World production of steel in 1963 was estimated at 422 million net tons. During the same year, steel production in the United States was 109 million tons, or 26 percent of the world total; in Japan, 35 million tons, or 8 percent of the world total; and in Western Europe, 121 million tons, or 29 percent of the world total.[3]

U.S. production of stainless steel ingots in 1963 came to 1.2 million

---

[1] American Iron and Steel Institute, *Steel Facts,* Bulletin No. 182 (June 1964), p. 5.

[2] *The New York Times,* October 18, 1964.

[3] American Iron and Steel Institute, *Charting Steel's Progress in 1963* (New York: The Institute, 1964), p. 36.

tons. Domestic mills turned out 467,277 tons of stainless steel sheets, 41,527 tons of stainless steel plates, and 34,505 tons of stainless steel strip.[4]

U.S. imports of stainless steel were as follows:

	Total imports (net tons)	Imports from Japan (net tons)	Percent of total imports
Ingots	11,600	1,600	1.4%
Sheets	17,300	15,600	90.1
Plates.	114	112	98.2
Strip	1,890	470	24.8
	30,904 (100%)	17,782	57.5%

Sources: American Iron and Steel Institute, *Annual Statistical Report, 1963,* (New York: The Institute, 1964); U.S. Bureau of the Census, United States Import Statistics, Report FT 110, 1962 Annual, *United States Imports of Merchandise for Consumption: Commodity by Country of Origin* (Washington, D.C.: U.S. Government Printing Office, May 1963). From the latter source, detailed classifications were combined to the four broad categories used in the preceding table.

Total imports as a percent of U.S. production were: ingots, 0.9 percent; sheets, 3.2 percent; plates, 0.3 percent; and strip, 5.4 percent.[5]

Imports of stainless steel sheets and strip remained heavy in 1964 and, as in the previous year, came primarily from Japan. At hearings before the U.S. Trade Information Committee and the Tariff Commission in Washington in February, 1964, steel executives testified that one out of four U.S. stainless steel producers would be forced out of business if the present import trends continued.[6]

In general, the argument that the upsurge in steel imports was the result of "dumping" by foreign producers continued to be the major one advanced by U.S. steel producers. Importers, on the other hand, charged that small American steel fabricators were forced to turn to imports, because they had become victims of unfair pricing by the big integrated mills which not only supplied them with raw material but also competed with them on fabricated end products. The U.S. steel industry, the argument went on, was seeking protectionist laws to elimi-nate import competition rather than for protection from dumping. Im-

---

[4] American Iron and Steel Institute, *Annual Statistical Report, 1963* (New York: The Institute, 1964), p. 61. Production figures for carbon steel are given as follows: sheets, 32,257,328 tons; plates, 7,147,734 tons; strip, 1,386,199 tons.

[5] American Iron and Steel Institute, *Annual Statistical Report, 1963,* ibid., p. 61; and U.S. Bureau of the Census, United States Import Statistics, Report FT 110, 1962 Annual, *United States Imports of Merchandise for Consumption: Commodity by Country of Origin* (Washington, D.C.: U.S. Government Printing Office, May 1963).

[6] American Iron and Steel Institute, *Steel Facts,* Bulletin No. 181 (April 1964), p. 2.

porters maintained that such legislation would hurt the small American steel fabricator and eventually put him out of business. They charged that the U.S. steel industry, in seeking protectionist legislation, was trying to create the impression that imports were unpatriotic and that there was some stigma about foreign steel.[7]

The development of prices for stainless steel since 1957 is illustrated by the prices of sheets "AISI No. 304," which is typical for all flat rolled stainless steel, in the accompanying table.

In June, 1964, the American Iron and Steel Institute reported that

PRICES OF STAINLESS STEEL SHEETS NO. 304
(cents per pound)

Months/year	1957	1958	1959	1960	1961	1962	1963
1	53.25	55.00	55.00	55.00	52.00	52.00	48.00
2							
3							
4						50.00	
5						50.55	
6							
7	55.50						
8							45.25
9				52.00			
10						48.00	41.75
11							
12	55.50	55.00	55.00	52.00	52.00	48.00	41.75
Ø	54.38	55.00	55.00	54.00	52.00	50.27	45.97

Source: *Iron Age*, Annual Issue, January 2, 1964, p. 196. Reprinted by permission.

the combined domestic output of alloy and stainless steels in 1963 had jumped 15 percent over the 1962 tonnage made by U.S. mills and was expected to increase further in the years ahead because of the increasing usage in the automotive and transportation fields, in construction and contractors' products, and in consumer goods.[8]

COLUMBIA MANUFACTURING CO., INC. (A)*

In 1954, executives of the Columbia Manufacturing Co., Inc.,[1] a leading bicycle firm, had become increasingly worried by the sharply declin-

[7] *The New York Times*, October 18, 1964.

[8] American Iron and Steel Institute, *Steel Facts,* Bulletin No. 182 (June 1964), p. 7.

* © by the President and Fellows of Harvard College; all rights reserved.

[1] The Columbia Manufacturing Co., Inc., was the successor of the well-established Westfield Manufacturing Company, which for many years had produced bicycles

ing demand for domestically manufactured bicycles. This falling demand had been reflected in the industry by decreased unit production, reduced dollar sales, and increased percentage costs for production, administration, and marketing. At the same time, the public demand for foreign bicycles had increased, and imports had climbed substantially. By the end of 1954, these imports amounted to almost two fifths of the total new units available in the U.S. market. The top executives were considering various alternative courses of action in the face of this growing foreign competition.

BRIEF HISTORY OF BICYCLE INDUSTRY IN THE UNITED STATES

Up to World War II

Demand for bicycles had varied in the United States since the late 1870s when two-wheelers were first introduced. In the early years, bicycles, rather light in weight and with narrow tires, were very popular among adults as well as young people. The establishment of electric street railways and later the expansion of automobile manufacture into models which could be economically mass-produced provided effective and relatively inexpensive means of rapid transport for adults; consequently, the demand for bicycles by the late 1920s had become centered chiefly on recreational equipment for children.

This market for bicycles, drastically reduced by the impact of the Great Depression, began to revive following the introduction in 1933 of the somewhat less expensive but rather heavy bicycles with balloon tires. During the late 1930s the demand for this type of bicycle increased rapidly, and the unit production of "balloons" in the United States came to greatly exceed that of the formerly widely accepted "lightweights." By 1936 the total volume of bicycle production in the United States was the highest, at 1.2 million units, than it had been since about the turn of the century.

1942–54

During the years of World War II, few bicycles were produced in the United States. The major activities of bicycle companies at that

---

under the brand name Columbia. Information for a series of four cases presenting problems met by the firm from 1948 to 1964 was provided by Mr. Norman A. Clarke, president of the company. Since the early 1930s Mr. Clarke had been associated in the business with his father, who preceded him as its chief executive. For simplicity in the case presentations, the company will be identified as the Columbia Manufacturing Co., Inc., throughout this case series.

time involved projects related to the war effort. Immediately after the war, however, the firms turned back to the assembling of bicycles to satisfy a pent-up demand for such equipment. As indicated in Exhibit 1, production rose to its highest peak ever, almost 2.9 million units,

Exhibit 1
U.S. PRODUCTION OF BICYCLES: 1880–1954

Year	Units	Year	Units
1880	6,000	1935	656,828
1885	30,000	1936	1,242,076
1890	125,000	1937	1,130,736
1895	800,000	1938	870,379
1897	1,998,000	1939	1,252,029
1899	1,182,691	1940	1,313,116
1904	250,487	1941	1,854,351
1909	233,707	1942 (war production)	560,848
1914	398,899	1943 (war production)	178.938
1919	479,163	1944 (war production)	172,965
1921	216,464	1945 (war production)	554,655
1923	486,177	1946	1,652,923
1925	303,446	1947	2,875,000
1927	255,456	1948	2,794,516
1929	307,845	1949	1,483,009
1930	289,791	1950	1,963,716
1931	260,029	1951	1,918,923
1932	205,000	1952	1,930,307
1933	320,000	1953	2,083,439
1934	524,234	1954	1,554,233

Source: Material for this exhibit taken from company records.

in 1947. In the following seven years, however, the annual volume subsided to a level between roughly 1.5 million and 2 million units. As shown in Exhibit 2, the decline in production in part reflected a substantial increase in the supply of imported bicycles.

Manufacturing methods in the industry

The production of bicycles in the United States, while the end result of the activities of only a few firms, depended to a large degree on the manufacture of component parts by other specialists. Thus, while the end producers might fabricate such parts as frames, forks, and handlebars and finally assemble complete bicycles, they procured many components and accessories from other manufacturers. Since few parts usually were produced on the premises, capital investment in plant facilities frequently was relatively small in relation to sales volume and number of employees.

Because bicycle firms served as assemblers of components variously procured, an important function in a bicycle firm involved (1) the selection of reliable suppliers of such special parts as multiple speed gears,

Exhibit 2
U.S. PRODUCTION AND IMPORTS OF BICYCLES: 1947–54
(in units)

Year	Domestic production	Imports	Total supply*	Imports as a percentage Of total supply (percent)	Imports as a percentage Of domestic production (percent)
1947	2,875,000	19,758	2,894,758	0.7	0.7
1948	2,794,516	16,774	2,811,290	0.6	0.6
1949	1,483,009	15,935	1,498,944	1.1	1.0
1946–49 Avg.	2,201,362	24,826	2,226,188	1.1	1.0
1950	1,963,716	67,789	2,031,505	3.4	3.5
1951	1,918,923	176,644	2,095,567	8.4	9.2
1952	1,930,307	245,763	2,176,070	11.3	12.7
1953	2,083,439	592,999	2,676,438	22.2	28.5
1954	1,554,233	963,667	2,517,900	38.3	62.0

* Supply equals the sum of domestic production and imports.
Source: Material for this exhibit based on data taken from *Supplementary Brief* dated March 16, 1964, Bicycle Manufacturers Association of America before the U.S. Tariff Commission hearings held on bicycles, March 2, 1964, in accordance with the provisions of section 225(b) of the Trade Expansion Act of 1962.

chains, brakes, saddles, spokes, wheels, tires, pedals, and lights, and (2) the negotiating of contracts with these companies.

Domestic competition

During the period 1947 to 1954 a total of nine firms produced substantially all the bicycles manufactured in the United States. Companies equaling or surpassing the Columbia firm in size included the Huffman Manufacturing Company, of Dayton, Ohio; Murray Ohio Manufacturing Company, of Cleveland, Ohio; and Arnold Schwinn & Company, of Chicago, Illinois. Competition among these companies was strong particularly for large national accounts.

Nevertheless, these firms formed a closely knit trade group in the interests of protecting and furthering the activities of the domestic bicycle industry as a whole. All nine companies were members of the American Bicycle Manufacturers Association. Together they formed the Bicycle Institute of America, Inc., among other things, to conduct institutional advertising campaigns and to compile periodically comprehensive industry statistics on production, shipments, inventories, and related matters. The presidents of member companies frequently visited with each other to discuss developments in the national and international bicycle market.

All firms were usually represented at major bicycle fairs both within the United States and abroad.

Tariff regulations

In 1930 the United States had imposed a 30 percent *ad valorem* tariff on all types of bicycles. Prior to World War II, imports had accounted for less than 1 percent of total domestic sales. The 30 percent rate remained in effect until 1939 when it was reduced to 15 percent pursuant to a bilateral trade agreement with the United Kingdom.

In 1948, under the General Agreement on Tariffs and Trade (GATT), the duty on lightweights, or English-type bicycles, was reduced to 7½ percent *ad valorem,* while the rates on all other bicycles remained unchanged.

A BRIEF HISTORY OF THE COLUMBIA
MANUFACTURING CO., INC.

Early years

The Columbia Manufacturing Company traced its origin to the year 1877, when a bicycle designed by Albert Pope was produced and marketed under the trade name Columbia by the Pope Manufacturing Company. The Pope firm was founded in Boston but moved its manufacturing facilities to Hartford, Connecticut, shortly thereafter. Around 1900 the firm moved from Hartford to Westfield, Massachusetts, where it continued to assemble bicycles. Over following years its production and distribution pattern paralleled that for the U.S. bicycle industry as a whole. In the 1890s and the early decades of the 1900s, the company established a leading industry position in the American bicycle market by adopting such innovations as diamond, camelback, and twin-bar frames; pneumatic bicycle tires; coaster brakes; cushion, spring, and truss forks; and lightweight bicycles with narrow tires. In 1954 the company's plant facilities consisted of several multistory red-brick buildings that were over 50 years old.

The 1940s

During World War II, while the Columbia firm engaged chiefly in the production of munitions. it still assembled a small quantity of bicycles each year for use by the armed services. Then as soon as the war ended, the company once more concentrated all its efforts on bicycle production. By 1946 it was working at prewar capacity level, turning out in excess of 250,000 units per year. In 1947 and 1948 the company's production rose to levels respectively 22 percent and 40 percent higher than in 1941.

Commenting on the development of the bicycle market since the 1920s, Mr. Norman A. Clarke, president of the company, said,

> The market for adult bicycles has been lagging ever since Henry Ford came out with his Model-T.[2] Up until that time American manufacturers produced primarily a roadster, or lightweight, bicycle. When the Model-T came on the market, we lost our volume business and bicycles became kids' toys. We went into an unbelievable variety of bike sizes, shapes, trims, decorations, and gadgetry to appeal to the kids. The functional bicycle went out of the picture, although we continued to make a few. After the war we experienced not only a pent-up demand and an expansion of the juvenile bicycle market but also, for the first time in many years, an expansion of the upperage bicycle market. Adults became interested primarily in lightweights, whereas children preferred the more rugged, heavier balloon-tire bike with chrome fenders, tanks, and many other accessories.

The line of bicycles produced during the late 1940s included both models equipped with balloon tires and the so-called lightweight wheels. These two classifications of bicycles, balloon tire and lightweights, reflected largely design differences rather than distinct differences in weight. Balloon-tire models traditionally were designed with curved bar frames, while lightweight models had triangular frames of straight tubing. Frame sizes ranged from 13 inches to 23 inches for children and adults. Models were assembled with (or without) variable speed hubs, hand or coaster brakes, "tanks" containing horn and headlights, and many other accessories. As far as tires were concerned, sizes ranged from 16 inches to 26 inches, and the dimensions ranged from a cross-sectional diameter of $2\frac{1}{4}$ inches for balloons to $1\frac{3}{8}$ inches for lightweight models.

The firm had national distribution of its products, most of the bicycles being sold under the Columbia brand name. Important volume also had resulted, however, from sales to large retail organizations for their own private label.

1949–54

In 1949, the company experienced a drastic slump in the demand for its products. Unit output fell to 74 percent of the plant's 1941 produc-

---

[2] In the period 1906–13 Henry Ford, who started his career as a bicycle mechanic, pioneered mass-production methods for the manufacture of motor cars which could be popularly priced. The Model-T Ford designed to sell for less than $1,000 was introduced in 1908. After 1911, there was a sharp increase in Ford production. "By 1923 half of the 10 million passenger cars in the United States were Ford automobiles. . . . It is not too much to say that Ford had become an agent of social change." (See William Greenleaf, *Monopoly on Wheels* [Detroit: Wayne State University Press, 1961], pp. 237–38.)

tion level, and the company lost money. During the same year total domestic production of bicycles dropped to 1.5 million units from the 2.8 million units of the preceding year.

Mr. Clarke believed that this market decline was due in part to satisfaction of the pent-up demand caused by the war, and in part to tariff concessions on bicycles granted by the U.S. government under the General Agreement on Tariffs and Trade of 1948. In regard to the latter and the significance of foreign-made bicycles in 1954, Mr. Clarke commented at some length:

European manufacturers of bicycles have always used modern mass-production methods. In England the bicycle industry is the seventh largest in the country. Recently British bicycle makers have turned out 5 million units per year, Germany has produced 3 million units, while the United States has had a capacity for only 2 million units.

When the duty went down to 7½ percent, the British manufacturers, who had just lost their big market in India, turned their full attention to the U.S. market, which was growing fast after the war. And they started to bring in the bicycle they had always made, that is, an adult lightweight bike, designed for transportation, the kind of bike we had stopped making in the late 1920s. In Europe, the bicycle had continued to be a transportation means for the worker. European manufacturers never went into producing all kinds of funny-sized and funny-shaped kid bicycles. So they came with a well-designed, efficiently produced lightweight adult bicycle of high quality and low manufacturing cost and at a greatly reduced rate of duty. Nearly all the bicycles we were producing in the United States were heavy balloon-tire bicycles.

Immediately a fad developed for the lightweight, which consumers started to call "English bikes." But, more important, the Europeans were able to make bicycles at a much lower cost, enabling them to sell in the American market at a price that was between $7 and $8 below our prices at the wholesale level. So American parents were able to buy imported lightweight bikes for themselves and for their children at the same prices as our models, or even below [see Exhibits 3 through 6].

In 1950, Columbia's production volume improved over that of the previous year, reaching 89 percent of the 1941 output level. This trend continued, and by the end of 1953 the company had regained the 1941 sales production volume. Mr. Clarke explained that this improvement of sales amidst stiffening foreign competition had been achieved largely through rigorous cost cutting and price reductions. "But profits became almost negligible," he commented.

One year later, in 1954, the company's sales volume once again began to falter. By year's end, production was down by 50 percent, and the firm suffered a loss. Columbia's American competitors also were severely affected. For the domestic industry as a whole losses of over $0.5 million

Exhibit 3
PRICES OF DOMESTIC AND IMPORTED BICYCLES: 1949–54

Year	British light-weights with gears, over 25 inches, weighing less than 36 pounds	American light-weights with gears, over 25 inches, weighing less than 36 pounds	German balloon-tire bicycles, over 25 inches	American balloon-tire bicycles, over 25 inches
	Average foreign invoice price (unit value)*	Average factory price (unit value)	Average foreign invoice price (unit value)*	Average factory price (unit value)
1949	$29.63	$45.32	Not available	$35.24
1950	23.58	44.83	$29.08	34.70
1951	25.42	44.79	21.54	33.43
1952	24.79	43.05	25.31	33.15
1953	25.57	45.36	20.99	34.42
1954	24.53	41.91	18.35	32.63

* The average costs of importing a bicycle, including ocean freight, insurance, entry, and delivery to the importer's warehouse was $4.44 per unit in 1954. If these costs are added to the invoice value of a British bicycle, for instance, average landed costs, duty included, were $30.81 in 1954 at a duty rate of 7½ percent *ad valorem.*

Sources: U.S. Tariff Commission, *Bicycles, Report to the President (1955);* U.S. Tariff Commission, *Bicycles, Report to the President (1958); Application for Investigation and Public Hearing and Imposition of an Absolute Import Quota with Respect to Bicycles,* dated January 11, 1957, Bicycle Manufacturers Association of America before the United States Tariff Commission; Percy W. Bidwell, *What the Tariff Means to American Industries* (New York: Harper & Bros., 1956), p. 79.

Exhibit 4
APPROXIMATE UNIT MANUFACTURING COSTS
(of all U.S. manufacturers of 26-inch balloon-tire
bicycles in 1954)

Raw materials	$ 2.00
Purchased parts and components	16.00
Direct labor and factory overhead	8.00
Manufacturing cost per unit	$26.00

Source: Company records.

were sustained in 1954 in contrast to achieved net operating profit before taxes of approximately $5 million in 1950.

The drastic drop in sales and the associated problems of ineffective use of plant and staff and lowered opportunity for profits were of great concern to all members of Columbia's top management group who frequently discussed the problems besetting the industry and their own firm. Following the sharp deterioration in Columbia's sales volume, management described the company's financial position as "getting tougher by the day."

Overall organization of the Columbia Manufacturing Co., Inc.

The major executives, all of whom reported to the president, included two sales managers, the treasurer, the factory manager, the purchasing agent, and the advertising manager (see Exhibit 7). Commenting on the company' organization, Mr. Clarke said, "We are a small company, and the executives have worked closely together for many years. Although we have a formal organizational structure, our relationships are pretty much informal. Emphasis is on getting the job done and not on who reports to whom." Problems of product design changes and industrial engineering were generally handled by Mr. Clarke in close cooperation with his factory manager, who in turn was assisted by the chief engineer.

Exhibit 5
NET SALES, OPERATING EXPENSES, AND PROFITS OF NINE
UNITED STATES PRODUCERS OF BICYCLES,* 1937 AND 1947–54
(net sales = 100 percent)

Item	1937†	1947	1948	1949	1950	1951	1952	1953	1954
Cost of goods sold:									
Direct materials. . . .	62.4%	58.3%	57.9%	58.3%	57.1%	58.3%	58.9%	58.5%	56.1%
Direct labor	12.3	13.9	13.5	12.6	13.4	12.8	12.5	14.0	13.7
Factory overhead . . .	13.3	14.2	14.5	17.0	16.1	15.9	16.1	18.5	20.2
Net cost of goods sold‡.	87.1	86.1	85.9	87.7	86.4	86.4	87.7	88.8	91.3
Gross profit	12.9	13.9	14.1	12.3	13.6	13.6	12.3	11.2	8.7
General, administrative and selling expense	6.5	4.7	5.1	7.7	6.5	6.0	6.2	7.1	9.7
Net operating profit . .	6.4	9.2	9.0	4.6	7.1	7.6	6.1	4.1	–1.0
Net sales (in millions). .	$19.9	$81.0	$85.8	$47.0	$62.6	$64.6	$64.9	$72.3	$51.9

* In some instances the firms manufactured other items in addition to bicycles or bicycle parts. These data relate to the bicycle operations only and are expressed as percentages of net sales of bicycle and bicycle parts.
† Includes data for eight companies only.
‡ The net cost of goods sold percentages have been influenced either upwards or downwards by an inventory adjustment varying between the extremes of –2.2 percent of net sales in 1953 and +1.3 percent in 1954. A positive inventory adjustment indicates a decrease in total inventories during the year, and a negative adjustment indicates an increase.
Source: Compiled from reports submitted to the U.S. Tariff Commission by individual companies. U.S. Tariff Commission, *Bicycles (1955), Report to the President* (Washington, D.C., 1955), Appendix Table 6.

Purchasing activities

The purchasing agent was assisted by two buyers and two clerk-typists. Procurement of hardware, such as bolts, nuts, screws, and bearings, was assigned to one buyer. Procurement of all other operating supplies was assigned to the second buyer. The purchasing agent, in

Exihibit 6
U.S. IMPORTS OF BICYCLES, BY TYPE
(1939 and 1946–54)

Year	Units			Percent	
	Light-weight	Balloon-tire	Total	Light-weight	Balloon-tire
1939	10,716		10,716	100	0
1946	43,956		43,956	100	0
1947	18,018		18,018	100	0
1948	16,108		16,108	100	0
1949	15,053		15,053	100	0
1950	59,019	6,210	65,229	90	10
1951	121,627	44,591	166,218	73	27
1952	211,328	32,380	243,708	87	13
1953	522,599	68,858	591,457	88	12
1954	742,145	208,382	950,528	78	22

Note: This table does not include small bicycles, classified in the tariff schedule as having wheels with a diameter of not over 19 inches. Imports in this category have never exceeded 15,000 machines annually.

Source: Percy W. Bidwell, *What the Tariff Means to American Industries* (New York: Harper & Bros., 1956), p. 81. Reprinted by permission.

Exihibit 7
ORGANIZATION CHART

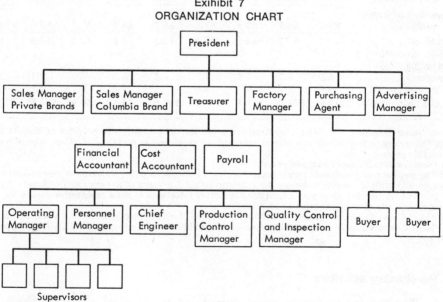

addition to his supervisory activities, was in charge of steel purchasing. Buying of parts and components was done by the president. "When the negotiations with our parts suppliers are finished," said Mr. Clarke, "the purchasing department takes over and handles the technical and administrative work."

Possible solutions to Columbia's problems

It was the opinion of most company executives that if the deterioration of sales and profits could not be checked within a year or two there was little hope of staying in the bicycle manufacturing business. In searching for ways to deal with the intense foreign competition, members of management concentrated their attention on a number of alternative courses of action which they believed were open to the company:

1. In a joint effort with other members of the industry association, seek tariff relief from the government (through an escape-clause action under section 7 of the Trade Agreements Extension Act of 1951) by establishing that the imports caused or threatened to cause serious injury to domestic bicycle producers.
2. Improve production efficiency through capital investments designed to modernize facilities and streamline production processes.
3. Build manufacturing facility overseas and phase out Westfield plant.
4. Move Westfield plant to a southern state offering lower wage rates.
5. Add foreign-made bicycles to the company's existing product line.
6. Persuade U.S. bicycle parts manufacturers to cut prices.
7. Buy bicycle parts from overseas.
8. Diversify into other products.

Alternative 1. Mr. Clarke recalled the industry's unsuccessful attempt in 1951 to obtain an increase in the rates of duty and the establishment of an import quota on bicycles so as to curb the flow of lower priced foreign bicycles into the U.S. market. In its investigation of the industry the Tariff Commission found: that imports were largely confined to the lightweight bicycle which had traditionally played a minor role in the product lines of U.S. manufacturers; that imports the balloon-tire bicycles which represented the bulk of U.S. companies' sales were small; and that imports posed therefore no threat to the domestic industry.

In view of the developing situation on imports Mr. Clarke wondered whether a second attempt to establish higher tariff walls might be more successful, and, if so, whether the rates would be set high enough to have any significant impact upon the volume of imports.

Alternative 2. The major operations in the production of bicycles included fabrication of steel strip into tubing, forming of frames, forks, handlebars (bending, cutting, shaping, welding brazing) assembly of major components painting, assembly of additional parts and accessories, and packing. Mr. Clarke estimated that the installation of a fully conveyorized assembly line, a new wheel-assembly system, automatic paint spray equipment, automatic wheel fork brazing, and more modern packaging machines at a cost of approximately $800,000 would cut unit costs by approximately $1.35. Mr. Clarke was extremely doubtful, however, whether he would be able to persuade the top executives of the firm to approve a capital investment of such magnitude in face of an explosive growth of imports, a large price differential between the company's products and foreign bicycles which would not be completely bridged by the investment, and relatively small profit margins with which the company would continue to work. "We have exhausted all possibilities of cleaning out deadwood, introducing new work methods, reducing overhead—in short, cutting cost without a major outlay of funds," said Mr. Clarke. He added: "There are definite limits to the cost reductions which we can achieve in our manufacturing process because close to 50 percent of our total costs represents material costs for parts purchased from outside suppliers."

Alternatives 3 and 4. Although Mr. Clarke fully recognized the economic advantages realizable in the long run by moving the plant away from Westfield and particularly by setting up manufacturing operations overseas, he all but discarded this particular course of action.

This company has been in Westfield for over 60 years. It is by far the largest factory in town, which means a lot to the people living here. We have an obligation to our employees and to the town to solve our problems right here—and not in Alabama or Great Britain or Germany. I suppose we could have left Westfield some years ago to head off the struggle we are in now. But I must say that I am rather proud of still employing 500 people of this community. I just cannot buy the economist's argument—and we have been given the advice by certain government economists—that maintaining our plant here is nonsensical. I like to see smoke coming out of chimneys right here. If it were just a matter of economic analysis, sure, we'd go to England tomorrow. But there are other considerations. Now, if this thing became a matter of going out of Westfield or going out of business, my thinking might change, but in the meantime we must explore thoroughly every other possible solution that will ensure the plant's survival in Westfield. After all, in addition to having obligations to our people, we have over $3 million invested in our facilities here.

Alternative 5. Mr. Clarke thought that by adding a line of foreign-made lightweights to the company's own product line the problem of heavily sagging sales might well be overcome. On the other hand he recognized that there might be dangers inherent in adopting such a policy if it developed later that the imported line, after having been firmly incorporated in the company's marketing program, continued to take a larger and larger share of total sales. "We might involuntarily wind up being an importer or distributor rather than a manufacturer," Mr. Clarke stated. "Moreover, after we have established a firm market for the imported line, what would keep the foreign manufacturer from selling the same bike, but without our Columbia label, directly to our customers at a lower price? Or, conversely, what would keep our large customers, the national chains, from going directly to the foreign producer, if they can get the same bike for less money?"

Alternative 6. In 1954, U.S. bicycle manufacturers purchased parts from approximately 50 domestic suppliers, ranging in size from companies with three or four dozen employees to divisions of large national corporations. Mr. Clarke was not certain how these suppliers would react to a request for a general price reduction in view of the company's and, for that matter, the industry's inability to meet prices of foreign competitors. He recalled the strong appeals which executives of some of the large companies had recently made to him to "Buy American" and thought that if these suppliers propounded such a procurement policy, cooperation through downward price revisions might well be expected from them. Mr. Clarke was not sure, however, whether the cost structure of small suppliers would permit them to reduce prices in order to maintain their markets.

Alternative 7. To replace domestic parts suppliers with foreign parts producers was another course of action which looked promising to Mr. Clarke at first glance. From visits to European bicycle fairs as well as sales literature coming into his office regularly from major foreign suppliers, he was well aware that some parts could be purchased at a much lower cost from abroad than from domestic sources, despite a 30 percent tariff rate on all bicycle parts. Thus, for instance, an English firm had quoted c.i.f. prices for coaster brakes which, after adding all cost of landing including duty, came to $1.73 per unit as compared with $2.68 per unit charged by a large manufacturer in the United States. Similar price differences obtained for other parts, such as chains from which the company was paying 26 cents per foot and which could be bought from a German firm for 8.7 cents per foot. (Each bicycle required approximately 5 feet of chain.)

Mr. Clarke believed, however, that there were many other considerations that made the purchase of foreign parts something less than a clear choice. Thus, for instance, he knew that many of the company's executives, including himself, disliked the idea of putting foreign parts into the company's bicycles that were being marketed as "Made in U.S.A." and under a trade name that was a symbol for the American bicycle industry. Mr. Clarke also knew that some of his competitors viewed with disfavor the use of imported parts in domestically produced bicycles, partly for emotional reasons, and partly because there was a feeling that the solution to the industry's problems lay in fighting for higher tariffs and, in doing so, enlisting strong support from the large parts manufacturers. These competitors argued that a practice of procuring parts from abroad would jeopardize any success before the Tariff Commission as well as any cooperation by the domestic parts industry.

Apart from such strategy considerations affecting his company as well as the industry as a whole, Mr. Clarke was concerned with several other questions that he thought the purchasing of parts from overseas manufacturers would raise. Thus, he recognized that if his company began to shift to international sources of supply and his major competitors followed suit, many of the large domestic suppliers, for whom bicycle parts constituted only a very small portion of their business, would sooner or later withdraw from the market. Such a development, Mr. Clarke thought, was undesirable because of the resulting total dependency of his company on foreign suppliers and the disappearance of American technical innovations in bicycle parts. Mr. Clarke believed that the large domestic parts manufacturers possessed superior R.&D. facilities and a wealth of technical know-how. Moreover, Mr. Clarke was wondering whether foreign bicycle manufacturers would seize upon such a development by putting pressure on the parts manufacturers in their countries to restrict in one way or another the supply of parts to U.S. bicycle manufacturers. Finally, Mr. Clarke was concerned with the impact of foreign parts upon the company's inventory level as well as on the ability of retailers to make rapid repairs. Mr. Clarke was under the impression that many jobbers and large chains were reluctant to carry the larger inventories which would become necessary if his company decided to switch to foreign parts. He knew that with domestic suppliers a two weeks' to one month's supply was adequate, whereas the use of foreign parts would necessitate keeping up to three months' supply on hand to preclude any disruptions in production or customer service.

Alternative 8. Mr. Clarke had not given much thought to the development, production, and distribution of products unrelated to the bicycle business. Although he believed that the matter of diversification needed attention, he was aware of the financial and managerial constraints which the deterioration of the company's bicycle market had placed upon the prospects of taking on entirely new products. But more importantly, Mr. Clarke was far from being convinced that the bicycle market was lost for good, and he thought that it would be extremely difficult to simultaneously get back into the bicycle business and start a move toward diversification away from bicycles.

COLUMBIA MANUFACTURING CO., INC. (B)*

In 1954 the Columbia Manufacturing Co., Inc., a leading U.S. bicycle manufacturer, had experienced a severe drop in sales, the second such

---

reduction in a six-year period. Production, of necessity, had been cut back to about half the level attained just before World War II, and the company had sustained a substantial loss. Meanwhile, the aggregate domestic production of bicycles had fallen from a level of around 2.7 to 2.8 million units in the years 1947 and 1948 to slightly less than 1.5 million in 1949; then, following a rise to a level of between 1.9 and 2.0 million units in the years 1950 and 1953, had decreased to about 1.5 million units in 1954. Aggregate profits for the industry had dropped from approximately $5 million in 1948 to a loss in excess of $0.5 million in 1954.

Company management attributed the loss of business to imports of bicycles from foreign countries. They believed that such imports reflected a rapidly developing juvenile and adult market for lightweight (30–36 pounds), or "English-type," bicycles, favorably priced, since production costs in Europe were comparatively low. The wholesale prices of imported lightweight bicycles were $7 to $8 below Columbia prices for balloon-tire bicycles and approximately $17 below their prices for lightweight bicycles.

The English-type imported machines featured diamond-shaped frames, multiple-speed gear built into the hub, narrow tires, and caliper brakes attached to the handlebars and operating on the rims of both front and rear wheels. Total bicycle imports, which had been in the vicinity of 17,000 units, or 0.6 percent of domestic production in 1948, had risen to 964,000 units, or 64 percent of domestic production in 1954. Of these 964,000 bicycles, close to 655,000, or 68 percent, were 26" lightweights, brought in primarily for the United Kingdom.

By contrast over 90 percent of the bicycles manufactured in the United States were of the heavier (45 pounds) balloon-tire type, featuring frames of curved bar or "cantilever" design, coaster brakes, wide tires, and "tanks" containing horns and lights but usually not equipped with variable-speed hubs.

Alarmed by the rising tide of low-price imported bicycles, domestic producers had consulted together and decided to attempt for the second time to have tariff levies increased and an absolute import quota established. Accordingly, in June, 1954, members of the Bicycle Manufacturers Association of America had filed an application for relief under the escape clause in section 7 of the Trade agreements Extension Act of 1951.

In March, 1955, after hearings and investigation, the Tariff Commission had issued a report in which it concluded that bicycles were being imported into the United States in such increased quantities as to cause serious injury to the domestic industry.[1]

---

[1] At the hearings, foreign producers argued, among other things, that import competition was caused by the failure of American manufacturers to produce lightweight bicycles and that the foreign producers had created a new market by selling

The commission recommended to the President of the United States that the minimum *ad valorem* duty rates be raised from 7½ percent on lightweights and from 15 percent on other types of bicycles to 22½ percent on *all* types of bicycles. By proclamation effective in August, 1955, President Eisenhower raised the minimum *ad valorem* rate to 11¼ percent on lightweights and to 22½ percent on all other types.

Columbia's executives were satisfied with the rate increase to 22½ percent on bicycles other than lightweights but deeply concerned about the President's decison to limit the increase on lightweights to one half the rate recommended by the commission. Mr. Clarke thought that an increase of 3¾ percent *ad volorem* was too small to bring the prices of imported bicycles up to a level where his company could compete effectively with foreign manufacturers.

He believed that to recover lost sales volume other steps would have to be taken. Turning once more to his list of eight proposed approaches (see Columbia Manufacturing Co., Inc. (A) case), Mr. Clarke looked at the remaining seven suggestions, five of which were directed toward lowering expenses and thus enabling the firm to be more competitive. Three of these economy measures had been considered and rejected in 1954. They involved: moving the plant away from Westfield to some region where operating costs were lower—either (*a*) to one of the southern states, or (*b*) out of the country; and gaining economies through the purchase of foreign-made component parts. The remaining two suggestions for production economies had a greater appeal to management, however: (1) plant modernization, while requiring capital outlay, might eventually bring lowered units costs; (2) across-the-board price cuts might be negotiated with suppliers of component parts.

The remaining two of the eight original proposals related to merchandise policy. One was to add foreign-made lightweight bicycles to the Columbia line, while the other was to seek diversification through manufacture of articles other than bicycles.

The first of these merchandise policy suggestions ran counter to the general policy that had been adopted by the domestic bicycle industry. In concert with other major American producers, the Columbia Manufacturing Company had continued to de-emphasize lightweight bicycles in its advertising and marketing program. Instead, all selling effort had been concentrated on the balloon-tire models. Mr. Clarke said, "We

lightweights to adults who would not have bought bicycles otherwise. (*Brief for Certain Importers of British Bicycles before the U.S. Tariff Commission,* Investigation No. 37 [Washington, D.C., November 26, 1954], pp. 104–10, mimeograph.) American manufacturers rejected this argument by insisting that a bicycle is a bicycle "notwithstanding the many variations in form, type, style, weight, accessories, and appearance." They added: "There is only one major difference between the bikes made in America and those coming from any foreign source. That single difference is price." (*Brief of the Applicants, American Manufacturers, before the U.S. Tariff Commission,* Investigation No. 37 [Washington, D.C., November 26, 1954], pp. 8 and 13, mimeograph.)

were afraid that any advertising for lightweights would merely help the foreign manufacturers to sell more machines, because the prices for our lightweights were even higher than those for balloon-tire models [see Exhibit 3 of case (A)]. So, although we made the lightweight, we kept playing it down, insisting that it was a somewhat dangerous bicycle because of its lighter tubing and lack of coaster brakes."

Since the domestic emphasis was still on the manufacture and promotion of the heavier wheels, Mr. Clarke was not eager to add imported lightweight wheels to his line, although he kept that step in mind as a future possibility. The second merchandise policy proposal, diversification, would require research into products that could be made using existing plant equipment and employee skills. Mr. Clarke believed that thought definitely should be given to the matter.

Meanwhile, management decided to modernize the plant and to try to negotiate price cut with suppliers of bicycle components.

The plant investment program, which was started in the summer of 1955 for completion by the end of 1956, called for a new wheel assembly system, automatic paint spray equipment, automatic wheel-fork brazing equipment, complete mechanized assembly lines, and new packaging machinery at an estimated cost of $800,000. Mr. Clarke expected that this investment would reduce costs by approximately $1.35 per unit. Although he realized that the modernization program by itself would not bring Columbia's price level down to that of foreign manufacturers, he believed that, if increased plant effectiveness were combined with a general decrease in the cost of purchased parts and an increase in the duty rate on imported bicycles leading to a higher price of such imports, the company could about overcome the price differential between Columbia and foreign-made bicycles.

Negotiations to obtain price concessions from the major parts suppliers were undertaken by Columbia directly and also on an informal basis at industry conventions and similar occasions by the Bicycle Manufacturers Association representing all members, including Columbia. The argument advanced by the bicycle manufacturers was that, if they could not lower the cost of purchased parts substantially and through such economies be able to offer their finished products at prices matching those for imported bicycles, foreign competitors, whose market share was approaching 50 percent, would drive domestic bicycles completely out of the market. Such a development, the argument continued, would also lead to a collapse of the parts suppliers' market and, in turn, force the suppliers out of business. Although the bicycle manufacturers made no specific suggestions to the suppliers with respect to the size or the terms of the visualized price reduction, Columbia executives hoped that the aggregate reductions would be sufficiently large to bring Columbia's prices on bicycles "within shooting distance of foreign competition," as Mr. Clarke put it.

These negotiations with many suppliers, however, proved to be unsuccessful. "I suppose these companies were too busy with their major product lines to be really concerned with our problem; they kept their prices where they always had been," commented Mr. Clarke.

Throughout 1955 the volume of imported bicycles continued to increase. By year's end, a total of 1.2 million units had been brought into the United States (as compared with 963,000 units in the previous year), constituting approximately 70 percent of the domestic production volume. Since the higher duty rates had not gone into effect until August, 1955, management thought that statistics for that year would not permit any final conclusions as to the impact of the new rates on the flow of bicycle imports. But the opinion persisted among company executives that no decisive decrease in imports was to be expected in the foreseeable future from the raised tariff.

Moreover, management became much concerned with a marked shift in the composition of the import volume; while in 1950 only 6,000 baloon-tire models had been imported, constituting 10 percent of all imports, such models accounted for 30 percent of all imports at the end of 1955. Columbia manufactured primarily bicycles of this type. Mr. Clarke said, "Obviously, even the new tariff rate of 22½ percent on balloon-tire bicycles, which is higher than the one for lightweights, had no effect on imports thus far [see Exhibit 1]."

By the end of 1955, Columbia's sales had improved by only 4 percent

Exhibit 1
U.S. IMPORTS OF BICYCLES BY TYPE
(1939 and 1945–55)

	Units			Percent of total	
Year	Light-weight	Balloon-tire	Total	Light-weight	Balloon-tire
1939	10,716	–	10,716	100	–
1946	43,956	–	43,956	100	–
1947	18,018	–	18,018	100	–
1948	16,108	–	16,108	100	–
1949	15,053	–	15,053	100	–
1950	59,019	6,210	65,229	90	10
1951	121,627	44,591	166,218	73	27
1952	211,328	32,380	243,708	87	13
1953	522,599	68,858	591,457	88	12
1954	742,146	208,382	950,528	78	22
1955	851,500	360,000	1,211,500	70	30

Note: This table does not include small bicycles classified in the tariff schedule as having wheels with a diameter of not over 19 inches. Imports in this category have never exceeded 15,000 machines annually.

Source: Percy W. Bidwell, *What the Tariff Means to American Industries* (New York: Harper & Bros., 1956), p. 81. Reprinted by permission.

over the previous year, although the company came close to its break-even point. In view of the growing foreign competition, Mr. Clarke was convinced that no significant change would take place in Columbia's volume of sales or profits unless new and different action were taken. He therefore once more reviewed the list of alternatives prepared in 1954 and held lengthy discussions with members of the executive group. Once again the ideas of moving the plant or of buying foreign-made components were dismissed. Decision was reached, however, to find some new line that could be produced in the Westfield plant using the existing skills of the engineering and employee group. After an extensive search for a product that would require no additional investment and would fit easily into the company's bicycle business, management decided in 1956 to develop a line of school furniture utilizing the plant's tubing bending, welding, and brazing facilities.

Mr. Clarke also decided to explore the possibility of adding a line of foreign-made lightweights to the Columbia line of bicycles. While planning how to approach the matter, however, he learned that two of the firm's domestic competitors who had recently started to sell imported bicycles under their respective private labels were experiencing difficulties with their foreign suppliers. After the two American firms had built up a sizable sales volume for the foreign-made lightweights, salesmen of the European producers had begun to call on the American manufacturers' customers, who seized upon the opportunity to buy the same bicycle without an American label at a lower price. Realizing that Columbia's large customers were likely to follow the same practice, Mr. Clarke, by the fall of 1955, had dropped the idea of selling foreign-made bicycles under the Columbia label.

Instead, in the fall of 1955, Mr. Clarke began to consider seriously the production of a so-called middleweight bicycle, featuring narrow tires, coaster brakes, and a light frame of curved bar or "cantilever" design. This, he thought, would be a compromise between the English-type bicycle and the American balloon-tire model. He knew that one of his larger competitors had successfully tested a middleweight bicycle late in 1954, and he wondered if Columbia, by developing a line of bicycles of such design, might be able to recapture the share of the market that it had lost to foreign competition.

Following a thorough analysis of the industry's sales volume of middleweights and upon completion of the necessary design work, Mr. Clarke decided early in 1956 to divert a substantial proportion of the company's manufacturing capacity to the production of such middleweights. This decision was carried out, and by the summer of 1956 production of middleweight bicycles was in full swing.

Imports of lightweight wheels continued at a high level, however; and in addition to an increasing quantity of imported balloon-tire machines, there were some German-made middleweight models entering the domestic market at prices below those of the Columbia lines. This development led Mr. Clarke to the conclusion that he would have to cut his production costs further by buying at least some favorably priced imported components.

In explanation of his changed attitude toward foreign purchasing, Mr. Clarke commented as follows:

Management's policy to abstain from buying foreign-made parts in order to enlist the help of large American parts suppliers in the industry's fight for tariff protection did not work. Neither did the "Buy American" approach. We have not received any support from the large manufacturers of parts, and we have failed to get more than a small and inadequate increase in the rate of duty on bicycles.

Despite the various measures that we took,[2] our sales continued to be inadequate. Profits were nominal at best. Our middleweight line was very successful, but already the West Germans were copying it, as well as the balloon-tire models, and were beginning to sell both types of bicycles in increasing quantities in our market. And they sold them at a much lower price. Judging from the past two or three years, I think it would be foolish to pin any hopes for solving our problem on tariff protection.

I thought that the time had come to stop waving the flag and recognize that this company and this industry would not survive unless we not only cut our costs for middleweights and balloon-tire bicycles drastically but also started making lightweights at a price that would be competitive with the prices for imported lightweights. Now, the only way we could accomplish this was by putting foreign parts on our bikes. And, regardless of how the industry felt about it, that's what I was going to do. Whether the arguments that we had raised against such a policy three years ago were valid or not was, in my mind, no longer an issue [see Columbia Manufacturing Co., Inc. (A) case]. We simply had no other choice left.

Organization for purchasing

Columbia's purchasing department was staff with a purchasing agent, who reported to the president, two buyers, and two clerk-typists. The purchasing agent had overall responsibility for the operation of his department with particular emphasis on the procurement of all raw material and major components. Purchase of supplies and hardware and the scheduling of purchased parts against blanket orders were done by the buyers. Long-term contracts for parts and components, constituting the bulk of all purchases, were many times negotiated by Mr. Clarke alone or by Mr. Clarke and the purchasing agent; and, from this point on, the purchasing department's activities were confined to order confir-

---

[2] The venture into manufacturing school furniture had been worthwhile. Within a year of the introduction of this activity, sales of desks and chairs had accounted for approximately 3 percent of Columbia's volume. Management had been satisfied with the profit margins on those products and had estimated that by 1962 or 1963 furniture would make up about 15 percent of the total business.

mation, order follow-up, importing procedure, invoice checking, and record keeping.

Foreign buying

In July, 1956 Mr. Clarke went to Frondenberg, Germany, to negotiate a contract for drive chains with Union Sils, a large manufacturer of such parts. Previous tests in Westfield of samples of the product had indicated that the chain's tensile strength was roughly 500 pounds higher than that of U.S.-made chain that Columbia had been buying at 26 cents per foot, delivered plant.

After four days of plant inspection, further material testing, and conferences with the vendor's engineers, Mr. Clarke placed an order for a 12-months supply, or 1 million feet, of standard drive chain. The terms of the contract provided that the price was to be 6.1 cents per foot, c.i.f. Boston, Mass.; payment was to be on a 90-day open account basis; and shipments were to begin in September, 1956, according to release schedules, to be specified. Adding duty at the rate of 30 percent, other costs of entry, such as customs broker fees, and trucking charges, Mr. Clarke estimated that the total costs for imported chain would be between 8.7 cents and 9 cents per foot. As each bicycle required 5 feet of chain, Mr. Clarke calculated that the use of German chain would cut Columbia's cost by about 85 cents per bicycle.

Mr. Clarke commented:

After I had checked out the engineering aspects and satisfied myself with the product quality, it did not take much to come to terms with Union Sils because I had known the president of the company for many years. Although we never had bought anything from him, we had met regularly to trade exhibitions, and he had visited with us here in Westfield at least once a year. Also, being a large manufacturer, we had kept abreast of developments in the bicycle and bicycle-parts industry throughout the world through subscription to all major foreign trade magazines, regular participation in international bicycle fairs since the early 1950s, and personal contacts with the top management of the major foreign parts suppliers. So, when we decided to abandon our policy to buy U.S.-made parts only and to switch to international purchasing, we knew exactly which parts manufacturers we wanted to deal with and what people we wanted to see. There was no problem of hunting for sources of supply.

Encouraged by arrival of the first shipments of chain on the promised dates, by the ease with which his purchasing departments handled the custom's procedures, and by Union Sils' strict adherence to quality standards, Mr. Clarke made a second trip to Germany in the late fall of 1956, this time to negotiate a contract with the same firm for a year's supply of pedals, front wheel hubs, and spokes. After spending a week in the vendor's plant inspecting manufacturing processes and testing materials, Mr. Clarke placed an order for 400,000 pedals at 43 cents per pedal, delivered plant; 200,000 front wheel hubs at 38 cents per hub, delivered plant; and 30 million spokes and nipples at $7.20 per 1,000 units, delivered plant. (The terms of the contract were the same as those of the earlier chain agreement.) The approximate prices that Columbia had been paying to American suppliers were: pedals, 50 cents per unit; front wheel hubs, 51 cents per unit; spokes and nipples, $9 per 1,000 units.

While in Germany, Mr. Clarke went to Schweinfurt to visit Fechtel & Sachs, another large manufacturer specializing in coaster brakes. Fechtel & Sachs also had been supplying Columbia with price quotations and samples of their coaster brakes, and through visits in Westfield the managing director of Fechtel & Sachs was well known to Mr. Clarke. The most recent price quotation on coaster brakes had been $1.35 per unit, c.i.f. Boston, as against $2.68 per unit, delivered plant, which Columbia was paying to an American supplier. The company was now making an offer at $1.33 per unit, c.i.f. Boston, which, in Mr. Clarke's calculation, would work out to $1.75, delivered plant.

Mr Clarke knew well that the production of coaster brakes required a great deal of engineering and manufacturing competence because of close tolerances and high performance requirements of the brake drum's rolling surface—a competence that American parts suppliers had demonstrated to Columbia over many years. Before making a decision to place an order with Fechtel & Sachs, Mr. Clarke therefore was particularly careful in inspecting plant facilities, manufacturing operations, and quality control procedures. Satisfied with his investigations, Mr. Clarke signed a contract for the purchase of 190,000 coaster brakes for delivery as required by Columbia between January and December, 1957, and on a 90-day open account payment basis.

Following his return to Westfield, the executive made more detailed calculations which confirmed that the contracts with Union Sils and Fechtel & Sachs would cut Columbia's production cost by approximately $2.20 per bicycle (in addition to $1.35 per bicycle upon completion of the company's plant modernization program in the early part of 1957).

Mr. Clarke realized that these reductions would diminish but not eliminate the price differential of $7 to $8 that existed between imported lightweights and Columbia's middleweights and balloon-tire models. He, therefore, restudied recent price quotations by foreign manufacturers on other parts and listed the following possibilities of purchasing: from a Swedish firm, tires at delivered-plant prices of $3.40 per unit, as compared with $3.79 for U.S.-made tires; from a Dutch supplier, saddles at 89 cents per unit, as compared with $1.14 for American saddles; from a British source, rims at $2 per pair, as compared with $2.20 charged by American vendors; from an English parts maker, lamps at 54 cents per unit, as compared with 70 cents for an equivalent domestic product; and from an Italian manufacturer, reflectors at 4 cents per unit, as compared with 6 cents paid to U.S. parts suppliers. Such reduction would, in his view, enable him to cut prices of Columbia middleweights and balloon-tire bicycles to a level where the company would be "back in the ball park" in competing with imported lightweights.

Mr. Clarke further estimated that if he decided to emphasize lightweights in Columbia's product mix, he would be able to purchase from Raleigh Industries, Britain's largest bicycle manufacturer, three-speed gear mechanisms at $6 per unit, delivered plant, as compared with higher prices for U.S.-made two-speed gear mechanisms that were then being used on Columbia's lightweight models. (American parts suppliers did not make three-speed gear units, although one company had quoted units at $11.) Caliper brakes, another characteristic component of lightweights, were not made in the United States; so Columbia would have to purchase from abroad for this reason rather than for lower prices.

Although Mr. Clarke was convinced that his company had no choice but to buy parts from international sources of supply, he wondered whether it was realistic to translate the price differentials into reduced manufacturing costs without making allowance for other considerations that might have a bearing on the magnitude of cost savings. Specifically, Mr. Clarke began to think about the impact of an almost complete switch from domestic to foreign suppliers (1) on the company's level of inventories and also on the volume of parts stocked by the company's customers, both at the jobber and retail level, (2) on the continued availability of domestic "backstop" sources of supply, and (3) on the long-run pricing policy of the European parts suppliers.

1. In procuring parts from domestic vendors, Columbia had rarely kept on hand more than a two weeks' supply. In many instances, even a one week's supply had proven to be sufficient.[3] Mr. Clarke commented:

If we replace domestic parts with foreign parts, we have to recognize that it takes six weeks to get the material from the European factory into our plant. If our operations are geared to such a shipping distance and if we have no alternative sources of supply in this country, we must carry at least a three-month supply, because there can be factory strikes abroad, shipping strikes, changes in sailing schedules, and dock or tugboat strikes in American ports. Assuming that we have to buy on a letter-of-credit basis, we will have our money tied up in a four-and-a-half-month supply of parts.

My calculations show that our inventories necessary to support an uninterrupted production of, say, 12,000 bicycles per week would increase by $800,000 to $1 million. In addition, I expect that we would have to carry replacement parts for certain items over the first two or three years, because I know that domestic parts distributors, as well as our customers, will be reluctant to stock components for foreign parts. Now, for some items, such

---

[3] Columbia was buying parts from American suppliers on a 2-percent, 10th prox. basis.

as pedals, tires, or spokes, this won't be necessary because imported parts are identical with American parts; for example, if a pedal breaks or wears out, it can be replaced with a pedal made in this country. But for other items, such as coaster brakes or variable-speed gears, we will have to carry inventories, at least initially, to ensure quick repair service for our products. I expect that this will tie up at least another $50,000 to $100,000.

The company executives believed that by careful use of its resources it could handle the financial requirements of the larger inventories, recognizing, however, that there would be periods of strain.

2. Mr. Clarke knew that two of Columbia's large competitors had begun to buy coaster brakes from abroad. He expected that, if Columbia decided to buy from Europe essentially all parts not made in its own plants, the remaining six members of the Bicycle Manufacturing Association could be expected to follow suit. Mr. Clarke thought that such a development most likely would lead to a withdrawal of American parts producers from the market because of lack of sufficient volume of business to operate profitably. He believed that the ensuing unavailability of alternative sources of supply in the domestic market would pose a real threat to the American bicycle industry, since prolonged interruptions in the flow of parts from Europe conceivably could occur for many reasons.

3. By the same token, Mr. Clarke wondered whether a withdrawal of American parts manufacturers from the market and the resulting increase in dependency of his company and others upon foreign sources might induce European suppliers sooner or later to raise prices by export cartel arrangement or otherwise. The exercise of pressure by Euopean bicycle manufacturers on the European parts producers to restrict in one way or another the supply of parts to American bicycle producers as American bicycles made with foreign parts became competitive with European-made bicycles was a distinct possibility in Mr. Clarke's view.

The chief executive of Columbia was not sure to what degree these three aspects, and possibly others, should influence his decision on whether to substitute European for all domestically purchased components. He believed, however, that such considerations were too significant to be dismissed lightly.

The selection of buying channels and the many technical and procedural aspects of international purchasing, on the other hand, presented no particular problems in Mr. Clarke's opinion. His views follow:

We are a big enough company to make a direct contact with the foreign manufacturer. Some of the European firms have signed up with exclusive agents in the United States in their efforts to break into the American market. In these cases we would have to deal with the agents for a while, but I would try to bypass them as quickly as possible. I believe strongly in dealing directly with the foreign producers, because it guarantees the most effective and efficient communication. Besides that, it fosters personal relationships and friendships.

If technological or administrative problems develop, such as rejections or fouled-up shipping schedules or diverging contract interpretations, I like to call directly on the president of the European company and work out the problems with him. I just wouldn't want any third party in between. And, based on our limited experience in foreign buying so far, I believe this approach has worked out quite well.

As far as doing business and handling transactions on an international level is concerned, I also think that our purchasing department has done a good job, and I would not expect any difficulties with direct imports from this angle.

Of course, I firmly believe that we should deal only with large, well-known firms and stay away from the small foreign supplier, even if he may offer a somewhat lower price.

COLUMBIA MANUFACTURING CO., INC. (C)*

During the year 1956, Columbia's sales volume had climbed encouragingly, and the prospects of ending the year with a small profit were good. On the other hand, the firm's executives realized they were so close to the break-even point that even a minor reversal of the sales trend could wipe out any gains. Since Mr. Clarke believed strongly that all possibilities of cost reductions outside of using foreign-made parts had been exhausted, he decided to substitute foreign suppliers of bicycle components for domestic suppliers whenever net savings on purchased parts could be achieved.

Mr. Clarke believed it wise to restrict the contracts for individual parts to as few foreign producers as possible in view of the risk of communication difficulties, the rather complicated shipping procedures, and the relatively high transportation costs encountered when purchasing outside the country.

"In order to simplify the foreign buying as much as possible, particularly as far as shipping schedules are concerned, and to get maximum bargaining power as well as maximum cooperation from the European companies, we usually let it be known that we were prepared to give them all of our business for a particular item," Mr. Clarke commented.

On this third trip to Europe, Mr. Clarke was accompanied by his chief engineer and his purchasing agent. Together they visited the chosen firms and thoroughly examined each manufacturer's engineering capability, production facilities, and product quality. Mr. Clarke then placed orders with about 12 European manufacturers for a substantial part of Columbia's 1957 requirements for tires, saddles, rims, lamps,

---

reflectors, caliper brakes, and variable-speed gear units.[1] All purchase orders were written on a 90-day open account basis. Mr. Clarke specified delivery schedules for the first quarter of 1957 and advised the suppliers that releases for the remaining three quarters would be specified at a later date.

As in previous years the company continued to manufacture such parts as frames, fenders, forks, handlebars, handlebar stems, braces, cranks sprockets fittings, and kickstands. Mr. Clarke explained, "These parts were not available from foreign sources at a cost savings to us. Only parts common to bicycles everywhere and standardized throughout the world were cheaper in Europe. With respect to specialty items, such as front forks which vary from one model to another, foreign parts manufacturers are not competitive. If we take a special design to a European company and ask them to give us a quote, the price would be much higher than our manufacturing costs or, for that matter, the price of domestic suppliers." He added, "When we finally decided to change our procurement policy, we moved fast, so that by the end of 1957 we would be able to produce a quality bicycle at a price that would be reasonably near the prices for foreign bicycles imported into the United States."

Meanwhile, as predicted by Mr. Clarke, the 1955 tariff increase had provided only moderate protection against foreign-made bicycles. In 1956, imports had dropped to 1.1 million units from the 1955 high of 1.2 million. Then in 1957, the first full year with the new raised tariff rates, imports had declined to 750,000 units. This level, while less than two thirds of the former import peak, was still uncomfortably high. Mr. Clarke observed, "The number of bikes that were brought into the United States from abroad in 1957 still made up 30 percent of the entire domestic market, and there were absolutely no indications that this percentage would decrease any further."

By the end of 1957, over 50 percent of the purchased parts for some Columbia models were obtained from Western European vendors. Consequently, the Federal Trade Commission advised Columbia that it could no longer label its products as "Made in U.S.A."

Although output for 1957 dropped 5 percent below the 1956 volume, the company showed net profits on sales (after taxes) of approximately 3 percent.

By late 1957, all nine major American bicycle manufacturers were importing parts on a large scale from Western European countries. Domestic production of bicycles in 1957 rose to 1.9 million units from 1.7 million units in the preceding year (see Exhibit 1). Mr. Clarke remarked,

---

[1] Contracts had been negotiated previously for coaster brakes, chains, pedals, front wheel hubs, and spokes. [See Columbia Manufacturing Co., Inc. (B) case.]

Exhibit 1

U.S. PRODUCTION AND IMPORTS OF BICYCLES: 1947–57

Year	Units			Imports	
	Domestic production	Imports	Total supply*	Percent of total supply	Percent of domestic production
1947	2,875,000	19,758	2,894,758	0.7	0.7
1948	2,794,516	16,774	2,811,290	0.6	0.6
1949	1,483,009	15,935	1,498,944	1.1	1.0
1946–49 Avg.	2,201,362	24,826	2,226,188	1.1	1.0
1950	1,963,716	67,789	2,031,505	3.4	3.5
1951	1,918,923	176,644	2,095,567	8.4	9.2
1952	1,930,307	245,763	2,176,070	11.3	12.7
1953	2,083,439	592,999	2,676,438	22.2	28.5
1954	1,554,233	963,667	2,517,900	38.3	62.0
1955	1,749,322	1,223,990	2,973,312	41.2	70.0
1956	1,761,702	1,174,214	2,935,916	40.0	66.6
1957	1,906,973	749,780	2,656,753	28.2	39.3

* Supply equals the sum of domestic production and imports.
    Source: Material for this exhibit was based on data taken from *Supplementary Brief,* dated March 16, 1964, submitted by the Bicycle Manufacturers Association to the U.S. Tariff Commission in re Hearings on Bicycles held March 2, 1964, in accordance with the provisions of section 225(b) of the Trade Expansion Act of 1962.

There is no question in my mind that the survival of my company hinged upon the use of foreign-made parts in our products. Had we not started to buy parts from overseas, the British and German bicycle producers would have dominated the American market within a few years. All our other defensive measures taken together could not have stopped them. In this sense the question that we and other members of the BMA had raised regarding any undesirable effects or disadvantages of foreign buying were academic. It was a question of doing it or going out of business.

Imports of bicycle parts amounting in 1949 to less than $0.5 million had climbed by 1957 to nearly $20 million, or close to 40 percent of the domestic market for bicycle parts. As a result, two of the four largest parts producers and a number of the 50-odd smaller suppliers discontinued manufacture of such parts.

Columbia's sales and profits continued to increase through 1960, when the production volume reached the company's 1953 level (which was the last year prior to the company's 50 percent loss of sales volume). Total domestic production of bicycles rose to nearly 2.6 million units in 1960 from 1.9 million units in 1957, while the ratio of imports to the total domestic market remained approximately 30 percent. Average net profits on sales for the American bicycle industry as a whole rose to about 5 percent (after taxes).

Throughout the period 1953–60, Columbia's sales of balloon-tire bicycles declined persistently. In 1953 bicycles of this type had accounted for approximately 95 percent of total sales, while lightweights contributed about 5 percent of sales. By 1960, middleweights accounted for approximately 94 percent of the company's sales volume, and lightweights 6 percent.

In 1959–60 Mr. Clarke decided to start emphasizing lightweight bicycles in the company's sales programs, since he believed that, if his company was to go beyond recovering lost ground and expand its business in aggressive competition with foreign producers, it had to sell lightweights at prices fully competitive with those of English imports.

Columbia's experience with foreign buying

Regularly in the fall of each year Mr. Clarke went on a four-week trip to Europe to place purchase orders for the company's parts requirements for the following year. After several years of experience, the president believed that the technical and administrative problems associated with Columbia's foreign procurement were tolerable in light of the continued large savings in material costs. Mr. Clarke said:

To buy parts over such a long distance and from foreign nationals creates certain problems, such as misinterpretation of letters or of order specifications. We have repeatedly received material with European standard threads, although we thought we had given thoroughly detailed specifications for American standards. At other times, we have received large shipments of spokes mixed together in different lengths, which created a considerable sorting problem, whereas with a domestic supplier we simply would have sent the spokes back. Recently we found that the white plastic covers of a batch of imported saddles developed yellow stains because on the type of rubber used for the padding. This, of course, is the kind of problem that can just as easily occur with a domestic vendor; but, when it happens with an overseas vendor, rejection and replacement problems can become quite involved and costly.

Also, some time ago, we experienced problems with the European type of plating, which was inferior to our standards and which created some arguments with the supplier involved. But, generally speaking, problems of quality are rare, which I think is largely due to the fact that we buy strictly standard items that have been used on bicycles throughout the world for many years. We do not buy anything made to our specifications or novel or different from standard bicycle equipment. The incidence of damage in transit is much higher, of course, if parts come across oceans rather than by rail or truck from a domestic plant. For example, in recent months we have received shipments of rims with such extensive damage and in such frequency that we are thinking about buying them again from a domestic source, although they are more expensive.

In 1961 Columbia lost the account of a large national department store chain to a European bicycle manufacturer, and sales dipped to 78 percent of the company's 1960 sales level. Since the prices of Columbia's middleweight and lightweight bicycles were still approximately $3 above those for German-made middleweights and British-made lightweights, the loss of the account gave Mr. Clarke new impetus to seek further material cost reductions. Thus, during his purchase negotiations in Europe for the company's 1962 production requirements, Mr. Clarke for the first time seriously explored the possibility of purchasing from several smaller manufacturers of component parts—firms that on previous occasions had offered lower prices than those that Columbia was paying to the large European suppliers. Satisfied with his investigations and negotiations, Columbia switched its orders for spikes, pedals, hubs, and saddles to smaller companies and, in some cases, to concerns in countries such as Italy and Spain not previously used as suppliers. Mr. Clarke estimated that these changes would cut Columbia's material costs by close to 45 cents per unit. He commented "Although we originally stayed away from smaller and less well-known companies, I thought that by now I had gained sufficient experience in foreign buying to avoid any real pitfalls that might result from switching to small vendors. During my trips to European countries and dealings with European firms since 1956, I learned enough to spot unsuitable or incompetent vendors.

Following this shift of orders among European parts suppliers, Mr. Clarke believed that he would be unable to reduce material costs further in this manner without jeopardizing material quality and continuity of supply.

Purchase of Japanese parts and components

In the summer of 1963, executives of one of the largest U.S. distributors of bicycles approached Mr. Clarke to see whether Columbia lightweight bicycles could be purchased at the same prices the distributor was paying to a British manufacturer. "These men told me they had experienced certain delivery and service problems with the foreign producer that would make it desirable for them to change from imported to domestic bicycles if no price differential existed," said Mr. Clarke. He continued:

They told me that they hoped, since the prices for our bicycles were so close to the foreign prices, that we might be able to do something to eliminate the remaining difference.

There seemed little doubt that if we could meet the foreign price these executives were prepared to place a substantial part of their 1964 orders with us. They would not disclose the price difference, but I knew that we were off by about $2.50 per unit. I replied that, if they were to approve the use of Japanese parts, Columbia might be of real interest to them. After much discussion by the distributor's purchasing heads, the executives came back a few weeks later and told us that they would welcome a bid for many tens of thousands of bicycles made partially with Japanese parts.

In addition to being concerned about a generally critical attitude of other American bicycle producers toward using Japanese parts, Mr. Clarke wondered about the quality of such parts as well as the ability of the Japanese parts producers to supply the volume needed by Columbia and to adhere rigorously to delivery schedules. Although Columbia had tested samples of Japanese multiple-speed gear units and found them satisfactory, management was inclined not to take product quality, and particularly consistency in product quality, for granted on the basis of samples.

Mr. Clarke also believed that the issue of purchasing Japanese parts was further complicated by the longer shipping and communication distance, as compared with European companies, which, in his view, increased not only the lead times but also the chance of disruptions in the flow of supplies. The Japanese offers specified irrevocable letters of credit as method of payment, which, according to Mr. Clarke, was a requirement by the Japanese government rather than a practice followed by the parts manufacturers.

If we placed orders with Japanese firms, the uncertainties with respect to quality, delivery, and general vendor reliability would be great. If, after having received an order for nearly 100,000 bicycles at a price that is between $2 and $3 below our current prices, something went wrong with the Japanese parts, this company might face a serious financial problem considering the fact that we just managed to get it back on a profitable basis.

COLUMBIA MANUFACTURING CO., INC. (D)*

In the summer of 1963, after Columbia Manufacturing Co., Inc., had been invited by one of the largest U.S. bicycle distributors to submit a bid for many tens of thousands of lightweight bicycles to be made partially with Japanese parts in order to meet prices currently paid by the distributor for British-made bicycles, Mr. Clarke, president of Columbia, decided to go to Japan to negotiate with Japanese bicycle parts manufacturers. He was interested particularly in buying three-speed gear mechanisms but also planned to look into the possible purchasing of other parts including tires and hubs. Mr. Clarke believed that a trip to the Orient was warranted to satisfy himself with respect to the ability of the Japanese firms to supply parts not only in large quantities but also of a consistently high quality and within the time limits dictated by Columbia's 1964 production schedules.

Mr. Clarke spent 10 days in the plants of the largest parts manufacturers in Japan, inspecting production facilities and quality control procedures, testing samples of the products in which he was interested, and negotiating prices and other terms and conditions with Japanese executives.

Satisfied with the results, he returned to Westfield and decided to submit a bid to the large distributor offering 26-inch Columbia lightweight bicycles, equipped with Japanese-made three-speed gear units, tires, and hubs, at a price that, in Mr. Clarke's estimation, would exceed by $1 the price (including transportation costs and duties) paid by the distributor for British lightweights. Mr. Clarke reasoned that the distributor would have to make some allowance for the fact that the British bicycles were delivered with the front wheel disassembled and also for the fact that buying from Columbia involved a 45-day supply of bicycles whereas buying from England necessitated carrying a three- to four-month supply. After some further price negotiations in which the distributor sought and obtained from Mr. Clarke an additional price concession of approximately 15 cents, Columbia received a letter of intent to buy the distributor's annual requirements of lightweights in 11 different models for 1964 delivery.

The company, in turn, placed orders with two Japanese firms for the supply of 100,000 three-speed gears, 240,000 tires, and 250,000 front hubs; also many thousands of caliper brakes, lamps, generators, and approximately 1.4 million feet of chain. As the first shipment of 10,000 gear units, 20,000 tires, and 10,000 hubs were reported ready for shipment in November, 1963. Mr. Clarke sent his factory manager to Japan to inspect the products. The factory manager spent one week in the plants of the suppliers testing random samples and then approved the shipment. Mr. Clarke commented:

In addition to the supplier's inspection and our examination, a Japanese government-sponsored inspection association went through the shipment before it left Japan. The quality of the parts was excellent, and the people that had warned us about Japanese quality were consistently proved wrong. We were scared stiff when the first parts arrived in Westfield, but no rejection problems developed. Had we received parts of inferior quality, we would have had a big problem on our hands, particularly since the parts were paid for.

Subsequent shipments arrived in Westfield on time and also proved to be of satisfactory quality. As a result, Columbia placed additional orders with the same suppliers for chains and lamps for delivery in the second half of 1964.

Within five weeks following the break of the news within the American bicycle industry that Columbia was buying parts and components from Japan, many major producers negotiated purchases of components with Japanese firms. Mr. Clarke said, "The net result was that, by the end of 1964, most large U.S. distributors of bicycles will have shifted back from various European manufacturers of bicycles to American manufacturers. Imports will have decreased by approximately 400,000 units, and domestic production will have increased by approximately 900,000 units." (See Exhibit 1.)

Exhibit 1
U.S. PRODUCTION AND IMPORTS OF BICYCLES: 1947–64*

	Units			Imports	
Year	Domestic Production	Imports	Total Supply†	Percent of Total Supply	Percent of Domestic Production
1947...................	2,875,000	19,758	2,894,758	0.7	0.7
1948...................	2,794,516	16,774	2,811,290	0.6	0.6
1949...................	1,483,009	15,935	1,498,944	1.1	1.0
1946–49 Avg...........	2,201,362	24,826	2,226,188	1.1	1.0
1950...................	1,963,716	67,789	2,031,505	3.4	3.5
1951...................	1,918,923	176,644	2,095,567	8.4	9.2
1952...................	1,930,307	245,763	2,176,070	11.3	12.7
1953...................	2,083,439	592,999	2,676,438	22.2	28.5
1954...................	1,554,233	963,667	2,517,900	38.3	62.0
1955...................	1,749,322	1,223,990	2,973,312	41.2	70.0
1956...................	1,761,702	1,174,214	2,935,916	40.0	66.6
1957...................	1,906,973	749,780	2,656,753	28.2	39.3
1958...................	2,104,549	823,914	2,928,463	28.1	39.2
1959...................	2,562,325	1,013,794	3,576,119	28.3	39.5
1960...................	2,584,622	1,186,596	3,771,218	31.5	45.8
1961...................	2,579,093	1,085,239	3,664,332	29.6	42.1
1962...................	2,954,215	1,266,790	4,221,005	30.0	42.9
1963...................	3,116,263	1,348,000	4,464,263	30.0	43.2
1964*.................	4,000,000	1,000,000	5,000,000	20.0	25.0

* Estimates by company executives.
† Supply equals the sum of domestic production and imports.
Source: Material for this exhibit was based on data taken from *Supplementary Brief*, dated March 16, 1964, submitted by the Bicycle Manufacturers Association to the U.S. Tariff Commission in re Hearings on Bicycles held March 3, 1964, in accordance with the provisions of section 225(b) of the Trade Expansion Act of 1962.

Sales and profits of Columbia rose sharply in the first 10 months of 1964, and Mr. Clarke anticipated that the company's production volume for the entire year would exceed the previous all-time record by 34 percent.

SUFFOLK POWER CORPORATION (A)

Suffolk Power Corporation was building three additional generating stations to serve its rapidly expanding energy market. To link these stations with the total area grid, a new method of carrying the power lines using ornamental tubular poles instead of towers had been adopted. Suffolk had had no previous operating experience with poles and decided to subcontract the design engineering, fabrication, and erection of the new line.

For the first phase engineering design, Mr. Carter, the director of purchasing, faced the responsibility of deciding with which supplier the business was to be placed after his staff had developed the information needed. He was aware that Suffolk had only three years in which to complete the entire project, and yet he had to ensure high-quality work.

Company background

Suffolk Power Corporation had been established before the turn of the century and was now one of the largest power utilities in the eastern United States. It serviced a highly industrialized area from ten fossil-fueled plants. It was expanding into nuclear generation. With assets of over $3 billion and demand doubling every decade, it had already earmarked funds to increase its kilowatt capacity from 8.4 million to 13 million over a four-year period.

The company was well known for its advanced technology and its good public relations. Both purchasing and engineering departments were centralized and located in the head office in the area's largest city. The new construction program was a heavy strain on both the professional and financial resources of the company, placing increased emphasis on the use of qualified people and suppliers outside the corporation.

Transmission line background

Although Suffolk was stepping up its older lines to 230 KV, by management decision and in accordance with the technological trend, 345 KV was adopted for the new line. It was to link the new generating stations in Addison, Smithfield, and Mesa Valley with the area grid, some 140 miles all told. As the atomic plants came on stream, voltages twice as high were foreseen.

Until now, Suffolk had used structural steel towers exclusively for carrying its power lines. (See Exhibit 1.) These were strong but visually prominent and attracted adverse comments from a public daily growing more aesthetically sophisticated. A relatively new development in the transmission field was the introduction of the ornamental tubular power pole. (See Exhibit 2.) Approximately 200 miles of line using these poles had been installed with good success in various parts of the country. Most installations were relatively short sections in densely populated areas. A line using poles cost twice as much as the conventional towers but was still substantially cheaper than underground installation. Con-

Exhibit 1

scious of the great strides made in power pole design and use, Suffolk management decided to specify poles for the new line.

Because of the volume of conversion and projected expansion work Mr. Carter and the project engineers knew that the tower manufacturers and erection companies with whom they had dealt in the past would not have the capacity to handle all the elements of the new pole concept. Furthermore, with no experience in 345KV or pole suspension, Suffolk had to rely on the know-how of others for the new line and needed the services and guidance of competent subcontractors.

Exhibit 2

The total job involved three major phases:

1. Engineering design called for layout as well as a functional pole specification and project guidance.
2. Pole manufacture involved a manufacturing proposal consisting of a specific design to meet the functional specifications as well as manufacturing volume and schedule deadline capabilities.
3. Pole installation involved excavation foundation setting, pole erection, and line stringing. Preliminary cost estimates for the total project were as follows:

> Phase 1—Engineering—$250,000–$300,000
> Phase 2—Pole Manufacture—$15 million
> Phase 3—Installation—$13 million

Mr. Carter and the chief engineer were not satisfied that any individual supplier could handle the total contract well. They decided, therefore, to subcontract each phase to a reliable source of high expertise within that phase, so that optimum overall benefits would accrue to Suffolk. The first sourcing decision dealt with the engineering phase.

Design engineering selection

All through the spring and half of the summer Mr. Oliver Dunn, the buyer, worked with the transmission engineering section of the system engineering department of the company to establish parameters and locate a suitable design source. By late July he was able to make his recommendation to the director of purchases. (See Exhibit 3.)

Exhibit 3
SUFFOLK POWER CORPORATION (A)
QUOTATION SUMMARY

Description: Design 140 miles 345KV transmission line for Addison-Smithfield-Mesa Valley
Recommended Vendor: Pettigrew Associates, New York, N.Y.
Location: Their Premises   Using Department: General Engineering
Buyer: O. Dunn.   Total Value: Established $290,000 Salaries
                                  + Burden
P.O. No: Date: Approval:

Additional Information:
1. The transmission section of our general engineering department is unable to perform the design work of all the planned transmission work for the next three years, and it is necessary to contract some portions of this work. Travers & Bolton are already assigned the conversion of the 120KV to

230, and it is recommended that this 140-mile Addison-Smithfield-Mesa Valley 345KV be contracted to some competent engineering firm.

2. We had sessions with each of three below mentioned engineering firms to acquaint them with our needs and learn of their capabilities. The work they will perform is as follows: make route sections; make subsurface investigations; make electrical hardware and general project designs; and furnish miscellaneous specifications, drawings, and technical data required to procure the right of way, hardware, structural steel and for the awarding of contracts for construction. It is estimated this work will total 12,300 man-hours. There would also be approximately $24,000 worth of computer services and general out-of-pocket expenses in addition to the man-hours.

3. Bid comparison is:

Supplier	Estimated man-hours	Basic average cost per man-hour (w/o fringes)	Approximate fringes (assumed same for all)	Overhead & profit	Estimated $/hour
Travers & Bolton	14,350	$10.00	20%	67½%	20
Crown Engineering . . .	–	$10.00	20%	80%	21.60
Pettigrew Associates . .	12,190	$10.00	20%	85%	22.20

It is recommended that this contract be awarded to Pettigrew even though their cost per hour is higher than the others. Total cost will be influenced by the capability and productivity of the company chosen, and, therefore, Pettigrew may not cost us any more; it is the desire of Suffolk management to have Pettigrew perform such a job with Suffolk as our first experience with them. Both T&B and C.E. have done considerable work for Suffolk.

It was normal practice at Suffolk to provide a very brief summary for the director of purchases on all major contracts. A large file containing detailed information was built up by the buyers and purchasing agents involved. Normally, some preliminary discussions were held as the project progressed, so that Mr. Carter was reasonably informed by the time the official recommendation was prepared. Should he wish to see more information he could request the file at any time.

All three of the engineering firms considered were large and engaged in a wide variety of engineering consulting services. Travers & Bolton and Crown Engineering had both done considerable work for Suffolk in the past and had performed satisfactorily. Pettigrew Associates had its head office in New York and maintained branches in ten American cities. Pettigrew employed over 3,800 people, had a good credit rating, and had annual sales in excess of $80 million per year. Suffolk had never used Pettigrew in any of its projects. All three engineering firms had some tubular pole experience with short-line sections in other parts of the country. Aside from the design requirements, the consulting engineering firm was also expected to evaluate bids from pole manufacturing and erection subcontractors.

SUFFOLK POWER CORPORATION (B)

Suffolk Power Corporation was building three additional power generating stations to serve the rapidly expanding energy market. To link these stations to the existing area grid, a new method of carrying the power lines using ornamental tubular poles, instead of towers, had been adopted. The second phase of the project involved pole manufacture to a functional engineering design with parameters. Mr. Carter, director of purchasing, had to evaluate the proposal from his purchasing supervisor as to which supplier should be chosen. [For company and transmission line background see Suffolk Power Corporation (A).]

Bidding procedures—preselection

Mr. Carter had given the responsibility to recommend a pole manufacturer to Gordon Yarrow, supervisor of materials purchasing. Gordon had the consulting engineers' services and the experience of his own engineering department to assist him. The consulting engineering firm on the project had been selected in August, and by early spring of the following year it had furnished Suffolk with functional specifications for the poles, cross-arms, and hardware. Suffolk engineers recommended that quotations should first be obtained on the most pressing portion of the line linking Addison to Smithfield. This amounted to about half of the total project distance. The expectation was that the experience gained on this first section would guide the contracts on the remaining half. Mr. Yarrow had to ensure a start on the 345KV line by the fall. This left not much time in which to develop pole prototypes and to perform the engineering tests in advance of erection. The number of potential suppliers was severely limited by two major requirements. Each supplier had to have a design computer program and a large press-brake for heavy metal.

First progress report

In May, after extensive negotiations with eight potential suppliers, Gordon Yarrow was able to give his superior a brief run-down on his progress. He told Mr. Carter he had encountered quite a spread in prices and that there were disturbing gaps in engineering information in some cases, but he believed the time-table could be met.

MR. CARTER: Try anyone abroad? There's a lot of high voltage experience on the outside, but perhaps it's mainly tower transmission?

GORDON YARROW: I don't know about that so much, but I've one bid definitely in the ballpark from a Canadian outfit, and what looks like rather a wild one from Japan. I think we can whittle these quotes down to a few fairly quickly when we get together with the engineers as some of them are a bit off the mark on first inspection.

MR. CARTER: Good. I take it that you don't think it will be necessary to let the consulting engineer see all the quotes, but only those that look most likely?

GORDON YARROW: Exactly, I shall let you know the outcome of our preliminary selection after I see our project engineers, and then we'll get the consulting engineer's evaluation of the remainder.

Mr. Yarrow then went over all detailed information and prices in the following weeks with the system engineering department and reported rejection of four bidders for the following reasons (see Exhibit 1).

JORDAN POLE CO.: *Q.* Use a zinc metallic finish and do not galvanize. Prices not firm, based on all rates in effect at time of delivery. Design not satisfactory; two-section bolted pole. No Charpy impact value furnished. Would have to add to test costs.

H. B. SMITHERS, INC.: *R.* Price too high. No previous experience in transmission but only in street light poles. Some questionable manufacturing techniques that we feel can be corrected. Excellent prospect for future requirements.

MARTIN AND STEVENSON: *S.* Price too high. Best qualified on basis of experience but did not provide weights, drawings, or details or alternate prices on standard base plate.

KYUSHIMO, INC.: *T.* Price highest (100 percent over low). No previous experience in high voltage transmission poles but provided the most information on design, drawing specifications, etc. Japanese source.

He then sent engineering information only (no prices) on the four remaining bidders to Suffolk's engineering consultants for a complete analysis of the bids on the basis of the requested design, a comparison of designs frunished, and exceptions to specifications.

Consultant's analysis

The engineering consultant's analysis were combined in six documents.

1. Covering letter (see Exhibit 2).
2. Design points considered (see Exhibit 3).
3. Pole data comparison (see Exhibit 4).
4. Comparison of designs (see Exhibit 5).
5. Comments on exceptions to specification by Henry Nelson Company, (see Exhibit 6).
6. Recommendations (see Exhibit 7).

Exhibit 1

QUOTATION SUMMARY—POLES AND ARMS 345KV LINE
ADDISON-SMITHFIELD SECTION

Quantity: 390 type 3A, 61 type 3B, 24 type 3C, 7 type 3D, 8 type 3E. Total 490

						Bidders		
	M Molson, Inc.	N Norris Steel Co.	O Structures Cdn., Ltd.	P† Henry Nelson Co.	Q Jordan Pole Co.	R H. B. Smithers, Inc.	S Martin & Stevenson	T Kyushimo, Inc.
Bid (in $000)	$5,600	6,040*	6,160*	6,974*	5,940*	7,930*	9,580*	9,940*
Extra for Nelson base	350							
Escalation	63	Firm	Firm	125	307	Firm	118	Firm
Total	$6,013	6,040	6,160	7,099	6,247	7,930	9,698	9,940
Revised total							8,025	

* On basis of Nelson base design.
† Recommended on basis of past service; engineering preference; delivery.
  Buyer: G. Yarrow

Approval:

Exhibit 2
LETTER FROM CONSULTING ENGINEER

Mr. A. Northrup,
Transmission Projects Engineer,
Suffolk Power Corporation.

Dear Mr. Northrup:

Re:

Addison-Smithfield-Mesa Valley 345KV Line
Design Evaluation, Steel Poles

As requested in your letter, we have evaluated the design information submitted by bidders *M*, *N* and *O*. We compared the designs with the Henry Nelson Company design which was previously submitted. We also considered the exceptions to the specifications proposed by the Nelson Company.

We have concluded after reviewing all the information furnished that the designs should be rated: Bidder *P* (Nelson); Bidder *O* (Structures Canadian, Ltd.); Bidder *M* and Bidder *N*. However, if Nelson is permitted to make their proposed exceptions to the specifications, we believe that their fabricated structure would be inferior to the structure proposed by Structures Canadian, Ltd.

Accordingly, our recommendation is:

1. Award the contract for poles to Nelson Company, provided they will accept the terms and conditions of the bid specification.
2. Award the contract to Structures Canadian, if unable to obtain a satisfactory agreement with the Nelson Company on the bid specification.

We were not requested to comment on any item other than the design features of steel poles. However, since H. Nelson Company is presently behind schedule on another project we are concerned with, we believe you may wish to review this area with them as well as with other suppliers. In this respect, we have not considered the experience or quality control procedures of the various fabricators, since we understand you will make this evaluation.

If you need any additional information, please let us know.

Yours very truly,

Robert Jason
Project Engineer

Project engineer's review and discussions on capabilities

At the end of May, Gordon Yarrow agreed with Mr. Northrup of transmission projects that the latter should meet with bidders *M*, *N* and *O* (Structures Canadian, Ltd.) to resolve the engineering and fabricating capabilities of each. This was not necessary for bidder *P* (Henry Nelson Company) as he was already working for Suffolk.

When the engineer had concluded his meetings, he called the supervisor of material buying to that effect. "Be right over," said Gordon Yarrow, "I'm very anxious to learn what transpired.

Exhibit 3
STEEL POLES ADDISON-SMITHFIELD—SECTION 345KV
DESIGN POINTS CONSIDERED

	P H. Nelson	N Norris Steel	M Molson, Inc.	O Structures Canadian
		Rating of bidders		
Number of field splices	1	2	1	2
Lap of field splices	1	*	2	2
Arm connection details	1	3	2	1
Welding procedures	2	1	1	1
Anchor bolt cage dimensions	1	1	2	1
Ease of erecting	1	3	1	2
Protective coating	1	1	1	1
Exceptions of specifications	2	1	1	1
Electrical clearance	1	*	*	*
Weight of poles	1	*	*	*

* Insufficent information.
Note: Numbers indicate order of preference.

"Sit down, Gord," said Mr. Northrup, greeting the purchasing department representative cheerfully and at the same time sweeping aside a pile of blueprints to make more room on his desk.

YARROW: How did you make out?

NORTHRUP: Not too bad. At least let me say it's pretty clear in my mind what we should do. Let's take our Canadian friends first. They're prepared to order a 40', 2,000 ton press now with a July delivery promised and probable operation by August.

YARROW: But we're after 108 poles by October 1.

NORTHRUP: Precisely. So they suggested subcontracting these along with the required test poles. This, of course wouldn't do because the whole purpose of the test is to prove out the fabrication as well as the design.

YARROW: Have they made poles like this before? I know they are competent enough in other structures.

NORTHRUP: No. And there would be a certain risk in placing an order this size with them. Still, they indicated a thorough understanding of the engineering and manufacturing details, and we have some confidence in their ability based on past structural experience.

YARROW: What did you think of bidder M?

NORTHRUP: They, too, had three representatives present, but their engineering was incomplete and left much unanswered. The designs covered only the 150' 3A and 3B poles and nothing on the remaining three types. Because of their press brake size, all sections greater than ½" thickness would have to be made in shorter sections.

YARROW: Meaning welding?

NORTHRUP: Right. And circumferential welds are so critical in the stability of the pole, it would be better if they were avoided.

Exhibit 4

POLE DATA COMPARISON ON 3A-130s ADDISON-SMITHFIELD-MESA
VALLEY-345 K.V. LINE

	Bidders			
	P H. Nelson	N Norris Steel	M Molson, Inc.	O Structures Canadian
Weight of pole and anchorage	42,905 #	N.S.	39,752	N.S.
Size of pole at ground line	46.7"	47.1" P.P.	48.4"	50" P.-P. = 46.2"
Plate thickness at ground line	½"	9/16"	9/16"	9/16"
D/t at ground line	93.5	84.0	86.0	82.1
Ground line design moment	4,740*	N.S.	4,240*	4,724*
Height to top of pole shaft	130'	130'	127.5'	130'
Number and size of anchor bolts	20 @ 2¼"	20 @ 2¼"	20 @ 2¼"	20 @ 2¼"
Length of anchor bolts	8'-0"	9'-0"	9'-0"	9'-6¼"
Shape	Octagon	Octagon	12 sides, irregular	Octagon
Coating	Galvanized	Galvanized	Galvanized	N.S.
Number of field splices	3	4	3	4
Deflection @ 25 psf wind	83.4"	N.S.	N.S.	N.S.

Materials	ASTM	Yield	ASTM	Yield	ASTM	Yield	ASTM	Yield
a. Anchor bolts	A615-Gr	75	A615	75	N.S.	75	A615	75
b. Base plates	A588	55	N.S.	(55 (42	N.S.		N.S.	50
c. Pole shafts	A572	65	N.S.	65	A572	65	N.S.	60
d. Arms	A572	65	N.S.		N.S.		N.S.	60

N.S. = Not shown on drawings
* Foot Kips

YARROW: So this leaves us with bidder *N*. Things any brighter there?

NORTHRUP: Not really. While their fellows told me that they had a 30′ 1,500-ton press in transit and could have it operating in five days after delivery, I don't like the underdesigning of the arm attachment and cross-arms. However, they agreed to review these. The lengths of the sections as shown on the designs can't be made in a single piece because of the length of

Exhibit 5

COMPARISON OF DESIGNS—BIDDERS *M, N, O, P.*

STEEL POLES—345KV LINE ADDISON-SMITHFIELD-MESA VALLEY

As shown in the comparison sheet for the 3A–130 pole, the nominal dimensions at the ground line are essentially the same for the four suppliers with the exception that *P* (Nelson) shows a ½″ plate thickness for the bottom plate section whereas the others show ⁹⁄₁₆″. This may tend to increase the weight of the poles supplied by *N, O* and *M*. A direct weight comparison cannot be made since *P* (Nelson) was the only fabricator to show structure weights. The increased weight is not important from a design standpoint, but a significant increase or decrease in weights will affect steel erection costs.

Pole splices

For the 3A–130, Nelson and *M* have three field splices while the *N* and *O* poles have four. All splices are slip joint type. Although the number of field splices is not important from a design standpoint, it is expected that the additional splice required for the *N* and *O* poles will result in somewhat higher erection costs than would the Nelson and *M* poles.

As may be noted from the drawings, the length of the lap splices for all the fabricators is different. Nelson provides the longest, followed by *O* and *M*. *N* did not show their lap dimensions. The specifications did not specify a particular lap dimension. However, the generally accepted criteria is to lap the joints by 1½ times the tube diameter. For the 3A–130 beginning at the pole top and poceeding down, *P*'s (Nelson's) lap to diameter ratios are 1.66, 1.82, 1.90. Ratios for *O* and *M* are approximately 1.50. It is believed that the additional lap on the Nelson pole is a more conservative approach and offers a somewhat larger safety factor in the area of the pole splices. This is desirable due to necessary tolerances in making field splices.

Arm connection details

Since the details submitted by all suppliers except Nelson are incomplete, we have regarded the information from *N, O* and *M* as schematic only. We rate the arm designs in this order: Nelson, *O, M, N.* In comparing the arm connections details of the four suppliers, it may be noted that the Nelson arm is connected to the pole shaft by four large bolts. The arms on the other designs are also bolted to the pole shaft and are similar to each other. However, the *N, O* and *M* arm connections utilize smaller bolts than Nelson's, and therefore more bolts are required. This will increase costs of construction somewhat.

Exhibit 5 (*Continued*)

The Nelson connection detail also has the advantage in that arms for the 3A type can be used on the other type pole shafts. This is desirable in some instances to achieve longer span lengths. Interchangeable arms were not required by the specifications and from a structure design standpoint should probably not be considered in this evaluation. However, from a line design standpoint, the interchangeable arms are desirable. It is believed, however, that any of the fabricators could make their arms interchangeable without any increased fabrication costs if they are asked to do so before the contract for supplying poles is awarded.

Anchor bolt patterns

All anchor bolt cages for a particular type of pole would be interchangeable with exception of the *M* design. *M* has not based his anchor bolt pattern on the drawings submitted with the bid documents.

Ladder details

Nelson and *M* were the only two to show any ladder details. We believe that satisfactory ladder details could be worked out with any of the fabricators.

Electrical clearance

With the exception of Nelson, the arm details are not sufficient to determine electrical clearances.

Construction consideration

Since the contract for steel erection has already been signed based on the Nelson design, we believe that a fair analysis must also include our comments on the possible increased construction costs which may be incurred by Suffolk Power due to the changing of pole designs. Some of these comments are already mentioned above.

1. Number of splices. It is believed that it will cost approximately $200 to make the additional splice required on the *N* and *O* poles. This price may be increased somewhat if it is necessary for the contractor to purchase different jacking equipment.

2. Arm connections. It is believed that the *N*, *M* and *O* connections will cost about $30 to $50 more than the Nelson connections.

3. Structure weights. Nelson is the only fabricator to provide structure weights. However, the others have proposed somewhat thicker plates in the bottom sections of the poles. This may increase steel erection costs. We have not attempted to determine the overall increase in project costs should the poles be other than Nelson's. We would be happy to do so if it would be helpful or desirable.

Exhibit 6
COMMENTS ON EXCEPTIONS TO SPECIFICATIONS
IN NELSON COMPANY'S BID

Exception 1

The exception to the method of shipping would relieve Nelson of the responsibility for poles during shipment from the southern factory to your storage yards.

Exception 2

No comment.

Exception 3

In Nelson's alternate bid, no material could be rejected on the basis of low Charpy values shown on the mill test reports or by sampling or anything but the thickest plate of the heat. Similarly, in their alternate bid, welding materials or techniques would not be subject to rejection because of low Charpy results, which is inconsistent with the intent of the specifications.

Exception 4

Excessive bolt projections represents a hazard to installation and maintenance personnel and would also increase construction costs.

Exceptions 5 and 6

Under Nelson Company's proposed welding and inspection specifications, the puchaser would be prohibited from using radiography to determine weld quality, even for the purpose of clarifying the interpretations of ultrasonic indications or for use where ultrasonic inspection cannot be made. Only visual or magnetic particle inspection would be permissible for any welds except the pole shaft to base plate weld and the longitudinal welds at the lap joints. Some welds, such as the arm to butt plate welds, are virtually impossible to adequately inspect after they are completed and require inspection while the work is being performed; most inspection techniques except radiography are of questionable value following galvanizing; all inspection would have to be made in the fabricator's plant. Henry Nelson company proposed inspection procedures are less stringent than AWS–D1.0.69 in allowing $\frac{3}{16}''$ or smaller defects regardless of spacing.

Exception 7

Nelson's conditions of sale give the purchaser only five days from unloading to make claims for damaged or defective material. The warranty clause is unclear in that it can be interpreted to mean that Nelson has one year in

Exhibit 6 (*Continued*)

which to make corrections but no provision for correcting defective material unless found in the five-day inspection period. It is our understanding that the intent is to provide a one-year warranty, but the words do not so state.

Escalation clause

Delays in delivery that are not caused by the purchaser should not be charged to the purchaser.

Exhibit 7
RECOMMENDATIONS FOR STEEL POLES ADDISON-SMITHFIELD SECTION

Our recommendations based on the information submitted for review are:

1. Award the contract for supplying the poles to Henry Nelson Company provided they will accept the terms and conditions of the specifications.
2. Award the contract to bidder O (Structures Canadian, Ltd.) if unable to obtain a satisfactory agreement with Nelson's.
3. Require that Structures Canadian provide arm details such that the 3A-type arms can be used on the 3B-type pole shaft.
4. Before awarding the contract to Structures Canadian, determine working hole arrangements, hot line maintenance requirements, and ladder details.
5. Require additional splice design overlap which will allow for a minus tolerance in field erection and still maintain the required splice overlap dimensions.
6. Resolve questions on design features such as designation of steels to be used in fabricating the poles, arm attachment plate details, electrical clearances, and data to be shown on drawings.
7. Perform time studies on steel pole assembly and erection activities to determine any increase or decrease in erection costs between Nelson and Structures Canadian poles which may be incurred by the erector.

If you should award the contract to bidder M or N, our comments would be essentially the same as for Structures Canadian. However, we may have some additional comments regarding their proposed arm connections.

the brake. This would require either more lap field splices or circumferential welds, neither of which is desirable, particularly the latter. I really would question giving an order of this magnitude to an inexperienced supplier.

YARROW: Well, you have serious reservations about all of them. I'm a little sorry. I was hoping we could have uncovered a more positive new source of supply. I take it, then, that you favor the present supplier, Henry Nelson?

NORTHRUP: Let me put it this way, and I'll confirm it in writing, based on engineering and fabricating experience, our first recommendation is Nelson's. However, the exceptions to our specifications would have to be resolved.

Next would be the Canadians, provided they fabricated all poles in their plant and delivery schedules could be worked out. Our third choice is bidder *N*, but design details must first be resolved. And we're still concerned about their lack of experience in heavy steel fabrication.

YARROW: And bidder *M*?

NORTHRUP: Can't recommend them, based on the engineering data supplied. Considerable engineering work would be required in order to supply the missing information.

YARROW: O.K., many thanks. We're reviewing all the bids because there are still a lot of loose ends to be tied together. I'll be seeing a lot of you in the next month or two.

Purchasing recommendation

On July 2, Gordon Yarrow made his recommendation to the director of purchasing, Mr. Carter. He supplied the consultant's analyses and explained what had transpired to his chief. "We wanted to encourage competition and develop local suppliers as you instructed," he said. "Engineering and purchasing met several times with representatives of bidders *M*, *N* and *O*." He related the engineer's side of it and said, "It is all here, confirmed by Tony Northrup," and he laid the report on the desk. "Then I summarized the bids, including the four we rejected earlier on, and here is how it looks (see Exhibits 1 to 7)."

Mr. Carter studied the figures briefly and said, "Thanks, Gordon. I have a meeting with the executives now, so I'll go over this later and get back to you tomorrow. I'll give you a call, probably in the morning." The two went their separate ways.

Next day the two resumed their discussion. "I see what you mean when you talked of a large price spread," said the senior man, "I can't understand how bidder *S*—that's Martin & Stevenson—were so far out of line. After all, with their experience, they shouldn't have, in the first place, tried to get away without drawings, weights, and alternatives. Were they not really interested?"

"It's hard to say" replied Gordon Yarrow. "But we went back at them and got into all that detail. As a result they revised their design and prices from $9,698,000 to an estimated $8,025,000 including steps and tests. We also considered buying the Canadian design, but they ran into labor troubles and withdrew their quote. Also gave serious consideration to buying Nelson's design and having companies such as *M* and *N* requote on the basis of using it."

"Why?"

"Because they have excellent shop facilities but they lack engineering ability and experience in this area. We inspected their plants. Bidder *M*, as you will recall, is making some of our low voltage poles—the 120 KVs—and is running into manufacturing difficulties. Bidder *N* had a hard job to come through with a test pole for this line. All in all, we felt it was the better part of wisdom to stay with someone more tried and true. Mind you, both these companies have potential and with more experience should be considered on future requirements."

"So that leaves Nelson?"

"Yes, Mr. Carter. The exceptions pointed out by our consultants have been resolved with them. In addition they will release to us for unrestricted use, the designs on all the 345KV poles."

SUFFOLK POWER CORPORATION (C)

Suffolk Power Corporation was building three additional generating stations to serve the rapidly expanding energy market. To link these stations with the total area grid a new method of carrying the power lines using ornamental tubular poles instead of towers had been adopted. Suffolk lacked experience with poles and decided to subcontract the design engineering, fabrication, and erection of the new line. [For company background and line project information and the selection of engineering consultants see Suffolk Power Corporation (A). For selection of pole manufacturers see Suffolk Power Corporation (B).]

Having selected its consultants for its first 345KV transmission line and placed its order for the fabrication of the poles and hardware, Suffolk Power was ready to locate a suitable contractor to do the foundation work, erect the poles, and string the lines.

Purchasing and engineering had been pursuing this concurrently with the search for a fabricator as Suffolk wanted to get started on the line by the fall. Mr. Gordon Yarrow, supervisor of materials purchasing, was responsible to the director of purchasing, Mr. John Carter, for the negotiations.

Construction selection

One company, T. D. Rapier, had done almost all Suffolk's transmission work for over the last five years, but, with the consultant's help, a good cross section of qualified line builders had been invited to bid. In addition several foundation companies were asked to quote on the subgrade work. This helped to test the market to determine whether foundation contractors could build foundations cheaper than line builders. Mr. Carter reserved the right to award separate contracts for above and below grade work.

Two meetings were held with the bidders, one for the line builders and another for the foundation contractors at which all aspects of the job were fully discussed. The unit prices were based on current wage rates and working conditions and were subject to adjustment by a percentage equal to .80 times the percentage change in the average wage rates.

By September the consulting engineers were able to provide purchasing with an evaluation of the bidding and computations enabling the attached summary to be compiled (see Exhibit 1).

Exhibit 1

SUFFOLK HYDRO 345 KV TRANSMISSION LINE—ADDISON-SMITHFIELD-MESA VALLEY

COMPARISON OF BIDS

Bidder	Line construction	Foundations installation	Total
Line contractors			
(D)	$7,850,640	$8,846,608	$16,697,248
(E)	6,352,984	7,436,185	13,789,169
(F)	6,898,440	6,296,413	13,194,853
(G) T. D. Rapier	6,247,560	6,332,312	12,579,872
(H) McTaggart Construction	7,238,950	4,612,134	11,851,084
(I)	6,032,012	No Bid	
Consulting engineer's prior estimate	7,958,400	5,102,400	13,060,800
Foundation contractors			
(J)		12,295,929	
(K)		6,494,394	
(L)		5,866,896	

Notes:
1. Two line contractors and one foundation contractor declined to bid.
2. The two lowest line constructors, Rapier and McTaggart, were evaluated, plus the possibility of a split award to (L) for foundations and (I) for above grade work. However, McTaggart is recommended for the following reasons:

    a. Lowest bid.
    b. Highly experienced. Built thousands of miles of line in mountain, desert, and swamp. Experience included 230, 345, 500 and 750KV construction.
    c. Presently working for several other power companies.
    d. Recommended by our design engineers and consultants.
    e. Have done considerable work in this state through a subsidiary although not for Suffolk.

THE DETROIT EDISON COMPANY

Introduction

In 1966 the Booker T. Washington Association of Detroit contacted The Detroit Edison Company to solicit discussions with their Purchasing Department, as to the desirability of the white business community placing business with Detroit based black-owned businesses. There were a number of meetings and, with each, a growing understanding within Edison of the special attention the Edison Buyers would have to exert if there was to be an Edison business relationship with black suppliers. Immediately following one of these meetings, there was the costly and unnerving Detroit race riot of July, 1967.

Exhibit 1
THE DETROIT EDISON COMPANY
(organization chart—purchasing department)

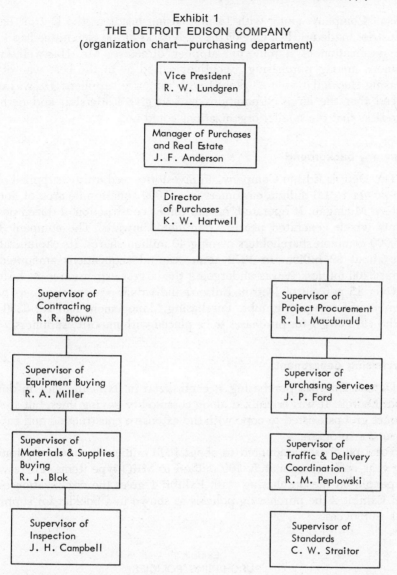

Following this, the non-profit organization, Economic Development Corporation (EDC), was formed in Detroit, under the auspices of 15 of Detroit's largest companies, to aid the growth of minority business locally. EDC's basic belief had been that private business and financial communities were best equipped to help minorities. One of the aims of EDC, therefore, was the encouragement of corporations to buy the products and services of minority firms. To this end, a sub-division of EDC was formed in 1968, called the Industrial Purchasing Committee (IPC). Mr. Kenneth W. Hartwell, Director of Purchases at The Detroit

Edison Company, along with 14 purchasing heads of the Detroit based industries made up IPC. One of the early tasks of the committee had been the publication of a minority supplier directory. Mr. Hartwell knew opinions among purchasing executives varied as to the best way of increasing the dollar volume placed with minority suppliers. He was convinced that the large corporations had to give leadership and perhaps take risks that the smaller organizations could not.

Company background

The Detroit Edison Company, an investor-owned utility, supplied electric power to 1.6 million customers in a 7,600 square mile area of Southeastern Michigan. It operated, or had under construction, a dozen power plants which generated nearly 11 million kilowatts. The company had 167,000 common shareholders owning 40 million shares. Its capitalization was about $2 billion. In 1972 alone, capital acquisitions amounted to about $400 million. It was undergoing the largest expansion in its history.

Over 15 percent of Detroit Edison's individual power consumers were members of minority groups. Purchasing Management had set $350,000 as the 1973 target for purchases to be placed with minority suppliers.

Purchasing department

Detroit Edison's purchasing is centralized in its head office in downtown Detroit. It was organized along commodity buying lines, but special project groups existed to cope with the extensive construction and capital expansion program.

Total purchases amounted to about $340 million in capital equipment per year and approximately $60 million in MRO type items. There were 80 people on the purchasing staff. Exhibit 1 gives the organization chart and Exhibit 2 the purchasing policies as shown in a booklet for suppliers and employees.

Exhibit 2
PURCHASING POLICIES

The following policies govern our business relationships with the Company's suppliers. They are necessarily broad enough to allow for the reasonable exercise of judgment and discretion.

1. Develop and maintain the maximum competition compatible with the quality and service required by the Company and the degree of reliability we desire in our suppliers.
2. Develop and maintain dependable sources of supply—ask for quotations only from those suppliers from whom we are willing to buy.
3. Deal fairly—avoid favoritism and make each transaction both a good buy for the Company and a satisfactory sale for the supplier.

4. Do not bargain with suppliers—obtain each bidder's best price on his first quotation; don't ask for a second quotation to meet a competitive bid.
5. Pay no premium for reciprocal business—award orders to the lowest bidder, provided the elements of quality, service, delivery, and reliability are equal.
6. Keep prices confidential—do not divulge prices to competitors.
7. Receive supplier representatives promptly and courteously.
8. Establish good relationships with supplier representatives—this can be better accomplished when incidental social expenses are shared equally by buyer and seller.
9. Do not accept gratuities—it is not in accordance with Company policies and has no place in our purchasing transactions.

Minority business development

The United States government had, among other measures, encouraged the support of businesses operated or owned by minority groups for a number of years. The Small Business Administration and the Office of Minority Business Enterprise were the administration's main means of implementing its policy.

Mr. Hartwell, early in 1973, realized that his department had to undertake special steps if it were to satisfy his and Management's wishes to place a significant amount of business with minority suppliers.

Buying from minority sources

Mr. Hartwell had made a special effort as a member of the IPC, to become better acquainted with the question of buying from minority sources. His information included publications, as well as direct contact with purchasing managers outside and inside that organization. At a recent special meeting of the local National Association of Purchasing Management chapter a number of participants voiced the opinion that just because the government advised purchasing from minority sources this was hardly sufficient reason for a purchasing manager to risk his company's dollars where it did not make good business sense.

Mr. Hartwell heard from several colleagues in the automotive field that a very aggressive approach to minority source development had resulted in the placement of significant volumes of business. He also heard from many others that, despite genuine efforts, results had been largely disappointing. Mr. Hartwell talked informally with a number of purchasing managers and buyers inside his own organization and he found that his buyers were largely conditioned to being sold by suppliers. When he asked the mill supplies buyer why a certain black supplier was not considered, this typical buyer voiced the following contentions:

1. That no representatives of the minority supplier had called on him, and he therefore had no idea at all of their interest in Edison, which

he believed was reason enough to assume that if a man doesn't think enough of his products to tell others about them, then the buyer is not willing to risk the Company's dollars on him.

2. He admitted that he did send inquiries to other outfits with whom he had never dealt before, but he had done so because they were listed in trade directories, or he had learned about them from others, and he was generally satisfied that they could meet the Company's needs. To gain the same information about minority suppliers seemed to be impossible, as he had no directories nor anyone with whom he could discuss this matter.

3. He reasoned that even if he did turn up a black supplier, he would have to be extra cautious except if he were a dealer for an established product.

4. He had not considered that he or the Company could go out of the way to encourage such suppliers, because he was well aware that the Company would not pay a premium in price, or lower the quality or service standards just to do business with minorities. The extent of his Company's willingness to find other ways to help minorities had not been evident, even though he knew the government had been encouraging the business community to deal more with minority groups.

Mr. Hartwell realized that purchasing from minorities was not exactly a high priority matter with his staff, but before taking further action he wanted to get the subject more into the open.

Mr. Peplowski, an experienced buyer, had recently taken part in an invaluable incident of doing business with minorities and this had excited him. The Company's normal distributor of some electrical fittings had announced a price increase of the products they distributed, which were manufactured by a certain company. When this increase was questioned by Mr. Peplowski, the answer was not too convincing as to the need to increase this price, so he had developed the names of other Detroit outlets for these same products. One of these companies was a minority business, and they offered the same items for the same forthcoming period 15 percent lower than the longtime supplier.

Mr. Hartwell asked Mr. Peplowski if he would head a special committee of four buyers, to investigate the ways to motivate the other buyers in this program. At the first meeting, he explained that the Company was anxious to deal properly with the problem of minority suppliers and not merely to give it lip service. He announced that Purchasing Management had adopted a goal of doing $350,000 of business with minorities in 1973. He also said he believed firmly in the desirability of this program and that the target could be met. Success would lead to a more stable community and this was not only in the best interest of Detroit Edison but of every Detroit resident as well. He frankly said that he did not know how to proceed, but thought open discussion would be useful. He asked what difficulties had been encountered in making a buying approach to minorities. Typical replies were:

"No one contacted the purchasing department." "They lacked financial stability." "There was no qualified minority supplier of major equipment." "Lack of persistence in selling, perhaps because they didn't know whom to contact and were too shy to inquire." "They don't know how to cost and bid a contract." "Often don't know enough about a product to sell professional purchasing agents."

Mr. Peplowski reported that approximately $50,000 had been expended during the previous year on minority businesses, mainly in painting, cleaning and appliance parts. This figure may have been greater, as there may have been much more business that had gone their way and not been recorded. He further stated that it may not be known if some suppliers are in the minority group.

Mr. Hartwell could see that one of the difficulties was in locating these people. He knew that EDC published a directory, and wondered if there might be others. When asking those present how many possessed such a directory, only one or two hands went up. Also, only a few hands went up when questioned as to how many kept records of minority purchases. He thanked the participants and asked for suggestions from all present to meet the target for 1973. He realized, however, he would have to take a strong position to get a significant change in the department. He knew he himself had to undertake the tasks of writing a policy for top level company approval and the outline of a positive action plan which would assure meeting his objectives.

7 SOME PROBLEMS IN SOURCE SELECTION

One might think that after a vendor had been found who could meet all the requirements, the search would be over. Such is not the case. Shall the buyer, in buying a given item, rely upon a single supplier, or utilize several? Shall the buyer buy directly from manufacturers or through distributors? Shall the buyer confine orders to local sources? Consider minority groups and environmental and political concerns? What shall be done about the problem of commercial bribery in any one of its various forms? To understand the difficulties involved in making a final selection of source, it is necessary to consider some of these problems. In doing so, we shall assume that adequate investigation has been made of the vendor's financial standing, general reputation for fairness, and capacity to meet the requirements as to quality, quantity, and delivery, and that prices are not unreasonble.

Concentration of purchases with one source

Shall the purchasing officer, in buying any given item, rely upon a single supplier, or utilize several? The answer to this question must be the very unsatisfactory one, "It all depends."

Briefly, the arguments for placing all orders for a given item with one supplier are as follows:

a. The supplier may be the exclusive owner of certain essential patents or processes and, therefore, be the only possible source. Under such circumstances the purchaser has no choice, provided that no satisfactory substitute item is available.

b. A given supplier may be so outstanding in the quality of product or in the service provided as to preclude serious consideration of buying elsewhere.

c. The order may be so small as to make it just not worthwhile, if only because of added clerical expense, to divide it.

d. Concentrating purchases may make possible certain discounts or lower freight rates that could not be had otherwise.

e. The supplier is more cooperative, more interested, and more willing to please having all the buyer's business. This argument, of course, loses much of its weight if even the total order amounts to but little or, although fairly large, represents but a very small proportion of the seller's total sales.

f. A special case arises when the purchase of an item involves a die, tool, mold charge, or costly set-up. The expense of duplicating this equipment or set-up is likely to be substantial. Under such circumstances, probably most buyers confine their business to the possessor of the die, tool, or mold.

g. When all orders are placed with one supplier, deliveries may be more easily scheduled.

h. The use of the stockless buying or systems contracting concept provides many advantages which are not possible to obtain unless business is concentrated with one or at best a very few suppliers.

On the other hand, there are strong arguments for diversification— provided, of course, that the sacrifice is not too great:

a. It is the more common practice among the majority of buyers to use more than one source, especially on the important items.

b. Knowing that competitors are getting some of the business tends to keep the supplier more alert to the need of giving good prices and service.

c. Assurance of supply is increased. Should fire, breakdowns, or similar accidents occur to any one supplier, deliveries can still be obtained from the others.

d. Even should floods, railway strikes, or other widespread occurrences develop which may affect all suppliers to some extent, the chances of securing at least a part of the goods are increased.

e. Some companies diversify their purchases because they do not want to become the sole support of one company, with the responsibility that such a position entails.

f. Assigning orders to several suppliers gives a company a greater degree of flexibility, because it can call on the unused capacity of all the suppliers instead of only one.

Numerous examples exist showing the advantages of one approach over another. A typical example favoring sole sourcing was as follows.

A very high-quality custom printer found that none of the company's ink suppliers could satisfactorily meet the exacting requirements of the unusual jobs the firm was called on to perform. A special arrangement with one supplier which involved extensive research and development resulted in a satisfactory, but expensive, product. Since the printer was in a position to pass ink costs to its customers who were more interested in quality and delivery than price, the printer found working with this one source advantageous in several ways. To protect against shortages, strikes, and other interference, the supplier agreed to maintain a special inventory in both the supplier's and customer's plant. When market shortages developed in 1974, the supplier put all customers except this printer on quotas.

A typical example favoring multiple sourcing was the purchaser of recreational equipment. One supplier, a sole source for a large segment of equipment, was strongly favored by engineering and production and had provided excellent service over the years. However, prices had increased substantially despite large volume increases. Only when a second source was brought in by the purchasing agent, over strong initial engineering and production objections, did the first supplier become concerned over price performance. Both suppliers performed well and competed strongly with the result that savings over the following five years ran into millions of dollars.

Genuine concern exists among purchasing executives as to how much business should be placed with one supplier, particularly if the supplier is small. It is feared that sudden discontinuance of purchases may put the supplier's survival in jeopardy, and, yet, the purchaser does not wish to reduce flexibility by being tied to dependent sources. One simple rule of thumb is that no more than a certain percentage, say 20 or 30 percent, of the total supplier's business should be with one customer. For small purchasers the mirror image of this problem may well exist in terms of a maximum percentage of total purchases with one supplier.

If a decision is made to divide an order among several vendors, there is then the question of the basis on which the division is to be made. The actual practice varies widely. One method is to divide the business equally. Another is to place the larger share with a favored supplier and give the rest to a second vendor. The second supplier is usually fully aware, even if not actually told, that he is an alternate. He accepts the business, however, because he needs volume, because it fills off-peak production periods or because he hopes that he may secure a larger share at some later date. When reciprocity is practiced, the division may be made as a reward (or lure) and may be based on the proportionate volume of sales obtained from the suppliers in question. There is, and can be, no common practice or "best" method of procedure.

Purchase through manufacturer or distributor

The question sometimes arises whether to purchase from a manufacturer directly or from some middleman. In a great many cases no such issue is involved. Occasionally, however, pressure is brought to bear, by various types of trade associations particularly, to induce the purchaser to patronize the wholesaler, or jobber, or mill supply house. The real issue involved here is closely related to buying from local sources. The question is not primarily one of proximity to the user's plant but rather one of buying channels.

Many arguments advanced in favor of purchasing through the middleman are equally applicable to purchasing from a manufacturer located near the point at which the goods are to be used. For example, the purchasing officer for a candy manufacturing company had been buying transparent gelatin paper from a wholesale distributor. This distributor had up to that time been able to render the better service, with the price practically identical. It appeared likely, however, that there might be a shortage in the supply of this item and also that the manufacturer might undertake direct distribution. In the event of a shortage, the buyer felt that those who bought directly from the manufacturer would probably receive preference on their orders. His belief that this situation might develop was so pronounced that he abandoned the use of the wholesale distributor and purchased directly from the manufacturer.

Another example may be cited to illustrate an opposite decision. An insurance company decided to purchase loose-leaf binders from a wholesale distributor and, when urged by the manufacturer to purchase directly at a lower price, refused to do so. The basis for this action was that the manufacturer had neglected to notify the wholesale distributor of his intention to canvass the latter's customers directly, and the purchasing director thought it was unethical of him to change his policy without notifying the distributor. The purchasing director did, however, notify the manufacturer that he would continue to use that company's product, although refusing to buy directly.

Another illustration of change in distributors may be found in the case of the purchasing officer for a company which made addressing machines. He bought glue directly from a manufacturer, even though the local wholesaler could make more prompt delivery than the manufacturer and quoted the same price; his reason was that the wholesaler occasionally followed the very unwise policy of substituting glue inferior in quality to that demanded by the buyer's specifications. Since appearance did not indicate quality, this substitution was rather easy to effect. Although brands were usually marked on the barrels, occasionally they were indistinct; and if the supplier wished to deceive, he could alter the brand markings. The purchaser felt that refusal to give further orders for glue to the wholesaler would be a warning to guard against substitutions on the other products which he continued to purchase from it in the future.

The justification for independent middlemen is to be found in the economic services which they render. If a wholesaler is carrying the products of various manufacturers and spreading his marketing costs over a great variety of items, he may be able to lay down the product at the buyer's plant at a lower cost, particularly when the unit of sale is small and customers are widely scattered or when the demand is irregular. Furthermore, he may carry a stock or goods greater than a manufacturer could afford to carry in his own branch warehouse and therefore be in a better position to make prompt deliveries and to fill emergency orders. Again, he may be able to buy in carload lots, thus effecting a saving in transportation charges, with a consequent lower cost to the buyer than if the purchaser were buying in a smaller quantity in an attempt to procure his requirements directly. There are other important services rendered by the middleman which make him not infrequently a very justifiable source of supply for the purchasing officer.

Local sentiment may be strongly in favor of a certain jobber. Public agencies are particularly susceptible to such influence. Generally, concerns that sell through jobbers tend, as a matter of policy, to buy whenever possible through jobbers.

On the other hand, some large organizations often seek ways of going around the supply house, particularly where the buyers' requirements of supply items are large, where the shipments are made directly from the original manufacturer instead of from the middleman's stock, and where no selling effort or service is rendered by the wholesaler. Some manufacturers operate their own supply houses to get the large discount. Others have attempted to persuade the original manufacturers to establish quantity discounts—a practice not unlike that in the steel trade.

Still others have sought to develop sources among small manufacturers not having a widespread distributive organization. Some attempts have been made to secure a special service from a chosen middleman, such as an agreement whereby the latter would add to his staff "two people exclusively for the purpose of locating and expediting nuisance items in other lines."

Most steel warehouses do the bulk of their business in general steel products. The great majority of the tonnage is in carbon grades, with alloys and stainless steel accounting for a small portion of the total warehouse business. In some instances other metals are stocked.

The warehouses do not offer their customers any price advantage over mill purchases. The mills give warehouses no price protection in the form of trade discounts, and a steel warehouse operator buying steel must pay exactly the same price for a given quality and quantity as would any of his customers placing an identical order. For the most part a warehouse must obtain its margin to cover operating costs and profits from buying in large quantities and reselling at the proportionately higher prices specified for small quantities.

Heavy inventories must be carried, for example. There may be as many as 600 items in a stock of carbon bars when qualities, finishes, and sizes are all taken into account. Similarly, it may be desirable to stock 1,000 different items of mechanical tubing. The average warehouse is likely to carry between 1,000 and 2,500 tons of steel. A very large warehouse will stock as many as 10,000 items, adding up to 25,000 or 30,000 tons of steel.

In addition to carrying a wide selection of inventory for their customers, the warehouses usually maintain a rather elaborate delivery system as a part of their services. Most warehouses have facilities for shearing and cutting steel to the customer's specifications. Indeed, some warehouses do a substantial amount of "readying" of steel for customer use. For this service, of course, they make an additional charge.

Certainly, the warehouses cannot cut their services if they hope to improve their position. If anything, they must improve the quality of the services they offer as sources of supply in competition with mills. With the margin picture in mind, the problem of volume assumes increasing importance.

Stockless buying or systems contracting

Many companies which buy the type of item sold by mill supply houses, jobbers, and wholesalers have found that the use of the stockless buying concept has resulted in lower prices, better service, less paper work, elimination or reduction of inventories and stockroom storage space (see Chapter 3). Usually the buyer's requirement for a family of related items is purchased from one source or at the most two sources.

Systems contracting may well disrupt some of the normal trade patterns. For example, a buyer may request a vendor to carry certain lines to complete the systems contract of a group or class of items. This may force the vendor to make arrangements with additional manufacturers to switch sources and to add to the product line. The impact of stockless buying arrangements has been felt in a number of areas according to L. Groeneveld.[1] It leads to the merging of ordering and inventory systems with extensive use of telephone, teletype, and Data-Phone. The next logical step is the integration of DP systems. Reliance on one source and one channel reduces dual channels and more service is usually provided by the seller. Assurance of 24-hour or 48-hour delivery in packages which can be directly delivered to the ultimate user is fairly common. Additional services include inventory and record keeping, assembly of related items, an acquisition service, and technical services. Standardization is normal along with simplification. Most systems contracts are renewed regularly. The economic order quantity concept is no longer relevant. Distributors are becoming more sophisticated and managerial representation in negotiations becomes essential. The popularity of blanket contracting is, therefore, creating a new set of relationships in the marketplace with substantial impact on both buyer and seller.

---

[1] L. Groeneveld, "The Implications of Blanket Contracting for Industrial Purchasing and Marketing," *Journal of Purchasing*, vol. 8, no. 4 (November 1972), pp. 51–58.

Geographical location of sources

Shall purchases be confined as largely as possible to local sources, or shall geographical location be largely disregarded? Seventy-five percent of buyers *prefer* to buy from local sources, and a substantial percentage of these indicate that they are willing to pay more or accept less satisfactory quality or service to do so. This is particularly true of the larger companies.

This policy rests on two bases. The first is that a local source can frequently offer more dependable service than one located at a distance. For example, deliveries may be more prompt both because the distance is shorter and because the dangers of interruption in transportation service are reduced; savings in freight may mean a lower price; knowledge of the buyer's peculiar requirements, as well as of the seller's special qualifications, may be based on an intimacy of knowledge not possessed by others; there may be greater flexibility in meeting the purchaser's requirements; and local suppliers may be just as well equipped as to facilities, know-how, and financial strength as any of those located at more distant points. Thus, there may well be sound economic reasons for preferring a local source to a more distant one.

A second basis for selecting local sources rests on equally sound, although somewhat less tangible, grounds. The purchasing agent and local company owe much to the local community. The plant is located there, from it is drawn the bulk of the labor force, and often a substantial part of its financial support, as well as a notable part of its sales, is local in character. The local community provides the company's personnel with their houses, schools, churches, and social life. To recognize these facts is good public relations, which have financial as well as social value. Therefore, if a local source of supply can be found that can render a buyer as good a value as can be located elsewhere, it should be supported.

This policy has two complicating elements. One is that the purchasing agent's primary responsibility is to buy well. Emotion should rarely supplant good business judgment, for to do so is, in the long run, to render the local community a poor service indeed. A second complication arises through the difficulty of defining "local." Technological changes have affected not only the size and distribution of the centers of population but also the commercial and business structure, resulting, among other things, in a widening of market areas and hence the sources from which supplies can be obtained. These boundaries are constantly expanding. Sellers can now profitably cover a much wider area than they once could. With radio and television, increased national advertising, and wider newspaper coverage, "local promotion" has taken on a new meaning. Improved packaging, improved roads, and speedier delivery by truck and plane have had a similar effect. Therefore, what once might properly have been called "local" has, for many areas and many items become provincial or national. There is no easy rule by which a buyer can decide the economic boundaries of the local community. The answer can be found only in the good judgment of the purchasing officer.

The great number of mergers which have occurred in recent years, and the development of the conglomerate type of corporation have absorbed many successful local companies into national companies. As and when the management of the local company moves into the national headquarters, some of the advantages of dealing with a local company may be lost.

Despite the validity of the arguments for giving preference to local sources, it would be folly to carry them too far. The wisdom of stimulating healthy competition, the assurance which comes from having a diversity of sources, actual inefficiency of local sources—these and many other reasons lead purchasing officers to seek a proper balance with reference to the geographical location of suppliers. No vendor should expect to get orders merely because he represents a local firm. Mr. W. G. Morse, formerly purchasing agent for Harvard University, has said, "I am asked to buy because the dealer is a Harvard graduate; because at some time or other he made gifts to Harvard; because it is his policy to employ Harvard men; because he happened to pay rent to Harvard; and because Harvard is in Cambridge." No reliable vendor is likely to seek business on such grounds as these.

Reciprocity

Under what circumstances, if at all, shall reciprocity be practiced? A workable, though none too exact, definition of reciprocity is as follows: "Reciprocity is the practice of giving preference in buying to those vendors who are customers of the buying company as opposed to vendors who do not buy from the company." This broad statement, however, is scarcely the form in which the problem arises. Much fruitless criticism has been advanced on the part of those who apparently do not fully realize that so far as purchasing departments, at least, are concerned, reciprocity is not a debatable policy to the extent that it involves purchasing requirements under conditions which will result in substantially higher prices or inferior service. Purchasing directors do debate the issue as to how far it can be practiced, *assuming that conditions of price, service and quality are substantially the same;* there is, however, very little attempt to defend placing orders with a company, even a valued customer, when these conditions are out of line with those available from other sources.

The use of reciprocity as a basis for obtaining sales is a practice of long standing, the essential soundness of which has been argued pro and con at great length. It is probable that the policy originated simply from a desire to increase goodwill. Quality, service, and price being equal, it was natural for a company to distribute some of its orders for materials and supplies among its better customers as a friendly gesture of appreciation, realizing that at no added cost to itself it might strengthen good relations already existing. A great many companies still follow the practice only for this purpose. There are many others that refuse to practice it, even to this extent, because they are not satisfied that in the long run it is essentially sound. Others do not feel the need of it, as, for instance, those who do a large amount of special order business, have an outstanding reputation for service, or sell a product widely recognized as superior. On the other hand, many companies have come to use it as a basis for soliciting and even for demanding orders. Thus, a definite issue on policy has developed. Should sales depend solely on the ability of the sales force to obtain orders without any assistance from the purchasing department, or should the purchasing power of the company be used as a means to increase the sales volume and presumably the net profits of the company even at some added cost or sacrifice at other points?

Reciprocity is not, in the last analysis, either a purchasing or a sales problem; it is a management problem—and management can build an excellent case for reciprocity. Thus, there are cases—real or fancied—in which a company is, to all intents and purposes, forced to practice reciprocity to survive.

But reciprocity may be practiced from choice rather than necessity. And why not? After all, reciprocity means that the sales department gets some business it might not otherwise have, and if care is exercised in handling, it should be profitable business. This business is particularly important to the management of a company whose product, although wholly satisfactory, is not one of outstanding superiority and whose distributors or customers must therefore be secured on some other basis. Of course, to the sales department both of the purchasing company and of its supplier the reciprocal orders may have come rather easily and at little or no cost to either of them. Yet orders are orders. "But," some purchasing officer says, "my purchasing department often has to pay a higher price for the material we buy. My company's real profit on the transaction is less than appears in the sales record because part of the cost of getting this business has been charged to me." This statement may be true. But as a management question the whole issue is one of comparative costs. Thus, to add $1,000 to the cost of material purchased in return for a sales order on which the profit would otherwise have been $1,500 will cut the actual net return to $500. But there is still a profit of $500 on a sale that might not otherwise have been made at all, to say nothing of the additional volume over which to spread overhead costs. Furthermore, when the supplier is given an order, his goodwill toward the buyer has been increased. The sales department of the purchaser then finds it easier to get an order the next time; and the supplier, in an effort to prove that the confidence was warranted, will do his utmost for the buyer.

The case against any general use of reciprocity rests on the belief that the practice is at variance with the sound principles of either buying or selling. Whatever else may be said, the sale of a product must, in the last analysis, be based on the qualities of the product sold and of the service attending the transaction. There is only one permanent basis for a continuing customer-supplier relationship: the conviction on the part of the buyer that the product of a particular seller is the one best adapted to his need and is the best all-around value available. As long as the sales department concentrates its attention on this appeal, it will find and retain permanent customers. Every sales manager will concede this argument, at least in theory. But if it be sound sales policy for one company, it is equally sound for the sales departments of the companies with which it has business relations. In other words these companies should be required to sell not on the shifting sands of direct price cutting, free deals, good fellowship, or fear, but on the firm foundation of a better product at a fair price. And if it is the business of the purchasing officer to place orders on this latter basis, he should not be required by the management of his company to compromise his responsibility in order to aid a sales department unable or unwilling to stand on its own feet. The whole issue is not one of encroachment by one department upon the prerogatives of another, but it is one of the essential nature of the two functions. When management endorses the practice, it is often quite as unaware of the inconsistency of its policy as when boasting of a one-price sales policy, on the one hand, and urging the purchasing officer to break any price a seller may offer him, on the other. Reciprocity, even as a sales policy, is a dubious practice. Although its proponents urge that it can be defended as sound sales promotion, supplementing rather than supplanting more basic sales appeals, considerable skepticism exists on this score.

When all other arguments have failed, the defenders of reciprocity rest their case on the assertion that all they are requesting is that when quality, service, and price are equal, the customer of the company be given preference. Few purchasing officers would object to reciprocal buying on this basis. When reciprocity really means this, the controversy vanishes into thin air; there is nothing left to argue about. But, in practice, it seldom does. Actually, abuse is practically certain to creep in, and any policy almost inevitably leading to abuse is open to serious question, quite regardless of the theoretical arguments pro and con. For instance, buyers are urged to buy from X not because X is a customer but because X is Y's customer and Y is our customer, and Y wants to sell to X. Moreover, seldom is the sales department or the customer content with an even break. The sales manager, unable to sell his product on its own merit and unable or unwilling to cut prices, asks the purchasing department to make up for his deficiencies by making sales for him and by absorbing any differential in cost incurred, which would be to the discredit of the purchasing department.

It is apparently true that to a greater or less degree reciprocity is found in nearly every type of manufacturing business as well as in banking institutions and insurance, public utility, transportation, and construction companies. It is among manufacturers of industrial goods, however, that the practice is most common. It appears to be particularly prominent among manufacturers of machinery and other iron and steel products, electrical supplies, paper and printing, chemicals (including paints) and nonferrous metals, petroleum, and rubber.

Reciprocity is not a practice in which but a single seller and a single buyer are involved. In the past, most of the discussions on the wisdom of the policy have apparently assumed not merely that such simple relationships are typical but that they constitute the only circumstances under which the issue arises. Such is, in fact, far from true, for about 44 percent of the purchasing officers' replies to a questionnaire indicated that their companies engaged to a greater or less extent in what may be called "three-way reciprocity" or in even more complicated forms. Thus, a manufacturer of sheet metal sells his product to a manufacturer of oil drums. The sheet metal manufacturer, having no use for the drums, buys its oil from a customer of the drum manufacturer. Again, a construction company is often under pressure from the owner of the proposed building to buy from a particular material supplier because that supplier happens to be a purchaser of the owner's product or a stockholder. The construction company may also feel pressure from the engineer or architect and at the same time want to satisfy other owners who have been clients in the past or may become so in the future. Indeed, a great deal of ingenuity has been exercised in the use of reciprocity when the manufacturing requirements of the seller are such as to prelude purchasing the products sold by an actual or a potential customer.

Even the purchasing department may take the initiative in developing reciprocal relations by using its contacts for their sales possibilities. In fact, in many cases the purchasing officer goes out of his way to assist customers from whom he is not in a position to buy by suggesting other companies, obligated to his own, to which his customers may go. Sometimes, instead of relying on mere suggestion, a purchasing department goes further in its efforts to ensure that a relationship is established between its customers and its suppliers. Although the principles underlying these indirect reciprocal relationships differ in no essential particular from two-way reciprocity, nevertheless it is true that more vigorous objection is raised to the extended policy than to the simpler form. From the standpoint of the sales department, it is clear that the more involved the relationships become, the greater is the difficulty of checking up on the effectiveness of the policy. There also is a quite understandable resentment on the part of the purchasing officer toward having various forms of indirect pressure brought to bear upon him.

Trade relations departments

The term "trade relations" is sometimes used synonymously with the word reciprocity. Actually, trade relations has only come into common business usage since the end of World War II. It is generally defined as an organizational device that is designed to centralize information and records so that full analysis can be made of the buying and selling relationships of a company. Without such organization, particularly in a decentralized multidivision company, it is virtually impossible to administer any consistent companywide policy concerned with reciprocity. Companies which have established a trade relations department usually assign the organization to one of three places: as a staff position under the president or some other general management executive; under the top marketing or sales executive; as a staff job under the top purchasing executive.

The advocates of the use of a formal trade relations organization emphasize that trade relations enters a situation only after it is determined that price, quality, and service are acceptable to the companies involved. The role of the trade relations manager is that of advisor, consultant, analyst, and commercial relations expert.

Reciprocity, trade relations and the antitrust laws

Generally speaking there is no body of law relating directly to reciprocity. In three cases decided in the decade of the 1930s, the Federal Trade Commission condemned the use of purchasing power to *coerce* reciprocal purchases.[2] In the absence of threats or other types of coercion the use of reciprocity was not regarded as illegal.

Whether or not the substantial increase in the number of companies instituting trade relations departments in the late 1950s had any bearing on the increased interest of federal antitrust authorities in reciprocity in the early part of the 1960s is open to question. The fact is, however, that on April 12, 1961, a federal indictment was obtained against the Electro-Motive Division of General Motors charging that General Motors had coercively used the placement of its large rail shipments to monopolize the manufacture and sale of railroad locomotives. (The indictment was dismissed December 28, 1964.)

---

[2] *Waugh Equipment Co. et al.* (1931) 15 FTC 232; *Mechanical Manufacturing Co. et al.* (1932) 16 FTC 67; *California Packing Corporation et al.* (1937) 25 FTC 319.

A case against Ingersoll-Rand Company in 1963 sought to stop the company from acquiring three manufacturers of underground coal mining machinery whose combined share of the market was 30 percent. In issuing a preliminary injunction the federal district court stated:

> It is not overly speculative to assume that the judicious use of its steel purchasing power by Ingersoll-Rand could immeasurably increase the sales by the acquired companies of machinery and equipment to the coal-mining companies which acutely need the continued goodwill of the steel industry.

In 1965, the Supreme Court expressed its views on reciprocity in considering mergers under Section 7 of the Clayton Act in a decision of the U.S. Supreme Court against Consolidated Foods.[3] The court held that Consolidated had overtly used reciprocity to promote Gentry, Inc. (an acquired company), sales. Such use of Consolidated's purchasing power was held to have given Gentry an unfair advantage over competitors. The court ordered Consolidated to divest itself of Gentry.

Other recent government antitrust actions against certain corporate mergers have been based on the charges that the consummation of the merger would result in conditions where the use of reciprocity could create unfair competition in an industry.

These actions and decisions regarding reciprocity and trade relations activities raise a question as to the advisability of having a formalized trade relations department.

Attitude toward gratuities

How shall the purchasing manager deal with the problem of excessive entertainment and gifts in any one of their varied and subtle forms? Here is a practice that seeks, through gifts, entertainment, and even open bribery, to influence the decision of persons responsible for making a choice between suppliers.

There can be no justification for accepting such gratuities. Fortunately, the purchasing manager today is not open to any general criticism on this basis. Such, of course, is not always the case. In extreme form some companies have been practically forced into bankruptcy through excessive inventories built up with a total disregard of market trends to satisfy obligations incurred through direct and indirect bribery. In some instances this bribery has been quite open; in others, it has been due to stupidity and incompetence of the individual buyer. Sometimes the buyer has been permitted to benefit from a speculative stock or commodity account (carried by the seller of supplies for the buyer) giving the buyer margin facilities which he would not otherwise have

---

[3] The case is *FTC* v. *Consolidated Foods* (1965) 380 U.S. 592.

been entitled to receive; in some cases he has even been allowed to trade and reap the benefit of all the profits, while all losses have fallen on the party sponsoring the account.

Such attempts to influence decisions unfairly are directed not only toward purchasing personnel. Work managers, foremen, and others in production or engineering who are directly responsible for or largely influence decisions regarding types of materials to be procured are also approached. In such cases, even though the purchasing officer himself is not directly influenced, the work of his department is perforce affected, and the efficiency with which that work is done may in no small measure be minimized.

So serious do some companies consider this whole problem that they forbid any employee of the company to receive any gift, no matter how trivial, from any supplier, actual or potential.

It is, of course, difficult always to distinguish between legitimate expenditures by suppliers in the interest of goodwill, and illegitimate expenditures made in an attempt to place the buyer under some obligation to the vendor. In these borderline cases, only ordinary common sense can provide the answer. It is not to be expected that a small gift at Christmas time of but nominal value need subject the recipient to adverse criticism. Or a salesman calls on a purchaser and invites him out to lunch so they may discuss a transaction without losing time or as a matter of courtesy. Such action is presumed to be in the interests of goodwill, although the cost of the lunch must be added to the selling expense. An attractive but inexpensive gift may be given by the vendor's company to adorn the desk of the procurement officer. The vendor's name appears on the gift, and therefore it is construed as advertising. The salesman may send a box of cigars after a deal has been completed, merely as an expression of personal appreciation, paying for them himself. It is but a step from this type of effort to secure goodwill to the spending by a salesman of his company's funds to entertain a prospective buyer at a dinner, followed perhaps by a theater party. The custom of giving simple gifts may develop into the granting of much larger ones. It is because of the difficulty of drawing the line between these different situations and because of an appreciation of the desire to keep the buyer wholly without any sense of obligation toward a possible vendor that some companies, as has been indicated, refuse to permit their employees to accept gifts of any sort. The purchasing officer himself, of his volition, not infrequently refuses to allow salesmen to pay for his luncheon or at least insists upon paying for as many luncheons as do the prospective sellers. These situations are referred to because of the difficulty, and yet the necessity, of drawing some practical line between bribery, on the one hand, and the legitimate development of goodwill, on the other. In a seller's market there is usually a pronounced drop in gift and entertainment spending by suppliers.

There are several basic reasons why purchasing managers disapprove of gifts or other incentives to buyers. In the first place, money expended on gifts is usually added to the cost of selling and ultimately charged to the purchaser in the form of higher prices. Second, such selling practices tend to reduce the importance of quality, service, price, and similar factors in favor of entirely personal considerations. In the third place one of the most harmful economic consequences is the tendency to restrain free competition on a proper basis. When carried to extremes, as it has been in some industries, commercial bribery has the effect of causing competition in quality, service, and price to give way to competition in corruption.

Aside from its economic aspects, the practice of commercial bribery is involved in many legal cases. Fundamentally, the rulings on commercial bribery rest on the doctrine of agency. Any breach of faith on the part of the agent, who has always been recognized by law as keeping a fiduciary position, is not permitted; therefore, the agent's acceptance of a bribe to do anything in conflict with the interests of its principal is not permitted by law.

A number of decisions bearing on the matter of bribery have been handed down. Thus, the U.S. Circuit Court of Appeals for the Sixth Circuit has rendered a decision affirming an order of the Federal Trade Commission against the Grand Rapids Varnish Company prohibiting the practice of commercial bribery. From a strictly legal point of view, there seems to be some question on the liability of a vendor when gifts are made to the employees without the employer's consent as against those cases in which he is aware of what is being done. Sixteen or more states have laws making commercial bribery a criminal offense.

The evils of commercial bribery are more far-reaching than would at first appear.[4] Although originating with only one concern, bribery is likely to rapidly become a practice of the entire industry. A producer, no matter how superior the quality of his goods or how low his price, is likely to find it extremely difficult to sell in competition with concerns practicing bribery. The prices paid by the buyer who accepts bribes are almost certain to be higher—in some cases, two or three times as much as they would be under other circumstances. Defects in workmanship or quality are likely to be smoothed over by the buyer who accepts bribes and hidden from his employer. Materials may be deliber-

---

[4] See Twinplex Sales Company, Federal Trade Commission Docket 1292 (1927), Vol. XI, *Federal Trade Commission Decisions*, p. 57, in which case rewards were offered to the salesmen employed by retail dealers without the knowledge or consent of their employers. See *T. C. Hurst & Son.* v. *Federal Trade Commission*, 268 Federal Reporter 874 (1920), involving tampering with the employees of the purchaser without his knowledge or consent so as to cause the employees to favor the goods of the briber. As distinguished from these, see *Kinney-Rome Company* v. *Federal Trade Commission*, 275 Federal Reporter 665 (1921), in which the employers consented to the premiums offered by the manufacturer.

ately damaged or destroyed to make products of some manufacturers who do not offer bribes appear unsatisfactory. There is no occasion for going further into an analysis of this practice. It takes many forms, but regardless of the guise in which it appears, there is nothing to be said for it.

There is a noticeable trend away from Christmas bottles, fishing trips, sporting event tickets, and other enticements that were common up to about 1960. Hopefully, this trend will continue, and, perhaps, this will be a small side benefit of recent sellers' markets.

Before a purchasing manager can make final choice of vendor, a decision on all the important questions of policy just discussed must be reached: whether to patronize a single or several souces of supply; whether to buy directly from the manufacturer or through a distributor; whether to buy wholly from local sources; to what extent, if at all, to practice reciprocity; what weight to give social, political, and environmental concerns; and how to deal with the problem of commercial bribery. Having formulated a policy with reference to these matters the basis has been laid for settling the specific issues as they arise later on. Most purchasing managers are compelled sooner or later to take a position on these issues and, having done so, have gone a long way toward selecting their sources.

Joint purchasing with supplier

Sometimes a purchasing manager buys for a supplier certain materials required by the latter for manufacturing or processing items sold to the purchaser as finished material or component parts. Sometimes a procurement executive with a highly organized department and huge buying power, operating in the same raw material market as are smaller suppliers, believes he can purchase more efficiently than they can. Since the suppliers would realize substantial savings on raw material purchases, some of these savings might be passed along to the purchaser. Although the purchasing department will incur some additional expense, there would be a net gain to both parties in the transaction. The close relationship that would exist between the suppliers and purchasers, furthermore, would enable purchasers to know more about the production costs of those companies and to ascertain whether or not it was paying a fair price for the products. The purchaser would, moreover, be sure of the quality of the raw material used and would increase his own buying power; with a reduction in the number of buyers in the market of the raw materials, there would be less false activity and thus greater price stability. This last reason is rather important. Not infrequently when a large company requests bids from individual suppliers, they in turn enter the material markets to make inquiries about prices and quantities available. If six suppliers are bidding on an offer, their preliminary inquiries for material required to fill the prospective order will be multiplied six times.

Purchasing for company personnel

Still another problem faced by most purchasing departments is that of the extent to which it is justified in using its facilities to obtain merchandise for employees of the company or for its executives at better terms than they could individually obtain through their own efforts. Many companies not only sell their own merchandise to their employees at a substantial discount and also allow them to buy at cost any of the merchandise bought by the company for its own use but go even further and make it possible for employees to obtain merchandise which the company itself neither makes nor uses.

There are many reasons why a company should pursue a policy of employee purchasing. Under certain circumstances, of course, it is imperative that a company make some provision for supplying its employees with at least the necessities of life, a condition particularly true in mining and lumbering towns. A policy of employee purchasing, it is also argued, provides the means for increasing real wages at little or no cost to the company. It may increase the loyalty of the employees to the organization and thus form a part of the general company policy with reference to old-age pensions, thrift plans, and so on. Many times, in fact, the employees feel they are entitled to any considerations or advantages the company can obtain for them. Furthermore, whatever the procurement manager may think about the general practice, it is often somewhat difficult to refuse a request from one of his firm's top executives to "see what can be done about a discount."

Many companies, on the other hand, have steadfastly refused to adopt such a policy. For one thing, if used as a wage expedient, it is still true that there is some additional expense connected with it. It is argued that the employees prefer cash if increases in wages are called for. There is also a feeling that such a wage policy is inequitable, because only those in a position to take advantage of the discounts made possible by the company realize the wage increases. As a matter of fact, even for those who do buy through the company, there is some question of just how much prices are really reduced compared with the prices of the chain store, the supermarket, the discount store, and other low-cost distributive outlets. Furthermore some ill will toward the company may be aroused, since the ordinary retailer is likely to feel that the manufacturer, if selling to its employees from its stock, is entering into direct competition with the retailer or at least is bringing pressure on him to grant discounts to the manufacturer's employees.

Thus, quite aside from the policy an individual company may follow under the peculiar circumstances surrounding it, the question may well be raised as to how far this whole program of employee purchasing is in the social interest. Are employees generally entitled to all the immediate advantages in the way of price reductions or allowances that their employers can obtain for them, regardless of the effect upon the distributive machinery through which such merchandise commonly passes? Do price allowances of this sort undermine our marketing structure by diverting a substantial volume of consumer products from the regular and normal channels through which they should flow into those considered socially uneconomical?

To what extent are wholesalers and retailers engaged in distributing goods entitled, through legislation or otherwise, to protection against "irregular channels"? And what, after all, are "regular channels" of distribution? Are consumers' cooperatives in this category? Are department stores regular channels for the distribution of automobiles; or chain grocery stores for cosmetics; or drugstores for confectionery? The answers to these questions are by no means clear.

Unfortunately, few people realize how difficult it is for a purchasing department to handle numerous small requests of a personal nature. It is a time-consuming and unrewarding task, since a complete market search is almost impossible, and any quality, price, or service troubles arising from the purchase are always brought back to those involved.

Social, political and environmental concerns

Recognition has come, rather belatedly, that certain noneconomic factors may have a significant bearing on procurement sourcing decisions. These fall into the social, political, and environmental areas.

Social. Most organizations recognize that the carrying on of its existence may affect the social concerns of society. It is possible to address some social problems through purchasing policy and actions. For example, it is possible to purchase from agencies employing addicts and the physically and mentally handicapped certain items or services which assist in the employment of these people. It is possible to purchase from suppliers located in low-income or certain geographical areas of high unemployment. The U.S. Federal Government has tried in a variety of ways to encourage purchasing from minority suppliers. [See also the Southern Power Corporation (B) case.] Most larger organizations recognize the problems and opportunities present through the exercise of purchasing power in the social area. It is not easy for a hard-nosed purchasing manager, used to standard, low-risk, reputable sources, and extensive competition, to consider dealing with the high-risk sources often represented by this class. Most purchasing managers agree that the "deal" must make good business sense and that an arrangement based on charity will sooner or later collapse. Without purchasing initiative to at least seek out those suppliers who might have reasonable potential, it is unlikely that much can or will be accomplished. Too many of the potential sources are small, have few resources, and low marketing skills. Recognition of supplier weaknesses and the willingness to be of assistance are, therefore, necessary ingredients. Normally, sources like these will be local allowing for personal contact, watchfulness, and support through the development stage.

Political. The basic question in the political area is: should the acquisition area be seen as a means of furthering political objectives? Public agencies have long been under pressure of this sort. "Buy local" is a common requirement for city and state purchasing officials. "Buy American" is a normal corollary requirement. The recent attempt by the Canadian Government to direct the department of supply and services to spread purchases across the country, approximately in line with population distribution is another example. For military purposes the U.S. Federal Government has a long-standing tradition of support and development of a national supply base to afford protection in the case of conflict.

The question always arises as to how much of a premium should be paid to conform with political directives. Should a city purchasing agent buy buses from the local manufacturer at a 12 percent premium over those obtainable from another state or other country? In early 1974 the American steel industry warned its public buyers that Buy American restrictions had better be lifted, because the industry would not be in a position to satisfy total domestic demand in the foreseeable future.

For private industry political questions are also present. Should the corporation support the political and economic aims of the governing body? In the construction industry there has often been a form of patronage. The contract is awarded on the basis of specified subcontractors who might otherwise not have received the business. Governments have little hesitation on large business deals to specify that a minimum percentage should have domestic content. In the aerospace industry, for example, foreign plane orders are often contingent on the ability to arrange for suitable subcontracting in the customer's home country. It is interesting that governments have no fear to tread where private industry is forbidden to walk. Multinationals often find themselves caught in countries with different political views. American companies have not been allowed to trade with Cuba. American subsidiaries in other countries face strong national pressure to export to Cuba or the USSR the same products that the American parent is not allowed to sell from American soil. The same holds for purchasing from countries with whom trade is not encouraged by the government. American subsidiaries frequently find themselves caught between the desire of the local government to encourage local purchases and the U.S. Government which encourages exports from the parent or the parent's suppliers. The growing role of government in all business affairs is likely to increase difficulties of this kind in the future. Their resolution is far from easy and will require a great deal of tact, understanding, and freedom to make decisions in which the political consideration may be an overriding factor.

Environmental. Although environmental concerns are not new to our society, genuine purchasing concern as a potential area of influence is. The first problem is: should our organization purchase materials, products, or equipment which may directly or indirectly increase environmental concerns? Should the purchasing group raise the environmental question when others in the organization fail to do so?

The second problem is: Should we purchase from sources, domestic or international, that we know are not following sound environmental practices? These are not easy questions answered glibly out of context. It is possible to evade the issue by putting government in the control seat, saying, "as long as government allows it, it must be all right." A practical purchasing consideration is that government may shut down a polluting supplier with little notice, endangering supply assurance. The report of the Club of Rome reinforces the potential dangers of pollution to our world and the real question in the environmental, as in the political and social areas is: should our organization take a positive stand on this issue?

BIBLIOGRAPHY

ALEXANDER, RALPH S.; CROSS, JAMES S.; AND HILL, RICHARD M. *Industrial Marketing.* 3d ed. Homewood, Ill.; Richard D. Irwin, Inc., 1967.

ALJIAN, GEORGE W., ed. *Purchasing Handbook.* 3d ed. New York: McGraw-Hill Book Co., 1973.

AMERICAN MANAGEMENT ASSOCIATION. "Trade Relations Defined," *Management Bulletin,* No. 19. New York, 1962.

AMMER, DEAN S. "Realistic Reciprocity," *Harvard Business Review,* January-February 1962.

BOLTON, RALPH A. *Systems Contracting: A New Purchasing Technique.* New York: American Management Association, 1966.

CARPENTER, O. W. "What's Good and Bad about Reciprocity?" *Industrial Marketing,* July 1962.

NATIONAL ASSOCIATION OF PURCHASING AGENTS, INC. "The Purchasing Agent's Role in Trade Relations," *Guide to Purchasing.* New York, 1965.

CASES FOR CHAPTER 7

WESTERN CHATHAM CHEMICAL CORPORATION*

In the fall of 1964, Mr. Franklin Stephens, corporate director of purchases of the Western Chatham Chemical Corporation, held a conference of divisional purchasing directors and purchasing agents of the corporation. The corporation, with an annual sales volume in excess of $500 million, comprised three major decentralized divisions, operating 15 manufacturing plants scattered throughout the United States.

During the period 1954–64, the Western Chatham Chemical Corporation expanded rapidly as a result of sharing in the growth of the nation's economy. During this period, it successfully met competitive pressures, introduced new products, and diversified its operations by acquisition of several small and medium-size companies.

A major problem confronting Mr. Stephens in the decentralized structure of purchasing operations in this period of expansion was the ever continuing need to improve the system of communications within the diverse, far-flung purchasing departments of the three divisions and the plants. During 1954–64, the number of buyers and other purchasing personnel in the purchasing operations increased about 75 percent. As one means of communication, he held periodic conferences of key purchasing personnel. As another he had sponsored the preparation of a comprehensive *Procurement Policies Manual,* which was widely distributed to all personnel having relationships with suppliers' representatives. But techniques of conveying information on basic procurement policies to newly hired buyers and purchasing personnel were particularly difficult to implement.

In the fall, 1964, conference, Mr. Stephens devoted one of the conference sessions to the subject of the difficult ethical problems in buyer-supplier relationships. Mr. Stephens, age 51, and holding a degree from a well-known Eastern technical school, was especially concerned about three prevalent practices involving business ethics that were clearly looming down the line throughout industry, as well as in government.

One was the custom of accepting invitations to business lunches, dinners, and entertainment proffered by suppliers' representatives. Another was the exchange of gifts at Christmas and other holidays. Mr. Stephens read in a trade paper a summary of a survey of the practice of giving Christmas gifts to customers in the sales departments of over 100 companies, indicating a steady growth in this practice. Also, stemming from this practice, he read of the aggressive selling of business gifts, which was becoming "big business" with sales running into several hundred millions of dollars a year.

A third practice causing him considerable concern was one brought forcibly to his attention at a national trade convention of machinery and equipment builders. He was visiting a "hospitality suite" of one of the suppliers in a hotel housing registrants at the convention, where he became engaged in a conversation with a Mr. Lowe, a salesman of a large supplier of maintenance and repair products. Mr. Lowe said, among other things, that he had called on the Western Chatham Chemical Corporation's purchasing departments periodically over the past two or three years without ever having been able to obtain an order. Suddenly he asked Mr. Stephens, "To whom, and how much, do I have to pay to get a chance at some of your company's business?" When Mr. Stephens tactfully tried to elicit specific information from Mr. Lowe, he became evasive and abruptly left, saying he was feeling ill.

Although this was the first time Mr. Stephens personally had run into such a question, he had frequently read in the trade papers that buyers had been charged with receiving payments of fixed percentages on purchases from suppliers. He told the men at the conference that he recognized that Mr. Lowe had been imbibing heavily and may not have been thinking rationally, but, on the other hand, there was the implication that the salesman may have been voicing an opinion based on a rumor he had heard in the trade. If this were the case, Mr. Stephens believed there were several possible reasons for such a rumor: (1) A disgruntled employee of Western Chatham may have been trying to "get even" for either a real or an imaginary grievance. (2) A disgruntled supplier's salesman may have been trying to cover his inability to sell to Western Chatham. Or (3) a company buyer might be dishonest and might be accepting kickbacks from suppliers.

Mr. Stephens said his first reaction was to cope with this rumor by sending a letter to all the suppliers on the purchasing departments' vendor lists restating the corporation's position on basic policies in the matter of relationships with suppliers. He drafted the following letter but decided to withhold action on it until the corporation's purchasing executives had an opportunity to discuss it at the conference:

GENTLEMEN:

Our company has always endeavored to conduct its relationships with its suppliers on the basis of sound business principles. We recognize and appreciate the important part our suppliers play in the successful operation of our company.

Recently it has come to my attention that at least one supplier's representative who has not been successful in his efforts to obtain orders from us has expressed the opinion that "it is necessary to pay someone to get business at Western Chatham." At the moment I do not know whether this statement represents the opinion of one individual or whether it is a view shared by others. I do know it is contrary to the basic policies we have adopted to control the activities of our purchasing departments.

Fundamentally, we try to make every effort to obtain adequate competition on all purchases and then to award our business on the basis of merit without favoritism. Likewise, we recognize that the continuing and long-range business health of our suppliers is an essential element in assuring adequate sources of supply for our operations.

In achieving these objectives, we try to conduct our day-to-day relationships with suppliers and potential suppliers on a high standard of business ethics. While we recognize that there is a widespread practice in American business of giving "business gifts," we have not permitted the acceptance of any gifts by our employees. Regardless of the value of a gift, unnecessary questions with respect to the integrity of both the donor and the recipient can arise when a gift is accepted.

Business luncheons are a part of a normal business day and may be accepted by our buyers as long as they reciprocate in being host. We have requested that our people avoid the acceptance of business entertainment or other forms of hospitality, unless it is a situation that is mutually advantageous and can be reciprocated.

If any supplier's executive believes that he, or his representative, has been treated in a manner other than outlined in this letter, I shall welcome the opportunity to discuss the situation.

Sincerely yours

After reading the letter to the group, Mr. Stephens said he was not certain that sending such a communication to all the suppliers would accomplish a constructive result. He asked the group for their opinions on how to handle the situation.

SOUTHERN CHEMICAL PRODUCTS, INC.*

Introduction

On June 15, 1965, Mr. William Todd, director of purchasing of Southern Chemical Products, Inc., of New Orleans, Louisiana received a wire from Puritan Chemicals of Knoxville, Tennessee, in which he was informed that the price at which Puritan was selling muriatic acid to Southern Chemical's Tulsa plant in Oklahoma was to be raised from $19.50 to $26.50 per net ton effective July 1, 1965. Although Mr. Todd had been aware of talk in trade circles about an expected sharp increase in demand for the chemical in the Tulsa region due to stepped-up buying by steel mills, he considered the price change "unjustified, arbitrary, and unacceptable." The director of purchasing observed:

Puritan has been an important customer of Southern Chemical for some years. Frankly, we might have swallowed a price boost of, say, $2 or $3 per ton in view of our trade relationships with the firm. But pushing it to $26.50 per ton is outrageous. The magnitude of the price increase left us no choice but to reject the increase completely and with determination.

Southern Chemical's Tulsa plant was depending on Puritan as the sole source of supply for the acid under an annual contract covering the year 1965.

Company background

Southern Chemical Products was an industrial company producing and marketing commodity chemicals and chemical intermediates and specialities. Over 95 percent of the company's 700-odd products were sold primarily to industrial markets both in the United States and abroad. Sales were over $190 million in 1964, with net profits after taxes amounting to over $12 million. The company employed approximately 7,000 persons in over 30 geographically dispersed plants.

Commodity chemicals, sold principally to other large chemical producers, such as Puritan, accounted for approximately 40 percent of sales in 1964. Products included alcohols, benzenes, chloroform, camphor, esters, ketones, purines, phenols, acetate and oxalic acids, caustic soda and potash, amines and ammonia. In addition to other chemical companies, Southern Chemical's customers for commodity chemicals included petroleum companies, food processors, pulp and paper manufacturers, textile companies, and steel mills.

Muriatic acid

Southern Chemical's Tulsa plant used muriatic acid, 20° Baume (31.45 percent Hcl), for purification of NaCl brines fed to electrolytic cells. This application called for a low concentration of heavy metals, iron, and other impurities. Strict and consistent adherence to specifications was important for the prevention of improper cell operation and also for storage in rubber-lined equipment. The specifications set up by Southern Chemical chemists required that the acid be essentially colorless liquid (35 APHA max.), with iron content of 1 ppm. max., hydrochloric acid content of 31.45–32.56 percent, sulfate content of 50 ppm. max., arsenic content of 0.2 ppm. max., and lead content of 1 ppm. max.

The Tulsa plant preferred to purchase the material as a prime asset rather than as a by-product of ethyl silicate

Southern Chemical—Puritan trade relations

Southern Chemical Products and Puritan Chemicals had been buying from, and selling to, each other a variety of commodity chemicals for a number of years. Thus, for instance, in 1960 Puritan had bought from Southern commodity chemicals amounting to $1.636 million, while Southern had placed orders with Puritan totaling $847,000. Between 1960 and 1964 this balance had changed as Southern doubled its purchases from Puritan to reach a total of $1.798 million, whereas the latter firm's purchases from Southern had increased during the same period from $1.636 million to a total of $2.477 million by 1964 (see Exhibit 1). Of the two companies, Puritan was by far the larger one, with sales of $1.8 billion and net earnings after taxes of $159 million in 1964.

Exhibit 1
TRADE RELATIONSHIPS WITH PURITAN
CHEMICALS, 1960–64
(dollars in thousands)

Year	Purchases by Puritan from Southern Chemical	Purchases by Southern Chemical from Puritan
1960	$1.637	$0.847
1961	1.592	1.247
1962	2.232	1.677
1963	2.244	1.729
1964	2.477	1.798

Source: Company records.

Puritan employed approximately 74,000 persons in over 60 domestic and overseas plants.

Procurement of muriatic acid

The need to purchase muriatic acid for Southern Chemical's Tulsa plant had arisen in November, 1963, when the plant discontinued its own production of the material because of an unfavorable cost structure. By the end of 1963, the company's director of purchasing had negotiated a contract for 1964 with Puritan for the supply of "the buyer's requirements of muriatic acid estimated at 4,000 tons and not to exceed this quantity without the seller's consent" at $19.50 per net ton, delivered Tulsa plant. The contract specified that shipments were to be made from Puritan's plants in Springfield, Missouri, or Dallas, Texas, by tank truck. The terms and conditions under which Puritan accepted the contract stated, among other things, that "price . . . may be revised as of the beginning of a new quarterly period commencing on the first of January, April, July, and October . . . by a written notice from the seller not less than 15 days prior to the date on which the new quarterly period is to commence. . . ." Puritan had further stipulated that:

. . . the buyer's written objection to a price revision served upon the seller prior to its effective date shall permit the buyer to purchase elsewhere quantities due during the ensuing quarterly period if the buyer is able to purchase from a responsible U.S. manufacturer and to furnish the seller with satisfactory written evidence of a bona fide offer, and the seller shall have elected not to meet such offer in which event the seller shall be released from his obligations. . . .[1]

---

[1] These and other terms and conditions were printed on the back of Puritan's contract forms.

Because of high transportation costs for the acid over long distances, Mr. Todd had been severely restricted in the choice of sources of supply. With the exception of Lee Chemical Company, a jobber in Nashville, Tennessee, that had solicited the plant's muriatic acid business late in 1963, he had been unable to locate other suppliers with plants sufficiently near Tulsa to sell to Southern Chemical at prices competitive with those of Puritan. Mr. Todd said:

The nearest supplier quoted us a price of $30 per ton delivered plant. The only way to get the acid at competitive prices over a longer distance might have been by barge. This we ruled out because we had no facilities for unloading. Of course, the price we were paying to Puritan was very advantageous, and, in this sense, the absence of other suppliers was not considered to represent a particular problem at the time the contract was negotiated. In fact, when Lee Chemical solicited the business, I told them that we were very satisfied with our supplier. Normally a buyer doesn't shop around for deals as long as he is convinced that the existing source of supply is excellent.

Unloading facilities available at the Tulsa plant required that the acid be shipped by tank trucks. The material supplied by Puritan was pumped by the truck driver from the truck into storage. Tank cars, by contrast, required additions to the existing railroad siding to reach the acid storage area, and the use of company yard crews. Plant engineers had estimated that the additional investment and labor required would add costs of up to $1 per ton of acid. The engineers had also noted that this cost figure presumed a full utilization of the facilities which could only be achieved by switching other incoming liquid chemicals from transport by tank truck to transport by tank car. The question of whether such switching would create other production problems had not been examined by the engineers. Tank car schedules were considered less flexible than truck schedules.

Developments subsequent to Puritan's announced price increase

Following the receipt of the wire sent by Puritan, Mr. Todd telephoned the general sales manager of Puritan's chemical division producing and marketing the acid and expressed his deep dissatisfaction with the price increase. The director of purchasing commented: "I told the man in no uncertain terms what I thought about the $26.50 price and that we refused to accept it. But I made little headway, and at the end of our conversation it was perfectly clear that we couldn't just talk Puritan into rescinding the increase."

On June 17, 1965, Mr. Todd, by letter, invited the Lee Chemical Company to submit a price quotation for muriatic acid and to indicate available tonnage, lead time, and means of delivery. On June 21, Lee Chemical submitted a bid of $22.15, delivered Tulsa by tank car. The quotation indicated that Lee could deliver up to 3,500 tons per year and that the first shipment could arrive at Southern Chemical's Tulsa plant within four days following the signing of a contract. In a cover letter accompanying the quotation, Lee's president stated that a contract would have to be signed on a must-take basis for no less than 3,000 tons. The offered acid was a by-product from a chlorination process. The specifications given by Lee were as follows:

Appearance	Clear
Color--APHA	40–50
HCl^2.	31.5%
Free Cl	Nil
Organics	5–7 ppm.
Fe.	0.8 ppm.
Ni	Nil
Arsenic	Nil

In discussing Lee's quotation with the general production manager of Southern's industrial chemical division and the production manager of the Tulsa plant, Mr. Todd encountered considerable skepticism. He observed:

Because Lee was a jobber and the real source of supply was unknown, the production people were extremely wary of quality problems. The minimum-requirement and must-take features met with no enthusiasm, and delivery by rail was considered inadequate. There was no argument that the price was good. But we were all quite aware of the fact that disregarding the unreasonable price boost, Puritan was a top-rate supplier. And no one likes to dump an excellent supplier for some unknown outfit that might not be able to meet delivery schedules or adhere to specifications.

At the request of Southern Chemical, Lee submitted to the Tulsa plant a quarter sample of the acid, which was analyzed and found to meet specifications. In a memorandum to Mr. Todd, the plant manager emphasized, however, that short of a trial run with a full tank truck the production department remained unconvinced about Lee's material quality and that delivery by tank car, as well as the minimum-requirement and must-take conditions, was unsatisfactory.

One June 22, Mr. Todd arranged for a meeting with Puritan representatives in which he reiterated in strong language his company's unwillingness to accept the announced price increase. He disclosed to the Puritan representatives that, as a result of Puritan's action, he had sought and received a highly attractive, competitive offer for the supply of acid. He, however, was careful to avoid searching questions by the Puritan representatives regarding any details of the offer and to avoid identifying the source of supply. Mr. Todd gained the impression that the Puritan representatives seemed particularly anxious to get information leading to an identification of the alternate source of supply. They pointed out that their company's action was strictly within the bounds of the terms and conditions of the contract and reminded Mr. Todd that the contract called for the supply by Puritan of the Tulsa plant's *entire* muriatic acid requirement. The representatives stated their belief that this condition prevented Southern from using a second supplier during the term of the contract. They emphasized through the meeting that any serious consideration of an alternate source of supply for the acid by Southern was likely to have detrimental effects on the company's trade relationships with Puritan. Mr. Todd commented:

There was no direct suggestion that we might lose some of Puritan's business, of course. Reciprocal business today is not handled on the basis of cold turkey deals, at least not in our business. But when the other guy keeps wondering about how this or that could have an adverse impact on trade relations, you know perfectly well what he is talking about. I pointed out to them that we had more tremendous efforts since 1960 to increase our purchases from Puritan and would continue to do so. As far as the clause "buyer's requirements" was concerned, I took the position that this meant the Tulsa plant's requirements *from Puritan* rather than the plant's total requirements of the acid. I made it quite clear that we saw nothing in the contract that would compel us to stay with Puritan as the exclusive supplier for the Tulsa plant during 1964. Of course, I must admit that the term "buyer's requirements" was ambiguous and open to different interpretations. It was loose language that I should have caught at the signing of the contract. But, then, our relationships with the major chemical producers in the United States to whom we sell and from whom we buy are of a long-range nature, and the ties are frequently quite closely knit, so that the fine print on contract forms is not too important. At any rate, the meeting produced no results, and Puritan stuck with the new price.

On the following day (June 23), Mr. Todd contacted the president of Lee Chemical and informed him that, although the small sample of acid submitted by Lee had been found satisfactory, the production department of the Tulsa plant had expressed considerable concern over the need for a consistent adherence to specifications, particularly since there was no knowledge of the producer of the acid. In addition, he pointed out that any price in excess of $19 per ton was unsatisfactory, that delivery by tank car was viewed with disfavor by the Tulsa plant, and that the minimum-requirements and must-take conditions attached to the quotation represented a significant obstacle to a serious consideration of the offer. Shortly after this conversation, Mr. Todd received a letter from the jobber offering a new price of $21 per ton delivered by truck. The letter pointed out, however, that the minimum-requirements and must-take conditions could not be dropped in view of the favorable price. The letter furthermore suggested that Southern Chemical accept a full tank truck of acid for a trial run. After conferring with the Tulsa plant manager, Mr. Todd ordered from Lee such a tank truck for testing purposes, and it arrived at the plant on June 28.

On July 1, before the Tulsa plant had tested the new trial shipment of acid, Mr. Todd received a letter from Puritan informing him that the announced price increase had been canceled and that shipments of the acid would continue at $19.50 per ton. The letter reemphasized that under the existing contract Puritan was to supply all of the Tulsa plant's muriatic acid requirements. Mr. Todd communicated Puritan's price rescission to the Tulsa plant. In response, the plant manager suggested that Mr. Todd drop the jobber from further consideration in light of Puritan's action and also in view of Lee's insistence on delivery of at least 3,000 tons of acid on a must-take basis. The plant manager pointed out to Mr. Todd that the total quantity offered by Lee was not sufficient to fill the plant's needs, thus forcing Southern to rely on a second supplier even if a contract with Lee were to be signed.

On July 9, the director of purchasing sent a memorandum to the Tulsa plant manager inquiring about the results of the trial run with the carload of acid supplied by Lee. Mr. Todd concluded the memorandum with the following statement:

In thinking about the present and also the future supply situation, with respect to muriatic acid for your plant, I cannot help but think that if it had not been for Lee's offer, Puritan would now charge $26.50 per ton and this price would probably be the basis for the imminent negotiations for 1966.

It was not until August 10 that Mr. Todd received a memorandum from the Tulsa plant manager stating that the results of the trial run had been satisfactory. The plant manager added that while he could not be absolutely certain, he had good reason to believe that the jobber was buying the acid from the National Chemical Corporation of St. Louis. This information was of interest to Mr. Todd, since he knew that Puritan was a large buyer of several commodity chemicals produced by National Chemical.

Before Mr. Todd came to a conclusion about how to proceed with the offer made by Lee, he received a phone call from Lee's president, who was anxious to learn about the results of the trial run. Upon being informed by Mr. Todd that the results had been satisfactory, the president of Lee expressed his desire to sign a contract, indicating that he would be prepared to take a partial requirement contract of less than 3,000 tons and to drop the must-take condition. He reiterated that he considered a price of $20.50 per ton delivered tank truck to be a very competitive price and that he was also prepared to sell at $19.50 per ton delivered tank car.

Early in September, while Mr. Todd was still undecided as to how to continue negotiations with Lee, Puritan representatives informed him that their company was extremely anxious to sign a contract for 1966 in view of tightening supply. The representatives offered a price of $19.50 per ton and told Mr. Todd that they would allow him three days to accept the offer on an "entire requirements basis." They also informed him that Puritan was prepared to increase the dollar volume of purchases from Southern in 1966 by approximately $200,000 through the placement of orders for several chemical commodities not previously purchased from Southern.

THE CROSS ARMS

Suffolk Power Corporation was building three additional generating stations to serve the rapidly expanding energy market. To link these stations with the total area grid a new method of carrying the power lines using ornamental tubular poles instead of towers had been adopted. Suffolk was unfamiliar with poles and decided to subcontract the design engineering, fabrication, and erection of the new line. [For company background, line project information, and the selection of engineering consultants see Suffolk Power Corporation (A). For selection of pole manufacturers see Suffolk Power Corporation (B). For selection of foundation and erection contractors see Suffolk Power Corporation (C).]

Work on the Addison-Smithfield section of the new power line was progressing well. All of the poles had been manufactured, tested, and received. Foundation work was 30 percent complete, and 10 percent of the poles had been erected. None of the wire had been strung yet. The engineering consultants had completed their assignment. The graceful new poles had already attracted favorable attention from Suffolk employees and the public.

On February 24, on a clear, crisp day, almost two years after the board of directors had approved the new line, the bad news hit like a thunderbolt. The cross arms on several of the newly installed poles were hanging limply along the pole for no apparent reason! Consternation struck Suffolk headquarters. Weather conditions during the last month had been ideal. The previous night there had been only a slight breeze. Engineering tests of poles and cross arms showed that all specifications had been met. The installation contractor had followed proper procedures as far as anyone could tell.

A helicopter was used to inspect all poles, and no visible defects appeared on the cross arms which had not collapsed. Although speculation abounded, no one could assign a cause for the defects. Suffolk engineers dismantled the stricken poles and took sections into the laboratory. No one was sure how long it would be before an explanation could be found. Mr. Carter, director of purchases, wondered what action, if any, he should take with respect to the three subcontractors used on the project. The engineering consultants, the pole manufacturer, and the erector had all been involved at various stages. Whether all or any were to blame for the current mishaps was not clear. Within 24 hours of the first report of cross arm failure, three additional poles showed cross arms collapse.

FORMEX, LTD.

In November, 1973, Mr. Smith, president and general manager of Formex, Ltd., was obliged to reconsider the purchasing function in his enterprise. Recent shortages in the paper industry had thoroughly upset the traditional picture for his company. Mr. Smith had in the past based his supplier's choice mainly on price because paper had been a buyer's market. With a new quota system starting in January, 1974, he was left with only one supplier for his paper requirements, and he was terribly upset about the implications for his firm.

Company background

Formex, Ltd., was a small firm located in Montreal, Quebec. It was incorporated in 1954. In 1965 a new management group took over the business, and in less than eight years sales climbed from half a million to $9.7 million. The recently introduced quota system threatened to reduce sales below the 1973 level, however. The president attributed the past success of his firm to: (1) lower prices; (2) aggressive sales force; and (3) personalized service.

Formex had approximately 600 active customers located in the prov-

Exhibit 1
FORMEX, LTD.
(organization chart)

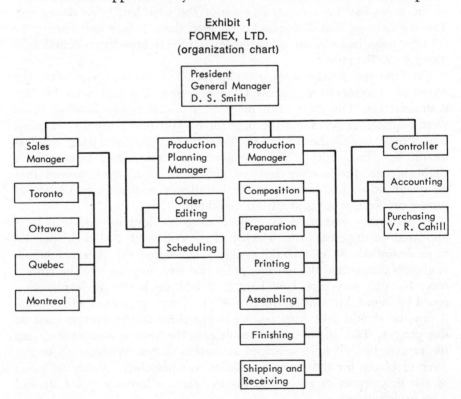

Exhibit 2
DATA FOR 1972 ON THE MAJOR BUSINESS FORMS COMPANIES
(millions of dollars)

	Total sales	Sales in Canada	Products[1]
Moore Corp., Ltd.[2]	500	50	Business forms (92.4%) Custom packaging (5.6%) Machinery (2%)
R. L. Crain, Ltd.[3]	24	24	Business forms Systems Machinery
Drummond Business Forms, Ltd.[4]	16[5]	16	Business forms Machinery

[1] Sales distribution by product is not available for R. L. Crain, Ltd., and Drummond Business Forms, Ltd. Business forms are the principal sales source.
[2] Moore is the world's largest producer of business forms.
[3] The company is associated with Standard Register Company of Dayton, Ohio, the second largest in the United States, and has exclusive Canadian rights for the sale of Standard's forms-handling and business equipment.
[4] Subsidiary of Uarco, Inc., the third largest business form company in United States.
[5] Estimated.

inces of Quebec and Ontario. Its sales volume was distributed as follows: 15 percent governmental customers (federal, provincial, and municipal); 30 percent financial institutions; 45 percent commercial or industrial enterprises; and 10 percent data centers or data processing companies.

Nine percent of Formex's products were custom made. They were of five types: register forms, continuous forms custom, continuous forms standard, snap out set, and sales books. The company organization included 260 employees (see Exhibit 1).

Formex had three major competitors: Moore Corporation, Ltd., a leader in the international market; R. L. Crain, Ltd., a national firm; and Drummond Business Forms, Ltd., a smaller size company situated in Drummondville, Quebec (see Exhibit 2 for more details on these companies). Other business forms competitors were mainly local with sales in the $.5–$5 million range. Mr. Smith thought all business forms producers were in the same position regarding the paper situation.

Purchases and paper suppliers

The range of production purchases required by Formex was not broad. It included about 15 kinds of items: paper, carbon, ink, plates, films, etc. Paper and carbon accounted for more than 90 percent of these purchases. In 1973, paper purchases amounted to $2,450,000 and carbon to $875,000. In paper, three variables could lead to hundreds of combinations; there were seven major colors, five common weights, and widths varying from 8 to 30 inches. Carbon requirements included two colors, five sizes, and two categories (typing or manual). There was some scarcity of carbon fabric. But the carbon market situation was less serious than the paper situation. Carbonless-paper, known as NCR carbon, although very expensive, could possibly be used as a substitute.

In eastern Canada, there were four suppliers for bond paper: E. B. Eddy, Domtar, Abitibi Paper, and Rolland Paper (see Exhibit 3

Exhibit 3
FINE PAPER PRODUCERS

	Rolland Paper Co.	Abitibi Paper Co.	Domtar, Ltd.	E. B. Eddy Co. *
Percent of fine paper market in Canada†	16%	30%	25%	19%
Fine paper sales (millions of dollars).	46	83	70 (est.)	53 (est.)
Fine paper production (thousands of tons).	115	177	n.a.	n.a.
Capacity of operations				
(1972)	80%	79%	n.a.	n.a.
(1973)	97%	97%	n.a.	n.a.
Total sales (millions of dollars).	46	308	561	1,137‡
Total net profit (millions of dollars)	1.3	8.5	17	19
Earnings per share (dollars)	.73	.43	1.14	1.61
R.O.I.	4.7%	4.6%	n.a.	n.a.
Share price range (dollars)	3.10–7.87	$9^{1}/_{4}$–$14^{7}/_{8}$	$11^{3}/_{4}$–$18^{3}/_{8}$	$13^{3}/_{4}$–$20^{1}/_{8}$

  * Subsidiary of George Weston, Ltd.
  † These four companies represented 90 percent of the fine paper industry output.
  ‡ George Weston, Ltd.
  Sources: *Annual Reports,* Financial Post Cards.

for selected data on these producers of fine paper). These producers were all integrated, except Rolland which had to buy its raw materials. In the past, Formex had never purchased from Domtar (see Exhibit 4 for the paper purchases distribution by supplier from 1971to 1973).

Exhibit 4
PAPER PURCHASES DISTRIBUTION BY SUPPLIER

	1971	1972	1973
Rolland Paper Company	40%	60%	80%
Abitibi Paper Company	60%	40%	15%
E. B. Eddy Company.			5%

Past paper situation

From 1968 through 1972 the fine paper market was severely depressed. Two main factors combined to create a number of poor years for the Canadian fine paper producers: weakness of fine paper demand as the economy slowed down in 1969 and much stronger competition after the lowering of Canadian tariffs. In 1967 federal authorities decided on a 40 percent reduction of tariff on all fine paper products to be implemented gradually on a five-year basis, and in 1969 Canada accelerated this reduction by eliminating the adjustment period. As a result, fine paper manufacturers found themselves competing with imported products, notably American, which could be produced at a much lower unit cost. Furthermore, over-capacity of American mills and a lower level of U.S. economic activity exercised a downward pressure on fine paper prices which was extended to the Canadian market.

During these years, all of Formex's paper suppliers were offering essentially the same quality, service, and delivery. Price discounts were the only differentiation. These discounts increased from $6 in 1970 to $30 per ton in 1972. "The scope of our purchasing function was quite limited and the methods used rudimentary," explained Mr. Smith. Because of the large amounts involved, he negotiated prices personally and selected suppliers.

Purchasing process

Purchase orders were sent on a day-to-day basis depending on needs, which varied with the orders received from customers. A Formex salesman obtained an order and gave it to the order editing department. This department verified if all details were registered correctly and checked prices from the price list. Then the order was referred to the scheduling department which had to plan all necessary steps and requirements to complete the order. Normal delivery promises ranged from seven to nine weeks. There was a final check by the accounting department before the order could follow the normal steps mentioned in the schedule. If required materials were not available in stock, supervisors of the different production departments sent requisitions, signed by the production manager, to the purchasing department.

Mr. Cahill was in charge of the buying operations and looked after all documentation. Mr. Smith decided with whom the paper business would be placed and at what price. Then Mr. Cahill sent out the purchase order accordingly. Paper purchases were usually received within two weeks. Other items like ink, plates, films, and supplies he purchased on his own. For a few items normally carried in inventory, the shipping and receiving department determined minimum levels of inventory and safety stocks. Mr. Smith said that most purchasing decisions were based on guesstimates. "The purchasing function in our industry," added Mr. Smith, "has always been a neglected one, and, unfortunately, this was reflected in our attitude with our suppliers. We could compel them to do almost anything we wanted, and I must admit we took too much advantage of the situation."

The new paper situation

In the fall of 1972 prices in the fine paper industry started rising as the market grew stronger. From September, 1972, to October, 1973, Formex faced six successive price increases which varied from 60 percent to 80 percent depending on paper grades. The acceleration of the North American economy spurred demand for fine paper. This demand growth was so strong that shortages appeared in September, 1973, and U.S. producers, who had been active in Canada, decided to concentrate their efforts on their domestic market. This provided a strong and impressive turnabout. The Canadian paper manufacturers had had their problems in the past and were obviously anxious to regain some of their losses.

For the first three months of 1973 Mr. Smith placed 60 percent of his paper purchases with Rolland and 40 percent with Abitibi. In April he decided to concentrate all his purchases with Rolland who offered him a better deal. "I was also trying to do some hedging," said the president, "as the three other suppliers were expecting labor problems because of labor contract terminations." In the summer Mr. Smith realized that the rules of the game were changing, and in July he reached an understanding with the E. B. Eddy sales representative that Formex would order 2,000 tons during the following 12 months. No specific details on grades and monthly quantities were agreed to at the time. In September E. B. Eddy went on strike and stopped its shipments. At the same time Rolland reduced its own shipments to help furnish, with the other paper producers, E. B. Eddy's customers during its strike. In the beginning of October, a week after the strike was over, E. B. Eddy's sales representative told Mr. Smith that he could not furnish Formex any paper during the next year.

In mid-October, the four paper producers announced to their customers a new quota system starting in January, 1974. Abitibi Paper at first agreed to give Formex a quota for 1974 equal to its purchases in 1973, i.e., 1,025 tons. Two weeks later, Abitibi cut this to 515 tons, and the following week it notified Mr. Smith that it could supply nothing. Mr. Smith had received a circular letter from Abitibi explaining some of the difficulties faced by suppliers (see Exhibit 5). Rolland Paper offered to meet its 1973 quota of 5,500 tons.

In November, 1973, Mr. Smith was, therefore, left with only one supplier for all his paper requirements. This company had a major labor agreement which expired on April 30, 1974. The volume offered was well below Formex's needs. In addition, Formex was now obliged to forecast its needs well in advance. For example, December 1 would be the deadline to order all January requirements. Rolland would not guarantee a delivery date or monthly order quantity. This would cause Formex's own delivery cycle to stretch to 12 weeks and Mr. Smith was wondering how his customers would react to this.

"I learned much from this market reversal," said Mr. Smith, "and I promised myself not to pay back when the paper situation changes." He also wondered if this might not be an opportune time to reorganize the purchasing function, as he thought the responsibilities should not fall exclusively on himself.

Exhibit 5
CIRCULAR LETTER FROM ABITIBI TO ITS CUSTOMERS

ABITIBI PROVINCIAL PAPER, Toronto-Dominion Center, Toronto, Canada M5K 1B3 a division of Abitibi Forest Products, Ltd.
Phone 416-866-4200

For Personal Contact Dial: 866–4230

October, 1973

To our customers:

To the consternation of all of us, the supply and price situation in fine papers over the past year has been changing at an unprecedented rate. As one of those being asked to pay the higher price, you are undoubtedly concerned, possibly confused, and probably irritated. We as a manufacturer of fine papers think that you are entitled to an explanation of what is going on. Some of this may be self-evident or part of a story you have heard too often in recent months.

Last February we wrote a letter trying to forewarn you of the likely course of events. Having done so, we cannot pretend that at that time we had any idea that the situation would be as it is today. Since the beginning of this year there has been a fantastic change in paper markets. Prices have increased as never before, some grades have become in short supply, and it is impossible to predict what the market might be a few months hence.

We cannot help but ask what has caused this abrupt change. We should perhaps put "paper" in perspective by suggesting that it is not the only commodity which has been subject to rapid price escalation or short supply in recent months. Further, it is important to remember that many paper grades, but, more importantly, their raw material, pulp, are internationally traded commodities, and their price, not unlike copper, sugar, or soybeans, is determined by worldwide supply and demand situations. Whether we like it or not there is now a world shortage of pulp, and the price has escalated and probably will continue to do so.

Exhibit 5 (*Continued*)

How much of this pulp shortage is due to insufficient capacity is difficult to say. Some figures indicate that capacity is sufficient to look after likely demand through 1974. This, however, presupposes that unfavorable weather and reluctant workers do not prevent the wood from coming out of the forests and that there are no strikes in the mills or transportation tie-ups. We know from 1973 that we should assume none of these. It is quite safe to say that pulp is not going to be in free supply in the next few years and the price may well go substantially above present levels.

Pulp, the major raw material of fine paper, has increased since the beginning of this year from $160/ton to a possible level of $265/ton January 1, 1974, an increase of 66 percent. There are various spot prices in Europe and elsewhere $40 to $50/ton higher than this. Unless we are prepared to keep pace, we can only expect greater shortages in our mills.

One must ask why these pulp shortages exist, since we have the forest resources to supply the wood. If there is a pulp shortage now and a growing one in the future, it must be because too little new capacity has come on stream. This deficiency in turn has been caused by inadequate return on the capital required to install such capacity. Regardless, the time required for the installation of new pulp mills is such that we are not likely to see significant new production for three to four years.

So much for pulp. Surely, all the paper supply and price problems are not caused by the pulp situation. Quite true, but pulp is the primary raw material in the manufacture of fine paper. Price and availability of printing and writing grades are tied very closely to the market pulp situation. There are, however, other major cost factors. Fine paper is relatively labor intensive compared, for instance, with newsprint, and we are looking at a 10-percent increase in labor costs. Items such as starch, clay, and numerous chemicals have not simply kept pace with the cost of living; they have in some cases almost doubled in price in the last year. The cost and availability of energy is a source of concern to us and to all industries.

There is undoubtedly a general awareness that fine paper manufacturers have not been in a healthy financial state in the years 1968 through 1972. Fortunately, this is showing some improvement. Progress is being made through better mill operation, and, by working closer to capacity, high overheads are being more completely absorbed. Some marginal grades have been eliminated or priced more realistically, and certainly the experience of the past five year has made us more efficient. To this extent we are getting into better shape, and, hopefully, some of the earnings statements are beginning to reflect this fact. However, our general price levels, incredible as the increases may appear, have not kept pace with costs. It is quite simple to add up a paper mill's cost increases and demonstrate that these have not been fully covered by the rise in product selling prices. Escalation in costs is occurring so rapidly that it is not being recovered in pricing before the next round takes place. There is an inherent danger in this situation that we will start to anticipate increases and thus ensure their occurrence.

Price is one problem, but availability of supply, today and in the near future, is of equal, if not greater concern. It is difficult to convince a customer who cannot get what he wants, when he wants it, that there is no paper

Exhibit 5 (*Continued*)

shortage. There should, however, be ample paper to go around. Not always in the grades desired but in qualities and quantities to satisfy the needs of our respective customers. Figures indicate that domestic mill shipments have jumped this year by some 17 percent against a normal growth rate of about 5 percent.

Imports have also increased by about 40 percent. This would seem to be out of all proportion to the increase in consumption of printed matter and would perhaps indicate that, at some level, there is inventory building, panic buying, or simply a vast pipeline-filling operation going on.

This suggests that the present shortage may be artificial in terms of today's market. It does not tell us that supply will be sufficient to look after demand, one, two, or three years hence. That we will have shortages through to 1975–1976, there can be little doubt. What is the Paper Industry doing about it?

The answer is difficult. For five years or more the Industry has not shown sufficient return to justify investment in added capacity. Today, the Industry is not generating, internally, sufficient profit to finance new machines. Further, the investment community has an uncanny memory for a record of low earnings and irresponsible expansions. Outside capital is going to be slow in returning to our Industry. In any event, even if new machines were on the drawing board today, it would be 1976–1977 before they could be producing effectively.

What, then, is the outlook and what can be done about it? It is obvious that there will be growing shortages of some grades of fine paper, and this may be accentuated by a greater refinement of producers' product lines. Attempts will be made to maximize production by reducing the number of grades, colors, and basis weights being manufactured. There will also be greater stress on improved paper machine deckles and the movement of standard sizes. We believe, however, that in 1974 printers should be able to get the paper required to run their presses. If it becomes necessary to introduce allocations to ensure a fair distribution of our product we will not hesitate to do so.

We believe, also, that there will be continuing price increases, hopefully, at a more modest rate as market pulp prices reach their effective maximum and as some of the steam goes out of other inflationary pressures.

Under these conditions it would seem wise that you plan your paper requirements as far ahead as possible and order intelligently. It need hardly be said that you should keep pricing to your customers on as flexible a basis as possible.

There have been frequent occasions in recent weeks when we have failed to live up to original commitments. We hope our customers will understand that we are not adopting a cavalier attitude towards our servicing responsibilities, nor are we using present conditions as a crutch. The fact is that we often do not know from one day to the next what pulps and other raw materials will be available to us and machine schedules are being adjusted constantly.

In conclusion, we would like to ask for your patience and continued cooperation. While it may not be readily apparent, we *are* trying to reflect our cost increases in new prices as fairly and as modestly as possible. At the same time, however, we as an industry must demonstrate that we can generate

Exhibit 5 (*Concluded*)

the return on capital that will justify the investment in added papermaking capacity to look after *your* long-term paper requirements. Herein is the dilemma which we must all help solve.

Your respectfully,

ABITIBI PROVINCIAL PAPER.

T. H. Birchall/d   Vice-President.

8 PRICE POLICIES

The determination of the price to be paid is one of the major decisions to be made by the purchasing agent. Indeed, the ability to get a "good price" is sometimes held to be the prime test of a good buyer. If by "good price" is meant greatest value, broadly defined, this may well be true. But if this is interpreted as meaning the very lowest attainable unit price or that price is a residue factor, to be considered only after the underlying elements of technical fitness and quantity have been determined, then the statement is by no means correct.

Importance of price

A sound price policy must rest on the basis that price is an important element in any purchase. A purchaser must give a great deal of attention to obtaining as reasonable a price as possible. There is no reason to apologize for emphasizing price or for giving it a place of importance among the factors to consider. The purchaser is rightly expected to get the best value possible for the organization whose funds are spent. Any price quoted should be analyzed, irrespective of who the supplier is or what the item may be. In the final analysis the price paid by the purchaser is as much a factor in the final decision as to what is the "best buy" as are the technical properties of the product. However, because price is an integral and coordinate factor in a sound purchasing decision, because it is itself a variable, and because the purchasing agent is a specialist in matters of price, we do need to devote special attention to the problems involved in price determination.

Relation of cost to price

Every purchasing manager believes that a fair price should be paid to vendors. But what does a "fair price" mean? A "fair price" is the lowest price that ensures a continuous supply of the proper quality, where and when needed. A fair price makes it possible for the user to be reasonably assured of a material cost such that, an end product or service can be sold in a competitive market at a profit or can be provided in a noncompetitive market at a satisfactory cost benefit ratio over the long run. This statement calls for some elaboration.

A "continuous supply" is possible in the long run only from a vendor who is making a reasonable profit.

The vendor's total costs, including a reasonable profit, must, in the long run, be covered by total sales. Any one item in the line, however, may never contribute "its full share" over any given period but even for such an item the price paid should at least cover the direct costs entering into it.

A fair price to one seller for any one item may be higher than a fair price to another and an equally satisfactory substitute item.

Both may be "fair prices" as far as the buyer is concerned, and the buyer may advisedly pay both prices at the same time.

Merely because a price is set by a monopolist or is established through collusion among the sellers does not, in and of itself, render that price unfair or excessive. Likewise, the prevailing price need not necessarily be a fair price, as, for example, when such price is a "black" or "gray" market price or when it is depressed or raised through monopolistic or coercive action.

The purchasing manager is called upon continuously to exercise judgment as to what the "fair price" may be under a variety of circumstances. To determine this "fair price," he or she must have experience and common sense. In addition to these qualifications, some people seemingly possess an intuitive ability to judge prices—and the suppliers offering them—to an unusual degree; others appear to possess far less of this particular capacity. In part, of course, accuracy in weighing the various factors which culminate in a "fair and just price" is a matter of capitalizing on past experience. Regardless of experience, however, some people have an almost uncanny ability to determine a "good" price. They apparently follow no rule or definite procedure in arriving at these decisions and if called upon to justify their conclusions would have great difficulty in doing so. They have a certain "feel of the market" which is at once both sensitive and accurate. Perhaps the possession of this "native ability" and the cultivation of it constitute one of the reasons why some people make good purchasers while others are better designers or advertising executives.

Meaning of "cost"

Assuming that this concept of a fair price is sound, we are faced almost immediately with the question as to the relationships between cost and price. This relationship is not easy to define. Clearly, over the long run to stay in business every supplier must cover total costs, including overhead, and receive a profit. Unless these costs, including profit, are covered, eventually the vendor must be forced out. This reduces the number of sources available to the buyer and may cause short supply, higher prices, less satisfactory service, lower quality, and other unfortunate consequences. Every purchasing manager recognizes this fundamental economic principle.

But this broad statement leaves unanswered a whole series of difficult questions, once one undertakes to apply it to a particular transaction. Thus, what is to be included in the term, "cost"? At times it is used to cover only direct labor and material costs, and in times of depressed business conditions, many a seller is willing merely to get this amount back rather than not make a sale at all. Or the cost may mean direct labor and material costs with some contribution (whatever can be obtained) toward overhead. Cost may mean actually incurred cost in the form of cost outlay, or it may mean incurred plus anticipated costs. Obviously, these future costs are only estimates. If the "cost" for a particular item includes overhead, is the latter charged at the actual rate (provided it can be determined) or is it charged at any average rate? In the latter case it may, for the particular item in question, be far from the actual. These and many more questions regarding the use of the term "cost" will occur to every cost accountant.

Most knowledgeable businessmen realize that the determination of the cost of a particular manufactured article is not a precise process. However, it is common practice to refer to the cost of an article as a very precise figure. Fundamentally, in manufacturing industries there are two basic classifications of costs—direct and indirect.

Direct costs are usually defined as those which can be specifically and accurately assigned to a given unit of production, i.e., materials, such as ten pounds of steel; or labor, 30 minutes of a person's time on a machine or assembly line. However, under accepted accounting practices the actual cost of the specific material used may not be the cost that is charged in figuring direct material costs. Because the price paid for material may fluctuate up or down over a period of time, it is common practice to use a so-called standard cost. Some companies use a standard cost for materials the last price paid in the immediately prior fiscal period. Other companies use an average price for a specific period.

Indirect costs are costs which are incurred in the operation of a production plant or process but which normally cannot be allocated directly to any given unit of production. Some examples of indirect costs are rent, property taxes, machine depreciation, expenses of general supervisors, power, heat and light.

Classification of costs into variable, semivariable, and fixed categories is a common accounting practice and a necessity for any meaningful analysis of price/cost relationships. Most direct costs are called variable because they vary with the units produced. For example, a product which requires 10 pounds of steel for 1 unit will require 100 pounds for 10 units. Semivariable costs may vary with the number of units produced but are partly variable and partly fixed. For example, more heat, light, and power will be used when a plant is operating at 90 percent of capacity than when operating at a 50 percent rate, but the difference is not directly proportional to the number of units produced. In fact, there would be some costs for heat, light, and power if production were stopped completely for a period of time.

Fixed costs generally remain the same, or within narrow limits regardless of the number of units produced. For example, real estate taxes will usually remain the same for a given period of time regardless of whether 1 unit or 100,000 units are produced. There are several accounting methods for allocating fixed costs. A common method is to apply a percentage of direct costs in order to determine the cost of factory overhead for purposes of figuring the manufactured cost of each unit. It is obvious that full allocation of fixed expenses will depend on accuracy of the forecast of production and the percentage used. It is also obvious, that as full production capacity is reached, the percentage rate charged to direct costs will be the lowest that it is possible to charge in order to provide for all fixed charges.

From the foregoing, we can define cost as so many dollars and cents per unit based on average cost for raw material over a period of time, direct labor costs, and an estimated volume of production over a period of time on which the distribution of overhead is calculated.

If this definition of the term "cost" is acceptable, then a logical question to ask is, whose cost is it to be? Some manufacturers are more efficient than others when producing items of a similar nature. Usually all sell the same item at about the same price at any one time. But should this price be high enough to cover only the most efficient supplier's costs, is it to cover the "bulk-line" producer, or should it cover the costs for all of the vendors?

Furthermore, it must be clear that cost does not determine market price at any time. When a seller insists the price must be as quoted because of costs this position is not really justified. In the final analysis goods are worth and will sell for what the market will pay.

Moreover, no seller is entitled to a price that yields profit merely because the vendor is in business or assumes risk. If such were the case, everyone in business would be automatically entitled to a profit regardless of costs, quality, or service. Unless a seller can supply a market with goods that are needed and desired by users and can supply them with reasonable efficiency, that seller is not entitled to get a price that even covers "cost."

One might be tempted to conclude from what has been said thus far regarding cost that the use of costs as a basis for determining fair price is a waste of time. Such a conclusion would, of course, be entirely fallacious. An approximation of vendor's costs is very important to a buyer. Stress has been placed in our discussion of quality determination on the significance to both buyer and supplier of the development of cost and value analysis. This type of analysis obviously rests on a knowledge of cost.

Techniques for price cost analysis

Reconizing the importance of cost, it is common practice for the purchasing manager to make the best estimate possible of supplier's costs as one means of judging the reasonableness of the price offered. Many larger corporations have their own cost-price analysts to help purchasing managers do a better job. They assist not only in identifying high-cost areas, but also may identify small vendors who, without realizing their own costs, are attempting to merchandise below cost. (See also Chapter 15 on purchasing research.) This estimate must be based on such data as are available. The prices of raw material entering into the product are commonly accessible, and the amounts required are also fairly well known. For component parts, catalog prices often offer a clue. Transportation costs are easily determined. Competitive quotations and the prices last paid for the item, if previously purchased, are enlightening. The buyer's own engineers should give evidence as to processing costs. Burden and general overhead rates can be approximated, if they are considered at all.

One method of estimating the reasonableness of quotations normally used in value analysis is to reduce price to a per pound or per property basis. For example, this part cost us $7.80 per pound, and it costs $120.00 to transmit 1,000 foot pounds of torque. The average cost is determined by classification of the various types of equipment according to material contents manufacturing processes, and other variables. Through comparison with a standard thus formed for the particular class of equipment in question, an estimate of a fair price is secured. In judging the reasonableness of bids actually received, some buyers subtract all the known costs from the bids and compare the results with those on previous quotations. An illustration may aid in making this procedure clear.

A piece of equipment, more or less special in makeup, was quoted at a price equivalent to 70 cents a pound for the complete equipment. It was substantially an assembly of gray-iron castings, copper tubes, structural steel, and steel bars. The buyer proceeded to "break down" the price. She estimated the castings at 20 cents a pound, copper at 90 cents a pound, structural steel at 15 cents a pound, and steel bars at

25 cents a pound. By the use of weighted averages of the pound-price figure for each component, she determined that 38 cents a pound represented a fair value for the material manufactured but unassembled. This gave her a chance to question the quoted price and negotiate a substantial reduction.

Many companies have found it advantageous to locate price/cost specialists in the purchasing function. Price can be broken down into direct material, direct labor, overhead, general and administrative expenses, and profit.

Overhead costs generally consist of indirect costs incurred in the manufacturing, research, or engineering facilities of the company. It is important to know how these costs are distributed to a given product. If overhead is allocated as a percentage of direct labor costs and there is an increase in labor costs, overhead costs can be unduly inflated unless the allocation percentage is changed.

The growing tendency for industry to become more capital intensive has increased the relative percentage of overhead versus direct labor and materials. Since some items in the overhead are attributable to the location of the supplier such as local real estate taxes, and others are properly seen as depreciation or investment at varying technological and economic risk levels, the analysis and allocation of these costs to individual products is particularly difficult.

General and administrative expense includes selling, promotion, advertising, executive salaries, legal expense, and so forth. Frequently, there is no justification for the supplier to charge an advertising allocation in the price of a product manufactured to the buyer's specifications.

Material costs can be estimated from a bill of material, a drawing, or a sample of the product. The buyer can arrive at material costs by multiplying material quantities per unit by raw material prices. Sometimes a material usage curve will be helpful. The purpose of the curve is to chart what improvement will occur from buying economies and lower scrap rates as experience is gained in the manufacturing process. Use of price indices and maintenance of price trend records is standard practice.

Direct labor estimates are not made as easily as material estimates. Even though labor costs are normally labeled direct for machine operators and assembly line workers, in reality, they tend to be more fixed than most managers care to admit. Most organizations prefer not to lay-off personnel, and there are strong pressures on them to keep the so-called "direct labor" force reasonably stable and employed. This means that inventories and overtime are often used to smooth fluctuations in demand and also that labor cost becomes at least semivariable and subject to allocation.

Product mix, run sizes, and labor turnover may affect labor costs substantially. The greater the mix, the shorter the lot size produced, and the higher the turnover, the greater direct labor costs will tend to become. These three factors alone may create substantial cost differences between suppliers of an identical end product. Geographical considerations also play a large part as differences in labor rates do exist between plant locations. Such differences may change dramatically over time as the rapid increases in direct labor rates in Japan, Puerto Rico, and Germany have demonstrated. The sound cost analyst will attempt to recreate a supplier's real labor costs, taking the above considerations into account.

The learning curve

The learning curve provides an analytical framework for quantifying the commonly recognized principle that one becomes more proficient with experience. Its origins lie in the aircraft industry in World War II when it was empirically determined that labor time per plane declined dramatically as volume increased. Subsequent studies showed that the same phenomenon occurred in a variety of industries and situations. Although conceptually most closely identified with direct labor most experts believe the learning curve is actually brought about by a combination of a large number of factors which include:

1. The learning rate of labor.
2. The motivation to increase output of labor and management.
3. The development of improved methods, procedures, and support systems.
4. The substitution of better materials, tools, and equipment or more effective use of materials, tools, and equipment.
5. The flexibility of the job and the people associated with it.
6. The ratio of labor versus machine time in the task.
7. The amount of preplanning done in advance of the task.
8. The turnover of labor in the unit.

We know the learning curve happens; its presence has been empirically determined a sufficient number of times that its existence is no longer in doubt. The reasons for it sound plausible enough; yet it is still not possible to determine a priori just what the learning rate should be for a brand new product or a novel task.

The learning curve may be expressed mathematically as follows:

$$Y_x = K(X)^n$$

and

$$T_x = \sum_{i=1}^{x} (Y_i)$$

Where:

Y_x = the man-hours required for the single unit X.

T_x = the cumulative total man-hours required from the first unit through unit X.

X = the number of the unit for which the man-hours are being determined.

K = the man-hours for the first unit.

n = log r/log 2.

r = improvement ratio or learning rate (90 percent, etc.), expressed as a decimal (.90, etc.).

The learning curve has tremendous implications for cost determination, management by objectives, and negotiation. For example, let us take a 90-percent learning curve. Suppose we wish to purchase 800 units of a highly labor intensive, expensive product which will be produced by a group of workers over a two-year period. The first 100 units have been produced at an average labor time of 1,000 hours. With a 90-percent learning curve the average labor time for the first 200 units would drop to 900 hours. Figure 8–1 shows the calculations.

Figure 8–1
LEARNING CURVE EXAMPLE

Units produced	Cumulative labor hours	Average labor hours per unit
100	100,000	1,000
200	180,000	900
400	324,000	810
800	583,200	729

These figures may be plotted on rectangular coordinates as shown in Figure 8–2.

Figure 8–2
NINETY PERCENT LEARNING CURVE EXAMPLE

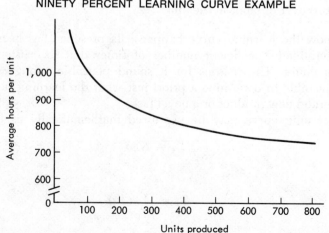

Using logarithmic coordinates this curve is a straight line as shown in Figure 8–3.

It is important to recognize that the choice of learning curve, be it 95, 90, 85, or 80 percent or any other figure, is not an exact science.

Figure 8–3
NINETY PERCENT LEARNING CURVE EXAMPLE

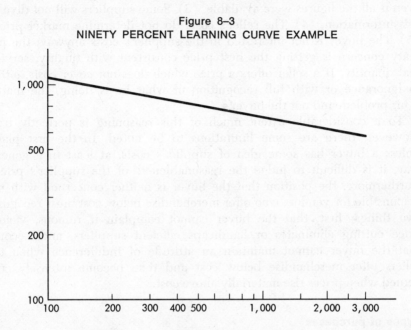

The new product situation can be compared to other situations where the same or similar circumstances were deemed to have taken place. It can be readily established afterwards what really happened and what the actual curve was. It is also possible to wait for some preliminary production data which can then be used to plot the curve since, theoretically only two points are required to fix the curve's location. Thus, for new products and relatively short runs, actual production information may be requested on the first significant run and renegotiation requested on the basis of actual data if uncertainty exists as to which learning curve is appropriate.

The learning curve or improvement function implies that improvement never stops, no matter how large the volume becomes. This goes counter to most industrial engineering philosophy which puts labor on a time standard which presumably does not change with volume unless the method is changed or other significant changes occur in the job.

The potential of the learning curve in materials management has not yet been fully explored. It is a powerful concept and very much in the purchaser's favor. Progressive discounts, progress payments, shortened lead times, and better value should be planned and obtained through its use.

Some purchasing managers believe they are not justified in going very far into the costs of suppliers. They take this position for several reasons: (1) In many cases suppliers do not know their costs, and it would be useless to inquire into them. (2) The interpretation of costs calls for an exercise of judgment, and differences of opinion would arise even if all the figures were available. (3) Some suppliers will not divulge this information. (4) The seller's costs do not determine market prices. (5) The buyer is not interested in the supplier's costs anyway; the primary concern is getting the best price consistent with quality, service, and quantity. If a seller offers a price which does not cover costs, either in ignorance or with full recognition of what he is doing, the matter is his problem and not the buyer's.

To a considerable extent much of this reasoning is perfectly true. However, there are some limitations to be noted. In the first place, unless a buyer has some idea of supplier's costs, at least in a general way, it is difficult to judge the reasonableness of the supplier's prices. Furthermore, the position that the buyer is neither concerned with nor responsible for vendors who offer merchandise below cost must recognize two things: first, that the buyer cannot complain if ruinous, vicious price cutting eliminates or handicaps efficient suppliers, and, second, that the buyer cannot maintain an attitude of indifference when the sellers offer merchandise below cost and then become intensely concerned when prices rise materially above cost.

Types of purchases

Analysis of suppliers' costs is, however, by no means the sole basis for deciding upon the reasonableness of a quoted price. What other means can be used? Much depends upon the type of product being bought. Four general classes may be considered:

1. Raw materials. This group is made up of the so-called sensitive commodities, such as copper, wheat, crude petroleum, and jute.

2. Special items. This group includes items and materials which are special to the organization's product line and are, therefore, custom ordered, as well as purchases of equipment and of a nonrepetitive nature.

3. Standard production items. This group includes such items as bolts and nuts, many forms of commercial steel, valves, tubing, and the like, whose prices are fairly stable and are quoted on a basis of "list price with some discount."

4. Items of small value. This group includes items of such small comparative value as not to justify the expenditure of any particular effort to check price prior to purchase.

Sensitive commodities. For the sensitive commodities, the price at any particular moment is in some respects less important than the trend of the price movement. The price can be determined readily in most instances because many of these commodities are dealt in on well-organized markets; and to the extent that such quoted prices are a fair reflection if market conditions,[1] the current cash price is known and is substantially uniform for a given grade. With commodities of this sort, however, a company's requirements are usually sufficiently adjustable, so that an immediate order is seldom a necessity, and purchase can be postponed if the trend of prices chances to be downward.

The trend of price is a matter of importance in the purchase of any type of commodity, but it is particularly important with this first group. Moreover, insofar as "careful and studious timing" is essential to getting the right price, both the types of information required as a basis for such timing and the sources from which the information can be obtained differ from those necessary in dealing with other groups of items.

Special items. Special items include a large variety of purchased parts or special materials peculiar to the organization's product or service. Make or buy is always a significant consideration on these items because of their proprietary nature. Prices are normally obtained by quotation because no published price lists are available and can be analyzed by a variety of cost/price techniques. Subcontracts are common and the availability of compatible or special equipment, skilled labor and capacity may be significant factors in determining price. Since large differences may exist between suppliers in terms of these factors and their desire for business, prices may vary substantially between bidders. Each product in this group is unique and may need special attention of its own. A diligent search for suppliers willing and able to handle its special requirements including an advantageous price may pay off handsomely.

Equipment and nonrepetitive purchases are also normally processed individually with extensive use of quotations.

Standard production items. The third group of items in our classification includes those standard production items whose prices are comparatively stable and are likely to be quoted on a basis of list less certain discounts. This group includes a wide range of commodities commonly obtainable from a substantial list of sources. The inventory problems related to this class of requirements are largely routine. Changes in price do, of course, occur, but they are far less frequent than with raw materials and are likely to be moderate in range. Prices are usually obtained from catalogs or similar publications of vendors, supplemented by periodic discount sheets.

It should not be concluded from this that such purchases are unimportant or that the prices quoted should not be examined with care. Quite the contrary is true. The items are important in themselves; the annual dollar volume of purchases is often impressive; and real attention needs

---

[1] It is common knowledge among buyers, however, that the published quotations, even for such commodities, are often open to question as to their accuracy.

to be paid to the unit price. When a requisition is received by the purchasing department, the first procedure would commonly be to refer to past purchase records as the first source of information. If the material in question has been regularly purchased or orders have been placed for it recently, an up-to-date price record and catalog file will give all the information pertaining to the transaction, such as the various firms able to supply the commodity, the firms from which purchases have been made, and the prices paid. This information will be sufficiently recent and reliable to enable the buyer to place the order without extended investigation. However, if the buyer does not feel justified in proceeding upon the basis of the information thus provided, a list of available suppliers from vendor files, catalogs, and other sources can be assembled and quotation requests can be sent to selected sources.

The importance of catalogs has already been discussed. From the standpoint of price data, their chief weakness arises from the difficulty of keeping the information up to date.

One of the best sources for current prices and discounts is representation. Few manufacturers rely wholly upon catalogs for sales but follow up such material by visits from their personal representatives. Much useful data can be obtained from such visits. The buyer learns of price revisions, which may well be noted in the appropriate catalog, ascertains the probable date of publication of new editions, and is assured that the corporation is on the proper mailing lists. In some lines confidential discounts, usually based on quantity, are found to exist. Advance notice of intended price changes sometimes is given. It is the buyer's duty to be alert to the possibilities of such information in order that full advantage may be taken of them.

Items of small value. The fourth group into which commodities have been classified for the purpose of price determination includes such items of small value, comparatively speaking, as not to justify any particular effort to analyze the price in detail. Every purchasing department has numerous items of this sort to buy from time to time; yet these items do not in themselves justify a catalog file, even when such catalogs are available, nor do they bulk large enough to warrant sending out inquiries for individual quotations. Actually, the pricing problem on such items is handled in a variety of ways. The following constitutes an excellent summary of these procedures:

It is common practice to send out unpriced orders for such items. Another common practice is to indicate on the order the last price paid, this price being taken from the record of purchases or past purchases, if the last purchase is not too far back. Other purchasing agents have made a practice of grouping these small items under some contract arrangement or on a cost-plus basis with suppliers who undertake to have the materials on hand when needed, and who are willing to submit to periodical checking as to the fairness of the prices they charge.

In most cases sources of supply for these small items are local, and current prices are often obtained by telephone and then placed upon the face of the purchase order so that they become a part of the agreement of purchase. The most common practice of all, however, is perhaps to depend upon the integrity of the suppliers and to omit any detailed checking of the proper price on items of small value. Many purchasing agents believe that their best assurance is the confidence they have in their carefully selected sources of supply, which is such that they feel secure in relying upon the vendors to give them the best available price without requiring them to name the price in advance, and without checking it when the invoice is received.

Another and final method for controlling the price element for these small items consists of the practice of "spot-checking." This means the selection of an occasional item which is carefully investigated to develop the exact basis upon which the supplier is pricing a given class of items. It is obvious that the discovery of unfair or improper prices by such spot checks is considered a reason for discounting the source of supply who is discovered to be taking advantage of the nature of the transaction in his pricing.

Perhaps a more effective way to buy items of small value, such as are included in the MRO groups, is to use the stockless buying-systems contracting techniques described earlier.

The use of quotations and competitive bidding

Quotations are normally secured when the size of the proposed commitment exceeds some minimum dollar amount. They may be sought for the purpose of checking on prices already being paid for items currently purchased from an established source or for the purpose of adding new sources of supply to those already being used. Governmental purchases must commonly be on a bid basis. In the latter case the law requires that the award shall be made to the lowest responsible bidder. In industrial practice, bids may be solicited with a view to selecting those firms with whom negotiations as to the final price are subsequently carried on.

The extent to which competitive bidding is relied upon to secure an acceptable price varies widely. On the one hand, it is a common practice for buyers of routine supplies, purchased from the same sources time after time, to issue unpriced orders. The same thing occasionally happens in a very strong seller's market for some critical item when prices are rising so rapidly that the vendor refuses to quote a fixed price. Wherever at all possible, however, prices should be indicated on the purchase order. In fact, from a legal point of view, a purchase order *must* either contain a price or a method for its determination if the contract is to be binding.

When it is decided to ask for competitive bids, certain essential steps in procedure are called for. These are a careful initial selection of dependable, potential sources, an accurate wording of the request to bid, the submission of such inquiries to a sufficient number of suppliers to assure a truly competitive price, the proper treatment of such quotations, once received, and a careful analysis of them prior to making the award.

The first step is to select possible vendors from whom quotations are to be solicited; the procedure amounts, in fact, to a preliminary sorting of the sources of supply. It is assumed that the bidders must (1) be qualified to make the item in question in accordance with the buyer's specifications and to deliver it wthin the desired date, (2) be sufficiently reliable in other respects to warrant serious consideration as suppliers, (3) be numerous enough to ensure a truly competitive price, but (4) not be more numerous than necessary. The first two of these qualifications have been adequately considered in our discussion of sources. The *number* of suppliers to whom inquiries are sent is largely a matter of the buyer's judgment. Ordinarily, at least two vendors are invited to bid. More often, perhaps, no more than three are invited to submit bids. A mere multiplicity of bidders does not, of course, ensure a truly competitive price, although under ordinary circumstances it is an important factor, provided that the bidders are comparable in every major respect and provided each is sufficiently reliable so that the buyer would be willing to purchase from him.

At any rate, the first step is clearly to draw up a list of acceptable potential suppliers to whom requests to bid will be sent. In general, it is a good rule to exclude from such a list the names of the firms with which it is unlikely that an order would be placed, even though their prices were low. Occasionally, some vendor may more or less insist upon being given an opportunity to quote, and it may be good diplomacy on the part of the buyer to accede to this request. So, too, it is wise to test out new and untried suppliers for the purpose of locating new sources. Sometimes bids are solicited solely for the purpose of checking the prices of regular suppliers or for inventory-pricing purposes.[2] It should be remembered, however, that a company is always put to some expense—at times, a very considerable one—when it submits a bid, a cost that it should not be asked to bear without good reason. Moreover, the receipt of a request to bid is always something of an encouragement to the vendor and always carries with it the implication that an order is possible, unless the inquiry specifically states that no order is contemplated. For a variety of reasons, therefore, purchasers should not lightly solicit quotations.

Having settled upon the companies that are to be invited to bid, a general inquiry is addressed to them in which all the necessary information is set forth. A complete description of the item or items involved,

---

[2] Occasionally, a purchaser may solicit bids even though he has selected a supplier in advance of receipt of quotations. In such a case, bids are obtained in order to provide a ready answer to unsuccessful bidders. Such a practice, of course, is not to be commended.

the date on which these items are wanted, the date by which the bid is to be returned, and similar information is included. In many instances, however, telephone inquiry is substituted for a formal request to bid.

Subsequent to the mailing of an inquiry but prior to the announcement of the award, bidders are naturally anxious to know how their quotations compare with those of their competitors. Since sealed bids, so commonly used in governmental procurement, are not looked upon with favor or commonly used in private industry, the purchaser is in a position to know how the bids, as they are received, compare with one another. However, if the bids are examined upon their receipt, it is important that that information be treated in strictest confidence. Indeed, some buyers deliberately keep themselves in ignorance of the quotations until such time as they are ready to analyze the bids, thus being in a position truthfully to tell any inquiring bidders that they do not know how the bid prices compare. Even after the award is made, it is probably the better policy not to reveal to the unsuccessful bidders the amount by which they failed to meet the low price.

Firm bidding

The reason for this confidential treatment of bid price information is its connection with a problem practically all buyers have to face, namely, that of "firm bidding." Most firms have a policy of notifying suppliers that original bids must be final and that revisions will not be permitted under any circumstances. Ostensibly, exceptions are made only in case of obvious error. Actually, revisions are so common that in some lines of business it is contended by sales managers that a strict policy of firm bidding cannot be followed.

A specific example will indicate what frequently happens. It relates to the experience of a buyer who received, in response to a request for bids on a certain installation, quotations accompanied by a very complete set of specifications. Of the bids which were returned, the lowest price quoted was $17,000, while the others varied up to $20,500. The purchaser was unable to reconcile these prices with his own estimate on the basis of any possible errors which he might have made in his own calculations. He believed, therefore, that each contractor had set his price so as to allow an extra margin of profit, in the expectation of being allowed to revise that price if his bid proved to be too high and yet retain a margin of profit. The buyer decided not to accept any bid immediately. Within a week following receipt of the bids, representatives of each of the contractors went to the buyer in an attempt to learn just where their respective bids stood in relation to the others. He answered them only telling the representative of that contractor whose bid was the lowest that it was the lowest received up to that time and by telling the others that theirs were not the lowest.

Upon receiving this information, each contractor whose bid was high asked for permission to submit a new bid and indicated that he would reduce his price. In two cases, the proposed reduction was as much as 20 percent of the original quotation. The contractor whose bid had originally been lowest learned, not from the buyer himself but through contacts outside, that other contractors were quoting new prices which were lower than his original price, whereupon he asked permission to quote a new figure on his bid. In all cases the contractors asked for the opportunity of placing lower bids for the entire job, without attempting to ascertain in just what parts of the specifications their respective bids might have been too high.

In the buyer's opinion the fact that each contractor had thus attempted to lower his original bid was a reasonable confirmation of the theory that each had originally sought too large a profit margin, with the expectation that if others underbid him, he could still cut his price and receive the contract. The purchaser believed that if he allowed the contractors to juggle figures on this first contract, he must expect a similar bargaining procedure on each of four transactions which were contemplated in the near future. He therefore declared void all bids on these first specifications for equipment and sent out requests for new bids which were to be final, unless the purchaser suggested changes for some particular reason.

The bids returned upon the second request were more nearly uniform than those submitted upon the first request, approximating the price which the purchaser had expected to pay. The range between the lowest and the highest of these bids was $1,500. For each of these bids the purchaser compared the prices of the separate items in the list to ascertain, if possible, the causes for the variations in the total contract prices. He found several instances in which some one contractor had quoted a price for a particular item widely different from the prices quoted by the others for that same item. In such cases, believing that the variation was evidence of a misunderstanding of the specification for that item by the contractor whose price was out of line, the purchaser explained the specification to that contractor. If he found that there had been a misunderstanding of the requirement, he then gave the contractor the privilege of changing his price on that item, whether the price was too low or too high. Two of the contractors found it advisable to lower their prices on one item each, while one contractor raised his price on one item, the specification of which he had misunderstood. After allowing such changes to be made, the purchasing officer accepted the lowest bid of $14,200, this price to include the installation of the equipment.

Every purchasing director can relate instances of this sort from experience. Particularly in times of falling prices, suppliers, extremely anxious to get business, try by various devices to assure themselves that their bids will be the lowest. It must be said, too, that they have not infrequently been encouraged in this procedure by those purchasers who have acceded to requests that revisions be made. Unfortunately, it is also true that there are buyers who deliberately play one bidder against another and who even seek to secure lower prices by relating imaginary bids to prospective suppliers. The responsibility for deviations from a policy of firm bidding must be laid at the door of the purchaser as well as of the supplier.

Theoretically, a policy of firm bidding is sound, and in practice it should be deviated from only under the most unusual circumstances. To those who contend that it is impossible to adopt such a policy, the answer is that it actually is the practice followed in many concerns. The advantages of firm bidding as a general policy, however, need no particular explanation. If rigidly adhered to, the practice is the fairest possible means of treating all suppliers alike. It tends to stress the quality and service elements in the transaction instead of the price factor. Assuming that bids are solicited only from thoroughly honest and dependable suppliers and that the buyer is not obligated to place the order with the lowest bidder, it removes from suppliers the temptation to try to use inferior materials or workmanship, once their bid has been accepted. It saves the purchaser time by removing the necessity of constant bargaining with suppliers over price.

In the experience of the purchaser cited above, all bids were rejected at one stage in the negotiations. This practice is resorted to from time to time under a number of circumstances. It may be caused by buyers who obviously do not understand the specifications, which are either loosely or poorly drawn. It may happen when it is felt that all the prices quoted are too high.

The market

Thus far, discussion of price has been, largely, from a purchaser's point of view. However, the purchaser's influence over the price set by suppliers may be relatively small. If any or a combination of the following factors hold, such as: if the purchasing organization is large relative to the supplier, if a buyer's market exists, and if the purchasing personnel are unusually capable, the influence of the purchaser in price setting may be significant.

Depending on the commodity and industry the market may vary from almost pure competition to oligopoly and monopoly. Obviously, pricing will vary accordingly. Most firms are not anxious to disclose just how prices are set for competitive reasons, but two traditional approaches have been the cost and the market approach.

The cost approach

The cost approach to pricing holds that the price should be a certain amount over direct costs and allow for sufficient contribution to cover indirect costs and overhead and leave a certain margin for profit. Many refinements exist in economic theory depending on the nature of the marketplace and the specific cost behavior. For the purchaser the cost approach offers a number of opportunities to seek low-cost suppliers, to suggest lower cost manufacturing or buying alternatives, and to question the size of margin over direct costs. Negotiation may be a particularly useful tool along with cost analysis techniques.

The market approach

The market approach implies that prices are set in the marketplace and may not be directly related to cost. If demand is high relative to supply, prices are expected to rise; when demand is low relative to supply, prices are expected to decline. This, too, is an oversimplification, and a large variety of conditions hold in economic theory to explain variations of this theme. J. K. Galbraith holds that large multinational multiproduct firms have such a grip on the marketplace that pure competition does not exist and that prices will not drop even though supply exceeds demand. In the market approach, the purchaser must either live with prevailing market prices or find ways around them. If the decision is that nothing can be done to attack the price structure directly, it may still be possible to select those suppliers who are willing to offer nonprice incentives, such as inventory, technical service, good quality, excellent delivery, transportation concessions, and early warning of impending price and new product changes. Negotiation may well center on items other than price, therefore.

There are a number of ways around market pricing. One is for the purchaser to seek the same product in a different market where the price is lower. In the past this has often meant purchasing from foreign sources. As the tendency to world trade increases and multinational firms grow, substantial differences between markets may well disappear, allowing only for freight and tariff differentials.

Many economists hold that substitution of like but not identical materials or products is one of the most powerful forces preventing a completely monopolistic or oligopolistic grip on a market. For example, aluminum and copper may be interchanged for a number of applications provided certain price relationships hold. The aluminum and copper markets are, therefore, not independent of one another. The purchaser's ability to recognize these trade-offs and to effect organizational design and use changes to take advantage of substitution will be one determinant of flexibility. Make or buy is another question, of course. If access to the raw materials, technological process, and labor skills is not severely restricted, one alternative may well be for an organization to make its own requirements to avoid excess market pricing.

Sometimes, purchasers hope to use long-term contracts as an inducement for the supplier to ignore market conditions. This approach may be successful in certain instances, but it is normal for suppliers to find ways and means around such commitments once it becomes obvious that the prevailing market price is substantiallly above that paid by some long-term customers.

Government intervention

During recent years the role of government in price setting has changed dramatically in North America. In many other parts of the world government's involvement in market pricing has been commonplace for a number of years. In North America, where belief in private enterprise and the market mechanism has been particularly strong, the increasing degree of government intervention has been viewed with considerable alarm by many industrialists. The role of government has been twofold. Not only has the government taken an active role in determining prices as part of an anti-inflationary battle, but also in the ways that buyer and seller are allowed to behave in agreeing on prices. The price control role is likely to vary with economic, political, and international conditions. The energy crisis and the dramatic increase in fossil fuel prices have created a very serious challenge for the American government and American business. Since other governments are active in price control and have in a number of situations created dual pricing for domestic use and exports, it is difficult to see how North American governments will be able to ignore their position. Prices may be determined by review or control boards or by strong moral suasion. They are likely to be augmented by governmental controls like quotas, tariffs, and export permits. The purchaser's role in affecting the price of items which are under direct government control may vary. Any purchaser may try to influence government directly. Substitution is still a possibility. The temptation of a gray or black market may well present itself, particularly if the governmental official price is so low that producers are loathe to supply all the quantities the market needs. In the 1970s the phenomenon of copper scrap is a good example of what happens. With the price of virgin copper under control at 60 cents a pound and a world price of at least 90 cents a pound and higher, copper scrap, which was not price controlled, rose to as high as $1.30 a pound domestically. The purchaser is in a very difficult position when supplies are not sufficient to meet internal demand and the pressure to acquire the additional needs at almost any price is extremely strong.

The trading acts

The government has also taken an active interest in how buyer and seller agree on a price. The government's position has largely been a protective role to prevent the stronger party from imposing too onerous conditions on the weaker one or preventing collusion so that competition will be maintained and the interests of the American public protected. Antitrust legislation holds any business practice which hinder competition or restrain trade are illegal. Both the Justice Department and the Federal Trade Commission are concerned with antitrust and may be called on for assistance by a buyer suspecting seller collusion, unfair pricing practices, or other discriminatory behavior. The Sherman Act, Clayton Act, Robinson Patman Act, and the Federal Trade Commission Act all bear on antitrust and pricing issues.

From a buyer's standpoint bringing a seller to the government's attention has few advantages. Since most of the time government's reaction is relatively slow, the need for the item may be gone and conditions may be substantially changed by the time the complaint is decided. Most sellers would view the lodging of a complaint as a particularly unfriendly act making it difficult for both the individual person and the organization to maintain a reasonable future relationship with the particular vendor. For this reason, complaints are not common, and most are probably lodged by governmental buying agencies rather than public corporations.

BIBLIOGRAPHY

ALEXANDER, RALPH S.; CROSS, JAMES S., AND HILL, RICHARD M. *Industrial Marketing,* 3d ed. Homewood, Ill.: Richard D. Irwin, Inc., 1967.

ALJIAN, GEORGE W., ed. *Purchasing Handbook.* 3d ed. New York: McGraw-Hill Book Co., 1973.

BACKMAN, J. *Pricing: Policies and Practices.* New York: National Industrial Conference Board, Inc., 1961.

CONTRACT MANAGEMENT INSTITUTE. *Incentive Contracting in the Aerospace Industry.* Washington: Contract Management Insitute, 1965.

DEPARTMENT OF DEFENSE. *Defense Contract Audit Manual.* Washington: Defense Contract Audit Agency, 1969.

DEPARTMENT OF DEFENSE. *Manual for Contract Pricing (ASPM #1),* Washington: Government Printing Office, 1969.

FITZPATRICK, ALBERT A. *Pricing Methods of Industry.* Boulder, Colo.: Pruett Press, 1964.

GWU GOVERNMENT CONTRACTS PROGRAM. *Incentive Contracting* Monograph No. 7. George Washington University, 1963.

GWU GOVERNMENT CONTRACTS PROGRAM. *Cost Determination* Monograph No. 8 George Washington University, 1964.

JORDON, R. B. "Learning How to Use the Learning Curve," *Bulletin at the National Association of Accountants,* January 1958, pp. 27–39; June 1958, pp. 77–78.

TUCKER, SPENCER A. *Cost Estimating and Pricing with Machine Hour Rates.* New York: McGraw-Hill Book Co. 1961.

WESTING, J. H.; FINE, I. V.; ZENZ, GARY JOSEPH. *Purchasing Management,* 3d ed. New York: John Wiley & Sons, Inc., 1969.

CASES FOR CHAPTER 8

AKON LIFE INSURANCE COMPANY

Mr. Stan Clark, director of purchasing was surprised to receive from his fuel oil supplier a contract cancellation charge amounting to $4,900.

The Akon Life Insurance Company's head office building in the downtown area of a central Illinois city had switched from oil to gas usage in April of 1972. Earlier in the year the Air Management Branch of the state government had informed Akon that the smoke from its chimney was leaving unacceptable levels of sulphur and oil particles on the surrounding buildings. Akon's heating system used bunker oil burners which were very efficient but did not burn cleanly enough to pass the Air Management Branch standards. The alternatives were to switch to a more costly lighter oil, switch to gas, or increase the height of the present chimney by 20 feet. However, due to the present structure of the chimney, only the rebuilding of a new one was feasible. If the company was to switch to gas, the chimney would in any case have to be relined. If a new chimney were to be built, the cost would be $200,000. The alternative to use light oil would be operationally too expensive. The company's board of directors, being pollution conscious, favored any alternative which would reduce pollution from the chimney. Consolidated Gas had in the last part of 1971 laid a major gas line near Akon's building, thus facilitating gas usage by Akon. For the above reasons, the building services committee recommended conversion to gas.

These developments had put Mr. Stan Clark in a difficult position. The gas company, interested in selling summer consumption, had pressured Akon to begin gas usage April 1 or wait a full 12 months for service. The present bunker oil contract with its supplier, Quality Fuels, ran from July 1 to June 30. Mr. Clark, therefore, had to cancel the oil contract three months early. Quality Fuels, after being notified of this, had presented Akon with the cancellation charge.

Mr. John Steward, sales manager for Quality Fuels came to Mr. Clark's office to outline the cancellation problem for his company. He explained that his company was now stuck with a high-cost product since the wholesale price of bunker oil had recently declined. He also added that his company would incur storage charges at their port termi-nal which now would not be covered. He confirmed his calculation of the cancellation charge in a memo which he left with Mr. Clark (see Exhibit 1).

The gas contract

The building services committee had determined that operationally gas and bunker oil would be approximately equivalent in costs. Although bunker oil generated more B.T.U.'s per gallon, the wholesale price had climbed from 6.8¢ to 11.9¢ in 1971 and had recently declined slightly. This situation was not expected to change in the near future. The burner conversion to gas was estimated at $45,000. The conversion and the relin-ing of the chimney were scheduled and completed by April 1, 1972.

The committee had negotiated an "interruptible contract" with Con-solidated Gas. This meant that the gas company could interrupt gas usage at any time up to a maximum of 40 days a year. For this eventuality, Akon had to buy and store light oil to burn in the place of gas if the need arises. The winter months would most probably be interrupted if the winter should turn out to be an exceptionally cold one. In such a situation, if the general demand became too great to maintain adequate pressure on the gas lines from summer stored reserves, the gas company would be forced to shut down large single users.

The oil contract

Quality Fuels had been a supplier of bunker oil to Akon for the last 30 years. Akon's annual usage totaled 500,000 gallons. This was delivered on a staggered basis throughout the year. Generally by April most of the contracted oil was used, leaving about 40,000 gallons for the last three months. However, the winter had been a particularly warm one, leaving by April 140,000 gallons unused.

Mr. Clark had put the bunker oil contract out to tender as usual and received four quotes on the 71–72 oil contract. Most quotes were within ½¢ of one another, but only Quality Fuels would give a fixed price con-tract. Because an uncertain market price situation existed, most suppliers were unwilling to commit themselves to a fixed price contract.

Quality Fuels submitted a price of 12.4¢ a gallon based on 500,000 gallons. Quality in turn had to buy in advance to ensure delivery and availability of navigational season price fixed at 12.4¢ a gallon. By April, however, the wholesale price of bunker oil had dropped almost 2¢ a gal-lon. As mentioned, Quality Fuels did not feel obligated to absorb the price drop since it would have to resell the oil at a competitive loss.

Mr. Clark attempted to determine the legal justification of the cancel-lation charge by asking for a professional opinion from Mr. Duff, the

Exhibit 1

Attention: Mr. Stan Clark,
              Purchasing Manager.
Re: Notice of Termination April 1, 1972 of
       Bunker Fuel Oil Agreement
       versus P.O. No. 53006 for 500,000 gallons
       supply to June 30, 1972.

As I indicated in our telephone conversation last week, we are extremely
disappointed to learn that circumstances have made a decision necessary which
is resulting in the changing of your main fuel supply from bunker oil to
natural gas by about April 1, 1972.

We regret that the decision was not to go to light industrial fuel oil. However,
it is realized that we were struggling with a high-cost product last year,
and any improvement in our cost picture comes too late for consideration
of your engineering people. In addition, the consumption would be increased
by about 25 percent.

As mentioned, while we are prepared to accept the situation and are reluctant
to bring it up—we do face the unpleasant fact of having approximately
140,000 gallons of bunker oil left in stock. This product was sold to you
on the basis of our 1971 lake navigation season cost f.o.b. our port terminal
plus storage, handling, transportation, administration, and profit. None of
these revenues will now accrue to us on the portion of the 500,000 gallons
we provided but which you will not now require. To March 22, 1972, we
have delivered approximately 360,000 gallons. Normally, such gas installations
are scheduled to coincide closely with the contract year and avoid this surplus
fuel oil problem.

Due to a radically changing supply picture with which you have been made
familiar, we are able to start purchasing our 1972 bunker oil requirements
at 1.85¢/gallon less than last season. In addition, our gross margin, made
up of the items referred to above, amounts to 2.05¢/gallon less the portion
we will not actually pay out in labor/wages—transportation charges. If we
allow the full amount for these items which is of questionable merit from
the point of view that we provided the physical facilities, which are not
going to be used entirely as planned, it would reduce the figure to 1.46¢/gal-
lon or a combined total of 3.51¢/gallon × 140,000 gallons approximately
not taken, an amount of $4,900.00 involved in short terming the supply agree-
ment. It may be left at this figure or adjusted if you wish to take the actual
last delivery. However, we presume you will burn down the supply in the
storage tanks in preparation to the switch to light industrial fuel oil for standby,
so that deliveries during the last week may be very limited, if any at all.

I trust this will provide sufficiently detailed information for consideration
by your company of paying the amount involved.

Yours sincerely,
J. Steward,
Sales Manager,
Quality Fuels.

company solicitor. He had examined the contract with Quality Fuels and found it legal and binding. (See Exhibit 2.) The purchase order specified that Akon would purchase 500,000 gallons of fuel from Quality during the 12 months ending June 30, 1972, but did not clearly specify

Exhibit 2

PURCHASE ORDER   No. 53006

Quality Fuels Company Limited   All invoices and correspondence must show this
118 Clearwater Avenue   order number and be sent to:
Southbury, Illinois   Akon Life Insurance Company

Date: July 1, 1971

Please supply the following:

Quantity	Description				Unit Price	Total Price
500,000	Imperial Gallons of Bunker "6C" Fuel Oil with specifications as follows:				$0.1240 per Gallon Delivered	
	Gravity A.P.I. @ 60°	12.0	B.T.U. per	Gal	181,000	
	Flash Pensky °F	175	Sulphur max.		2%	
	Viscosity (Furol @ 122°F)	200	B.S. & W. %		0.8%	
	Pour Point °F	30 to 40	Vanadium Content Max.		18 parts per Million	
	The quoted price may change and any price increase must be submitted in writing 30 days prior to the increase and if this new price is not approved the contract may be cancelled by the buyer by 30 days written notice.					

(In the event of this order not being filled as and at the time indicated we reserve the right to reject)

Deliver to: Akon Life Insurance Company   Delivery Date:.
            268 Featherbraid Avenue   As requested within the next 12 months
            Southbury, Illinois   ending June 30, 1972.

                                        Mr. Stan Clark
                                          Signature

the penalties for failing to do so. Mr. Clark had gathered from his conversation with Mr. Duff that Quality Fuel would very likely be awarded some amount for cancellation charges if the matter were taken to court but that the amount of the award would be uncertain.

Possible bases for agreement on cancellation terms

While considering how to determine a mutually agreeable basis for cancellation, Mr. Clark took into account the fact that the new gas burners might have to be switched to light industrial oil for up to 40 days during mid-winter. It was possible that this requirement for light industrial oil could reach 100,000 gallons annually. He wondered if a meeting with the Quality Fuels representative might result in some arrangement to transfer the unpurchased Bunker C gallonage into a commitment to buy the necessary light industrial oil from Quality Fuels in the future.

The possibility of making such an arrangement appealed to him because, if the $4,900 were paid directly as a cancellation charge, existing accounting procedures would place this amount in the heating fuel expense account. Mr. Johns, chief heating engineer had flatly refused to have this charge included in his budget. He said to Mr. Clark that after doing business with Quality Fuels for over 30 years, they "owed" the Akon Life Insurance Company at least that much.

Mr. Clark recognized the need to be fair with a supplier of 30 years, such as Quality Fuels, by dealing in terms which that supplier himself considered to be fair. This attitude had in the past built excellent supplier relations upon which Akon prided itself. He knew that Akon wanted to continue such satisfactory relations as part of a public relations image needed for a company which marketed an intangible product such as life insurance.

Mr. Clark was unsure about the possibility of resolving this situation satisfactorily with all parties concerned.

LOCAR CORPORATION

Mr. John Palmer, manager of purchasing for Locar Corporation, became in early 1973 increasingly concerned about the shortage of supply of PL75, a major pipe resin. Several PL75 suppliers had approached Mr. Palmer requesting long-term supply contracts. Mr. Palmer was attempting to assess the advisability of such a commitment for Locar Corporation.

Company background

Locar, a long established company in Cincinnati, Ohio, sold industrial piping and plumbing supplies. The company's four plants were located in the eastern United States. A series of regional warehouses provided an extensive distribution system which serviced customers throughout the domestic U.S. market. Total company sales for 1972 exceeded $150 million; piping products totaled $51 million. PL75 pipes and fittings made up 80 percent of piping products sales by Locar. Locar had experienced rapid growth; total company sales had increased at 20 percent a year and were expected to continue at that rate for at least the next four years. The corporate five-year plan called for pipe and fitting sales to exceed $120 million by 1976.

PL75 piping

Locar used PL75 in the manufacture of piping products. Compounds and stabilizers were added to the PL75 polymer, which was then extruded into pipe and pipe fittings (see Exhibit 1). The manufacturing cost of PL75 pipe amounted to 35 percent of its selling price.

Exhibit 1

STAGES IN PLASTICS MANUFACTURING*

Stage:	Basic chemicals	Monomers	Polymerization	Compounding	Processing	Fabricating	Finishing
Activities:	Petroleum is converted to *petrochemicals* such as: ethylene, benzene, propylene, acetylene.	Petrochemicals plus other chemicals are converted into *monomers* such as: ethylene, vinyl-chloride, acrylonitrile, styrene, propylene	One or more monomers are polymerized to form *polymers* or copolymers such as: polyethylene polyvinyl-chloride styrene-acrylonitrile butadiene, copolymer polystyrene polypropylene	Plasticizers, stabilizers, color pigments, antioxidants, inhibitors, and other chemicals are sometimes added to the base polymers to form *compounds* suitable for use by processors or as coatings for paper, wood, etc., or in paints and adhesives	The plastics *compounds* are *formed* into a variety of solid shapes such as sheets, tubes, rods, film, and other shapes, by the heat and/or pressure of casting, molding extrusion, or other means of processing. This step may provide a finished product, such as plastic pipe	These solid shapes may be *fabricated* by thermoforming, machining, etc., to create plastics articles such as toys or appliances.	In some cases there is a *finishing* step, such as the printing of surface designs on vinyl film.

	Chemical			Physical and Mechanical			
Process:							
State:	Gases and liquids	Mostly liquids	Solids and slurries	Solids and slurries	Solids	Solids	Solids
Customers:	Monomer manufacturers	Polymerizers	Processors		Fabricators and end users	Finishers and end users	End users
Important trends and improvements:	New and larger manufacturing facilities which will lower costs through economies of scale.	New manufacturing processes which will lower prices through greater efficiencies and use of lower cost raw materials.	New techniques of copolymerization and stereospecific polymerization which allow producers to create polymers with specific sets of processing and end-use characteristics.	New and more effective additives which expand the range of usefulness of plastics.	New processing equipment and techniques which can produce very large and stress-free parts.	Use of butt welding of large plastics parts is extending the range of shapes which may be made out of plastics.	New plating methods which increase the environmental resistance and eye-appeal of plastics. New graphic finishing techniques such as wood graining which will allow plastics to compete as decorative items.

* Modern Plastics Encyclopedia

PL75 polymer was a versatile nonburning resin used in significant quantities in nearly every major segment of the pipe market (see Exhibits 2 and 3).

Pipes produced from PL75 had remarkable long-life characteristics. Chemically, these pipes had not yet been known to break down or deteriorate. Another reason for the enthusiastic adoption and use of PL75 piping and plastic piping in general was the ease of installation and fastening of the pipe joints with a cement. This made resin piping far superior to cast iron and copper piping which required soldering.

Exhibit 2
PLASTIC PIPE BY APPLICATION AND BY RESIN*
SALES AND USAGE
(in million pounds)

Item	1969	1975	1980	Percent annual growth 1980/69
Pipe by Application				
Portable water.	170	325	500	10.3
Agriculture and irrigation	94	145	175	5.8
Electrical conduit.	49	78	124	8.8
Drain and sewer.	54	92	148	9.6
Drain, waste and vent	64	120	172	9.4
Oil and gas.	39	76	150	13.0
Process industries.	30	52	88	10.3
Structural, mechanical and miscellaneous	15	36	60	13.4
Total.	515	924	1417	9.6
Pipe by Resin				
PL75.	251	498	789	11.0
Polyethylene	111	176	243	7.3
PL80.	64	98	136	7.1
Styrene-rubber	58	90	144	8.6
Thermosets	27	55	89	11.4
Other resins	4	7	16	13.4
Total.	515	924	1417	9.6

PLASTIC PIPE AND FITTINGS SALES

Item	1957–59	1960–62	1963–65	1966–68	1969	1975	1980
	(in million pounds)						
Pipe.	49	79	153	320	515	924	1417
Fittings.	6	11	26	60	100	191	298
Pipe and fittings.	55	90	179	380	615	1115	1715
Dollars per pound.	.73	.69	.65	.61	.55	.52	.50
	(in million dollars)						
Pipe.	29	44	77	144	206	352	515
Fittings.	11	18	40	88	132	228	345
Pipe and fittings.	40	62	117	132	338	580	860

* *Plastic Pipe, August 1970*, T-18, Predicasts, Inc., 200 University Circle Research Center, Cleveland, Ohio 44106.

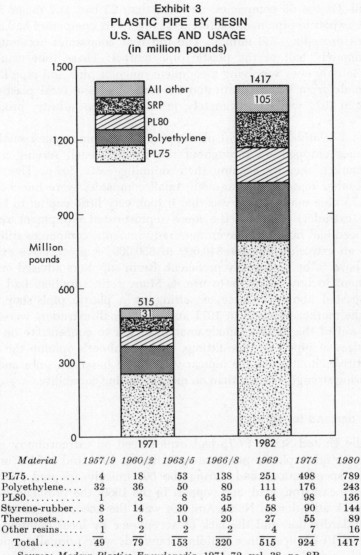

Exhibit 3
PLASTIC PIPE BY RESIN
U.S. SALES AND USAGE
(in million pounds)

Material	1957/9	1960/2	1963/5	1966/8	1969	1975	1980
PL75..........	4	18	53	138	251	498	789
Polyethylene....	32	36	50	80	111	176	243
PL80..........	1	3	8	35	64	98	136
Styrene-rubber..	8	14	30	45	58	90	144
Thermosets.....	3	6	10	20	27	55	89
Other resins.....	1	2	2	2	4	7	16
Total........	49	79	153	320	515	924	1417

Source: *Modern Plastics Encyclopedia*, 1971–72, vol. 38, no. 8B.

However, PL75 pipe during manufacture was difficult to stabilize during
the extrusion process. The larger the diameter of the pipe or fitting,
the more technically competent the extruder had to be. Much of the
future market growth would be toward larger pipe sizes and pipe applications which required a high degree of extrusion ability.

The plastic pipe industry

Nationally, the plastic pipe industry consisted of about 60 companies
in 1971 which shared a business volume of approximately $600 million

at retail. Of the 60 companies, no more than 25 had any major market impact as plastic pipe manufacturers; as few as six companies had annual volumes exceeding $30 million. The top four companies accounted for approximately half of the plastic pipe market. These four companies were the only ones supplying a complete range of pipe and pipe fittings. Pipe made from PL75 constituted 50 percent of the total plastic pipe market in 1971 with approximately one third of the industry processing PL75.

With a relatively high cost of shipping plastic pipe, many small pipe companies cropped up throughout the country, each serving a small local market, thereby keeping their shipping costs down. There were several other reasons why so many small companies were bunched into the PL75 pipe market. One was that it took very little capital to become a pipe extruder. Although the more sophisticated equipment recently introduced had raised the investment requirements, companies still could set up an extrusion line for $40,000 to $50,000. A prospective extruder didn't have to be technically proficient. Resin suppliers advised on what equipment to buy and how to use it. Many resin suppliers had in the past boasted about the ease of setting up a plastic pipe shop.

As the market matured in 1971 and 1972, small extruders were being forced out of the market, amalgamated, or left to concentrate on a few small sizes of pipe and pipe fittings. In Mr. Palmer's opinion the future competitive situation in the industry would be based on sales and merchandising strengths rather than on manufacturing capability.

Future demand for PL75

In the United States PL75 had experienced an extraordinary growth along with other plastic pipe materials during 1971 and 1972. European building specifications had during the 60s quickly adopted resin pipe to replace cast iron, lead, and copper. In the 1960s the problems holding back quick adoption in North America were the needs for greater product standardization and the lack of acceptance by local building codes for use of PL75 pipe. Since building standards were normally controlled by local as well as state or federal agencies, the job of gaining plastic piping acceptance was time-consuming. This approval process was just beginning to snowball in 1972. Market expansion of PL75 was forecast to continue at a rapid rate. In 1971, *Modern Plastics,* an industry publication, predicted U.S. industry use of PL75 for piping to reach 1 billion pounds by 1982. In early 1973, *Modern Plastics* anticipated the 1-billion mark would be overshot as early as 1977.

Growth rates of 30 percent, however, were felt to be unrepresentative "accelerated advances." Mr. Palmer expected that after 1974, a steady growth would stabilize between 10 and 12 percent per year for PL75 pipe.

Some experts in the market predicted a glut on the market of resins including PL75 by 1975, but the manufacturers of PL75 polymer strongly denied this. R. J. Abramowitz[1] stated in a recent joint article in *Modern Plastics*[2] in regards to PL75 polymer, the following:

SUPPLY-DEMAND

For the near term, PL75 polymer will be kept in reasonable balance with demand, with some debottlenecking types of expansion expected in 1972–73 before any major new capacity commitments. A continued high growth rate in pipe and favorable rulings on the ecology scene for rigid bottles could tighten the supply situation in late 1972 or in 1973.

Supply of PL75 polymer

Suppliers of PL75 had built up loyalties with their customers over the years when the market was soft and prices were low. However, since the beginning of 1973, they had set quotas for all their present customers, thereby making PL75 still available to many small extruders. Mr. Palmer thought that in a few years these loyalties would be terminated.

At the same time other polymer suppliers, who were also extruders of PL75, had stopped selling PL75 polymer during the last year and were using all of their own production.

Suppliers located within a 1,000-mile radius were considered by Mr. Palmer to be within the maximum shipping distance. Since PL75 was delivered in bulk by rail or truck, all current contracts were f.o.b. Locar plants. Suppliers further than 1,000 miles away would not submit an f.o.b. quote. Within this shipping distance, Mr. Palmer estimated that 15 potential suppliers of PL75 polymer existed. If suppliers were to be switched or lost, freight charges could play a critical role in alternative supplier selections.

Locar purchases and suppliers of PL75

Locar started extruding resin pipe in 1963. Increasing quantities of PL75 had been purchased since then. Past purchases, future demand, forecasts, and price increases are oulined in Tables 1 and 2.

In 1973, five companies supplied Locar with PL75. Clark and Solvay had supplied PL75 to Locar since 1963. These two companies also supplied other chemical stabilizers and compounds to Locar in addition to PL75 and were considered by Mr. Palmer to be "old, reliable sup-

---

[1] R. J. Abramowitz, L. T. Friedman, and R. V. Lucky, *Business Managers* (Burlington, N.J.: Hooker Chemical Corporation).

[2] *Modern Plastics Encyclopedia 1972–1973*, vol. 49, no. 10A, p 102.

Table 1
PL75 PURCHASE FORECASTS BY LOCAR
(volume—millions pounds)

1969	*			
1971		*		
1972			*	
1973				*
1974				35
1975				47
1976	20 million	35 million	45 million	60 million

* Year forecast was made.

Table 2
PL75 ACTUAL PURCHASES AND PRICES PER POUND

	Volume (in million pounds)	Price per pound (paid by Locar)
1950	—	45¢
1963	3	8
1970	12	10
1971	15	10.5
1972	20	11
1973	(28) projected to year end	12

pliers." The other three companies had supplied PL75 only and were relatively new having commenced business with Locar during the last three years. One of these three, Imperial, manufactured PL75 polymer and also extruded industrial food and beverage piping made of PL75. Table 3 outlines the percentages and volumes expected to be supplied by these five companies for 1973.

Table 3
1973 SUPPLY OF PL75 TO LOCAR

Company	1973 capacity (in million pounds)	Locar purchases (in million pounds)	Value
Clark	85	8.4	$1,008,000
Solvay*	60	8.4	1,008,000
Imperial*	20	5.6	672,000
Acro	40	2.8	336,000
Albis	60	2.8	336,000
		28.0	$3,360,000

* Capacity available for sale. Other capacity exists which is used within the company.

Prices were the same from all five suppliers. Mr. Palmer noted that with the general tightening of supply, the price had quickly settled to a common level. Until 1973 it had been standard industry practice to buy on a hand-to-mouth basis at the current market price.

Long-term contract proposals

In February, 1973, Mr. Palmer was stunned by the rapid alteration of the supply situation. Within the same week three of the present suppliers (Clark, Solvay and Imperial) had approached Mr. Palmer with proposals to supply Locar with present and future requirements of PL75.

Clark, a large international producer of a wide range of chemical products was generally perceived as a leader in the monomer and polymer field. Clark had asked for a five-year contract extending until 1978 with escalation clauses for labor, energy, and feedstock based on a current price of 12¢ a pound. Clark pointed out the danger of future capacity shortages by showing Mr. Palmer projected capacity and sales figures. (See Exhibit 4.) Minimum contract volumes would be based on Clark's

Exhibit 4
DOMESTIC PRODUCTION AND TOTAL SALES
AND USAGE OF PL75 RESINS
THREE MONTHS MOVING AVERAGE

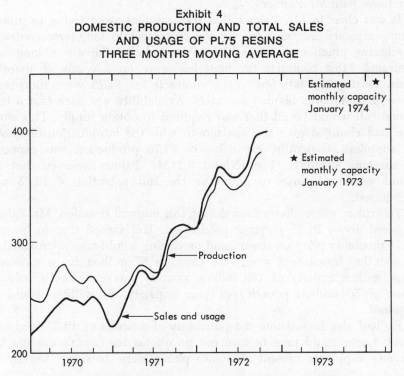

Source: Society Plastic Institute (in millions of pounds by month).

present percentage of Locar's total purchases (30 percent) projected over Locar's 60 million pounds forecast. The commitment would be on a firm volume guaranteed contract with an escalated price. Locar would be contractually obligated to pay for that volume at the agreed price. A cancellation penalty was available which would amount to 60 percent of the selling price at the time of cancellation. Clark's sales representative stated that without this long-term contract no supply guarantees could be given after August, 1973.

Solvay, another large international concern, manufactured PL75 polymer as a raw material for some of its own end products as well as selling the polymer on the open market. Solvay's proposal was similar to Clark's except that they were asking for a three-year contract instead of a five-year contract.

Imperial, like Solvay, was a large international corporation selling a wide range of end products using PL75 polymer. Imperial asked for a purchase agreement which could be mutually dropped at any time. Mr. Long wondered if Imperial's reluctance to offer a long-term contract indicated that Imperial was planning to use all production of PL75 polymer itself within a few years.

Acro and Albis, both small PL75 polymer producers, had not asked for any special considerations and had not initiated discussions of future purchases with Mr. Palmer.

It was clear to Mr. Palmer that the suppliers were trying to protect future capacity increases by signing customers to long-term contracts. Purchasing practice at Locar had never included the use of long-term contracts. Most contracts for materials were on a yearly or monthly basis. During the last few years, contracts for PL75 were short-term, three or six months blanket contracts. Availability was such that a telephone call would be all that was required to obtain supply. This situation had changed over the last month with the introduction of quotas by suppliers. Generally, expansion of PL75 production was expected to continue strongly. (See Exhibit 5.) Mr. Palmer believed that demand would continue to climb as the full potential of PL75 was recognized.

To explore other alternatives during this unusual situation, Mr. Palmer inquired about PL75 polymer production. He learned that to bring a PL75 monomer plant on-stream and producing would take approximately 18 months. Investment would be close to $7 million for a monomer plant with a capcity of 150 million pounds per year. For a polymer plant of 50 million pounds per year capacity, $4 million would be required.

He had also looked into the possibility of contracting PL75 feedstock which Locar could then in turn put on quotas for Locar's existing five polymer suppliers. Present monomer plants were, however, heavily in-

Exhibit 5
WORLD PL75 POLYMER PRODUCTION BY COUNTRY*
(in billion pounds)

Country	1960–62	1963–65	1966–68	1969	1975	1980
United States	1.04	1.62	2.31	3.03	5.50	8.10
Japan	.64	.96	1.56	2.31	5.31	9.30
West Germany	.44	.73	1.12	1.62	2.75	4.00
USSR	.07	.11	.26	.33	1.00	3.00
Italy	.35	.62	.86	.94	1.90	3.00
United Kingdom	.24	.39	.51	.57	1.10	1.80
France	.27	.44	.57	.82	1.45	2.30
Netherlands	.02	.04	.09	.15	.55	1.00
Spain	.03	.06	.12	.18	.30	.50
All Other	.52	.91	1.47	2.11	5.00	10.30
Total	3.62	5.88	8.87	12.06	24.86	43.30
Nine Major Countries (Percent)	85.6	84.5	83.4	82.5	79.9	76.2

* *World Plastics Markets* T-21, May 1971. Predicasts Inc., 200 University Circle Research Center, Cleveland, Ohio 44106.

vested in by the petrochemical companies, making any control over the feedstock difficult. These companies also controlled ethane, itself a by-product accounting for only 1 percent of their sales but a major component of the monomer. Unsure about Locar's present suppliers' reactions, Mr. Palmer hesitated to act in this area. He was uncertain about the dangers of becoming too deeply involved in the problems of polymer and monomer producers.

In a recent article Mr. Palmer had read that a laboratory had successfully developed a better manufacturing method for PL75 monomer. Should this method be proven commercially it might be expected to reduce the manufacturing cost of PL75 by about one cent per pound by 1976.

On March 5, 1973, Clark's sales representative telephoned Mr. Palmer to ask if he could bring his sales manager to a meeting on March 9 to discuss future business. Mr. Palmer knew that the long-term proposals would have to be decided upon before then. He was not sure if it was in his company's best interest to make the kind of commitment the suppliers were presently requesting. Nevertheless, he was most anxious to assure adequate supply for the future.

SOUTHERN POWER CORPORATION (A)

Mr. Hanley, director of purchasing for Southern Power Corporation, faced an interesting problem on the insulation contract for a new nuclear reactor. Specifications were somewhat vague and subject to further changes. Firm bids requested from four contractors showed a wide variation in price. Mr. Hanley was, therefore, considering the use of a special contract allowing for price variation and incentive.

Company background

Southern Power Corporation was one of the larger electrical utilities in the southern United States. It employed over 8,000 people and had annual operating revenues in excess of $750 million per year. Annual plant and equipment expenditures exceeded $400 million. Purchases of noncapital items and fuel were over $180 million per year.

The insulation job

The insulation job for the new nuclear plant presented a difficult purchasing problem. The job involved coating of beams, ceilings, and piping and was subject to rigid inspection procedures. Access to some areas might be difficult, and the amount of material which might be required could not be easily determined. Not all construction details were clear yet, and Mr. Hanley had expressed some misgivings in going out for fixed bids when the contract came up. Al Williams, manager of contracts suggested that, if suppliers objected strongly to a fixed bid, something else might be worked out. Al preferred a fixed bid from a budgeting and ease of management point of view.

Special efforts were taken to assure that only reliable sources would quote. Four suppliers were approached, and, although none objected to using a fixed bid, the results showed a large price variation. Bob Cunningham, Inc., was high bidder at $225,000. Next came Hughes Corporation at $204,000 and Rennie Construction at $165,000. Stillcamp Construction was low bidder at $103,000.

Al Williams discussed the bids with Mr. Hanley.

"I'm really unsure about using fixed bids on this new insulation job," said Mr. Hanley. "The scope and definition of this installation is still quite vague, leaving me very uneasy about these bids we received." Al Williams thought Stillcamp Construction might "get clobbered" once they got into the actual job and were subjected to Southern's high expectations. He raised this possibility with the sales manager of Stillcamp who replied that Stillcamp had included a safety margin in its bid. According to all of Stillcamp's calculations they felt they could meet a target price about 10 percent below the bid price. The sales manager confided that he thought his bid was on the high side rather than low. When Mr. Williams reported this rather startling finding to Mr. Hanley, Mr. Hanley wondered: "Perhaps we should be working on a form of incentive contract instead. You see, they're sure they're on the high side and that they can do better. We're sure they're on the low side and may get hurt. From everything we know, they're a good supplier, but they wouldn't be able to stand a bid loss if they turn out to be wrong. If they're willing to share some of the gains with us if they do better than the fixed bid, perhaps we can assist them a bit if they go over." Does this mean we'll have to go out for new bids all over again?" asked Mr. Williams. "Why don't we think about that while we work out a scheme?" replied Mr. Hanley.

The new proposal

Al Williams was intrigued by Mr. Hanley's remarks. As manager of contracts he had become aware of a number of situations where fixed bids did not seem to make sense from either the buyer's or the seller's point of view. He also realized that the frequency of contracts involving specification uncertainty was increasing. He wondered, therefore, if the insulation contract might not be an excellent vehicle for testing a different approach. Compared to most contracts in his office, the dollar volume was relatively low. All four suppliers were technically sound. The element of risk was, therefore, not particularly great. If, however, a new approach could be found it might be applied to a number of larger dollar contracts in the future.

Al Williams and one of the purchasing agents worked on the problem for several weeks and developed a scheme for Mr. Hanley's approval. It was a substantial departure from the traditional fixed bid approach, and the two originators were proud of their ideas.

The proposal called for a base price around which the contract provisions resolved. Suppliers would calculate the base price using detailed estimates of labor, material overhead, a contracting fee, and profit. Actual costs incurred, carefully audited, would form the basis for final price paid. If total actual costs were less than the base price, Southern and the contractor would share in the savings. Sixty percent of the savings would go to Southern, 40 percent to the contractor.

The contractor would also bid an adjustment price above the base price. If actual costs incurred exceeded the base price but were below the adjustment price, Southern would pay all direct costs and overhead but no additional fee and profit. Should actual costs exceed the adjustment price, Southern would pay additional direct materials and labor only, but no overhead, fee, or profit.

The two designers of this scheme had used the Stillcamp bid as an example of how the system might work (see Exhibits 1 and 2).

Exhibit 1
SOUTHERN POWER CORPORATION

Memorandum for File

Subject: Martin Lee Insulation Contract

A variety of factors make it desirable for Southern to ask the bidders on the insulation work at our Martin Lee Power Plant to consider bidding an alternate to the lump sum price mentioned in their previous bids. This alternate bid is on the basis of sharing in savings up to base, contractors loss of profit mark-up for all costs between base and adjustment price, contractors loss of profit and overhead for costs over the adjustment price. Southern would like to evaluate the potential of such a contract using both the lump sum and time and material method of performing this work. Therefore, the alternate bid is to be on the following basis:

1. The bidders stipulate a base price from which the basic contract will center. (This could be your lump sum bid of the previous quotation) **$103,000**

    The actual work to be performed on a time and material basis with the following items being established before the contract starts:

    a. Labor—including all expenses based on labor (including all hourly supervision) .... **$ 48,500**
    b. Materials, cost to Contractor **36,500**
    c. Overhead—including all home, office and field cost not a part of labor
        1 a. above
        (1) Overhead—labor (including all other supervision) .... 10% **4,850**
        (2) Overhead on material .... 10% **3,650**
    d. Profit (about 10%) **9,500**
    e. Total or base price **$103,000**

2. If the contractor experiences cost of any of the items listed above that results in a total bill less than the base price, the savings would be shared between Southern and the contractor on the basis of 60 percent of the savings to Southern and 40 percent to the contractor.

3. If the cost of work reaches and starts to exceed the *base price*, Southern is to pay only the additional direct labor and taxes, insurance and benefits, cost of material and overhead as defined in 1 *a, b* and *c* above. The contractor offers as a limit to this arrangement the following adjustment price:

    $115,000

4. If the cost of the work exceeds adjustment price Southern is to pay all direct labor and those items of taxes, insurance, and benefits directly based on labor payroll plus cost of items included in 1 *a* and *b* above but the contractor is to receive no compensation for overhead or profit, items *c* and *d* in 1. above.

5. All extra work to the contract which is not a part of the current bid in current drawings or specifications will be bid on by the contractor as a *lump sum* or *base price*. These individual amounts will be added to the *base* and *adjustment prices* as they occur and the accounting will remain on a time and material basis.

Since it had been normal Southern practice in the past to reject all bidders on a contract if a major change in specifications or bidding procedure was planned, Al Williams thought he should go out for new bids from all four suppliers. He asked Mr. Hanley to review the plan and to give it approval as soon as possible so that he could get going on the insulation contract.

Exhibit 2
SAMPLE CALCULATIONS TO SHOW
IMPACT OF INCENTIVE FORMULA

Situation A—Contractor Performs Below Base Price

Actual costs incurred:	Labor	$40,000
	Material	32,000
	Total	$72,000
	Overhead allowed (10%)	7,200
	Profit allowed	7,200
	Total job cost	$86,400

Original base price: $103,000
Actual job: 86,400

Difference . . . . $ 16,600
Therefore, incentive earnings to contractor @ 40% . . . . $ 6,640
Therefore, savings to Southern @ 60%   9,960
Therefore, final job cost to Southern $103,000 − $93,040 = ...   93,040
Therefore, total contractor profit = $7,200 + $6,640 = ...   13,840

Situation B—Contractor Performs Above Adjustment Price

Actual costs incurred:	Labor	$ 66,000
	Material	47,000
	Total	$113,000
	Overhead incurred	11,300
	Profit at 10%	11,300
	Total job theoretical price	$135,600

Southern's final job cost would be:

To adjustment price:	$115,100		
Labor and material	96,000	Actual labor and material	$113,000
Overhead allowed	9,600	Less labor and material covered	
Profit allowed	9,500	under adjustment price.	96,000
Total	$115,100	Additional labor and material	
		allowed.	$ 17,000

Therefore, final job cost to Southern $115,100
                                                          17,000
                                                        ─────────
                                                        $132,100
Therefore, final profit to contractor . . . . $ 9,500

CARLYN CORPORATION

In the spring of 1974 Mr. Bill Thomas, purchasing manager for Carlyn Corporation, became increasingly concerned about the purchase of MS-7, a special ingredient used in Stimgro, one of his company's new products. It appeared that a major cost increase might threaten the product's profitability, and Bill Thomas was anxious to explore any alternatives which promised at least some cost relief.

Carlyn Corporation was the U.S. subsidiary of Carlyn International, a U.K. based producer of veterinary products and feed additives. Total U.S. sales in 1974 were expected to be about $5 million with profits before taxes of about $200,000. The Carlyn plant located in Chicago employed about 70 hourly rated people. The premises were leased, and primary activities involved the mixing of ingredients and the bottling and packing of finished products. About half of the $3 million worth of ingredients were imported from the U.K. parent, the remainder and all packaging were purchased in the U.S. The executive team consisted of Mr. Peters, president and treasurer, Mr. Grove, sales manager, Mr. Thomas, purchasing manager, and Mr. Harper plant manager. Carlyn Corporation occupied a special niche in the U.S. market, concentrating on poultry medicines and feed additives. In 1971 Carlyn had introduced Stimgro, a feed additive for turkeys, which had shown unusual promise in promoting rapid, healthy development in birds less than one month old. Sales prospects appeared extra promising, and, had it not been for the introduction several months later of a competitive product from Blondin, Carlyn might have captured the total U.S. market. By 1974 Carlyn and Blondin had about equal shares in the Stimgro market with annual sales of about $350,000 each.

Carlyn imported the two primary ingredients for Stimgro from its U.K. parent and mixed and packaged them in the Chicago plant. The manufacturing cost for Stimgro is shown in Exhibit 1.

Exhibit 1
1974 STIMGRO MANUFACTURING COST/KG

MS-7 (500 grams)	$25.00
Other ingredients (500 grams)	12.00
Packaging	1.00
Labor	2.00
Overhead	5.00
Total	$45.00

Carlyn's selling price of Stimgro was $90.00 per kilogram.

Mr. Thomas had tried to find a North American source for MS-7 over the past few years but had found that all potential sources, pharmaceutical, and specialty chemical firms had declined serious interest. They claimed the volume was far too low, and the price would have to be at least $200.00 per kilogram before they could be persuaded to manufacture MS-7.

Blondin

Blondin Corporation was a U.S. owned manufacturer of products similar to those marketed by Carlyn. Blondin's range of products was greater than Carlyn's, and its annual sales volume was about $12 million. Blondin had originally obtained its MS-7 from a U.K. competitor of Carlyn International, but in the spring of 1974 it had placed orders for equipment to manufacture its own MS-7. This action had surprised Mr. Thomas because, like Carlyn, Blondin had been relatively poorly prepared to take this step. For example, the North American market demand for MS-7 was limited to its use by Carlyn and Blondin. Although future growth might show a healthy increase, total market demand for 1974 certainly did not warrant the $250,000 investment Blondin had to make.

Moreover, MS-7 was tricky to produce requiring very careful temperature, pressure, and timing control. The main equipment item was a large glass-lined autoclave ingeniously instrumented and constructed to deal with the unusual demands of MS-7 extraction. The autoclave was normally a fairly general purpose type of equipment in the chemical industry. However, the special conditions required for the manufacture of MS-7 made this reactor a special purpose tool, certainly overdesigned and overengineered for the other uses to which Blondin might apply it. MS-7 manufacture was a batch production process, and the expected capacity of the equipment was about 40,000 kilograms per year based on one shift operation.

In Mr. Thomas' eyes, Blondin's action affected his own purchases of MS-7, which up to this point had been at an advantageous transfer price from the U.K. parent. Although the exact impact was still not entirely clear, Mr. Thomas expected at least a 40 percent increase in his laid down cost. He had no doubt that Blondin would aggressively seek customs protection from undervalued MS-7 imports and that at least a 20 percent duty would be applied on the American selling price.

In May, 1974, Mr. Thomas, therefore, requested information from the parent company concerning manufacturing costs of MS-7. He added several other data from his own knowledge and prepared the following summary:

SUMMARY OF MS-7 COST AND PRICE DATA

Minimum equipment outlay	installed $250,000
Delivery on equipment	9–12 months
U.K. normal market price	$56.00/kg.
Our laid down current cost from Carlyn U.K.	$50.00/kg.
Carlyn (U.K.) out of pocket cost (material, labor and variable overhead)	$40.00/kg.
Estimated minimum laid down cost in Chicago after Blondin starts production	$70.00/kg.

Mr. Thomas went to see Mr. Grove, Carlyn's sales manager, to discuss possible sales requirements for the future. Mr. Grove said:

It's really anybody's guess. First, it depends on the popularity of turkeys. We are banking on continued growth there. Second, as soon as the feed companies can develop a suitable substitute for our product, they will go for it. We appear to be very expensive on a weight basis, although research and actual results show we represent excellent value. It takes such tiny quantities of Stimgro to improve the overall quality of a mix that it is difficult to believe it could have any impact. More competition can enter this market any day. We are just not large enough in the U.S. market to have any strong promotional impact. Each of our product lines is specialized, of relatively small volume, in an area where the big firms choose not to operate. Should a larger firm enter this market, they could flatten us. Blondin's entry after Stimgro took us by surprise, and those bastards stole half of our market already. Now you tell me how to turn this into a reasonable forecast.

Mr. Thomas replied:

I'm glad that's your problem and not mine, Frank. Any time you feel you're ready to put some figures down, please let me know, because it may become very important for us in the near future.

In looking over past figures, Mr. Thomas estimated that the second half of 1974 requirements would total about 1,000 kilograms of MS-7. In June, 1974, Mr. Thomas decided that he had better think out the effect that Blondin's decision to make MS-7 might have on his future purchasing strategy.

9 PRICE POLICIES (CONTINUED)

Determination of most advantageous bid

When the bids have been submitted and are ready for comparison, the question arises which should be selected. The lowest bid is customarily accepted.[1] The whole objective of securing quotations and bids from various sources is to obtain the lowest price, and the purpose of accompanying such requests with detailed descriptions of specifications and statements of requirements is to assure the buyer that he receives the same items or services irrespective of whom the supplier may be. Governmental contracts are required by law to be granted to the lowest bidder unless very special reasons can be shown for not doing so.

In many cases the lowest bidder may not receive the order. Information received by the buyer subsequent to the request for quotations may indicate that the firm submitting the lowest bid is not reliable or dependable. Even the lowest bid may be higher than the buyer believes justifiable. Or there may be reason to believe that collusion existed among the bidders.

There are other reasons why the lowest bid is not always accepted: plant management, engineering, or using departments may express a preference for a certain manufacturer's product. Possibly a slight difference in price may not be considered to compensate for the confidence insured by a particular supplier's product, whereas a larger difference in price might outweigh the other considerations. A small difference in price may not seem to justify the buyer in changing from a source of supply that has been loyal and satisfactory over a long period; yet the issuance of inquiries and the receipt of quotations may have been considered essential by the buyer for assuring that the company was receiving the proper price treatment. Reciprocity may likewise enter into this situation.

---

[1] This statement is made on the assumption that the lowest bid comes from a reliable supplier; presumably, of course, only reliable firms have been invited to bid.

In any one of these cases the purchaser may feel justified either in rejecting all bids or in awarding the order to some company other than the lowest bidder.

Selecting the supplier, once the quotations are received, is not a simple matter of listing the bidders and picking out the one whose price is apparently low, because the obvious price comparisons may be misleading. Of two apparently identical bids, one may actually be higher than the other. One supplier's installation costs may be lower than another's. If prices quoted are f.o.b supplier's plant, the transportation charges may be markedly different. One supplier's price may be much lower because he is trying to break into a new market or is trying to force his only real competitor out of business. One vendor's product may require tooling which must be amortized. One supplier may quote a fixed price; another may insist on an escalator clause that, probable price trends considered, is likely to push his price above his competitor's firm bid. These and other similar factors are likely to render a snap judgment on comparative price a mistake.

Negotiation necessary between buyer and seller

Unless the order is awarded strictly on the basis of the lowest bid received, a certain amount of negotiation between buyer and seller is necessary before arriving at a final agreement on price. This negotiation is a perfectly natural procedure and quite to be expected. Indeed, no small part of the special function of a purchasing agent lies in the ability to negotiate skillfully. Of course, negotiation covers the suitability of the product, the qualifications of the vendor, as well as the fairness of the price.

Reasonable negotiation is expected by buyer and seller alike. A reasonable discussion with a vendor as to price, a fair inquiry into costs, a request to justify the quotation—all these are surely desirable. It is within reasonable bounds of negotiation to insist that a supplier:

1. Keep prices in line with those of qualified competitors.
2. Does not take advantage of a privileged position.
3. Make proper and reasonable adjustment of claims
4. Compete on the same terms as qualified competitors.
5. Be prepared to consider the special needs of the buyer's organization.

Price haggling. Negotiating a fair price, however, should not be confused with "price haggling" for which there is little justification. Purchasing agents generally frown upon haggling wherever it appears and properly so, for in the long run the cost to the buyer far outweighs any temporary advantage which may be obtained. For a purchaser to tell a sales representative that he or she has received a quotation that was not, in fact, received or that is not comparable; to fake telephone calls in the sales representatives presence; to leave real or fictitious bids of competitors in open sight for a sales representative to see; to mislead as to the quantity proposed to buy; to make much over very minor differences in price—these and similar practices are illustrations of that "sharp practice" so rightly condemned by the Code of Ethics of the National Association of Purchasing Management.

Collusive bidding. A buyer also may reject all bids when satisfied that the suppliers are acting in collusion with one another. In such cases the proper policy to pursue is often difficult to determine. Various possibilities, of course, suggest themselves. Legal action is at times possible but is seldom feasible because of the expense, delay, and uncertainty of the outcome. Often, unfortunately, the only apparent solution is simply to accept the situation with the feeling that there is nothing that can be done about it anyway. Another possibility is to seek new sources of supply either inside or outside the area within which the buyer customarily has secured materials or services. Resort to substitute materials temporarily, or even permanently, may be an effective means of meeting the situation. Another possibility is to reject all the bids and then to attempt, by a process of negotiaton or bargaining with one or another of the suppliers, to have the price reduced. If circumstances make the last alternative the most feasible, a question of ethics, of course, is involved. Some purchasing officers are likely to feel, when collusion among the vendors exists, that it is just as ethical for them to attempt to force down suppliers' prices by means which would not ordinarily be adopted as it is for the suppliers to attempt to force prices up beyond reasonable limits.

Revision of price upward. All negotiation need not result in a lower price. Occasionally, there may be revision upward of the price paid, even after a contract has been awarded on the bid basis. Some buyers are willing to cooperate with vendors experiencing unforeseen increases in cost of such magnitude that substantial losses will result if a price adjustment is not made. When a purchaser cooperates in granting increases not required by the purchase contract, the buyer is in a position to request decreases in prices if unforeseen events occur which result in the vendor's being able to produce the material or product at a substantial saving. In seller's markets, pressure is strong on buyers to allow upward price revisions. This is an opportunity for the buyer to request justification in the form of detailed cost breakdown. Such information can be valuable for future negotiations.

Adjusting purchases to meet fixed costs

Frequently, an organization is unable in the short term to raise the selling price of its own products, and yet the prices of the components and raw materials fluctuate. Animal feeds, candy, flour, and many other products are examples of this. If it is possible to change the mix of ingredients without adversely affecting the quality, taste, nutrition, or performance of the final product, there may be an opportunity to buy in some markets which are low to substitute for at least some of the high-cost ingredients. Linear programs have been developed for a number of animal feeds, for example, in an effort to maintain nutrition with a large number of formulations. The rapidly fluctuating prices of ingredients force the manufacturer to plan production according to market availability and prices. If all ingredients rise substantially in price at the same time, as is common at a time of shortages, such substitutions will not solve the problem, and the manufacturer will be forced to raise prices or absorb the extra costs despite the difficulties associated with each action.

Guarantee against price decline and providing for escalation

The guarantee against price decline is frequently provided in contracts for goods bought on a regular recurring basis and for process materials. The contract usually specifies a price in effect at the time the contract is negotiated and provides for a reduction during a subsequent period if there is a downward price movement in the marketplace. In essence the buyer has a right to place orders elsewhere for materials originally included in the contract if offered a lower net price by a reputable manufacturer for material of equal quality and in like quantity. The original contractor has the right to demand proof of the lower price offer and to meet the price. If the material is purchased from another source, the quantity so purchased will be deducted from the total quantity agreed upon in the contract.

The buyer is more likely to be influenced by such guarantees when they are offered in an effort to overcome reluctance to buy, induced by a fear that prices are likely to drop still further. As a matter of practical purchasing policy, guarantees against price decline raise no particular issue, although, from a marketing point of view, there are some serious questions as to the extent to which they should be granted.

Escalator clauses. Guarantees against price decline and escalator clauses are two common methods of price-adjustment. The actual wording of many of escalator clauses provides for either increase or reduction in price, if costs change. Clauses providing for escalation came into common use during World War II because suppliers believed that their future costs were so uncertain as to make a firm quotation either impossible or, if covering all probable risks, so high as to make it unattractive, and perhaps unfair, to the buyer.

Escalator clauses aroused a great deal of debate, into which we need not go. Underlying all of them, of course, was the assumption that costs, whatever they might be in the future, should be covered. Whether the same suppliers would have been equally willing to relate selling price to current cost on a falling market or to assume losses incident to risk as readily as they took gains is open to considerable question. Doubtlessly both vendor and buyer fully realized the strategic bargaining position in which the former found himself. As a rule, procurement officers resisted the use of escalator clauses as far as possible and acquiesced in their use only under pressure.

In any analysis of any particular escalator contract there are several general and many specific problems—such as the proportion of the total price subject to adjustment; the particular measures of prices and wage rates to be used in making the adjustment; the methods to be followed in applying these averages to the base price; the limitations, if any, on the amount of adjustment; and the methods for making payment— which will be encountered. At times of price stability, escalation is usually reserved for long-term contracts on the principle that certain costs may rise and that the seller has no appreciable control over this rise. At times of inflation, shortages, and sellers' markets, escalation becomes common on even short-term contracts as sellers attempt to assure themselves the opportunity to raise prices and preserve contribution margins. Finding a meaningful index to which escalation may be tied is a real problem in many instances. Since most escalation is automatic once the index, the portion of the contract subject to escalation, the frequency of revision, and the length of contract have been agreed to, the need for care in deciding on these factors is obvious.

The following is an illustrative escalator clause:

a) *Labor.* Adjustment with respect to labor costs shall be made on the basis of monthly average hourly earnings for the (Durable Goods Industry, subclass Machinery), as furnished by the Department of Labor (hereinafter called the Labor Index). Adjustments shall be calculated with respect to each calendar quarter up to the completion date specified in contract. The percentage increase or decrease in the quarterly index (obtained by averaging the Labor Index for each month of the calendar quarter) shall be obtained by comparison with the Labor Index for the basic month. The basic month shall be_____, 197... The labor adjustment for each calendar quarter as thus determined shall be obtained by applying such percentage of increase or decrease to the total amount expended by the contractor for direct labor during such quarter.

b) *Materials.* Adjustment with respect to materials shall be made on the basis of the materials index for Group (VI. Metals and Metal Products), as furnished by the Department of Labor (hereinafter call the Materials Index). Adjustments shall be determined with respect to each calendar quarter up to the completion date specified in contract. The percentage of increase or decrease in the quarterly index (obtained by averaging the Materials Index for each month of the calendar quarter) shall be obtained by comparison with the Materials Index for the basic month. The basic month shall be _____, 1974... The material adjustment for each calendar quarter shall be obtained by applying to the aggregate amount of the firm quotations for materials received by the contractor during such quarter the percentage of increase or decrease shown by the Materials Index for that quarter during which the material was purchased.[2]

A buyer who uses escalator clauses must remember that one legal essential to any enforceable purchase contract is that it contain either a definite price or the means of arriving at one. No contract for future delivery can be enforced if the price of the article to be delivered is conditioned entirely upon the will of one of the parties. Reasonable as this legal principle is, the purchasing agent would be well advised to seek advice of counsel in case of doubt, since considerable controversy has arisen over its interpretation. The clauses cited above would appear to be adequate. So, too, are those clauses authorizing the seller to change his price as his costs of production change, provided that these costs can be determined reasonably from the vendor's accounting records and these records are, by contract, open to the buyer. On the other hand, the following clause has been held unenforceable: "The prices and terms shall be as shown in the company's current price sheet and as established from time to time by the company. . . . Prices and discounts are subject to change without notice." Similarly, a contract containing this clause has been held void because of indefiniteness of price: "As a basis for price agreement it is agreed that all prices shall be on the basis of actual cost of manufacture plus the general average of profit, and that from said price a deduction of 20% shall be made to establish a net price."

Discounts

No discussion of price negotiations or of the relation of cost to price would be complete that did not include some reference to the issues involved in using various kinds of discounts. These discounts really fall into two classes. The first class consists of inside prices, free details, and various other forms of price concessions that are not always defensible either legally or commercially. The second class consists of ordinary cash, trade, and quantity discounts which are thoroughly legitimate, fair, and profitable.

The line of distinction between these two classes is difficult to draw, for it is not always easy to define what is legitimate and what is not. Moreover, there may be a question at times as to whether the decision is to be made from the point of view of the buyer or of the seller. Human judgment and a fair ethical code—vague though those terms are, they represent very real concepts—must be relied upon for a verdict. Clearly, there are certain types of apparent price concessions, such as

---

[2] For further clauses see the Carlyn (D) and Midwest Utilities cases.

"inside prices," for which no responsible purchasing agent should even ask and which under most circumstances should be refused if offered. A vendor who offers an "inside price" to one buyer will offer a similar or lower price to another. A seller who will not be open and aboveboard in his pricing policy is not one with whom a purchaser can afford to do business on any terms.

The second class of discounts warrants more attention.

Cash discounts. Cash discounts are commonly granted by virtually every seller of industrial goods, although the actual terms of the discount are largely a matter of individual trade custom and vary considerably from one industry to another. The essential purpose of a cash discount is to secure the prompt payment of an account.

Most sellers expect buyers to take the cash discount. The net price is commonly fixed at a point which will yield a fair profit to the vendor and is the price the vendor expects the great bulk of his customers to pay. Those who, for one reason or another, are unable to pay within the time limit are penalized and are expected to pay the gross price. It may be noted, however, that variations in the amount of cash discounts are frequently made without due regard for the real purpose for which such discounts should be granted and are used, instead, as merely another means of varying prices. If a buyer secures a cash discount not commonly granted in the past, he may be sure that the net result is merely a reduction in the price, regardless of the name under which such reduction is made.

On the other hand, a reduction in the size of the cash discount is, in effect, an increase in the price.

Cash discounts, therefore, sometimes raise rather difficult questions of price policy; but provided that they are granted on the same terms to all buyers and provided that postdating and other similar practices are not granted some buyers and denied others then the interest which the purchasing officer has in cash discounts is confined largely to being sure that they are called to the attention of the proper financial managers. The purchaser cannot ordinarily be held responsible for a failure to take cash discounts, since this matter depends upon the financial resources of the company and is, therefore, a matter of financial rather than one of purchasing policy. The purchaser should, however, be very careful to secure such cash discounts as are customarily granted. It is, too, a part of the buyer's responsibility to see to it that inspection is promptly made, that goods are accepted without unnecessary loss of time, and that all documents are handled expeditiously so all discounts quoted may be taken.

Cash discounts have generally become less popular in the last decade. This may have been partly caused by buyers who insisted on paying the discounted price but not within the discount period. The practice of sending invoices ahead of the actual goods also has not helped this situation. Lastly, most sellers have raised their prices, and removing cash discounts has been a somewhat less painful way of doing so.

Trade discounts. Trade discounts are granted by manufacturers to a buyer because he is a particular type of distributor or user and they are not tied to any quantities that may be bought. In general, they aim to protect the distributor by making it more profitable for a purchaser to buy from the distributor than directly from the manufacturer. The justifications that exist for granting trade discounts to protect the channels through which merchandise may move are not questions we need to discuss here.[3] However, the procurement manager is interested in the efficient distribution of merchandise. When a manufacturer has found that various types of distributors can sell his merchandise in a given territory more cheaply than he can, he usually relies on their services. To ensure that his goods will move through the channels selected, he grants the distributors a trade discount approximating the cost of doing business. If the manufacturer's ability to sell efficiently in that territory depends on policy, the buyer can have no particular objection to it; in fact, the practice ensures that continuance of the source of supply which would not otherwise be open.

However, trade discounts are not always used properly. Protection is sometimes granted distributors not entitled to it, since the services which they render manufacturers, and presumably customers, are not commensurate with the discount they obtain. Generally speaking, buyers dealing in small quantities, who secure a great variety of items from a single source, or who depend on frequent and very prompt deliveries, are more likely to obtain their supplies from wholesalers and other distributors receiving trade discounts. With the larger accounts, manufacturers are more likely to sell directly, even though they may reserve the smaller accounts in the same territory for the wholesalers. Some manufacturers refuse to sell to accounts purchasing below a stipulated minimum. Many have found it profitable to segregate accounts on some basis and reserve the large ones for their own solicitation.

Quantity discounts. Quantity discounts are those granted for buying in particular quantities and vary roughly in proportion to the amount purchased. From the seller's standpoint, the justification for granting such discounts is usually that quantity purchasing results in savings

---

[3] The legal status of the trade discount under the Robinson-Patman Act is open to some doubt. Properly used and in the absence of other incriminating acts, however, there should be no real question about it, in spite of the fact that there have been no direct court decisions on its legality, and few unqualified decisions can be drawn from the actions of the Federal Trade Commission. The intent of the Robinson-Patman Act was to strengthen federal antitrust laws forbidding price discriminations injuring competition or fostering monopoly. Before competition can exist, buyers must compete; and buyers compete when they sell to the same customers. Industrial buyers who purchase for their own consumption or for processing or fabrication may compete with one another but can scarcely be said to compete with mill supply houses.

to the seller, enabling him to grant to the buyer who has made such savings possible a lower price than he would otherwise be able to quote. These savings may be of two classes: first, savings in marketing expense and, second, savings in production expense.[4]

In the late 1940s, the Federal Trade Commission in administering the Robinson-Patman Act, from time to time proceeded against buyers who were alleged to have knowingly received lower prices from sellers than their competitors. It is obvious that in most cases it would be extremely difficult for the buyer to prove the seller had cost savings in selling to the buyer which could justify the lower price.

In one case the Federal Trade Commission found the Automatic Canteen Company of America, a large buyer of candy and other confectionery products for resale through automatic vending machines, guilty of receiving prices as much as 33 percent lower than prices quoted other purchasers. The commission did not attempt to show that the price differential exceeded any cost saving that sellers may have enjoyed in their sales to Canteen, or that Canteen knew, or should have known, that they did.

In 1953, the U.S. Supreme Court ruled in the case of the Automatic Canteen Company of America that:

1. The mere inducement of receipt of a lower price is not unlawful.
2. It is lawful for a buyer to accept anything which it is lawful for a seller to give.
3. It is only the prohibited discrimination a buyer may not induce or receive.
4. It is not unlawful for a buyer to receive a prohibited discrimination unless he knows or, as a reasonably prudent buyer, should know that the differential is prohibited.

The court concluded that to prove cost justification according to the Federal Trade Commission's accounting standards would place a heavy burden on a buyer—would require a study of the seller's business and "would almost inevitably," to quote the court, "require a degree of cooperation between buyer and seller, as against other buyers, that may offend other antitrust policies, and it might also expose the seller's cost secrets to the prejudice of arm's-length bargaining in the future." The court added: "Finally, not one, but as here, approximately 80 different sellers' costs may be in issue." The court dismissed the case against Automatic Canteen.

While the above decision and subsequent ones clarified the buyer's

---

[4] The U.S. Supreme Court in May, 1948, ruled in the case of the Morton Salt Company (68 S. Ct.) that no wholesaler, retailer, or manufacturer whose product is sold to the public through these channels may grant quantity discounts unless they can be justified by (a) lower costs "due to quantity manufacture, delivery, or sale" or (b) "the seller's good-faith effort to meet a competitor's equally low price." Furthermore, it ruled that the Federal Trade Commission need not prove that discounts are discriminatory. The burden of proof is on the seller to prove he is not violating the law.

position to a degree, there is no clear-cut pattern the buyer can follow and be sure of being in the clear when accepting prices which are substantially below prices paid by his competitors to the same supplier for similar quantities and services.

The savings made possible in marketing expense arise from such facts as that it may be no more costly to sell a large order than a small one, that the billing expense is the same, and that the increased cost of packing, crating, and shipping is not proportional. When these circumstances exist, a direct quantity discount not exceeding the difference in cost of handling the small and the large order is probably justified.

It is also urged that there are substantial savings which may lower production costs as a result of securing a large order instead of a small one. For instance, it is said that placing orders in advance of the time when actual production begins is an aid in production planning. The larger orders also are considered more valuable in reducing the overhead expense than are the smaller ones.

From the buyer's point of view, the question of quantity discounts is intimately connected with that of inventory policy. While it is true that the larger the size of a given order, the lower the unit price is likely to be yet the carrying charges on the buyer's larger inventory are likewise more costly. Hence, the savings on the size of order must be compared against the increased costs of the inventory.

The quantity discount question is of interest to many buyers for a second reason, namely, all quantity discounts, and especially those of the cumulative type, tend to restrict the number of suppliers, thereby affecting the choice of source. (See also Chapter 5.)

It is not necessary to discuss the theory and practice of quantity discounts at length. Since there is real justification for quantity discounts when properly used the buyer should undertake to obtain such discounts whenever possible. Ordinarily, they come through the pressure of competition among sellers. Furthermore, an argument may be advanced that such discounts are a matter of right. It may be said that the buyer is purchasing goods or merchandise; not crating or packing materials, nor transportation. The seller presumably should expect to earn a profit not from those wholly auxiliary services but rather from manufacturing and selling the merchandise processed. These auxiliary services are necessary; they must be performed; they must be paid for; and it is natural to expect the buyer to pay for them. But the buyer should not be expected to pay to the supplier of the merchandise more than the actual cost of these auxiliary services; it is the merchandise on which the manufacturer should expect to earn profit. Plausible as that argument is, it is probably sounder to say that the purchaser is buying marketing service rather than a given quantity of merchandise. If so, the supplier is entitled to a percentage of profit on the entire marketing costs, including these auxiliary services.

When an attempt is made to justify quantity discounts on the basis that they contribute to a reduction of production costs through providing a volume of business large enough to reduce the overhead expenses, somewhat more cautious reasoning is necessary. It is true that in some lines of business the larger the output, the lower the overhead cost per unit of product. It may also be true that without the volume from the large customers, the average cost of production would be higher. It should be borne in mind, however, that the small buyers may bring in a greater total proportion of the company's business than do the large. So far as production costs are concerned, therefore, the small buyers contribute even more toward that volume so essential to the production per unit cost than does the larger buyer.

Another phase of the production argument is the contention that large customers ordering early in the season, or even prior to the time actual production of a season's supply begins, should be granted higher discounts because their orders keep the mill in production. Such a buyer probably may be entitled to a lower price than one who waits until later in the season to place his order. However, such a discount, since it is justified by the early placement of an order and therefore should be granted to every buyer placing an order at his early period regardless of the size, is not properly a quantity discount but may be considered a time discount.

Cumulative discounts. Quantity discounts may be based on a single order or on purchases made over a period. Another type of quantity discount is cumulative and varies in proportion to the quantity purchased; however, instead of being computed on the basis of the size of the order placed at any one time, it is based on the quantity purchased over a period. Such discounts are commonly granted as an incentive to a company for continued patronage. It is hoped they will induce a purchaser to concentrate purchases largely with a single source rather than distribute them over many sources, thus benefiting the company offering the discount. Generally speaking, it is wise for the purchaser not to scatter orders over too large a number of sources. If undue dependence upon the single source is dangerous, distributing one's orders over many sources is uneconomical and costly. No one supplier, under such circumstances, is so likely to give the same careful attention to the buyer's requirements as he would if he felt he was getting the larger portion of the purchaser's business.

The use of cumulative discounts is more applicable to some lines of business than it is to others. With perishable merchandise, such as the products of the National Biscuit Company, for example, the use of cumulative discounts provides an incentive for the purchaser to buy in as large quantities as is reasonable and at the same time obviates the danger of deterioration in the quality of the product which would be present were excessive amounts to be stocked at any one time. The purchaser will not stock in large amounts such items as electric refrigerators and other goods involving substantial inventory expense. A quantity discount on a single order might not, therefore, prove particularly stimulating. A discount based on the number of such items purchased at three-, six-, or nine-months' intervals might be very helpful. Although these illustrations do not apply to the purchaser who procures materials and equipment for internal use, they exemplify the purpose for which cumulative discounts are given. The use of such discounts, however, involves some dangers, and many concerns do not look upon them with favor; others that have used them have now abandoned the practice. Among the objections constituting particularly a marketing rather than a purchasing problem, the following may be mentioned: uncertainties as to the amount of discount to grant a new customer; doubt as to whether the discount rate earned shall be applied to purchases of the following year or to the purchases of the past year; the irritation likely to arise when a customer finds he is almost in the next higher discount bracket but not quite eligible for such higher classification; and the danger that purchasers may overstock in an effort to get into the higher rating without any permanent benefit accruing to the seller.

This discussion of discounts has oversimplified the nature of the problem. The discount structure not only in many individual companies but also in whole industries is extremely complicated—far more so than is reasonably justified. From the standpoint of the buyer, the whole purpose of the price discount is defeated when it becomes so intricate as to render it impossible to compare the various quotations offered. There is something wrong about a situation so complicated as to require the use of special discount tables and slide rules to figure out the final results of a system of list prices and discounts. The fault rests with the sellers. In some cases it is the result of plain bad judgment. In other instances there can be little doubt that the confusion is deliberate.

Cancellation of contracts

One phase of the price problem to which reference should be made is the cancellation of contracts. It is mentioned here because, in practice, cancellations usually occur during a period of falling prices. At such times, if the price has declined since the placing of the order, there is a tendency for some buyers to take advantage of all sorts of loopholes in the purchase order or sales agreement to reject merchandise. To avoid the completion of the transaction, they take advantage of technicalities which under other circumstances would be of no concern to them whatever. One can have sincere sympathy with the buyer with a contract at a price higher than the market without being protected by a guarantee against price decline. There is little justification, however, for the purchaser who follows a cancellation policy continuously. The contract should be considered a binding obligation. The practice referred to is an instance of so-called shrewd business, which one may hope is becoming less and less prevalent as the years go by. There may be occasions when a buyer justifiably seeks to cancel the contract, but to do so merely because the market price chances to have fallen is, in most instances, not one of them.

In what has been said about discounts, reference has been made to the legitimate and illegitimate use of such concessions. There is possibly a place for cash discounts. Trade discounts, as far as they are necessary to the well-being of a desirable source of supply, have their proper place. Quantity discounts may be properly earned and justified. It should be noted, however, that in every case discounts may be used illegitimately. They may be used to grant price concessions, to pursue a policy of price cutting under a guise of legitimate business practice, or of playing certain types of buyers against others. Indeed, the Robinson-Patman Act holds the buyer as well as the seller guilty of violation of the law where discriminatory price concessions are made available to some customers but not to others.

One-price policy

On the other hand, a one-price policy on the part of a supplier, in accordance with which he charges the same price to all types of customers buying the same type of goods, in the same quantity, and under substantially the same conditions, is sound marketing policy.[5] Where failure to maintain a one-price policy exists, the inference is sometimes drawn that the fault is to be laid at the door of the purchaser. In contradiction to this assertion, there is probably no progressive purchasing executive who does not favor a one-price policy, properly conceived and soundly executed. The issue is not one of ethics; it is one of plain, good business judgment. The buyer is interested in getting a good price but is at least as much, and perhaps even more, interested in knowing that he is paying the same price that competitors are paying.

It must be understood that with a one-price policy the seller may quote a price lower than a competitor. It is good purchasing policy to seek from every desirable source as low a price as is reasonable and profitable. When the vendor quotes a price to a purchaser, the latter wants to be assured that that vendor is quoting the same price to everyone else who is buying under the same circumstances. The sales representative who comes in from a selling trip and says a certain customer could not be sold unless a lower price was quoted is following the course of least resistance in selling. Such a practice indicates to the buyer the seller's lack of confidence in his own merchandise. This,

---

[5] Note that this does not mean vendor agreement that all sellers necessarily charge the same price. The "one-price" referred to is that of a particular supplier.

of course, does not apply to such purchases as those of construction and other engineering projects—each of which is more or less individual in its nature.

There is one other phase of this pricing problem that should be mentioned. Selling methods are dependent primarily upon buying motives and buying habits. To know and to understand the latter is to act wisely with reference to the former. It is, therefore, a most interesting business anomaly that concerns are frequently inconsistent within their own organizations on points where they seem essentially sound in their dealings with others. A one-price policy is generally conceded to be good. Many a firm boasts of its strict adherence to a one-price policy under every circumstance when dealing with its customers. Yet some of these same concerns insist that their purchasing officials use every device within their power to force exceptions from their suppliers' quoted prices. Such multiprice policies are encouraged by sales departments primarily and by the general management, almost always against the wishes of the procurement executives. If a one-price policy is good for one, it is good for all.

The problem of identical prices

It is not at all unusual for the buyer to receive identical bids from various sources. Since such bids may indicate intensive competition, on the one hand, and discrimination or collusion, on the other, the purchaser must take care in handling such situations. R. H. Wolf lists eight factors which tend to make identical or parallel prices suspect:[6]

1. Identical pricing marks a novel break in the historical pattern of price behavior.
2. There is evidence of communication between sellers, or buyers, regarding prices.
3. Sellers refuse to sell at a higher price even if a buyer makes the offer.
4. Meetings are held which result in "artificial" standardization of the product.
5. Identical prices are submitted in bids to buyers on complex, detailed, or novel specifications.
6. Identical prices result from adherence to an "artificial" delivered pricing system.
7. Parallel pricing is associated with an "open price plan" or "price reporting plan" carried on by the industry's trade association.
8. Deviations from uniform prices are not ignored or endured in the same way as changes in the weather but become the matter of industry-wide concern—the subject of exhortations, meetings, and even organized sanctions.

---

[6] R. H. Wolf, "Purchasing in a World of Identical Prices," *Journal of Purchasing*, vol. 2, no. 1 (February 1966), p. 82.

According to Wolf, the purchaser can take four different types of action to discourage identical pricing. The first is the encouragement of small sellers who form the nonconformist group in an industry and are anxious to grow. The second is to allow bidders to bid on parts of large contracts, if they feel the total contract may be too large. The third is the encouragement of firm bidding without revision. And the fourth is to choose criteria in making the award, so as to discourage future identical bids. "Drawing names from a hat, sharing the business among all the identical bidders, or dividing the business according to the historic market shares of the bidders are not conducive to breaking a pattern of identical bidding because such procedures are exactly what the firms hope will be done if bids are identical."[7]

Various alternatives of awarding the bid are available. It may be given to:

1. The smallest supplier.
2. The one with the largest domestic content.
3. The most distant firm forcing it to absorb the largest freight portion.
4. The firm with the smallest market share.
5. The firm most likely to grant nonprice concessions.

"President Kennedy issued Executive Order No. 10936 on April 24, 1961, which directed the gathering and analysis of identical bids received by federal and local levels of government."[8] The Department of Justice must be informed of identical bids on contracts exceeding $10,000 by all agencies purchasing for the federal government. State and local purchasing agents were asked to report identical bids over $1,000. Of course, this is another alternative. Although most industrial purchasing managers are reluctant to use the courts to address identical bids, governmental employees are required to report them, and their action has had significant results.

Negotiation strategy

As the status of the purchasing function in well-managed companies has increased in importance, a more professional attitude has developed in the people responsible for the operation of the function. As the professional competence of the personnel has increased, greater use has been made of the more sophisticated tools available to the business decision-making executive. One of the tools, negotiation, is as old as the first contract between two human beings, but only in recent years has formal study been undertaken to analyze the various elements involved in negotiations so as to postulate what leads to successful negotiation. Certainly

---

[7] Ibid., p. 86.
[8] Ibid., p. 83.

research findings from the field of psychology have helped to provide a better understanding of people and how they may react in a negotiation relationship.

The discussion of some of the elements and considerations which affect the price of an item in this and the preceding chapter make it obvious that negotiation can be a valuable technique to use in reaching an agreement with a supplier on the many variables affecting a specific price. This is not to say that all buying-selling transactions require the use of negotiations. Nor is the intention to indicate that negotiation is used only in determining price. Normally there is little purpose to be served to attempt to negotiate price for proprietary items. Reaching a clear understanding of time schedules for deliveries, factors affecting quality, methods of packaging, and so forth may require negotiations of equal or greater importance than those applying to price.

A list of some of the various kinds of purchasing situations in which the use of negotiations should prove of value follows:

1. Any written contract covering price, specifications, terms of delivery, quality standards, and so forth.
2. The purchase of items made to the buyer's specifications. Special importance should be attached to "first buys" as thorough exploration of the needs of the buyer and the supplier will often result in a better product at a lower price.
3. When changes are made in drawings or specifications after a purchase order has been issued.
4. When quotations have been solicited from responsible bidders and no acceptable bids have been received.
5. When problems of tooling or packaging occur.
6. When changing economic or market conditions require changes in quantities or prices.
7. When problems of termination of a contract involve disposal of facilities, materials, or tooling.
8. When there are problems of accepting any of the various elements entering into cost type contracts.
9. Problems arising under the various types of contracts used in defense and governmental contracting.

The process of negotiation is often referred to as an "art" which requires the development of certain skills. Harold Bloom has stated:

The techniques of negotiation are the same as those used for any communication of ideas. Since negotiation involves either convincing the other party that you are right or reaching agreement which will maximize the benefits to both parties, communication skills become absolutely essential.[9]

---

[9] Harold Bloom, "Principles and Techniques of Negotiation," *Guide to Purchasing* (New York: National Association of Purchasing Management, 1966).

While this book is not the place to explore the knowledge which has been developed about negotiation, a brief summary of the important steps in developing a strategy for negotiation follows:

1. Develop the objectives it is hoped to achieve through negotiation.
2. Accumulate all the facts pertaining to the subject of the negotiations. Attempt to recognize the needs of the other party.
3. Develop acceptable alternative plans which include objectives that will be acceptable if accomplished.
4. Obtain acceptance from interested executives in other departments.
5. Brief all persons on your team who are going to participate in the negotiations.
6. Conduct a dress rehearsal for your people who are going to participate in the negotiations.
7. Conduct the actual negotiations with an impersonal calmness.
8. Recognize the need and plan for recesses from time to time.
9. Always leave a line of retreat open.

Successful negotiators usually are extroverts who can express themselves well and analyze the position of the other party to a negotiation and who have quick minds. A pleasant personality and a sense of humor go a long way in keeping negotiation sessions functioning.

Research into negotiation has not been extensive thus far, for obvious reasons. Most sellers and buyers are not anxious to have observers present during negotiations. Since considerable parallels exist between negotiation in purchasing and in labor relations, a large body of knowledge is, in fact, available. Some interesting observations by C. Karrass[10] dispel some of the old myths held about the negotiation process. Mr. Karrass holds that deadlock or the threat of it can be very effective in forcing a party afraid of deadlock into agreement. He also believes in status as a powerful tool. It is no contest between a president and a clerk. This is another powerful argument for top management status for procurement. Certainly marketing personnel have never shied away from using the vice president of marketing, the president, or even the chairman of the board as negotiators on key business deals. Lastly, the negotiator must have confidence in his or her negotiation skills. A skilled negotiator can spot lack of confidence and turn it to his or her own advantage. Although experience is a tremendous asset, and negotiation skills are learnable, a confident inexperienced negotiator may well do better than an inconfident experienced one.

G. I. Nierenberg[11] has developed a "Need Theory" of negotiation.

---

[10] Karrass, Chester, *The Negotiating Game* (New York: World Publishing Co., 1970).

[11] G. I. Nierenberg, *Fundamentals of Negotiating* (New York: Hawthorn Books, Inc.), 1973.

He identifies six categories in which the negotiator has progressively decreasing amount of control. These are:

1. Negotiator works for the opposer's needs.
2. Negotiator lets the opposer work for his needs.
3. Negotiator works for the opposer's and his own needs.
4. Negotiator works against his needs.
5. Negotiator works against the opposer's needs.
6. Negotiator works against the opposer's and his own needs.[12]

The risk for the negotiator increases from category 1 to 6. These categories when combined with Maslow's need hierarchy of seven basic needs (Homeostatic, Safety and Security, Love and Belonging, Esteem, Self-Actualization, To Know and Understand, Aesthetic) form a grid which may be used to plan the appropriate approach and techniques for the particular negotiation at hand.

BIBLIOGRAPHY

ALJIAN, GEORGE W., ed. *Purchasing Handbook*. 3d ed. New York: McGraw-Hill Book Co., 1973.

BAGOT, J. KEITH. *The Profit Potential of Purchasing Negotiations*. New York: American Management Association, Purchasing Division, 1968.

BROWN, LOUIS MORRIS. *How to Negotiate a Successful Contract*. Englewood Cliffs, N.J.: Prentice-Hall, Inc., 1955.

DE ROSE, LOUIS V. *Negotiated Purchasing: The Key to More Profitable Buying*. New York: Materials Management Institute, 1962.

HEINRITZ, STUART, AND FARRELL, PAUL V. *Purchasing*. Englewood Cliffs, N.J.: Prentice-Hall, Inc., 1965.

INTERNATIONAL BUSINESS MACHINES CORPORATION. *The Learning Curve: A Tool of Negotiation*, 1961.

KARRASS, CHESTER. *The Negotiating Game*. New York: World Publishing Co., 1970.

KROEKER, HERBERT T. *Negotiation Techniques in Contract Pricing*. Columbus: Ohio State University, 1960.

NIERENBERG, GERARD I. *The Art of Negotiating*. New York: Hawthorn Books, Inc., 1968.

NIERENBERG, GERARD I. *Creative Business Negotiating: Skills and Successful Strategies*. New York: Hawthorn Books, Inc., 1971.

PACE, DEAN FRANCIS. *Negotiation of Defense Contracts*. New York: John Wiley & Sons, Inc., 1969.

RULE, GORDON W. *The Art of Negotiation*. Washington, D.C.: Department of the Navy, 1963.

SHERMAN, STANLEY N. *Contract Negotiation*, Washington, D.C.: George Washington University, 1969.

---

[12] Ibid., p. 91.

WESTING, J. H.; FINE, I. V.; ZENZ, GARY JOSEPH. *Purchasing Management.* 3d ed. New York: John Wiley & Sons, Inc., 1969.

CASES FOR CHAPTER 9

AIR AND GAS COMPRESSORS, INC. (A)*

Introduction

In November, 1962, Mr. Charles M. Linscott, director of steel purchases of Air and Gas Compressors, Inc., was concerned about the relatively high price that his company was paying for stainless steel to the Olle Skrede Steel Works Co. Ltd., of Upsala, Sweden. Air and Gas Compressors, Inc., (AGC) was a large U.S. producer of compressors and related equipment, with manufacturing divisions in over ten foreign countries. The firm's annual worldwide requirements for high-quality special stainless steel were in excess of 2,000 tons. In the recent past, 60 percent of the stainless steel purchased had been supplied by the Olle Skrede Steel Works at $2.21 per pound, f.o.b. mill, while 40 percent had been shipped by the Stanley Steel Products Co., Ltd., a smaller mill in Glasgow, Scotland, at $1.76 per pound, f.o.b. mill. Repeated attempts in the summer and fall of 1962 by AGC to obtain price concessions from the Olle Skrede Steel Works had been unsuccessful "Each time we negotiated with the Swedish executives we were told that price reductions were out of the question because of high equipment costs to be amortized" said Mr. Linscott. It was this experience which stimulated the purchasing executive to consider new approaches to the deadlocked price negotiations with the Swedish mill and also to review the overall steel procurement policy that AGC had been pursuing over the past several years. (For some structural and operational aspects of the European steel industry, see the Appendix.)

Air and Gas Compressors, Inc.

Air and Gas Compressors, Inc., was one of the world's leading producers of industrial compressors, offering lines of single or multistage reciprocating compressors, rotary blowers, steam and water-jet blowers or exhausters, and hydraulic compressors, with a range of pressures from a few ounces to 5,000 pounds per square inch (psi) and capacities to about 10,000 cubic feet per minute (cfm). The company also produced high-vacuum pumps for medium and extreme vacuums and in all capacities, as well as centrifugal and axial fans for a maximum pres-

---

* All names and any other data that would identify the company have been disguised. © by the President and Fellows of Harvard College; all rights reserved.

sure range of about 1 psi and for small and large capacities. In 1960, the company had acquired a large international manufacturer of refrigerating machinery and also a large producer of two-cycle combustion engines.

AGC maintained its headquarters and largest manufacturing plant in Bismarck, California. In addition, the company conducted manufacturing operations in more than ten overseas countries, and its distribution system extended to many more countries outside the Iron Curtain. In the fiscal year 1961–62, consolidated sales were $503.7 million, with net earnings of $61.3 million (after taxes). Consolidated assets were $342.8 million, and employment stood at 21,675.

Purchasing organization

Each of the company's manufacturing divisions maintained its own procurement organization, headed by a director of purchasing who reported to the general manager of the division. Every divisional purchasing department was responsible for its division's procurement of materials other than raw materials common to all divisions. The headquarter's procurement organization, headed by a vice president, was responsible for placing large and long-term contracts for raw materials against which the divisional purchasing departments could draw as well as for formulating companywide procurement policy and facilitating and coordinating the work of the divisional purchasing departments.

Over the years the headquarters procurement organization had worked with the research and development divisions of variously located foreign mills to further the production of special steels required by AGC. In 1961, for instance, as described in the following pages, the company was purchasing special high-carbon steel from seven European suppliers, several of which had installed special cold-rolling mills to accommodate AGC's requirements.

High carbon steel procurement

In 1961, AGC had purchased in excess of 7,000 tons of special high-carbon cold-rolled steel strip designated by the company as XK404 steel and used in the production of various compressor parts and components, including valves. Prices (f.o.b. mill) ranged between 50 cents and 62 cents per pound. Of these purchases, 30 percent were made from the Olle Skrede Steel Works; 5 percent from the Sixten Berger Steel Company, Ltd., an alternate Swedish supplier in Goteberg; 15 percent from the Westdeutsche Stahlwerke, GmbH, a German steel producer in Hagen, Westphalia; 5 percent from the Essener Edelstahl HG, KG, an alternate German source of supply in Essen, Westphalia; 20 percent from the British Stanley Steel Products Co.; 20 percent from an American steelmaker; and 5 percent from a French mill. All these mills were relatively small in size and concentrated on the production of special steels. The largest one, the Olle Skrede Steel Works, had an annual capacity of less than 100,000 tons of specialty steels. AGC was buying carbon steel on a one-year contract basis at firm prices. Each fall Mr. Linscott, using sales forecasts compiled by the operating divisions, estimated the company's total steel requirements for the coming year and negotiated orders with the mills in accordance with such estimates.

Because of the special mechanical properties and extremely high degree of uniformity required of the high-carbon steel, AGC's central metallurgical research laboratory had worked closely over the years with the supplier's R & D organizations, and particularly with the research laboratory of Olle Skrede Steel Works, in developing special steel microstructures not found in other commercially produced steel and also in developing special methods and techniques of temper rolling and roller leveling unknown in other commercial applications.

Each of AGC's four major suppliers had built a special rolling mill for the production of AGC's special steel at costs ranging from $1 million to $3 million, depending on size. Mr. Linscott commented:

Three or four decades ago when we became a large user of this steel, we had to develop sources of supply for it. None of our suppliers were originally able to produce XK404 without the technical and metallurgical requirements that we supplied. Today these mills sell this type of steel to our competitors both in the United States and in Western Europe. But the volume of our purchases is so large that they would find it very difficult to operate their special rolling mills profitably without our orders. We buy over one half of the world output of this particular type of specialty steel.

In recent years AGC had been paying approximately 50 cents per pound for steel purchased in Europe and about 62 cents per pound for steel bought in the United States. Mr. Linscott explained:

Although prices for domestic steel were higher, we developed a source of supply within the United States to provide protection against shortages in supply and also against price increases from abroad. The 12-cent price differential has always been regarded as a kind of insurance premium against pressure of one sort or another from the European steel mills. Also, over the past decades the danger of war has greatly contributed to our desire to have a domestic source of supply available.

For many years AGC had pursued a policy of paying one price to a mill, regardless of the country into which the steel was shipped. Mr. Linscott said:

If we buy from Westdeutsche Stahlwerke for our division in Germany and also for our divisions is Switzerland or Mexico, we will pay only one price. When the one-price policy was first adopted we took the mills' c.i.f. prices for shipments to the United States, reduced them to f.o.b. mill prices, and insisted that we would pay no more than that plus transportation and other shipping charges, which varied, of course, with the destination. Since most European steel mills maintain a differential between domestic and export prices, our one-price policy was resented by the mill executives, but our decision prevailed.

The prices that AGC was paying for carbon steel were negotiated prices and reflected AGC's dominant position as a buyer in the total market for XK404 special steel. Each year, prior to the signing of contracts, the director of purchasing met separately with the top executives of each supplier to negotiate and set quantities, prices, and approximate delivery schedules. Mr. Linscott said:

Over the many years in which we have been buying this particular type of steel we have developed a fairly detailed and accurate picture of each mill's production costs, although we have little information with respect to individual cost items. The prices paid by us to the various mills are based on their respective production costs plus a fair profit, as we have defined that term. Generally speaking, the mills' profits are close to 10 percent on sales. In determining a fair profit figure, we were guided by the idea that our orders should be a little more attractive than any other business with which the mills could replace our orders, assuming that such other business was available.

In 1961, following several visits to AGC's manufacturing divisions in Western Europe and extensive discussions with the divisional executives, the director of purchases recommended to AGC's board of directors that both the German and Swedish alternate suppliers of XK404 steel be dropped from AGC's vendor list, and he obtained their consent. Mr. Linscott commented:

The executives of our German and Swedish divisions, which received large shares of the shipments of the two German and the two Swedish mills, respectively, were strongly opposed to a reduction in their national sources of supply. They favored maintaining two suppliers in each country in order to ensure competitive prices and services, continuity of supply, and flexibility in the XK404 steelmaking capacity available to them for AGC products. My position was determined by three considerations: First, I had always been convinced that, while there may be competition with respect to service and quality, national mills within one European country do not compete with each other on a price basis. An analysis of the prices paid by our German division to the two German mills over many years indicated not only identical prices but also perfectly synchronized timing of any price changes. Second, with the rapidly progressive economic integration of Western European countries and the emergence of a supranational market, the need for alternate sources of supply within a national economy to ensure a continual stream of supply in case of political conflicts no longer existed; I was convinced that the remaining Swedish mill could serve as a backup source of supply for the remaining German mill, and vice versa. Finally, and this was perhaps the most crucial consideration, by dropping one mill in each country and thus allowing each of the remaining mills to increase sales volume to us substantially, we could encourage them to modernize their rolling mills, produce more efficiently, and consequently lower prices.

In May, 1961, AGC had notified Essener Edelstahl and Sixten Berger of its decision to drop them as suppliers. In recognition of the mills' needs for time to adjust to this decision, the company had indicated to each mill a specific quantity of steel it would buy and left it to the mills to specify the time period over which they would prefer to make delivery. Mr. Linscott commented:

Each mill could have supplied this volume in approximately five months, but they both stretched it out to about 12 months, so that our relationships with them were terminated in April, 1962. When we took on these two mills as suppliers in the early 1950s, they were already making small quantities of steel, similar to our XK404 grade, which they were selling to other compressor and engine manufacturers. In contrast to the Olle Skrede Steel Works and the Westdeutsche Stahlwerke, our major suppliers, the two eliminated vendors had not installed special mills upon our request. Thus we had no commitments to them, legal or moral, with respect to the disposition or utilization of their rolling equipment beyond the termination of our contracts.

Simultaneously with the elimination of the two alternate suppliers, AGC had reached agreements with the Olle Skrede Steel Works and also with the Westdeutsche Stahlwerke specifying increases of AGC's annual purchase volume of carbon steel from each mill, the construction of more efficient rolling mills at a cost of approximately $500,000 for the German concern and $4 million for the Swedish company, and a price reduction of 2.25 cents per pound following the completion of the installations in early spring of 1962.[1]

Stainless steel procurement

In the summer of 1962, AGC incorporated a revolutionary stainless steel flapper valve of advanced design into most of its products. This production change created an explosive demand by AGC's manufacturing divisions for a certain stainless steel that had been specially developed for AGC.

Prior to this time, in order to keep the unusually high R&D costs for the new specialty stainless steel at a minimum, the company had limited the number of steel mills participating separately in the research work to two, i.e., the Olle Skrede Steel Works and Stanley Steel Products Co. These two mills had installed, at a cost ranging from $1 million to $2 million, special annealing equipment needed in the production

---

[1] The new rolling mill of the Swedish company was only partially used for the production of AGC special stainless steel.

of AGC's special stainless steel. The process called for the use of the same cold-rolling mills employed in the manufacture of AGC's high-carbon steel.

In the original selection of suppliers for the costly development and subsequent production of the new stainless steel, neither Olle Skrede nor Stanley Steel had been AGC's first choice; AGC executives believed that another well-known Swedish mill with a capacity of 50 to 60 tons a month was best equipped to undertake the required research work and to produce the steel in the desired high quality within a reasonable period of time. There was evidence, however, that this mill had already signed an R&D agreement with one of AGC's competitors for the development of stainless steel used in the production of flapper valves. Mr. Linscott said:

We felt that under these circumstances we would have little, if any, protection against a transfer of R&D data to our competitor. The mill could not keep work done for us from being transferred to any competitor having an R&D contract with it. In addition, because of prior commitments, this mill would have had little capacity for us. The best bet for security would have been a mill supplying only AGC, but there was none. The best bets for quality were companies supplying us already with carbon steel and also producing stainless alloys. This is where the Olle Skrede mill and Stanley Steel Products Co. came into the picture. Both companies had been doing a substantial portion of their total special carbon steel business with us. In fact, we were buying well over 50 percent of the total production of each of these companies. Furthermore, both mills had done R&D work for us, and to our knowledge we never lost confidential information through them.

When AGC began to place large orders for the special stainless steel with the two mills, the purchasing director followed his long-standing policy of seeking prices based on production costs plus a fair profit. Neither of the mills, however, possessed any experience in producing the material on a large-scale basis; and this lack of experience and the resulting uncertainties with respect to rejection rates made it extremely difficult for mill executives to estimate production costs.

"Stanley Steel Products Co. agreed to base its price for stainless steel on the project production costs despite the uncertainties involved in the estimates," said Mr. Linscott. "The price which they suggested and which we accepted with no reservation was $1.76 per pound, f.o.b. mill." He continued:

We estimated production costs in two ways. First, we knew the costs of the additional raw materials required for stainless steel, which was principally chrome, because we kept careful track of chrome prices in the world markets. We were also aware of the mill's lower yield factors by knowing the size of a melt and through our accumulated data on the average delivery per melt in the past. It was our policy to insist on receiving from the mill the entire product of a melt. Second, after examining some summary figures on costs and yields supplied to us by Stanley, we knew that the mill was in fact pricing on the basis of estimated costs. We knew how the mill's price for stainless steel stood in relation to the carbon steels which we had been buying from them for a long time and for which we had developed fairly accurate cost figures over the years. We had some control over the costs of a melt by specifying the type of raw material, the type of furnace, and the type of melting procedures to be used. The bulk of the costs, about 75 percent of the total, was in the cold-rolling sequences and in the scrap loss during these sequences, and there was some control by us over rolling costs because we could always buy hot-rolled steel and have it converted by a "custom roller." We knew how Stanley's price for carbon steel stood competitively with those of the other suppliers, including the Swedish mill, and we also had a good idea that Stanley's price was at a minimum for an acceptable level of profit as a result of several rounds of negotiation during which the mill executives had indicated a price point at which they would no longer be interested in our business. But most important, we had a lot of respect for Stanley's cost control system, which we knew quite well. On the basis of all these factors, we were confident that Stanley's price of $1.76 per pound was reasonable and that the Swedish price was too high, instead of the Swedish price being correct and the British price being too low.

The managing director of the Olle Skrede mill, on the other hand, refused to use cost estimates as a basis for our price negotiations. Instead, he argued that the steel was similar to AISI-recognized stainless steel grade 440A, which sold at approximately $2.24 per pound in the world markets late in 1962, and he insisted that considering the absence of any prior experience with large-scale production runs and the likelihood of high rejection costs, the price should be set at market.

Because of the differential between the Swedish and the British price, we took every pound we could get from the British mill. But Stanley Steel Products could supply no more than 40 percent of the total quantity needed; and an increase in, and modernization of, the mill's cold-rolling capacity would have taken nearly two years and cost several million dollars.

Since we needed the stainless steel badly, we had no choice but to accept the Swedish price set at $2.21. Because of Olle Skrede's new rolling mill built in 1961, capacity was no problem. The Swedish executives knew, of course, that the capacity of the British mill was fully utilized and that we had not developed any other source of supply. From U.S. import statistics and from contacts with some of our competitors who made it a practice to reveal to one vendor the prices they were paying to another, the Swedish executives knew how much we were paying to the British mill. They hoped, however, that the heads of the British mill, being aware of the market price of 440A grade steel and its similarities with our material, and knowing that we could not turn to a third source immediately, would raise their price to $2.21. We knew that one Swedish mill had contacted the British mill in an effort to persuade the British to raise their price. In order to prevent such a development, we talked repeatedly to Stanley executives about our basic understanding that prices would be based on costs plus a fair profit and that we expected the mill to adhere to this understanding. We did get assurance that the price would remain at $1.76 per pound.

Shortly after the first large-scale orders for stainless steel had been executed by the British and the Swedish mills, Mr. Linscott learned from the managing director of Stanley Steel Products Co. that the original cost estimates for the production of the new material had turned out to be in line with actual production costs. Equipped with this information, Mr. Linscott approached the executives of the Olle Skrede Steelworks to renegotiate the price of $2.21 on the basis of the Swedish mill's actual production costs. Mr. Linscott commented:

Without disclosing the price we paid to the British mill we told the Olle Skrede executives that the British price was substantially lower, although the British mill was of smaller capacity than that of Olle Skrede and thus was likely to have higher unit production costs. We further told them that no price changes were requested by the British concern after actual production cost figures became available, indicating that the mill's first cost projections upon which the price was based had been largely correct. But the Swedish executives rejected the idea of price cuts, and dodging the subject of production costs altogether, claimed that Olle Skrede was charging less than the market price for 440A grade steel, which was at that time slightly above $2.24 per pound.

Several months later the director of steel purchases tried for the third time to obtain price concessions from the Swedish mill's managing director, but his efforts were not successful.

Changes in steel procurement policy

In considering alternative approaches to the problem of inducing the Olle Skrede Steel Works Co. to lower its prices for AGC's stainless steel to a level at which AGC was buying from the Stanley Steel Products Co., Mr. Linscott concluded that his company would have to develop, if only temporarily, additional sources of supply for the material. He said:

Since we were not in a position to reduce our quantity of purchases from Olle Skrede, there was no other way of getting the Swedish mill executives to reduce their price to a level more closely related to the mill's production costs. The question with which we were faced was, therefore, what other potential suppliers were available to provide the high quality, the sizable tonnage, and the fair price that we were looking for?

The development of an additional source of supply in Sweden which was appealing to AGC executives because of the superior R&D facilities and production know-how characteristic of Swedish specialty steel producers was ruled out because of identical prices charged by Swedish mills through the operation of a national and government-supported price-setting committee in which all major mills were represented. U.S.

mills were regarded as capable of delivering any required tonnage but unable to meet foreign prices and quality standards.[2] Mr. Linscott commented:

U.S. steel suppliers priced on the basis of costs but took, in some cases, less profit than they would have liked to in order to be reasonably close to imported steel prices. But, in our price inquiries, we found that their price would be approximately 25 percent above the best prices of overseas mills delivered to our U.S. plants and approximately 40 percent above foreign prices if they were to supply to our overseas plants. Other things being equal, we would have preferred using domestic suppliers, which would have allowed us to carry less inventory, which cost us about 5 percent out of pocket per year plus possible obsolescence costs. Domestic suppliers would also have insured us against long-term disruptions in supply, which could not have been compensated for by carrying large inventories. Of course, the risks of long-term interruption of supply from foreign mills located in different countries were related to global conflict, and we did not attempt to protect against this eventuality. As far as prolonged dock strikes, embargoes, and the like, were concerned, our U.S. plants were protected not only by a three-months' inventory but also by our willingness to resort to air shipments through second nations. At any rate, we would have preferred to have a U.S. mill as our first source of supply if a price and a quality could have been secured that would meet our criteria. But such a source was just not available. Japanese mills selling through trading companies were becoming interested in our business, but their initial prices were above the best overseas prices. The Japanese steel executives with whom we had contact indicated to us that they would meet and beat any price, if we told them what the competitive prices were. This we would not do.

Knowing that Westdeutsche Stahlwerke had sufficient cold-rolling capacity for stainless steel because of the installation of the new mill in 1961, Mr. Linscott believed that the German firm could be effectively utilized. He estimated that special additional annealing and tempering facilities needed by the German mill would require an investment of approximately $250,000. Since the Westdeutsche Stahlwerke had not participated in the complex laboratory research work on the steel's microstructure and mechanical treatment—and thus lacked the valuable experience which both the British and Swedish suppliers had accumulated prior to large-volume production—the purchasing executive believed that the German mill would initially be faced with substantial manufacturing problems. "The installation of the needed equipment would require approximately six months, and I would not expect quantity production within the first three months following the start-up of the stainless steel mill," remarked Mr. Linscott.

Although he had not formally discussed the production of stainless steel with the managing director of the German mill, Mr. Linscott had

---

[2] Small test supplies of stainles steel received by AGC from an Amercian mill were found to be of inadequate quality.

received indications that the mill would be prepared to sell the material at a price between $1.90 and $1.96, f.o.b. mill, Mr. Linscott commented:

The Westdeutsche Stahlwerke had historically priced below the Swedish mills, probably using a sliding-percentage formula to determine price. I believe that the indicated price reflected the mill's estimate of production costs. Because of the German mill's cost structure and lack of technical know-how with respect to the type of material we need, I could not expect to obtain a price that would match the British price. If we went ahead and asked the Westdeutsche Stahlwerke to build a mill and at a later time decided for one reason or another not to develop the company as a permanent source of supply for stainless steel, we would, of course, be prepared to pay for the special annealing and tempering facilities installed at our request.

In considering the various alternative strategies that Mr. Linscott regarded as being open to AGC, he also became concerned with the effect that any significant drop in volume of business with the Olle Skrede Steel Works Co. could have upon their interest in performing R&D work for AGC. He stated:

We are not concerned about R&D work from other suppliers to the extent that it should seriously influence our source of supply selection. Capacity-wise we could handle two or three steel suppliers. Two sources of supply would be a minimum from the viewpoint of sound purchasing policy and in order to meet the required quantities. Any additional source would be justified on the basis of better quality, greater assurance of supply, and a significant contribution to competitive pricing. When we first marketed the flapper valve, price competition for the stainless steel was not as important as moving surely and quickly to meet our quantity needs and doing this with a minimum of technical effort diverted from our other development activities.

Appendix: Some aspects of the European steel industry[3]

. . . Since World War II West European nations have given increased attention to the problems of cartels and business concentration. Most of these countries have adopted within the last decade national laws condemning or regulating cartels which operate within their respective economies. Moreover, the European Coal and Steel Community (1952) and the European Economic Community (1958) have adopted antitrust regulations which seek to guarantee a free market economy.

The Treaty of Paris, signed in January, 1952, brought into fruition a long-sought goal urged by political leaders in Western Europe as well as the United States. It created the European Coal and Steel Community (ECSC), which established a single open market for coal and steel in place of a whole series of national markets restrained by governmental and private barriers. The countries included are the Federal Republic of Germany (West Germany), France, Belgium, Luxembourg, Italy, and the Netherlands.

---

[3] The following excerpts were taken from various industry journals and other publications, identified at the end of each quotation.

The Coal and Steel Community is considered the forerunner of the European Economic Community. Antitrust laws are an important part of the Paris treaty. Cartels which fix prices, control output, or allocate supplies are condemned. Mergers are regulated and firms of dominant size which "abuse their position" are penalized.

Even though cartels which restrain competition are condemned by the treaty, the High Authority—the supranational governing body of the ECSC—is empowered to authorize cartel agreements "to specialize in the production, or to engage in the joint buying or selling of specified products." Under this power, some 40 cartel arrangements had been authorized between 1952 and 1961. They range from specialization agreements for production of particular types of steel products to joint selling agreements in the coal and steel industry.

International business can find some important clues to how Common Market policies toward industrial concentrations are shaping up in three major recent decisions of coal and steel regulating bodies: one prohibits definitely the rebirth of a national cartel that would have a clearly dominant position; another requires the dissolution of a government-dominated cartel organization; the third authorizes the creation of a joint venture between EEC giants on the grounds that the combined output of the joint subsidiary will not represent a dangerously large share of the market.[4]

So far as what one might call the "legal position" of the steel industries of the six ESC countries is concerned, all come under the free enterprise system. Before the Community was established, no body such as Britain's Iron and Steel Board existed for any of them, but that does not mean that there are no differences between the conditions and the working of this system of free enterprise in the various countries.

Take, as an example, the position in France and in Belgium. For several years the French steel industry has been engaged in what is known as "concerted economy," by which the programmes and objectives of different sectors of the economy are viewed together at high level. This review is the work of the Commissariat General du Plan whose head—prior to his joining the Coal and Steel Community—was M. Jean Monnet. Obviously the State enters the discussion and plays an important role in granting capital for investment purposes and there is no doubt that to a certain extent this system prevents private enterprise having completely free play—a fact reflected in the fixing of French steel prices.

Belgium has no comparable system. During the past year there has been a tendency towards some kind of "programmation," but this is purely indicative for private sectors.

A further difference exists elsewhere in the community, in that you find direct participation by State and public bodies in the property of steel works. In the Netherlands, for instance, the steel companies were founded by private groups, the City of Amsterdam and the Dutch Government. This has no effect, however, on the way in which such a concern is managed. To all intents and purposes it is a privately-run industry. Italian State intervention

---

[4] Joint Economic Committee, U.S. Congress, Study Paper No. 4, "Private Trade Barriers and the Atlantic Community" (Washington, D.C.: U.S. Government Printing Office, 1964), pp. 1–2.

is perhaps more extensive. After the war—as with other industrial sectors—a specialized financial holding was created to take over State participation in certain steelworks. Finsider has played a very big part in the remarkable post-war expansion of the Italian steel industry and now controls nearly 54% of all Italian production.

* * * * *

While the ECSC Treaty contains rules governing the forms of competition regarding price, it also contains quite severe basis regulations ensuring the reality of this competition. In principle, all agreements between companies which hamper the free play of competition in the common market are forbidden. The High Authority has power to make exceptions to this general rule only in certain rare cases and always safeguarding the maintenance of competition in the market.

If this provision has raised—and still raises—problems regarding coal, it has up to now, at least, not caused any major difficulty to the steel industry. This is all the more noteworthy in that up to the Second World War, the West European steel industries had for the most part lived under a cartel regime. Admittedly, since the beginning of the ECSC these industries have on the whole known a period of expansion contrasting with the difficult situation in the "thirties" and one cannot say what the future holds for us in this direction.

The principal limitation in competition and the freedom of enterprises on the steel market that can be found in the ECSC are the result of the actions of public authorities and not of agreements between companies. The most striking example has been in France, where on the occasion of the devaluations in recent years—despite the high costs they had to incur—French companies were only allowed to raise their prices to an inadequate extent, thereby creating at least at certain moments a rather serious disturbance in the Common Market. In fact, French companies lack complete freedom as regards price; the government possesses effective measures for putting pressure on them and so obtaining quite strict discipline in respect of French general economic policy.

While the rules applicable to agreements and restrictive practices have raised no difficulties for steelworks, the problems of concentration, mergers and so on, have given rise at certain times to quite considerable controversy.

All mergers of enterprises above a certain size must be submitted to the High Authority, which decides whether the operation is liable to give the firms in question dominating positions in the market, and in Article 66, the High Authority has the right to forbid the proposed operation or lay down conditions to prevent any harmful effects.

Nevertheless, it may be said that the powers of the High Authority, generally speaking, are limited to directing and organizing competition in the market. It intervenes regarding prices only in exceptional cases of excessive rises or falls, whilst in addition it holds certain powers to fix production quotas in time of recession or to distribute the supplies in the event of shortage. These powers cannot be exercised without the agreement of the Council of Ministers, which is composed of representatives of all the governments of member countries.

There are certain additional powers governing investment. The High Authority must be informed of all projects above a certain size and may express its observations regarding the schemes, but these observations involve practical consequences only when the Authority recognizes that the scheme submitted is not practicable without a subsidy or other form of Government help, in which case the enterprise can have recourse only to its own capital for financing it. Indeed, the powers of High Authority are quite moderate and seem to me to be well short of the rights held by the Iron and Steel Board in respect of the British steel industry. . . .[5]

The capacities of melting shop and rolling mills cannot be increased gradually in line with the gradually increasing demand for steel. Modern plants to replace obsolete ones have to be built for much higher capacities than previously because of technical progress and considerations of profitability.

The German steel manufacturers, like their foreign colleagues, are always faced with the following question when making decisions on development. Should a new plant be installed early and a certain amount of excess capacity be tolerated during a transitional period, or should they delay, and accept their temporary inability to meet the entire home demand from domestic production? Bearing in mind just how difficult it is to regain a lost market, and also the fact that it is still impossible to coordinate development plans internationally, it has not been possible to avoid such excess capacities in transitional periods—and they still cannot, for the time being, be avoided. It would, however, be desirable if international cooperation particularly in this field could be considerably extended. There is no reason why the exchange of manufacturing capacity by hire rolling and similar arrangements, the forming of joint enterprises and the joint operation of plants should stop at national boundaries.[6]

German steelmakers, in a bid to meet intense international competition, are steadily coming together.

Concentration has been the overriding factor in two key operations which have changed the pattern of the Ruhr steel industry in the past few months:

Integration of two major subsidiaries by the August Thyssen group which now becomes the world's third biggest steel concern with an annual production of over 14 million tons—more than half the total British steel output.

Proposed establishment by four top Ruhr companies of a central office in Essen to coordinate their combined rolling mill program.

*   *   *   *   *

One of the developments in the German steel industry in the past few months has been the exceptional extension of the Thyssen group. After long and wearisome negotiations with the Steel High Authority, the August Thyssen-Huette AG of Duisburg-Hamborn has at last been granted permission to integrate two more of its subsidiaries—the third and fourth—into the

[5] P. van der Rest, Chairman of the Belgian Steel Federation, "Europe's Steel Industry," *Steel Review*, October, 1961, pp. 8, 12, and 14. Reproduced by permission of the publisher.

[6] Herbert W. Köhler, Director of the German Iron and Steel Federation, "Prospects for German Steel," *Steel Review*, April, 1963, p. 8.

parent concern. These are the important Phoenix Rheinrohr AG, of Duesseldorf, and Germany's biggest iron trading company, the Handelsunion AG, also of Duesseldorf.

* * * * *

The Thyssen group is now virtually as big as the pre-war Vereinigte Stahl-werke but its proportion of the total German steel production is considerably less. As a yardstick it must be emphasized that although Thyssen is now the world's third largest, and Europe's largest, steel producer its output is only a quarter of that of United States Steel. Mergers such as that completed by Thyssen are, however, in no way exceptional and merely follow the modern European pattern.

The Thyssen operation merely follows similar moves by other groups in both Germany and France.

Four companies—Mannesmann AG with their new Huckingen plant; Huet-tenwerk Oberhausen AG, which belongs to the Gutehoffnungshuette; Hoesch AG with its Westfalenhuette plant; and the Dortmund-Hoerder Huettenunion, which belongs to the Dutch Hoogovens steel group—have agreed to coordinate their production programs for merchant bars and sections.

A new Rationalization Office is to be set up in Essen to control and coordi-nate the combined rolling mill program. Agreement to set up this joint enter-prise—the idea of the Hoesch chief Willy Ochel—was reached after negotia-tions lasting more than a year.

All incoming orders will pass through this office, which will distribute them among the four plants on the basis of the most economic utilization of the combined capacity. Main aim will be to achieve the biggest possible production run of steel of any single dimension and thereby maintain the existing level of employment.

This will doubtless cause difficulties in the case of customers who desire their contract to be fulfilled by a specified plant or who have special manufac-turing wishes.

Service to customers of the individual companies will be maintained as before, but spare parts deliveries for so-called "rejects" may be provided from any of the plants in the group.

There will, however, be no joint sales organization. Contacts between mer-chants or other consumers and the plants will remain unchanged. The new office will have no responsibility either for obtaining orders or ensuring delivery.

Accordingly there will be no joint accounting between the undertakings, each plant being responsible for that section of the orders which it carries out. The plan still awaits the approval of the High Authority in Luxemburg.

It would be possible to extend this arrangement to the production of wire rods but scarcely to sheets and other flat products where the needs of the customer tend to vary greatly.[7]

. . . During the past years steel prices within the European Coal and Steel Community were generally not determined by free market forces; other-

---

[7] "Europe's Biggest Steel Group," *German International*, vol. VIII, no. 11 (No-vember 1964, p. 29). Excerpts reproduced by special permission of the publisher, Heinz Moller–Verlag.

wise the price differentials from one member country to another for comparable rolling mill products would have dwindled. Furthermore, steel mills would have been unable to realize export prices that were higher than those charged to domestic customers. It must be considered, however, that since the formation of the ECSC demand has generally been upward. When temporary interruptions in this demand trend occurred and supply exceeded demand—as for example between summer of 1953 and spring of 1954—steel prices did become competitive. During that period a number of mills decided to sell in the Common Market below their list prices and to undercut the minimum prices to customers in countries outside the ECSC that were set by the 1953 export cartel agreement of Brussels.

✽   ✽   ✽   ✽   ✽

. . . The price policies pursued by the individual steel mills show frequently a conspicuous identity. The High Authority of the ECSC is aware of the fact that prices are formed under the principle of price leadership. But the High Authority does not intervene as long as the mills conform with the regulations of the ECSC Treaty pertaining to the publication of price lists, and as long as no other discriminations or abuses occur. . . .[8]

AIR AND GAS COMPRESSORS, INC. (B)*

Introduction

Air and Gas Compressors, Inc. (AGC) was a large U.S. producer of compressors and related equipment with manufacturing divisions in over ten foreign countries. In 1962, the company was purchasing a high-quality special stainless steel from the Olle Skrede Steel Works Co., Ltd., a Swedish mill, at $2.21 per pound, f.o.b. mill, and from the Stanley Steel Products Co., Ltd., a British mill, at $1.76 per pound, f.o.b. mill. AGC's annual worldwide requirements of the steel were in excess of 2,000 tons. The steel that was developed by the company in close cooperation with the two mills in separate research efforts for the production of a flapper valve had required not only sizable research funds but also the installation of specialized annealing and tempering facilities at the suppliers' plants. Because of the high R&D costs and the need for costly specialized production equipment, the company had limited the development of sources of supply to these two mills. (For further details and background, see the Air and Gas Compressors, Inc. (A) case.)

In November of 1962, Mr. Charles L. Linscott, director of purchases of AGC, was considering various approaches to bring about a reduction in the price paid to the Swedish mill. The company had initially accepted

---

[8] Alfred Nies, "Internatiale Kartelle" (Unpublished dissertation, Wirtschaftschochschule Mannheim, Mannheim, Germany, 1959). Reproduced by permission of the author.

* All names and any other data that would identify the company have been disguised. © by the President and Fellows of Harvard College; all rights reserved.

the differential between the British and the Swedish prices in view of the high uncertainties involved in estimating the production costs of the special steel without any production experience and also in view of an explosive growth in the demand for the company's new stainless flapper valve that had required all the steel AGC could obtain.

After having gained experience, the executives of the British mill had indicated to AGC that the mill's original cost estimates had been sufficiently accurate to warrant keeping the price at $1.76 per pound. The Swedish mill executives also continued to charge their original price of $2.21, which they justified by pointing to the world market price of $2.24 per pound for steel similar to the special product made for AGC. Several rounds of price negotiations conducted by Mr. Linscott had been unsuccessful in reducing the Swedish price which Mr. Linscott considered to be unreasonably high in view of the experience with the British mill. Shifting orders from the Swedish mill to the British mill had not been possible because of limitations in the latter mill's cold-rolling capacity. The executives of the British mill had indicated no interest in expanding this capacity to produce more steel for AGC.

Because of the resoluteness with which the Swedish steel executives had been refusing to consider any price change, Mr. Linscott had concluded that his company would have to develop, if only temporarily, additional sources of supply for the steel. In this manner it might be possible to persuade the management of the Olle Skrede Steel Works to lower prices to the level at which AGC was buying from the British mill.

Actions taken by Mr. Linscott

Of the various alternatives that the director of steel purchases considered open to the company, he chose to develop the Westdeutsche Stahlwerke, a German specialty steel producer, as a third source of supply. This mill had been supplying carbon steel to AGC's German manufacturing subsidiary for many years. The Westdeutsche Stahlwerke offered a price of $1.95 per pound, which Mr. Linscott accepted. Upon AGC's request, the German mill installed in the spring of 1963 special annealing and tempering facilities at a cost of approximately $250,000. As had been expected by Mr. Linscott, the German company experienced considerable production problems for nearly four months following the start-up of the new equipment in the fall of 1963. The Germany company had not participated in the development of the special steel and possessed little experience in the production of the type of steel required by AGC.

In January, 1964, Olle Skrede Steel Works announced to AGC a price reduction from $2.21 per pound to $1.88 per pound. Mr. Linscott commented:

Since the quality problems with the German mill were still not completely resolved early in 1964 and the price of $1.95 was not competitive, we discontinued our efforts to get the stainless steel from this mill. We offered to pay the mill for the special facilities installed upon our request but were told that this was not necessary in view of other uses to which the facilities could be put.

Several months prior to the price reduction by the Olle Skrede Steel Works, Mr. Linscott had been contacted by a Swedish businessman who acted as an independent agent for the Tokyo Steel Company, Ltd., a large Japanese steel producer. The agent had had considerable experience in the pricing policies of the Swedish steel industry through his work with a government-supported association of major Swedish mills. He had offered Mr. Linscott Japanese stainless steel for $2.07 per pound, f.o.b. mill. A small sample submitted by the agent had been analyzed by the company's research laboratory and found to be of satisfactory quality. In its report the laboratory pointed out, however, that the sample was most likely of Swedish rather than Japanese origin.

Mr. Linscott knew from trade circles and public sources that Japanese steel mills were making vigorous efforts to increase their share of the world market for high-quality stainless steel. Traditionally, Swedish producers had held a leading position in this market. Already Japanese firms had developed a high-grade stainless steel for camera shutters, with the result that some large international camera makers had shifted their sources of supply from Sweden to Japan. Although Mr. Linscott was not convinced that the Tokyo Steel Company could produce the high-grade steel required for AGC's flapper valves at a price below that of the British mill, he decided to pursue with caution the offer made by the Swedish agent. In April, 1963, he ordered a 500-pound sample of the offered steel. Laboratory tests showed that while the steel's microstructure was satisfactory, other deficiencies, such as inadequate response to hardening and insufficient uniformity in thickness, existed. In contrast to its first report, the laboratory indicated that the larger sample appeared to have been produced in Japan.

In a meeting held in November, 1963, Mr. Linscott communicated the results of the testing to the Swedish agent, who responded by stating that any quality problems could be overcome if AGC made available the required technical specifications. The agent offered a new price of $1.67½ per pound, f.o.b. mill. Mr. Linscott concluded the meeting with the remark that while his company was not too interested in pursuing the offer, he would give it some further consideration.

In the ensuing months Mr. Linscott took no further action with respect to the Japanese steel offer. During this time, he learned that the Tokyo Steel Company was one of many subsidiaries of a large diversified industrial combine that also operated a company manufacturing compressors and two-cycle combustion engines. Upon further investigation Mr. Linscott learned that the product line offered by this company was small and accounted for an insignificant percentage of the total Japanese market. Mr. Linscott commented:

At about the time this matter came to our attention I had a call from the Swedish agent telling me that a group of executives of the Tokyo Steel Company wanted to tour our plants and meet with our technical people to become better acquainted with our steel needs. When I mentioned to the agent that the Tokyo Steel Company belonged to an industrial group that was also in the compressor and two-cycle combustion engine business, the agent replied that I had probably been misinformed. I made it quite clear at that point that while we might be prepared to meet with the mill representatives, such meeting would have to take place away from our plants.

In January, 1964, Mr. Linscott received a communication from a New York-based Japanese trading company informing him that the Swedish agent no longer represented the Tokyo Steel Company and that further negotiations should be conducted with the trading company.

Several weeks later Mr. Linscott met with representatives of the trading company in New York City to explore further the purchase of Japanese steel. During this meeting, which was also attended by a representative of the Tokyo Steel Company, Mr. Linscott emphasized that the quality of the steel samples thus far had been unsatisfactory and that furthermore the price of $1.67½ per pound was "not encouraging." The director of purchases then spoke at some length of AGC's long-standing policy to maintain extremely close and intimate relationships with steel mills once they were selected as suppliers. He commented:

I left no doubt that we would consider direct communication without interpositioning of any third party as an absolute prerequisite for doing business with the mill. I then closed the meeting by saying that under the given circumstances the prospects of placing orders with the mill were poor but that we should keep in touch.

In January, 1964, the Tokyo Steel Company advised Mr. Linscott that a new sample was being sent to AGC with a request for analysis and testing. The mill reconfirmed its previous offer to supply the steel at $1.67½ per pound, f.o.b. mill. Upon examination of the sample by AGC's research laboratory, Mr. Linscott advised the mill that while there were some quality improvements, the deficiencies found in the previous samples had not been entirely overcome and that certain other problems, such as the appearance of rolled-in particles, had appeared. The director of purchases also expressed dissatisfaction with the unchanged price quotation.

In November, 1964, Mr. Linscott received a letter from the Tokyo Steel Company informing him that the mill had assigned an engineer to a newly established office in New York City to act as "technical coordinator" between AGC and the mill. In response Mr. Linscott expressed his satisfaction with the establishment of a direct contact on technical matters and urged the mill to bypass the trading company also with respect to commercial matters. Approximately four weeks later the mill advised Mr. Linscott that all further negotiations should be conducted directly with the mill.

Toward the end of January, 1965, Mr. Linscott met in New York with the mill's technical coordinator and several high-level executives who had flown in from Tokyo to discuss with AGC the supplying of steel. Disclosing for the first time that AGC was interested in purchasing as much as 50 tons per month, Mr. Linscott asked for a new price quotation. Before the meeting was adjourned, the Japanese offered a price of $1.19 provided AGC agreed to take a minimum delivery of 50 tons a month and provided further that the firm made available to the mill the technological information necessary to produce steel in the quality required. The Japanese representatives indicated that they would be prepared to assign to the New York office a metallurgist to cooperate with AGC's production department and research laboratory in overcoming the quality problems that had shown up in the samples. The representatives also indicated that they would be prepared to install at their own expense any new annealing and tempering facilities that AGC might consider necessary to meet specifications. A further condition that the mill representatives attached to the offer was an agreement that AGC would not purchase stainless flapper valve steel from any other Japanese mill. In return, the Tokyo Steel mill proposed to meet fully AGC's requirements before selling the steel to AGC's competitors. The representatives emphasized that they would expect to give AGC return guarantees to treat as highly confidential any technical information supplied by AGC to the mill. Before departing, the Japanese executives extended an invitation to AGC's management to visit with the mill's management in Tokyo for further discussions and inspection of the mill's production facilities.

NEGOTIATION PREPARATION

Mr. Thomas thought he had three main alternatives of action in purchasing MS–7 once Blondin's equipment went into operation.

1. He could continue to buy from the parent company.
2. Carlyn could start manufacturing MS–7 itself.
3. He could purchase MS–7 from Blondin.

The fourth alternative of buying MS–7 elsewhere in North America appeared unrealistic because of MS–7's special properties.

The main disadvantage of the first alternative was that Carlyn would have to pay U.K. market price plus duty, plus exchange and transportation instead of the former preferred price. Mr. Thomas thought this might increase his laid down cost to at least $70.00/kg. The main advantage of this action would be the staying with a reliable high-quality preferred supplier and the U.K. parent company would continue to reap the benefits of the American business.

The second alternative was not too attractive in view of the uncertainty of demand, the relatively high cost of the equipment, the manufacturing skills required, and the lack of space in the Carlyn operation. This alternative would, however, mean that Carlyn should be able to operate on approximately the same cost structure as Blondin.

The third alternative also had its drawbacks. Mr. Thomas knew that he would have difficulty persuading his fellow company officers to buy from Blondin, a direct competitor on at least four of Carlyn's products. He knew that Blondin would be in the driver's seat regarding the setting of price, and he might end up losing out on three counts. First, by helping Blondin get some volume going on the reactor, he would enable them to achieve production savings and efficiencies. Second, by paying a price over Blondin's cost, he was putting Stimgro at a cost disadvantage to Blondin's competitive product. Third, he would be heavily dependent on the goodwill of Blondin, who would be a sole source on a vital item. One advantage to buying from Blondin was the elimination of the investment risk. Another was the shortening of supply line. Perhaps the strongest point in favor was that it seemed to make economic sense. Why should both Blondin and Carlyn end up with expensive pieces of equipment running at an uneconomic level when they could pool their resources and requirements?

Mr. Thomas decided he would prefer to go after alternative three. He knew he could always buy from the parent company so that supply was at least assured. He also knew his fellow managers at Carlyn would never go for a deal with Blondin in which Carlyn paid a premium price. He, therefore, went back to his original cost and price figures to see if he could set some targets to use in discussion with the other Carlyn managers. He concluded that Blondin's out of pocket cost would probably be about $40/kg. He guessed Blondin would be anxious to charge the U.K. market price laid down in the United States which would be around $70/kg. He knew as long as he got a better price than $70/kg, he would be better off than with alternatives 1 and 2. He summarized his position as follows:

Summary of Our MS–7 Position

Maximum price: $70–75/kg.
Would possibly settle for as high as $65/kg.
Would strongly prefer: $50/kg (present cost).
Should offer: $44/kg (10 percent better than their out-of-pocket cost)

N.B.: The only way in which this can be sold is on the basis of a mutual sharing of the benefit.

Mr. Thomas thought he was now ready to discuss the proposition with the other Carlyn executives. An informal atmosphere existed among Carlyn's top team, and all major moves in any area were normally fully argued out before action was taken. Deliberations could be initiated by any individual with any other at any time. The group normally lunched together at least once a week, at which time shop talk was also normal.

It was common knowledge among all members of Carlyn's executive team that there was no love lost between Frank Grove and Blondin. Mr. Thomas knew that Frank in his capacity as sales manager saw Blondin daily as an adversary and had taken an extremely strong dislike of their aggressive marketing tactics. Mr. Thomas knew that Frank would strongly oppose any proposition which would involve buying anything from Blondin. He also knew that approaching the president or the production manager first would produce the automatic question: "Have you talked to Frank about this yet?" For this reason he thought he might as well talk to Frank first on the basis that if Frank would veto any approach to Blondin, there would not be much point in pressing this alternative further. He, therefore, went to Frank's office to see what he might be able to accomplish. Their conversation went like this:

Mr. Thomas: Frank, remember I asked you about Stimgro a while ago?

Mr. Grove: Sure, Bill, what's on your mind now?

Mr. Thomas: Well, did you know that Blondin had ordered their own equipment to start making MS–7 in the U.S.?

Mr. Grove: No, but so what? We're getting a good deal from the U.K., so why should we care what Blondin is up to?

Mr. Thomas: As soon as they get into operation, they will be able to force us to pay U.S. market dutiable and dumpable instead of our present prices.

Mr. Grove: How much are we talking about?

Mr. Thomas: At least $70/kg as opposed to our present $50.

Mr. Grove: That's too darn much. How much do you figure Blondin's cost will be to them?

Mr. Thomas: This depends on how you figure it. Their straight out-of-pocket cost should be around $40/kg. At their present volume their return on investment after tax is practically negligible.

Mr. Grove: I'm glad to hear that, but what are you leading up to?

Mr. Thomas: If Blondin can't really make any money making their own MS–7, neither can we, right?

Mr. Grove: I guess so.

Mr. Thomas: O.K., then we are automatically forced to pay at least $70 and you've already said that's too much.

Mr. Grove: I suppose the parent wouldn't mind that at all, but it would certainly give us a rough time on our Stimgro costs and profits.

Mr. Thomas: That's the way I figure it, too. That's why I would like a chance to play a long shot to see if we can't keep our cost down.

MR. GROVE: What are you talking about?

MR. THOMAS: I think we should go to Blondin and offer to buy our MS–7 from them. It . . .

MR. GROVE: (interrupting) Holy cow, have you gone crazy? Do you know what you are saying? For ten years I have been fighting those guys, and we are in with Stimgro and guess who else tried to horn in on a good deal. That's like the U.S. buying its atom bombs from Russia. Man, you sure come up with some real wild ones every once in awhile. Why don't you just forget about the whole thing, and, if and when Blondin gets their equipment going, we'll just have to pay the parent a bit more. After all, it's not as if we are shoving the dough down the drain.

MR. THOMAS: Now, just a minute. If I could get the stuff at a good price elsewhere in the U.S. would you care?

MR. GROVE: Well, now, that's something different altogether. If you can get a good price elsewhere in the U.S. I'm all for it.

MR. THOMAS: Fine, unfortunately, there is no chance of that. You know as well as I do that Blondin and we are the only users. But, if I could get a good price from Blondin, why shouldn't we take it?

MR. GROVE: *If* the old lady hadn't picked up the dime between the railway tracks, she would still be alive today.

MR. THOMAS: Sure, I am not guaranteeing a thing. I don't know if I can get a good price from Blondin. As a matter of fact, I have a feeling they might not be too anxious to sell to us, period.

MR. GROVE: And why not?

MR. THOMAS: Because we are their competition, too. If they feel they've got an advantage over us by making their own MS–7, why should they let us in on a good deal?

MR. GROVE: Because with us they might have a better total deal than without us.

MR. THOMAS: Exactly, that's why I want a chance to try them out. I want to sell them on the basis that we both share in the benefit from pooling our requirements. I have a feeling they may be worried about their efficiency at the low volume they are turning out, and we could double their volume.

MR. GROVE: Suppose, just suppose, and I am not committing myself to a thing here now, that Blondin let us talk to them, what makes you so sure they will give us a good deal?

MR. THOMAS: As I have said before, Frank, I can't guarantee a thing. They may just be too obstinate to give us even a chance of proposing anything. On the other hand, if we don't try it, we'll never know.

MR. GROVE: You really are a persistent joker. Just give it a chance, Bill, and tomorrow Blondin's trucks are delivering the stuff, and the next day we have a merger on our hands.

MR. THOMAS: No, sir, I want to approach this on a straight business basis. It so happens they are the only U.S. supplier of a product we need. Why we need that product should have nothing to do with them.

MR. GROVE: How much do you think we could get it for?

MR. THOMAS: I really don't know. Theoretically, we are better off as long as their price is lower than $70 or $75/kg. I would like to settle for less than $65.00. As a starter I think we should offer $44.00.

MR. GROVE: That starter is going to give us a really warm reception at Blondin.

MR. THOMAS: What do you mean?

MR. GROVE: Well, with that kind of an offer they are really going to wonder who is doing whom a favor.

MR. THOMAS: You are probably right. However, it's always easier to come up than to get down. Do you really think Blondin might give us a rough time?

MR. GROVE: I am positive. Unless you offer them $100/kg. and a gold-plated key to our plant.

MR. THOMAS: Have you got any idea on how we might pitch this thing to them?

MR. GROVE: The only way would be to hit their top man. If he doesn't buy it, no one else in their organization will.

MR. THOMAS: That sounds like a good idea. Whom do you think should talk to him?

MR. GROVE: Bill, I know you can talk an old lady on a bus into giving her seat up for your briefcase, but I figure it's got to be our top man versus theirs.

MR. THOMAS: I fully agree. Let's go talk to the old man.

MR. GROVE: Now, just a minute . . . I was just hypothesizing . . .

MR. THOMAS: Sure you were, but we have gone too far now to drop this thing.

MR. GROVE: The old man will never go for it.

MR. THOMAS: Let's go and see.

MR. GROVE: Remember, this is your idea, not mine. How do you feel knowing the knife is coming and no anesthetic?

MR. THOMAS: It scares me to pieces, but I know you always enjoy a good side show.

The "old man," Mr. John Peters, president of Cato of Canada was to Mr. Grove's surprise fairly quickly won over to the general idea. He did want to enlist the ideas of Bob Harper, the production manager, and he instructed Grove, Harper, and Thomas to think ahead and to predict possible future demands so that he could have some idea of the length of period that a deal might be settled on. He said:

If I were in Blondin's shoes, I would insist on a fairly long contract if the price seems favorable. I would insist on a reasonable guarantee of sufficient volume to make the deal at least half attractive. Then we might be talking a contract lasting as long as five or six years. Before I commit Carlyn to that kind of deal I want some indication of what our volume would be over that period. We don't want to find ourselves in the boat that we are committed to buy if we should be making it ourselves, for example.

Subsequently, Mr. Harper determined that the minimum production volume he would like of MS–7 to warrant plant expansion, labor training, etc., would be 20,000 kg. of MS–7 a year. Mr. Grove forecasted the following demands for the next six years.

```
1975 . . . . . . . . . . . . . .    4,000 Kg.
1976 . . . . . . . . . . . . . .    6,000 Kg.
1977 . . . . . . . . . . . . . .    9,000 Kg.
1978 . . . . . . . . . . . . .    13,000 Kg.
1979 . . . . . . . . . . . . .    18,000 Kg.
1980 . . . . . . . . . . . . .    23,000 Kg.
```

On the basis of their forecast, Mr. Harper, Mr. Grove, and Mr. Thomas thought that the maximum contract length should be five years. Mr. Peters agreed. Mr. Peters warned the other three that he saw his main role as that of an ice breaker. He said:

All I want to do is feel them out and possibly agree on a price. Bill Thomas and you guys can take over after that and clean up all the details.

MIDWEST UTILITIES

Mr. Lloyd Harbison, director of purchases for Midwest Utilities, was concerned about a major nuclear reactor contract. This $37 million contract extended over six years. Four suppliers had submitted bids including, as was normal practice, escalation clauses for labor and materials. Each contractor had used different indices tied to materials and labor, making direct comparison of the quotes difficult. A regression analysis of the past trend of these indices showed past annual increases ranging from 2.7 to 3.5 percent. Because of the magnitude of the contract and the major impact of the escalation clauses, Mr. Harbison had requested advice from Professor Roy Jones, a well-known economist. Professor Jones was surprised to see that escalation was even considered. He argued that improved productivity should offset future increases in labor and materials. Mr. Harbison knew he would have great difficulty persuading the four bidders to accept this productivity argument, but he was anxious to keep escalation, if any, to a minimum.

Company background

Midwest Utilities was a privately owned large supplier of electrical power serving a highly industrialized area of about 6,000 square miles in the midwestern United States. Total assets exceeded $4 billion and kilowatt capacity totaled about 10 million kilowatts. In response to the rapidly increasing demand for power, Midwest had moved into nuclear power in the 1960s and was planning at least five nuclear additions between 1970 and 1984.

Nuclear installations

The nuclear power unit under consideration in 1972 was to be installed in the Alta plant, for which an earlier similar power unit had already been contracted in 1970 and which was expected to be completed by 1975. The extended contract time on nuclear power units necessitated the use of progress payments, and for the utility the impact of the carrying cost of money was considerable.

The Alta 1 unit cost about $36 million and was expected to provide a capacity of approximately 1.1 million kilowatts. J&E Engineering had been awarded the Alta 1 job which included escalation clauses for labor and material.

In view of the volume of nuclear work ahead, Midwest was anxious to seek as many qualified suppliers as possible and at the same time assure a favorable price on each unit. For Alta 2 four possible suppliers were approached on June 15, 1972, by Joe Walton, equipment buyer, who sent out an inquiry along with extensive specifications and drawings (see Exhibit 1). Suppliers were requested to reply by August 15, 1972, on the understanding that the contract would be awarded by November, 1972.

Exhibit 1
MIDWEST UTILITIES

June 15, 1972

Copies sent to: J & E Equipment
                  Malton Electric
                  Durnford Corporation
                  Ermi, Inc.

Gentlemen:

Subject: Inquiry No. B-2624
           Nuclear Steam Supply System and Nuclear Fuel Supply for Unit
           No. 2 for Alta Atomic Power Plant and a Two-Unit Unspecified
           Site

Please submit a complete and detailed quotation, in quadruplicate, by no later than August 15, 1972, to furnish each of the following:

One (1) 3300 Mwt—Nuclear Steam Supply System (NSSS) and associated Nuclear Fuel Supply for Unit No. 2 Alta Power Plant.

Two (2) 3300 Mwt—NSSS and associated Nuclear Fuel Supplies for a new Unspecified Site.

Options for two (2) additional identical NSSS and associated Nuclear Fuel Supplies for the Unspecified Site.

The above units are to have a guaranteed nominal nameplate rating of 1,100,000 electrical kilowatts, but the bidders may submit quotations on larger units as an alternate.

The Scope of Supply for these units shall be in strict accordance with the enclosed:

1. Midwest Specification 4194—1, dated 5/4/72, "NSSS and Nuclear Fuel, Alta Unit Two and Unnamed Two-Unit Nuclear Power Plant."
2. Midwest Specification 4194–3, dated 5/1/72, "Controls and Instrumentation for the NSSS, Nuclear Power Plant."

Exhibit 1 (*Continued*)

3. Midwest Specification 4148–A, dated 3/8/66, Addendums A, B, and C, "Horizontal and Vertical A.C. Electric Motors."

Inquiry No. B-2624

4. Midwest Specification 4178, dated 2/5/69, Addendum A, "460 Volt A.C. Motors."
5. Midwest Drawings:

6M–2263	3M–2287
5M–2278	3M–2288
5M–2279	6M–2290 sheet 2
3M–2285	3M–2300
3M–2286	

The scheduled date for Contract Award is approximately October–November 1972.

The commercial operating dates for the units have been established as follows:

Alta Unit 2—October 1, 1979
Unspecified Site Unit 1—October 1, 1980
Unspecified Site Unit 2—April 1, 1982
Optional Units:
Unspecified Site Unit 3—October 11, 1983
Unspecified Site Unit 4—April 1, 1985

The following requirements should be considered when preparing your proposal:

1. Proposals are requested for "equipment only" including technical direction on erection.
2. Itemize the "equipment only" prices, and state in detail the basis for escalation (if any). Include protection for a downward trend in the market. Also furnish total estimated escalation for each of the five (5) units specified above and the basis and accuracy for your estimate.
3. Submit quotations covering the initial fuel loading and fuel for a second core or for sufficient fuel to operate for six years on a requirement basis. Except for the initial fuel loading, the quote shall be on a batch by batch basis. Refer to Division 3—Nuclear Fuel Supply, Page 17, of Midwest Specification 4194–1 for additional information on fuel supply requirements.
4. Please note that we are preparing a "NSSS Commercial Specification" for transmittal to you in the very near future. This document will incorporate the commercial aspects for the purchase of this equipment, and all exceptions to this specification will be resolved and/or negotiated prior to contract award.
5. Do not include any cost for state sales and/or use tax. The state sales tax status will be determined at the time the contract is awarded. Your quotation *must* include, however, all other taxes and fees.
6. Furnish schedules and dates of key points for required Midwest decisions on design, fabrication, and/or erection.

Exhibit 1 (*Concluded*)

7. Rail facilities are available at both Alta and the Unspecified Site. Barge receiving facilities will be available at Alta 2 and for the Unspecified Site. It is required that all equipment be shipped f.o.b. plant site.
8. During the preaward period, Midwest may perform an in-depth audit of the bidders Quality Assurance Program to assess compliance with the requirements of Appendix B of 10 CFR 50.

If you have any questions concerning this inquiry, please fee free to contact me on 851-1099, extension 4839.

Sincerely,

Joe R. Walton
Buyer
Equipment Buying

JRW:bc
Enclosures (6) Six ccs all applicable specifications and drawings.

A nuclear reactor system could be considered as 60 percent mechanical equipment, including heat exchangers and piping and 40 percent electrical equipment and wiring.

Alta 2 bids

The four suppliers submitted acceptable proposals by August 15, 1972. The contract price for each was almost identical at $37 million. Differences existed primarily in the escalation bases and percentages chosen. Two of the bidders were mechanical contractors who would subcontract the electrical equipment. J&E Engineering (company no. 1—see Exhibit 2) estimated labor at 55 percent of contract cost and used the primary metals index for escalation base. J&E estimated material at 35 percent and used two indicators, the iron and steel index and the nickel index, for escalation here. Ermi, Inc., (company no. 4) was the only bidder to estimate labor at 45 percent and material at 45 percent. Total employment was used as the index for labor escalation and the composite price of finished steel for the material. The two other bidders Malton Electric (company no. 2) and Durnford Corporation (company no. 3) were electrical equipment manufacturers. Both had chosen labor escalation clauses tied to the electrical equipment and supplies index. Both had estimated labor at 55 percent of the total contract and material at 35 percent. Malton had specified steel mill products for the material index and Durnford the metal and metal products index.

The confusion of indexes used made direct bid comparison difficult. Mr. Harbison, therefore, requested that two steps be undertaken. First, he requested the purchasing research group to analyze the individual indexes proposed by the four bidders, to establish a trend line, if possi-

Exhibit 2
SUMMARY OF CONTRACT BIDS ON ALTA 2
SHOWING THE VARIATIONS IN ESCALATION

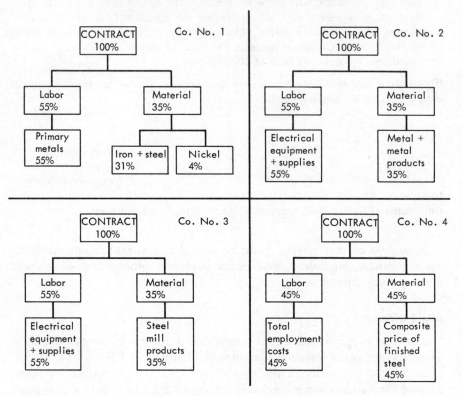

ble, and to calculate the impact on each of the four bids over the length of the contract. Second, he wanted expert outside advice on the use of escalation. Although Midwest had allowed escalation on its Alta 1 nuclear contract (see Exhibit 3), he was particularly concerned about its possible impact and its future use on additional nuclear units.

Exhibit 3
SELECTED CLAUSES FROM THE ALTA 1 CONTRACT
WITH J&E ENGINEERING

A. Price

The purchaser shall pay to the Seller $35,983,211.00 (contract price) for the materials and equipment furnished and services performed by the Seller pursuant to this contract.

B. Terms of Payment

Progressive terms of payment shall apply to the system as follows:

1. Purchaser shall make consecutive monthly deposits on account of the contract price, adjusted as provided in Section C below, at the percentages listed below in Column 3. Such deposits shall be refundable to Purchaser as provided in Article XII. The monthly deposits shall commence on October 1, 1969.

Exhibit 3 (*Continued*)

| Monthly deposit no. (column 1) | Number of deposits (column 2) | Percent of price | |
		Monthly (column 3)	Cumulative (column 4)
1–6	6	1	6
7–18	12	2	30
19–24	6	3	48
25–30	6	4	72
31–36	6	3	90
	36		

2. The balance of the contract price, adjusted as provided in Section C below and consisting of the customary retention of 10 percent of the contract price, shall be paid in two equal payments as follows:

5%—30 days after date of shipment as defined in Section D below.

5%—30 days after successful completion of the 100-hour output performance test or on October 1, 1975 (as extended by delays established to the fault of Seller), whichever occurs first.

3. In the event of any change in the contract price the new price shall be considered as having been in effect since April, 1969, for the purpose of payment.

4. If the Seller's performance of the work is significantly delayed, the Purchaser and the Seller will mutually agree on an adjustment of the deposit schedule which will equitably reflect the effect of such delay provided that to the extent that such delay is nonexcusable as provided in Article XII.B, then price adjustment as defined in Article V.C. below shall not apply to that portion of the agreed adjustment of the deposit schedule which is a result of the delay so caused.

C. Price Adjustment

The contract price specified in Section A above is subject to adjustment upward or downward for changes in labor and material cost indices at the times when deposits are due and as of the date of shipment for payments due after the date of shipment. Such adjustments shall be determined as set forth in this Section C.

1. Definitions. For the purpose of this provision, the following definitions apply:

a. The "Labor Index" shall be the Average Hourly Earnings in the Electrical Equipment and Supplies Industry (SIC 36) as finally determined and reported for the month in question by the Bureau of Labor Statistics of the U.S. Department of Labor in the publication "Employment and Earnings."

b. The "Materials Index" shall be the Steel Mill Products Index (Code 1013) as finally determined and reported for the month in question by the Bureau of Labor Statistics of the U.S. Department of Labor in the publication "Wholesale Prices and Price Indices."

Exhibit 3 *(Continued)*

  c.   The "Base Labor Index" shall be determined by averaging the Labor Indices for the months of March, April, and May, 1969.

  d.   The "Base Materials Index" shall be determined by averaging Materials Indices for the months of March, April, and May, 1969.

2.   Adjustment for Labor Costs

  a.   For the purpose of price adjustment, 55 percent of the contract price and of each deposit and payment to be made on account thereof shall be deemed to represent the labor content.

  b.   The labor content of each deposit shall be adjusted for any increase or decrease in labor costs. The adjustment for labor shall be equal to the percent by which the Labor Index for the month in which such deposit is due is greater or less than the Base Labor Index.

  c.   The labor content of each part of the contract price due after the date of shipment shall be adjusted for any increase or decrease in labor costs. The adjustment for labor shall be equal to the percent by which the Labor Index for the date of shipment is greater or less than the Base Labor Index.

3.   Adjustment for Material Costs

  a.   For the purpose of price adjustment, 35 percent of the contract price and of each deposit and payment to be made on account thereof shall be deemed to represent the material content.

  b.   The material content of each deposit shall be adjusted for any increase or decrease in material costs. The adjustment for material shall be equal to the percent by which the Materials Index for the month in which deposit is due is greater or less than the Base Materials Index.

  c.   The material content of each part of the contract price due after the date of shipment shall be adjusted for any increase or decrease in material costs. The adjustment for material shall be equal to the percent by which the Materials Index for the date of shipment is greater or less than the Base Materials Index.

4.   General

  a.   In the event of any change in the contract price the new price shall be considered as having been in effect since April, 1969, for purpose of price adjustment.

  b.   For billing purposes, each periodic deposit and each payment shall include a tentative adjustment calculated in the manner prescribed above but based upon the Seller's estimate for the Labor Index and the Materials Index at the time such deposit or payment is due. Any further adjustment which may be required shall be made at the time the Indices are first published in final form. Billing rendered on the basis of indices published in such final form shall not be revised for a subsequent Index revision which may occur. Should the Indices specified in Paragraphs 1 *a* and 1 *b* above be discontinued, or should the basis of their calculation be modified, proper Indices shall be substituted by mutual agreement of the parties.

  c.   The Base Labor Index shall be determined to the nearest second decimal place. The Base Materials Index shall be determined to the

Exhibit 3 (*Concluded*)

nearest first decimal place. In either case, if the next succeeding digit
is five or more, the preceding digit shall be raised to the next higher
figure.

    d. Both labor and material adjustments shall be calculated to the nearest
one tenth of 1 percent.

D. Shipment Date Defined

For the purpose of Sections B and C above, the phrase "date of shipment"
shall mean the date the bill of lading is signed by the carrier covering the
last to be shipped of the following items: reactor vessel, recirculation pumps
(complete set) and control rod drive mechanisms (complete set).

Exhibit 4
CAPITAL GOODS REVIEW

Indexes of Equipment Prices and Hourly Labor Costs (section A);
Ratio of the Equipment Index to the Labor Index and the
Long-Term Trend of the Ratio (Section B)*
(indexes 1929–100)

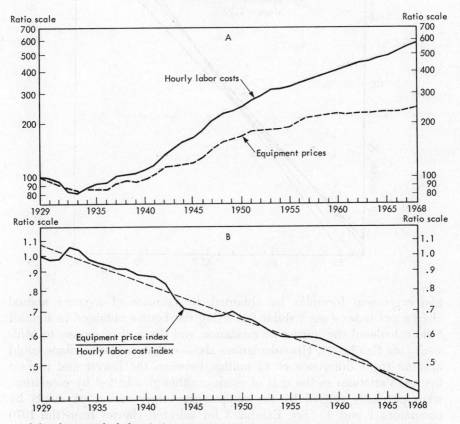

* A mimeographed description of sources and methods is available on request. The
figures for 1968 are, of course, estimates.

Computations of escalation concepts

Bill Morris in purchasing research spent several weeks gathering data from various sources on the indexes proposed by the four bidders. Most of the information was available from the Bureau of Labor Statistics in Washington, D.C. (See Exhibits 4, 5, 6 and 7.) Using the computer

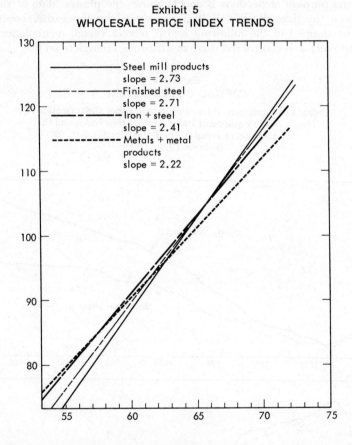

Exhibit 5
WHOLESALE PRICE INDEX TRENDS

Steel mill products
slope = 2.73
Finished steel
slope = 2.71
Iron + steel
slope = 2.41
Metals + metal
products
slope = 2.22

and regression formulas he obtained an estimate of average annual charge per index (see Exhibit 8). Using the figures obtained in Exhibit 8 he calculated the impact of escalation and the cost of money to Midwest (see Exhibit 9). His calculations showed that escalation alone could account for a difference of $1 million between the lowest and highest figures. Variations in the cost of money, although affected by escalation, were primarily caused by the request for larger earlier payments by companies 1 and 4. (See Exhibit 3 for selected clauses from the 1970 Alta 1 contract with J&E Engineering, showing progress payment rates and the use of escalation.)

Exhibit 6
AVERAGE HOURLY EARNINGS

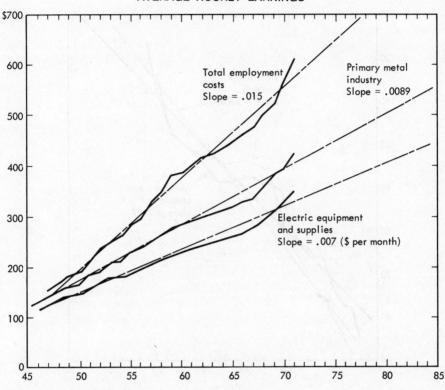

Total employment
costs
Slope = .015

Primary metal
industry
Slope = .0089

Electric equipment
and supplies
Slope = .007 ($ per month)

The outside consultant's view on escalation

Mr. Harbison was anxious to improve his understanding on the use of escalation in view of the large number of capital projects planned by Midwest. In the past he had not questioned the validity of escalation as it was a fairly standard concept, and he had accepted its use as a necessary evil of doing future business. He instructed Bill Morris to find an outside expert so that the Midwest purchasing staff might benefit from his opinion. Bill Morris checked a number of sources and found out that Professor Roy Jones, employed at an internationally recognized local university, was considered one of the best economic experts on this subject. When Professor Jones visited Midwest he was surprised to see that escalation was even considered for the nuclear reactor at Alta 2. He claimed his calculations showed significant productivity increases in most industries through technological and management advances, removing the necessity for escalation altogether. He argued that the electrical industry as a whole had done extremely well in keeping consumer prices down on all appliances and saw no reason why the

Exhibit 7
WHOLESALE PRICE INDEXES

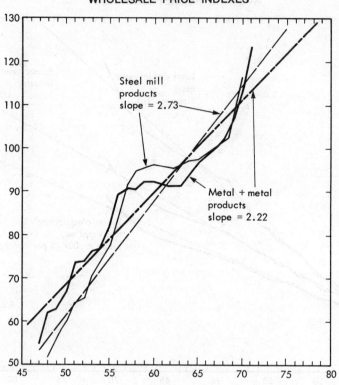

Exhibit 8
COMPUTATIONS OF ESCALATION CONCEPTS

	Percent change per year in labor	Percent change per year in material		Total percent change per year
Concept no. 1	2.12	Iron and Steel	.79	3.07
		Nickel	.16	
			.95	
Concept no. 2	1.96		.83	2.79
Concept no. 3	1.96		1.04	3.00
Concept no. 4	2.15		1.31	3.46

Computations based on the 10-year period, 1960–1970.

same principle could not be applied to large electrical equipment. In view of the popularity of nuclear reactors volume savings alone should warrant price decreases rather than escalation. The idea that escalation allowed for protection against increases in cost beyond management's control was not correct, according to Roy Jones. He said most labor

Exhibit 9
ESCALATION AND COST OF MONEY ANALYSIS
(average bid—$37,000,000)

	Company no. 1	Company no. 2	Company no. 3	Company no. 4	Maximum difference
Escalation	3,054,017	3,588,165	3,296,244	4,099,476	1,045,459 (34%)
Cost of money (including interest on escalation)	10,113,639	8,598,680	8,421,131	9,795,280	1,691,508 (20%)

and material costs were controllable through sound management and design. How Midwest could persuade its suppliers to drop escalation charges was a problem Professor Jones could not answer.

Conclusion

Mr. Harbison was pleased with the work of Bill Morris and the advice of Professor Jones. He realized that the dollar impact of escalation was substantial and had largely been ignored in the past. In view of the short time left before the contract was to be awarded, he knew he would have to move quickly. His impression was that all four bidders believed escalation was legitimate and necessary, contrary to Professor Jones' opinion. He, therefore, wondered what he should do.

VERNON TOOL CORPORATION

On March 5, 1973, Mr. Ted Long, corporate purchasing manager for Vernon Tool, received a call from Benson Fuels, a supplier of propane. Benson Fuels requested a 1¢ per gallon increase in the contract price due to extra freight charges that were being incurred. Mr. Long was surprised by the call since Benson Feuls was a new supplier for a very short-term contract. He knew he, therefore, had to respond quickly on this request.

Mr. Long recalled that on February 15, 1973, Mr. John Bruce, purchasing agent at Vernon's No. 4 plant in Tennessee, had requested help in obtaining a propane supplier. The natural gas company supplying this plant had exercised its right to interrupt service and had advised Mr. Bruce that it would be unable to resume supply before the end of March. In response to Mr. Bruce's call Mr. Long had immediately searched the marketplace and had been able to arrange with Benson Fuels to supply all the propane needed for the six-week period. In 1971 and 1972 there had been frequent short interruptions lasting anywhere from a few hours to one or two days. Plant management had not worried about these interruptions as Mr. Bruce had used a local standby supplier for small quantities of propane. However, this supplier was unable to meet the unexpectedly large demand created by the six-week natural gas interruption.

Vernon's No. 4 plant produced aluminum castings and needed fuel for general heating and firing of the furnaces. A fuel shortage would cause furnace shut-downs and costly start-up problems. Without any natural gas or propane the plant would have to close completely.

Company background

Vernon, a manufacturer of plastic products, chemical compounds, and related ferrous and nonferrous materials operated throughout the United States. Divided into four divisions, the company had 36 plants, many located in the Mississippi Valley.

Total company sales had climbed to $360 million in 1972. (Profits after tax had averaged 10.5 percent of sales over the last three years.) The company had set ambitious sales and profit targets for 1975 based on a growth rate of 20 percent a year.

Purchasing at Vernon

Corporate purchasing was a relatively new group in the organization. (See Exhibit 1.) Prior to 1968 purchasing was decentralized with a

Exhibit 1
VERNON TOOL CORPORATION

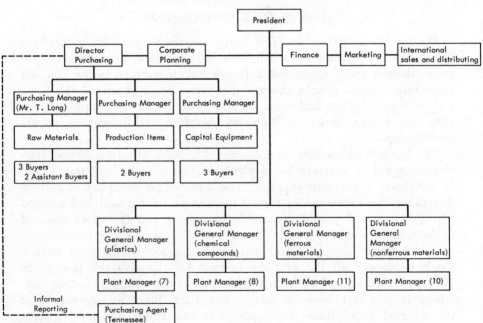

purchasing manager for each division. Since its formation in 1968, the corporate group saw its contribution to the organization increase with amalgamation of company purchases, improvements in contract negotiations, coordination or disposal of surplus equipment, market research and an active role in corporate planning. In 1972 Vernon's total purchases totaled $90 million. Corporate purchase orders accounted for $60 million of this amount.

Corporate purchasing was responsible for raw materials and supplies common to several plants. Plant purchasing was responsible for releases against corporate orders, expediting, and M.R.O. items. Fuel was presently considered an M.R.O item. Corporate purchasing generally acted as "back-up for local purchasing." Plant purchasing was also the training field for new people coming into purchasing at Vernon. Each plant's purchasing agent reported directly to the plant manager. Liaison between plant purchasing and Mr. Ted Long was informal.

Mr. Long thought a dual responsibility existed between plant and corporate purchasing to make each other aware of changing supply and market conditions. He considered communication, although informal, important at Vernon. Plant purchasing people within a division met periodically to discuss common problems, and a corporate purchasing manager was usually in attendance. Corporate purchasing had plans underway to publish quarterly a purchasing newsletter dealing with current business trends and company developments.

Vernon's normal corporate purchasing policy was to pay fair market prices and not to haggle. Suppliers were expected to make a reasonable profit on their sales to Vernon.

Natural gas contract

The natural gas contract for No. 4 plant had been negotiated yearly since the plant was acquired by Vernon in 1967. It had always contained a clause for interruptions. In 1972, the cut-off temperature had been raised to 46° from 32°. That is, any time the temperature dropped at the Tennessee plant below 46°, the gas company could exercise its service interruption clause. There was no specified time limit to the extent of the interruption. In other states Vernon plants were not as sharply affected by shortages as shown by the 26° cut-off temperature evidenced in their natural gas contracts. The natural gas company explained that regional shortages throughout the United States had forced the company to put its large users on reduced quotas. In recent years, natural gas usage in the surrounding rural area had increased significantly when farmers responded to the utility's marketing promotions to use natural gas as the fuel for corn and grain kilns. In case of interruption, Vernon's No. 4 plant required 8,000–9,000 gallons of propane as a substitute per day, six days a week. This the local propane standby supplier could only afford to supply for one or two days before his regular customers would suffer.

Natural gas shortages

"Domestic natural gas reserves are finite. The realization of this for the industry and the consumer was just late in coming," Mr. Long said. "Regional shortages have already been encountered and are likely to increase in the future. Natural gas, just like oil and coal, is under new pressures from governmental regulations, which in the case of natural gas have kept the price low, resulting in its increased acceptance and use. In recent years this low price caused consumption to skyrocket. By the beginning of the 70s all easily accessible reserves were tapped. The need for large investments in natural gas as well as other fossil fuels is growing. Exploration for new reserves must be undertaken. Negotiations with other countries must be started to develop alternative sources of supply for the increasing demand. The present reserve shortage is bringing a major reassessment to the whole supply and price structure." (See Exhibit 2.)

Exhibit 2
THE NATURAL GAS INDUSTRY*

It seems difficult to believe that at one time natural gas was regarded as a waste product. In the 1930s no one explored for gas since it had no market and obviously no commercial value. If drillers were unlucky enough to strike gas, they burned it—flared it in the field for quick disposal. It was not until after World War II that technology permitted the construction of pipelines from the Gulf Coast and Texas to the northern areas of the United States. During the period 1945–1970 the industry invested some $17 billion to extend high-pressure transmission pipelines into all of the lower 48 states. The truly contemporary nature of the gas industry is illustrated by the fact that Vermont was the last of our states to receive natural gas in 1966. Because of tight regulation natural gas was priced low and quickly developed a strong competitive advantage over coal and oil. Some measure of national gas growth can be gained from comparing 1970 reserves and production to those of 1946. In 1946 natural gas production was 4.9 trillion cubic feet and estimated reserves were 159.7 TCF. This resulted in a reserve/production ratio of 32.5 years supply. In 1971 the supply had further decreased to about a 12.6 ratio. In other words, assuming no new gas discoveries, we will simply run out of domestic supply in 12 to 13 years. If the Alaskan fields had not been discovered, our current reserves would be 26 TCF less or about 252 TCF. This reserve would have been the lowest since 1957. Although we are told that substantial gas fields remain undiscovered, there is no assurance that even if we accelerate drilling programs we will uncover them. The two major gas producing states both reported a decline in proven reserves in 1971. Louisiana's proven reserves de-

* Source: U.S. Investment Security Note, Morgan and Stanley Company.

Exhibit 2 (Continued)

clined from 83 TCF to 78.6 TCF, and Texas reserves fell from 106.4 TCF to 101.5 TCF. Our total U.S. proven reserves are less today than they were in 1964 even though demand has risen almost 45 percent.

The natural gas industry: The problem of price

The natural gas pricing structure has been a study in futility. It has been (and remains) an unwanted illegitimate offspring for which all parties disclaim responsibility. The gas industry regards the past and present rate structure

ESTIMATES OF NATURAL GAS RESERVES IN THE U.S.
(in trillions of cubic feet)

	Total discoveries	Production	Estimated reserves at year end
1971	9,825,421	22,076,512	278,805,618
1970	37,196,359	21,960,804	290,746,408
1969	8,357,004	20,723,190	275,108,835
1968	13,697,008	19,373,428	287,349,852
1967	21,804,433	18,380,838	292,907,703
1966	20,220,432	17,491,073	289,332,805
1965	21,319,279	16,252,293	286,468,923
1964	20,252,138	15,347,028	281,251,454
1963	18,164,667	14,546,025	276,151,233
1962	19,483,959	13,637,973	272,278,858
1961	17,166,422	13,378,649	266,273,642
1960	13,893,979	13,019,356	262,326,326
1959	20,621,252	12,373,063	261,170,431
1958	18,896,718	11,422,651	252,761,792
1957	20,008,055	11,439,890	245,230,137
1956	24,716,114	10,848,685	236,483,215

as an iniquitous invasion of the free enterprise concept. Regulatory agencies under political pressure have attempted to give consumers cheap energy while enabling the industry to earn only enough to quiet their objections and accordingly been able to please no one. Consumers are increasingly unhappy over curtailment of new customer service and rightly see the day when existing gas customers will be rationed. The control of natural gas prices must go down as one of the biggest regulatory failures. Although the original intent was to protect the consumer, the final outcome will be just the opposite. Regulation of a finite natural resource from the consumer side of the fence can only hasten the day of shortage. The basic problem was that the natural lubricant of price was not allowed to function between supply and demand. The historic pricing structure was allowed to hold down supply while encouraging demand. Obviously, at some point in time, the stress created by this artificially lopsided supply/demand situation would become great enough to force a drastic change. At a recent seminar devoted to the energy crisis, M. A. Adelman, professor of economics of the Massachusetts Institute of Technology, advocated the use of price to balance the supply/demand equa-

Exhibit 2 *(Continued)*

tion. Professor Adelman outlined three consequences that would result from letting prices float free: (1) An increase in exploration and reserves. (2) A lowering of demand. (3) A partial restructuring of gas demand to the presently less critical areas of coal and oil. In the face of a critical shortage of any commodity, an artificially based price level that encourages use and more rapid depletion of supplies makes no sense at all.

The present natural gas pricing structure appears confusing to say the least. The problem can be traced back to 1938 with the passage of the National Gas Act. In effect, Congress ordered the Federal Power Commission to regulate the price of interstate gas. The FPC took the position that it had only the authority to regulate pipeline prices but not wellhead prices. The matter was taken to the Supreme Court which in 1954 ruled that the FPC must regulate not only the transportation but also the price of the gas itself. Thus, the FPC began active regulation of the industry from wellhead through pipelines to the consumer. It should be noted that this covered interstate gas, not intrastate gas. A producer was subject to FPC regulation only if his output crossed state lines. It is doubtful if anyone could view the present pricing situation as anything but strange.

At this point, we should differentiate between "old" gas and "new" gas— already established reserves and newly discovered fields. The price of interstate old gas is about 18.2 cents per thousand cubic feet (Mcf). In 1971 the FPC allowed a ceiling of 26 cents per Mcf on new interstate gas. Currently, intrastate gas is being contracted in the 35 to 60 cent per Mcf range, and prices appear likely to go higher. With the strong probability of an impending shortage, many companies are now arranging for the importation of liquified natural gas (LNG) from distant foreign fields at prices ranging from $1.00 to $1.50 per Mcf. It would seem that the 18–19 cent price level for old interstate gas is not quite realistic in the face of 26 cent per Mcf new interstate gas, 35 to 60 cent intratstate gas and $1.00 to $1.50 for imported liquified natural gas. These price differentials already illustrate the extent of the shortage. Gas (or any other commodity) at any price is far more preferable than cheap but unavailable reserves. In the case of LNG, investment in development, facilities, transportation, and marketing will also be heavy.

With not only willingness but eager pursuit of contracts for foreign gas at over $1.00 per Mcf., it would seem that the FPC will have difficulty in keeping old gas at 18 or 19 cents. With an acute shortage now visible, one would expect that the regulatory commissioners should take all necessary steps to allow the industry an economic climate in which it could aggressively step up exploration. As with electric utilities, the gas industry experienced decreasing rates through regulatory order in the early and mid-1960s. Along with electric utilities, gas producers, transporters, and distributors are encountering more sympathetic hearings in their requests for rate relief.

Estimates of undiscovered gas supplies in the lower 48 states and Alaska indicate that our present reserves could be multiplied three or four times. This assumes, of course, that the industry would be willing and able to invest enormous sums of money in exploration. To date, the industry has been lacking in the economic incentive to accomplish this most necessary

Exhibit 2 (*Continued*)

task. As was pointed out elsewhere in this report, in 1969, Congressional tax legislation added some $500 million in new taxes to the petroleum industry. This could hardly have been called a new incentive to spend the money needed to solve the problem. In addition to economic factors, the industry has been beset by environmental problems. The proposal for a pipeline from the Alaskan North Slope has been bogged down in environmental controversy. This delay in construction will, at best, vastly increase the ultimate cost of the project (with consumers finally forced to pay the bill) and, at worst, will further contribute to the shortage of fuel and further aggravate our balance of payments.

GAS WELL STATISTICS

	Average cost per well ($000)	Average cost per foot ($)	Average depth feet per well	Wellhead price per mcf (¢)
1971				18.2
1969	154.3	25.88	6,034	16.7
1968	148.5	24.05	6,177	16.4
1967	141.0	23.05	6,116	16.0
1966	133.8	21.75	6,151	15.7
1965	101.9	18.35	5,552	15.6
1964	104.8	18.57	5,641	15.4
1963	92.4	17.19	5,373	15.8
1962	97.1	18.10	5,366	15.5
1961	94.7	17.65	5,366	15.1

Source: National Petroleum Council

As can be seen from the table, gas wells have become increasingly more expensive to drill. Offshore drilling has added to costs considerably. Drilling in 300 feet of water requires an $8 million drilling rig that costs about $9,000 per day to operate. The platform to handle production costs another $2.7 million. Exploration is increasingly moving into deeper waters. Some drilling activities now take place as far as 200 miles at sea. It is estimated that the Gulf area contains over 140 trillion cubic feet of gas undiscovered. If all these resources could be identified, it would only, however, add six to seven years to total U.S. reserves. As gas reserves become depleted, drillers must venture farther and farther offshore as well as other remote and hostile environments at greater cost.

Liquified natural gas (LNG)

The development of the technology for the production and handling of liquified natural gas has now made foreign supplies available to U.S. consumers. Although the first patent involving the liquification of natural gas

Exhibit 2 (*Continued*)

was issued in 1914, it was only recently that large-scale commercial activity began. The first shipload of LNG was delivered to Boston in 1968 from Algeria. In 1969, LNG was exported from Alaska to Japan and in 1970 the first over-the-road shipment of LNG was made. Imports of LNG will rise in coming years to become an ever-important supplement to domestic production. LNG imports are projected to 0.3 trillion cubic feet in 1975, rising to 3 TCF in 1985 and over 4 TCF in 1990. If anything, these figures could prove to be quite conservative.

The liquification of natural gas results in its reduction in volume by more than 600-to-1. In the liquification process, natural gas is cooled to $-259°$ F whereupon it assumes a liquid form. In its liquid state, natural gas offers a convenience of transportation in either ship, truck, railcar or barge. Maintained at proper temperatures, LNG may be transported easily for long distances. Upon regasification or reforming with the application of heat, one cubic foot of liquid methane becomes the equivalent of 625 cubic feet of gaseous methane. The gas may then be fed into normal pipeline facilities for delivery to consumers.

The ships that transport LNG are virtually giant floating thermos bottles, as their cargo must be kept at $-259°$F during the voyage. These sophisticated cryogenic ships will have a capacity of some 5 million cubic feet of LNG and are expected to cost somewhere between $90 to $100 million each. In addition to the high cost for ships, investment must be made in foreign liquification facilities and domestic terminals and regasification plants. LNG contracts have been signed or are pending for imports from Alaska, Algeria, Canada, Ecuador, Indonesia, Nigeria, the North Sea, Trinidad and Venezuela.

In early November, 1972, three U.S. firms announced their study of a plan to import large quantities of natural gas from the Soviet Union in exchange for goods and services. The announcement indicated that investment in the project would perhaps run close to $40 billion. Under the plan, some 2 billion cubic feet of natural gas would be brought in to the U.S. East Coast each day from Siberian fields. A similar venture is being planned for the U.S. West Coast in competition with another group. If the plan is approved by both the U.S. and the Soviet Union, it would become the largest single construction project in history.

In addition to LNG, gas produced from coal will be an important supplementary source of fuel in future years. In addition to enlarging our gas supply, gasification would permit increased utilization of our vast coal reserves. Further, it would be independent of foreign sources of supply. The only currently available commercial gasification process is the Lurgi process whose output must be further refined to achieve pipeline quality gas. Two major efforts to develop gasification facilities are expected to be on stream in 1975 in New Mexico. Costs per Mcf are believed to be in the $.85 to $1.10 range. Assuming successful solutions to technical obstacles, the coal gasification process may supply about 1.4 trillion cubic feet of gas per year by 1985, about one half the expected LNG imports. Beyond 1985 gasification is expected to grow at a more rapid pace. By 1990, it is expected that the process will supply about 7 percent of the projected national gas requirement.

Exhibit 2 *(Concluded)*

SUMMARY OF 1970 WORLD NATURAL GAS
RESERVES AND PRODUCTION
(in billions of cubic feet)

Total production	Year-end reserves	R/P ratio	Percent world production	Percent world reserves
		North America		
		United States		
21,960.8	290,746	13.2	48.88	17.90
		Canada		
2,656.0	53,086	29.7	5.91	3.27
		Mexico		
665.0	12,000	18.0	1.48	0.74
		Central and South America		
2,635.4	53,850	20.4	5.86	3.30
		Western Europe		
2,882.9	154,761	53.7	6.41	9.52
		Africa		
1,405.3	188,920	134.4	3.13	11.63
		Oceania and Far East		
610.4	39,280	64.4	1.36	2.42
		Australia and New Zealand		
56.9	15,417	270.9	.15	.95
		Middle East		
2,885.2	351,862	122.0	6.43	21.67
	U.S.S.R., Eastern Europe and Mainland China			
9,167.4	463,980	50.6	20.41	28.58
44,925.3	1,623,902	36.1	100.00	100.00

Source: Bureau of Natural Gas, Federal Power Commission.

New propane supplier

Mr. Long was able to find an alternative propane source, Benson Fuels, after an extensive search. Benson held a large number of commercial accounts throughout western Tennessee. Actually, Benson turned out to be the only company with supplies capable of meeting the daily demand at Vernon's No. 4 plant. Mr. Long signed a corporate contract with Benson, specifying that the weekly requirements until the end of March would total 300,000 gallons. The contract would last six weeks, from February 19 until the end of March 1973. It contained no escalation clauses and specified that all delivery schedules and supply procedures would be handled by Mr. Bruce, the purchasing agent at the plant. Any difficulties arising from the contract would require Benson to deal with Mr. Long directly. Mr. Long had forwarded a copy of the contract to Mr. Bruce. Benson Fuels had agreed to supply the propane at a premium price of 16.75¢ a gallon. Local freight was to account for 3.0¢ of the premium and profit another 1.25¢. Normally, freight was a major price component of propane. For example, propane near the well heads in Texas cost 7.5¢ a gallon. In the past the plant had paid from 12.5 to 12.75¢ a gallon in Tennessee. Mr. Long felt that due to the locally tight supply condition he was fortunate to obtain the required propane at the 4.25¢ premium.

Request for price increase

Benson Fuels, after supplying propane for two weeks, approached Mr. Long on March 5, 1973, and requested an additional 1¢ per gallon, claiming that it was incurring extra daily freight charges. Benson's sales manager explained that he was supplying No. 4 plant from two terminals. The western one was farther from the plant and also had a 15 percent higher labor cost for handling propane than the eastern terminal. Delivered by tanker truck and pumped into the company's storage tank, Benson's deliveries came almost daily. Each tanker truck contained approximately 10,000 gallons. An erratic schedule of deliveries had forced Benson to use the western terminal more than expected when contract costs had been calculated. During those two weeks it was not uncommon for Benson to receive a call as late as 9:00 P.M. with an urgent request for delivery first thing in the morning. The eastern terminal was invariably booked with other work for the day, forcing Benson to make longer hauls for the western one.

Mr. Long telephoned Mr. Bruce at the No. 4 plant inquiring into the supply problem with Benson. Mr. Bruce explained that it had been difficult to monitor a safety zone in the 12,000 gallon storage tank. Weather combined with some variations in production made it difficult to forecast exact propane usage. Whenever the 90 percent empty mark in the storage tank appeared, Mr. Bruce put a telephone call through to Benson. Mr. Bruce was not certain as to what corrective action could be taken.

Conclusion

Mr. Long talked with the divisional general manager responsible for No. 4 plant during the afternoon concerning the requested price increase. The divisional general manager stated that the plant manager at No. 4 was in a very tight cost and profit squeeze and unable to afford any price increase.

Mr. Long was concerned about the request from Benson but was reluctant to alter the terms of the contract. Under Vernon's decentralization policy, each plant was a profit center, and the price increase would have to be absorbed by the plant. Mr. Long, as corporate purchasing manager, negotiated the contract on behalf of the plant and could, therefore, only make recommendations to the parties involved.

In view of this, Mr. Long wondered what action he might take in the present situation. Mr. Long was not sure if his decision might be affected by future corporate purchasing plans which called for all company fuel requirements to be placed in Mr. Long's hands. He, therefore, wondered what stance he should take for the following year on propane purchases for all the five regional plants. Corporate propane needs for five regional plants in Tennessee totaled 500,000 gallons a month during the summer and 800,000 a month in winter. If standby propane for all the plants had to be arranged additional volumes approaching 900,000 gallons a month might be required at times.

THE VERBAL AGREEMENT

Mr. John Peters, president of Carlyn Corporation, visited Mr. Doug Warden, executive vice president of Blondin on July 9, 1974. They knew each other reasonably well, and Mr. Peters quickly got down to business.

Mr. Peters: Doug, I have come to you to discuss a proposition which I think makes a lot of sense for both of our companies. Are you interested?

Mr. Warden: John, all I have to lose is some time. Your start intrigues me. What have you got up your sleeve?

Mr. Peters: It has to do with MS–7. We know you are preparing to make your own, and we would like to help you make it a success.

Mr. Warden: What do you know about MS–7 that we don't know?

Mr. Peters: Perhaps not much. Maybe it's more a matter of what we both know. And that is that your present volume is way below a reasonable efficiency level for the investment you are shelling out.

Mr. Warden: Suppose that's true, we would still be prepared to meet our growing sales requirements in the future.

Mr. Peters: Sure, but that's going to take time. Now you know that our parent has been supplying us with MS–7. We have all of their cost figures and experience behind us, and we know pretty well what your situation looks like from a financial and production point of view. That's why we were a little surprised to see you get into it. However, now that you are in the game it's probably wise to make the best of it. I want to be frank with you. We have no real interest in starting our own MS–7 manufacture because it is tricky, and our volume just doesn't warrant it. On the other hand, if we have to, we will. And then two of us are fiddling around with expensive equipment inadequately loaded. What I want to propose to you is that, since you have taken the step to start manufacture, you supply both of us with MS–7 instead of just yourself. I am willing to make a long-term commitment to you, four or five years, if necessary, but I want a good price in return.

Mr. Warden: John, there is a heck of a lot of sense to what you are saying. I have been worried a little about our return on this investment.

If your volume comes in with ours, we could certainly expect better operating efficiency. What are you willing to offer?

MR. PETERS: We are prepared to offer $44/kg.

MR. WARDEN: You must be kidding. You know that the current U.K. laid down price in the U.S. is close to $60/kg.

MR. PETERS: That may be, but that's certainly not what we have been paying. Look, if it really interests you, I'll tell you what we figure your variable cost is, and that's around $40. Now everything you make on top of that is contribution to your fixed expenses. That's why we are willing to give you a 20-percent contribution. We think we should approach this from a sharing of the benefits point of view rather than a market price proposition. What's market price anyway, with only two customers?

MR. WARDEN: (After requesting a file from his secretary and scribbling on paper) Excuse me, John, I had to check a few things myself. Let's not kid ourselves, if I let you have the stuff at $44 my sales and production managers would kill me. At that price the sharing of the benefit you talk about is too one-sided. Now I know we can start horse trading and end up frustrated and feeling foolish. I'll be honest with you. I like the premise of your proposition. I like the idea. I don't like the price you quoted. Now, I am not going to beat around the bush. I'll quote you what I think is a very good deal. You either take it or leave it. If you take it, we can settle a few details later. If you leave it, you'll never be able to buy MS-7 from us.

MR. PETERS: You are not giving me much choice but go on.

MR. WARDEN: First, the length of time. You want five years, we'll give you five years. Now the price. I'm probably crazy, but I'll let you have it for $50/kg, f.o.b. our plant in St. Paul, Minnesota. Agreed?

MR. PETERS: Doug, you drive a hard bargain. If you feel that you need $50 to feel satisfied about our sharing agreement, $50 it is, and good luck to both of us.

MR. WARDEN: Fine.

MR. PETERS: What I would like to suggest to you is that our Mr. Bill Thomas in purchasing get together with whoever you want to assign this to on your end to agree on further details. Is this acceptable to you?

MR. WARDEN: This is agreeable. Since our equipment will not be coming in until late October, I would appreciate holding off on any follow-up until the beginning of October because we have our annual plant shut-down still coming up, and we are trying to introduce another new product which will take a lot of our staff's time until early October. Is this okay with you?

MR. PETERS: It's a little long, and I would like to get this thing tied up as soon as possible, but I guess we can wait until October in view of your special circumstances. I'd like to wish you good luck with your new product provided it's not going to compete with one of ours.

MR. WARDEN: Thanks. No, this new one isn't another rival. Thank you for coming, John. I am sorry I don't have more time to spend with you now.

MR. PETERS: I want to thank you too. I'm glad we got a deal. Goodbye, Doug.

MR. WARDEN: Goodbye, John.

10 FORWARD BUYING AND SPECULATION

From the discussion up to this point, it should be clear that the determination of the proper price to pay is often far from being a simple task. It is even more difficult when the problem becomes one not merely of buying for immediate and known requirements but of buying for some period well in advance of these needs. Yet this is a situation with which every company is faced. Under what circumstances and to what extent is forward buying justifiable?

It must be noted that a real distinction exists between what may be termed ordinary forward buying, speculative buying, and a policy which is, in effect, little short of gambling. While the border line between these three concepts at times is often difficult, if not impossible, to draw, they are by no means the same thing. Furthermore, the basic thinking of top management with reference to forward buying will be reflected in its procurement policy. If the management feels that its primary source of profit is to be derived from speculative purchases of raw material, it is likely to gear not only its procurement activities to that end but its sales, merchandising, and financial policies as well.

FORWARD BUYING VERSUS SPECULATION

All forward buying involves some risk and is to some degree unavoidable. In what may be termed ordinary forward buying, purchases are largely confined to actually known requirements or to carefully estimated requirements for a limited period of time in advance. The essential controlling factor is need. Anticipated trends are not disregarded but play a minor part in determining the amounts to buy. Thus, the inventory of an item may be controlled by a maximum-minimum method based on usage experience. Yet even here, when the reorder point is reached, the amount to be bought may be increased or decreased in accordance both with probable use and with the price trend, rather than automatically reordering a given amount. Temporarily, no order may be placed at all. On the other hand, a quantity somewhat larger than usual may be ordered. But the essential controlling factor is known need.

This may be true even where purchases have to be made many months in advance, as in the case of seasonal products, such as wheat, or those that must be obtained abroad, such as jute or carpet wools. Obviously, the price risk increases as the lead time grows longer, but the basic reason for these forward commitments is assurance of supply to meet production requirements, and only secondarily price.

Speculation cannot be defined merely as risk assumption. All business is a risk, and every person who engages in it is a risk-taker. Risks, however, are of different varieties. All business people are specialists in certain types of risk and endeavor to shift the other necessary allied risks to someone else. Thus, a manufacturer shifts the risk of fire loss to a fire insurance company. The risk may be avoided by making the structure fireproof. By floating new bonds to some type of financial underwriter the financial risk of securing new capital is transferred almost entirely. The risk in which the manufacturer specializes is that of anticipating a public need for some particular type of commodity and of undertaking to meet that need by producing and marketing the commodity; profits result from the successful assumption of the manufacturing and marketing risk involved. The manufacturer is a risk-taker just as surely as the insurance company or the underwriter. However, the manufacturer plans to make his profit primarily from the assumption of a particular type of risk.

Is hand-to-mouth buying speculation?

"Hand-to-mouth buying" may or may not involve speculation. If by the term is meant reducing substantially the size of one's ordinary purchases in order to avoid a needlessly large investment in inventory, there is nothing speculative about it. Speculation enters only when a procurement officer buys even less than the usual rules of safety require in order to profit by the fall in price.

Ordinarily, hand-to-mouth buying is not interpreted as being of a speculative nature. As long as the purchasing manager does not interfere with the continuous operation of the production process through failure to have material available when called for, there is often much to be said for such a policy, even though it merely shifts certain elements of expense back to the supplier instead of avoiding them completely. From the buyer's point of view, there are definite risks in minimizing the inventory. Since the size of the orders is small, they must be placed more frequently. Unit prices on small lots are frequently higher than on large lots, partly because the costs to the seller on these small lots are greater and partly because the buyer is in a less advantageous bargaining position. In addition, small-lot shipments usually result in higher freight rates. Other handling costs are also increased because of the additional time spent in packing and unpacking and in shipping and receiving shipments. The smaller units may even necessitate revision of transportation and receiving methods and later of handling and storage. Storage and warehouse facilities may go unused, but their principal overhead costs continue. In many cases, small orders result in spoilage and breakdowns in delivery schedules because they receive less attention from the vendor. With starved inventories, it does not take much delay in receipt of materials to interfere with the vendee's production schedule. The company cannot then guarantee prompt deliveries of its finished products. In view of these facts, it becomes quite evident that hand-to-mouth buying involves elements of risk which, upon occasion, may well place it in the category of speculative buying.

As with many administrative questions, the final decision in any case becomes a balancing of factors. The higher costs which hand-to-mouth buying might necessitate may be of small import in the face of substantial price changes or costly shutdowns.

Speculation versus gambling

Just where the line of distinction between speculation and gambling is to be drawn is a matter of individual judgment. However, there are certain practices which cannot be classified in any other category than in the latter. If a person undertakes a venture in which there is virtually no chance to win, it is clear that that venture is not speculation. If a purchaser tries to guess what the market trend is likely to be for some commodity with which he or she has had no experience and practically no knowledge, he or she is a gambler. Others in the same category are those who, regardless of their experience with a particular commodity, lack adequate data upon which to forecast probable price movements. People who endeavor to anticipate price changes largely because of the thrill which they get out of such a practice are also to be placed in this same class.

The distinction between ordinary forward buying, speculative purchasing, and gambling should be reasonably clear. Although, in practice, the border line may at times be difficult to see, it is important to note that the three policies are quite different. The first policy is, in most cases, unavoidable. The second is debatable. If a company deliberately undertakes a policy of speculative buying, it is adopting a policy which it may feel is profitable but which cannot be harmonized with the purpose for which most manufacturing concerns are organized. The third is never to be condoned.

The organization for determination and execution of policy with regard to long-term commitments on commodites whose prices fluctuate widely varies considerably from company to company, depending upon its size, the extent to which it desires to speculate, and the percentage of total manufacturing cost represented by those volatile commodities. In some instances, the president exercises complete control, based almost wholly on personal judgment. In other cases, although the president assumes direct responsibility, an informal committee provides assistance. There are companies in which the financial officer controls the raw materials inventory.

Some companies have a person other than the purchasing agent, whose sole responsibility is over "speculative" materials and who reports directly to top management. In a very large number of firms the purchasing manager controls the inventory of such commodities. In a few companies almost complete reliance for policy execution is placed in the hands of an outside agency that specializes in speculative commodities.

The soundest practice for most companies would appear to be to place responsibility for policy in the hands of a committee consisting of the president or general manager and the purchasing manager. If the company employs an economist, he also should be on the committee. Actual execution of the broad policy as laid down should rest with the procurement department.

Such a procedure is equivalent to ensuring that full utilization is made of all the executive talent qualified to participate. Such participation is highly important. However, the emphasis should be not on details of actual buying but on policy, i.e., *broad company* policy involving purchasing; and it should be carried out in the interests of coordinating the various management functions concerned, thus providing those immediately in charge of the procurement of raw or semiprocessed materials with all pertinent information in order that the inventory of these materials may be controlled wisely. Such joint participation will also provide the production, sales, and financial executives with more dependable and timely information than they might otherwise have as to prices and price trends of the essential raw materials as well as of the plentifulness or scarcity of them—data which will prove of great value to them in meeting their respective responsibilities.

Objectives of forward and speculative buying

The objectives of forward and speculative buying, as we have defined them, of course, are not always identical. However, since the one policy is likely to merge imperceptibly into the other, we shall list the objectives together. One purpose of buying ahead may be to ensure an available supply. Some commodities are marketed only during a particular season, although their use is constant throughout the year. To assure a supply of a particular grade or type of wheat, a flour miller may have to buy and store a year's supply at one time. In some localities iron ore, coal, and limestone are purchased months ahead for stock to carry through the winter and spring while the waterways are frozen.

Another objective in ordinary forward buying may be simply that of keeping costs as low as may reasonably be done. No great profit is expected by virtue of "buying low," nor is it likely that the savings on any particular purchase will be reflected in a lower selling price on the finished product. In all such buying, price trend is a secondary consideration anyway; it is watched, therefore, only for the purpose of keeping costs on ordinary purchases reasonably low.

One final objective of future buying must be mentioned—the hope of securing an out-and-out speculative profit. It is immaterial whether part or all of the material bought is resold "as is" or is processed and sold as a finished product at a price based on raw material values substantially above those existing when the raw material was obtained. Either of these operations has as its objective the securing of speculative profit, and it is around this policy that most of the controversy concerning the wisdom of so-called speculative buying centers.

This question is not one which can be decided by reference to authority, nor is it a question to which a categorical answer can be given. Like so many other questions involving business policy, the answer is to be found in the circumstances which surround a given situation; until these circumstances are known, therefore, it would be unwise to attempt to lay down a general rule. It is true that so-called speculation has been most strongly condemned by a great many people, Thus it is said:

At best, any speculation, in the accepted meaning of the term, is a risky business, but speculation with other people's money has been cataloged as a crime. The position of a purchasing agent is a fiduciary one. His office should contain no throne for the Goddess of Chance. Its incumbent is a trustee for the wise employment of the funds belonging to the stockholders of the company. It is not within his province to expend any portion of those funds with the main object of future and uncertain gains, but only to provide for the immediate needs of the property, to the best advantage possible at the time, and to keep the investment in unused materials, the value of which is subject to fluctuations, at the lowest point consistent with safety of operation and economical maintenance.

Costs of speculation

In the long run, the question of whether or not a manufacturing concern should speculate is a matter of the comparative costs of gains resulting from such activity and of the effect of such gains—or losses—upon the profits from the remaining activities of the company. These speculatvie activities may consist of buying in advance of requirements or, on the contrary, of starving one's stock down to the least possible amount. To buy materials to be held for rising prices necessarily involves certain distinct costs which must be set off against any gains which may accrue. These costs must include interest on the money invested in the commodity, dangers of obsolescence and of deterioration, storage costs including allowances for fire and theft, handling charges, and the profits which might have been made had the money been otherwise used. It is clear that some of these costs are not borne directly by all concerns engaged in speculation. For example, the transaction may consist simply of an order for future delivery at a price stipulated at the time the order is placed. In this event, some of the costs may be shifted to the supplier. Whether so shifted or not, they must be borne and must enter into a balancing of the gains against the costs.

On the other hand, if a concern starves its inventory down to the lowest possible point consistent with continued operation, there are other costs which must also be met, the nature of which has already been discussed. In view of these costs—tangible and intangible—it is evident that hand-to-mouth buying is speculation whenever it results from a desire to avoid being in possession of large stocks of goods in the face of falling prices or an attempt to carry unusually low stocks temporarily in order to profit by an anticipated drop and subsequent rise in price. Consequently, in spite of the belief on the part of many people that hand-to-mouth buying is just the opposite of speculative buying, it may in fact be of essentially the same nature.

Control of forward buying

Whether or not the reader agrees with this position, there can be little dissent from the proposition that some safeguards should be set up with a view to ensuring that the administration of a speculation will be kept within proper bounds. Just what these bounds will be varies, of course, from one company to another and to some extent with the materials involved. The following checks set up by one leather company are given merely as an illustration: (1) Speculative buying must be confined to those hides which are used in the production either of several different leathers or of the leathers for which there is a stable demand. (2) Daily conferences are held among the president, treasurer, sales manager, and hide buyer. (3) Orders for future delivery of leather are varied in some measure in accordance with the company's need for protection on hide holdings. Since the leather buyer is willing to place orders for future delivery of leather when prices are satisfactory, this company follows the practice of using unfilled orders as a partial hedge of its hide holdings. In general, the policy is to have approximately 50 percent of the total hides which a company owns covered by sales contracts for future production of leather. (4) A further check is provided by an operating budget which controls the physical volume of hides rather than the financial expenditures and which is brought up for reconsideration whenever it is felt necessary. (5) There is, a final check which consists of the use of adequate and reliable information, statistical and otherwise, as a basis for judging price and market trends.

This particular company does not follow the practice of hedging on an organized commodity exchange as a means of avoiding undue risk, though many companies, including some leather companies, do. Nor does this company use any of the special accounting procedures, such as last-in, first-out or reproduction-cost-of-sales, in connection with its forward purchases.

However, these various control devices, regarded as a unit rather than as unrelated checks, should prove effective. They are obviously not foolproof, nor do they ensure absolutely against the dangers inherent in buying well in advance. However, elasticity in the administration of any policy is essential, and, for this one company at least, the procedure outlined combines reasonable protection with such elasticity.

All such checks are designed in order that the combined judgment of those responsible for management may be exercised for the prevention of loss. It has already been pointed out that a firm which operates to any substantial extent in the speculative markets without adequate financial backing is, in effect, gambling. A company always anticipates a profit from such operations, or it would not engage in them. Yet losses do occur because mistakes are made, and luck does not favor the speculator consistently. No company should permit its resources to be so far committed to the uncertainties inherent in all speculative buying as to endanger its existence if heavy losses are incurred. Since losses are inevitable, ample reserves and reasonable caution are essential.

In manufacturing operations requiring large quantities of certain raw materials whose prices fluctuate widely, the risks involved in buying ahead may under some circumstances be substantially minimized through the use of the commodity exchanges. We must therefore devote some attention to these organizations, even though there is no need here to enter into a discussion of their technical operations and even though such organized exchanges exist for only a limited number of commodities.[1]

THE COMMODITY EXCHANGES

The prime function of an organized commodity exchange is to furnish an established marketplace where the forces of supply and demand may operate freely as buyers and sellers carry on their trading. An exchange which has facilities for both cash and futures trading can

---

[1] See J. B. Baer and O. G. Soxon, *Commodity Exchanges and Futures Trading* (New York: Harper & Bros., 1949); L. Belveal, *Commodity Speculation with Profits in Mind* (Wilmette, Ill.: Commodities Press, 1967); Chicago Board of Trade, *Commodity Trading Manual* (Chicago, 1966); Gerald Gold, *Modern Commodity Futures Trading* (New York: Commodity Research Bureau, 1966); Merrill Lynch, Pierce, Fenner and Smith, Inc., *How to Buy and Sell Commodities* (New York, 1969); H. B. Arthur, *Commodity Futures as a Business Management Tool* (Boston: Division of Research, Harvard University, 1971).

also be used for hedging operations. The rules governing the operation of an exchange are concerned primarily with procedures for the orderly handling of the transactions negotiated on the exchange, providing, among other things, terms and time of payment, time of delivery, grades of products traded, and methods of settling disputes.

In general, the purposes of a commodity exchange will be served best if the following conditions are present:

enough volume of a business so that no one buyer or seller can
1. The products traded in are capable of reasonably accurate grading.
2. There is a large enough number of sellers and buyers and a large
    permanently influence the market.

In order for a commodity exchange to be useful for hedging operations, the following conditions should also be present:

1. There must be trading in "futures"—the buying or selling of the commodity for delivery at a specified future date.
2. A fairly close correlation between "basis" and other grades.
3. A reasonable but not necessarily consistent correlation between "spot" and "future" prices.

All of these conditions usually are present on the major grain and cotton exchanges, and in varying degrees on the minor exchanges, such as those on which hides, silk, metals, rubber, coffee, and sugar are dealt in.

All these exchanges perform a real function. In most cases, the prices quoted on them and the record of transactions completed furnish some clue, at least, to the current market price and to the extent of the trading in those commodities. They offer an opportunity, some to a greater extent than others, of protecting the buyer against basic price risks through hedging. Purchasing officers have actually found at least some of the exchanges of great value in the purchase of some of their requirements, and the student may find ample expositions of them in any reliable book dealing with organized commodity exchanges.

Limitations of the exchanges

In spite of these advantages there are very definite limitations upon the value of these exchanges as a source of physical supply for the purchasing officer. One of the most important of these is that in spite of a reasonably satisfactory attempt to define the market grades acceptable on transactions completed on the exchange, the grading in many cases is not sufficiently accurate for manufacturing purposes. The requirements of a textile manufacturer concerning the character of the cotton which he is to use are likely to be very exacting. In fact, one may say that, in most cases, these requirements are so definite that even the comparatively narrow limits of any specific grade are too broad to serve his purpose. Moreover, the rules of the exchange are such that the actual deliveries of cotton made do not have to be of a specific grade but may be of any grade above or below basis cotton, provided, of course, that the essential financial adjustment is made. For the purpose of the cotton merchant or the cotton broker, these variables are of no practical importance. For him, therefore, the exchange serves a very useful purpose, but it is because his requirements are different from the requirements of the cotton textile manufacturer. In considerable measure this same rule holds true for wheat. Millers who sell patented, blended flours must have very definite types of wheat. These types can be most satisfactorily procured only by purchase through sample.

There are other reasons why these exchanges are not satisfactory for the purchasing officers who is endeavoring to meet actual physical commodity requirements. On some of the exchanges, no spot market exists. There also exists on some of the commodity exchanges a certain lack of confidence in the validity of the prices quoted. Crude rubber, for example, is purchased primarily by tire manufacturers. There are only a few of them, and they are very large buyers. Since there is the possibility, if not the probability, of a restricted number of buyers—all large—the demand aspect is such as to give no confidence that purchasing is done in a free, open, competitive market. The contrary situation prevails in the case of the hide exchange. The great bulk of hides sold are by-products of the packing industry, and the grading problem is a very real one. Because the supply of hides is owned by a limited number of sellers, an increase or a decrease in the price of hides, however, does not have the same effect upon supply that such changes might have upon the supply of some other commodities. The fact that the supply of hides is not so elastic as that of many other agricultural commodities also has a bearing upon the usefulness of the hide and skin exchange. It is not asserted that these sellers use their position to manipulate the market artificially any more than it is asserted that the buyers of rubber manipulate the market to their advantage. In these two cases, however, there is likely to be a serious question in the minds of those who might otherwise wish to use the exchange as to the accuracy with which the prices quoted really reflect supply and demand conditions.

The large producers of nonferrous metals in this country do not use the metal exchange as largely as they might. The producers are said to be opposed to the use of the New York metal market because they wish to retain full control of their product and to sell to consumers only. They are especially anxious to keep it out of the hands of speculators because their past experience has indicated that buyers have refused to recognize the contracts when prices were falling and because the producers sometimes have found themselves in the position of competing "with their own products." They therefore feel that, through constant contact with users, better service to both parties in matters of brand, price, and delivery is obtained than if they were to deal through those who are interested primarily in the exchange. It is said, for example:

> Larger producers are interested primarily in having a stable copper market, something to which dealers and speculators are not committed, as speculators depend for a profit upon a rise or a decline in prices, and hence are anxious to have a fluctuating market. . . . The whole machinery of the metal business in this country is not built on lines which would work well with a large speculative exchange.

Hedging

Perhaps the greatest advantage of the commodity exchanges to a manufacturer is that they provide an opportunity to offset transactions and thus to protect to some extent against price risks. This is commonly done by "hedging," which, broadly speaking, refers to transactions on the exchanges whereby a future sale or purchase of commodities is made to offset a corresponding purchase or sale on a spot basis. Hardy and Lyon say:

> The essence of a hedging contract is a coincident purchase and sale in two markets which are expected to behave in such a way that any loss realized in one will be offset by an equivalent gain in the other . . . The commonest type of hedging transaction is the purchase and sale of the same amount of the same commodity in the spot and future markets.[2]

Clearly, hedging can occur only when trading in futures is possible. A simple example of hedging to illustrate the above statement follows:

In the Cash Market	*In the Futures Market*
On September 1	
Processor buys	Processor sells
5,000 bushels of wheat shipped from country elevator at $4 per bushel (delivered Chicago)	5,000 bushels of December wheat futures at $4.10 per bushel
On October 20	
Processor sells	Processor buys
flour based on wheat equivalent of 5,000 bushels priced at $3.85 per bushel (delivered at Chicago)	5,000 bushels of December wheat futures at $3.95 per bushel
Loss of 15¢ per bushel	Gain of 15¢ per bushel

In the foregoing example it is assumed that the cash or spot price and the futures price maintained a direct correlation, but this is not always the case. Thus, there may be some gain or loss from a hedging operation when the spread between the spot price and the futures price does not remain constant. Hedging can be looked upon as a form of insurance,

---

[2] Charles O. Hardy and Leverett S. Lyon, "The Theory of Hedging," *Journal of Political Economy*, vol. xxi, no. 2, pp. 276–87.

and like insurance it is seldom that it is possible to obtain 100 percent protection against all loss, except at prohibitive cost. As the time between the spot and future declines, the premium or discount on the future declines toward zero (which it reaches when spot = future). On seasonal commodities, this decline in price differential usually begins six to eight months in advance. Under certain circumstances this phenomenon can make "risk-free" speculation possible. For example, when the speculator has access to a large amount of money, at least three times the value of the contract, and when a six- to eight-month future premium exceeds the sum of contract carrying cost and inventory and commission cost, the "speculator" can buy spot and short the future with a precalculated profit. Volume on the exchange should be heavy for this kind of operation.

While there are other variations to the techniques used in hedging, the one simple example is sufficient for our present discussion of forward and speculative buying.

For some commodities, notably wheat and cotton, the advantages of hedging are very real. It may be questioned, however, whether the opportunities afforded by these exchanges are utilized as largely as they might be. For instance, many country elevators which are not using the wheat exchanges could do so with benefit to themselves. It is probably true that too many buyers fail to realize the possibility of hedging against inventory or forward commitments or a falling market. They are quite willing to hedge requirements to protect themselves against forward sales, but they do not seem to appreciate the necessity of such hedges by sales of forward positions against physical inventory or future physical commitments. Large inventory losses can sometimes be avoided if the purchasing executive sees the opportunity and has the courage to take advantage of the organized markets as a means of protection under such circumstances.

The value to the manufacturer of hedging on exchanges other than those of wheat and cotton is a matter of considerable debate. Silk, rubber, and hide exchanges, among others, are used for hedging purposes, but it is difficult to determine to what extent. It is not simply that hedging does not always provide absolute protection; on this point there is no difference of opinion. The issues are of a different character and involve the question of the net advantage to the buyer. It must be recognized that successful hedging on an exchange is a procedure requiring a great deal of skill and experience on the part of the hedger and considerable capital resources. On the one hand this requirement suggests certain limitations imposed upon small manufacturers, and, on the other, it explains why companies using large amounts of a certain commodity will often own seats on the exchange which deals in that commodity. A representative of the firm may then be constantly on the watch for advantageous opportunities for placing, withdrawing, or switching hedges between months and can translate this judgment into action immediately. To be successful, the actual procedure of hedging calls for the close observation of accumulating stocks of the commodity, the consequent widening or narrowing of the spreads between prices quoted on futures contracts, and the resulting opportunities for advance opening and closing of trades. These factors are momentarily shifting on the exchanges. The skill of the hedger is reflected in the ability to recognize and grasp these momentary opportunities.

Even assuming that the buyer is in a position to exercise this judgment and that the company is able to afford the administrative expenses and margin requirements there are other factors to consider. A close student of the commodity exchanges has summarized his conclusions relative to hedging as follows:

Clearly it will not offset and should not offset expected basis gains or losses[3] . . . cash prices normally rise relative to future prices as the crop year advances. They usually rise also with any improvement in the quality or position of supplies and it is through these sources that merchants derive the major part of their trade profit. It follows that if the cash commodity deteriorates in quality or position or is carried from an old crop year to a new in years when the on-coming crop is large, the hedge will not offset the loss sustained. Hedging is designed to protect only against unforeseen major movements in price. After allowance has been made for any expected basis change in the relation of cash to futures, it should serve to offset these large and uncertain price movements. . . . These are price movements which could not be foreseen in advance. They are also movements caused by factors having a common influence on both cash and future prices. After due allowance has been made for those relative changes in the relation of cash to futures which may be expected, there remains a body of minor, unexpected changes in basis against which the future hedge will not protect. Sometimes these unexpected changes result in gains to the hedger and sometimes losses. Sometimes they are brought about by factors affecting the futures price and sometimes by factors affecting the cash. As a rule they are comparatively small

---

[3] "The cotton merchants had repeatedly stated that they were not so much interested in the actual price of cotton as quoted on the exchange or in the spot markets as they were in the 'basis,' i.e., the spread between the price of futures contracts in middling ⅞-inch staple cotton and the price received in the various sales and purchases of many lots of cotton of different types in different parts of the country. The merchant hedged each of his transactions and quoted his price to a mill as so much 'on' or 'off' the price of the futures contract which hedged the actual cotton. This premium or discount, known as the basis, resulted for any specific grade from the variation in price between it and the standard grade of middling ⅞-inch used for futures contracts. The variation was a result of the relative demand or lack of demand for the particular grade in question, the extent of the supply, the location of the cotton, and the extent to which it might be necessary to supply even-running lots of cotton of the precise grade desired by the mill. It was this spread and its variations which meant profit or loss for the merchant, even though he could protect the major part of his investment by hedging" (Deane W. Malott, *Problems in Agricultural Marketing* [New York: McGraw-Hill Book Co.], pp. 93–94).

though occasionally a relative and unexpected change of large proportions occurs. To some extent, these unexpected basis changes are neutralized by counter movements at other times thus minimizing their importance.

It thus appears that hedging may not always be helpful or advantageous to the purchaser for a manufacturing plant. While the advantages to be derived from the existence of definitely organized commodity exchanges are by no means to be minimized, the limitations upon their value to the great majority of purchasing officers are not to be disregarded. Aside from any other limitations, one obstacle to a wider use of the exchanges is the lack of understanding by manufacturers as to when and how to use them. Until this knowledge is gained, perhaps it is just as well that these industrial buyers proceed slowly. Another limitation is the vacuum effect when one of the relatively few large commodity brokers goes bankrupt, pulling some clients along.

Moreover, most brokers have not shown extensive interest in the industrial market. Most brokers probably will admit that they can barely afford to service a straight hedger, because they may have to send out six monthly position statements and four or more margin calls for a single round turn commission while their faithful "traders" will often maintain a substantial cash account and net them several round turn commissions per month with a minimum of bookkeeping.

Communication and perceptual difficulties exist between purchasers and brokers and opportunities to protect profit margins are being bypassed.

According to G. J. Zenz[4] many managers still view futures trading with suspicion and tend to blame past mistakes on the system rather than managerial errors of judgment. The large increases in commodity prices in recent years may well have sensitized a number of managers to the opportunities of future trading, where before there seemed little need to be involved.

Business cycles and price forecasting

Underlying the entire discussion of forward and speculative buying is the problem of the business cycle and of price forecasting. In addition to secular and cyclical changes there are, of course, the ordinary seasonal movements, very pronounced in some fields of business while practically nonexistent in others. These are looked upon more or less as the normal courses of events, and their influence is well recognized.

Some understanding of the nature of the business cycle should be part of the background of every purchaser. But, after all, it is only background, and the immediate task is much more specific. Theorists

---

[4] G. J. Zenz, "Use of Hedging in Purchasing," *Journal of Purchasing*, vol. 8, no. 2 (1972), pp. 47–53.

may argue about the causes of these fluctuations, and statisticians may evolve formulas and indices which will aid in foretelling price trends. The buyer cannot stop here, however, and must place definite orders at named prices. Academicians may analyze, but the buyer must act and is held responsible for the decision.

Sources of information regarding price trends

Upon what is the buyer's judgment as to price trends based? Roughly speaking, there are three general sources of information. One consists of the services of specialized forecasting agencies, such as the Babson Statistical Organization, Standard Statistics Company, Moody's Investors Service, and the Brookmire Economic Service. The second includes a wide variety of governmental and other published data which are generally available. The third comprises the highly unscientific—but nevertheless valuable, if properly weighted—information derived from salesmen and others with whom the buyer comes in daily contact.

Any extended discussion of these sources is out of the question in this volume and, moreover, is readily available elsewhere. The important thing to observe here is that all—even the highly organized and specialized forecasting agencies—are subject to marked limitations with respect to their value and dependability.

The second source of data consists of such material as the *Federal Reserve System Bulletin*, the *Survey of Current Business*, the *Journal of Commerce, Business Week, Barron's*, and the *Wall Street Journal*. Trade magazines are also very helpful in particular industries. They are typified by such publications as *Iron Age*, the *Oil, Paint, and Drug Reporter*, and *Engineering News Record*.

One of the most valuable publications in this connection, although available only to members, is the weekly *Bulletin* of the National Association of Purchasing Management. The Business Survey Committee of the association provides a most useful service in compiling a composite opinion of purchasing agents throughout the country on commodity prices, inventories, employment, and commodity price changes.

The third source of data, although wholly unorganized and quite unscientific, is the information coming to the buyer through the personal relationships with business associates. Advance information as to price changes, for example, can often be obtained through such channels.

Thus, from a great variety of sources the purchaser gathers information concerning business conditions and price trends, sifts and weighs it in the light of past experience and best judgment, and finally acts. If asked to tell why a particular decision was reached the buyer might well have difficulty in explaining. Often the buyer acts upon what appears to be only a "hunch," although, in fact, there is a substantial basis for that action. In the last analysis, it is judgment. The astonishing thing is not that the purchaser makes mistakes but that the buyer is right so much of the time. The record of the best "professionals" appears to be little better.

BIBLIOGRAPHY

ALJIAN, GEORGE W., ed. *Purchasing Handbook.* 3d ed. New York: McGraw-Hill Book Co., 1973.

ARTHUR, HENRY B. *Commodity Futures as a Business Management Tool.* Boston: Division of Research, Harvard Business School, 1971.

BRATT, E. C. *Business Cycles and Forecasting.* 5th ed. Homewood, Ill.: Richard D. Irwin, Inc., 1961.

BUTLER, WILLIAM F. *How Business Economists Forecast.* Englewood Cliffs, N.J.: Prentice-Hall, Inc., 1966.

DAUTEN, CARL ANTON. *Business Cycles and Forecasting.* 3d ed. Cincinnati, Ohio: South-Western Publishing Co., 1968.

WOLFE, HARRY DEANE. *Business Forecasting Methods.* New York: Holt, Rinehart & Winston, Inc., 1966.

CASES FOR CHAPTER 10

EXERCISE IN PRICE FORECASTING*

Select one of the commodities listed below and report on it, giving:

1. Name of commodity selected.
2. Specific grade of commodity on which price is quoted.
3. Price of the commodity as of the present time. (Where the quotation applies only to a particular city, that point should be named; thus, gum turpentine at Savannah, or prime western zinc at St. Louis, or No. 2 hard, winter wheat at Chicago.)
4. Specific source of this quotation. (If the quotation is obtained from a printed source, give the name of the publication, date, and page. In a few cases, where a quotation is not available from a published source, give the name or names of the individuals from whom the quotation was obtained and their connections.)
5. Anticipated price (on comparable basis with that used in paragraph 3 above) as of six months from the present date.

Analysis of the reasons for anticipating the forecasted price will be accepted but not required.

Coconut oil, crude	Print cloth
Cotton linters	Rubber smoked sheets
Flaxseed	Sugar, raw
Hides (cattle)	Tin, pig
Paper, newsprint	Wool, carpet
Paper, waste (No. 1 mixed)	Wool tops

COMMODITY PURCHASING GAME

In this game you will have the chance to try your skill as a commodity purchaser. You will be using information similar in type to that available to Mrs. Martin, the purchasing manager of a well-known chocolate bar corporation.

Because raw material accounts for 50 percent of the cost of producing a chocolate bar, the purchasers in the chocolate bar business have a great deal of responsibility on their shoulders.

Among other functions, Mrs. Martin, at the beginning of each month has to decide how many pounds of cocoa should be purchased during the coming weeks of that month. When doing this, she takes into account the expected need of the production department, the time of the year, the inventory on hand, the cost of short supply, the cost of carrying inventory and, finally, the commodity market trends, more specifically, cocoa.

You will be able in this game to make similar decisions, although the game will be a simplified version of the actual situation. The most important features of this simplification are first, it will not be possible for you to buy cocoa after the first day of the month (you are allowed to purchase cocoa only once a month—on the first day); and, secondly, it will not be possible for you to buy cocoa on the futures market.

Cocoa need

Company sales, and industry sales in general, are very much influenced by seasonal factors. Because the chocolate has a tendency to melt in the warm months of the year, sales usually slow down during the summer months and rebuild very quickly in the fall when the manufacturers start their promotion again. For the last six years, July has been the slowest month for sales and September the biggest.

Because chocolate bars have a limited shelf life, and because it is company policy to supply freshly made chocolate bars to the retailers, it is company practice not to stockpile finished goods. Actually chocolate bars sold in one month have to be produced in that same month.

In the last five years, the company's cocoa need has grown almost constantly. Cocoa requirements have increased 200 percent in this five-year period. Last year's cocoa purchases were 4.76 million pounds. An average of the cocoa requirements for the last three years, broken down per month, is shown in Exhibit 1. The curve shown is only the average of the experience of many years. In any given year, the monthly percentage of total need might vary ± three percentage points from what is given by the curve. For example, January's figure of 10 percent is really the mid-point of a low of a possible low of 7 percent and a possible high of 13 percent.

From past experience, Mrs. Martin knows that the production department uses approximately 60 percent of the total yearly cocoa purchases in the last six months of the year. And, moreover, 55 percent of this last six months' need is used in September and October.

Production scheduling is done on a weekly basis. Mrs. Martin has no precise idea of what the actual total monthly production need for cocoa will be on the first day of that month, other than from her judgment of need level of prior periods and from consideration of the general shape of the need curve shown in Exhibit 1.

Exhibit 1
COCOA NEED PER MONTH BY THE PRODUCTION DEPARTMENT

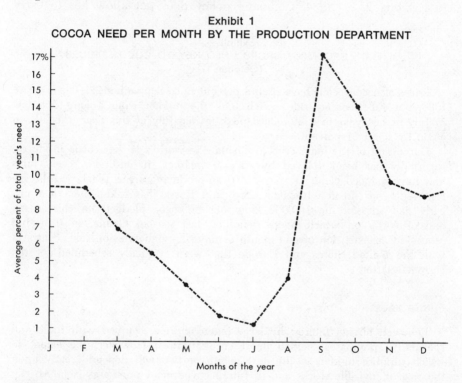

Months of the year

Raw material

Cocoa, the basic raw material in chocolate, has an especially volatile price, and there is no way to hedge completely against the wide price swings. Chocolate comes from cocoa beans, a crop subject to wide production fluctuations with a stable and generally rising demand. Furthermore, it takes 7 years for new cocoa trees to come into production (15 years to reach full production), and drought and disease can sharply reduce supply in a matter of months or even weeks.

Using the company's expected sales and expenses for the year, Mrs. Martin estimates that when she pays 24 cents a pound for cocoa, the contribution per pound purchased to profit is 6.5 cents, and any increase in the price paid for cocoa has a direct reverse effect on the amount of contribution and vice versa. (If she pays 25 cents per pound, then the contribution would be one cent less or 5.5 cents, and so on.)

In order to be as efficient as possible in her predictions of future cocoa prices, Mrs. Martin keeps informed by means of trade journals; she follows the futures market closely and studies the past performance of cocoa prices.

As of October 1, Mrs. Martin has assembled the information given in Exhibits 2, 3 and 4. Company policy does not allow her to carry

Exhibit 2
SIZE OF UPCOMING CROPS HOLD KEY TO COCOA PRICES
(October 1)

Prices of cocoa beans have risen 8 percent since September 22. The increase follows a roller-coaster ride which took the market from a long-time low in July of last year to a 39-month peak in mid-July of this year, then down again by some 21 percent.

Harvesting of the main crop in Ghana, the world's largest cocoa producer, reportedly has been delayed by adverse weather. In addition, recent rains may have reduced yields in several African-producing areas. Black pod disease reportedly has hit the Brazilian crop, and Russia has told Ghana it wants early deliveries of the 100,000 long tons of cocoa pledged for this season and of cocoa on which Accra defaulted last season. Ghana, in turn, has requested an extension of one month or more for deliveries on sales contracts with the United States and Europe that were originally scheduled for the current quarter.

Future boost

Renewed buying interest by large manufacturers, coupled with trade and speculative purchases, helped boost cocoa futures. However, the extent to which supplies tighten in the next month or two will depend greatly upon the size of invisible stocks and of future government purchases from African growers, who have been given an incentive through purchase price increases by the Cocoa Marketing Boards.

The current New York spot prices of Accra (Ghanaian) cocoa beans, at 24 cents per pound compares with quotes of 22.25 cents on September 22, 16.75 cents a year ago, and a peak 28.25 cents on July 14 of the current year. During the ten-week price slump, the open interest in New York cocoa futures shrank from a record 38,054 contracts (30,000 pounds each) on August 10 to fewer than 28,700 contracts; it now aggregates 29,500 contracts.

On the New York Cocoa Exchange, the December future currently is selling at around 22.52 cents, up from 20.22 cents on December 22. The March option is quoted at around 23.11 cents, against 20.92 cents on September

Exhibit 2 *(Continued)*

22. The May future is selling at 23.54 cents. The distant December option is at 24.72 cents.

British bean experts

According to London's Gill and Duffus, Ltd., unfavorable weather held this year's world cocoa bean crop to 1,214,000 long tons, 20 percent below a year earlier. In the face of this dip, relatively attractive prices and rising incomes are expected to push the current year's world cocoa bean grindings (not to be confused with actual consumption) to a record 1,414,000 long tons, 83,000 (6.2 percent) above that of last year.

Allowing 1 percent for loss in weight, output seems to be lagging anticipated grindings by a record 212,000 long tons. This being the case, the October 1 world carry-over of cocoa beans, which is estimated at around 366,000 long tons, is barely a three-month supply. Nine years ago, a similar drop to a three-month supply saw prices averaging 34 cents, far above the current market.

On the eve of the coming season, the trade lacks accurate information on the size of the major new African crops. During recent months, African governments have sold ahead a large portion of the prospective new main crop at prices well above those of a year ago. Ghana's advance sales are placed above 275,000 long tons, some 100,000 more than last year, at prices ranging between 23 cents and 26 cents a pound.

Prior to the recent reports of adverse weather, the trade generally estimated the coming season's world cocoa output at around 1,300,000 long tons, some 60,000 to 86,000 tons above last season. This includes this year's prospective main and mid crops in Ghana of between 435,000 and 475,000 long tons versus 410,000 tons last year, and a record 572,000 long tons two years ago. Guess estimates for Nigeria range between 200,000 and 210,000 tons, against 182,000 last season, and a record 294,000 tons two years ago but may fail to account fully for losses due to the country's tribal unrest. Output from the Ivory Coast is tentatively forecast at between 120,000 and 150,000 tons, up from 112,000 tons last season, and close to its record of 145,000 tons.

Bad weather and pod rot, a fungus that causes seed to rot, have caused the experts to drop their estimates on the Brazilian crop to 130,000 or 135,000 long tons, down from 158,000 tons of last season. Recent reports indicate that the crops in other Latin American countries also will lag last season's levels, which may drop next season's yields for our southern neighbors some 60,000 to 75,000 tons below the 283,000 tons of last year. Adding everything together, the coming season's cocoa bean harvest is likely to range between 1,250,000 and 1,350,000 long tons, which would be a good deal smaller than the current year's anticipated world cocoa bean grindings.

How closely output matches next year's consumption is the key to the cocoa market. Bulls on cocoa believe that prices have not been high enough long enough to discourage the steady rise in usage. They attribute the July to September slump mainly to forecasts of increased crops, tight money, and the large open interest which invited volatile prices.

Exhibit 3
COCOA SPOT PRICE AND
COCOA FUTURES MARKET
(October 1)

Spot Price: 24.0 cents per pound

Futures market

December	22.52
March	23.11
May	23.54
July	23.92
September	24.31
December (next year)	24.72

Exhibit 4
PAST PERFORMANCE OF COCOA ON THE COMMODITY MARKET

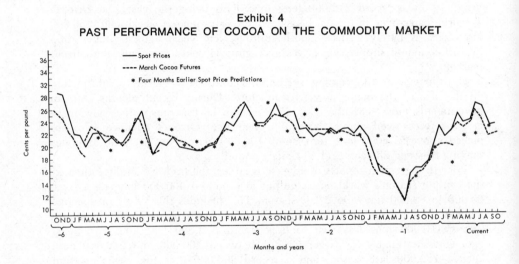

an inventory of more than 1,200,000 pounds of raw cocoa in her monthly ending inventory. The company is short of funds, and the president is not anxious to exceed borrowing limits set by the bank.

Costs involved

In deciding on purchasing alternatives, Mrs. Martin bears in mind several costs which she knows to be fairly accurate. These costs are inventory costs and stock-out costs.

(A) *Inventory costs.* Storage cost for one pound of raw material is 0.2 cents per month. This amount takes into account interest on tied-up capital, insurance against breakage of finished product or deterioration of raw material, and direct handling expense. Mrs. Martin knows that over the period of a season, inventory carrying charges can reasonably be calculated on the basis of inventory on hand at the end of each month.

(*B*) *Stock-out costs.* Mrs. Martin also considers stock-out costs. A stock-out cost occurs whenever the production demand for raw cocoa in a particular month is greater than the available raw cocoa in inventory. For example, if 50,000 pounds of raw cocoa are on hand at the beginning of the month, 50,000 pounds are purchased, and the need during the month totals 110,000 pounds, then a stock-out of 10,000 pounds occurs. The company then has to place rush orders for raw cocoa and, consequently, is forced to pay a three-cent per pound premium.

Mrs. Martin's commission

The president of the company was convinced that incentives for executives were important. Therefore, part of Mrs. Martin's salary was based on her performance as a cocoa purchaser. She received a 5 percent commission on the monthly net contribution to profits.

Net Monthly Contribution = Monthly contribution less
monthly stock-out costs
(or monthly inventory carrying costs)

Closing inventory target

At the end of the game, each group is expected to have a closing inventory of 200,000 pounds of raw cocoa. Every group who fails to reach this 200,000 pound target will be penalized in the following way.

a. For every pound in excess of the aforementioned target:

As in every other month, the company will have to pay an inventory carrying cost, and, moreover, there will be an extra charge of 2.8 cents per pound over the 200,000 pound target.

b. For every pound short in relation to the aforementioned target:

The company will have to pay 3.0 cents per pound and will have to buy sufficient cocoa at the September 1 spot price to bring the inventory level to 200,000 pounds.

How to play the game

In the actual conduct of this game, teams will be used to make the purchasing decisions normally made by Mrs. Martin. On the first day of each month, each team will be required to decide on the quantity of cocoa to be purchased. This decision will be made by the team by whatever means it chooses. Thus, a prediction from a plot of past months' performance might be used by some teams, a pure guess by others. In making the decision, teams will want to consider both the possibilities of future needs and the inventories now on hand as well as their forecast of cocoa spot prices behavior.

After each team has made its purchasing decision for the coming month, the instructor will announce what the month's need has been. Given this information, teams will then be able to calculate, using Exhibit 5, all of the necessary costs and, finally, the "net commission of the purchaser."

The object of the game is to increase as much as possible the purchaser's cumulative commission over 12 months. This means that teams will have to decide whether it would be cheaper in the long run to incur some inventory or stock-out costs, depending on their predictions of the cocoa behavior on the commodity market. At the end of each month, every team's results will be shown on the screen in front of the class and, at the end of the 12th month, the class will discuss each team's method of predicting sales and cocoa prices. Teams will probably find it advantageous to split the work of making sales estimates, calculating costs and profit, and estimating the next period cocoa spot price.

Exhibit 5
RESULT FORM

	Stock on hand at start of month in lbs. = ending inventory of previous month	Purchases in lbs.	Total available for production in lbs. (3 = 1 + 2)	Production requirements in lbs.	Ending inventory in lbs. (5 = 3-4) Cannot be less than 0 or greater than 1,200,000 lbs. Penalty for any excess of $1,000 in commission	Stock-out in lbs. (6 = 4 - 3) if greater than (0)	Stock-out costs (7 = 6 × $.03)	Inventory carrying costs (8 = 5 × $.002)	Contribution per lbs. purchased ($.065 - ($SPOT - $.24))	Total monthly contribution (10 = 2 × 9)	Total monthly costs (11 = 7 + 8)	Net monthly contribution (12 = 10 - 11)	Monthly commission on contribution (13 = 5% × 12)	Cumulative commission 14 = 13 + 14 previous month
	1	2	3	4	5	6	7	8	9	10	11	12	13	14
August	50M	350M	400M	450M	0	50M	$1,500	0	3.5¢	$12,250	$1,500	$10,750	$537	($537)
September	0	1,100M	1,100M	900M	200M	0	0	$400	6.4¢	$70,400	$400	$70,000	$3,500	($4,037)
October	200M													
November														
December														
January														
February														
March														
April														
May														
June														
July														
August														
September														

Exhibit 5 (*Continued*)

If (15) is less than 200,000 lbs. {

15. Stock at end of September
    (15) = (5) of September _____

16. Purchases in quantity _____

17. September contribution per pounds purchased
    ($.065 – ($SPOT – $.24)) _____

18. Final added contribution
    (18) = (16) x (17) _____

19. Extra cost
    (19) = line (16) x $.03 _____

20. Net September contribution
    (20) = (18) – (19) _____

21. September commission
    (21) = (.05 x (20)) – (13) of September _____

22. Total cumulative commission
    (22) = (21) + (14) (August) _____

If (15) is greater than 200,000 lbs. {

23. Extra cost
    (23) = ((15) – 200,000) x $.028 _____

24. Net September contribution
    (24) = (12) of September – (23) _____

25. September commission
    (25) = (.05 x (24)) _____

26. Total cumulative commission
    (26) = 25 + (14) (August) _____

Summary of important points to remember when playing the game

1. Purchases can be made only on the first day of the month.
2. You cannot buy cocoa on the "futures market."
3. It is a company practice to purchase at least all the production requirements of the current month on the first day of that month.
4. It is not possible to carry an inventory of more than 1,200,000 pounds of raw cocoa.
5. At a purchased price of 24 cents per pound, the cocoa will bring a contribution to profit of 6.5 cents. This contribution is directly related to the purchased price. (A one-cent increase in the cost results in a one-cent decrease in the contribution, and vice versa.)
6. There is an inventory carrying cost and a stock-out cost which are

directly deducted from the contribution amount to give the net contribution.

7.   There is a closing inventory target of 200,000 pounds.

Result form used

To make the keeping of results easier for each team, a form has been distributed (see Exhibit 5). The exact steps in using this form are shown on the form itself.

Concluding result form

Because there is a closing inventory target of 200,000 pounds, you will be required to fill the concluding result form (see Exhibit 5) at the end of September. The steps in filling this form are as shown on the form itself.

Example

Each team member should carefully trace the proceedings as outlined in the following example so that he fully understands all of the steps involved in playing and recording the game.

Mrs. Martin has already used the "Result Form" to record the operating results of the two months prior to October. On August 1, Mrs. Martin had to decide how may pounds of cocoa should be purchased. Knowing the spot price on August 1 was 27 cents a pound, she thought, after consulting the trade journals and studying the "futures market," that the prices would go down; therefore, she decided to purchase cocoa to supply the need of the current month only. She then consulted the production need curve and came to the conclusion that the need of that month would be approximately 300,000 pounds. Knowing that she had 50,000 pounds of cocoa in inventory, and wanting to keep a safe margin, she purchased 350,000 pounds of cocoa at the price of 27 cents per pound. She then entered the following figures on the "Result Form."

Column (1)   = 50,000 pounds (from column (5) previous month)
Column (2)   = 350,000 pounds
Column (3)   = 400,000 pounds
Column (9)   = $.035 = $.065 − ($.27 − $.24)
Column (10) = $12,250

At the end of the month of August Mrs. Martin received from the production department the exact figure of the month's requirements, 450,000 pounds. Since there were only 400,000 pounds of cocoa in inventory, the company had had to make a last minute order to another user of cocoa at a premium of $.03/lb. With this information, Mrs. Martin could now calculate her net commission according to the company's norms. She entered the following figures on the "Result Form."

Column (4)   =   450,000 pounds
Column (5)   =   0   pounds
Column (6)   =   50,000 pounds
Column (7)   = $ 1,500
Column (8)   = $ 0
Column (11) = $ 1,500
Column (12) = $10,750
Column (13) = $ 537
Column (14) = $ 537

On September 1, she received the latest information on the cocoa market (spot price, futures market, and trade news), and she went through the same process to purchase the raw cocoa for the month of September.

Start of the game

The game proper starts on October 1. At the beginning of the game there are 200,000 pounds of cocoa on hand. It is now up to each team at this time to decide on the coming year's purchases and, thus, start playing the game. We will assume that the cumulative commission of $4,037 to the end of September has been paid to Mrs. Martin and that each team will start again from zero. Please use Exhibit 6 as the sample for your group's reporting form which should be handed in to the instructor each period.

Exhibit 6
REPORT FORM

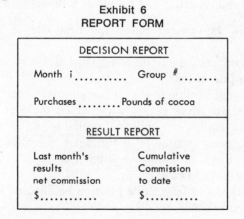

DECISION REPORT

Month i .... Group # ....

Purchases .... Pounds of cocoa

RESULT REPORT

Last month's results net commission	Cumulative Commission to date
$	$ ....

References

From the *Guide to Commodity Price Forecasting*[1] with permission from the Commodity Research Bureau, Inc.

JILER, MILTON W.   "Understanding the Commodity Futures Markets"; pp. 5–22.

SHISHKO, I.   "How to Forecast Cocoa Price," pp. 98–108.

───────
[1] M. Jiler, ed., *Guide to Commodity Price Forecasting* (New York: Commodity Research Bureau, Inc., 1967).

11 PROCUREMENT OF MAJOR EQUIPMENT

We have been concerned thus far primarily with the procurement of materials, component parts, and supplies. We turn now to the purchase of major equipment.

In most companies it is clear-cut that decisions involving the purchase of major equipment are closely controlled at the top executive level. It is by no means so clear-cut that most companies have a well-thought-out equipment policy which goes beyond a consideration of comparative annual operating costs and wear write-offs. Many interrelated problems should be considered if a sound equipment policy is to be formulated. Some of these problems are stated briefly as follows:

1. Will the new equipment make the best use of available capital funds?
2. Will a desired return on invested capital be received if the new equipment is purchased?
3. Is the equipment flexible in that it has alternate uses?
4. Are technical advances being made which make it likely that more advantageous equipment will be available at an early date?
5. Will the necessary volume be maintained to realize fully the operating cost advantages of the new equipment?
6. What is the effect of taxes?
7. Will the company's competitive position be affected if the new equipment is not purchased?

These problems raise questions which often are not answered easily and, in fact, may raise doubts about the feasibility of having a stated equipment policy rather than considering each new equipment purchase separately.

DEFINITION OF MAJOR EQUIPMENT

Throughout this discussion, the term "equipment" will be applied broadly to those items the cost of which is more properly chargeable to a capital account than to expense. They are essential "durable" or "capital" goods, as contrasted either with supplies or with those raw materials or fabricated parts which are purchased for direct incorporation into the product that the company is manufacturing for sale. We shall exclude, however, building and similar construction, which, although both "durable" and "capital," falls for quite obvious reasons into a class by itself. We shall include all classes of power machinery (such as electrical generators, boilers, and internal combustion and steam engines), construction machinery (such as concrete mixers, dredges, steam shovels, and derricks) transportation equipment (such as trucks and elevators), and industrial machinery, both general (such as machine tools, blowers, and pumps) and special (such as looms, various types of shoe repair machinery, and airplane engines). Any complete list of such equipment will be extremely long and varied; this fact must constantly be borne in mind since, although the questions relating to any particular piece of equipment will be common to all types of capital goods, the degree to which any broad conclusion will apply must vary with each individual case.

A useful classification of equipment is the division into multipurpose and single purpose. Multipurpose equipment may have a variety of uses, may be used in several or many industries, tends to have longer technological life, and may have considerable salvage value. Fork lift trucks, certain classes of computers, and standard lathes are typical examples.

Single purpose equipment is designed to do one or several operations well, normally, substantially better than a multipurpose piece of equipment could. On the other hand, its specificity limits its potential use, and its usefulness is closely tied to the need for the operations it performs. Such special equipment is normally limited to one industry and may even be limited to one customer. The purchaser's specifications are important, requiring extensive consultation between the technical personnel of both buyer and supplier. The salvage value of special equipment may be low, and chances are that the need for the tasks disappears before the equipment is physically worn out. Minor or accessory equipment is normally used in an auxiliary capacity and tends to be of much lower dollar value. Its cost may not even be capitalized, and much of it tends to be standardized. Small pumps and motors are typical examples.

The special problems involved in the purchase of equipment, as contrasted with raw materials and supplies, grow out of the character of the product and the purpose for which it is bought. Equipment represents "capital goods." It does not itself enter into the product being manufactured, as does the raw material. The engineer who recommends the acquisition of a piece of equipment may do so for a variety of reasons. The engineer may believe that manufacturing efficiency will be improved because of greater speed of output or less variation in the product or greater ease and simplicity of operation, lower maintenance cost, greater versatility of use, lower labor cost, greater dependability, lower power cost, longer life resulting from less depreciation and/or obsolescence. The above reasons tend to be for the sake of efficiency or economy. Other reasons for having equipment may be that they are a necessity by law or a form of insurance. For example, safety equipment as specified by OSHA, such as roll-proof cabs on skidders, and firefighting equipment, may do little to increase operating efficiency. Antipollution equipment may well decrease operating efficiency and increase costs but is an environmental necessity. Emergency stand-by equipment such as an emergency power plant, an idle lathe in a veneer plant, and an extra crusher at a mine are only purchased to protect against the eventuality that the prime equipment or source may fail. An item of equipment seldom stands by itself—it is operated in conjunction with people and other machines as part of a system; hence, layout must be considered as well as the people and other types of equipment already in use. It is probable that the engineer's conclusions are based on a systems approach.

In the first instance, decisions as to either the replacement of equipment or the purchase of new, untried equipment are normally engineering decisions, based on the ascertainment of a need that usually originates in the engineering or production department, not in the procurement department. They are, moreover, based presumably on a careful analysis of past costs and in most cases on estimates of future ones.

Special problems of equipment buying

Major equipment procurement raises special problems. Some of the more important of these follow.

1. The buying of equipment usually requires that substantial amounts of money be expended for a single purchase. Sometimes the sum is so large as even to call for a special form of financing, such as a bond issue or payment on the installment plan. Occasionally, leasing may be resorted to, one reason among several being the inability of the would-be user to raise the necessary funds for outright purchase. It is true, of course, that some equipment items are comparatively inexpensive and that the financing of such purchases requires only very incidental outlays, as compared with the necessary expenditure for raw materials or fuel. Even in such instances, however, the necessary funds are tied up for much longer periods of time, and the capital turnover is considerably slower in the case of equipment purchase.

2. Because of its comparatively long life and the investment involved, equipment items, particularly those of a major character, are likely to be bought less frequently than other types of industrial purchases.

3. The final cost of equipment is more difficult to determine with exactness than, for example, the final cost of raw materials. The latter figure can be ascertained with reasonable definiteness. The initial cost of equipment, however, is but part of the total cost, which involves a whole series of estimates, such as the effects of idle time, of obsolescence, of maintenance and repair, of displaced labor, and even of direct operation factors. Some of these items may never be known exactly, even after experience with the particular piece of equipment in question. Moreover, many of the costs, such as insurance, interest, and obsolescence, continue even when the equipment is not in actual use. The income to be derived is also problematical, and, thus, even when it is possible to compute approximate costs, it is often difficult to determine how soon they will be met. These comments are particularly applicable to so-called nonproductive equipment, such as cranes and hoists.

4. Equipment purchases are often less affected by current price trends than, for instance, are raw materials. The demand for industrial equipment more than the demand for any other type of industrial goods is a derived demand. Pricewise, the best time at which to buy is, therefore, particularly hard to determine. "Only when the need and the justification of the equipment has been established is there a possibility that its actual purchase may be delayed or hastened by price considerations." Since equipment is not commonly bought until needed, it is seldom bought during periods of business recession, although prices for equipment normally are low at such times and many good arguments can be advanced for buying then. Aside from absence of immediate need, manufacturers in periods of slack business tend to watch their assets carefully. Also, it is true that labor may be cheaper during recessions, and there is less incentive to substitute machinery for labor. The reverse conditions prevail in times of prosperity. The purchase of equipment following the close of World War II and the inflationary period of the late 1960s and early 1970s are excellent examples.

5. The purchase of equipment frequently involves problems concerning the wisest method of disposition of the displaced item, a consideration which almost never arises in connection with materials or supplies.

6. A decision to purchase equipment, especially major items, is therefore likely to require a careful consideration of many factors involving broad management policy. The decision, once made, may well commit the company in a rather definite fashion to a series of other decisions of a comparatively permanent nature, such as the type of product to be manufactured, the method of its production, and the cost of operation. Put in other words, it is much easier "to get in and out" of a situation involving the purchase of raw materials than one involving the purchase of major equipment. Furthermore, the company's labor policies may be affected. Questions of financial policy, such as bond issues and alternative uses for available funds, may be involved. In short, equipment

questions are likely to be procurement decisions of prime importance to management.

We turn now to a brief conideration of some of the specific problems involved in equipment procurement decisions. There are many of them, inevitably, but for purposes of our present discussion, we shall consider only the following:

1. The general principles which should control the selection of equipment.
2. The cost factors immediately applicable.
3. The problem of engineering service.
4. The timing of the purchase.
5. The selection of the source.
6. Some legal questions.
7. The financing of the purchase.
8. The disposition of obsolete or replaced equipment.
9. The purchase of used equipment.
10. Leasing.

General principles which should control the selection of equipment

The selection of major equipment is clearly based upon due consideration of a wide range of factors, so coordinated that the net result is efficient manufacture of the desired product at the lowest net cost per unit. To achieve this, it is necessary to analyze not only the price of the particular equipment in question but also such elements as plant layout, kind of power used, types of machines used for other operations, and the like. In short, the proposed installation must be looked upon as an integral part of an established production process; and its coordination with the existing plant facilities must be obtained, even though extensive changes may be required to effect economical production.

Decisions as to equipment purchases involve in part engineering and production considerations and in part factors largely outside the scope of these functions. From the former standpoint, there are six commonly recognized reasons for purchase: economy in operation, increased productivity, better quality, dependability in use, savings in time or labor costs, and durability. To these safety, pollution, and emergency protection should be added.

Beyond these engineering questions are those which only the marketing department, purchasing department, financial department, or general management itself can answer. Are style changes or other modifications in the present product essential or even desirable? Is the market static, contracting, or expanding? Does the company have the funds with which to buy the machine which theoretically is most desirable, or is it necessary, for financial reasons, to be satisfied with something that is perhaps less efficient but of a lower initial cost? What should be done in a case in which the particular equipment most desirable from an engineering standpoint is obtainable only from a manufacturer who is not thoroughly trustworthy or perhaps is on the verge of bankruptcy? Such questions are quite as important in the final decision as are the more purely engineering ones, and they are not questions which the engineer is qualified to answer. This merely emphasizes once more the many-sided nature of the problem and the many types of judgment required in reaching a sound solution of it.

Importance of cost factors

Once the need for new equipment has been determined, one of the first questions to be considered is that of the cost. To arrive at the right answer to cost is likely to be difficult, calling for a careful balancing of several factors. For example, among the facts called for are the following: Is the equipment intended for replacement only or to provide additional capacity? What is the installed cost of the equipment? Will its installation create problems of plant layout? What will be the maintenance and repair cost? Are accessories required, and, if so, what will their cost be? What will be the operating cost, including power and labor? What is the number of machine-hours the equipment will be used? Can the user make the machine in his own plant, or must it be bought outside? At what rate is the machine to be depreciated? What financing costs are involved? If, as is usually the case, the equipment is for production, what is the present cost of producing the product for which it is intended as compared with obtaining the item from an outside supplier and as compared with the cost of producing the unit with the new equipment?

Since the middle 1950s, there has been a substantial growth in the use of quantitative methods in the analysis of capital investment and capital equipment purchases. Research in mathematics and the increasing availability of computers have provided tools for a depth of economic analysis not feasible in the past. The increased sophistication of business managers in using such concepts as "discounted cash flow," "return on investment," and "present value" in making capital equipment and investment decisions has probably resulted in greater understanding and improved decisions.[1]

Life cycle costing

The Department of Defense has strongly encouraged the use of Life Cycle Costing (LCC) as a decision approach to capital investments.

---

[1] For an explanation of these concepts, see George Willard Terborgh, *Business Investment Management* (Washington, D.C.: Machinery and Allied Products Institute, 1967).

ilosophy behind LCC is relatively simple. The total cost of a f equipment goes well beyond the purchase price or even its l cost. What is really of interest is the total cost of performing the intended function over the life time of the task or the piece of equipment. Thus, an initial low purchase price may mask a higher operating cost, perhaps occasioned by higher maintenance and downtime costs, more skilled labor, greater material waste, more energy use, or higher waste processing changes. Since the low bid would favor a low initial machine cost an unfair advantage may accrue to the supplier with possibly the highest life cycle cost equipment.

The Logistics Management Institute defines LCC as "the total cost of a system during its operational life."[2] It is the inclusion of every conceivable cost pertaining to the decision that makes the concept easier to grasp theoretically than practice in real life. Since many of the costs are future ones possibly even 10 to 15 years hence of a highly uncertain nature, criticisms of the exactness of LCC are well founded. Fortunately, computer programs are available varying from simple accounting programs, which compute eight of the LCC from projected life cycles, to Monte Carlo simulation of the equipment from conception to disposal. The computer allows for testing of sensitivity, and inputs can be readily changed when necessary. The normal emphasis, particularly in governmental acquisition, on the low bid finds, therefore, a serious and preferable alternative in LCC. The experience with LCC has shown in a surprising number of instances that the initial purchase price of equipment may be a relatively low percentage of LCC. For example, computers, if purchased, seldom run over 50 percent, and most industrial equipment falls into the 20-percent–60-percent range.

There are eight steps in LCC formulation. In practice, one may combine some of the following eight steps:[3]

1. Establish the operating profile.
2. Establish the utilization factors.
3. Identify all cost elements.
4. Determine the critical cost parameters.
5. Calculate all costs at current prices.
6. Escalate current labor and material costs.
7. Discount all costs to base period.
8. Sum up all discounted and undiscounted costs.

An interesting example provided by Kaufman includes two automatic palletizers X and Y for which the critical costs are shown in Table 1.[4]

The result of this study was that palletizer X with a substantially

[2] *Logistics Management*, Institute Report, 4C-5, April 1965.

[3] R. J. Kaufman, "Life Cycle Costing: Decision Making Tool for Capital Equipment Acquisitions," *Journal of Purchasing*, vol. 5, no. 3, (August 1969).

[4] Ibid., p. 25.

Table 1
CRITICAL COST PARAMETERS

	Palletizer X			Palletizer Y		
Cost parameter	Value	CL %	Srce	Value	CL %	Srce
Acquisition cost.	$200,000	100	mfgr	$170,000	100	mfgr
Equipment life	12 years	100	mfgr	12 years	100	mfgr
Initial engineering.	$3,000	100	mfgr	$2,000	100	mfgr
Installation cost	$3,000	100	mfgr	$4,000	100	mfgr
Manning	⅓ man	100	mfgr	½ man	100	mfgr
MTBF	500 hrs	80	ee	100 hrs	90	ee
MTTR	.5 hrs	80	ee	2.0 hrs	90	ee
PM cycle	16 hrs	100	mfgr	16 hrs	100	mfgr
PM downtime	.5 hrs	100	ee	.84 hrs	70	ee
Time between overhauls	2 years	100	mfgr	2 years	100	mfgr
Cost to overhaul	$1,000	80	ee	$3,000	100	ee
Parts cost per year	1%, NOHY	60	ee	2%, NOHY	70	ee
(Percent of acquisition cost)	2%, OHY	60	ee	2.5%, OHY	80	ee
Input power	3.0 kw	90	mfgr	5.0 kw	100	mfgr

CL   = Confidence level
Srce   = Source of information
NOHY = Nonoverhaul year
OHY   = Overhaul year
ee   = Engineering estimate
mfgr   = Manufacturer
kw   = Kilowatt
MTTR = Mean time to repair
MTBF = Mean time between failure
PM   = Preventive maintenance

higher initial purchase cost of $200,000 (versus Y at $170,000) showed a lower LCC of $289,000 versus $306,000 for Y. Since this company intended to purchase six machines the magnitude of the savings, beyond the normal return on investment of the equipment, amounted to about $100,000.

Regardless of how simple or how complicated the costing approaches to the problem may be, it must never be overlooked that human judgment must always be called upon for the final answer. In the last analysis, the problem is one in financial values and in human relations. The answers, therefore, are not to be found on the slide rule, in the mathematician's brain, or in the engineer's office, although all three may well provide essential data. But they provide only the raw data, with a clue to the solution. Whether to buy or not to buy is a matter of business judgment.

Problem of engineering service

Most sellers of major equipment maintain an intimate and continuing interest in their equipment after it is sold and installed. Two major questions are involved in providing engineering service: why the service is given and accepted, and what the cost of such service is.

Technical sales service is provided by a vendor to a potential or actual purchaser of equipment, to determine the designs and specifications of the equipment believed best suited to the particular requirements of the buyer and also to ensure that, once bought, the equipment functions properly. It is nearly always related to the "individualized buying problem of particular users." Some sellers feel that the equipment they sell is so complicated or requires such fine adjustment that none but their own experts can either install the machines or service them after installation. The vendor may feel further that the buyer's operatives need to be specially trained, perhaps for weeks or months, before they can be trusted to handle the equipment themselves. Occasionally, equipment is sold which carries with it a production guarantee, an additional reason for supervising both the installation and the operation of the equipment. Even after this initial period, the seller may provide for regular inspection to ensure the proper operation of the machine.

In many instances, services of these various types are thoroughly warranted; and it is to the best interests of buyer and seller alike that they be offered by the vendor and utilized by the purchaser. Smaller companies may well be most in need of such assistance because they are unable to employ their own consulting engineers. Furthermore, regardless of the size of the company making the purchase, the greater the amount either of presale or postsale service rendered by the seller, the greater the responsibility of the latter for proper and satisfactory performance.

There is, however, another side to this question of sales service. For one thing, the prospective buyer may ask for and receive a great deal of presale service and advice without real intention of buying or knowing full well that the firm providing the service will under no circumstances receive an order. Not only is such a procedure unethical, but the buyer who pursues it will sooner or later find the organization's reputation for fair dealing has seriously suffered.

Yet abuses are by no means confined to the buyers. It is well known that salesmen often solicit requests for export consulting service from buyers without any real inquiry as to whether or not a sale is likely to materialize. Furthermore, the theory that such services are mutually advantageous is not always substantiated by the facts. The seller's claims as to the necessity of vendor-supervised installation and instruction are not always warranted.

The problem of engineering service is really twofold, both phases, however, involving cost. The first phase relates to the method followed by the seller in charging for presale service. Such service is clearly a matter of sales promotion, and, when no subsequent sale results or when the profit on the sale is insufficient to cover fully the cost of the service, some other means of caring for it must be found. If the total costs of all such service are borne only by the firms which actually do buy, the price paid will appear unduly high; yet this method may prove the only feasible way of handling the charge. The problem is complicated further when a firm produces two lines of product, one requiring service and the other not. If presale service cost is charged into general sales promotion overhead, clearly the one product is likely to be overpriced and the other underpriced; this situation places the seller in an awkward competitive position. One suggestion that has been made for meeting this problem is that a specific charge, either a flat fee or one computed on the basis of actual cost, be made for presale engineering service, the recipient of the service paying this charge irrespective of whether or not a purchase is made subsequently.

The second phase of the problem relates to postsale engineering service. The prime abuse of postsale services arises from those firms which insist upon furnishing it and upon charging for it, whether or not the buyer feels a need for it. Such charges naturally become a part of the price paid for the equipment, irrespective of whether they are included in a single quotation or are billed to the purchaser separately. When the service is really needed, no objection to such charges can be raised by the buyer, provided, of course, that they are fair. The purchaser must see to it, however, that the service actually is necessary and that the charges are legitimate and reasonable. Such considerations are matters of price negotiation and should be settled before the purchase contract is signed.

Timing of the purchase

The determination of the proper time at which to make a purchase of equipment is significant although its importance varies both with the amount of money involved and with the character of the item. One requiring a large expenditure naturally receives more attention than one necessitating only a small sum; the purchase of a piece of "productive" equipment such as a turret lathe is likely to be more carefully considered than the purchase of a "nonproductive" item such as a desk, although both are, properly speaking, "equipment."

Productive equipment, particularly of an expensive nature, is usually bought on a basis of known requirements. The equipment is bought only when, after an analysis of all cost and other factors, it appears probable that the purchase will "pay for itself" within a definite period of time. The exact length of this period naturally varies widely both with company policy and with the item in question. It may range from six months to several years or more. Obviously, in spite of all the formulas, this evidence is often somewhat difficult to produce, since it calls for judgment as to future sales and prices as well as cost figures.

For one thing, the need for expansion is normally felt during prosperous periods. Demand may be artificial, in the sense that it is caused by contracting ahead or by purchasing in advance of immediate requirements or through fear of inability to obtain supplies when needed, and is greatest at such a time. Pressure from the sales force through complaints that orders are not filled promptly, from the production department, which is compelled to work overtime, and from stockholders, who demand that the company get its share of the business—all these lead to the expansion. During periods of recession, this need is not apparent. Furthermore, the funds available during the prosperous periods are not available in a period of recession, even if the managers were willing to invest in equipment at such a time. True, during prosperous times a concern might set aside money to be used for plant improvements or expansion in a time of recession. Actually, this is seldom done partly because it is difficult to invest money in such a way that the company will receive a satisfactory profit and still be able to liquidate the investment without being forced to take an inordinate loss. Expansion thus occurs during times that are already prosperous and thus still further promotes overcapacity and overproduction, even though from some points of view the reasons do not appear entirely logical.

Selection of the source

Selection of the proper source requires careful consideration in any purchase of major equipment. In the purchase of raw materials and supplies, quick delivery and the availability of a continuous supply are important reasons for choosing a particular supplier. These characteristics are not so important in equipment purchases. The reliability of the seller and a reasonable price are, of course, important, regardless of what is being bought. But, as contrasted with raw materials, what may be called "cooperation" in selecting the right type of equipment, proper installation, common interests in efficient operation—in short, a long-continuing interest in the product after it is sold—becomes very important. So, too, does the availability of repair parts and of repair services throughout the entire life of the machine. Satisfactory past relationships with the equipment supplier weigh heavily in the placing of future orders.

During the 1960s and early 1970s there was a substantial increase in foreign-made capital equipment sold in North America. Whether this was caused primarily by availability, price, technology, or other reasons is not entirely clear. The difficulties of obtaining service from nondomestic manufacturers may be considerable even for such simple reasons as poor translations of service manuals.

Normally, the interest of operations, engineering, or technical personnel in capital equipment is such that their source preference is a normal rather than unusual problem with which the purchaser must cope.

Manufacture of a needed item may at times be quite possible, particularly of comparatively simple standardized equipment, such as a coal crusher. Furthermore, it may be the most economical method of procedure, even though a payment for the use of some patented feature is involved. The basic questions involved in "make or buy" have been covered in another chapter and need not be reviewed here, even though the manufacture of a piece of equipment does call for some modification in the application of the generalizations there laid down.

Some legal questions

Attention should also be directed to the legal questions that arise in connection with equipment buying, although no attempt will be made to discuss them here. The danger of liability for patent infringement constitutes one such problem. The extent of liability for accidents to employees is another. Again, the equipment sales contracts and purchase agreements are often long and involved, offering many opportunities for legal controversies. Various forms of insurance coverage are used and are often subject to varying interpretations. Any purchased machine must comply fully with the safety regulations of the state in which it is to be operated, and these safety regulations vary greatly in the different states.

As of recently the Federal Government OSHA requirements have to be followed. The question of consequential damages is a particularly touchy one. Should the seller of a key piece of equipment be responsible for the loss of sales and contribution when the machine fails because of a design or fabrication error? Such losses may be huge for the buyer. In one company gross revenue of $1 million per day was lost for six months because of the failure of a new piece of equipment costing $800,000! These and many other situations exist which call for careful scrutiny and interpretation by qualified legal counsel. The importance of this phase of equipment buying should not be overlooked.

Financing of the purchase

Before any commitment to buy a major item is authorized, careful thought must be given not only to the desirability of the purchase but also to the means by which payment is to be provided. Regardless of what else may be said for the equipment, unless it can be paid for, obviously no action can be taken.

When the financial budget is set up, it is customary to make provision for two types of capital expenditure. The first type covers probable expenditures which, although properly chargeable to some capital account, are still too small to be brought directly to the attention of the finance committee or controller. Customarily, some limit is fixed, as, for example, $500 or $1,000.

The second type includes expenditures for larger amounts. These are also provided for in the budget, because large sums are involved and because the practice may induce those responsible for such purchases to plan their equipment needs well in advance. The inclusion in the budget, however, constitutes neither an authorization to spend that amount of money nor an approval of any specific equipment acquisition. This authorization must be obtained subsequently from the appropriate executives concerned, and their specific approval is given only after they have examined carefully a preliminary, although detailed, analysis of the project. To secure such authorization, a formal appropriation request is called for, giving a detailed description of what is to be bought, estimates of the costs involved, the savings likely to result, the causes which have created the need, the effect of the purchase upon the organization as a whole, and whatever other information those initiating the request feel is pertinent or the financial authorities may request. In the light of these facts, together with the data regarding other financial requirements of the company and its financial position, a decision is made as to the wisdom of authorizing the particular expenditure under consideration.

In years past, no major capital expenditure was possible unless the company either had the necessary funds on hand or could secure them through what may be termed the "orthodox channels." More recently, however, the sellers of equipment have made possible purchase on a deferred payment plan, and today there are very few types of standardized machinery that cannot be secured on this basis. The wisdom of buying equipment on such a plan is, of course, a matter which each individual company must decide for itself and then only with reference to the particular purchase in question. Two general comments only will be made at this point.

In the first place, it is undoubtedly true that such financial arrangements have made it possible for some manufacturers to secure needed equipment more promptly than they otherwise could. Improvements in both design and type are continually being made in almost all kinds of machinery and other equipment. If a manufacturer is to continue to compete effectively, one means of keeping costs down is to reduce, as far as possible, the disadvantages of operating with obsolete equipment. But, although fully cognizant of the need for new machinery, a manufacturer may not be able to raise enough cash to pay for the purchase. Deferred payment plans or leasing may make it possible to meet this problem.

In the second place, before placing an order on a deferred payment basis, the purchaser must be doubly sure that the purchase is really wise. Installment selling is essentially a device by which sellers develop a market much more intensively than they could otherwise—often, it should be added, to the disadvantage of buyer and seller alike. From the buyer's angle, the anticipated savings may never develop, or at least are materially less hoped for. Again, the buyer may be tempted not only to replace existing equipment but, either through additional machines or through the acquisition of equipment of greater capacity, to overexpand. The financing charge may be excessive and, in any event, must always be considered in arriving at the total cost. Finally, the danger that the new equipment may become obsolete before it is paid for will be greater in the case of installment purchases, because of the longer time over which payment is made. From the seller's standpoint, we need only point out that if such sales are made unwisely, it is quite possible that the market may be overdeveloped, with all the attendant problems.

An interesting variation of the deferred payment plan has developed in recent years, particularly in some industries, based on the theory that the payments to the seller are dependent upon and proportional to the anticipated savings.

Leasing, a popular method of financing equipment, is described at the end of this chapter.

Disposition of obsolete or replaced equipment

This problem takes various forms—all resolving themselves into a decision as to the most economical and profitable method of disposition. One procedure is to trade in the old machine on the new, the vendor making an allowance and assuming the burden of disposing of it as best he can. A second procedure is to sell the old equipment to a used equipment dealer directly. A third method is to find a direct buyer. A fourth method is to sell the old machine as scrap. A fifth method is to destroy the machine to assure no one else will have access to it.

The responsibility for disposing of the displaced machines commonly rests on the purchaser. This responsibility is clear when dealing directly with prospective users or with used equipment dealers. Trade-in allowances raise a somewhat different problem, in that all such allowances are likely to be price concessions on the new equipment instead of being based solely upon the actual market value of the machine traded in. The responsibility for excessive allowances of this nature rests essentially on the seller and not on the buyer. The latter may go too far in getting price concessions. The chief abuse of the trade-in practice has been committed not by buyers but by sellers.

The purchase of used equipment rather than new often raises some interesting issues. In general, the same rules of evaluation apply as in the case of new equipment. One important difference, however, may be that, ordinarily, manufacturers' services and guarantees do not apply to such purchases. The value of these intangibles is difficult to determine.

Many buyers would say that they are more important with used equipment than with new and that their value may be greater than any differential in price. The matter, however, is one of individual judgment as applied to each particular purchase.

Procurement of major equipment—used and leased

In our discussion of equipment purchases thus far, it has been largely assumed that the buyer was acquiring new equipment. An alternative to such a procedure is the purchase of used equipment.

Why used equipment comes on the market

Used equipment comes onto the market through a variety of reasons. One obvious result of the modernization of a plant is the disposition of the displaced equipment. It can, of course, as a last resort, be demolished and sold as scrap. It may be possible, however, to utilize at least some of the machinery in some other department or plant of the company. But if this is not feasible, then the equipment may be sold at a price yielding a return well above the scrap value.[5] In addition to this somewhat general reason, there are other explanations as to the appearance of used equipment on the market. Some of these may be listed as follows:

1. Loss of contracts.
2. Change in process or in line of manufacturing.
3. Obsolescence in a specific use.
4. Insufficient productivity to meet the needs of the original owner.
5. Trade-in on a new machine.
6. Inadequacy to meet new requirements.
7. Discontinuance of entire manufacturing operations because of bankruptcy, insolvency, death of owner, etc.

Sales contract terms

Having used equipment either to sell or to buy, a manufacturer has at least two problems. The first relates to the terms of contract. Here there are three choices: (1) The equipment may be disposed of "as is," and perhaps "where is." A sales "as is" means that the contract carries essentially "no warranty, guarantee, or representation of any kind, expressed or implied, as to the condition of the item offered for sale." "Where is," of course, is self-explanatory. (2) The equipment may be

---

[5] The sale of used equipment to a potential competitor at a price well below that paid for new machines, particularly if done in large blocks, thereby making it possible for a potential competitor to start up in business with a low capital investment, is something that bothers many businessmen.

sold with certain specific guarantees, preferably expressed in writing. This practice is found more generally among used equipment dealers, though they sometimes may offer equipment "as is." (3) Finally, the equipment may be sold "guaranteed and rebuilt." The desirable interpretation placed on this is that the equipment has been rebuilt or is in condition equivalent to that of a rebuilt machine and is invoiced as such; that it has been tested; and that it carries a binding guarantee of satisfactory performance for not less than 30 days from the date of shipment.

Organization of used equipment market

The next query relates to the channels through which the equipment is bought and sold. Here, too, there are various alternatives. Briefly, they are:

1. Trade-in as partial payment on new equipment.
2. Direct sale to a user.
3. Sale through a broker or liquidating agent.
4. Sale at auction.
5. Sale to a dealer in used equipment.

Trade-in as partial payment on new equipment. Generally speaking, manufacturers of equipment are unwilling to accept used equipment as part payment on new. Under certain circumstances, however, in the interest of customer goodwill, they may be willing to assist a prospective buyer of new equipment to locate a buyer for the used. This is most likely to be the case (1) when the item to be sold is noncompetitive with anything manufactured by the seller or (2) when the buyer is a regular customer of the particular equipment manufacturer. When the seller is unable to make delivery of a new item in time to meet the buyer's requirements, he may even go so far as not only to suggest a market for the equipment to be replaced but to indicate where it may be possible to locate a piece of used equipment of the type sought.

It must be recognized, however, that, except in the obvious case of direct sale to user, the utilization of one of these channels does not necessarily preclude the use of another. Thus, a used machine may be sold by the owner to a dealer, who in turn sells to another user. Or a liquidating agent may sell either to a dealer or to a user and may do so either directly or through an auction. Although direct purchase from the seller is an important method of acquisition, in the brief description which follows, major attention will be devoted to the dealer, probably the most important single agency in the market.

Direct sale to user. Direct sale through the company's own organization is often a profitable method of disposal. Through advertising in trade journals or some other media, the attention of potential buyers may be attracted to the offer, and negotiation initiated either by mail or by direct visitation. Used equipment is frequently disposed of in this manner. Since this procedure eliminates the use of an intermediary, it suggests a saving of the latter's profit. Finding a buyer, moreover, often does not appear to be a serious problem, particularly since the potential buyers are likely to be somewhat limited in number and the seller ordinarily has a sales organization already set up. However, experience has shown that in many cases the "saving of the middleman's profit" is illusory and that direct sale actually is time-consuming, troublesome, and ineffective so far as securing as high a return as can be secured through other methods is concerned. This is particularly true when, for instance, an entire plant is being closed down and the equipment sold.

Sale through broker.   Brokers, in theory at least, do not take title to the equipment in which they are interested but seek only to bring buyers and sellers together. In fact, however, they may act in the capacity both of brokers and of dealers, though obviously not for the same equipment. Used equipment brokers are more important in some industries than in others. Comparatively few of them, for instance, specialize in general machine tools, largely because of the multiplicity of regular dealers. Brokers frequently employ personal selling and advertising to liquidate equipment and commonly realize a commission of 10 to 15 percent on the gross sale.

Sale at auction.   Auction firms vary in type and character. Some are highly reputable. Others are not always so regarded. One type of auction firm is the trader who buys stock and auctions it off. This type of firm frequently has representatives both at its own sales and at other auctions to encourage bidding and to acquire good machines that, for one reason or another, do not bring high prices on the day of the initial auction. While the auction commission is less than that for a broker, the price realized on the merchandise frequently is lower, inasmuch as it is impossible to bring together in a local region as many interested buyers as can be reached through direct-mail advertising. On the other hand, by the use of the auction method, it is possible at times to realize higher prices because it gives play to the emotional factors involved when bidders openly compete against one another. (See Figure 11–1.)

From the standpoint of the buyer, both equipment and material can often be obtained economically through an auction sale. However, to buy well calls for a rare degree of ability on the part of the bidder, since it requires an intimate knowledge of one's requirements, judgment as to the economic worth of the items, an understanding with management in advance as to the amount of funds available, and skill in the difficult art of bidding.

Sale to dealers.   There are many types of dealers who buy and sell used machinery tools and other used equipment. Certain dealers act

Figure 11–1*
AUCTIONS

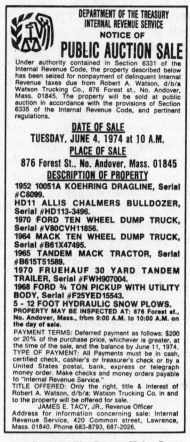

DEPARTMENT OF THE TREASURY
INTERNAL REVENUE SERVICE

NOTICE OF

PUBLIC AUCTION SALE

Under authority contained in Section 6331 of the Internal Revenue Code, the property described below has been seized for nonpayment of delinquent Internal Revenue taxes due from Robert A. Watson, d/b/a Watson Trucking Co., 876 Forest st., No. Andover, Mass. 01845. The property will be sold at public auction in accordance with the provisions of Section 6335 of the Internal Revenue Code, and pertinent regulations.

DATE OF SALE
TUESDAY, JUNE 4, 1974 at 10 A.M.

PLACE OF SALE
876 Forest St., No. Andover, Mass. 01845

DESCRIPTION OF PROPERTY
1952 10051A KOEHRING DRAGLINE, Serial #C8099.
HD11 ALLIS CHALMERS BULLDOZER, Serial #HD113-3496.
1970 FORD TEN WHEEL DUMP TRUCK, Serial #V80CVH11856.
1964 MACK TEN WHEEL DUMP TRUCK, Serial #B61X47495.
1965 TANDEM MACK TRACTOR, Serial #B615T51589.
1970 FRUEHAUF 30 YARD TANDEM TRAILER, Serial #FWH907004.
1968 FORD ¾ TON PICKUP WITH UTILITY BODY, Serial #F25YED15543.
5 - 12 FOOT HYDRAULIC SNOW PLOWS.
PROPERTY MAY BE INSPECTED AT: 876 Forest st., No. Andover, Mass., from 9:00 A.M. to 10:00 A.M. on the day of sale.
PAYMENT TERMS: Deferred payment as follows: $200 or 20% of the purchase price, whichever is greater, at the time of the sale, and the balance by June 11, 1974.
TYPE OF PAYMENT: All Payments must be in cash, certified check, cashier's or treasurer's check or by a United States postal, bank, express or telegraph money order. Make checks and money orders payable to "Internal Revenue Service."
TITLE OFFERED: Only the right, title & interest of Robert A. Watson, d/b/a: Watson Trucking Co. in and to the property will be offered for sale.
   JAMES E. TACY, JR., Revenue Officer
Address for information concerning sale: Internal Revenue Service, 420 Common street, Lawrence, Mass. 01840. Phone 683-8793, 687-2026.

* Source: *The Boston Globe*, June 2, 1974.

as brokers in handling some sales, while at other times they purchase outright. Another class of dealers stock new as well as used machines, but many—perhaps most—dealers specialize only in used equipment. In addition, many dealers rebuild equipment. The largest dealers of this type maintain plants which manufacture parts for used machinery, and they also employ an engineering staff to design improvements for the rebuilt machines. They then offer the machines "rebuilt," including guarantees which often are more comprehensive than those given by new machinery manufacturers. A large number of dealers stock used machinery in warehouses and sell to manufacturers and other dealers. Still a different type is the merchant who buys machinery by placing a deposit against it and then sells it before moving it from the premises were it was purchased, thus eliminating the necessity of warehousing.

Plants about to be closed down or liquidated following bankruptcy are sometimes bought by another type of large buyer, a speculator who attempts to keep a liquidated plant in operation for a time. Often these plants are operated only long enough to process the material on hand.

A used equipment dealer may acquire used equipment from several sources. Many large manufacturing firms ask a dealer to inspect a plant that is being closed down and to make an offer for the machinery which it contains. While some of these firms have previous buying or selling relations with the dealer, others are influenced by the dealer's advertising[6] or by customers' recommendations. In prepared trade journal advertising and on sales brochures, a dealer may indicate a willingness to buy any quantity of good used machinery and offer to send a representative to inspect such equipment. The dealer may also invite firms that are contemplating the purchase or sale of surplus equipment to write for sales bulletins, which outline the services which the dealer offers.

Some large used equipment companies do not undertake to repair and rebuild the equipment they purchase, but instead they have the machines overhauled and repaired by various organizations that specialize in specific types of machines. They believe that no one dealer can adequately rebuild the machines which these larger companies handle. Such concerns, moreover, do not acquire the real estate when they purchase entire plants but concentrate only on the machinery and equipment contained therein. It is obviously difficult to keep track of the fluctuating real estate values in the many different cities in which some companies operate, and they consequently prefer to stick to the line in which they specialize.

While many purchasing officers say they are opposed to purchasing used equipment, virtually all do buy it in larger or smaller quantities. The policy varies widely from company to company. Some apparently buy it only under unusual circumstances, while others buy used equipment in preference to new whenever a satisfactory purchase can be made.

Reasons for buying used equipment

Some of the reasons for the purchase of used equipment follow:

1. When price is important either because the differential between new and used is vital or the buyer's funds are low.
2. For use in a pilot or experimental plant.
3. For use with a special or temporary order over which the entire cost will be amortized.
4. Where the machine will be idle a substantial amount of time.

---

[6] Trade journals often carry regularly an entire section devoted to the advertisements of firms having used equipment for sale. One example is the "Clearing House" of *Iron Age*.

5. For use of apprentices.
6. For maintenance departments (not production).
7. For better delivery when time is essential.
8. When a used machine can be easily modernized for relatively little or is already the latest model.
9. When labor costs are unduly high.

Leasing equipment

It was pointed out earlier that purchasing used equipment was one of two alternatives to purchasing new equipment, a second being leasing equipment. Some attention needs to be directed to this possibility.

Since the end of World War II, there has been a substantial increase in the number and diversity of manufacturers of capital equipment who lease as well as sell their equipment. Those who advocate leasing point out that the concept of leasing involves payments for the *use* of the assets rather than payment for the privilege of *owning* the asset.

Short-term rentals are a special form of lease with which everyone is familiar. Short-term rentals make a lot of sense when limited use of the equipment is foreseen and the capital and/or maintenance cost of the equipment is significant. Often an operator can be obtained along with the piece of equipment rented. The construction industry is a good example where extensive use is made of short-term rentals.

Most lease contracts can be drawn to include an "option to buy" the equipment involved after some stated period. It is important for anyone considering the lease of capital equipment to be sure that the latest Internal Revenue regulations are understood. On October 15, 1955, the Internal Revenue Service announced its position on ascertaining the tax status of leases as follows:

In the absence of compelling factors of contrary implication the parties will be considered as having intended a purchase and sale rather than a rental, if one or more of the following conditions are covered in the agreement:

1. Portions of periodic payments are specifically applicable to an equity to be acquired by the lessees.
2. The lessees will acquire title upon payment of a stated amount of rentals.
3. The total amount which the lessee is required to pay for a relatively short period constitutes an inordinately large proportion of the total sum required to be paid to secure transfer of title.
4. The agreed rental payments exceed the current fair-rented values.
5. The property may be acquired under a purchase option which is nominal in relation to the value of the property at the time when the option may be exercised, as determined at the time of entering into the original agreement, or which is a relatively small amount when compared with the total payments which are required to be made.

6. Some portion of periodic payments is specifically designated as interest or is otherwise recognizable as the equivalent of interest.

Unless the lease rental payments are allowed to be treated as an expense item for income tax purposes, some of the possible advantages of the equipment lease plan may not be realized.

In the past, some large manufacturers of machines and equipment employing advanced technology have preferred to follow a policy of leasing rather than selling their equipment. Government antitrust actions have aimed at giving the user the right to determine whether he wished to lease or purchase. The leasing may be done by the manufacturers of the equipment, by distributors, or by companies organized for the specific purpose of leasing equipment.[7] At times, as in the construction industry, an owner of equipment who has no immediate use for his equipment may lease or rent it to other concerns that may have temporary immediate need for it.

Types of leases

There are two main types of lease, the financial and the operational. The financial lease is primarily financial in nature and may be of the full payout or partial payout variety. In the full payout form the lessee pays the full purchase price of the equipment plus interest and, if applicable, maintenance, service, record keeping, and insurance charges on a regular payment plan. In the partial payout plan there is a residual value to the equipment at the end of the lease term and the lessee pays for the difference between original cost and residual value plus interest and charges.

The financial lease cost is made up of the lessor's fee, the interest rate and the depreciation rate of the equipment. The lessor's fee depends on the services offered and may be as low as .25 percent of the gross for straight financing without other services. The interest will depend both on the cost of money to the lessor and the credit rating of the lessee. The depreciation normally varies with the type of equipment and its use. For example, trucks are usually depreciated over a five-year period.

The operational lease is in its basic form noncancellable, has a fixed term which is substantially less than the life of the equipment and a fixed financial commitment which is substantially less than the purchase price of the equipment. Service is the key factor in the operational lease with the lessor assuming full responsibility for maintenance, obsolescence, insurance, taxes, purchase, and resale of the equipment, etc. The charges for these services must be evaluated by the lessee against other alternatives which may be open.

---

[7] See Henry G. Hamel, *Leasing in Industry* (New York: National Industrial Conference Board, 1968), for a full discussion of professional lessors.

Categories of leasing companies

According to J. P. Matthews[8] careful analysis of how the lessor will profit from the leasing arrangement is vital in obtaining a satisfactory price. Since most leasing companies have standard procedures for calculating leases but are seldom willing to disclose these or the vital figures behind them, it behooves the buyer to search carefully before signing. Since lessors are more likely to disclose competitors' procedures and figures than their own, the search need not be seen as an impossible task. Matthews identifies four major different structures of leasing relationships, each with its special implications. (See Figure 11–2.)

Figure 11–2
FOUR LEASING STRUCTURAL RELATIONSHIPS

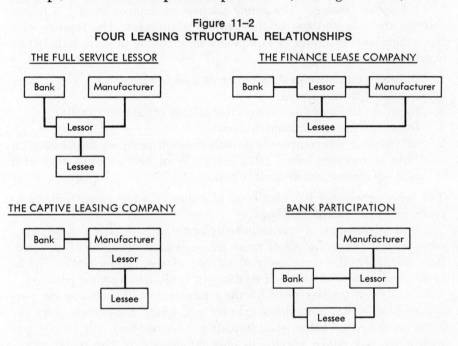

1. The full service lessor. Full service lessors are most common in the automotive, office equipment, and industrial equipment fields. The lessor performs all services, purchases the equipment to the buyer's specifications, and has its own source of financing. This type of lessor generally obtains discounts or rebates from the equipment manufacturers which are not disclosed to the lessee. Profits are also obtained on the maintenance and service charges which are included in the lease rate. Care should be taken on long-term leases which contain an escalation provision to allow such escalation only on that portion of the lease on which costs might rise.

---

[8] J. P. Matthews, "Equipment Leasing: Before the Cash-Flow Analysis, What Else?" *Journal of Purchasing,* vol. 10, no. 1, (February 1974), pp. 5–11.

2. *The finance lease company.* This type of lessor does not purchase or maintain the equipment, so that the lessee deals directly with the equipment manufacturer. The lessor frequently has access to funds at close to prime rate and is able to make its profit by lending above this. Occasionally, if a relatively short lease is involved, the lessor may wish to profit from the resale value of the equipment and may offer unusually low lending rates. A profitable lessor may benefit from the investment tax credits and depreciation which to a less profitable lessee may be meaningless. When a lessee has already reached the limits on its investment tax credits because of large capital expenditures but the lessor is not yet at the limit, leasing may similarly benefit both.

3. *Captive leasing.* The prime purpose of captive leasing is to encourage the sale and use of the parent's equipment. The reasons why the original manufacturer of equipment may choose to lease rather than to sell are several.

1. To secure either wider distribution or a higher margin.
2. To reduce the credit risk.
3. To sell a full line or to increase the volume of sales of supplies.
4. To control the secondhand market.
5. To stabilize the company's growth through securing distribution in times of recession when sales, especially of new as contrasted with used equipment, are difficult to make.

The lease agreement has also been of value to some manufacturers in protecting their patent position.

These advantages, of course, usually apply only in part and to somewhat special situations. All of them are somewhat debatable. But where they do apply, the company making use of the leasing device, while at the same time well aware of its dangers, is often in a strong position.

Obviously, a transfer price for the equipment holds between the parent and the lessor. Sometimes a lessor will quote a 2-percent sales tax figure on the rental value when in reality the lessor may only be charged with a use tax which applies to only 50 percent of the rental value. A lessee might expect to gain at least a 1-percent benefit from negotiation here.

4. *Bank participation.* There are advantages to bank participation in cases where the lessee has a good credit rating. The bank may be willing to finance part of the lease at rates slightly over prime, because it is a low-risk and low-nuisance lease. The lessor looks after the purchasing, servicing, and disposal of the equipment, relieving the bank of tasks it normally has little expertise in.

Advantages and disadvantages

We are here more concerned, however, with the user of the equipment, particularly the company with option to lease or buy. Without undertaking to elaborate upon them, for they are self-evident, the advantages of leasing may be listed as follows:

1. Burden of investment shifted to supplier.
2. Small initial outlay (may actually cost less).
3. Availability of expert service.
4. Risk of obsolescence reduced.
5. Adaptability to special jobs and seasonal business.
6. Test period provided before purchase.
7. Lease rentals are expenses for income tax purposes.

On the other hand, there are certain equally clear disadvantages:

1. Final cost likely to be high.
2. Surveillance by lessor entailed.
3. Less freedom of control and use.

Many leases are definitely one-sided in their terms, placing virtually all the risks on the lessee. These terms, therefore, need to be watched with the utmost care. For instance, what are the arrangements for replacing equipment when obsolete or no longer serviceable? Is the lessee in fact free to buy supplies anywhere, such as paper for copying machines? Are the actual charges what they appear to be? Are there onerous limitations on either the maximum or the minimum output or other such operational factors as the number of hours per day or number of shifts the equipment may be used or on using attachments? What limitations, if any, are there to the uses to which the equipment may be put?

Evaluation of advantages and disadvantages

To evaluate these advantages and disadvantages is no easy task. Take, for example, the matter of cost. A buyer might be tempted to assume that if the purchase price equaled approximately five times the annual rental charged, this would be an excessive price for leasing. Yet, before coming to this conclusion, the buyer must remember that the annual rental in dollars includes more than merely recovering the cost of the equipment, since the lease rate presumably includes allowances for such charges as service and maintenance, insurance, and interest. Moreover, should the buyer purchase the equipment not only these charges would be assumed but the very intangible risks of depreciation and obsolescence.

Or take the moot question as to the freedom of a lessor to buy supplies from someone other than the owner of the leased equipment:

In some cases manufacturers of both supplies and basic equipment have used their equipment installations as a method of promoting the sale of supplies by leasing the equipment at very low annual rates in order to secure the lessee's orders for supplies. From the user's standpoint this may have an important impact on purchasing. Selection of supplies may be based more upon the evaluation of the basic equipment installation than on the price and quality of supplies from competing sources. . . .

Users must recognize that their choice of equipment introduces certain pressures for purchasing supplies and auxiliary equipment from the equipment manufacturer. A lease may serve to accentuate such pressures. . . . The effective performance of the machine, as well as its cost of maintenance and repair, *may be materially* affected by the type of supplies used. Obviously, the vendor's reputation is threatened if his equipment does not live up to performance claims. Consequently it may be argued that if his own supplies are used, the equipment will operate at maximum efficiency. . . . But under the lease, the argument will be more forceful, since the lessor can show that he has a *direct* interest in the particular equipment installation.

A lessor assumes a great interest and responsibility for the servicing of leased equipment. Since ownership remains with the lessor under the lease, he must take precautions against damage to his equipment resulting from improper use by the lessee. If an improper supply item is used, it may increase the amount and cost of servicing required. If the rental is based upon units of output, the use of inferior supply items can reduce the lessor's revenue from the lease. In either case, the lessor can argue that he has a direct interest in the type of supplies purchased by the user. . . .

Even if it is assumed that there is no contractual agreement concerning the purchase of supplies, and that the lessor does not actively push the argument that his own supplies are essential for the maximum performance of the equipment, this purchasing consideration still exists. The user should anticipate that there will be an inclination to assume that supplies provided by the company who makes the equipment will be superior for use with that particular type of equipment. . . .[9]

Quite aside from any weighing of the specific advantages and disadvantages and beyond the actual terms of the lease, any prospective lessee of equipment needs to exercise the utmost care in passing judgment on the lessor. Is the lessor:

1. Reasonable and fair in dealings with customers?
2. Devoting as much attention and money to research as alleged?
3. Strong financially?
4. Fully protected by patents?
5. If a sole source, prone to be arbitrary in the periodic adjustment of rental and other fees?

What effect would a fire in the lessor's plant have on the repair and servicing requirements of the user?

There is neither formula nor theory which can provide the right

[9] See Wilford J. Eiteman and Charles N. Davisson, *The Lease as a Financing and Selling Device.* Report No. 20 (Lansing, Mich.: Bureau of Business Research, School of Business Administration, University of Michigan, 1951), pp. 80 and 100–101.

answer to all these questions. The solution to each particular problem can be found only in the sound judgment of the procurement personnel within the buyer's organization.

BIBLIOGRAPHY

ALJIAN, GEORGE W., ed. *Purchasing Handbook.* 3d ed. New York: Mc-Graw-Hill Book Co., 1973.

HAMEL, HENRY G. *Leasing in Industry.* New York: National Industrial Conference Board, 1968.

MACHINERY AND ALLIED PRODUCTS INSTITUTE. *Leasing of Industrial Equipment.* Washington, D.C., 1965.

NATIONAL ASSOCIATION OF PURCHASING AGENTS. *Leases versus Buying.* New York, 1963.

VANCIL, RICHARD FRANKLIN. *Leasing of Industrial Equipment.* New York: McGraw-Hill Book Co., 1963.

WESTING, J. H. FINE, I. V.; AND ZENZ, GARY JOSEPH. *Purchasing Management.* 3d ed. New York: John Wiley & Sons, Inc., 1969.

CASES FOR CHAPTER 11

LINK SAND AND GRAVEL COMPANY

Mr. F. Wheeler, purchasing manager at Link Sand and Gravel was considering a proposal submitted to him by a local construction equipment leaser. Link was in the market to buy a wheel tractor scraper for its new quarry operation. Two decisions had to be made; one, which scraper model would suit the jobs best; and, two, should the scraper be purchased or leased.

Company background

Link operated a number of sand and gravel quarries throughout Ohio. Scrapers were used to remove the overburden and deliver the mixed sand and gravel to a sorting and screening plant. In the Wellfeld sand and gravel pit operation, an average scraper load carried 80 percent sand and 20 percent gravel. Sand after being sorted into different grades was sold for $10.00 to $17.00 a ton. The Wellfeld pit, typical of most Link sand and gravel quarries, used two scrapers, three loaders, and six large trucks.

In 1972 Link had annual sales of $43 million. The company had purchased 76 pieces of equipment valued at approximately $4 million in 1972. The expected life of this equipment was between three and five years. Mr. Wheeler and the company treasurer had worked out the optimum tax credits and trade-in values of the company's $18 million worth of capital equipment.

The Wellfeld operation

In 1971 Link had purchased an elevator scraper to replace a grader and loader. The $150,000 elevator scraper had proved to be a poor purchase. Substantial downtime and increased maintenance had skyrocketed operating costs. The resulting production tonnages were 60 percent of the estimated 1 million ton target for the first operating year. The pit superintendent and general manager suggested that the scraper be traded in and replaced with a simple scraper tractor capable of producing one million tons a year. It had to be able to operate in dirt, sand, and gravel and be free of maintenance problems. Mr. Wheeler estimated that any piece of capital construction equipment would use 95 percent of its purchase price in parts and maintenance costs over its expected life. The Wellfeld pit was very rugged, limiting equipment life to a maximum of five years.

Search for the right scraper

Mr. Wheeler requested information and costs of scrapers from various manufacturers. The Wellfeld pit superintendent went to a number of other quarry operations to see what equipment was most popular and what type of equipment problems they were having. Caterpillar was known in the trade as the Cadillac of construction equipment, and the test results shown by Caterpillar in their testing fields warranted a Wellfeld on-site demonstration. Caterpillar had three scrapers which would be considered for the job. (See Exhibit 1.) Caterpillar model 633 had a purchase price of $143,000; model 637 cost $120,000, and model 627 cost $84,000. All purchase prices included options but no taxes. The pit superintendent was pleased with all three scrapers.

The Wellfeld quarry was 40 miles from the nearest company maintenance depot. On site maintenance was very expensive, therefore making unscheduled downtime an important consideration. An hour of downtime was estimated to cost the company $23. The company accountant had recently pointed out to Mr. Wheeler that investment in capital equipment must be recouped in three years in order to take the maximum tax credits. He also estimated that the company's cost of capital was 8.5 percent. Internal sources of funds were becoming increasingly scarce.

The lease alternative

Mr. Wheeler contacted Contract Leasing Company who had done business with Link previously on a satisfactory basis. Arrangements were

Exhibit 1

![CATERPILLAR] CATERPILLAR

MORE PLUS VALUES OF CAT TANDEM POWERED PUSH-PULL SCRAPERS

TRACTOR FEATURES...

Semi-automatic 8-speed tractor transmission (standard on 637 and 657B, optional on 627). Highly efficient in the cut, haul and fill. Operator has option of automatic or manual power shifts in six haul road speeds, manually selects from two torque converter speed ranges to meet high rimpull needs.

Transmission hold pedal (semi-automatic transmission) locks machine in the gear in use—allows operator to maintain high engine RPM. For added hydraulic power and to prevent unwanted upshifts on favorable grades.

Tractor differential lock reduces tire spin and improves traction on wet or slippery surfaces. Engaged by foot pedal.

Constant speed steering through working engine RPM range combines with stabilizing action of follow-up mechanism to give automotive "feel" to steering.

Louvered radiator guard (637, 657B) directs radiator heat to right side of tractor and away from operator compartment.

Cushion Hitch (optional on 657B, 637) absorbs road shocks, allows faster usable road speeds. Cuts haul road "washboarding," reduces wear and tear on machine parts. Combines with torsionflex seat for smooth ride.

SCRAPER FEATURES...

Low wide scraper bowl picks up big loads fast. Wide cutting edge gathers volume loads from shallow cuts, incoming earth meets low resistance because the bowl is shallow.

Outboard-mounted scraper bowl cylinders (637, 657B) reduce stress on draft frame. Trunnion mounting allows fore, aft and sideways movement which eliminates bending forces that shorten cylinder, seal and rod life.

Power down apron slices through and holds hard materials. Double-acting hydraulic cylinder exerts powerful force. Apron lip protected from lodged rocks by hydraulic relief valve.

Positive bulldozer ejection dumps wet or sticky material. Powered by fast double-acting hydraulics. Detent allows operator to take hand from control lever during ejector return. Lever automatically snaps to "hold" when ejector reaches rear position.

Positive down-pressure on bowl provides penetrating force on cutting edge. This reduces load time in hard materials and prevents the bowl from riding over and on blocky material which can accelerate bowl wear.

Multiple speed scraper transmission combines multi-speed gear box with torque converter. Accurately balances scraper engine to speed and load requirements.

Automatic positive locking type differential on scraper reduces wasteful tire spinning and rutting. Aids traction.

Horn and light alert operator to malfunction of rear engine cooling and lubrication systems or transmission synchronization problems.

TRACTOR AND SCRAPER FEATURES...

Four cycle engines for tractor and scraper have high torque rise and excellent lugging characteristics, can burn non-premium, high energy fuels.

Exhaust muffler combines with silencing effect of turbocharger to keep engine noise to a minimum.

Fuel filler opening accepts adapter for high speed pressurized fueling attachments.

Automatic dust ejector uses engine exhaust gases to remove 95% of foreign matter from air entering the precleaner. Air cleaner requires less servicing time and effort.

XT-3 hydraulic hose made by Caterpillar will outlast any other make hose in high pressure, high temperature, high flexing applications. Significantly reduces hydraulic system downtime.

Multiple system hydraulic tank supplies all needs: steering scraper operation, Cushion Hitch and Push-Pull. One sight gauge checks all, simplifies servicing.

Variable rate tractor and scraper retarders (637, 657B, optional on 627) Tandem powered units provide virtually double retarding capacity over comparable single drive units—increasing downhill performance.

Separate brake circuits for tractor and scraper assure reserve braking is always available at one axle.

Automatic emergency braking automatically engages if brake pressure drops below safe operating level.

VARIOUS SCRAPER TYPES

PUSH-PULL SCRAPERS
3 sizes...dual struck loading capacities from 28 to 64 cu. yd. (22-49 m³)

High returns from modest added investment. Team-load two tandem powered scrapers then separate on-the-go for haul. Can also be loaded separately by usual pusher.

TANDEM POWERED SCRAPERS
4 sizes...struck capacities from 14 to 40 cu. yd. (11-31 m³)

The added power and traction pay important productive dividends on a surprisingly wide range of jobs.

STANDARD SCRAPERS
6 sizes...struck capacities from 14 to 40 cu. yd. (11-31 m³)

Powerful engines, advanced transmissions and low, wide bowls make these machines the most productive units of their type on the market.

ELEVATING SCRAPERS
3 sizes...struck capacities from 11 to 32 cu. yd. (8.4-25 m³)

These units self load—eliminate a pusher and unproductive wait time. Another point worth considering: these are the most *durable* elevating scrapers you can buy.

made to bring a 637 model scraper to the Link Sand Pits at Wellfeld and substantiate previous manufacturer's operating figures. The results were favorable, and Contract Leasing outlined a proposal to lease and maintain any one of the three models for the Wellfeld quarry. (See Exhibit 2.) Mr. Wheeler thought that the reputation of a leaser was

Exhibit 2

To:	Link Sand & Gravel Co., Ltd.,	From:	Contract Leasing, Ltd.,
	R.R. 1,		192 Eglington Avenue,
	Wellfeld, Ohio.		Wellfeld, Ohio.

We propose to rent to you the following equipment subject to the terms described below:

1—Caterpillar 633 Wheel Tractor-Scraper, Cushion-Hitch, series C, 32 cubic yard elevating scraper, semiautomatic, power shift transmission, direct electric starting, muffler, emergency brake system, ROPS fully enclosed cab, heater, windshield wiper, defroster fan, scraper floodlight, driving lights, 33.25-35 32 PR, Michelin tires. Elevator extended one foot to include 14 flights and scraper modified with sideboards and miscellaneous wear shields to adapt it for operation in gravel.

Base rental rate $5,170.00 per month plus any applicable taxes, from date of delivery until equipment is returned to Lessor, or satisfactory notification of rental termination is received. This rate is based upon 3,000 hours use in one year as measured by Sangamo Tachograph. If machine is rented in excess of 3,000 hours per year, all excess hours shall be on the basis of $20.00 per hour. Credit *will be issued* for use under 3,000 hours per year at $10.00 per hour; maximum 400 hours credit.

Minimum rental charge $62,040.00 based upon a guaranteed 12-month rental at the base rental rate renewable for a second year at the same rate.

1—Caterpillar 627 Wheel Tractor-Scraper, Cushion-Hitch, push-pull, series C, 20 cubic yard heap capacity, semiautomatic power shift transmission, direct electric starting, muffler, emergency brake system, ROPS fully enclosed cab, heater, windshield wiper, defroster fan, scraper floodlight, driving lights, 29.5-29 28 PR, Michelin tires.

Base rental rate $3,000.00 per month plus any applicable taxes, from date of delivery until equipment is returned to Lessor, or satisfactory notification of rental termination is received. This rate is based upon 3,000 hours use in one year as measured by a Sangamo Tachograph. If machine is rented in excess of 3,000 hours per year, all excess hours shall be on the basis of $12.00 per hour. Credit *will be issued* for use under 3,000 hours per year at $6.00 per hour; maximum 400 hours credit.

Minimum rental charge $36,096.00 based upon a guaranteed 12-month rental at the base rental rate renewable for a second year at the same rate.

1—Caterpillar 637 Wheel Tractor-Scraper, Cushion-Hitch, push-pull, series C, 30 cubic yard heap capacity, elevating scraper, semiautomatic power shift transmission, direct electric starting, muffler, emergency brake system,

Exhibit 2 (*Continued*)

ROPS fully enclosed cab, heater, windshield wiper, defroster fan, scraper floodlight, driving lights, 33.25-35 32 PR, Michelin tires.

Base rental rate $4,512.00 per month plus any applicable taxes from date of delivery until equipment is returned to Lessor, or satisfactory notification of rental termination is received. This rate is based upon 3,000 hours use in one year as measured by a Sangamo Tachograph. If machine is rented in excess of 3,000 hours per year, all excess hours shall be on the basis of $18.00 per hour. Credit *will be issued* for use under 3,000 hours per year at $9.00 per hour; maximum 400 hours credit.

Minimum rental charge $54,144.00 based upon a guaranteed 12-month rental at the base rental rate renewable for a second year at the same rate.

Terms:

100 percent of the base monthly rental rate is payable monthly in advance. Monthly billings are to be recognized as an *estimate* of the actual use charges. Every 90 days, commencing 120 days after delivery to the Lessee, a supplemental invoice (or credit memo) will be issued adjusting the estimate for cumulative *Total Actual Use*. These supplemental adjusting invoices will be due for payment within ten days of receipt. Should a "credit balance" develop in excess of one "monthly estimate," Lessor will remit a check in the amount of such excess, insofar as these refunds do not infringe on the minimum annual guarantee or actual use charges.

Lessor will deliver and pick up machine at Link Sand and Gravel, Ltd. Lessee is to assume full responsibility for the equipment during the rental period and will return machine in as good condition as received, less wear incident to normal use in the hands of a competent operator and while operated in the manner the equipment was designed for. Lessor will be responsible periodically to inspect the machine and advise Lessee immediately if this requirement is not being met. Lessor is to deliver equipment in good working order. Lessor is to furnish all filters, parts, and labor necessary for maintenance and repairs necessitated either by normal wear and tear or by internal equipment failures, except that Lessee will assume full responsibility for all fuel and lubricants and for the proper lubrication of the equipment while renting machine. The scraper linkage rollers and pins will be pressure lubricated twice per shift.

Lessee will be responsible for all breakdowns and repairs occasioned by operator negligence or external job factors, except for those resulting from some poor design, weakness, or failure in the machine itself. No repairs are to be made by the Lessee without the specific permission of the Lessor. Lessor assumes no liability for loss or damage on account of accidents, delays due to defective material, engine or transmission troubles, delays in the delivery or removal of equipment or resulting from interruption of business or other consequential loss. Lessee agrees to indemnify Lessor against all loss, damage, expense, and penalty arising from any action on account of personal injury or damage to property occasioned by the operation, handling or transportation of this equipment during the rental period, unless due to some weakness of failure on the machine itself. Lessor reserves the right, if Lessee is in default under the terms of this agreement, or if in the Lessor's

Exhibit 2 (*Concluded*)

opinion the equipment is being damaged in excess of ordinary wear and tear, to take possession of the machine upon 24 hours notice.

Lessor agrees to perform all possible repairs during Lessee's nonworking hours and in case of long delays resulting from serious breakdowns. Lessor will endeavor to furnish a replacement machine on a "no extra charge" basis.

Location:

This rental rate is predicted on use of this machine in the Link Sand pit at R.R. 1 Wellfeld, Ohio.

Safety:

Unit will be equipped to meet applicable OSHA safety standards.

Production and Cost:

Based upon a field time study of one of our present 627s in your Link Sand pit we have arrived at hourly production over an approximate 1,800-foot one-way haul distance. These production figures, plus an annual production capability based upon 3760 hours per year, are listed below. To present reasonable costs we projected an average rental cost based upon 3,000 hours of use in a year at the base rental rate plus 760 hours at the "extra" rate. The average annual hourly cost is listed in the table below.

	Cat 627	*Cat 637*	*Cat 633*
Hourly production			
(tons per Hour)	255 TP Hour	370 TP Hour	385 TP Hour
Annual production	TP	TP	TP
(3,760 hours)	958,545 Year	1,390,830 Year	1,447,215 Year
Average hourly rental cost	$12.03	$18.04	$20.54
Operator (category II)	7.50	7.50	7.50
Fuel (16¢ per gallon)	3.62	4.40	3.17
Total operated cost	$23.15	$29.94	$31.21
Cost per ton (in cents)	9.08	8.08	8.12
Total rental costs	$45,232	$67,830	$77,230

the critical dimension in leasing. There were never enough guarantees and warranties in equipment leasing. Manufacturing warranties, tire warranties, and other parts problems were difficult to handle when purchasing equipment but were compounded when a leaser was involved.

DEANS BREWERY (A)

In February, 1968, Mr. Simpson, chief engineer at Deans Brewery, Trinidad, was completing the design of a new bottling line. The last remaining major issue dealt with the materials handling situation at the end of the line. Currently, the company was using manual labor to put the full cases of beer on pallets. Mr. Simpson was considering the possibility of using automatic equipment.

Company background

Deans Brewery was located in the southern Caribbean island of Trinidad. Founded by John Deans in 1924, the company had established a high reputation. Deans beer had also become a favorite with tourists, and as a result a modest export business to the United States had started in 1959. In February, 1968, sales reached the highest level in the company's history. However, in 1967 the sales increase had been well below the trend average. Four sales peaks occurred during the year: Carnival,[1] Christmas, Easter and Independence.[2] Carnival was the highest sales period, but each peak caused the company to operate on tight schedules during which Deans hired more labor and scheduled extra shifts.

Brewing process

Beer brewing started with extraction of sugar from malt by an enzymic process. This suger was boiled with hops, producing a sterilized and concentrated solution. The resins extracted from the hops during boiling acted as a preservative and gave the beer its bitter flavor. The hops were then removed, and the solution was cooled to a temperature of $50°F$ for bottom fermentation lasting seven days, during which yeast converted the sugar to alcohol and CO_2. After fermentation the beer was cooled to $30°F$ and stored for ten days (during which the yeast dropped out) and then roughly filtered through diatomaceous earth. After 24 hours storage it was put through a polish filtration process and was artificially carbonated ready for bottling. After bottling and case packing, the beer was stored in the finished goods warehouse ready for delivery to retail outlets.

Current operating in bottling and warehousing

The bottling department and warehouse were part of the same building separated by a wire fence (see Exhibit 1). The current bottling line had a capacity of 400 bottles per minute and usually operated two eight-hour shifts, five days a week at 85-percent efficiency. For the past three months it had run at three shifts per day. This had meant that maintenance, previously done at night, had begun to interfere with production time. The third shift was difficult to staff and supervise, but the expanded bottling capacity would eliminate this need. At 1,000 bottles per minute demand could be met by a one-shift operation with occasional overtime.

---

[1] Carnival took place two days before Ash Wednesday, which normally occurred during February and occasionally in early March.

[2] Trinidad gained its independence from Britain on August 31, 1962.

Exhibit 1
WAREHOUSE LAYOUT SHOWING PROPOSED AUTOMATIC
PALLETIZING SYSTEM

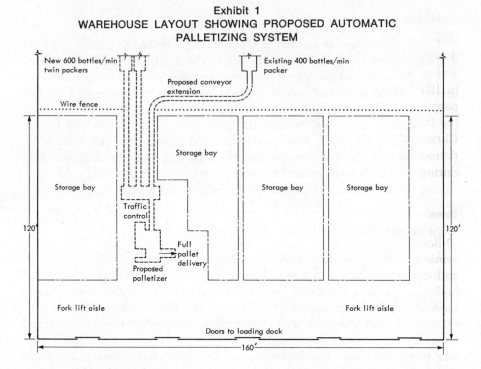

The last operation on the current bottling line was the manual stacking of full cases (24 bottles per case) on wooden pallets. Each case weighed 45 pounds, and each pallet held 40 case (5 layers high of 8 cases per layer). Two men were employed at this task; normally it took 7½ seconds to load each case. Each man loaded his own pallet and earned $40.00 a week.[3]

Currently two fork lift trucks carried the full pallets to the warehouse. Fork lifts cost $15,000 each and drivers earned $70.00 a week. The company owned 12 trucks and usually had at least two in the repair shop at any one time. Fork lift operators stacked the pallets three high in the warehouse. The warehouse (ceiling height 15½ ft.) had four storage bays in total, and usually two were being unloaded while the other two were being loaded. Space was reasonably plentiful except before peak sales periods when extra pallets were stacked in the aisles for inventory build-up.

New bottling line

The bottling line which Mr. Simpson had designed called for major changes in the bottling shop. Line capacity was to be increased by

---

[3] In 1698: $2.00 Trinidadian = $1.00 U.S.

600 bottles per minute with the addition of twin packers which would unload onto two exit conveyors. Aside from this a new empty bottle conveyor feed-in system was planned and would occupy all existing space between the bottling shop and the warehouse. As a result it would be necessary to move the unloading and palletizing operation into the warehouse. (See Exhibit 1.) The required conveyor system from the three lines in bottling to the warehouse for hand loading of pallets would cost $18,000 including installation. One advantage of the move to the warehouse was the shortening of the fork lift route. Mr. Simpson calculated that turnaround time from the new location would range from 35 seconds to 3 minutes and would probably average 1 minute.

Automatic palletizer

Mr. Simpson was considering the possibility of substituting an automatic palletizer for the hand loading operation in the new location (see Exhibit 2). The machine's operation was similar in concept to the manual loading procedure. It would take eight cases at a time and feed them onto the pallet in a predetermined pattern. The pallet was then lowered for the next layer. The full pallet was put onto the discharge conveyor which could hold up to three full pallets. The machine required one operator whose primary function was to make sure the machine shut off in case of trouble and to clear jams if they occurred at the feed-in point. He would probably be paid $50.00 per week. The palletizer would require a different feed-in system from manual loading because of the counting operation and machine height.

Mr. Simpson was considering two different makes of equipment, Perrin and Clark. He had received literature on both and had talked with sales representatives and also with executives in North American breweries. He was not sure how to choose between the two makes. Mr. Simpson wanted a palletizer which could handle 45 cases per minute, operate on a 50-cycle electrical supply, load at least 40 cases per pallet and have a stacking pattern identical to the present system. Both Perrin and Clark sales representatives said they could produce satisfactory equipment.

Perrin Conveyors, Ltd., was a Canadian subsidiary of an American firm. It handled all Canadian and Commonwealth sales and operated relatively autonomously from its parent. For over 50 years Perrin had enjoyed a high reputation for its conveyor systems which were light, easy to install, durable, and efficient. An additional feature was the ready convertibility of all conveyors to any of three basic types—live roller, gravity, or belt. Perrin had designed and manufactured many of the conveyor systems for Canadian grain handling and mineral processing installations. Perrin manufactured a variety of materials handling equipment including palletizers, although it had never built one which

Exhibit 2
AUTOMATIC PALLETIZER AND PALLET STACKING PATTERN

Palletizer Operating in a Different Company

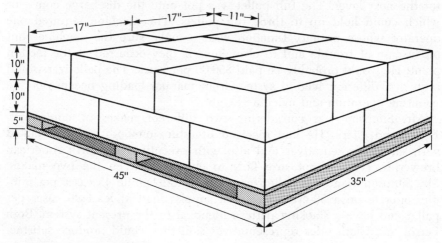

Pallet Stacking Pattern

met all of Mr. Simpson's specifications. Maximum capacity was determined by the number of cases the machine could handle in a given amount of time, and Perrin had never manufactured a unit faster than 40 cases per minute. In answer to Mr. Simpson's request, Perrin had said they would design a machine especially for him, which could handle 45 cases per minute and stack 5, 6, or 7 layers high with 8 cases per layer. The machine would be strictly mechanical, consisting of gears, belts, etc., and would not require a foundation of any sort. It would require an air line at a pressure of 120 psi. which exceeded the 90 psi. in the current general shop lines, and, therefore, a separate small compressor would have to be added at a cost of about $400. Perrin would supply a skilled technician for ten days to help with installation after delivery. The equipment would carry a standard guarantee of one year. Deans Brewery had purchased Perrin conveyors in the past and had been fully satisfied. Perrin's quotation for the palletizer was $54,000,[4] including the air compressor.

Clark Loading Systems was an American company of high reputation in the palletizer field. It could supply a standard model which met all of Mr. Simpson's specifications and could stack five, six or seven layers high. The Clark palletizer would be hydraulic, with few mechanical parts, requiring a 12-foot hole in the floor for the piston in the pallet lift. The general shop air line pressure would be sufficient for the machine. Service and guarantee terms would be the same as Perrin's. Clark also manufactured conveyors which tended to be heavier, bulkier, and more difficult to install than Perrin's but which also enjoyed an excellent reputation for quality and durability. Clark quoted a price of $68,000 for the palletizer.

If Mr. Simpson decided to use an automatic loader, he would have to combine the three exit lines into one line for delivery into the loader. He had asked both Perrin and Clark to quote on a traffic control system to join the lines. This system would have to jockey the cases into the single line and automatically count out eight cases for delivery to the loader for each layer on the pallet.

Clark indicated that a traffic control unit would cost $12,000, plus $10,000 for conveyors leading from the end of the bottling lines to the control unit and from the unit to the loader. Perrin quoted $12,000 for the control and $8,000 for the conveyors.

Two mechanics would have to be trained to service a loader, and Mr. Simpson felt training could be done when one of the suppliers' technicians was at Deans for installation and start-up. A palletizer was not a complex machine, and servicing should not be difficult for a skilled mechanic. Spare parts would be available from the makers, but with normal maintenance costs would be negligible. Mr. Simpson felt that two of the mechanics already employed to service the bottling shop at about $60 per week could be trained to handle a palletizer as part of their regular duties.

Both palletizers under consideration would require electric power from lines extended into the warehouse from the bottling department. Each palletizer had a 12.75 h.p. motor; power consumption would probably cost $500 per year.

Installation costs would be substantial for either palletizer-conveyor

---

[4] All prices quoted represent landed cost to Deans, including freight and duty but not including installation.

system. Mr. Simpson estimated that a total Perrin System with traffic control could be installed by a local engineering contractor for $15,000. A complete Clark system would require $18,000.

Mr. Simpson wondered if he should change to a seven-layer pallet if an automatic palletizer were purchased, but he was not sure how he could quantify the advantages and disadvantages of such a move. In any case he wanted to find the best system possible for handling finished goods. Mr. Simpson was concerned about his lack of familiarity with this kind of equipment, but he realized he could not turn easily for help elsewhere. It had been standard practice at Deans Brewery to justify certain investments on the basis of meeting future demand. These investments would also have to show a reasonable return in the long run.

CARMEN CANNING COMPANY (D)

The Carmen Canning Company, Ltd., was the major fruit juice canning company in Jamaica. For many years, the company had made its own cans and covers from imported tin steel sheet.

In January, 1968, the plant manager, Mr. James Thompson, learned that press manufacturers were offering new machinery for cover making. These new presses were capable of higher speed production and required less maintenance than the existing equipment in the cannery. Mr. Thompson gathered further information and in July, 1968, was ready to weigh all pros and cons carefully. If he wanted to convert to the new processes, he would have to present a feasibility report to the board of directors meeting in September. If he did not wish to invest at this time he would still have to explain his reasons to the president who had been interested in this study right from the start.

Company background

In 1940, the Carmen Canning Company began operations with a plant in Christiana, Manchester Parish, Jamaica, an area of large fruit groves. The company was a subsidiary of International Canneries, with head offices in London, England.

The new cannery processed 60,000 cases of orange juice (4 dozen 14 fl.oz. tins per case) in 1941 and employed 60 production workers. In 1942 the employees voted for representation by the Fruit Workers Union (F.W.U.). During the following eight years the company grew slowly because of difficulties in getting adequate supplies of fresh oranges and because of sluggish post-war demand.

Steady expansion came in the 1950s as the Jamaican economy prospered. New equipment increased capacity and versatility. In 1953 grapefruit juice, paw-paw nectar, and mango nectar were produced for the first time. The export market proved profitable, and by 1957 production had climbed to 300,000 cases. With the exception of a few slow years, the 1960s followed the same pattern, and in 1967 volume had grown to a million cases.

Past company policy had been not to lay off workers displaced by technological changes. In 1967 there were 172 production workers including 36 females. Wages were the highest paid by any company in the area, except for those paid by a bauxite company about 15 miles away. The average hourly wage at the cannery was 8/- for men and 4/- for women.[1] Employees received time-and-a-half for the first three hours of overtime each day (double-time for over three hours) and a shift premium of 6d per hour.[2]

The five major production departments were juicing, processing, can-making, filling, and packing. Processing was the only department operating three shifts; all the others operated one eight-hour shift five days per week with overtime when necessary.

Plant operations

Product flow started from fruit receiving through juicing to processing and filling. In processing, nine storage tanks held juices for direct delivery to three filling machines in the filling department. An overhead conveyor carried tin cans from can-making to the filling room. From the filling room, a conveyor transported the canned juices to the packing room for labeling and case packing, sealing, and palletizing for delivery to the finished goods warehouse. (See Exhibit 1.) During 1967 packing room production exceeded one million cases.

Can-making

Can-making was divided into two major operations: the press shop for cover punching and the tin shop for can fabrication. (See Exhibits 1 and 2.) In the press shop a scroll shear cut tin steel sheet into strips from which the seven presses punched out the covers.

In the tin shop, sheet for the can bodies was cut on the automatic sleeve former and fed into one of the three body makers which formed the cylindrical portion of the can. An elevator and gravity feed runway carried the bodies to the automatic flangers and to the seamers. In the flanger the edges on both ends of the cylinder were turned out

---

[1] In 1968: £1 = one pound Jamaican = 20/ = 20 shillings = $2.40 U.S. 12d = 12 pence = 1/ = 1 shilling = $0.12 U.S.

[2] Government regulations stipulated that female employees could not work before 6 A.M. or after 10 P.M. but could work shifts between 6 A.M. and 10 P.M. Women could only work 200 overtime hours per year unless the company requested permission from the Jamaican Ministry of Labour.

Exhibit 1
PRODUCT FLOW

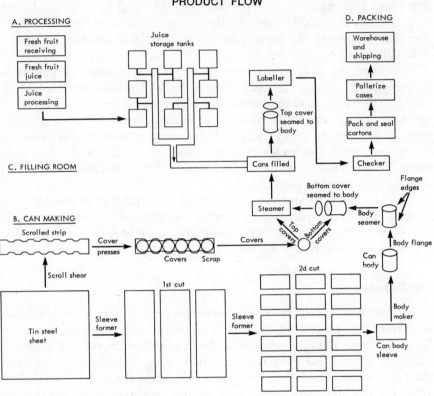

so that covers could be attached to the can. The seamer attached the bottom covers. The runways from each of the three seamers led to a mixing operation, and a single overhead conveyor carried the cans to the filling room.

The press shop present operations

Seven single die presses produced the top and bottom covers. Five of the presses were installed in 1940, and two (nos. 6 and 7) were added in 1959 and 1962 (see Exhibit 2). With these two additions, space had become tight in the department and in the resulting layout change press no. 1 was squeezed between the Blake body-maker and flanger.

The presses punched the covers from strips which had been cut from tin steel sheets on the scroll shear (see Exhibit 3). The presses punched out 8 covers from each strip or 64 covers out of each sheet.

The fork lift operator transported each full case (53,000 covers) to

Exhibit 2
LAYOUT: TIN SHOP AND PRESS SHOP

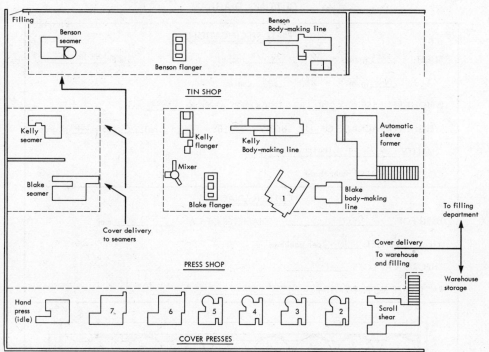

the body-making seamer, filling room seamers or warehouse as production required. Exhibit 4 gives the production record in the press shop for the month of July, 1968.

A total of 11 people were employed in the press shop (see Exhibit 5). Two women operated every two machines: one to feed the scrolled strips and one to remove the cover blanks. When labor was available, two additional women operated press no. 1. One full-time mechanic performed regular maintenance on the presses. Every 50,000 covers, he removed the upper die on each press for sharpening and realignment with the lower die. The mechanic normally required 30 minutes to perform these repairs. Every three months, both upper and lower dies had to be replaced at a cost of £26 (£10 lower die, £16 upper die). The company kept a stock of six complete die sets. Two scrap collectors gathered the waste material from each scrolled strip; the company received £ ⅔ per ton of scrap. Scrap in July, 1968, amounted to seven tons per week. Two women operated the scroll shear.

Mr. Thompson and his management team forecasted a 5-percent increase in production for 1968. During 1967 the press operators had worked an average of ten hours overtime per month to meet the packing'

Exhibit 3
TIN STEEL SHEET SPECIFICATIONS AND SCROLL SHEET CUTTING DIAGRAM

PLATE SPECIFICATIONS

SHEET: 25 7/16 inches   X   30 1/8 inches   SIZE: 19 No. 2

646 m.m.   X   765 m.m.

WEIGHT PER BASE BOX 80 LBS: THICKNESS APPROX. 0.229 m.m.

WEIGHT PER PACKAGE OF 112 SHEETS = 219 LBS = 100 kg.net 228 LBS = 104 kg.gross

QUALITY: 0.75 lb. Electrolytic

COST: 2 shillings per sheet

CUTTING DIAGRAM

USED FOR: Covers   DIAMETER OF CAN: 73 mm

YIELD PER SHEET: 64 per package

THEORETICAL LOSS: 21.6%

FACTORIES SUPPLIED WITH: Carmen

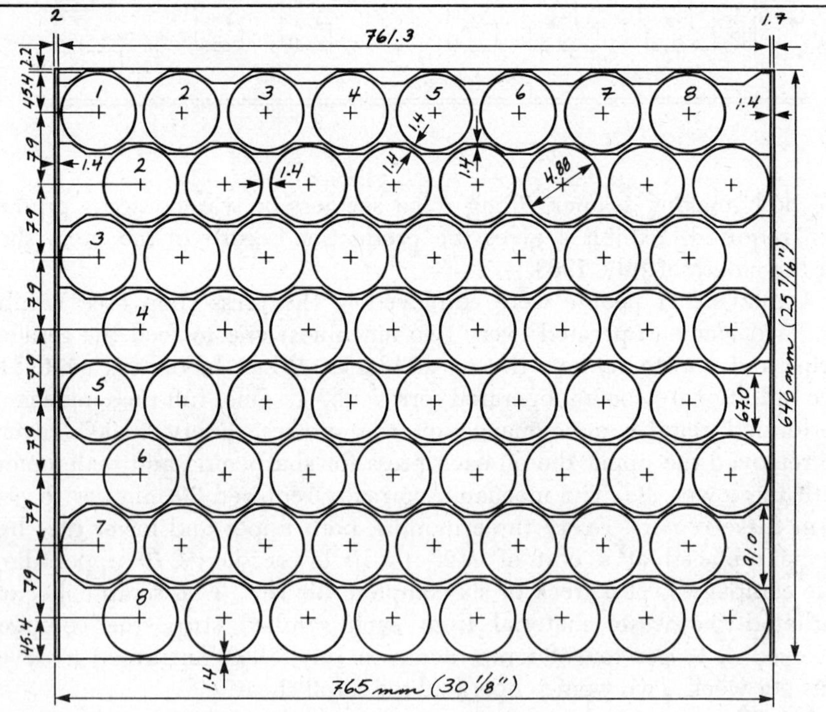

Exhibit 4
PRESS SHOP ACTUAL PRODUCTION, JULY, 1968.

Shift: 7:30 A.M. to 12 Noon—1 P.M. to 4:30 P.M.
Working Days: 21
Average Packing Room Demand: 405 cartons per hour (48 cans/carton)

Press number	1	2	3	4	5	6	7
Days worked	16	21	21	21	21	21	21
Hours overtime	0	11	12	4	2	8	4
Cases produced (53,000 covers per case)	10	21	19	16	21	26	21

Exhibit 5
PRESS SHOP EQUIPMENT AND LABOR EMPLOYED

Equipment	Year installed	Theoretical output (units per/min)	Cost £	Present market value £	Operators Female	Operators Male
Scroll shear	1940	150 (strips)	1,000	150	2	
Presses nos.						
1	1940	140 (covers)	500	70	2	
2	1940	140 "	500	70	2	
3	1940	140 "	500	70		
4	1940	140 "	500	70	2	
5	1940	140 "	500	70		
6	1959	160 "	700	80	2	
7	1962	160 "	700	80		
						2 (scrap men) 1 (mechanic)

room demand. By July, 1968, overtime in this department had climbed to over 40 hours. Mr. Thompson became concerned with this rising cost situation and had written to the technical advisers in the head office for details on new cover-making presses. From the information he received on four possible models, Mr. Thompson felt the German Kort press would be the best choice. It had the lowest cost, highest productivity, and shortest delivery date of the suggested models.

The Kort press

The Kort press was a high-speed, twin die press with a rated capacity of 240 covers per minute from each die. Operating efficiency was 92 percent. The purchase price was £8,000 c.i.f. per unit plus £120 for

Exhibit 6
TIN STEEL SHEET SPECIFICATIONS AND SCROLL SHEET CUTTING DIAGRAM

PLATE SPECIFICATIONS

SHEET: __31 1/4__ inches   X   __37 1/16__ inches   SIZE: __19 No. 4__

__794__ m.m.   X   __942__ m.m.

RATIO 1 TO 4,1360

WEIGHT PER BASE BOX __80 lbs.__ THICKNESS APPROX. __0.22 m.m.__

WEIGHT PER PACKAGE OF 112 SHEETS = __331__ LBS = __150__ kg.net __351__ LBS = __160__ kg.gross

QUALITY: __to be specified on order__

COST: __3 shillings__ per sheet

CUTTING DIAGRAM

USED FOR: __Covers__   DIAMETER OF CAN __73__ m.m.

YIELD PER SHEET: __100__ per package

THEORETICAL LOSS: __18.6%__

FACTORIES SUPPLIED WITH: _____

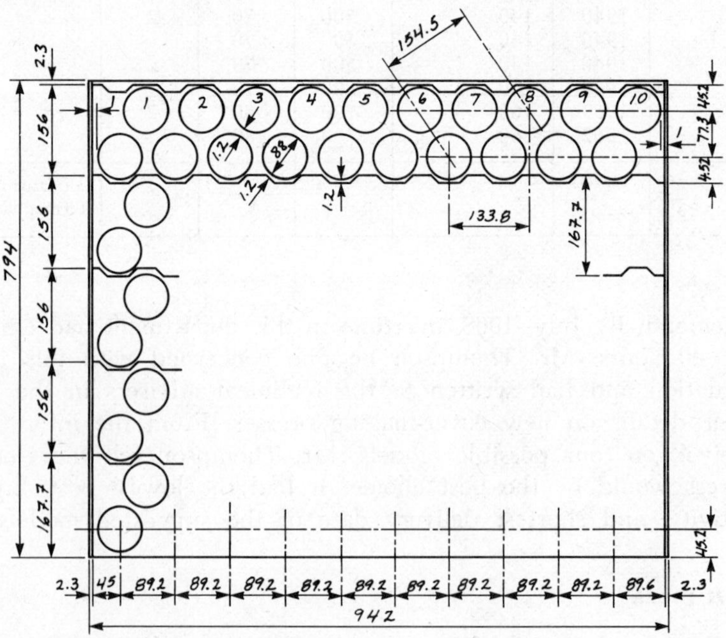

dies (£40 each upper die, £20 each lower die). Manufacturing specifications guaranteed a production of 2.5 million covers from each die before routine maintenance was necessary. At this point, die sharpening would take about 15 hours. Complete die replacement would be necessary approximately every six months. Three people could easily operate the equipment: one woman to feed the scrolled strips, one woman to remove the covers, plus one male scrap collector. It was also possible for the same three operators to run two new presses placed side by side. At present volume scrap from two new presses would be about five and a half tons per week. The mechanic would only be needed over a weekend period to perform the die maintenance when required.

The operation of the new press was similar to the present presses except that the Kort was designed to take larger scrolled strips and produced ten covers per strip (100 covers per sheet) (see Exhibit 6). This would mean buying a larger size tin steel sheet and replacing the present scroll shear. A new scroll shear would cost £7,500 c.i.f. and would require two operators. Total installation costs would be £125 (£75 for the press, £50 for the shear).

Conclusion

International Canneries, Ltd., required feasibility studies for all capital budgeting projects. In cases of equipment acquisitions, assets were depreciated over a five-year period. Money was available on a priority basis which included the rate of return and qualified statements justifying spending needs.

Mr. Thompson was aware that with a small change in the present press shop layout, three operators could run all existing presses and maintain present production levels. A recently completed work study in the press department had confirmed this.

Mr. Thompson wished to avoid overtime or multiple shift operations as much as possible. "There is a continuing trend toward greater mechanization," he said. "I am not anxious to hire additional people now and then find they are no longer required next year or the year after. Even though the union contract allows us to lay off workers with less than three years seniority without severance pay, this company is not anxious to create ill will in the community and with its workers."

HUDSON BAY MINING AND SMELTING COMPANY

Late in March, 1969, Mr. Harold McKenzie, vice president, development of Hudson Bay Mining and Smelting Company, was reviewing the alternative proposals regarding the selection of process equipment for the company's new potash mine in Saskatchewan. Mr. William

Schultz, who had been in charge of the mining studies that had been carried out, was eager to bring new technology into the mine operation for which an outline design had been prepared. However, there was strong pressure among the management personnel in the company to go with proven process equipment and not expose the company to the risk of substantial financial losses. Mr. McKenzie had until April 10 to come to a decision on the choice of mining equipment. This date was the last possible on which the equipment could be ordered for delivery on schedule in September, 1970.

The company mining operation

Hudson Bay Mining and Smelting Company is one of the larger and more successful nonferrous mining companies in Canada. It was formed in 1927 to exploit the Flin Flon copper/zinc deposit in Northern Manitoba. Operations started in 1930, the top 300 feet of the ore body being mined by open pit methods, while the lower parts were mined underground. Since 1937 all ore has been derived from the underground mine. At Flin Flon the company has built up extensive processing facilities. In addition to the mines the company operates a zinc refinery and a copper smelter.

Unlike other mining companies, Hudson Bay Mining and Smelting did not integrate forward into metal fabricating and processing. Rather, it plowed back retained earnings into exploration in northern Manitoba, Saskatchewan, Northwest Territories, the Yukon, and British Columbia. Its policy at that time was to discover its own mines and develop them. Subsequently, several other ore bodies were discovered, and the company managed to retain its ore reserve position. In 1930 ore reserves totaled 17.6 million tons. However, by the end of 1968 more than 60 million tons of ore had been mined, and ore reserves at the year end were still over 17 million tons. Major operating statistics are presented in Exhibit A–1 in the Appendix.

Diversification of interests

Hudson Bay Mining began moving into secondary industry soon after effective control of the company was acquired in 1962 by Anglo-American Corporation of Canada, Ltd. In 1965 the company acquired all the issued and outstanding shares of Zinc Oxide Company of Canada, Ltd., a manufacturer of zinc dust and zinc oxide for the paint and chemical industries. Hudson Bay Diecastings, Ltd., was established as a wholly owned subsidiary in 1965 to manufacture zinc based die castings for the automotive and appliance industries.

In 1966 Hudson Bay Mining moved into the natural gas and oil industry by acquiring a controlling interest in Francana Oil and Gas, Ltd.

One of Francana's assets was a controlling interest in Sylvite of Canada, Ltd., a valuable potash property near Rocanville, Saskatchewan. In 1968 Hudson Bay Mining acquired all property and assets of Sylvite and proposed to develop it as an operating division. At this time the company had no personnel with experience in potash mining or marketing.

Potash mining

1. **Potash: (KCl).** The development of modern farming techniques has led to an increasing demand for fertilizers. Farmers have turned to chemical compounds, some produced synthetically to provide needed nitrogen, phosphate, potassium, and trace elements in soil. A good source of potassium, potash has become a widely used fertilizer ingredient, and demand for the chemical soared during the 1950s and the early 1960s. In Saskatchewan the chemical occurs in a potash-enriched ore bed which varies in grade over different areas. The potash is mixed in with other salts but can be easily separated by mechanical methods.

2. **Potash mining in Canada.** Up to the early 1960s, the main source of potash in North America was in deposits around Carlsbad in New Mexico. International Minerals and Chemicals, Inc., and other companies mined and distributed the product throughout North America. In the 1950s the presence of reserves of potash in Saskatchewan had been indicated during exploration drilling for oil in the province. However, at that time, no decision was made to extract the mineral as the New Mexico sources were adequate to meet demand.

During the latter half of the 50s demand for potash as a fertilizer increased dramatically and companies were encouraged to explore the extent of the Saskatchewan resources. Exploration delineated a massive ore body underlaying nearly one quarter of Saskatchewan with mineable reserves exceeding 5 billion tons. The potash was located in a 9' thick blanket at a depth of 3,000' which extended over the area shown in Appendix Exhibit A–2. Studies to determine the feasibility of economically extracting the ore were started by several firms. A major obstacle to develpment of the reserves was the presence of a water-bearing layer of rock above the potash (see Appendix Exhibit A–3). However, Potash Company of America sunk a shaft and commenced production. The total investment was approximately $50 million. It was not long before the mine was flooded and work ceased. At this point in time German technology in shaft development came to the rescue. The Germans were able not only to sink a shaft, but also to seal off the water-bearing layer from it by use of special construction techniques.

Once this major problem was overcome several large companies began mining and processing operations. International Minerals and Chemicals started a major mine at Esterhazy, followed by Noranda and several other companies (see Exhibit A–4). Throughout the early 1960s demand continued to rise (see Exhibit A–5). In 1968 the management of Hudson Bay Mining decided to develop their potash reserves as part of the company's long-term growth strategy.

Potash mining and processing

The schematic flow chart of a typical Saskatchewan potash mine is shown in Exhibit 1.

Exhibit 1

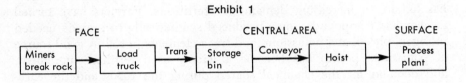

The conventional method for mining potash is a batch process operation. The actual mining of the ore takes place 3,000 feet below ground level in long passages called rooms. In the rooms, machines called "miners" break ore from the rock face. They are propelled forward and backwards by a very sophisticated drive mechanism that allows them to advance into the area that they are mining, enabling rotors mounted on the front to break off the ore. Each machine has two rotors, similar to an ordinary wood bit that rotate and bite into the rock due to the pressure applied by the advancing miner. These rotors are each approximately eight feet in diameter, and the face of each rotor is made up of many small carbide cutting tools. The action of the rotors on the rock causes it to fall away, and it is then picked up from the ground by a gathering head loader and discharged into a large truck for hauling to a central collection conveyor which carries the ore to the foot of the mine shaft.

From the foot of the mine shaft, the ore is hoisted to the surface and placed in storage until it is processed. The processing operation is a continuous operation and requires a continuous feed of ore. Hence, a buffer stock is held on the surface to ensure continuous plant operations.

An output of 2.3 million tons of ore from the mine will produce approximately 1.2 million tons of potash. To mine this amount of ore every year conventionally requires three shifts working with a total mine staff of approximately 170 men. The organization of this staff is shown in Exhibit 2.

The Sylvite project

1. Organization. After an initial outline study, the board of directors of Hudson Bay decided to proceed with a mining complex capable

Exhibit 2
ORGANIZATION CHART—FIVE 2 ROTOR BORERS

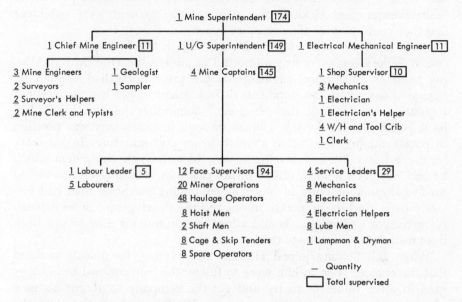

1 Mine Superintendent [174]

1 Chief Mine Engineer [11]   1 U/G Superintendent [149]   1 Electrical Mechanical Engineer [11]

3 Mine Engineers   1 Geologist   4 Mine Captains [145]   1 Shop Supervisor [10]
2 Surveyors   1 Sampler   3 Mechanics
2 Surveyor's Helpers   1 Electrician
2 Mine Clerk and Typists   1 Electrician's Helper
                                                                           4 W/H and Tool Crib
                                                                           1 Clerk

1 Labour Leader [5]   12 Face Supervisors [94]   4 Service Leaders [29]
5 Labourers   20 Miner Operations   8 Mechanics
                          48 Haulage Operators   8 Electricians
                          8 Hoist Men   4 Electrician Helpers
                          2 Shaft Men   8 Lube Men
                          8 Cage & Skip Tenders   1 Lampman & Dryman
                          8 Spare Operators

                                                          — Quantity
                                                          [ ] Total supervised

of producing 1.2 million tons of potash per year and costing in total about $70 million. This output would require mining 2.3 million tons of ore per year. The complex would consist of a mine and surface processing plant. Services to the complex could be obtained without much difficulty, and no problems were expected with transportation, electricity, or water supplies. The project was broken down into the following phases, with corresponding investments as shown:

1. O/H + other capital..........$10 million
2. Process plant................$30 million
3. Shaft development............$20 million
4. Underground mine............$10 million

Mr. J. S. Warwick, former superintendent of mines at Flin Flon was appointed general manager of the project by the board of directors. Each of the subprojects was to be under the control of an engineer or manager who would ultimately head the operation of his own section of the complex.

At the time the company decided to develop its potash bearing ore reserves, early in 1968, little experience was available within Hudson Bay Mining which the company could draw on to plan the development of the mine. Hence, Mr. Warwick decided to look outside for experienced personnel. There were several companies that offered mine engineering consultancy services, and the management of Hudson Bay selected one of these, A. J. Serke and Co., to work for the company in the planning of the mine and the processing plant. This company had been involved in several previous potash mine developments in Saskatchewan, and Hudson Bay Mining management were confident that they could provide the necessary expertise.

Early in April, 1968, Mr. McKenzie had learned that Bill Schultz, one of Serke's engineers was interested in joining the Hudson Bay Mining team as chief mine engineer for the project. He had worked on several of the potash developments in Saskatchewan and had an excellent reputation for "getting the job done." Soon after he was hired, Bill let it be known that he felt a break-through in technology was possible in potash mining, leading to a much lower cost structure. In his work for the industry Bill had developed some ideas for new equipment which he had not been able to utilize in his past jobs. The innovations would involve the manufacture of much larger mining machines than had formerly been used in the potash mines and the development of an extensible conveyor system that would allow the continuous flow of ore back from the mining machine to the hoisting shaft.

When Bill Schultz joined Hudson Bay Mining, he quickly realized that the choices open to him were to follow the conventional technology used in other mines or to try and get the company to accept his new ideas on a continuous mining process. He felt that by the time the company's operation came on stream, the other operations in Saskatchewan would have realized many production efficiencies and would make it difficult for the new operation to compete.

For the new operation to be able to compete effectively, he felt that it was necessary to utilize his production concept. Using these methods, Bill hoped to reduce the labor content of the mining operations substantially. A possible organization chart is shown in Exhibit 3. Realizing that he had to have some proof of the feasibility of the new technology, Bill decided to ask several equipment suppliers if the concept was capable of being put into operation.

He approached three mining equipment suppliers, Joy Manufacturing, MARCO (the mining division of a large industrial company), and National Mines Service, Inc., and asked them if they would be interested in designing and developing the new mining equipment. Joy indicated that it would not be interested in developing the miners but would be willing to develop the conveyor system. National Mines Services (N.M.S.) indicated that it would be interested in designing the whole system but would require $50,000 just to cover its design costs to produce a design outline and a price for the equipment. MARCO were interested in designing the miners but required $30,000 to determine a price and a rough design. Consequently, in July, 1968, Bill and Mr. Warwick approached Mr. McKenzie for $100,000 to cover these preliminary design studies.

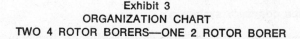

Exhibit 3
ORGANIZATION CHART
TWO 4 ROTOR BORERS—ONE 2 ROTOR BORER

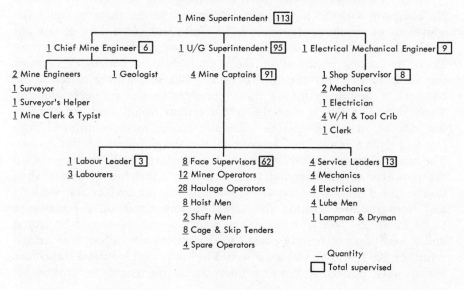

The last date on which conventional mine equipment could be ordered was April 1, 1969. Therefore, Hudson Bay Mining had up to nine months to explore the feasibility of the new technology. Mr. McKenzie decided that it would be worthwhile to investigate the new concepts, and so the company initiated what proved to be two design competitions. The first was for the miners in which only MARCO and N.M.S. were competing. The second was for the conveyor system in which seven companies expressed an interest. These were: National Mines Services, Joy Manufacturing, Roydon, Ltd., Smithson-Mathers, Tolman-Browns, Stel Trak, and Mine Conveyor Company. The deadline for the submission of prices and designs was set as January 9, 1969. In parallel with the design competition, Hudson Bay Mining also carried out a study to determine the cost of the conventional system.

Design of the conventional system

If the company decided to go ahead with the conventional mining systems, it would be either MARCO or N.M.S. who would be responsible for the manufacture of the miners. Except for a few design modifications, the machines would be of a standard design and be built to order for Hudson Bay Mining. Along with their proposals for the new machines, both companies prepared prices for the standard miners.

Design of the conveyor system

Seven companies showed interest in designing the conveyor system. No company had the technology that would permit them to build the conveyors as required. However, Bill Schultz had given a lot of thought to the design of such conveyors and had patented several inventions. These inventions would allow the manufacture of conveyors to meet the needs of the new system. Therefore, Bill was willing to allow the competing companies to use these concepts in the conveyor designs. There was no certainty that the actual system would work when built, nor whether it could operate efficiently under mine conditions. Both Joy and N.M.S. took keen interest in the development of the system. The main element in the system was a floating "end" that permitted the conveyor to be extended from 0 feet to 4,000 feet long and then disassembled with a minimum of effort when the end of the working had been reached. During the actual mining operation the conveyor could move 200 feet with the miner before operations would be halted and a new piece of belting placed in the conveyor to allow it to extend a further 200 feet. The conveyor would be supported by metal stanchions which were placed at ten-foot intervals as the conveyor progressed.

Design of the miner

MARCO and National Mines Services were to present their version of the miners to Hudson Bay Mining management on January 9, 1969. At this presentation they were to have major design outlines, prices, and a scale model of the machine. From April, 1968, until January, 1969, Bill Schultz spent much time working with the two companies. There were many problems and uncertainties, but gradually designs were developed, and on January 9, 1969, the presentations were made. Both MARCO and N.M.S. presented machines that differed only marginally in price, but N.M.S. had far more detailed design data on the machine than had MARCO.

The new miners operated on the same principle as the smaller machines currently in use in other mines, but, instead of having only two rotors, the new machines had four. New drive, control, and structural designs were required, and each company had different concepts of how these should be developed.

Each company's proposal contained detailed drawings and a complete specification for the machines. Although the companies could not be certain of having eliminated all major design flaws, they were reasonably certain that the miners would perform as specified. Bill Schultz estimated that there was a slight chance at most that either machine would not work given the present designs. However, the real problem was not whether or not the machines would work; it was more a case of how well they would work. This could not be determined until the machines were actually in operation.

Report on the proposed system

Once the data on the alternatives had been gathered, Bill Schultz prepared a report which was submitted in March, 1969, to the project general manager, Mr. Warwick. This report was then passed to Mr. McKenzie for a final decision. Extracts from this report are appended below. Bill included cost and performance data for the alternative systems. Realizing the importance of the suppliers in the process of development, he also included a personal evaluation of the companies based on his personal experience.

Following the decision on the systems, it would be necessary to commit at this stage $1.5 million to develop and build the chosen system. To have the equipment available on site in Saskatchewan in September, 1970, it was necessary to place orders immediately for several long delivery components and raw materials. If the new miners were selected, it would be necessary to commence detail design activities on the subassemblies and control systems required. There would be over 40 engineers and designers working on the system, and the suppliers would be committing a substantial part of their design and manufacturing capabilities to the machine.

As he read Bill's report, Mr. McKenzie wondered how he should evaluate the proposal and, in choosing the equipment, on what criteria he should base his decision.

APPENDIX: EXCERPTS FROM REPORT ON PROPOSED MINING SYSTEM SUBMITTED BY W. SCHULTZ TO J. S. WARWICK

RECOMMENDATIONS
It is recommended that Sylvite:

1. Purchase two National Mine Service Marietta 780AW4 mining machines and one National Mine Service Marietta 780A mining machine with Tamper motors at the best possible price which can be negotiated.
2. Purchase one Joy extensible conveyor, and proceed with the demonstration, testing, debugging program previously discussed, negotiating in advance terms covering Sylvite's prior right, testing program, and purchase price of subsequent units.
3. Sylvite adopt as a general organizational operating plan the capital equipment schedule, manning schedule, and mining layout presented in this report.

✻   ✻   ✻   ✻   ✻

PART I—ECONOMICS

This part is a complete economic appraisal of the effect of using a wide 4-rotor machine in a progressive type operation as opposed to duplicating the operation of IMC-K2 with minor improvements without regard to equipment manufacturer.

* * * * *

Miners: five small, or two large and one small

1. Based on a 365-day year operation, the number of 2-rotor boring machines required is 5, using 1 machine as a spare and development machine.
2. Based on a 365-day year operation, the number of 4-rotor boring machines required is 2. In this case a 2-rotor machine is considered necessary as a spare and development machine.
3. Tonnage cut in a 24-hour period by a 4-rotor machine is approximately three times the tonnage cut by a 2-rotor machine operating under the same standard conditions.
4. The actual percentage cutting time in any 24-hour period is virtually the same for both types of machines.

* * * * *

TOTAL COST TO MINE COMPARISON

Description	2-Rotor	4-Rotor
Operating labor comparison	$0.57/ton	$0.38/ton
Operating and maintenance cost comparison	$0.67/ton	$0.62/ton
Depreciation mine equipment	$0.51/ton	$0.56/ton
Depreciation small equipment.	$0.12/ton	$0.12/ton
Depletion cost mine development and small development	$0.275/ton	$0.275/ton
	$2.145/ton	$1.955/ton

Miner capacity: The miner capacity can be defined as *tons of ore* produced per cutting hour. Factors affecting the miner capacity are:

1. Type, design and make of mining machine including electrics.
2. Design and condition of cutting tools.
3. Possible penetration rate under permissable load depending on the ore characteristics, (hardness of minerals, grain size, crystal form, backing of crystals, etc.).
4. Horsepower.

* * * * *

Labor:
1. Supervisory staff cost comparison per year:

	No.	2-Rotor cost	No.	4-Rotor cost
Total	15	$124,500	10	$93,000/year

Assumes 365 days per year, 3-shift operation.

2. Maintenance crew cost comparison:

No.	2-Rotor cost	No.	4-Rotor cost
15	$109,500	11	$83,000

3. Production crews cost comparison:

	No.	Cost	No.	Cost
Mine foremen	12	120,000	8	80,000
Miner operators	20	160,000	12	96,000
Haulage operators.	48	336,000	28	196,000
Spare operators	8	48,000	4	24,000
Others	57	423,000	41	311,000
Total	145	1,087,000	93	707,000

✿   ✿   ✿   ✿   ✿

4. Face equipment capital cost comparison:

Description	Quantity	2-Rotor ($×1,000)	Quantity	4-Rotor ($×1,000)
Boring machine +3,000 feet of miner cable 5		1,726.0	1-2-rotor 2-4-rotor	2,916.0 (Note 1)
Extensible conveyor installed 3		930.0	3	930.0
Loaders installed 3		225.0	2	150.0
Miscellaneous		737.0		760.0
Total installed cost		3,618.0		4,756.0

Note 1: The price of $2,916,000 shown is for the N.M.S. 4-rotor mine. If the MARCO miners were to be chosen the price would be $2,825,000.

✿   ✿   ✿   ✿   ✿

5. Total capital cost comparison:

Description	2-Rotor	4-Rotor
Face equipment	3,618.0	4,756.0
U/G haulage conveyors.	1,743.0	1,425.0
Storage and reclaim.	800.5	800.5
Ventilation and safety	208.5	193.5
Power distribution	482.8	442.8
Mobile service equipment	600.4	547.6
U/G shops and warehouse	229.9	229.9
Level stations	170.0	170.0
Construction overhead	401.0	401.0
	8,254.1	8,966.3

Revised upward see estimate dated March, 1969.
$8,966.3 becomes $9,350.0

✿   ✿   ✿   ✿   ✿

Supplier Evaluation:
    MARCO versus N.M.S.
Finance:

1. MARCO is a division of a major industrial corporation. Financing is impeccable. . . . Question of profit orientation at the expense of quality.
2. National Mine Services . . . privately held . . . currently delivering nine units in Saskatchewan . . . good at IMC, delivered to schedule . . . bad at another operation . . . two strikes at National Mine Services Plant . . . other company did not monitor operations too closely.

Manufacturing:
    Total world market for the 2-rotor miner is about 20 per annum. MARCO and N.M.S. are the only companies in the world with any real capability. Current order back logs are:

N.M.S. 14.
MARCO 2

In Saskatchewan the total machine population is:

Capacity

N.M.S. 16 M/C's—2162 T.P.D.
MARCO 23 M/C's—2026 T.P.D.

Personnel:
    MARCO personnel . . . difficult to work with, . . . self centered. National Mine Services personnel are very cooperative and enthusiastic.

❉   ❉   ❉   ❉   ❉

I INTRODUCTION

In August, 1968, seven manufacturers expressed a genuine interest in the development of a new extensible conveyor to be used in conjunction with our continuous boring machine.

To this date, six out of the seven have presented proposals at varying stages of design and detail.

It is the purpose of this report to evaluate those six proposals with regards to design and cost and to make the necessary recommendations.

❉   ❉   ❉   ❉   ❉

II RECOMMENDATIONS AND CONCLUSIONS

It is recommended that Joy Manufacturing be engaged to manufacture a prototype extensible conveyor, as per their proposal.

There is no doubt in saying that out of the six proposals presented, Joy has come up with the best prototype design, the most detail to evaluate, and the best price.

Joy have not given us a firm price on additional units, but it is hoped that negotiations prior to any contract for the prototype would result in a firm price on additional units.

Also, at this time the necessary arrangements regarding our potential patent rights will have to be negotiated and agreed upon, particularly licensing arrangements for future users.

❉   ❉   ❉   ❉   ❉

EXTENSIBLE CONVEYOR PROPOSALS—PRICING COMPARISON

Supplier	Firm price	Can. funds	F.O.B.	Length	Less	Test	Taxes	Duty
National Mine Services	$220,000	$237,600	Minesite	2,000 ft.	Motors, belting, chutes	Labor $10/hr/man Eng. $15/hr/man + $124,000 U.S.	Extra	
Roydon, Ltd.	Want approval on design before pricing or testing information.							
Smithson-Mathers	Prototype unit only—complete with testing. None yet $150,653.15		Factory	2,480 ft.	Belting will provide @ 50,496.74 no chutes.	Price included in protype unit at their site.	Extra	
Mine Conveyor, Ltd.	No projection on a completed protype. None yet			500 ft.	Drills, chutes	$131,000 (in U.K.) (6–10 wks. trial work).	Extra	Included
Joy Manufacturing	a. Test unit		Galt	800 ft. for test only		$160,365.00	Extra	
	b. Completed prototype $188,293		Galt	1,700 ft.	Everything included		Extra	
Tolman-Browns	No proposal and no apparent interest.							
Stel Trak	Very sketchy rush type design—no prices available.							

Exhibit A–1
MAJOR OPERATING STATISTICS HUDSON BAY MINING AND SMELTING COMPANY
(all figures in 000's)

	Operating revenue	Net earnings	Dividends	Copper prod/tons	Ore reserves (tons)
1962	49,396	11,302	8,273	37,023	14,934,000
1963	57,224	11,737	8,963	37,301	15,115,500
1964	56,377	13,095	9,652	40,417	16,627,400
1965	61,702	15,990	10,342	38,726	16,842,400
1966	69,112	19,116	11,170	38,268	16,765,300
1967	72,351	16,718	11,000	38,403	16,884,600
1968	79,700	21,134	11,551	41,660	17,612,300

Exhibit A–2
POTASH DEPOSITS IN SASKATCHEWAN AND MINE LOCATIONS

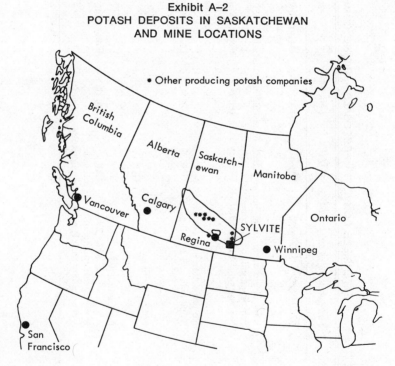

Distribution of potash reserves

Exhibit A–3
CROSS SECTION VIEW OF A TYPICAL
SASKATCHEWAN MINE

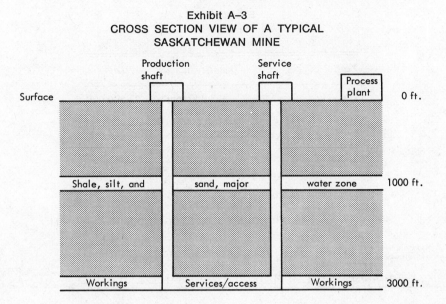

Exhibit A–4
POTASH MINES IN SASKATCHEWAN AND CAPACITY

Mine	Location on stream	Date	Cost (in million dollars)	KCl capacity (million tons per year)
IMC-KI	Esterhazy	1962	65	2.00
Kalium	Belle Plaine	1964	50	0.75
P.C.A.	Saskatoon	1965	50	0.70
IMC-K$_2$	Esterhazy	1967	65	2.50
Alwinsal	Lanigan.	1968	60	1.0
Alan	Alan	1968	80	1.5
Cominco*	Vanscoy	1969	65	1.20
Noranda*	Viscount	1970	81	1.20
Duval*	Saskatoon	1969	63	1.00

* Indicated underdeveloped.

Exhibit A–5
CANADIAN POTASH PRODUCTION
1963–1967

Year	Quantity mined	Value
1963	383,000 tons	22,500,000
1964	858,351 tons	31,162,000
1965	1,491,000 tons	55,970,000
1966	1,990,000 tons	62,665,000
1967	2,383,000 tons	67,396,000

Exhibit A–6
SIDE VIEW OF THE PROPOSED CONVEYOR AND MINER SYSTEM

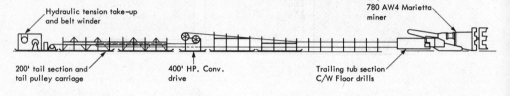

Hydraulic tension take–up
and belt winder

780 AW4 Marietta
miner

200' tail section and
tail pulley carriage

400' HP. Conv.
drive

Trailing tub section
C/W Floor drills

12 PROCUREMENT BY MANUFACTURE

The "make or buy" question is an interesting one because of its many dimensions. Almost every organization is faced with it continually. For manufacturing companies the make alternative may be a natural extension of activities already present or an opportunity for diversification. For nonmanufacturing concerns it is normally a question of services rather than products. Should a hospital have its own laundry, operate its own dietary, security, and maintenance services, or should it purchase these outside? Becoming one's own supplier is an alternative that has not received much attention in this text so far, and yet it is a vital point in every organization's procurement strategy.

Make or buy—the strategy

What should be the attitude of a company toward this issue of "make or buy?" It is probably true that most companies do not have a consciously expressed policy with reference to this issue but prefer to decide each separate problem as it arises. Perhaps, if the problem arises frequently enough, a series of such decisions is equivalent to a policy; on the other hand, if the question is never raised, that very fact may in itself be indicative of the company's attitude. In any event there apparently are concerns which lean toward the doctrine of self-support to the extent of making for themselves the things they need, whenever possible, and thereby becoming largely independent and self-sustaining industrial units. On the other hand, there are concerns which believe that companies specializing in the production of a definitely limited line are better able to provide the quality and economy necessary for economical procurement than can a company producing such items as a sideline to its major interests.

The strategic dimensions of the make or buy question are far reaching. "What kind of an organization or company do we want to be?" is a fair starting question. If the opportunities in the environment can be matched against the strengths and weaknesses of the firm, a preliminary stance on make or buy is likely to result. An organization seeing an environmental need for certain products may be anxious to make if it has considerable manufacturing skills. If the opportunity is primarily of a marketing nature and the firm is weak on the manufacturing side, it might not be wise to take a strong "make" stance. If it were possible to discuss the question in the aggregate for the individual firm, the problem should be formulated in terms of: "What should our organization's objective be in terms of how much value added as a percentage of final product or service cost and in what form?" Such a goal might never be reached or agreed on because of factors beyond the control of the decision makers. For example, vertical integration may be forced on a concern to protect its sources of key raw materials, even though the executive might have preferred purchasing these requirements on the open market. Political, social, and environmental concerns may also affect the desired stance. Despite the difficulties of formulating a strategic stance, an attempt to develop one may well have significant benefits. Few organizations recognize the quality of their materials management function as one variable to be considered. A strong purchasing group, capable of assuring supply at reasonable prices would favor a "buy" tendency when other factors are not of overriding importance. For example, one corporation found its purchasing ability in foreign markets such a competitive asset that it deliberately disinvested itself of certain manufacturing facilities common to every competitor in the industry.

In some ways it is rather futile to discuss this issue as a matter of general policy, only because in the last analysis the problems always resolve themselves into specific situations; each case must be settled on its own merits. This statement holds, whether we are considering individual companies or individual items required by a given company. The best that can be done, therefore, is to outline the advantages or objectives of procurement by manufacture; attempt to note the dangers; and, finally, try to reach some useful generalizations.[1]

Direct control of sources of supply

There are situations in which the manufacturer, although not actually engaged in producing certain articles, has nevertheless established relationships with suppliers that at least approach a degree of control approaching that maintained by one of its own departments. Three such types of control may be cited.

The first involves the purchaser's inspection at the plant of the supplier; this procedure normally means inspection of goods in process of manufacture. Such control is particularly evident when quality specifications are rigid and when transportation charges on the completed prod-

---

[1] One of the most thoroughgoing and useful treatments of the topic is that of James W. Culliton, *Make or Buy*. 4th reprint (Boston: Harvard Business School, Division of Research, Business Research Study, No. 27, 1956).

uct are high. Closely allied to inspection at the point of origin is the use of specifications covering the material and the method of manufacture. This practice has already been discussed.

The second type of semimanufacturing control is illustrated by the practice of certain companies which, without going to the extent of actually engaging in manufacturing operations themselves, have in one form or another sought to develop a satisfactory source of supply. Long-term contracts have been made and the manufacturers assured that, as long as they maintained quality, service, and reasonable price, they would be given the company's business. Purchasing departments have taken pride in conducting relationships with such suppliers in a fair and just manner, at times even paying higher prices than might be available elsewhere in order that a particular supplier might meet production costs. Under such a stimulus, these supplying companies have, in turn, continued as sources of supply for many years. They have occasionally installed special machines at a substantial cost in order to meet the specific requirements of the buyer. The savings from production economies have not infrequently been passed along to the buyer. In one instance the director of purchases for a manufacturer of cosmetics was informed by one of the major can manufacturing companies that its research department had developed a leak-proof and airtight can which the cosmetics manufacturer had long been seeking. The latter was informed that large numbers of the cans could be obtained at a reasonable price, provided the buyer was willing to make a five-year contract and that under these circumstances no charge would be made for the special machinery which would be required. The contract was accepted, with the provision that it could be canceled at the end of any year upon the payment by the cosmetics manufacturer of a sum equal to the unamortized value of the machines. The provision was also made that if changes occurred in the price of tin and the wages of labor, the contract price would be adjusted fairly to reflect such changes. The cancellation clause was inserted with particular thought of the possibility of changes in styles, a discontinuance in the type of can called for in the contract, or a reduction in the quantity required. The container manufacturer, moreover, was willing to transfer the patents to the cosmetics manufacturer.

A third type of "halfway measure" exists when the manufacturer buys the material which is to go into the product and has it shipped directly to a concern which fabricates that material and ships the finished product to the "buyer."

Reasons for manufacture instead of purchase

There are many specific reasons that may lead a manufacturer to produce rather than purchase required items. These include:

1.   Occasionally, such small quantities of a special item may be required to make production of it by a vendor prohibitive because of the cost.

2.   Manufacture may be undertaken as a means to secure the desired quality. The quality requirements may be so exacting or so unusual as to require special processing methods that vendors cannot be expected to provide. Also, in a strong seller's market, vendors tend to grow careless and, although quite capable of meeting the specifications, simply do not do so. On the other hand, vendors may be selling only a quality far above that which would fully satisfy the need in question and may, at the same time, have so satisfactory a volume at the higher level as to have no interest in a lower grade. If any one of these various situations exists, the user may feel forced to start manufacturing the item. This decision may be quite sound. Before undertaking the experiment, however, the user should carefully reexamine specifications, check on inspection procedure and methods, and make every reasonable effort to secure the active cooperation of a vendor. If the manufacturer still decides to "make rather than buy," it is assuming responsibility for producing and maintaining a quality not obtainable from anyone else.

3.   Manufacture may be undertaken as a means of greater assurance of supply. Under some circumstances, a closer coordination of the supply with the demand is possible when the item is manufactured by the user. A certain degree of self-sufficiency appears attractive, since it theoretically involves a freedom from transportation difficulties and costs and from interruption of delivery by vendors confronted with labor difficulties or "acts of God." A delayed delivery through the fault of no one in particular may close down an entire department. Of course, this argument is not valid when the items in question are obtainable from a variety of sources, including numerous local ones. On the other hand, when but one qualified supplier exists—even though located geographically nearby—there is a substantial risk of delayed deliveries. True, the very type of difficulties the manufacturer is seeking to avoid may arise equally in connection with those sources from which he has to buy the material he himself will manufacture. The danger, however, may well be less, and under most circumstances, therefore, it is probably true that there is a somewhat greater assurance of supply when the item is manufactured by the user.

4.   In some industries, manufacturers find it essential to make their own equipment because no suitable suppliers exist or because they wish to preserve technological secrets. One large chemical firm owns its own equipment making plant where about 60 percent of all corporate requirements are manufactured. Experimentation in recent years showed it was possible to subcontract certain parts of equipment to various vendors leaving final assembly and manufacture of particularly "sensitive" components to the corporation's own shop.

5. It may be cheaper to manufacture than to buy. There are conditions under which a company may temporarily or even permanently produce certain items more cheaply than they can be bought, due consideration being given to transportation and other costs. Thus, a company may, quite by accident, discover a new process by which it can produce some item at a substantially lower cost than its regular suppliers, although the latter may specialize in the manufacture of that particular item. So, too, a company may be able to acquire, at an exceptionally low price, certain equipment with which it can manufacture some part at a cost below that of its past suppliers. Also, the volume of certain items used may be so large that it is possible to manufacture them at a production cost as low as that of any accessible supplier and thus to save an amount equivalent to the latter's marketing expense and profit. The lower cost in any one of these cases may be real, computed in accordance with the best accounting practice, and not merely a juggled cost computed to justify a decision actually made on quite different grounds. The circumstances making it possible for a company to operate under these lower costs are usually peculiar to the company; few, if any, generalizations can be made concerning them. Furthermore, the required volume of a company manufacturing some of its own supplies may so change with time altering markedly the conditions prevailing when the original decision was made.

6. Particularly in depression or recession the manufacturer with idle equipment may undertake production, rather than buy, to use surplus production facilities. Even in more normal times, when items of satisfactory quality can be obtained from reliable suppliers, manufacture by the company itself may be undertaken as a means of increasing the total volume of production over which the overhead burden can be distributed.

The make or buy decision can be an integral part of the overall production plan of a company. Any organization wishing to smoothe production or employment can use make or buy as one alternative. If a significant portion of total requirements is purchased, it may be possible to ensure steady running of the corporation's own facilities, leaving the suppliers to bear the burden of fluctuations in demand. If making is normally preferred and buying is only resorted to when all other alternatives to capacity expansion have been exhausted, it theoretically appears attractive. In reality, such subcontracting would occur normally at very busy times, making it difficult to find suitable and willing vendors. A number of interesting models have been developed using make or buy in the production smoothing context. Few still recognize the difficulties of jumping in and out of the marketplace on short notice.[2]

---

[2] B. Shore, "Quantitative Analysis and the Make-or-Buy Decision," *Journal of Purchasing*, vol. 6, no. 1 (February 1970), pp. 5–11.

7. Occasionally, although the cost of manufacturing an item may not be any lower for a user than those of vendors from whom it could buy, yet those vendors, through collusion, legislative protection, or unwise pricing policy, may be asking an exorbitant price. A concern that is manufacturing even a small part of its requirements is in a strategic position to bargain with such suppliers. Its employees have had experience in making the article, and the company has a record of cost data that can be used effectively with vendors. The latter know that although the buyer may be reluctant to go further in making this particular item, the buyer can and will do so if necessary.

8. Still another reason for manufacturing an item formerly purchased is to protect the personnel of the company and to maintain the organization. This same contention is used as an argument against abandoning manufacture, once undertaken, in favor of buying outside.

9. Competitive, political, social, or environmental reasons may force a company to make even when it might have preferred to buy. When a competitor acquires ownership of a key source of raw material, it may force similar action. Many countries insist that a certain amount of processing of raw materials be done within national boundaries. A company located in a high unemployment area may decide to make certain items to help alleviate this situation. A company may have to process further certain by-products to make them environmentally acceptable. In each of these instances, cost may not be of overriding concern.

10. Finally, there is a purely emotional reason. The management of some companies appears to take an unreasonable pride in mere size. Bigness and self-sufficiency seem to these executives to be interrelated. Quite aside from any legal questions, it is by no means self-evident that these objectives can be justified. For one thing, no company can ever be entirely self-sufficient. Furthermore, the more completely integrated an industrial organization is, the more complex, diverse, and difficult become its administrative problems and the thinner its supervisory talent is likely to be spread. Clearly, too, concentration primarily on size is bound to divert attention from the proper task of operating the business most efficiently. Nevertheless, there can be no doubt that the desire for size lies behind many a decision to manufacture instead of to buy.

Dangers involved in decision to manufacture

Thus, there is an imposing list of reasons for undertaking, under the proper circumstances, to manufacture certain items rather than to purchase them. Many times the reasoning in favor of such a policy is cogent and the conclusions are sound. It is also true, however, that not infrequently a company will succumb to the temptation to make its own items under conditions which do not warrant doing so and without full appreciation of the dangers involved in the decision.

One of the dangers faced by a company in launching upon a general policy of producing for its own use is lack of administrative or technical experience in the production of the items in question. These items are often substantially unlike those which the company is manufacturing for sale. They have been bought from companies which presumably have considered their manufacture sufficiently specialized to necessitate devoting the company's entire attention to the production of that line. What is now proposed assumes that the purchaser can produce this item as a sideline and can do a better job than the original manufacturer. The company undertaking manufacture lacks the experience of the supplier, and the project may require new types of skilled labor, new supervisors, and new equipment; moreover, every time another unrelated production unit is added to the original organization, there is bound to be some loss of cohesion and unity resulting in new technical operating and executive problems. In short, the company may well be launching upon a type of business not originally contemplated, without experience and frequently without adequate or qualified personnel.[3]

The extent to which this argument applies, of course, varies widely with circumstances. To attempt to apply it to some situations would, because of the trivial nature of the item and the simplicity of the manufacturing operation, be quite foolish. But under other circumstances it is so important that often the failure of the company itself can be traced to an inability to recognize this danger.

There may be a definite loss of goodwill that could have an adverse effect upon the sales volume of the company in a number of ways. If reciprocity plays a part in the selling program, the effect of ceasing to buy an item is obvious. The salesmen from the former suppliers cease to call. To sever business relations with former suppliers may arouse their actual resentment. This may prove particularly serious if the displaced supplier is one through whom the manufacturer's finished product was sold as well as one from whom the manufacturer had bought. The erstwhile buyer will find competitors prompt to take advantage of the

---

[3] The problem is simplified somewhat by virtue of the fact that a marketing problem is not involved; at least, none is intended. Actually, a marketing problem may develop. If the company's requirements for the particular item in question subsequently become less than originally contemplated after auxiliary facilities have been built up to meet the larger demand expected, it naturally follows that the company has the option of producing a volume beyond its own requirements and disposing of the surplus in the general market or of finding itself with equipment which is excessive as far as its own needs are concerned. Under these circumstances the company may actually be confronted by a marketing problem as well as by a technical and an administrative one.

ill will created. Finally, too, such action is likely to raise the question in the minds of those companies from which other items are still bought as to how long it will be before they, in turn, are dropped.

Frequently, certain suppliers have built such a reputation for themselves that they have been able to build a real preference for their component as part of the finished product. Normally, these are branded items which can be used to make the total piece of equipment more acceptable to the final user. For example, most diesel engine manufacturers buy Bosch or Simms injection pumps, not because they are cheap, or difficult to manufacture, but because the ultimate consumers want them. The manufacturer of road grading equipment and other construction or mining equipment frequently let the customer specify the power plant brand and see this option as advantageous in selling their equipment.

Companies wishing to maintain a leading position in their industry must be constantly engaged in some form of research so their product may be continually improved and production costs reduced. A concern that specializes in manufacturing a major line can do this. A company in which that product is merely a sideline can rarely afford to devote the same attention to it; consequently, no matter how great an advantage existed originally, it is likely to be only a matter of time before the company in which such an item is a sideline finds itself outclassed both as to product and as to cost. There are, it is true, some items so standardized in nature and in method of manufacture as to have remained unchanged over many years, but their number is limited.

This last argument becomes more serious when, as is natural, the new department comes, perhaps unconsciously, to look upon itself as being in a favored position; in other words, it enjoys a "protected status." This attitude having once been established, every conceivable argument is advanced for retaining the department. The new department is seldom under the same competitive pressure either to keep costs down or to keep the product up to date, as is the independent supplier.

Closer coordination of inventory with requirements is one of the arguments advanced for manufacturing rather than buying. Actually, this result is not as easy to obtain as might at first appear. To get the lowest costs, the production department must manufacture in the quantities set by the most economical run. It is possible that this quantity may be well above reasonable requirements. The alternatives are either higher costs or excessive inventory.

A lack of flexibility in selecting possible souces and substitute items is likely to result. As a purchaser the company is able to buy from anyone, to obtain the best existing price, to shift from one source to another whenever conditions warrant, or, indeed, with the greatest freedom to cease using the product at all. Such is not the case once a concern has committed itself to a policy of procurement by manufacture.

Some problems in costing

Whether or not a particular company can manufacture at a cost lower than that at which a given item can be bought is a question often very difficult to answer. The question is not whether this cost is lower than that of a high-cost supplier but rather whether it is lower than that of the firm (or group of firms) that set the actual market price. Indeed, it is frequently possible to obtain from a low-cost producer (as distinguished from the marginal one) a price that is lower even than the market price and at a profit to both buyer and seller, especially if such a producer is seeking additional volume or for some other reason finds the purchaser's business particularly attractive.

Further, it is always a moot question as to what *cost* really is. The answer depends upon what cost data are available, the purpose for which they are collected, and the form in which they are to be kept. Standard costs, for example, may be most helpful for control purposes and of no value whatsoever in attempting to answer the question: "At what cost can one manufacture a particular brass stamping or a metal container of given material and specification?" If new equipment is bought for the purpose, how is depreciation to be handled? Shall the usual burden of overhead factors be considered in arriving at a comparative cost figure? Since many costs vary with volume of output, what volume figure is to be used? Shall it be present or future volume? For total requirements or only for part? And if for only part, then how much? What allowance shall be made for the additional expense incurred by the purchasing department, if manufacture is undertaken, for such operations as assembling the new raw materials and performing the extra inspection required? Also, what allowance shall be made for the necessary training of the production personnel and the effect of the new product on the major production lines? Clearly, there are many debatable questions that must be settled before any progress at all can be made in actually arriving at a definite figure.

Normally, direct variable costs include labor and materials. Variable overhead costs may include: indirect labor and fringe benefits, social security taxes, overtime premiums, additional supervisory costs, additional power and security costs, equipment depreciation, and others. Fixed costs may include several of the above plus general taxes, building repair and depreciation, administrative costs, insurance, and others. The difficulty in deciding whether making or buying is justified on a cost basis lies in the identification and quantification of those costs relevant to the decision. Normally, in the short term, variable costs are of most concern. In the longer term fixed costs may become important. It is also useful to recognize that a difference exists between the individual decision and the cumulative effect of many make or buy decisions over a period of time. Since future costs are almost always uncertain, probabilistic estimates need to be made in any longer term make or buy decision. An interesting probabilistic model developed by D. A. Raunick and A. G. Fisher attempted to quantify such factors as the loss of trade secrets, employee morale, and communications and control if subcontracting were used instead of making. This allowed the calculation of a rate of return on investment with a probabilistic range permitting managers to make the decision with quantitative recognition of the risk involved.[4]

Experience has made it amply clear that once management has definitely committed itself to a policy of procurement by manufacture, it is not difficult for costs to be figured to justify both the original decision and a continuance of the practice.

Thus, it becomes increasingly evident that the decision on whether to procure by manufacture or by purchase is often a most difficult one to make and that the decision to manufacture, once made, is likely to place the company in a position from which it is difficult to withdraw.

If an examination is made of the reasons why the problem is brought up in the first instance, it will often be discovered that it arises out of a temporary condition. The plant may be operating below capacity because of temporary business conditions. Vendor's current prices may appear out of line. The immediate needs of quality, volume, or service cannot be filled satisfactorily by suppliers at the moment. Or in a reverse situation, a war or some other unusual condition may force a company to concentrate on processes in which it is peculiarly qualified to a degree far beyond what is either necessary or desirable under ordinary circumstances, with the result that it has to "farm out" or subcontract many items it commonly both could and would produce in its own plant. Or it may, in such extraordinary situations, have requirements for such subcontractable items far beyond what it is able to produce with its available equipment and manpower and, in consequence, be forced to "buy" where it normally would have "made." Such conditions may appear, and doubtlessly are, serious for the moment; but in many cases it is only a comparatively short time before the situation has been corrected.

There may be good reason for a company to undertake manufacture if the item is required in large volume, is substantially of the same nature as the regular product, is adapted to the existing productive facilities, is capable of production by the company at a cost low enough to allow a saving over the price charged for the item by a supplier, and is not protected by patents so sizable royalties have to be paid.

From this analysis of the problems involved in arriving at "make or buy" decisions, certain generalizations appear justifiable, although, as in all generalizations, exceptions must be made. Clearly it can be said

[4] D. A. Raunick and A. G. Fisher, "A Probabilistic Make-Buy Model," *Journal of Purchasing*, vol. 8, no. 1 (February 1972), pp. 63–80.

that only in rare instances will any one argument be so conclusive as to dictate an obvious decision. Consequently, in most cases the solution will be a compromise based on judgment as to the course of action most conducive to the company's best interest. In a real sense, therefore, the correct answer to the question: "What is preferable, make or buy?" is that "it all depends upon circumstances." Nevertheless, balancing all the arguments, the burden of proof in most situations rests on those urging "make" rather than "buy." Dr. Culliton states the case well:

Most of the arguments *for* making appear to be weaker than those *for* buying. They appeared weaker because in many instances they seemed to smack of rationalization. The argument, for example, that the impossibility of buying necessitates making was rarely used as a current argument but only in explanation of previous decisions to make. And quite frequently the conditions which were claimed to have rendered buying impossible changed with embarrassing rapidity. The number of instances in which a company *had* to make was small.

This implies that in many instances where corporations began making, not because they had to but because they wanted to, the decision was wrong and that those corporations would be better off if they bought certain things now being made. This conclusion is based on several grounds.

Make or buy problems are considered as unusual by many business executives, even though every purchase and every manufacturing schedule implies a decision to buy or to make. In other words, any executive machinery for discovering make or buy decisions is practically nonexistent. Consequently, the only make or buy problems ordinarily to receive any attention are those that come to management's attention by way of an accident, an emergency, or as the result of the addition of an entirely new final product to the company's line.

Closely allied to the failure to recognize make or buy problems was the failure to review decisions once they were made. Companies were especially lax in reviewing those decisions which had led to the adoption of a make program.

There is a general lack of attention to other possible solutions to the problem. A company, for example, claimed that it was unable to buy the quality needed. Yet, its procurement efforts were devoted almost entirely to negotiations with one supplier, despite the fact that there were several well-equipped prospective suppliers that, in appearance at least, were only too anxious to work on the kind of technical problems faced by the company. Failure to secure from one supplier what was wanted offered an excuse for following a course of action already desired by the company. The real reasons were based principally upon the management's pride and desire to boast of the large number and variety of products which the company made.

Finally, relatively few companies seem to give any attention to the change in their organization which will be caused by the addition of something new. A company's production men often favor a new program in the belief that they would be able to meet all the problems without loss of efficiency in their regular jobs.

This last fact is a dramatic comment upon the narrow point of view many people take with respect to limitations in their own ability. The same fact is frequently overlooked by executives themselves when they keep adding new functions to their portion of the business, with little thought to the possibility that their efforts might be less effective. . . .[5]

BIBLIOGRAPHY

CULLITON, JAMES W. *Make or Buy.* 4th reprint. Business Research Study No. 27 Boston: Harvard Business School, Division of Research, 1956.

GROSS, HARRY. *Make or Buy.* Englewood Cliffs, N.J.: Prentice-Hall, Inc., 1966.

HEINRITZ, STUART F., AND FARRELL, PAUL V. *Purchasing: Principles and Application.* 5th ed. Englewood Cliffs, N.J.: Prentice-Hall, Inc., 1971.

OXENFELDT, ALFRED R. *Make or Buy: Factors Affecting Decisions.* New York: McGraw-Hill Book Co., 1965.

STEINER, GEORGE A. *Industrial Project Management.* New York: MacMillan, 1968.

WESTING, J. H.; FINE, I. V.; ZENZ, GARY JOSEPH ET AL. *Purchasing Management.* 3d ed. New York: John Wiley & Sons, Inc., 1969.

CASES FOR CHAPTER 12

ERICSON-MORGAN INDUSTRIES, INC.

Recent problems with piston pin suppliers had created a tight supply situation resulting in unreliable deliveries. In view of this Mr. H. Irwin, manager of purchasing for Ericson-Morgan, had to decide whether or not he should propose to top management that the company further investigate the possibility to manufacture piston pins instead of purchasing them.

Company background

Ericson-Morgan, an international company, sold automotive parts to the domestic O.E.M. (original equipment market) and to the international as well as domestic replacement market, sometimes known as the "aftermarket." In 1972 sales of $65 million were split 25–75 respectively, between these two markets. Over the years, the company had expanded with the rapidly advancing automobile market and was now a major auto parts supplier. The company had four manufacturing plants in the United States, one in Canada and one in Europe. Approximately 50 percent of the products sold by Ericson-Morgan were directly manu-

---

[5] Culliton, *Make or Buy,* pp. 98–99.

factured by company plants. The remaining 50 percent were purchased and resold as part of the company's product line. Piston pins represented 15 percent or $9.75 million of the company's auto parts business. Piston pin sales were split, $8,800,000 to the aftermarket and $950,000 to the O.E.M. market. Piston pin sales, like other company products, had been experiencing a 15-percent annual growth rate over the last four years.

Piston pins

Piston pins were used in gas combustion piston engines for automobiles and trucks. A piston pin resembled a steel cylinder, approximately $1/3''$ long with a $5/8''$ diameter that could either be formed as an extruded blank or produced on a screw machine. Extrusion was substantially lower in cost of the two methods due primarily to the one step "blanking" nature of the process. The cylinder blank was then further machined to the process, the cylinders were heat treated to very close hardness tolerances.

Ericson-Morgan had purchased $3.1 million worth of piston pins in 1972. The average purchase price was 32¢ per pin. Size and volume purchased changed the price from 18¢ to 54¢ per pin. Ericson-Morgan sold 50 different sizes of pins. Twelve pin sizes topped the 100,000 mark. Twenty-five pin sizes called for more than 50,000 pins. Order volumes ranged from 2,000 to 700,000 pins of one size.

In the United States, there were five suppliers of piston pins, four of which were small and did specialty work on high-cost, low-volume orders. The fifth supplier, Craig Manufacturing, was large and supplied a substantial share of the O.E.M. market. Craig supplied 85 percent of Ericson-Morgan's piston pin business; two smaller suppliers had 10 percent and 5 percent respectively. Prices in 1972 had remained constant, but in 1973 a price increase of at least 5 percent or 6 percent was expected by Mr. Irwin.

Future demand for piston pins

Mr. Irwin felt that piston pin purchases would increase substantially over the next few years. In Europe, especially, the aftermarket was increasing rapidly as a result of the growing number of supermarket type stores for automobile replacement parts. Previously, European automobile manufacturers had monopolized the auto part replacement business by controlling the distribution system. In addition, domestic U.S. auto sales had hit unexpected new highs in the previous two years, resulting in a significant increase in demand for auto parts in both the O.E.M. and the aftermarket. At some point in time major changes to the piston engine would be made because of ecological antipollution legislation. Mr. Irwin felt that this or other advances into the piston market like the rotary engine were "too far down the road" to worry about. He did not expect a large proportion of the O.E.M. business to be affected before 1977. The aftermarket would then lag a signicant number of years past that date. Piston pin customers, such as engine rebuilders or specialty garages, were expected to be in business for a long time to come.

Ericson-Morgan had, until now, considered the feasibility of making or buying pins based only on the amount of return that would be generated from the invested capital for such a project. Reliability of supply had in the past never been an issue.

Delivery problems

Craig, a division of a large corporation, had been experiencing new equipment problems and had found it difficult to meet the general increase in demand for piston pins. This had resulted in a one- to two-month backlog of orders. Craig was attempting to train workers to operate the special production equipment for the last 18 months but was not entirely successful. Competition was unable to take up the slack since Craig's prices and quality were highly superior. Craig had a reject rate that was less than 1 percent. In 1972 Craig's total sales had amounted to $100 million. The company also competed with Ericson-Morgan in the aftermarket for piston pin sales as well as other automotive parts.

Located 300 miles from Ericson-Morgan's main plant and head office, Craig Manufacturing was accessible to Ericson-Morgan's engineering and purchasing people. Close contact was maintained, and Craig's progress was continuously monitored. Recent correspondence and field visits to Craig indicated that the company would resolve its backlog orders and the resulting unreliable deliveries within the next year. Similar assurances had been given by Craig's managers a number of times over the last two years. Craig management felt that once these production problems were solved, future capacity and deliveries would no longer present difficulties.

The old make or buy proposal

In 1966, the purchasing department had recommended to the vice president of operations that he further investigate the making of piston pins at Ericson-Morgan. At that time the study which cost hundreds of man-hours in engineering and production studies revealed that pins made entirely by screw machines would cost 30 percent more than 1966 purchased prices. On a few large-volume standard pins the prices would, however, be competitive. Capital investment would have been a substantial $4 million for plant and equipment. If extrusion equipment were purchased to make blanks, the net additional investment would amount to another $2 million. Other more favorable investments for company funds at that time resulted in the shelving of this proposal.

The new make or buy situation

In a recent meeting of the management committee reviewing new company undertakings, Mr. Irwin as member of the committee had raised the question of making piston pins. The vice president of operations said that presently Ericson-Morgan controlled 40 percent of the aftermarket in piston pins and expected at least to hold onto that share. Any market share loss would critically hurt company sales growth targets. He subsequently stated that delivery of piston pins and not profit should be the primary consideration for the make or buy consideration.

During 1972 a new plant was built by Ericson-Morgan, making extra production space available. Screw machine equipment was also available in the surplus equipment stock. Mr. Irwin thought the necessary engineering and production capabilities were available in the organization. In discussion with engineering and production personnel, Mr. Irwin learned that, in house, 90 percent of the piston pin requirements could be met. The other 10 percent would have to be purchased from an outside supplier because of their low volume and extreme size dimensions.

Engineering estimated that, in 1973, additional capital investment would total $200,000 to start the production of piston pins. The required lead time to set up production was estimated at six months.

The chief engineer said that a continuing problem was deciding upon standard blanking sizes. Once a standard cylinder wall thickness was established, five or six different piston pins could be finish machined from one blank. The number and size of blank determined, therefore, major production costs and, hopefully, savings.

A pin costing 32¢ previously purchased on an average run of 50,000 would have a primary material and blanking cost of 16¢ per pin. Finish machining would cost 5¢ and heat treating another 2¢ per pin. The cost, however, depended upon the size of run for any particular pin. Production runs under 50,000 pins could boost the cost by at least 40 percent. Engineering's primary cost projections could be met with the in-house use of screw machines. Extrusion equipment would reduce the primary material and blanking cost from 16¢ to 11¢ per pin for a 50,000 production lot. This difference would continue to increase as the production lot increased. Extrusion equipment was very expensive; however, one option was to have the blanks extruded by an outside supplier. Mr. Irwin thought that Pearson, Inc., a well-known local extrusion company, would have the capabilities and capacity required.

In 1972 Pearson, Inc., had sales of $20 million and were expanding at a 20 percent sales and profit growth rate. A majority of its business was with the big three automobile manufacturers. Pearson, Inc., had followed a policy in recent years of not committing itself to low volumes for any type of business. Any quantity over 50,000 would offer no "difficulty" in cost or delivery. Mr. Irwin estimated Pearson's prices for blanks would be close to Ericson-Morgan's variable manufacturing costs, using screw machines for volumes over 50,000.

Conclusion

Mr. Irwin was expected to report his findings and recommendations at the next management committee meeting. A number of factors at this time were very disconcerting to Mr. Irwin. First, with the long lead time required for the manufacture of piston pins, when should preparation for production be made in order to avoid a sudden shortage of supply? Secondly, Craig had stated that it hoped to be back on schedule within the next year but could still not promise anything definite in the way of delivery time. The one- to two-month delivery delays had caused low inventory stocks of specific pin sizes and slow delivery for Ericson-Morgan customers. Delivery, quality, and availability of piston pins were primary considerations in the O.E.M. and aftermarket. Thirdly, Mr. Irwin realized that if Ericson-Morgan should stop buying from Craig, this might help solve much of the current crisis and allow Craig to offer better service to Ericson-Morgan's competitors or its own customers. Finally, he was not sure if Ericson-Morgan could meet the high quality standards or efficiency set by Craig Manufacturing.

CHELMSFORD TOY COMPANY

Mr. Tom Denton, materials manager at Chelmsford Toy Company, was investigating alternate means of supply for a new plastic blister enclosure. Several years earlier Chelmsford had introduced a successful new line of toys called Micro Monsters in a tent package. For a variety of reasons a plastic blister was considered an improvement on this earlier tent package. Mr. Denton was seriously considering a local workshop for the retarded as a supplier for the new plastic blister. He was uncertain about the problems associated with catapulting such a workshop into this type of business and how his future alternatives of supply might be affected.

Company background

Chelmsford Toy was a large well-known manufacturer of quality toys sold under the Chelmsford label. It produced a full range of toys, although it was best recognized for its line of dolls. Chelmsford was known in the industry as an aggressive merchandiser, and it had secured wide distribution in a large number and variety of retail establishments from coast to coast.

Packaging history and development

The highly successful Micro Monster line used a package composed of a card with tapering cutouts. Two monsters were enclosed in each pack. By folding the thin cardboard over the two toys and stapling it at the top, a "tent" was formed, approximately 3¾" by 4¼" with a ½" wide floor. This could be displayed free standing or on a wire bar rack for which it was prepunched. The package was attractive, simple, cheap, and different from its competitors'. The fit was snug enough around the Micro Monsters to require some effort in removal. The packaging operation was largely a manual one utilizing automatic staplers. There were three different sizes of package to accommodate the range of shapes of Micro Monsters. Total volume had grown to six million toys a year using three million packages. Each "tent" cost about 3.6¢.

The marketing manager had recently talked with Tom Denton indicating that an improved package was necessary for Micro Monsters. Retailers complained that youngsters were prying the monsters out of the packages hanging on the display racks. The small size of the monsters made them easy to hide. The tent also did not permit full display of the monsters inside.

Mr. Denton proposed a blister type of enclosure and discussed various possibilities with several suppliers. He wanted a unique package that would not require high-cost skilled labor and which could be manufactured to meet sudden variations in demand. One of his suppliers, Green Plastipackers, Inc., had suggested an interesting option and supplied several prototypes made on a hand tooled mold. It was a clear plastic enclosure made from transparent 7.5 mil P.V.C. sheeting formed on a vacuum mold. A graphics card printed on both sides and the twin monsters could be placed in position by hand. The plastic enclosure was then folded together and heat sealed. This gave a completely enclosed, pilfer-proof display that could be either free standing or hung on a wire counter rack (see Exhibit 1). One tremendous advantage of the blister pack was that only one size could handle the full range of Micro Monsters. The printed card inserts could still vary to contain different merchandising information.

Green's proposal

Green was well known in the packaging trade for selling domestically manufactured and imported plastics and other wrappers. To promote packaging material sales Green's had started selling and leasing equipment produced by others for forming, wrapping, slitting, and sealing.

Exhibit 1
PROPOSED MICRO MONSTER PACKAGE

Green's also supplied packaging advice and packaging expertise. During the last decade Green had begun manufacturing machines of its own design. Chelmsford had purchased from and consulted with Green's in the past and found it to be a thoroughly knowledgeable and reliable supplier.

Green recommended one thermoforming machine, one die cutter, and at least three heat sealers as the minimum necessary equipment. This semiautomatic machinery was a well-known American line widely used for medium production demands, and it was carried in stock by Green. The equipment was demonstrated to Tom Denton. It did not require a highly skilled operator as automatic timers governed the cycles of the forming machine. The flat mold bed could accept any mold up to 24″ by 36″ and 2″ to 3″ in depth. The thermoforming machine occupied a floor space of 4′ by 8′ and was little more than desk height. It contained its own vacuum pump and provision for water supply for cooling molds, but the small compressor stood separately. The die cutter, approximately the size of the mold bed, was adjacent to the thermoformer head. Heat sealers could be placed at sorting tables as required.

The operating procedure was as follows. An operator manually drew the film over top of the mold from a 100-foot roll of P.V.C. mounted on the left hand side of the machine. The glass-topped cover was manually lowered over the film, locking it in place and shearing it off the roll. Heat was applied automatically, then the vacuum, which sucked and stretched the soft film skin-tight over the mold. An air blast was applied automatically, both to release the film from the mold and to cool it. Next, the cover released automatically. The operator moved the molded sheet manually to the adjoining die press cutter which sectioned it automatically. Cut sections of two joined halves were manually removed by another operator to the sorting tables where workers inserted the monsters in their blister cavities and the graphics card in the surrounding space. They then folded over the section in the middle and applied it to a three-point heat sealer. Others packed the twin toys into cartons.

Green's sales manager estimated that after two weeks under their supervision (supplied free) an experienced operator could reach the maximum of nine sheets per minute made from a 24-impression mold. Each sheet would yield 12 packets. Chelmsford would be responsible for the design and purchase of the mold from others. The cost of a 24-impression mold was estimated at $2,000. Green Plastipackers quoted $15,000 for all of the equipment and were prepared to offer a conditional sales contract over a three-year period or less on annual payments of one third of the principal plus a $7\frac{1}{2}$ percent carrying charge per annum.

When he asked about service and maintenance, Tom Denton was told that this was included, providing that the film was bought from Green. Current P.V.C. material costs were estimated at $15.00 per 1,000 blisters. The sales manager explained that his company had found it best for long-term satisfaction to operate on this basis, but he emphasized that he had to meet prevailing competition in plastics. If the P.V.C. was not bought from Green, maintenance and service could be purchased on an hourly rate basis of $25.00 per hour.

Green also had a more automated line available involving automatic feed of the sheet P.V.C., transfer to the die cutter and conveyor to filling, folding, and sealing. It had a capacity of 25 sheets per minute with a 64-unit mold processing 750 blisters per minute. Cost of this equipment was about $90,000. The mold would cost about $5,000.

The first alternative—make own

Tom Denton discussed the new blister package proposal with Lyle Stanley, Chelmsford's plant manager. Lyle was concerned about the changeover as he currently employed about the equivalent of ten women full time on the tent packaging line. Actually, the line was not operating on a daily basis. Normally, about 30 or 40 employees would work for about a week and produce a month's output. Then the workers would switch to other packaging jobs. He favored purchasing the highly automated line proposed by Green but doubted he could get approval for that large an expenditure on a still unproven design. He also hoped the same line could be used for other products. He estimated he would need at least one machine operator and 36 packers for the less automated line when it was running. With a card insert price of $4.00 per thousand, P.V.C. raw material cost of $15.00 per thousand and direct labor of $20.00 per thousand, he figured his direct variable cost at $39.00 per thousand. Normally, factory overhead was assessed at 230 percent of direct labor and was composed of 34 percent—fringe benefits, 20 percent—supervision, 120 percent—materials handling, maintenance, suppliers, power and heat, and 55 percent—fixed charges, such as depreciation, insurance and taxes.

Commercial packagers

Mr. Denton obtained quotations from several commercial firms specializing in custom packaging. For the blister package, card insert, filling, closing, and packing in Chelmsford supplied cartons, the lowest quote was from Jarnes, Inc. Jarnes was a medium-sized local firm of good reputation, and Mr. Denton was satisfied he would receive a quality job. Jarnes quoted $75.00 per thousand blisters on a guaranteed volume of at least 2 million blisters per year. Jarnes would purchase the card inserts with Chelmsford specified graphics. Chelmsford would own and supply the mold.

The association for the retarded

Mr. Denton was considering a third alternative, the Association for the Retarded. The Association operated several workshops within a 20-mile radius of the Chelmsford plant. The largest of these, employing about 50 people, was located only several blocks from Chelmsford's main warehouse. Mr. Denton had used this workshop for a variety of small packaging jobs in the past, often on an overflow basis, and had always been pleased with the quality and prices of the jobs done. In discussion with Chelmsford's president Tom Denton found that he was not averse to placing business with charitable institutions, although no company policy existed on this matter.

The Association had a progressive board of directors dedicated to make its charges active and happy members of the community. It was confident that its drive to expand its industrial section would go a long way to meeting the foregoing criteria. (See Exhibit 2.)

Exhibit 2
THE ASSOCIATION FOR THE RETARDED TREASURER'S REPORT

It is of interest to note the percentage breakdown and change in our sources of funds over the three-year period—the latter year being based upon budget estimates.

Exhibit 2 (*Continued*)

	Two years ago (actual)	Last year (actual)	This year (budgeted)
Operating costs	$1,020,000	$1,391,240	$1,795,000
Recoveries:			
Government grants and subsidies	36%	37%	44%
United Way	30	25	19
Parents fees	17	17	21
Donations, local campaigns and membership fees	6	5	4
Sale of goods including Christmas cards	10	12	9
Use of capital funds	1	4	3

Operations:

The above table shows a dramatic change in our total actual spending and our budgeted spending. Furthermore, there are significant changes in the sources of our operating funds. It must also be pointed out that a high proportion of recovery from Parents and Users is actually government allowance money, which in turn emphasizes that the Association is highly dependent upon government financing.

It is impossible for the United Way monies to keep up with our present rate of expansion, and in our opinion every effort must be made to increase future recoveries from our industrial sales program. To do this, we will need additions to our managerial resources which, although very competent, are becoming strained. We believe this can be accomplished by mobilizing volunteer sales and production-oriented people.

Capital funds:

You will note that our description of these has been changed to show, as clearly as possible, the amount of funds available for general use, as compared to specifically designated funds.

General capital available, at December 31 last year, to cover new projects and potential deficits was approximately $250,000.

Future expansion of services:

There is increasing pressure to spend money on:

a. Additional residences
b. More workshop space to accommodate:
  1. More workers.
  2. Better production equipment.
  3. More storage space for materials and finished product.

Thus, capital spending priorities must be carefully established.

The bricks and mortar of these facilities are not the only priorities to be considered. In the end it is people that make things happen, and we must carefully plan our expansion based on the capability of our staff to cope with the additional demands. If this is neglected, then the quality of our programs and services to the people we serve will suffer due to the overstretching of our human resources.

Mr. Denton visited Mr. Watts, the administrative director, to explore the new packaging proposal.

WATTS: First of all, let me tell you that we are determined to become as self-sufficient as possible. We have to absorb about 70 workers annually, aged about 20–23 years. Our cost deficit has been running to $500 per worker per annum, which the United Way met, but it is now becoming too much for them. So our only answer is to generate more business to close the gap. We have been digging into capital to improve our workshop facilities, and we are hungry for almost any kind of work.

DENTON: How do you cost your jobs?

WATTS: That's an interesting question. It was difficult to find a basis for measurement. Conventional time and motion studies and profit and loss factors were no good. We settled on a job-day return basis which gave us an earnings target for costing contracts. We ran a pilot project at one of our larger workshops, the one near your warehouse. We kept the shop going at full pressure under normal factory conditions for the study.

DENTON: How did your labor force react to that?

WATTS: Very well. Absenteeism dropped because each worker was anxious to see how well he did against the target, and a sense of competition was established. We also evolved a set of ideal factory conditions for us. One hundred workers and 20,000 square feet of space is just about right. Below this, efficiency drops. Mind you, these fellows have to be organized more than normal people. Fifty percent normality is high. We need lots of jig work, for instance, but their ability to use equipment under close supervision is good. We've had to employ normal trained artisans rather than social service people as supervisors, because they must watch the work and the inmates. Another thing, everything has to be inspected, and is. No statistical checks for us. That's why we turn out better quality than an automated factory. Furthermore, we are flexible. If you need a rush job done, we can transfer people from any of our other workshops on short notice. Shortage of labor is one problem we don't have.

My philosophy is that we're not looking for handouts. I'm willing to sign a contract with normal safeguards for you for anything within our capabilities. Just tell me what you're after, and we'll quote.

Mr. Denton then explained to Mr. Watts the nature of the new blister package. He requested Mr. Watts to supply a full quote based on using Green's equipment and materials with Chelmsford supplied molds and cardboard inserts. He suggested Mr. Watts contact Green directly to see if his labor force might be capable of operating the equipment and whether Green might be able to offer training assistance.

Two weeks later, Mr. Watts quoted the following prices based on an annual order quantity of 3 million blisters.

Empty blisters ready for filling....................$20.00/thousand.
Fully packed blisters using Chelmsford supplied molds,
inserts and packing cartons.........................$35.00/thousand.

Green would guarantee the packaging materials costs for the duration of this contract.

Tom Denton discussed the workshop quote with Lyle Stanley who expressed doubt about the contract. Lyle also wondered if he would have to supply quality control personnel to assure workshop performance.

Lastly, Lyle Stanley was worried he might lose shop flexibility if Micro Monster packing were done outside the plant.

Conclusion

Mr. Denton was pleased with the Association's quote as it would mean that a superior package could be obtained at almost the same price as the current "tent." Moreover, the quote was about 40 percent below the lowest commercial suppliers. He was not happy about the plant manager's reaction to the proposal. He also wondered if he might not be encouraging the Association to enter an area of risk taking not traditionally encountered. The new process was highly material and machine dependent, and the Association's real strengths lay in simple, labor intensive tasks. Moreover, marketing had just issued its forecast of Micro Monster sales for the coming year, and it called for 4 million packages. Finally, Tom Denton was not convinced that Chelmsford's long-term manufacturing strengths should lie in the packaging area.

13 THE SALVAGE OF SURPLUS, OBSOLETE, WASTE, OR SCRAP MATERIALS

Managers have long been concerned about the effective and efficient handling of the salvage of surplus, obsolete, and waste and scrap materials generated within the firm. In recent years, salvage problems have become more complex, as well as more important, as companies have become larger, more diversified in product lines, and more decentralized in management. More recently, a new dimension has been added to the overall salvage problem, the need to develop and use new methods to avoid the generation of solid waste products and better means of salvaging and disposing of other wastes which are discharged into the air and waterways, causing pollution.

While it is the purpose of this chapter to analyze and discuss the purchasing department's role in disposition of surplus and waste, the alert purchasing executive must also keep abreast of the new technology concerned with avoiding and eliminating causes of wastes which result in pollution.

The salvage of all types of materials in U.S. industry is big business. It is estimated that sales of scrap and waste materials of all types are in excess of $6 billion per year. Not only does the sale of scrap and waste result in additional income for the seller, it also prevents pollution and serves to conserve raw material resources and energy. For example, every ton of iron and steel scrap recycled saves $1\frac{1}{2}$ tons of iron ore, 1 ton of coke and $\frac{1}{2}$ ton of limestone.

Sources of waste and surplus

No matter how well a company may be managed, some excess, waste, scrap, and obsolete material is bound to develop. Every organization tries, of course, to keep such material at a minimum. But, try as they may, this can never be wholly successful. The existence of this class of material is the result of a wide variety of causes, among which may be mentioned overoptimism in the sales forecast; changes in design and specifications; errors in estimating mill usage; inevitable losses in processing; careless use of material by factory personnel; overbuying resulting from attempts to avoid the threat of rising prices or to secure quantity discounts on large purchases.

We are not now concerned with the methods by which excess, waste scrap, and obsolete material may be kept at a minimum, for these have already been discussed in connection with proper inventory and stores control, standardization, quality determination, and forward buying. The immediate problem has to do with the disposition of these materials when they do appear. In attacking it, we first need to distinguish among the four categories in question.

Excess of surplus material

Excess (or surplus) material is that stock which is in excess of a reasonable requirement of the plant. It arises because of errors in the amount bought or because anticipated production did not materialize. There are various ways in which such material may be handled. In some cases it may be desirable merely to store it until required, particularly if the material is of a nonperishable character, if storage costs are not excessive, and if there is a reasonable expectation that the material will be required in the future. Occasionally it may be substituted for more active material. Or, if the company operates a number of plants, it may be possible to transfer the excess to another plant. There are times, however, when these conditions do not exist and when fairly prompt sale is desirable. The chances for change in the style or design may be so great as to diminish considerably the probability that this particular material may be required. Or, it may be perishable. Factory requirements may be such as to postpone the demand for large amounts of this material so far into the future that the most economical method is to dispose of it and repurchase at a later date.

Many companies set some rough rule of thumb by which to determine when a stock item is to be classed as "surplus." Thus, according to one manufacturing organization:

Generally speaking, the question of excess material should be decided on a six-month basis. Customarily, the excess would be that amount of material on hand which represents more than a six-months' supply. There are exceptions, however. Some material deteriorates so rapidly that any quantity on hand greater than two or three months' supply be treated as excess material. In other cases, where it takes six months or longer to procure new material, more lengthy supply periods are frequently essential.

This rule suggests that all materials should be grouped into rough classifications, and normal requirement and supply periods established for each. Mere classification in itself is not sufficient. As with all classes of material considered in this chapter, systematic, physical stock-taking, continuous review of inventory records, and occasional "cleanup campaigns" are also necessary.

Another source of excess material usually appears upon the completion of a construction project. The company just referred to covers this situation as follows: "All new material for a specific property on order and not used on the project in question constitutes an inventory and must be treated as such. As soon as the work is completed, all new, unused material should be transferred immediately to the custody of the stores department. The original cost of the material should be charged to "Reclamation Stores" which is an unclassified segment of the Stores Account and credited to the property order or authorization." Provision is also made for the proper accounting of used material created or resulting from demolition work carried on in conjunction with construction projects.

In the case of one large manufacturing company, if the sales department has definitely obligated the company to make a certain quantity of an item, or has set up a sales budget for that quantity subsequently accepted by the management, and later finds itself unable to dispose of its quota, the losses sustained on the excess material are charged to that particular item or sales classification. The same practice is followed if the sales department, by virtue of recommending a change in design, creates an excess of material. This company feels that the loss should not be absorbed generally or distributed over other departments.

Obsolete material

Once material has been declared obsolete, it is wise to dispose of it for the best price that can be obtained. Obsolete material differs from excess stock in that whereas the latter presumably could be consumed at some future date, the former is unlikely ever to be used inside the organization which purchased it. Material becomes obsolete as a result of a change in the production process or when some better material is substituted for that originally used.

Although material may be obsolete to one user, this need not mean it is obsolete for others. An airline may decide to discontinue using a certain type of airplane. This action makes not only the plane, but also the repair and maintenance parts inventory, obsolete. Both may have substantial value to other airlines or users of planes.

What are "scrap" and "waste"? Scrap and waste material differ from excess or obsolete stock since they cannot properly be classified as new or unused. The former terms are sometimes used indiscriminately, and from the standpoint of their disposition no harm results by so doing.

However, the causes which produce them and their effect on costs are very different. "Scrap" is a term which may be applied to material or equipment which is no longer serviceable and has been discarded. It includes such items as worn machinery, old tools, and the like. In such cases, scrap arises because the company is replacing old machines with others which are more modern and more productive. A concern buying new machines, tools, and other equipment normally maintains a depreciation charge intended to cover the original cost of such items, so that the value of a machine has been written off by the time it is finally discarded. Such a depreciation charge normally covers an obsolescence factor as well as ordinary wear and tear. Actually, however, a discarded or scrapped machine may still have a value for some other manufacturer in the same type of business or in some other industry. It consequently may be disposed of at a price which will show a profit in many instances. This replacement of old or obsolete machines by others capable of larger production at the same or lower cost provides a profit-making opportunity not to be overlooked.

Another form of scrap is represented by the many by-products of the production process, such as fly from cotton spinning, warp ends from weaving, and metal scrap from boring and planing machines. Start-up adjustment scrap is frequently significant, and, in industries like paper making, paper converting, printing, polyethylene pellet manufacture and many others, it is one major reason for a significant price increase for small custom orders. The faster and the more automated the equipment, the higher the start-up scrap will be as a percentage of the total material used in small orders. Commonly, items of this class, which are quite unavoidable, are considered a form of scrap; such material may frequently be salvaged and handled in one of several ways, to which reference will be made later. In the metal industries, the importance of scrap in this form has a definite bearing on costs and prices. For instance, a selection from forgings, stampings, or castings may depend upon the waste weight. The waste weight to be removed in finishing plus labor costs of removing it may make a higher priced article the better value. In turning brass parts, the cost of the material (brass rod) may be greater than the price of the finished parts, because the recovered brass scrap is such an important element in the cost. Indeed, so valuable is scrap as an element in cost that it is not unusual for the purchase contract on nonferrous metals to include a price at which the scrap will be purchased by the supplier.

Waste has been defined as material or supplies the original forms of which have been changed during the production process and which "through carelessness, faulty production methods, poor handling, or other causes have been spoiled, broken or otherwise rendered unfit for further use, so far as concerns the particular manufacturing process." This definition is not entirely adequate. There is a form of waste not due to obsolescence and yet not a result of carelessness or poor handling. Waste, for example, may be brought about by the fact that the material is not up to specifications, because of faulty machinery or breakdowns or because of chemical action not foreseen.

Theoretically, waste should not exist. Actually, however, there probably will never be a time when some waste will not exist in every plant. This statement does not mean that every effort should not be made to reduce the waste factor to the lowest possible point. Its reduction can be brought about in a great many ways, such as the installation of new processes, by improved production layout, and by employee motivational programs.

Some differences of opinion may exist between accountants and engineers as to the exact definitions of scrap, excess, and waste. From the standpoint of the purchasing manager who has to dispose of the material, these differences are secondary. The commercial term "scrap" is for all practical purposes all-inclusive and as such can be used in a general discussion of the problem.

Value of reclaimed scrap. In one respect, it is surprising that more attention has not been given by more companies to the whole problem of scrap. The reasons are probably several. One of the most important is that scrap is suggestive of something which has no value and which the junkman can take away—in other words, something which a company is willing to sell if it can get anything for it, but which, if not, it is willing even to pay somebody to haul away. Another reason, is that many concerns are not large enough to maintain scrap and salvage departments, since the amounts of scrap they have do not appear great enough to warrant particular attention. Yet scrap may well be a source of potential profit.

An illustration may be in point. A man purchased old burlap and other items from the salvage department of a large organization. He then called on the sales department of the same company and disposed of the material at a substantial profit. He made $20,000 in these transactions merely because the salvage and the sales departments of the same company were not cooperating.

At times of raw material shortages scrap is likely to have very high prices. The example of copper scrap at $1.30 per pound compared to the government controlled price of 60¢ has already been mentioned. The director of purchases of a large equipment manufacturer said in early 1974 that he had about 40 tons of a special bronze alloy scrap in the yard, and he received telephone calls from potential buyers from all over North America.

England found in 1973 and 1974 that its domestically controlled price of waste rags of about $60 per ton was well below that of the European market, resulting in an exodus of this material for which a special domestic collection program had been set up to encourage local manufacture of toilet tissue. The result was a shortage of raw materials for the English mills, and a tissue shortage forcing imports of an item that could well have been manufactured locally.

The disposition of all kinds of scrap materials should always be so handled as to reduce the net loss to the lowest possible figure or if possible achieve the highest potential gain. The first thought, therefore, should be to balance against each other the net returns obtained from each one of several methods of disposition. Thus, excess material can frequently be transferred from one plant of a company to another of the same company. Such a procedure involves little outlay except for packing, handling, and shipping. At other times, by reprocessing or reconditioning, the material can be salvaged for use within the plant. Such cases clearly involve a somewhat larger outlay, and there may be some question as to whether, once the material has been so treated, its value, either for the purpose originally intended or for some substitute use, is *great* enough to warrant the expense. Since the decision whether to undertake the reclamation of any particular lot of material is essentially one of production costs and of the resultant quality, it should be—and commonly is—made by the production or engineering departments instead of by the scrap department. The most the purchasing manager can do is to suggest that this treatment be considered before the material is disposed of in other ways. In some companies there is created, within the manufacturing department, a separate salvage or "utilization" division to pass upon such questions as possible reclamation. Indeed, the place of the "salvage engineer" is well established among many larger firms. This salvage division is, as has been indicated, primarily a manufacturing rather than a sales division and is concerned with such duties as the development of salvage processes, the actual reclamation of waste, scrap, or excess material, and the reduction of the volume of such material.

Marketing of scrap. If the material is such that profitable reclamation is not possible, other opportunities present themselves. It may be sold to a local scrap dealer. It may be sold, either directly or through a broker, to some large consumer, as a great deal of steel scrap is sold. It may be sold back to the original supplier, who may resell it "as is" or who may be in a more strategic position for its reclamation than the seller.

The Elimination of Waste Committee of the American Society of Mechanical Engineers some years ago developed a *Dictionary of Waste Elimination* in which it points out four important alternative methods for disposing of scrap:

(1) Can the material be used, either "as is," or with economical modification, for any purpose other than that for which it was purchased? e.g., substitution for similar grades and near-by sizes, and shearing or stripping sheet metals to obtain narrower widths. (2) Can it be returned to the Manufacturer or Supplier from whom it was purchased, either for cash or for credit on other

purchases? (3) Can any other manufacturer use the material either "as is," or with economical modifications? It should be noted that sales can often be made direct to other users, and there are surplus materials dealers in most cities who either purchase such material outright or dispose of it on a commission basis. (4) Can the material be reclaimed or modified for use by welding? Welding has become a very important factor in disposing of materials to advantage. Defective and spoiled castings and fabricated metal parts can be reclaimed at little expense, short ends of bar stock, pipe, etc., can be welded into working lengths and worn or broken jigs, fixtures, and machine parts can be built up or patched. Furthermore, castings and fabricated metal parts can be reduced in size by either the arc or acetylene cutting process.

If all of these fail, the material will have to be salvaged. . . . A major point to keep in mind is the fact that metals for salvage should be broken, sheared, or torched to small charging size, because they then command a much better price than can be obtained for large materials. Also before proceeding with the dismantling of finished apparatus and assembled parts, it should be determined that the salvage value will exceed the cost of labor and overhead—otherwise, the material should be disposed of as mixed scrap.

Different kinds and grades of material . . . should be kept separate and clean at the source because it is expensive to separate them when mixed. . . .

Standardization with consequent reduction of grades, sizes, shapes, etc., will accomplish more in the way of waste prevention than any other single thing.

When scrap is sold, careful attention should be given to the selection of a buyer and to the procedure for handling the sale. The yellow pages of the telephone directory provide lists of dealers who buy scrap and waste products. The *Waste Trade Journal*[1] which is published weekly provides price information for most waste and scrap products for the major markets in the United States. *The Waste Trade Directory*[2] published annually provides comprehensive coverage of all segments of the market.

Should the procurement department be responsible for the sales of salvaged materials?

The question of where the responsibility for the management of salvaging operations should be placed in an organization is rather difficult to answer. In large companies where substantial amounts of scrap, obsolete, and waste materials are generated a separate department may be justified. The manager of such a department could report to the general manager or the production manager. The limited surveys which have been made to determine the location of salvage disposal responsibility

---

[1] Published by Atlas Publishing Co., 130 W. 42nd St., New York.
[2] Ibid.

have indicated that between 50 and 90 percent of the companies responding depend on the procurement department to handle salvage sales. There are other reasons for holding the purchasing manager responsible for scrap and salvage which perhaps are more forceful. These include: (1) knowledge of probable price trends, (2) contact with salesmen is a good source of information as to possible users of the material, (3) familiarity with the company's own needs may suggest possible uses for the material within the organization, (4) placing the responsibility for this task upon the purchasing manager broadens one's outlook by giving some idea of the problems and points of view of vendors.

In conglomerate and highly diversified and decentralized types of organizations, there is great need for the coordination of salvage disposal if the best possible results are to be obtained. Where a corporate procurement department is included in the home office organization structure, even if only in a consulting relationship with the various divisions of the company, available information and records and established channels of communication should help to ensure that salvage materials generated in any part of the company are considered for use in all parts of the company before being offered for sales outside the company.

The general conclusion which we may draw is that except in the cases of companies with separate salvage departments, management has found the purchasing department, because of its knowledge of materials, markets, prices, possible uses, etc., in a better position than other departments of the company to salvage what can be used and to dispose of what cannot.

Procedure for disposing of scrap

The procedure for handling the disposal of waste and scrap is important. One writer has said:

In connection with the selling and delivery of the material, a system should be set up which will be consistently followed and will afford the company protection against all possible loss through slipshod methods, dishonest employees and irregular practice on the part of the purchaser of by-products. All sales should be approved by a department head and cash sales should be handled through the cashier and never by the individual whose duty it is to negotiate the sale. All delivery of by-products sold should be effected through the issuing of an order form and sufficient number of copies made to provide a complete record for all departments involved in the transaction. The shipping department should determine the weight, count, etc., and this figure should go to the billing department without going through the hands of those who negotiate the sale.

Any department responsible for the performance of this function should maintain a list of reputable dealers in the particular line of scrap and waste to be disposed of and should periodically review this list. At frequent intervals the proper plant official should be instructed to clean up the stock and report on the weights and quantities of the different items or classes of items which he has for disposal.

A common procedure is to send out invitations to four or five dealers to call and inspect the lots at the factory and quote their prices f.o.b. factory yard. Such transactions are usually subject to the accepted bidders' check of weights and quantities and are paid for in cash before removal. Not infrequently, acceptable and dependable purchasers with whom satisfactory connections have already been established are relied upon as desirable purchasers, and no bids are called for from others. In some cases, it has been found desirable for the purchasing department, in order to maintain a record of such sales, to issue a formal purchase order on the production department giving the particulars, such as the dealer's name and address, the weights, prices, shipping instructions, and terms, and requesting that department to issue a regular sales order on the factory for delivery as arranged.

After the purchasing department has been notified that the buyer has accepted and paid for the shipment, a copy of the order on the production department is marked with the date and amount of payment, stamped "COMPLETED," and filed away in a special folder. For future reference, these sales of scrap and waste are recorded on a special card or sheet designed for that purpose.

A disposal example

Scrap disposal is still a managerial attitudinal problem, since most waste can be disposed of profitably by use of imaginative resourcefulness. The following example concerns a large forest products company which acquired a logging-lumber-veneer-flooring operation that was on the verge of bankruptcy. The waste in this operation (which the former management was not even aware of) was incredible. The new manager soon called a meeting of all salaried personnel at which he stressed two major points:

1. "We don't have any problems—only opportunities to solve a few difficulties"; and
2. "There is no such thing as scrap, because there is a buyer for everything at the right price."

He concluded by telling the staff he expected them to provide him with the means of profitably disposing of all "by-products" within two months. The following is a list of the accomplishments within three months of this meeting:

1. Two years before the takeover, the state Department of Lands

and Forests had insisted that some areas be "clean cut" and reseeded to birch. Balsam fir and spruce were just being cut and left to rot. A visit to a newsprint company resulted in an offer of $26 per cord for this pulpwood delivered to their plant. Contractors were hired to cut and deliver it for $22, resulting in a profit of $4 per cord to the company, plus a 100 percent saving of the former cost of selling the spruce and balsam fir.

2.   A trucker had been hired to draw away veneer "cores," and nobody knew how to dispose of them. A gang saw was installed to cut them into boards which were automatically the right length for crating veneer, saving the veneer mill from having to buy crating material from the saw mill. Surplus cores were treated and sold as ornamental fence posts at $1.00 each.

3.   There had been a sometimes dangerous fire in the sawdust pit for seven years. Fighting it was futile because the water only caused spontaneous combustion in about three weeks time (with an even larger pile of sawdust). The company was too far away from any of its chipboard plants to transfer the sawdust economically, and it did not "produce" enough to make a chipboard plant on location feasible. The company lent a small entrepreneur enough money to set up a little fireplace-log plant on the premises, and he subsequently paid $5 per ton for the sawdust.

4.   A plant visit to a fine paper manufacturer resulted in an offer of $28 per ton for hardwood chips from the veneer and flooring mills which had previously been dumped in the sawdust pit.

5.   Cut-offs from the flooring mill which had formerly been thrown into the sawdust pile were shipped some distance for $40 per ton (delivered) to a manufacturer of hardwood floor tiles.

6.   Slabs from the sawmill which had formerly been chipped and dumped in the sawdust pit were end-cut and sold to a distributor who stored them for a year (to air dry) and then resold them to campers for firewood over a radius of about 50 miles. He bought them for $4 per "estimated" cord (and made a killing by reselling them for about $32 per cord). This distributor initiated negotiations to cut up the "slash" in the bush at the same price for the same purpose. This would be pure windfall profit—and would leave less debris in the logging areas.

BIBLIOGRAPHY

ALJIAN, GEORGE W., ed.   *Purchasing Handbook*. 3d ed. New York: McGraw-Hill Book Co., 1973.

AMMER, DEAN S.   *Materials Management*. 3d ed. Homewood, Ill.: Richard D. Irwin, Inc., 1974.

WESTING, J. H.; FINE, I. V.; ZENZ, GARY JOSEPH ET AL.   *Purchasing Management*. 3d ed. New York: John Wiley & Sons, Inc., 1969.

CASES FOR CHAPTER 13

GOODLAND PLASTICS CO., LTD.

When the new president decided suddenly to drop the line, Mr. Allan, manager of purchasing, Goodland Plastics Company, realized in November that he had some 75,000 pounds "PL" clear film left on his hands, normally about a three-month supply.

This biaxially oriented plastic was not made in North America. The Japanese manufacturer, eager to penetrate the North American market, had agreed to a price about 25 percent below European competition. Only this enabled the operation of fabricating and printing wrappers to customers' requirements, mainly in the food industry, viable. But after three years "PL" failed to realize the "miracles" predicted for it, and in the face of revitalized competition from long-established cellophane and the new polyesters it had lost ground.

Normal lead time had been eight–ten weeks from the Orient. Mr. Allan used to order every two months on the basis of firm production orders, in a variety of thicknesses and widths. The price varied by the thickness. The material was supplied in rolls of 2,000 and 4,000 meters, weighing approximately 125 kg. and 200 kg. gross.

The bulk of the stock consisted of 18 micron, 48", 4,000 meters. Mr. Allan estimated his average quoted price to be U.S. 70¢ a pound, f.o.b. delivered, duty (17 percent) paid. The material was in a heated warehouse, but the inventory carrying cost had not yet been calculated.

When examining the possibilities of finding a buyer for this now obsolete inventory, the purchasing manager was aware of several constraints:

a. Goodland also manufactured other film from resins but had no facilities for reworking extruded stock.
b. The company had publicly announced its intention to abandon "PL."
c. He could not guarantee the machinability or printability of the film to a third party less well-equipped and knowledgeable than the experienced Goodland Company. This put him at a disadvantage opposite original manufacturers of competitive plastics.
d. Goodland had a "quality house" reputation to protect.

CANADIAN BROADCASTING CORPORATION

In the fall of 1972 Mr. Roland Chaput, manager of the purchasing and supply services for the French network of the Canadian Broadcasting Corporation faced the second major disposal of furniture within six months. This furniture had become surplus following the moving of several services of the corporation into the new $75 million administrative and production complex in Montreal, called la Maison de Radio-Canada. Mr. Chaput wondered about the best way to dispose of this furniture. The experience of selling about 2,000 pieces of furniture to employees six months earlier had been time-consuming, and he thought all alternatives should be considered before a decision was made.

The corporation

Established by Parliament, the Canadian Broadcasting Corporation (CBC) aimed to provide a distinctively Canadian broadcasting service for a relatively small population spread over a very large territory. According to this mission CBC operated two national television and radio networks for the French and English Canadians. CBC staff numbered over 9,000 employees. In 1972 the corporation's total expense amounted to $233 million. CBC was financed mainly by public funds, supplemented by commercial revenue accounting for approximately 25 percent of the corporation's total income. All public funds provided were subject to Parliament approval.

Moving into la Maison de Radio-Canada

The rapid expansion of television in the 1950s produced a problem of scattering of production facilities among numerous locations within the same community. In Montreal, la Maison de Radio-Canada grouped several services which were dispersed until then in 22 different buildings throughout the city. The new 25 story offices and studios complex was one of the largest broadcasting centers of the world, headquarters of the CBC's French services, and production center for the French television and radio network. The building, prominent in the Montreal skyline on the east of the city's center, included a number of special architectural features. All offices contained attractive new furniture chosen to match the architecture and the office design concept.

The moving of approximately 3,000 employees into la Maison de Radio-Canada started in the autumn of 1971. This operation was planned over a 14-month period following the termination of leases in existing locations. As the move proceeded, the obsolete furniture released from the various buildings was sent to the rehearsal studios of the new complex. By the beginning of March, 1972, these rooms were completely full, and the balance of the old furniture had to be shipped directly to rented warehouses. Mr. René Bergevin, director of general services, requested the first disposal in mid-March, 1972. Half of the total moving operations were then completed. Mr. Bergevin gave Mr. Chaput the responsibility to clear all of the furniture occupying the rehearsal studios, as the production activities would soon require this space. He also asked Mr. Chaput to try to give priority to employees interested in purchasing any of the furniture.

The first disposal

Mr. Chaput knew the disposal was a large job. There were hundreds of furniture pieces involved. In the past, Mr. Chaput had occasionally looked after the disposal of certain assets but only on a small scale. He felt procedures previously used would no longer be practical. Normally, disposal involved only a few articles at a time. The corporation's administration manual described instructions to follow in such circumstances (see Exhibit 1). Usually, a placard informed employees of the

Exhibit 1

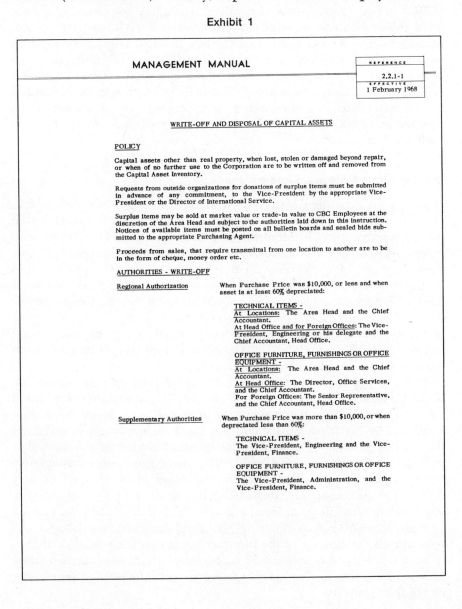

MANAGEMENT MANUAL

REFERENCE
2.2.1-1
EFFECTIVE
1 February 1968

WRITE-OFF AND DISPOSAL OF CAPITAL ASSETS

POLICY

Capital assets other than real property, when lost, stolen or damaged beyond repair, or when of no further use to the Corporation are to be written off and removed from the Capital Asset Inventory.

Requests from outside organizations for donations of surplus items must be submitted in advance of any commitment, to the Vice-President by the appropriate Vice-President or the Director of International Service.

Surplus items may be sold at market value or trade-in value to CBC Employees at the discretion of the Area Head and subject to the authorities laid down in this instruction. Notices of available items must be posted on all bulletin boards and sealed bids submitted to the appropriate Purchasing Agent.

Proceeds from sales, that require transmittal from one location to another are to be in the form of cheque, money order etc.

AUTHORITIES - WRITE-OFF

Regional Authorization — When Purchase Price was $10,000, or less and when asset is at least 60% depreciated:

TECHNICAL ITEMS -
At Locations: The Area Head and the Chief Accountant.
At Head Office and for Foreign Offices: The Vice-President, Engineering or his delegate and the Chief Accountant, Head Office.

OFFICE FURNITURE, FURNISHINGS OR OFFICE EQUIPMENT -
At Locations: The Area Head and the Chief Accountant.
At Head Office: The Director, Office Services, and the Chief Accountant.
For Foreign Offices: The Senior Representative, and the Chief Accountant, Head Office.

Supplementary Authorities — When Purchase Price was more than $10,000, or when depreciated less than 60%:

TECHNICAL ITEMS -
The Vice-President, Engineering and the Vice-President, Finance.

OFFICE FURNITURE, FURNISHINGS OR OFFICE EQUIPMENT -
The Vice-President, Administration, and the Vice-President, Finance.

Exhibit 1 (*Continued*)

REFERENCE
2.2.1-1
EFFECTIVE
1 February 1968

MANAGEMENT MANUAL

AUTHORITIES - DISPOSAL

Once the write-off of the asset has been authorized, and, subject to Section 30, Broadcasting Act, authority to dispose of Capital Assets is delegated to:

- The Local Purchasing Agent, when the depreciated value of the asset to be sold or traded is $5,000. or less.

- The General Purchasing Agent, when the depreciated value of the asset to be sold or traded is in excess of $5,000.

- The originator of the write-off request when the item is to be disposed of by means other than sale or trade.

WRITE-OFF PROCEDURE

Budget Unit Head	1.	Completes section 1 of CBC 70A, retains copy 7 for follow up and forwards six copies to Chief Accountant.
Chief Accountant	2.	Notifies Plant Accountant in order to obtain all information necessary for completion of section 2 of CBC 70A; retains copy 6 for follow up and forwards five copies to Regional Inspection Officer.
Regional Inspection Officer	3.	Obtains estimate of current market value and when applicable an estimate of repair.
	4.	Completes section 3 of CBC 70A and forwards all five copies to Area Head.
Area Head	5.	Completes required portion of section 4 of CBC 70A and: (a) If not approving request, sends all five copies to Chief Accountant or (b) If not approving request, returns copy 2 to Budget Unit Head and remaining copies to Chief Accountant.
Chief Accountant	6.	Signs required portion of section 4 of CBC 70A and: (a) If approved, sends 4 copies to Operations Engineer (technical items) or Director, Office Services (furniture, furnishings and office equipment). (b) Sends copy 5 to Plant Accountant whether request is approved or not.
Operations Engineer or Director, Office Services	7.	Completes section 5 of CBC 70A and if approving of disposition, forwards all copies to Plant Accountant.
	8.	Suspends write-off procedure when item is suitable for use at another location. Advises those who have already signed the document and the

---

sale, conditions attached to it, and gave them an opportunity to bid. Some days were granted to allow employees to see the goods, and a deadline was set for the bids (see Exhibit 2). On the stipulated date, bids were opened in front of witnesses. Goods were sold to the highest bidder, but management did not bind itself to sell more than one item to one employee.

In the present case, Mr. Chaput thought the first thing to do was to draw up an inventory of the furniture for sale. These data would

Exhibit 1 (*Concluded*)

MANAGEMENT MANUAL

REFERENCE
2.2.1-1
EFFECTIVE
1 February 1968

		Plant Accountant. Ascertains within 30 days if there is a requirement at any other location.
	9.	Informs all concerned, when there is a requirement and arranges with Budget Unit Head for transfer of the item through local stores.
Plant Accountant	10.	Completes section 6 of CBC 70A and: (a) When the purchase price of asset was in excess of $10,000, or it has been depreciated less than 60%, forwards all four copies to the Vice-President, Administration or the Vice-President Engineering, as applicable, through the Vice-President, Finance. (b) When the purchase price was $10,000, or less and asset is at least 60% depreciated, retains copy 1 of CBC 70A and forwards one copy each to the Budget Unit Head, the Chief Accountant and the appropriate Disposal Agent.
Vice-President, Engineering or Vice-President, Administration and Vice-President, Finance	11.	Completes section 7 of CBC 70A and forwards all five copies to Plant Accountant for distribution.
DISPOSAL PROCEDURE		
Disposal Agent (sale or trade)	1.	Disposes of items in manner suggested in section 1 of CBC 70A.
	2.	Obtains bids from prospective purchasers.
	3.	When trade-in is involved, records purchase order number of new item on CBC 869 in order that trade-in value be reinstated on records.
	4.	Completes CBC 869 in quintuplicate, retains one copy and forwards one copy each to the Budget Unit Head and Chief Accountant, and two copies to Plant Accountant together with any proceeds from sale.
Budget Unit Head (other then sale or trade)	5.	Disposes of item in manner suggested in section 1 of CBC 70A.
	6.	Completes CBC 869 in triplicate, retains one copy and forwards one copy each to Chief Accountant and Plant Accountant.
Plant Accountant	7.	After disposal, takes necessary accounting action and when applicable, forwards one copy of CBC 869 together with any proceeds from the sale to the Chief Accountant, Head Office.
	8.	Request explanations or reasons for delays when CBC 869 has not been received within sixty days of the authorization.

---

be necessary for the official request of write-off and disposal according to the manual's instructions. He formed five teams of two men, all unionized employees in the purchasing and stores operation, to produce the list and to arrange the furniture for display. This task required five evenings of overtime, six hours per evening for all ten men. The list showed there were over 2,000 items. The corporation used an asset identification program in which each piece of furniture had its own

Exhibit 2
PLACARD SPECIMEN
For Sale: Used Vehicles

Canadian Broadcasting Corporation offers to its employees six (6) motor vehicles hereafter described:

1	Truck	Fargo	1955–2 tons	CBC 411–33
1	Truck	Fargo	1961–2 tons	CBC 411–60
1	Truck	Fargo	1961	CBC 411–52A
1	Familial	Plymouth	1963–Fury II	CBC 411–70
1	Familial	Plymouth	1964–Fury II	CBC 411–76
1	Familial	Ford	1964–Country Sedan	CBC 411–77R

These vehicles are on display on working days from 9:00 A.M. to 5:00 P.M., at the T.V. Technical Equipment Center, entrance on Papineau Street.

Written bids will be received in the Purchasing Agent Office until Friday, January 25, 1971, at 5:00 P.M. Be so kind as to write down your employee number.

Sales will be held according to the following conditions:

1. No guarantee is given as for condition and useful purpose of the mentioned vehicles.
2. CBC reserves the absolute right without any obligation:
    A. To reject all bids or one of their number.
    B. To withdraw in part or in total the items for sale.
3. Total cash payment before taking of possession, plus 8 percent provincial tax, and transport are chargeable to purchasers.

Montreal, Quebec
January 7, 1971.

numbered metal tag. Most pieces had no book value as they were totally depreciated; others had never been capitalized (Exhibit 3 illustrates one page of that list).

The official request for write-off and disposal involved five signatures for authorization from the request originator up to the vice president finance in Ottawa. This could easily take two months, and Mr. Chaput was urged to remove the furniture from the rehearsal studios as fast as possible. He communicated this problem to his superiors who granted him full power to proceed and promised their cooperation. In less than ten days all necessary signatures were gathered, and he was able to prepare the sale (see Exhibit 4).

The next thing to do was to draw a price list for the goods as bidding would not be feasible (see Exhibit 5). Mr. Chaput was helped by two of his men for this task. The prices related to the physical state of the furniture, depending if in excellent, good, or poor conditions. "This operation was done to the best of our knowledge," said Mr. Chaput.

Exhibit 3
ONE PAGE OF INVENTORY LIST

H.O. REF. No. REF. S.e.	PURCHASE DATE DATE D'ACHAT M	Y/A	ASSET TAG No. PLAQUE MATRICULE	OBJECT OBJET	COST/PRIX	NET BOOK VALUE VALEUR COMPTABLE NETTE	WRITE-OFF No. N° DE DÉSAFFECTATION	W.O. CODE CODE O.E.	TRANS. CODE
			DESK SGL TER DROT HEAD		1/2 X 30		0102	0	93
	03	61	065257	501-1 0870	65.45	.00			
	03	59	077909	501-11 0870	65.00	.00			
			DESK SGL TED		1/2 X 30				
	06	58	076453	501-11 0870	72.50	.00			
	03	59	062447	501-16 0870	65.45	.00			
	02	54	068466	501-16 0870	76.08	.00			
	03	61	065271	501-16 0870	76.07	.00			
	03	61	065211	501-16 0870	76.07	.00			
	03	61	064262	501-14 0870	76.07	.00			
	03	61	065200	501-16 0870	76.07	.00			
	03	61	065829	501-16 0870	76.07	.00			
	11	55	067056	501-16 0870	65.45	.00			
			TABLE TELEPHONE						
			065101	0870	.00	.00			
			063588	0870	.00	.00			
			062821	0870	.00	.00			
			061038	0870	.00	.00			
			066244	0870	.00	.00			
			147407	0870	.00	.00			
			068420	0870	.00	.00			
			059041	0870	.00	.00			
			060416	0870	.00	.00			
			065435	0870	.00	.00			
			061479	0870	.00	.00			
			061087	0870	.00	.00			
			158838	0870	.00	.00			
			071932	0870	.00	.00			
					790.28	.00			

TEMP. 0.850 BIL. (11/70)

"Our goal was to fix reasonable prices," he added, "and we used our experience from past disposals and current market information."

He also prepared sale labels, in the form of prenumbered stickers to be fixed to each item. Mr. Chaput designed the sticker which was composed of three sections (see Exhibit 6). The printing job cost $200. Only the A section would stick to the article, and the B and C sections

Exhibit 4
REQUEST FOR WRITE-OFF AND DISPOSAL

CAPITAL ASSET Request for Write-off and Disposal	BIENS D'ÉQUIPEMENT	Demande de désaffectation et de liquidation

1. IDENTIFICATION DATA/SIGNALEMENT

Location and Department Lieu et service	Description/Désignation	Asset Tag No./Plaque matricule
501	MOBILIER DE BUREAUX	DIVERS

Make/Marque	Model/Modèle	Serial No./No. de série
DIVERSE	—	—

WRITE-OFF REASON / RAISON: ☒ 0 Obsolete/Désuet ☐ 1 Lost/Perdu ☐ 2 Stolen/Volé ☐ 3 Damaged beyond repair/Irréparable ☐ 4 Other/Autre

RECOMMENDED DISPOSAL / SORT PROPOSÉ: ☒ Sale/Vente ☐ Trade-in/Échange ☐ Scrap/Rebut ☐ Dismantle for parts/Démontage pour conserver les pièces ☐ Donated/À donner ☐ Other/Autre

MATERIALS OR SPARE PARTS AFFECTED / ENTRAÎNE DÉSUÉTUDE DE MATÉRIELS OU PIÈCES: ☐ yes/oui ☐ no/non

Estimated value/Valeur estimative	Storekeeper notified/Magasinier prévenu
NULLE	☐ yes/oui ☐ no/non

Comments/Observations

28-3-72 Date   Originator/Requérant

2. REGIONAL INSPECTION REPORT ON CONDITION OF ASSET/RAPPORT DE L'INSPECTION RÉGIONALE SUR L'ÉTAT DU BIEN

Comments/Observations   Estimated present worth / Estimation de la valeur actuelle

28-3-72 Date   Regional Engineer or Officer-in-Charge — Office Services / Ingénieur régional ou Responsable des Services de bureau

3. REGIONAL AUTHORIZATION/AUTORISATION RÉGIONALE

28/3/72 Date   Chief Accountant/Chef comptable   28/3/72 Date   Area Head/Chef de secteur

4. CONCURRENCE WITH DISPOSAL RECOMMENDATION/ACCORD SUR LA RECOMMENDATION

CONCURRENCE APPROUVÉ: ☒ yes/oui ☐ no/non ☐ usable at/utilisable à   Name of Location/Lieu

Comments/Observations

30/3/72 Date   Operations Engineer or Director, Office Services / Ingénieur à l'exploitation ou Directeur des Services de bureau

5. SUPPLEMENTARY AUTHORIZATION REQUIREMENT/AUTORISATION SUPPLÉMENTAIRE AU BESOIN

PURCHASE PRICE IN EXCESS OF $10,000 OR LESS THAN 60% DEPRECIATED / PRIX D'ACHAT DÉPASSANT $10,000 OU BIEN AMORTI DE MOINS DE 60%	TECHNICAL/TECHNIQUE	FURNITURE, FURNISHINGS, OFFICE EQUIPMENT / AMEUBLEMENT ET ÉQUIPEMENT DE BUREAU
	Date Vice-President, Engineering / Vice-président à l'Ingénierie	Date Vice-President, Administration / Vice-président à l'administration

6. FINANCIAL AUTHORIZATION/AUTORISATION FINANCIÈRE

Comments/Observations

4/4/72 Date   Vice-President, Finance/Vice-président aux finances

7. WRITE-OFF DATA (to be completed by Chief Accountant)/DONNÉES COMPTABLES (À remplir par le Chef comptable)

PURCHASE DATE/DATE D'ACHAT M	Y/A	ASSET TAG NO. PLAQUE MATRICULE	OBJECT OBJET	COST/PRIX	NET BOOK VALUE VALEUR COMPTABLE NETTE	WRITE-OFF NO. No DE DÉSAFFECTATION	DATE FINALIZED DATE D'EXÉCUTION M/J M Y/A	W.O. CODE CODE O.E.	TRANS. CODE
		voir liste attachée				0102			93

CBC 70 A BIL. (2/70)   Punched/Poinçonné   Verified/Vérifié par

would be torn off by the person interested in buying the article. The buyer would then complete the *A* section and would keep the *B* and *C* sections to hand to the cashier when paying. The price and description of the article would already be filled in on the *B* and *C* sections. The cashier would only have to write down the buyer's name and social insurance number and to check the method of payment on the *B* section. The cashier would stamp the *C* section and would give it back to the

Exhibit 5
EXCERPT FROM THE PRICE LIST

Description	Condition and price		
Desks	Excellent	Good	Poor
Suite 3 no. 1750 double pedestal desk, 56" × 30"	$22.00	$16.00	$10.00
Suite 1 no. 1753 flat top desk, 56" × 30" with 1765 side unit, 30" × 18"	20.00	14.00	8.00
Suite 1 no. 1753, flat top desk, 56" × 30", oak	25.00	18.00	12.00
Flat top desk 60" × 30" with side unit and book case	30.00	22.00	15.00
Tables			
Table, 354/20T, rols rim	$12.00	$ 8.00	$ 3.00
Table, telephone, 317/17, rols rim	6.00	4.00	2.00
Table, 360/34T, rols rim	18.00	12.00	4.00
Bookcases			
Closed bookcase, 376-BC, rols rim	20.00	12.00	6.00
Open bookcase, 31-67-0	10.00	6.00	2.00
Closed bookcase, 31/67-D	18.00	11.00	4.00
Chairs			
Side chair, 177-S, walnut	3.00		
Arm tilter chair, 468 1/4	10.00		
Arm chair, 177-A	5.00		

Exhibit 6
SALE LABEL

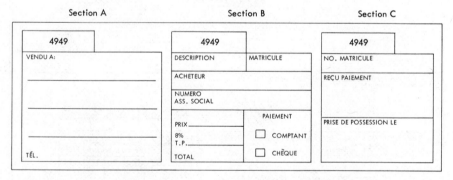

buyer as receipt. At the exit a clerk would also stamp the C section to confirm the taking of possession when customers carried out the articles. It took another week of evening overtime for the same teams that had done the inventory listing to fill out the labels and to stick one to each article.

Mr. Chaput then fixed the sale date and did the necessary advertising to all Montreal employees. The dates were set from April 17 to April 21 from 6 p.m. to 11 p.m. He also made arrangements with the accounting service to get two cashiers for each sale evening and with the security service to get a sufficient number of agents. Furthermore, the five teams of workers were asked to help the buyers carry the furniture out during the sale period and to unscrew the asset tag number from each piece when it was carried away.

Five hundred employees attended the sale. Ninety percent of the furniture was sold, and the rest was given to Les Disciples D'Emmaüs, a charitable organization. The disposal report showed proceeds of $7,926.29 (see Exhibit 7). It took five additional evenings with the help

Exhibit 7
DISPOSAL REPORT

CAPITAL ASSET – DISPOSAL REPORT / BIENS D'ÉQUIPEMENT – RAPPORT DE LIQUIDATION

Location / Lieu	Date	Write off No. N° de désaffectation
Montréal	28/6/72	no. 102

☒ Sale / Vente	Sold to/Vendu à	Date	Proceeds/Montant perçu
	Au Personnel de la Société	17-21 Avril	$7,926.29
☐ Trade in/Reprise	Traded to/Repris par		Trade in value/Valeur de la reprise
			Date

| ☐ Other disposal Autre mode de liquidation | Comments/Observations | | |

| ☐ Disposal completed as authorized Liquidé selon l'autorisation | ☐ Disposal not completed as authorized (Detail reasons below) Liquidé non selon l'autorisation (Préciser ci-dessous) | Asset tag No. Plaque matricule | Punched and verified Poinçonné et vérifié |

Comments re actual disposal:/ Observations sur la liquidation effective

Tel qu'autorisé sur la demande de Désaffection no. 102
Le montant ($7,926.29) ci-haut mentionné a été remis
au Chef de la Comptabilité Générale au moment de la vente.

R. Chaput

CBC 869 BIL. (12/68)   Disposal agent / Liquidateur

---

of three workers (always on overtime) to clear out the studios, as the buyers were allowed an extra period to take possession of the merchandise.

The second disposal

During the following six months the remaining departments moved into la Maison de Radio-Canada. Their furniture was transported to rented commercial warehouses, as there was no storage space at the new building available for this purpose. By the end of October, 1972, Mr. Bergevin asked Mr. Chaput to recommend a way of disposing of this lot. Mr. Bergevin was anxious to terminate the warehouses charges which amounted to about $1,000 per month. Mr. Chaput estimated that the second lot was approximately equal to the first. Taking an inventory in the warehouses would not be easy as the furniture was piled high to the ceiling. This would also make it extremely difficut to hold an employee sale like the last one. Moreover, Mr. Chaput was not certain the employees would be interested to the same extent as during the first disposal. Finally, he realized that obtaining approval signatures might not be as quick this time as the last when studios were tied up.

14 THE LAW AND THE PURCHASING FUNCTION

The competent professional buyer does not require the training of a lawyer but should possess an understanding of the basic principles of commercial law. Such understanding should provide recognition of problems and situations which require professional counsel and also the knowledge to avoid legal pitfalls in day to day operations.

Legal authority of the purchasing officer

What is the essence of the purchasing officer's legal status? Briefly put, it may be said that he has authority to attend to the business of purchasing in accordance with the instructions given by his employer. These instructions are usually broad in their character. In general, there should be, and in all progressive organizations there is, a clear understanding as to what the purchasing officer is expected to do. Attention has already been called to the necessity for a clear understanding of his duties simply as a matter of good business policy. The reasons for this clear understanding, cogent as they are from other points of view, are strengthened by virtue of the fact that the law assumes an agreement between the agent and his employer as to the scope of the authority. Presumably, the purchasing officer performs these assigned duties to the full extent of his capacity. In other words, the purchasing officer has a right to expect from his employer a clear understanding as to what his duties and responsibilities are, and he, in turn, may be expected to perform these duties to the best of his ability in an honest, careful manner. So long as he does this, his obligations to his employer, from a legal point of view, are fulfilled. In agreeing to render service to an employer, there is no implied agreement that he shall commit no errors. "For negligence, bad faith, or dishonesty, he is liable to his employer; but, if he is guilty of none of these, the employer must submit to such incidental losses as may occur in the course of the employment." Such losses are incidental to all vocations. Although, by special stipula-

815

tion, the agent may assume responsibility to his principal for this type of risk, including, indeed, even honest mistakes in the extension of credit, such arrangements are rare. Nevertheless, when a man accepts an appointment to serve as an agent for the principal, there does exist the implication that he possesses the necessary skill to carry on the work that he undertakes. In some cases, a very high degree of skill is demanded, and when a man accepts an appointment under such circumstances he implies that he has the necessary skill. There are, of course, many possible modifications of this general statement. The purchasing officer becomes liable to his employer when he damages the latter through active fault or through negligence, particularly if this negligence arises in connection with the duties imposed upon him. In this connection it may be noted that many difficulties arise in an attempt to define what negligence is, although, in general, it may be said to constitute an "omission of due care under given circumstances."

Since the purchasing officer is acting as an agent for the company which he represents, it follows that he is in a position to bind the company within limits. Actually, of course, the power of an agent to bind his principal may greatly exceed his right to do so. His right is confined by the limits assigned to him, in other words, in accordance with his actual authorization; his power to bind the principal, however, is defined by the *apparent* scope of his authority, which in the case of most purchasing officers, is rather broad. Furthermore, if he is to avoid personal liability, it must be made clear to the person with whom he is dealing that he is acting as an agent. In fact, the law requires that he go further if he is not to be held personally liable; not only must he indicate the fact that he is acting as an agent but also the person with whom he is dealing must agree to hold the principal responsible, even though the latter is at the moment unknown.

The actual authority delegated to an agent is not limited to those acts which, by words, he is expressly and directly authorized to perform. Every actual authorization, whether general or special, includes by implication all such authority as is necessary, usual, and proper to carry through to completion the main authority conferred. The extent of the agent's implied authority must be determined from the nature of the business to be transacted. These powers will be broad in the case of one acting as a general agent or manager. It is the duty of the third person dealing with the agent to ascertain the scope of the agent's authority. Statements of the agent as to the extent of his powers cannot be relied on by the third party. Any limitation on the agent's power which is known to the third person is binding on the third person.

Personal liability of the purchasing officer

It would appear that there are certain conditions under which the purchasing officer may be held personally liable when signing contracts.

(1) when he makes a false statement concerning his authority *with intent to deceive* or, in other phraseology, when his misrepresentation has the natural and probable consequence of misleading; (2) when he performs without authority a damaging act, even though believing he has such authority; (3) when he performs an act which is itself illegal, even on authority from his employer; (4) when he willfully performs an act which results in damage to anyone; (5) when he performs damaging acts outside the scope of his authority, even though the act is performed with the intention of rendering his employer a valuable service. In each of these cases the vendor ordinarily has no recourse to the company employing the agent, since there existed no valid contract between the seller and the purchasing firm; and since such a contract does not exist, the only recourse which the vendor commonly has is to the agent personally. However, should the question arise as to who may be sued on contracts made within the apparent scope of the agent's authority but beyond his actual scope, because of the fact that there were limitations on the latter unknown to the seller, it may still follow that the principal can be held. Under these circumstances, the agent has probably put himself in the wrong and is, of course, answerable to his principal. He may also be answerable to the seller with whom he has dealt, on the ground of deceit, on the charge that he is the real contracting party, or for breach of the warranty that he was authorized to make the precise contract he undertook to make for the principal.

Moreover, suits have been brought by sellers against purchasing managers when it was discovered that the latter's principal was for some reason unable to pay the account. For example, such conditions have arisen (1) when the employer became insolvent or bankrupt; (2) when the employer endeavored to avoid his legal obligations to accept and pay for merchandise purchased by the purchasing manager; or (3) when the employer became involved in litigation with the seller, whose lawyers decided that the contract price could be readily collected personally from the purchasing manager.

Although a purchasing officer should never attempt to replace the services of a competent lawyer by his own actions, the alert buyer and purchasing manager should keep informed about court decisions and changes in laws which affect his actions. Purchasing trade publications normally report court decisions and major changes in laws which have an impact on the proper performance of the buying function.

The purchase order contract

There are many federal, state, and local statutes which relate to purchasing, but the Uniform Commercial Code covers most of the transactions involving purchase and sale of goods and services. The UCC resulted from the joint efforts of the American Law Institute and the

Conference of Commissioners on Uniform State Laws. Since the first publication of the Code in 1952, with subsequent revisions and refinements in 1958 and 1962, all of the states have enacted the code into law, except for the state of Louisiana.

Anyone that has had any exposure to commercial law knows that a valid contract is based on four factors:

1. Competent parties—either principals or qualified agents.
2. Legal subject matter or purpose.
3. There must be an offer and an acceptance.
4. There must be a consideration.

The purchase order is generally regarded as containing the buyer's offer and becomes a legal contract when accepted by the vendor. Many purchasing managers have designed the purchase order form with a copy that includes provision for acknowledgement or acceptance. There has never been universal agreement on how detailed the terms and conditions which are printed on the purchase order should be. Some companies use forms that use the reverse side to spell out all the complete terms and conditions which apply to any transaction. Some companies may include a separate printed sheet detailing terms and conditions applying to the order. Some companies provide only for the very basic items necessary for a valid offer and depend on the provisions of the UCC for proper legal coverage. The purchasing officer should depend on the professional legal counsel responsible for handling legal matters for the company in determining the policy to be followed.

An "offer" can be equally valid if made by a vendor, either in writing or verbally. Such an offer becomes a legal contract when accepted by the buyer.

Regardless of whether an offer is made by the buyer or the vendor it can be modified or revoked before it is accepted. However, an offer in writing that includes an assurance that the price would remain firm for a specified period may not be revoked prior to the expiration of the period.

The courts have generally held that advertisements and price lists do not constitute legal offers unless specifically directed to the buyer or unless an order placed on the basis of the advertisement or price list is specifically accepted by the vendor.

Acceptance of orders

Since the purchase order form or the sales contract is intended to include all the essential conditions surrounding the transaction, it is customary to include in the agreement a statement such as, "Acceptance of this order implies the acceptance of conditions contained thereon."

The purpose of such a provision is, of course, to make all the conditions legally binding upon the seller and to avoid cases in which the seller advances the defense that he was not aware of certain conditions. Statements similar to that indicated are found in practically all purchase agreements, to give warning that there are conditions attached, either on the front or on the reverse side of the contract.

It is important to observe, however, that ordinarily only those terms and conditions which appear *above* the signature of the purchasing officer may be considered a part of the contract. To append at the foot of the purchase order and below the signature of the contracting parties an additional condition or to append below the signature a statement to the effect that the conditions cited on the reverse side are to be considered as incorporated in the contract is likely to have no binding effect, and such conditions may not be considered by the courts as part of the agreement.

Having placed an order with a vendor, the purchasing officer wishes to assure himself that the order has been accepted. To obtain such assurance, it is customary for him to insist upon a definite acknowledgment, usually in written form. It is not uncommon to incorporate as a part of the contract a clause requiring that the acceptance be made in a particular manner, in which case a form is enclosed with the order and the purchase order contains a clause which stipulates: "This order must be acknowledged on the enclosed form."

The question sometimes arises as to when an offer either of sale or of purchase has been accepted. As a matter of law, the person making an offer may demand, as one of the conditions, that acceptance be indicated in whatever manner he may specifically designate. Ordinarily, however, when an offer is made, the offerer either expressly or impliedly requires the offeree to send his answer by post or telegraph; and when the answer is duly posted or telegraphed, the acceptance is communicated, the contract being complete from the moment the letter is mailed or the telegram is sent.

Sometimes the vendor may use an acknowledgement form of its own design which upon detailed examination may conflict with some of the conditions stated in the purchase order. Often in such situations, a careful detailed examination is not made in comparing *all* conditions stated in the offer with *all* conditions stated in the acceptance. If litigation subsequently occurs between buyer and seller the UCC may resolve the question through the provisions of (UCC 2-207) (C) which states:

Conduct by both parties which recognize the existence of a contract is sufficient to establish a contract for sale although the writings of the parties do not otherwise establish a contract. In such case the terms of the particular contract consist of those terms on which the writings of the parties agree, together with any supplementary terms incorporated under any other provisions . . . [of this statute].

Under the terms of this provision, the conflicting conditions of both offer and acceptance are disallowed and the applicable provisions of the UCC apply.

Purchases made orally

Most professional buyers have occasion to place orders over the telephone or orally in person. Such oral orders are enforceable contracts without written notation if the materials or equipment are suitable for use only by the purchaser. However, the UCC specifies that:

1. Normally there must be some written notation if the value of the order is $500.00 or more.
2. If the seller supplies a memorandum which is not in accordance with the buyer's understanding of his oral order, he must give a notice of objection to the supplier within ten days if he wishes to preserve his legal rights.

Authority of vendor's representatives

Another obviously important consideration relates to the authority of the salesman representing a company with which the purchasing officer is transacting business. Subject to the many exceptions arising out of varying circumstances, it may be said that the courts have consistently held that although an employer is bound by all the acts of his agent while acting within the scope of the employment, yet a salesman's ordinary authority is simply to solicit orders and to send them to his employer for ratification and acceptance. It therefore behooves the purchasing officer to know definitely whether the salesman with whom he is doing business has or does not have the authority to conclude a contract without referring it to the company which he represents. Although a vendor does not authorize his salesmen to enter into binding contracts and although the company may do nothing to lead others to believe that its representative has such power, yet if the salesman does enter into a contract with a buyer, the contract is likely to be held valid unless the seller within a reasonable time notifies the buyer that the salesman has exceeded his authority. In other words, a contract results because the conduct of the employer is interpreted as acceptance. Should any doubt arise in the mind of the purchasing officer, he should be assured that the individual signing the contract for the vendor company is authorized to do so, regardless of whether the person making such claim be the salesman or someone else. Should someone claim the right to bind the seller or lead the purchasing officer to believe that he has that right to such an extent that it influences the decision of the buyer, the purchaser generally has the somewhat dubious privilege of holding the individual personally liable.

In passing, it may be well to indicate that false statements on the part of the seller or his representative regarding the character of the merchandise being purchased cause the contract to become voidable at the option of the other party.

It is true that this "undoubted right" to rely upon vendors' statements is at best a highly qualified right, the value of which depends upon the circumstances surrounding the transaction. It is of value insofar as the misstatement can be relied upon as a breach of warranty, a condition broken, or a fraud, and, in any event, has no good effect on the purchaser's title. However, it may be said that, aside from any legal question which is involved under ordinary circumstances, the seller is likely to be sufficiently jealous of his reputation and goodwill to make substantial concessions, even though he feels that technically he is right.

One important right which the buyer has is that of inspecting the goods before he accepts them. The purpose of this rule, of course, is to give the buyer an opportunity to determine whether or not the goods tendered comply with the contract description. It is well established that a buyer who inspects goods before entering into a contract of sale is put on his guard and is expected by law to use his own judgment with respect to quality, quantity, and other characteristics of the merchandise. The court is prone, however, to recognize circumstances which may affect the purchaser's ability to judge the accuracy of the vendor's statements. Thus, it has been held:

In order to vitiate a contract of sale on the ground of fraudulent representations, such representations must relate to an existing fact, material to the contract, and upon which the other party has a right to rely and did rely to his injury. If the means of information as to the matters alleged to be misrepresented are equally accessible to both parties, they will be presumed to have informed themselves, and if they have not done so they must abide by the consequences of their own carelessness.

From this statement, it would seem to follow that where a purchaser accepts merchandise after his own inspection, either as to quality or quantity, he would ordinarily be debarred from raising an issue with respect to these points. Also, as has been pointed out elsewhere, a vendor cannot be held responsible for the failure of equipment to perform the work which the buyer expected of it, if the latter orders merely upon material specifications and without indicating to the seller the purpose to which the equipment or goods are to be put.

The courts have generally held that if a purchaser is not sufficiently experienced to be able to judge adequately the goods which he inspects, or if he relies upon a fraudulent statement made by a seller and purchases in consequence of that fraudulent statement, he may then rescind the contract or hold the vendor liable for damages.

As previously stated, a purchasing officer is personally liable for the commission of any illegal act, and this liability holds even though he is unconscious of the illegality of the act and though it is done under the direction of the employer. An officer is not likely to commit an illegal act consciously; but under stress of severe competition he may, in an effort to secure as favorable terms as possible for his company, and perhaps to strengthen the bargaining power of other purchasers in a position similar to his own, run afoul of the law unintentionally. For example, it is well to remember that the antitrust acts apply to buyers quite as much as to sellers. The U.S. Supreme Court has held that these acts are applicable to all attempts to restrain trade, even though the restraint is exercised upon those not engaged in the same line of business and though based upon purchasing activities rather than selling activities, provided that the net result of the act is to restrain competition by virtue either of restricting normal activities among potential sources of supply or of seriously handicapping the sales efforts of the competitors of the buyer. A notable case in this connection is that of *George Van Camp & Sons Co.* v. *American Can Co. et al.*[1]

Cancellation of orders and breach of contract

Once a contract is made, it is expected that both parties will adhere to the agreement. Occasionally one or the other seeks to cancel the contract after it has been made. Ordinarily this is a more serious problem for the seller than it is for the buyer, although occasionally a seller may wish to avoid complying with the terms of an agreement, in which event he may merely refuse to manufacture the goods or he may delay the delivery beyond the period stipulated in the agreement. The rights of a purchaser under these circumstances depend upon the conditions surrounding the transaction. Speaking broadly, it may be said that the seller is likely to be able, without liability, to delay delivering purchased goods when the buyer orders a change in the original agreement which may have the result of delaying the seller in making delivery; if, after delayed shipment, the purchaser agrees to accept delivery; and also under certain other conditions.

It is clear that if the seller fails to make delivery by the agreed time, the purchaser may without obligation refuse to accept delivery at a later date.[2] However, the attempt to secure what the buyer might consider reasonable damages resulting from a breached sales contract is likely to be full of difficulty, owing to the fact that the courts experi-

---

[1] Supreme Court 112. See also *American Can Co.* v. *Ladoga Canning Co.*, 44 Federal Reporter (2d) 763.

Judge Brandeis, in a dissenting opinion, in the case of *United States* v. *American Column & Lumber Co. et al.* (42 Supreme Court 114), said: "Restraint of trade may be exerted upon rivals; upon buyers *or upon sellers;* upon employers or upon employed."

[2] See footnote 1.

ence a good deal of trouble in laying down rules for the guidance of the jury in estimating the amount of damages justly allowed a buyer who sustains financial losses resulting from a seller's failure to fulfill a contract of sale. If there be a general rule, it may be said that the damages allowable to a purchaser if a seller fails to deliver goods according to contract are measured by the difference between the original contract price and the market value of the merchandise at the time when and at the place where the goods should have been delivered. The amount of damages which the buyer can collect for breaches of warranty on the part of the seller therefore will be tremendous.

The seller, in his turn, is sometimes confronted by an attempted cancellation on the part of the buyer. It is not unusual, therefore, to find in the sales contract the following clause: "This contract is not subject to cancellation." As a matter of fact, the inclusion of such a clause has little practical effect, unless, indeed, it is intended merely to indicate to the purchaser that if he does attempt to cancel, he may expect a suit for breach of contract. From a legal point of view, the seller is in no better position that he would have been had this clause been omitted. Moreover, even if an order for merchandise contains a clause by the terms of which the purchaser is notified that the seller will not accept cancellation, the purchaser is legally privileged to cancel the order at any time before the seller legally accepts the order by acknowledgment or by any other act.

However, in a very strong seller's market, where the breach of contract by the seller is related to failure to deliver on a promised date or even to abide by the price agreed upon, the alternatives open to the buyer are almost nil. The latter still wants the goods, and he may be unable to acquire them from any other supplier any sooner or at any better price. Much the same restriction, in fact, exists even where the contract provides for the option of cancellation by the buyer. The purchaser wants goods, not damages or the right to cancel. Since his chances of getting them as promptly from any other supplier are slight, he is likely to do the best he can with the original vendor, provided, of course, that bad faith as to either price or delivery is not involved.

Warranties

Over time the rules governing warranty negotiations between the buyer and seller have advanced from "caveat emptor" (let the buyer beware) to the legal provisions of the UCC which recognizes three types of warranties:

a. Express warranty.
b. Implied warranty of merchantability.
c. Implied fitness for a particular purpose.

Essentially, express warranties include promises, specifications, samples, and descriptions pertaining to the goods which are the subject of the negotiation.

Implied warranty of merchantability has to do with the merchantable quality of goods, and the UCC statutes applying have developed out of mercantile practices.

Accepted trade standards of quality, fitness for the intended uses, and conformance to promises or specified fact made on the container or label are all required as measurement of marketable quality.

Implied warranty of fitness for a purpose usually results from a buyer's request for material or equipment to meet a particular need or accomplish a specific purpose. If the buyer provides detailed specification for the item requested, the seller is relieved of any warranty of fitness for a purpose. There would be a warranty on the part of the seller that his product would meet the buyer's detailed specifications.

Acceptance and rejection of goods

The acceptance of goods is an assent by the buyer to become the owner of the goods tendered by the seller. No unusual formalities are necessary to indicate that the buyer has accepted the goods. Any words or acts which will indicate the buyer's intention to become the owner of the goods are sufficient. If the buyer keeps the goods and exercises rights of ownership over them, he will be held to have accepted them, even though he may have expressly stated that he has rejected them. If the goods tendered do not comply with the sales contract, the buyer is under no duty to accept them; but if the buyer does accept the goods, he does not thereby waive his right to damages for the seller's breach of contract. If the buyer does accept goods which do not comply with the sales contract, he must notify the seller of the breach within a reasonable time after the buyer knows or ought to know of such breach.

The question as to whether or not to reject goods delivered under a particular order may arise from various causes and may be dealt with in a variety of ways. For instance, the goods may not have been delivered on time; may have been delivered in the wrong amount; may not have been in proper condition; or may actually fail to meet the specifications. The problem for the purchasing officer is what to do under such circumstances. The important thing to keep in mind is that it may be safely presumed that the purchaser wants the goods. A suit at law, therefore, is not desirable, even though the buyer is granted any one of the commonly recognized judicial remedies for breach of contract, such as money damages, restitution, or insistence upon performance, because, aside from the fact that it is goods the buyer wants, legal action is uncertain and the outcome costly; it may be long drawn out and may cause the loss of a friendly supplier. The procurement officer therefore usually seeks other means of adjustment. Several courses are clearly open to him. The first question, of course, is one as to the seriousness of the breach. If not too serious, a simple warning to the vendor not to repeat this failure may be quite adequate. If somewhat more stringent action is called for and if the goods received are usable for some purpose, even though not quite up to specifications, a price adjustment can frequently be worked out to the mutual satisfaction of the buyer and the seller. Sometimes the goods, though not usable in the form received, may be reprocessed or otherwise made usable by the vendor, or perchance by the purchaser at the vendor's expense. If the goods happen to be component parts, they may be replaced by the supplier. If some sort of equipment is involved, or even processed material that is incapable of being efficiently used in its present form, the vendor may correct the defects at the user's plant. Or, as a last resort, the goods may be rejected and shipped back to the supplier, usually at the vendor's expense.

Needless to say, where the original difficulty arose from breach of contract pertaining to quantity or time of delivery, the method of dealing with the problem is not an engineering matter, and some, at least, of the procedures suggested above will not apply.

Protection against price fluctuations

Cancellations can, of course, be the direct result of action by the buyer. They arise in two ways:

The first of these methods of cancellation—or attempted cancellation—is rarely to be commended. It comes about because the buyer, if compelled to live up to his agreement, would lose money. Conditions in his plant may have altered, or sales may have fallen off. Therefore, he no longer wants the goods he contracted for. The market price may have dropped, and he finds that he could now buy the goods for less than he agreed to pay. Faced with these conditions, he seeks some form of relief. He becomes extremely watchful of deliveries; and he rejects goods which arrive even a day late, although he would ordinarily have accepted them without question. Inspection is tightened up, and the slightest failure to meet any detail in the specifications is seized upon as an excuse for rejection. Such methods are not to be commended and are never followed by a good procurement officer.

The second form of cancellation may arise in a perfectly legal and ethical manner as far as the *price aspects* are concerned, through evoking a clause—occasionally inserted in purchase contracts—which seeks to guarantee against price decline. Particularly in periods of declining prices and in purchasing goods subject to price fluctuations, it is in the interests of the buyer to be protected against what might be considered unreasonable prices. Occasionally, too, a long-term contract is drawn up which leaves the ascertainment of the exact price open until some deliveries are called for under it. To meet these conditions, various clauses are incorporated in purchase contracts. Thus:

You warrant that the prices named herein are as low as any net prices now given by you to any customer for like materials, and you agree that if at any time during the life of this order you quote or sell at lower net prices similar materials under similar conditions such lower net prices shall from time to time be substituted for the prices named herein.

These stipulations against price decline are not confined to purchase agreements, and under some circumstances the buyer may receive price reductions upon the seller's initiative. An example of this type of clause is the following:

Should the purchaser at the time of any delivery, on account of this contract, be offered a lower price on goods of equal quality and in like quantity by a reputable manufacturer, he will furnish the seller satisfactory proof of same in which event the seller will either supply such shipment at the lower price or permit the buyer to purchase such quantity elsewhere and the quantity so purchased elsewhere will be deducted from the total quantity of this contract. Should the seller reduce his prices during the terms of this contract. the buyer shall receive the benefit of such lower prices.

Legally such clauses are ordinarily enforceable and frequently work to the buyer's advantage. Actually, the administrative problems involved in seeing to it that these clauses are lived up to and enforced are substantial. The moral effect doubtlessly is greater than the legal.

Standardization of contract forms

To avoid many of the pitfalls which the purchasing officer may unwittingly encounter, as well as to create a contract which satisfies the mutual demands of both vendor and purchaser most adequately, efforts have frequently been made to bring about some standardization among the contracts which are in use. Arguments in favor of such a standard contract scarcely need any elaboration. However, in spite of the advantages, it is doubtful whether standard contracts would solve the real problem. Whether this statement be true or not, the very general feeling among men engaged in purchasing is that such contracts are neither feasible nor desirable. The fact that this group of men is opposed to a suggested change is not to be considered lightly; and although it need not be a deciding factor, in this case there is good reason to believe that a standardized form is not practical. The most that could be expected, under any circumstances, would be the development of a standard contract which would relate to the purchase and sale of specific types of materials or equipment as between two similar companies.

In practice, purchase agreements differ to such an extent, not only between one industry and another but within the same type of industry, that almost no generalizations can be drawn. It is highly desirable that a company should give the closest attention to the type of agreement which it uses. It is also desirable that a company should make a thorough study of the types of agreements used by other organizations confronted by essentially the same problems. It is possible that a good deal of simplification could be effected without undue restriction of the rights of the buyer.

Title to purchased goods

The professional buyer should have a clear understanding of when the title of goods passes from the seller to the buyer. Normally, there will be an agreement on the f.o.b. (free on board) point, and the buyer receives title at that point. Moreover, the UCC code in section 2–401 states that "title of goods cannot pass under a contract for sale prior to their identification for the contract." On capital goods it is particularly important for tax and depreciation reasons to establish title before the tax year end.

In some instances the buyer is given possession of the goods prior to the passing of a legal title. This is known as a "conditional sales contract," and the full title passes to the buyer when full payment is made. This procedure permits a buyer to obtain needed material without payment until a future time.

Unless a buyer furnishes specifications which infringe on a patent, the seller has the basic responsibility for providing a guarantee that there is no patent infringement on the products he sells.

Commercial arbitration

Regardless of the type of contract, disputes will sooner or later arise. These disagreements are always annoying, and, for reasons that have been given, it is not usually advantageous to go to law with them. In the majority of cases they are settled by some compromise. Occasions do arise when such compromises cannot be effected. It is to meet these situations, and yet to avoid the necessity for resorting to a court of law, that arbitration clauses are frequently included in commercial contracts. It may be said, however, that, merely because the contract includes a provision calling for arbitration, the purchasing officer does not so fully cover himself as many have believed. Many purchasing officers have deceived themselves on this point. There are prepared arbitration clauses which are valid, irrevocable, and enforceable under the arbitration laws[3] of certain states, notably: New York, New Jersey, Pennsylvania, Massachusetts, California, Louisiana, Connecticut, Rhode Island, New Hampshire, Arizona, Oregon, Ohio, and Wisconsin; and for matters

---

[3] The *Code of Arbitration Practice and Procedure* of the American Arbitration Association contains full information as to the arbitration laws of the various states.

cognizable in the federal courts, there exists the Federal Arbitration Law. Even in states which do not have such laws, it is possible to demand arbitration if provision is made for the necessary procedure in the contract, if, as is to some extent the case in Washington and Colorado, there is a statute making *"future* disputes" the subject of binding arbitration agreements. The use of arbitration clauses in contracts enforceable under these laws is a reasonable measure of protection against costly litigation. To ensure this protection, a writer has called attention to the following queries which should be made with reference to arbitration clauses which it is proposed to incorporate in commercial agreements:

1.   Is your clause in proper form under the appropriate arbitration laws? Unless properly drawn it may not be legally valid, irrevocable, and enforceable.

2.   Does your clause fully express the will of the parties or is it ambiguous? If it is uncertain in its terms, the time and expense involved in determining the scope of the clause and the powers of the arbitrators under it, may destroy its value or increase costs.

3.   Does your clause assure the appointment of impartial arbitrators? If a person serving as arbitrator is an agent, advocate, relative, or representative of a party, or has a personal interest in the matter being arbitrated, the award rendered may be vacated by the court on the ground of evident corruption or partiality on the part of an arbitrator.

4.   Does your clause provide adequately, by reference to the rules of an Association or otherwise, for a method of naming arbitrators, thus safeguarding against deadlocks or defaults in the proceedings? If not, the actual hearing of the dispute may be unduly delayed and the practical value of the arbitration be defeated.

5.   Is your clause intended to apply to appraisals or valuations or as an aid to price fixing agreements? If so, it may have no legal validity and may not be enforceable.

Federal statutes

Although the Uniform Commercial Code plays a major role in the business dealings between buyer and seller, virtually every state has its own statutes governing fraud and periods of limitation.

An ever-increasing number of Federal laws have varying degrees of impact on the performance of the purchasing department. Many of the statutes mentioned below apply primarily to purchasing activities performed in connection with government contracts.

Anti-Kickback Act
Armed Services Procurement Act
Buy American Act
Consumer Product Safety Act
Contract Work Hours Standards Act
Davis Bacon Act (minimum wages for public works employees)

Miller Act (bonds of contractors for public buildings)
Occupation Safety and Health Act
Renegotiation Act of 1951
Robinson-Patman Act
Small Business Act
Sherman Anti-Trust Act
Truth in Negotiations Act
Vincent-Trammel Act (profit limitations)
Walsh-Healy Act (minimum wages and maximum hours of work)
Wunderlich Act (government contracts judicial review)

BIBLIOGRAPHY

ALJIAN, GEORGE W., ed. *Purchasing Handbook*, 3d ed. New York: McGraw-Hill Book Co. 1973.

BUNN, CHARLES. *An Introduction to the Uniform Commercial Code.* Charlottesville, Va.: Michie Co., 1964.

COCCIA, MICHEL A. ET AL. *Product Liability: Trends and Implications.* New York: American Manufacturers Association, 1970.

DEPARTMENT OF THE ARMY. *Procurement Law.* Army Pamphlet 27-153. Washington, Department of the Army.

DEPARTMENT OF THE NAVY. *Navy Contract Law.* Washington: Government Printing Office.

HEINRITZ, STUART F., AND FARRELL, PAUL V. *Purchasing.* Englewood Cliffs, N.J.: Prentice-Hall, Inc. 1965.

LEE, LAMER, JR. AND DOBLIS, DONALD W. *Purchasing and Materials Management.* New York: McGraw-Hill Book Co., 1971.

LUSK, HAROLD F. *Business Law.* UCC ed. Homewood, Ill.: Richard D. Irwin, Inc. 1966.

MURRAY, JOHN E., JR. *Purchasing and the Law.* Purchasing Management Association of Pittsburgh, Penn. 1973.

SINGER, H. HALLECK AND MICKLEN, CHARLES M. *The Laws of Purchasing*, Danville, Ill.: Interstate Printers & Publishers, 1964.

TREADWAY, LYLE E., AND AFFLECK, G. *Guide to Purchasing.* New York: National Association of Purchasing Management Inc., 1967.

WESTING, J. H.; FINE, I. V.; ZENZ, GARY JOSEPH ET AL. *Purchasing Management*, 3d ed. New York: John Wiley & Sons, Inc., 1969.

WINCOR, RICHARD. *The Law of Contracts.* Dobbs Ferry, N.Y.: Oceana Publications, Inc., 1970.

CASES FOR CHAPTER 14

JONES & BOND

Mr. Carter, director of purchases for Suffolk Power Corporation, had just received a legal opinion from Jones & Bond regarding the cross arm failure on a new power line. Suffolk had run into major problems during the erection phase of the new ornamental tubular poles, and Mr. Carter was anxious to assure early safe operation of the line. He was not sure on how to proceed with respect to repairs and recovery of additional costs since three different suppliers had participated in the project. [For company and power line background information and the selection of engineering consultants see Suffolk Power Corporation (A). For selection of pole manufacturers see Suffolk Power Corporation (B). For selection of foundation and erection contractors see Suffolk Power Corporation (C). For cross arm failure see The Cross Arms.]

At the time of the cross arm failure it was not clear what caused the problem. Only after extensive engineering tests which lasted almost three months was the prime cause found. Had the conductors been strung immediately or had the insulators been installed, as had been normal practice in all other tubular steel pole erections in this country, failure of the arms within a month of installation would not have occurred.

Mr. Carter had advised all three suppliers involved of the difficulties as soon as they arose. All three expressed concern and also claimed their part of the job could not have been responsible and that all work had been done to specifications. All offered to be of any assistance they could and gave a number of suggestions throughout the research phase. All of the work on the line was halted until the reason for the failure was clear. Once the real cause was found, engineering was able to make recommendations for repair and strengthening which would prevent reoccurrence of the same difficulties (see Exhibit 1). Purchasing had obtained preliminary estimates showing an additional cost of about $1.8 million (see Exhibit 2). Mr. Carter had written a letter to Suffolk Power's

Exhibit 1
SUFFOLK POWER CORPORATION SYSTEM ENGINEERING DEPARTMENT

Memorandum:

Re: Replacement of Henry Nelson Company—345KV Cross Arms—Addison-Smithfield-Mesa Valley

It is required that all the groundwire and conductor cross arms on the line be removed and replaced by modified or new cross arms. It is the purpose of this correspondence to review the problems that have occurred and to outline a specific specification for the handling of these damaged cross arms. We will also continue the procedures for the installation of new cross arms on poles already erected and on new poles which have not been erected.

Through an extensive engineering research program, it was determined that the existing Nelson Company cross arms have low fatigue properties. The existing cross arm will fail by low velocity wind induced (aeolian) vibration which can cause a fatigue failure in less than a month. Secondly, the cross arm can fail by fatigue over a period of approximately 15 years by the continuing reversal of stresses due to the galloping of the conductors.

Exhibit 1 (*Continued*)

The problem of aeolian vibration can be resolved by the use of dampening devices mounted on the ends of the cross arms. Examples would be the use of insulator strings on the conductor cross arms and stockbridge dampers on the groundwire cross arms. The problem of designing for galloping requires the reduction of the stress level at the weldment of the cross arm shaft to the cross arm baseplate. This can be accomplished by the use of stiffener bars on existing cross arms which have been fabricated but not erected. It can be accomplished on the damaged arms by the use of new thicker baseplates for the conductor cross arms. On new cross arms to be fabricated, there will be some of both of the types previously described.

The field specifications for the removal and replacement of groundwire and conductor cross arms shall be accomplished by adhering to the following items:

1. All the existing cross arms shall be removed. The end of the attachment plate at the small end of the arm shall be marked with an "x." On the end of the arm attachment plate on the large end of the cross arm, the word "repair" shall be marked in paint.

2. All nuts on the arm attachment bolts shall be torqued. This includes both the inner and outer nuts. The groundwire nuts ($1\frac{3}{4}$" $\emptyset$) shall be torqued to a minimum of 600 foot-pounds and the conductor nuts ($2\frac{1}{2}$" $\emptyset$) shall be 1600 foot-pounds.

3. The cross arms shall be mounted so the centerline of any arm is within 5° of the bisector of the line deflection angle. If shims are required to obtain this tolerance, then they shall be used.

4. The damaged cross arms shall be hauled to nearest available marshalling yard and stored until enough arms are available for shipment to the supplier.

5. All groundwire cross arms that are installed on the poles shall be dampened immediately by the installation of a stockbridge damper on the attachment plate on the end of the cross arm. It is recommended that the damper designed for 954 MCM 54/7 conductor be used. As an alternative, the 159 MCM 12/7 stringing block can be used.

6. All conductor cross arms that are installed on the poles shall be dampened immediately by the installation of the insulator string on the attachment plate on the end of the arm. The strings may be left vertical or can be caught off by stringing lines to the pole.

7. A record of the type of cross arms used on each pole shall be kept by the steel inspector. The conductor cross arms will have either stiffener bars or a $2\frac{3}{4}$" baseplate. The groundwire cross arms will either be galvanized or sealed and painted. This log should be sent to the transmission engineer monthly.

The field specifications for the installation of cross arms on poles which have not been erected shall be the same as the previous specification except for the omission of items 1, 2, and 5 which are not relevant.

John R. Ward,
Engineer Transmission

Exhibit 2

SUFFOLK POWER CORPORATION ADDISON-SMITHFIELD-MESA VALLEY

Structures Canadian (M-225700) Nondamaged—Quantity 1,245—Conductor Arms Only

Strip flange plate and approximately 12″ of the shaft, reinforce flange plate with grillage, seal 4″ diam inspection hole in flange plate, plug two drain holes in arm shaft and paint base area, and minimum of 6″ of galvanized shaft surface three coats special paints—prime, intermediate, and finish.

Original estimate 1,307 @ $138.60 ea.

Actual count 1,245 @ $150 ea.	$186,750.00
Plus nonproduction extra	11,976.00
62 grills, surplus @ $14.81 ea.	918.22
Subtotal	$199,644.22
Estimated duty, brokerage, etc.	9,000.00
Estimated freight	23,650.00
Total	$232,294.22

(Average cost per arm $186.35)

Structures and Canadian (M-225700) Damaged Arms—Quantity 1,310— Ground and Conductor Arms

Remove flange plate, strip arm approximately 12″, use new 1½″ flange plate on groundwire arms and new heavier 2¾″ flange plate on conductor arms, plug remaining drain hole, paint three coats special paint—prime, intermediate, and finish.

Estimated quantity

340 groundwire @ $170.32 ea.	$ 57,908.80
970 conductor @ $270.00 ea.	261,900.00
Storage of arms, 1,310 @ $10.25 ea. (if necessary)	13,427.50
Subtotal	$333,236.30
Estimated duty, brokerage, etc.	15,000.00
Estimated freight	24,890.00
Total	$373,126.30

(Average cost per arm:
groundwire $217.64
conductor $300.84)

Henry Nelson Company (M-034100, M-123600)—Quantity 3,007

At Henry Nelson we have both groundwire and conductor arms in various stages of fabrication. At the time the procedures for repair were finalized, they were as follows:

	A Groundwire	B Conductor
1. Galvanized, nondamaged, ready to ship	(107)	93
2. Fabricated, nondamaged, ungalvanized	69	140
3. Not started	672	2,033

Repair Procedure:

Item 1.   Groundwire: No repairs made, accepted as is.
              Conductor: Same as S.C., nondamaged.

Exhibit 2 (*Continued*)

Item 2. Groundwire: Seal hole in flange plate, plug drain holes, and paint instead of galvanizing.

Conductor: Same as groundwire above except also reinforce flange plate with grillage.

Item 3. Groundwire: Fabricate to new specifications—no holes, no galvanizing, paint.

Conductor: Same as groundwire above except also reinforce 1377 flange plate with grillage and fabricate 656 with new 2¾" base plate. (Since 2" base plate material is already on hand for entire order, it is more economical to cut 656 plates into ¾" × 2" bars for grillage and replace with 2¾" plate as needed.)

	Quantity	Cost	Total
1A	107	None	–
1B	93	$240.00	$ 22,320.00
2A	69	120.00	8,280.00
2B	140	200.00	28,000.00
3A	672	52.85	35,515.20
3B	1,377	130.00	179,100.00
	656	62.50	41,000.00
			$314,215.20

McTaggart Construction (estimated by D. Fox):

To remove damaged arms and replace with new or repair arms per pole . . . . $	4,000.00	$6,000.00
Average $5,000.00 × 164 poles	820,000.00	

Engineering Research Costs:

Conservative estimate . . . . $	100,000.00
Summary of Estimates:	
Damaged arm repair	
1,310–Structures Canadian . . . . $	373,126.30
Nondamaged arm repair	
1,245–Structures Canadian	232,294.22
3,007–Henry Nelson	314,215.20
Contractor–remove and replace	820,000.00
Research costs.	100,000.00
Total.	$1,839,635.72

legal firm, Jones & Bond summarizing the situation to date (see Exhibit 3). Jones & Bond had met with Mr. Carter five days later and confirmed their statements in this meeting by letter the following day (see Exhibit 4). Twenty-six months had now passed since the beginning of the three-year project (see Exhibit 5). Suffolk Power Corporation was facing tremendous demand pressures for more power and simultaneously had not received particularly favorable treatment with rate increase requests.

Exhibit 3
SUFFOLK POWER CORPORATION DIRECTOR OF PURCHASES

Memorandum to: Mr. T. R. Bond

Subject: Ornamental Poles and Arms

The company has experienced a most unfortunate failure of the eight arms of each of its first 345KV ornamental tubular steel pole transmission line. The failure results in our believing that we should try to recover our losses from two or all of the three contractors involved in (1) engineering, (2) designing and fabricating, and (3) erecting these poles and arms.

We purchased the engineering assistance from Pettigrew Associates of New York, N.Y. This contract issued two years ago covered the technical assistance we needed to: lay out the line circling our service area from Addison to Smithfield to Mesa Valley substations; the drawing up of specifications for our use in obtaining bids on the poles, arms and appurtenances; and their assistance to us in the evaluation of the bids on poles and arms when received.

Pettigrew Associates performed the services required by this contract according to the original schedule, and we had no idea that there was any difficulty with any of their performance until failure of the arms occurred. An analysis of the failure of the arms proved that failure was occasioned by what is known as the aeolian effect of wind on these free standing poles and arms. Had the insulators and cables been installed immediately as the poles and arms were constructed, there apparently would have been no failures; but our erection contractor chose to erect the poles and arms and then return months later to install the insulators and cables. It is well proven now that neither McTaggart Construction Company (our erector), the Nelson Company (the pole and arm fabricator), nor Pettigrew Associates (the engineer), or Suffolk knew of the possible low velocity wind induced vibration (aeolian) that could cause arm fatigue and failure. Pettigrew contends they did not draw up a detailed specification for poles and arms but rather a "performance" type specification.

Suffolk contends that the performance specifications should have included sufficient performance description to permit the poles to be erected without arm failure, and, if the aeolian effect existed and was a construction parameter that should have been avoided, they should have known it and so specified.

Suffolk awarded its contract for the designing, furnishing, and fabricating of poles and arms to the H. Nelson Company of Dallas, Texas. Our testing has proven that the poles and arms that Nelson Company designed and furnished to Suffolk would have withstood all of the performance requirements had we installed the insulators or some type of dampeners on the arms and not subjected them to the wind induced vibration in the freestanding condition. H. Nelson Company claims no knowledge of the aeolian effect. All arms need to be reworked and given more strength through the use of heavier materials; but this is not because of the aeolian effect but rather to strengthen the arms to withstand "galloping" conditions of the cables that develop in certain wind conditions. Perhaps Pettigrew Associates were derelict in not protecting us from this possible hazard also.

The McTaggart Construction Company in Indianapolis was awarded our contract for unloading of the poles and arms, installation of the foundations, erection of the poles and arms, and the stringing of the wire and cables.

Exhibit 3 (*Continued*)

In our discussions of the arm failure with McTaggart, we attempted to point out their contributing to the failure by not installing insulators or dampeners and/or the cables and wires immediately upon erection of the poles and arms. They claimed they have erected lattice steel towers and ornamental poles and arms for many years without any concern or knowledge of the aeolian effect of wind-induced vibration and, therefore, could not know they had such an erection hazard to contend with. They have put insulators on while erecting on other tubular pole jobs, but they did it because of other erection problems—not the wind vibration.

We have attempted to have each of these companies assume obligation for our losses but to no avail yet. The costs likely to be incurred are as follows:

a.	Rework of arms at Nelson Co.	$ 314,215.20
b.	Rework of a portion of the arms at Structures Canadian	605,420.52
c.	Installation costs to be paid to McTaggart Construction	820,000.00
d.	Suffolk's cost (study and processing)	100,000.00
	Total Cost	$1,839,635.72

Your immediate attention to this matter would be very much appreciated.

John Carter

Exhibit 4
JONES & BOND
ATTORNEYS AND COUNSELORS
CHICAGO, ILLINOIS

Mr. John Carter,
Director of Purchases,
Suffolk Power Corporation.
Dr. Mr. Carter:
Re: 345KV Transmission Pole Failures

This will confirm our opinion as expressed at the meeting held in your office on Monday. As you will recall, two basic legal matters were discussed, to wit: the possible bases of liability of the three parties involved and whether the Company would jeopardize its rights by proceeding to repair the poles without first consulting any of those parties.

Concerning the latter, if the Company is entitled to recover from anyone, it can reasonably expect to recover the cost of correcting the problem. The cost of doing so must be reasonable, and the repair must also be reasonably likely to correct the problem. In other words you cannot recover for a "gold plating" job, nor can you recover the cost of a repair which does not correct the problem. This right to recover is not affected by a failure to negotiate in advance with any party against which a claim might be made. If, however, any such party is consulted in advance of the commencement of a repair program and is given a chance to participate in determining the repair to

Exhibit 4 *(Continued)*

be used, the chances of later being required to defend either the necessity of that repair or its cost would be greatly reduced.

With respect to the liabilities of each party, the contracts and related documents have been reviewed in detail on the basis of the Company's findings that the cause of the damage to the pole arms was wind vibration, which can be substantially avoided by dampening the arms with conductors, rather than letting the bare arms stand. As stated at the meeting, the bases for potential liability of each party can be set out, and the Company can then assess the value of each on the basis of the known facts.

McTaggart Construction Company performed its services pursuant to a detailed contract which covered the work to be done but which did not provide any specific rights or remedies for a situation like the one now faced. In order to recover from McTaggart, whether on a theory of breach of contract or of negligence, it will be necessary to show that in erecting the poles, McTaggart did not exercise the degree of care, skill, and diligence that a reasonably competent contractor, purporting to be able to erect poles and lines, would have exercised. The McTaggart contract does not, in our opinion, impose any burden upon McTaggart for engineering or design adequacy.

As for Henry Nelson Company, their contract consists of a purchase order with detailed specifications attached thereto. There are no commercial terms, such as warranties, in the contract which relate directly to the arm failure problem. There are, however, four (4) possible bases of liability, which are:

1. *Faulty design:* this would require that Nelson be shown to have had general design responsibility and that the current problem is a result of faulty design. The principal problem in this area is that the contract appears to give Nelson the burden of designing to Pettigrew Associates' specifications only.
2. *Breach of warranty:* if Nelson had reason to know the use to which the poles would be put and to know that Suffolk was relying on Nelson's skill and ability to produce a product fit for that purpose, than there would be in the contract an implied warranty that the poles would be fit for the purpose for which they were intended to be used. The primary weakness here is that the poles may well be fit for their ultimate intended use, and it would be necessary to show that Nelson knew or had reason to know that the poles would be erected and left standing without conductors.
3. *Failure to detail assembly procedures:* Section 14 of the Pettigrew Specification indicates in part that "the Vendor shall provide sketches indicating assembly procedures and the most desirable attachment points for raising the structures." With the benefit of hindsight, it can be argued that this includes the responsibility to direct that the arms be hung with conductors, although there seems to be general agreement that this is not necessarily what 14 was intended to cover.
4. *Failure to comply with the National Electrical Safety Code:* 24 of the Pettigrew specification requires compliance with the N.E.S.C., and it appears that there may be some basis for asserting that Nelson did not comply. This depends, as I understand it, largely upon whether the rele-

Exhibit 4 (*Concluded*)

vant section of the N.E.S.C. can be construed as covering poles erected without conductors.

Finally, as regards Pettigrew Associates, the Company has a contract pursuant to which Pettigrew is selected ". . . to perform the Engineering and Design Services in connection with (the) Addison-Smithfield-Mesa Valley 345KV Transmission Line Project." Article I provides that Pettigrew will ". . . furnish complete project administration for coordinating and expediting the Work" and is to perform services ". . . of the highest professional character . . ." with Pettigrew being ". . . fully responsible to Suffolk for the correctness of the engineering design and related data . . . ," which included pole design. In addition, Pettigrew evaluated all bids, including designs offered, and recommended the award to H. Nelson. If it can be shown either that the engineering design and related data were not correct or were not of the highest professional quality, then the Company should have a sound cause of action against Pettigrew. I might add that the term "incorrect" can readily be construed to include omissions. As for the professional quality ground, it would be necessary to introduce expert testimony or evidence, or both, to establish that a top-quality engineer would have at least considered the wind vibration problem.

Depending on the facts which you are able to establish, the Company may have a cause of action against one or more of the parties involved. We would be pleased to assist you further, should you so request, in progressing any claim the Company may wish to make.

Yours very truly,
T. R. Bond

Exhibit 5
SUFFOLK POWER CORPORATION
TIMETABLE FOR THE NEW ADDISON-SMITHFIELD-MESA VALLEY
POWER LINE

Year 1:

March	Management approves use of ornamental tubular steel poles for the 140-mile line.
April–July	Preliminary work and search for engineering consultant.
August	Pettigrew Associates selected as consulting engineers to prepare pole specifications, line layout, and assist in selection of manufacturer and erection.

Year 2:

March	Pettigrew Associates submits pole specifications and line layout.
April–July	Engineering and purchasing evaluation of manufacturing of poles for the first half of the line.
July	H. Nelson selected as the pole manufacturer.
June–September	Engineering and purchasing evaluation of foundation and erection contractors.
September	McTaggart Construction chosen for both foundation and erection of the new line.

Exhibit 5 (*Continued*)

October	Delivery of test poles by H. Nelson. Tests prove poles meet specifications.
January	Installation starts. New poles draw favorable employee and public attention.
February 20	H. Nelson completes manufacture of poles for Addison-Smithfield section.
February 24	First cross arm failure noted. Purchasing notifies all three suppliers. All deny blame.
February 26	All project work halted.
Year 3:	
March–April	Continuing pole cross arm failures. Engineering search for causes.
May 11	Engineering determines reason for failure.
May 25	Purchasing determines repair costs.
May 25	Mr. Carter sends memo to Jones & Bond for a legal opinion.
May 30	Jones & Bond representatives meet with Mr. Carter.
May 31	Letter from T. R. Bond confirming legal opinion.
Year 4:	
April 30	Project deadline.

Mr. Carter was not sure where the extra funds to repair the cross arms would come from. The very high demand for capital in the corporation made it imperative that every avenue be explored to recover the extra costs to be incurred on the line. Workers had expressed fear about working near and with the poles. Since on time completion and safety were also both of the highest priority, Mr. Carter wondered what action to take next.

MAYFAIR COUNTY BOARD OF EDUCATION

Mr. Fraser Lewis, supervisor of purchasing for the Mayfair County Board of Education (see Exhibit 1), Mayfair, Ontario, Canada, listened thoughtfully to the supervisor of caretaking, Bob Oxford, outline his plans for the cleaning of ten new and near-new schools:

"As you know, Fraser, we are trying to find a flexible balance in the systems between the Caretakers' Association and outside contractors. We find no fault with the Association people but, naturally, they want an exclusive if they can get it, even though they are not actually a union. However, this depends on their doing a proper job, and there's nothing like a bit of competition to ensure keeping everyone on his toes. Even if we do contract for schools one to ten, we are large enough to be able to transfer existing staff to other schools without anyone suffering, especially at the rate we are expanding. As you remember, we don't need to employ our own caretaking staff for new schools, under our agreement."

"Fine," said Fraser Lewis. "This will run into quite a bit of money, so we'll have to advertise for tenders as well as approach firms we already know. We'll ask for bids on all or some of the schools and reserve the right to accept any combination. I think the board is still sticking to the policy of using our own forces, providing costs are pretty close?"

"That's right," replied the caretaking supervisor. "By the way, I'll send you the usual sequare footage specification information and work up costs for you when required. As it's nearly April now, perhaps you'll get this rolling quickly?"

"No problem, Bob. Send the material to Lin Godfrey who handles this buying for me."

Fraser Lewis smiled ruefully as he remembered this phone call which had been the starting point of the new cleaning contract. He had a high regard for Bob Oxford, who had formerly managed a national caretaking firm. It was not at the end of November, and the supervisor of caretaking was breathing down his neck. He would have to make a drastic decision soon. He phoned his caretaking buyer. "Lin, let's run through the caretaking tender file again to refresh my memory. Bob Oxford is furious about the Carlon situation."

"Well, here's the run-down, Fraser," said Godfrey, seating himself and opening a thick file. "On April 9, I advertised for tenders (see Exhibit 2). In addition, I sent it to about 15 firms we know. Some we had dealt with, including Carlon, and, of course, we asked for references and supplied complete specs. The prospective contractors had to examine the schools."

"What was Carlon's reputation?" interjected Lewis.

"Well, let's put it this way," said the buyer, "He's done a little for us in the past reasonably well, but he's held some really important contracts for the federal government and quite an array of well-known industrial firms. I'd rate him adequate. Certainly not by any means low enough to exclude him from consideration, but not a leader like Smithers who walked off with the low bid on eight of the ten original schools. Smithers has done quite a bit of work for us before and always well."

"Did we get the usual bid bonds to ensure that the companies would go ahead if awarded a contract?"

"Yes, for 10 percent of the overall bid." (See Exhibit 3.)

"And what about performance bonds for 10 percent of the contract value,"

"All O.K.," replied Godfrey, "as far as Smithers is concerned (see Exhibit 4). Actually, Carlon's isn't in our file, but I have Surety's agreement to bond them for performance if they were successful (see Exhibit 5). This was the situation," he continued. "I had all my figures from half a dozen people by April 24 (see Exhibit 6). Some of them go all over the shop. Smithers was lowest on schools 1, 3, 4, 5, 6, 7, 8 and 9 and Carlon on 2 and 10."

"None of the bidders bothered to be present at the opening read-out on May 7, but somehow Carlon knew where he stood. That was obvious from subsequent conversations. It so happened that Carlon was about $2,300 below the next man on School No. 2 and $4,100 lower on School No. 10. In both cases Smithers was the competition." By June 6 we agreed internally to withdraw School No. 2—a large one—because Bob Oxford's cost estimates showed his own forces to be within 2 percent of outside bids (see Exhibits 7 and 8). Actually, with your approval I issued the appropriate purchase orders on June 15. We told the board in our recommendation of June 20 that we had given eight schools to Smithers and only one to Carlon.

"When did Carlon react?" asked Mr. Lewis.

"Their sales manager phoned me at the end of June," said the buyer, "and confirmed it on July 6, asking leave to withdraw his quotation." (See Exhibit 9).

"And when did I write him about his obligations?" asked Mr. Lewis. "On July 13," said Mr. Godfrey. "Here it is." (See Exhibit 10.)

"Then nothing further transpired until September when Bob Oxford's men noted sloppy work in School No. 10. He sent them a registered letter at the end of that month (see Exhibit 11) and received verbal assurances of improvement but complained again by letter a month later (see Exhibit 12) and go renewed assurance and a very temporary improvement. However, last week he was fed up and sent in one of his assistant superintendents with a team for a detailed inspection which proved the inefficiency of the cleaning. Some floors needed complete refinishing. Bob Oxford is mad. All he wants is to get these blank, blank people out."

"To tell you the truth, Fraser, this Carlon outfit has been around long enough to know what they are doing. I think they're trying to weasel and should be nailed. They know what a performance bond means."

"Thank you, Lin," replied the purchasing supervisor, "I'll think it over."

Fraser Lewis knew that it was bad for a firm's reputation to have to call on surety to make-up for a deficiency, yet to release the contractor from his responsibilities would affect the board's posture on future tendering. He wondered if all reasonable avenues of avoiding an unpleasant show-down had been explored.

Exhibit 1
MAYFAIR COUNTY BOARD OF EDUCATION—GENERAL INFORMATION

The board was one of the largest in Canada and fast expanding. It controlled 143 schools with 78,000 pupils. The average cost of a school was $5 million. The operating budget was $75 million; the capital budget about $22 million for new buildings.

Exhibit 1 (*Continued*)

ORGANIZATION CHART

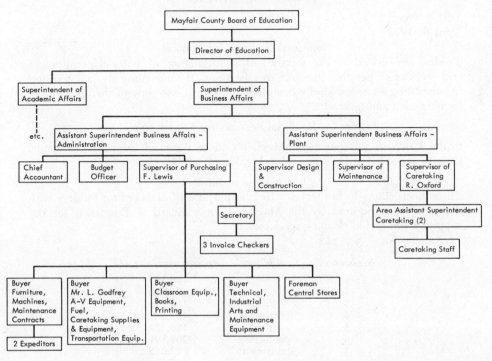

Purchasing Information:

Purchasing expenditures for supplies and equipment were $9–10 million annually.

The tendering policy was:

$500 and under	Verbal quotation
$501 to $1,000	Verbal quotation plus written confirmation
$1,001 to $5,000	Formal quotation
Over $5,000	Publicly advertise for tenders

Usually three quotations were required except when only small amounts were involved or there was too limited a number of suppliers. Tenders were opened by purchasing and the amounts read out to those contractors attending the opening. Mr. Lewis approved all tenders and also signed all orders over $5,000. He reported this decision at regular reporting board of trustees meetings.

Unionization of contractors' labor was not demanded.

All things being equal, suppliers in or nearest the boards' territory were favored.

Abnormal bids were only drawn to suppliers' attention if there was an obvious error. Rebidding was permitted once in this event. However, a bidder could withdraw his tender up to the moment of opening.

The range of bids in this case did not raise any thought of a mistake in Mr. Godfrey's mind. Spreads of 25 percent were quite common. Sometimes contractors preferred to bid high deliberately rather than not show interest.

Exhibit 2
MAYFAIR COUNTY BOARD OF EDUCATION
MAYFAIR, ONTARIO

Tender No. 14
April 9, 1973

Janitorial Services for Schools

Tenders are invited for the supply and/or installation of materials, equipment and services as per the attached specifications. If your company is interested in submitting a tender, kindly complete and return one copy of the appropriate forms, sealed and marked:

Tender for Janitorial Services for Schools, No. 14

to the Purchasing Department, Mayfair County Board of Education, Mayfair, Ontario, on or before 3.00 p.m. Monday, May 7, 1973.

Instructions to Bidders

These instructions to bidders are for the purpose of acquainting bidders with the conditions required by the Mayfair County Board of Education for the supply of contracted cleaning services.

1. Locations

School no.	Address	Approx. area in sq. ft.
1		180,550
2		173,800
3	map	169,644
4	obtainable	152,680
5	from	180,384
6	purchasing	209,801
7	department	77,015
8		110,616
9		130,897
10		60,500

2. Bid Bond

The contractor, when submitting his bid, shall include attached to the tender form, a bid bond in the amount of ten percent (10%) of the contract sum, said bond to be in effect for 30 days.

3. Agreement to bond

The contractor shall be required to enclose a letter from a bonding or surety company certifying that they are prepared to provide a performance bond if they are successful in obtaining the contract. The performance bond shall be in an amount equal to ten percent of the total contract price.

4. Length of contract

The length of term of this agreement shall be for the period commencing Labor Day, 1973, and ending at the conclusion of yearly services in the summer holidays of 1974 as outlined in the attached specifications. It should be noted that summer clean up will have to be individually scheduled for each school to accommodate summer use of schools.

5. Number of schools to be bid

The contractors may bid on any or all of the schools listed.

6. Subcontracting

Subcontracting of any portion of the work outlined in these specifications will not be permitted without the prior written consent of the Board.

Exhibit 2 (*Continued*)

Any work undertaken by subcontractors shall be under the terms and conditions as set forth in this specification and the use of subcontractors shall in no way relieve the contractor of his responsibilities.

7. Examine the schools

The contractor shall be required to examine all of the schools being tendered by him prior to bidding to familiarize himself with the existing individual conditions. Failure to do so shall not relieve the contractor of his responsibilities.

8. Products

All bidders are required to provide a list of the materials and equipment to be used in the performance of this contract. This list should include such items as floor finishes and waxes, soaps and detergents, stripping agents, germicidal agents, bowl cleaners, abrasive cleaners, furniture polishes, etc. All materials must be of a high quality and must meet the standards required by the Mayfair County Board of Education. The successful bidder will be required to submit samples for approval.

9. References

Firms submitting tenders shall be actually engaged in this type of work and shall supply a resume indicating the size and experience of their respective firms including a list of clients. The size and type of buildings being serviced should be indicated and the length of time for which they have had a contract.

10. Insurance

The successful bidder will be required to provide the Board with written proof of insurance coverage of not less than $500,000 public liability and $500,000 property damage.

11. Bonding

All employees of the successful bidder shall be covered by a fidelity bond in the amount of not less than $5,000.

12. Workmen's compensation

The contractor must be in good standing with the Workmen's Compensation Board and the Unemployment Insurance Commission and provide the Board with a certificate to this effect with his tender.

13. Invoicing procedures

The contract will be paid each month in arrears before the end of the succeeding month, providing that invoices are submitted to the Board on the first of each succeeding month. There will be eleven equal payments, each one equal to one eleventh of the total contract price. The final payment will be withheld until the yearly services as outlined in Appendix A have been completed to the Board's satisfaction.

The Board reserves the right to withhold part or all of the payment for any invoice if, in the Board's opinion, the portion of the contract for which the invoice was submitted was not performed up to the standard required in this specification.

14. Labor laws

It shall be the contractor's responsibility to be aware of all current or impending legislation relating to Provincial Employment Standards concerning minimum wages, vacation pay, termination of employment, etc.

Exhibit 2 (*Continued*)

15. Safety

Contractors shall be aware of all governing local municipal regulations relating to employee's safety and fire regulations and are required to acquaint their staff with this information.

16. Additional information

All queries and requests for additional information or instructions for visiting the schools are to be directed to the Purchasing Department, attention, Mr. L. Godfrey.

General Conditions
Contract Cleaning

1. Intent

It is the intent of this specification to provide and outline the terms and conditions necessary to provide a complete evening cleaning service in the schools listed in the Instructions to Bidders.

2. Work involved

The work included in this specification includes the supply of all the necessary personnel, cleaning supplies, miscellaneous supplies, cleaning equipment, supervisory staff, etc., to carry out the work as outlined in this specification.

3. Termination

The contract may be terminated by the Board for just cause as determined by the Board. One month's notice of termination shall be given in writing by the Board using registered mail.

4. Areas to be serviced

The areas to be serviced are the complete premises including the teaching and the administration areas, corridors and stairwells, gymnasiums, washrooms, change rooms, cafeteria and food service areas, shops, storage and service areas. Not included are swimming pool areas and mechanical rooms.

5. Services to be provided

Provide all the necessary working personnel and supervision to carry out all of the work outlined in the specification. The contractor shall be required through regular supervision by the contractor's supervisory staff, to ensure that all of the services to be provided in this contract are carried out to the Board's satisfaction. The contractor shall be prepared from time to time to reschedule his personnel to suit the operation of groups using the schools in the evenings.

Cleaning services—See Appendix A.

Supplies—See Appendix B.

6. Security of buildings

The contractor shall be responsible for the security of the buildings during those hours in which his forces are in the buildings. The contractor shall further be responsible for ensuring that all doors and windows are locked when his staff leaves the building. The contractor has an obligation to notify designated Board personnel of any unusual occurrence in any building where his forces are working which could adversely affect the security and/or safety of the building.

Exhibit 2 (*Continued*)

7. Hours of service
   On regular school days the work involved in this contract should be carried out between 4:00 P.M. and 12:00 midnight. Regular service is not required on statutory holidays, regular school holidays or weekends.

8. Yearly services
   Yearly services as outlined in Appendix A should not commence until July 1, 1974 and be completed by no later than August 30, 1974. These services may have to be scheduled to suit organizations using the schools during the summer and performed at a time agreeable to the Supervisor of Caretaking for Mayfair County Board of Education.

9. Uniforms
   Contractor's forces should wear a uniform of design and quality acceptable to the Board. It is essential that these forces present a neat, tidy appearance at all times.

10. Equipment
    This contractor shall be required to supply all of the necessary tools and equipment required to carry out the work of this contract, i.e., scrubbing machines, vacuum cleaners, brooms, mops, miscellaneous tools, etc., and to maintain in good, safe working order.

11. Cleaning methods
    Only those methods generally acceptable to the trade as being good practice shall be used in this contract. The recommendations of both manufacturers of building products and supplies of cleaning agents, waxes, finishes, etc., shall be adhered to unless mutually agreed upon by the contractor and the Board as being suitable for the particular condition of the school.
    It should be pointed out in particular that hardwood flooring in gymnasiums should be serviced only as outlined in Appendix A. If the contractor deems that any further treatment is required, it should only be performed after consultation with the Supervisor of Caretaking for Mayfair County Board of Education. The use of "hot" stripping solutions on any flooring or surface is prohibited. Floors must be maintained at a high level of cleanliness at all times and therefore, the cycles outlined in Appendix A may have to be adjusted to suit each school condition as experience indicates.

12. Storage facilities
    The Board shall provide adequate storage facilities for the contractor's supplies and equipment.

13. Supervision
    This contract will come under the direct supervision of the Supervisor of Caretaking for Mayfair County Board of Education, his Assistants, and the Board Head Caretaker or Building Supervisor in charge of each school.

14. Contractor's staff
    The contractor shall be required to provide trained and qualified staff to undertake the work as outlined in this specification. In each school the contractor shall appoint a lead hand to be the responsible person. This person should be able to converse in and understand English. The Board reserves the right to demand the dismissal of any employee

Exhibit 2 (Continued)

engaged in this contract if, in the Board's opinion, his or her conduct has been of an unacceptable nature.

Appendix A: Contract Cleaning
Specification A: Services

Nightly services to include:
1. Empty and wipe clean all waste receptacles and place or dispose of contents as specified.
2. Empty and damp clean all ash trays and cigarette stands.
3. Dust, using chemically treated dust cloths, all office and classroom furniture such as desks, tables, cabinets, telephones, shelves, benches, window and partition ledges, and all other office and classroom equipment and furniture.
4. Remove all obvious finger marks and stains from walls, doors, partitions, around light switches, etc.
5. Clean and polish all door hand pushplates.
6. Remove all stains from all desk and table tops in all classrooms, cafetoriums, lunchrooms, and offices.
7. Clean all glass doors.
8. Wash, using germicidal soap, all chairs, tables, waste containers, etc., in health departments (if required)
9. Empty all pencil sharpeners.
10. Damp clean all chalk rails.
11. Wash and disinfect all drinking fountains.
12. Thoroughly clean, disinfect, and polish all washroom fixtures such as sinks, toilets, urinals, mirrors, etc.
13. Replenish all washroom dispensers, towels, tissues, soaps, napkins, deodorants, etc.
14. Damp clean all shower walls and fixtures.
15. Clean all benches in change rooms.
16. Spot clean all vinyl covered chairs or benches.
17. Remove, clean, and reposition all door mats.
18. Vacuum and spot clean all carpets and rugs.
    Floors
19. Completely dust mop all floor areas, using an approved method of dust control.
20. Wash all washrooms, change rooms, shower areas, and locker rooms, using germicidal detergent.
21. Damp mop all terrazzo hallways and stairs, and all cafetoriums, serveries and staff lunchrooms, using a neutral soap.
22. Remove all spillages, liquid stains, etc., from all other floor areas.
23. Incinerate garbage or place in designated area as required.

Service twice per week:
1. Spray buff all tiled floor areas in all general offices including vice principals', guidance offices, health department areas and staff dining rooms and lounges.
2. Spray buff waiting rooms and principals' offices.

Exhibit 2 (*Continued*)

Weekly services:
1. Treat and polish all desk and table tops in principals', vice principals', library, general, and private offices.
2. Spot clean all doors of lockers.
3. Thoroughly wash and disinfect all shower walls.
4. Clean and polish all kick plates on doors, using stainless steel cleaner.
5. Spray buff floor areas in cafetoriums and tiled hallways at top of each staircase.
6. Clean all stair risers.

Service every two weeks:
1. Completely recondition (spray buff or scrub and rewax) all tiled hallways and corridors.
2. Disinfect all telephones.
3. Completely recondition (spray buff or scrub and rewax) all tiled floors not previously scheduled. (Includes all classrooms, laboratories, seminars, etc.)

Monthly services:
1. Thoroughly wash all floors in trade rooms.
2. Vacuum or dust all venetian blinds.

Service every three months:
1. Recondition (spray buff or clean and wax) all grainwood and hardwood floors in gymnasiums.
2. Completely wash all walls and partitions in all washrooms (if required).
3. Clean all glass in all entrances and lobbies on first floor levels.

Service every six months:
1. Window Cleaning
   a. All entrances and lobbies on second and third floor levels (where applicable).
   b. Both sides of all windows encompassing open court areas (where applicable).

Service once per year:
1. Clean all windows on all floors on all sides. (Double windows taken apart.)
2. Completely strip and recondition all tiled terrazzo and concrete floor areas.
3. Clean all baseboards, door ends, cove mouldings, etc.
4. Clean and treat all desks, chairs, benches and other classroom and office furniture, using germicidal agents.

Appendix B: Contract Cleaning Supplies

1. Board supplied items
   The following items will be purchased by the Board and supplied to the contractor.

   > Hand towels
   > Toilet tissue
   > Dispenser napkins
   > Sanitary disposal bags
   > Hand soap
   > Garbage bags

Exhibit 2 (*Concluded*)

2. Contractor supplied items
The following items shall be supplied by the contractor.
All the necessary soaps, detergents, solvents, waxes, finishes, bowl cleaners, etc., to perform this contract. Also equipment as specified in general conditions.

Exhibit 3
BID BOND

WPUR 113

C.C.A. DOCUMENT NO. (S) 20

NUMBER **00000.11111**

The Canadian Surety Company
HEAD OFFICE   TORONTO

A Member of Transamerica Corporation

BID BOND

No. $

KNOW ALL MEN BY THESE PRESENTS THAT   **Carlon Cleaning Co. Ltd.**

as Principal

hereinafter called the Principal, and   **The Canadian Surety Company**

a corporation created and existing under the laws of Canada and duly authorized to transact the business of

Suretyship in Canada as Surety, hereinafter called the Surety, are held and firmly bound unto

Mayfair County Board of Education   as Obligee

hereinafter called the Obligee, in the amount of   **Thirty-Six Thousand Four Hundred and Eighty** _____

_____ Dollars

(**$36,480.00**   ) lawful money of Canada, for the payment of which sum, well and truly to be made, the Principal and the Surety bind themselves, their heirs, executors, administrators, successors and assigns, jointly and severally, firmly by these presents.

WHEREAS, the Principal has submitted a written tender to the Obligee, dated the   **7th**
day of   **May**   19 73 , for Janitorial Services at 10 Schools.

NOW, THEREFORE, THE CONDITION OF THIS OBLIGATION is such that if the aforesaid Principal shall have the tender accepted within sixty (60) days from the closing date of tender and the said Principal will, within the time required, enter into a formal contract and give the specified security to secure the performance of the terms and conditions of the Contract, then this obligation shall be null and void; otherwise the Principal and the Surety will pay unto the Obligee the difference in money between the amount of the bid of the said Principal and the amount for which the Obligee legally contracts with another party to perform the work if the latter amount be in excess of the former.

The Principal and the Surety shall not be liable for a greater sum than the specified penalty of this Bond.

Any suit under this Bond must be instituted before the expiration of six months from the date of this Bond.

IN WITNESS WHEREOF, the Principal and the Surety have Signed and Sealed this Bond this   **7th**
day of   **May**   19 73 .

SIGNED and SEALED
In the presence of

_____ (Seal)
Carlon Cleaning Co. Ltd.
Principal

The Canadian Surety Company

Attorney in Fact

42056 (8/72)
ENDORSED BY: R.A.I.C., A.C.E.C., E.I.C., C.C.A., S.W.A.C.   APPROVED BY: INSURANCE BUREAU OF CANADA

Exhibit 4
PERFORMANCE BOND

WPUR 113

THE GUARDIAN INSURANCE COMPANY OF CANADA ☐
ROYAL EXCHANGE ASSURANCE ☐
UNION INSURANCE SOCIETY OF CANTON, LIMITED ☐

HEAD OFFICE: 25 ADELAIDE STREET WEST, TORONTO 105, ONTARIO

BOND No.
1234567

PERFORMANCE BOND
(CANADIAN CONSTRUCTION ASSOCIATION APPROVED FORM)

AMOUNT: $ 26,720

KNOW ALL MEN BY THESE PRESENTS, that   Smithers Cleaning Company Limited

as Principal, hereinafter
called the Principal, and   The Guardian Insurance Company of Canada   as Surety, hereinafter
called the Surety, are held and firmly bound unto   Mayfair County Board of Education
as Obligee, hereinafter called the Obligee, in the amount of

Twenty-six thousand, seven hundred and twenty -- Dollars ($ 26,720   ) lawful
money of Canada, for the payment of which sum, well and truly to be made, the Principal and the Surety bind themselves, their heirs, executors, administrators, successors and assigns, jointly and severally, firmly by these presents.

WHEREAS, the Principal has entered into a written contract with the Obligee,
dated the   **4th**   day of   September   19 73 ,

for supply of contracted cleaning services at the following schools:-

Numbers 1, 3, 4, 5, 6, 7, 8, 9.

in accordance with the plans and specifications submitted therefor which contract, plans and specifications and
amendments thereto, to the extent herein provided for, are by reference made part hereof and are hereinafter referred
to as the Contract.

NOW, THEREFORE, THE CONDITION OF THIS OBLIGATION is such that, if the Principal shall promptly
and faithfully perform said Contract (including any amendments thereto, provided such amendments do not collectively
increase the amount to be paid to the Principal by more than 10% of the amount of the Contract except with the
written consent of the Surety) then this obligation shall be null and void; otherwise it shall remain in full force and
effect.

Whenever the Principal shall be, and declared by Obligee to be, in default under the Contract, the Obligee having
performed Obligee's obligations thereunder, the Surety may promptly remedy the default, or shall promptly

(1) Complete the Contract in accordance with its terms and conditions or

(2) Obtain a bid or bids for submission to Obligee for completing the Contract in accordance with its terms and
conditions, and upon determination by Obligee and Surety of the lowest responsible bidder, arrange for a
contract between such bidder and Obligee and make available as work progresses (even though there should
be a default or a succession of defaults under the contract or contracts of completion arranged under this
paragraph) sufficient funds to pay the cost of completion less the balance of the contract price; but not
exceeding, including other costs and damages for which the Surety may be liable hereunder, the amount
set forth in the first paragraph hereof. The term "balance of the contract price", as used in this paragraph,
shall mean the total amount payable by Obligee to Principal under the Contract, less the amount properly
paid by Obligee to Principal.

Any suit under this Bond must be instituted before the expiration of one (1) year from date on which final payment
under the Contract falls due.

The Surety shall not be liable for a greater sum than the specified penalty of this Bond.

No right of action shall accrue on this Bond to or for the use of any person or corporation other than the Obligee
named herein or the heirs, executors, administrators or successors of the Obligee.

IN TESTIMONY WHEREOF, the Principal has hereto set his hand and affixed its seal, and the Surety has
caused these presents to be sealed with its corporate seal duly attested by the signature of its Administrative Manager
this   **4th**   day of   September   19 73 .

SIGNED, SEALED and DELIVERED
In the presence of

Smithers Cleaning Company Limited   (Seal)
(Principal)

Guardian Royal Exchange   (Seal)
(Surety)

Form No. 2804

Exhibit 5
AGREEMENT TO BOND

---

101 Richmond Street West, Toronto 1, Ontario
Suite 402, (416) 864-9680

WPUR 113

A Member of
Transamerica Corporation

The Canadian Surety Company

May 7th, 1973.

AGREEMENT TO BOND NO. 0000011111

TO _____ Mayfair County Board of Education _____

_____ Carlon Cleaning Company Limited _____
is submitting a tender in writing to

_____ Mayfair County Board of Education _____

for   Janitorial Services at 10 Schools _____

THE CANADIAN SURETY COMPANY undertakes and agrees with

Mayfair County Board of Education
to furnish a Performance Bond within sixty days from the
closing date of said tender for   10 % of the tender price
but not exceeding

Thirty-Six Thousand, Four Hundred and Eighty —————————— 00/100
DOLLARS provided that within sixty days of closing date
of tender, the said tender is accepted and

_____ Carlon Cleaning Company Limited _____
shall enter into a contract for performance of the said work.

THE CANADIAN SURETY COMPANY
BY:

_____
Attorney-in-Fact.

Exhibit 6
JANITORIAL SERVICE
(tender summary in $1,000's)

| School | Square feet | Present cost | Bidder | | | | Smithers E | Carlon F |
			A	B	C	D		
1	180,550	49.8	49.2	48.2	–	46.9	39.7L	44.6
2	173,800	44.4	47.8	–	53.0	45.2	45.2	42.9L
3	169,644	44.6	46.2	48.3	51.7	52.3	39.4L	41.8
4	152,680	41.4	41.6	42.1	–	39.7	32.7L	39.4
5	180,384	46.5	49.6	51.7	55.0	46.4	36.7L	44.6
6	209,801	50.0	59.8	–	–	49.9	45.8L	51.4
7	77,015	21.2	26.2	20.8	–	21.1	20.1L	21.5
8	110,616	25.5	33.2	30.9	–	28.6	24.2L	29.0
9	130,897	–	39.3	–	–	31.7	28.6L	34.2
10	60,500	20.6	26.0	–	–	25.7	19.5	15.4L

April 24, 1973.

Exhibit 7
CLEANING COST ESTIMATE
(comparative caretaking costs for one year)

No. 2 Secondary School . . . . 173,800 sq. ft.

Cost Using Board's Own Forces

1.	1 Building supervisor (maximum).	$10,064
2.	1 Head caretaker (average).	8,768
3.	3 Assistants (average $7,676)	23,029
4.	Projected increase (7% of 1,2,3).	2,930
5.	Fringe benefits (8% of 1,2,3,4)	3,583
6.	Floater costs (2% of 1,2,3,4,5)	968
7.	11 Cleaning ladies at $2,254 each.	24,795
8.	Fringe benefits (3% of 7)	744
9.	Material costs–1¢ per sq. ft. (173,800).	1,738
10.	Administration–1¢ per sq. ft.	1,738
11.	Depreciation on equipment (20% of $1,430)	286
	Total	$78,643

June 6, 1973.

Exhibit 8
CLEANING COST ESTIMATE

No. 2 Secondary School . . . . 173,800 sq. ft.

Cost Using Contract Cleaning

1. Contract price	$42,937
2. 1 Building supervisor	10,064
3. 2 Assistant caretakers.	15,353
4. Projected increase (7% of 2 & 3)	1,779
5. Fringe benefits (8% of 2,3,4)	2,176
6. Floater costs (2% of 2,3,4,5)	587
7. 1 Cleaning lady at $2,254	2,254
8. Fringe benefits (3% of 7)	68
9. Material costs (.125¢ per sq. ft.).	217
10. Administration (1¢ per sq. ft.).	1,738
Total	$77,173

June 6, 1973.

Exhibit 9
LETTER FROM CARLON

CARLON CLEANING COMPANY, LIMITED
P.O. Box LX 70, Toronto, Ontario

July 6, 1973.

Mr. L. Godfrey,
Mayfair County Board of Education,
Mayfair, Ontario.

Dear Mr. Godfrey:

Referring to our telephone conversation last week, please take note that Carlon Cleaning Company, Ltd., wishes to withdraw its quotation of April 20, 1973, covering Janitorial Services to your Public School No. 10.

Our company quoted on the ten schools offered in your tender and was low bid in two cases, Schools Nos. 2 and 10. We would have been able to provide janitorial services had we been awarded both schools, as supervisory and other operating costs could have been split between them. The Board's decision not to award us the contract for School No. 2 leaves us little choice but to withdraw our quotation for the remaining School No. 10. Therefore, we are returning your purchase order number 93346 of June 15, 1973.

We sincerely hope that our decision will not disqualify our company from any further tender calls of your Board.

Thanking you in advance for your understanding.

Yours sincerely,
Carlon Cleaning Company, Limited,

Thomas Inglis,
Sales Manager.

Exhibit 10
REPLY TO CARLON

Mayfair County Board of Education

Mayfair, Ontario.
July 13, 1973

Mr. Thomas Inglis,
Sales Manager,
Carlon Cleaning Company, Ltd.,
P.O. Box LX 70,
Toronto, Ontario.

Dear Mr. Inglis:

Your letter of July 6, 1973, to Mr. L. Godfrey requesting withdrawal of your tender covering Janitorial Services at Public School No. 10 has been referred to me.

I would like to draw to your attention the fact that, included with your tender, was a bid bond which reads in part:

> Now, Therefore the condition of this obligation is such that if the aforesaid Principal shall have the tender accepted within sixty (60 days from the closing date of tender and the said Principal will, within the time required, enter into a formal contract and give a good and sufficient bond to secure the performance of the terms and conditions of the contract, then this obligation shall be null and void; otherwise the Principal and Surety will pay unto the Obligee the difference in money between the amount of the bid of the said Principal and the amount for which the Obligee legally contracts with another party to perform the work if the latter amount be in excess of the former.

> The Surety shall not be liable for a greater sum than the specified penalty of this Bond.

The difference between your tender and the next lowest is $4,100. If the services are not carried out by your company according to specifications, we shall have to refer the matter to your surety company for the extra cost to complete the work. This may not be in your best interest.

Please advise.

Yours truly,

F. Lewis,
Supervisor of Purchasing.

Exhibit 11
LETTER TO CARLON

Mayfair County Board of Education

Mayfair, Ontario.
September 27, 1973.

Mr. Arthur Dale,
Operations Manager,
Carlon Cleaning Co., Ltd.,
P.O. Box LX 70,
Toronto, Ontario.

Re: Contract for Cleaning Services—Public School No. 10.

Dear Mr. Dale:

This letter will put on record our experience of the service your company has provided at School No. 10 since the beginning of your contract until the present time.

I personally inspected the interior of this school prior to the commencement of your contract and found it to be in a very clean condition. Since then, a steady deterioration in the general cleanliness of the school has been noted by the Principal and the Caretaker. Notes have been left daily for your staff to see regarding specific complaints. Your Mr. Johnson was called in by the Principal on September 21, and he agreed that the condition of the interior of the building had deteriorated since your company had assumed the cleaning contract and that some changes would have to be made.

At the Principal's request, Mr. Riddell, Assistant Supervisor of Caretaking, inspected the school this morning. His report to me read as follows:

1. None of the classroom floors had been swept.
2. Desk tops had not been cleaned.
3. Washroom floors had neither been swept or washed.
4. Toilet seats had not been washed.
5. There was no indication that any "spray buffing" had been carried out on the floors the previous night.

This, Mr. Dale, is a very poor situation, and one which requires immediate attention by your company. I would expect an immediate drastic improvement in the quality of the service your company is providing and a firm assurance from yourself that this type of experience will not be repeated.

Yours very truly,

Mayfair County Board of Education.
R. Oxford, Supervisor of Caretaking.

Exhibit 12
LETTER TO CARLON

Mayfair County Board of Education
Mayfair, Ontario

October 30, 1973.

Mr. Arthur Dale,
Operations Manager,
Carlon Cleaning Co., Ltd.,
P.O. Box LX 70,
Toronto, Ontario.

Re: Contract Cleaning Services—Public School No. 10

Dear Mr. Dale:

It has again become necessary to write to you regarding the condition of Public School No. 10, where cleaning services are presently being provided by your company. The school premises were inspected once more by my Assistant Supervisor on the morning of October 26, 1973. His report follows:

1. Room 29—floor dusty, desk tops dirty, corners dirty.
2. Music Room 28—risers not swept.
3. Large Gym—floor not swept.
4. Locker Rooms—toilets not cleaned, floors not swept.
5. Industrial Arts Room—floor not swept properly, bradley basin not cleaned.
6. Rooms 21–26 inclusive—floors poorly swept, desk tops dirty, chalk ledges dirty, corners of floor dirty.
7. Rooms 12–17 inclusive—desk tops sticky, floors not properly swept.
8. Art Room—floor needs refurbishing.
9. Rooms 3–9 inclusive—floors and desk tops in poor condition (the lunch room is particularly bad).
10. Library—table tops dirty, black base dirty.
11. Office—counter top dirty, dusting could improve.
12. Staff Room—there appeared to be a white film on the floor, tables dirty.
13. Corridors—dull, there is some kind of film all over.
14. The spray buffing program is not being carried out according to specifications.
15. Washrooms—urinals had been poorly cleaned.

As you can see, Mr. Dale, there has been no improvement since my letter of September 27, 1973. I would expect you to get in touch with me as soon as possible, as I do not feel that I can authorize payment for your October invoice.

I believe we should also talk about the future of your contract, as no apparent effort is being made by your company to live up to the specifications. You will remember that we offered to cooperate with you in rescheduling your

Exhibit 12 (*Continued*)

help, receiving your assurance that this would enable you to do a satisfactory job. This has not been the case.

I will await your early reply.

Yours very truly,
Mayfair County Board of Education.
R. Oxford,
Supervisor of Caretaking.

THE CONTRACT

Mr. John Peters, president of Carlyn Corporation, returned from his July 9, 1974, visit to Blondin with a feeling of satisfaction. He had just finished negotiating what he considered a good price for the purchase of MS–7. He called Messrs. Harper, Grove, and Thomas into his office on the morning of July 10 to tell them the good news. He finished his account by instructing Mr. Bill Thomas, purchasing manager, "to carry the ball from here on in." He also said: "Bill, Blondin asked us to stay away from them for awhile because they won't start up till later on anyway and because they are all busy on a new product introduction right now. So there is no hurry on this thing, but they want you to get in touch with them in October." Mr. Thomas replied: "That suits me just as well, anyway, with holiday season coming up and everything else, I'll have things ready to roll in October for sure."

For the remainder of July and all of August the MS–7 file lay unattended, but early in September Mr. Thomas decided he had better start getting ready for his October meeting with Blondin. He knew that a formal contract should be drawn up, and on the basis of a friend's purchasing advice he felt it would be useful if Carlyn presented a contract at his first meeting with Blondin. This would mean some extra preparatory work for him now, but it could speed-up final agreement on all terms later on. He was, therefore, wondering what type of initial contract to use.

Early in 1973 Mr. Thomas had become concerned about his lack of knowledge in the design of formal purchase contracts. Through his membership in the National Association of Purchasing Management, he had become acquainted with Mr. Tom Shaw, director of purchases of Major Chemicals and generally known in the trade as a highly competent negotiator. He voiced his dissatisfaction to Mr. Shaw at a committee meeting they both attended, and Mr. Shaw invited Mr. Thomas to Philadelphia to see what Major Chemicals could do to help. In March, 1973, Mr. Thomas visited Major Chemical's purchasing department, and he was tremendously impressed. Mr. Shaw had arranged a number of appointments with various experts in contracts at Major, and Mr. Thomas spent a whole day learning from the "pros."

At the end of the day Mr. Shaw offered Mr. Thomas a sample blank contract which Major had found useful. Mr. Thomas had altered this contract slightly by substituting his own company's name on it (see Exhibit 1). He also had a few comments typed up resulting from his conversations during this Major visit (see Exhibit 2).

Although Mr. Thomas had felt much better about his contract knowledge after his visit to Major, he did not have the opportunity to use the sample contract itself in 1973 or the first part of 1974. He could see that an opportunity arose with the MS–7 deal, and he decided to try it out. As soon as he got started, however, he began to wonder what exactly to put down and what terms to insist on. He began to wonder if what applied to Major really applied to Carlyn. Yet, he was intrigued and decided he should give it a try. This meant he should decide whether price adjustments should be allowed, and, if so, what index to use. He also wondered if the meet or release and most favored nations clauses had any meaning in his case where only one buyer and one supplier existed. He saw these as some of his obvious problems, but he realized that others would crop up as he got involved more deeply.

Exhibit 1

A General Guide to Negotiations and Form of
Agreement for Contracts of Short Duration and
Periodic Price Adjustment Provision
(Special provisions for individual cases to be added)

THIS AGREEMENT made and entered in this _____ day of _____ 19____ by and between _____ (hereinafter referred to as "SELLER") and CARLYN CORPORATION, INC., CHICAGO, ILLINOIS, (hereinafter referred to as "BUYER").

WITNESSETH:

The SELLER agrees to sell and deliver and the BUYER agrees to purchase and accept the material specified herein upon the following terms and conditions:

1. MATERIAL:
(Describe material in general terms, e.g., tubular containers, sulphuric acid, caustic soda, etc.) as specifically set forth in Schedule "A" attached hereto and made a part hereof.
2. SPECIFICATIONS:
The material(s) delivered by SELLER to BUYER hereunder shall meet the specifications set forth in Schedule "A" attached hereto and made a part hereof.

Exhibit 1 *(Continued)*

3. QUANTITY:

_____ percent of BUYER'S requirements for its _____ plant(s). SELLER to supply additional _____ percent of BUYER'S requirements if so requested by BUYER. Total annual requirements estimated at _____.

4. PRICE:

In accordance with Schedule "B" attached hereto. The basic price(s) stated herein may be adjusted:

Yearly
Semiannually ⎬ by SELLER for subsequent periods
Quarterly

in accordance with market conditions providing the BUYER is notified in writing a minimum of fifteen (15) days prior to the commencement of the

Quarter
Semiannual period
Annual period

Such price(s) shall be paid for all materials ordered hereunder on or after the date they become effective, unless subsequently again revised by the SELLER as provided herein. If any proposed increase is unacceptable to BUYER and SELLER is unwilling to offer the material at a price which is acceptable to BUYER, then BUYER shall have the right either to cancel from the agreement any portion of the material to be supplied hereunder so affected by the increase or to cancel this agreement in its entirety, providing BUYER gives SELLER written notice thereof on or before the effective date of the proposed price increase.

Notwithstanding the provisions of this clause 4 it is accepted by the parties that from time to time revisions may be made to the specifications on the request of either party. Any change in the specifications or the price arising out of such revisions is to be agreed upon mutually by the parties before such changes in specifications or price become effective.

5. TERM OF PAYMENT:

_____ % _____ days from date of monthly invoice.
Net _____ days from date of monthly invoice.

6. MEET OR RELEASE:

Should BUYER be offered any of the material specified hereunder of at least equal quality or material which BUYER considers equivalent at a lower delivered cost on a 100-percent contained basis to BUYER than the effective price hereunder and/or under more favorable terms or conditions, then SELLER shall either supply such quantities of material at the lower competitive price and/or under the improved terms or conditions offered to the BUYER or permit BUYER to purchase elsewhere such quantities, and this will result in a corresponding reduction of the BUYER'S obligations under this agreement.

7. MOST FAVORED NATIONS:

Should the SELLER during the term of this contract, sell or offer to

Exhibit 1 (*Continued*)

sell any of the materials specified hereunder or materials which BUYER considers equivalent at a lower price than that in effect hereunder or under more favorable terms or conditions, the SELLER undertakes to notify the BUYER at once of the detail and timing of the sale or offer including the period for which either is effective, and the quantity involved and BUYER shall receive the benefit of such lower price or more favorable terms or conditions at BUYER'S option either for similar quantities or for the period they are effective or offered to be effective.

8.   MEASUREMENT OF QUANTITY DELIVERED:

The amount of material deemed to have been delivered shall be determined by _____.

9.   SHIPPING METHOD:

The above material shall be shipped in

SELLER'S	Tank cars
BUYER'S	Tank trucks
	Other (specify)

10.   SUSPENSION:

If at any time the material delivered hereunder is not in accordance with the specifications set forth therefor or if delivery is not in accordance with BUYER'S instructions or if SELLER refuses or is unable to supply for any reason, BUYER reserves the right to purchase elsewhere until such time as SELLER demonstrates to BUYER'S satisfaction that said conditions have been corrected. Any quantities so purchased elsewhere will reduce BUYER'S obligations hereunder.

11.   TERM OF CONTRACT:

_____ to _____

12.   FORCE MAJEURE:

No liability hereunder shall result to either party from delay in performance or nonperformance caused by circumstances beyond the control of the party affected, including, but not limited to, act of God, fire, flood, war, government regulation, direction or request, accident, labor trouble or shortage of or inability to obtain material, equipment, or transportation. Deficiencies in deliveries hereunder due to such causes shall not be made up by the SELLER except by mutual agreement in writing. During periods of force majeure BUYER is entitled to receive a share of the available production in the proportion that BUYER'S contracted deliveries bear to the total contractual deliveries of the SELLER.

13.   PATENTS:

SELLER warrants that the use or sale of the materials delivered hereunder will not infringe the claims of any AMERICAN patent.

14.   ASSIGNMENT:

This agreement is not assignable or transferable by either party without the written consent of the other party.

15.   ENTIRETY:

This agreement constitutes the entire contract of sale and purchase of the material(s) hereunder.

Exhibit 1 (*Concluded*)

Failure on the part of either party in any one or more instances to insist upon the keeping, performance, or observance of any of the terms, conditions, or provisions of this contract shall not be construed or interpreted, and shall not operate, as a relinquishment of such party's rights to require the future keeping, performance, or observance of any such terms, conditions, or performance.

16. DEFAULT AND TERMINATION:

If either SELLER or BUYER shall fail to perform any of the covenants or obligations imposed upon it by the contract then in such event the other party may at its option terminate said contract by proceeding as follows: the party not in default stating specifically the default and requesting the defaulting party to remedy such default within thirty (30) days; if within said period of thirty (30) days the party in default does remedy the said default and fully indemnify the party not in default for any and all consequences of such breach, then the contract shall continue in full force and effect. In case the party in default does not so remedy the default or does not indemnify the party giving notice for any and all consequences of such breach, within said period of thirty (30) days, then at the option of the party giving notice, the contract shall terminate. Any termination of the contract pursuant to the provisions of this paragraph shall be without prejudice to the right of the SELLER to collect any amounts then due to it for material delivered prior to the time of termination and shall be without prejudice to the right of the BUYER to receive any materials which it has not received but for which it has paid prior to the time of termination, and without waiver of any remedy to which the party not in default may be entitled for breach of the contract.

By _____
Title _____

CARLYN CORPORATION INC.
By _____
Title _____

March, 1973

Exhibit 2

Some Special Comments Concerning Contracts
by Major Chemical's Purchasing Staff

1. Never commit yourself to a major contract without legal opinion.
2. It is useful to draw up your own contract before the supplier has a chance to submit his own as a basis for discussion.
3. A contract is never a one-way street. Both parties have to live with it.
4. Usually draw up contracts for purchases one year and over in length.
5. Do not allow price adjustment on one-year contracts if you can help it, if supplier wants price adjustment only on that portion of cost subject to change. For example, if he argues his labor costs may go up and labor is 20 percent of total cost, keep him tied to this 20 percent of total cost as the only portion subject to change. Also find a reasonable

Exhibit 2 (*Continued*)

index to tie price increases to. Historical review must be carried out, and supplier may offer alternatives.

6.   Try to sign "requirements" contracts without a firm commitment to take or pay but may have to settle for as low a commitment as you can get. Sometimes it's useful to sign up for 90 percent of requirements and to leave 10 percent for competition. At the end of a contract ask for a period of time to evaluate other sources and allow for deliveries from other suppliers.

7.   Sometimes it is useful to ask the seller for a price on his uncommitted plant capacity if he has any just in case you underestimated your requirements.

8.   It may be useful in some cases to ask the supplier to carry a certain minimum amount of inventory as part of the overall agreement to assure a reasonable continuity of supply under other than force majeure situations.

9.   Sellers occasionally want forecasts more than a year ahead. Make it clear that you are willing to give these only as the best indication you have to date but that you do not consider yourself bound in any way by them. Forecasts of this kind can be made in quarters for the following year and in annual amounts for succeeding years.

10. A contract is exactly what you make it. As long as you deal with a reputable supplier you may never have to pull it out. You can request his cost figures if this is what you agreed to, and on "requirements" contracts the seller can come and see that you are using the proper percentage of material. There must be mutual trust on each side.

15 PROCUREMENT RESEARCH, PLANNING, BUDGETS, AND OBJECTIVES

Introduction

The huge sums of money spent annually for all kinds of research by government, industry, and educational institutions, since the beginning of World War II, have resulted in an explosion of knowledge and technology that has accelerated rates of change in all aspects of life. Business organizations have become larger and more complex, resulting in a demand for ever-increasing degrees of sophistication and advanced training for business managers.

Scientific research has produced new metals, new textiles, new plastics, new sources of energy, and new understanding of our universe. Research in mathematics and quantitative methods has developed new concepts and tools for the analysis of business problems. Research in the behavioral sciences has opened new areas of understanding why people behave the way they do. New concepts have been developed to aid in organizing and supervising human activity to encourage greater achievement.

In a rapidly changing environment, experience has taught us that change can be best managed if we plan for change. Most human achievement results from some kind of a plan. The plan may be in a man's head and be very informal, or it may be carefully developed step by step and formalized in writing and charts. Research and planning proceed hand in hand. Most research is preceded by careful planning, and the results obtained from research are best utilized by developing an appropriate plan.

Procurement research

There has been a steady growth in the number of companies which have added research staffs to their procurement departments since the early 1950s. A research study published in 1963 reported that approximately one third of the 304 companies participating in the study had purchasing research staffs.[1]

The purpose of the purchasing research staff is to investigate systematically all purchasing and associated techniques which have a capability of improving procurement performance. Obviously this is an objective which has the possibility to be helpful to all companies regardless of size. Because of cost considerations, purchasing research staffs are seldom found in small companies. However, many small company purchasing departments have been organized to do value analysis studies and thus are performing a type of research. Experience in companies which have made use of purchasing research indicates that it is difficult for an employee with line purchasing duties also to be responsible for research projects unless work loads are so arranged that there is adequate time planned for research activities.

Worthwhile research requires competent employees, access to information, and the necessary time to search out information and to make appropriate analysis. While most communities in which companies are located have library facilities, it is desirable for a procurement department to acquire a library of reference material specifically concerned with the purchasing function. The relatively small investment required for a library will be justified by the convenience and time saving inherent in having reference and source material close at hand. An adequate purchasing library usually includes current trade journals concerned with the purchasing function and the industries which the company operates in or has close association with; directories of all types that refer to sources of supply and industry associations; suppliers' catalogs and other publications providing technical and commercial information about materials and products; all types of economic information concerning general business conditions as well as conditions in the suppliers' industries; textbooks concerned with procurement, materials management, general management; and handbooks for accounting, production, marketing and purchasing. The National Association of Purchasing Management maintains a reference library supervised by a competent librarian at its New York headquarters.

The types of research projects which are most frequently undertaken are:

1. Value analysis studies.
2. Purchasing procedures and systems studies.
    a. Forms design.
    b. Use of data processing systems.

---

[1] Harold E. Fearon, and John H. Hoagland, *Purchasing Research in American Industry*, Research Study 58 (New York: American Management Association, 1963).

      c.   Improved contracting procedures to reduce inventory investments, reduce paper work, reduce prices, and obtain supplier cooperation.

      d.   Developing and updating a purchasing manual.

      e.   Study of negotiating strategies.

3.   Vendor and source development studies:

      a.   Methods for evaluating vendor performance.

      b.   Vendor attitude surveys.

      c.   Analysis of vendor marketing strategies.

      d.   Study of production innovations in vendor industries.

      e.   Location of new sources of supply, both domestic and foreign.

4.   Commodity and product studies:

      a.   Short- and long-term studies of supply and demand factors for commodities purchased.

      b.   Pricing studies and forecasts.

      c.   Make or buy studies (see Chapter 12)

      d.   Buy or lease (see Chapter 11)

      e.   Development of purchase price index.

      f.   Logistics studies to determine efficient methods of transportation, effect of packaging alternatives and the like.

      g.   Life cycle costing studies.

5.   Special projects:

      a.   Establishing overall procurement department objectives.

      b.   Developing long- and short-term procurement plans.

      c.   Assisting new product development.

      d.   Standardization studies.

The above listing of subjects which may help to improve the performance of the procurement function is not all inclusive, but it provides some indication of the breadth of the challenge which exists.

Value analysis will be described in further detail next because of its importance in procurement and its unique purchasing origin.

Value analysis, value engineering

L. A. Miles, the "Father of Value Analysis," developed the initial set of techniques which founded this new concept of purchasing research. It was H. Erlicher, vice president of purchasing for G.E. who provided the impetus towards V. A. Erlicher noticed during World War II that many material substitutions not only lowered product cost but also improved product quality. He observed: "This happened so often by accident we decided to try to make it happen on purpose." He gave Miles the task of finding ways to accomplish this.

L. D. Miles coined the phrase *Value Analysis* for the set of tools and their order of application. Many others have built on his contribution to create the most powerful concept available to achieve value. To Miles value analysis and value engineering were synonymous terms. Some people make the distinction that value engineering applies to products and services while they are still in the design stage, whereas value analysis is applied for products and services which have existed for some time.

According to Miles : "Value Analysis/Value Engineering is a functionally oriented scientific method for improving product value by relating the elements of product worth to their corresponding elements of product cost in order to accomplish the required function at least cost in resources."[2]

The following excerpts from an excellent article[3] on a special value project at a Westinghouse subsidiary describes a number of issues related to V.A. The authors acknowledge with special thanks the assistance of Mr. Jack Prendergast, president of Value Programs for Industry, Inc., much of whose material is also reproduced here.

Value analysis does not mean merely cost improvement. To appreciate this, take the example where, in the design of the high and low voltage windings of a transformer, a choice of insulating material must be made. Here, the fundamental requirement is that the insulation must have sufficient dielectric strength to handle the potential difference.

Now the choice could be between a low cost material of given thickness or a high cost material of less thickness. The important thing to note is that the high cost material should not be ruled out without careful consideration. It could be that the reduced HV winding resulting from its use may reduce the overall cost of the complete design. This would be cost improvement. However, it is also possible that its use may vastly improve overall performance at little additional cost (i.e., improve value). And this might be the paying proposition.

Perhaps the best way to bring out the difference between cost improvement and value improvement is to look at the Value Ratio.

Mathematical value

Value Ratio is defined as:

$$VR = \sum \frac{\text{use} + \text{esteem}}{\text{cost}} \gtrless 1$$

for the producer

and

$$VR = \sum \frac{\text{use} + \text{esteem}}{\text{price}} \gtrless 1$$

for the customer

---

[2] L. D. Miles, *Technique of Value Analysis and Engineering* (New York: McGraw-Hill, 1961).

[3] R. A. Simon, "The Time Shrinkers," Product Design and Value Engineering, Southam Business Publication, February 1967.

where:

>   use = the power of a thing to serve an end
>   esteem = the power of a thing that makes us desire its possession

When we talk about Cost Improvement we are talking about manipulating to our advantage the denominator of the VR. Thus, if we can decrease cost we're pushing the VR further in excess of 1, which means the Value of the product (or service) is greater.

But there are two more variables which could be (in fact, should be) tackled—use and esteem—which will achieve the same aim.

Optimum design results from simultaneous manipulation of the three variables to provide lowest cost and apt use and esteem.

Which is what Value Analysis is all about.

But does VE work?

Value engineering or value analysis is not just a new gimmick. As the following figures indicate, it has proved its worth many times over.

The American Ordinance Association made an independent study of 125 VA/VE projects, and came up with the staggering conclusion that in *addition* to a reduction in cost as a result of the projects, the following benefits accrued:

76% Reduced lead time
39% Weight reduction
90% Improvement in productibility
21% Improvement in performance
38% Improvement in quality
46% Improvement in reliability
40% Improvement in maintainability

But there is a catch, as with all good things, to VA. It requires a much more disciplined approach and conscientious effort than with conventional methods. It can only work with inputs from everywhere—from sales, marketing, manufacturing, engineering and procurement, in fact anyone who is likely to effect any influence on the finished product. And it is important that all these people make their decisions in parallel. Because we are concerned with the cost for the given overall function, we have to make sure that any decision to make a change within the system (say by engineers) doesn't produce a change in another field which results in an overall deleterious effect on the VR.

Collapsing time

Married with VA, as previously mentioned, is Time Compression. This is simply making everything happen at once, and is a particularly important part of VISTA 67.[4]

---

[4] *VISTA 67*, page 66. Two task force major products.

Although it sounds like wishful thinking to say, "Let's make four–five weeks become four–five days," TOP 66 has demonstrated that such a thing is possible. One of the outputs of that program actually resulted in the building of a transformer core for a small power transformer in four days when normal cycle time is four weeks!

It is made possible by generating what could be called "total environment." That is:

a.   Subjecting the participants to no extraneous distractions.
b.   Having everything on hand when it is needed.
c.   Having the participants go through the same paces at the same time so there can't be duplication of effort or time wasted while each discipline catches up on background before taking over from the previous discipline.
d.   Giving participants the authority to call in expert assistance from inside or outside the organization as it is needed.

And this means Task Force.

Task force

The Task Force concept is probably most familiar in military context where it is used for building an effective fighting force. But a more general description is supplied by A. F. Kee, Value Programs Manager of Value Programs for Industry, Inc. On the suppliers' day of VISTA 67, Kee said, "The value task force is a catalyst in the activity of removing unnecessary costs from a product or system. A task force is created from a group of three to fifty people, who are gathered together for a specific purpose, provided specific objectives—profit targets, cost targets—given a target date to create needed urgency, and disbanded when objectives are met."

An important aspect of the Value Task Force is that it is just not any old group which is selected to do the job. Because people are a necessary part of the system, they too must be value engineered into the scheme. They have a definable function which is intimately related to a component function of the project, and only slightly less related to every other component function. In this way, each person becomes complementary within his team, and each team becomes complementary within the whole task force.

"But isn't that really a committee?" is a question which could be asked at this stage.

The answer must be no, despite the similarities of: (a) both being transitory expedients for solving a problem, and (b) both being disbanded when the problem is solved to satisfaction.

There are two significant differences, however.

Firstly, the group is completely work oriented. This means:

a.   Full-time assignment for the personnel—there can be no interference from normal duties.
b.   Full attention and concentration to the limit of the environment created is desired, and a positive contribution from every member of the team is expected.

Design improvements in a stator core such as this are expected as a result of the VISTA program.

c. Each person on the team is there because he has essential know-how—he is not, like many committees, there because the project happens to interest him, or affect him, or because of political expedient.

Secondly, the task force has very real authority and responsibility. This means:

a. It has a well-defined mission, a leader and a projected termination date.
b. It has the authority to implement its decisions without interference from outside the task force.
c. It bears full responsibility—because there is no authority outside the team, there is no-one to "pass the buck" to; a conclusion must be reached and positive action taken—thus there can be no hedging about its effectiveness; it either succeeds or fails.
d. It is not primarily an education device
e. It is not merely a sales gimmick.

Structure of task force

The structure of the Task Force is determined by the structure of the object of consideration, with particular emphasis on function rather than hardware. Thus, within the Task Force there are a number of teams, each oriented to a specific major function which is contributory to the overall function. Within each team there are a number of specialists, each handling specific aspects which contribute to an understanding and will lead to a conclusion concerning the team's function.

The first step, then, in creating a Task Force is to break down the object under consideration into its major functional areas. That is, in the case of the vertical water wheel, to understand the structure of the Task Force we must understand the structure of the water wheel itself.

Ideally, of course, we should not allow ourselves to start off by saying too much about hardware. The object of the exercise is to make a profit by selling a function. That the function is manifested in the form of hardware is incidental.

Westinghouse, however, because they recognize that the vertical water wheel generator is still a salable commodity, at least for the time, have accepted it as the means of achieving the basic function of "converting mechanical to electrical energy" as a starting point.

What is a vertical water wheel generator then?

It is primarily a rotating dynamo-electric machine which generates voltage and causes current to flow in armature conductors in a magnetic field. This means we can:

a. Rotate armature conductors in a stationary magnetic field so that the conductors will cut magnetic flux lines, or

b. Rotate a magnetic field so that magnetic flux lines cut stationary armature conductors.

Westinghouse have, from experience, accepted the further limitation that for the large powers and high voltages under consideration, the second method is better.

Examination of Figure 15–1 reveals the essential structure of the vertical water wheel system. In fact, the VISTA 67 program is essentially concerned only with the generating function. But to understand the function breakdown of the generator implies an overall understanding of the whole system.

The arrangement is basically very simple. The rotating water turbine blades, drive via a vertical shaft, the rotor assembly consisting of a rotor rim supported on the spider (which is virtually the spokes of the wheel). The rim carries individual electro-magnets on magnetic steel poles. The electro-magnets supply the magnetic fields for the generating function.

The armature—in which the rotor rotates—has armature coils embedded in the magnetic steel stator core. The stator core is clamped around the outside and secured to the powerhouse by the stator frame.

The rotating assembly is supported by a huge thrust bearing and located radially with a guide bearing, the whole bearing structure located and secured to the powerhouse by the lower bracket as shown in Figure 15–1.

Other parts include the enclosure with upper bracket supporting the deck plates, and the air-to-cooling-fluid heat exchangers around the outside of the frame.

Figure 15–1
SECTION VIEW OF ONE CONFIGURATION OF WATER
WHEEL AND GENERATOR

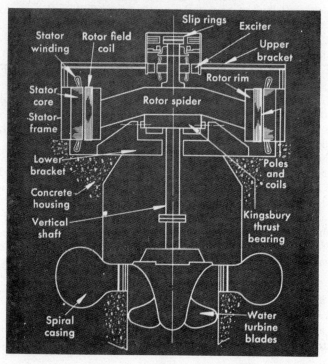

For field excitation of the electro-magnets of the main generator, either the dc can be fed through slip rings from an exciter at the top of the vertical shaft (as shown here), or a separate static exciter can be used.

Constructing the teams

With this understanding, the next step is to carry out what is called the Mathetics Design, or Function Tree. As was said before, the teams are constructed strictly in parallel with the function they represent, and this is the purpose of the mathetics design. Formally designated as "identifying materials," "extrapolating functional areas" and "designating required skills," the function tree starts with the overall basic function, "to convert rotational mechanical energy into electrical energy" at the tree trunk and then branches out into various components, their functional area, basic function, and sub-functions. On the basis of this (Figure 15–2) the type of skills needed to handle all aspects of a particular function area are immediately apparent. Thus a team profile can be drawn up, and the best people available to represent the desired disciplines can be chosen.

With plenty of room and facilities, members of the VISTA 67 task force find a good working environment in Westing-house's conference center at Hamilton.

Figure 15–2

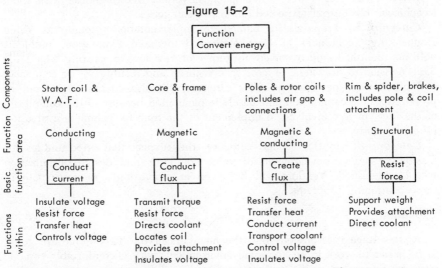

The function tree establishes functions and sub-functions of components contributing to the prime function.

Figure 15–3

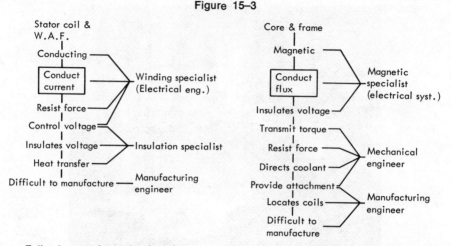

Following on from the function tree, this process of derivation of skills allows function structure to select team structure.

The method is apparent from Figure 15–3. The important thing to notice with the technique is that the function *dictates* the structure of the teams within the Task Force, and to some extent even the individuals within the teams.

Aims

Given their Task Force, what specifically does Westinghouse wish them to achieve? The outputs expected fall in two categories:

Category A. Proposals for immediate implementation through the Value Engineering Techniques of Cost Analysis/Functional Evaluation; problems will be identified and resolved in terms of revision to existing Standards data, revision to drawings, process specifications and manufacturing sequences and purchasing specifications. This category will also contain an output of proposals which cannot be immediately implemented because of the complexity of the idea, money involved to implement or the time for complete evaluation by model study, etc.

Category B. In this second category, they expect that opportunities for feasibility studies, development of value standards and design optimization will be identified. Vendors will be given an opportunity to participate in these continuing programs.

Education

At this stage it is obvious that the members of the Task Force are going to be asked to work in an abnormal environment, with uncomfortable copious resources, unaccustomed authority and responsibility, and completely alien techniques. Education and guidance are therefore two very essential aspects of a program such as VISTA 67.

This is where Value Programs for Industry, Inc., comes in.

Very successful as Value Program consultants in the States, this firm is headed by energetic, enthusiastic, down-to-earth Roy E. Fountain. With his vice president Jack Prendergast, he has taken the concept of Value Analysis and spun it into a workable technique complete with standard forms, lecture programs and unobtrusive overseeing.

Called in for the job of running VISTA, he and colleague Jim Parker (who presently is Task Force manager) spent three months preparing the necessary groundwork. Although the VA methods are fundamental, obviously there is a need to tailor the program to suit the size of the task, and the personalities, and talents involved. Schedules had to be made, lectures planned and a massive volume, the VISTA 67 handbook, prepared which would include the lecture material, examples, standard forms, and a vast amount of background data.

Then they went to work. Preliminary education of personnel varied in depth and duration, from 100 hours for the value engineers to 5 hours for managers (including district representatives). For members of the task force, lectures continued through the program, each subject injected into the procedure when it did most good, that is when it was needed to complete the next step in the chain of preferred activity.

The program length was decided on. It was to go a projected twelve weeks, at which time the force should have developed the ideas, generated

Figure 15–4

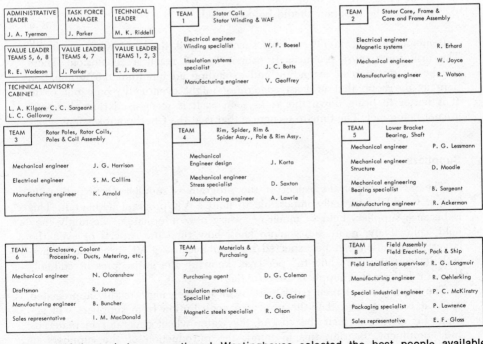

By use of the techniques mentioned, Westinghouse selected the best people available in the above configuration for their task force.

proposals, and completed drawings and designs to the stage of implementability. The program started on November 7, 1966, and will continue through February 11, 1967.

To give some idea of the detailed thought which went into the planning of VISTA 67, a précis of the schedule is given in Table 15–1.

Checkpoints

One thing that can immediately be seen from the general format of this schedule is the way the lecture material has been woven into the fabric of the work plan to achieve the best possible output. Subjects are introduced at a carefully considered stage of developments, i.e., when the techniques are needed for application to the problem in hand; which means, at the point of greatest need; which means, at the point of most intense interest.

This of course is an extension of the VE-TF-TC (Value Engineering—Task Force—Time Compression) concept of having all possible requirements on hand at the time they are wanted.

The schedule in Table 15–1 points up two very important aspects of a program such as VISTA 67. The first is the Checkpoints which crop up at carefully planned points in the timetable. Basically the Checkpoint is an assessment of three things:

a.   Whether steps to date have been satisfactorily completed.
b.   What stages are yet to be done.
c.   Whether the program should be continued.

Remembering that a TF can only succeed or fail, the last is very important. The task force *must* produce. It cannot fail to reach a conclusion. There can be no question of extending and extending ad infinitum the termination date in the hope that at least *something* might eventually come out of it. It is better to bring down the ax as soon as it is recognized that objectives are not being met. The time to recognize that is at the Checkpoint sessions.

Suppliers

The second important aspect of the program is supplier participation. In fact, it would be virtually impossible to hold a VE program without it. This is because suppliers hold so much necessary new information. Certainly they hold, collectively, many times more know-how than the experts of even the largest corporation can be expected to. And because a VE program implies, with its emphasis on "how-to" per cost, knowing the entire present state-of-the-art it follows that suppliers are essential.

The importance of their participation can be even more readily appreciated when it is recognized that the projected contribution from suppliers will account for about one half the cost of the water wheel generator in materials and equipment. Bearing this in mind, the introduction of the suppliers to the VISTA 67 program was handled with care.

On September 15, 1966, a Specialty Suppliers' Day was held at Canadian Westinghouse in Hamilton. Its purpose was to tell suppliers what the objects of VISTA 67 are and how they can be achieved, and in particular what role the suppliers were to play.

It was a full day, from 8:15 A.M. to 4:30 P.M., during which time all the important points had to be imparted to these important people. Being potential participants in the VE program immediately made it imperative that they be initiated into the VE methodology. To work with the teams in the future, they had to be re-oriented to think, along with the task force members, in terms of "function" and "value."

Thus, of necessity, the day imposed a lot of educational material on the supplier representatives. After the introductory addresses, lectures were given on value, value leadership planning, analytical and creative value techniques, and the role of the supplier in a value task force. It laid out in some detail the concept, mission, schedule, and mechanics of VISTA 67. It gave targets and stated the ways these could be achieved.

In particular, the demands of the task force on the suppliers was explicitly stated. Needed were:

a. New developments both in hand and envisaged—to be presented in display form for the members of the TF to pick over and with expert explanation from the suppliers on hand.
b. The prices of these developments.
c. Quotations with speed.
d. Provision of their best technical services available.
e. Prototypes for feasibility tests.

Advantages to suppliers

These may sound like fairly solid demands in light of the fact that there can, by the very nature of the program, be no guarantee that all this work will result in any business, and that in any case there can be no talk of hardware changing hands until well after the end of the Task Force schedule.

But there are advantages that more than offset any feeling of being "used" that the suppliers could have. Not the least telling argument for supplier participation was put forward by Jack Hishon, Purchasing Agent for Canadian Westinghouse.

"The task force approach," he said, "can work well for you since it brings out the new design more rapidly and tends to result in earlier returns on your sales efforts. It slices through the communications barrier that unfortunately sometimes appears to exist between you and the design people. It slashes through much of the red tape of the market place and puts you face to face with the decision-makers. It provides a unique opportunity to sell in an environment specifically created to assist you to the utmost."

If the suppliers view the whole deal as a panacea to their selling problem, an opportunity to pour their products willy-nilly into a massive project and with little effort make much profit, then they will be disappointed.

Table 15–1
VALUE LEADERSHIP TASK FORCE—THE SCHEDULE FOR VISTA 67

Week	Activity	Comments
1	Lectures: Value Task Force goals and mechanics Cost problems, analysis, and targeting Habits and attitudes VISTA project work: Problem identification Application of cost analysis techniques Graph plotting Cost targeting	After each daily session, homework "Human" oriented lectures intimately concerned with breaking down communications barriers and establishing desired behavior, run throughout the program
2	Lectures: Function evaluation techniques Human relations Cost targeting and value control How to combine cost analysis and function evaluation techniques VISTA project work: Function identification and evaluation Evaluation of function areas	Problem set to demonstrate technique of developing a standard of value for a function (see later)
3	Lectures: The creative approach Collective genius Blast, create, and refine Developing ideas Make or buy? Economic challenge VISTA project work: Group brainstorming Blast, create, and refine Developing ideas	An important question in Value Analysis
4	Lectures: Don't be a hermit Preparing Task Force proposals VISTA project work: Specialty suppliers consulting and display Project work continued Checkpoint 1	That is, exploit everything the specialty supplier has to offer Invaluable inputs in the form of new products, techniques, and ideas Also a very important phase, interjected throughout the program
5	Lectures: Overcoming roadblocks VISTA project work: Anticipating and planning to overcome roadblocks More supplier consulting and display More project work	

Table 15–1 (*Continued*)

Week	Activity	Comments
6	Lectures: Put a $ sign on the main ideas Tools quantities and set-ups VISTA project work: More project work More from suppliers	
7	Lectures: Specifics not generalities VISTA project work: Suppliers Project work Checkpoint 2	A further estimate of team success
8	Lectures: Introduction to new way of thinking VISTA project work	A look back at Top 66–lesson from the past By this stage project work dominates time
9	Lectures: Procedure to be followed for the week How to sell ideas VISTA project work: Project work Group brainstorming Idea development	The emphasis here is on recycling analysis and evaluation Recycling cost analysis and function evaluation on proposed designs
10	Lectures: Learning and behavior Operant conditioning and behavior reinforcement VISTA project work: Checkpoint 3	Film Aids to getting your ideas implemented The final success assessment
11	Project work continued	
12	Lectures: Goals we have attained through the Task Force and what we hope to accomplish in the future Team reports Task Force summary What next after the Task Force? Value leadership and profit improvement Display period and discussion	All these take place on the last day–a wrap-up Including proposals, date of implementation, follow-on organization, and cost targets versus identified achievement Organizing for value leadership Future plans

If they view it as a straight forward, convenient sales opportunity, and recognize the benefits it offers, of being efficient and merit-orientated, then they will get the most out of it. By normal sales methods, they could never hope to get so many of their products in front of so many key people, who are not only ready to listen, but *need* to listen, who are not only prepared to act but have the *authority* to act. All this, and the knowledge that implementation is not a nebulous possibility but a planned necessity makes for a hard-to-beat sales climate.

And more advantages

Of course there is the additional plus to the suppliers of having their representatives learn the basics of VE and TF, and the opportunity to work, almost as closely at the members of the Task Force, in such a program. If they accept the VE/TF/TC concept as being the coming thing, then they must realize the value of participating.

And, if nothing else, they will get a free, objective, value-orientel apprasial of their wares and technical services. They will learn what VE-oriented companies arc coming to expect from them and make the most out of future programs. Perhaps it may even stimulate some suppliers to begin VISTA type programs of their own.

Finally, again from the suppliers' viewpoint, there are two outputs of VISTA 67 of particular value. These come in the form of two documents generated by the task force which will be of lasting importance to both members and suppliers alike. They are:

The function catalog—which lists various functions required and tabulates value standards for achieving those functions.

"Where used" file—tabulating all places where a specific element is used.

In this way, if the supplier can define the function of his product, Westinghouse can supply a comprehensive list of applications for that function.

The tools

An essential feature of successful task force and a prerequisite for time collapsing is the instant availability of everything which could conceivably be called for during the proceedings. Thus, the working area, in the conference room of the Hamilton company, is fitted out with wall charts, photographs, a colored cutaway of a pre-VISTA water wheel generator, telephones and lecturn. The teams are well spread out with plenty of room to lay out data sheets and drawings, which incidentally can be drawn up on the spot by the drafting members of the force.

Not the least of their valuable tools consists of a section in the rear of the VISTA 67 handbook referred to as "Resources." This wad of seemingly more-than-essential facts and figures points out the wealth of detail which is needed to make such a program tick over effectively.

The first section of this is devoted to "Comparative Cost Information"—a compilation from experience, price lists, ad information catalogs and literature. The contents of this section alone runs something like this:

1. Cost/lb criteria (these are listed alphabetically by process and material).
2. Metals (listed alphabetically—giving cost/lb, cost/in³ and density).
3. Metals (listed in order of cost/lb—giving cost/lb and cost/in³).
4. Materials (nonmetallic—listed alphabetically and giving cost/lb, cost/in³, and density).
5. Product prices (listed alphabetically—giving cost/lb and the value of other important parameters where applicable; this is a listing of cost per unit dimension of finished product, which is so comprehensive it includes things like missiles and shavers).
6. Reference data.

   a. Formulae—(all the standard equations and more for areas, volumes, c of g's, etc.).
   b. Conversion factors for weights and measures.
   c. Properties of materials (giving an alphabetic listing of materials—from acetal to zirconium).

The second, third, and fourth sections of the compilation are no less valuable. The List of Technical Specialists for example is a necessary part of the philosophy of Task Force. If talent is required beyond the scope of the group, a quick scan of this section will yield who are the experts in that specialty (whatever it might be) and where they can be reached NOW.

Following that is a checklist of speciality materials and products and processes to alleviate the possibility of missing out on a possible solution because of thinking like, "I've never heard of a material (or process) which could handle *that* way-out idea of mine, so I'll skip it."

Finally there is a section of Cost Reduction Ideas, little prodding reminders of methods, old and new, of the industry. To manufacture a part for example it says you can:

Fabricate it	Permanent mold it
Diecast it	Roll and weld it
Extrude it	Roll form it

And it suggests checking on the lesser known methods such as: lost wax casting, electroforming, powder metallurgy.

Value job plan

An essential part of TF applied to VA is that the approach be organized. With Value Programs for Industry, Inc., this means following their Value Job Plan, which consists of these phases:

1. Information phase
2. Speculative phase
3. Analytical phase
4. Program planning phase
5. Program execution phase
6. Summary and conclusion phase

And the schedule for achieving this organized approach is something like in Figure 15–5.

To aid members of the TF in keeping to the schedule, and to follow the technical procedures through to their logical conclusion without missing

Figure 15–5
VALUE PROGRAMS FOR INDUSTRY'S VALUE JOB PLAN
AND TASK FORCE SCHEDULE

The Value Job Plan

1. Information phase	4. Program planning phase
2. Speculative phase	5. Program executive phase
3. Analytical phase	6. Summary & conclusion phase

Task force schedule

1st week	2nd	3d	4th	5th	6th	7th	8th	9th	10th

Information phase — What is it? What does it cost? What does it do? — Cost analysis / Function evaluation — Get all the facts / Information – / Best source

Speculative phase — What else will do the job? — Creative approach / Blast and refine / Develop ideas — Don't be a hermit / Use specialty materials / Products & processes / Use standard or specials

Analytical phase — What will that cost? — Work on specifics – not generalities / Overcome roadblocks

Planning phase — $ Sign on ideas

Execution phase — Use your judgment / Spend money as your own / Human relations / How to sell ideas

Summary & Conclusion

a step, Value Programs for Industry, Inc., has generated the chart shown in Figure 15–6. The Value Problem Solving Process chart is always with them. It is in their project folders, and a copy of it is displayed prominently in the conference room where they work.

It can be appreciated how important the first phase in the Value Job Plan will be to the success of the mission. The information phase sets the tone of the subsequent work. Depending on the thoroughness of approach, it will provide either a mind-cramping back-drop or an unfettered backdrop which will reflect the tenor of the future phases; it will define, either crisply or flaccidly, the problems to be concentrated on.

The techniques applied in this phase, then, must be comprehensive in their span and disciplined in their application. Cost Analysis and Function Evaluation are two very fundamental techniques employed.

Figure 15–6
THE CORRECT VALUE PROBLEM SOLVING PROCESS

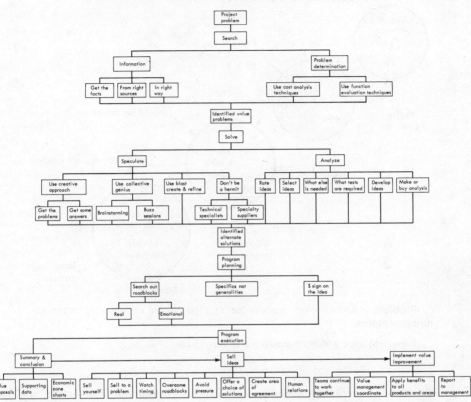

Copyright 1966 Value Programs for Industry, Inc.

CA and FE

To locate *high* costs is the purpose of Cost Analysis, and is achieved by looking at the problem from seven separate angles:

1. Analyze costs.
2. Analyze cost elements.
3. Analyze cost increments.
4. Analyze cost per year.
5. Analyze cost per pound.
6. Analyze cost per dimension.
7. Analyze cost per property.

These are achieved, quickly and efficiently, by completing a standard copyrighted cost analysis form from Value Programs for Industry, Inc. A worked example done for a control assembly is presented in Figure 15–8. The ringed figures in this chart identify high cost areas which must receive particular attention.

Figure 15–7

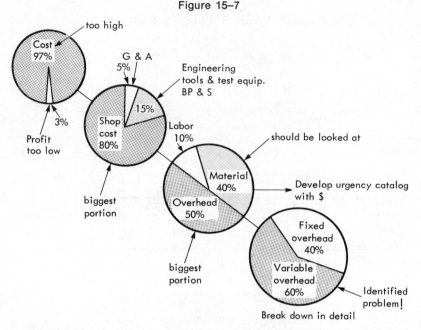

**Problem indentification process as applied to an engineering manufac-
turing problem.**

To locate *unnecessary* costs is the purpose of Function Evaluation, and
is achieved by looking at the problem from five separate angles:

1.   Evaluate by comparison.
2.   Evaluate function.
3.   Evaluate functional areas.
4.   Evaluate the basic function.
5.   Evaluate functions scientifically.

An example of the standard forms used for this procedure is given in
Figure 15–9. The virtue of employing this type of technique has already
been demonstrated in the function tree, where such an evaluation enabled
the function definitions to choose the skills required.

Cost targeting and value control are two further areas of consideration
in the information phase. Logical steps suggested for attaining these criteria
could be:

Cost targeting:
   Establish price.
   Establish profit.

Figure 15–8

EXAMPLE 1

Name JOHN SMITH   Team No 12   Sheet 1 of 1

SUPPORTS PROPOSAL: No. (S)

TECHNIQUES of COST ANALYSIS	1 COST		QUANTITY		4 COST	5 COST	6 COST 7
	UNIT		LOT SIZE		YEAR	=	DIM PROP
	$178.31	EACH × 1000 ANNUAL USAGE = √178,310					

DESCRIPTION CONTROL ASSEMBLY	2 MATERIAL	(110.31) 62% Tot.	% Av.	WEIGHT	DIM PROP
DRAWING # K7947590	LABOR	$16.38 9% Tot.	% Av.	136#	
	OVERHEAD	$51.62 29% Tot.	% Av.	(√.31) = $

ITEM	OPERATION	$	$	$	$	$		
BRACKET		(40.00)	1.91	9.10		51.01	(51,010)	7 (7.30)	30IN³ 1.70
CONTROL		(27.00)				27.00	(27,000)	12 (2.34)	270½ .10
BASE		(15.42)	.25	.61		16.28	(16,280)	20 .81	80IN² .21
ENDS (2)		4.92	.34	.82		6.08	6,080	20 .31	40IN² .15
SIDES (2)		6.72	.15	.36		7.23	7,230	26 .24	60IN² .12
GUSSETS (4)		2.94	.13	.31		3.38	3,380	10 .34	20IN² .16
COVER		4.26	.28	.64		5.18	5,180	20 .26	80IN² .07
SEAL STRIP (2)		.82				.82	820	4 .21	8FT .10
SEAL (2)		5.79				5.79	5,790	8 .75	
BOLTS (16)		.64				.64	640	4 .16	
WASHERS (16)		.32				.32	320	2 .16	
NUTS (16)		.48				.48	480	3 .16	
ASSEMBLE			4.20	(12.40)	16.60		(16,600)		
ASSEMBLED UNIT						14681	146,810	136 1.04	
MASK, PAINT		1.00	1.00	3.00	5.00		5,000		
PAINTED UNIT						14581	145,810	136 1.07	
TEST			8.12	(24.38)	32.50		(32,500)		
COMPLETED UNIT		110.31	16.38	51.62		178.31	178,310	136 1.31	

A worked example of applying Value Programs for Industry's cost analysis sheets to identify high cost areas, which are circled.

Establish cost target for item using:

a. Comparative cost.

b. Component using percentage.

c. Component using judgment.

d. Component using cost analysis.

Figure 15-9

Copyright 1965. Voice Programs for Industry, Inc.

Name_____   Table No._____ Date_____ Seminar

TECHNIQUE 2 – EVALUATE FUNCTION

(1) WHAT IS THE ITEM?_____				
(2) WHAT DOES IT DO?		(3) WHAT ELSE WILL DO THE JOB?	(4) WHAT WILL THIS COST	(5) WHAT DOES IT PRESENTLY COST?
VERB	NOUN			

A work sheet of Value Programs for Industry Inc., used by the VISTA task force to evaluate function.

Value Control:
Establish value standard for item:

 a. Product function value standard—based on commercial products that will perform function.
 b. Artful value standard for large assemblies or systems.
 c. Artful value standard for assemblies or small devices.
 d. Artful standard for parts.
 e. Basic function value standard based on material, based on material and shape, based on a combination of several materials and/or shapes.

Again standard forms are used extensively to help obtain the cost target. Further, by plotting price trend and cost trend of an item, over the years, and extrapolating, one can come to a conclusion about profit margins and the order of cost target one should aim for to stay in the game.

Standard of value

The process of establishing a standard of value is an interesting exercise. A sample problem is that of a weight to be supported by a tensile supporting member. The data, preliminary calculations, and problem statement are given below. As indicated, this procedure enables you to find, for a particular application, the material which offers the best value (i.e., in this case, the lowest ρ^p/S_t ratio) and therefore to establish a plot of the cost per relevant parameter versus basic function parameter.

Given:

(1) $$W = SA$$

where

W = Weight to be supported (in tension) in pounds. (Neglect weight of supporting member)
S_t = Allowable tensile strength in psi.
A = Area of supporting member in square ins.

(2) $$C = Al\rho P$$

where

C = Cost in cents
l = Length of supporting member in feet
ρ = Density of weight-supporting member. (For steel, 0.283 lb/in.[3])
P = Price in cents/pound of weight-supporting material

Solving equations (1) for Area:

(3) $$A = \frac{W}{S_t}$$

Substituting equation (3) into (2):

(4) $$C = \frac{W}{S_t} l\rho P$$

Dividing by length:

(5) $$\frac{C}{l} = \frac{W}{S_t} \rho P$$

The variables with respect to material are:

$$\frac{\rho P}{S_t}$$

Search for the material with the lowest ratio of:

$$\frac{\rho P}{S_t}$$

(This has been done for you—see Figure 15–10.)

Problem:
Calculate weight (W) that can be supported and cost/unit length (C/l) for diameters of ½, 1, 1½ and 2 inches. Read values for tensile strength and price from Figure 15–10. (Check that the equations are dimensionally correct.) Plot cost/unit length versus weight on log-log paper.

Figure 15–10

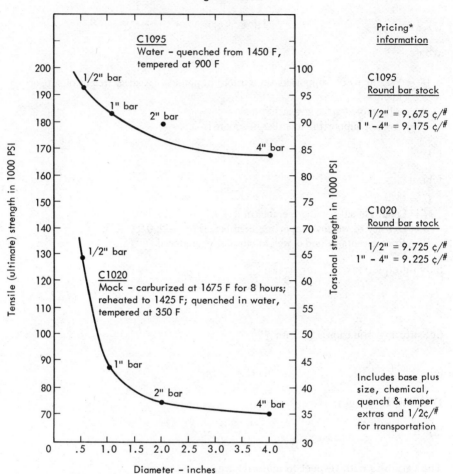

Data sheet from "Modern Steels and Their Properties," Bethlehem Steel, 6th Edition 1961, for use with the value standard problem given in the text.

Notice in the cost analysis the step of establishing cost elements. For this a breakdown of costs through its natural levels to the selling price can be indicative. Further illumination is then provided by the problem identification process proper as shown in Figure 15–7. Using such a procedure, the problem areas stand out a mile, and the steps to be taken become well defined.

In the speculative phase the method of developing an idea is important to the members of the Task Force. Value Programs for Industry reckon the process should run something like this:

Given the idea, the question, "Will it work?" should be asked. Following this, the answer to that question will determine the structure of further questions, thus:

Answer	2d stage question	3d stage question
No	Why not?	How can we overcome that objection?
Yes and No	What is the partial solution as distinct from the remaining problem? What is the new problem?	How can we solve this problem?
I don't know. I'll have to test it. I'll have to check.	Who will investigate?	When do we reconvene?

Probably the most important aspect of this procedure is in the third stage question, "How can we overcome this objection?" Without it a good idea could die at the hands of a categorical "No" uttered from a preconditioned pattern of thinking.

As a further aid to idea development still more standard forms are used. They list the idea, advantages, disadvantages, and action. Again this is a useful defense against our human nature. Listing the disadvantages, especially of our own idea, comes in the category of Charles Darwin's system of writing down the arguments of his contemporaries which were in disagreement with his own—otherwise he would forget them!

The most important aspects of the analytical phase of the Task Force schedule lie in the reminders:

Don't be a hermit.
Use specialty materials, products and processes.
Use standard or specials.

. . . which emphasize the importance of not rejecting expensive "specials" until their *value* has been determined (remember the transformer winding example given previously?). This is where the impact of the detailed work presented for the TF members in the "Resources" section of their handbooks is very likely to be felt.

By the planning phase, ideas should have jelled well enough to permit major decisions about implementation. Difficulties should be well defined and a dollar sign should be on all ideas.

For execution, the economic zone chart is the tool applied to establish a priority system for implementation of value proposals, based on economic merit. The zone criteria of course should be based on the specific needs of your business. To insure effective implementation, it is suggested that a specific percentage of engineering time (for example: 30 percent) be set aside to work on the proposals falling in zone 1, followed by adjusted percentages for the other zones (see Figure 15–11).

In the same manner, contribution to profit resulting from sales versus total effort can be plotted. By comparing this to contribution and effort for value proposals, it will be clearly indicated where effort should be expended, i.e., in the area of sales or implementing value proposals.

Figure 15–11

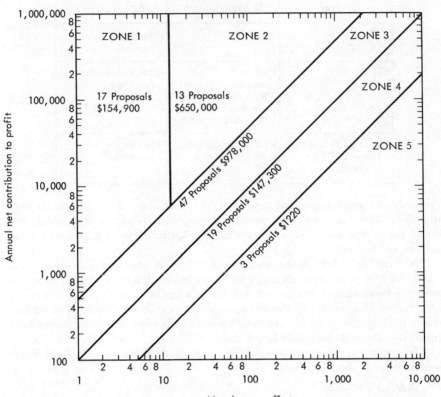

The economic zone chart is recommended by Value Programs for Industry Inc., to establish priorities of execution in the final stages of Task Force.

Zone 1—Fewer than 12 hours to implement results greater than $500/year/man-hour
Zone 2—More than $500/year/man-hour and requiring more than 12 hours to implement
Zone 3—Implementation return of more than $100/year/man-hour
Zone 4—Implementation return of more than $20/year/man-hour
Zone 5—Implementation will require reappraisal of expense required to achieve the best 75% of cost gains

Way-out

This then is the pattern, tools, methods of the members of the VE oriented TF at Canadian Westinghouse, Hamilton. The relatively short term results expected have already been stated. The possible long term effects are immeasurable.

Sitting in on one of the TF's advanced design VE session is like listening to a science-fiction writers convention. If many of the possible suggestions at this meeting were to be carried out it is doubtful many people would be able to recognize a vertical water wheel any longer.

"Use spider arms to circulate air."
"Combine turbine and spider functions."

"Have we investigated ceramics, oxides for insulation?"

"Let's talk of the possibilities of hydrostatic bearings of 12×10^6 lbs."

"Why oil in hydrostatic bearings? Why not high pressure water straight from the penstocks?"

Thinking like this can hardly be accused of being "cramped."

But then, that's what TF and VE are all about!

Procurement planning

The determination of objectives is an important part of the overall procurement planning operation. Most procurement plans are made to coincide with the corporate fiscal year, with the recognition that changes may have to be made as the year progresses.

The actual planning process starts with information derived from the annual sales forecast, production forecasts, and general economic forecasts. The sales forecast will provide a total measure of the requirements of materials, products, and services to be acquired by the activities of the procurement function; production forecasts will provide information on the location at which the materials, products, and services will be required; and the economic forecast will provide information useful in estimating general trends for prices, wages, and other costs.

It is obvious that some objectives will have to be revised to meet the changes indicated by the broad forecasts. In most procurement operations less than 20 percent of the items purchased account for over 80 percent of the dollars spent. In breaking down the broad forecast into specific plans, the next step is to make price and supply availability forecasts for each of the major items (the 20 percent of all items which account for 80 percent of total purchase expenditures).

The estimates of material consumption are broken down into time periods, monthly and quarterly. These quantities are checked against inventory control procedures which take into account lead time and safety stocks. These estimates are then related to the price trend and availability forecasts for the material under consideration, and a buying plan is developed. If the forecasts predict ample supplies of the material and a possible weakening in prices, a probable buying policy will be to reduce inventories and others to the lowest level which is economically feasible. On the other hand, if the forecasts predict the possibility of short supply and increasing price trends, prudence will require a buying policy which will ensure that adequate stocks are on hand or are covered by contract, and the possibility of forward buying is considered.

The procedure outlined above is used for both raw materials and component parts. In forecasting trends which will affect the availability and price of component parts, consideration has to be given to the conditions expected to be present for the period being forecasted in the industries in which the parts suppliers operate.

The 80 percent of the items purchased which account for 20 percent of the dollars spent in the average procurement function can be classified into related product groups. The pattern of analysis followed in forecasting for the major items can be used for the related product groups.

After the monthly and quarterly unit quantities and estimated dollar costs for each item or related product group are tabulated and modifications made as a result of developing a buying plan, individual buyers make an analysis of the items for which they are responsible to determine if further modifications in prices should be made because of the objectives which they have established to guide their activities for the period of the forecast.

Special projects such as the construction of new facilities or the planning for the manufacture of new major products not previously produced by the company may create uncertainty as to the time periods when new equipment or products will be needed making planning difficult.

According to A. J. D'Arcy[5] there is a tremendous value in preparing plans, not only on the aggregate, but also for individual items. He stresses the need for careful preparation including data gathering from many sources (See Figure 15–12).

Unless the plan is prepared in written form much of its contribution is lost. A sample plan for wooden pallets is shown in Figure 15–13.[6]

Figure 15–12
QUESTIONS TO BE ASKED IN DEVELOPING A WRITTEN PROCUREMENT PLAN FOR RAW MATERIALS

1. What are the short- and long-term objectives of the business involved?
2. Quantity required at each using location—by months for the next one to two years?
3. What specification applies at each location? What alternative might be considered?
4. Storage capacity available at each location? What ideas do we have on how much inventory to carry? Is inventory limited by storage facilities, working capital, deterioration with age?
5. Method of delivery preferred at each location? What alternative methods of delivery can be considered without new investment or with new investment? What is the maximum quantity per delivery?
6. Consumption and price by location, by month, for previous one or two years?
7. Current suppliers at each location, price being paid, and quantity supplied for previous one or two years? Production department performance evaluation of current suppliers?
8. Prospective suppliers, their plant locations, capacities, and processes? Desirable features of prospective suppliers relative to current suppliers? Is supply regularly available or subject to seasonal or other factors?

---

[5] A. J. D'Arcy, "Planning for Buying," *Journal of Purchasing*, vol. 7, no. 3 (August 1971), pp. 24–32.

[6] Ibid., pp. 30, 31, and 32.

Figure 15–12 (*Continued*)

9. Total industry capacity/demand ratio for the product for past one or two years, with estimate of expected demand in next few years, by end use?
10. Supplier labor review—renewal date on labor contract?
11. Process economic data, such as estimated production cost, raw material cost, co-product values, batch sizes, yields, make-versus-buy? Rank suppliers from lowest to highest cost producers. Relative profitability of suppliers?
12. Objectives for value improvements sought in new buying period?
13. Preferred quantity statement in new agreement, i.e., fixed quantity or percent of requirement, or fixed monthly minimum or fixed monthly maximum?
14. Specifications and methods of analysis to be described in contracts for use in receiving and accepting material?
15. Preferred length of contract period? What alternatives might be considered?
16. Is any option desired for contract extension?
17. Preferred terms of payment?
18. Method of invoicing?
19. What points of discussion must be explored between technical production men in buyer or seller organization?
20. What technical service might we require?
21. Who will provide transportation equipment? What alternatives should be considered?
22. Are suitable freight rates currently in effect? Do any new rates have to be established? Evaluate for each supplier.
23. Will all material move in bulk equipment or will some be required in containers? If so, how should it be packed?
24. Will purchases be negotiated or determined by bidding?
25. Distribution cost from the various suppliers' plants to each consuming location?
26. Do we want multiple suppliers for each consuming location?
27. How do we want to write our inquiry?

Figure 15–13
PROCUREMENT PLAN FOR WOODEN PALLETS
(October 1, 1970, to October 1, 1971)

1. Supplier:
    Mall Lumber Company
    Ashland, Kentucky
    Borne Wood Products, Inc.
    Manfred, West Virginia
    State Pallet Company
    Columbus, Ohio
    Walter Company
    Knoxville, Tennessee
    Burk Corporation
    Montgomery, West Virginia

Figure 15–13 (*Continued*)

The Vocational Rehabilitation Center
State Board of Vocational Education

2. Past and Present Purchases

During the past 12 months, Mall Lumber Company has furnished 95 percent of our total requirements. The Vocational Rehabilitation Center has furnished a few pallets on a spot basis. In recent months, Borne Wood Products, Inc., has become a supplier, mainly due to quality, and currently is furnishing approximately 50 percent of our requirements.

3. Future Purchases (based on estimated requirements)

Borne Wood Products:

Type	Percentage of usage	Dollar volume
DF-10	100% (2,500)	$ 5,225.00
Double face warehouse	100% (1,000)	3,970.00
5454	70% (20,000)	40,400.00
		$49,595.00
	Less 1%	495.95
		$49,099.05

Mall Lumber Company:

Type	Percentage of usage	Dollar volume
No. 1	100% (700)	$ 1,155.00
No. 2	100% (700)	1,379.00
7AC	100% (1,000)	2,070.00
5426	100% (5,000)	6,650.00
5454	30% (6,000)	13,500.00
Notched	100% (4,500)	9,630.00
Design no. 3	100% (600)	2,508.00
Design no. 3 except 42×42	100% (1,500)	5,715.00
Design no. 2	100% (400)	1,336.00
FC cylinder	100% (1,200)	1,980.00
		$45,923.00
	Less 1%	459.23
		$45,463.77

Vocational Rehabilitation Division

Due to the nature of Vocational Center's work, it is impossible to determine their production ability. Since they are local and have assisted us in past emergency requirements, we will favor them with spot business occasionally at the same or lower prices than those from our regular suppliers. This business will be very minimal and is not reflected in percentages shown for Borne and Mall.

4. Reasons for Business Distribution

Quality and service play a major part in the distribution of business to pallet manufacturers. However, in obtaining bids, we find that the low bidder also offers the best quality in the critical areas. List of offers follows. Borne will furnish all 5,454 pallets used at South Hadley (20,000). This is due not only to price but also the fact that other suppliers have been unable to furnish acceptable quality for use with our automatic palletizer. Mall

Figure 15–13 (*Concluded*)

will furnish 5454 pallets to our Huntington, W. Va., warehouse (5,000) at a price 15¢ cheaper than the nearest bidder.

Both Borne and Mall offer good engineering assistance and will be in a position to furnish pallets during inclement weather. Borne's quality is exceptionally good while Mall's ranges from fair to good. Price is also a determining factor in the distribution.

5. Buying Techniques

Individual types in quantities of 2,000 or more per year will be purchased on yearly or semi-yearly requirement orders. This will simplify ordering and releasing procedures, eliminate paper work, and expedite deliveries. All other pallets will be purchased on a spot basis.

6. Objectives

There is a definite shortage in our area of dependable pallet manufacturers who can offer quality pallets and service. A contributing factor is the Viet Nam war situation which is requiring heavy government purchases for unitized shipments to Southeast Asia. Another factor is the small manufacturer's lack of capital to make quality and service improvements. With this in mind, our objectives are:

1. Maintain good buyer-vendor relations with existing vendors.
2. Continue our search for new suppliers.
3. Improve quality in needed areas; investigate foamed plastic pallets.
4. Change from spot orders to blanket orders when requirements are increased.

7. Savings

The inclusion of Borne as a supplier will result in a $5,603.40 annual savings. Mall has been supplying 5,454 pallets to our Huntington, W.Va., warehouse at the same price as those delivered to South Hadley. Because of geographical location, we have succeeded in getting that price lowered from $2.29 to $2.25 per pallet, with a resultant $237.60 annual savings. Total annual savings under this procurement program will be $5,841.00.

8. Offers from Pallet Manufacturers

Type	Annual usage	Borne	Mall	State	Walter	Burk
No. 1	700	$1.83	$1.65	$1.90		
No. 2	700	2.09	1.97	2.07		
7AC	1,000	2.07	2.07	—		
5426	5,000	1.93	1.33	1.80		
5454	20,000 (S.C.)	2.02	2.29			
	5,000 (Hunt.)	2.40	2.25			
DF-10	2,500	2.09	2.11			
Notched	4,500	2.17	2.14	2.25	No Bid	No Bid
Design no. 3	600	4.87	4.18	5.75		
Design no. 3 except						
42 × 42	1,500	4.23	3.81	4.50		
Design no. 2	400	3.78	3.34	4.00		
Double face						
warehouse	1,000	3.97	4.18	4.25		
FC cylinder	1,200	2.10	1.65	1.68		

PERT and CPM

Within the past 15 years, new planning techniques have been developed which are useful in complex situations in which many variables and interrelationships are present. The Critical Path Method (CPM) provides for determining the sequence of all tasks required from the start to the completion of a project. An arrow diagram is used to show graphically the interrelationship between tasks for any project and hence determine the longest or critical path required to complete a project. An estimated time requirement is assigned to each task.

The Program Evaluation Review Techniques (PERT) was developed by the U.S. Navy in cooperation with others for the purpose of reducing the development time for the Polaris Ballistic Missile System. PERT is similar to CPM in that each technique uses a network to diagram graphically the sequence of tasks, which in PERT terminology are called "events." Events are also defined as being "highly identifiable points in time." The network lines connecting events are known as "activities" and represent the elapsed time required to complete an event. Unless stated otherwise, activities are stated in 7-day calendar weeks with an assumed 40-hour work week. Figure 15–14 shows a simple PERT network diagram.

Figure 15–14
SIMPLE PERT NETWORK

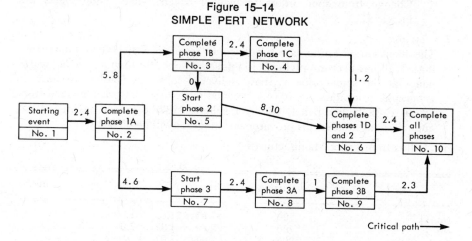

Critical path ⟶

When the time interval "activity" to accomplish an event is uncertain, an estimate of the longest time and the shortest time expected is shown on the activity line by number, i.e., 5, 8, where eight weeks is the longest time and five weeks the shortest time that may be required to complete an event.

In this example phases 1 and 2 were related to internal data gathering for a procurement plan, and phase 3 involved some external information seeking from three different sources.

Rules for the effective use of the CPM and PERT techniques have been developed and reported in the rather substantial amount of literature which has been published explaining their techniques.

Modeling the procurement function

Many of the operations research techniques developed for the materials function are highly specific and deal with short-term decisions and problems. Corporate models have also been developed like CORSIM[7] (Corporate Simulation Model) and LREPS[8] (Long Range Physical Distribution System Model). The value of such models may potentially be very high. It allows managers to ask questions like, "What if we make this decision, what is likely to happen?" and expect some reasonable answers before having made the decision. Table 15–2 provides a

Table 15–2

SUMMARY OF EXPERIMENTAL FACTORS

Target Variables	Environmental Variables
Service to production	Supplier environment
Total system cost	Technology
System flexibility	Product demand environment
Production level	

Controllable Variables	Design Options
Production order characteristics	Actual and pseudo
Material/parts mix	Tracked materials and components
New materials/parts	As desired
Supplier mix	Actual and pseudo
Facility network	Manufacturing plants
	Material centers
	Consolidated shipping points
Inventory policy	Reorder point, replenishment, and hybrid for the tracked products
Transportation	Common carrier, private, and contract (truck, rail, air, water)
Communications	Centralized-decentralized (computer, teletype, mail, telephone)
Materials handling	Automated-mechanized
Purchasing policy	Actual and pseudo programs
	Vendor selection
	Multinational and national
	Single and multiple sourcing
Material quality	Actual and pseudo

* Source: O. K. Helferich and R. M. Monczka, "Development of a Dynamic Simulation Model for Planning Materials Input Systems: Formulation of the Conceptual Model," *Journal of Purchasing*, vol. 8, no. 3 (August 1972), pp. 24.

[7] W. B. Lee, "Corporate Simulation Models and Purchasing Decision Making," *Journal of Purchasing*, vol. 8, no. 4 (November 1972), pp. 5–16.

[8] O. K. Helferich and R. M. Monczka, "Development of a Dynamic Simulation Model for Planning Materials Input Systems: Formulation of the Conceptual Model," *Journal of Purchasing*, vol. 8, no. 3 (August 1972), pp. 17–33.

summary of experimental factors for LREPS which deals with the very difficult problem of long-range planning.

Figures 15–15[9] and 15–16,[10] provide dimensions of the material input network. Conceptually, it is, therefore, possible to model long-range

Figure 15–15
GENERAL DESCRIPTION OF THE MATERIAL
INPUT-USER FIRM SITUATION

Material Input System
  Manufacturing control centers (MCC)
    Multilocation
    Each produces full line or less
  Material centers (MC)
    Multilocation
    Full or partial line
    Remote or adjacent
  Consolidated shipping point (CSP)
  Transportation
    Common carrier
    Private
    Contract
  Inventory
    Reorder point, replenishment, and hybrid at MCC and MC
  Communications
    Computer, teletype, mail, telephone
  Material handling
    Automated or manual
Material Profile
  Multimaterial requirements
  Key material groups for each supplier by commodity classifications
  Actual or pseudo*
  Existing or new
Supplier Profile
  Multisupplier classifications
  Total U.S. market
  Individual or agglomerated supply
  Purchase order characteristics—actual or pseudo*
Demand Profile
  Multiproduct manufacturing
    Actual or pseudo*
    New or existing
    Key product groups by class of trade
  * Simulated based on past experience.

materials planning. Although the usefulness of this approach is difficult to determine empirically in the short term, such models could be of valuable assistance in detecting long-range problems and testing alternate strategies.

When the planning job is completed it is then possible to submit to top management estimates of total dollars to be spent in the acquisition

---

[9] Ibid., p. 21.
[10] Ibid., p. 22.

Figure 15–16
ECHELONS AND TYPICAL CHANNELS OF THE MATERIAL SUPPLY NETWORK

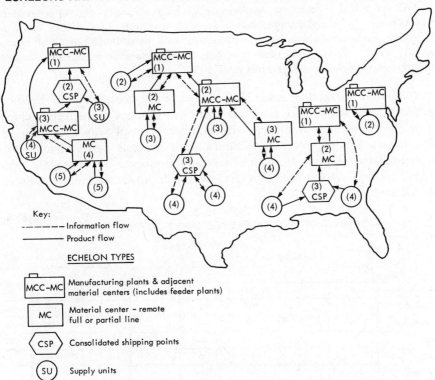

Key:
------- Information flow
————— Product flow

ECHELON TYPES

MCC–MC	Manufacturing plants & adjacent material centers (includes feeder plants)
MC	Material center – remote full or partial line
CSP	Consolidated shipping points
SU	Supply units

Note: Number in ( ) indicates level facility is in particular commodity supply channel.

of materials, products, and services monthly, quarterly, and for the fiscal year. After top management has approved the procurement plan, it is usually incorporated in the total company plan and in the financial planning for cash requirements and flows.

When the approved procurement plan is returned to the procurement department, it is used as a basis to prepare a procurement budget.

Input-output analysis

According to M. F. Elliott-Jones[11] input-output analysis may have substantial promise in the next few decades as a procurement and market research concept. The use of I-O tables, models, and techniques will permit the analyst to determine market shares and trends, develop forecasts, and provide an insight into material use the prices not easily accomplished by other means.

---

[11] M. F. Elliott-Jones, *Input-Output Analysis: A Nontechnical Description* (New York: The Conference Board, 1971).

During recent years, one of Wassily Leontief's major contributions to economics—input-output analysis—has shown signs of finally becoming a practical tool of empirical economics. Availability of large capacity digital computers has allowed this development, and a growing inventory of statistics has furthered it. Presently, a number of economists anticipate development of input-output (I-O) during the next two decades comparable with development of aggregative econometric models since 1950.[12]

Industrial marketing research becomes more complex as a finished product becomes farther removed from the product or material which a seller produces and also as the number of applications or uses of the seller's product increases. Input-output analysis helps identify the intermediate transactions which normally disappear in aggregate economic models. An example of a Compressed Input-Output table is shown in Table 15–3.[13]

Table 15–3
SAMPLE OF A COMPRESSED INPUT-OUTPUT TABLE

				Purchases by:				
	Agriculture	Manufacturing I	Manufacturing II	Services	Imports	Total intermediates	Final demand	Total output
Agriculture	15	100	75	40	—	230	220	450
Manufacturing I		50	200	100	—	350	400	750
Manufacturing II	5	170	35	140	—	350	250	600
Services	20	30	40	20	—	110	390	500
Imports	10	100	50	20	—	180	–180	—
Value added	400	300	200	180	—			
Total inputs	450	750	600	500	—	1220	1080	2300

(left margin label: Sales by:)

Notes: The table may be read across rows: sales by the row sector to the sector named in the column. Or the table may be read in columns: purchases by the column sector from the row sector. Total sales to nonfinal users: the row sum of sales by a sector to every other using sector. Final demand consists of consumption, investment: exports, and government spending. Total output is the sum of sales by the row sector to all intermediate users, and final users. The column sum of final demands is equivalent to GNP, in this example 1,030 units.

Procurement budgets

In addition to the procurement plan which is concerned with projecting the need for the acquisition of materials, products, and supplies required by the production facilities in manufacturing the products to be sold by the marketing department, as anticipated by the sales forecast, a budget should be prepared for all of the expenses incurred in the operation of the procurement function. Such expenses include: salaries and wages; space costs including heat and electricity; equipment costs

[12] Ibid., p. 1.
[13] Ibid., p. 4.

for desks, office machines, files, and typewriters; data processing costs including computer usage or time-sharing charges; travel and entertainment expense; educational expenditures for personnel who attend seminars and professional meetings; postage, telephone, and telegraph charges; office supplies; subscription to trade publications and funds to provide additions to the purchasing library; and a contingency fund for miscellaneous expenses.

A good starting point is to review the actual operating expenditures for the previous fiscal period. If a budget was in effect for the previous fiscal period a comparison between budget and actual expenditures may point up problem areas. An attempt should be made to reconcile any substantial differences. Actually, expenditures should be compared with budget estimates on a monthly basis as soon as figures are available. This procedure is one means of controlling operating expenses and detecting problem areas promptly.

After reviewing the past procurement department operating expense history, a budget should be prepared for the next fiscal period. The new estimates should include provision for salary increases, personnel additions or deletions as anticipated by the requirements of the procurement plan. New estimates of all other expenses required in the efficient operation of the department should be made in keeping with the requirements of the purchasing plan. The final budget should be coordinated with the total company budget with the executive responsible for the companywide budget.

Procurement objectives

Much has been written in recent years about the concept "management by objectives." This text is not the place to explore the full details of what is required to adopt and implement an effective management by objectives program. Companies which have used the concept to improve operations have learned that it usually requires a substantial period of time, often several years, to develop the climate of managerial philosophy which is essential to full implementation of the concept.

The chief procurement executive or materials manager has the basic responsibility for determining general objectives for the function and the coordination of such objectives with the strategic objectives of the company as a whole. Once the overall objectives or targets are outlined, they are handed to the subordinates not as a directive but as general guidelines for subordinates who have decision-making authority to use in establishing the objectives which will govern their activities for some period of time. When properly administered the individual's objectives act as a motivating force to give direction to work and subsequently a basis for appraising performance. The more responsibility the individual exercises in establishing and implementing objectives, the greater the opportunity for the motivation of employees and the individual's satisfaction which comes from a sense of accomplishment and achievement.

The establishment of objectives for a procurement department is a procedure which is specific to a given company at a particular period in time. The services of a competent purchasing research analyst or a purchasing research staff can be of great assistance in selecting objectives which will provide the greatest payback for the efforts expended. An example of selecting an objective may help to clarify the foregoing.

The XYZ Company marketed a new product which had been carefully market tested and gave promise of becoming an important source of revenue for the company. Several months after the product had been placed in national distribution, complaints about the failure of the product to perform to specification were received. New orders declined sharply. A thorough investigation disclosed that some of the component parts failed after a period of several months' operation. It was suspected that failure was caused by inferior quality of the parts in question. An overall objective of improving the consistency of quality of all purchased components was established. Individual buyers were asked what means they could select which would help to implement the accomplishments of the overall objective. Included in the individual suggestions were:

Review of quality control methods of the suppliers.
The introduction of a "zero defects" program.
Location of new sources of supply.
The adoption of a statistical quality control system.

A review of the specifications with suppliers to determine if requirements caused unusual production problems, followed up with cooperative efforts with company engineers and quality control people.

Management by objectives

The research and planning procedures discussed in this chapter provide a framework for improving the performance of the procurement activities of a company. Careful research and planning will provide a better understanding of the job which has to be done. The use of the "management by objectives" concept should provide a means to implement the planning process, motivate the personnel responsible for operating any plan developed, and provide a mechanism for appraising results. In the final analysis a good plan should help to do a better job, but it is the attitude and ability of the people on the job which will obtain maximum results. In recognition of this fact, permission has been obtained from Professor Alva F. Kindall to quote[14] his five-step

---

[14] Alva F. Kindall, *Personnel Administration: Principles and Cases* (Homewood, Ill.: Richard D. Irwin, Inc., 1969). Reprinted by permission, pp. 412–15.

program for effective use of management by objectives to achieve company goals.

Step one: Position description areas of accountability responsibilities. In *step one*, the individual occupant of a position or job discusses his job description with his superior, and the occupant defines his areas of accountability—his responsibilities. He then outlines the *results* he is responsible for attaining in return for the pay he receives.

Since the occupant of a position or job knows more about what he does than anyone else, he should be given the opportunity to write his own position description. Obviously, the occupant should discuss his position description with his immediate superior to make certain that the two are in complete agreement on the responsibilities and duties of the occupant of the position.

Step two: Individual goals. In *step two*, having obtained complete agreement of his superior on the duties of a position or job, the occupant should then prepare a list of goals that he believes would represent reasonable performance in each of his areas of responsibility for, say, the next six months, or the next year. In other words, the occupant *plans* his activities for the forthcoming period, in accordance, of course, with the overall goals of his unit and his organization.

In establishing his own performance goals, the occupant must know the goals of the organization for which he works and the goals of his particular organizational unit. Every organization imposes certain constraints on individual activities, and these constraints must be communicated to the individual by the organization. Thus, an individual can set reasonable, manageable, and stretch goals for himself only when he knows the goals of his overall organization and the goals of his unit. This means that the organization must implement its program in the overall *planning* and must make its plans and objectives known to the individual.

Also included in an individual's goals for the forthcoming period should be his own personal goals for self-development.

No management, however, should attempt to introduce such a goal-setting program until it is firmly convinced that individuals will respond to this freedom and trust by establishing higher goals for themselves than those management would have imposed upon them from above. The fact that individuals will respond in this fashion has been proved over and over again in programs that are well conceived and administered.

Step three: Agreed-upon goals. In *step three*, the occupant discusses his goals with his immediate superior until they are in complete agreement on the goals. This third step is the most tricky and the most complicated in the entire procedure. For one thing, the moment a superior asks a subordinate to raise or lower a goal that he has set for himself, the goal then becomes the superior's, not the subordinate's. On the other hand, if some crisis exists that requires immediate action on the part of a subordinate, the superior obviously may have to change a subordinate's goal. But such action should be necessary only under emergency conditions.

In *step three*, the superior should act in the role of questioner, advisor, counselor, trainer, developer, and even "warner." The superior should not play the role of God or judge!

Step four: Standards, or checkpoints. In *step four*, the superior and the subordinate jointly establish the standards, or checkpoints, to be used by both parties during the course of the forthcoming period and at the end of the period to determine the subordinate's success in attaining his objectives. Examples of such checkpoints are due dates, sales, financial and cost figures, statistical data, and comparisons.

Step five: Results. In *step five*, the *results* of a person's performance become known: either he has attained or exceeded his goals or he has failed to attain his goals. The mere attainment or failure to attain a goal is not of significance in itself. The important consideration here is: what has the person *accomplished?* Obviously, a man who establishes extremely high goals for himself and then almost attains them has accomplished more than a man who originally established low goals and then exceeded them. Judgment must be used in assessing *accomplishments.* The superior's task in *step five* is to eliminate negative accomplishments and to reward appropriately positive accomplishments.

Negative accomplishments are warning signals that something must be done. Perhaps the subordinate needs training or development. Maybe he needs additional help or new equipment. Or he could be misplaced in his position. After a superior has exhausted all means of help and guidance and the subordinate continues to produce negative accomplishments, he must make efforts promptly to transfer the subordinate into a position in which he can produce positive accomplishments. If the person fails this opportunity, he may have to be retired early or even discharged. For his own welfare and for the good of an organization, a person should not be continued in a position in which he cannot attain positive accomplishments.

On the other hand, the superior should appropriately reward a subordinate who has produced *positive accomplishments* by periodical salary increases and promotions.

In all of these five steps, no mention has been made of *personality traits.* No effort has been made to try to determine *why* a man produces certain results. The *cause* of a man's activities is not explored; he has not been put on a couch and psychoanalyzed. Instead, a person is judged on the basis of his *results*—his *accomplishments.* If a man has serious (not imagined) personality deficiencies, he will inevitably have negative accomplishments. The administrator, by eliminating negative accomplishments, automatically eliminates those with personality deficiencies. The task of identifying and improving serious personality deficiencies should be left to the professional when such advice is sought by the individual.

In the superior-subordinate relationship, judgmental statements on personality should *never* be communicated to the individual, and they should *never* be recorded on written forms or documents. Confine such statements to summaries of *actual results.* This principle applies to both positive and negative judgmental comments.

BIBLIOGRAPHY

ALJIAN, GEORGE W., ed. *Purchasing Handbook.* 3d ed. New York: McGraw-Hill Book Co., 1973.

ALLEN, GEORGE R. *Value Engineering—Its Development and Application.* Washington, GWV, 1968.

AMERICAN MANAGEMENT ASSOCIATION. *Value Analysis—Value Engineering.* Edited by William D. Falcon. New York, 1964.

AMERICAN SOCIETY OF TOOL AND MANUFACTURING ENGINEERS. *Value Engineering in Manufacturing.* Englewood Cliffs, N.J.: Prentice-Hall, 1967.

AMMER, DEAN S. *Materials Management.* rev. ed. Homewood, Ill.: Richard D. Irwin, Inc., 1968.

CAMERON, BURGESS. *Input-Output Analysis and Resource Allocation.* Cambridge, Mass.: Harvard University Press, 1968.

CLAWSON, ROBERT H. *Value Engineering for Management.* New York: Auerbach Publishers, Inc., 1970.

COLLIER, JAMES R. *Effective Long Range Business Planning.* Englewood Cliffs, N.J. Prentice-Hall, Inc., 1968.

DEPARTMENT OF DEFENSE. *Value Engineering.* DOD 5010.8H Washington: Government Printing Office, 1968.

ELECTRONIC INDUSTRIES ASSOCIATION. *Value Engineering.* Elizabeth, N.J.: Engineering Publications, Inc., 1959.

ELLIOTT-JONES, M. F. *Input-Output Analysis: A Nontechnical Description.* New York: The Conference Board, 1971.

FALLON, CHARLES. *Value Analysis to Improve Productivity.* New York: John Wiley & Sons, Inc., 1971.

FARAG, SHAWKI M. *Input-Output Analysis: Applications to Business Accounting.* Center for International Education and Research in Accounting, 1967.

GAGE, W. L. *Value Analysis.* London: McGraw-Hill Publishing Co., Ltd., 1968.

GOLDMAN, THOMAS A. *Cost Effectiveness Analysis: New Approaches in Decision Making.* New York: Praeger, 1967.

HECKERT, JOSIAH BROOKS. *Business Budgeting and Control.* 3d ed. New York: Ronald Press Co., 1967.

LEONTIEF, WASSILY. *Input-Output Economics.* New York: Oxford University Press, 1966.

LYDEN, F. V. AND MILLER, E. G., eds. *Planning Programming, and Budgeting: A Systems Approach to Management.* Chicago: Markham Publishing Co., 1968.

MILLER, ROBERT W. *Schedule Cost and Profit Control with Profit.* New York: McGraw-Hill Book Co., 1963.

MYLES, L. D. *Techniques of Value Analysis and Engineering.* 2d ed. New York: McGraw-Hill Book Co., 1972.

MUDGE, ARTHUR E. *Value Engineering: A Systematic Approach.* New York: McGraw-Hill Book Co., 1971.

NATIONAL ASSOCIATION OF PURCHASING AGENTS. "Value Analysis." *Guide to Purchasing.* New York, 1965.

NATIONAL ASSOCIATION OF PURCHASING AGENTS. *Cutting Costs by Analyzing Values: A Practical Purchasing Program.* rev. ed. New York, 1963.

National Association of Purchasing Management. *Standardization Manual.* New York, NAPM, 1958.

National Association of Purchasing Management. *Value Analysis: An Aid for the Buyer.* New York, NAPM, 1960.

Reuter, Vincent G. "The Success Story of Value Analysis, Value Engineering," *Journal of Purchasing,* vol. 4, no. 2 (May 1968), p. 63.

Richardson, Harry W. *Iuput-Output and Regional Economics.* New York: Halsted Press, John Wiley & Sons, Inc., 1972.

Ridge, Warren J. *Value Analysis for Better Management.* American Management Association, Inc., 1968.

Schlesinger, James R. *Defense Planning and Budgeting: The Issue of Centralized Control.* Washington: Industrial College of the Armed Forces, 1968.

Valentine, Raymond F. *Value Analysis for Better Systems and Procedures.* Englewood Cliffs, N.J.: Prentice-Hall, Inc., 1970.

Van De Water, J. "New Concepts in Value Buying," *Purchasing.* Value Analysis Issue. May 18, 1964, pp. 35–75.

Westing, J. H.; Fine, I. V., and Zenz, Gary J. et al. *Purchasing Management.* 3d ed. New York: John Wiley & Sons, Inc., 1969.

CASES FOR CHAPTER 15

MODEL ALUMINUM CORPORATION*
Function of a Purchase Research Staff in a Complex Organization

In September, Mr. Brodie was assigned the position of manager of the purchase research department of the Model Aluminum Corporation, a large producer of ingots and finished aluminum shapes. Mr. Brodie's official job objective was to "formulate programs designed to increase efficiency and accomplish the maximum potential effect of each dollar expended for purchased goods and services." Annual expenditures for purchases by the Model Aluminum Corporation were $1 billion, going to 35,000 suppliers. Mr. Brodie decided to undertake whatever type of program seemed to offer a possibility of increasing purchasing efficiency or obtaining maximum values from purchasing expenditures. He believed that if possible it was essential not to limit the function of purchase research by strict definition, but rather to provide staff service wherever needed and allow the success of the programs to determine the ultimate size and objective of his department. Six months after becoming manager, Mr. Brodie was attempting to evaluate the development of the department so as to decide how long to wait before asking for personnel to assist him.

In addition to Mr. Brodie's special talents and interests, three factors helped to determine the function of the purchase research department during the first six months of its operation: (A) the size and complexity of the materials management function; (B) the type of materials purchased by the aluminum industry, and (C) the status of Mr. Brodie in the headquarters organization.

A. The great size of the Model Aluminum Corporation presented three types of problems to Mr. Brodie: (1) the difficulty of servicing a department of 50 buyers; (2) the need to consider the extent to which the company's purchasing power could influence a commodity market; and (3) the importance of coordinating purchase research with other staff and supervisory groups located in other departments of the central office.

1. The central purchasing department in Chicago consisted of: (a) a staff group which established corporationwide policies and (b) a department of 50 buyers which purchased all materials for the two major divisions consolidated with headquarters as well as common materials for the eight other divisions (see Exhibit 1). Mr. Brodie was thus located

Exhibit 1

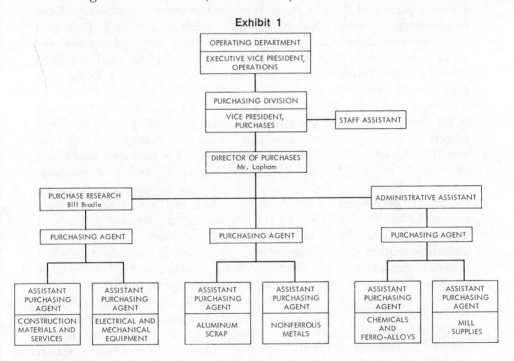

in the same office as the executives who determined corporation purchase policies for all the operating divisions and in the same department as the 50 buyers who purchased two thirds of the corporation's materials. The great number of buyers made it impossible for Mr. Brodie to work closely with each one without additional personnel in his department. He did not wish to develop a staff, however, until experience indicated what type of purchase research would be most effective. For this reason, his actual working contacts were with the six assistant purchasing agents and the three purchasing agents rather than the 50 buyers themselves.

2. The great purchasing power of the corporation in certain commodity markets such as scrap aluminum, steel, manganese, and coal made it essential to direct purchase research toward long-range pricing policies in addition to achieving the lowest immediate price. For example, corporation purchasing executives wished to keep prices as low as possible, but were aware of the danger of forcing certain prices excessively low with the resulting unstable markets and excessive pressure on suppliers. In many cases, pricing decisions had to be made too quickly to rely on the top economic policy advise of the senior executive committees. For this reason, purchase research was requested to undertake the evaluation of long-range price and supply conditions in the commodity markets.

3. Furthermore, due to the size of the central office, analysis and research staffs had already been developed in other departments of the headquarters group in Chicago, some of which undertook projects that could be considered to fall into the objectives of purchase research as broadly defined. Four staff groups in particular did work that was related to Mr. Brodie's assignment: (a) the staff assistant to the vice president of purchases accumulated data relating to price changes of the major materials. He issued regularly to all management personnel in the department above the rank of assistant purchasing agent historical reports of recent price movements and economic changes; (b) the accounting department, which processed invoices for payment, could provide considerable data concerning the historical pattern of purchase orders, including the dollar value of different product classifications, the market percentage of individual suppliers, and certain other characteristics of the transactions; (c) the engineering department maintained a group of "consultant" metallurgists and mechanical engineers who undertook certain standardization and value analysis projects of different materials grades; and (d) the sales division maintained a large market analysis department, which undertook supply-demand studies of raw materials at the request of certain operating divisions in the field. Due to the existence of these related staff activities and the need to develop communication with many different executives, buyers, and plant personnel, Mr. Brodie considered that one major objective of purchase research would necessarily be the liaison with other departments of the corporation.

B. The type of materials purchased by the aluminum industry placed further restrictions on the type of research Mr. Brodie undertook. Of the $1 billion annual purchases, almost $600 million were for seven raw materials, refractory materials, scrap aluminum, steel, coal and coke, natural gas, zinc, and manganese. Although economic commodity studies could be made of these materials, Mr. Brodie considered it to be difficult to make cost savings in their purchase through ordinary value analysis methods. Savings through cost analysis were limited because the price of these materials was determined more by market pressures than by production costs. Savings through product analysis were difficult to achieve through a headquarters staff because of the specialized metallurgical knowledge required to change a grade of ore without making the aluminum-making process more difficult or influencing the physical and chemical characteristics of the finished aluminum. In addition to the seven major raw materials, $200 million was expended for new plant construction, electric power generating equipment, and for miscellaneous raw materials. Value analysis of capital equipment purchases was usually delegated to a field purchasing agent who could work closely with the design engineers at the location of the construction. Another $200 million was expended for maintenance, repair, and operating supplies such as valves, pumps, and hand tools, which presented opportunities for value analysis. Although they constituted a wide range of purchases and so lacked the possibility of great dollar savings from a single cost reduction that could be obtained in mass production industries, Mr. Brodie believed that considerable results could be obtained from effort devoted to this area.

C. A third characteristic that helped determine the function of the purchase research department was the status of Mr. Brodie in the organization. Three factors had placed Mr. Brodie in a position that tended to emphasize other purchase research activities rather than cost reductions through value analysis, which would require close contact with the buyers. First, the willingness of purchasing executives to support purchase research gave the function a status on the executive rather than the operating level of the organization (see Exhibit 1). Second, the desire of the vice president of purchases to have a highly placed staff man who was relieved of the pressure of day-to-day work resulted in some pressure on Mr. Brodie to devote time to advanced policy and requirements planning for the department. Third, the need to maintain the line authority of the assistant purchasing agents together with the large size of the buying department seemed to make direct contact inadvisable between Mr. Brodie and the buyers. Instead, it was decided that a description of any projects which the buyers were anxious to have investigated were to be submitted through channels to their purchasing agents and eventually to Mr. Lapham, the director of purchases. Under this plan, Mr. Lapham was then to select those projects he considered important and submit them to Mr. Brodie for investigation. Mr. Lapham thus acted as the program director for purchase research, using his key position in the department to assign problems he considered most essential to the organization. At the same time that projects were submitted to him from the buyers, Mr. Lapham also received notice of purchasing problems through his committee meetings with other executives in the company. For example, the manufacturing, the coal, and the appropriations committees met biweekly and the general superintendents' committee met bimonthly. Through these meetings and through the quarterly profit objective conferences, Mr. Lapham detected cost trends and materials management problems that could be investigated by Mr. Brodie.

Before coming to the purchasing department, Mr. Brodie had had considerable staff experience in the Model Aluminum Company. He had set up a sales evaluation system for the aluminum wire division and had spent two years in the finance department in the headquarters office. Mr. Lapham considered his broad staff experience throughout the company to be ideally suited for Mr. Brodie's new assignment and stated that it had taken almost two years to find the proper man for the job. Upon accepting the position, Mr. Brodie pointed out that he was new to purchasing and had no engineering training. For this reason, he preferred to work under the broadest possible definition of purchase research so that he could use his staff experience to advantage, rather than limiting his function to operating problems that might involve technical knowledge. "I'm not an operational man," he said, "I want the flexibility to develop anything that management feels should be developed to increase the control over purchases." Mr. Lapham agreed that it was best to let the new program undertake whatever projects seemed most promising during the first year without restricting the scope of its operations in advance. "This is a long-range project" said Mr. Lapham. "I don't expect results for more than a year. We'll let Brodie do whatever he wants and see by trial and error what the best kind of projects are. That way, he'll settle in through actual experience."

During the first six months in his new assignment and without the assistance of any personnel other than stenographic help, Mr. Brodie undertook five types of projects: (1) development of management systems and reports, (2) the establishment of a clearinghouse for purchasing information, (3) long-range economic commodity studies, (4) investigations into particular contract or product problems at the request of any of the 50 buyers, and (5) value analysis projects.

1. The development of management systems and reports required Mr. Brodie to determine what kinds of information useful to the supervision of the department could be assembled from the order processing system in current use. The general accounting division maintained a business machine department which processed invoices from IBM cards and submitted to Mr. Lapham summary reports of the dollar value of various purchase classifications. Mr. Brodie studied the code punched on the cards from the invoices and initiated two new reports using existing data: an inventory commitment report showing stocks on hand and on order for the six most important raw materials, together with

price changes from the previous month; and a supplier's market report, showing the percentage of the company's business given to each supplier in the most important categories of purchases. In addition, Mr. Brodie decided that the use of five-digit code on the IBM cards was inadequate to give a sufficiently close breakdown of purchases by category and dollar value. He therefore studied the advisability of using a nine-digit code for the major purchases so that studies could be made of the costs of alternate shipping containers, means of transportation, or premium grades of material with different physical or chemical properties.

2. Since Mr. Brodie believed that one objective of the purchase research function should be to establish communication between the buyers and the people outside their department whose work related to theirs, he began to accumulate published data about sources of supply. By reading through the important supplier industry magazines and house organs, he believed he could come across useful information about new product developments, the plant expansions of suppliers, and the market conditions in supplier industries. This information was to be published in a bulletin called *Vendors' Notes* and distributed to buying and other interested personnel.

3. Shortly after Mr. Brodie became manager, the sales department of one of the operating divisions had requested that a commodity study of sulfur be made by the market analysis department of the headquarters sales division. When the study was completed, a copy was submitted to Mr. Lapham who then suggested to Mr. Brodie that he personally undertake a similar study on a larger scale to investigate the zinc situation. When Mr. Brodie accepted the request, he had in mind a full-scale investigation of the mining companies' cost of production, the pricing practice of the industry, the long-range supply-demand trends and research into all factors in the international market that affected the commodity price.

4. Since Mr. Brodie wished to make the buyers feel that he was available for help, he sometimes undertook investigations directly for them if circumstances indicated that the project was not a difficult one. The established procedure, however, required that the buyers refer their requests for purchases research service through their purchasing agents to Mr. Lapham, who would then assign the projects to Mr. Brodie. Despite the variety of his research projects, therefore, Mr. Brodie had little personal contact with the 50 buyers. His most direct contact with them was to review the cost savings reports which the buyers submitted so as to evaluate their claims for cost reductions.

5. Although the buyers' cost savings reports indicated a variety of methods of making cost reductions, their principal emphasis was on negotiations with suppliers. Mr. Brodie wished to originate cost reductions of his own through value analysis projects requiring changes in specifications and designs. Mr. Brodie had received reports of metallur-

gical studies made by company engineers to determine the cost and performance characteristics of the various grades of ore which accounted for almost 60 percent of the annual purchases. Since he was not an engineer, however, it was difficult for him to participate in value analysis projects in highly technical areas such as metallurgy. Mr. Brodie therefore decided that a cost reduction program through the standardization of maintenance, repairs, and operating supplies would be less difficult to undertake without technical knowledge. For this reason, he selected as a test item the purchase of valves which accounted for $2 million of annual expenditures and began to evaluate the possibility of cost savings in a project that would eventually require supplier surveys and visits with requisitioning and using personnel throughout the corporation.

During his first seven months on the job, Mr. Brodie had spent a considerable amount of time in addition to working hours studying purchasing reports and developing the various projects he had started. He stated, "I can staff up eventually when I am sure what kind of assistance I need. What I've got to do now is to prove what the job can do by getting out some successful projects. When I've actually proved what can be done, it will be easy enough to get the help I need."

Mr. Brodie recognized that although the original objective of his job had been to make cost reductions in purchases, his value analyses were actually only a portion of the research projects. Part of this result, he believed was due to the difficulty of establishing effective contact between the buyers and the plant personnel who specified and used materials. He reasoned that value analysis could be effective only if cost and performance characteristics were investigated concurrently. The buyers, however, had little contact with the plant personnel. There were two groups in headquarters, however, who did have active contact with plant operations—the "consultant" engineers and the cost accountants.

Due to the highly technical nature of their work, it was difficult for Mr. Brodie to work closely with the engineers. The cost accountants, however, had effective access to the plants and could make the kind of analyses that Mr. Brodie wanted.

The accounting department of the Model Aluminum Corporation was the only one in which headquarters executives had both line authority over their field representatives in the plants and constant contact with them. As a management service group, the cost accountants often organized savings programs and evaluated the results of the projects. Many of the cost accountants were industrial engineers who could work directly with the operations problems facing plant personnel. In addition, the accounting headquarters maintained tabulating equipment with which to process complicated information from the field. For these reasons, the reports of the accounting department carried considerable weight with management executives and their evaluation of savings resulting from cost reduction programs were regarded as official.

Both Mr. Lapham and Mr. Brodie believed that the purchase research function would have to be defined more precisely as soon as the results of its initial programs could be evaluated. Mr. Brodie believed that the most important problem currently facing the development of value analysis was the need to establish close working relationships with the personnel who defined materials specifications and those who used the delivered supplies. Since his early attempt to make use of the facilities of the accounting department to establish contact with the plants had thus far met with indifferent success, he hoped to increase their interest in value analysis in the future. One possible solution, he believed, was to help organize a companywide cost reduction program under the supervision of the accounting department in which purchasing personnel could participate. On the other hand, a program of such magnitude might be difficult to organize without help from key executives in other departments. Mr. Brodie was not sure whether the relationship he needed could best be established by a companywide cost reduction program, by committee relationships through the senior executives, or through the slow development of informal contacts between himself and the accounting supervisors. As the scope of purchase research increased, Mr. Brodie felt the need to be more pressing to obtain personnel to assist him. On the other hand, he believed that until such problems were resolved as his relationship with the accounting department and a definition of the type and extent of value analysis projects that should be made, it was impossible to determine what kind of personnel should be hired to assist in the program.

GENERAL ELECTRIC COMPANY*

In 1948 Larry D. Miles was assigned the task of organizing a value analysis service for the purchasing operations of the General Electric Company. Within six months he and his assistant had worked out the elements of a method of analysis to reduce the price of purchased subassemblies through design changes in the blueprints and specifications. For the next five years the principal effort of Mr. Miles and his staff was directed to the problem of developing value analysis throughout the corporation from headquarters without exercising direct supervision over divisional operations.

The value analysis assignment had originated in 1948 through the "consulting" function that headquarters purchasing executives often assumed. Due to the great scope and diversity of the General Electric Company's activities, operating responsibility had been delegated to the 80 divisional managers throughout the United States. The divisional managers were responsible for hiring personnel, establishing new product designs, and maintaining their sales volume and profit. It was the policy of the headquarters purchasing group not to exercise either direct or functional control over the divisional purchasing departments, so as not to undermine the authority of the divisional managers. However, due to the great scope of the procurement activities, the purchasing department maintained both operating and staff personnel at headquarters to assist divisional purchasing personnel when necessary. The 40 headquarters buyers purchased materials such as steel, copper, aluminum, lumber, and chemicals that were common to most divisions, and they undertook long-range studies of the supply and demand prospects of the most important materials. The headquarters purchasing office compiled information on new materials and processes from trade publications and from disseminating bulletins on government orders affecting price and allocation of critical materials. There were also a number of staff specialists in the general headquarters office who could assist the divisions in matters such as packaging, tooling, space utilization, and engineering plant layout. The senior executives of the headquarters purchasing department established materials management policies for the entire corporation and made appraisals of the divisional purchasing operations at the invitation of the divisional managers. In the course of these appraisals, headquarters purchasing executives often made special services available to the divisions.

In visiting divisional plants during 1947, headquarters purchasing executives had noted a number of cases in which purchase prices could be reduced through changes in the quality of materials specified for procurement. For example, a buyer at one division had been unable to obtain sufficient quantities of asbestos. Certain production foremen were quick to register complaints about the shortage to the divisional management. When the problem was investigated in detail, it was found that the asbestos was used solely as a nonburning floor covering to catch paint drippings. Conferences with paper suppliers revealed that many types of nonburning paper were readily available at a much lower cost than asbestos. The plant safety engineer refused to accept a paper substitute, however, because fire regulations specifically required asbestos. Fire department representatives were then invited to a special demonstration of the nonburning paper provided by the supplier's sales engineers. Since the test proved conclusively that certain nonburning papers were safe for use in the plant, the fire regulations were subsequently revised to allow the substitution to be made, and the purchase price of floor covering was substantially reduced.

Examples such as that of the asbestos floor covering convinced headquarters executives that considerable savings could be made in the price of purchased materials if specialists were available to devote their full attention to the proper specification of materials. The headquarters purchasing office decided to assign an experienced man to the problem of value analysis to determine the analytical methods that could be developed, the extent of the potential savings, and the kind of facilities that could be made available to assist the divisions. Larry Miles, a purchasing agent in the headquarters office, was asked to explore the problem on a provisional basis early in 1948.

Mr. Miles was an experienced mechanical engineer and had worked for many years as a designer of technical products before transferring to the purchasing department. He immediately selected as an assistant a methods man who was familiar with shop practice and could deal with practical production problems. Rather than working with new products at an early stage of design, Mr. Miles decided to make an intensive examination of a complete purchased assembly already on the market and ready for larger volume production. There were three reasons for this approach: (1) modification of a completed assembly would give a clear-cut cost comparison between the price of a typical unit as designed and purchased through the regular divisional organization and as modified by an independent group who could evaluate design and procurement factors concurrently; (2) Mr. Miles and his assistant were technically trained personnel interested in the details of component specifications and assembly methods; and (3) Mr. Miles believed that to be of service to the divisions, a headquarters analysis staff had to make specific suggestions after intensive study of a single project rather than working with general cost trends and summary statistics.

The first product analysis occupied several months while Mr. Miles and his assistant made detailed investigation of the blueprints and specifications of each component part, interviewed new vendors, and visited buyers, design engineers, and salesmen connected with the original assembly. The product contained 115 component parts, and design modifications were suggested on 35 of them. Exhibit 1 is a page of the final report illustrating the suggested changes in procurement of one of the components. The complete report was submitted to the divisional manager responsible for the product, with the understanding that the conclusions would be considered advisory only and that no subsequent follow-through action would be taken by headquarters. The divisional manager then assigned to his own engineers and buyers the task of deciding which suggestions would be incorporated in the new design. Meanwhile, Mr. Miles used the project to demonstrate to the headquarter's buyers at a three-month series of weekly meetings the kind of methods that he and his assistant had developed to analyze product value.

By the fall of 1948, therefore, the value analysis division had been able to demonstrate a method of cost reduction through design modification. The method had three principal characteristics: (1) it emphasized design changes rather than price reductions through negotiations with suppliers; (2) it attacked the technical problem of product performance

Exhibit 1

February 14, 1948

Elbow Assembly
K-5002520 G1
26, 400 used per year (CW2 and CW3)

	Cost/C		
	Material	Labor	Shop Cost
Present	$10.26	$1.11	$14.79 incl. K-5043630-2 flare nut
Potential	4.90		5.25

Comments:

1. A vendor quotes the above price for a straight fitting instead of an elbow. The fitting would have a self-flaring feature, eliminating the separate flare nut since the nut is part of the fitting. The straight fitting can be used if a 1/8″ tube is used on the control instead of two-diameter tube.

2. Another vendor quotes on a standard straight flare fitting with orifice as follows:

$$\begin{array}{lr}
30,000 \text{ lots.} \dots \dots \dots \dots & \$2.25/C \\
10,000 \text{ lots.} \dots \dots \dots \dots & 3.90 \\
5,000 \text{ lots.} \dots \dots \dots \dots & 5.00 \\
2,000 \text{ lots.} \dots \dots \dots \dots & 8.25
\end{array}$$

This fitting requires flare nut 5043630 P2 at a material cost of $4.28/C which must be added to the above prices to compare with the present costs as listed. No tool charge is involved in either quotation.

Expected Effective Date:

Record of Actual Cost Decreases:

    Date   New Shop Cost   Reduction

If Not Adopted: Why and by whom found unsuitable.

Purchasing Department
Value Analysis Division

---

so as to grasp the opportunity of using completely different materials to meet the underlying quality requirements; (3) it made considerable use of specialty suppliers who could quote lower prices by employing their own machine tools or production techniques. The problem that then had to be solved was to determine the function of a central value analysis staff in the headquarters purchasing office of General Electric Company.

The initial project had demonstrated that considerable time and effort was necessary to accomplish results with a single project. The magnitude of the analysis task, together with a policy of decentralization, made it obviously undesirable to organize product modification under a large headquarters group equipped to investigate all major products of the corporation. Two other alternatives remained: the analysis staff could act as a consulting service available to make selected studies whenever the divisional managers chose to use it; or it could act as a central training unit to develop value analysis staffs within the divisions.

The consulting type of service was frequently requested by the divisions during 1948. For example, in September, 1948, the Cleveland division became concerned over the prospect of excessive cost for television tube components for 1949 because market demand was then increasing far more quickly than the technical and production facilities of suppliers. The divisional manager estimated an extra cost of $4 million due to excessive handling, almost 50 percent rejects, and inadequate equipment for the 600,000 tubes annually required by the company. The price of the glass envelopes was considered to be far too high since the raw materials costs constituted only 10 percent of the purchase price. The divisional buyers, however, had been unable to reduce the price by negotiation due to the lack of additional suppliers, the shortage of envelopes, and the increasing cost of new capital equipment needed by the suppliers to expand their production.

At a meeting with the president of one of the suppliers, Mr. Miles and the divisional executives learned that the efficiency of glass tube production was low principally because the glass company lacked knowledge of television tube requirements while the General Electric engineers lacked knowledge of glassmaking problems. The value analysis division was, therefore, invited to investigate the cost of the elements of production. The investigation revealed that the most substantial savings would occur if the glass components could be purchased separately from the suppliers and sealed within the General Electric plant where the electronic engineers could develop specifications suited to tube requirements in close conjunction with the mechanical engineers who designed high-speed production equipment. The resulting production analysis and the larger production runs subsequently convinced the suppliers that they could reduce their unit prices one half, and the projected sealing program promised further savings of 40 percent.

It therefore became evident in 1949 that central value analysis could serve those divisions requesting help for major projects provided that headquarters analysts were careful not to antagonize the operating personnel who subsequently had to work out the decisions made. One particular advantage of this system seemed to be that intensive product analysis from a fresh point of view could often reopen negotiations with suppliers that seemed to be at an impasse. In addition, the headquarters analysts could act as a liaison group to help the divisional manager bring together the buyer, engineers, salesmen, and production foremen who might otherwise work independently. On the other hand, the time and effort necessarily consumed in the television tube project indicated the limited number of projects that a small group in headquarters could undertake by itself unless the analysts used took the opportunity to train divisional personnel.

As constituted in 1949, the headquarters value analysis group changed its emphasis somewhat. It acted as a consulting service but began to use its facilities primarily to interest divisional managers in the program and to train their personnel to do analysis work in the plants. Although the value analysis group was subsequently requested to undertake major projects for the primary purpose of making cost reductions on a particular product, the policy of the group was to use these projects as far as possible to train new men in the methods of analysis and to attract wider interest in value analysis throughout the corporation. Mr. Miles employed three methods of increasing the training value of central value analysis: (1) personal interviews to interest divisional managers in participating in his program; (2) training selected divisional personnel through detailed product modifications at the headquarters value analysis office; and (3) disseminating materials information both to divisional engineers and trained value analysts.

In dealing with the divisional manager, Mr. Miles felt he had to demonstrate the service his staff could provide, while taking little more advantage of his position in headquarters purchasing than if he represented an independent consulting company. He often telephoned a divisional manager to ask for an hour of his time to prove the extent of cost savings through value analysis. During his presentation he would demonstrate value analysis through examples of cost savings made on other projects, using product samples to illustrate certain design changes. He would then explain that the objective of the program was to train personnel with a technical background to form a value analysis group in the divisional purchasing departments to suggest design modifications of their products. Mr. Miles would then ask the divisional manager to select a project for analysis, preferably a product already marketed and ready for design changes to eliminate "bugs," simplify construction, or use special manufacturing equipment for large volume production. If the divisional manager agreed to the proposal, he would select one of his men to be sent to headquarters for three-months' training with Mr. Miles's group, using a divisional product as a sample for value analysis.

By 1950 Mr. Miles had three trained analysts assigned to his headquarters group, each of whom worked with a trainee for three months on a divisional product. Mr. Miles could, therefore, train a maximum of 12 analysts per year by this means. He therefore limited the training to one project from each divisions, to expand the program into as many divisions as possible until there were a sufficient number of analysts throughout the corporation. During the training period his men were allowed to travel anywhere, talk to any engineer or buyer from whom they could receive useful information, and discuss manufacturing and design problems with any vendor whom they believed could be of assistance. When the project was finished, each component on which specification changes were proposed was described in detail, showing the suggested revisions, the proposed suppliers, and the dollar value of the potential savings. The analyst then returned to his division and submitted the suggestions for the regular operating personnel to approve or disapprove. Mr. Miles made it a policy not to follow up these suggestions from headquarters, nor to inquire into the working problems of the value analysts in the divisions, nor to keep records indicating the cost savings resulting from headquarters initiative.

The major influence of headquarters on divisional value analysis was through the dissemination of publications especially prepared by Mr. Miles's group for the use of operating personnel. "New Materials News" (see Exhibit 2), which was a monthly six-page notice of new technical developments available through suppliers, was distributed to design engineers throughout the corporation to keep them informed of new materials specifications. "Value News" (Exhibit 3) was a single sheet distributed weekly to engineering, purchasing, and production personnel dramatizing cost savings resulting from analysis methods to interest them in supporting the divisional value analysts. The headquarters set up an exhibition room containing company products illustrating different degrees of purchase value as well as vendor samples of new materials or components such as special fastenings, alloys, and plastics. The exhibits were used both to demonstrate efficient product design to visitors and to prepare slides for illustrated talks to be used for training and promotional purposes. Mr. Miles's group had two main sources for such information on new materials. One source was salesmen's presentations, which were often made to the headquarters analysts for subsequent publicity throughout the corporation. The other was the information supplied by headquarters specialists in tool design, packaging, and the cataloging of trade magazine information. This information was used increasingly to release public information describing the value analysis program. Articles were written for such publications as the *General Electric Review*, the *Monogram* (the company magazine of the Canadian General Electric Company, Ltd.), *The American Machinist*, and for *Purchasing* magazine. Mr. Miles himself gave many illustrated lectures to purchasing agents' association meetings and to business or engineering college classes, and served on the committee of the National Association of Purchasing Agents that published the bulletin, *Cutting Costs by Analyzing Values*.

In 1952, the value analysis program had attracted enough attention to interest divisional managers in sending more trainees than Mr. Miles's three-man staff could work with personally at headquarters. The group therefore stopped all projects for one month and assembled a class of 60 men for a formal training course. Although the value analysts were

Exhibit 2

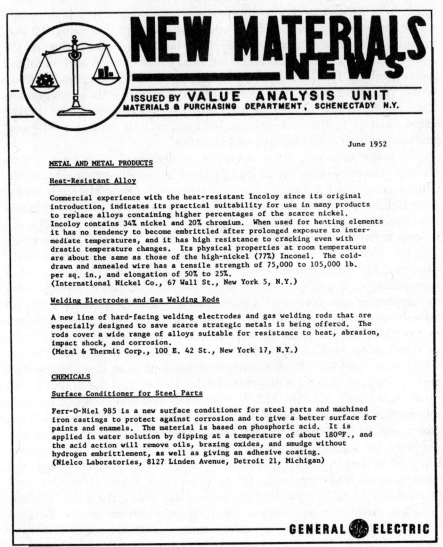

to be assigned to divisional purchasing departments, the trainees were largely design engineers and shop methods men rather than buyers. One method used to demonstrate value analysis was class discussion of a previous analysis project, such as the one made of a single pivot pin ⅜ inch in length. The price of the pin, which was a single component of the Telechron clock, had been reduced from $3.45 per thousand to $1.79. The method of investigation, as presented to the training class, is described in Exhibit 4.

Exhibit 3

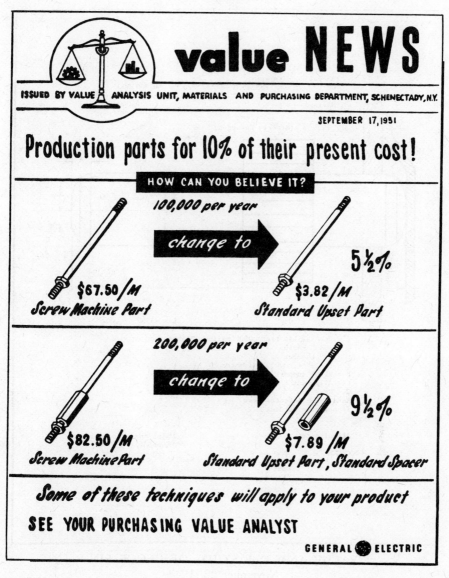

By March, 1953, most of the effort of the central value analysis division was devoted to training divisional analysts. By the end of the year, it was expected that 120 men would have received the class training and 25 men the in-station training directly with Mr. Miles's staff. Although he disseminated information about new materials as often as possible to the divisional analysts, Mr. Miles considered it to be a basic policy of the division neither to keep summary figures indicating the

Exhibit 4

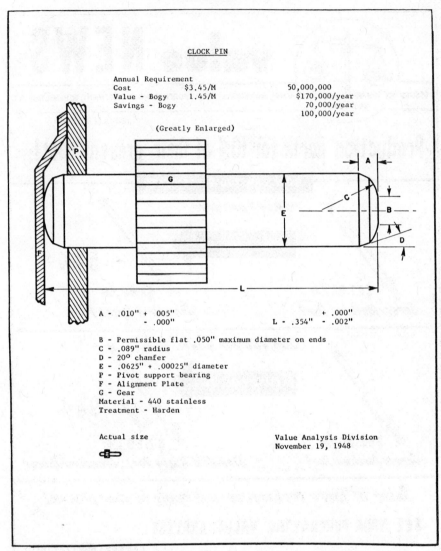

CLOCK PIN

Annual Requirement
Cost $3.45/M   50,000,000
Value - Bogy 1.45/M $170,000/year
Savings - Bogy   70,000/year
                               100,000/year

(Greatly Enlarged)

A - .010" + .005"   + .000"
          - .000"   L - .354" - .002"

B - Permissible flat .050" maximum diameter on ends
C - .089" radius
D - 20° chamfer
E - .0625" + .00025" diameter
P - Pivot support bearing
F - Alignment Plate
G - Gear
Material - 440 stainless
Treatment - Harden

Actual size   Value Analysis Division
                           November 19, 1948

VALUE ANALYSIS STUDY OF CLOCK PIN
November 22, 1948

Questions raised by the discussion group and tentative answers, to be reviewed with the product engineer.

1. Why does it cost $3.65 instead of $1.45 per M?
   Because of the ±0.001″ length tolerance, the 2½ tenths *OD* tolerance, the chamfer-radius-end construction, the 440 stainless steel, and the hardening.

2. What purpose does the pin serve?
   It is the pivot used to support the pinions and gears in the electric clock. Several of them are used in each clock.

Exhibit 4 (*Continued*)

3. How is it made now?

    We don't know exactly. We do know that it is cut off too long and is made of material over the desired diameter. Then, after hardening, the ends are ground to length, and the *OD* is ground to size. The vendor says there are 12 operations in the making of this pin.

4. Could the entire unit be made smaller in order to save material on all parts?

    We don't know, we'll ask that of the engineer.

5. How is the gear put on to the pin?

    Pressed on. The pinions are made from thin laminated carbon steel which are blanked in a small punch press and pressed directly on to the pin. Gears and pinions are held in place by friction with the pin.

6. Why is stainless used?

    To avoid corrosion.

7. How much does the stainless material only cost?

    $0.45 per M pieces.

8. How much would carbon steel cost?

    Around $0.10 per M.

9. Why use No. 440 stainless which is twice as hard to machine as the others?

    Because it has 100 points of carbon and can be satisfactorily hardened.

10. Why harden it?

    In pressing on the tight gears and pinions, the surface is sometimes otherwise slightly scored and, unfortunately, on the pin this is the bearing surface so that it provides a very poor bearing surface with erratic and short life. The sole function of the hardening is to avoid damage to the pin surface while the gears are being pressed on. Since the pins are running in copper bearings, it is felt that the steel would be sufficiently hard for good bearing operations even without hardening.

11. If the gears are carbon steel and they do not corrode or rust, why would the pins?

    That is something we don't quite understand—we have tried carbon steel for the pins and it does corrode. The gears are made of a very thin cold rolled steel, and it seems probable that the supplier must use some rust inhibitor in his process which is good enough. If we acid clean, or otherwise thoroughly clean the pinion steel, they too will rust.

12. Why chamfer *D*?

    To provide entry into the gear.

13. Why chamfer both ends?

    To save labor. Otherwise each pin must be picked up and examined before it is used to locate it with proper end up.

14. Why the flat *B*?

    The flat presses against the end plate and locates the pin axially. It is desirable for the flat surface to be a minimum in order to reduce end friction.

15. Why the radius *C*?

    The radius is for the purpose of connecting the chamfer to the flat.

Exhibit 4 (*Continued*)

16. Why have both the chamfer *D* and the radius *C* when the combined length of both is 0.010 and may, within tolerances, be as little as 0.005"?
A chamfer or suitable radius is necessary to provide entry into the gear and a small end bearing surface is necessary to limit end friction. We presume that the other details best fit into the manufacturing arrangement of the supplier who helped to work it out. A desirable end from this viewpoint would be a semispherical surface. However, such surface would extend clear back into the bearing *P* and eliminate the cylindrical portion which is now the bearing surface.

17. Why only ±0.001" on the length tolerance when it is observed from actual assembly that there is an end plate of around 0.015" on each pin?
We are advised that due to the build-up of tolerances there may be friction between gear faces if more than 0.001" is allowed. We are further advised that the tolerance on the studs which separate the end plates is ±2" and that if it were more economical to hold them to a closer tolerance than the pins, the tolerances might be reversed allowing ±0.002" on the pin and making the stud to ±0.001" without adversely affecting the assembly.

18. Why only 2½ tenths diameter tolerance?
To provide dependable interference fit when mounting the gears and pinions.

19. There are other ways of providing the features which have been discussed. In general what prompted this particular design?
We understand that the part has quite a history, that it was made by ourselves and possibly others, but one vendor showed particular interest in an aptitude for the job and it is probable that some of the design details are prescribed to coincide with his manufacturing processes.

20. Can wire be purchased to the diameter tolerance required?
Yes.

21. Will automatic screw machines cut it off to ±0.001" length tolerance?
Probably not. We would expect ±0.003 from them.

22. How close will wire forming equipment shear it into length?
Good equipment will hold ±0.002".

23. Why not cut it off on a form cutter which will provide in one operation the necessary chamfer radius and end flat?
It might work—the problem would be to cut it off to the tolerance of ±0.001" and the maintenance of the form cutter.

24. Some cutoff methods would normally leave a small tip in the center—wouldn't it be desirable to do so?
We would expect so providing the tip was close enough controlled so that the distance from end to end of the tips would come within the length tolerance.

25. I believe that an abrasive cutoff machine can be obtained which will cut to a tolerance of ±0.001". Why not use it and tumble the parts to provide the necessary radius for entry into the gear?
Let's determine if such a machine is available. There are certain problems. Ordinarily such a part tumbled before hardening would secure

Exhibit 4 (*Concluded*)

a slight dumbbell shape at the end which would cause looseness of the gears after they have been pressed on. The tumbling might be done after hardening but would be slower and a somewhat different operation. We have a most outstanding tumbling laboratory in West Lynn, however, and they advise that they believe they could prescribe a tumbling cycle which would not produce a dumbbell effect.

26. If the wire is bought to exact diameter tolerance, hardening becomes a problem. Could it be gas hardened or hardened in some other manner which did not produce discoloration or other undesirable surface conditions on the material?
   We don't know. That should be investigated.

27. We have one supplier who is doing such a spectacular job to millions of small parts somewhat similar to this. Don't you believe that if we put the problem up to him and went into these details with him that he would find a way to do it for around $1 or $1.50 per M?
   Possibly—we'll try it.

Value Analysis Division
Purchasing Department

results of central value analysis projects nor to evaluate the effectiveness of the divisional analysts once they had graduated from his program. For this reason, despite the growing number of value analysts working in the divisional plants, no attempt was made by the experienced analysts in headquarters to help solve the organizational problems involved in establishing analysis groups in the divisions.

WAYFARER BOARD OF EDUCATION

Introduction

Mr. G. Feltar, controller of purchasing for the Wayfarer Board of Education, was concerned about the impact of the four-year-old budget control system on his supply operations.

He was occasionally criticized by the schools for slow deliveries and red tape but considered that his department was being faulted, not by its own inefficiency, but rather by the intricate controls he had to enforce.

Decreasing enrollments had led to budget cuts, and the board deemed tight control over purchases to be a critical factor in its fight to conserve funds.

Although most educational expenditures were determined by the state a large item over which the board exercised complete discretion was the $9 million purchasing budget. Approximately one third was spent on equipment and two thirds on general supplies.

The board was one of the largest in the state of Indiana, employing 3,000 teachers, 700 support staff, and operating 70 elementary and 15 secondary schools.

The budget year

The budget year ran from January 1 to December 31. However, the annual budget was not approved by the board until early March, causing a rush of orders in March. At that time most departments start ordering materials, especially equipment and supplies for elective programs such as a school's new camera club. Another rush occurred in November when the final purchases were requested to finish the budgets for that year. A third rush of orders was in June when teachers ordered everything to be ready for the next school year, September 1.

In January, Mr. Feltar received board approval to buy 75 percent of last year's annual budget for general supplies. This allowed him to purchase between then and March 1. This 75 percent, however, did not include equipment. Many items were once-only purchases which required the annual budget approval before they could be bought. The budget did vary substantially from year to year. Last year, for example, no equipment purchases were allowed. It was impossible under this system to buy on next year's budget before January 1 or carry over an unused budget amount into the following year. During these peak order times there was virtually no prompt delivery. If a principal telephoned and asked where his purchase order was in the process, or whether or not an order would be approved by the computer in time for him to switch it to another budget, Mr. Feltar often could not answer since he could not readily locate the order.

Purchasing at the board

Each school had numerous budgets, sometimes totaling fifty or more. Mr. Feltar came in contact primarily with the custodial, furniture, physical education, science, commercial, vocational and general supply budgets. His department (see Exhibit 1) handled all the actual purchases. All custodial, physical education, and some general supplies were shipped to the central warehouse. The remaining supplies were sent directly to the schools. The services which acted as courier for the schools' mail, delivering it to the post office or the administrative offices, would also distribute warehouse supplies. Most mail arrived every second day from secondary schools and twice a week from elementary schools, varying in some degree with the size of the school.

The warehouse, with an inventory of $150,000 made up primarily

Exhibit 1
WAYFARER BOARD OF EDUCATION

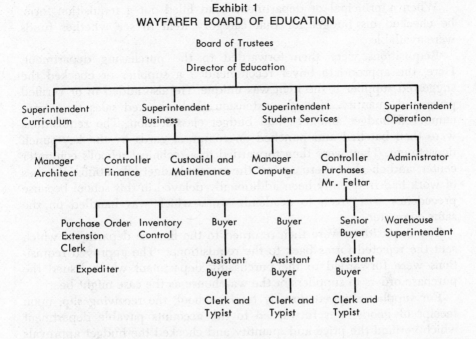

of standard school supplies, also handled special physical education and art equipment which schools could use on a loan basis. The warehouse provided prompt delivery on standard items and to some degree allowed purchasing to buy in economical quantities. Generally, delivery time from the warehouse was two weeks. Mr. Feltar thought ideally this should be one week.

The schools received weekly and, at times, daily printouts on how they stood in regard to their budgets, but still about 2 percent-5 percent of the purchase orders were rejected due to lack of funds.

Sometimes it was necessary to make budget transfers. All budget transfers had to be approved at the Board of Trustees' meeting. If a transfer involved more than $1,000, approval had to be obtained before any action was initiated, but transfers under $1,000 were automatically approved at the next regular board meeting. A principal could resubmit a previously rejected requisition with a new budget number, noting the transfer status of the item.

The purchasing procedure

A budget committee of the Board of Trustees determined yearly the per student expenditure for supplies and allocated dollar appropriations for replacement and purchase of capital equipment. The resulting guidelines were then discussed and approved by the board's trustees.

When a principal or department head filled out a requisition form, he checked his budget for that category item to see whether funds were available.

Requisitions were then forwarded to the purchasing department. Here, the appropriate buyer recommended a supplier or checked the suggested supplier if the item was unique. He also added in or verified price and quantity. Next the extension clerk checked sales tax, unencumbered budget amounts, and budget classification. The requisitions were then batched and punched on computer cards by the key-punch department. They were then forwarded to a technical school's computer center, and checked there against the master budget allocations. Batches of work had frequently been additionally delayed in this school because precedence was given to academic work which was handled on the same computer.

The requisitions were then returned to the finance department which sent the rejected forms back to the requisitioner. The approved requisitions were forwarded to the purchasing department which issued the purchase orders to suppliers or the warehouse as the case might be.

For supplies shipped directly to the school, the receiving slip, upon receipt of goods, was forwarded to the accounts payable department which verified the price and quantity and checked the budget approvals on the purchase order. Most invoices were paid promptly and all discounts taken. Mr. Feltar had, however, encountered situations where "When am I going to get my money?" arose. If he had helped a principal by ordering before budget approval was obtained and the service or goods had been delivered, the supplier had to wait until a budget transfer was completed.

Normally, the purchase cycle with suppliers took three weeks. At the end of the budget year this increased to five weeks. A tracer was sent out if an order was misplaced or the supplier did not ship. If a teacher complained about slow delivery, a tracer was also used.

Mr. Feltar explained that it was extremely difficult to locate orders. The purchasing department handled 33,000 purchase orders and 7,000 warehouse releases. The board had approximately 1,000 suppliers. Sixty percent of the dollar purchases were called on tender, taking the form of yearly contracts. In a recent computer survey of 10,000 purchase orders, 20 percent were under $10.00; 39 percent under $25.00; 56 percent under $50.00 and 72 percent under $100.00. Of these 10,000 orders, 2,200 were between $100.00 and $500.00 per order.

Areas of concern

Everyone in the purchasing department was under considerable pressure to live up to the "service department" expectation that the rest of the board held of purchasing. Mr. Feltar had to handle frequent "misunderstandings" between finance clerks, key-punch operators, and purchasing personnel, including the purchase order extension clerk. These "misunderstandings" were becoming more personal and created at times an unpleasant atmosphere. Mr. Feltar recognized that some of these difficulties were a direct result of the budgetary system and had introduced a number of ideas to alleviate the strain.

Mr. Feltar believed that the large number of purchase orders could be reduced, thereby decreasing the purchase order cycle time. He devised a mini-order system for school principals who would fill out the mini-order and send it directly to a supplier with a copy to the purchasing department. These were to be used only for small-dollar and low-quantity items which were not carried in the board's warehouse. Mr. Feltar had had little success from these mini-orders. Their usage was low and when they were used they were applied incorrectly. Mr. Feltar thought the users did not familiarize themselves enough with the orders. The users said they saw little advantage in using them.

In the past all requisition forms had the purchase order number printed upon them. If a principal phoned the purchasing department for approval he could use a requisition and subsequently quote its number to a supplier. If a budget problem occurred later, purchasing was stuck. Mr. Feltar now proposed to dispense with prenumbered requisition forms, forcing principals to phone him for a purchase order number and resulting approval.

Another area of concern was the increased use of petty cash. Under the prevailing system, a school had up to $150 in cash for small emergencies. A minimum dollar requirement per receipt was set at $10.00. Once the money was used up, the receipts were totaled and forwarded to the finance department. The petty cash would then be replenished. No fixed yearly amount was set as long as there were funds available in the user's budget. Mr. Feltar realized that if a school needed some supplies in a hurry it would resort to using petty cash. This resulted in paying the generally higher retail price. Provincial sales tax was also paid on purchases which could have been avoided if handled on the board's purchase orders.

With the warehouse superintendent reporting directly to Mr. Feltar, a request for items that were in stock could be, if necessary, expedited quickly. Mr. Feltar, after receiving an urgent request, would telephone the order through and let the paper work "catch-up." This "special" expediting involved risks to Mr. Feltar. If it was early in the year, the paper work would certainly receive budget approval, but as the year progressed and the budgets approached their ceilings, the required approvals would become more uncertain. The time delays encountered in schools obtaining their supplies were generally lengthening. The paperwork was taking three to five weeks to complete its cycle. On the whole, the warehouse delivery could not be reduced from two weeks since all orders had to go through the computer system. Thus, depending upon the time of year and the delivery from suppliers, time estimates for receiving goods were unreliable. Moreover, supplies for school programs seemed always to be required "yesterday."

Cooperation and individual school priorities were ever-present hurdles to cross. Mr. Feltar would at times try to help a principal find a budget in some other school to cover an essential request. However, this was a difficult and delicate thing to carry out.

Mr. Feltar was convinced that the service image of his department was slipping in the schools (see Exhibit 2), but he could not easily define what actions to take or recommendations to make to remedy this.

Exhibit 2

Secondary school teachers complained about a lack of trust and consultation by administration, expressing a desire to influence decisions regarding academic standards, examination policy, pupil-teacher ratios as well as curriculum matters.

They expressed harsh dissatisfaction with the business services department of the board, particularly the purchasing system, contending that bureaucratic delays and tight budgeting procedures are often harmful to their programs.

They also charged the administration with encouraging too much permissiveness both in discipline and educational standards. Most would like to see schools offer a more structured approach to education than is found at present with regard both to discipline and standards.

The main thrust of secondary school teachers' opinion, the report says, favors decentralizing administrative and decision-making processes, bringing them as far as possible to the individual school.

Administrators surveyed agreed that the school should be regarded as the key operational unit in the system, recognized that up-dating of teachers should be part of the normal working day of the teacher, and proposed a continuous program in human relations for all personnel.

Source: Taken from the *Wayfarer Journal*, October 31, 1972.

M.E.C. CORPORATION

In early March, 1974, Mr. Jack Allison, assistant manager of purchasing and traffic department, was made responsible for administering the purchasing savings program for the following year by Mr. Robert Cochrane, the department manager, who was due to retire in the near future. The savings program had been in effect for a number of years without change, and Jack Allison wondered if the 1973 savings of some $150,000 on an eligible outlay of $12 million could not be considerably improved. Therefore, he instituted a review of methods, procedures, and attitudes to determine what course to adopt for the coming year.

M.E.C. Corporation was part of a large conglomerate which had been formed in 1966. M.E.C. produced a wide range of electrical products for the measurement and control of industrial processes. M.E.C. had started in 1926 and had been privately owned until 1966. It had an excellent reputation for quality in the trade. M.E.C. operated with a high degree of autonomy. The conglomerate's corporate headquarters were primarily concerned with financial planning. M.E.C.'s sales totaled about $30 million in 1973 and were expected to reach $40 million by 1976. M.E.C. was divided into two sales divisions, industrial and utilities. Each accounted for about half of total sales.

Purchasing at M.E.C.

Total purchases at M.E.C. were about 40 percent of sales and were the responsibility of Mr. Cochrane, director of purchases, who had been in his post for 22 years. Mr. Cochrane planned to retire in July, 1975, and had recently brought in Jack Allison, an engineer, who had previously worked in quality control and design at M.E.C. There were two purchasing agents and six buyers. For production purchases the department was organized into the same divisions as corporate sales: industrial and utilities (see Exhibit 1 for organization chart). Production purchases in-

Exhibit 1
M.E.C. CORPORATION
(organization chart)

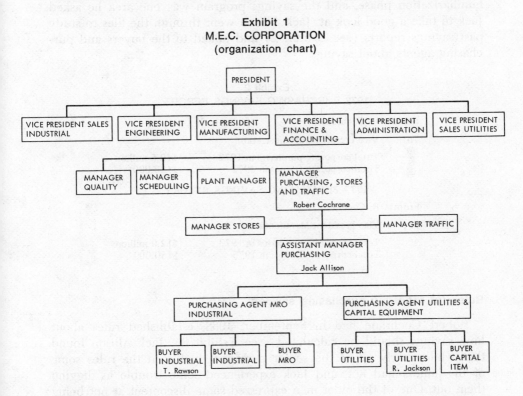

cluded raw materials like copper, steel, aluminum, and purchased parts like castings, stampings, and a wide variety of electrical and electronic items.

In April, 1973, the vice president of manufacturing took over responsibility for purchasing from the vice president administration who claimed that personnel and industrial relations matters prevented him from giving the purchasing function the necessary time.

Robert Cochrane told his assistant that before 1973 when he responded to the vice president administration, his reports of total savings realized used to elicit little interest.

"I think they do some cash flow projections up top," said the department manager casually, "but I guess our small savings are not that important. At any rate, they've never asked for savings forecasts. However, I think that the vice president of manufacturing will show more practical enthusiasm."

Savings in purchasing

Jack Allison had been given complete freedom to become acquainted with all facets of the purchasing operation. Robert Cochrane had thought it useful to give a few specific projects to Jack to work on during his familiarization phase, and the savings program was one area he asked Jack to take a good look at. Jack Allison went through the files to study past savings reports (see Exhibit 2) and talked to the buyers and purchasing agents about savings.

Exhibit 2
1972 PURCHASING SAVINGS REPORT

From: R. Cochrane

To: Vice President Administration

Total corporate purchases in 1972	$10.5 million
Total corporate savings in 1972	$120,000

1973 PURCHASING SAVINGS REPORT

From: R. Cochrane

To: Vice President Manufacturing

Total corporate purchases in 1973	$12.0 million
Total corporate savings in 1973	$150,000

Rules for reporting purchasing savings

Robert Cochrane had in September, 1968, established rules about how savings should be calculated (see Exhibit 3). Jack Allison found that while nearly all of the senior personnel had seen the rules some of the juniors had not, and Jack experienced some trouble in digging them out. One of the older men expressed some discontent at not being able to claim savings for more than one year ("They're still real enough after 12 months," he growled), but few held any strong opinions on

Exhibit 3
RULES FOR REPORTING PURCHASING SAVINGS

1. The material must have been purchased before.
2. Savings apply to orders placed within the calendar year under consideration.
3. Savings due to mixed contribution by purchasing and the personnel of other departments may not be claimed by the buying staff.
4. Savings are: *a.* The improvement over the old unit price multiplied by the projected annual usage at the time the first new order is placed, less tooling investment, if any.
   b. On indirect material where no forecast is available, utilize the one-time saving and any reorders in the same calender year.
5. Savings may not be carried beyond one year. If a one-time, several-year commitment is made, credit may be claimed for the first year's estimated consumption.
6. Savings reports for the current calendar year must be submitted to me prior to January 31.[1] of the next year.

R. Cochrane,
Manager, Purchasing, Stores,
and Traffic

Date: September, 1968.

[1] M.E.C. Corporation's financial year-end was at the end of February.

---

them. One man said cynically that he doubted whether such reports were even read. "Has management heard of purchasing?" he inquired innocently. One of the purchasing agents thought that avoidance of cost increases through negotiation should also be included.

Savings report forms

Jack Allison studied the slender file of forms from previous years and discussed one of the cases (see Exhibit 4) with Mr. Cochrane. He mentioned that there were no supporting documents attached and wondered to what extent the claims were checked.

"Oh, the divisional buyers have a pretty good idea of what's what," said the manager, "so I never required them to clutter up their claims with a lot of documentation. However, as you know, all savings must be due to their efforts only. It's purchasing skills I'm demonstrating."

Jack Allison discussed the same savings report with T. Rawson, the buyer who had submitted it. "Would we work closely with production scheduling in such instances?" he asked. "For example, where did the consumption forecast come from?"

Rawson assured him that previous orders gave him a good idea of standard usage as it was a repetitive item, and that was how they usually derived their annual consumption for calculating claims. Of course,

Exhibit 4
BUYER'S SAVINGS REPORT

Division ___SERVO___   Date: August 21/73

1. M. E. C. part number: 15723

2. Description: 9V Nickel Battery Enclosure

3. Yearly usage: 240,000

4. Purchase order no. (if applicable)   S54754-1010

5. Savings Accomplished:
    Previous price: 93.6¢
    New unit price: 72.0¢
    Savings per unit: 21.6¢
    Savings this order: $51,840
    Savings per year: $51,840

6. How Was Saving Accomplished?
    Through the efforts of Ralph Jackson and myself placing orders simultaneously to
    earn the next price break and going a little long (with Division's agreement) on
    inventory.

7. Comments: It is my opinion that without interdivisional exchange of buying
    intelligence on common commodities this saving would not have come about.

                                        Submitted by: T. Rawson
                                        Approved: R. Cochrane
                                        Date: August, 1973

scheduling had cleared the requisition, but he never encouraged the
operations people to pry into what he considered was purchasing's business. "It's just as well not to get these production guys involved in
our commercial dealings with suppliers," he said seriously, "or before
you know it you have back-door selling on your hands."

Motivation

Jack Allison found that the savings program played a relatively small
part in the buyers' plans. It was something to be reported when the
situation arose. Furthermore, he noted that higher in the buying echelon
interest was desultory, as large orders were automatically handled by
the seniors. Even Mr. Cochrane used to take a hand in the negotiation
of equipment until the last year or so. The seniors skimmed the cream
off. Relatively little attention was given to value analysis techniques.

Organization

Some cases of the two divisions buying the same material or components at different times without one buyer being conscious of the other's

efforts had come to light. Separate savings reports treating with the same commodity brought this to Jack Allison's attention.

Jack Allison had noted the buyers' reluctance to talk about their savings expertise outside of the department and wondered how necessary this secrecy was. It made him recall his own ignorance of what purchasing was doing when he was a member of the design or quality groups at M.E.C. He also wondered what action, if any, he should take now that the savings program had become his responsibility.

16 PROCUREMENT DEPARTMENT REPORTS TO MANAGEMENT, APPRAISING PROCUREMENT DEPARTMENT PERFORMANCE, AND STRATEGY

Reports to management

The importance of good communications in achieving optimum results in the operations of a business is being given increasing recognition by top management. As the tempo of business activity has quickened and companies have become larger, more diversified and more decentralized in operations, information, and the proper communication of information, has become essential in the development of managerial controls.

In Chapter 3, many of the information flows which directly affect the decision-making activities of procurement personnel were explored. These information flows can be broadly classified as originating from the interface relationships with other functional areas within the firm and contacts with the outside worldwide marketplace. In Chapter 15 we studied the process of developing a procurement plan, establishing objectives for the department and personnel, and constructing a budget to provide for the operating expenses of the procurement department. Inasmuch as the procurement plan and the budget are submitted to top company management executives for approval, they provide the basic reports about expected procurement activity for the forecast period or periods. The accuracy of the projected plans and strategies is checked when reports on the actual performance of the procurement task are made.

934

Operations reports

It is not practical in the space available to give a detailed explanation of all the types of procurement reports which might be useful under all circumstances. Emphasis on what information is essential to report will vary with the type of industry. In the past, too many purchasing executives limited their reports to a tabulation of the figures showing:

1. Total dollar volume of purchases.
2. Total dollars spent for department operating expenses.
3. Total number of purchasing orders issued.

In some instances these figures were related to each other by calculating average figures and percentages to show:

1. Average dollar cost of the purchase orders written

$$\frac{\text{Dollar cost of operating department}}{\text{Number of P.O. written}}$$

2. Operating costs as a percentage of total dollar volume of purchases.
3. Operating costs as a percentage of total dollar volume of sales.

It is probably true that comparing the above figures and ratios with similar figures for previous periods of the same length as the period currently reported provides some perspective on what is happening in the procurement function. However, these reports are of little use in furnishing information that will provide a basis for the evaluation of how effective the procurement function is in providing the materials and equipment needed at the lowest net cost, considering quality, service, and the needs of the user. It should be noted that the lowest net cost is not necessarily the lowest price.

Data processing equipment, when properly programmed, is capable of providing information promptly and in a form that facilitates analysis of most procurement activities.

What to report, the frequency of reporting, and how to report, are decisions which require careful analysis. In some situations top management specifies the type of report, the frequency, and whether the report is to be written or presented orally. The personality of major executives, the type of organization structure, and the nature of the industry have an influence on decisions affecting reporting procedures. Good reporting is important to the status and effective operation of the procurement function because of the insights obtained from the analysis required in preparing reports, the information presented, and the opportunity to broaden the understanding of management of the results to be obtained by effective procurement.

In general, procurement operation reports which are prepared on a regular basis; monthly, quarterly, semiannually, or annually can be classified under the following headings:

1. Market and Economic Conditions and Price Performance
2. Inventory Investment Changes
3. Procurement Operations and Effectiveness
4. Operations affecting Financial Administration

A brief statement of the kinds of information included in reports in each classification follows:

Market and Economic Conditions and Price Performance
1. Price trends and changes for the major materials and commodities purchased. Comparisons with standard costs where such accounting methods are used.
2. Changes in demand-supply conditions for the major items purchased. Effects of labor strikes or threatened strikes.
3. Lead time expectations of major items.

Inventory Investment Changes
1. Dollar investment in inventories classified by major commodity and materials groups.
2. Days' or months' supply and on order for major commodity and materials groups.
3. Ratio of inventory dollar investment to sales dollar volume.
4. Rates of inventory turnover for major items.
5. Total floor space required for inventory.

Procurement Operations and Effectiveness
1. Cost reductions resulting from purchase research and value analysis studies.
2. Quality rejections rates for major items.
3. Number of out-of-stock situations which caused interruption of scheduled production.
4. Number of change orders issued, classified by cause.
5. Number of requisitions received and processed.
6. Number of purchase orders issued.
7. Employee work load and productivity.
8. Transportation costs analysis

Operations Affecting Administration and Financial Activities
1. Comparison of actual departmental operating costs to budget.
2. Cash discounts earned and cash discounts missed.
3. Commitments to purchase, classified by types of formal contracts and by purchase orders aged by expected delivery dates.
4. Changes in cash discounts allowed by suppliers.

Special project reports

From time to time there is need to prepare special reports to bring to the attention of top management or to various functional managers matters which concern the best interests of the firm. The alert procurement executive who has an appreciation for the key position he occupies in the flow of information may have the opportunity to detect changes in trends of market practices or long-term supply situations, as well as in other areas of interest. Procurement departments having purchasing research staffs are in a favored position to prepare special reports.

Effective report presentation

Reports which are not read are a wasted effort. Reports consisting solely of a tabulation of figures often have little meaning to anyone except the compiler of the report. There are a number of good textbooks available on effective report writing, and a procurement executive would be well advised to keep such a book handy for reference.

A good starting point in preparing any report is for the writer to try and put himself in the position of the person who is expected to read the report—what information is important to him in performing his job. Some of the fundamentals common to all reports are the need for clarity of presentation, simple and concise statements, and carefully checked information to ensure accuracy. A title should be used which clearly describes the nature of the report.

Most busy executives when reading a report prefer to see a brief summary of the important information, and, if appropriate, conclusions, at the beginning of the report. This procedure alerts the reader to what follows in the main body of the report. Recommendations, when appropriate, appear at the end of the report. Short statistical tabulations are usually included in the body of the report or may be shown graphically by pie charts, bar charts, or graphs. Lengthy statistical tabulations should be provided in an appendix and are identified and analyzed in the body of the report.

Provisions should be made in any system which issues regular reports to check from time to time to learn if the reports are useful to the recipients. All too frequently reports continue to be issued because of habit rather than because they serve a useful purpose.

APPRAISING PROCUREMENT DEPARTMENT PERFORMANCE

Need for appraisal

Few man-made organizations operate at full effectiveness. The company which is successful over time recognizes this fact of life and strives constantly to improve all aspects of its operation. Ideally in a highly competitive environment only the efficient survive. Actually, legislative attempts to protect the rights of free competition from the excessive use of economic power often results in some degree of protection for the less-efficient organizations.

An increasing number of company managements have recognized that a properly organized procurement function staffed by competent employees is capable of contributing to the profits of the firm. Along with this recognition has come an awareness of the desirability of periodic appraisals of the performance of the procurement function. As mentioned in Chapter 1, the average U.S. manufacturing company spends approximately 56 percent of its total sales income in the procurement of materials, supplies, components, and outside services. Savings made in procurement expenditures flow directly to profit. In a free economy profits are the lifeblood of business operation and a necessity for continued progress. Thus, there is a continuing need for appraisal of procurement performance with the purpose of improving effectiveness.

Problems of appraising efficiency

It is one thing to recognize the need for performance appraisal and quite a different situation to develop meaningful methods for measuring performance. For years prior to 1950 various committees of the National Association of Purchasing Management worked diligently to develop a uniform statistical method of evaluation which would apply generally to procurement activities. It was finally concluded no one method would fit all situations. Shortly after the end of World War II the U.S. Air Force employed as consultants industrial procurement executives who were acknowledged experts in their respective fields. These consultants were grouped in teams to make intensive performance evaluation surveys of the procurement activities of the major prime contractors producing aircraft and other military equipment for the Air Force. These contracts involved billions of dollars in procurement expenditures annually.

In the decade of the 1950s, increasing attention was given to developing new methods for the evaluation of the procurement function. Many large corporations developed methods which met their specific needs. Some of the corporate evaluation plans were reported in the purchase trade journals. The accounting profession expressed its interest and published results of research projects.[1]

Continued interest in the subject of evaluation into the 1960s is evidenced by the publication of a comprehensive report by the American Management Association.[2] Over 200 companies cooperated in the study,

---

[1] Two of the best reports are: Institute of Internal Auditors, *The Internal Audit and Control of a Purchasing Department*, Research Report No. 2 (New York, 1955); *Purchasing Policies and Procedures* (Arthur Andersen and Company, 1960).

[2] F. Albert Hayes, and George A. Renard, *Evaluating Purchasing Performance*, AMA Research Study 66 (New York: American Management Association, 1964).

and 75 percent indicated that some method of evaluation was used.

Research in organization theory and human behavior in organizations has produced greater understanding of how to organize for effective results. We have learned about the importance of clearly defining the purpose, the objectives or goals, we expect a function and the employees in that function to achieve. A major problem in many organizations has been the lack of clearly defined objectives for the procurement department and its personnel. Unless it can be determined what is to be evaluated the question of how to make an evaluation has little meaning.

Procedures to be used in evaluation

There are essentially two approaches which can be taken in evaluating the performance of the procurement function:

1. The continuing evaluation which compares the operating results reported periodically with the procurement plan, budget, and objectives established for the department and personnel.
2. The outside audit made by someone outside the department or the company.

While these two approaches are not mutually exclusive, it works out in general practice the company that has been progressive in its concepts of organization and has recognized the need to staff the procurement department with highly competent people, there is less need to call on consultants from outside the company to participate in the evaluation process, at least on a regular basis. Managements of companies having well-established internal auditing departments obtain substantial help in evaluating various functional operations when internal auditors use a broader approach than just checking for integrity. Working cooperatively with the chief procurement executive and his staff, the auditors can help in making objective appraisals in areas such as:

1. Work load allocations.
2. Procurement department relationships with other departments, procedures, problem areas and the like.
3. Relationships with vendors—vendors' attitudes toward the company and toward the buyers.
4. Adherence to policies and procedures as detailed in company policy statements and manuals.

Procedure to be used by an outside consultant

When an outside consultant is used for evaluation purposes, careful inquiry should be made to assure that the consultant has the specific expertise and breadth of experience needed for the job to be done.

After a selection is made, a conference should be arranged between the consultant, the chief procurement executive and the executive to whom he reports. A broad outline of the areas to be investigated should be agreed to by those attending the conference.

Contact with top management. Clearly, for an outside consultant, the place to begin is with whoever represents top management, presumably the president or in some cases the general manager. He shall probably want to talk to the other top executives of the company sooner or later, but he does not start with them. Quite aside from assuring himself that he has the complete cooperation of the president, there are various things he needs to learn at the outset:

1. What is the scope and responsibility of the department *as the president understands it?* This qualification is important because there are many instances in which confusion exists between the various levels of administration concerning just who is responsible for what. Often, too, it will be found that the authority is not in fact exercised by those who are supposed to be exercising it.

2. Who is responsible for the determination of procurement policy concerning such important matters as inventory control, speculative buying, reciprocity, and the like? Are these policies set by the president or by some inner council of which the procurement officer is not a member, or does the latter participate at all times?

3. Does the procurement officer hold his own on those occasions when he is called upon to sit in the top councils, or, on the contrary, does he contribute little? Does he have a broad understanding of business problems? Does he exercise responsible judgment on matters within, as well as outside, his own sphere when called upon to do so? Does he command the respect of other top executives?

4. If the procurement officer is not rated a top executive, on what occasions is he called in for advice, and is the advice worthwhile when he does give it?

5. Is there more than one purchasing department in the company, and, if there are several, what are their respective responsibilities?

6. Does the president himself keep in touch with the procurement policy and its administration and, if so, to what extent?

What is learned from the president (and other top executives) will give us an indication of the attitude toward the importance of procurement and of the degree to which there is confidence in the procurement organization and personnel. Of course, both of these will need to be checked on later. In addition to this information, partly in the form of facts and partly in the form of impressions, there will be some very useful clues to be followed as the investigation proceeds.

Interview with head of procurement division. The second step would probably be a preliminary interview with the head of the procurement department. There are several obvious reasons for such an interview, including the desirability of explaining why the consultant has been called in at all and making it clear that his whole attitude is one of cooperation and constructive assistance rather than one of seeking things that are wrong.

The main purpose of the interview, of course, is to make at least a tentative evaluation of the character and ability of the man who is presumably responsible for the policy, personnel, organization, and procedures of the department. What sort of a man is he? Is he thoroughly familiar with, and a student of, materials and manufacturing processes? Does he have at least some familiarity with business problems and practices beyond those directly related to procurements? Does he try to operate his department singlehandedly, or does he delegate authority wherever possible? Is he tactful, yet able to come to a decision with firmness? Does he have a receptive mind and an ability to gather information wherever it may be found and to screen out the useful from the worthless? To what professional associations does he belong? What magazines does he read of a trade, general business, and broad cultural nature, either regularly or occasionally? Does he give the impression of being honest, fair, vigorous, and pleasant? All these characteristics and others that will readily suggest themselves to the reader will go to make up the consultant's final judgment of the capacities of the head of the department.

Indeed, it is inevitable that, as a result of such conversations, certain definite impressions will be formed. Although the final result will be a matter of judgment in any case, there is need to be most careful in crystallizing impressions too early and without adequate information. Preliminary opinions must be treated *as* preliminary—to be checked and rechecked later on. The importance of all this cannot be overestimated, for, with the possible exception of the size-up of the president of the company himself, the qualifications of the head of the department constitute the most important single element in our whole analysis.

Remaining steps in investigation. From this point on, the exact order of the investigation is not important. Actually, it is unwise to attempt to lay out too rigid a program. What the next step will be should depend upon what was learned at the previous step. The significant thing is that a wide range of points should be checked, not the order in which this is done. Thus, sooner or later we shall need to form judgments on the following points:

Points for judgment in appraisal

Is the organization of the department based on sound principles? Is the organization as it appears on paper the real, working organization? Are the lines of responsibility drawn with reasonable appreciation for the nature of the tasks and of the personnel available? These and many other organizational questions have been discussed earlier, and we need not review them here. Much of the required data on these points will be gained from the president himself or from the head of the department. But the information as to how well the organization works and whether it actually functions in the way that either the president or the head of the department *thinks* it does will be disclosed only by further study at the lower echelons within the department.

Is the physical layout of the department well planned? Is office space planned for the efficient performance of the work? Are there adequate reception room facilities to handle the salesmen and other callers? Do buyers have facilities where they can talk with salesmen without unnecessary interruptions? Proper office working facilities are not only important in building employee morale but also in obtaining the best possible attitude from the outsiders calling on the buyers and others in the department.

Is there a reasonably well-defined procurement policy? Is there a policy that is accepted by the president, as well as by other top executives, such as the sales, production, and engineering managers, and that is actually followed within the procurement department itself? Policies are often extremely hard to define, frequently still harder to follow, and bound to change from time to time. None of these facts provides excuses for the department's not having something approaching that somewhat vague concept called "general policy."

Moreover, the statement of policy should be written and rather widely distributed, not only among the members of the department itself but throughout the entire company and even among the suppliers. All of these groups should actually have a permanent copy of the statement in their possession. For they should not only know and understand it but also have immediate access to it for reference purposes. In no other way can the best results of full cooperation be expected. Furthermore, such general familiarity with the policy of the procurement department makes close integration with the policies of other departments more probable and necessary modifications easier to effect. It may also be added that the mere writing of such a statement helps to define policy in the minds of those responsible for carrying it out and keeps them "on their toes" in the observance thereof. Moreover, to reduce a company's policies and procedures to writing is one of the best of all means of ensuring that the department head has carefully, critically, and constructively thought his way through the objectives, policies, and administrative problems confronting his organization. If it accomplished no other purpose than this, it would be worthwhile.

Are the procedures reasonable? There are two good reasons for checking the procedures in some detail. One is to be able to judge their adequacy. The other is equally important for our purposes: the experience of some consultants is that there is *no surer way of locating clues to departmental problems* than going over the procedures with the greatest of care. There, if anywhere, general weaknesses will be disclosed.

The number of small orders and the volume of rush orders, for instance, are very revealing types of information. An analysis of the purchase orders and a comparison of them with the corresponding requisitions will indicate both the completeness of the latter and the independence exercised in placing the former. It will be revealing, too, to learn something of the extent of carload orders as against less-than-carload orders, of the distribution of suppliers as between local suppliers and those from out-of-town, of the degree of reliance on supply houses as against manufacturers, and of the total number of suppliers used. The very forms themselves are clues to the familiarity of the personnel with the "tools of the trade." So, too, is the filing system: how promptly can documents be located and inquiries, both those originating within and those originating without the department, be answered? What records—vendor, purchase order, contract, quotation, price, or other—are kept? To what extent are the records that are kept used?

So one might go on almost indefinitely. Procedures and forms are, as a rule, very dull things; and to most people they are, indeed, very elementary and routine. But for an evaluator of efficiency there is no greater source of "leads" than a study of procedures. Here, too, it would be well to find out whether the department has a formal written description or manual of procedure. This is quite revealing, because the preparation of a manual leads to exactness in thinking, to certainty of responsibility, and to smoothness of operation, although, of course, it can also have undesirable effects if it becomes too much of a "bible" and serves to cut down flexibility and initiative.

Importance of a manual of procedure

In the discussion of the last three points—policy, organization, and procedures—reference has been made to the use of formal statements and manuals. Because of their importance, it would be well to elaborate before going on with our analysis.

In addition to the reasons already indicated as pointing to their desirability is the fact that the carefully prepared, detailed statements of organization, of duties of the various personnel, and of procedures and filing systems (including illustrative forms, fully explained) are of value not only to the senior members of the department but even more so to newcomers. A manual is almost an essential for a well-conceived in-training program for junior members. Furthermore, it adds an element of flexibility in facilitating the transfer of personnel from one job to another in case of vacation, illness, or the temporary overburdening of a particular segment of the organization. And, finally, the manual is useful in explaining to those not in the department what and how things are done.

Some procurement officers feel that because their departments are not so large as are those in bigger companies or because the number of personnel is limited, there is no special need for a manual. They feel that everyone knows all that would commonly be put in a manual anyway and that hence there is no need for writing it all down. This argument overlooks the benefits gained in the actual task of preparation.

Preparation of a manual

The preparation of a manual is a time-consuming and somewhat tedious task, to be sure, but one well worth what it costs. In setting up the project, it is well to bear in mind that unless the work is carefully planned and well done, is accurate, and is reasonably complete, it might almost as well not be done at all. Careful advance planning of the coverage, emphasis, and arrangement is essential. So, too, is a clear definition of the purposes sought in issuing the manual and the uses to which it is to be put, for both of these have bearing on its length, form, and content.

Very early in the project the writer will have to decide whether the manual is to cover only procurement policy or is to include also a description of the organization and the procedure, and if the latter, in how much detail. In reaching a decision on these matters, it is strongly recommended that a collection of manuals now in use be made. Fortunately, excellent sample manuals that will serve as guides can be obtained from any number of companies.

When the general outlines have been determined, the actual writing may be undertaken. This work need not be done all at one time, but section by section as the opportunity presents itself. It is also well to have the work thoroughly discussed and very carefully checked, not only by those within the department itself but by those outside this group, such as engineering and production personnel, whose operations are directly affected by procurement operations. When a section is completed, that portion may well be made the basis for a department discussion forum, not only for the sake of spotting errors and suggesting modifications before the material is actually reproduced but also to ensure that everyone understands its contents. This should all be done prior to issue. When reproduced, a loose-leaf form generally may be found preferable, to allow for revisions as they come along. Another worthwhile step is to have the president of the company write a short foreword, endorsing the policy and practices of the department, defining its authority, and generally giving his approval.

What is the personnel policy?

Investigation of the personnel program should start with an analysis of the work to be done, including the size of the total work load and the way in which various tasks with similar characteristics can be combined. From this analysis it should be possible to make estimates of how many people are required and the educational and experience qualifications such people should have. A comparison of these findings with the actual members of the department and their job assignments should provide a basis on which to begin an evaluation of personnel policy.

Selection of personnel. The next query is whether the people on the various jobs are personally qualified for the work they are doing. This, in turn, calls for several other lines of inquiry. One concerns the *manner of selection.* Is there a fairly definite understanding of the qualifications? What are the personal characteristics wanted? What academic training is expected? What experience background is called for? From what sources are new personnel recruited? The answers to each of these and similar questions will, of course, vary with the particular circumstances. Thus, if a potential buyer is being sought, most companies will look for a man of analytical ability and good judgment, of honesty, and, of course, of pleasing personality who is neat in appearance, willing to work, loyal, and patient. He is more likely that not to be a college graduate, specializing preferably, but not necessarily, in science or engineering. If, in addition, he has had business school training, so much the better. The important thing about his academic training, however, is not how much or on what subject but how thorough it has been. The man should have had some experience in a stock room or factory, and a little selling experience would help. The selection of such a man, in the case of most companies, would be made from within the company itself rather than from outside.

Replacement program. Again, does the department have a regular *replacement program?* Too often there is a failure to have the personnel distributed among the various age groups, with the result that all the buyers are older men who will retire at about the same time and—to make the matter even worse—with no trained personnel coming along behind them.

In-training. Another significant check point in the personnel program is the *training after employment.* Newcomers to the department have much to learn about procurement, particularly in view of the basic principle that purchasing calls for specialized training. Under such circumstances, the new man is likely to have a good deal of difficulty in learning a new job in any office where he gets no particular help but must depend on the information that he picks up by trial and error or from his office mates, all of whom are busy with their own work. This means that the head of the department should actively encourage and take a continuing interest in the training of these new men. Either in some sort of an evening class or by means of an in-training program, help should be provided.

Is there an on-the-job training program? It must be said that many procurement departments lack one. This is a most serious omission. Such a program may well be built around the manuals to which reference has already been made. Study of the principal items purchased by the company should be conducted, perhaps with the aid of motion-picture films. So, likewise, study of the products and processes of the particular company will fill in many a gap. Reading assignments, films, regular written reports, group discussions and even occasional outside lectures will all serve, in proper proportions, to keep up the interest and measure the progress. The head of one large department says: "I believe a report by each trainee should be submitted *monthly,* or at the end of a particular assignment if less than a month. But do not prescribe the form and contents of these reports. Give the trainee freedom of action and thought. This will bring out his originality and will increase the value of the report as a yardstick of ability."

Older members of the department should also be encouraged to remember that one's education is never completed and that experience is by no means always the best teacher.

Compensation plan. But a personnel program must cover more than selection and training. What, for instance, is the *compensation plan?* Are the men adequately paid? Is there a definite system for advancements, and, specifically, what are the young man's chances for advancement in rank and in responsibility? Does the department have enough people to do the work properly and still keep everyone reasonably busy? What is the general morale of the personnel, including the attitude of each toward the others, toward the head of the department, and, of course, toward the company itself?

All of these elements may be passed in review in determining how well a department is functioning. The list is suggestive rather than complete.

What is the record of the department with respect to prices paid? By a reasonable amount of the right kind of spot-checking, it is quite possible to determine whether the prices paid have been consistently at, below, or above the market. Particular attention should be devoted to the purchases of materials that are most important dollarwise. What has been the department's performance in getting deliveries on time? Has material arrived by the dates requested by the stores and production departments, or at least by the dates promised by the buyers to those departments? Have the buyers secured promised shipping dates from suppliers, and have the materials gone forward on those dates? Both of these—prices paid and deliveries—are obviously important points to check, and a reasonable effort should be made to learn whether or not all is being done that could be expected.

Insofar as the department is responsible for inventory control, the following points must be looked into with great care: What evidences are there of "dead stock"? Have operating departments been handicapped by lack of material through the procurement department's fault? Are there adequate controls on forward purchases? Are inventory policies and purchasing policies closely integrated administratively? An examination into these possibilities involves a study of the inventory policy itself, including the standards that are set, the devices for controlling the inventory, and the soundness of the judgment of those responsible.

What is the attitude of other departments? Another check point of great importance relates to the attitude of the other departments of the company toward the procurement department and their feeling concerning its efficiency. Does the department have a reputation for being capable, alert to its opportunities, and helpful? Evidence on this score is one of the things which is often better obtained by an outside consultant than by an insider, unless the latter be of the internal auditor type—and not always even then.

Attitude of suppliers. Related to this factor is the evidence of supplier goodwill, in particular. This, like intracompany goodwill, should be a factor of real concern. The fact that it is, of course, clearly one of the things that can least be reduced to any sort of a statistical measure is not important. Fortunately, considering its significance, it can be gauged by an intelligent person who is sensitive to the reactions of others.

Here, then, are some of the areas for checking, which point in the direction of efficiency or its lack. Out of a study of them will come a definite picture of the department's operation to one who knows purchasing principles and the purchasing departments of other companies; the study will reveal how well the department is doing, whether it is measuring up to all that might be expected of it.

By following check points of the type outlined in the foregoing, by gaining clues from cost and other statistical data, and by the proper use of reports, it would appear that general management can make an appraisal of the efficiency of a department.

Quite obviously the department administrator himself also must continually appraise his own work as well as that of his organization. True, his judgments on these matters may not coincide with those of the executive head of his company, and they may not be wholly unbiased. Yet, provided that the administrator is a good man, he can accomplish much. If he is too busy with other matters (though evaluation is part of good administration), handicapped by inertia, deficient in the ability to judge these things, or lacking in knowledge of the policies and procedures of other companies, then he is not a good man.

There is much to be said at the same time, in favor of an occasional outside check on the department. The much abused internal auditor and the outside consultant can bring a point of view which is very difficult for one who is continually "on the job" to get, and this is of value both to top management and to the department head himself.

The latter gains because the independent critic can judge even better than he the degree of cooperation and the confidence in the department expressed by other departments of the business. Inefficient methods, otherwise easily overlooked, are spotted. The psychological effect of knowing an examination is to be made is excellent. The fact that the personnel in the department are forced to review and justify what they do helps considerably. At the same time, constructive and helpful suggestions should be forthcoming from the examiner, and full credit should be given for what is commendable. And the consultant or internal auditor frequently makes it possible for the department head to secure the approval of the management group for any changes he happens to desire, simply because of the fact that his recommendations have the support of a representative of the management from "outside."

The performance of any department might be improved by such analysis. Yet management probably has the most to gain from the independent appraisal of a department like procurement, whose efficiency is inherently difficult to evaluate and whose real function is not always well understood. Any assistance that management can get which will enable it to specify the contributions it has a right to expect from such a department, to segregate the particular function from the other major activities of the business, and to evaluate more adequately the company policies in that area should profoundly better the individual company concerned and, by and large, the complete structure of the economy as a whole.

Procurement strategy

Over the past 75 years the procurement function has slowly evolved from a clerical type function to one which requires complex processes to provide information for effective decision making by professional buyers. This change has in turn stimulated the development of procurement strategies to maximize the effectiveness of the performance of the function.

A procurement strategy is made up of substrategies all of which are conceived by using all available information to project a plan which is directed to the achievement of a specific purpose. Some of the more common substrategies are:

1. The strategy of supplier development, selection and evaluation.
2. The strategy of buying: (a) the use of negotiation, (b) competitive bidding, (c) systems contracting, (d) national contracts, (e) foreign buying, (f) forward buying, (g) hand-to-mouth buying.
3. The strategy of cost reduction through value analysis and standardization.

The careful development of a procurement strategy is a difficult task but necessary if the full potential of the procurement function is to be achieved.

BIBLIOGRAPHY

ALJIAN, GEORGE W., ed. *Purchasing Handbook.* 3d ed. New York: McGraw-Hill Book Co., 1973.

EDWARDS, M. G. AND HAMILTON, H. A., ed. *Guide to Purchasing,* vol. 1. New York: National Association of Purchasing Management, 1969.

GALLAGHER, W. J. *Report Writing for Management.* Reading, Mass.: Addison-Wesley Publishing Co., 1969.

HAYES, F. ALBERT, AND RENARD, GEORGE. . *Evaluating Purchasing Performance.* New York: American Management Association, 1964.

HEINRITZ, STUART F., AND FARRELL, PAUL V. *Purchasing.* 5th ed. Englewood Cliffs, N.J.: Prentice-Hall, Inc., 1971.

LEE, LAMAR, JR., AND DOBLER, DONALD W. *Purchasing and Materials Management.* New York: McGraw-Hill Book Co., 1971.

WESTING, J. H., FINE, I. V., AND ZENZ, GARY JOSEPH. *Purchasing Management.* 3d ed. New York: John Wiley & Sons, Inc., 1969.

CASES FOR CHAPTER 16

UNIVERSAL TYPEWRITER, INC. (A)*

In the summer of 1959, top management of Universal Typewriter, Inc. (UTI), with headquarters in Hartford, Connecticut, had become increasingly concerned with the adequacy of the company's organization for procurement and the effectiveness of the purchasing operations. Consequently, Mr. Wesley Greiner, a staff methods engineer, was asked to conduct a study of the company's organization of the procurement function for its seven domestic and Canadian plants. Mr. Greiner was to submit his findings and conclusions to top management by the end of the year. In addition to presenting an analysis evaluation of the performance of the purchasing organization, he was to recommend changes that he believed necessary to improve such performance.

Company background

Universal Typewriter, Inc., was a large multinational manufacturer of a full line of standard typewriters. The company also produced bookkeeping and adding typewriters as well as typewriters for special requirements, such as writing from right to left or using special symbols. In

---

1958 worldwide sales amounted to over $600 million, with a net income of about $16 million. Universal had been one of the world's leading companies in the industry for many decades, conducting sales activities not only in the domestic market but also in many foreign countries. Altogether, the company employed nearly 80,000 people throughout the world.

The company maintained production and assembly plants in the United States, Canada, England, Belgium, Austria, Sweden, Argentina, Mexico, and a number of Far East countries. Plants in the United States and Europe accounted for over 80 percent of the company's total manufacturing volume. The European plants exported heavily into many parts of the world, including the United States. Manufacturing or assembly activities in a number of foreign countries had been established since World War II principally to overcome national import or currency exchange restrictions.

Competition

By 1958, although the company still held a leading position in the world's markets for typewriters, rapidly intensifying foreign competition had made heavy inroads into the company's business, cutting its share of the U.S. market from approximately 60 percent to approximately 30 percent. Foreign-made typewriters retailed in the United States generally at between 40 percent and 65 percent of the price of the lowest priced Universal standard front stroke type-bar machine equipped with a standard keyboard.

Corporate strategy

Early in 1958 Universal's top management began to develop long-range strategic plans to halt the accelerating erosion of the company's markets, particularly in the United States, and to reverse the general decline of a company that had been recognized in the early days of mechanical writing machines as one of the leading international industrial organizations. Initially, these plans were designed to:

1. Rebuild the typewriter business by producing electric machines of advanced design and with new features, such as automatic margin setting and touch control and by withdrawing from the market a number of older models.
2. Reduce manufacturing costs through modernization and specialization of the company's generally aged and outmoded plant facilities.
3. Reduce selling costs by shifting from single-channel distribution to multiple-channel distribution.[1]

---

[1] Traditionally, the company had distributed its products through specialized office equipment outlets only.

4. Eliminate excessive assets to improve the firm's return on investment and to free funds for investment in new products.
5. Cut back the company's heavy reliance on typewriters to about 50 percent of total sales by diversifying from a one-product company to a multiproduct company, which was to be accomplished primarily through acquisitions.

By the summer of 1959, although the full impact of implementing the new strategy was not yet felt, management believed the company had taken the first successful steps toward reestablishing its competitiveness in the domestic and international typewriter market. The firm had already rapidly developed a substantial sales volume for the newly designed electric models. It had invested over $50 million in plant modernization. The company had made a promising start in significantly reducing the assets required to support a given level of business. And it was well launched on its program of product diversification, having entered into the production and distribution of other office machines and data processing equipment such as accounting machines, dictating machines, teleprinters, duplicating machines, and analog computers.

Company organization

Strongly conditioned by its long history as a one-product company, Universal for many decades had been organized for two broad functions, manufacturing and sales, as shown in Exhibit 1. Sales units throughout the world were grouped by geographical location under the jurisdiction of four sales executives, who maintained their offices at company headquarters in Hartford, Connecticut, and reported to the vice president of sales and distribution. All manufacturing units were under the jurisdiction of a vice president in charge of production. Other administrative operations—such as finance and accounting and labor relations—were also centered at the headquarters under the jurisdiction of vice presidents. Throughout the organization each sales office, usually headed by a sales director, reported to one of the four sales executives at the Hartford headquarters. Similarly, each manufacturing plant, ordinarily headed by a works manager, reported to the vice president of production.

Coordination of relationships between the manufacturing and sales units in both domestic and foreign markets was effected at the company's executive offices. Below the vice presidential level little, if any, formal communication existed between the sales organization and the manufacturing organization. Characteristic of the working relationships between headquarters and the national and international operating units was a close control of all operations through headquarter executives. This control was maintained by requiring comprehensive reports of each oper-

Exhibit 1
PARTIAL ORGANIZATION CHART, 1959

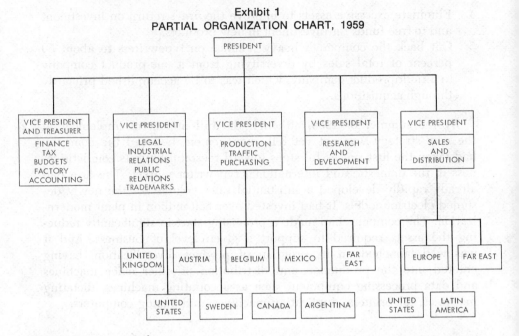

Source: Company records.

ating unit, covering such items as unit sales and dollar sales volume, petty cash flows, salesmen's expenses, and inventory movements. The report system was designed primarily to enable operating expense analysis for each sales and manufacturing unit. Thus, the focus of the headquarters financial control activity was on costs exceeding standard percentage ratios. Profitability of the firm as a whole, expressed as return on investment, was determined at the corporate level. Under this system of reporting, there was a time lag of about three months due to the processing time required for the comprehensive data flowing from the operating units to headquarters. Feedback of performance information by the home office to the operating units occurred generally if profit margins were regarded as too low or if operating expenses were too high; according to some executives it was not always easy to pinpoint the cause of unsatisfactory operating results.

The company operated under a board of directors comprising seven "inside" members and one "outside" member.

For several decades through the late 50s, the company had been managed by a president who had been highly regarded for his ability to keep the company's liquidity at a relatively high level at all times, even during the years of the Great Depression. Liquidity and conservation of assets continued to be major company objectives. In the late 50s, Mr. Harvey S. Marple, who had joined the company in 1948 when he was in his middle thirties, was appointed president and chief executive officer.

Organization for procurement

At the headquarters offices Universal maintained a central purchasing department that served the company's North American manufacturing plants in Rhode Island, Massachusetts, Tennessee, and North Carolina, and in Canada.[2] The department was headed by a purchasing agent, who reported to the vice president of production. Under the purchasing agent's responsibility was a staff of 35 employees comprising 3 assistant purchasing agents, 4 buyers, 14 clerks, 3 supervisors, 5 secretaries, 5 typists, and 1 receptionist. (See Exhibit 2 for organization chart of pur-

Exhibit 2
ORGANIZATION CHART—CENTRAL PURCHASING DEPARTMENT

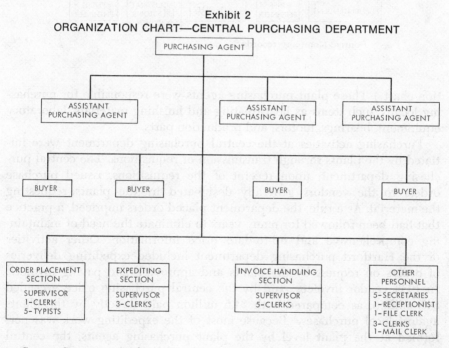

Source: Company records.

chasing department.) The central purchasing department was responsible for procuring such items as raw materials, component parts, services, operating supplies, maintenance supplies, capital equipment, office furni-

---

[2] The company's overseas manufacturing units were generally not serviced by the Hartford central purchasing organization, although the procurement activities of the foreign units were closely controlled by the home office. Upon request, the central purchasing department bought materials from domestic sources for shipment to foreign-based plants.

ture, and stationery supplies for all domestic manufacturing units. Although the formal organization chart did not provide for purchasing departments at the factory level, each plant operated with one or more purchasing agents who reported to the plant superintendent, the controller, or the chief engineer. (See Exhibit 3 for a typical plant organiza-

Exhibit 3
TYPICAL PLANT ORGANIZATION CHART

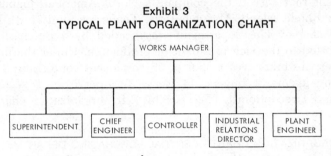

Source: Company records.

tion chart.) These plant purchasing agents were responsible for purchasing locally such items as heat-treating and finishing materials, laboratory equipment, bearings, motors, and production parts.

Purchasing activities at the central purchasing department were initiated by the plants through transmission of requisitions. The central purchasing department, upon receipt of the requisitions, issued purchase orders to the vendors generally designated by the plants requesting the material. As a rule, the department placed orders unpriced, a practice that had been followed for many years to eliminate the need of maintaining comprehensive and up-to-date price information. Other activities of the Hartford purchasing department included expediting deliveries of orders on request by the plants and approving and paying invoices. In 1958 vendor invoices paid by the central purchasing office exceeded $45 million, as compared with $4.5 million paid directly by the plants against local purchases.[3] Because most of the expediting work was performed at the plant level by the plant purchasing agents, the central purchasing department had no particular follow-up procedures other than maintaining copies of acknowledgment of orders placed. In order to avoid undue delays in paying trade obligations, vendor invoices for purchase orders placed by the central purchasing department were generally paid by the department subsequent to delivery as specified by the purchase order without notice of receipt of the ordered material from the plants.

Although purchase orders were generally placed by the central pur-

---

[3] Cash discounts taken during the year at the central purchasing office amounted to ½ percent of the total dollar amount.

chasing department, it was customary for the plant engineering departments to select the vendors on the basis of past experience with vendor performance. (See Exhibit 4 for the table showing point of vendor selection and point of purchase for selected materials, parts, and equipment.)

Exhibit 4
POINT OF VENDOR SELECTION AND POINT OR PURCHASE
FOR SELECTED MATERIALS, PARTS, AND EQUIPMENT

Classification	Point of vendor selection	Point of purchase
Aluminum	Plant, engineering dept.	Executive office
Heat treating & finishing	Plant, engineering dept.	Plant, purchasing dept.
Laboratory equipment	Plant, engineering dept.	Plant, purchasing dept.
Hardware, purchased tools	Plant, engineering dept., and executive office	Executive office
Electric parts	Plant, engineering dept.	Executive office
Bearings and bearing lube	Plant, engineering dept., and purchasing dept.	Plant, purchasing dept.
Rubber mold parts	Plant, engineering dept., and executive office	Executive office
Name plates	Executive office	Executive office
Screws, screw machine parts	Plant, purchasing dept., and executive office	Executive office
Cartons	Plant, purchasing dept., and executive office	Executive office
Chemicals and paints	Plant, purchasing dept., and executive office	Executive office
Electrical steel and steel bars	Executive office	Executive office
Patterns and die cast molds	Plant, engineering dept.	Executive office
Tools, dies, jigs, perishable tools	Plant, engineering dept.	Executive office
Production parts	Plant, engineering dept.	Executive office
Rhode Island plants, production parts	Plant, engineering and production depts.	Plant, engineering and production depts., and executive office
Export, commodities	Plant, engineering dept., and executive office	Executive office

Top management, however, selected vendors of large-volume raw materials, such as steel, that were used by more than one UTI plant.

Plant purchasing agents were responsible for: (1) editing, approving, and transmitting requisitions to the central purchasing department; (2) assisting plant engineers in negotiating with vendors; (3) expediting orders; (4) buying emergency items; (5) paying invoices for plant-issued purchase orders; and (6) maintaining inventory control cards, requisition and purchase order files, and bookkeeping records.

In 1958 Universal used nearly 4,000 vendors. The company's plants in Rhode Island and Massachusetts relied heavily on local vendors. Although the southern plants bought from local vendors, most of their orders were placed with vendors located in the Northeast because of lack of what management considered suitable vendors in southern states. Of the approximately 4,000 vendors used in 1958, slightly less than half received orders amounting to $1,000 or less each. The purchase order volume was relatively high for most of the manufacturing units. Thus, for instance, the Massachusetts plant in one year issued requisitions for approximately 7,000 local orders amounting to less than $20 each. Plant purchasing agents believed that, while it was the plant's responsibility to obtain the most favorable prices through continued negotiations with vendors, it was the task of the central purchasing department to combine the plant's orders in quantities to reduce the overall volume of purchase orders and, in the case of commodities commonly used by two or more plants, to take advantage of "national discounts."

Time intervals ranged from a minimum of three days to a maximum of ten days between the issuance of requisitions at a plant and the issuance of purchase orders at the central purchasing department. Because of the geographic dispersion of the plants, certain delays in the issuance of orders by headquarters were regarded as inevitable. (See Exhibit 5 for the distances between the plants and the central purchasing

Exhibit 5
GEOGRAPHICAL DISTANCE OF DOMESTIC PLANTS FROM COMPANY
1959 HEADQUARTERS AND ESTIMATED 1960 PURCHASING
VOLUME BY PLANT

Plants	Distance from central purchasing department	Estimated 1960 purchase dollar volume
Massachusetts	100 miles	$ 4,550,000
Rhode Island (Plant 1)	40 miles	10,400,000
Rhode Island (Plant 2)	35 miles	10,400,000
North Carolina (Plant 1)	800 miles	1,950,000
North Carolina (Plant 2)	800 miles	13,000,000
Tennessee	1,000 miles	6,500,000

Source: Company records.

department, and the volume of purchases issued by the plants.) When materials were needed urgently, however, plant purchasing agents avoided delay by placing orders directly with vendors. Also, company executives believed the volume of purchase orders issued directly by the plants had increased since the introduction of some of the new products. At the end of each month, all plants prepared comprehensive lists of all materials received from or returned to suppliers. These lists, sometimes referred to by purchasing personnel as "laundry lists," were used by the Hartford purchasing department as source documents for updating purchasing order files. In addition to the central purchasing department staff of 35, the company employed a total of 48 persons in the various purchasing offices at the plant level. Total annual salary costs for the entire purchasing organization were $431,057 in 1958. (See Exhibit 6 for breakdown of salary costs.)

Exhibit 6
NUMBER OF PERSONNEL AND ANNUAL SALARY COSTS
OF PURCHASING ORGANIZATION, CLASSIFIED BY
GEOGRAPHICAL LOCATION, 1958

Location	Number of employees	Annual salary costs
Massachusetts (1 plant)	16	$ 92,820.00
Rhode Island (2 plants)	20	96,120.00
North Carolina (2 plants)	9	42,117.00
Tennessee (1 plant)	3	13,000.00
Hartford, Conn. (Headquarters)	33	187,000.00
Total	81	$431,057.00

Source: Company records.

Although the company had no training programs, management thought the purchasing personnel at headquarters were intimately familiar with the company's purchasing practices and work procedures because of their many years of service with the company. Partly because of this familiarity with all aspects of the purchasing system and partly because of the long existence of the centralized purchasing department and centralized control of all purchasing activities at headquarters, management had not considered it necessary to develop written purchasing policies or to formalize purchasing procedures or responsibilities through the issuance of manuals. Similarly, no need had been felt at company headquarters to issue written directives governing interdepartmental relationships and supplier relations. Because the plants had been using essentially the same local suppliers for many years, and because the buyers at company headquarters had little or no contact with most of the local suppliers, the central purchasing department had left the task of evaluating vendor performance to plant purchasing and engineering personnel. Furthermore, company officials believed that a thorough knowledge of the nature and actual use of purchased materials was essential in rating the performance of suppliers. Although buyers at company headquarters had extensive administrative experience, they had as a rule no engineering or technical training and therefore knew little about the use to which purchased commodities were put. Plant engineers and plant purchasing agents, who had expressed themselves as having been generally satisfied with their suppliers for many years, appraised the performance of vendors without formal procedure, applying criteria they had found useful over the years.

Total annual purchases for the two Rhode Island plants amounted to nearly $30 million, as compared to about $2 million for the company's smallest plant. (See Exhibit 7 for table showing total dollar volume

Exhibit 7
DOLLAR VOLUME OF PURCHASES BY PLANTS
FOR THE FIRST SIX MONTHS OF 1959

Plant	Dollar volume
Rhode Island (2 plants)	$18,104,247
Tennessee and North Carolina (3 plants).	2,602,268
Canada (1 plant)	2,105,642
Massachusetts (1 plant)	1,246,994
Foreign.	69,549
Total.	$24,128,700

Source: Company records.

of purchases for the six domestic plants and the Canadian plant in the first six months in 1959.) The combined dollar volume of purchases for these seven plants exceeded $50 million annually. Production parts accounted for 35 percent of the company's total dollar volume of purchases for the seven plants in the first six months of 1959; steel accounted for 10 percent; wire and cable accounted for 5 percent; and each of the remaining categories of materials accounted for less than 5 percent. (See Exhibit 8 for table showing the dollar volume of purchases classified by materials and cross-classified by plant usage.)

As indicated by data in Exhibits 7 and 8, the two plants in Rhode Island accounted for a substantial share of the total purchases and for an average of 70 percent of the purchases of the three most significant categories, production parts, steel, and wire and cable.

Material costs represented offering proportions of total production costs for various products manufactured by Universal, as shown in Exhibit 9.

Mr. Greiner's identification of the problem

In studying Universal's purchasing practices, procedures, and organization, and in visualizing the company's future procurement requirements, Mr. Greiner came to the conclusion that the basic procurement problem of the company was the proper allocation of purchasing responsibility. To give perspective to his investigation of Universal's purchasing operations, he spent considerable time searching through the available literature to study the writings of both academicians and practitioners

Exhibit 8

DISTRIBUTION OF DOLLAR PURCHASES BY CLASS OF MATERIAL, TOGETHER WITH AN INDICATION OF THE DEGREE OF
USAGE OF THE SEVERAL MATERIALS IN THE FIRM'S NORTH AMERICAN PLANTS AND OVERSEAS

(first six months of 1959)

Class of Materials	Purchases		Usage — Percent of Total Purchases of Each Material					
	Dollar Volume	Percent of Total	2 Plants in R.I.	3 Plants in Tenn. & N.C.	1 Plant in Mass.	1 Plant in Canada	Export*	Total
Production parts	$ 9,278,663	38.4%	71%	7%	6%	6%	9%	99%
Steel	2,515,144	10.4	60	–	3	6	30	99
Wire and cable	1,142,995	4.7	88	–	–	7	3	98
Operating supplies	1,005,269	4.2	28	16	14	5	36	99
Die castings	983,871	4.1	88	–	–	6	5	99
Capital equipment	785,255	3.3	34	9	13	9	32	97
Aluminum	712,981	3.0	16	–	–	–	83	99
Operating equipment	643,587	2.6	31	9	15	11	44	99
Cartons	637,636	2.6	32	40	2	–	15	99
Finishing materials	607,734	2.5	7	75	3	9	5	99
Molding compound	568,247	2.4	90	–	–	10	–	100
Jigs, dies, cages	539,379	2.2	39	–	13	1	46	99
Oil	464,471	1.9	19	17	12	37	14	99
Paper, tape, forms, etc.	453,779	1.9	32	4	5	4	55	100
Felt	378,991	1.6	1	93	7	4	1	99
Abrasives	334,931	1.4	8	23	7	6	54	98
Grey iron castings	266,393	1.1	96	–	2	–	1	99
Machine tool parts	229,564	1.0	23	16	5	14	41	99
Castings	225,295	0.9	–	91	8	–	–	99
Rubber	208,763	0.9	16	–	–	9	–	100
Chemicals	163,482	0.7	16	9	14	11	50	100
Pig iron	151,845	0.6	–	–	–	8	92	100
Office machines rented	147,483	0.6	13	7	–	17	60	100
Glue	142,218	0.6	–	73	–	12	1	99
Oil resale	138,437	0.6	–	–	–	–	100	100
Miscellaneous	1,402,367	5.8	–	–	–	–	–	100
Total	$24,128,780	100.0%						

* Including Canada.

Source: Company records.

Exhibit 9
SELECTED PRODUCT LINES CLASSIFIED BY MANUFACTURING LOCATIONS, 1959

Product line	Plant						Material as a percent of product cost
	Mass. A	R.I. B	N.C. C	R.I. D	N.C. E	Tenn. F	
Standard typewriters (manual).		x					30
Standard typewriters (electric).			x				34
Electric office machines				x			60
Molded products				x			60
Servomotors.				x			13
Other motors					x		51
Electronic data processing systems					x		55
Woodwork						x	55
Other products	x						60

Source: Company records.

on the subject of how to organize a company's procurement function. During the course of this research, however, he remained somewhat bewildered by the writers' frequently ambiguous use of the terms *centralization* and *decentralization* and was uncertain about how to label Universal's existing purchasing organization. He believed the basic arguments for centralized and decentralized purchasing in companies with geographically dispersed plants could be summed up as follows:

Arguments for Decentralized Purchasing

1. Decentralized purchasing gives a plant manager full jurisdiction over purchasing, which is essential if a plant is operated as a profit center and particularly if material costs constitute an important part of the total product cost.
2. Decentralized purchasing reduces costly order-processing procedures, cuts down lead times, provides great flexibility in meeting emergency requirements, cuts inventory requirements, and improves production scheduling.
3. Decentralized purchasing affords purchasing agents on-the-spot, close-touch relationship with production, which is essential in planning and buying effectively if a plant has unique materials requirements or operating conditions.
4. Decentralized purchasing makes purchase know-how and advice always readily available to the engineering department (as, for example, in cases of "make-or-buy" decisions).
5. Decentralized purchasing gives purchasing people, working within the plant environment, an opportunity for intimate familiarity with the techni-

cal properties and the uses of the materials being bought; persons working at distant corporate headquarters are less likely to develop such knowledge.

6. Decentralized purchasing gives purchasing agents authority and responsibility, leading to higher employee motivation and work satisfaction and, possibly, to higher profits.

7. Decentralized purchasing gives purchasing agents the opportunity to develop local supply sources, which should be used if a company's management discerns a social responsibility to the community in which the plant operates.

Arguments for Centralized Purchasing

1. Centralized purchasing avoids duplication of effort and working at cross purposes from one plant to another.

2. Centralized purchasing permits consolidation of orders for material commonly used by two or more plants, resulting in greater buying power and more favorable national contracts and trade agreements.

3. Centralized purchasing permits establishment of and adherence to unified purchasing policies, practices, and procedures, as well as product standards.

4. Centralized purchasing recognizes that procurement is a major corporate function which should not be subordinated organizationally.

5. Centralized purchasing permits correlation of each plant's resource acquisition cycle, resulting in improved companywide material flows (including interplant flows).

6. Centralized purchasing permits development of greater knowledge and skills by procurement officers specializing in buying a limited number of parts and materials on a large scale for all plants.

7. Centralized purchasing facilitates development and effective utilization of trade relations (reciprocity).

As Mr. Greiner was pondering the question of what might constitute the most effective organization for Universal's domestic procurement operations over the years ahead, he came across many references in trade journals pointing to the future potential use of electronic data processing systems in industrial purchasing. He noted that these references were frequently accompanied by comments suggesting that, in order to realize the greatest overall benefit to the company, the use of EDP in purchasing might well call for the integration of the purchasing function with other functions, such as receiving, material control, traffic, inventory control, and even production control. Mr. Greiner noted also that such integration was thought by some writers to require the eventual creation of highly centralized materials management. In thinking about his report to management recommending changes in the distribution of procurement responsibilities and changes in the procurement process, he was uncertain to what extent he should be guided in his recommendations by a possible future use of EDP in Universal's purchasing activities.

UNIVERSAL TYPEWRITER, INC. (B)*

In the summer of 1959 Mr. Wesley Greiner, a staff methods engineer for Universal Typewriter, Inc., was assigned the task of analyzing the company's organization for procurement for its domestic and Canadian manufacturing units. Mr. Greiner was to submit to management by the end of the year a report of his findings, including recommendations for a program of reorganization, if he came to the conclusion that such reorganization was warranted.

Universal was a large multinational manufacturer of standard typewriters. In 1958, worldwide sales amounted to over $600 million and net income to about $16 million. Since the early 1950s, foreign competition had been cutting heavily into Universal's markets, particularly in the United States; and by 1958 the company's market share had fallen from about 60 percent to about 30 percent. Early in 1958, top management had begun to develop long-range strategic plans to meet the mounting competitive pressures. These plans were designed to: (1) rebuild the typewriter business by producing electric models of advanced design and by withdrawing from the market a number of older models; (2) reduce manufacturing costs through modernization and specialization of the company's generally aged and outmoded plant facilities; (3) reduce selling costs by shifting from a single channel of distribution to multiple channels of distribution; (4) eliminate excessive assets to improve return on investment and to free funds for investments in new products; and (5) cut back the company's heavy reliance on typewriters to about 50 percent of total sales by diversifying from a one-product company to a multiproduct company primarily through acquisitions.[1]

Control of all company operations throughout the world was centralized at headquarters in Hartford, Connecticut. In line with the company's operating philosophy, Universal maintained at headquarters a central purchasing department, which placed all purchase orders, except those for emergency requirements, for one Canadian and six domestic plants; handled the accounts payable; and procured material upon request for overseas operating plants. Initial negotiations with suppliers of many commodities were generally conducted at the plant level by the engineering departments with the assistance of the plant purchasing agents. Contracts for basic materials, such as steel, however, were negotiated on a companywide basis by top management. In addition to providing assistance to the plant engineers, plant purchasing agents were responsible for editing, approving, and transmitting requisitions to the central purchasing department; expediting deliveries of orders; buying emergency items; paying for plant-issued purchase orders; and keeping inventory and general purchase records.

---

* © by the President and Fellows of Harvard College; all rights reserved.

[1] See Universal Typewriter, Inc. (A) case for description of company background and organization.

In 1958 the company bought from approximately 4,000 suppliers. Total procurement volume for the company's domestic and Canadian plants exceeded $45 million, with production parts, steel, and wire and cable accounting for the bulk of all material expenditures.

In relation to total production costs, material costs varied from one product to the next. Thus, while the cost of materials had been relatively small for typewriters, such cost represented a significantly higher proportion of total costs for such items as electronic office machines and analog computers that were added to the firm's product portfolio under the new diversification policy.

Mr. Greiner's report and recommendations to management

On December 28, 1959, Mr. Greiner submitted his report on the study of the company's procurement system with a covering memorandum. The latter read as follows:

MEMORANDUM

To: Mr. William James Lee, Vice President—Manufacturing
From: Mr. Wesley Greiner

Attached hereto is the report on my study of the purchasing function of our company. All of the six domestic operating plants were visited. The Canadian plant was not visited in view of the recent decision to make their purchasing efforts largely independent of the central purchasing department. It is hoped that the study will be of benefit in determining the future course of purchasing.

Excerpts from the study follow:

I.   The Purchasing Problem

The stature of the purchasing function in a manufacturing company can usually be measured by the factor of the cost of purchases in the end products. Traditionally, in our company typewriters have dominated our product line and the ratio of purchases in the product cost has been low.

Our present product line is diversified, and the cost of purchases in the product cost has become a dominant factor. This cost factor has caused attention to focus on the manner in which our purchasing is being conducted.

Our present purchasing system comprises a central purchasing department in Hartford, Conn., and local purchasing departments in all the plants. In late years there has been a distinct trend in our plants to conducting their own purchasing without reference to Hartford. This trend is most evident in plants with product lines characterized by high material costs. The result of this has been for the Hartford purchasing function to become more of a centralized typing center than a centralized purchasing office. The most apparent weaknesses in our present system are:

1.   A lack of a manual on purchasing policies and procedures; therefore, a lack of understanding both in the Hartford office and in the plants as to the specific responsibilities of each.

2. The inevitable loss of time in purchase order placement as a result of routing the requisitions to Hartford.
3. A duplication of effort relative to record keeping at headquarters and at the plants.
4. The placement of unpriced purchase orders as the rule, rather than as the exception, which indicates lack of close control of purchasing.
5. The lack of local area blanket purchase orders, which would reduce the work load and the cost of purchasing. A survey at the Rhode Island plant revealed that in 1959 a total of 7,000 purchase orders would be issued to vendors in the area, where the dollar value of the orders averaged $20 or less.
6. The lack of knowledge in the Hartford office of the actual end use of the purchased commodities.
7. A lack of understanding existing at the plant levels relative to the role of purchasing. Functions are being performed, such as receiving or invoice approval, which are not proper responsibilities of purchasing. And, conversely, other departments are expending time and effort on negotiations with vendors which should be done by purchasing.
8. The lack of training programs to enable the study and mastery of advanced techniques of purchasing.
9. Too large a number of vendors used by our company. In 1958 a total of about 4,000 vendors was used. Of this number, 2,500 received orders from us each amounting to $1,000 or less.
10. A lack of suitable vendors in the South. Over 40 percent of our 1960 expenditures will be for our three southern plants. Vendor services, transportation costs, and purchase costs should be to our advantage if southern vendors can be developed.

Before advocating change, it may be well to note briefly the various forms of purchasing structures in other multiplant manufacturing companies in this country, as reported in the literature. These companies are structured as follows:

1. Completely centralized . . . . 25% of companies
2. Completely decentralized . . . . 15% of companies
3. Partially centralized and partially decentralized . . . . . . 60% of companies

The most essential factors needed for successful operation of a completely centralized purchasing function are two in number: one, similarity of product lines; two, similarity of purchases. A further factor, of secondary importance, is the close proximity of the plants to the purchasing office. Until recent years, our product lines and purchases met the essential conditions of centralized purchasing, but this statement is not true for our present operations.

The completely decentralized purchasing of multiplant companies has been the least successful of the three purchasing systems. General Electric was among the first to decentralize purchasing and has freely admitted that this method has serious shortcomings. GE is now studying regional purchasing with the thought of combining common requirements of plants in a given area.

The third form of purchasing, wherein the advantages of both centralization and decentralization are combined into a purchasing function, had the largest number of adherents and is adding to its number with each passing year.

This structure usually provides for completely integrated purchasing functions at the plants and a central purchasing service facility at the home office. The plant purchasing agent is responsible to the works manager for the performance of his department and to the director of purchases at the home office for carrying out company policy and procedures. The principal strong points of this combination system are:

1. It provides the works manager with greater control over his costs. This control is particularly pertinent when the purchases are a dominant factor of product cost, and when local area purchases are a large part of the total expenditures.
2. It allows companywide policy to be established and maintained. This is a responsibility of the central purchasing services.
3. It allows systematic audit and evaluation of the plant purchasing functions by the central purchasing service.
4. It provides better vendor relationships for the plants, because the plant purchasing agent will be more familiar with the plant needs than the central purchasing staff can be. This is especially true when the plant is a considerable distance from the home office.
5. It eliminates the delays inherent in order placement by the central office.
6. It provides for economical purchasing of companywide common items by placing the responsibility for national contracts and trade agreements on the central purchasing services.
7. It enhances goodwill in the plant communities, as more local purchasing will result. This is not to the detriment of the company, as local prices are audited by the central purchasing services.

II.   Point of Purchase

In considering whether the operational level of our purchasing should be at the home office or at the plants, the following factors are pertinent:

1. Dollar volume of purchases.
2. Product lines and the percent of purchases in the product cost.
3. Type of purchases.
4. Geographical location of the plants, major areas of supply, and estimated future volume.
5. Cost of the purchasing function.
6. Evaluation of the purchasing function.

Typewriter production in the future will account for only one third of our purchase costs. A high proportion of our total procurement volume was for the Rhode Island plants, where a wide range of products is produced. As our product lines continue to diversify, purchased materials and components will become increasingly the dominant factor in our product costs. Twenty-three percent of the dollar volume of our purchases is for commodities that should receive the special attention of the central purchasing services—these commodities are: steel; operating supplies; cartons; oil; paper; forms, etc.; abrasives and chemicals. The distance between the Hartford central purchasing department and the southern plants impedes close liaison and incurs delays in the transmission of documents. The southern plants will have expenditures of some $60 million to $70 million in 1960, which is over 40 percent of our total purchasing volume. The area of supply must be studied with a view to reducing the distance between our vendors and our plants and providing the most economical purchasing.

As indicated in Exhibit 1, a decentralization of the purchasing function

Exhibit 1

COMPARISON OF PRESENT SALARY COSTS OF EXISTING PURCHASING ORGANIZATION WITH ESTIMATED SALARY COSTS OF PROPOSED DECENTRALIZED PURCHASING ORGANIZATION

Location	Present salary costs (1958)	Present number of personnel	Estimated salary costs (under decentralized purchasing)	Estimated number of personnel
Massachusetts	$ 92,820	16	$ 76,934	12
Rhode Island	28,000	7	55,000	11
Rhode Island	68,120	13	55,000	11
North Carolina	10,257	3	20,000	4
North Carolina	31,860	6	41,860	8
Tennessee	13,000	3	20,000	5
Hartford, Conn.	187,000	35	55,000	6
Total.	$431,057	83	$323,794	57

Source: Company records.

according to the recommendations made below would bring about annual savings of over $100,000 in salaries.

III.   The Recommendations

1. That our purchasing structure be changed to provide integrated purchasing departments at the plants and a central purchasing services facility in Hartford.
2. That the plant purchasing agents be responsible to:
   a. The plant works manager for the proper performance of their departments.
   b. The director of purchases in the Hartford office for compliance with company policies and procedures.
3. That the central purchasing services consist of:
   a. Director of purchases.
   b. Two commodity specialists. These men would specialize in commodities common to the needs of our plants.
   c. One buyer. This man would handle the necessary purchasing for foreign requirements and the home office.
   d. Two clerical personnel for office services.
4. That the responsibilities of the central purchasing services be:
   a. To establish and maintain uniform purchasing policies through the medium of a companywide purchasing manual.
   b. To perform continuing audit of the purchasing activities of the plants. This would be accomplished by:

(1) Receiving a copy of all purchase orders placed by the plants.

(2) Receiving monthly plant purchasing performance reports.

(3) Periodic visits to the plants and to principal vendors, in order to have direct knowledge of the plant purchasing operations.

c. To negotiate contracts and trade agreements for commodities in common use at two or more plants when such action would reduce the net price. The plants to release orders against these contracts or agreements and to have the option of buying independently if they can improve on the terms applicable to their requirements.

d. To advise plants of price trends of major commodities.

e. To make special studies or assistance available to the plants upon request.

f. To conduct a continuing training program in order to provide our purchasing personnel with knowledge of the latest techniques of purchasing. This would involve:

(1) Periodic meetings of the plant purchasing agents and the central purchasing services personnel. These meetings could be rotated among the plants in order to familiarize the plant purchasing agents with the purchasing facilities and the purchasing problems at our plants.

(2) The central purchasing services personnel and the plant purchasing agents holding membership in the purchasing associations in their areas.

HANNA CHEMICALS, INC.

The executive vice president of Hanna Chemicals of Canada, Mr. L. Doucet, had just received a task force report assessing the strengths and weaknesses of the purchasing function. He was now wondering what action to take next. He could ask for a special meeting with the task force to discuss its findings. He could reject the report and/or ask for more or different information. He could also put the report on the agenda for the executive council.

Company background

Hanna Chemicals was a large American-owned international producer of chemicals and related products. It was well known for its aggressiveness in consumer products but also produced a large range of agricultural and industrial chemicals. Subsidiaries were located in eight countries. Consolidated annual sales exceeded $2 billion. Subsidiaries operated reasonably autonomously of the parent company. The president of each subsidiary reported to the president of international operations of Hanna Chemicals and was held responsible for subsidiary profits and return on investment.

Hanna Chemicals of Canada operated a dozen plants divided among the three divisions, agricultural chemicals, plastics, and industrial products. Annual purchases for all three divisions combined totaled about $70 million. Mr. John Keiler was in charge of the corporate purchasing function which bought common items. John Keiler reported to the vice president administration. Each division had its own purchasing department with a line operating responsibility to the local plant manager. Informal liaison was maintained between John Keiler and the managers of the divisional purchasing departments.

The task force

Mr. Bill White, corporate vice president of purchasing for Hanna Chemicals, had found that subsidiary management was often ill informed on the purchasing function and its potential. He thought the international market, in particular, presented opportunities, provided appropriate liaison between various Hanna subsidiaries and corporate purchasing could be established. Bill White had requested an opportunity to speak to the executive council of Hanna Chemicals of Canada to discuss corporate ways and means to explore the potential of the international marketplace. The Canadian president had granted the request, and a meeting had been held in early March, 1973.

Bill White had brought Ross Prout, international purchasing manager in central purchasing along with him and both gave an impressive audiovisual presentation to the Canadian executives. The result was that the executives recommended a task force be formed to study the Canadian purchasing operations.

The report of the task force follows.

REPORT OF PURCHASING TASK FORCE

Background

At a meeting on March 6, 1973, with the executive council, Messrs. W. R. White and R. Prout, Hanna corporate purchasing, provided background information on Hanna Corporation's international purchasing activities and suggested areas for study and consideration which might be advantageous to Hanna Chemicals of Canada's purchasing activities.

As a result of this meeting, the executive council directed that a purchasing task force be formed with the following members:

D. R. Masters	Chairman (vice president administration HCC)
J. L. Keiler	Member (purchasing manager HCC)
R. W. Prout	Member (international purchasing manager HCUS)
P. S. Blackstone	Member (manager, agricultural chemicals HCC)

Terms of reference

On March 27 and May 29, 1973, the executive council approved the following terms of reference for the task force:

1. Examine and evaluate the efficiency of the purchasing function of Hanna Chemicals of Canada (HCC).
2. Determine ways by which the efficiency of the purchasing function might be improved with particular reference to cost and/or efficiency justifications for increased coordination of purchasing effort between Hanna Chemicals of Canada and the central purchasing department, Hanna Chemicals Corporation.
3. To make recommendations for such improvements to the executive council.

Method

In order to obtain basic data on the purchasing activities of the company, a product group purchasing survey was completed by the head office purchasing department and the purchasing departments of the product groups. A file of these surveys is available from members of the task force.

In addition, the task force visited the head office purchasing department and the purchasing departments of plastics, Toronto; agricultural chemicals, Vancouver; industrial products, Montreal. During these visits the survey data was reviewed with the product group purchasing personnel and suggestions for possible improvements of purchasing efficiency were reviewed and discussed. Details of locations and personnel involved in these meetings are available from members of the task force.

When the task force findings and recommendations were complete, the results were discussed with the product group purchasing managers of the three divisions.

The task force held 11 meetings, and the minutes of these meetings are available from task force members.

Scope of purchasing in Hanna Chemicals of Canada

The purchasing function in Hanna Chemicals of Canada has considerable dollar responsibility. Excluding intercompany and intracompany transactions and the purchase of energy and petroleum, the various purchasing departments in 1972 were responsible for buying $72.1 million of goods and services. Of this total, head office purchasing negotiated and committed $27 million ($18 million in raw materials and packaging; $9 million in construction and equipment)—the balance was committed by the product groups.

In 1972 the company's purchasing activities were carried out by 62 full-time employes operating at four major locations including the head office purchasing. Thirty-four of these employees were purchasing managers, purchasing agents, and buyers, the remaining consisted of support staff. The operating cost of the company purchasing function last year was $609,000.

Findings and recommendations

As a result of the meetings heretofore mentioned and the close examination of the purchasing function throughout the company, the task force was able to compile a list of findings. These findings represent a critical or negative list in that they summarize what (in the opinion of the task force) is lacking in the present system. No attempt has been made to catalog those practices and policies which are right and effective.

The recommendations of the task force flow from the findings, and they represent the steps which are recommended to change or supplement the existing purchasing practices and improve the effectiveness of the company purchasing activities.

The findings and recommendations have been recorded in this report under subjects, and there is a correspondence between the findings and the recommendations.

The subject headings are:

1. Organizational structure
2. Policies, practices, procedures
3. Planning
4. Personnel, status, selection, development qualification
5. Management information

Findings of the task force

1. Organizational structure. The organization structure of the purchasing function is generally decentralized, and responsibility for purchasing resides within the product group organization; exceptions to this general rule are commodities common to all groups which are purchased by head office purchasing (example: automobiles, fuel oil, gasoline, tires) and certain specific items which have historically been committed by head office purchasing (example: methanol, phenol, caprolactam).

2. Policies, practices, procedures. There is no policy statement or definition of the purchasing function and responsibility in the current *Policies, Practices, and Procedures Manual* of HCC.

Purchasing policies and practices are presently to be found in several sources, the HCC: *Policies, Practices, and Procedures Manual, Purchasing Manual, Accounting Manual;* the *U.S. Purchasing Manual,* and in the policies, practices, procedures manuals of some of the product groups. There are no uniform policies, practices and procedures to guide the purchasing function of HCC. While a high degree of cooperation exists between the head office purchasing department and the product group purchasing departments, the relationships between these purchasing groups is not formalized by organization or by direction.

While the product groups sometimes inform head office purchasing of major expenditures, $50,000 and over, there is no formal procedure which requires such notice. Consequently, the full resources of the company's purchasing organization do not bear on these major expenditures.

An analysis of last year's major raw material and packaging purchase activities indicates relatively little interference and involvement between the purchasing departments of HCC and the U.S. corporations. In some 50 purchase commitments, each of $100,000 or more and aggregating about $37 million in 1972, central purchasing was involved in some $7 million only. HCC head office purchasing negotiated and committed approximately $18 million of these purchases and for value analysis purposes discussed these informally with central purchasing personnel. (Some of the products involved were packaging, polyethylene resin, coal tar pitch, dicup and isopropyl alcohol.)

The above, supported by discussions with the product group purchasing personnel, indicates a limited awareness and appreciation of the resources available in central purchasing. Communication between the product groups and central purchasing was minimal; between HCC head office purchasing and the Corporation, highly selective.

3. *Planning.* While most of the purchasing departments (head office and product groups) prepare business plans, there is a considerable variation in the content and the purpose of such plans. In many cases it is questionable as to the value of such plans as a blueprint for future action.

The preparation of procurement plans for major purchases of $100,000 per annum or more is not followed in HCC. This practice has been in effect in central purchasing for ten years and has proven an effective means of integrating purchasing activities with business center plans and objectives.

4. *Personnel—status, selection, development, qualification.* The role of the purchasing personnel varies with the product group and ranges from a true procurement manager to a paper processor.

With some exceptions, personnel have generally occupied positions in the purchasing function for many years and have not kept pace with professional development taking place within the industrial purchasing field.

There has been very little mobility of personnel between the purchasing function and other functional areas of the company. Nor has there been any significant transfer of purchasing personnel from product group to product group, even within the purchasing function.

Within the total purchasing function there has been little opportunity for purchasing personnel to get together and exchange ideas. The materials management program is creating a closer relationship among product groups by providing an opportunity for head office and product group personnel to collectively discuss the advantages of common procurement of some commodities.

Qualifications of personnel actively engaged in the company's purchasing activities are varied. According to the personnel records, the educational level of the 34 purchasing managers, purchasing agents, and buyers is as follows:

13 completed grade 11
11 completed grade 12
 9 completed grade 13
 1 completed grade 11 and has 10 credits toward Bachelor of Commerce.

Less than half have pursued supplemental courses in purchasing.
With the exception of plastics, no training programs for purchasing personnel exist within the company.

5. *Management information.* Some product groups prepare periodic reports on the purchasing function for review by their respective managements. There is considerable variation in the scope and distribution of such reports. No company-wide reporting system exists to provide management with information on dollar value of purchases, operating costs, accomplishments or deficiencies, future plans and objectives.

Flowing from these findings are the following recommendations.

Recommendations of the task force

1. *Organizational structure.* The task force discussed at length the advantages and disadvantages of centralized and decentralized purchasing and agreed that neither form by itself would optimize HCC's purchasing activity.

It is the opinion of the task force that the most effective purchasing organization for HCC is a blend of both concepts.

It is therefore recommended that HCC design an organization to provide:

>   *a.*   An effective head office purchasing department with functional responsibility for all of the company's purchasing activities and with capabilities commensurate with such responsibility:
>
>   *b.*   Competent purchasing departments at the product group level responsible for most of the actual purchasing commitments;
>
>   *c.*   Clearly defined responsibilities and scope of activities for the head office purchasing and product group purchasing departments.

The following detailed recommendations reflect this view.

2. *Purchasing policy, practices, procedures.* It is recommended that HCC issue a policy statement on the purchasing function to reflect the following specific suggestions:

Authority for company purchasing should be delegated to the manager of the head office purchasing department hereafter referred to as the manager of purchasing, and the product group purchasing managers. This authority will include responsibility for the commercial aspects of all purchasing commitments for raw materials, energy, packaging, supplies, equipment, construction, and services and for the commercial aspects associated with the disposal of surplus materials, equipment, and scrap.

It is recognized that the purchasing department will call upon the resources of the company and the corporation to assist in the negotiation of major purchase contracts. Typical of this are contracts involving power, ethylene, refinery gas, and petrochemical feedstocks.

These commercial aspects are to include the development of new sources of supply, selection of qualified bidders, obtaining and evaluating quotations, negotiation of prices and terms and conditions, preparation of purchase documents, award and administration of the purchase order or contract.

In the performance of these duties, HCC purchasing personnel will be guided by the policies and guidelines set forth in a HCC policies and procedures manual to be prepared as a supplement to the *U.S. Corporate Purchasing Policies and Procedures Manual.*

It is understood that in the discharge of these purchasing responsibilities, the purchasing departments will act in support of the various functional activities of the company, such as operations, maintenance, engineering, research and development, marketing to satisfy requirements of maximum value based on price, quality, service, and delivery.

Purchases specifically assigned by HCC management to other departments are excluded from the responsibility of HCC purchasing. These exceptions should be defined by HCC management and should include advertising services, real estate transactions, insurance, taxes, communications, and transportation services.

While product group purchasing personnel will continue to report to their appropriate management, the total purchasing function, head office and product group, should be viewed as a company-wide function. The following sections define the views of the Task Force on the division of purchasing responsibilities between head office and product groups.

Product group purchasing responsibilities

Product group purchasing departments will:

A. Make all purchases of materials and services required by the respective product groups and which are not included as those purchases which will be made by head office purchasing.

B. Make whatever short-term commitments necessary to continue operations under emergency conditions.

C. Schedule deliveries for all commitments and expedite such deliveries as required.

D. Process and administer adjustment and damage claims on all commitments.

E. Perform such other duties as product group management require.

Head office purchasing responsibilities

A. Head office purchasing will be responsible for the purchase of raw materials, packaging, supplies, equipment, construction, and services where one or more of the following conditions exist:

1. Competition between using locations for the purchase of similar material could result in higher prices and delivery conflicts.

2. The overall company requirements are sufficient to reflect more favorable prices or other contract terms.

3. A material is produced as a by-product or co-product of other materials that are purchased by head office purchasing.

4. The existence of a supplier serving a number of using locations makes a uniform company position desirable.

5. Specialized knowledge of a commodity or market that has been developed within head office purchasing will provide better value.

6. A purchase commitment requires coordination with HCC management and/or U.S. central purchasing, which coordination and document preparation cannot be readily handled at the product group location.

7. Preparation and steering of all contracts requiring approval of the executive council, including securing of resource department clearances.

8. A purchase commitment contains potential legal, tax, insurance, auditing, or similar problems that cannot be readily solved by the person at the product group location.

9. Duration of the purchase commitment covers a period of 18 months or more.

B. To insure that HCC receives full benefit of company and corporate buying strengths, the product group purchasing departments should discuss with head office purchasing, all purchases of $50,000 or more annually, prior to requesting quotations. In such instances the product group purchasing department concerned and head office purchasing will agree as to which department will handle the transaction.

C. The manager of purchasing (HCC) will represent Hanna Chemicals Corporation in purchases from Canada for shipment to other corporation global locations and will represent HCC in the integration of HCC's purchase requirements into the corporation's global purchasing activities. Since many of HCC's purchases are similar to those purchased globally by the corporation, HCC head office purchasing department and central purchasing will coordinate their efforts on major purchases to best utilize the assets of each. Specifically, HCC head office purchasing will discuss those purchases in excess of $100,000 per year with central purchasing to determine the method of purchase and degree of participation that will bring maximum benefits to both HCC and the corporation. It is recognized that in some cases head office purchasing—HCC will delegate responsibility for this communication to the product group concerned. Central purchasing will also be contacted on lesser value commitments when their knowledge of the global markets would assist HCC in obtaining better values. The criteria for central purchasing participation will be based solely on the ability to bring additional value to the purchase.

D. In order to control the authorization for making purchase commitments, it is recommended that the manager of purchasing review with the appropriate product group the number of personnel and the dollar limits which attend these authorizations. It is also recommended that any future changes in such authorizations be referred to the manager of head office purchasing.

E. It is recognized that in the administration of the policies and procedures, differences will arise between the head office purchasing department and the individual product group purchasing departments. While it is expected that such differences will be resolved between the parties in the best interest of the company, it is recognized that there may be times when resolution of differences, even with the best of intentions, will be impossible. Where such differences of view cannot be reconciled, the matter will be resolved by the HCC officer responsible for the purchasing function of HCC.

3. *Planning.* It is recommended that specific procurement plans be prepared for materials with an annual value of $100,000 or more and where

such commodities do not form a part of an existing HCC procurement plan. The procurement plans should be prepared by the purchasing authority responsible for commitment of the purchase.

Procurement plans can be of considerable assistance in major construction projects, and it is recommended that the manager of purchasing be advised by the product groups of all major construction projects under consideration. In this way, the total corporate purchasing resource can participate at the conceptual developments of the procurement plans involved in such major projects.

It is recommended that HCC purchasing operations be committed to forward planning, goals, and budgets which are integrated with and in support of the overall objectives of HCC. The manager of purchasing, working with the group and purchasing managers should develop an annual purchasing plan which should include goals related to costs, staffing, cost reductions, and market conditions. Source of this information should be product plans and product group purchasing reports. Quarterly progress reports should be provided by the manager of purchasing to the executive council, and such reports should reflect the "goals" review of the product group purchasing managers.

4. Personnel—status, selection, development, qualification. Purchasing is an important company function responsible for over $70 million of expenditures in 1972. In the current climate of rising material costs efficient purchasing can often make the difference between a profit or loss situation. Because of the active competition for scarce materials such as the current crisis in coal and coke, the head of the various purchasing departments should act and have the status of decision-making managers, not "paper" handlers.

It is the impression of the task force that minimum attention has been given to the selection and development of purchasing personnel—the impression of professionalism is not in evidence! In a highly technical company such as Hanna Chemicals, there appears to be a lack of technically trained personnel engaged in purchasing activities. This deficiency implies that many other positions such as project engineers, product managers, and development personnel ara, in fact, purchasing materials, and equipment, thereby losing the value of purchasing coordination and specialization.

With this in mind the task force makes further recommendations:

A. The manager of purchasing, working with the general manager employee relations, will assist the product groups in the maintenance of a manpower and career plan for purchasing personnel; this would include assistance in the determination of qualifications, future needs, training, and rotational development.

The recent introduction within HCC of the personnel committee will provide a means for more extensive review of available personnel, qualifications, and rotation.

B. The manager of purchasing will assist in the write-up and periodic review of job descriptions which relate to the purchasing function. Following acceptance of the task force recommendations, all job descriptions relating to purchasing should be reviewed and up-dated.

C. In view of the government of Quebec's intention to make French the working language of the province, bilingualism is a qualification which should be considered as a requirement for most purchasing positions at the company's locations in Quebec.

D.   All product group purchasing managers should meet collectively at least once per year to discuss new systems and methods and to develop unified efforts and objectives. The managers of purchasing should visit each purchasing location a minimum of twice per year and more frequently when warranted.

E.   Since the manager of purchasing has considerable additional responsibilities under these proposals, it is strongly recommended that a technically qualified person be added to the head office purchasing department. This addition was approved for 1973, but to date the position has not been filled.

    5. *Management information.*   It is recommended that each product group purchasing location prepare a brief quarterly report for product group management and the manager of purchasing.

This report would report on the performance of the purchasing function; furnish statistical information on operating costs, workloads, staffing, and contributions to the business.

Such a report would make possible the dissemination of purchasing information and experiences among the various locations and permit a periodic review of progress on purchasing goals and objectives by the executive council.

    6. *Future review by the purchasing task force.*   It is recommended that if the executive council sees fit to implement any or all of these recommendations that the purchasing task force convene in June, 1974, to review and report to the council on the progress being made in the implementation of this report.

This report is endorsed unanimously by the members of the purchasing task force and is respectfully submitted to the executive council, December 17, 1973.

SIGNED
_____—Chairman
D. R. Masters
SIGNED
_____—Member
J. L. Keiler
SIGNED
_____—Member
R. W. Prout
SIGNED
_____—Member
P.S. Blackstone

INDEX TO CASES

SUBJECT INDEX

I

IBM, 382–97
IMPACT, 382–91
Information systems, 172–77
  external flows to purchasing, 174–75
  internal flows from purchasing, 175–77
  internal flows to purchasing, 172–74
Inspection, control of quality, 304–17
  adjustment and returns, responsibility
    for, 314–16
  computer programs, 314
  legal rights of buyer, 815–17
  method specified, 305–6
  operating characteristic curves, 313–14
  organization for, 306–8
  output inspection, 100%, 312–13
  process quality control, 311–12
  purpose of, 304–5
  quality capability survey, 308–9
  reasonable requirements for, 305
  records, 316–17
  rejected material, allocation of cost,
    314–16
  responsibility for, 307–8
  sequential sampling, 314
  statistical quality control methods,
    309–14
Inspection division
  functions of, 306–8
  location of, 306–8
  relation to procurement department,
    68, 162–64, 306–8
Installment payments for equipment purchases, 723–25
Inventory control, 356–400; *see also* Inventory policy, definition of
  data processing equipment, 382–98
    IMPACT, 382–91
    PICS, 391–98
  factors bearing on, 358–61
  forward buying as aspect of procure-
    ment function, 598–99, 687–701
  functions and forms, 361–73
    buffer inventories, 367–69
    cycle inventories, 366–67
    decoupling inventory, 370–71
    forms, 364–65
    framework, 365–66
    functions, 363–64
    implications for control, 371–73
    spare parts inventory, 369–70
    transit inventories, 366
    why exist, 362–63
  methods of, 358–61
  models, 375–82
    deterministic-fixed quantity, 375–78

Inventory control—*Cont.*
  models—*Cont.*
    fixed order quantity, with variation
      in demand and buffer inven-
      tory, 379–81
    fixed period, 377–78
    probabilistic, 378–79
    service level, 379
  price-discount problem, 373–75
  relation of economical purchase to pro-
    duction, 358–61
Inventory control methods, 356–400
  formulas for determining most eco-
    nomic purchase quantity,
    356–400
  relation to storeskeeping, 398–400
Inventory policy, definition of, 357–58
Invoice, checking as step in procurement
  procedure, 158–62

J–K

Jobbers versus manufacturer as source of
  supply, 544–47
Joint purchasing with supplier, 557–58
Karrass, C., 53, 639
Kaufman, R. J., 718–19
Kindall, A. F., 900

L

Laboratory and use tests, 297
Law and the purchasing function, 815–61
  acceptance
    of goods, 824–25
    of orders, 818–20
  cancellation of orders, breach of con-
    tract, 822–23
  commerical arbitration, 827–28
  commerical bribery, 554–57
  federal statutes, 828–29
  importance of purchase order con-
    tracts, 817–18
  legal authority of purchasing officer,
    815–16
  personal liability of purchasing officer,
    816–17
  protection against price fluctuations,
    825–26
  purchase made orally, 820
  salesmen's authority, 820–22
  standardization of contract terms and
    forms, 826–27
  title to purchase goods, 827
  warranties, 823–24
Lawrence, P., 53
Learning curve, use of, 587–90
Leasing as alternative to purchasing,
  advantages and disadvantages of,
  735–37

This book has been set in 10 and 9 point Caledonia, leaded 2 points. Chapter numbers are 48 point Baskerville and chapter titles are 18 point Baskerville. The size of the type page is 27 × 46½ picas.